McGraw-Hill

networks™

A Social Studies Learning System

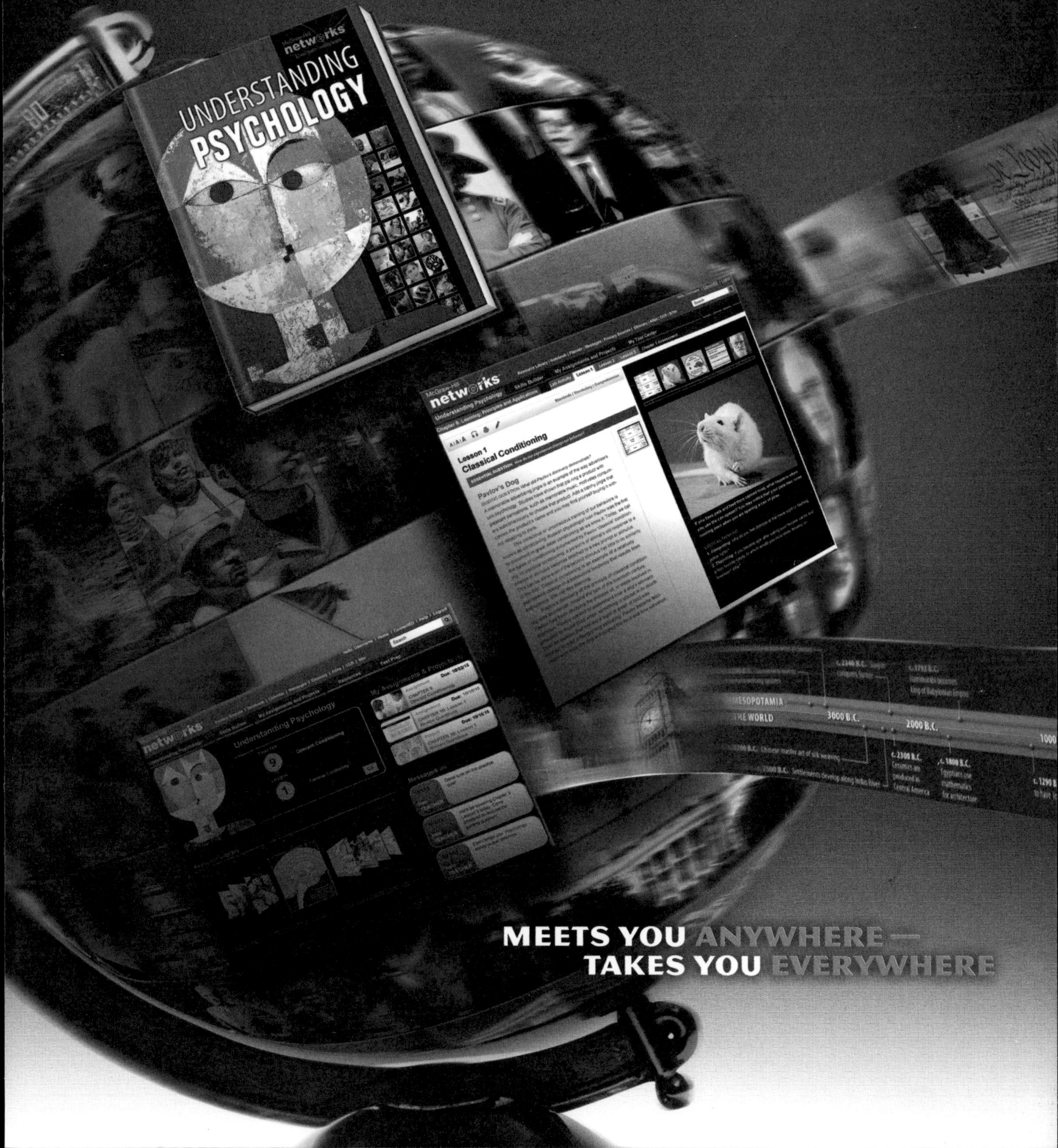

McGraw-Hill
netw⊙rks™

MEETS YOU ANYWHERE—
　　TAKES YOU EVERYWHERE

GO online

1. Go to *connected.mcgraw-hill.com*.

2. Get your User Name and Password from your teacher and enter them.

3. Click on your **Networks** book.

4. Select your chapter and lesson.

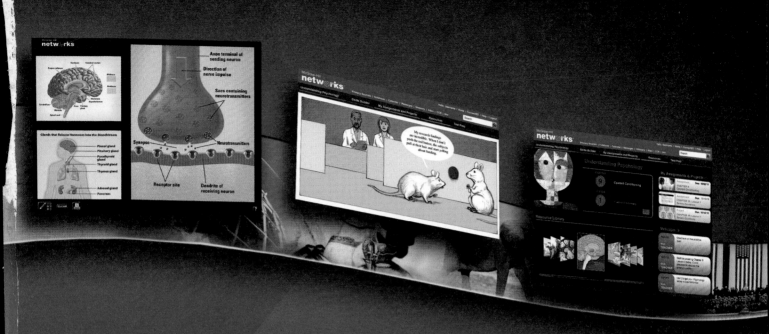

HOW do you learn?

Read • Reflect • Watch • Listen • Connect • Discover • Interact

start networking

WHAT do you learn?

History • Geography • Economics • Government • Culture

start networking

McGraw-Hill
networks™

MEETS YOU ANYWHERE — TAKES YOU EVERYWHERE

HOW do you make **Networks** yours?

Organize • Take Notes • Study • Submit • Message

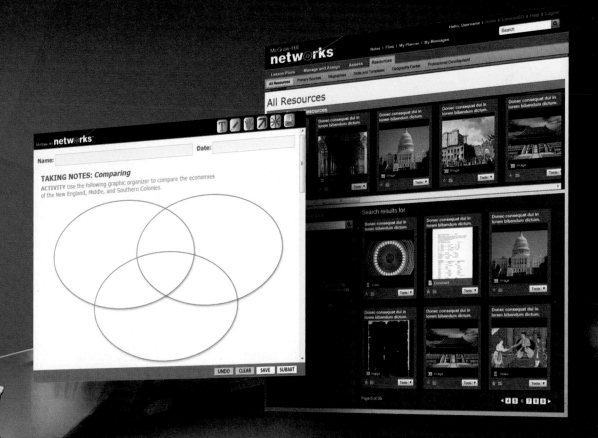

WHAT do you use?

Graphic Organizers • Primary Sources • Videos • Games • Photos

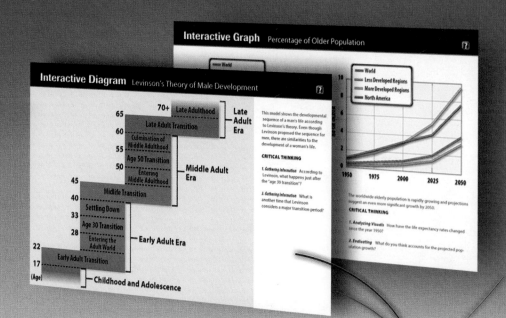

start networking

McGraw-Hill
netw⊙rks™

**MEETS YOU ANYWHERE —
TAKES YOU EVERYWHERE**

HOW do you show what you know?

Hands-On Projects • Foldables® • Print or Online Assessments

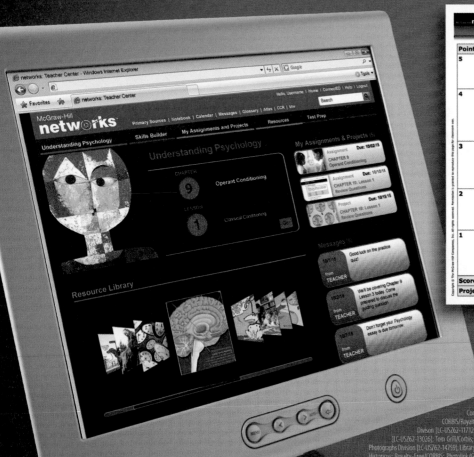

start netw⊙rking

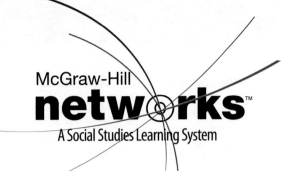

McGraw-Hill
netw⊙rks™
A Social Studies Learning System

UNDERSTANDING
PSYCHOLOGY

Richard A. Kasschau, Ph.D.

Mc
Graw
Hill
Education

Bothell, WA • Chicago, IL • Columbus, OH • New York, NY

AUTHOR

Richard A. Kasschau, Ph.D., is Professor of Psychology at the University of Houston. Dr. Kasschau is a fellow of the American Psychological Association, a former president of the Society for Teaching Psychology, a charter fellow of the Association for Psychological Science, and former chair of the Educational Testing Service task force that recommended the establishment of the Advanced Placement Exam in Psychology. He has written extensively for magazines, newspapers, and professional journals, and has over a dozen books to his credit, including the nation's first all-electronic college-level introductory psychology text. An award winning and distinguished teacher who has taught psychology for 48 years, Dr. Kasschau has twice won the University of Houston's Teaching Excellence Award.

Contributing Author

Jay McTighe has published articles in a number of leading educational journals and has co-authored ten books, including the best selling *Understanding By Design* series with Grant Wiggins. Jay also has an extensive background in professional development and is a featured speaker at national, state, and district conferences and workshops. He received his undergraduate degree from The College of William and Mary, earned a Masters degree from The University of Maryland and completed post-graduate studies at The John Hopkins University.

Photo Credits:

Cover (Main image) Senecio, 1922, oil on gauze, by artist Paul Klee. De Agostini Picture Library/Getty Images. (Thumbnails left to right, top to bottom) Jason Reed/Ryan McVay/Getty Images; Carlos Davila/Photographer's Choice/Getty Images; Ariel Skelley/Blend Images/Photolibrary; Ariel Skelley/Blend Images/Photolibrary; The Schlesinger Library, Radcliffe Institute, Harvard University; The Schlesinger Library, Radcliffe Institute, Harvard University; Thinkstock/Jupiterimages; Arthur S. Aubry/Photodisc/Getty Images; Hemis.fr/SuperStock; Films du Carrosse-Les Productions Artistes Associés/The Kobal Collection/Art Resource; Lewis J. Merrim/Photo Researchers, Inc.; Lars A. Niki; Lewis J Merrim/Photo Researchers/Getty Images; Lars A. Niki; Lewis J. Merrim/Photo Researchers, Inc.; Jeff T. Green/Getty Images News/Getty Images; ©Adrianna Williams/Corbis; DreamPictures/Blend Images/Getty Images; Robert Gray/Getty Images News/Getty Images; Image Source/Jupiterimages; Robert Gray/Getty Images News/Getty Images; Image Source/Jupiterimages; ©JLP/Jose L. Pelaez/Corbis; Ingram Publishing/SuperStock; ©JLP/Jose L. Pelaez/Corbis; Danita Delimont/Alamy; Ingram Publishing/SuperStock; Comstock Images/PictureQuest; Jon Feingersh/Blend Images/Getty Images; ©Adrianna Williams/Corbis; ©Rob Howard/Corbis; Image Source/SuperStock; Elizabeth Crews/The Image Works; ©Bettmann/Corbis; Sean Mcleod/Flickr/Getty Images.

Credits for pages M1–M6: M1: Omar Tobias Vega/Getty Images Entertainment/Getty Images; M2: (l to r)Robert Gray/Getty Images News/Getty Images, Plush Studios/Blend Images/Getty Images, AP Images, ©Farrell Grehan/Corbis; M3: (tl)Science Source/Photo Researchers, Inc., (tr)©Frans Lanting/Corbis, (bl)Ariel Skelley/Blend Images/Photolibrary, (br)Martin Rogers/Stone/Getty Images

McGraw-Hill Networks™ A Social Studies Learning System. Meets you anywhere—takes you everywhere. Go online. 1. Go to connected.mcgraw-hill.com. 2. Get your User Name and Password from your teacher and enter them. 3. Click on your networks book. 4. Select your chapter and lesson.

www.mheonline.com/networks

Send all inquiries to:
McGraw-Hill Education
8787 Orion Place
Columbus, OH 43240

ISBN: 978-0-07-663194-0
MHID: 0-07-663194-X

Printed in the United States of America.

3 4 5 6 7 8 9 QVS 17 16 15 14 13

CONSULTANTS AND REVIEWERS

ACADEMIC CONSULTANTS

Shirley DeLucia
Professor
Department of Education
Capital University
Columbus, Ohio

Judith R. Levine
Professor
Department of Psychology
Farmingdale State College
Farmingdale, New York

Randi Shedlosky-Shoemaker
Psychology Instructor
Department of Psychology
York College
York, Pennsylvania

Clarissa A. Thompson
Assistant Professor
Department of Psychology
University of Oklahoma
Norman, Oklahoma

Danelle Wilbraham
Lecturer of Psychology
Social Sciences Department
Wartburg College
Waverly, Iowa

Tom Daccord
Educational Technology Specialist
Co-Director, EdTechTeacher
Boston, Massachusetts

Justin Reich
Educational Technology Specialist
Co-Director, EdTechTeacher
Boston, Massachusetts

TEACHER REVIEWERS

Lisa Bernstein
Psychology Teacher
Hasbrouck Heights School District
Hasbrouck Heights, New Jersey

Kent Korek
Psychology Teacher
Germantown School District
Germantown, Wisconsin

Nancy Haynam
Social Studies Teacher
Westerville City Schools
Westerville, Ohio

Sara Heck
Teacher
Teays Valley Local School District
Columbus, Ohio

James May
Teacher
Harford County Public Schools
Bel Air, Maryland

Rich McKinney
Social Studies Teacher
Knox County Schools
Knoxville, Tennessee

Pam Watson Mueller
Psychology Instructor
Hazelwood School District
Florissant, Missouri

Steve Prince
Social Studies Teacher
Knox County Schools
Knoxville, Maryland

Adam Schwartz
Social Studies Teacher
Montgomery County Public Schools
Rockville, Maryland

Judi Shortt
AP Psychology Teacher
Edmond Public Schools
Edmond, Oklahoma

Carolyn van Roden
Social Studies Department Chair
Harford County Public Schools
Bel Air, Maryland

CONTENTS

CCSS This icon indicates where reading skills and writing skills from the *Common Core State Standards for English Language Arts & Literacy in History/Social Studies, Science, and Technical Subjects* are practiced and reinforced.

©Rob Howard/Corbis
CHAPTER 3

©Tim Pannell/Corbis
CHAPTER 4

CONTENTS

Patrick Giardino/age fotostock

CHAPTER 5

ranplett/the Agency Collection/Getty Images

CHAPTER 6

Shawn Van Daele/Flickr Select/Getty Images

CHAPTER 7

Stockdisc/Digital Vision

CHAPTER 8

CONTENTS

CONTENTS

Ryan McVay/Stone+/Getty Images

CHAPTER **14**

©Randy Faris/Corbis

CHAPTER **15**

Ron Chapple/Taxi/Getty Images

CHAPTER 16

SuperStock

CHAPTER 17

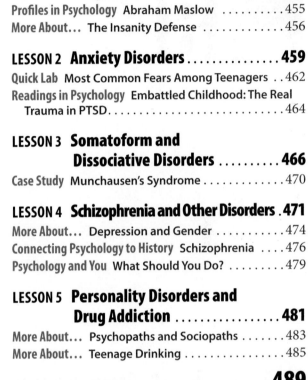

CONTENTS

©DLILLC/Corbis

CHAPTER **18**

Individual Interaction

Essential Questions

Why do people form bonds? • How do individuals develop judgments?

Hill Street Studios/Blend Images/Getty Images

CHAPTER **19**

Group Interaction

Essential Question

How can groups shape the behavior of individuals?

FEATURES

Analyzing Readings in Psychology

FOCUS on research Case Study

Psychology & YOU

Profiles in Psychology

More ABOUT...

FEATURES

Quick *Lab*

Connecting Psychology

Diversity in Psychology

Online Lab Activity

Interactive Self-Check Quiz

Complete the Self-Check Quiz as you finish reading each lesson. The quiz provides instant feedback on areas you may need to re-read to understand a main idea.

Chapter Video

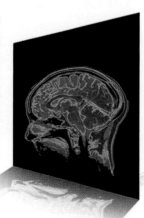

netw⊙rks ONLINE RESOURCES

Interactive Charts, Graphs & Tables

Chapter 1 A Personality Wheel
The Scientific Method
Where Psychologists Work
Test Your Intuitions

Chapter 2 Experimental Research
A Correlational Study
A Frequency Polygon and a
  Scatterplot

Chapter 3 Visual Preferences of Infants

Chapter 4 Juvenile Arrests in the United
  States
Average Annual Gains in Height

Chapter 5 Percentage of Older Population

Chapter 7 EEG Patterns for the Stages of
  Sleep

Chapter 9 How Social Learning Works

Chapter 10 Three Systems of Memory
Stages of Memory

Chapter 11 Decision Trees

Chapter 12 Maslow's Hierarchy of Needs
Range of Emotions
Percentage of Overweight
  Americans
Theories of Emotion

Chapter 13 Approaches to Reducing Test
  Anxiety
The Dove Counterbalance
  Intelligence Test

Chapter 14 Eysenck's Personality
Theories of Personality

Chapter 15 Fight or Flight Response
Types of Conflict Situations
Types of Coping Mechanisms

Chapter 16 Suicide Rates
Major Psychological Disorders
Types of Personality Disorders

Chapter 18 Triangular Theory of Love

Chapter 19 Group Polarization
Sociograms

Chapter 20 Attitude Formation Through
  Classical Conditioning
Theory of Planned Behavior

Chapter 21 Employment of Ph.D.
  Psychologists

Interactive Cartoons and Photos

Chapter 1 Rat Researchers

Chapter 2 Jane Goodall

Chapter 3 Role-Taking
Konrad Lorenz

Chapter 4 Changing Norms
Gender Roles
Margaret Mead and Samoa

Chapter 5 A View of Growing Older
Ceremonies Associated with
Death

Chapter 6 Hallucinations
Human Eye: Pupils Changing

Chapter 8 Service Dog

Chapter 9 Obedience Training
Edward Thorndike

Chapter 11 Language and Gender
Overcoming Wrong Assumptions
Overcoming Functional Fixedness

Chapter 12 Fear of Failure

Chapter 13 A World of Acronyms
Bubble Test

Chapter 14 Freudian Slips
Personality Characteristics
Personality Traits
Defense Mechanisms

Chapter 15 Stress Appraisals
Money and Stress

Chapter 16 Avoiding Happiness
PET Scans

Chapter 17 Humanistic Approaches to
  Therapy
Dorothea Dix

Chapter 18 Body Language
Standards of Physical
Attractiveness

Chapter 19 Conformity and Obedience
Milgram's Experiment

Chapter 20 Anti-Smoking Ad

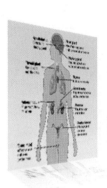
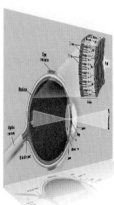
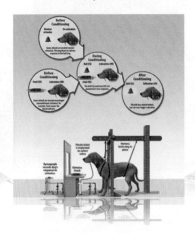
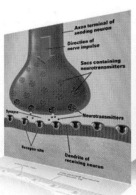
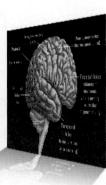

David H. Wells/The Image Works

Interactive Diagrams

Writing Skills

How to Find Main Ideas and Details

How to Find Resources on the Internet

How to Make an Outline

How to Manage Your Time

How to Paraphrase

How to Sequence Events

How to Summarize Information

How to Take Notes

How to Use What You Find on the Internet

How to Write a Letter

21st Century Skills

Analyze Political Cartoons

Creating a Bibliography: CMS Style

Creating a Bibliography: MLA Style

Getting a Job

How to Analyze the News

How to Recognize Historical Perspectives

How to Plan a Service Project

Read for Information

Social Studies Graphing Tool

Your Education: Jump-Start Your Future!

Psychology Skills

Designing an Experiment

Forming a Hypothesis

Identifying Cause-and-Effect Relationships

Interpreting Charts, Tables, Graphs, and Diagrams

Interpreting Statistics

Organizing and Analyzing Information

Reading and Making Graphic Organizers

Using the Scientific Method

Using Critical Methods of Inquiry

Writing a Research Report/Essay

Critical Thinking Skills

How to Analyze the News

How to Analyze Primary Sources

How to Analyze Visuals

How to Compare and Contrast

How to Distinguish Fact from Opinion

How to Identify Cause and Effect

How to Make Inferences and Draw Conclusions

How to Predict

SCAVENGER HUNT

NETWORKS contains a wealth of information. The trick is to know where to look to access all the information in the book. If you complete this scavenger hunt exercise with your teachers or parents, you will see the textbook is organized and how to get the most out of your reading and studying time. Let's get started!

1 How many chapters and how many lessons are in this book?

2 Where do you find the glossary and the index? What is the difference between them?

3 Where can you find primary sources in the textbook?

4 If you want to quickly find all the charts, graphs, tables, and diagrams about childhood development, where do you look?

5 How can you find where the book discusses early psychologist Wilhelm Wundt?

6 Where can you find a diagram illustrating Ivan Pavlov's famous experiment on classical conditioning discussed in Chapter 9?

7 Where can you find the content vocabulary for Chapter 14, Lesson 2?

8 Where can you find a quick guide to reading, critical thinking, research, writing, and basic psychology skills?

9 If you needed to know the Spanish term for schizophrenia, where would you look?

10 Where can you find a list of all the Quick Lab activities in the book?

Approaches to Psychology

ESSENTIAL QUESTIONS • *What are the goals of psychology?* • *How did psychology develop as a unique form of study?*

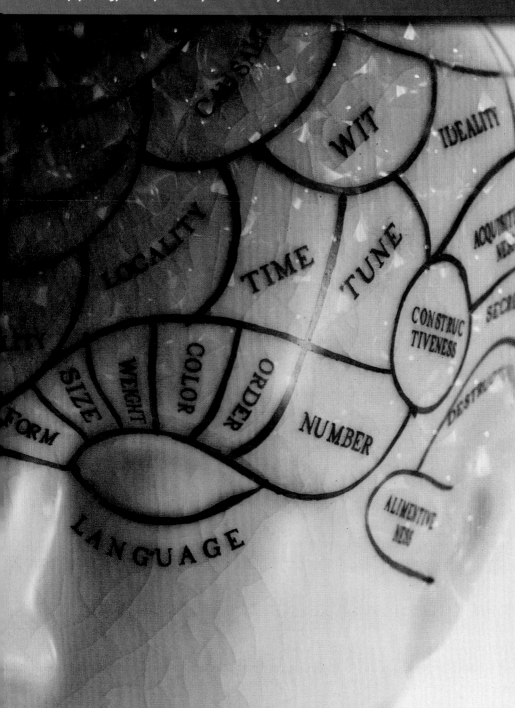

Psychology Matters...

During the nineteenth century, phrenology had many adherents. Phrenologists believed that they could predict future conduct and identify personality traits and mental disorders by the size and shape of a person's skull. Phrenology, which was the first system to attribute psychological behavior to localized regions of the brain, remained popular into the last century. Although discredited by scientific research, it did help focus attention on the brain, rather than the heart, as the seat of emotion.

◀ Phrenologists divided the brain into regions, each of which was believed to govern abilities or personality traits.

Jason Reed/Ryan McVay/Getty Images

1

Lab Activity

Color and Emotion

THE QUESTION...

RESEARCH QUESTION Do all people respond emotionally to color in the same way?

Have you ever seen a kitchen painted black? Or a living room painted bright purple? Probably not. Homebuilders know that people respond emotionally to color. Some colors seem to make us feel calm, while some make us anxious. A room painted the wrong color could be the difference between a peaceful breakfast every morning and a food fight.

We have these emotional responses to color every day. But do all people respond the same way? Let's study this emotional response with an experiment.

Psychology Journal Activity

Think about your emotional responses to different colors. Write about these feelings in your Psychology Journal. Some things to consider as you write: What is your favorite color? Why? Open your closet and look at the colors of your clothes. Are there one or two colors that you seem to favor? Are there any colors you'd never paint a room in your house? Why?

Carlos Davila/Photographer's Choice/Getty Images

FINDING THE ANSWER...

HYPOTHESIS People respond emotionally to color and do so in universal ways.

THE METHOD OF YOUR EXPERIMENT

MATERIALS labeled color samples of equal shape and size of the following colors: red, yellow, green, blue, purple, orange, brown, black, white, and gray; forms containing the names of each color, each with a checklist of the following emotions: Happy, Sad, Angry, Nice, Fearful, Safe, Excited, Bored

PROCEDURE Prepare your color samples to be presented in a digital slideshow. Present the slideshow to at least ten participants, drawn from as many different age groups and ethnicities as possible. You may choose to show your slideshow to each participant individually or all participants as a group. Have your participants view each color for five seconds and then record the emotional response the color makes them feel by selecting an adjective from their form.

DATA COLLECTION Gather the forms and tabulate the responses. Compare these responses with those of your classmates.

ANALYSIS & APPLICATION

1. How did the data support or reject the hypothesis?

2. What conclusions can you draw from the results about your everyday environment?

3. Do you think emotional responses to color are innate (natural) or are they learned? Think about the use of color in fashion or consumer products.

net**w**rks ONLINE LAB RESOURCES

Online you will find:

- An **interactive lab experience**, allowing you to put principles from this chapter into practice in a digital psychology lab environment. This chapter's interactive lab will include an experiment allowing you to explore issues fundamental to psychological study.

- A **Skills Handbook** that includes a guide for using the scientific method, creating experiments, and analyzing data.
- A **Notebook** where you can complete your Psychology Journal and record and analyze your experiment data.

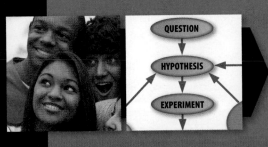

networks

There's More Online!

☑ **IMAGE** Friends and Behavior

☑ **DIAGRAM** The Scientific Method

☑ **SELF-CHECK QUIZ**

Reading HELPDESK ⓒⒸⓢⓢ

Academic Vocabulary

• insight • acquire

Content Vocabulary

• physiological
• cognitive
• psychology
• hypothesis
• theory
• basic science
• applied science
• empirical
• structuralist

TAKING NOTES:

Key Ideas and Details

LISTING Use a graphic organizer like the one below to list the main goals and characteristics of anthropology, sociology, and psychology.

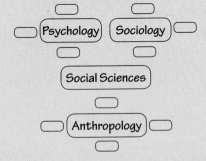

4

The Field of Psychology

ESSENTIAL QUESTION • *What are the goals of psychology?*

IT MATTERS BECAUSE

Why do people do the things they do? As the science that studies behavior and mental processes, psychology seeks to answer that question. Through the study of psychology we are able to understand and determine how the mind and body work together.

Gaining Insight into Behavior

GUIDING QUESTION *What insights can you gain by studying psychology?*

Behavior is a result of physiological and cognitive processes. **Physiological** processes are the normal physical activities, such as breathing, eating, and sleeping, which take place in any living organism. **Cognitive** processes involve conscious intellectual activity, such as thinking, reasoning, or remembering—all ways of processing information. Physiological and cognitive processes can affect each other. For example a lack of sleep can impair our ability to think. Similarly we can will ourselves to stop breathing temporarily or to go without food for extended periods of time.

Psychology is the scientific study of behavior and mental processes. Such study can involve both animal and human behaviors. When applied to humans, psychology covers everything that people think, feel, and do. Psychologists differ in how much importance they place on specific types of behavior. For example some psychologists believe that you should study only behavior that you can see, observe, or measure directly. While psychologists may differ on which types of behavior are important, they agree that the study of behavior must be systematic. The use of a systematic method of asking and answering questions about why people think, act, and feel as they do reduces the chance of false conclusions.

Consider the story of the blind men and the elephant. A long time ago, three blind men on a journey came across a sleeping elephant. Being blind, they could not see what was blocking their way, so they set about to discover what they could about the obstacle. Each man put his hands on a different section of the elephant, examining it in great detail and with much thought. The first man, having felt the elephant's trunk, described a creature that was long, worm-like, and quite flexible. "No, no! You must be mistaken," said the second man, who was seated astride the elephant.

"This creature is wide, very round, and does not move very much." The man who was holding one of the elephant's tusks added his description of a small, hard, pointed creature.

Each of these men was correct in his description of what he felt, but in order to understand the elephant fully, they needed to combine their accumulated knowledge. The study of human behavior is similar. We cannot rely on simplistic explanations. In order to understand our observations, we have to combine the results of many psychological studies. We all like to think we understand people. We spend time observing others (and ourselves) and form conclusions about people from our daily interactions. Sometimes the conclusions we draw, however, are not accurate because we are not systematic in our efforts.

Psychology can provide useful **insight** into behavior. For example suppose a student is convinced that he is hopelessly shy and doomed forever to feel uncomfortable in groups. Then he learns through social psychology that different kinds of groups tend to have different effects on their members. He thinks about this. He notes that although he is miserable at parties, he feels fine at meetings of the school newspaper staff and in the group he works with in the chemistry laboratory. In technical terms, he is much more uncomfortable in unstructured social groups than in structured, task-oriented groups. Realizing that he is uncomfortable only in some groups brings him relief. He is not shy; he just does not like unstructured groups. He is not alone in his feelings—and thinking about his feelings helps him gain confidence in himself.

☑ READING PROGRESS CHECK

Explaining How does psychology provide insight into behavior?

physiological having to do with an organism's physical processes

cognitive having to do with an organism's thinking and understanding

psychology the scientific study of behavior that is tested through scientific research

insight the act or result of being aware of the inner nature of things

Psychology involves gaining new perspectives on your own behavior and that of others.

▶ CRITICAL THINKING

Predicting Consequences
How could the study of psychology help us better appreciate those around us?

Ariel Skelley/Blend Images/Photolibrary

The Goals of Psychology

GUIDING QUESTION *How do psychologists avoid false conclusions?*

In the scientific and systematic study of humans and animals, psychologists have several goals. Overall, psychologists seek to do four things—describe, explain, predict, and influence behavior. The first goal for any scientist or psychologist is to describe or **acquire** information about the behavior studied and to present what is known. Once the facts have been understood and restated, a better study of the behavior in question can begin. From this point, psychology begins to take on the nature of a true scientific study.

Hypothesis and Theory

While a description is an important first step, psychologists are not content simply to state the facts. Rather they also seek to explain why people (or animals) behave as they do. Such explanations can be called psychological *principles*—generally valid ideas about behavior. Psychologists propose these explanations as hypotheses. A **hypothesis** is an educated guess about some phenomenon. It is a researcher's prediction about what the results of a study are expected to be.

As research studies designed to test each hypothesis are completed, more complex explanations called theories are constructed. A **theory** is usually a complex explanation based on findings from a large number of experimental studies. Theories change as new data improve our understanding, and a good theory becomes the source of additional ideas for experiments. A number of theories taken together may validate or cause us to alter the principles that help explain and predict observed behavior.

The third goal of psychologists is to predict, as a result of accumulated knowledge, what organisms will do. In the case of humans, this is often accomplished

acquire to get or obtain

hypothesis an assumption or prediction about behavior that is tested through scientific research

theory a set of assumptions used to explain phenomena and offered for scientific study

Test your intuitions about behavior by answering true or false to the statements below.

Test Your Intuitions
1. The behavior of most lower animals—insects, reptiles and amphibians, most rodents, and birds—is instinctive and unaffected by learning.
2. A child learns to talk more quickly if the adults around the child habitually repeat the word he or she is trying to say, using proper pronunciation.
3. Slow learners remember more of what they learn than fast learners.
4. On average, you cannot predict from a person's grades at school and college whether he or she will do well in a career.
5. Most stereotypes are completely true.
6. The largest drug problem in the United States, in terms of the number of people affected, is marijuana.
7. Psychiatry is a subdivision of psychology.
8. Most developmentally disabled people also have psychological disorders.
9. Nearly all the psychological characteristics of men and women appear to be inborn; in all cultures, for example, women are more emotional and sexually less aggressive than men.
10. No reputable psychologist takes seriously such irrational phenomena as ESP, hypnosis, or the bizarre mental and physical achievements of Eastern yogis.
11. The best way to get a chronically noisy child to settle down and pay attention is to punish him or her.
12. In small amounts, alcohol is a stimulant.
13. A third or more of the people suffering from severe psychological disorders are potentially dangerous.
14. Highly intelligent people, geniuses, tend to be physically frail and socially isolated.

Answers
All of the statements in the table are false. As you read the different chapters in Understanding Psychology, you will learn more about the correct answers to these statements and the research that psychologists have conducted to demonstrate why these statements are false.

6

by predicting a behavior, or what a person will think or feel in various situations. By studying descriptive and theoretical accounts of past behaviors, psychologists can predict future behaviors.

Influence

Finally some psychologists seek to influence behavior in helpful ways. These psychologists conduct studies with a long-term goal of finding out more about human or animal behavior. They are doing **basic science**, or research. Other psychologists are more interested in discovering ways to use what we already know about people to benefit others. They view psychology as an **applied science** and are using psychological principles to solve more immediate problems.

Psychologists who study the ability of infants to perceive visual patterns are doing basic research. They may not be concerned with the implication their findings might have on crib design. Psychologists studying rapid eye movement in sleep research are also involved in basic science. If they discover that one individual has a sleep disturbance, they will try to explain the situation but not how to correct it. That is a job for applied scientists, such as clinical psychologists, industrial psychologists, counseling psychologists, or engineering psychologists.

An example of a psychologist involved in applying psychological principles rather than discovering them is a consultant to a toy manufacturer. A toy manufacturer tries to develop toys that appeal to children. The manufacturer may apply, or use, psychological principles when designing those toys. Since the transfer of findings from basic to applied science can be tricky, the distinction between basic and applied science is important. The following example illustrates this.

Psychologists doing basic research have found that babies raised in institutions such as orphanages become delayed in physical, intellectual, and emotional development. Researchers believe this is because they have nothing to look at but a blank, white ceiling and white crib cushions, and are handled only when they need to be fed or changed. However, we have to be very careful not to apply this finding too broadly. Even though children who lack stimulation tend to develop poorly, it does not follow that providing infants with maximum stimulation will cause them to grow up emotionally sound and intellectually superior. Quite the contrary, most babies do best with a medium level of stimulation. Even more significantly, social interaction seems much more important than visual stimulation. Research has shown that development is more likely to result from long-term interactions with a responsive caregiver. Basic science provides specific findings—what happens in one study conducted at one time and in one place.

☑ READING PROGRESS CHECK

Differentiating Define the concepts of theory and principle and explain the differences between the two.

The Scientific Basis of Psychology

GUIDING QUESTION *What is the purpose of the scientific method?*

Ancient Greek philosophers attempted to explain the workings of the mind. Aristotle based his theories about mental processes on observation. In the seventeenth and eighteenth centuries, philosophers such as John Locke tried to be as objective in explaining mental operations as Sir Isaac Newton was in explaining the laws of physics. Their efforts were hindered by a lack of experimental methods and theoretical ideas.

The development of the scientific method used experimental and mathematical techniques to formulate and test scientific hypotheses. Many **empirical** sciences,

Psychology & YOU

Why You Overreact

Your friend makes a simple comment about your hair or clothes, and you blow up, getting very angry and feeling deeply hurt. Why? Emotions occur as the result of a physical stimulation paired with some social or personal event. If an emotional event occurs but you do not have a physical reaction—such as a pounding heart or a tense stomach—you will not feel that emotion in the usual sense. Yet consider the following situation: You just drank two cans of caffeinated soda. Your heart is beating hard and your stomach is tense. Then your friend makes a critical comment. When you hear the comment, you get angry—but you get angrier than usual because your body is already stimulated. If you are very tired, you may react mildly or not at all to an emotional event.

basic science the pursuit of knowledge about natural phenomena for its own sake

applied science discovering ways to use scientific findings to accomplish practical goals

empirical based on observation or experiment

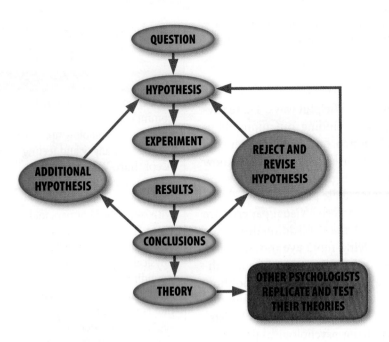

QUESTION

HYPOTHESIS

EXPERIMENT

ADDITIONAL
HYPOTHESIS

REJECT AND
REVISE
HYPOTHESIS

RESULTS

CONCLUSIONS

THEORY

OTHER PSYCHOLOGISTS
REPLICATE AND TEST
THEIR THEORIES

structuralist a psychologist who studies the basic elements that make up conscious mental experiences

which derive knowledge from experiment and observation, use mathematical tools borrowed from statistics. This is especially true of the social sciences, which are those fields of study devoted to the individual, social, and cultural aspects of human behavior.

The social sciences include cultural anthropology, sociology, and other branches in addition to psychology. Cultural anthropology relies on the collection, analysis, and explanation of data from research in the field. Sociology examines the interactions of human societies and their constituent parts, such as institutions, communities, and population group. Psychology focuses on the individual and individuals in groups rather than groups or cultures.

To ensure that data are collected accurately, psychologists rely on the scientific method. In psychology, facts are based on empirical data. Data are obtained from methods such as experiments, surveys, and case studies. This means that psychologists reach their conclusions by identifying a specific problem or question, formulating a hypothesis, collecting data through observation and experimentation, and analyzing the data.

Systematic Procedure and Research in Psychology

The scientific basis of psychology goes back many years. Today people are very sophisticated about scientific procedures, but that has not always been true. Wilhelm Wundt is credited with setting up the first psychology laboratory in Leipzig, Germany, in 1879. He proposed that psychological experience is composed of compounds, much like the compounds found in chemistry. Psychology, he claimed, has two kinds of elements—sensations and feelings. Wundt tried to test his statements by collecting scientific data.

Wundt is generally acknowledged as establishing psychology as a separate, formal field of study. Although he was trained in physiology—the study of how the body works—Wundt wanted to study the human mind by modeling his laboratory research on research in the natural sciences.

As a **structuralist**, interested in the basic elements of human experience, Wundt developed a method of self-observation called introspection. In carefully controlled situations, trained participants reported their thoughts, and Wundt tried to map out the basic structure of thought processes. Wundt's experiments were important historically because he used a systematic procedure to study human behavior. This approach attracted many students who carried on the tradition of systematic research.

Although Wundt's methods proved cumbersome and unreliable, the importance of Wundt's work is the procedure he followed, not the results he obtained. He called the procedure "introspection," and in psychology it led to what we now call the scientific method. Whereas Wundt's introspection was subjective—an individual observes, analyzes, and reports his or her own mental experiences—the scientific method developed as an objective method of observation and analysis. Researchers thus are better able to share and retest findings.

Although psychologists use the scientific method to test and support many theories, many questions about behavior still remain unanswered. Established psychological theories are continually reviewed and revised. New theories and technological developments are constantly generating new questions and new psychological studies.

Why Study Psychology?

As you begin your study of psychology, you will find that it is different from any of your other classes. This is because psychology is connected to both the social sciences, such as history or economics, and the natural sciences, such as biology and chemistry. As a social science, psychology explores the influences of society on individual behavior and group relationships. As a natural science, psychology looks for biological explanations for behavior. You will learn more about the social and biological aspects of human behavior as you draw from the course material to gain insight into your life and the lives of those around you.

In your study of psychology, you will learn to think like a scientist. Scientists constantly question their own assumptions and look for alternative evidence and conclusions. Scientists, including psychologists, use the scientific method as a problem-solving tool. It teaches them to think critically by encouraging open-mindedness, intellectual curiosity, and evaluation of reasons. Using the scientific method will help you think critically and be objective when applying principles to everyday issues, people, and problems. The scientific method consists of five steps that help the scientist integrate theory and research, as well as compare empirical—or factual—data with common sense ideas. Using the scientific method will help you think like a psychologist.

In your psychology course, you will also need to solve problems through individual research or group projects—whether they are the projects in this textbook or other activities your teacher may assign. To begin any project, you need to establish goals—what you want to accomplish, how you will accomplish it, and by when. Intermediate goals address parts of the problem that must be solved in order to arrive at the terminal goal—the final solution to the problem. Use intermediate goals to establish a time line for completing the assignment, which will help you keep track of your progress. As you work, monitor and evaluate your work for schedule, accuracy, and whether it is focused on the final goal. Ask yourself: Are things working as expected? Do I need to adjust anything?

✔ READING PROGRESS CHECK

Inferring How would an unexpected result to an experiment affect the original hypothesis?

LESSON 1 REVIEW

Reviewing Vocabulary
1. *Summarizing* What is the difference between a theory, a hypothesis, and a principle?

Using Your Notes
2. *Comparing and Contrasting* Use the notes you completed during the lesson to compare and contrast the goals and characteristics of psychology and those of sociology and anthropology. What distinguishes psychology?

Answering the Guiding Questions
3. *Assessing* What insights can you gain by studying psychology?

4. *Explaining* What is the purpose of the scientific method?

5. *Analyzing* How do psychologists avoid false conclusions?

Writing Activity
6. *Informative/Explanatory* Write a short essay on how a psychologist doing basic science and a psychologist practicing applied science might differ in their approaches to the issue of Internet addiction. Assess the value of each approach.

7. *Informative/Explanatory* Research the work done by psychologist and animal scientist Temple Grandin into the behavior of cattle and pigs. Write a paragraph on how her research has affected the design of meat processing plants.

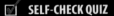

LESSON 2

A Brief History of Psychology

Academic Vocabulary

- alternative
- contemporary

Content Vocabulary

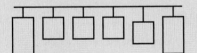

- functionalist
- psychoanalyst
- behaviorist
- humanist
- cognitivist
- psychobiologist

TAKING NOTES:

Key Ideas and Details

FINDING THE MAIN IDEA Create a time line of the order in which the following approaches to the study of psychology developed.

ESSENTIAL QUESTION • *How did psychology develop as a unique form of study?*

IT MATTERS BECAUSE

The study of human behavior began with the ancient Greeks. With the development of scientific methods, the field of psychology began to evolve. Since the mid-nineteenth century, society has been affected in many ways by the development of scientific psychology.

Historical Approaches

GUIDING QUESTION *How do the four historical perspectives on psychology relate to one another?*

Phrenology—the practice of examining bumps on a person's skull to determine that person's intellect and character traits—became a practice in the United States in the mid-1800s. Although this pseudoscience appears ridiculous to us, modern scientists credit phrenology for encouraging study into the role of the brain in human behavior. Phrenology may have inspired scientists to consider the brain, instead of the heart, as responsible for human behavior. Psychology has come a long way since the days of studying bumps on heads.

In the fifth and sixth centuries B.C., the Greeks began to study human behavior and decided that people's lives were dominated not so much by the gods as by their own minds: people were rational. These early philosophers attempted to interpret the observable world in terms of human perceptions—objects were hot or cold, wet or dry, hard or soft—and the influence of these qualities on people's experiences. The Greek philosophers did not rely on systematic study, but they did set the stage for the development of the sciences, including psychology, through their reliance on observation as a means of knowing their world.

In the mid-1500s, Nicolaus Copernicus (1473–1543) published the idea that the sun, not Earth as was previously thought, is the center of the universe. Later, Galileo Galilei (1564–1642) used a telescope to confirm predictions about star position and movement, all based on Copernicus's work. These and other individuals of the Renaissance were beginning to refine what would become the modern concept of experimentation through observation.

Seventeenth-century philosophers popularized the idea of *dualism*, the idea that the mind and body are not acting together but separately and distinctly. The French philosopher René Descartes (1596–1650) disagreed, however, proposing that a link existed between mind and body. He reasoned that the mind controlled the body's movements, sensations, and perceptions. His approach to human behavior was based on the assumption that the mind and body influence each other to create a person's experiences. Exactly how this interaction takes place is still being studied today.

By the nineteenth century, biologists had announced the discovery of cells as the building blocks of life. Chemists later developed the periodic table of elements, and physicists made great progress in furthering our understanding of atomic forces. Many natural scientists were studying complex phenomena by reducing them to simpler parts. It was in this environment of emerging modern science that the science of psychology was formed. The history of psychology is a history of **alternative** perspectives. As the field evolved, various schools of thought arose to compete and offer new approaches to the science of behavior.

Functionalism

Recall that William James (1842–1910) taught the first class in psychology at Harvard University in 1875. James is often called the "father of psychology" in the United States. It took him 12 years to write the first textbook of psychology, *The Principles of Psychology*, published in 1890. James speculated that thinking, feeling, learning, and remembering—all activities of the mind—serve one major function: to help us survive as a species. Rather than focusing on the structure of the mind as Wundt did, James focused on the functions or actions of the conscious mind and the goals or purposes of behaviors. **Functionalists** studied how animals and people adapt to their environments. Although James was not particularly interested in experimentation, his writings and theories are still influential.

Inheritable Traits

Sir Francis Galton (1822–1911), English mathematician and scientist, wanted to understand how heredity, or biological traits passed from parents to children, influences abilities, character, and behavior. Galton traced the famous ancestors of various eminent people and concluded that genius is a hereditary trait. He did not consider the possibility that the tendency of genius to run in distinguished families might be a result of the exceptional advantages that also tend to surround such families. Galton suggested that "good" marriages should be encouraged to supply the world with talented or "fit" offspring and eliminate the birth of less desirable offspring. Scientists all over the world later recognized the flaws in Galton's theory: heredity, along with environment, influences intelligence.

The data Galton used were based on his study of biographies. Not content to limit his inquiry to indirect accounts, however, he went on to invent procedures for directly testing the abilities and characteristics of a wide range of people. These tests were the ancestors of modern personality and intelligence tests. Galton began his work shortly before psychology emerged as an independent discipline. Even so, his theories became central aspects of the new science. In 1883 he published *Inquiries into Human Faculty and Its Development,* considered the first study of individual differences. Galton's writings raised the question of behavior as determined by heredity or environment—a subject that remains controversial today.

Gestalt Psychology

A group of German psychologists, including Max Wertheimer (1880–1943), Wolfgang Köhler (1887–1967), and Kurt Koffka (1886–1941), disagreed with the principles of structuralism and behaviorism. They argued that perception is more than the sum of its parts—it involves a "whole pattern" or, in German, a *Gestalt*. For example, when people look at a chair, they recognize the chair as a whole rather than noticing its legs, its seat, and its other components. A chair is not seen as simply wood and cushions.

Mary Whiton Calkins
1863–1930

Mary Whiton Calkins, a female pioneer in psychology, contributed greatly to the field of psychology despite numerous obstacles. In the 1800s, North American universities barred women from Ph.D. programs. Despite this, Harvard's William James admitted Calkins into his graduate seminar. When Calkins joined the seminar, all the other students dropped it in protest, so James tutored her alone.

Calkins petitioned Harvard to admit her as a Ph.D. candidate. Harvard refused and, instead, held an informal examination for her. Calkins completed the requirements for the doctoral degree and outperformed all her male counterparts on the examination. When Radcliffe University offered her the doctoral degree, she refused to accept the compromise.

Calkins served as a full professor of psychology at Wellesley College and became the first female president of both the American Psychological Association (APA) and the American Philosophical Association.

▶ **CRITICAL THINKING**

Drawing Conclusions How might Calkins's experiences have helped other women?

alternative different

functionalist a psychologist who studies the function (rather than the structure) of consciousness

contemporary modern or current

psychoanalyst psychologist who studies how unconscious motives and conflicts determine human behavior, feelings, and thoughts

CARTOON ⌄

RAT RESEARCHERS
Psychologists might differ in their approaches, but all agree that the study of human behavior must be systematic.

▶ **CRITICAL THINKING**

1. *Interpreting* How have the roles of researcher and subject been reversed in this cartoon? Explain your answer.

2. *Analyzing Visuals* Which of the many different approaches or subfields of psychological study is most likely shown in this cartoon? Which subfield of psychology do the rats represent?

Another example includes the perception of apparent motion. When you see fixed lights flashing in sequence as on some neon signs, you perceive motion rather than individual lights flashing on and off. Gestalt psychologists studied how sensations are assembled into perceptual experiences. This approach became the forerunner for cognitive approaches to the study of psychology.

✅ READING PROGRESS CHECK

Explaining How did phrenology contribute to the development of psychology?

Contemporary Approaches

GUIDING QUESTION *What common element are all the contemporary approaches to psychology studying?*

Many ideas taken from the historical approaches to psychology are reflected in **contemporary** approaches to the study of psychology. The most important approaches to the study of psychology today are the psychoanalytic, behavioral, humanistic, cognitive, biological, and sociocultural approaches. While the first psychologists were interested in understanding the conscious mind, Sigmund Freud (1856–1939), a physician who practiced in Vienna until 1938, was more interested in the unconscious mind. He believed that our conscious experiences are only the tip of the iceberg, that beneath the surface are primitive biological urges that are in conflict with the requirements of society and morality. According to Freud, these unconscious motivations and conflicts are responsible for most human behavior. He thought that they were responsible for many medically unexplainable physical symptoms that troubled his patients.

Freud used a new method for indirectly studying unconscious processes. In this technique, known as *free association,* a patient said everything that came to mind—no matter how absurd or irrelevant it seemed—without attempting to produce logical or meaningful statements. The person was instructed not to edit or censor his or her thoughts. The role Freud assumed, that of **psychoanalyst**, was to be objective; he merely sat and listened and then interpreted the associations. Free association, Freud believed, revealed the operation of unconscious processes. Freud also believed that dreams are expressions of the most primitive unconscious urges. To learn more about these urges, he used *dream analysis*—basically an extension of free association—in which he applied the same technique to a patient's dreams.

While working out his ideas, Freud took extensive notes on all his patients and treatment sessions. He used these records, or case studies, to develop and illustrate a

comprehensive theory of personality. In many areas of psychology today, Freud's view of unconscious motivation remains a powerful influence. Even so, it is controversial, and modern psychologists may support, alter, or attempt to disprove it. The technique of free association is still used by psychoanalysts, and the method of intensive case study is still a major tool for investigating behavior. A *case study* is an analysis of the thoughts, feelings, beliefs, experiences, behaviors, or problems of an individual.

Behaviorists

Russian physiologist Ivan Pavlov (1849–1936) charted another new course for psychological investigation. In a now famous experiment, Pavlov rang a tuning fork each time he gave a dog some meat powder. The dog would normally salivate when the powder reached its mouth. After Pavlov repeated the procedure several times, the dog would salivate when it heard the ring of the tuning fork, even if no food appeared. It had been conditioned, or trained, to associate the sound with the food.

Those psychologists who stressed investigating observable behavior became known as behaviorists. Their position, as formulated by psychologist John B. Watson (1878–1958), was that psychology should concern itself only with the *observable* facts of behavior. Watson further maintained that all behavior, even apparently instinctive behavior, is the result of conditioning, or situational training, and occurs because the appropriate stimulus is present in the environment.

Although it was Watson who defined and solidified the behaviorist position, it was B.F. Skinner (1904–1990) who popularized the concept of changing behaviors through repeated rewards or punishments. Skinner attempted to show how his laboratory techniques might be applied to society as a whole. In his classic novel *Walden Two*, published in 1948, he portrayed his idea of Utopia—a small town in which conditioning, through rewarding those who display behavior that is considered desirable, rules every conceivable facet of life.

behaviorist a psychologist who analyzes how organisms learn or modify their behavior based on their response to events in the environment

Humanists and Cognitivists

Humanistic psychology developed as a reaction to behavioral psychology. In the 1960s, humanists such as Abraham Maslow, Carl Rogers, and Rollo May described human nature as evolving and self-directed. Humanistic psychology differs from behaviorism and psychoanalysis in that it does not view humans as being controlled by events in the environment or by unconscious forces. Instead, the environment and other outside forces serve as a background to internal growth. The humanistic approach emphasizes that each person has a unique individual identity and the potential to develop fully. This potential for personal growth and development can lead to a more satisfying life.

Since 1950, cognitive psychology has benefited from the contributions of people such as Jean Piaget, Noam Chomsky, and Leon Festinger. Cognitivists focus on how we process, store, retrieve, and use information and how this information influences thinking, language, problem-solving, and creativity. They believe behavior is more than a response to a stimulus. Behavior is influenced by a variety of mental processes, including perceptions, memories, and expectations.

humanist a psychologist who believes that each person has freedom in directing his or her future and achieving personal growth

cognitivist a psychologist who studies how we process, store, retrieve, and use information and how thought processes influence our behavior

Psychobiologists

This viewpoint, today often referred to as *behavioral neuroscience*, emphasizes the impact of biology on behavior. Psychobiologists study how the brain, the nervous system, hormones, and genetics influence our behavior. PET, CT, fMRI, and MEG/MSI scans are the tools used by psychobiologists. Psychobiologists have found that genetic factors influence a wide range of human behaviors. Recently, psychobiologists have discovered a link between chemicals in the brain and behavior. For example, researchers found that autistic children share a genetic defect in regulating the chemical serotonin, which plays an important role in brain functioning. In many ways, our behavior is the result of our physiological makeup.

psychobiologist a psychologist who studies how physical and chemical changes in our bodies influence our behavior

Quick Lab

WHY DO YOU DO WHAT YOU DO?
Throughout the course of a day, you perform many activities. Why?

Procedures

1. Observe and keep careful notes of your behavior on a particular day.
2. You may want to make a chart listing each action, such as "woke to the alarm clock's ring," "ate breakfast," and "yelled at younger brother."

Analysis

1. Beside each behavior you have noted, list what caused your behavior. For example, "I woke up at 7:00 A.M. because school starts at 8:00 A.M., and I hate being late. I ate breakfast because I was hungry."
2. Using the behaviorist approach, describe how rewards and punishments affected each of the behaviors on your list.

Sociocultural Psychologists

The newest approach to psychology involves studying the influence of cultural and ethnic similarities and differences in behavior and social functioning. For example, a sociocultural psychologist considers how our knowledge and ways of thinking, feeling, and behaving are dependent on the culture to which we belong. Psychologist Leonard Doob illustrated the cultural implications of a simple, reflexive behavior—a sneeze. Doob asks, "Will [the person who senses the urge to sneeze] try to inhibit this reflex action? What will he say, what will bystanders say, when he does sneeze? What will they think of him if he fails to turn away and sneezes in their faces? Do they and he consider sneezing an omen and, if so, is it a good or bad omen?" To answer such questions, we would have to understand the cultural context in which the sneeze occurred, as well as the cultural beliefs associated with the sneeze.

Sociocultural psychologists also study the impact and integration of the millions of immigrants who come to the United States each year. The character of the U.S. population is rapidly changing. By the year 2025 it is estimated that Americans of Hispanic origin will make up almost 17 percent of the population, while those of African American and Asian descent will make up nearly 22 percent. Psychologists study the attitudes, values, beliefs, and social norms and roles of these various racial and ethnic groups. They also study methods to reduce intolerance and discrimination.

The sociocultural approach is also concerned with issues such as gender and socioeconomic status and is based on the idea that these factors impact human behavior and mental processes. For instance, how might you be different if you had been born female instead of male, or male instead of female? Would you be different if you had been born in poverty or into an extremely wealthy family?

☑ **READING PROGRESS CHECK**

Contrasting How do cognitive psychologists differ from behavioral psychologists?

LESSON 2 REVIEW

Reviewing the Vocabulary

1. ***Contrasting*** What distinguished the psychoanalysts' approach from those of earlier psychologists?

2. ***Identifying*** What are some issues a sociocultural psychologist would study?

Using Your Notes

3. ***Describing*** Using the notes you took during the lesson, write a brief description of each contemporary psychological approach to understanding human behavior.

Answering the Guiding Questions

4. ***Comparing*** How do the four historical perspectives on psychology relate to one another?

5. ***Making Connections*** What common element are all the contemporary approaches studying?

Writing Activity

6. ***Informative/Explanatory*** Consider the following question: Why do you sometimes daydream in your classes? Write a short essay, comparing how the various approaches to the study of psychology would address the question.

Case Study

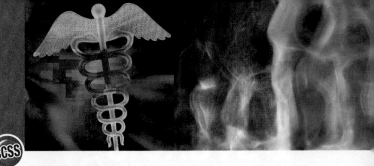

The Four Humors

Period of Study: Around B.C. 150

Introduction: Hippocrates (460–375 B.C.), often referred to as the "father of medicine," became one of the first people to claim that illness had natural, not supernatural, causes. Hippocrates associated the four elements—earth, air, fire, and water—with four humors in the body. He associated earth with phlegm (mucus), air with blood, fire with yellow bile, and water with black bile. Humans with balanced humors were healthy; an imbalance among the humors resulted in sickness. Galen (A.D. 130–200) extended Hippocrates' theory by making connections between the various humors and specific personality characteristics.

Hypothesis: Galen identified four personality characteristics called *melancholic, sanguine, choleric*, and *phlegmatic*. Galen associated these four characteristics with the four basic substances, or humors, that were thought to fill the body at that time. Each humor was thought to give off vapors that rose to the brain. An individual's personality could be explained by the state of that person's humors.

A PERSONALITY WHEEL

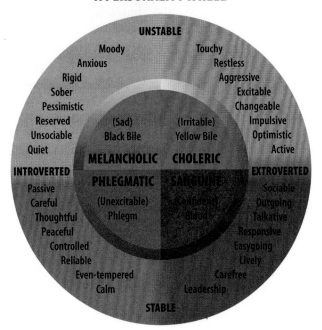

PRIMARY SOURCE

❝ *The churning humors, with their alternating cycles of hot and cold and wet and dry, were the microcosm of physical processes in the world at large, driven by the same fundamental laws that govern the production of rain, for instance, or the change from summer to fall. Time, place, climate, season, weather, temperament, age, diet, and habits were all indicators of health or disease, and also suggested the means for diagnosis and treatment.* ❞

—K. Dickson, *World Eras* (2001)

Method: Doctors might diagnose someone who was pale and cowardly as having excess phlegm. Cheerfulness and generosity resulted from a surplus of blood. Laziness and gloominess were associated with cold and dryness, or black bile. A violent person had too much choler, or yellow bile. A perfect personality resulted when none of the four humors dominated. At that time, treatment of a psychological disorder involved restoring balance among the humors. Doctors gave patients poisonous herbs that caused vomiting, a sign that the imbalanced humor was leaving the patient's body. Balancing the diet could also balance the humors.

Results: The theories of Hippocrates and Galen proved unfounded, and their prescribed treatments for various disorders did not prove reliable. The relationship between physical makeup and personality has not been firmly established. One's mental state can make the symptoms of an illness more distressing, or factors such as stress can inhibit recovery. However, the dominance of, say, black bile in the system does not lead to depression. Galen's notion, though, that a healthy personality is a balanced one may indeed be sound.

Analyzing the Case Study

1. ***Explaining*** According to Galen's hypothesis, how are a person's physical and mental states related?

2. ***Describing*** How did Galen treat psychological disorders?

3. ***Analyzing Visuals*** According to the personality wheel, would an optimistic person be stable or unstable?

4. ***Evaluating*** What part of Galen's theory was incorrect? How can his original theory be used today as a prescription for a healthy personality?

Reader's Dictionary ⒸⒸⓈⓈ

An Experiment in the Seventh Century B.C.

Assyrians: people of an empire in the Middle East, c. 650 B.C.

spontaneously: arising naturally, without external influence

Phrygians: people of an ancient country located in Anatolia, or present-day Turkey

innate: existing in an individual from birth

The Wild Boy of Aveyron

inarticulate: incapable of understandable speech

erratic: strange; not normal

These excerpts describe two experiments. The first experiment, related in *The Story of Psychology*, took place in an ancient time, when humans were just beginning to question the origin of their own thoughts. The second excerpt appeared in *History of Psychology* and details the attempts of one scientist to change the behavior of a wild boy.

An Experiment in the
Seventh
Century B.C.

By Morton Hunt

PRIMARY SOURCE

A most unusual man, Psamtik I, King of Eqypt. During his long reign, in the latter half of the seventh century B.C., he not only drove out the **Assyrians**, revived Egyptian art and architecture, and brought about general prosperity, but found time to conceive of and conduct history's first recorded experiment in psychology.

The Egyptians had long believed that they were the most ancient race on earth, and Psamtik, driven by intellectual curiosity, wanted to prove the flattering belief. Like a good psychologist, he began with a hypothesis: If children had no opportunity to learn a language from older people around them, they would **spontaneously** speak the primal, inborn language of humankind—the natural language of its most ancient people—which, he expected to show, was Egyptian. To test his hypothesis, Psamtik commandeered two infants of a lower-class mother and turned them over to a herdsman to bring up in a remote area. They were to be kept in a sequestered cottage, properly fed and cared

for, but were never to hear anyone speak so much as a word. The Greek historian Herodotus, who tracked the story down and learned what he calls "the real facts" from priests of Hephaestus in Memphis, says that Psamtik's goal "was to know, after the indistinct babblings of infancy were over, what word they would first articulate."

The experiment, he tells us, worked. One day, when the children were two years old, they ran up to the herdsman as he opened the door of their cottage and cried out, *"Becos!"* Since this meant nothing to him, he paid no attention, but when it happened repeatedly, he sent word to Psamtik, who at once ordered the children brought to him. When he too heard them say it, Psamtik made inquiries and learned that *becos* was the Phrygian word for bread. He concluded that, disappointingly, the **Phrygians** were an older race than the Egyptians.

We today may smile condescendingly; we know from modern studies of children brought up under conditions of isolation that there is no **innate** language and children who hear no speech never speak. Psamtik's hypothesis rested on an invalid assumption, and he apparently mistook a babbled sound for an actual word. Yet we must admire him for trying to prove his hypothesis and for having the highly original notion that thoughts arise in the mind through internal processes that can be investigated.

The Wild Boy of
Aveyron
by David Hothersall

In 1799 [Phillipe] Pinel was asked to examine a wild boy, believed to be about twelve years old, who had been found by three hunters in the woods of Saint-Serin near Aveyron in southern France. From reports of hunters who had caught glimpses of him, it was believed that he had lived in the woods for some years. He was virtually naked, covered with scars, dirty, and **inarticulate**. Apparently he had survived on a diet of acorns and roots. He walked on all fours much of the time and grunted like an animal. News of the capture of this wild boy caused a sensation in Paris. The newly formed Society of Observers of Man arranged for him to be brought to the capital for study.… Taken to Paris in 1800 and exhibited in a case, the wild boy sat rocking back and forth and was completely apathetic. He was a great disappointment to the hordes of curious spectators.…

After examining the boy, Pinel concluded that far from being a noble savage, the boy was an incurable idiot. Despite this conclusion, one of Pinel's assistants, Jean-Marc-Gaspard Itard (1744–1835), undertook to care for the wild boy and to try to educate him. First he

gave him a name, Victor, and then made a working assumption that Victor's behavior was due to his social isolation rather than the result of brain damage or some other organic condition. Itard had five aims:

1st Aim—To interest him in social life by rendering it more pleasant to him than the one he was then leading, and above all more like the life which he had just left.

2nd Aim—To awaken his nervous sensibility by the most energetic stimulation, and occasionally by intense emotion.

3rd Aim—To extend the range of his ideas by giving him new needs and by increasing his social contacts.

4th Aim—To lead him to the use of speech by inducing the exercise of imitation through the imperious law of necessity.

5th Aim—To make him exercise the simplest mental operations upon the objects of his physical needs over a period of time, afterwards inducing the application of these mental processes to the objects of instruction.

So Itard undertook Victor's rehabilitation. With the assistance of Madame Guerin, Itard succeeded, after truly heroic efforts, in teaching Victor to pay attention, to keep clean and to dress himself, to eat with his hands, to play simple games, to obey some commands, and even to read and understand simple words. However, despite all their efforts, Victor never learned to talk. At times he showed signs of affection, but often, and especially under stress, his behavior was **erratic**, unpredictable, and violent. Victor learned simple discriminations, but when they were made more difficult, he became destructive, biting and chewing his clothes, sheets, and even the chair mantelpiece (a broad, flat piece of wood used to make the back of a chair). After working with Victor for five years, Itard gave up hope of ever attaining his goals. Victor's background and the "passions of his adolescence" could not be overcome. Victor lived with Madame Guerin until 1828, when he died at the age of forty.

Analyzing Primary Sources

1. *Identifying Central Issues* What was Psamtik's hypothesis? Why was it invalid?

2. *Finding the Main Idea* Why was Psamtik's experiment important even though his hypothesis was flawed?

3. *Analyzing Ethical Issues* Do you think Itard's experiment was worthwhile? Why or why not?

netw☉rks

There's More Online!

☑ **CHART** Divisions of the APA

☑ **IMAGE** Psychologists at Work

☑ **GRAPH** Where Psychologists Work

☑ **SELF-CHECK QUIZ**

LESSON 3

Psychology as a Profession

Reading **HELP**DESK (CCSS)

Academic Vocabulary

• **analyze**   • **environment**

Content Vocabulary

• **psychologist**
• **psychiatry**

TAKING NOTES:

Key Ideas and Details

ORGANIZING Use a graphic organizer like the one below to name several specialty fields of psychology.

Specialty Fields of Psychology

ESSENTIAL QUESTION • *What are the goals of psychology?*

IT MATTERS BECAUSE

The science of psychology includes subfields in areas from biology to sociology. Psychologists study the juncture between brain function and behavior and the juncture between the environment and behavior. Psychologists follow scientific methods, and they are creative in the way they apply their findings.

Psychologists and Psychiatrists

GUIDING QUESTION *How do clinical and counseling psychologists differ?*

Psychologists are people who have been trained to observe, **analyze**, and evaluate behavior. Some psychologists conduct research in a lab setting, while others work with individuals in a practice. They usually have a doctorate degree in psychology. There are many different fields of psychology. The principal ones are described in this lesson.

Clinical and counseling psychology are the largest areas. Clinical psychologists help people deal with their personal problems. They work mainly in private offices, mental hospitals, prisons, and clinics. Some specialize in giving and interpreting personality tests designed to determine whether a person needs treatment and, if so, what kind. (About one-half of all psychologists specialize in clinical psychology.) Counseling psychologists usually work in their own office, in schools, or industrial firms advising and assisting people with the problems of everyday life. They help people adjust to challenges. In most states a doctorate is required to be a clinical or counseling psychologist.

People often confuse the terms *psychologist* and *psychiatrist*. These are different professions. **Psychiatry** is a specialty of medicine. After a student completes medical school, he or she continues training in psychiatric medicine and learns to treat people with disturbed behavior. A psychiatrist is a medical doctor who can prescribe medication or operate on patients. Sometimes a psychologist works with a psychiatrist in testing, evaluating, and treating patients.

☑ **READING PROGRESS CHECK**

Contrasting How does a psychiatrist differ from a psychologist?

Subfields of Psychology

GUIDING QUESTION *How does experimental psychology differ from the other subfields?*

As the field of psychology has grown and expanded, it has steadily been divided into a number of additional subfields, or specialties. Each subfield focuses on a specific subset of the study of psychology or the study of human life. Though each subfield might differ in the subject it covers, all psychology specialists approach their work and study with the same attention to detail and the same commitment to accuracy and ethics.

There are almost as many subfields in psychology as there are human interests. Some psychologists provide therapy and counseling, while others conduct research and apply their results to solving real-world problems. A career in one of the subfields of psychology depends on your interests and which type of work setting you would most likely enjoy. Psychologists work with individuals, groups, data, and systems. They can be found in any number of settings, such as schools, marketing firms, law offices, sports rehabilitation clinics, hospitals, as well as in research facilities.

For students interested in working with children, especially in the areas of education and human development, one of the following subfields might prove satisfying. School psychologists, educated in principles of human development, clinical psychology, and education, help young people with emotional or learning problems. Educational psychologists deal with topics related to teaching children and young adults, such as intelligence, memory, problem-solving, and motivation. Specialists in this field evaluate teaching methods, devise tests, and develop new instructional devices. Sport psychologists help athletes set goals and deal with issues of motivation, anxiety, and other factors of competition.

psychologist a scientist who studies the mind and behavior of humans and animals

analyze to study the nature of something by closely examining the parts that make it up

psychiatry a branch of medicine that deals with mental, emotional, or behavioral disorders

Schools
School psychologists give psychological tests, supervise programs for students with special needs, and may help teachers implement classroom strategies.

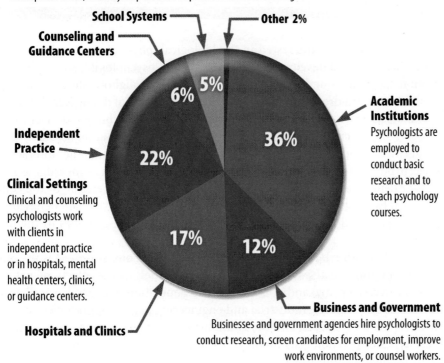

School Systems — **Other 2%**
Counseling and Guidance Centers
6% — 5%

Independent Practice → 22%

Clinical Settings
Clinical and counseling psychologists work with clients in independent practice or in hospitals, mental health centers, clinics, or guidance centers.

Academic Institutions
Psychologists are employed to conduct basic research and to teach psychology courses. — 36%

17% — 12%

Hospitals and Clinics

Business and Government
Businesses and government agencies hire psychologists to conduct research, screen candidates for employment, improve work environments, or counsel workers.

Source: American Psychological Association Research Office

‹ GRAPH

WHERE PSYCHOLOGISTS WORK
Most psychologists in the United States are engaged in clinical psychology.

▶ CRITICAL THINKING

1. *Analyzing Visuals* In which two settings do the majority of clinical and counseling psychologists work?

2. *Theorizing* Why do you think academic institutions account for the largest percentage of psychologists?

Diversity in Psychology

CULTURE AND THE INDIVIDUAL

What is culture? Behavioral scientists define it as the full range of learned human behavior patterns, including language and the way people perceive family relationships and gender roles. Cultural beliefs include the rules we live by, from table etiquette to our ethical beliefs, and the value we place on our cultural artifacts—all the objects that we use, make, and build. All of us are affected by the culture we live in. Each of us has a unique identity, but each of us is also a product of our culture. As members of various subcultures within a larger culture, we reflect our society's cultural diversity. These diverse subcultures reflect our national, ethnic, and racial differences. Cultural diversity also reflects our differences in gender, sexual orientation, and age and our different interests, tastes, abilities, and status.

In recognition of the diverse society in which we now live, the American Psychological Association adopted new *Ethical Principles and Code of Conduct* in 2003. The "old rules" were based on a monocultural (that is, single culture) perspective, whereas the "new rules" recognize a multicultural (that is, many cultures) perspective. Under these new rules, psychologists evaluate such factors as race, disability, fluency in English, social status, and sexual orientation.

▶ CRITICAL THINKING

1. **Drawing Conclusions** Pick two cultural groups and imagine that they have to trade places for one day. What do you think the members of these groups would learn about each other? Do you think they might treat each other differently?

2. **Evaluating** How do the APA's "new rules" help to eliminate cultural bias?

▲ Festivals and parades are opportunities for cultural expression.

Many students are interested in the biological, physical, or social factors of human behavior and development. Developmental psychologists study physical, emotional, cognitive, and social changes that occur throughout life. Specialists in this field study children, the elderly, and even the process of dying. Rehabilitation psychologists work with people with developmental disabilities or victims of accidents or violence, helping them with issues of personal adjustment, pain management, and coping skills. Health psychologists study the interaction between physical and psychological health factors. They may investigate how stress or depression leads to physical ailments such as ulcers, cancer, or the common cold. Psychobiologists study the effect of drugs or try to explain behavior in terms of biological factors, such as electrical and chemical activities in the nervous system.

environment the objects or conditions that surround something or someone

The relationship between people and their physical **environment** is the purview of environmental psychologists. They may look at the effects of natural disasters, overcrowding, and pollution on the population in general as well as on individuals and families. Industrial and engineering psychologists are concerned with people's work spaces, and the relationship between humans and machines. These types of psychologists might study and develop methods to boost workplace production, improve working conditions, train and place employees, or reduce accidents in the workplace.

Lars A. Niki

20

Psychologists interested in the relationships between human behavior and social factors might consider the social and forensic subfields. Social psychologists study social behavior and interpersonal relationships, especially how groups influence individual behavior and how people form attitudes towards others. Some social psychologists study consumer attitudes and preferences while others are interested in public opinion and devote much of their time to conducting polls and surveys. Forensic psychologists work in legal, court, and correctional systems. They assist police by developing personality profiles of criminal offenders or help law-enforcement officers understand problems like abuse.

Finally, some psychologists are experimental psychologists. These psychologists perform research to understand how humans (and animals) operate

∨ CHART

DIVISIONS OF THE APA
The divisions of the APA represent areas of psychological specialization.

▶ CRITICAL THINKING

1. **Speculating** Where might the work of a clinical psychologist fall?

2. **Assessing** Which division would most likely study effects of war?

Divisions of the American Psychological Association (APA)

1. Society for General Psychology	20. Adult Development and Aging	39. Psychoanalysis
2. Society for the Teaching of Psychology	21. Applied Experimental and Engineering Psychology	40. Clinical Neuropsychology
3. Experimental Psychology	22. Rehabilitation Psychology	41. American Psychology-Law Society
4. vacant	23. Society for Consumer Psychology	42. Psychologists in Independent Practice
5. Evaluation, Measurement, and Statistics	24. Society for Theoretical and Philosophical Psychology	43. Society for Family Psychology
6. Behavioral Neuroscience and Comparative Psychology	25. Behavior Analysis	44. Society for the Psychological Study of Lesbian, Gay, Bisexual, and Transgender Issues
7. Developmental Psychology	26. Society for the History of Psychology	45. Society for the Psychological Study of Ethnic Minority Issues
8. Society for Personality and Social Psychology	27. Society for Community Research and Action: Division of Community Psychology	46. Media Psychology
9. Society for the Psychological Study of Social Issues - SPSSI	28. Psychopharmacology and Substance Abuse	47. Exercise and Sport Psychology
10. Society for the Psychology of Aesthetics, Creativity and the Arts	29. Psychotherapy	48. Society for the Study of Peace, Conflict, and Violence: Peace Psychology Division
11. vacant	30. Society of Psychological Hypnosis	49. Society of Group Psychology and Group Psychotherapy
12. Society of Clinical Psychology	31. State, Provincial, and Territorial Psychological Association Affairs	50. Society of Addiction Psychology
13. Society of Consulting Psychology	32. Society for Humanistic Psychology	51. Society for the Psychological Study of Men and Masculinity
14. Society for Industrial and Organizational Psychology	33. Intellectual and Developmental Disabilities	52. International Psychology
15. Educational Psychology	34. Society for Environmental, Population and Conservation Psychology	53. Society of Clinical Child and Adolescent Psychology
16. School Psychology	35. Society for the Psychology of Women	54. Society of Pediatric Psychology
17. Society of Counseling Psychology	36. Society for the Psychology of Religion and Spirituality	55. American Society for the Advancement of Pharmacotherapy
18. Psychologists in Public Service	37. Society for Child and Family Policy and Practice	56. Trauma Psychology
19. Society for Military Psychology	38. Health Psychology	

Source: American Psychological Association, 2012.

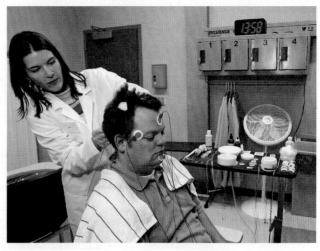

All psychologists, no matter what their area of expertise, are interested in theories about behavior and mental processes.

▶ **CRITICAL THINKING**

Making Inferences Which type of psychologist do you think is at work in each photo?

physically and psychologically. Experimental psychologists do everything from testing how electrical stimulation of a certain area of a rat's brain affects its behavior, through studying how disturbed people think, to observing how different socioeconomic groups vote in elections. Experimental psychologists supply information and research used in psychology.

The American Psychological Association (APA), founded in 1892, is a scientific and professional society of psychologists and educators. It is the major psychological association in the United States and is the world's largest association of psychologists. The APA is made up of 54 divisions, each representing a specific area, type of work or research setting, or activity. Some divisions are research-oriented, while others are advocacy groups. Together they are a cross section of the diverse nature of psychology. The APA works to advance the science and profession of psychology and to promote human welfare.

What psychologists think about, what experiments they have done, and what this knowledge means form the subject of this text. Psychology is dedicated to answering some of the most interesting questions of everyday life: What happens during sleep? How can bad habits be broken? Is there a way to measure intelligence? Why do crowds sometimes turn into mobs? Do dreams mean anything? How does punishment affect a child? Can memory be improved? What causes psychological breakdowns? In trying to answer such questions, psychologists tie together what they have discovered about human behavior, thoughts, and feelings in order to look at the total human being. The picture is far from complete, but some of what is known will be found in the chapters that follow.

☑ **READING PROGRESS CHECK**

Contrasting How does developmental psychology differ from educational psychology?

LESSON 3 REVIEW

Reviewing the Vocabulary
1. *Determining Importance* What do experimental psychologists do? Why is their work important?

Using Your Notes
2. *Describing* Using the notes you took during this lesson, write a brief description of each specialty.

Answering the Guiding Questions
3. *Comparing* How do clinical and counseling psychologists compare?

4. *Differentiating* How does experimental psychology differ from the other subfields?

Writing Activity
5. *Informative/Explanatory* Create a pamphlet that answers some basic questions concerned with psychology as a profession, for example: What is psychology? What is the difference between psychiatry and clinical psychology? What kinds of jobs can I get with a psychology degree?

(l)Lewis J. Merrim/Photo Researchers, Inc.; (r)Jeff T. Green/Getty Images News/Getty Images

Directions: On a separate sheet of paper, answer the questions below. Make sure you read carefully and answer all parts of the question.

Lesson Review

Lesson 1

1 *Defining* What is psychology?

2 *Listing* What are four goals of psychology?

3 *Summarizing* What are the steps of the scientific method?

Lesson 2

4 *Analyzing* What factors did Francis Galton fail to take into account in his studies?

5 *Describing* How did Freud make use of free association in psychoanalysis?

6 *Comparing and Contrasting* Compare and contrast functionalism and behaviorism.

Lesson 3

7 *Identifying* Which branches of psychology are the largest?

8 *Differentiating* What is the difference between a clinical psychologist and a counseling psychologist?

9 *Describing* What kind of background do school psychologists typically have?

21st Century Skills

Review the chart below, which illustrates contemporary approaches to psychology. Then answer the questions that follow.

Approach	What influences behavior	Sample research question
Psychoanalytic Psychology	Unconscious motivations	How have negative childhood experiences affected the way I handle stressful situations?
Behavioral Psychology	Events in the environment (rewards and punishments)	Can good study habits be learned?
Humanistic Psychology	Individual or self-directed choices	Do I believe I can prepare for and pass the test?
Cognitive Psychology	How we process, store and retrieve information	How does caffeine affect memory?
Biological Psychology	Biological factors	Do genes affect your intelligence and personality?
Sociocultural Psychology	Ethnicity, gender, culture, and socioeconomic status	How do people of different genders and ethnicities interact with one another?

10 *Drawing Conclusions* Which psychological approach would be most likely to look for a genetic reason for behavior? Explain your answer.

11 *Formulating Questions* What other questions might a cognitivist study?

Need Extra Help?

If You've Missed Question	1	2	3	4	5	6	7	8	9	10	11
Go to page	4	6	8	11	12	13	18	18	19	14	14

Directions: On a separate sheet of paper, answer the questions below. Make sure you read carefully and answer all parts of the question.

Critical Thinking Questions

12 *Synthesizing* Write your own definition of psychology. Is your definition different from one you would have written before reading the chapter? Put the definition in your Psychology Journal and read it at the end of the course to see if you still agree with it.

13 *Theorizing* Do you think human behavior is free or determined? Defend your answer using theories from the different approaches to psychology.

14 *Contrasting* Consider the issue of fear of the dark. How would the work of a psychologist involved in basic science and a psychologist involved in applied science differ in regard to the study of this issue?

15 *Drawing Inferences* Do you think that humanistic psychology presents an optimistic world view? Explain.

16 *Drawing Conclusions* Why is it fair to say that psychology is a young science? As it is a young science, why should we study its history?

Exploring the Essential Questions

17 *Synthesizing* Write a brief essay in which you discuss the goals of psychology and its development as a unique form of study in the late nineteenth century.

College and Career Readiness

18 *Research Skills* Create an advertisement for a psychology clinic. In the ad, describe the services of the types of psychologists that work at your clinic. Research and include at least six types of psychologists, such as clinical, environmental, and so on. When creating your ad, keep in mind the types of problems that people might want to bring to the clinic. You may want to create a magazine, newspaper, or Internet ad. Be sure to monitor and evaluate your project for time lines, accuracy, and goal attainment.

Research and Technology

19 *Synthesizing* Use the Internet to research careers in psychology. Choose one field of psychology and detail the education, experience, and skills needed for a job in that field. Present your research in the form of an informational pamphlet.

DBQ Document Based Questions

Use the document below to answer the following questions.

PRIMARY SOURCE

"*In the two works of Aristotle in which there is mention of dreams, they are already regarded as constituting a problem of psychology. . . . The dream is defined as the psychic activity of the sleeper, inasmuch as he is asleep. Aristotle was acquainted with some of the characteristics of the dream-life; for example, he knew that a dream converts the slight sensations perceived in sleep into intense sensations . . . , which led him to conclude that dreams might easily betray to the physician the first indications of an incipient physical change which escaped observation during the day.*"

—*from* The Interpretation of Dreams *by Sigmund Freud, 1900*

20 *Defining* According to Freud, how did Aristotle define dreams?

21 *Identifying* What is the importance of dreams?

Psychology Journal Activity

22 *Informative/Explanatory* Review your entry in your Psychology Journal for this chapter. After learning about the scientific method in this chapter, can you think of a way you have ever used it to understand your emotions? Was your initial study on responses to color based on the scientific method?

Need Extra Help?

If You've Missed Question	**12**	**13**	**14**	**15**	**16**	**17**	**18**	**19**	**20**	**21**	**22**
Go to page	4	13	7	14	10	6	18	19	13	13	8

Psychological Research Methods and Statistics

ESSENTIAL QUESTIONS • *How do psychologists gather information?* • *What can influence the results of experiments?*

networks

There's More Online about psychological research methods and statistics.

CHAPTER 2

Psychology Matters...

Psychologists learn about what they do not know by carefully and systematically collecting information through research. This research assumes many different forms. Sometimes it can be simple, as with questionnaires or surveys. Sometimes it is highly specialized and requires years of experience to do properly, as with brain scans. Regardless of the form it takes, all psychological research attempts to explain and predict why people behave, feel, and think as they do.

◄ One way of gathering data is by using sensors to measure brain activity.

Adrianna Williams/Corbis

25

Lab Activity

The Questionable
Eyewitness

THE QUESTION...

RESEARCH QUESTION Are memories a reliable source of information?

Have you and a friend ever been witness to an event where later you were unable to agree about what happened? You both saw the same thing, you both have all your senses, and you both have it pretty together. How could your stories be so different? The answer lies partly in the complex workings of memory. The things you saw with your eyes—the evidence— are only the beginning of the story. This information goes into your brain and gets turned into memories.

Eyewitnesses give testimony in courts every day. But how reliable are their memories? Let's study this phenomenon in an experiment of being an eyewitness.

Psychology Journal Activity

Think about your memory and your ability to transform everyday experiences into memories. Describe a recent event that you saw or an encounter you had with another person. Write about this in your Psychology Journal. Some things for you to consider as you write: Do you think you have a good memory? Do your memories feel firm or vague? What details can you remember about that particular event or encounter? Do you think you would make for a good eyewitness in court?

FINDING THE ANSWER...

HYPOTHESIS Memory alone is an unreliable source of information.

THE METHOD OF YOUR EXPERIMENT

MATERIALS   surveys, pens

PROCEDURE   Recruit a friend to help you with this experiment. Host a meeting for the purpose of creating a class presentation, asking ten classmates to help you prepare. These classmates will be your participants. Prepare the one friend that you recruited to purposefully interrupt your presentation. Prior to the meeting create ten details (e.g., clothing, eyewear, spoken words, etc.) that can be used later to identify your friend. After a minute of your presentation has passed, your friend should enter the room, create a loud or otherwise rowdy interruption, and leave. This interruption should last no longer than five to ten seconds. Prior to your experiment, create a list of ten questions regarding details of the interruption. After the incident, ask half of the participants to complete the survey immediately. A day later ask all of the participants to complete the survey.

DATA COLLECTION   After you have gathered the surveys, compare what they wrote. Circle all details that all witnesses agree upon. Underline the details that at least two of the eyewitnesses included.

ANALYSIS & APPLICATION

1. Did the results support the hypothesis?

2. Briefly analyze the similarities and differences in the eyewitness accounts.

3. Suppose you are a judge hearing two different eyewitness testimonies. How would these results affect your judgment?

4. If you want to be a good eyewitness, what is the best strategy for remembering events correctly? How can this same strategy be useful for scientists conducting experiments?

net**w**orks   ONLINE LAB RESOURCES

Online you will find:

- An **interactive lab experience**, allowing you to put principles from this chapter into practice in a digital psychology lab environment. This chapter's lab will include an experiment allowing you to explore issues fundamental to psychological research.

- A **Skills Handbook** that includes a guide for using the scientific method, creating experiments, and analyzing data.
- A **Notebook** where you can complete your Psychology Journal, and record and analyze your experiment data .

networks

There's More Online!

☑ **CHART** A Correlational Study

☑ **CHART** Experimental Research

☑ **SELF-CHECK QUIZ**

LESSON 1

What Is Research?

Reading **HELP**DESK

Academic Vocabulary

• specific   • constitute

Content Vocabulary

• naturalistic observation
• case study
• longitudinal study
• cross-sectional study
• correlation
• variable
• experimental group
• control group

TAKING NOTES:

Integration of Knowledge and Ideas

CONSIDERING ADVANTAGES AND DISADVANTAGES Use a graphic organizer similar to the one below to list the different types of research methods and state the advantages and disadvantages of each one.

Type of Research Method	Advantages	Disadvantages

ESSENTIAL QUESTION • *What can influence the results of experiments?*

IT MATTERS BECAUSE

Have you ever heard of the expression "garbage in—garbage out"? This expression means that the results you get cannot be better than what you put in. If you build a house with poor materials, the results will be poor, regardless of your building skills. Likewise, when doing research, psychologists must gather and use accurate data in order to obtain correct results.

Approaches to Research

GUIDING QUESTION *Why is it important that samples be representative?*

Psychologists collect information somewhat like most people do in everyday life—only more carefully and systematically. When you ask a number of friends about a movie you are thinking of seeing, you are basically conducting an informal survey. Of course, there is more to doing scientific research than asking friends what they think. Like all scientists, psychologists use the scientific method to systematically obtain new knowledge. Following the scientific method helps improve the accuracy and validity of research findings. When research is accurate and valid, it measures what it is supposed to measure.

Pre-Research Decisions

Researchers must begin by asking a **specific** question about a limited topic or hypothesis. The next step is to look for evidence. The method a researcher uses to collect information partly depends on the research topic. For example, a social psychologist who is studying the effects of group pressure is likely to conduct an experiment. A psychologist who is interested in personality might begin with intensive case studies. Whatever approach to gathering data a psychologist selects, the psychologist must make certain basic decisions in advance.

Samples

Suppose a psychologist wants to know how the desire to get into college affects the attitudes of high school juniors and seniors. It would be impossible to study every junior and senior in the country. Instead, the researcher would select a sample, a relatively small group out of the total *population* under study—in this case, all high school juniors and seniors.

(l)Robert Gray/Getty Images News/Getty Images; (r)Image Source/Jupiterimages

Psychologists want the results of their research to have *external validity*. This means that the results can be generalized to a larger population. To increase the probability that results will have external validity, the sample must be *representative* of the population a researcher is studying. For example, if you wanted to know how tall American men were, you would want to make certain that your sample did not include a disproportionately large number of professional basketball players. Such a sample would be *nonrepresentative*; it would probably not represent American men in general.

There are two ways to avoid a nonrepresentative sample. One is to take a purely *random sample* so that each individual has an *equal chance* of being selected. For example, a psychologist might choose every twentieth name on school enrollment lists for a study of schoolchildren in a particular town. This sample is random because the psychologist selects individuals purely by chance. Random sampling is like drawing names out of a hat while blindfolded.

The second way to avoid a nonrepresentative sample is to deliberately pick individuals who represent the various subgroups in the population that is being studied. For example, the psychologist doing research on schoolchildren might select students of both sexes, of varying ages, of all social classes, and from all neighborhoods. This is called a stratified sample. In a *stratified sample*, subgroups in the population are represented proportionately in the sample. For example, if about 30 percent of schoolchildren in the United States are ages 5–8, then in a stratified sample of schoolchildren in the United States, 30 percent of those studied should be ages 5–8.

☑ **READING PROGRESS CHECK**

Explaining What are the two basic ways that a psychologist might select a representative sample for a survey?

Research Methods

GUIDING QUESTION *What role do control groups play?*

The goals of research are to describe behavior, to explain its causes, to predict the circumstances under which certain behaviors may occur again, and to control certain behaviors. Psychologists use various methods of research to accomplish each of these goals. Some research methods require sophisticated equipment and tools, while others require only pen and paper. Studies that monitor humans or animals in their natural setting may use electronic monitoring technology. The type of research and the goals of the experiment determine what tools the psychologist will use.

Studies

Research studies can be divided into either qualitative studies or quantitative studies. Qualitative studies focus on examining a limited number of participants in depth whereas quantitative studies examine a large number of participants, but for a more limited purpose. Before they begin their research, psychologists must decide which type of study, qualitative or quantitative, will best answer the research questions they are attempting to answer.

Researchers need to know how people and animals behave naturally, when they are not conscious of being observed. To obtain such information, a psychologist uses **naturalistic observation**. The cardinal rule of naturalistic observation is to avoid disturbing the people or animals you are studying by concealing yourself or by acting as unobtrusively as possible. Otherwise you may observe a performance produced because of the researcher's presence.

Robert Gray/Getty Images News/Getty Images

More
ABOUT...

Sampling Errors

To predict the presidential elections of 1936, the *Literary Digest* mailed 10 million ballots as a poll (a survey of citizens' votes). With 23 percent responding, the *Literary Digest* predicted Alfred M. Landon would win comfortably. However, Franklin D. Roosevelt won with 61 percent of the popular vote! The *Digest* sampled mainly owners of telephones and cars and members of clubs. This resulted in a significant over-sampling of the wealthy, who preferred Landon in the election. These, and other sampling errors, created one of the greatest polling fiascoes of all time.

specific relating to a particular category

naturalistic observation research method in which the psychologist observes the subject in a natural setting without interfering

case study research method that involves an intensive investigation of one or more participants

longitudinal study research method in which data are collected about a group of participants over a number of years to assess how certain characteristics change or remain the same during development

cross-sectional study research method in which data are collected from groups of participants of different ages and compared so that conclusions can be drawn about differences due to age

correlation the measure of a relationship between two variables or sets of data

---

GRAPH ∨

A CORRELATIONAL STUDY

These graphs display possible correlations between the different activities and a final grade in a psychology course.

▶ **CRITICAL THINKING**

1. *Analyzing* How does time spent studying psychology correlate to the final grade?

2. *Identifying Cause and Effect* Is there a cause-and-effect relationship between the two variables in the middle chart? Why or why not?

A **case study** is an intensive, qualitative study of a person or group. Most case studies combine long-term observations with diaries, tests, and interviews. Case studies can be a powerful research tool. Sigmund Freud's theory of personality development was based on case studies of his patients. Jean Piaget's theory of intellectual development was based in part on case studies of his own children. By itself, however, a case study does not prove or disprove anything. The results cannot be generalized to anyone else. The researcher's conclusions may not be correct. Case studies, though, provide a wealth of descriptive material that may generate new hypotheses that researchers can then test under controlled conditions with comparison groups.

One of the most practical ways to gather data on the attitudes, beliefs, and experiences of large numbers of people is through surveys. A survey may consist of interviews, questionnaires, or a combination of the two. Interviews allow a researcher to observe the participant and modify questions if the participant seems confused by them. On the other hand, questionnaires take less time to administer and the results are more uniform because everyone answers the same questions. Questionnaires also reduce the possibility that the researcher will influence the participant by unconsciously frowning at an answer the researcher does not like. In interviews, there is always a danger that participants will give misleading answers in order to help themselves gain approval.

When conducting **longitudinal studies**, a psychologist studies the same group of people at regular intervals over a period of years to determine whether their behavior and/or feelings have changed and if so, how. These are examples of qualitative studies. Longitudinal studies are time-consuming and precarious; participants may disappear in midstudy. Longitudinal studies, however, are an ideal way to examine consistencies and inconsistencies in behavior over time. A good example was the New York Longitudinal Study. Psychologists followed 133 infants as they grew into adulthood, discovering that children are born with different temperaments.

An alternative approach to gathering data is cross-sectional studies. In a **cross-sectional study**, psychologists organize individuals into groups on the basis of age. Then, these groups are randomly sampled, and the members of each group are surveyed, tested, or observed simultaneously. Because they typically involve large numbers, these are quantitative studies. Cross-sectional studies are less expensive than longitudinal studies and reduce the amount of time necessary for the studies.

In 1995 researchers from Stanford University conducted a cross-sectional study in which they showed three-, four-, six-, and seven-year-olds a picture of a serious-looking woman. The psychologists then asked the participants what they thought the woman was thinking about. The psychologists found that the older

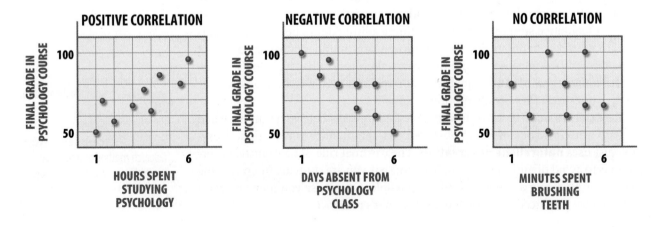

children seemed to have a clearer picture of mental processes. From this discovery, the psychologists proposed that as children mature, their understanding of mental processes improves.

Correlations and Explanations

A researcher may simply want to observe people or animals and record these observations in a descriptive study. More often, however, researchers want to examine the *relationship* between two sets of observations—say, between students' grades and the number of hours they sleep.

Scientists use the word **correlation** to describe how two sets of data relate to each other. For example, there is a *positive correlation* between IQ scores and academic success. High IQ scores tend to go with high grades; low IQ scores tend to go with low grades. On the other hand, there is a *negative correlation* between the number of hours you spend practicing your tennis serve and the number of double faults you serve. As the hours of practice increase, errors decrease. In this case, a high rank on one measure tends to go with a low rank on the other.

It is important to keep in mind that a correlation describes a relationship between two things. It does not mean, though, that one thing causes the other. In some cases, a third factor exists that may account for the observed correlation. Correlations do not identify what causes what. For example, although you might detect a positive correlation between sunny days and your cheerful moods, this does not mean that sunny days cause good moods.

Experiments

Why choose experimentation over other research methods? Experimentation enables the investigator to *control* the situation and to decrease the possibility that unnoticed, outside **variables** will influence the results. When conducting experiments psychologists use the scientific method. Every experiment begins with a hypothesis, or an educated guess, about the expected outcome. In creating a hypothesis a researcher will have some evidence for suspecting a specific answer. In a hypothesis, a psychologist will state what he expects to find. The hypothesis also specifies the important variables of the study.

In designing and reporting experiments, psychologists think in terms of variables, conditions and behaviors that are subject to change. There are two types of variables: independent and dependent. The *independent variable* is the one experimenters change or alter so they can observe its effects. If an effect is found, the *dependent variable* is the one that changes in relation to the independent variable. For example, the number of hours you study, an independent variable, affects your performance on an exam, a dependent variable.

Participants who are exposed to the independent variable are in the **experimental group**. Participants who are treated the same as the experimental group, except that they are not exposed to the independent variable, make up what is called the **control group**.

variable any factor that is capable of change

∨ CHART

EXPERIMENTAL RESEARCH

Psychology is an experimental science. Psychologists follow the scientific method when conducting experimental research.

▶ **CRITICAL THINKING**

1. *Interpreting* What are the dependent and independent variables of this experiment?

2. *Analyzing* What has the researcher done to increase the probability that this experiment will be externally valid?

STEP 1: ASK RESEARCH QUESTION
• Does watching violence on TV lead to aggressive behavior?

STEP 2: FORM A HYPOTHESIS
• People who watch violent TV programs will engage in more acts of violence than people who don't.

STEP 3: DETERMINE VARIABLES
• People watch violent TV programs (independent variable);
• People engage in aggressive acts (dependent variable).

STEP 4: EXPERIMENT (TESTING)
A: Participants (randomly assigned to groups)

EXPERIMENTAL GROUP
• Spends four hours a day watching violent programs

CONTROL GROUP
• Spends four hours a day watching nonviolent programs

B: Measure aggressive behavior (dependent variable) of experimental and control groups

STEP 5: COMPARE MEASUREMENTS

STEP 6: INTERPRET RESULTS AND DRAW CONCLUSIONS

Jane Goodall
1934-

Jane Goodall, a British zoologist, became known for her naturalistic observations of chimpanzees in the wild. In 1960 she began her research at what is now Gombe Stream National Park in Tanzania. By living among the chimpanzees, she won their trust, observing their daily activities and writing detailed reports. Goodall discovered while doing 30 years of research that chimps make and use tools more than any species except humans. Goodall also witnessed the first known instance in which one group of chimps systematically killed another group, even though the first group's survival was not threatened. The scientific method Goodall used in her observations follows the same principles psychologists use when conducting research on humans.

▶ **CRITICAL THINKING**

Inferring What type of study did Jane Goodall use during her years of research?

experimental group the group to which an independent variable is applied

constitute to make up or form

A control group is necessary in all experiments. Without it, a researcher cannot be sure the experimental group is reacting to what the participants think they are reacting to—a change in the independent variable. By comparing the way control and experimental groups behaved in an experiment the researchers can determine whether the independent variable influences behavior and how it does so.

Keep in mind, the results of any experiment do not **constitute** the final word on the subject. Psychologists do not fully accept the results of their own or other people's studies until the results have been *replicated*—that is, duplicated by at least one other psychologist with different participants. Why must psychologists meet this requirement? Because there is always a chance that a study may have hidden flaws.

Ethical Issues

Ethics are the methods of conduct, or standards, for proper and responsible behavior. In 1992 the American Psychological Association published a set of ethical principles regarding the collection, storage, and use of psychological data. These ethical principles, which the APA amended in 2010, include the following guidelines for psychologists to follow when conducting research:

- Using recognized standards of competence and ethics, psychologists plan research so as to minimize the possibility of misleading results. Any ethical problems are resolved before research is started. The welfare and confidentiality of all participants are to be protected.
- Psychologists are responsible for the dignity and welfare of participants. Psychologists are also responsible for all research they perform or that is performed by others under their supervision.
- Psychologists obey all state and federal laws and regulations as well as professional standards governing research.
- Except for anonymous surveys, naturalistic observations, and similar research, psychologists reach an agreement regarding the rights and responsibilities of both participants and researcher(s) before research is started.
- When consent is required, psychologists obtain a signed, informed consent before starting any research with a participant.
- Deception is used only if no better alternative is available. Under no condition is there deception about (negative) aspects that might influence a participant's willingness to participate.
- Other issues that are covered include sharing and utilizing data, offering inducements, minimizing invasiveness, and providing participants with information about the study.

Today, before starting a new research project, psychologists must obtain permission from an ethics committee. This requirement includes research being conducted at all types of institutions, including colleges, hospitals, and public and private research facilities. These committees have names such as the institutional review boards (IRBs) or research ethics committees (RECs.)

Animal Research

Another ethical issue of ongoing concern and debate is the use of animals in research. Many psychologists, both historical and contemporary, have conducted research with animal subjects to answer many fundamental questions about both human and animal behavior. In addition, psychologists often use animals when conducting research that cannot be carried out on humans. Using animals allows psychologists and other scientists to control the test subject's environment, such as food intake, in ways that would not be possible to do with humans. To address concerns regarding proper treatment of animal subjects, safeguards have been established to ensure that animal research is conducted ethically.

The Institutional Animal Care and Use Committee (IACUC) serves as an information resource for institutions such as universities and research facilities on the care of animals used in either research or education. Those institutions that receive federal funding for their research are required to have a committee that makes certain the specified guidelines are followed. The IACUC Web site contains links to organizations that provide specific instructions for the ethical treatment of laboratory animals. For example, there are specific rules regarding housing, feeding, the conditions under which animals may be subjected to pain, and so forth. The IACUC site also hosts a forum in which member institutions can share information concerning the ethical use of laboratory animals with one another. Researchers have attempted to balance the rights of animals with the need to advance the health of humans through research. While some people oppose subjecting animals to pain for research purposes, others point to the enormous gains in knowledge and reduction in human suffering that have resulted from such research.

When ethical concerns require that participants provide informed consent, they are required to sign written forms.

▶ **CRITICAL THINKING**

Explaining What should the researcher do to make certain that participants are providing "informed consent"?

control group the group that is treated in the same way as the experimental group except that the experimental treatment (the independent variable) is not applied

☑ **READING PROGRESS CHECK**

Applying Give an example of a situation in which changing the amount of an independent variable would affect a dependent variable.

LESSON 1 REVIEW

Reviewing Vocabulary

1. *Defining* What does the term *correlation* mean?

2. *Explaining* Why do psychologists always develop a hypothesis at the beginning of a research project?

Using Your Notes

3. *Considering Advantages and Disadvantages* Review the notes that you completed during the lesson to describe the different types of research methods, including the advantages and disadvantages of each one.

Answering the Guiding Questions

4. *Analyzing* Why is it important that samples be representative?

5. *Interpreting Significance* What role do control groups play?

Writing Activity

6. *Informative/Explanatory* You and your classmates are planning to conduct research that involves small animals. Write a set of ethical guidelines to be used by all students during the experiment. In addition to this, write a paragraph explaining why ethical guidelines are important in conducting research on animals or humans.

There's More Online!

☑ **SELF-CHECK QUIZ**

Reading **HELP**DESK

Academic Vocabulary

• **eliminate** • **evaluate**

Content Vocabulary

• **self-fulfilling prophecy**
• **single-blind experiment**
• **double-blind experiment**
• **placebo effect**

TAKING NOTES:

Integration of Knowledge and Ideas

Comparing and Contrasting Use a graphic organizer like the one below to show the similarities and differences between single-blind and double-blind experiments.

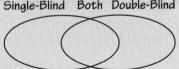

Single-Blind   Both   Double-Blind

LESSON 2

Problems and Solutions in Research

ESSENTIAL QUESTION • *How do psychologists gather information?*

IT MATTERS BECAUSE

Have you ever thought about the different factors that might affect your score on a test? Perhaps you think you will do poorly because you did not sleep well the night before. Maybe the chairs are uncomfortable. Research results can be influenced in similar ways. Psychologists must be aware of such influences and try to reduce or eliminate them.

Avoiding a Self-Fulfilling Prophecy

GUIDING QUESTION *Why must experimenters keep their own expectations from influencing their experiments?*

A math teacher thinks a particular student will be above average in algebra because the student's older sister excelled in the class. The student thrives under the extra attention and praise that the teacher gives him. This is what we mean by a self-fulfilling prophecy. A **self-fulfilling prophecy** involves having expectations about a behavior and then acting in some way, usually unknowingly, to carry out that behavior. In everyday life, we consciously or unconsciously make our expectations known to others. We give cues, such as nodding and raising our eyebrows. Others pick up on those cues and act as expected. Psychologists must be aware of such cues when conducting experiments. They must not allow their expectations to influence their results. In this lesson, we will examine common problems psychologists confront in research.

Single- and Double-Blind Experiments

Suppose a psychologist wants to study the effects of a tranquilizer drug. She might give the drug to an experimental group and a substitute drug that has no effect to a control group. The next step would be to compare their performances on a series of tests. This is a **single-blind experiment**. The participants are "blind" because they do not know if they have received the real drug or the substitute. If the participants taking the substitute report feeling its effects, it means their expectations have played a role and they felt the effects because they believed they were taking a tranquilizing drug, not because of the drug itself.

In another scenario, the researcher will not know who takes the drug or the substitute. She may, for example, ask the pharmacist to number rather than label the pills. Only after she scores the tests does she go back to the pharmacist to learn which participants took the tranquilizer and which took the substitute. This is a **double-blind experiment**. Neither the participants nor the researcher knows which participants received the drug. This **eliminates** the possibility that the researcher will unconsciously find what she expects to find about the effects of the drug. As a consequence, the researcher remains free of bias.

The Placebo Effect

When researchers **evaluate** the effects of drugs, they must always take into account a possible placebo effect. The **placebo effect** is a change in a patient's physical state that results solely from the patient's knowledge and perceptions of the treatment. The placebo is a type of treatment, such as a drug or injection, that resembles medical therapy but has no actual medical effects.

In one double-blind study, researchers divided hospitalized psychiatric patients into two experimental groups and a control group. The experimental groups received either a "new tranquilizer" or a "new energizer" drug. The control group received no drugs. After six weeks the researchers evaluated the experimental groups. Fifty-three to eighty percent of the experimental groups reported that they had benefited from the drugs. Yet all the drugs were placebos. The participants had reacted to their own expectations about the effects of the drugs. Neither the researchers nor the patients were aware that the drugs were placebos until after the experiment.

☑ **READING PROGRESS CHECK**

Synthesizing Why would a researcher conduct a double-blind experiment?

self-fulfilling prophecy
a situation in which a researcher's expectations influence that person's own behavior, and thereby influence the participant's behavior

single-blind experiment
an experiment in which the participants are unaware of who received the treatment

double-blind experiment
an experiment in which neither the experimenter nor the participants know which participants received which treatment

eliminate to remove or get rid of

evaluate to determine the significance of

placebo effect a change in a participant's illness or behavior that results from a belief that the treatment will have an effect rather than from the actual treatment

Diversity in Psychology

CULTURALLY SENSITIVE RESEARCH

Cultural factors that influence our identity include religion, education, and the importance of family. These views affect nearly every aspect of our lives, including our views on politics, art, and our economic behavior. Some cultures see family interests as more important than individual desires. Because the family's needs take precedence over self, individuals from these cultures are likely to bypass opportunities that might disrupt the family. Other cultures, however, see individual goals as supremely important. As a result, meeting individual goals takes precedence over others.

To help psychologists adjust therapy based on an individual's cultural background, the APA has developed a document titled "Guidelines on Multicultural Education, Training, Research, Practice, and Organizational Change for Psychologists." By using these guidelines a psychologist will have a better understanding of an individual's cultural background, and therefore be better able to treat him or her.

▶ **CRITICAL THINKING**

1. ***Identifying Perspectives*** Give two examples of how people's culture can affect their identity.

2. ***Analyzing*** Why is it important that psychologists understand how cultural diversity influences human behavior?

▲ A respectful appreciation for another's cultural background is important for balanced therapy and psychological research.

The Milgram Experiment

GUIDING QUESTION *Why can the Milgram experiment be classified as a single-blind experiment?*

In the 1920s, industrial psychologists conducted studies on productivity at a General Electric plant in Hawthorne, Illinois. The participants were eight assembly-line workers. First, the psychologists gradually increased the room lighting and observed an increase in productivity. Then, the participants were permitted to take rest breaks. This also increased productivity. Next, the psychologists reduced the lighting levels, and again productivity increased. No matter the changes to independent variables, productivity, the dependent variable, increased. Why? It turns out the participants realized they were receiving special attention. This motivated them to work harder. The results of this experiment apply to work situations today.

Stanley Milgram wanted to determine whether participants would administer painful shocks to others when an authority figure instructed them to do so. Milgram studied 1,000 males, including college students and adults in various occupations. He told them he was studying the effects of punishment on learning.

Milgram introduced each volunteer "teacher" to someone posing as a learner. The teacher watched the learner try to recite a list of words that he supposedly had memorized. Each time the learner made a mistake the teacher was ordered to push a button to deliver an electric shock. The teachers were told that the shocks would gradually increase from mild to a dangerous 450 volts. The teachers did not know the shocks were false because the learners displayed pain and begged to end the shocks. Although the task seemed difficult for them, 65 percent of the volunteers pushed the button until the shocks reached maximum severity.

The results implied that individuals could easily inflict pain on others if directed by an authority figure. Later, Milgram informed the volunteers that there had been no shocks. Milgram's experiment was a single-blind experiment because the participants did not know they were not administering a shock. Critics raised the following questions. How would you feel if you had been one of Milgram's participants? Did Milgram violate ethical principles? Was Milgram's deception appropriate? Did the information gained outweigh the deception? Today, before the start of any experiment, the researcher is required to submit a plan to a Human Subjects Committee that approves or rejects the ethics of the experiment.

Researchers at Swarthmore College hypothesized that Milgram's findings were due, in part, to the fact that his participants were mostly middle-aged, working-class men. Most had probably served in the military during World War II and thus had experience obeying orders. Young, liberal, highly educated Swarthmore students would obey less. Yet, surprisingly, 88 percent of the Swarthmore undergraduates administered the highest level of shock!

It is important to remember that the Milgram experiment was conducted prior to the development of the APA Code of Ethics. In fact, the experiment itself was a major reason pressure grew to develop the code.

☑ READING PROGRESS CHECK

Drawing Conclusions Would the Milgram experiment have worked if the researchers had not used deception? Why or why not?

LESSON 2 REVIEW

Reviewing Vocabulary

1. *Describing* What is one method a psychologist could use to avoid self-fulfilling prophesies in their research?

2. *Explaining* What is a placebo? How can the placebo effect lead to incorrect results in an experiment?

Using Your Notes

3. *Contrasting* Review the notes that you completed during the lesson to describe how a double-blind experiment is different from a single-blind experiment.

Answering the Guiding Questions

4. *Identifying Central Issues* Why must researchers keep their own expectations from influencing their experiments?

5. *Classifying* Why can the Milgram experiment be classified as a single-blind experiment?

Writing Activity

6. *Informative/Explanatory* Write a paragraph describing an experiment that could result in the placebo effect. Use as much detail as possible in your description.

Case Study

The Case of Clever Hans

Period of Study: 1911

Introduction: A horse, Clever Hans, grew famous throughout Europe for his startling ability to answer questions. Taught by his owner, Mr. von Osten, Hans seemed to be able to add, subtract, multiply, divide, spell, and solve problems, even when his owner was not around. Oskar Pfungst decided to investigate the humanlike intelligence of the horse.

Hypothesis: Two different hypotheses are involved in this case. First, Mr. von Osten, believing that horses could be as intelligent as humans, hypothesized that he could teach Hans some problem-solving abilities. Pfungst, on the other hand, believed that horses could not learn such things and, while investigating this theory, developed a hypothesis that Hans, the horse, was reacting to visual cues to answer questions.

PRIMARY SOURCE

" [This story] is a document of the very first consequence in its revelation of the workings of the animal mind as disclosed in the horse. Animal lovers of all kinds, whether scientists or laymen, will find in it material of greatest value for the correct apprehension of animal behavior. Moreover, it affords an illuminating insight into the technique of experimental psychology in its study both of human and animal consciousness."

—*From Prefatory Note by James. R. Angell,* Clever Hans *by Oskar Pfungst (1911, p. vi)*

Method: Mr. von Osten, a German mathematics teacher, started by showing Hans an object while saying "One" and at the same time lifting Hans's foot once. Von Osten would lift Hans's foot twice for two objects, and so on. Eventually Hans learned to tap his hoof the correct number of times when von Osten called out a number. For four years, von Osten worked with Hans on more and more complex problems, until Hans was able to answer any question with a numerical answer that was given to him. Upon hearing of the amazing horse, Pfungst grew skeptical and investigated the claim by retesting Hans. Pfungst soon discovered that Hans responded correctly to questions only when the questioner had calculated the answer first. Then Pfungst realized that Hans's answers were wrong when the horse could not see the questioner.

To test his hypothesis, Pfungst fitted the horse with blinders. The horse failed to answer the questions. Eventually Pfungst realized that the questioner would unknowingly give Hans clues as to the right answer. For example, the questioner would lean forward to watch Hans's foot. This was a cue for Hans to start tapping. Pfungst observed that "as the experimenter straightened up, Hans would stop tapping, he found that even the raising of his eyebrows was sufficient. Even the dilation of the questioner's nostrils was a cue for Hans to stop tapping." Questioners involuntarily performed these actions, and Hans responded to the visual signals. Hans needed to see the questioners in order to answer correctly.

Results: Von Osten believed that he had been teaching the horse to solve problems when in fact he had been teaching Hans to make simple responses to simple signals. Pfungst had uncovered errors in von Osten's experiments. Von Osten had been unintentionally communicating to Hans how he expected the horse to behave. Pfungst had learned the truth by isolating the conditions under which Hans correctly and incorrectly answered questions. He had carefully observed the participant's reactions under controlled conditions.

Analyzing the Case Study

1. ***Drawing Conclusions*** How does this case study illustrate the concept of a self-fulfilling prophecy?

2. ***Analyzing Perspectives*** Use both the primary source quote and the information in this case study to summarize the hypotheses of both von Osten and Pfungst, noting any discrepancies you may find between them.

3. ***Problem-Solving*** If Pfungst had not come along to find the truth, how could we discover today how Hans answered the questions?

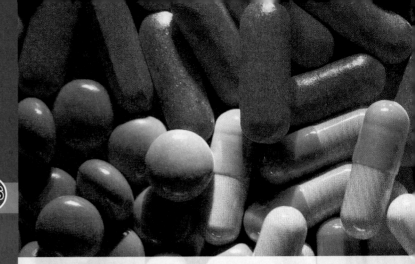

Reader's Dictionary · ⓒⓒⓢⓢ

fallacious: incorrectness of reasoning or belief

psychogenic: having a psychological origin or cause rather than a physical one

seminal: strongly influencing later developments

analgesia: inability to feel pain

hyperalgesia: abnormally heightened sensitivity to pain

Most people are familiar with the use of placebos in clinical trials and the possibility of a placebo effect. However, the opposite of the placebo effect, the "nocebo" effect, is not as well known. If the power of suggestion can cause positive effects, it is not surprising that suggestion may also have negative effects. This article discusses these contrasting responses.

The Amazing Power
of the
Placebo Effect

By Jamie Hale

Placebo effects have been shown in many different areas in science. Sometimes placebo effects have been shown to mimic or even exceed effects produced by active treatments (such as therapies or medications).

The definition of *placebo* is an inert, inactive, fake, sham, dummy, non-therapeutic, pseudo, or spurious substance or procedure presented as a treatment for any of a number of conditions.

In general, the placebo effect can be defined as a positive effect that occurs after receiving treatment (interaction, therapy, medication), even when the treatment is inert (inactive, fake).

The placebo effect is a ubiquitous phenomenon. We all experience some degree of the placebo effect on a regular basis.

The power of the placebo effect is illustrated in the movie classic, *The Wizard of Oz*. The wizard didn't actually give the scarecrow a brain, the tin man a heart, and the lion courage, but they all felt better anyway (Stanovich, 2007).

It can be expected that the benefits obtained from any treatment are at least partially due to placebo effects. "[S]ubjects typically know they are getting some kind of treatment, and so we may rarely be able to measure the actual effects of a drug by itself. Instead, we see the effects of treatment plus placebo effects that are shaped by the subjects' expectations. We then compare those effects with the effects of placebo alone" (Myers and Hansen, 2002).

A common statement heard when discussing placebo effects goes something like this: *it's not real, it's the placebo effect, it's just in your head.* This is an erroneous viewpoint. Placebo effects often produce robust neurobiological and other physiological effects that are very real. This **fallacious** assumption can be at least partly attributed to the belief that the mind and body are somehow separate.

In [a] video segment on YouTube, Paul Bloom, a cognitive scientist and author, talks about the mind versus the brain. He maintains that although the mind and the brain are "one and the same," most people intuitively "at a gut level think the mind is separate from the brain."

According to Bloom, "The mind is a product of the brain. The mind is what the brain does." Considering

PHOTO: Comstock Images/PictureQuest; TEXT: © 2012 Psych Central

them separate entities may be derived from belief in dualism–that the soul is an immaterial entity separate from the body (another subject for another day).

Possible mechanisms contributing to the placebo effect include:

- Suggestions and expectations
- Classical conditioning
- Anxiety reduction hypothesis

Other mechanisms are sometimes mentioned when explaining the constituents of the placebo effect, but the three mentioned are probably the mostly widely discussed. Of course, in many conditions they overlap and their interaction shapes the placebo effect.

Nocebo is sometimes referred to as "placebo's evil twin," or the "negative placebo effect." It's also sometimes described as "the other side of placebo." The *nocebo effect* can be defined as a negative effect that occurs after receiving treatment (therapy, medication), even when the treatment is inert (inactive, sham).

It is important to note that negative effects seen when taking active substances, reported as drug side effects, can often be at least partly attributed to a combination of effects from the substance's constituents (specifics), and those from nocebo effects (non-specifics).

Studies suggest that nocebo effects can contribute appreciably to a variety of medical symptoms, adverse events in clinical trials and medical care, and public health "mass **psychogenic** illness" outbreaks. Primary

mechanisms of the nocebo effect that are often discussed include negative suggestions and expectations. However, other mechanisms are often involved with the negative response.

The term nocebo, Latin for "I will harm," was chosen by Walter Kennedy, in 1961, as the counterpart of placebo, Latin for "I will please" (Kennedy, 1961). The term was introduced a few years after Henry Beecher published his **seminal** paper on the placebo effect (Rajagopal, 2007).

Kennedy emphasized that there's no such thing as a "nocebo effect," there's only a "nocebo response." Some individuals use the terms interchangeably while others differentiate. The same can be said concerning placebo; some researchers distinguish between placebo effect and placebo response. Those distinctions will not be discussed in this article. For the sake of our present discussion let's assume the terms are synonymous.

Kennedy claimed that a nocebo reaction was subject-centered and that the term nocebo reaction specifically referred to "a quality inherent in the patient rather than in the remedy" (Kennedy, 1961).

Stewart-Williams and Podd argue that using the opposing terms placebo and nocebo is counterproductive (Stewart-Williams, & Podd, 2004). There are two key problems when dichotomizing the terms.

First, the same treatment (substance) can produce **analgesia** and **hyperalgesia**. Analgesia by definition would be a placebo while hyperalgesia would be a nocebo. A second problem is that the same effect may be desirable for one person while undesirable for others. In the former case, the effect would be a placebo, and in the latter, a nocebo.

In their criticism of the placebo nocebo dichotomy, Stewart-Williams & Podd go on to discuss two more major problems. Refer to these researchers' work, *The Placebo Effect: Dissolving the Expectancy Versus Conditioning Debate*, published in the *Psychological Bulletin* for a detailed discussion.

The research on nocebo effects is expanding, and with this new body of research we will be able to gain more knowledge on the other side of the placebo effect.

Analyzing Primary Sources

1. *Identifying* Why is it inaccurate to say that the placebo effect is "all in your head"?

2. *Speculating* What are some of the risks of listing the possible side effects of a medication?

3. *Identifying Central Issues* What are the two problems with having the opposite terms "placebo" and "nocebo"?

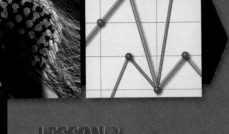

networks
There's More Online!

☑ **CHART** A Frequency Distribution

☑ **CHART** A Frequency Polygon

☑ **CHART** Kate's Data

☑ **DIAGRAM** Measures of Central Tendency

☑ **GRAPH** A Normal Curve

☑ **GRAPH** A Scatterplot

☑ **GRAPH** Standard Deviation

☑ **SELF-CHECK QUIZ**

Reading **HELP**DESK

Academic Vocabulary

• statistics   • significant

Content Vocabulary

• descriptive statistics
• frequency distribution
• normal curve
• central tendency
• standard deviation
• variance
• correlation coefficient
• inferential statistics

TAKING NOTES:

Key Ideas and Details

Categorizing Fill in a graphic organizer like the one below to list the two basic categories of statistics. Then identify the tools researchers use for each category.

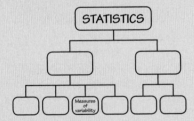

LESSON 3
Statistical Evaluation

ESSENTIAL QUESTION • *How do psychologists gather information?*

IT MATTERS BECAUSE

Long ago, just after Johns Hopkins University began admitting female students, someone reported a real shocker: Thirty-three and one-third percent of the women at Hopkins had married faculty members! The raw figures, however, gave a clearer picture. Only three women were enrolled, and one of them had married a male faculty member. Not all people use statistics honestly. In order to allow statistics to validly support a hypothesis, psychologists must collect meaningful data and evaluate them correctly.

Descriptive Statistics

GUIDING QUESTION *How is the central tendency used to evaluate data?*

How many times have you been told that in order to get good grades, you have to study? A psychology student named Kate has always restricted the amount of TV she watches during the week, particularly before a test. She has a friend, though, who does not watch TV before a test but who still does not get good grades. This fact challenges Kate's belief. Although Kate hypothesizes that among her classmates, those who watch less TV get better grades, she decides to conduct a survey to test the accuracy of her hypothesis. Kate asks 15 students in her class to write down how many hours of TV they watched the night before a psychology quiz and how many hours they watched on the night after the quiz. Kate collects additional data. She has her participants check off familiar products on a list of 20 brand-name items that were advertised on TV the night before the quiz. Kate also asks her participants to give their height.

When the data are turned in, Kate finds herself overwhelmed with the amount of information she has collected. Her data are presented in the graphic organizer you can see on the following page. How can she organize it all so that it makes sense? How can she analyze it to see whether it supports or contradicts her hypothesis? The answers to these questions are found in **statistics**, a branch of mathematics that enables researchers to organize and evaluate the data they collect. We will explore the statistical procedures that help psychologists make sense out of the masses of data they collect.

Before	After	Grade*	Products	Height
0.0	1.5	5	2	71
0.5	2.5	10	4	64
0.5	2.5	9	6	69
1.0	2.0	10	14	60
1.0	2.5	8	10	71
1.0	1.5	7	9	63
1.5	3.0	9	7	70
1.5	2.5	8	12	59
1.5	2.5	8	9	75
1.5	3.0	6	14	60
2.0	3.0	5	13	68
2.5	2.5	3	17	65
2.5	3.5	4	10	72
3.0	3.0	0	18	62
4.0	4.0	4	20	67

* Highest grade possible is 10.

< CHART

KATE'S DATA
Kate's data show the number of hours of television watched before and after the quiz, the grade on the quiz, the number of products recognized, and participants' height in inches.

▶ **CRITICAL THINKING**

1. *Analyzing* How much television did the two students with the best grades watch before the quiz?

2. *Analyzing* What grade did the shortest student receive?

When a study such as Kate's is completed, the first task is to organize the data in as brief and clear a manner as possible. For Kate, this means that she must put her responses together in a logical format. When she does this, she is using descriptive statistics, the listing and summarizing of data in a practical, efficient way, such as through graphs and averages.

Distributions of Data

One of the first steps researchers take to organize their data is to create frequency tables and graphs. Tables and graphs provide a rough picture of the data. Are most of the scores bunched up within a small range of results or are they spread out along a broader range? What score occurs most often? What are the high and low scores? Frequency distributions and graphs provide researchers with their initial look at the data.

Kate is interested in how many hours of TV her participants watched the night before and the night after the quiz. She uses the numbers of hours of TV viewing as categories, and then she counts how many participants reported each category of hours before and after the quiz. She has created a table called a frequency distribution. A frequency distribution is a way of arranging data so that we know how often a particular score or observation occurs.

What can Kate do with this information? A common technique is to figure out percentages. This is done by dividing the frequency of participants within a category by the number of participants and multiplying by 100. Before the quiz, about 13 percent of her participants (2 divided by 15) watched TV for 2.5 hours.

statistics the branch of mathematics concerned with summarizing and making meaningful inferences from collections of data

descriptive statistics the listing and summarizing of data in a practical, efficient way

frequency distribution an arrangement of data that indicates how often a particular score or observation occurs

Hours	Frequency Before*	Frequency After*
0.0	1	0
0.5	2	0
1.0	3	0
1.5	4	2
2.0	1	1
2.5	2	6
3.0	1	4
3.5	0	1
4.0	1	1
Total	15	15

* Number of students

< CHART

A FREQUENCY DISTRIBUTION
This data arrangement shows how often a score or observation occurs.

▶ **CRITICAL THINKING**

1. *Analyzing* How many students watched three or more hours of television before the quiz?

2. *Explaining* Why is this frequency distribution an example of a descriptive statistic?

On the night after the quiz, 40 percent watched 2.5 hours of TV (6 divided by 15). If you are familiar with the use of percentages, you know that test grades are often expressed as percentages (the number of correct points divided by the total number of questions times 100). Sometimes frequency distributions include a column giving the percentage of each occurrence.

It is often easier to visualize frequency information in graph form. Since Kate is interested in how much TV her classmates watched, she decides to graph the results. Kate constructs a histogram. *Histograms* are very similar to bar graphs except they show frequency distribution by means of rectangles whose widths represent class intervals and whose areas are proportionate to the corresponding frequencies. Another kind of graph is the frequency polygon or frequency curve. Instead of boxes, a point is placed on the graph where the midpoint of the top of each histogram bar would be. Then the points are connected with straight lines.

Frequency polygons are useful because they provide a clear picture of the shape of the data distribution. Another important feature is that more than one set of data can be graphed at the same time. For example, Kate might be interested in comparing how much TV was watched the night before the quiz with the amount watched the evening after the quiz. She can graph the "after quiz" data using a different kind of line. The comparison is obvious; in general, her participants watched more TV on the night after the quiz than on the night before the quiz. Imagine that Kate could measure how much TV everyone in Chicago watched in one night. If she could graph that much information, her graph would probably look something like the graph "A Normal Curve." A few people would watch little or no TV, a few would have the TV on all day, while most would watch a moderate amount. Therefore, the graph would be highest in the middle and taper off toward the tails, or ends, of the distribution, giving it the shape of a bell.

This curve is called the **normal curve** (or bell-shaped curve). Many variables, such as height, weight, and IQ, fall into such a curve if enough people are measured. The normal curve is symmetrical. This means that if a line is drawn down the middle of the curve, one side of the curve is a mirror image of the other side.

It is an important distribution because of certain mathematical characteristics. We can divide the curve into sections and predict how much of the curve, or what percentage of cases, falls within each section.

Measures of Central Tendency

Most of the time, researchers want to do more than organize data. They want to be able to summarize information about the distribution into statistics. For example, researchers might want to discuss the average height of men or the most common IQ test score. One of the most common ways of summarizing is to use a measure of **central tendency**—a number that describes something about the "average"

normal curve a graph of frequency distribution shaped like a symmetrical, bell-shaped curve; a graph of normally distributed data

central tendency a number that describes something about the "average" score of a distribution variance

GRAPH ∨

A FREQUENCY POLYGON

This graph shows the number of hours of TV watched the night before and after the quiz.

▶ CRITICAL THINKING

1. *Comparing* How do the two lines compare?

2. *Analyzing* At what two points do the lines meet?

FREQUENCY (NUMBER OF STUDENTS)

Hours of TV watched before quiz

Hours of TV watched after quiz

HOURS OF TV

score. We will use the grades from "Kate's Data" chart in the following examples.

The *mode* is the most frequent score. In a graphed frequency distribution, the mode is the peak of the graph. The most frequently occurring quiz grade is 8; that is, more students received an 8 than any other score. Distributions can have more than one mode. The data for height presented in "Kate's Data" chart have two modes: 60 and 71. Distributions with two modes are called *bimodal*.

When scores are put in order from least to most, the *median* is the middle score. Since the median is the midpoint of a set of values, it divides the frequency distribution into two halves. Therefore, 50 percent of the scores fall below the median, and 50 percent fall above the median. For an odd number of observations, the median is the exact middle value.

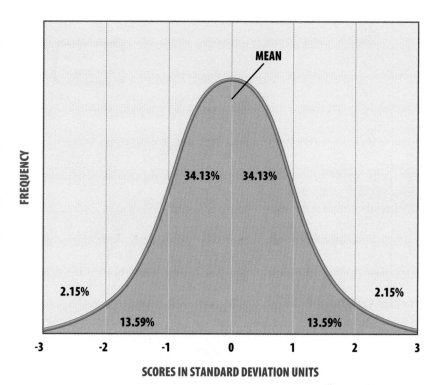

The *mean* is often thought of as an average and is the most commonly used measure of central tendency. To find the mean (or $\bar{X}$), add all the scores and then divide by the number of scores. The mean equals the sum of the scores on variable X divided by the total number of observations. For the quiz grades, the sum of the scores is 96, and the number of scores is 15. When 96 is divided by 15 our result is a mean quiz grade of 6.4. The mean can be considered the balance point of the distribution, like the middle of a seesaw, since it reflects all the scores in a data set. If the highest score in a data set is shifted higher, the mean will too. If we change the highest quiz grade from 10 to 20, the mean changes from 6.4 to 7.1.

^ GRAPH

A NORMAL CURVE
The maximum frequency lies in the center of a range of scores in a perfect normal curve. The frequency tapers off as you reach the edges of the two sides.

▶ CRITICAL THINKING

1. *Analyzing* Where is the mean located in a normal curve?

2. *Analyzing* What percentage of students fall within one standard deviation of the mean?

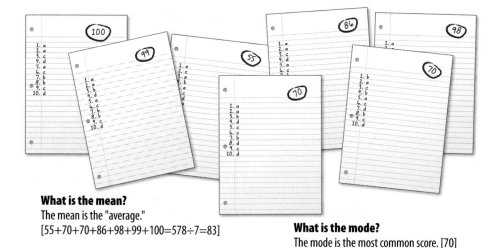

What is the mean?
The mean is the "average."
[55+70+70+86+98+99+100=578÷7=83]

What is the mode?
The mode is the most common score. [70]

What is the median?
The median is the middle score after the scores are ranked highest to lowest. [86]

< DIAGRAM

MEASURES OF CENTRAL TENDENCY
It is often useful to summarize a set of scores by identifying a number that represents the center, average, or most frequently occurring number of the distribution.

▶ CRITICAL THINKING

1. *Comparing* If your score matched the median on the last psychology quiz, how did you do in comparison to your classmates?

2. *Analyzing* If your score was 92 on the last psychology quiz, how would that affect the mean?

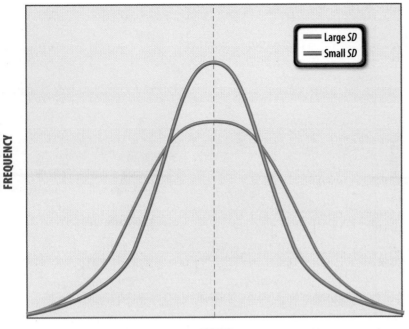

Large SD

Small SD

FREQUENCY

SCORES

standard deviation a
measure of variability that
describes an average distance of
every score from the mean

variance a measure of
variability that is the mean of the
squares of the deviations from the
mean of the set of data

correlation coefficient
describes the direction and
strength of the relationship
between two sets of variables

Measures of Variability

Distributions differ not only in their average score but also in terms of how spread out, or how variable, the scores are. The "Standard Deviation" graphic on this page shows two distributions drawn on the same axis. Each is symmetrical, and each has the same mean. However, the distributions differ in terms of their variability. Measures of variability provide an index of how spread out the scores of a distribution are. Commonly used measures of variability include range, variance, and standard deviation.

To compute the *range*, subtract the lowest score in a data set from the highest score and add 1. The highest quiz score is 10 and the lowest is 0, so the range is 11, representing 11 possible scores 0–10. The range uses only a small amount of information, and it is used only as a crude measure.

The **standard deviation** is a better measure of variability because, like the mean, it uses all the data points in its calculation. It is the most widely used measure of variability. The standard deviation is a measure of distance. It is like (but not exactly like) an average distance of every score to the mean of the scores. This distance is called a *deviation* and is calculated: $X - \overline{X}$. Scores above the mean will have a positive deviation; scores below the mean will have a negative deviation. To find the standard deviation, you must find the **variance**. A variance shows how measured data vary from the mean of a set of data. The variance is the mean of the squares of the deviations from the mean of the set of data. The standard deviation is the square root of the variance. The size of the typical deviation depends on how variable, or spread out, the distribution is. If the distribution is very spread out, deviations tend to be large. If the distribution is bunched up, deviations tend to be small. The larger the standard deviation, the more spread out the scores, which is shown in the "Standard Deviation" graph.

Correlation Coefficients

A **correlation coefficient** describes the direction and strength of the relationship between two sets of observations. The most commonly used measure is the Pearson correlation coefficient (*r*). A coefficient with a plus (+) sign indicates a *positive correlation*. This means that as one variable *increases*, the second variable also *increases*. For example, the more you jog, the better your cardiovascular system works. A coefficient with a minus (-) sign indicates a *negative correlation*; as one variable *increases*, the second variable *decreases*. For example, the more hours a person spends watching TV, the fewer hours are available for studying. Correlations can take any value between +1 and –1 including 0. An *r* near +1 or –1 indicates a strong relationship (either positive or negative), while an *r* near 0 indicates a weak relationship. Generally, an *r* from ±0.60 to ±1.0 indicates a strong correlation, from ±0.30 to ±0.60 a moderate correlation, and from 0 to ±0.30 a weak correlation. A correlation of ±1.0 indicates a perfect relationship between two variables and is very rare.

To get an idea of how her data look, Kate draws some scatterplots. A *scatterplot* is a graph of participants' scores on the two variables, and it demonstrates the direction of the relationship between them. The graphic "A Scatterplot" illustrates one of Kate's correlations. Note that each point represents one person's score on two variables, one plotted on the X-axis and the other on the Y-axis.

☑ **READING PROGRESS CHECK**

Identifying What is the purpose of a correlation coefficient?

Inferential Statistics

GUIDING QUESTION *Why are inferential statistics important to experimenters?*

The purpose of descriptive statistics is to describe the characteristics of a sample. Psychologists, however, are not only interested in the information they collect from their participants, but they also want to make generalizations about the population from which the participants come. To make such generalizations, they need the tools of inferential statistics. Using **inferential statistics**, researchers can determine whether the data they collect support their hypotheses, or whether their results are merely due to chance outcomes.

Probability and Chance

If you toss a coin in the air, what is the probability that it will land with heads facing up? Since there are only two possible outcomes, the probability of heads is 0.50. If you toss a coin 100 times, you would expect 50 heads and 50 tails. If the results were 55 heads and 45 tails, would you think the coin is fair? What if it were 100 heads and zero tails?

When a researcher completes an experiment, there are lots of data to analyze. The researcher must determine whether the findings from the experiment support the hypothesis (for example, the coin is fair) or whether the results are due to chance. To do this, the researcher must perform statistical tests, called measures of statistical significance. When researchers conclude that their findings are statistically **significant**, they are stating, at a high level of confidence, that their results are not due to chance.

Statistical Significance

For many traits in a large population, the frequency distribution follows a characteristic pattern, called the normal curve. For example, if you measured the heights of 500 high school students chosen at random, you would find very few extremely tall and very few extremely short people. The majority of students would fall somewhere in the middle. Suppose Kate wants to know if her classmates watch more TV than the "average American." Since daily TV viewing is probably normally distributed, she can compare her results to the normal distribution if she knows the population's mean number of TV viewing hours.

inferential statistics numerical methods used to determine whether research data support a hypothesis or whether results were due to chance

significant results that are unlikely to have occurred by chance

∨ **GRAPH**

A SCATTERPLOT
When there is little or no relationship between two variables, the points in the scatterplot do not seem to fall into any pattern.

▶ **CRITICAL THINKING**

1. *Drawing Conclusions* What conclusions can you draw from this scatterplot?

2. *Calculating* Would the correlation for this scatterplot be closer to 0 or closer to −1?

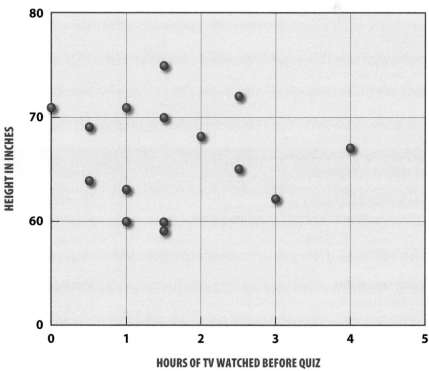

HEIGHT IN INCHES

HOURS OF TV WATCHED BEFORE QUIZ

Quick Lab

DO SOME PEOPLE REALLY HAVE PSYCHIC POWERS?
A well-known psychic sometimes begins his performance by saying the following: "Think of a number between 1 and 50. Both digits must be odd numbers, but they must not be the same. For example, it could be 15 but it could not be 11. Please choose a number and I will tell you what number you are thinking of."

Procedure
1. Develop a hypothesis that explains how the psychic is performing this feat. (Hint: The psychic uses statistics, not magic.)
2. Try out the psychic's act on several of your classmates and record their responses.

Analysis
1. Based on the psychic's directions, which numbers can be used and which numbers will most likely be used?
2. How do your observations support or contradict your hypothesis?

When psychologists evaluate the results of their studies, they ask: Could the results be due to chance? What researchers really want to know is whether the results are so extreme, or so far from the mean of the distribution, that they are more likely due to their independent variable and not due to chance.

The problem is that this question cannot be answered with a yes or no. This is why researchers use some guidelines to evaluate probabilities. Many researchers say that if the probability that their results were due to chance is less than 5 percent (0.05), then they are confident that the results are not due to chance. Some researchers want to be even more certain, and so they use 1 percent (0.01) as their level of confidence. When the probability of a result is 0.05 or 0.01 (or whatever level the researcher sets), we say that the result is *statistically significant*. It is important to remember that probability tells us how likely it is that an event or outcome is due to chance, but not whether the event is *actually* due to chance. When does a statistically significant result *not* represent an important finding? Many statistical tests are affected by sample size. A small difference between groups may be magnified by a large sample and may result in a statistically significant finding. The difference, however, may be so small that it is not a *meaningful* difference.

✓ READING PROGRESS CHECK

Explaining What does it mean when a psychologist says that research results are "statistically significant"?

LESSON 3 REVIEW

Reviewing Vocabulary
1. ***Defining*** What does the term *normal curve* mean?

2. ***Explaining*** How does the standard deviation measure the variability of scores?

Using Your Notes
3. ***Categorizing*** Review the notes that you completed during the lesson to define the two basic categories of statistics and provide examples for each category.

Answering the Guiding Questions
4. ***Analyzing*** How is the central tendency used to evaluate data?

5. ***Interpreting Significance*** Why are inferential statistics important to the interpretation of experiments?

Writing Activity
6. ***Argument*** Consider the following statement: "Correlation implies causation." Write a paragraph in which you argue for or against this statement. Give specific reasons for your opinion. In your writing, include at least one example that supports your opinion.

Directions: On a separate sheet of paper, answer the questions below. Make sure you read carefully and answer all parts of the question.

Lesson Review

Lesson 1

1 *Identifying* Describe two methods a researcher can use to avoid obtaining a nonrepresentative sample.

2 *Making Predictions* What is a correlation? What kind of correlation would you expect between students' grades and class attendance?

3 *Analyzing* Why should psychologists question the results of an experiment that they have conducted for the first time?

Lesson 2

4 *Synthesizing* How do you think self-fulfilling prophesies might strengthen stereotypes about a specific cultural or racial group? Give an example in your answer.

5 *Explaining* How can the expectations of the participants bias the results of an experiment? How can the expectations of the experimenter bias the results?

6 *Summarizing* What was the hypothesis of the Milgram experiment? Did the results support this hypothesis? Explain your answer.

Lesson 3

7 *Identifying* Describe the three measures of central tendency and the two measures of variability. What do measures of variability tell a psychologist about research results?

8 *Explaining* What information is provided by a correlation coefficient about the data?

9 *Applying* Various kinds of statistics are used in sports. Provide examples of the statistics used in a specific sport.

21st Century Skills

Using Graphs Study the graph below. Then answer the questions that follow.

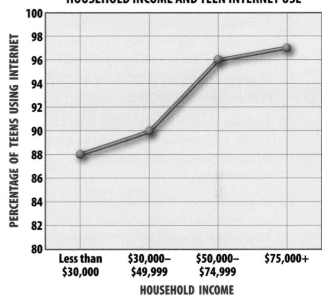

HOUSEHOLD INCOME AND TEEN INTERNET USE

(y-axis: PERCENTAGE OF TEENS USING INTERNET, 80–100)
(x-axis: HOUSEHOLD INCOME — Less than $30,000; $30,000–$49,999; $50,000–$74,999; $75,000+)

10 Is this an example of quantitative or qualitative research? Why?

11 What type of correlation is shown between household income and percentage of teens using the Internet?

Exploring the Essential Question

12 *Interpreting Significance* With a partner, create an oral presentation in which you explain the major factors that influence research results. Choose a specific research project to illustrate your points. Your presentation should explain how factors such as non-random sampling and the absence of a control group can cause results to lack external validity. You also should discuss different techniques for obtaining representative samples. Create a slide show to accompany your presentation.

Need Extra Help?

If You've Missed Question	1	2	3	4	5	6	7	8	9	10	11	12
Go to page	29	31	32	34	34	36	42	44	41	29	30	29

Directions: On a separate sheet of paper, answer the questions below. Make sure you read carefully and answer all parts of the question.

Critical Thinking Questions

13 *Making Decisions* Explain how you might conduct an experiment that tests the following hypothesis: You can raise blood pressure by making a participant anxious. Discuss the possible biases of your experiment.

14 *Contrasting* Explain how quantitative research methods differ from qualitative research methods. Describe two quantitative and two qualitative research methods discussed in this chapter and explain how their results might be presented graphically.

15 *Analyzing* Define descriptive statistics. Define inferential statistics. Why is each one important? Provide examples of each type, including the three measures of central tendency.

16 *Evaluating* Explain the difference between a single-blind and a double-blind experiment. Evaluate each one's effectiveness in preventing self-fulfilling prophecies and the placebo effect.

College and Career Readiness

17 *Research Skills* Use the Internet to conduct research to investigate the effects of cultural bias on research results. Try to locate suggestions for avoiding such bias. Write a report on your findings.

Research and Technology

18 *Exploring Issues* With a partner, use the Internet or other appropriate resource to locate the American Psychological Association's Guidelines for Ethical Conduct in the Care and Use of Nonhuman Animals in Research. Study the guidelines and then prepare a short oral presentation summarizing what you learned. Discuss both the pros and cons of such research. At the end of your presentation, state your own opinions about whether nonhuman animals should be used in basic and applied research, and, if so, whether the APA guidelines are appropriate.

DBQ Analyzing Primary Sources

Use the document to answer the following questions.

PRIMARY SOURCE

"*In many cases, withholding the intervention from the control group is ethical, since being in the study leaves them just as well off as they would have been had they not participated in the study. However, for vulnerable populations (e.g., students with disabilities) this may not be as straightforward. If researchers have good reason to believe that an intervention will benefit their study participants, denying this intervention to a control group may raise ethical questions. Conducting a pre-post test study addresses this ethical concern by offering the intervention to all study participants.*"

—*National Center for Technology Innovation*

19 *Evaluating* In what kinds of situations might an experimental study be halted?

20 *Making Generalizations* What does this document say about the importance of evaluating how a control group is affected by the research topic?

Psychology Journal Activity

21 *Informative/Explanatory* Review the entry in your Psychology Journal in which you described a recent event you witnessed or an encounter you had with another person. After learning in this chapter about the importance of carefully collecting information and separating fact from opinion, how have your ideas about your memory changed? Make a new entry describing these changes. Was your initial response about memory accurate? Why? If it was not accurate, how would you change it?

Need Extra Help?

If You've Missed Question	**13**	**14**	**15**	**16**	**17**	**18**	**19**	**20**	**21**
Go to page	31	29	41	34	35	32	32	31	26

TEXT: National Center for Technology Innovation (NCTI), American Institutes for Research (AIR)

Infancy and Childhood

ESSENTIAL QUESTIONS • *How do our abilities change from birth to childhood?*
• *What impact do parents have on the development of their children?*

Psychology Matters...

According to Greek mythology, the goddess Athena sprang full-grown from the head of her father Zeus. While it may seem efficient to skip childhood and adolescence, imagine what your life would be like today if you had missed those early steps. The process that brought you to your present stage of development helped make you the person you are today. In this chapter, we will learn about the development that occurs prior to birth, during infancy, and into childhood.

◀ Childhood is a time of rapid growth and development. Families provide an ideal setting for nurturing this growth.

Rob Howard/Corbis

49

CHAPTER 3

Lab Activity

Learning
Languages

RESEARCH QUESTION How do we acquire language?

Have you ever heard someone say that a toddler is like a sponge? In fact, a toddler's capacity for language is amazing: By the time a child is two years old, she will acquire many hundreds of words; if raised in a household where adults speak in two languages, she will acquire both with the same speed as a child who is exposed to just one.

However, how we acquire a second language later in life is a different cognitive process. We can learn to read, write, and speak fluently in a second language, but we are no longer "sponges." For most of us, it takes a lot of effort to learn a new language or to increase our vocabulary once we leave childhood. Two of the most common ways to learn a new word are with memory exercises or with physical activity. Is one method better than the other?

Psychology Journal Activity

Think about how you learn new words, whether in a foreign language class or in a favorite subject. Write about this experience in your Psychology Journal. Some things to consider as you write: Is learning new words difficult for you, or does it come easily? Do words in some subjects come more easily than in others? What tricks do you use when you are learning new words?

FINDING THE ANSWER...

HYPOTHESIS New words are easier to memorize when paired with a physical activity.

THE METHOD OF YOUR EXPERIMENT

MATERIALS   paper and writing utensils for six people

PROCEDURE   Invent and define five new words. These invented words must be verbs and must be simple actions that one can do in everyday life. Example: "snorfle" might mean to hold your nose closed for three seconds. Next, recruit six people. Randomly divide them into two groups of three, and place each group in two different rooms. The three people assigned to Group A must spend five minutes memorizing the five new words and their definitions. The three people in Group B must learn the five new words by acting them out repeatedly for five minutes, for example, pinching their noses closed for three seconds and saying "snorfle."

DATA COLLECTION   At the end of the five minutes, hand each person a blank sheet of paper and a writing utensil and ask them to write the words and definitions. Count the number of correct answers from Group A and average their scores. Do the same for Group B's scores. Does one group's results suggest that their learning method was more successful than the others?

ANALYSIS & APPLICATION

1. Did the results support the hypothesis?

2. What are some of the benefits of learning words with physical activity? With memory exercises?

3. If young people learn language better through physical activity than by memorization alone, how might schoolwork be different in the future?

networks   ONLINE LAB RESOURCES

Online you will find:

- An **interactive lab experience**, allowing you to put principles from this chapter into practice in a digital psychology lab environment. This chapter's interactive lab will include an experiment allowing you to explore issues related to infancy and childhood.

- A **Skills Handbook** that includes a guide for using the scientific method, creating experiments, and analyzing data.
- A **Notebook** where you can complete your Psychology Journal, and record and analyze data collected in your experiments.

Infancy and Childhood **51**

netw○rks

There's More Online!

☑ **CHART** Flowering of Language

☑ **CHART** Visual Preference of Infants

☑ **DIAGRAM** Physical and Motor Development

☑ **IMAGE** Visual Cliff

☑ **SELF-CHECK QUIZ**

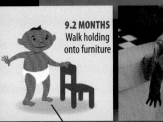

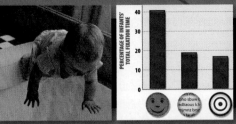

9.2 MONTHS
Walk holding onto furniture

Reading HELPDESK CCSS

Academic Vocabulary
- **capacity**
- **symbol**

Content Vocabulary
- **developmental psychology**
- **grasping reflex**
- **rooting reflex**
- **telegraphic speech**

TAKING NOTES:
Key Ideas and Details

SEQUENCING Use a graphic organizer like the one below to identify ways in which humans develop from conception through early childhood.

> Early Childhood
>> Infant
>>> Newborn Development
>>>> Fetal Development

LESSON 1
Physical, Perceptual, and Language Development

ESSENTIAL QUESTION • *How do our abilities change from birth to childhood?*

IT MATTERS BECAUSE

Human development is remarkable for the speed with which it takes place. In a mere three years, a human will move from a one-celled organism to a living, breathing, responsive child fully capable of walking, talking, thinking, and making its likes and dislikes clearly known. These complex and fascinating first steps into life involve numerous changes in physical and mental development.

Fetal and Newborn Development

GUIDING QUESTION *How are the capabilities of newborns measured?*

Developmental psychology is the study of how humans mature and why they develop as they do. Developmental psychologists study the following main issues: continuity versus discontinuity, stability versus change, and nature versus nurture. Psychologists studying continuity versus discontinuity ask the question: How much developmental change occurs gradually over time, and how much occurs in a series of clearly defined steps or stages? The question asked by psychologists studying the stability versus change issue is: Do various traits, such as shyness or extraversion, remain stable and consistent through life or do they change over time? Finally, on the question of nature versus nurture, psychologists ask: How much of development is the result of inheritance (heredity), and how much is the result of what we have learned?

Some psychologists believe that most of our behaviors are the result of genetics or inheritance. Others believe that most of our behaviors are the result of experience and learning. Separating biological and environmental causes of behavior is very complicated. Usually behavior develops as a result of the interaction of both heredity and environment. For example, Attention Deficit Hyperactivity Disorder (ADHD), which leads to the inability of children to stay focused on tasks, is a developmental disorder that demonstrates the close relationship between biological and environmental causes of behavior.

Fetal Development

Human development begins long before an infant is born. Over the span of roughly 40 weeks, a fertilized egg develops into a newborn baby. This development is rapid and complex. By the end of the first week, the embryo consists of more than 100 cells. By Week 2, these first cells are no longer alike. They are developing into a variety of cell types, including bone, muscle, nerve, and blood cells. Arteries and veins are forming by the end of Week 2. By the end of Week 4, the embryo consists of millions of cells and has the beginnings of eyes, ears, a brain, and a face. The heart and nervous system also begin development.

By the end of Week 5, the embryo has all its internal organs. The brain continues to develop during this period, and by Week 8 the number of nerve cells in the brain is increasing at the rate of 100,000 cells per minute. By the end of the first trimester, which is the first three months of development, the embryo is called a fetus and is continuing to grow at an amazing rate. At this time the fetus is about 3 inches long and looks like a tiny adult. The next several weeks are crucial as the organs develop and the fetus grows in size. Expectant mothers can feel strong movement and kicking—even hiccuping—inside them during the final stages of pregnancy. It is common for a fetus to suck its thumb, even though it has never suckled at its mother's breast or had a bottle.

Although protected in its mother's womb, the developing fetus remains vulnerable to factors that can harm its growth. Environmental factors, such as the mother's exposure to radiation, mercury, lead, or other contaminants, may damage the developing organs, particularly the brain. Exposure to diseases such as rubella, especially in the first month of pregnancy, can cause physical or mental damage in the early stages of the development of the embryo. In addition, a mother's use of alcohol, drugs, or nicotine can harm the developing fetus. Fetal alcohol syndrome, producing physical and mental damage in the fetus and behavioral difficulties in childhood, is one of many possible results.

Biological factors can affect the developing fetus, too. Some birth defects are caused by genetics. Conditions such as sickle cell anemia, Tay-Sachs disease, and Down syndrome are all hereditary. Sickle cell anemia can lead to heart deformities. Tay-Sachs disease usually leads to death within three to four years after birth.

developmental psychology the study of changes that occur as an individual matures

∨ DIAGRAM

PHYSICAL & MOTOR DEVELOPMENT
Infants achieve milestones in motor development at different times but in the same order. This chart shows the average ages when milestones are achieved.

▶ **CRITICAL THINKING**

1. **Analyzing Visuals** At what age would you expect an infant to start standing? To start walking?

2. **Interpreting** What test might a pediatrician use to measure the development of a three-month-old infant?

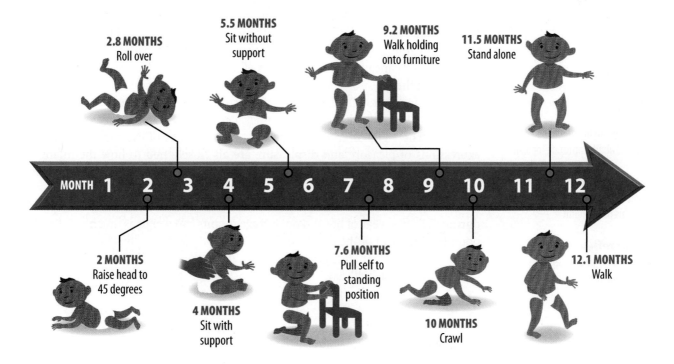

2.8 MONTHS Roll over

5.5 MONTHS Sit without support

9.2 MONTHS Walk holding onto furniture

11.5 MONTHS Stand alone

MONTH 1 2 3 4 5 6 7 8 9 10 11 12

2 MONTHS Raise head to 45 degrees

4 MONTHS Sit with support

7.6 MONTHS Pull self to standing position

10 MONTHS Crawl

12.1 MONTHS Walk

The *rooting* and *sucking* reflexes, present in all human infants, gradually decline in strength. The *grasping* reflex disappears during the first six months in those infants where it is present at birth. The Moro, or *startle*, reflex is quite unusual. An infant lying on its back when startled by a loud noise out of sight above his or her head will show a very complex response. The arms will spread out at right angles to the body and grasp upwards, and the legs will spread outward and pull in.

Now consider this situation. What would happen if someone ran a thumbnail right up the center bottom of your foot? Your toes would curl, and your foot would withdraw. Before her first birthday, an infant will do exactly the opposite—the toes flare outward, and the foot presses against the stimulus. This is called the *Babinski* reflex. Pediatricians use the shift in the Babinski from infantlike to adultlike form around the first birthday as a sign of normal neurological development.

capacity an individual's mental or physical ability, aptitude, or skill

grasping reflex an infant's clinging response to a touch on the palm of his or her hand

rooting reflex an infant's response in turning toward the source of touching that occurs anywhere around his or her mouth

Down syndrome produces varying levels of mental retardation. The developmental disorder ADHD seems to begin during fetal brain development; the brain scans of affected children are different from those of other children. The disorder may run in families, which suggests a genetic component, though its exact cause is not yet clear. Researchers continue to explore the possibility that some developmental disorders, such as ADHD, are the result of a combination of genetic, environmental, and physiological factors.

Newborn Development

While 40 weeks is the normal period needed for a human baby to develop, some are born before that time. If the baby is born before Week 37 it is considered premature. Although the baby's organs are formed by Week 5, the next 35 weeks are needed for the organs to grow and develop to the point that the fetus can survive after birth. The more time these organs have to grow, the better the chance of a premature baby's survival. Babies born as early as 17 weeks can survive, but they are more likely to have serious health difficulties. Because their organs are not fully formed, premature babies are subject to heart defects, respiratory problems, blindness, and brain damage. Hospitals with neonatal intensive care units are equipped to deal with the special needs of dangerously premature infants.

Newborns have the ability at birth to see, hear, smell, and respond to the environment. These abilities allow them to adapt to the world around them. Psychologists have found that birth puts staggering new demands on a baby's **capacity**, or ability, to adapt and survive. Newborns go from an environment in which they are protected from the world to one in which they are assaulted by it. From the moment it is born the newborn is confronted by bright lights, loud sounds, unfamiliar touches, and temperature extremes. The newborn is capable of certain automatic, coordinated movement patterns, called reflexes, that help them respond to their new environment. Reflexes can be triggered by the right stimuli. Many, but not all, infants are born with these reflexes.

The **grasping reflex**, for example, is a response to a touch on the palm of the hand. Infants can grasp an object, such as a finger, with enough strength that they can be lifted into the air. Also vital is the **rooting reflex**. When alert newborns are touched anywhere around the mouth, they will move their head and mouth toward the source of the touch. In this way the touch of a mother's breast on her newborn's cheek guides the infant's mouth toward her nipple. The sucking that follows such contact is one of the infant's most complex reflexes. The infant is able to suck, breathe, and swallow milk twice a second without getting confused.

How do we measure the capabilities of newborn infants who cannot speak or understand the questions of curious psychologists? One reasonable way to answer these questions is to take advantage of the things infants *can* do. What they can do is suck, turn their heads, look at things, cry, smile, and show signs of surprise or fright. The vigor of an infant's sucking, the patterns of eye movements, and expressions of pleasure and displeasure are all closely tied to how the infant is being stimulated. By measuring these behaviors while stimulating the infant in different ways, we can infer how the infant perceives the world.

Infants on average weigh 7.3 pounds at birth. Their weight can grow rapidly during their first year of life and on average infants can weigh as much as 20 or 25 pounds by the end of the first year. This first year also sees substantial growth in length. From birth, infants grow about 1 inch per month during their first year of life. By their first birthday, infants are on average 1.5 times longer than their length at birth. The changes that happen in the first years of life are substantial. In the space of two years, the grasping, rooting, searching infant will develop into a child who can walk, talk, and feed herself or himself. This transformation is the result of both maturation and learning.

Maturation

Infants will begin to lift their heads at about 3 months, smile at 4 months, and grasp objects at 5 to 6 months. Crawling appears at 8 to 10 months. By this time infants may be able to pull themselves into a standing position, although they will fall if they let go. They will begin to walk 3 or 4 months later, tentatively at first, but gradually acquiring a sense of balance. Psychologists call this complex growth process maturation.

Maturation is as important to development as learning or experience, especially in the first years. Unless children are persistently underfed, severely restricted in their movements, or deprived of human contact and things to look at, they will develop more or less according to this schedule. Purely as a matter of efficiency, it is worthwhile to wait until an infant reaches *maturational readiness* before pushing that infant into mastering new skills. No amount of coaching will enable children to walk or speak before they are physiologically ready.

The process of maturation becomes obvious when you think about walking. Infants lack the physical control walking requires. By the end of the first year, however, the nerves connected to the muscles have grown and the infant is ready to walk. By recording the ages at which thousands of infants first began to sit upright, to crawl, and to try a few steps, psychologists were able to develop an approximate timetable of maturation. This schedule helps doctors and other health professionals spot potential abnormalities. If a child has not begun to talk by the age of 2½, a doctor will recommend tests to determine if something is wrong.

Elizabeth Crews/The Image Works

The visual cliff study demonstrated that infants display the ability to perceive depth. Though some, such as the infant at left, demonstrate little fear of it. Researchers found that infants' heart rates increased as they approached the perceived drop-off of the visual cliff.

▶ **CRITICAL THINKING**

Hypothesizing Why do you think researchers measured the infants' heart rates during this experiment?

VISUAL PREFERENCE OF INFANTS

Three- or four-month-old infants show a strong preference for faces and patterns, suggesting that infants are born with and develop visual preferences.

▶ **CRITICAL THINKING**

1. *Assessing* For which circle did infants show the least preference? Why do you think this was so?

2. *Interpreting* Why do you think infants showed the greatest visual preference for the face image?

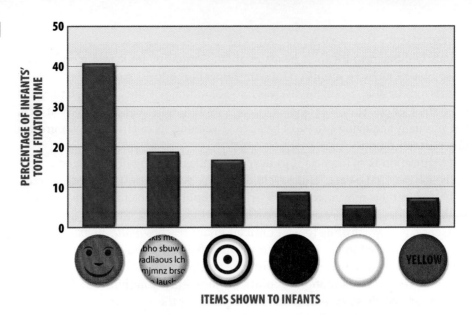

PERCENTAGE OF INFANTS' TOTAL FIXATION TIME

ITEMS SHOWN TO INFANTS

One of the facts to emerge from this effort, however, is that the maturational plan inside each child is unique. The average infant starts walking at 12 to 13 months. Some, though, are ready at 9 months, and others delay walking until 18 months. Each infant also has his or her own temperament. Some infants are extremely active from birth and some are quiet. Some are cuddly and some are stiff. Some cry a great deal and some do not. Although no two infants are exactly alike and no two mature according to the same timetable, most infants progress through the same sequential steps. Identifying similarities and differences in growth patterns is one of the many challenges for developmental psychologists.

Perceptual Development

Newborns can do more than grasp and suck. They also look at their bodies and at their surroundings. In the early months of life, the human brain continues to develop, and external experiences directly influence changes in the infant's perceptual development. That is, the newborn's brain continues to "wire" itself in response to its environmental stimuli, such as light, color, and movement. Different areas of the brain develop as the infant matures to support different processes of perception, such as vision, hearing, taste, touch, and smell, as well as perception of movement, color, and depth. Auditory perception—especially voice recognition—is in place at birth, while brain areas implicated for vision continue to develop after the baby is born.

In 1961 researcher Robert Fantz showed infants different faces and discovered that babies have a preference for looking at human faces and patterned materials. Infants also benefit greatly from being touched by their parents. A pair of experimenters devised the visual cliff to determine whether infants have depth perception. The visual cliff is a platform, part of which has a checkerboard pattern. The other part consists of a sheet of glass with the checkerboard pattern a few feet below it. This creates the view of a clifflike drop-off. Whereas very young infants seemed unafraid, older infants (6 months and older) who were experienced at crawling refused to cross over the cliff. The older infants had explored the world, apparently finding that drop-offs are dangerous. Also, researchers found that there were changes in the heart rates of very young infants as they would crawl farther, implying that newborns are born with some perceptual capabilities.

✔ READING PROGRESS CHECK

Describing What tests would you expect a physician to make regarding the developmental progress of a three-month-old baby?

Language Acquisition

GUIDING QUESTION *What steps are involved in learning language?*

Language and thought are closely intertwined. Both abilities involve using representations or **symbols**. We are able to think and talk about objects that are not present and about ideas that are not necessarily true. A child begins to think, to represent things to himself, before he is able to speak. The acquisition of language propels the child into further intellectual development.

Many psychologists argue that language is a learned behavior, while others claim it is inborn. Some psychologists claim there is a critical period, or a window of opportunity, for learning a language. Humans *may* have a sensitive period early in life in which acquisition of language is easier.

symbol something that stands for or suggests something else; a visible sign of something invisible

How Children Acquire Language

In the beginning, infants and toddlers learn the signs of communication—whether by hand or by mouth. As they grow, they will slowly develop their vocabulary and understanding of grammar. During the first year of life, the average child makes many sounds, beginning mostly with cooing sounds. These sounds develop into a babble that includes every sound humans can make—Chinese vowels, Xhosa clicks, German rolled *r*'s, and English *o*'s. Late in the first year, the strings of babble begin to sound more like the language the child hears. Children imitate the speech of their family members, and are greeted with approval whenever they say something that sounds like a word. In this way children learn to speak their native language, though they could just as easily learn any other.

The leap to using sounds as symbols occurs sometime early in the second year. The first attempts at saying words are primitive. "Ball" usually sounds like "ba," and "cookie" may even sound like "doo-da." The first real words usually refer to things the infant can see or touch. Often they are labels or commands ("dog!," "cookie!"). By the time children are 2 years old, they have a vocabulary of 500 to 1,500 words. Near the end of the second year, they begin to join words into two-word phrases. From about 18 months to 5 years of age, children are adding approximately 5 to 10 words a day to their vocabulary.

At age 2, though, a child's grammar is still unlike that of an adult. Children use **telegraphic speech** such as "Where apple?" or "Daddy fall." They leave out words or use the wrong verb tense but still get the intended message across to the listener.

telegraphic speech the kind of verbal utterances in which words are left out, but the meaning is usually clear

⌄ CHART

FLOWERING OF LANGUAGE
Between the ages of 2 and 5, the typical child learns an average of 10 words a day—nearly 1 word every hour awake!

▶ CRITICAL THINKING

1. *Analyzing* When should new parents expect to hear their baby's first word?

2. *Predicting* When a pediatrician is measuring the capabilities of a three-year-old, what level of speech would he or she expect to hear?

Age	Language Abilities	Example
1 year	Babbling begins and increases; by year's end, infant masters sounds of own language and usually says his or her first word	baba mama
2 years	Infant will progress to saying dozens of words; begins to speak in paired words; to ask a question, child issues a declaration in a rising tone; to negate something, child uses nouns with a negative word	Allgone ball. More ball. Jenny go? No ball.
3 years	Child acquires more grammatical knowledge; says appropriate sentences; uses simple declaratives; produces correct negative sentences; average size of vocabulary is over 5,000 words	I eating. I'm eating Don't go.
4 years	Child uses more grammatical rules and future tense; asks questions in adult form; average vocabulary is about 9,000 words	Will Jenny go? I can't go. Why is Jenny crying?
5 years	Child uses more complex clauses; joins two or more ideas in one sentence; has problems with noun/verb agreement	I see what you did.

Source: Adapted from *Developmental Psychology* by Howard Gardner, 1963.

As psychologists have discovered, 2-year-olds already understand certain rules. They place words in the same order adults do. At first children imitate the correct verb form: "Daddy went yesterday." Once children discover the rule for forming past tenses, they replace the correct form with sentences like "Daddy *goed* yesterday." When the correct form appears, the child has shifted from imitation to rule-based language. By age 4 or 5, children have a several thousand word vocabulary.

Scientists have long known that areas in the left hemisphere of the brain are used for learning how to speak and understand language. Several other areas of the brain are also involved in processing language. Studying babies who were born prematurely can begin to explain the brain's role in language development. Children born prematurely may have a more difficult time with language as it becomes more complex. One study found that preterm babies can show normal language development until they are around age 2, while language is fairly simple. Research using brain imagery suggests that the brain can create neurological connections that help compensate for the babies' early development. As language becomes more complex, however, it appears that the brain is limited in its ability to compensate.

Animals and Language

We have been able to learn much about language acquisition from animal research. Psychologists believe that chimpanzees develop at least as far as 2-year-old humans, as they will look for a toy or a bit of food that has disappeared. They can represent the existence of that toy or bit of food mentally. Can they be taught to "talk" about it? Beatrice and Allen Gardner raised a baby chimp named Washoe in their home and taught her to use American Sign Language. At 3½ years of age, Washoe knew at least 87 signs that could represent words such as *food*, *dog*, and *toothbrush*. By age 5, Washoe used more than 160 signs. Chimpanzees have been trained on special typewriters connected to computers. One chimpanzee, Panzee, used a special computer keyboard with symbols to communicate with humans.

The chimps use only some aspects of the human language. Chimps use words as symbols but do not apply grammatical rules. The ability to arrange symbols in new combinations to produce new meanings is especially well developed in the human brain. The rules for such organization of symbols are called *grammar*. Grammatical rules are what make the sentence "the rhinoceros roared at the boy" mean the same thing as "the boy was roared at by the rhinoceros." It is in our unique ability to use such grammatical rules that we surpass the simpler language of the chimpanzee.

☑ **READING PROGRESS CHECK**

Explaining What is the role of the brain in language acquisition?

LESSON 1 REVIEW

Reviewing Vocabulary

1. *Identifying* Describe two reflexes that infants display.

2. *Making Connections* How is telegraphic speech different from grammatical speech?

Using Your Notes

3. *Comparing* Use your notes to compare the development of a fetus with development in early childhood.

Answering the Guiding Questions

4. *Stating* How can the capabilities of newborns be measured?

5. *Listing* What steps are involved in learning language?

Writing Activity

6. *Informative/Explanatory* Research the neonatal intensive care options available at hospitals in or near your community. Visit the Web site of the hospital to learn the level and scope of care available for premature infants. Then, research how environmental factors assist in brain development of a premature baby. Assess the level of care provided by your hospital, and present your findings in an essay.

Case Study

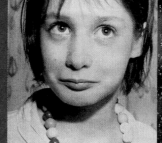
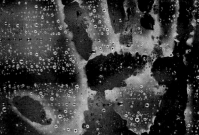

Too Late for Words: The Case of Genie

Period of Study: 1981

Introduction: In 1970 an unusual and unfortunate discovery was made in California. A 13-year-old girl known as "Genie" had spent all 13 years of her life locked in a room isolated from the world. Her parents had kept her harnessed to a potty-chair, which allowed only small movements of her hands and feet. At night Genie was put in a type of straitjacket and forcefully placed in a wire cage. Her parents refused to communicate with her in any way and demanded Genie's siblings avoid any form of communication with her as well. Genie was discovered by a combined effort of people in social services and the police. When she was discovered, she had no bowel or bladder control, could not chew solid food, had severely damaged posture from years of sitting, and she could not speak or understand language. After nursing her back to physical health, Genie's caregivers called upon psychologists to evaluate her mental and emotional conditions, as well as to begin teaching her how to communicate.

Hypothesis: The unfortunate case of Genie provided psychologists with some clues in defining whether language can be learned at any point in time or if there is a specific stage of development in which humans need to learn language and communication skills. The control of language has been traced to the left hemisphere of the brain. However, much evidence suggests a window exists in early childhood that allows language to be learned easily.

Method: Placed in a hospital, Genie was described as "a pitiful, malformed, incontinent, unsocialized, and severely malnourished creature." Genie was given tests that were designed to measure social maturity and school-level placement. She scored at a level equal to that of a normal 1-year-old. As time passed, Genie learned to recognize her written name. After 7 months passed, she began to develop spoken use of the phrases "stopit" and "nomore," one-word utterances similar to what toddlers use. One-word use progressed to two

words. However, Genie's development was slower than that of a toddler with similar language skills.

Results: Genie made limited progress in language development. After 7 years had passed, she had acquired as much language skill as a normal child learns in 2 to 3 years. When she was 24 years old, she had the language skills of a 5-year-old. Even though Genie learned much about language, she could not fully understand grammar or the use of pronouns and was unable to control the pitch of her voice. Perhaps Genie's window for learning language had passed; thus her brain could only understand language in a simplified form. The physical, emotional, and mental abuse that Genie sustained during her first 13 years of life undoubtedly played key roles in her development.

PRIMARY SOURCE

Noam Chomsky, of the MIT Department of Linguistics & Philosophy, suggested that language is an ability born with all people. He hypothesized that people are born with an understanding of the rules, which he calls "Universal Grammar." These rules provide people with the ability to build and use human languages.

"The most striking aspect of linguistic competence is what we may call the 'creativity of language,' that is, the speaker's ability to produce new sentences, sentences that are immediately understood by other speakers although they bear no physical resemblance to sentences which are 'familiar.'"

—*Noam Chomsky*

Analyzing the Case Study

1. *Identifying Cause and Effect* Why was Genie unable to speak coherently or understand language when she was found?

2. *Assessing* Describe Genie's ability to learn to use language properly. How much progress in language development did Genie make? Explain.

3. *Drawing Conclusions* What conclusions can you draw from this case and your study of the chapter regarding a window of opportunity to learn language? Are the results conclusive? Explain.

4. *Integrating Information* What does the case of Genie demonstrate about Chomsky's hypothesis?

networks

There's More Online!

- ☑ **IMAGE** Imprinting
- ☑ **IMAGE** Parental Scaffolding
- ☑ **TABLE** Piaget's Stages of Cognitive Development
- ☑ **TABLE** Tasks to Measure Conservation
- ☑ **SELF-CHECK QUIZ**

Reading **HELP**DESK CCSS

Academic Vocabulary

- invariably • research

Content Vocabulary

- schema
- assimilation
- accommodation
- representational thought
- conservation
- egocentric
- imprinting

TAKING NOTES:
Integration of Knowledge and Ideas

SUMMARIZING Use a table like the one below to record the level of cognitive and emotional development in a child at each age.

Age	Cognitive Development	Emotional Development
1 – 12 months		
12 – 24 months		
2 – 4 years		
5 – 7 years		

LESSON 2

Cognitive and Emotional Development

ESSENTIAL QUESTION • *How do our abilities change from birth to childhood?*

IT MATTERS BECAUSE

If you have a younger brother or sister, you may remember times when your parents insisted that you let the younger one play with you and your friends. No matter how often you explained hide-and-seek to your 4-year-old brother, he spoiled the game. Why couldn't he understand that he had to keep quiet or he would be found right away?

Cognitive Development

GUIDING QUESTION *What are the stages of cognitive development in children?*

A newborn baby is not simply a small adult. A baby develops physically, mentally, and emotionally on the road to adulthood. Just as the body grows in size, strength, and ability, so too does the brain. The human brain develops most rapidly during the early years of childhood. This brain development allows children to learn and understand the world around them. This is called cognitive development—the construction of thought processes, such as thinking, recalling, and analyzing.

Spend just a little time with a child and it will become obvious that children think differently from adolescents and adults in numerous ways. It could be said that children form their own hypotheses about how the world works. In order to better understand the cognitive development of children, Swiss psychologist Jean Piaget (1896–1980) chronicled the development of thought in his own daughter, whom he referred to as "L.," more than 80 years ago. According to Piaget, intelligence, or the ability to understand, develops gradually as the child grows. The sharpest, most inquisitive 4-year-old simply cannot understand things that a 7-year-old grasps easily.

What accounts for the dramatic changes between the ages of 4 and 7? Piaget spent years observing, questioning, and playing games with babies and young children—including his own. He concluded that young children think in a different way than older children and adults; they use a different kind of logic. A 7-year-old is completely capable of answering the question "Who was born first, you or your mother?" but a 4-year-old is not capable of answering this same question. Intellectual development involves quantitative changes, or growth in the *amount* of information as well as qualitative changes, or differences in the *manner* of thinking.

Understanding the world involves the construction of **schemas**, or mental representations of the world. Each of us constructs intellectual schemas, applying them and changing them as needed. We try to understand a new or different object or concept by applying it to one of our preexisting schemas, or by changing one of our schemas to fit the object. We employ two different processes when using existing schemas or developing new ones: assimilation and accommodation. In the process of **assimilation**, we try to fit the new object into this schema. In the process of **accommodation**, we reverse this process and change our schema to fit the characteristics of the new object.

For example, suppose a child encounters a new block. The block fits his schema for other blocks he has encountered before. The child has stacked blocks before and can easily assimilate the new block into his existing stacking schema. Suppose he then encounters an open box. He may at first try to fit the box into his stacking schema but finds that a block just falls inside the box. Now his stacking schema must be altered to accommodate this new object. Assimilation and accommodation work together to produce intellectual growth and allow us to use our schemas in a variety of new ways. When events do not fit into existing schemas, new and grander schemas have to be created. The child begins to see and understand things in new ways.

Object Permanence

An infant's understanding exists only in the here and now. For infants, the sight of a toy, the way it feels in their hands, and the sensation it produces in their mouths are all that they know about the toy. They do not imagine it, picture it, think of it, remember it, or even forget it. When a toy is hidden from an infant, the infant acts as if the toy has ceased to exist. The infant does not look for it. Instead, the infant grabs whatever else he or she can find and plays with that new object, or he or she may simply start crying. At 7 to 12 months this pattern begins to change. When you take the infant's toy and hide it under a blanket while he or she is watching, the infant will search for it under the blanket. However, if you change tactics and put the toy behind your back, the infant will continue to look for it under the blanket—even if that infant was watching you the whole time.

You cannot fool a 12- to 18-month-old quite so easily. A child this age watches closely and searches for the toy in the last place she saw you put it. Suppose you take the toy, put it under the blanket, conceal it in your hands, and then put it behind your back. A 12-month-old will act surprised when she does not find the toy under the blanket—and keep searching there. An 18- to 24-month-old will guess what you have done and walk behind you to look. She knows the toy must be somewhere.

This is a giant step in intellectual development. The child has progressed from a stage where she apparently believed that her own actions created the world, to a stage where she realizes that people and objects are independent of her actions. Piaget called this concept object permanence. A child who lacks object permanence will reach for a visible toy but not for one that is hidden behind a barrier—even if the child has seen someone place the toy behind the barrier. A child who has object permanence, however, will reach for a toy he or she has seen being placed behind a barrier. The concept might be expressed in this way: "Things continue to exist even though they cannot be seen or touched." Understanding object permanence signifies a big step in the second year of a child's life.

Profiles in Psychology

Jean Piaget
(1896–1980)

Jean Piaget sought to answer one question in his life work: How does knowledge grow? To answer this question, Piaget spent his time watching and playing with thousands of children. He told them stories and listened to their stories. He invented problems for them to solve and asked them what they dreamed about.

Piaget discovered that children develop logic and think differently at different ages. Piaget's theory challenged the behaviorists' view that the environment determines behavior. He stressed a child's role in gaining knowledge.

Some of Piaget's findings are being questioned today. Even so, he is still considered the greatest child psychologist of the twentieth century.

▶ **CRITICAL THINKING**

Contrasting How would a behaviorist's view of object permanence differ from Piaget?

schema a conceptual framework a person uses to make sense of the world

assimilation the process of fitting objects and experiences into one's schemas

Representational Thought

The achievement of object permanence suggests that a child has begun to engage in what Piaget calls **representational thought**. The child's intelligence is no longer one of action only. Now, children can picture (or represent) things in their minds. At 14 months of age, Piaget's daughter demonstrated this. When she was out visiting another family, she happened to witness a child throwing a temper tantrum. She had never had a temper tantrum herself, but the next day she did—screaming, shaking her playpen, and stamping her feet just as she had seen the other child do. She had formed so clear an image of the tantrum in her mind that she was able to create an excellent imitation of it a day later. To Piaget, this meant that his daughter was using symbols. Soon she would learn to use a much more complex system of symbols—spoken language.

The Principle of Conservation

More complex intellectual abilities emerge in childhood. Between the ages of 5 and 7, most children begin to understand what Piaget calls **conservation**, the principle, or rule, that a given quantity does not change even when its appearance is changed in some way. For example, if you have two identical short, wide jars filled with water and you pour the contents of one of these jars into a tall, thin jar, a child under 5 will say that the tall jar contains more water than the short one. If you pour the water back into the short jar to show the amount has not changed, the child will still maintain that there was more water in the tall container. Children under 5 do not seem to be able to think about two dimensions such as height and width at the same time. They do not understand that a change in the width of the small glass is made up for by a change in the height of the tall glass.

Conservation happens because children use centered thought, or thought focused on one feature or aspect of a problem. Centered thought also results in largely **egocentric** thinking. Egocentric thinking refers to seeing and thinking of the world from your own standpoint and having difficulty understanding someone else's viewpoint and other perspectives. Egocentrism lessens as children age. By age 7, the same child from the above example will tell you that the tall jar contains the same amount of water as the short one.

TYPE OF CONSERVATION		
LENGTH COMPARISON		**CHILD IS ASKED** *Which stick is longer?*
		**PRECONSERVING CHILD** will say that one stick is longer.
FIRST DISPLAY The child agrees that the sticks are of equal length.	**SECOND DISPLAY** The experimenter moves one stick to the right so it is closer to the child.	**CONSERVING CHILD** will say that the sticks are the same length.
AMOUNT COMPARISON		**CHILD IS ASKED** *Do the two pieces have the same amount of clay?*
		**PRECONSERVING CHILD** will say that the long piece has more clay.
FIRST DISPLAY The child acknowledges that the balls have equal amounts of clay.	**SECOND DISPLAY** The experimenter rolls out one of the balls.	**CONSERVING CHILD** will say that the two pieces have the same amount of clay.

Stage	Approximate Age	General Characteristics
Sensorimotor	Birth–2 years	Behavior consists of simple motor responses to sensory stimuli; lacks concept of object permanence
Preoperational	2–7 years	Lacks operations (reversible mental processes); exhibits egocentric thinking; lacks concept of conservation; uses symbols (such as words or mental images) to solve simple problems or to talk about things that are not present
Concrete operations	7–11 years	Begins to understand concept of conservation; still has trouble with abstract ideas; classification abilities improve; masters concept of conservation
Formal operations	11 years–onward	Understands abstract ideas and hypothetical situations; capable of logical and deductive reasoning

Piaget's Stages of Cognitive Development

Piaget described the changes that occur in children's understanding in four stages of cognitive development. In the *sensorimotor stage*, the infant uses schemas that primarily involve his body and sensations. That is, during the first two years of the child's life, learning is done through movements and the sensations that result from them. A child can only form schemas for objects that they are seeing, hearing, or touching at that time. It is during this stage that the development of object permanence happens.

The *preoperational stage* emerges when the child begins to use mental images or symbols to understand things. Children use symbols in their play, for example, riding a broom as if it were a horse. Language also develops during this stage and children have an egocentric view of the world. During this stage, roughly between the ages of 2 and 7, children learn concrete concepts such as counting or classifying objects, but most of their thought is in the present and concrete thought, rather than thinking of abstract thought, or the past or future.

By the third stage, *concrete operations*, children are able to use logical schemas, but their understanding is limited to concrete objects or problems. During this stage, from about ages 7 to 11, children no longer focus on one feature of an object as they did in the preoperational stage, such as the height of a glass. They also begin to be able to see things from another person's viewpoint and imagining things or events that can happen outside of their own lives.

In the *formal operations stage*, usually over the age of 11, the person is able to solve abstract problems and think about ideological or abstract issues. They are able to speculate about what is possible in the future. According to Piaget, development through these four stages depends on both the maturation of the nervous system and on individual past experiences. Everyone goes through the stages in the same order, but not necessarily at the same age.

Piaget was considered one of the most influential and groundbreaking psychologists of his time, and since then, researchers have continued to build upon his ideas. However, many psychologists today think that although Piaget was accurate in his description of the sequence of cognitive stages, there is much about the development of children that he did not consider. For example, many contend that children in the preoperational stage are not as egocentric as Piaget proposed, and that they are able to consider situations that are not part of their concrete lives. They can have sympathy for others and understand their viewpoint. Some argue that Piaget's theories underestimate the ability of developing children, especially infants. Others think that, when it comes to the formal operational stage, Piaget's theories overestimate the abilities of teens; as their brains continue to develop, teens need more time to slowly develop abstract thinking and logic. Piaget's stages are now recognized as a framework of ideas to be explored in more depth, rather than the final word in children's cognitive development.

∧ TABLE

PIAGET'S STAGES OF COGNITIVE DEVELOPMENT
Piaget stressed the active role of the child in gaining knowledge. He also stressed the differences in the way a child thinks during different stages of maturity.

▶ CRITICAL THINKING

1. *Analyzing Visuals* At which of Piaget's stages do children lack the concept of conservation?

2. *Drawing Conclusions* Based on this chart, why would it be difficult for a 7-year-old child to understand the concept of algebraic variables?

egocentric a young child's inability to understand another person's perspective

According to Vygotsky's theory, adults provide children with supportive problem-solving methods.

▶ **CRITICAL THINKING**

Making Connections What kind of scaffolding might a parent or teacher provide while a child is learning to read?

A Different Approach: Lev Vygotsky

Russian psychologist Lev Vygotsky (1896–1934) had another perspective from which to study child development. Like Piaget, Vygotsky believed that children develop slowly in stages until they can function independently and feel confident enough to think for themselves. However, in contrast to Piaget's emphasis on the internal origin of schemas, Vygotsky emphasized an external origin of cognitive development, taking into account the culture the child comes from and the social relationships and interactions the child is exposed to. Vygotsky considered a child's surroundings a critical aspect of his or her development.

One of Vygotsky's concepts is the zone of proximal development, in other words, children learn from watching and working with others. The guidance and encouragement a child gets from her teacher or parent—and even from her siblings and peers—provides a scaffold, or support, for that child to perform a task. For example, when a child is learning to ride a bicycle, an adult is usually running alongside, holding the bicycle steady while the child learns to pedal and steer. When the child is ready, the adult provides less and less support until the scaffolding is no longer needed and the child is able to do the task alone. Then, too, while an adult models and encourages behavior such as learning to read or write, that adult is also providing scaffolding for the child to experience important ideas of the culture, such as the way people should interact with one another and form social relationships. Then, too, a child who is being taught something is not only learning an idea or task, but is also learning to solve problems and apply reasoning skills on his or her own.

In contrast to Piaget's belief that a child's cognitive development must precede learning, Vygotsky argued that social learning tends to precede cognitive development. According to Vygotsky, a child develops with the help of social and cultural interactions, and not just the maturation process of the brain as Piaget described. For this reason, cultural differences can be seen in the stages of a developing child. For instance, a child raised in a culture where there is more access to technologies and modern conveniences will quickly learn about those things, no matter what stage of development she is in.

☑ **READING PROGRESS CHECK**

Stating At what age should a child begin to understand the concept of object permanence?

Emotional Development

GUIDING QUESTION *How does attachment affect emotional development?*

While the child is developing the ability to use his body, to think, and to express himself, he is also developing emotionally. He begins to become attached to specific people and to care about what they think and feel. A child's emotional development is as important as his cognitive and physical development. It is the desire to connect with others that motivates a child to learn. How well a child learns, as well as the quality of the relationships that child has with others, depends in large part on the child's sense of emotional attachment and security.

Experiments with Animals

Experiments with baby birds and monkeys have shown that early in life there is a maturationally determined time of readiness for attachment. If the infant is too young or too old, the attachment usually cannot be formed, but the attachment itself is a kind of learning. If the attachment is not made, or if a different attachment is made, the infant will develop in a different way as a result.

Konrad Lorenz (1903–1989) became a pioneer in the field of animal learning. Lorenz discovered that baby geese become attached to their mothers in a rapid, virtually permanent learning process called **imprinting**. A few hours after they struggle out of their shells, goslings are ready to start waddling after the first thing they see that moves. Whatever it is, they usually stay with it and treat it as though it were their mother from that time on. Usually, of course, the first thing they see is the mother goose. Yet Lorenz found that if he substituted himself or some moving object like a green box being dragged along the ground, the goslings would follow that. Lorenz's goslings followed him wherever he went and ran to him when frightened, showing the importance of imprinting for survival.

Imprinting is hypothesized to have a critical period that is strongest about 13 to 16 hours after birth. A critical period is a time in the cycle of development when animals and humans are best able to learn a skill or behavior. Goslings are especially sensitive just after birth, and whatever they learn during this critical period makes a deep impression that resists change. If a gosling has imprinted on a human being instead of a goose, it may or may not correct its imprinted response when later exposed to its actual mother goose.

Imprinting inherited tendency of some newborn animals to follow the first moving object they see

The experimenter, Konrad Lorenz, was the first moving object the goslings saw after they hatched, so they became imprinted on him.

▶ **CRITICAL THINKING**

Making Connections How is imprinting related to survival?

An American psychologist, Harry Harlow (1905–1981), studied the relationship between mother and child in a species more similar to humans, the rhesus monkey. His first question was: What makes the mother so important? He tried to answer this question by taking baby monkeys away from their natural mothers as soon as they were born. Harlow raised the monkeys with two surrogate, or substitute, mothers. Each monkey could choose between a mother constructed of wood and wire and a mother constructed in the same way but covered with soft cloth. In some cases, the cloth mother was equipped with a bottle; in others, the wire mother was so equipped.

The results were dramatic. The young monkeys became strongly attached to the cloth mother, whether it gave food or not, and for the most part ignored the wire mother. If a frightening object was placed in the monkey's cage, the baby monkey would **invariably** run to the cloth mother for security, not to the wire mother. It was the touching—physical contact—that mattered, not the feeding. Harlow referred to this as *contact comfort*. He concluded that the young monkeys clung to the cloth mothers because of the need for contact comfort.

Human Infants

Is there a sensitive period when infants need to become attached to a caregiver, as Lorenz's experiments suggest? Some psychologists would answer this question with a firm "yes." Infants begin to form an attachment to their mothers, or to a surrogate mother, at about 6 months, when they are able to distinguish one person from another and are beginning to develop object permanence. Attachment is a deep, caring, close, and enduring emotional bond between an infant and caregiver. This attachment seems to be especially strong between the ages of 6 months and 3 years. By 3 years, the child has developed to the stage where he is able to remember and imagine his parents or caregivers and maintain a relationship with them in imagination even if they are absent.

When an attachment bond to one person has been formed, disruption can be disturbing to the infant. For example, when a 1-year-old child encounters a stranger, that child may display anxiety even when the mother is present. If the mother remains nearby, this anxiety, known as *stranger anxiety,* will pass. *Separation anxiety* occurs whenever the child is suddenly separated from the mother. If the separation persists over time, the child may then come to develop certain psychological disorders. Securely attached children are generally more sociable, well-adjusted, happier, and more cooperative. They often do better in school because they get along well with their peers and adults. Insecure attachment in infants is often a predictor of disorders in adolescents.

Mary Ainsworth, with John Bowlby, studied attachment in families. Ainsworth devised a technique called the Strange Situation to measure attachment. In this technique, mothers and children underwent a series of episodes that sometimes involved the mother leaving and coming back into the room when a stranger was present and when a stranger was not present. From her **research**, she found there were three patterns of attachment in children: *secure attachment, avoidant attachment,* and *resistant attachment.* Psychologists have since identified a fourth attachment, called *disorganized attachment.* The behaviors involved in evaluating attachment are the effort to maintain nearness to a caregiver and anxiety when separated from the caregiver.

invariably always

research a careful study of a subject, especially in order to discover new facts or information

Children with secure attachments are able to balance the need to explore their world with the need to be close to their parent or caregiver.

▶ **CRITICAL THINKING**

Making Connections What signs of resistant attachment is the child in this picture showing?

Lifesize/Getty Images

Infants who demonstrate secure attachment balance the need to explore and the need to be close. A securely attached infant may protest mildly when her mother leaves, but welcomes her back when she returns and is free of anger. An infant with avoidant attachment may be somewhat distressed at her mother's departure, play well by herself while she is away, but avoid or ignore her mother when she returns. An infant with resistant attachment is not upset when her mother leaves, but rejects her or acts angrily when she returns. An infant with disorganized attachment behaves inconsistently. She seems confused and acts in contradictory ways. This attachment seems to be the least secure attachment. Mothers who are sensitive and responsive tend to have securely attached infants. Affection and reliability are also important characteristics in developing a securely attached child. However, there is a complex interplay between caregivers and infants.

Ainsworth further identified three stages of attachment. During the first three months of life infants experience the initial attachment phase, where they attach themselves indiscriminately to caregivers. Around three or four months, infants move to the attachment-in-the-making phase, where infants develop preferences for familiar figures. Beginning at six or seven months, infants enter the clear-cut attachment phase in which they become more dependent on primary caregivers.

Attachment can become a loaded issue for families with children in daycare. With most mothers working at least part time, many children spend part of their day in a caregiving situation outside of their own home. Infants form attachments to their caregivers in daycare, particularly if the ratio of children per daycare worker is low and the quality of the stimulation the environment provides is high. Infants cared for at home and those in daycare are almost equally likely to form secure attachments with their caregivers.

✓ **READING PROGRESS CHECK**

Paraphrasing How does a securely attached child respond to his mother when she returns after an absence?

LESSON 2 REVIEW

Reviewing Vocabulary

1. *Making Connections* How do experiences alter our schemas? Describe two processes of change of schemas in Piaget's theory.

2. *Understanding Relationships* How is imprinting different from attachment?

Using Your Notes

3. *Synthesizing* Review the notes you completed during the lesson. Write a description of the cognitive and emotional development of a healthy, well-adjusted three-year-old child.

Answering the Guiding Questions

4. *Listing* What are Piaget's stages of cognitive development in children?

5. *Identifying Cause and Effect* How can attachment affect emotional development?

Writing Activity

6. *Informative/Explanatory* Write an observation-style paragraph describing the behavior of a child who displays an avoidant attachment reaction to his or her mother's separation and return.

Reader's Dictionary

Making Smarter Computers by Teaching Them to Think Like Children

causal: expressing or indicating cause

intuitive: without obvious inference or rational thought

Babies Remember Even as They Seem to Forget

milestone: a significant point in development

inkling: a vague idea

What can young children teach us about cognitive development? Children as young as infants may provide insights into the processes of learning and remembering. In these related articles, researchers have chosen to study infants and young children in order to gain insights into how we learn and how human development can help advance the technology we use.

Making Smarter
Computers
by Teaching Them to Think Like Children
By Lauren Gravitz

PRIMARY SOURCE

Rather than using computers to help children learn, one group of researchers at the University of California, Berkeley, is far more interested in using children to help computers learn. In cognitive development labs at the university, psychologists are using puppets, flashing toys, lollipops, and a variety of other tools to determine how young children—some not even talking yet—make calculations in their head that help them understand the world around them. By studying how the kids' fast-growing brains process information, the psychologists and their computer-scientist colleagues hope to create computers that think and react in more human-like ways.

While people constantly assess one another's mental state and use it to inform how they interact with each other, computers aren't yet able to evaluate a user's mood. But imagine if your computer could interpret facial expressions and tone of voice so as to read your frustration level, or put two-and-two together to understand that you work more slowly before you've had your morning coffee, it would be a huge leap forward for artificial intelligence.

"We're trying to understand what makes human beings such good learners. We learn language, **causal** relationships, and new concepts from small amounts of data," says Tom Griffiths, director of the university's computational cognitive science lab. "And children are particularly interesting because they're doing the largest amounts of learning. In just a few years, a child is going to speak a language, understand causal relationships in the world around him and learn concepts, like TV and computers, that haven't appeared anywhere in our evolutionary history."

The cognitive psychologists are testing infants, toddlers, and preschoolers to better understand how they figure out the world around them. One of the psychologists had toddlers watch her while she tasted different foods while making faces, then showed that the children were capable of empathy and could pick up on her preferences. Another one showed that even babies who can't yet speak seem to be capable of calculating odds ratios. When the researcher showed them two jars of candy, with different proportions of black and pink lollipops in each, then removed one from each without showing them the color, the infants almost always crawled toward the hidden pop removed from the primarily pink jar.

Figuring out how kids' developing brains make these calculations could lead to more **intuitive** computers that can interact more sensitively, intelligently, and responsively, in applications ranging from language learning, online tutoring and call-answering, to research labs in need of smarter processing power. "We have computer scientists, but we don't have computers that are scientists. That kind of causal reasoning and discovery is still something humans can do that computers can't," Griffiths says.

Babies
Remember
Even as They Seem to Forget

Johns Hopkins University

Fifteen years ago, textbooks on human development stated that babies of six months of age or younger had no sense of "object permanence"—the psychological term that describes an infant's belief that an object still exists even when it is out of sight. That meant that if mom or dad wasn't in the same room with junior, junior didn't have the sense that his parents were still in the world.

These days, psychologists know that isn't true: for young babies, out of sight doesn't automatically mean out of mind. But how much do babies remember about the world around them, and what details do their brains need to absorb in order to help them keep track of those things?

A new study led by a Johns Hopkins psychologist and child development expert has added a few pieces to this puzzle. Published in a recent issue of the journal Psychological Science, the study reveals that even though very young babies can't remember the details of an object that they were shown and which then was hidden, the infants' brains have a set of built in "pointers" that help them retain a notion that something they saw remains in existence even when they can't see it anymore.

"This study addresses one of the classic problems in the study of infant development: what information do infants need to remember about an object in order to remember that it still exists once it is out of their view?" said Melissa Kibbe, a post-doctoral researcher in the Department of Psychological and Brain Sciences at the Krieger School of Arts and Sciences at Johns Hopkins, who collaborated with colleague Alan Leslie at Rutgers University on the study. "The answer is, very little."

The team found that even though infants cannot remember the shapes of two hidden objects, they are surprised when those objects disappear completely. The conclusion? Infants do, indeed, remember an object's existence without remembering what that object is. This is important, Kibbe explains, because it sheds light on the brain mechanisms that support memory in infancy and beyond.

"Our results seem to indicate that the brain has a set of 'pointers' that it uses to pick out the things in the world that we need to keep track of," explains Kibbe, who did the majority of the work on this study while pursuing her doctorate in Leslie's laboratory at Rutgers. "The pointer itself doesn't give us any information about what it is pointing to, but it does tell us something is there. Infants use this sense to keep track of objects without having to remember what those objects are." In addition, the study may help researchers establish a more accurate timeline of the mental **milestones** of infancy and childhood.

In the study, six-month-olds watched as a triangle was placed behind a screen and then as a second object (a disk) was placed behind a second screen. Researchers then removed the first screen to reveal either the expected original triangle, the unexpected disk, or nothing at all, as if the triangle had vanished completely. The team then observed the infants' reactions, measuring how long they looked at expected versus unexpected outcomes. In the situation where the objects were swapped, the babies seemed to hardly notice a difference, Kibbe said, indicating that they didn't retain a memory of that object's shape. In their minds, a triangle and a disk were virtually interchangeable.

However, when one of the objects had disappeared, the babies were surprised and gazed longer at the empty space, indicating that they expected something to be where something was before. "In short, they retained an **inkling** of the object," said Leslie, of Rutgers.

Analyzing Primary Sources

1. *Analyzing* Why did the researchers discussed in the first article study learning in young children rather than adults?

2. *Contrasting* How did the findings of the researchers in the second article contradict previous ideas of object permanence?

3. *Speculating* How might the researchers in the first article use the findings discussed in the second article?

networks

There's More Online!

☑ **DIAGRAM** Erikson's Theory of Psychosocial Development

☑ **DIAGRAM** Freud's Theory of Psychosexual Development

☑ **CARTOON** Gender Roles

☑ **TABLE** Kohlberg's Stages of Moral Development

Reading HELPDESK (CCSS)

Academic Vocabulary

• theory   • issue

Content Vocabulary

• socialization
• identification
• sublimation
• role taking

TAKING NOTES:

Key Ideas and Details

ORGANIZING Use a graphic organizer like the one below to organize information on parenting styles and families as you read.

Parenting Style	Role of Parents	Role of Children

LESSON 3

Parenting Styles and Social Development

ESSENTIAL QUESTION • *What impact do parents have on the development of their children?*

IT MATTERS BECAUSE

Have you ever been seated near families with small children in a restaurant? If one child spent the entire meal crying, whining, or complaining, what were your thoughts? Chances are you did not blame the child but instead blamed the parents for this disruptive behavior. If a child at another table was quiet, content, and well behaved, you may have even compared the parents of the two children. You were evaluating parenting styles because of the children's behavior.

Parenting Styles

GUIDING QUESTION *What are the four types of parenting styles?*

The way in which children seek independence, and the ease with which they resolve conflicts about becoming adults, depends largely on the parent-child relationship. Diana Baumrind observed and interviewed nursery school children and their parents. Parenting styles may differ across cultures and groups, and Baumrind's research focused on European-American children. Follow-up observations when the children were 8 or 9 led to several conclusions about the impact of four distinct parenting styles, or methods, on children.

In authoritarian families, parents are the bosses of the home. The parents do not believe that they have to explain their actions or demands to their children. In fact, such parents may believe that their children have no right to question any parental decisions. Authoritarian parents are more likely to utilize strong disciplinary methods, including frequent spankings.

In democratic or authoritative families, children participate in decisions affecting their lives. There is a great deal of discussion and negotiation in such families. Parents listen to their children's reasons for wanting to go somewhere or do something and make an effort to explain their rules and expectations. The children make many decisions for themselves, but the parents retain the right to veto plans of which they

(l)LEMOINE/age fotostock; (r)Robin Nelson/ZUMA Press/Corbis

disapprove. The discipline in these families will probably be balanced between strict enforcement and gentler methods of securing compliance, mixing spanking, time out, and loss of privilege with verbal cues and encouragement.

In permissive or laissez-faire families, children have the final say. The parents may attempt to guide the children but give in when the children insist on having their own way. Or the parents may simply give up their child-rearing responsibilities—setting no rules about behavior, making no demands, voicing no expectations, virtually ignoring the young people in their house. Discipline in the permissive family might be given only in moments of extreme frustration, making it much less effective than where the boundaries are well-established and maintained. Psychologists have recently identified a fourth parenting style: uninvolved parents. These parents were typically egocentric in their child rearing and seemed uncommitted to their roles and quite distant from their children.

Effects of Parenting Styles

Numerous studies suggest that adolescents who have grown up in democratic or authoritative families are more confident of their own values and goals than other young people. This seems to come from two features—the *establishment of limits* on the child and *responding* to the child with warmth and support. The children of democratic families are more likely to want to make their own decisions with or without advice. There are several reasons for this: First, the child is able to *assume responsibility gradually.* He or she is not denied the opportunity to exercise judgment, as in authoritarian families, or given too much responsibility too soon, as in permissive families. Second, the child is more likely to *identify with parents* who love and respect him or her than with parents who treat him or her as incompetent or who seem indifferent. Finally, through their behavior toward the child, democratic parents *present a model of responsible, cooperative independence* for the growing person to imitate.

Although the style parents adopt in dealing with their children influences adolescent development, it would be wrong to conclude that parents are solely responsible for the way their children turn out. Children themselves may contribute to the style parents embrace, with consequences for their own personal development. Parents may adopt a laissez-faire attitude simply because they find that style the easiest way to cope with a teenager who insists on having his or her own way. Adolescents experiencing rapid physical and emotional changes may force their parents to make major adjustments in their parenting style.

Developmental issues such as ADHD, autism, Asperger syndrome, or other special needs also impact parenting styles. Even though a child may have reached an age at which a democratic parenting style would provide more responsibility, the child may not be ready to accept this responsibility. The ADHD child may need to be required to take medicine to relieve his or her symptoms. The child may need special therapy. In such situations, the parents may feel ineffective or overwhelmed by their child's needs. In some cases, this may lead to mistreatment.

Child Abuse

Child abuse includes the physical or mental injury, sexual abuse, negligent treatment, or mistreatment of children under the age of 18 by adults entrusted with their care. Accurate statistics are difficult to compile, since many incidents of child abuse go unreported. In 2010 more than 2.6 million cases of child abuse were reported. After investigation, an estimated 700,000 children were confirmed as victims of actual abuse or neglect situations.

Child abuse is viewed as a social problem that results from a variety of causes. Many abusive parents were themselves mistreated as children, suggesting that these parents may have learned an inappropriate way of caring for children. Such

Nature versus Nurture

Researcher Judith Rich Harris argues that other than the genes parents contribute to their children, they can have little to no impact on what kind of adult the child will become. Harris claims that peer groups, not parents, teach children how to behave in the world. So, according to her, the only influence parents have over their children is by choosing the environment in which their children meet other peers. Critics claim that there is a strong relationship between parenting styles and social development. They argue that although two children may share the same parents, they may be treated differently by them and, thus, turn out differently.

One of the most controversial aspects of parental discipline relates to the use of corporal punishment, particularly spanking. While people agree that beating a child is unacceptable, there are differences of opinion over whether spanking is the same as beating. One viewpoint asserts that a light spanking can prevent the child from doing something harmful. Another view holds that no form of physical punishment is effective and it will damage a child's self-esteem. All sides agree that, if a parent has a history of abuse, anger issues, or a tendency to over-discipline, corporal punishment should be avoided. Praise and positive reinforcement of good behavior minimize the need for discipline. Some nonviolent disciplines include time outs and loss of privilege. To be effective and avoid confusion appropriate methods of discipline should be used consistently.

theory a plausible or scientifically acceptable general principle or body of principles offered to explain phenomena

socialization the process of learning the rules of behavior of the culture within which an individual is born and will live

parents tend to use the harsh physical discipline that they saw their own parents using. Many abusive parents have little patience with their children. Often they have unrealistic expectations.

Overburdened and stressed parents are more likely to abuse their children. Low-birthweight infants and those children who are hyperactive or mentally or physically disadvantaged experience a higher than normal incidence of abuse. One reason for this higher incidence may be that such children are less responsive and more difficult to care for, thus making greater demands on and providing fewer rewards for the parents. Social-cultural stresses such as unemployment and lack of contact with family, friends, and groups in the community are other factors associated with child abuse.

Abuse has many developmental effects for its victims. It may rob children of their childhood and create a loss of trust and feelings of guilt. In turn, this may lead to antisocial behavior, depression, identity confusion, loss of self-esteem, and other emotional problems. Every state and most counties have social services agencies that provide protective services to children. They have legal authority to investigate reported incidents of child abuse.

Several strategies show promise in reducing child abuse. For example, parent education for abusive parents enables them to learn new ways of dealing with their children. By providing information about resources and a support system for these families, communities may reduce the incidence of child abuse. States, counties, cities, and private organizations provide protection for children in abusive situations. They also offer family counseling to help parents learn to discipline without abuse. Childhelp and the American Humane Association provide hotlines, literature, and information on child abuse.

✓ **READING PROGRESS CHECK**

Specifying According to research on European-American children, which parenting style seems to lead to more confident children?

Social Development

GUIDING QUESTION *What central themes are shared by Freud and Erikson's theories?*

As a child develops, he or she grows physically, mentally, emotionally, and socially. Researchers who study this development argue over how much is impacted by nature and how much by nurture. Psychologists also debate stability versus change and continuity versus discontinuity. Do our traits remain static from birth or do they change? Does change occur slowly over time or in a series of distinct steps? Most **theories** involve steps. Learning the rules of behavior of the culture in which you are born and grow up is a process known as **socialization**. To live with other people, a child has to learn what is considered acceptable and unacceptable behavior. This is not as easy as it sounds. Some social rules are considered very important and are inflexible. Other social rules leave room for individual decisions, so that sometimes there seems to be a gray area between right and wrong.

Some rules change from situation to situation. Some apply to certain categories of people. For example, some rules for boys in our society are different from the rules for girls. We tend to encourage boys to express aggression but not fear; traditionally, girls have been raised to express emotions but not ambitions. Of course, the rules for feminine behavior have changed over the years. Learning what the rules are—and when to apply or bend them—is, however, only one dimension of socialization. Every society has ideas about what is meaningful, valuable, worth striving for, and beautiful. Every society classifies people according to their family, sex, age, skills, personality characteristics, and other criteria. Every culture has notions about what makes individuals behave as they do. In absorbing these notions, a child acquires an identity as an individual member of a society, a member of different social categories, and a member of a family. Acquiring these identities is the second dimension of socialization.

Finally, socialization involves learning to live with other people and with oneself. Anyone who has seen the shock on a 2-year-old's face when another child takes a toy he wants, or the humiliation a 4-year-old experiences when she discovers she is unable to hit a baseball on the first try, knows how painful it can be to discover that other people have rights and that we all have limitations.

Freud's Theory of Psychosexual Development

Sigmund Freud believed that all children are born with powerful sexual and aggressive urges. In learning to control these impulses, children acquire a sense of right and wrong. The process—and the results—are different for boys and girls. According to Freud, in the first few years of life, boys and girls have similar experiences. Their erotic pleasures are obtained through the mouth, sucking at their mother's breast. Weaning the child from nursing is a period of frustration and conflict—it is the child's first experience with not getting what he or she wants. Freud called this the *oral stage* of development. Later the anus becomes the source of erotic pleasure, giving rise to what Freud called the *anal stage*. Through toilet training the child learns to curb freedom and establish social control.

A major conflict comes between the ages of 3 and 5, when children discover the pleasure they can obtain from their genitals. As a consequence, they become extremely aware of the differences between themselves and members of the opposite sex. In this *phallic stage*, according to Freud, the child becomes a rival for the affections of the parent of the opposite sex. The boy wants to win his mother for himself and finds himself in hostile conflict with his father. The girl wants her father for herself and tries to shut out her mother. These struggles take place on an unconscious level. Generally, the child and the parents do not have any clear awareness that it is going on. In this process, which is called **identification** with the aggressor, the boy takes on all his father's values and moral principles. Thus, at the same time that he learns to behave like a man, he internalizes his father's morality. The girl also goes through this process and begins to identify with her mother. She feels her mother's triumphs and failures as if they were her's and internalizes her mother's moral code.

Freud believed that at about age 5 or 6, children enter a *latency stage*. Sexual desires are pushed into the background, and children explore the world and learn new skills. This process of redirecting sexual impulses into learning tasks is called **sublimation**. Ideally, when one reaches the *genital stage* at adolescence, one derives as much satisfaction from giving pleasure as from receiving it. For Freud, personality development is essentially complete as we enter adolescence. Today, relatively few psychologists believe that sexual feelings disappear in childhood, or that Freud's stages are the norm.

identification the process by which a child adopts the values and principles of the same-sex parent

sublimation the process of redirecting sexual impulses into learning tasks

⌄ **DIAGRAM**

FREUD'S THEORY OF PSYCHOSEXUAL DEVELOPMENT

Freud identified traits common to various age groups and organized these into five stages of psychosexual development.

▶ **CRITICAL THINKING**

1. ***Reading Charts*** At what stage do children compete with their parents?

2. ***Determining Central Ideas*** What is the central theme of Freud's theory?

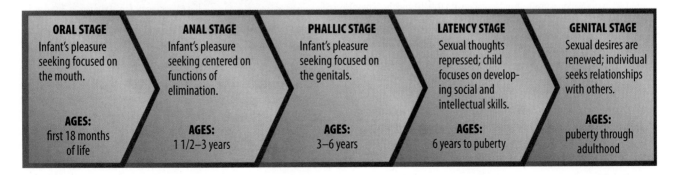

ORAL STAGE	ANAL STAGE	PHALLIC STAGE	LATENCY STAGE	GENITAL STAGE
Infant's pleasure seeking focused on the mouth.	Infant's pleasure seeking centered on functions of elimination.	Infant's pleasure seeking focused on the genitals.	Sexual thoughts repressed; child focuses on developing social and intellectual skills.	Sexual desires are renewed; individual seeks relationships with others.
AGES: first 18 months of life	AGES: 1 1/2–3 years	AGES: 3–6 years	AGES: 6 years to puberty	AGES: puberty through adulthood

Erikson's Theory of Psychosocial Development

Erik Erikson (1902–1994) took a broader view of human development than Freud in terms of both time and scope. Although he recognized the child's sexual and aggressive urges, he believed that the need for social approval is just as important. Erikson studied what he called *psychosocial* development—life periods in which an individual's goal is to satisfy desires associated with social needs. Although Erikson believed that childhood experiences have a lasting impact on the individual, he saw development as a lifelong interactive process between people (see Erikson's Stages of Psychosocial Development).

issue a problem or worry

Erikson argued that we all face many crises as we grow from infancy to old age, as we mature, and as people expect more from us. Each of these crises represents an **issue** that everyone faces. The child, adolescent, or adult may develop more strongly in one way or another, depending on how other people respond to his or her efforts. For example, the 2-year-old is delighted with his newfound ability to walk, to get into things, to use words, and to ask questions. The very fact that he has acquired these abilities adds to his self-esteem, and he is eager to use them. If the adults around him applaud his efforts and acknowledge his achievements, he begins to develop a sense of autonomy, or independence. However, if they ignore him except to punish him for going too far or being a nuisance, the child may begin to doubt the value of his achievements. He may also feel shame because the people around him act as if his new desire for independence is bad.

✅ **READING PROGRESS CHECK**

Listing What are the three dimensions of socialization?

Connecting Psychology to Civics

PUBLIC SERVICE AND DEVELOPMENTAL HEALTH

Less than fifty years ago, mental illness was regarded as the result of parenting styles and family dynamics. As a result, families with a mentally ill member tended to be ashamed of the fact. Medical professionals often isolated the mentally ill individual from his or her family and kept family members out of the loop on the individual's care. Gradually, however, science and medicine identified underlying genetic and/or medical causes of mental illness. Mental illness has become a medical issue, to be treated with drugs and ongoing therapy. As the viewpoint regarding causes changed, so too did family involvement in the care of mentally ill family members.

The government has taken a role in researching mental illness and in connecting families with professional help. Families, parenting styles, government intervention, and medical understanding of mental illness intersect in the National Institute of Mental Health (NIMH) and the National Alliance for the Mentally Ill (NAMI). NIMH funds research into all aspects of mental illness. This organization also generates interventions, education, and training for parents and other caregivers dealing with issues surrounding childhood maltreatment and abuse, mental illnesses, and developmental difficulties and disorders children face, such as autism and ADHD. The NIMH Web site (www.nimh.nih.gov) provides information on mental illness through publications as well as audio and video resources. NAMI exists to provide education and resources for individuals and their families.

▲ Today, children with special needs like this young girl are often given support in regular classrooms thanks to NIMH and NAMI.

▶ **CRITICAL THINKING**

1. *Drawing Conclusions* Do you think that the NIMH and NAMI provide an important public service? Explain.

2. *Identifying Cause and Effect* How has changing awareness of mental illness changed the part played by families in caring for the mentally ill?

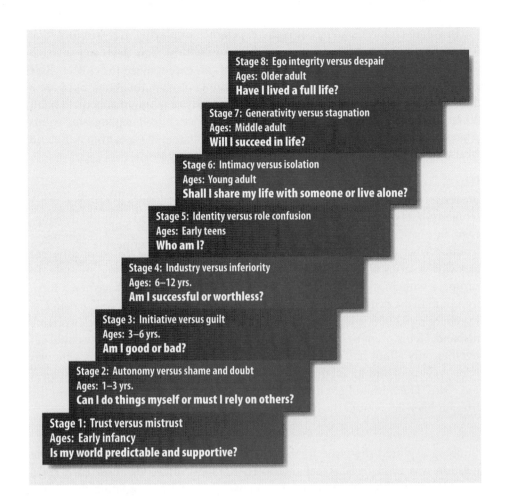

< DIAGRAM

ERIKSON'S THEORY OF PSYCHOSOCIAL DEVELOPMENT
According to Erikson, a child encounters a psychosocial challenge at each stage. If the child successfully resolves the issue, the child develops a positive social trait and progresses to the next stage.

► **CRITICAL THINKING**

1. *Analyzing Visuals* What issues concern a child in the first year of life?

2. *Analyzing Ideas* How are the issues of a child in Stage 4 different from those of a child in Stage 3?

Stage 8: Ego integrity versus despair
Ages: Older adult
Have I lived a full life?

Stage 7: Generativity versus stagnation
Ages: Middle adult
Will I succeed in life?

Stage 6: Intimacy versus isolation
Ages: Young adult
Shall I share my life with someone or live alone?

Stage 5: Identity versus role confusion
Ages: Early teens
Who am I?

Stage 4: Industry versus inferiority
Ages: 6–12 yrs.
Am I successful or worthless?

Stage 3: Initiative versus guilt
Ages: 3–6 yrs.
Am I good or bad?

Stage 2: Autonomy versus shame and doubt
Ages: 1–3 yrs.
Can I do things myself or must I rely on others?

Stage 1: Trust versus mistrust
Ages: Early infancy
Is my world predictable and supportive?

The Cognitive-Developmental Approach

GUIDING QUESTION *What occurs in the stages of moral development?*

Both Freud and Erikson stress the emotional dynamics of social development. Their theories suggest that learning social rules is altogether different from learning to ride a bicycle or to speak a foreign language. Many psychologists disagree. They believe children learn the ways of their social world because they are rewarded for conforming and because they copy older children and adults in anticipation of future rewards. In other words, social development is simply a matter of learning and imitating.

Theorists who emphasize the role of cognition or thinking in the development of children view the growing child differently. Learning theory implies that the child is essentially passive—a piece of clay to be shaped by experience. The people who administer rewards and punishments and serve as models do the shaping. Cognitive theorists see the child as the shaper. Taking their cue from Jean Piaget, they argue that social development is the result of the child's acting on the environment and trying to make sense out of his experiences. The games children play illustrate this.

Games and Play

Children's games are serious business. When left to their own devices, youngsters spend a great deal of time making up rules. This enables them to learn for themselves the importance of agreeing on a structure for group activities. A child can relax and enjoy himself without fear of rejection as long as he does not break the rules. The world of play thus becomes a miniature society, with its own rules and codes. Games also teach children about aspects of adult life in a nonthreatening way.

In young children's games, it is the experience of playing, not winning, that counts. Much of the children's play involves **role taking**. Youngsters try on such adult roles as mother, father, teacher, storekeeper, explorer, and rock star. Role taking allows them to learn about different points of view firsthand. Suppose a child plays a mother opposite another child who plays a whiny, disobedient baby. When she finds herself totally frustrated by the other child's nagging, she begins to understand why her mother gets mad. You are unable to cook even a pretend meal when the baby keeps knocking over the pots and pans.

Moral Development

Lawrence Kohlberg's studies show just how important being able to see other people's points of view is to social development in general and to moral development in particular. Kohlberg studied the development of moral reasoning—deciding what is right and what is wrong—by presenting children of different ages with a series of moral dilemmas. Kohlberg gave the following example: In Europe, a woman was near death from cancer. One drug might save her, a form of radium that a druggist in the same town had recently discovered. The druggist was charging $2,000, ten times what the drug cost him to make. The sick woman's husband, Heinz, went to everyone he knew to borrow the money, but he could get together only about half of what it cost. He told the druggist that his wife was dying and asked him to sell the drug cheaper or let him pay later. But the druggist said, "No." The husband got desperate and broke into the man's store to steal the drug for his wife. Should the husband have done that? Why?

Stages of Moral Development

Kohlberg explored the issue further in a 1969 study. While the answer to the question was immaterial, what interested Kohlberg most was how each child arrived at a conclusion. He wanted to know what sort of reasoning they used. After questioning 84 children, Kohlberg identified six stages of moral development. He then replicated his findings in several different cultures.

In stage one, children are totally egocentric. They do not consider other people's points of view and have no sense of right and wrong. Their main concern is avoiding punishment. A child in this stage will say that the man should steal because people will blame him for his wife's death if he does not, or that he should not steal because he will go to jail when he's caught.

Stage	Level	Orientation	Reference Group	Example
1	Pre-conventional	Obedience and punishment	Self	It's OK for Heinz to steal if he doesn't get caught.
2		Instrumental relativist	Immediate family	Stealing the drug helps his wife.
3	Conventional	Good boy/Nice girl	Extended family	His in-laws will respect him if he steals the drug.
4		Law and order	Self-serving view of society	It's illegal to steal.
5	Post-conventional	Social contract	Interactive view of society	It's OK to steal because the druggist is charging too much.
6		Universal ethics principle	Balanced cost/benefit analysis of self/society	If the situations were reversed, would the druggist steal from Heinz?

Children in stage two have a better idea of how to receive rewards as well as how to avoid punishment. Youngsters at this level interpret the Golden Rule "do unto others as you would have them do unto you" as "help someone if he helps you, and hurt him if he hurts you." They are still egocentric and premoral. They evaluate acts in terms of their consequences, not in terms of right and wrong. A child who is in stage two might support Heinz stealing the drug to help his wife, but he might oppose Heinz's theft because it would harm the druggist.

In stage three, children become acutely sensitive to what other people want and think. A child in this stage will say that the man in the story should steal because people will think he is cruel if he lets his wife die, or that he should not steal because people will think he is a criminal. In other words, children want social approval in stage three, so they apply the rules other people have decreed literally and rigidly.

In stage four, a child is less concerned with the approval of others. The key issue here is law and order—a law is seen as a moral rule and is obeyed because of a strong belief in established authority. For example, a woman may stay married because she took a vow, or a driver may obey the speed limit when no police are around. Moral thinking here, as at stage three, is quite rigid. For a child in stage four, Heinz should not steal the drug only because it is against the law. In the remaining two stages, people continue to broaden their perspective.

The stage-five person is primarily concerned with whether a law is fair or just. He believes that laws must change as the world changes, and that laws are never absolute and should not be followed rigidly. For a stage-five child, Heinz's theft could be excused because the druggist was unfairly charging too much. The important question for an individual in stage five is whether a given law is good for society as a whole.

Stage six involves an acceptance of ethical principles that apply to everyone, like the Golden Rule. A moral imperative such as the Golden Rule cannot be disobeyed or broken; they are more important than any written law. People at a stage-six level of development may sometimes find themselves obeying their principles despite great personal sacrifice.

Kohlberg's research demonstrated that while the levels are not strictly tied to the age of an individual, there are some correlations. He found that most adolescents and adults reason conventionally, although postconventional reasoning is the highest level he identified. However, if a person reaches the post-conventional level, he or she is most likely to reach it during adolescence. Of the adolescents he studied, Kohlberg found that 20 percent reached stage-five reasoning while about 5 percent reached stage six.

^ TABLE

KOHLBERG'S STAGES OF MORAL DEVELOPMENT
Each stage of Kohlberg's theory is cognitively more complex than the last.

▶ **CRITICAL THINKING**

1. *Interpreting* Why would a child in the first stage choose to listen to his or her parents?

2. *Assessing* Which stage has the most rigid sense of right and wrong?

Children learn to respect the feelings of others through caring for a pet.

▶ **CRITICAL THINKING**

Drawing Conclusions Which stage and orientation of moral development are these girls exhibiting?

Critics of Kohlberg, such as Carol Gilligan, point out that there is a gender bias in Kohlberg's theory. Gilligan theorizes that boys and girls use different principles when they are deciding between what is right and what is wrong. She argues that girls have been socialized to consider the needs of others and to avoid one-dimensional judgments. Girls are taught to be empathetic and caring, whereas boys are taught the goal of justice and fairness. Therefore, girls might argue that both stealing and letting Heinz's wife die are wrong, while boys might argue that life has greater value than property. Using these arguments, Kohlberg would place boys at higher levels of moral development. While Gilligan and others recognize the different reasoning that is employed, they would disagree that this indicates a lower level of moral development.

Other researchers suggest the need for studying the development of racial identity, as well as how racial identity interacts with gender and sexual orientation identities. William Cross followed the progression of racial identity for African Americans through a series of five steps, moving from a point of racial unawareness to a point of multicultural concern for all "oppressed groups." Janet Helms developed one of the first racial identity models for whites. Her work focused on six statuses in the development of a white racial identity. In the first three statuses, an individual moves away from the point of having a racist frame or perspective, and in the final three statuses, the individual develops a white identity that is nonracist and willing to confront racism in everyday life.

To reach the highest levels of moral development, a child must first be able to see other people's points of view. Yet this understanding is no guarantee that a person will respect the rights of others. Thus, the development of thinking or cognitive abilities influences moral development.

☑ **READING PROGRESS CHECK**

Contrasting How does a cognitivist's view of social development differ from Freud's view?

Photodisc/Getty Images

LESSON 3 REVIEW

Reviewing Vocabulary
1. *Defining* Describe role taking in children's play.

Using Your Notes
2. *Comparing* Review the notes that you completed during the lesson. Compare the role of parents and children in authoritarian and permissive families.

Answering the Guiding Questions
3. *Differentiating* Identify and describe the three types of parenting styles.

4. *Comparing* What central themes are shared by Freud's and Erikson's theories?

5. *Describing* List Kohlberg's stages of moral development and describe what occurs in each.

Writing Activity
6. *Informative/Explanatory* Go to a public place where you can observe children, such as a playground, park, or shopping mall. Note the interactions between parents and children and among the children as they play. Record your observations. Write about your analysis of the different parenting styles you observed.

Directions: On a separate sheet of paper, answer the questions below. Make sure you read carefully and answer all parts of the question.

Lesson Review

Lesson 1

1 *Describing* Describe capacities newborns display.

2 *Identifying* Identify biological and environmental influences on development of the prenatal brain.

3 *Summarizing* Summarize the typical stages of language development in children.

Lesson 2

4 *Defining* What is egocentric thinking?

5 *Drawing Conclusions* Explain imprinting in relation to Lorenz's geese. What would most likely have happened if the first thing the goslings saw was a dog?

Lesson 3

6 *Interpreting Significance* Define socialization and explain why it is so important to development.

7 *Identifying* Use Erikson's Stages of Psychosocial Development to match the following items:

Ego integrity vs. _____

Identity vs. _____

Autonomy vs. _____

Intimacy vs. _____

Initiative vs. _____

   a. shame and doubt

   b. role confusion

   c. isolation

   d. despair

   e. guilt

8 *Understanding Perspectives* Max is a very outgoing 3-year-old. In the stability versus change issue, suggest how each viewpoint would say he might behave as an adult.

College and Career Readiness

9 *Reaching Conclusions* Write a caption for the image that describes the type of parenting style this picture demonstrates. How does this style of parenting affect the children? Based on this image, describe this family when the girl is 16.

10 *Finding the Main Idea* Explain the views of Cross, Helms, and Gilligan in relation to Kohlberg's stages of moral development.

Critical Thinking Questions

11 *Making Connections* Describe fetal brain development and its role in relation to the developing fetus.

12 *Synthesizing* Review the concept of continuity versus discontinuity and use this to identify and evaluate limitations of one of the stage theories discussed in this chapter.

Need Extra Help?

If You've Missed Question	1	2	3	4	5	6	7	8	9	10	11	12
Go to page	54	56	57	62	65	72	75	72	71	78	53	72

Directions: On a separate sheet of paper, answer the questions below. Make sure you read carefully and answer all parts to the question.

13 *Making Inferences* Based on what you have learned about development, should young children be treated as "little adults"? Why or why not?

14 *Evaluating Information* Determine how well your beliefs agree with those of your parents. How much do you think your early social training impacted your beliefs?

15 *Analyzing Concepts* Describe typical play activities for boys and girls. Use the theories of social development to explain why these play styles are typical.

Exploring the Essential Question

16 *Using Context Clues* Select and print out a short story, poem, or song lyrics that addresses growing up. Identify instances in which the subject meets a psychosocial challenge, such as "Am I good or bad?" or "Who am I?" or "Have I lived a full life?". Label with the age range or stage of psychosocial development and draw a picture that represents that child's (or parent's) stage.

21st Century Skills

17 *Understanding Relationships Among Events* How does the maturation process explain why a 4-month-old infant cannot be taught to walk?

18 *Decision Making* Review the nature versus nurture issue. Do you think development is the result of heredity (nature) or learning (nurture) or both? Why?

19 *Time, Chronology, and Sequencing* Using Piaget's stages, create a time line that tracks the cognitive development of a child.

Research and Technology

20 *Evaluating* How do advertisements or products aimed at children contribute to the choices a child has for role-taking? Look through magazines and newspapers, watch television commercials, listen to the radio, and use the Internet. Present your findings in an illustrated, captioned poster.

DBQ Analyzing Primary Sources

Use the document below to answer the following questions.

PRIMARY SOURCE

"*Children are influenced by the model for behavior set by adults in their environment. When adults use physical punishment, children are likely to learn that this behavior is the desirable choice in discipline. Spanking, hitting and slapping are not effective and are damaging to the self-respect and self-esteem of children. There are many healthier and more effective forms of discipline that can be taught and utilized as alternatives to physical punishment.*"

—*American Humane Child Protection Position Statements, 16*

21 *Constructing Arguments* Agree or disagree with this statement and explain your reasoning. Be sure to identify alternate methods of discipline and parenting, and evaluate their effectiveness versus physical punishment.

Psychology Journal Activity

22 *Informative/Explanatory* Review your entry in your Psychology Journal for this chapter. What did you learn in this chapter about childhood development that relates to how you learn new words or foreign languages? Don't forget to address the importance of one's environment and surroundings.

Need Extra Help?

If You've Missed Question	**13**	**14**	**15**	**16**	**17**	**18**	**19**	**20**	**21**	**22**
Go to page	60	72	75	60	55	72	60	76	71	50

Adolescence

ESSENTIAL QUESTIONS • *How do physical changes impact emotional development?* • *How does culture influence behavior?*

Psychology Matters...

Adolescence is an exciting and confusing time when the body and mind are constantly changing. Neither children nor adults, adolescents experience a slow shift from childhood pursuits to more adult ways of thinking and behaving. Friendships and peer groups play an ever more important role in the development of identity. In this chapter we will better understand what happens in this transition from childhood to adulthood.

◄ Some friendships are based on similarities. Some are based on differences.

Adam Hester/Photographer's Choice RF/Getty Images

81

Lab Activity

The Internet Generation

THE QUESTION...

RESEARCH QUESTION Do adolescent males and females use the Internet differently?

Adolescents today are members of what is often referred to as the "Internet Generation." Your generation has earned this title because, unlike the generations that preceded you, you and your friends have never been without the World Wide Web. As the vast majority of you have never been without it, your generation uses the Internet fearlessly and for almost any task or pastime imaginable.

You have all shared the experience of growing up with the Internet. But do you use it in similar ways? Is there a difference between male and female adolescents in how they make use of the Internet? We will conduct an experiment to find out.

Psychology Journal Activity

Think about how the time adolescents spend online might affect their development. Write about this in your Psychology Journal. What are some examples of Internet resources or Web sites that have had an effect on you? How have your attitudes and decisions been swayed by what you've seen and heard online?

FINDING THE ANSWER...

HYPOTHESIS Male and female adolescents spend equal amounts of time online, but they spend that time online differently.

THE METHOD OF YOUR EXPERIMENT

MATERIALS survey regarding Internet usage, pens

PROCEDURE Create ten surveys regarding Internet usage. Your survey should include two question sections. The first should ask questions regarding time spent on the Internet, including the number of hours spent online, what types of devices are used to access the Internet, and where the Internet is accessed (i.e. at home, school, or elsewhere). The second question section should ask questions regarding how the participant spends their time on the Internet. Include the following activities on your question list: playing games, watching videos, doing homework, chatting with friends, writing or reading emails, writing or reading blog posts, visiting social media Web sites, visiting forums and chat groups, or shopping. You may choose to add other activities as you desire. Administer your survey on an individual basis to a group of at least ten participants, ensuring you have an equal number of males and females and that the entire participant group is between the ages of 15 and 17.

DATA COLLECTION Create a single report that includes at least one graph depicting your results. As a class, compare your results and discuss the similarities or differences exhibited between the genders.

ANALYSIS & APPLICATION

1. Did your results support the hypothesis? Is there a correlation between gender and Internet usage?

2. Evaluate your data, looking for other trends. Did you notice a concentration of participants in a specific activity? What about a connection between time spent online and specific activities?

3. How might certain online activities affect adolescents' pictures of themselves as they grow older?

netw⦿rks ONLINE LAB RESOURCES

Online you will find:

- An **interactive lab experience,** allowing you to put principles from this chapter into practice in a digital psychology lab environment. This chapter's lab will include an experiment allowing you to explore issues fundamental to adolescence.

- A **Skills Handbook** that includes a guide for using the scientific method, creating experiments, and analyzing data.
- A **Notebook** where you can complete your Psychology Journal and record and analyze data from your experiment.

networks

There's More Online!

- ☑ **CARTOON** Changing Norms
- ☑ **DIAGRAM** Glands that Release Hormones
- ☑ **GRAPH** Average Annual Gains in Height
- ☑ **SELF-CHECK QUIZ**

Reading **HELP**DESK 〈CCSS〉

Academic Vocabulary

- physical
- conform

Content Vocabulary

- initiation rites
- menarche
- spermarche
- asynchrony

TAKING NOTES:

Key Ideas and Details

COMPARING AND CONTRASTING
Create a Venn diagram similar to the one below to identify reactions to physical changes that are common to both male and female adolescents. Also identify the differences in the reactions of the two genders to early and late maturation.

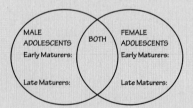

MALE ADOLESCENTS
Early Maturers:
Late Maturers:

BOTH

FEMALE ADOLESCENTS
Early Maturers:
Late Maturers:

LESSON 1
Physical and Sexual Development

ESSENTIAL QUESTION • *How do physical changes impact emotional development?*

IT MATTERS BECAUSE

Adolescence is complicated. Significant physical, mental, and emotional changes occur during this volatile transition period. Developmental psychologists find this is a time ripe for psychological research. It is a period of vast mental and physical change and no two teenagers cope with these changes in the same way.

Theories of Adolescence

GUIDING QUESTION *Why has adolescence been characterized as a time of "storm and stress"?*

Adolescence is the transition period between childhood and adulthood. Some define it in psychological terms: a time period of mixed abilities and responsibilities in which childlike behavior changes to adult like behavior. In some societies, adolescence is not recognized as a separate stage of life; individuals move directly from childhood to adulthood.

In our society, adolescence is looked upon as a time of preparation for adult responsibilities. There are many **initiation rites**, or rites of passage, that mark admission into adulthood. These rites include informal celebrations such as birthdays—at 16 or 18 or 21—as well as more formal events such as bar mitzvahs and bat mitzvahs, graduation from high school or college, and even weddings. Young people assume many of the new burdens of adulthood just when they are undergoing complex **physical** and emotional changes that affect them both personally and socially. The end of adolescence and the beginning of adulthood is often blurred because it varies for each person.

Psychologists have developed contradictory theories of adolescent development and the nature of the adolescent experience. Controversy has raged since 1904, when G. Stanley Hall presented his pioneering theory of adolescence. Hall saw the adolescent as representing a transitional stage. Being an adolescent for Hall, figuratively speaking, was something like being a fully grown animal in a cage, an animal that sees freedom but does not know quite when freedom will occur or how to handle it. Thus, the adolescent was portrayed as existing in a state of great "storm and stress," as a marginal being, confused, troubled, and highly frustrated.

Through the years many psychologists and social scientists have supported Hall's theories, but there have been others who disagree, some strongly. These theorists regard adolescence as a period of growth that flows naturally from the period of childhood that precedes it and into the period of young adulthood that follows.

One major proponent of this latter theory was Margaret Mead. In a series of classic anthropological studies in the late 1920s and early 1930s, Mead found that in some cultures, adolescence is a highly enjoyable time of life and not at all marked by storm and stress. She believed that adolescent storm and stress was a by-product of an industrialized society. Mead proposed that culture might play a role in adolescent development.

Other studies conducted since then have tended to support Mead. They point to a relative lack of conflict in the lives of adolescents and a continuous development out of childhood that is based on individual reactions to their culture. In 1988 a report indicated that adolescence may be a difficult time period, but only 11 percent of adolescents encounter serious difficulties. About 32 percent have sporadic problems, while 57 percent enjoy basically positive, healthy development during the teenage years.

Although adolescence may not be as crisis-ridden as some psychologists think, few would deny that there is at least some stress during that period. Great physical, mental, and emotional changes occur during adolescence. As psychologist Robert Havighurst pointed out, every adolescent faces challenges in the form of developmental tasks that must be mastered. Among the tasks that Havighurst lists are the following:

1. Accepting one's physical makeup and acquiring a masculine or feminine gender role
2. Developing appropriate relations with age-mates of both sexes
3. Becoming emotionally independent of parents and other adults
4. Achieving the assurance that one will become economically independent
5. Deciding on, preparing for, and entering a vocation
6. Developing the cognitive skills and concepts necessary for social competence
7. Understanding and achieving socially responsible behavior
8. Preparing for marriage and family
9. Acquiring values that are harmonious and appropriate

Although the tasks present challenges, adolescents generally handle them well. Most face some stress but find ways to cope with it. There are, of course, exceptions. A small percentage of young people experience various storms and stresses throughout their adolescent years. Another small group confronts the changes all adolescents experience with no stress at all. Perhaps the only safe generalization is that development through adolescence is a highly individualized and varied matter.

initiation rites ceremonies or rituals in which an individual is admitted to new status or accepted into a new position

physical of or relating to the body

In our society, various initiation rites mark the passage from adolescence to adulthood.

▶ **CRITICAL THINKING**

Hypothesizing How do you think celebrations like this one help adolescents make the transition to adulthood?

Adolescents undergo complex physical and emotional changes that affect them personally and emotionally.

▶ **CRITICAL THINKING**

Identifying Cause and Effect Give an example of a way that physical changes in adolescence might affect behavior.

The pattern of development a particular adolescent displays depends upon a great many factors. The most important of these include the individual's adjustment in childhood, the level of adjustment of his or her parents and peers, and the changes that occur during adolescence. This time period is marked by major physical, social, emotional, and intellectual changes.

✔ **READING PROGRESS CHECK**

Contrasting How do Hall's and Mead's theories of adolescence differ?

Physical Development

GUIDING QUESTION *How can physical development affect emotional development?*

Until recently, scientists believed that the structure of the brain changed very little after the age of 5 or 6, and that the amount of gray matter actually started dropping at about the age of 3. However, new research has shown that the brains of teens are different from those of both children and adults. This research shows an increase in gray matter at the onset of adolescence. This is followed by a sizable loss in the frontal lobes for about a decade starting in the mid-teens. Well developed frontal lobes are necessary in order to voluntarily restrain impulses. The fact that these lobes are late in maturing may partly explain why many teens are prone to risky behavior. As the frontal lobes mature, scientists believe that the abilities being used become "hard-wired" and retained, while others are lost.

Not only does the physical structure of the brain change during adolescence, the way it works also is altered. Chemicals called neurotransmitters carry nerve impulses from one brain cell to another. These must be properly balanced if the brain is to work correctly. During early adolescence, the quantities of several important neurotransmitters change. The neurotransmitter serotonin, for example, is responsible for regulating moods. In the early teen years, serotonin levels decrease. Scientists know that low levels of serotonin can lead to mood swings and aggressive behavior. At about the same time, another neurotransmitter, dopamine, becomes more active. A higher level of dopamine can cause individuals to seek out more exciting and dangerous experiences. These changes can help explain why teens engage in unsafe behavior more often than children and adults.

Another concern is that because the brain is undergoing such dramatic changes during this time, it is especially vulnerable to drugs. Chronic use of drugs that alter mood, such as methamphetamines, is likely to cause permanent damage. Marijuana has been shown to decrease teens' ability to perform higher-level thinking skills. Mood-altering drugs in general can disrupt the way in which the brain develops during this vital time.

Sexual maturation, or puberty, is the biological event that marks the end of childhood. Hormones trigger a series of internal and external changes. These hormones produce different growth patterns in boys and girls. Some girls start to mature physically as early as 8, while boys may start to mature at age 9 or 10. On average, girls begin puberty between ages 8 and 10. The age for boys entering puberty is typically between 9 and 16. Just before puberty, boys and girls experience a growth spurt.

The growth spurt is a rapid increase in weight and height. It reaches its peak at age 12 for girls and just after age 14 for most boys. The growth spurt generally lasts two years. Soon after the growth spurt, individuals reach sexual maturity. At about the age of 10, girls rather suddenly begin to grow. Before this growth spurt, fat tissue develops, making the girl appear chubby. The development of fat tissue is also characteristic of boys before their growth spurt. Whereas boys quickly lose this fatty tissue, progressing into a lean and lanky phase, girls retain most of it and can even add to it as they begin to enter their growth spurt.

Once their growth spurt begins, girls can grow as much as 2 to 3.5 inches a year. During this period, a girl's breasts and hips begin to fill out, and she develops pubic hair. Sometime between the ages of 10 and 17 she has her first menstrual period, or **menarche**. Another 12 to 18 months will pass before her menstrual periods become regular and she is capable of conceiving a child, although pregnancies do sometimes occur almost immediately following menarche. Most societies consider menarche the beginning of womanhood.

At about 12, boys begin to develop pubic hair and larger genitals. Normally, between the ages of 12 and 13 they achieve their first ejaculation, or **spermarche**. Their growth spurt begins 24 to 27 months later than that of girls and lasts about 3 years longer. Once their growth spurt begins, boys grow rapidly and fill out.

menarche the first menstrual period

spermarche period during which males achieve first ejaculation

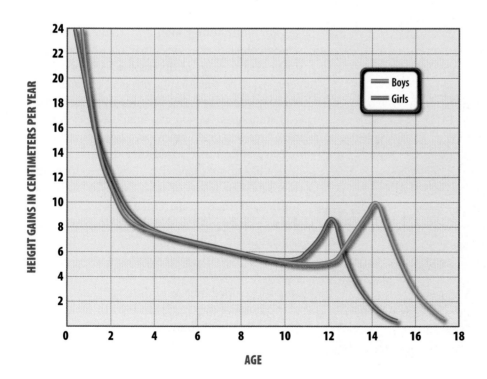

HEIGHT GAINS IN CENTIMETERS PER YEAR

AGE

Boys
Girls

< GRAPH

AVERAGE ANNUAL GAINS IN HEIGHT
Hormones controlled by the endocrine system can cause dramatic growth spurts; a boy may experience a yearly increase of 4–6 inches (10–15 cm), while a girl may increase 3–5 inches (8–13 cm) in height.

▶ **CRITICAL THINKING**

1. *Analyzing Visuals* When does the growth spurt occur in girls? In boys?

2. *Analyzing Visuals* About how many centimeters do girls gain in height at the peak of their growth spurt? About how many do boys gain?

They develop the broad shoulders and thicker trunk of an adult man. They also acquire more muscle tissue than girls and develop a larger heart and lungs. Their voices gradually deepen, and hair begins to grow on their faces and later on their chests and on their axilla, or armpit.

The rate and pattern of sexual maturation varies so widely that it is difficult to apply norms or standards to puberty. In general, however, girls begin to develop earlier than boys and for a year or two may tower over males their same age. This period of adolescent growth can be an awkward one for both boys and girls because of **asynchrony**—the condition of uneven growth or maturation of bodily parts. For example, the hands or feet may be too large or small for the rest of the body. As the adolescent grows older, however, the bodily parts assume their correct proportions relative to one another.

The average age of menarche varies between women of different countries. The onset of menarche appears to be earlier in countries where the life expectancy is longest. It has dropped in developed countries over the last century as living conditions have improved. Good nutrition appears to play a large part. Poor nutrition affects the amount of body fat and appears to delay menarche. A higher birth weight, as well as rapid weight gain up to age 7, corresponds to an earlier age of menarche. Interestingly, literacy rates appear to have a correlation to menarche. In countries where there is a high rate of illiteracy, children are more likely to be in the work force, where they expend more energy than they would if they were at school. This disrupts fat accumulation and delays menarche.

asynchrony the condition during adolescence in which the growth or maturation of bodily parts is uneven

conform to act in accordance with prevailing standards or customs

Rapid physical changes occur during adolescence. Normally the changes that occur in adulthood are gradual.

▶ **CRITICAL THINKING**

Analyzing Why do you think there are psychological reactions to physical growth?

Reactions to Growth

In general, young people today are better informed than they were two or three generations ago. Most do not find the signs of their sexual maturation upsetting. Nevertheless, the rather sudden bodily changes that occur during puberty make all adolescents somewhat self-conscious. This is particularly true if they are early or late to develop. Adolescents usually want to be accepted by their peers. They **conform** to ideals of how a male or female their age should act, dress, and look.

For both young men and women, there is a strong correlation between having a negative body image and feelings of depression. Adolescents are very aware of these rapid physical changes. They are very concerned that they measure up to idealized standards. As you can imagine, very few ever meet these expectations. Most adolescents mention physical appearance when they discuss what they do not like about themselves. Most tend to evaluate themselves in terms of their culture's body ideal. Youths of both sexes are particularly sensitive about any traits they possess that they perceive to be sex-inappropriate. For example, boys tend to be disturbed by underdeveloped genitalia, lack of pubic hair, or fatty breasts. Girls are likely to be shy about underdeveloped breasts or dark facial hair.

Individual differences in growth greatly affect the personality of young adolescents. For example, research indicates that boys who mature early have an advantage. They become heroes in sports and

leaders in social activities. Other adolescents look up to them; adults tend to treat them as more mature. As a result, they are generally more self-confident and independent than other boys. Some late-maturing boys may withdraw or develop behavioral problems. The effects of late maturation for boys may last into young adulthood.

Variations in the rate of development continue to have an effect on males even into their thirties. Those who matured earlier have been found to have a higher occupational and social status than those who matured later. The correlation between rate of development and social status begins to weaken, however, as males enter their forties.

With girls, the pattern is somewhat different. Girls who mature early may feel embarrassed rather than proud of their height and figure, at first. Some begin dating older boys and take charge with people their own age. Late-maturing girls tend to get along with their peers more easily. In their late teens, girls who matured early may be more popular and have a more favorable image of themselves than girls who matured slowly.

Why does physical growth have such powerful psychological effects? According to one widely held theory, the psychological reactions to physical growth may be the result of a self-fulfilling prophecy. For example, the boy who believes he does not meet his culture's physical ideal may think less of himself and not pursue success as doggedly as the next person. His belief actually helps bring about the failure he feared.

Sexual Attitudes

Adolescence is also the time when an individual develops attitudes about sex and expectations about the gender role he or she will fill. Early sexual maturity and cultural patterns of sexual behaviors have changed from one generation to the next generation. For example, the average age of marriage is about 27 years, some five years later than it was in the 1950s and about 13 years after sexual maturation.

Attitudes affect the way we feel about sex and the way we respond sexually. Around the world there are wide variations in what children are told about appropriate sexual behavior and how they respond. In some societies children are kept in the dark about sex until just before they are married, whereas in others preadolescent children are encouraged to engage in sexual play in the belief that such play will foster mature development.

∧ CARTOON

CHANGING NORMS
Adolescent rebellion can often introduce behaviors which later become the norm for society.

▶ **CRITICAL THINKING**

1. *Interpreting* What does the woman mean by telling the young woman "You're not going out like that!"?

2. *Contrasting* How have attitudes about display of the body changed in the past 30 years?

Attitudes about sex have changed from those of previous generations. The increase of sexual awareness and activity of today's teens has raised many questions over the role of family, religion, and government in providing information and guidance about sex. The Youth Risk Behavior Surveillance Report of 2009 states that each year, approximately 757,000 pregnancies occur among women aged 15 to 19. An estimated 9.1 million cases of sexually transmitted diseases occur each year among people aged 15 to 24. While the U.S. teen birth rate in 2009–2010 of 34 births per 1,000 teens aged 15–19 was significantly lower than the most recent peak rate in 1991 of 61.8 per 1,000, it is still higher than in other developed countries. For example, the teen birth rate in Canada in 2009 was about one-third of the U.S. rate. Teen pregnancies and births continue to be societal issues. Studies show that children of teenage mothers are more likely to become teenage parents themselves, to do poorly in school, and to serve time in prison.

The United States has the largest rate of teenage births of any developed nation. After declining for a decade, the U.S. teen pregnancy rate began to climb again. At least part of the reason for this is the fact that media and popular culture celebrate pregnancy. Mothers-to-be are encouraged to show off their "baby bumps." Unmarried teen mothers appearing in television reality shows, magazine covers, and movies can make teen motherhood seem glamorous.

Fear of sexually transmitted diseases, especially HIV/AIDS, has also affected sexual attitudes. On average, more than 38,000 people in the United States were diagnosed with AIDS each year from 1999 through 2008. The number of people living with AIDS in the United States has more than doubled from 1996 to 2008. Risk of HIV infection is not limited to intravenous drug use and homosexual sex. All sexually active people are at risk. However, condoms are highly effective in preventing sexual transmission of HIV as well as other sexually transmitted diseases. To be effective, condoms must be used correctly and consistently.

An increasing number of teens are examining the risks of sexual behavior and deciding that the only safe choice is abstinence from sexual intercourse. *Abstinence* is a choice to avoid harmful behaviors including premarital sex and the use of drugs and alcohol. By choosing abstinence, teens hope to avoid unwanted pregnancies, sexually transmitted diseases, and loss of self-respect.

☑ **READING PROGRESS CHECK**

Contrasting How do female and male growth spurts differ?

LESSON 1 REVIEW

Reviewing Vocabulary

1. *Explaining* What do menarche and spermarche have to do with physical development?

Using Your Notes

2. *Comparing and Contrasting* Use your notes to compare and contrast the common reactions of male and female adolescents to the physical changes they are experiencing.

Answering the Guiding Questions

3. *Analyzing* Why has adolescence been characterized as a time of "storm and stress"?

4. *Analyzing Cause and Effect* How can physical development affect emotional development?

Writing Activity

5. *Informative/Explanatory* Think back over the stages of your life from childhood to the present. Which were the best and worst years of your life and why? Summarize your thoughts in a few paragraphs. Compare your responses to your classmates, and as a class debate whether adolescence is a time of "storm and stress."

Case Study

Early Maturation

Period of Study: 1992

Introduction: In 1986 a 9-year-old Brazilian girl, Maria, gave birth to a healthy 7-pound daughter. Sexual development normally begins around age 11 in girls. Maria suffered from a hormone imbalance that produced premature puberty, or *precocious puberty*, a disorder that tends to affect more girls than boys. Children who start puberty prematurely are tall for their age because their hormones trigger early growth spurts. However, they never achieve their full height potential because their skeletal growth soon stops.

When she gave birth, doctors estimated that Maria's body was like that of a normal 13- or 14-year-old girl. Her case inspired psychologists to study psychological factors in the maturation of females.

PRIMARY SOURCE

Early puberty is not healthy for children for many reasons. Often, children with Precocious Puberty look older. . . . They are expected to act as old as they look and this is confusing for children. This in combination with other factors leads to a time of great stress.

—The Magic Foundation

Hypothesis: Psychological factors, including stressors revolving around family, social relationships, and school, will cause an earlier menarche in some females.

Method: Researchers conducted a longitudinal study on a group of 16-year-old girls. Psychologists assessed the living conditions in which the participants grew up, including the absence of a father, mother, or both; family conflict; and parental marital difficulty.

Results: The study found that females who grow up in stressful family conditions experience behavioral and psychological problems that induce earlier pubertal onset, leading to reproductive readiness. Stressful conditions caused a slower metabolism, resulting in weight gain and triggering early menarche.

Further studies have indicated that girls who experience precocious puberty may go through periods of moodiness or irritability, while boys may become aggressive. These children may also become self-conscious about their bodies. Treatment for precocious puberty is usually aimed at changing the hormonal imbalance in the body through drug therapy. Psychologically, the behavior of children usually becomes more age-appropriate as their bodies return to normal development.

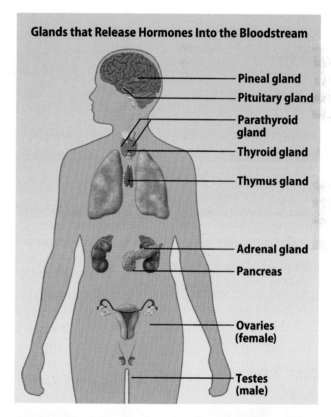

Glands that Release Hormones Into the Bloodstream

- Pineal gland
- Pituitary gland
- Parathyroid gland
- Thyroid gland
- Thymus gland
- Adrenal gland
- Pancreas
- Ovaries (female)
- Testes (male)

Analyzing the Case Study

1. *Finding the Main Idea* How could a 9-year-old child give birth?

2. *Drawing Conclusions* Based on their research, what might psychologists conclude about Maria's early living conditions?

3. *Evaluating* How does the quotation support the assertion that early puberty is not healthy? Based on the quotation and the case study, do you think that drug treatments are warranted to stop precocious puberty and early fertility? Why or why not?

PHOTO: Andersen Ross/Blend Images LLC; TEXT: The MAGIC Foundation

networks

There's More Online!

- ☑ **CHART** Identity Categories
- ☑ **CHART** Kohlberg's Model of Moral Development
- ☑ **IMAGE** Introspection
- ☑ **IMAGE** Margaret Mead
- ☑ **SELF-CHECK QUIZ**

LESSON 2

Personal Development

Reading **HELP**DESK

Academic Vocabulary

- authority
- unique

Content Vocabulary

- rationalization
- identity crisis
- social learning theory

TAKING NOTES:

Key Ideas and Details

DIFFERENTIATING Use a chart similar to the one below to describe the characteristics of each category of Marcia's identity theory.

Identity Status	Characteristics

ESSENTIAL QUESTION • *How do physical changes impact emotional development?*

IT MATTERS BECAUSE

During adolescence, many changes are occurring in ways of thinking and feeling. Becoming an adult involves much more than becoming physically mature, although that is an important part of the process. During the transition from childhood to adulthood, people try on different roles, seeking answers to the questions, "Who am I?" and "What do I believe?" Gradually a sense of self begins to develop.

Cognitive Development

GUIDING QUESTION *What makes adolescents prone to think idealistically?*

During adolescence, the thinking patterns characteristic of adults begin to emerge. Developmental psychologist Jean Piaget described this as *formal operations* thinking. From about age 11 or 12, most people's thinking becomes more abstract. For example, the adolescent can consider the answer to a hypothetical question such as "What would the world be like if people lived to be 200?" An adolescent can entertain such hypothetical possibilities in a way that a young child cannot. This ability expands the adolescent's problem-solving capacity. A teenager who discovers that her car's engine has a knock can consider a number of possible causes and systematically test various adjustments and auto parts until she finds the root of the problem. This is the same ability that a scientist must have to conduct experiments.

With the comprehension of the hypothetical comes the ability to understand higher level thinking, contemplate abstract principles, and deal with analogies and metaphors. Not only is this capacity important for studying higher level science and mathematics, but it also leads the adolescent to deal with abstractions in his or her own life, such as ethics, conformity, and phoniness. It allows for introspection—examining one's own motives and thoughts. In an example of abstract, introspective thinking, one adolescent noticed, "I found myself thinking about my future, and then I began to think about why I was thinking about my future, and then I began to think about why I was thinking about why I was thinking about my future."

Rationalization

These new intellectual capacities also enable the adolescent to deal with overpowering emotional feelings through **rationalization**. In rationalization, an individual tries to explain an unpleasant feeling or behavior in such a way as to preserve self-esteem. After failing a test, for example, an adolescent may rationalize that it happened "because I was overly worried about the date I might be going on next week." An 8-year-old is too tied to concrete reality to consider systematically all the reasons why he or she might have failed.

Rationalization grows out of the need for people to see themselves as decent and moral individuals. One study showed that adolescent smokers are very good at rationalizing their behavior—even better than adults who smoke. For example, they might say "there are lots of risks in life," "I'd rather have a short, good life than a long, boring life," or "I live healthy otherwise." All of these statements are designed to rationalize dangerous behavior.

Do all adolescents fully reach the stage of formal operations thinking at the same age? As you might suspect, just as there are variations in physical maturity, so there are variations in cognitive maturity. In general, the rate of mental growth varies greatly both among individual adolescents and among social and economic classes in this country. Regardless of their cultural background, the more education an adolescent has, the higher their reasoning stage will be. One study showed that fewer than half of the 17-year-olds tested had reached the stage of formal operations thinking.

Differences have also been noted among nations. Formal operations thinking is less prevalent in some societies than in others, probably because of differences in the amount of formal education available. People who cannot read and write lack the tools to separate thought from concrete reality, and hence they cannot reach, or do not need to reach, more advanced levels of thinking.

rationalization a process whereby an individual seeks to explain an often unpleasant emotion or behavior in a way that will preserve his or her self-esteem

Adolescents display an egocentrism—the tendency to be overly concerned with the sudden changes in their lives. Usually this period of intense introspection decreases as adolescents become young adults.

▶ CRITICAL THINKING

Identifying Cause and Effect Why does formal operations thinking bring about introspection in adolescents?

Idealized Thinking

The change in thinking patterns is usually accompanied by changes in personality and social interactions as well. For example, adolescents tend to become very idealistic. This is because, for the first time, they can imagine the hypothetical—how things might be. When they compare this to the way things are, the world seems a sorry place. As a result, they can grow rebellious. Some adolescents even develop a "messiah complex" and believe they can save the world from evil. In addition, the adolescents of each generation typically become impatient with what they see as the adult generation's failures. They do not understand why, for example, a person who feels a job compromises his or her principles does not just quit. For example, if a mother works for an engineering firm that damages the environment, her adolescent child might think she should simply find a different job.

HOW DOES THE MEDIA PORTRAY ADOLESCENTS?

Many television shows feature teenagers as the main characters. How are these teenagers featured? What are their concerns and how do they handle problems?

Procedure

1. Watch a television show that features teenagers as the main characters.
2. List the problems presented in the show, how you predict the teens will try to resolve them, and how the teens actually attempted to resolve them.
3. In small groups, identify and debate alternative solutions.
4. Select one alternative solution and implement it in a role-play of the show's protagonists. Create a video of the role-play and post it on the class site.

Analysis

1. View each group's video. In a report, discuss the pros and cons of each solution presented. Identify the solution you think was most effective in solving the problem. Support your choice.
2. How well did the show's characters' solutions compare with those of your classmates? Which solutions involved higher-level abstract thought and ethical considerations?

Little thought is given to hardships of changing jobs or to the fact that the new company's behavior might be just as questionable but perhaps in different ways. In other words, adolescents tend to be somewhat unrealistic about the complexities of life. Evidence suggests that adolescent risk-taking behavior may be based in underdeveloped self-regulation.

Psychologist David Elkind, a specialist in child and adolescent development, has conducted research to learn more about the thinking processes of young adolescents. Dr. Elkind notes that adolescents often overlook what may seem obvious to adults. Instead these young people may develop complicated solutions for common issues. This can lead to them making inappropriate choices. Because they have not yet fully developed the ability to see the world from others' perspectives, their views tend to be self-centered. For example, if they are extremely interested in baseball, they may assume this is true of everyone. According to Dr. Elkind, adolescents believe that they are always playing to an audience with an extreme interest in their individual activities and also believe that their feelings are unique and cannot be understood by anyone else.

Dr. Elkind has described some problems adolescents develop as a result of immaturity and abstract thought processes:

- **Finding fault with authority figures:** Adolescents discover that people they admired for years fall short of their ideals and let everyone know it. Suddenly a teen no longer wants to play tennis with her father and quits asking his opinion on current news events.
- **Argumentativeness:** Adolescents practice building their own viewpoints by arguing any problem that presents itself. This argumentativeness can lead to strained relationships with parents and other adults who see the adolescent as merely being difficult.
- **Indecisiveness:** Aware of many choices, adolescents often have trouble making even simple decisions. The fear of making a wrong decision may be so great that the adolescent avoids it by making no decision.
- **Apparent hypocrisy:** Adolescents have difficulty understanding an ideal and living up to it.
- **Self-consciousness:** Adolescents assume that everyone is thinking about the same thing they are—themselves! This leads them to avoid situations they think will be uncomfortable. For example, a young man who has a good voice may be willing to sing in a choir, but not to sing a solo.
- **Invulnerability:** Adolescents begin to feel special, that their experiences are unique, and that they are not subject to the same rules that govern everyone else. This special feeling of invulnerability underlies adolescent risk-taking behavior and self-destructive behavior.

✔ READING PROGRESS CHECK

Contrasting How does an adolescent's thinking differ from that of a child?

Moral Development

GUIDING QUESTION *What ability is key to reaching higher levels of moral thinking?*

Besides experiencing physical and cognitive changes, some adolescents, though by no means all, also go through important changes in their moral thinking. According to Lawrence Kohlberg, moral reasoning develops in three levels, which he subdivides into six stages.

The first level is preconventional morality. Infants are amoral; that is, they are unable to make moral judgments. Young children in the early stages of their moral development are very egocentric. Their notions of morality are primitive: they consider an act right or wrong depending on whether or not it elicits punishment. This is Stage 1 in Kohlberg's model. In Stage 2, children realize that there is not just one right view, but that different people have different viewpoints. At this stage, children look out for their own interests, considering an act right or wrong depending on whether it has positive or negative consequences for themselves. At this point, punishment is simply something to be avoided.

Kohlberg's second level of moral development is conventional morality. Children are usually at this point by the time they enter adolescence, although they may occasionally slip back to preconventional morality. Stage 3 is often referred to as the "good boy/good girl" stage. Children try to live up to the expectations of family members or close friends. They become interested in motives and intentions, and understand concepts such as love, trust, and concern for others. Stage 4 is commonly referred to as the "law and order" stage. At this stage, children become concerned with society as a whole. The emphasis is on obeying laws, respecting **authority**, and doing one's duty.

Many people never get beyond the conventional morality of Stage 4, and their moral thinking remains quite rigid. For those who do, however, adolescence and young adulthood are usually the periods of the most profound development as they transition to the third level of moral development, postconventional morality. Individuals who progress to Stage 5 become concerned with whether a law is fair or just. They believe that laws must change as the world changes and are not absolute. For example, an individual at Stage 5 might ignore a law to save a life.

authority a person who is in command or in charge

Kohlberg's Model of Moral Development		
Level I: Preconventional Morality		
Stage 1	Obedience or Punishment Orientation	Rules seen as fixed and absolute. Obeying rules is important to avoid punishment.
Stage 2	Self-Interest Orientation	Children see that there is room for negotiation. Decisions are based on "What's in it for me?"
Level II: Conventional Morality		
Stage 3	Social Conformity Orientation	There is a sense of living up to expectations of what "good boys" and "good girls" do.
Stage 4	Law and Order Orientation	By adulthood, people usually focus on law and order and following rules.
Level III: Postconventional Morality		
Stage 5	Social Contract Orientation	People sometimes disobey rules if they think them wrong or work to change laws that don't "work."
Stage 6	Universal Principles Orientation	At this point, people follow universal principles of ethics regardless of laws and rules.

< CHART

KOHLBERG'S MODEL OF MORAL DEVELOPMENT
Kohlberg argued that moral development followed a specific sequence.

▶ **CRITICAL THINKING**

1. *Interpreting* At which level are moral judgments based on consequences of behavior?

2. *Analyzing* At which stage are moral judgments based on rules that maintain moral order?

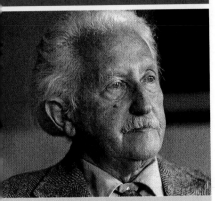

Erik Erikson
(1902–1994)

Born to Danish parents, Erik Erikson never knew his father. Erik's father left his mother before he was born. His mother married a German-Jewish pediatrician. Erikson felt that he did not belong. Mocked in synagogues because of his fair features and ostracized by non-Jews because of his faith, the development of an identity became one of the greatest concerns of Erikson's life.

Erikson traveled to Rome as an art student to study the works of Michelangelo, and this experience inspired him to study psychoanalysis with Anna Freud, Sigmund Freud's daughter. The success of therapy convinced Erikson to become an analyst.

Although Erikson never formally attained a degree in psychology, he taught at such institutions as Harvard and Yale. His major contribution to psychology was his identification of an eight-stage life cycle.

▶ **CRITICAL THINKING**

Making Connections What factors of Erikson's own childhood led to his interest in adolescence and identity development?

Individuals who reach Stage 6 are also concerned with making fair and just decisions. However, they differ from Stage 5 individuals in that they formulate absolute ethical principles, such as the Golden Rule, that they have worked through for themselves. They believe such moral laws apply to everyone, cannot be broken, and are more important than any written law.

Reaching higher levels of moral thinking involves the ability to abstract—to see a situation from another's viewpoint. That is why such moral development tends to occur in adolescence, when individuals gain the capacity for formal operations thinking. Not all adolescents who display such thinking simultaneously show higher levels of moral reasoning, though. In fact, only about 1 in 10 do. Thus, formal thought, while necessary for higher moral development, does not guarantee it. Interestingly, by the mid-1980s, Kohlberg began to question whether differentiating between Stages 5 and 6 was necessary. He concluded that only one stage—combining the key features of both stages—adequately identified the most advanced form of moral development and thinking.

Overall, psychologists agree that a person's moral development depends on many factors, especially the kind of relationship the individual has with his or her parents or significant others. Evidence shows that during high school, adolescent moral development does not progress much. During college, however, when the individual is away from home more and experiencing different cultures and ideas, more pronounced changes in moral development occur.

☑ **READING PROGRESS CHECK**

Contrasting What are the major differences between Stage 5 and Stage 6 of Kohlberg's moral development?

Identity Development

GUIDING QUESTION *How does Erikson's focus on individual development weaken his theory?*

The changes adolescents undergo affect many facets of their existence, so it is hardly surprising that these changes help to shape personality. Psychologists who have studied personality changes in adolescence have focused on the concept of identity. One psychologist in particular, Erik Erikson, has shown that the establishment of identity is key to adolescent development. His theory of how individuals arrive at an integrated sense of self has inspired a great deal of argument.

One issue that developmental psychologists still debate today is *continuity versus discontinuity*. Erickson viewed development as *discontinuous*—it proceeds in sequential stages. Moving on to the next developmental stage depends on successful completion of the previous stage. Other psychologists view development as *continuous*. Changes occur gradually over time.

Psychologists also disagree about the issue of *stability versus change*. Several studies have focused on determining to what degree development remains stable over time. For example, do behaviors or traits, such as shyness, stay the same? Or, do they change? Could a person become more or less shy over time? Studies suggest that many aspects of development do remain stable. However, evidence also supports the view that traits can and do evolve over a lifetime.

Erikson's Theory of the Identity Crisis

According to Erikson, building an identity is a task that is **unique** to adolescence. Children are aware of what other people think of them. They know the labels others apply to them, such as good, naughty, silly, talented, brave, and pretty. They are also aware of their biological drives and of their growing physical and cognitive abilities. Children may dream of being this person or that person, fictional or non-fictional, and act out these roles in their play. Yet they do not brood about who they are or where they are going in life. Children tend to live in the present. Adolescents, on the other hand, have begun to think about the future.

To achieve some sense of themselves, most adolescents must go through what Erikson termed an identity crisis—a time of inner conflict during which they worry intensely about their identities. Several factors contribute to the onset of this crisis, including the physiological changes and cognitive developments described earlier in this chapter, as well as awakening sexual drives and the possibility of a new kind of intimacy with the opposite sex. Adolescents begin to see the future as a reality, not just a game. They know they have to confront the almost infinite and often conflicting possibilities and choices that lie ahead. In the process of reviewing their past and anticipating their future, they begin to think about themselves. The process is a painful one that is full of inner conflict, because they are torn by the desire to feel unique and distinctive on the one hand and to fit in on the other. Only by resolving this conflict do adolescents achieve an integrated sense of self.

According to Erikson, adolescents face a crisis of identity formation versus identity confusion. The task of an adolescent is to become a unique individual with a valued sense of self in society. This issue is never completely resolved. The issue surfaces many times during a lifetime.

Adolescents need to organize their needs, abilities, talents, interests, background, culture, and peer demands to find a way to express themselves through an identity in a socially acceptable way. Identity forms when the adolescent can resolve issues such as the choice of an occupation, a set of values to believe in and live by, and the development of a sexual identity. The adolescent question is "Who am I?"

Role confusion is normal. It may be the reason why some adolescents' lives seem so chaotic. It also may explain why some adolescents are extremely self-conscious. Confusion is represented by childish behavior to avoid resolving conflicts and impulsiveness in decision making.

Marcia's View of the Identity Crisis

Erikson's theory finds support in the work of another psychologist, James Marcia. According to Marcia, Erikson is correct in pointing to the existence of an adolescent identity crisis. That crisis arises because individuals must make commitments on such important matters as occupation, religion, and political orientation. Using the categories of "crisis" and "commitment," Marcia distinguished four types of adolescent attempts to achieve a sense of identity. The first are *identity moratorium adolescents,* who are seriously considering the issues but have not made a commitment on any of the important matters facing them. These adolescents are trying to reach a compromise between their parents, society's demands, and their own abilities. They spend a lot of time trying to resolve difficult issues.

	Exploring identity issues	Not exploring identity issues yet
Decisions already made	Identity Achievement	Identity Foreclosure
Decisions not yet made	Identity Moratorium	Identity Diffusion

Source: Adapted from Kalat, 2005.

unique limited to a particular thing or person

identity crisis a period of inner conflict during which adolescents worry intensely about who they are

‹ CHART

IDENTITY CATEGORIES
Adolescent identity exploration can be divided into four categories.

▶ **CRITICAL THINKING**

1. *Interpreting* In which category would you place someone who is not actively concerned with his or her identity and is waiting until later to decide the issue?

2. *Making Connections* In which category would you place someone who has joined a political party in opposition to his or her parents' political choices?

The Samoa that Mead saw is now gone. Once a place in which most young people came of age with relative ease, Samoa has become a place where young people experience great difficulty in terms of finding a place in their society. As a result, they currently have one of the highest suicide rates in the world.

▶ **CRITICAL THINKING**

Comparing What are the cultural similarities and differences in the difficulties faced by young Samoans and Americans as they enter adulthood?

The second are *identity foreclosure adolescents.* This is an individual who has made a firm commitment about issues based not on their own choice but on the suggestion of others. This individual is becoming what others, such as parents, prepared him or her to become as a child. Individuals in this type often tend to be rigid and can find it difficult to change their beliefs.

The third type are *identity confused* or *diffused adolescents.* An individual of this type has not yet given any serious thought to making any decisions and has no clear sense of identity. This person has not yet chosen a career and is not concerned about it. An individual of this type is also not particularly concerned about the consequences of being directionless.

The fourth and final type are *identity achievement adolescents,* who considered many possible identities and have freely committed themselves to occupations and other important life matters. These individuals have examined several choices and made their decisions on their own terms, even if it is not what their parents may have wished. They may have reevaluated past beliefs when reaching their decisions. They tend to be flexible and are typically not overwhelmed if they face unexpected challenges or responsibilities.

These categories must not be too rigidly interpreted. It is possible for an individual to make a transition from one category to another, and it is also possible to belong to one category with respect to religious commitment and to another with respect to political orientation or occupational choice. Marcia's main contribution is in clarifying the sources and nature of the adolescent identity crisis.

Alternative Views

Although Erikson and Marcia insist that all adolescents experience an identity crisis, not all psychologists agree. The term "crisis" suggests that adolescence is a time of nearly overwhelming stress. It also implies that the adolescent transition to maturity requires a radical break with childhood experience. Many psychologists believe that adolescence is not strife-ridden, but a smooth transition from one stage of life to the next—especially following a healthy childhood.

One of the reasons Erikson may have arrived at his view is that he focused his study on disturbed adolescents who sought clinical psychiatric treatment. When adolescents attending school are selected at random and studied, critics point out that most show no sign of crisis and appear to be progressing rather smoothly through adolescence.

Psychologists and social scientists seeking an alternative to Erikson's theory have offered several other explanations for adolescent identity formation. A.C. Petersen, for example, argued that crisis is not the normal state of affairs for adolescents. When crises develop—as they do in a little more than 20 percent of all adolescent boys—the cause is generally a change in the external circumstances of an individual's life rather than a biological factor. Thus, a divorce in the family or a new set of friends may trigger teenage rebellion and crisis, but no internal biological clock dictates those events.

Social Learning View

Human development, in Albert Bandura's view, is one continuous process. At all stages, including adolescence, individuals develop by interacting with others. They observe and then model their behavior and emotional reactions to what they see around them. They adjust their behavior based on feedback received. For example, when an adolescent sees those around him cheering the local football team, he is likely to join in. However, if those around him respond negatively when he boos a referee, he will most likely not do so again. Therefore, adolescents are constantly adjusting their behavior to match those around them, especially those people whom they admire. Because of Bandura's emphasis on interaction in understanding adolescence and all other phases of human development, his approach is usually referred to as a **social learning theory** of development.

Margaret Mead also stressed the importance of the social environment in adolescent identity formation. On the basis of her studies in Samoa, for example, she concluded, like Bandura, that human development is more a continuous process than one marked by radical discontinuity. In that remote part of the world, adolescents were not expected to act any differently than they did as children or would be expected to act as adults. The reason was that children in Samoa were given a great deal of responsibility. They did not suddenly go from being submissive in childhood to being dominant later in life. Mead also pointed out that in Samoa, as in other nonindustrial societies, children had gender roles similar to those of adults and therefore did not experience the onset of sexuality as an abrupt change or a traumatic experience. The identity crisis, then, was by no means a universal phenomenon.

Personality development in adolescence is a complex phenomenon. It involves not only how a person develops a sense of self, or identity, but also how that person develops relationships with others and the skills used in social interactions. No one theory can do justice to all that is involved in the process of personality development. Erikson's emphasis on the adolescent's need for his or her own identity is an important contribution. In adolescence, self-esteem is influenced by the process of developing an identity. Self-esteem refers to how much one likes oneself. Self-esteem is linked to feelings of self-worth, attractiveness, and social competence. By focusing on the psychology of the individual, however, Erikson tended to ignore the influence of society. The studies of Bandura and Mead provide needed correctives. To arrive at a balanced picture of personality change and identity formation in adolescence, we must call upon all viewpoints.

✔ READING PROGRESS CHECK

Contrasting Distinguish between the two views of development as continuous or discontinuous.

Psychology & YOU

Good Looks Are Overrated

Often our opinions of ourselves relate to our looks. Many people actually think that they are better looking than others rate them. Also, any social advantages, such as popularity, seem to decline as people mature. This may be because plain people work harder to develop social skills, while their better-looking peers do not receive the automatic attention they once did. Having good looks is not the only way to earn self-respect. Researchers studied a group of boys from age 10 to early adulthood, finding that those with consistently high self-esteem were not necessarily the best looking. The most confident boys were the ones whose parents had set high standards yet showed respect for the boys' own decision making.

social learning theory
Bandura's view of human development; emphasizes interaction

LESSON 2 REVIEW

Reviewing Vocabulary
1. *Describing* Describe the social learning theory.

Using Your Notes
2. *Synthesizing* Use your notes to write a short summary of Marcia's identity theory.

Answering the Guiding Questions
3. *Analyzing* What makes adolescents prone to think idealistically?

4. *Identifying* What ability is key to reaching higher levels of moral thinking?

5. *Evaluating* How does Erikson's focus on individual development weaken his theory?

Writing Activity
6. *Informative/Explanatory* Select one of Dr. David Elkind's adolescent problems and characterize that problem in a narrative or fictional dialogue.

LESSON 3
Social Development

Academic Vocabulary

• **hierarchy**   • **phenomenon**

Content Vocabulary

• **clique**
• **conformity**
• **anorexia nervosa**

TAKING NOTES:

Key Ideas and Details

IDENTIFYING CAUSE AND EFFECT
Use a graphic organizer like the one below to describe three difficulties that adolescents might encounter.

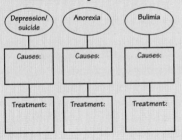

ESSENTIAL QUESTION • *How does culture influence behavior?*

IT MATTERS BECAUSE
Adolescents experience various changes in their social relationships. No longer a child though not yet an adult, the teenager must find a new role in the family—one that parents are not always ready to accept. He or she must also adjust to new, often more intense relationships with peers.

The Roles of Family and Peers

GUIDING QUESTION *How does the role of the family change during adolescence?*

Families in the United States have experienced marked changes in the past several decades. Prior to 1970, divorce was relatively uncommon. The typical American family had a wage-earning father who worked outside the home and a mother who worked within the home. Today, almost half of all marriages end in divorce, resulting in many single-parent families. More than half of all adult women are in the workforce, and families where both the mother and father are present usually have two rather than just one wage earners.

Regardless of these changes, one of the principal developmental tasks for adolescents is becoming independent of their families. Unfortunately, the means to achieve this status is not always clear, either to the adolescents or to their parents. First, there are mixed feelings on both sides. Some parents have built their lifestyles around the family and are reluctant to let the child go. Such parents know they will soon have to find someone else on whom to shift their emotional dependence. Also, parents whose children are old enough to leave home sometimes have to wrestle with their own fears of advancing age. In addition, many parents worry about whether their children are really ready to cope with the more difficult realities of life—worries that may often be shared by the adolescents themselves.

At the same time that young people long to get out on their own and try themselves against the world, they worry about failing. This internal struggle is often mirrored in the adolescent's unpredictable behavior, which parents may interpret as "adolescent rebellion." Against this background of uncertainty, which is almost universal, there are various family styles of working toward autonomy.

The Importance of Peer Groups

Adolescents can trust their peers not to treat them like children. Teenagers spend much of their time with friends—they need and use each other to define themselves. High schools are important as places for adolescents to get together, and they do so in fairly predictable ways. Most schools contain easily recognizable and well-defined groups. These groups are arranged in a fairly rigid **hierarchy**—everyone knows who belongs to which group and what people in that group do with their time. Early in adolescence groups are usually divided by sex, but later the sexes mix. Groups also usually form along class lines. Some school activities bring teenagers of different social classes together, but it is the exception rather than the rule that cross-class friendships are maintained.

Besides class, what determines whether an adolescent will be accepted by a peer group? Many studies have shown that personal characteristics are very important. These studies indicate that popularity is very much based on good looks and personality. With both sexes, athletic ability is also an important factor. Today many peer groups adopt very distinct styles to express themselves.

Belonging to a **clique**, or a small exclusive group of people within a larger group, is very important to most adolescents and serves several functions. Most obviously, perhaps, it fulfills the need for closeness with others. In addition, it gives the adolescent a means of defining himself or herself, a way of establishing an identity. The group does this by helping the individual achieve self-confidence, develop a sense of independence from family, clarify values, and experiment with new roles. For instance, members of cliques may imitate one another's clothing, speech, or hairstyles. By providing feedback, clique members not only help define who an individual is but also who he or she is not. Group membership separates an adolescent from others who are not in his or her group.

Of course, there are drawbacks to this kind of social organization. One of the greatest is the fear of being disliked, which leads to **conformity**—the "glue" that holds the peer group together. These group pressures often lead adolescents to avoid any behaviors they believe will be disliked by their group. Teenagers' fear of wearing clothes that might set them apart from others, for instance, is a well known example of this kind of behavior. Group pressures to conform, however, may also lead young people to do more serious things that run contrary to their better judgment.

hierarchy the classification of a group of people according to ability or to economic or social standing

clique a small, exclusive group of people within a larger group

conformity acting in accordance with some specified authority

As individuals progress from childhood to adolescence, peers become very important.

▶ **CRITICAL THINKING**

Hypothesizing Why are adolescents so heavily influenced by peers?

Tim Pannell/Corbis

Adolescence **101**

Some researchers claim that today's boys are in trouble and it is time to pay attention to how we are raising them. Why? Let us just look at the numbers. Males die in greater numbers in infancy than females. Boys are far more likely than girls to be told they have learning disabilities, to be sent to the principal's office, to be suspended from high school, or to commit crimes. In adolescence boys kill themselves five times more often than girls do. In adulthood they are being jailed at increasing rates, abandoning families, and are more likely to be the victims of or commit violence.

Some psychologists seek to explain these numbers by proposing that the way we parent and educate boys does not allow them to fully develop the capacity for emotional depth and complexity. As a result, boys are less capable than girls of meeting the challenges of adolescence successfully. In effect, we are not educating boys correctly. Their traditional survival qualities, such as physical strength and dominant personalities, no longer assure their survival or success.

Peer Groups and Families

Despite their tendency to encourage conformity, peer groups are not always the dominant influence in an adolescent's life. Both parents and peers exercise considerable influence in shaping adolescent behavior and attitudes. Peers tend to set the standards on such matters as fashion and taste in music. In addition, researchers have found that adolescents may consider the advice of peers on school-related issues to be more reliable than parental counsel.

When it comes to basic matters, however, involving marriage, religion, or educational plans, adolescents tend to accept their parents' beliefs and to follow their advice. Only in a few areas touching basic values—for example, drug use or sexual behavior—do differences exist. Even here the differences are not fundamental and represent only a difference in the strength with which the same basic belief is held. For example, adolescents may have more liberal views on premarital sex than their parents do.

Peer groups, then, do not pose a threat to parental authority. Even though parents spend less time with their adolescent children as the latter mature, their influence is still strong. Adolescents of both sexes tend to choose friends with values close to those of their parents. As a result, these peer groups are of immense help to the adolescent in making the transition from dependent child to independent adult. Thus, generational conflict is not nearly so pronounced as some researchers would have us believe.

On the other hand, psychologist Judith Rich Harris claims that peer groups, not parents, teach children how to behave in the world. So, the only influence parents are able to have over their children is by supplying the environment in which they meet peers. Harris argues that parents should live in a good neighborhood so their children associate with positive peers. Some psychologists passionately criticize Harris's theory. Critics claim that there is a very strong relationship between parenting styles and the social development of children and that the style is more important than the neighborhood.

✓ READING PROGRESS CHECK

Making Connections How do peer groups reinforce parental values for an adolescent?

Difficulties During Adolescence

GUIDING QUESTION *What parenting style is well equipped to respond to teenage depression?*

As you have seen in this chapter, adolescence is a time of transition. Since only about six or seven years separate older children from young adults, adolescence carries a great deal responsibilities involving change. But as Erikson pointed out, every stage of life brings with it unique challenges that are specific to that stage, whether it is old age, early childhood, or adolescence.

Given the great array of profound changes the adolescent must cope with involving his or her mind, body, emotions, and social relationships, it is natural and normal that most adolescents should experience some temporary psychological difficulties. The great majority, however, adjusts fairly quickly. Although some studies show that mental illness and suicide are relatively rare among adolescents, the rates of both have at times been high. Between 1950 and 1990, for example, the teenage suicide rate quadrupled. Since then, the rate has been in steady decline. Suicide figures, however, may be underestimated because medical personnel sometimes label a death as an accident to protect the victim's family.

The illusion of invulnerability—"Others may get caught, but not me!"—is a part of adolescent egocentrism. This illusion may lead adolescents to do things with their peers they would not do alone. This troubled minority often "acts out"

Types of crime	Number of juvenile arrests	Percent of juvenile arrests	Percent change, 2000–2009
All Types	**1,906,600**	**100.0**	**–9**
Violent crime	**85,890**	**4.5**	**–10**
Murder	1,170	.1	–7
Forcible rape	3,100	.2	–6
Robbery	31,700	1.7	–10
Aggravated assault	49,900	2.6	–11
Property crime	**417,700**	**21.9**	**–4**
Burglary	74,800	3.9	–10
Larceny-theft	317,700	16.7	–1
Motor vehicle theft	19,900	1.0	–20
Arson	5,300	.3	–17
Curfew	112,600	5.9	–15
Runaways	93,400	4.9	–14

Source: U.S. Department of Justice

< CHART

JUVENILE ARRESTS IN THE UNITED STATES
Crimes involving violence and property damage are the most frequently reported crimes involving juveniles. The arrest rates for both these types of crime have decreased over the past decade.

▶ **CRITICAL THINKING**

1. *Analyzing Visuals* Which of the two main categories of crime accounted for most juvenile arrests? How did arrests in this category change between 2000 and 2009?

2. *Identifying Cause and Effect* What factors contribute to juvenile delinquency?

problems in one of several ways. Acts of juvenile delinquency—running away from home, violent behavior, vandalism, alcohol and drug abuse, and underachievement at school—are frequently reported. Juveniles were involved in 15 percent of all violent crime arrests and 29 percent of all property crime arrests in the United States in 2003. Repeat offenders and the fact that many offenders are not caught make these data hard to interpret, though.

Most juveniles generally outgrow these tendencies as they mature, but unfortunately some do not. Those who do not outgrow these tendencies will often develop greater problems later in life, especially if they do not seek help or treatment. Adults, therefore, should not treat teenage delinquency lightly.

Teenage Depression and Suicide

The **phenomenon** of teenage depression is much more widespread than most parents or educators suspect. To many grownups who see adolescence as the best years of life, depression and youth may seem incompatible. What events trigger depression in adolescents? One major event is the loss of a loved one through separation, family relocation, divorce, or death. The adolescent may experience grief, guilt, panic, and anger as a reaction. If the teenager is not able to express these feelings in a supportive atmosphere, depression may result.

Another form of loss that causes depression is the breakdown of the family unit, often as a result of separation and divorce. Family members may be in conflict and unable to communicate well. In some cases, adolescents can find themselves "caught in the middle" between parents who have come to disagreements. Adolescents may be therefore deprived of the emotional support they need.

Unlike depressed adults, who usually look and feel sad or "down," depressed teenagers may appear to be extremely angry. They often engage in rebellious behavior such as truancy, running away, drinking, using drugs, or being sexually promiscuous. Often, depressed teenagers appear intensely hyperactive and frantic, traits that are frequently mistaken for normal behavior in teenagers. Parents and educators need to be aware of the warning signals of teenage depression and suicide. One warning signal is a change in the intensity and frequency of rebellious behavior. Others are withdrawing from friends, engaging in dangerous risk taking, talking about suicide, and excessive self-criticism. Frequently, the greatest danger of suicide occurs after a depression seems to be lifting.

Publicizing teen suicide does not seem to prevent it. In fact, publicizing suicide seems to encourage more suicidal behavior. The best way to deal with teenage

phenomenon an observable event

depression is to communicate with the teenager about his or her problems. Sometimes a caring, listening parent or a responsive, sensitive friend can help the youth deal with his or her concerns. In other cases, parents and their teenage child may need to seek professional help. This is particularly true when few channels of communication are open.

Eating Disorders

Eating disorders such as anorexia nervosa and bulimia nervosa affect many teenagers and young adults, especially females. Adolescents who develop eating disorders do not get the calories or the nutrition they need to grow. A serious eating disorder, **anorexia nervosa**, is characterized by refusing to eat and not maintaining weight. People suffering from this disorder are frequently perfectionists who do well in school. At the same time, they suffer from low self esteem. They have an intense fear of gaining weight or amassing fat. Anorexics have a distorted body image—they see themselves as overweight and fat even though they are underweight and thin.

When faced with the pressures of adolescence, some people develop abnormal eating patterns. Some psychologists suggest that anorexia represents a female's refusal to grow up. Girls who develop anorexia typically miss menstrual cycles. Other psychologists propose that anorexia is an attempt by teenagers to assert control over their lives at a time when so much seems beyond their control; teens are able to feel a sense of control when they deny their bodies' demands for food.

anorexia nervosa a serious eating disorder characterized by a fear of gaining weight that results in prolonged self-starvation and dramatic weight loss

Diversity in Psychology

BODY IMAGE AND EATING DISORDERS

"You've gained weight" is a traditional compliment in Fiji. In the 1990s a nicely rounded body was the norm on this South Pacific island. All that changed, though, with the arrival of television. Now girls in Fiji dream of looking like American TV stars—skinny. A 2007 study revealed that eating disorders are also spreading indirectly through social interaction. The risk of eating disorders among Fijian girls increased when friends in their social network were exposed to mass media.

Eating disorders are more common in industrialized countries, such as the United States, Canada, and as many countries in Europe, and Australia. Eating disorders affect more than 5 million Americans each year. More than 90 percent of sufferers are females between the ages of 12 and 25. However, abnormal eating attitudes in non-Western countries are increasing, due in part to the spread and influence of Western media.

Eating disorders have the highest death rate of any disorder. Health concerns have led to efforts to curb media promotion of unhealthy eating attitudes. The Media Watchdog program of the National Eating Disorders Association (NEDA) encourages advertisers to send healthy media messages about body size and shape. In 2012 some popular social Web sites announced that they would remove posts and information that could promote eating disorders. Also in 2012 Israel passed a law banning the use of underweight models in fashion shows and commercials. Lawmakers hope this will reduce eating disorders.

People needing help can find resources at the Web sites of NEDA and the National Institute of Mental Health (NIMH).

▲ An adolescent girl from the island of Fiji.

▶ **CRITICAL THINKING**

1. *Identifying Cause and Effect* What is your ideal body image? How has culture influenced your sense of the ideal body?

2. *Exploring Issues* What are the signs that someone has an eating disorder? How would you help someone with an eating disorder? Go to the NEDA Web site for information.

Alicia Fox/Alamy

Treatment for anorexics usually involves not just the individual but also her family, physician, and a nutritionist. It focuses on encouraging weight gain as well as dealing with psychological problems. No medication has yet proved effective in treating anorexia. Some people with anorexia recover after a single episode, while others have relapses. Still others suffer from a chronic form of the disorder.

Another serious disorder, bulimia nervosa, is characterized by binge eating followed by purging—vomiting, using laxatives, or rigorous dieting and fasting—to eliminate the calories taken in during the binge. The binge and purge cycle may be repeated several

times a week or many times a day. Bulimics usually engage in this behavior in private, often running the water while they are in the bathroom in an attempt to hide what they are doing. People suffering from bulimia nervosa are excessively concerned about body shape and weight. Unlike people with anorexia, bulimics usually appear to be healthy, and may even be overweight.

According to the National Institute of Mental Health, 1.5 percent of women report having bulimia nervosa at some time in their lives. The exact cause of bulimia is unknown. Many psychologists believe there are probably many components, including genetic, psychological, and cultural factors. Some psychologists suggest that bulimia may result from a teen's feeling of alienation during adolescence or a need to find approval from others. Some bulimics also experience depression, anxiety, and mood swings. Treatment involves therapy and the use of antidepressant drugs. Group therapy, in which individuals interact with others having the same condition, has proven helpful for some people.

Anorexia develops over time as a way of coping with emotional stress or pain, unhappiness, or other problems a person may have.

▶ **CRITICAL THINKING**

Exploring Issues How is anorexia nervosa treated?

☑ **READING PROGRESS CHECK**

Specifying How might teens show evidence of depression?

Reviewing Vocabulary

1. *Specifying* What are the symptoms of anorexia nervosa?

Using Your Notes

2. *Differentiating* Use your notes to write a short essay describing three difficulties that adolescents might encounter.

Answering the Guiding Questions

3. *Analyzing* How does the role of the family change during adolescence?

4. *Finding the Main Idea* What parenting style is well equipped to respond to teenage depression?

Writing Activity

5. *Informative/Explanatory* Create an informational pamphlet on a problem some teens encounter, such as eating disorders or depression. Include statistics and treatment suggestions. Consider where your pamphlet might be made available in order to reach the widest audience possible affected by your topic.

Reader's Dictionary

virulence: extreme bitterness
cacophony: a harsh sound
belie: to show to be false or wrong

Marya Hornbacher grew up in a comfortable, middle-class American home. At an early age, she remembers crying her heart out because she thought she was "fat." At age nine, she was secretly bulimic; at age 15, anorexic. In this excerpt, taken from her memoirs Wasted (1998), Marya describes her illness.

Wasted

By Marya Hornbacher

PRIMARY SOURCE

I became bulimic at the age of nine, anorexic at the age of fifteen. I couldn't decide between the two and veered back and forth from one to the other until I was twenty, and now, at twenty-three, I am an interesting creature, an Eating Disorder Not Otherwise Specified. My weight has ranged over the past thirteen years from 135 pounds to 52, inching up and then plummeting back down. I have gotten "well," then "sick," then "well," then "sicker," and so on up to now; I am considered "moderately improved," "psychologically stabilized, behaviorally disordered," "prone to habitual relapse." I have been hospitalized six times, institutionalized once, had endless hours of therapy, been tested and observed and diagnosed and pigeonholed and poked and prodded and fed and weighed for so long that I have begun to feel like a laboratory rat. . . .

I am not here to spill my guts and tell you about how awful it's been, that my daddy was mean and my mother was mean and some kid called me Fatso in

the third grade, because none of the above is true. I am not going to repeat, at length, how eating disorders are "about control," because we've all heard it. It's a buzzword, reductive, categorical, a tidy way of herding people into a mental quarantine and saying: *There.* . . . The question is really not *if* eating disorders are "neurotic" and indicate a glitch in the mind—even I would have a hard time justifying, rationally, the practice of starving oneself to death or feasting only to toss back the feast—but rather why; why this glitch, what flipped this switch, why so many of us? Why so easy a choice, this? Why now? Some toxin in the air? Some freak of nature that has turned women against their own bodies with a **virulence** unmatched in history, all of a sudden, with no cause? The individual does not exist outside of society. There are reasons why this is happening, and they do not lie in the mind alone.

This book is neither a tabloid tale of mysterious disease nor a testimony to a miracle cure. It's simply the story of one woman's travels to a darker side of reality, and her decision to make her way back. On her own terms. My terms amount to cultural heresy. I had to say: I will eat what I want and look as I please and laugh as loud as I like and use the wrong fork and lick my knife. I had to learn strange and delicious lessons, lessons too few women learn: to love the thump of my steps, the implication of weight and presence and taking of space, to love my body's rebellious hungers, responses to touch, to understand myself as more than a brain

attached to a bundle of bones. I have to ignore the cultural **cacophony** that singsongs all day long, Too much, too much, too much. . . .

I wrote this book because I believe some people will recognize themselves in it—eating disordered or not—and because I believe, perhaps naively, that they might be willing to change their own behavior, get help if they need it, entertain the notion that their bodies are acceptable, that they themselves are neither insufficient nor in excess. I wrote it because I disagree with much of what is generally believed about eating disorders, and wanted to put in my two cents, for whatever it's worth. I wrote it because people often dismiss eating disorders as manifestations of vanity, immaturity, madness. It is, in some ways, all of these things. But it is also an addiction. It is a response, albeit a rather twisted one, to a culture, a family, a self. I wrote this because I want to dispel two common and contradictory myths about eating disorders: that they are an insignificant problem, solved by a little therapy and a little pill and a pat on the head, a "stage" that "girls" go through—I know a girl whose psychiatrist told her that her bulimia was just part of "normal adolescent development"—and, conversely, that they must **belie** true insanity, that they only happen to "those people" whose brains are incurably flawed, that "those people" are hopelessly "sick."

An eating disorder is not usually a phase, and it is not necessarily indicative of madness. It is quite maddening, granted, not only for the loved ones of the eat-

"An eating disorder is not usually a phase, and it is not necessarily indicative of madness."

ing disordered person but also for the person herself. It is, at the most basic level, a bundle of deadly contradictions: a desire for power that strips you of all power. A gesture of strength that divests you of all strength. A wish to prove that you need nothing, that you have no human hungers, which turns on itself and becomes a searing need for the hunger itself. It is an attempt to find an identity, but ultimately it strips you of any sense of yourself, save the sorry identity of "sick." It is a grotesque mockery of cultural standards of beauty that winds up mocking no one more than you. It is a protest against cultural stereotypes of women that in the end makes you seem the weakest, the most needy and neurotic of all women. It is the thing you believe is keeping you safe, alive, contained—and in the end, of course, you find it's doing quite the opposite. These contradictions begin to split a person in two. Body and mind fall apart from each other, and it is in this fissure that an eating disorder may flourish, in the silence that surrounds this confusion that an eating disorder may fester and thrive. . . .

There were numerous methods of self-destruction available to me, countless outlets that could have channeled my drive, perfectionism, ambition, and an excess of general intensity, millions of ways in which I could have responded to a culture that I found highly problematic. I did not choose those ways. I chose an eating disorder. I cannot help but think that, had I lived in a culture where "thinness" was not regarded as a strange state of grace, I might have sought out another means of attaining that grace, perhaps one that would not have so seriously damaged my body, and so radically distorted my sense of who I am.

Analyzing Primary Sources

1. *Paraphrasing* Why did the author write this?

2. *Drawing Conclusions* According to the author, how do eating disorders rob the sufferer of an identity?

3. *Analyzing Primary Sources* What underlying causes of her disorder does the author reveal?

netw⊙rks

There's More Online!

☑ **CARTOON** Gender Roles

☑ **IMAGE** Gender Roles

☑ **IMAGE** Schema for Boys

☑ **IMAGE** Schema for Girls

☑ **DIAGRAM** Test Yourself

☑ **GRAPHIC ORGANIZER**

☑ **SELF-CHECK QUIZ**

LESSON 4

Gender Roles and Differences

ESSENTIAL QUESTION • *How does culture influence behavior?*

IT MATTERS BECAUSE

The first question asked of new parents is "Is the baby a boy or a girl?" Your sex greatly influences how you dress, move, work, and play. It can influence your thoughts and others' thoughts about you. Are there significant psychological differences between males and females? Do children learn gender identities or are they born different?

Gender Roles

GUIDING QUESTION *How do gender roles differ from gender stereotypes?*

Many people just take for granted the differences between boys and girls, claiming that "boys will be boys," or something similar. Pick up a magazine, turn on the TV, or look outside your window—**gender** stereotypes are everywhere. Some parents dress baby girls in pink and boys in blue, give them gender-specific names, and expect them to act differently.

Gender Identity

People often think of the words *sex* and *gender* as interchangeable. However, *sex* refers to biological status, whereas *gender* refers to the behaviors that a culture associates with people of a particular sex. There are a number of things that determine biological sex, including sex chromosomes, reproductive organs, and genitalia. Thus, if one has a vagina, one's sex is female; if a penis, male. In most cases, a person's sexual identity and gender identity are the same: males usually identify as male, and females as female. Such individuals are referred to as gender-normative. When males identify as females or females identify as male, they are said to be transgender.

Similarly, gender identity and gender **roles** are two different, though closely related, aspects of our sexual lives. Gender identity is one's sense of oneself as male, female, or transgender. Gender identity includes genetic traits we have inherited and may include some gender-linked behaviors as well. Between the ages of 2 and 3, most children learn to label themselves as boys or girls. By the age of 5, most children have learned the thoughts, expectations, and behaviors that accompany their gender role.

A person's **gender role** is defined partly by genetic makeup but mainly by the society and culture in which the individual lives. The gender role is a standard of how a person with a given gender identity is supposed to behave and includes the traditional behaviors that society expects of people because they are male or female. For example, in the United States, men were traditionally viewed as dominant, competitive, and emotionally reserved; women were viewed as submissive, cooperative, and emotionally responsive. These traits were considered appropriate for the different sexes. Today young people have a much broader view of what is appropriate behavior for males and females.

This broader view extends to sexuality. *Sexual orientation* is an individual's emotional and sexual attraction to the same sex (homosexual), the opposite sex (heterosexual), both sexes (bisexual), or neither sex (asexual). Sexual orientation is not limited to sexual behavior. It is a complex part of an individual's personality. Most psychologists believe that sexual orientation is shaped at an early age through interactions among biological, psychological, and social factors.

The strongest influence on a child's gender role development is the parents. Parents can directly influence this development, for example, by assigning housework to a daughter and lawn care duties to a son. The parents also can influence gender role development indirectly. If a mother is always the one who stays home from work when a child is ill, the child may develop the opinion that men's careers are more important than those of women.

Gender roles vary from one society to another, and they can change over time within a given society. Gender roles give social meaning to gender identity. However, not all societies agree on the roles the sexes should assume. Indeed, anthropologists have found that some societies reverse the roles that Americans traditionally give to men and women, while others assign to both sexes what we might consider masculine or feminine roles. Not only do gender roles vary among societies, but they also may change radically within a society, as we are witnessing today in the United States and Canada.

Gender Stereotypes

Sometimes gender roles become so rigid that they become gender stereotypes. **Gender stereotypes** are oversimplified or prejudiced opinions and attitudes about how men or women should behave. Media advertising often uses stereotypes to target specific genders and may shape children's idea of male or female.

gender relating to a person's sex, male or female

role a part played by a person

gender identity the sex group (masculine or feminine) to which an individual biologically belongs

gender role the set of behaviors that society considers appropriate for each sex

gender stereotype an oversimplified or distorted generalization about the characteristics of men and women

⌄ CARTOON

GENDER ROLES
Gender stereotypes are often applied to individuals regardless of their age.

▶ CRITICAL THINKING

1. *Analyzing Visuals* How does this cartoon depict gender differences?

2. *Identifying Cause and Effect* Why do you think the children switch activities?

Between the ages of 3 and 5, children gain ideas about which toys, clothes, or activities are appropriate for their gender.

▶ **CRITICAL THINKING**

Analyzing Visuals What have these children learned about their gender roles?

androgynous combining or blending traditionally male and female characteristics

The stereotype that men are rugged and women are sensitive is rooted in a time when division of labor was necessary for survival. Today, modern technology and birth control have freed women from duties associated with child rearing and childbearing for a large part of their lives. Sharp gender-role divisions are no longer necessary or appropriate, especially in the workplace. New concepts of what it means to be masculine and feminine are more widely accepted.

Changing Standards

Given these changing standards of acceptable gender roles, psychologist Sandra Bem argues that people should accept new **androgynous** roles—that is, roles that involve a flexible combination of traditionally male and female characteristics. She began her research by asking college students how desirable they considered various characteristics for a man and for a woman. Not surprisingly, she found that traits such as ambition, self-reliance, independence, and assertiveness were considered to be desirable for men. It was desirable for women to be affectionate, gentle, understanding, and sensitive to the needs of others.

These and other traits were then listed in a questionnaire called the Bem Sex Role Inventory. Bem asked people to rate how each of these traits applied to them on a scale from one (never or almost never true) to seven (always or almost always true). In a 1975 report, Bem described the results for 1,500 Stanford undergraduates: about 50 percent stuck to traditional sex or gender roles (masculine males or feminine females), 15 percent were cross-sexed typed (women who described themselves in traditionally male terms or men who checked feminine adjectives), and 36 percent were considered androgynous, in that they checked off both male and female characteristics to describe themselves.

In later studies, Bem found that the people whose responses indicated androgynous preferences were indeed more flexible. Such women were able to be assertive when it was required, as could traditional males, but traditional females could not. Such people were also able to express warmth, playfulness, and concern, as could traditional females, but traditional males could not. In our complex world, Bem argues, androgyny should be our ideal: there is no room for an artificial split between our concepts of feminine and masculine roles.

Androgyny is becoming an accepted ideal in our culture. One consequence of this shift is that adolescents who are developing into adults have more choices in the way they define themselves in life. In some ways, this shift toward more freedom in gender roles has resulted in greater personal responsibility. No longer limited by rigid gender-role stereotypes, young people are challenged to define themselves according to their talents, temperaments, and values. At the same time, not all people accept the more androgynous gender roles. Older people, especially, may still be guided by traditional ideas about gender roles.

☑ **READING PROGRESS CHECK**

Identifying When do children start to label themselves as male and female?

Ronnie Kaufman/Larry Hirshowitz/Blend Images/Corbis

Gender Differences

GUIDING QUESTION *What is one area in which genders differ significantly?*

Psychologists have found that most people do see differences between genders. Are these differences, though, real or imagined? Are these differences the result of cultural stereotypes, or do they show up in the actual behaviors of boys and girls? Over the years, psychologists have conducted research to find answers to these questions. They have examined gender differences within many societies and cultures across the globe.

Gender Differences in Personality

Are there differences between the sexes? Studies have found that besides the obvious physical differences, differences between males and females do exist. It is important to note that these differences, though, exist between groups of males and females. Individuals may or may not exhibit these differences.

One study found that males are more confident than females, especially in academic areas or in tasks stereotyped as masculine, such as math and science. Even when they achieve the same grades as men, women perceive themselves as less competent than males. The self-confidence of females rises, though, when they perform tasks in which they receive clear and direct feedback on their performance, especially that which they complete alone.

Many studies have also found that aggression, or hostile or destructive behavior, is one of the areas with the most significant differences between genders. Females engage in more verbal aggressive acts, while males participate in more physical aggression. Some researchers propose that women also think differently about aggression. The women studied said they feel guilty or have more anxiety about the dangers involved in aggressive behavior.

Differences in aggressive behavior can be observed by watching children at play. Males are more likely to use mock fighting and rough and tumble play including pushing and grabbing, while females tend to use indirect forms of aggression.

Males and females tend to express their aggression in different ways. Males are more likely to use physical means to show their aggression.

▶ CRITICAL THINKING

Analyzing How are these young adolescent males expressing aggression?

Kevin Muggleton/Corbis

Test A: Which two figures on the right are the same as the figure on the left? (Answers at bottom.)

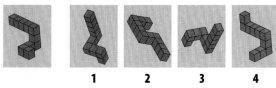

1   **2**   **3**   **4**

Test B: Cover the bottom box. Carefully study the top box for 1 minute. Then cover the top box, uncover the bottom box, and follow the instructions below.

Now note each item that remains in its original spot and each item that has been moved.

Source: Shepard & Metzler, 1971.

Answer to Test A: Figures 1 and 3 are the same as the figure on the left.

DIAGRAMS ^

TEST YOURSELF
In these tests of spatial abilities, most men would find Test A easier, while most women find Test B easier.

▶ **CRITICAL THINKING**

1. **Making Connections** How might biological theories explain gender differences of spatial ability?

2. **Identifying Perspectives** How might the social learning theory explain gender differences in spatial ability?

This may include such things as talking about or rejecting, ignoring, or avoiding the target of aggression.

What causes this physical aggression in boys? Starting at an early age, society encourages boys to be competitive and to settle conflicts through aggression. Evidence from studies of identical twins also indicates that men have lower levels of the neurotransmitter serotonin than women. Lower levels of serotonin have been associated with higher levels of aggression.

Another gender difference can often be detected in male and female verbal communication styles. Although popular stereotypes portray women as more talkative, studies have demonstrated that men actually talk more than women and interrupt women more while they are talking. Women talk more, though, when they have power in a relationship. Females are more likely to use *hedges* in speech, such as "kind of" or "you know." Women also use more *disclaimers*, such as "I may be wrong" or "I'm not sure." Finally, women use more *tag questions* at the end of sentences, such as "Okay?"

Men and women are frequently different in the ways they use nonverbal communication. Nonverbal communication involves providing information without using words. Instead of speaking, we use gestures, facial expressions, posture, and body language. Women are more likely to show submission and warmth, whereas men display more dominance and status. One way of showing submission nonverbally is by holding your limbs close to your body, for example, by crossing your legs. Dominance can be expressed by taking up more space, such as by stretching out your legs. More women than men are sensitive to nonverbal signals.

Gender Differences in Cognitive Abilities

You may have heard someone claim that females are better than males at verbal skills, while males excel at spatial and mathematical skills. In a 1988 study Janet Hyde and Marcia Linn examined 165 studies on verbal ability, finding that no measurable differences in verbal skills exist between males and females. If differences do exist, they are relatively small. When researchers examined mathematical abilities and gender, they discovered no significant differences between male and female abilities.

When researchers examine specific topics and age trends, some differences do appear. For example, males and females perform about the same in problem solving until high school. At that point, males outperform females. Men also tend to do better than females on tests of spatial ability that involve forming "mental maps"; however, women are better at tracking objects.

In conclusion, there are very few cognitive differences between males and females. The studies mentioned above should not limit the participation of males and females in specific areas, or be used as a basis for discrimination. The studies fail to reflect individual differences of ability and do not reflect an individual's motivations, past history, and ambitions.

✅ **READING PROGRESS CHECK**

Contrasting How do males and females differ in the way they show aggression?

Perspectives on Gender Differences

GUIDING QUESTION *How do nature and nurture affect gender differences?*

How gender differences develop is one of the many questions that fall into the *nature versus nurture* issue. While some argue that differences between sexes are biological, others propose that we learn gender differences from our environment. Today most psychologists agree that nature and nurture interact to influence gender differences. It is important to realize that even a minor biological difference can become greater if a child is rewarded for that difference. For example, if a boy is naturally more assertive than his sister, and his parents reward him for that behavior, his assertiveness will be strengthened.

Biological Theory

The biological theory of gender role development emphasizes the role of anatomy, hormones, and brain organization. Supporters of this theory state that regardless of what parents do, boys will tend to be more aggressive and girls will tend to be more sociable.

Supporters of this idea claim that differences in gender are the result of behaviors that evolved from early men and women. That is, men and women adopted certain behaviors throughout time in an attempt to survive. For example, men increased their chances of finding a mate and reproducing by adopting dominant and aggressive traits, while women increased their chances of raising children by being concerned, warm, and sensitive. Therefore, certain genetic or biological traits were formed in men and women.

Psychoanalytical Theory

According to Sigmund Freud, when a child identifies with a parent of the same sex, gender identity results. Little boys identify with their fathers, while girls identify with their mothers. This identification process occurs when children are between 3 and 5 years of age. Critics argue that identification seems to be the result, rather than the cause, of gender typing.

Social Learning Theory

The social learning theory emphasizes the role of social and cognitive processes on how we perceive, organize, and use information. For example, children learn their gender roles by observing and imitating models, such as their parents, friends, peers, and teachers. These models may respond to and reward certain behaviors in boys and different behaviors in girls.

For example, parents may buy rugged toy trucks for boys and soft dolls for girls. Parents may punish a girl for being outspoken and reward her for completing household chores. Parents may encourage a boy's high ambitions and independence but disapprove of him showing affection. In effect, these parents are rewarding or discouraging behaviors, depending on whether these behaviors match their views of traditional male and female gender roles.

Cognitive-Developmental Theory

The cognitive-developmental theory proposes that children acquire gender roles by interacting with their environment and thinking about those experiences. As they do this, children can learn different sets of standards for male and female behavior.

To learn about gender, a child must first begin to see himself or herself as male or female. Then the child begins to organize behavior around this concept. Through interaction with cultural influences, the child may begin to acquire societal preferences consistent with society's view of his or her perceived gender.

Traditionally girls were taught from an early age the homemaking skills they would need to care for their future husband and children.

▶ **CRITICAL THINKING**

Analyzing Visuals What might be different about this activity today?

gender schema a set of behaviors organized around how either a male or female should think and behave

If a child accepts these preferences, they combine in a gender schema. A **gender schema** is a mental representation of behavior that helps a child organize and categorize behaviors. A child develops a schema of how his or her gender should act and then behaves in accordance with or opposition to that schema. For example, a boy may watch a football game and then engage in rough play. A girl may begin to play with dolls if she believes that these are the kinds of toys girls play with. Under this theory, when children act in accordance with their schemas their confidence rises. When they act in ways contrary to their schemas they may feel inadequate.

Changing Gender Roles

The roles of women and men in society have changed dramatically and continue to evolve. For example, before the 1960s in the United States some women worked but few women were able to pursue careers. Most women grew up expecting to marry and quit work to raise children. By the mid-1980s, though, this had changed, with most women working outside the home. In 2010, 72 million women, almost 60 percent, are employed or looking for work and a growing percentage of women earn more than their husbands. For men and women, work provides income as well as a sense of accomplishment.

Despite the fact that more women are in the workforce, studies have shown that, in general, women do not advance as quickly as men and often occupy lower levels of leadership. Industrial/organizational psychologists propose that the inequality in the workplace may be the result of several factors. Companies may discriminate against women by not hiring or promoting them. Many women interrupt their careers for child care and in doing so miss opportunities for promotion and salary increases. Also, men and women may differ in their ambitions. That is, women may have been taught by society to set different goals. This is changing, however, as men become more involved in caring for their children and women's opportunities and earning power increase.

☑ **READING PROGRESS CHECK**

Explaining Which theories emphasize the role of how children are socialized in developing their gender identities?

LESSON 4 REVIEW

Reviewing Vocabulary
1. *Explaining* What is a person's gender schema?

Using Your Notes
2. *Describing* Use your notes to write a short essay describing the four theoretical perspectives on the origins of gender differences.

Answering the Guiding Questions
3. *Contrasting* How do gender roles differ from gender stereotypes?

4. *Contrasting* What is one area in which genders differ significantly?

5. *Analyzing* How do nature and nurture affect gender differences?

Writing Activity
6. *Argument* Select a TV program, advertisement, Internet site, or movie. Analyze the gender roles portrayed. Then, write a brief review of your selected media taking the representation of gender stereotypes into account.

netw⊙rks

There's More Online!

☑ GRAPHIC ORGANIZER

☑ SELF-CHECK QUIZ

Entering Adulthood

Reading **HELP**DESK (CCSS)

Academic Vocabulary

• encounter • intense

Content Vocabulary

• autonomy
• developmental friendship
• resynthesis
• comparable worth

TAKING NOTES:

Integration of Knowledge and Ideas

VISUALIZING Use a diagram similar to the one below to identify three ways that going to college stimulates change.

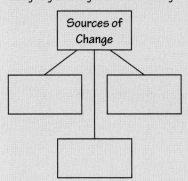

ESSENTIAL QUESTION • *How does culture influence behavior?*

IT MATTERS BECAUSE

Growing up involves gaining a sense of independence. Each person learns to make decisions, develop a value system, be responsible, and to care for himself or herself. Growing up is a process that starts long before an individual leaves home to live as a self-sufficient adult. Ultimately, it means separating from the family, both physically and emotionally.

Continuing Your Education

GUIDING QUESTION *What adjustments does going to college require?*

For many young Americans, college is a first big step toward this separation. As college students, individuals have more **autonomy** than they ever have. They are freer to make their own decisions, from when and what they eat to how to spend their time. College can be a liberating and stimulating experience. Yet it is also an experience that requires substantial adjustments to successfully navigate. As a result, many first-year college students feel an emotional upheaval called "college shock."

In 1969, Peter Madison spent nearly 10 years collecting data on how several hundred students adjusted to college. Each student provided a detailed life history and kept a weekly journal. Madison had classmates write descriptions of some of the students, and he tested and retested some at various points in their college careers.

Madison found that many students approach college with high, and often unrealistic, aspirations. For example, Bridget wanted to be an astronomer. She liked being different, and she considered astronomy an elite and adventurous field, but she did not know how many hard, unadventurous hours she would have to spend studying math to fulfill her dream. Keith planned to become a physician for humanitarian reasons. He had not thought about working in a hospital, however, or seeing people sicken and die.

These students, like many others, based their goals on fantasy. They did not have the experience to make realistic choices or the maturity to evaluate their own motives and needs. Their experiences during the first semesters of college led them to change both their minds and their images of themselves.

Sources of Change

autonomy ability to take care of oneself and make one's own decisions

How does going to college stimulate change? First, college may challenge the identity a student established in high school. A top high school student may go to a top college. Nearly everyone there is as bright as she is. Within weeks the student's identity as a star pupil has evaporated, and she may struggle to get average grades. Students who excelled in sports or other activities may have similar experiences.

encounter to come upon or meet with, especially unexpectedly

Second, students will **encounter** greater diversity in college than they ever have before—diversity in religious and ethnic backgrounds, family income levels, and attitudes. Suppose you develop a close relationship, and then discover that the person holds beliefs or engages in behavior you have always considered immoral. You may be badly shaken. You face a choice—abandon deeply held values or give up an important friendship. Madison called close relationships between people who force each other to reexamine their basic assumptions

developmental friendship friends force one another to reexamine their basic assumptions and perhaps adopt new ideas and beliefs

developmental friendships. He found that developmental friendships in particular and student culture in general have more impact on college students than professors do.

Instructors and assigned books can also create change. They can clarify thoughts that have been brewing in a student's mind. This was true of Keith. Keith did extremely well in pre-med courses, but he found he enjoyed his literature and philosophy classes far more. He began reading avidly. He felt as if each author had deliberately set out to put all his self-doubts into words. In time Keith realized that his interest in medicine was superficial. He had decided to become a doctor because it would give him status, security, and a good income. The self-image Keith had brought to college was completely changed.

Connecting Psychology to Economics

RECESSION AND FINANCIAL GOALS

Beginning in 2008, a financial crisis plunged world economies into recession. Millions of workers lost their jobs. Young people just entering the labor force had an especially hard time securing a job. They lacked the work experience to compete with laid-off workers who were also looking for employment. By July 2010, only about 31 percent of people ages 16 through 19 had jobs—a historic low. Retail stores and construction companies typically hire many young people, but jobs in these industries have dried up during the economic downturn.

Young people have also sometimes had to deal with their parents' unemployment. Their current financial insecurity has been coupled with concerns that they could not plan or provide for the future.

The good news is that, lacking job opportunities, more teens are choosing to stay in school. High school graduates who can't find jobs are seeing the value of continuing their education in college. With more skills to offer, college graduates can compete more successfully in the job market and earn higher pay over their work life.

Young adults learned an important lesson from the recession. A 2011 survey found that young adults, ages 18 to 34, were more likely than previous generations to say they wanted to save more, spend less, develop a budget, and pay down debts.

DreamPictures/Blend Images LLC

▶ **CRITICAL THINKING**

1. ***Making Connections*** Why do you think the recession influenced the financial goals of young adults?

2. ***Making Predictions*** Do you think young adults will follow these goals when the economy is booming again? Why or why not?

Coping With Change

Madison found that students cope with the stress of going to college in different ways. Some focus more narrowly when their goals are threatened by internal or external change. They redouble their efforts to succeed in the field they have chosen and avoid people and situations that might bring their doubts to the surface. Troy, for example, stayed in chemical engineering for three years, despite a growing interest in social science. By the time he realized that engineering was not for him, it was too late to change majors. He got the degree but left college with no idea where he was heading.

Others avoid confronting doubt by frittering away their time, going through the motions of attending college but detaching emotionally. Still others may keep their options open until they have enough information and experience to make a choice. Madison called this third method of coping **resynthesis**. This often involves a period of indecision, doubt, and anxiety. Students may try to combine the new and old, temporarily abandon the original goal, retreat, head in another direction, retreat again, and finally reorganize their feelings and efforts around an emerging identity.

✅ **READING PROGRESS CHECK**

Explaining Why do many students enter college with unrealistic aspirations?

The Working World

GUIDING QUESTION *Why is work satisfaction important?*

Graduating from college or high school involves thinking about and finding your first job and your career. But what is work? For one person work means loading 70,000 pounds on a five-axle truck, driving alone for several hours a day, perhaps for several days at a time, with only a few stops for food and fuel, talk, relief, and sleep. While alone in the cab, tension is constant; it is hard to suddenly brake a truck carrying thousands of pounds of cargo, so the driver must always think ahead. The work is wearing, yet the independence is rewarding.

For another person work means spending eight or nine hours a day at an advertising agency, dealing with clients and supervising commercial writers. This person earns good money, spends a great deal of time talking with people, and has plenty of opportunities to exercise his or her talents as a manager. All three are positive aspects of the job. Yet this person must also deal with deadlines and worry about whether millions of dollars' worth of ads will sell the products or not—and, subconsciously, whether it is worth the effort if they do.

For a third person work means training severely disabled children to use their muscles to grasp a spoon, to gesture in sign language, and perhaps to take a few steps. The job can be frustrating but there are also moments of **intense** personal satisfaction when a child makes progress. The point is that each person's work experience is different and each person reacts differently to a job as a result of his or her own personality.

resynthesis combining old ideas with new ones and reorganizing feelings in order to renew one's identity

intense to an extreme degree

⌄ **GRAPH**

EMPLOYMENT AND MEDIAN EARNINGS OF WOMEN, BY INDUSTRY

In 2009 the median weekly earnings of women was 80 percent of men's median weekly earnings. However, the percentage gap varied by occupation.

▶ **CRITICAL THINKING**

1. *Analyzing Visuals* The largest number of women work in what industry? About what percentage of men's pay do women earn in this industry?

2. *Comparing and Contrasting* In what industry do women earn the highest percentage compared to men? How would you describe the concentration of women in this industry compared to other industries?

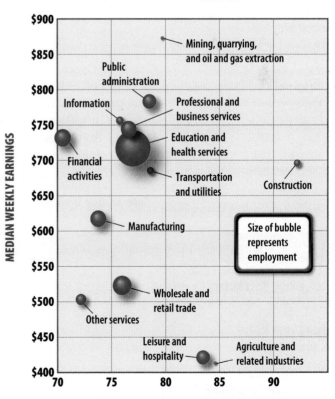

MEDIAN WEEKLY EARNINGS

Mining, quarrying, and oil and gas extraction
Public administration
Information
Professional and business services
Education and health services
Financial activities
Transportation and utilities
Construction
Manufacturing
Size of bubble represents employment
Wholesale and retail trade
Other services
Leisure and hospitality
Agriculture and related industries

WOMEN'S EARNINGS AS PERCENT OF MEN'S

Source: U.S. Bureau of Labor Statistics

Adolescence 117

Industrial/organizational psychologists explore what factors contribute to job satisfaction. This research is important because low job satisfaction is associated with high rates of employee absenteeism and turnover, which leads to lower productivity. Job satisfaction is simply the attitude a worker has toward his or her job. One study identified five major sources of work satisfaction.

1. *Resources:* The worker feels that he or she has enough available resources—help, supplies, and equipment—to do the job well.
2. *Financial reward:* The job pays well, offers good fringe benefits, and is secure.
3. *Challenge:* The job is interesting and enables the worker to use his or her special talents and abilities.
4. *Relations with coworkers:* The worker is on good terms professionally and socially with colleagues.
5. *Comfort:* Working conditions and related factors—hours, travel to and from the job, work environment, and so on—are attractive.

A career is a vocation in which a person works for at least a few years. Many people change careers several times in their lifetimes. Some workers retire from one career and start another. Many women step out of the job market to raise children and then reenter for a second career. If you are unhappy at a job, changing careers may provide the answer. Job shopping, or trying out several careers, is most common among people who have recently entered the labor force and are still trying to get a feel for the work that suits them best. Throughout your work life, you should acquire as many abilities and interests as you can and develop your interpersonal skills. View change as desirable and challenging. The broader your skills, abilities, and interests, the more occupations will be open to you.

comparable worth the concept that women and men should receive equal pay for jobs calling for comparable skill and responsibility

Jobs of comparable training, skill, and importance should be compensated at the same rate—this is **comparable worth**. In practice, however, many jobs traditionally held by females pay less than comparable jobs traditionally held by males. Moreover, men have tended toward higher-paid occupations, while women have tended (or been encouraged) toward lower-paid occupations. Overall, women face a considerable gap between their income and income received by men.

Many groups are working to achieve equal pay for comparable work. The National Organization for Women has made the upgrading of traditionally female jobs one of its highest priorities. Labor unions are also confronting the issue of pay equity. Congress has passed several major laws to prevent discrimination and income discrepancies between men and women. Most recently, the Lily Ledbetter Fair Pay Act of 2009 amended the Civil Rights Act of 1964 to allow a longer period of time in which to file lawsuits over equal pay for equal work.

☑ READING PROGRESS CHECK

Interpreting Significance What is comparable worth? Why is it important?

LESSON 5 REVIEW

Reviewing Vocabulary
1. *Explaining* Explain how going to college involves autonomy.

Using Your Notes
2. *Describing* Use your notes to write a short essay about how college can stimulate change.

Answering the Guiding Questions
3. *Finding the Main Idea* What adjustments does going to college require?

4. *Interpreting Significance* Why is work satisfaction important?

Writing Activity
5. *Informative/Explanatory* Your future happiness in the world of work depends on factors like what you are doing, where you work, who you work with, and why you are working there. Use these factors to write a description of careers that might suit you. Explain your choices.

Directions: On a separate sheet of paper, answer the questions below. Make sure you read carefully and answer all parts of the question.

Lesson Review

Lesson 1

1 ***Identifying Perspectives*** Describe G. Stanley Hall's theory of adolescence. Does the research of Margaret Mead support his position? Explain.

2 ***Analyzing*** What are the problems with defining the start and end of adolescence? Why do these problems exist?

Lesson 2

3 ***Finding the Main Idea*** What is the major criticism of Erikson's theory?

4 ***Explaining*** What is an example of rationalization and a reason it might occur?

Lesson 3

5 ***Describing*** How does the influence of parents over their children change during adolescence?

6 ***Constructing Arguments*** Why do adolescents form cliques? Do you think cliques serve a positive or negative purpose? Explain your answers.

Lesson 4

7 ***Analyzing*** Why might many people disagree with or oppose biological theories of gender differences?

8 ***Explaining*** According to the cognitive-developmental theory, how do children acquire gender roles?

Lesson 5

9 ***Drawing Inferences*** Why do developmental friendships have so much impact on a person?

10 ***Making Connections*** How do you think job satisfaction and job performance are related? Does good worker performance occur as a result of high job satisfaction, or is high job satisfaction a result of good worker performance? Explain your answers.

DBQ Analyzing Primary Sources

Use the document to answer the following questions.

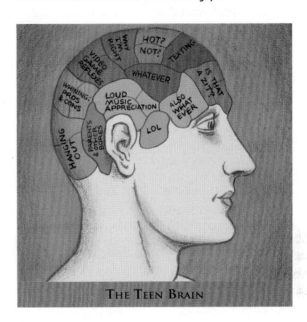

THE TEEN BRAIN

11 ***Analyzing Visuals*** According to this cartoon, what is most on the mind of teenagers?

12 ***Interpreting*** The cartoon is an exaggeration of what teenagers think about. What categories would you include in a more serious depiction of a teen brain?

Exploring the Essential Questions

13 ***Synthesizing*** Working with a small group, create a short brochure that will help prepare preteens for the changes they will experience as adolescents. Discuss physical changes and how these can impact teens emotionally. Also describe how culture can influence their behavior. Keep the tone upbeat, not scary. Find or create illustrations that help convey the main points to preteens.

Need Extra Help?

If You've Missed Question	**1**	**2**	**3**	**4**	**5**	**6**	**7**	**8**	**9**	**10**	**11**	**12**	**13**
Go to page	85	87	96	93	100	101	113	113	116	117	96	100	84

Directions: On a separate sheet of paper, answer the questions below. Make sure you read carefully and answer all parts of the question.

Critical Thinking Questions

14 *Comparing and Contrasting* Write five words or phrases that, in your opinion, characterize adolescence. Then ask an adult to also write five words or phrases. What are the similarities and the differences? What are some reasons for the differences?

15 *Drawing Conclusions* Which of the developmental tasks of adolescence do you think is the most difficult? Do you think that developmental task is continuous or discontinuous? Has it remained stable or changed over time? Explain your answer.

16 *Constructing Arguments* Do you think an individual with an androgynous gender role is healthier than one with a traditional gender role? Explain your answer.

17 *Drawing Conclusions* Erikson and Marcia insist that all adolescents experience an identity crisis. Do you agree? Explain your answer.

18 *Drawing Inferences* Do you think increasing autonomy can create positive or negative feelings in a college student? Why do you think so?

College and Career Readiness

19 *Reaching Conclusions* Select a career that you are considering right now. Go online to research the tasks involved in this career. A good place to start is the online Occupational Outlook Handbook. List aspects that you like about the career and aspects that concern you. Based on your research, assess whether this career is realistic for you. Summarize your assessment in a written report.

Research and Technology

20 *Interpreting* Advertisers often use gender stereotypes to promote products. Capture images from online advertising that promote products to young people. Use the images to create an electronic slideshow. On each slide, note the gender stereotype that the advertisement is using.

21st Century Skills

21 *Creating and Using Graphs, Charts, Diagrams, and Tables* Use the Internet to access the most recent National Vital Statistics Report, which is published by the Centers for Disease Control and Prevention. Using the data for the 10 leading causes of death, construct a bar graph for the top five causes of death for all races, genders, and age groups up to 19 years. How do some of the thought processes of adolescents help explain the leading causes of death in young people?

22 *Presentation Skills* Work with a partner to develop a skit of a situation that illustrates the conflict that Erik Erikson believes teenagers face in trying to be unique on one hand and to fit in on the other. Present your skit in class and discuss ways that teenagers can resolve conflict.

Psychology Journal Activity

23 *Informative/Explanatory* Review your entry in your Psychology Journal for this chapter. Was your understanding of the impact of the Internet on identity development accurate? After studying the chapter, how would you change your answer? Write a new entry in your journal reflecting what you have learned about identity development.

Need Extra Help?

If You've Missed Question	**14**	**15**	**16**	**17**	**18**	**19**	**20**	**21**	**22**	**23**
Go to page	84	92	110	96	115	115	109	102	97	82

Adulthood and Old Age

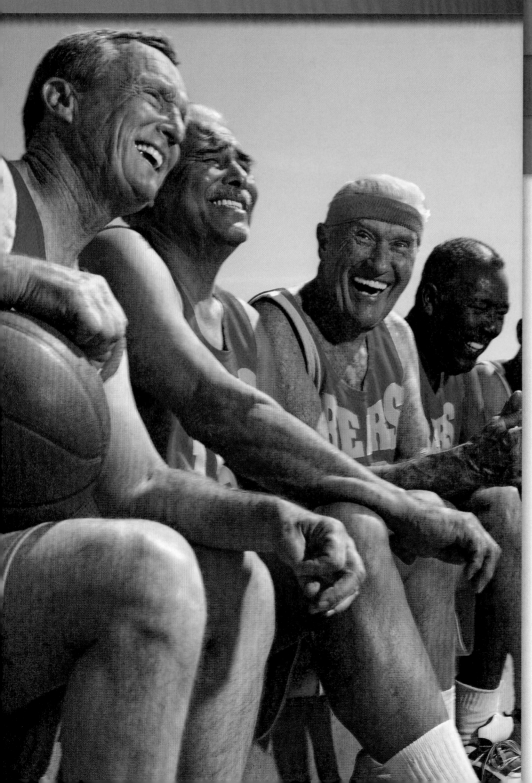

ESSENTIAL QUESTIONS • *How do cognitive abilities progress with age?* • *How do people manage life changes?*

Psychology Matters...

Adulthood is full of new experiences and challenges. In this stage of life you may get married, have children, find a career, and make new friends. All the while your body and mind will continue to change. As you enter middle adulthood you may find that your body requires more attention to keep in good shape. By old age, your strength will have decreased and you may find it harder to think as fast as you did in your youth. Despite these challenges, adulthood and old age can be very rewarding. Remaining healthy and happy as you age it becomes increasingly important to stay physically, mentally, and socially active, and get good, regular medical care.

◀ Physical and mental abilities may change as people age, but the capacity for friendship remains the same.

Patrick Giardino/age fotostock

Lab Activity

Age and Intelligence

THE QUESTION...

RESEARCH QUESTION Does cognitive ability change after adolescence?

The list of world champions in the game of chess reveals an interesting trend. Most of the winners are in their 30s. Why would this be? People of all ages play chess, and many people play the game into old age. Why wouldn't an older player's years of experience lead to more world championships for them? Perhaps it has something to do with the development of the human brain as we age.

Does intelligence decline as we get older? Or were all those chess players in their 30s just lucky? In this experiment, we'll run some tests and try to find out.

Psychology Journal Activity CCSS

Define the term "intelligence." Think about the difference between knowledge and intelligence. Write about this in your Psychology Journal. Consider some of the following points as you write: Which do you think hits its peak faster, knowledge or intelligence? As we get older, what do you think might happen to intelligence?

FINDING THE ANSWER...

HYPOTHESIS Cognitive abilities decline with each decade after adolescence.

THE METHOD OF YOUR EXPERIMENT

MATERIALS copies of a cognitive test, graphing paper

PROCEDURE Create your own set of thirty questions to test cognitive abilities. Your questions should be simple verbal exercises. For instance, you could instruct participants to select a word from a group of five words (*color, crayon, paint, yellow, rainbow*) that is most like a group of three words (*red, blue, green*). You may also use the Internet to find other cognitive abilities tests to use as a model. Once you have created or found a test to use, administer it to no fewer than ten participants. Screen your participants' ages so that your experiment includes at least one person in each decade of life from the teens to the 60s or 70s. Record the ages of your participants, their results on the cognitive test, and how long it took to complete their test. Your most important measurement will not be correct results, but time taken to complete your test.

DATA COLLECTION Use your data to create a three-column table that shows ages, test scores, and time needed to complete the test. Graph your results (with age on the x-axis and completion time on the y-axis).

ANALYSIS & APPLICATION

1. What conclusions can you draw? Does your data support the hypothesis? How does your data compare to that of your classmates? Are there variables that could have affected your results?

2. What were some of the challenges of running this experiment? How could you conduct the experiment differently to obtain more accurate results?

3. Seniors have recently been advised to do crossword puzzles and other mental exercises to maintain their cognitive abilities. How is this advice related to the Research Question?

networks ONLINE LAB RESOURCES

Online you will find:

- An **interactive lab experience**, allowing you to put principles from this chapter into practice in a digital psychology lab environment. This chapter's lab will include an experiment allowing you to explore issues fundamental to adulthood and old age.

- A **Skills Handbook** that includes a guide for using the scientific method, creating experiments, and analyzing data.

- A **Notebook** where you can complete your Psychology Journal, and record and analyze your experiment data.

netw◉rks

There's More Online!

☑ **DIAGRAM** How Our Bodies Age

☑ **DIAGRAM** Levinson's Theory of Male Development

☑ **IMAGE** Indian Wedding

☑ **SELF-CHECK QUIZ**

Reading **HELP**DESK **CCSS**

Academic Vocabulary

• adjust   • adapt

Content Vocabulary

• menopause
• generativity
• stagnation

TAKING NOTES:

Key Ideas and Details

CATEGORIZING Use a graphic organizer like the one below to label examples of ways people change during adulthood and old age in the areas of physical, cognitive, and social and personal development.

Physical	Cognitive	Social/Personal

LESSON 1
Adulthood

ESSENTIAL QUESTION *How do people manage life changes?*

IT MATTERS BECAUSE

For most people adulthood will be the longest period of their lives. It will be a time of many changes, such as marriage, divorce, parenthood, and the death of loved ones, as well as the physical and mental changes of aging. The way people adjust to and manage these life changes can affect their quality of life and the way they interact with others.

Physical and Cognitive Changes

GUIDING QUESTION *What physical and mental changes occur as we age?*

Early adulthood, or young adulthood, is considered the time between late teens and late twenties. At this time, our bodies are closer to that of an adolescent than that of a middle-aged person. Our physical strength is at its peak, and energy levels may also be high. During this period of adulthood, many mental changes occur as we adjust from being in school to being employed or finding a career. We may have changes in our schedules or work life that require us to adjust to going to bed earlier, getting up earlier, and dealing with more intimate personal relationships. We may have to adjust to living on our own or moving out of a parent's home and into a situation where we live with friends or other young adults. People in young adulthood may begin thinking about starting a family or having serious adult relationships with others.

In general, young adults are at their physical peak between the ages of 18 and 30. This is the period when we are the strongest, healthiest, and have the quickest reflexes. As the 30s approach, signs of physical aging are still not obvious. For most adults, the process of physical decline is slow and gradual—not at all noticeable month-to-month. For example, a 20-year-old manages to carry four heavy bags of groceries, while a 40-year-old finds it easier to make two trips. What is lost physically may be replaced by experience. For instance, a 60-year-old veteran racquetball player with decades of experience can still compete against a younger player, who may be faster but who is far less practiced.

What is the source of the physical changes that come with age? One theory claims that aging is the result of breakdowns in our bodies' cells. With time cells lose the ability to repair themselves, meaning aging is the result of normal wear and tear on our bodies. Another theory says our bodies age because our cells have preset biological clocks that limit the number of times they may divide and multiply. As cells reach that preset limit, the process of cell division occurs less accurately, or they simply begin to die. Either way, aging occurs.

In middle age, changes in appearance become noticeable. Body hair starts to turn gray in certain areas and for some, hair will begin to thin out. The skin will become somewhat dry and inelastic, and wrinkles will slowly form. In old age, muscles and fat that have built up over the years break down so that people often lose weight, become shorter, and develop more wrinkles, creases, and loose skin. Some physiological changes occur as we become older, and behavioral factors and lifestyle choices can affect psychological health.

The senses also change over time, requiring more and more stimulation. During their 40s, most people begin having difficulty seeing distant objects, having to **adjust** to seeing in the dark, or focusing on printed pages, even if their eyesight has always been good. Many experience a gradual or sudden loss of hearing in their later years. In addition, reaction time slows. If an experimenter asks a young person and an older person to push a button when they see a light flash, the older person will take about 20 percent longer to do so.

adjust to change to fit new conditions

Health Problems

Some of the changes we associate with growing older are the result of the natural processes of aging. Other changes result from diseases and from simple disuse and abuse. Our health reflects a life of making choices involving exercise, diet, and lifestyle. A person who eats sensibly, exercises, avoids tobacco, drugs, and alcohol, and is not subjected to severe emotional stress will look and feel younger than someone who neglects his or her health.

Three of the most common causes of death in later adulthood—heart disease, cancer, and cirrhosis of the liver—may be encouraged by the fast-moving lifestyle of young adults. Drug abuse—likely to peak in late adolescence or young adulthood and drop sharply after that—can easily become a problem. Other factors contributing to early death are inadequate diet and the effects of violence. Violent deaths may result from irresponsible accidents, a tendency to push the physical limits, and a social environment that encourages risk taking among young adults. All three of these contributing factors are psychological, although they ultimately have biological consequences.

Many cultures have traditions for significant life events such as weddings.

▶ **CRITICAL THINKING**

Analyzing Visuals What are some ways this couple demonstrates the commitment they are making to each other?

Marriage and Divorce

About 90 percent of adults in the United States will marry at some time in their lives. Forty to sixty percent of new marriages, though, end in divorce. Researchers who have performed longitudinal studies on married couples propose that success or failure largely depends on two factors: how couples resolve conflicts and how often they share intimate and happy moments.

Although happily married couples seem to argue just as much as unhappy couples, they argue more constructively. They listen to each other and focus on solving the problem. They also show respect for each other's views. Unhealthy ways of dealing with conflict include ignoring or denying conflict, exaggerating issues, and having ugly verbal fights.

Plush Studios/Blend Images/Getty Images

Psychologists who study adulthood and aging face a daunting task. This period of life can last many years, so conducting a longitudinal study would involve tracking a group of people over the course of decades. Because of the time and cost involved in this approach, researchers often opt to perform cross-sectional studies. These studies measure different age groups, or cohorts, at one time, and yield age differences. While this method is much more efficient, it is not without drawbacks. People from different cohorts develop in different historical and social time periods, and this can affect the results of a cross-sectional study. The differences observed between different cohorts that are not due to age, but rather different experiences are called the cohort effect.

menopause the biological event in which a woman's production of sex hormones is sharply reduced

While most couples in the United States marry for love, people in many parts of the world follow the tradition of having marriages arranged. Arranged marriages often prove more lasting than ones based on love alone, largely because society usually disapproves of breaking up an arranged union. Some researchers also believe that the union lasts longer because each person enters the union without expectations of personal happiness. Such arranged marriages usually provide strong family ties and, therefore, support on both sides.

Menopause and Sexual Behavior

Between the ages of 45 and 50, women typically experience a stage called the *climacteric,* which represents all of the psychological and biological changes occurring at that time. A woman's production of sex hormones drops sharply—a biological event called **menopause**. The woman stops ovulating (releasing eggs) and menstruating and therefore can no longer conceive children. Many women experience little or no discomfort during menopause. The irritability and severe depression some women experience during the climacteric appear to have emotional rather than physical origins. Women's uncertainty as to what to expect at menopause may be complicated by the changes in roles and relationships they are usually experiencing at this time.

One study shows that the negative effects of menopause are greatly exaggerated. Half of the women interviewed said they felt better, more confident, calmer, and freer after menopause than they had before. They no longer had to think about their periods or getting pregnant. They enjoyed sex as much as or more than they had before menopause.

A common stereotype of late adulthood holds that sexual activity declines or comes to a halt. However, studies have shown that sexual activity does not automatically decline with age. Indeed, there is no physiological reason for stopping sexual activity with advancing age. Most older adults who have an available partner maintain quite vigorous sex lives. Those who are inactive cite boredom with a partner of long standing, poor physical condition or illness (such as heart disease), or acceptance of the stereotype of loss of sex drive with aging.

Men do not go through a biological change equivalent to menopause. While the number of sperm declines gradually over the years, older men can father children. Psychologically it appears that older men go through age-related changes just as women do, with altered expectations about work and health, and the challenges that accompany an increased risk of illness and the death of parents.

Cognitive Changes

People are better at learning new skills and information, solving problems that require speed and coordination, and shifting from one problem-solving strategy to another in their mid-20s than they were in adolescence. These are considered signs of intelligence and are among the skills that intelligence tests measure.

At one time, many psychologists thought that intellectual development reached a peak in the mid-20s and then declined. The researchers used a cross-sectional design and found that scores on intelligence tests decreased with age. However, this was found to be a cohort effect. Further investigation revealed that some parts of these tests measure speed, not intelligence. An adult's reaction time begins to slow after a certain age. Intelligence tests usually penalize adults for this.

Even with a decline in speed, people continue to acquire information as they grow older. The ability to comprehend new material and to think flexibly improves with years and experience. This is particularly true if a person has had higher education, lives in a stimulating environment, and works in an intellectually demanding career. One researcher studied more than 700 individuals who were engaged in scholarship, science, or the arts. Although the patterns varied from

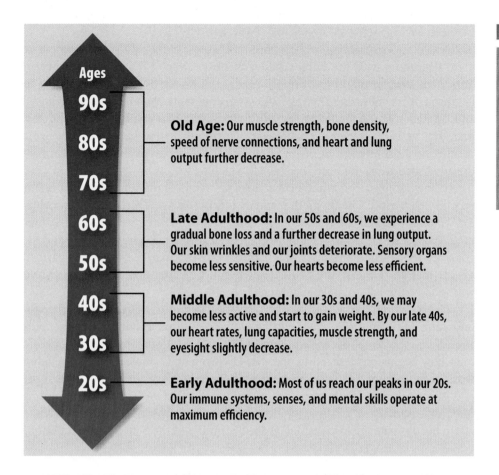

< DIAGRAM

HOW OUR BODIES AGE
Peak of physical ability is reached in the twenties. After this period the aging process slowly begins.

▶ **CRITICAL THINKING**

1. *Analyzing Visuals* At which stage of development are immune systems at peak efficiency?

2. *Categorizing* At about what age does late adulthood start?

Old Age: Our muscle strength, bone density, speed of nerve connections, and heart and lung output further decrease.

Late Adulthood: In our 50s and 60s, we experience a gradual bone loss and a further decrease in lung output. Our skin wrinkles and our joints deteriorate. Sensory organs become less sensitive. Our hearts become less efficient.

Middle Adulthood: In our 30s and 40s, we may become less active and start to gain weight. By our late 40s, our heart rates, lung capacities, muscle strength, and eyesight slightly decrease.

Early Adulthood: Most of us reach our peaks in our 20s. Our immune systems, senses, and mental skills operate at maximum efficiency.

profession to profession, most of the participants reached their peaks of creativity and productivity in their 40s, but in the humanities, such as history, foreign languages, and literature, most reached their peaks later in their 50s or 60s.

☑ **READING PROGRESS CHECK**

Summarizing What is one reason middle-aged people might receive lower scores on intelligence tests than younger adults?

Social and Personality Development

GUIDING QUESTION *How does stagnation represent negative development?*

An individual's basic character, or the way he or she **adapts** to situations, remains relatively stable over the years. Researchers are also convinced, however, that personality is flexible and capable of changing in response to new tasks. Researchers have given the same attitude and personality tests to individuals in late adolescence and again 10 or 15 years later. Many participants believed that they had changed dramatically, but the tests indicated that they had not. The degree of satisfaction they expressed about themselves and about life in general in their middle years was consistent with their earlier views. Confident young people remained confident, those prone to pessimism remained pessimistic, and passive individuals remained passive—unless something upsetting had happened.

Even though basic character remains relatively stable, people do face many changes in their lifetimes and will need to adjust accordingly. Adults encounter new developmental tasks, just as adolescents do. They too must learn to cope with problems and deal with new situations. Learning the skills needed to cope with change seems to occur in stages for both adult males and females.

adapt to change in order to meet the demands of a certain environment or circumstance

Levinson's Theory of Male Development

In the 1920s, Daniel Levinson proposed a theory for the adult development of men. Beginning with the Early Adult Transition at age 17, Levinson identified important *structures* and *transitions*, usually lasting for five years. According to Levinson, from about age 22 to age 28 a young man is considered, both by himself and by society, to be entering the adult world—he is not fully established as a man, but he is no longer an adolescent. During this time he will experience a conflict he must attempt to resolve between the desire to explore the options of the adult world and the need to establish a stable life.

Following Levinson's model, the years between 28 and 30 are often a major transitional period. The thirtieth birthday marks the Age Thirty Transition, during which the tentative commitments made in the first life structure are reexamined, and questions about the choices of marriage partner, career, family, and life goals are reopened, sometimes in a painful way. The man feels that any parts of his life that are unsatisfying or incomplete must be attended to now, because it will soon be too late to make major changes.

The searching of the Age Thirty Transition begins to be resolved as the second adult-life structure, called Settling Down, develops. Having probably made some firm choices about career, family life, and relationships, the 33-year-old man now begins concentrating on what Levinson calls "making it" in the adult world. Levinson found that approximately between the ages of 36 and 40, near the end of the Settling Down structure, there is a distinctive feeling of "becoming one's own man." Now it is time for a man to become fully independent, striving to attain his ultimate goals identified at the beginning of the Settling Down period.

Connecting Psychology to Economics

SOCIAL CLASS AND ADULT IDENTITY

Young adults are often working to establish themselves in the world and, if possible, advance their social status, or social class. As a result, this stage of life sees adults buying products that represent their class or the class they hope to enter. For some these purchases represent the "basics" of middle-class living, such as a modest car and home. For others, especially those hoping to enter a higher social class, these purchases can include expensive cars, clothing, and homes, as well as other luxury items such as unusual vacations and entertainment.

Social class remains an important part of an individual's identity throughout adulthood. Moving from one social class to another, however, can be difficult. Many people make purchases beyond their means, while some find class advancement difficult due to their economic circumstances. The resources of single-parent households, for instance, might be constrained in a very different way from someone without those same challenges.

▶ **CRITICAL THINKING**

1. *Analyzing* How might purchases of adults change as they age?

2. *Contrasting* How might a single parent's economic experience differ from that of a similar-aged person without children?

▲ The purchases we make are central to our class identity.

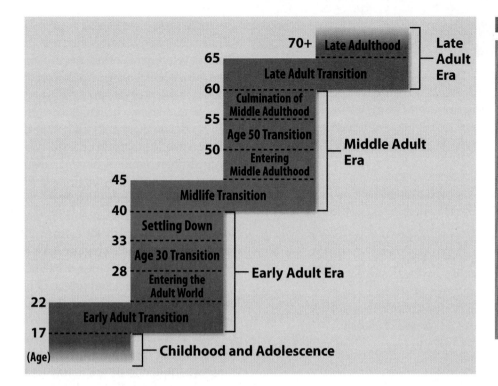

< DIAGRAM

LEVINSON'S THEORY OF MALE DEVELOPMENT
This model shows the developmental sequence of a man's life according to Levinson's theory. Even though Levinson proposed the sequence for men, there are similarities to the development of a woman's life.

▶ CRITICAL THINKING

1. *Gathering Information*
According to Levinson, what happens just after the Age Thirty Transition?

2. *Gathering Information* What is another time that Levinson considers a major transition period?

At about age 40, the era of early adulthood comes to an end and the Midlife Transition begins. Today this is most often called a "midlife crisis." From about age 40 to age 45, the man begins again to ask questions, but now the questions concern the past as well as the future. He may ask: "What have I done with my life?" "What have I accomplished?" "What do I still wish to accomplish?" At the end of this transition, he will have moved into the era of middle adulthood. How the man chooses to answer these midlife questions will prove his transition to be a success or a sign of trouble to come.

Upon reaching the late 40s and the Entering Middle Adulthood structure, true adulthood can be achieved. The man who finds satisfactory solutions to his life's transitional periods reaches a period of stability. He understands and tolerates others, and displays a sensitivity and concern for them. He is able to strike a balance between the need for friends and the need for privacy.

Often a successful Midlife Transition is accompanied by the man's becoming a mentor to a younger person. This event signals the attainment, in Erik Erikson's terms, of generativity. By **generativity**, Erikson means the desire to use one's wisdom to guide future generations. Generativity occurs for both men and women. The desire to "pass on knowledge" can take place directly, in the form of the relationship between a parent and child. It can also happen indirectly, as an older adult can form a mentoring relationship with a younger adult who is a close friend or in the same career.

The opposite of generativity—**stagnation**—can also occur. Instead of looking forward, adults may choose to hang on to the past, perhaps by taking part in the same sports or hobbies they did in youth. For those mired in stagnation the Middle Adult Era can be a time of extreme frustration and unhappiness. Instead of positive improvement, there is a mood of resignation to a bad situation. They may feel cut off from family and friends and believe that their future holds no promise. In the end, it is important to keep in mind that Levinson's eras and transitions are based on averages from many individual interviews. Nobody's life is likely to match Levinson's divisions exactly, and even though the theory was developed with men in mind, many women may go through these same stages regarding their families, careers, and lives.

generativity the desire, in middle age, to use one's accumulated wisdom to guide future generations

stagnation a discontinuation of development and a desire to recapture the past

Quick Lab

DO MEN AND WOMEN GO THROUGH THE SAME STAGES OF DEVELOPMENT?

The latest studies show that just as during adolescence, men and women also go through stages of development during adulthood. Are their experiences the same?

Procedure

1. Prepare a list of interview questions that address a person's attitudes about work, family relationships, and importance of physical attractiveness.
2. Arrange to interview, separately, a man and a woman who are middle-aged. Explain the purpose of your interview to them.

Analysis

1. What differences in attitudes or feelings did you detect between the man and the woman in your interview?
2. Based on your interviews, do you think men and women go through different stages of adult development? Explain. As a class compare your conclusions.

Female Development

While Levinson's study focused on male development, other researchers have focused on females. Adult women today face many of the same challenges as men, and some challenges that are their own. Some get married and have children, while others do not. Still others raise their families on their own. About 58 percent of women aged 16 and older work outside the home.

Unlike men, evidence does not support a midlife crisis for women. In fact, women may be facing difficulties earlier in adulthood. Some are balancing the roles of parent and career. Others may be waiting until their children are older to reenter the workforce or go back to college. Rather than a time of crisis, it is a time of opportunity for those who opted to have a family first.

A significant event in many women's lives is the moment the last child leaves the home. Contrary to popular belief, this event is not traumatic for all women, though it can be difficult for some. Psychologists have found that a stable marriage makes a difference. If a woman has a warm relationship with her husband, she may find the adjustment easier because of his support. If the woman is widowed or divorced, the transition could be more difficult.

Depression is common among middle-aged women. During the early years a woman may find a sense of worth from the roles of daughter, wife, and mother. These roles change as children grow, parents die, and marriages fail. With these changes some women experience a sense of loss and personal worthlessness. The onset of menopause, too, can trigger depression. Those who have defined themselves as child bearers may view themselves as useless. Some women, however, welcome this time of life. Career women can draw a new sense of self-esteem from their work. Many women find satisfaction in new activities and experiences, developing interests and friends apart from their children.

✅ READING PROGRESS CHECK

Comparing and Contrasting What are the similarities and differences in male and female adulthood development?

LESSON 1 REVIEW

Reviewing Vocabulary

1. *Identifying* What is menopause? What physical reactions does it cause? What potential emotional impact can it have?

Using Your Notes

2. *Summarizing* Review the notes that you completed during the lesson to summarize the social and personal changes that adults go through as they age.

Answering the Guiding Questions

3. *Explaining* What physical and mental changes occur as we age?

4. *Interpreting* How does stagnation represent negative development?

Writing Activity

5. *Informative/Explanatory* Write an essay comparing and contrasting challenges faced by adults and adolescents. Include real-life examples.

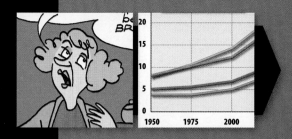
Reading **HELP**DESK CCSS

Academic Vocabulary
• function   • assumed

Content Vocabulary
• decremental model of aging
• ageism
• dementia
• Alzheimer's disease

TAKING NOTES:
Integration of Knowledge and Ideas

MAKING CONNECTIONS Use a graphic organizer like the one below to label the challenges faced in old age.

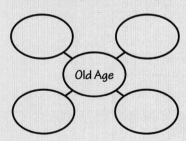

LESSON 2
Old Age

ESSENTIAL QUESTION • *How do cognitive abilities progress with age?*

IT MATTERS BECAUSE
The fear of growing old is probably one of the most common fears in our society. Many people fear that their physical and mental abilities will decline with age and that society will not value them as much as their younger counterparts. While cognitive and physical changes do take place in old age, there are many things that can help improve people's lives as they age.

Changes that Come with Aging

GUIDING QUESTION *What major changes in life situation affect older people?*

Many attitudes about aging are based on a **decremental model of aging**, which holds that progressive physical and mental decline is inevitable with age. In other words, your age is what makes you "old." In truth, there are numerous physical differences among the elderly, and these differences are less a matter of age and more a matter of genetic background and environment. The decremental view in our society is common in part due to ignorance and a lack of contact with older people. The result is a climate of prejudice against the old. A researcher coined the word **ageism** to refer to this prejudice. As with racism and sexism, ageism is based on myth rather than fact.

Stereotypes perpetuate widespread misconceptions about older people. Young people tend to believe that the old suffer from poor health, live in poverty, and are frequent victims of crime. The elderly, however, seldom see these as problems they experience on a personal level. Interestingly, they tend to think of them as problems for *other* older people. Such beliefs demonstrate the strength of ageism in society.

The notion that the elderly withdraw from life and sit around doing nothing is also very common. This, too, is a false picture. There are many musicians and actors who are good examples of active, older individuals, and many less well-known older people follow their lead. The majority of older Americans work or wish to work either for pay or as volunteers. Another misconception is that older people are inflexible or senile. Actually, rigidity is more a lifelong habit than a response to aging. The person who is rigid in old age was most likely rigid as a young adult.

Changes in Health

Physical strength and the senses decline about 1 percent a year through adulthood. Though most people over 65 consider themselves in good health, about 36 percent of American adults are obese. Good health in adolescence and adult life carries over into old age. Eating habits and exercise influence patterns of health and disease. An emphasis on a healthy lifestyle throughout adulthood will lead to physical wellness in old age.

All people, young and old, are subject to disease. About 80 percent of the elderly have at least one chronic disease, which is a permanent rather than temporary disability. The five most prevalent chronic diseases are heart disease, stroke, cancer, diabetes, and arthritis. In general, the major causes of death among the old are heart disease, cancer, and strokes. Most older people, though, believe their health is good. About 80 percent of noninstitutionalized adults aged 65 to 74 and 72 percent of those 75 and older rate their health as good to excellent.

The quality of health care for the elderly remains by and large inferior to that of the general population. The reasons for this are numerous. The elderly in the lower socioeconomic class tend not to take care of themselves or to seek out treatment when needed. Some doctors may prefer to administer to younger patients with acute diseases rather than to older patients with long-term chronic conditions that can only be stabilized, not cured. Some doctors hold stereotypical views of the elderly that can lead to misdiagnosis and improper treatment.

Some older adults who are no longer able to care for themselves live with relatives. For others, there are institutions such as nursing homes, but despite beliefs to the contrary only about 4 percent of people 65 and older live in them. Some of these nursing homes, however, have inadequate facilities. As more and more people each year reach late adulthood, it is crucial that there be a general overhaul of health care treatment for the elderly.

Changes in Life Situation

For younger people, transitions such as graduation, marriage, and parenthood are most often positive and enriching. In late adulthood, life's transitions such as retirement and widowhood are often negative, reduce responsibilities, and increase isolation. Perhaps the most devastating transition is the loss of a spouse. About 41 percent of women and 13 percent of men aged 65 and older are widowed. By the age of 75, nearly 22 percent of men and 60 percent of women are without a spouse.

Across the entire age spectrum, there are about four widows for every widower. All too often, the person loses not just a spouse but the support of friends and family, who cannot cope with the widowed person's grief or feel threatened by the survivor's new status as a single person.

The symptoms of depression are very common in older adults as many have suffered through the challenges common in this stage of life. Symptoms such as changes in weight, feelings of worthlessness, extreme sadness, inability to concentrate, and thoughts of death and suicide are often cited. Depression can often be amplified by habits formed over the course of adulthood such as an unhealthy lifestyle, poor nutrition, lack of exercise, loneliness, and poor methods of coping with stress.

On the positive side, older people today continue to learn and develop new skills more frequently than ever before. Some attend night school, local adult education classes, or take up new hobbies. It has become clear that in older adults some abilities such as nonverbal tasks and problem solving may decline, but other abilities remain normal and some even improve with age.

Changes in Sexual Activity

Just as young people tend to think sexual activity diminishes at midlife, they often believe it ceases altogether in old age. Yet the majority of people over the age of 65 continue to be interested in sex, and healthy partners enjoy sexual activity into their 70s and 80s. One psychologist commented that "Sexy young people mature into sexy middle-aged and elderly people." As with so many human behaviors, the best predictor of future behavior is past behavior. For the elderly with an available partner, the frequency and regularity of sexual activities during earlier years are the best overall predictor of such activities in later years. The reasons some do not engage in sexual activity are apparently related to poor health or the death of a spouse, rather than to a lack of interest or to a decrease in sexual **function**. Societal attitudes are another factor that discourages sexual expression by the elderly. Older people are not supposed to be interested in sex or be sexually active. Sexual relationships in old age—and even displays of affection—are often considered silly, improper, or even morally wrong.

People who live in this atmosphere may give up sexual activity because they believe they are "supposed to." On a more personal level, older people often encounter opposition from family and friends if they want to remarry after the death of a spouse. Children and family, too, may find the idea of love and sex in old age ridiculous or even vaguely disgusting. A change in our ideas may enable the older segment of our population to continue to enjoy a guilt-free, healthy sex life as they age.

Adjusting to Old Age

Many of the changes the elderly face make their adjustment to everyday life more difficult because they represent a loss of control over their environment. When older people are unable to maintain what they value most—good health, recognition in the community, visits from family and friends, a respect of privacy, leisure and work activities—the quality of their lives suffers dramatically, along with their self-image.

The loss of control is usually gradual, and it may involve both physical changes, such as becoming sick or disabled, and external circumstances, such as moving to a nursing home or losing a spouse. Losing a spouse is a terrible enough experience, but the emotional burden is only made worse if one loses friends and one's home as well. Those who experience a loss of control in old age often develop a negative self-concept. They can regain a sense of control and rebuild a more positive self-image if they are helped to make the best of those options available.

More

ABOUT...

Growing Old

Senior citizens in the United States may not be given much respect because they often lack social status and occupy the lower rungs of the economic ladder. In Japan that situation rarely develops because the able-bodied continue to work or to help their families in the home. For those who do live alone, the Japanese have established programs to assure that they receive daily visits or calls. To encourage the active involvement of all older citizens in social activities, the government subsidizes Elders Clubs and sports programs. Through these programs, the elderly supply each other with mutual support. In addition, they are guaranteed a minimum income, receive free annual health examinations, and are eligible for completely free medical care after age 70.

function use or purpose

Today, the average age of people in North America continues to creep upward while the number of children born continues to decrease. This may become a problem for your generation as it ages. Today's retirees can count on Social Security for funds—but will those funds be there when you retire? Social Security is not a personal retirement program; it is a tax-supported benefit. What workers pay in as a salary tax is paid right back out to today's retirees as a benefit. As the number of older people increases and the number of people in the workforce does not, two things are happening: Social Security taxes are increasing, and full retirement benefits, formerly available at age 65, will not be available until age 67, by the time you retire. Today's workers—this means you—should consider other funding sources for their retirement.

assumed thought to be true

dementia decreases in mental abilities, which can be experienced by some people in old age

In many cases people with confident, assertive personalities are often better at coping with life changes than more passive individuals because they are better able to clearly request the attention or care that they need.

In order to help the elderly adjust, society must make some basic changes. Older people champion this process by supporting organizations such as AARP, once known as the American Association of Retired Persons. These groups speak out and lobby on social issues that affect the elderly. Since the population over 65 is growing, social policy makers will need to continue to take the elderly into consideration. Attitudes toward older people are changing slowly, but positively. Eventually a time will come when old age will be considered the culmination of life, not simply the termination.

☑ **READING PROGRESS CHECK**

Summarizing What are some reasons for depression in older people?

Mental Functions in Old Age

GUIDING QUESTION *Why might older people have difficulty with problems that require the generation of new ideas?*

As people age, there are also changes in their mental functions, although there is much less decline in intelligence and memory than is commonly **assumed**. If you compare measures of intellectual ability for a group of elderly people with similar measures for younger people, you might see a difference—namely that older people do not score as well on cognitive tests. However, the older group of people will most likely be less educated and less familiar with test taking than younger people. Furthermore, there are many different types of mental skills and abilities that combine to produce intellectual functioning, and these abilities do not develop at the same rate or time across the life span. Factors such as physical health, vision, hearing, coordination, the speed or timing of intelligence testing, and attitudes in the testing situation all affect intelligence test scores.

John Horn has proposed two types of intelligence: *crystallized* and *fluid* intelligence. Crystallized intelligence refers to the ability to use accumulated knowledge and learning in appropriate situations. This ability increases with age and experience. Fluid intelligence is the ability to solve abstract relational problems and to generate new hypotheses. This ability is not tied to schooling or education and gradually increases in development as the nervous system matures. As people age and their nervous systems decline, so does their fluid intelligence. Thus, older people may not be as good at solving problems that require them to combine and generate new ideas. A decline in the nervous system affects reaction time, visual motor flexibility, and memory. Elderly people have more difficulty retrieving information from memory. If they are asked to recognize a familiar name or object, they cannot do so as well as younger people.

Dementia

A small percentage of people develop dementia in old age. **Dementia** is a collective term that describes conditions characterized by memory loss, forgetfulness, disorientation of time and place, a decline in the ability to think, impaired attention, altered personality, and difficulties in relating to others. Dementia has many causes—some forms are treatable, whereas others are not at this time.

For many years, it was believed that dementia was a normal part of aging and as such commonplace among the elderly. While a decreased cognitive functioning is normal, dementia is a condition diagnosed by a doctor and not a part of the normal developmental processes as described by Levinson and others.

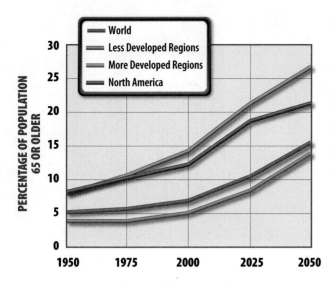

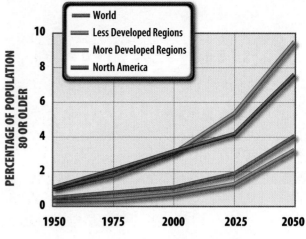

Alzheimer's Disease

The most common form of dementia is the neurological disease known as Alzheimer's. **Alzheimer's disease** is an affliction most commonly seen among the elderly. About 4.5 million people have this disease, and problems associated with it are the sixth leading cause of death among U.S. adults.

Alzheimer's is marked by a gradual deterioration of cognitive functioning. Early signs of the disease include frequent forgetfulness, poor judgment, increased irritability, and social withdrawal. Eventually Alzheimer's patients lose their ability to comprehend simple questions and to recognize friends and loved ones. Ultimately they require constant supervision and care, often from trained professionals. Rarely do patients die from the disease itself, but their weakened state leaves them vulnerable to a variety of other potentially fatal problems.

The causes of Alzheimer's are complex and still not completely understood. Genetic susceptibility plays a role. Other causes may involve life events. At present there is no cure for the disease. Many patients and their caretakers are offered supportive therapy that helps them learn to accept the relentless progression of the disease and the limitations it imposes on its victims.

 READING PROGRESS CHECK

Summarizing What are some ways that the mental functioning of an adult can decrease with age?

∧ **GRAPH**

PERCENTAGE OF OLDER POPULATION

The worldwide elderly population is rapidly growing and projections suggest an even more significant growth by 2050.

▶ **CRITICAL THINKING**

1. *Analyzing Visuals* How have life expectancy rates changed since the year 1950?

2. *Evaluating* What do you think accounts for the projected population growth?

Alzheimer's disease a condition that destroys a person's ability to think, remember, relate to others, and care for herself or himself

LESSON 2 REVIEW (CCSS)

Reviewing Vocabulary

1. *Inferring* Describe the decremental model of aging. Is this an accurate model of aging? Explain.

Using Your Notes

2. *Making Connections* Using the notes that you completed during the lesson, write a paragraph explaining how decreases in fluid intelligence might affect daily life for an elderly person.

Answering the Guiding Questions

3. *Discussing* What are the major changes in life situation that affect older people?

4. *Examining* Why might older people have difficulty with problems that require the generation of new ideas?

Writing Activity

5. *Informative/Explanatory* Create a "to-do" list that will help you successfully adjust to old age.

Reader's Dictionary (CCSS)

What's Behind the Phenomenon of Aging and Happiness

cognitive: related to thinking or reasoning

hypothesize: to form a hypothesis

Childhood music lessons may provide lifelong boost in brain functioning

visuospatial: ability to understand visual representations

neurodegenerative: a progressive loss of neurologic function

plasticity: ability to be altered

As we age, our cognitive processes also age. The first selection discusses why older people tend to have higher levels of happiness. In the second selection, researchers discuss the disparity in cognitive functioning between older people with and without music study backgrounds. Ultimately, differences in happiness level and cognitive functioning in older people are due to various life events.

What's Behind the
Phenomenon
of Aging and Happiness

by Adam Daley

PRIMARY SOURCE

Older people are generally happier, and some researchers believe it is because they tend to focus and remember more positive events while leaving behind negative ones, according to a study. These **cognitive** processes help older people control their emotions and let them see life more enthusiastically and in a sunnier light, researchers said.

"There is a lot of good theory about this age difference in happiness," said psychologist Derek Isaacowitz of Northeastern University, "but much of the research does not provide direct evidence" of the relationships between the phenomena and actual happiness.

Isaacowitz and Psychology Department Chair Fredda Blachard-Fields of the Georgia Institute of Technology said there needs to be more and better research on why the elderly are happier in a new article in the Perspectives on Psychological Science journal published by the Association for Psychological Science. Previous research reported that when older people are shown pictures of faces or situations, they tended to focus on and remember the happier ones more and the negative ones less. Other studies have shown that as people age, the more likely they were to seek out situations to lift their moods, such as cutting off friends or acquaintances who might bring them down. Researchers have also found that older adults are more likely to let go of loss and disappointment over unachieved goals to achieve greater emotional wellbeing.

However researchers said that there is still no evidence that can demonstrate direct links between these cognitive strategies that connects to the phenomena of aging and happiness. Researchers said that the results from previous studies are unclear and not straightforward. "When we try to use those cognitive processes to predict change of mood, they don't always do so," Isaacowitz explained. "Sometimes looking at positive pictures doesn't make people feel better." The authors said that a closer look at the studies reveals several contradictions.

Younger people actually make themselves feel better by magnifying the negative in others' characteristics or circumstances. Furthermore while some psychologists reported a relationship between higher scores on certain cognitive tests and the ability of older people to control their emotions, others have **hypothesized** that happiness in later life is caused by cognitive losses that force older people to concentrate on simpler and happier thoughts.

"It won't be as easy to say old people are happier. But even if they are happier on average, we still want to know in what situations does this particular strategy make this particular person with these particular qualities or strengths feel good," Isaacowitz said.

Childhood
Music Lessons

An APA press release

PRIMARY SOURCE

Those childhood music lessons could pay off decades later—even for those who no longer play an instrument—by keeping the mind sharper as people age, according to a preliminary study published by the American Psychological Association.

The study recruited 70 healthy adults age 60 to 83 who were divided into groups based on their levels of musical experience. The musicians performed better on several cognitive tests than individuals who had never studied an instrument or learned how to read music. The research findings were published online in the APA journal Neuropsychology.

While much research has been done on the cognitive benefits of musical activity by children, this is the first study to examine whether those benefits can extend across a lifetime, said Hanna-Pladdy, a clinical neuropsychologist who conducted the study with cognitive psychologist Alicia MacKay, PhD, at the University of Kansas Medical Center.

The three groups of study participants included individuals with no musical training; with one to nine years of musical study; or with at least 10 years of musical training. All of the participants had similar levels of education and fitness and didn't show any evidence of Alzheimer's disease.

All of the musicians were amateurs who began playing an instrument at about 10 years of age. More than half played the piano while approximately a quarter had studied woodwind instruments such as the flute or clarinet. Smaller numbers performed with stringed instruments, percussion or brass instruments.

The high-level musicians who had studied the longest performed the best on the cognitive tests, followed by the low-level musicians and non-musicians, revealing a trend relating to years of musical practice. The high-level musicians had statistically significant higher scores than the non-musicians on cognitive tests relating to **visuospatial** memory, naming objects and cognitive flexibility, or the brain's ability to adapt to new information.

The brain functions measured by the tests typically decline as the body ages and more dramatically deteriorate in **neurodegenerative** conditions such as Alzheimer's disease. The results "suggest a strong predictive effect of high musical activity throughout the lifespan on preserved cognitive functioning in advanced age," the study stated.

Half of the high-level musicians still played an instrument at the time of the study, but they didn't perform better on the cognitive tests than the other advanced musicians who had stopped playing years earlier. This suggests that the duration of musical study was more important than whether musicians continued playing at an advanced age, Hanna-Pladdy says.

"Based on previous research and our study results, we believe that both the years of musical participation and the age of acquisition are critical," Hanna-Pladdy says. "There are crucial periods in brain **plasticity** that enhance learning, which may make it easier to learn a musical instrument before a certain age and thus may have a larger impact on brain development."

Analyzing Primary Sources

1. *Finding the Main Idea* What are some cognitive strategies older people use to make themselves happier?

2. *Identifying* According to researchers, how might music study prevent the cognitive decline common with aging?

3. *Hypothesizing* In what ways does the research into cognitive strategies of older people and the later benefits of early music study seem contradictory?

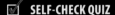

LESSON 3
Dying and Death

(l)Nicholas Kamm/AFP/Getty Images; (c)Bruno Morandi/Hemis/Corbis; (r)Lennox McLendon/AP Images

Reading **HELP**DESK

Academic Vocabulary

• component   • isolating

Content Vocabulary

• thanatology
• hospice

TAKING NOTES:

Key Ideas and Details

SEQUENCING INFORMATION Use a graphic organizer like the one below to describe the stages of dying.

Stage	Description
Denial	
Anger	
Bargaining	
Depression	
Acceptence	

ESSENTIAL QUESTION • *How do people manage life changes?*

IT MATTERS BECAUSE

At some time in their lives, everyone must face the idea of death and the death of loved ones. Death is one of the most feared stages of human development. However, psychologists who have studied death and dying describe stages that can help us cope with and understand the changes brought on by the process of death. This can help us to care for the dying as well as to come to grips with the concept of death.

Approaching Death

GUIDING QUESTION *Why do some people criticize the Kübler-Ross stages of dying?*

Dying and death are popular subjects for many poets and songwriters. Why does death mystify us? Death is inevitable. Death is not just biological. When a person dies, there are legal, medical, psychological, and social aspects that need attention. It is not very easy to even define death anymore because there are medical advances that cloud this issue.

Biological death becomes entangled with social customs. These customs include cultural attitudes toward death, care of the dying, the place where death occurs, and efforts to quicken or slow down the dying process. Death also has social aspects, including the disposal of the dead, mourning customs, and the role of the family. These social and cultural aspects of death are intertwined with our own thoughts and values about dying and death. Death may sound simple, but culturally and emotionally it is a confusing and complex process.

Stages of Dying

Once patients with a terminal illness have been informed of their condition, they must then cope with many changes as they approach death. Elisabeth Kübler-Ross did some pioneering work on how the terminally ill react to their impending death. Her investigations made a major contribution in establishing thanatology—the study of dying and death. Based on interviews with 200 dying patients, she identified five stages of psychological adjustment. The first stage is *denial*. People's most common reaction to learning that they have a terminal illness is shock and numbness, followed by denial. They react by saying, "No, it can't be happening to me," or "I'll get another opinion." They may assert that the doctors are incompetent or the diagnosis mistaken. In extreme cases, people may refuse treatment and persist in going about business as usual. Most patients who use denial extensively throughout their illness are people who have become accustomed to coping with difficult life situations in this way. Indeed, the denial habit may contribute to the seriousness of a condition. For example, a person might refuse to seek medical attention at the onset of an illness, denying that it exists.

During the second stage, *anger*, the reaction of dying people is "Why me?" They feel anger—at fate, at the powers that be, at every person who comes into their life. At this stage, they are likely to alienate themselves from others, for no one can relieve the anger they feel at their shortened life span and lost chances.

During the stage of *bargaining*, people change their attitude and attempt to bargain with fate. For example, a woman may ask God for a certain amount of time in return for good behavior. She may promise a change of ways, even a dedication of her life to the church. She may announce that she is ready to settle for a less threatening form of the same illness and begin to bargain with the doctor over the diagnosis. For example, if she submits gracefully to some procedures, might she be rewarded by being spared the next stage of the illness? This stage is relatively short and is followed by the stage of *depression*.

During depression, dying people are aware of the losses they are incurring such as the loss of body tissue, a job, or life savings. Also, they are depressed about the losses to come: they are in the process of losing everybody and everything. Kübler-Ross suggests that it is helpful to allow such people to express their sadness and not to attempt to cover up the situation or force them to act cheerfully.

Finally, patients *accept* death. The struggle is over, and they experience a sense of calm. In some cases, the approach of death feels appropriate or peaceful. They seem to become detached intentionally so as to make death easier.

Making Adjustments

Not all terminal patients progress through the stages that Kübler-Ross describes. Some people may go through the stages but in a different order, or they may repeat some stages. Critics note that individuals are unique and sometimes do not follow predictable patterns of behavior. For example, a person may die in the denial stages because he or she is psychologically unable to proceed beyond it or because the course of the illness does not grant the necessary time to do so. Kübler-Ross notes that patients do not limit their responses to any one stage; a depressed patient may have recurring bursts of anger. All patients preserve the hope that they may live after all. Camille Wortman and others have argued that Kübler-Ross's stages may simply identify the five most common styles of dealing with death, with no need to progress through stages.

Most people have trouble dealing with the thought of their own death, and they also find it difficult to deal with the death of others. What should we do when a loved one is approaching death? Like all people, dying people need respect, dignity, and self-confidence. Dying people need support and care. They require open communication about what is happening and help with legal and financial arrangements. What should we do after a loved one has died? Our society has developed certain standards that provide guidance on this point. For instance, in the 1800s, a widow or widower was expected to grieve for a long time. Today, society encourages people to try to get back to their normal lives. How long a person grieves depends on the person who is grieving.

✓ READING PROGRESS CHECK

Examining Why might a person not experience all of the stages of dying that Kübler-Ross describes?

Elisabeth Kübler-Ross
(1926–2004)

As a young woman, Dr. Kübler-Ross visited a concentration camp in Maidanek, Germany, after World War II. There she spoke to a young Jewish woman—a camp survivor—who had lost her entire family in a gas chamber. This woman was supposed to be the last one in the chamber, but there was no room, so she was spared. When Kübler-Ross asked how Nazi leader Adolf Hitler could commit such atrocities, the woman replied that there is a Hitler in every human. Kübler-Ross came to understand that depending on the circumstances, anyone could do horrible things.

After that experience Kübler-Ross sought to understand humans and human death. This eventually led her to develop a theory on the stages of dying. As a result of her studies, many people have been able to come to terms with death and help others die in peace.

▶ **CRITICAL THINKING**

Determining Cause and Effect
What life experience made Elisabeth Kübler-Ross become interested in understanding the stages of dying?

thanatology the study of dying and death

End of Life Adjustments

GUIDING QUESTION *What about hospice care makes it appealing?*

Discussing death is one of the few taboos left in twenty-first century America. The breakdown of extended families and the rise of modern medicine have insulated most people in our society from death and dying and partly as a result, they are often afraid to talk about it. In 1900 the average life span was less than 50 years, and most people died at home. Today Americans live on average to be 78 and they die in nursing homes and hospitals. Machines can prolong existence long after a person has stopped living a normal life.

Hospice Care

hospice a facility designed to care for the special needs of the dying

component one of the parts of the whole

A movement to restore the dignity of dying involves the concept of the **hospice**—usually a special place where terminally ill people go to die. The hospice is designed to make the patient's surroundings pleasant and comfortable—less like a hospital and more like a home. Doctors do not try to prolong life but to improve the quality of life. A key **component** of hospice care is the use of tranquilizers and other drugs to ease discomfort and relieve pain. The patient in a hospice leads the most normal life he or she is capable of and is taken care of as much as possible by family members.

Another form of hospice service features care for the elderly at home by visiting nurses, aides, physical therapists, chaplains, and social workers. Medicare now includes arrangements for providing and financing these hospice services. Many other insurance policies also include provisions for in-home hospice care and respite care. Growing rapidly in recent years, home-based hospice care is now a more frequently used service than inpatient hospice care in the United States.

Dealing with Grief

Once a person has died, the loved ones left behind may go through a distinct and emotional grieving process. Much like Elisabeth Kübler-Ross's five stages of dying, British psychologist John Bowlby established a framework for understanding how people tend to deal with grief, based on attachment.

The first stage of grief is *shock and numbness*. A person is at first stunned by the loss of a loved one or someone who they knew well. They may have trouble concentrating, or their judgment or functioning may be impaired. Depending on the attachment between the person and the deceased, this stage may last several hours to several weeks.

The staff of a hospice responds to the unique needs of the terminally ill by providing physical and emotional care.

▶ **CRITICAL THINKING**

Drawing Inferences How does hospice care help a person die with dignity?

Next in the grieving process, according to Bowlby, is *yearning and searching*. During this stage, the grieving person tends to withdraw from others, perhaps asking questions about life and death and yearning for the loved one that was lost. Guilt and anger over the loss of the person may happen in this stage. People who have spent most of their adult lives with a loved one and then lose that person may have an especially hard time with this stage, and it may last for several months.

The third stage, is a time of *disorientation and disorganization* that many people consider true grieving. The person may become depressed and the loss of their loved one becomes especially real in their minds. At the same time, they seem disoriented in their new reality.

Nicholas Kamm/AFP/Getty Images

For the Toraja people of Indonesia, funerals are elaborate and expensive events. Many families will save money for years in order to pay for a ceremony like the one shown on the left. In many cultures, the ceremonies associated with death help people begin the grieving process.

▶ **CRITICAL THINKING**

Considering Advantages and Disadvantages How might funeral ceremonies allow people to confront and accept the death of a loved one?

The fourth and final stage of grieving in John Bowlby's model is the *reorganization and resolution* stage. This is when the loved one finally gets over the **isolating** sadness of losing their loved one. They can feel joy again and feel more energy and confidence. They establish a new level of normality in their lives.

Similar to Kübler-Ross's stages of dying, some people experience Bowlby's grieving stages out of order, for different lengths of time, or may skip some stages altogether. Understanding the stages has been helpful for people going through the stages of grieving, as well as for counselors or analysts helping people through their grief. Bowlby has also adapted strong ideas of attachment to individuals such as family members. The more attached someone is to a loved one who dies, the more difficulty they may have grieving the loss of that person. This is especially true for spouses, children, or other loved ones who helped to make decisions regarding the loved one's end of life care.

isolating causing one to feel alone

☑ **READING PROGRESS CHECK**

Applying Why do some families choose hospice care over hospital care?

Bruno Morandi/Hemis/Corbis

LESSON 3 REVIEW

Reviewing Vocabulary
1. *Making Connections* Explain what thanatology is and why it is a subfield of psychology.

Using Your Notes
2. *Sequencing Information* Review the notes that you completed during the lesson to sequence the stages in the process of dying. Complete a similar chart outlining the stages of grieving as outlined by John Bowlby.

Answering the Guiding Questions
3. *Interpreting* Why do some people criticize the Kübler-Ross stages of dying?

4. *Examining* What about a hospice makes it appealing?

Writing Activity
5. *Informative/Explanatory* Research information on hospices and nursing homes. Based on your knowledge of this time of life, write a short essay evaluating the services these institutions provide.

Case Study

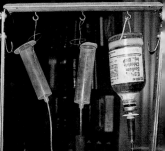

Psychologically Able to Decide?

Period of Study: 1960–ongoing

Introduction: In April 1999, a Michigan court jury sentenced Dr. Jack Kevorkian, a pathologist, to 10 to 25 years in prison. The conviction was based on Kevorkian's role in the assisted suicide of a 52-year-old man who suffered from Lou Gehrig's disease.

Kevorkian provided his "patient" with lethal drugs. The doctor claimed he had used this "method" in about 130 other cases. Kevorkian argued that the assisted suicides he performed were methods of euthanasia. Euthanasia is allowing a terminally ill patient to die naturally without life support, or putting to death a person who suffers from an incurable disease. The Michigan jury that sentenced Kevorkian ruled that Kevorkian was guilty of murder because he had injected the lethal drugs directly into his patient. (The Lou Gehrig's disease sufferer was unable to take the drugs himself.)

The controversy surrounding Kevorkian and assisted suicide are the most well-known examples regarding not only euthanasia but also an individual's right to die. Opinions and feelings vary on this sensitive topic. For those who believe a terminally ill individual does have the right to die, it is important to determine if that person is psychologically able to make that final decision.

For example, Janet Adkins, who had been diagnosed with Alzheimer's disease, was the first person to ask Kevorkian to assist at her death. Aware of the need to determine the patient's decision-making competence, Kevorkian recounted the method he used to assess her before providing his assistance:

PRIMARY SOURCE

❝*Without appearing too obvious, I constantly observed Janet's behavior and assessed her moods as well as the content and quality of her thoughts. There was absolutely no doubt that her mentality was intact and that she was not the least depressed over her impending death.*❞

—*Jack Kevorkian, Prescription: Medicide— The Goodness of Planned Death (1991)*

Hypothesis: How do you assess the psychological competence of a terminally ill person who desires death? This question must be resolved in a case-by-case manner and in accordance with the law. Medical doctors and psychologists must rely on the information gathered from past and present cases of those who were granted permission by either physicians or the court system to terminate life support.

Method: When a person is assessed for psychological competence, psychologists look for signs of depression, mental illness, and negative effects from any medication administered to them. If the terminally ill person does not show positive signs of these, the case is turned over to a physician, lawyer, court system, or any combination of these. From there, it is the legal decision of these authorities to allow the ill individual to follow through with the decision. This is the procedure used in adult cases. However, when the situation involves a child or teenager, the process is much more complex and emotionally difficult.

Results: Unfortunately experts cannot determine if a person who has opted to end life has made a psychologically sound decision. For this reason, among others, many oppose the idea that a person can terminate his or her own life. Those who support euthanasia believe it provides a release from the pain and anguish of a disease or condition of illness. They argue that it is unfair for others to grant or deny the choice of death because they have not experienced the pain and anguish of a terminally ill condition themselves.

Analyzing the Case Study

1. **Describing** What is euthanasia? Why is it controversial?

2. **Explaining** Why was Dr. Kevorkian convicted of murder?

3. **Evaluating Multiple Sources** Compare the excerpt about how Kevorkian assessed his patient with Kübler-Ross's stages of dying. In which stage did Kevorkian place his patient? How do you think that influenced Kevorkian's assessment that his patient was psychologically able to terminate her life?

4. **Argument** Do you think assisted suicide is "compassion" or "murder"? Conduct a webquest to gather information about euthanasia. Select a pro- or anti-euthanasia position and defend that position in a PowerPoint presentation. As a class compare your arguments.

Directions: On a separate sheet of paper, answer the questions below. Make sure you read carefully and answer all parts to the question.

Lesson Review

Lesson 1

1 *Identifying* Name three issues faced by women in the midlife period of adulthood.

2 *Describing* What is the cohort effect?

Lesson 2

3 *Applying* Describe how the "decremental model of aging" can lead to ageism.

4 *Summarizing* Describe some of the characteristics of Alzheimer's disease.

Lesson 3

5 *Expressing* List Kübler-Ross's five stages of psychological adjustment to death. What behaviors would you expect of someone at each stage?

6 *Specifying* What is a hospice designed to do? What types of people might stay in a hospice?

7 *Explaining* List Bowlby's four stages of grieving. What behaviors would you expect of someone at each stage?

Exploring the Essential Question

8 *Gathering Information* Interview an adult who is more than 50 years old. Ask this person to describe himself or herself physically, socially, intellectually, and emotionally at the ages of 20, 30, 40, and 50. Before the interview, list specific questions that would provide this information. Ask which age was his or her favorite and why.

21st Century Skills

The Aging Brain

Compare and Contrast The picture on the left is a cross-section of brain tissue from a healthy adult. At the right is a cross-section of brain tissue from an older adult suffering from Alzheimer's disease. Notice that the brain at right is shrunken in size and has lost white matter.

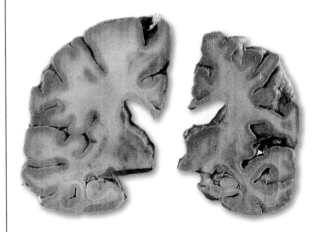

9 How might atrophy, or hardening of the brain, associated with Alzheimer's disease affect cognitive functioning?

10 How might an older person prevent a rapid decline of neuron connections in older age?

Need Extra Help?

If You've Missed Question	**1**	**2**	**3**	**4**	**5**	**6**	**7**	**8**	**9**	**10**
Go to page	130	126	131	135	138	140	140	124	135	134

Directions: On a separate sheet of paper, answer the questions below. Make sure you read carefully and answer all parts to the question.

Critical Thinking Questions

11 *Analyzing* Do you think an individual's personality basically remains the same throughout the individual's life, or is it capable of change during adulthood? Explain your answer.

12 *Drawing Conclusions* Do you think that people of other cultures necessarily experience a "midlife crisis"? Explain why you think they do or do not.

13 *Defending* Some people believe that dying people should not be told they are dying. Do you agree? Why or why not?

14 *Synthesizing* Dying and death have only recently become topics that are discussed openly. Given this growing openness, what changes do you see being made to make the adjustment to the prospect of dying less severe? What other changes do you think still need to be made?

College and Career Readiness

15 *Create and Analyze Arguments and Draw Conclusions* Explore the way that elderly adults are depicted in art and in the media. Bring in examples of art, literature, and newspaper or magazine articles that depict or describe the elderly. Display your chosen examples and present your findings to the class. In your report explain how these forms of media depict the elderly and how their treatment is fair or unfair.

Research and Technology

16 *Researching* Locate Web sites that address issues of middle adulthood and late adulthood. (The Web site for AARP is one such site.) Find out what kinds of information these sites offer. Evaluate the sites in terms of how they might benefit the lives of adults in middle and old age. Chart out your results and then provide a brief written summary.

DBQ Analyzing Primary Sources

Use the document below to answer the following questions.

PRIMARY SOURCE

" *This young woman had lost all her brothers and sisters, parents and grandparents in a gas chamber. She was the last one they tried to squash in, and there wasn't room for one more person, so they pulled her out. What she didn't understand was that she had already been crossed off the list of the living. They never got back to her. She spent the rest of the war years in this concentration camp swearing that she would stay alive to tell the world about all the atrocities that she witnessed.*

When the people came to liberate the camp, she said to herself, "Oh my God, if I spend the rest of my life telling about all these horrible things, I would not be any better than Hitler himself. I would plant seeds of hate and negativity. "

—*from an interview with Elisabeth Kübler-Ross, 1995*

17 *Concluding* How did the woman Kübler-Ross was talking about deal with the death of her loved ones?

18 *Interpreting* How do you think the woman's experiences changed her attitudes about her own death?

Psychology Journal Activity

19 *Informative/Explanatory* Review your entry in your Psychology Journal for this chapter. Was your initial understanding of the relationship between age and cognitive ability confirmed by what you learned in the chapter? How would you adjust your answer?

Need Extra Help?

If You've Missed Question	**11**	**12**	**13**	**14**	**15**	**16**	**17**	**18**	**19**
Go to page	127	128	138	138	131	125	140	139	122

Body and Behavior

ESSENTIAL QUESTIONS • *How do internal functions of the body affect behavior?*
• *How do changes in our body's processes lead to changes in our behavior?*

Psychology Matters...

Our body's systems work together, with the brain as a conductor, to pull off amazing feats. Climbing a mountain, reading a book, missing your grandmother, or writing a poem are all based on biological processes that take place within and between cells. The nervous and endocrine systems, produced by your genes, interact with the environment to produce your behaviors. Psychology includes the study of how these systems operate.

◄ An athlete gets the body in shape by practicing a move or action over and over again. The mind and body are working together and interacting with the environment.

Lab Activity

Reflexive Reaction

THE QUESTION...

RESEARCH QUESTION Does time spent playing video games improve our reflexes?

Have you ever watched a horror movie and gotten sweaty palms? That's your body and your mind working together. Have you ever woken up and been so sluggish you fumbled with your alarm clock? That's your body and mind *not* working together so well. The connection between mind and body is what allows us to get around and to form behaviors.

Researchers are finding that some of our everyday habits—especially the very repetitive ones—might have the ability to change how our bodies function. Perhaps these habits are even improving us.

Is it possible that playing video games improves our reflexes? This experiment will attempt to find out.

Psychology Journal Activity

Think about your daily habits and which ones are newer than others. Write about this in your Psychology Journal. Think about these questions as you write: Do you feel like everyday habits are physical or mental? Which do you think has a bigger role—your body or your mind—in forming your everyday habits?

FINDING THE ANSWER...

HYPOTHESIS Playing video games improves your reflexes.

THE METHOD OF YOUR EXPERIMENT

MATERIALS 12 inch ruler, ten surveys rating experience with video games

PROCEDURE Conduct the Ruler Drop Test with ten participants to test their reaction times. Hold the ruler at the end with 12 on it and let it hang down. Instruct participants to put their finger and thumb around the bottom end of the ruler. Tell them that you will drop the ruler (without advance warning) and that they should catch it as fast as they can. Measure the participant's reaction times by recording how far the ruler dropped (measuring from the top side of his or her thumb). The distance in inches or centimeters will represent their reaction times. Test each participant three times and find the average.

Next, ask each participant to fill in their survey with their age and gender, and to rate their experience with video games: a 1 means they spend more than 20 hours per week playing video games; a 2 means they play 5–20 hours per week; and a 3 means they play fewer than 5 hours per week.

DATA COLLECTION Analyze the data, noting any trends and relationships. Calculate the average reaction times (measured in inches) for the three different ratings.

ANALYSIS & APPLICATION

1. Did your results support the hypothesis?

2. What trends or relationships were you able to see in the data before you calculated the averages for each rating? Why were the data easier to analyze once you had the averages?

3. Why do you think playing video games might improve one's reflexes?

netw⬤rks ONLINE LAB RESOURCES

Online you will find:

- An **interactive lab experience**, allowing you to put principles from this chapter into practice in a digital psychology lab environment. This chapter's lab will include an experiment allowing you to explore issues fundamental to body and behavior.

- A **Skills Handbook** that includes a guide for using the scientific method, creating experiments, and analyzing data.
- A **Notebook** where you can complete your Psychology Journal and record and analyze your experiment data.

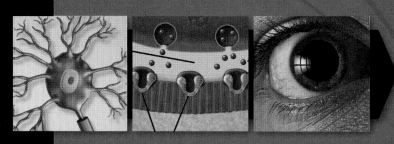

netwⓞrks

There's More Online!

☑ **DIAGRAM** Anatomy of Two Neurons

☑ **DIAGRAM** The Nervous System

☑ **DIAGRAM** The Synapse

☑ **SELF-CHECK QUIZ**

LESSON 1

The Basics of the Nervous System

ESSENTIAL QUESTION • *How do internal functions of the body affect behavior?*

Reading HELPDESK (CCSS)

Academic Vocabulary

• regulate • voluntary

Content Vocabulary

• **central nervous system (CNS)**
• **spinal cord**
• **peripheral nervous system (PNS)**
• **neurons**
• **synapse**
• **neurotransmitters**
• **somatic nervous system (SNS)**
• **autonomic nervous system (ANS)**

TAKING NOTES:

Key Ideas and Details

LABELING Use a graphic organizer like the one below to label, define, and describe the neuron's three basic parts.

1		
2		
3		

IT MATTERS BECAUSE

We can't do anything without our nervous systems. The nervous system allows us to think, move, create, and react to our environment. Messages are sent throughout the nervous system constantly. Learning about the nervous system helps us know how messages that are sent to and from the brain cause behavior.

How the Nervous System Works

GUIDING QUESTION *What are the three basic parts of a neuron?*

The nervous system is never at rest. There is always a job for it to do. It is working right along with you during the most demanding part of your day. Even when you are fully relaxed or sound asleep, your nervous system is busy **regulating** your body's functions. The nervous system controls your emotions, movements, thinking, and behavior. It is a part of almost everything you do.

Structurally, the nervous system is divided into two parts. The first part is the **central nervous system (CNS)**, which includes the brain and the **spinal cord**. The second part is the **peripheral nervous system (PNS)**, which is made up of the smaller branches of nerves that reach the other parts of the body. The nerves of the peripheral system transmit information back and forth from the organs to the central nervous system. The nerves of the peripheral system branch beyond the spinal column and range in thickness from the size of a pencil to almost microscopic in the body's extremities.

All parts of the nervous system are protected in some way. The brain is encased inside the skull and is also protected by several layers of sheathing. These layers of sheathing, which also protect the peripheral nervous system, not only protect the brain and nerves from physical damage, but also help to insulate them from extremities in temperature. The spinal cord is sheltered by the skeletal vertebrae of the spine. The bony protection of the vertebrae is vital to the spinal cord. An injury to the spinal cord could prevent the transmittal of messages between the brain and the muscles, and could result in paralysis.

Neurons

Messages to and from the brain travel along the nerves, which are strings of long, thin cells called **neurons**. Chemical-electrical signals travel down the neurons much as a flame travels along the fuse of a firecracker. The main difference is that unlike a firecracker, the neuron can be "fired" over and over again, hundreds of times a minute.

Transmission between neurons, or nerve cells, occurs whenever the cells are stimulated past a minimum point and emit a signal from other neurons or body sensors. The neuron is said to fire in accord with the all-or-none principle, which states that when a neuron fires, it does so at full strength. If a neuron is not stimulated past the minimum, or threshold, level, it does not fire at all.

Neurons have four basic parts: dendrites, the cell body, an axon, and axon terminals. Dendrites are short, thin fibers that protrude from the cell body that receive impulses, or messages, from other neurons. The dendrites are like antennae for the neuron. Along the dendrites are thousands of synapses receiving impulses for the neuron. These impulses are then sent to the cell body to be processed. The cell body integrates the signals, or impulses, from other cells. The cell body also contains the cell's genetic information, called DNA. This information is found in the nucleus of each cell in our bodies. In addition, the cell body provides metabolic support for the cell, meaning that the parts of the cell body work together to give the cell energy for continued support and maintenance. Without the reactions inside the cell body, the cell would not be able to maintain life.

regulate to control something

central nervous system (CNS) the brain and spinal cord

spinal cord nerves that run up and down the length of the back and transmit most messages between the body and brain

peripheral nervous system (PNS) nerves branching beyond the spinal cord into the body

neurons the long, thin cells of nerve tissue along which messages travel to and from the brain

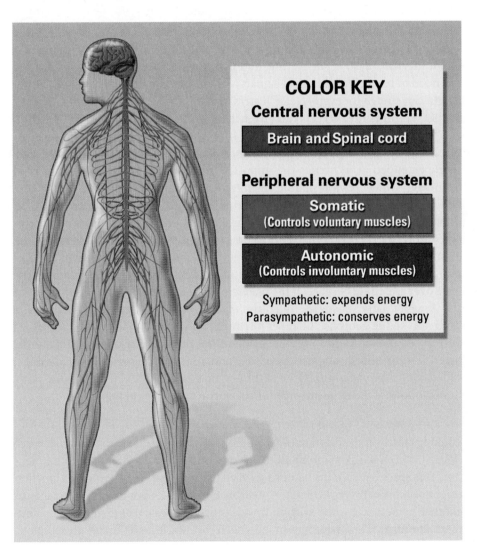

COLOR KEY

Central nervous system

Brain and Spinal cord

Peripheral nervous system

Somatic
(Controls voluntary muscles)

Autonomic
(Controls involuntary muscles)

Sympathetic: expends energy
Parasympathetic: conserves energy

<⟩ **DIAGRAM**

THE NERVOUS SYSTEM

The nervous system is divided into two parts: the central nervous system (CNS) and the peripheral nervous system (PNS).

▶ **CRITICAL THINKING**

1. *Gathering Information* What are the two main divisions of the peripheral nervous system?

2. *Comparing and Contrasting* What are the similarities and differences between the sympathetic and parasympathetic nervous systems?

ANATOMY OF TWO NEURONS

The human body contains billions of neurons. The neuron receives messages from other neurons via its dendrites. The messages are then transmitted down the axon and sent out through the axon terminals. The myelin sheath serves to protect the axon.

▶ **CRITICAL THINKING**

1. *Drawing Conclusions* What is the function of the dendrites?

2. *Gathering Information* What is the role of the myelin sheath?

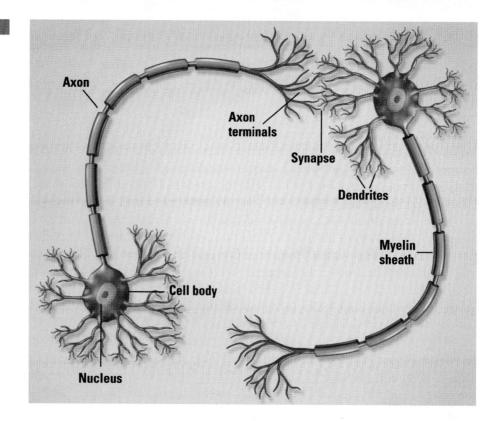

Axon

Axon terminals

Synapse

Dendrites

Myelin sheath

Cell body

Nucleus

There is a constant flow of chemical energy within the parts of the cell body. Body signals move from the cell body to the axons. The axons can reach to distant areas of the nervous system, delivering impulses to the parts of the body they are intended to reach. The electrical signals along axons usually move quickly, but in length can stretch to several feet. Clusters of axons may split into several branches so that their intended targets can be reached.

For example, a message may travel from the dendrite of a neuron, through the cell body, and then to the part of the body that reacts to that message. The single extended axon carries the impulses from the cell body toward the axon terminals, which release neurotransmitters to stimulate dendrites of the next neuron. The shape and structure of dendrites make them particularly easy to move, shape, or mold. This plasticity plays an important role in learning, memory, and recovery after spinal cord or brain injury. When new dendrites grow or existing ones grow new connections, long-term memory may improve. In addition, adaptive behaviors, learned behaviors, and retention of memories are possible over a lifetime because of the plasticity of dendrites.

A white, fatty substance called the *myelin sheath* insulates and protects the axon for some neurons. In cases of multiple sclerosis, the myelin sheath is destroyed, and as a result, the behavior of the person is erratic and uncoordinated. The myelin sheath also speeds the transmission of impulses. Small fibers, called *axon terminals*, branch out at the end of the axon. Axon terminals are positioned opposite the dendrite of another neuron.

Making Neural Connections

Looking closely at the diagram of the neuron, you can see that there is a small space or gap between the axon terminals of one neuron and the dendrites of another neuron. This space between the neurons is called the **synapse**. The synapse is a junction or connection between neurons. A neuron transmits its impulses or messages to another neuron across the synapse by releasing chemicals that are known as **neurotransmitters**. These neurotransmitters open chemical locks or "excite" the receptors.

synapse the gap that exists between individual nerve cells

neurotransmitters the chemicals released by neurons, which determine the rate at which other neurons fire

The neurotransmitters can excite the next neuron or stop it from transmitting altogether, which is called inhibition. With receptors only in the dendrites, the synapse allows signals to move in only one direction, from endfoot to dendrite.

Different types of neurotransmitters do different jobs for the body. Some, called excitatory neurotransmitters, excite the receptors and cause action among neurons. Others are inhibitory neurotransmitters, which prevent potential action among neurons. Glutamate is an excitatory neurotransmitter that plays an important role in memory, learning, and communication among receptors. Gamma-aminobutyric acid (GABA) receptors play a role in quieting the body and muscles. Both of these neurotransmitters play an important part in the effects of alcohol on the body. Glutamate receptors are slowed down when alcohol is consumed, and body functions are affected. GABA receptors work harder, which is what causes alcohol to work as a depressant that slows down the body. Other neurotransmitters have other effects on the body. Like glutamate, norepinephrine is involved in memory and learning. Endorphins inhibit pain.

The oversupply or undersupply of certain neurotransmitters has been linked to certain diseases. For instance, an undersupply of *acetylcholine*, a neurotransmitter involved in movement and memory, is associated with paralysis and Alzheimer's disease. An oversupply of *dopamine*, involved in learning, emotional arousal, and movement, is linked to schizophrenia, while an undersupply is linked to Parkinson's disease. An undersupply of norepinephrine and *serotonin* may result in depression. Medications that increase levels of norepinephrine are used to treat Attention Deficit Hyperactivity Disorder and hypotension as well.

Neural Activity

The intensity of activity in each neuron depends on how many other neurons are acting on it. Each individual neuron is either ON or OFF, depending on whether most of the neurons acting on it are exciting it or inhibiting it. The actual destination of nerve impulses produced by an excited neuron, as they travel from one neuron to another, is limited by what tract in the nervous system they are on. Ascending tracts carry sensory impulses to the brain, and descending tracts carry motor impulses from the brain.

There are different types of neurons. *Afferent* neurons, or sensory neurons, relay messages from the sense organs (including eye, ear, nose, and skin) to the brain. When you smell food cooking, afferent neurons stimulated in your nose react with a chemical signal to your brain. The brain may then be able to identify the smell without you being able to see or taste the food. *Efferent* neurons, or motor neurons, send signals from the brain to the glands and muscles. When you walk, move, exercise, or interact with your environment, efferent neurons help the brain coordinate the movement. *Interneurons* process signals, connecting only to other neurons, not to sensors or muscles. You may find interneurons connecting to either afferent neurons or efferent neurons.

✔ READING PROGRESS CHECK

Summarizing How does the nervous system send messages throughout the body?

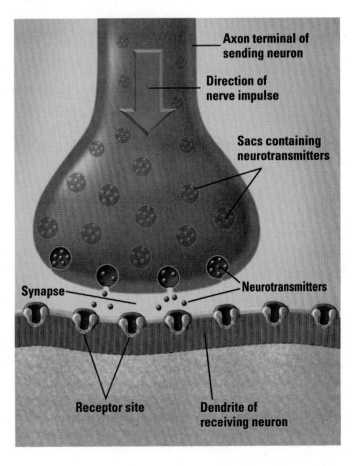

⌄ DIAGRAM

THE SYNAPSE

Neurons do not touch one another. Instead, a neuron sends its messages across a gap called a synapse by releasing neurotransmitters. These neurotransmitters are received by the dendrite of another neuron.

▶ CRITICAL THINKING

1. ***Sequencing*** How are neurons involved in sending a message to the brain to raise your arm to answer a question?

2. ***Drawing Inferences*** What transports neurotransmitters through the axon?

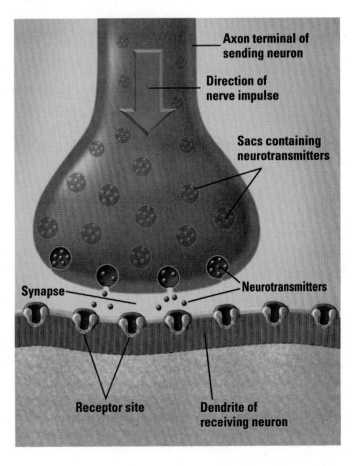

Axon terminal of sending neuron

Direction of nerve impulse

Sacs containing neurotransmitters

Neurotransmitters

Synapse

Receptor site

Dendrite of receiving neuron

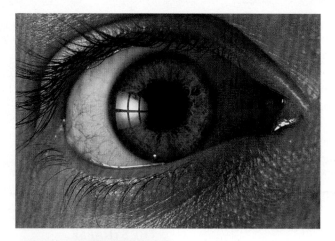

Voluntary and Involuntary Activities

GUIDING QUESTION *How do the sympathetic and parasympathetic nervous systems differ?*

Some of the actions that your body makes in response to impulses from the nerves are **voluntary** acts, such as lifting your hand to turn a page (which actually involves many impulses to many muscles). Others are involuntary acts, such as changes in the heartbeat, in the blood pressure, or in the size of the pupils. The term somatic nervous system (SNS) refers to the part of the peripheral nervous system that controls voluntary activities. The term autonomic nervous system (ANS) refers to the part of the nervous system that controls involuntary activities, or those that ordinarily occur automatically, such as heartbeat, stomach activity, and so on.

The autonomic nervous system has two parts: the sympathetic and parasympathetic nervous systems. The sympathetic nervous system prepares the body for dealing with emergencies or strenuous activity. It speeds up the heart rate to hasten the supply of oxygen and nutrients to body tissues. It constricts some arteries and relaxes others so that blood flows to the muscles, where it is most needed in emergencies and strenuous activity. It increases the blood pressure and suspends some activities, such as digestion. In contrast, the parasympathetic nervous system works to conserve energy and to enhance the body's ability to recover from strenuous activity. It reduces the heart rate and blood pressure and helps bring the body back to its normal resting state.

All of this takes place automatically. Receptors are constantly receiving messages, such as messages about hunger or the need to swallow or cough, that alert the autonomic nervous system to carry out routine activities. Imagine how difficult it would be if you had no autonomic nervous system and had to think about it every time your body needed to digest a sandwich or perspire.

☑ READING PROGRESS CHECK

Finding the Main Idea Which nervous systems are responsible for voluntary and involuntary activities?

When your pupils get larger in response to dim light, your body is performing an involuntary activity.

▶ **CRITICAL THINKING**

Categorizing What other involuntary activities take place in your body?

voluntary proceeding from one's own consent

somatic nervous system (SNS) the part of the peripheral nervous system that controls voluntary movement of skeletal muscles

autonomic nervous system (ANS) the part of the peripheral nervous system that controls internal biological functions

---

LESSON 1 REVIEW

Reviewing Vocabulary
1. *Defining* What is the difference between afferent and efferent neurons? What are interneurons?

Using Your Notes
2. *Diagramming* Using the notes you took during this lesson, create a diagram of the different parts of the nervous system.

Answering the Guiding Questions
3. *Describing* What are the three basic parts of a neuron?

4. *Applying* How do the sympathetic and parasympathetic nervous systems work?

Writing Activity
5. *Informative/Explanatory* Put your pen or pencil down and then pick it up. Write a paragraph identifying and describing the parts of the nervous system that caused those movements to happen.

152

netw⊙rks

There's More Online!

☑ **DIAGRAM** Brain Activity on a PET Scan

☑ **DIAGRAM** Cerebral Cortex

☑ **DIAGRAM** Functions of the Brain's Hemispheres

☑ **DIAGRAM** Parts of the Brain

☑ **SELF-CHECK QUIZ**

Reading **HELP**DESK ⒸⒸⓈⓈ

Academic Vocabulary

• **detect**   • **stimulate**

Content Vocabulary

• **hindbrain**
• **midbrain**
• **forebrain**
• **lobes**
• **electroencephalograph (EEG)**
• **computerized axial tomography (CT)**
• **positron emission tomography (PET)**
• **magnetic resonance imaging (MRI)**

TAKING NOTES:

Key Ideas and Details

LABELING Use a graphic organizer like the one below to label the parts of the hindbrain and forebrain.

Hindbrain	Forebrain

(c)Phanie/SuperStock; (r)Paul Burns/Blend Images/Corbis

LESSON 2

Studying the Brain

ESSENTIAL QUESTION • *How do internal functions of the body affect behavior?*

IT MATTERS BECAUSE

Even after centuries of study, parts of the human brain remain a mystery even to scientists. The knowledge we gain, the memories we have, and even the bodily functions that we rely on for life are managed and regulated in the brain. Understanding how the brain works can help us to understand the brain's effect on our lives.

The Three Brains

GUIDING QUESTIONS *What are the three parts of the human brain? What are the specializations of the left and right hemispheres of the brain?*

The brain is composed of three parts: the hindbrain, midbrain, and forebrain. The **hindbrain**, located at the rear base of the skull, is involved in the most basic processes of life. The hindbrain includes the *cerebellum, medulla,* and the *pons*. The cerebellum, located behind the spinal cord, helps control posture, balance, and voluntary movements; the medulla controls breathing, heart rate, and a variety of reflexes; the pons functions as a bridge between the spinal cord and the brain. The pons is also involved in producing chemicals the body needs for sleep.

The **midbrain** is a small part of the brain above the pons. It arouses the brain, integrates sensory information, and relays it upward. The medulla and pons extend upward into the midbrain. The medulla, pons, and midbrain compose most of the brain stem, and the reticular activating system (RAS) spans across all these structures. The RAS alerts the rest of the brain to incoming signals and is involved in the sleep/wake cycle.

The **forebrain**, covering the brain's central core, includes the *thalamus*, which integrates sensory input. The thalamus is a relay station for all the information that travels to and from the cortex. All sensory information with the exception of smell enters the thalamus. All information from the eyes, ears, and skin enters the thalamus and then is sent to the appropriate areas in the cortex. Just below the thalamus is the *hypothalamus*. It controls functions such as hunger, thirst, and sexual behavior. It also controls the body's reactions to changes in temperature, so when we are warm, we begin to sweat, and when we are cold, we shiver.

PARTS OF THE BRAIN

The brain is the largest, most complex part of the nervous system.

▶ **CRITICAL THINKING**

1. *Analyzing* What are the functions of the cerebellum?

2. *Gathering Information* In what part of the brain is the medulla located?

hindbrain a part of the brain located at the rear base of the skull that is involved in the basic processes of life

midbrain a small part of the brain above the pons that arouses the brain, integrates sensory information, and relays it upward

forebrain a part of the brain that covers the brain's central core, responsible for sensory and motor control and the processing of thinking and language

lobes the different regions into which the cerebral cortex is divided

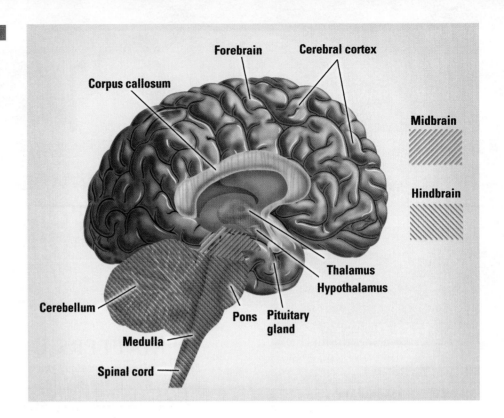

The higher thinking processes—those that make us unique—are housed in the forebrain. The outer layer of the forebrain consists of the *cerebral cortex*. The inner layer is the *cerebrum*. The cerebral cortex and cerebrum surround the hindbrain and brain stem like the way a mushroom surrounds its stem. The cerebral cortex gives you the ability to learn and store complex and abstract information, and to project your thinking into the future. Your cerebral cortex allows you to see, read, and understand this sentence. The cortex, or bark, of the cerebrum is the site of your conscious thinking processes, yet it is less than one-fourth-inch thick.

The *limbic system*, found in the core of the forebrain, is composed of a number of different structures in the brain that regulate our emotions and motivations. The limbic system includes the hypothalamus, amygdala, thalamus, and hippocampus. The amygdala controls violent emotions, such as rage and fear. The hippocampus is important in the formation of memories. If the hippocampus were damaged, it would be difficult to form new memories.

Lobes and Hemispheres

All of these parts are covered by the cerebrum. The cerebrum is really two hemispheres, or two sides. The cerebral hemispheres are connected by a band of fibers called the *corpus callosum*. Each cerebral hemisphere has deep grooves, some of which mark regions, or **lobes**. The occipital lobe is where the visual signals are processed. Damage to this area can cause visual problems, even selective or total blindness. The parietal lobe is concerned with information from the senses from all over the body. The temporal lobe is concerned with hearing, memory, emotion, and speaking. The frontal lobe is concerned with organization, planning, and creative thinking.

The front of the parietal lobe receives information from the skin and muscles. The number of touch sensors in an individual body part determines its sensitivity, and, along with the complexity of the part's movement, governs the amount of brain tissue that is associated with the part. The complex touch and movements of the hands, for example, involve more brain area than the more limited calves.

The somatosensory cortex, at the back of the frontal lobe, receives information from the touch sensors. The motor cortex sends information to control body movement. The more sophisticated the movements, such as those used in speaking, the bigger the brain area involved in their control.

The association areas mediate between the other areas and do most of the synthesizing of information. For example, association areas turn sensory input into meaningful information. Different neurons are activated when we see different shapes and figures. The association areas arrange the incoming information into meaningful perceptions, such as the face of a friend or a favorite shirt.

There is much concern that information about properties of the left and right hemispheres is misinterpreted. Popular books have oversimplified the properties of the two hemispheres. In reality, the left and right sides complement and help each other, so be aware of this as we list the properties of each hemisphere. The two hemispheres in the cortex are roughly mirror images of each other, and each of the four lobes is present in both hemispheres. The corpus callosum carries messages back and forth between the two hemispheres to jointly control human functions. Each hemisphere is connected to one-half of the body in a crisscrossed fashion. The left hemisphere controls the movements of the right side of the body. For most people, the left side of the brain is where speech is located. The left side also is specialized for mathematical ability, calculation, and logic.

The right hemisphere controls the left side of the body. Thus a stroke that causes damage to the right hemisphere will result in numbness or paralysis on the left side of the body. The right hemisphere is more adept at visual and spatial relations. Putting together a puzzle requires spatial ability. Perceptual tasks seem to be processed primarily by the right hemisphere. The right side is better at recognizing patterns. Thus, music and art are better understood by the right hemisphere. Creativity and intuition are also found in the right hemisphere.

In a normal brain, the two hemispheres communicate through the corpus callosum. Whatever occurs on one side is communicated to the other side. Some people have grand mal seizures, which is the most severe kind of seizure.

⌄ **DIAGRAM**

CEREBRAL CORTEX
Functions of the cerebral cortex are not fully understood. Below are areas important to behavior.

▶ **CRITICAL THINKING**

1. *Analyzing Visuals* What is the function of the motor cortex?

2. *Gathering Information* In which part of the brain are body sensations experienced?

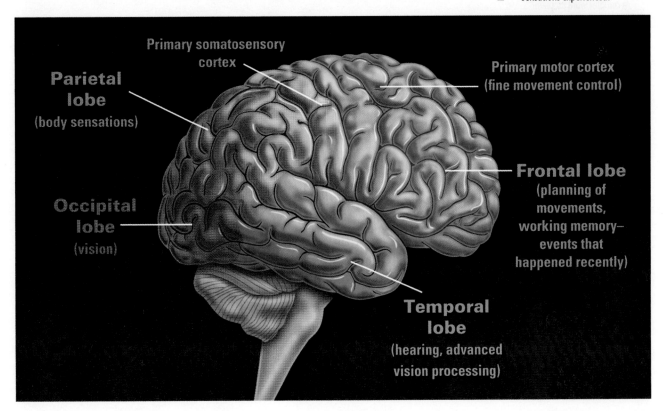

Primary somatosensory cortex

Parietal lobe
(body sensations)

Primary motor cortex
(fine movement control)

Occipital lobe
(vision)

Frontal lobe
(planning of movements, working memory—events that happened recently)

Temporal lobe
(hearing, advanced vision processing)

Separating the brain hemispheres has proven to lessen the number and severity of the seizures. As a result, the person has a split brain. The person has two brains that operate independently of each other. Since the corpus callosum is severed, there can no longer be any communication between the hemispheres. Studies have shown that normal functioning remains possible in such a situation.

Many psychologists became interested in differences between the cerebral hemispheres when split-brain operations were tried on epileptics like Harriet Lees. For most of her life Lees's seizures were mild and could be controlled with drugs. However, at age 25 they began to get worse, and by 30 Lees was having as many as a dozen violent seizures a day. An epileptic seizure involves massive uncontrolled electrical activity that begins in either hemisphere and spreads across both. To enable Lees to live a normal life, she and the doctors decided to sever the corpus callosum so that seizures could not spread.

Not only did the operation reduce the severity of seizures, but it also resulted in fewer seizures. Psychologists were even more interested in the potential side effects of this operation. Despite the fact that patients who had this operation now had two functionally separate brains, they seemed remarkably normal. Researchers went on to develop a number of techniques to try to **detect** subtle effects of the split-brain operation.

If a blindfolded man whose brain has been split holds a ball in his right hand, he would be able to say it is a ball. Place the ball in his left hand and he would not be able to say what it is. Information from the left hand is sent to the right hemisphere of the brain. Since the corpus callosum is severed, information cannot cross to the speech center in the left hemisphere.

Another experiment with split-brain patients involves tactile **stimulation**, or touch. In this experiment, objects are held in a designated hand but are blocked from the split-brain patient's view. Researchers project a word describing an object on a screen to either the right or left visual field. The patient's task is to find the object corresponding to the word they are shown. When words are presented

detect to find out or discover

stimulate to raise levels of interest, response, or activity

DIAGRAM ⌄

FUNCTIONS OF THE BRAIN'S HEMISPHERES
Being "right-brained" or "left-brained" is an exaggerated concept. We constantly use both hemispheres of our brain, as each hemisphere is specialized for processing certain kinds of information.

▶ **CRITICAL THINKING**

1. Assessing In what topics or activities does the right hemisphere specialize?

2. Analyzing What part of the brain would someone use to solve a complex word problem?

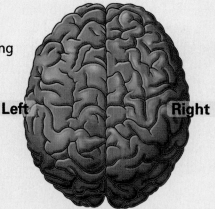

Front

Verbal: speaking, understanding language, reading, writing

Mathematical: adding, subtracting, multiplying, calculus, physics

Analytic: analyzing separate pieces that make up a whole

Left

Right

Nonverbal: understanding simple sentences and words

Spatial: solving spatial problems such as geometry, enjoying art

Holistic: combining parts that make up a whole

Back

Quick Lab

CAN YOU DETERMINE WHETHER THE LEFT OR RIGHT HEMISPHERE OF THE BRAIN IS DOMINANT?

The left hemisphere controls the movements of the right side of the body. This side of the brain is adept at language-related skills, mathematical ability, and logic. The right hemisphere controls the movements of the left side of the body. It is also the side that is more adept for creativity, intuition, and creative expressions such as art and music. Can you tell which side is dominant in people you know?

Procedure

1. Think about two of your friends or family members.
2. Compare them in terms of the areas that they seem to be most adept at—mathematics, logical thinking, musical ability, art, or speech.
3. Record your observations in a two-column chart.

Analysis

1. Based on your observations, which hemisphere seems to be dominant in each individual?

for the right hemisphere to see, patients cannot say the word, but they can identify the object with their left hand touching it behind the screen.

To explore emotional reactions in split-brain individuals, researchers designed a test to incorporate emotional stimuli with objects in view. In one of these experiments, a picture of a nude person was flashed to either hemisphere. When researchers flashed the picture to the left hemisphere, the patient laughed and described what she saw. When the same was done to the right hemisphere, the patient said nothing, but her face became flush and she began to grin.

Research on split-brain patients has presented solid evidence that each hemisphere of the brain is unique with specialized functions and skills. Individuals who have had split-brain operations remained practically unchanged in intelligence, personality, and emotions.

Using the Brain

Have you ever been told that people use only about 10 percent of their brains? It's a common belief, but scientists have proved that this myth is false. It is true that if we explored our brain's complete cognitive potential we could use a lot more of our brain's power than we use from day to day. But scientists are now discovering that our daily activities actually tap into a large portion of our brains. In fact, the brain uses about 20 percent of the body's total energy.

Think about when you ride a bicycle. You are coordinating the movement of your arms and legs. At the same time you are evaluating the environment around you, reading signs and interpreting what the signs mean to you. You are also calculating where you are and how far it is to your destination. Different parts of the brain are used to do this interpreting and thinking. Reading a stop sign uses parts of your brain associated with interpreting written language. Determining when you need to hit the brakes to stop in time, your brain connects to your legs and feet, coordinating smooth body movements and checking environmental factors around you at the same time. This coordination involves significant brain activity.

☑ **READING PROGRESS CHECK**

Understanding Relationships What is the difference between the left and the right hemispheres of the brain?

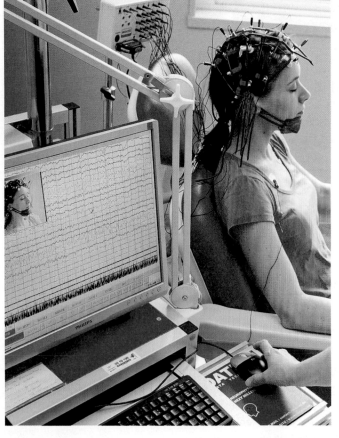

Scientists use an electroencephalograph (EEG) to measure brain waves.

▶ **CRITICAL THINKING**

Assessing What have psychologists observed about the electrical activity of the brain?

How Psychologists Study the Brain

GUIDING QUESTIONS *How can accidents that damage the brain instruct us in its functions? How do researchers use MRIs to learn about the brain?*

Mapping the brain's fissures and inner recesses has supplied scientists with fascinating information about the role of the brain in behavior. Psychologists who do this kind of research are called physiological psychologists, psychobiologists, or neuroscientists.

Some research techniques are better at studying the structure of the brain rather than its functions. Scientists must carefully choose which method they want to pursue for studying the brain, depending on what they want to find out. Working with human subjects must always be as ethical as possible to avoid any physical or emotional harm to the subjects.

In the past, an intrusive method called a lobotomy was used to treat severe mental illness. During this surgical procedure, an incision was made into the prefrontal lobe of the brain and nerve pathways in the brain were severed. While lobotomies had the effect of reducing anxiety and agitation in patients, it also produced other problems such as apathy and decreased ability to show emotion. The surgery was used widely in the United States from the 1930s to the 1960s because there were no medications or other ways to treat patients who suffered from severe mental illness. Today the procedure is very rarely performed because there are many other well-accepted and less intrusive ways to study the brain. The use of electrodes, lesions, and the study of damaged brains after accidents are less invasive, less intrusive, and even more effective.

Electrodes

Electrodes are wires that can be inserted into the brain to record electrical activity in the brain. By inserting electrodes in the brain, it is possible to detect the minute electrical changes that occur when neurons fire. The wires are connected to electronic equipment that amplifies the tiny voltages produced by the firing neurons. Even single neurons can be monitored. The electrical activity of whole areas of the brain can be recorded with an **electroencephalograph (EEG)**. Wires from the EEG are attached to the scalp so that millions upon millions of neurons can be monitored at the same time. Psychologists have observed that the overall electrical activity of the brain rises and falls rhythmically and that the pattern of the rhythm depends on whether a person is awake, drowsy, or asleep. These rhythms, or brain waves, occur because the neurons in the brain tend to increase or decrease their amount of activity in unison.

Electrodes may be used to set off the firing of neurons as well as to record it. Brain surgeon Wilder Penfield stimulated the brains of his patients during surgery to determine what functions the various parts of the brain perform. In this way he could localize the malfunctioning part for which surgery was required, for example, for epilepsy.

electroencephalograph (EEG) a machine used to record the electrical activity of large portions of the brain

When Penfield applied a tiny electric current to points on the temporal lobe of the brain, he could trigger whole memory sequences, including sound, movement, and color, that were clearer than usual memories. During surgery, one woman heard a familiar song so distinctly that she thought a recording was being played. Penfield discovered that by stimulating the same area of the brain again the same memory would be triggered.

One benefit of using electrodes is that scientists can map the parts of the brain where different cognitive activities take place. A drawback is that it cannot be used during everyday activities because the subject needs to be hooked up to the electrodes.

Lesions

Scientists sometimes create lesions by cutting or destroying part of an animal's brain. If the animal behaves differently after the operation, they assume that the destroyed brain area is involved with that type of behavior. For example, in one classic lesion study, two researchers removed a certain area of the temporal lobe from rhesus monkeys. Normally, these animals are fearful, aggressive, and vicious, but after the operation, they became less fearful and at the same time less violent. The implication was that this area of the brain controlled aggression. The relations revealed by this type of research are far more subtle and complex than people first believed. For this reason it is hard to apply the findings from animal studies to the working of the human brain.

Accidents

Accidents that resulted in brain injuries, while tragic, offered insight into how the brain functions. Psychologists try to draw a connection between the damaged parts of the brain and a person's behavior. One such case involved an unusual accident in 1848. Phineas Gage was a respected railroad foreman who demonstrated restraint, good judgment, and the ability to work well with other men. His crew of men was about to explode some dynamite to clear a path for the railroad rails. As Gage filled a narrow hole with dynamite and tamped it down, it suddenly exploded. The tamping iron had caused a spark that ignited the dynamite. The tamping iron, which weighed over 13 pounds and was over 3 feet in length, shot into the air! It entered Gage's head right below the left eye, and it exited through the top of his skull.

Gage survived the accident, but his personality changed greatly. He became short-tempered, was difficult to be around, and often said inappropriate things. Gage lived for several years after the accident. In 1994 psychologists Hanna and Antonio Damasio examined Gage's skull using the newest methods available. They reported that the tamping iron had caused damage to parts of the frontal cortex. They found that damage to the frontal lobes prevents censoring of thoughts and ideas.

In 2001 scans of Gage's skull were made but later lost. In 2012 neuroscientists rediscovered the data and reconstructed the scans. They created a composite image of a brain using scans of several men physically similar to Gage and used imaging software to position the virtual brain within the virtual skull. Then they traced the trajectory of the tamping iron through the skull and brain and were able to identify what areas of the brain had been affected by the accident. These neuroscientists found that while the frontal cortex indeed had been directly damaged by the iron, perhaps more important was the destruction of more than 10 percent of the white matter in Gage's brain. The significant loss of white matter connectivity is similar to the damage created by Alzheimer's disease or frontal lobe dementia and probably played an even greater role in his personality change.

Keystone/Hulton Archive/Getty Images

computerized axial tomography (CT) an imaging technique used to study the brain to pinpoint injuries and brain deterioration

positron emission tomography (PET) an imaging technique used to see which brain areas are being activated while performing tasks

Another unusual case took place in the nineteenth century. Dr. Paul Broca had a young patient who could only respond with hand gestures and the word "tan." Broca theorized that a part of the brain on the left side was destroyed, limiting the young man's communication processes. Many years later, researchers examined the young man's brain using modern methods. They discovered that Dr. Broca's theory was correct. The left side of the cortex, which is involved with the production of speech, was damaged. This area of the cortex is now known as Broca's area.

Another kind of brain damage, called Wernicke aphasia, occurs from damage of the temporal lobe. When this part of the brain is damaged, patients have trouble understanding spoken language. In addition, any sounds, phrases, or sentences that they try to speak themselves are not discernable. As a result of studying people with this type of damage, scientists can deduce that this part of the temporal lobe is associated with speech and language comprehension.

Studying people who have suffered accidents to the brain is a very useful way to figure out which parts of the brain affect our different behaviors. This gives us ideas about the structure of the brain, but there are still many things to learn about the function of the brain and how these areas might be repaired after they have been damaged.

Connecting Psychology to Geography

GLOBAL NUTRITION AND BRAIN DEVELOPMENT

Scientists have discovered that the health of a developing fetus is dependent largely on the diet and nutrition of the mother. For example, nutritional deficiencies during critical times of development can cause birth defects such as spina bifida and neural tube defects. Folic acid is needed early in pregnancy to reduce the chances of these abnormalities. This nutrient is found in leafy green vegetables, beans, nuts, grains, and citrus juices. A nutritious diet throughout the course of a woman's pregnancy is more likely to produce a fetus with a normally developing brain and organs. This will produce a healthy fetus as well as increase the baby's chance of survival after birth.

There are areas of the world, however, where obtaining proper nutrition can be difficult. Women in many less developed countries or remote areas do not have access to enough of the nutritious foods needed to develop a healthy fetus. For instance, remote areas of Africa, lack foods rich in nutrients such as vitamin A, iodine, and iron. Vitamin A has been linked to a vulnerability to malaria, a significant public health problem in Africa. Iodine deficiency is the largest preventable cause of developmental disabilities but can be successfully remedied if treated during the first six months of pregnancy. An iron deficiency, also termed anemia, is associated with low birth weights. Continuing to provide education about a balanced diet and increasing access to proper nutrition, both so important to the health of the mother and the brain development of the fetus, is crucial.

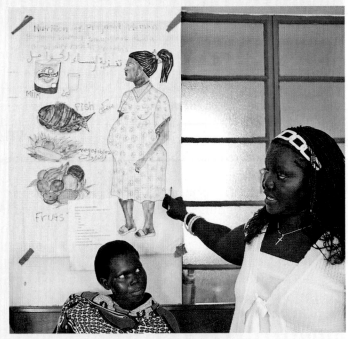

▲ Many less developed countries are increasing or hope to increase funding for education on proper prenatal care and nutrition.

▶ **CRITICAL THINKING**

1. *Assessing* What birth defects are the result of maternal nutritional deficiencies? Why is education on this topic of such importance for mothers in all parts of the world?

2. *Identifying Central Issues* How does maternal nutrition affect fetal health and brain development?

Disorders

Some disorders give us interesting information about the brain. For example, synesthesia is a disorder in which senses become confused and are given the impression of being other senses. For example, a person may see a number and associate it with a color. The number four may give the impression of being green every time it is seen. A song may produce a sense of smell for someone. With a disorder called prosopagnosia, a person cannot recognize familiar faces. They may see a relative or close friend many times, and never develop a sense of familiarity and recognition when that person is seen. Studying these disorders can give psychologists clues about how people create associations as they recognize or experience things such as objects, colors, or faces.

In addition to sensory disorders, the brain may also suffer degenerative disorders, or disorders that get worse over time. With Alzheimer's disease, the decline in memory and cognitive abilities is due to neural connections in the cerebral cortex. With Parkinson's disease, there is a decline of neural connections in the area of the brain associated with movement. When a person suffers a stroke, the flow of blood to the brain is disrupted, or there is bleeding within the brain. This may cause problems with muscular coordination or paralysis on one or both sides of the body. A study of degenerative diseases can show scientists how the brain ages and what effect changing neural connections may have on behavior.

Images

Dr. Paul Broca uncovered the connection between the brain and speech. Researchers proved Dr. Broca's theory using PET scans. Today psychologists and medical researchers are using this and other sophisticated techniques, including CT scans and fMRI scans. In the 1970s, **computerized axial tomography (CT)** scans were used to pinpoint injuries and other problems in brain deterioration. During a CT scan, a moving ring passes X-ray beams around and through a subject's head. Radiation is absorbed in different amounts depending on the density of the brain tissue. Computers measure the amount of radiation absorbed and transform this information into a three-dimensional view of the brain.

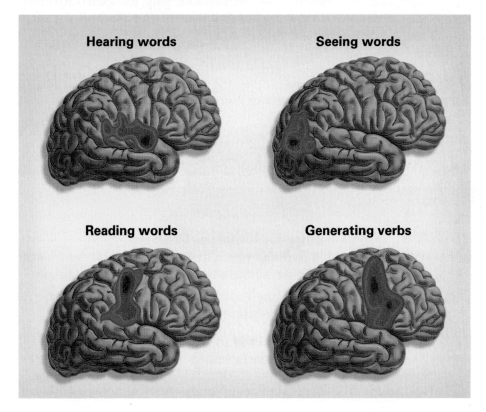

Hearing words

Seeing words

Reading words

Generating verbs

◄ DIAGRAM

BRAIN ACTIVITY ON A PET SCAN

A computer transforms the different levels of absorption by neurons of radioactive solution into colors. Red and yellow indicate maximum activity of neurons, while blue and green indicate minimal activity.

▶ **CRITICAL THINKING**

1. *Defending* Why would psychologists use a PET scan?

2. *Drawing Conclusions* Why do you think hearing and reading occur in different parts of the brain?

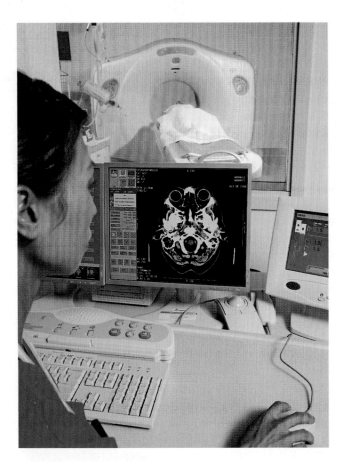

Magnetic resonance imaging (MRI) studies the activities of the brain.

▶ **CRITICAL THINKING**

Evaluating Why does an MRI of the brain give a more thorough picture than a CT or PET scan would give?

magnetic resonance imaging (MRI) a measuring technique used to study brain structure and activity

The **positron emission tomography (PET)** scan can capture a picture of the brain as different parts are being used. It involves injecting a slightly radioactive solution into the blood and then measuring the amount of radiation absorbed by blood cells. Active neurons absorb more radioactive solution than non-active ones. Researchers use the PET scan to see which areas are being activated while performing a task. PET scans show activity in different areas of the brain when a person is thinking, speaking, and looking at objects. The scan changes when one is talking and when one is looking at a piece of art. These pictures change as the activity changes.

Another process, **magnetic resonance imaging**, or **MRI**, enables researchers to study both activity and brain structures. It combines the features of both CT and PET scans. It involves passing nonharmful radio frequencies through the brain. A computer measures how these signals interact with brain cells and translates these signals into a detailed image of the brain. Researchers use MRIs to study the structure of the brain as well as to identify tumors or types of brain damage.

Researchers use a new technique of imaging, functional magnetic resonance imaging (fMRI), to directly observe both the functions of different structures of the brain and which structures participate in specific functions. The fMRI provides high-resolution reports of neural activity based on signals that are determined by blood oxygen level.

The fMRI actually detects an increase in blood flow to the active structure of the brain. So, unlike the MRI, the fMRI does not require passing radio frequencies through the brain. With this new method of imaging, researchers have confirmed their hypotheses concerning the functions of areas such as the visual cortex, the motor cortex, and Broca's area of speech- and language-related activities.

✓ **READING PROGRESS CHECK**

Making Connections What might scientists learn by studying images of the brain?

LESSON 2 REVIEW

Reviewing Vocabulary

1. *Defining* List and describe the main functions of the lobes of the human brain.

2. *Identifying* What are the functions of the thalamus and the hypothalamus?

Using Your Notes

3. *Diagramming* Using the notes you took during this lesson, write a paragraph explaining how damage to each of the three parts of the brain might affect activities of daily life.

Answering the Guiding Questions

4. *Describing* What are the three parts of the human brain? What are the specializations of the left and right hemispheres of the brain?

5. *Explaining* How can accidents that damage the brain instruct us in its functions?

Writing Activity

6. *Informative/Explanatory* A woman severely injured the right hemisphere of her brain. Write a scenario in which you describe two body functions that might be affected by the woman's injury.

Case Study

One Person . . . Two Brains?

Period of Study: 1979

Introduction: Victoria had experienced intense epileptic seizures since she was six years old. Doctors placed Victoria on medication that prevented seizures; however, after many years, the seizures returned with greater intensity. Weary and disgusted from living her life with the uncontrollable seizures, Victoria decided it was time to seek a new treatment.

Doctors suggested and Victoria opted for a split-brain operation. This involved separating the two brain hemispheres by cutting the corpus callosum. Split-brain operations disrupt the major pathway between the brain hemispheres but leave each hemisphere functioning almost completely independently. The procedure prevents the spread of seizures from one hemisphere to the other and reduces the incidence or shortens the duration.

The operation might result in other difficulties for Victoria, however. Researchers working with earlier patients who had undergone the procedure found that sometimes those patients acted as if they had a different personality in each hemisphere after the operation. One neuroscientist wrote:

PRIMARY SOURCE

❝[The patient] would sometimes find himself pulling his pants down with one hand and pulling them up with the other. Once, he grabbed his wife with his left hand and shook her violently, with the right hand trying to come to his wife's aid in bringing the left belligerent hand under control.❞

—*Michael Gazzaniga,* The Bisected Brain *(1970)*

Hypothesis: Researchers wanted to explore the degree to which the two halves of the brain could communicate and function on their own after the operation.

Method: Researchers asked Victoria to stare at a black dot between the letters HE and ART. The information from each side of the black dot would be interpreted by the opposite hemisphere in Victoria's split brain. Victoria's right hemisphere would "see" HE and her left would only "see" ART. When Victoria was asked what she had seen, she reported to have seen the word ART. The word ART was projected to her left hemisphere, which contains the ability for speech. She did indeed see the word HE; however, the right hemisphere could not make Victoria say what she had seen. With her left hand, though, Victoria could point to a picture of a man, or HE. This indicated that her right hemisphere could understand the meaning of HE.

Results: After some initial frustrations, Victoria developed new routines for everyday functions such as dressing, eating, and walking. Four months after her operation, she could easily remember and speak of past and present events in her life. Her reading, writing, and reasoning abilities were intact. Although the effects of her operation became apparent under special testing, they were not usually apparent in everyday life. Victoria, now free of her once-feared seizures, could live her life in full; split-brained but fundamentally unchanged.

Analyzing the Case Study

1. ***Explaining*** Why did Victoria choose to have a split-brain operation? What did the operation involve?

2. ***Identifying*** What questions did researchers set out to answer after Victoria's operation?

3. ***Applying*** Consider the quote from Gazzaniga. What problems do you think Victoria might encounter in everyday life?

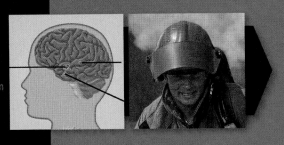

Reading **HELP**DESK

Academic Vocabulary

• beneficial   • impact

Content Vocabulary

• **endocrine system**
• **hormones**
• **pituitary gland**

TAKING NOTES:

Key Ideas and Details

CATEGORIZING Use a graphic organizer like the one below to list four types of glands in the endocrine system.

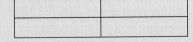

LESSON 3

The Endocrine System

ESSENTIAL QUESTION • *How do changes in our bodies' processes lead to changes in our behavior?*

IT MATTERS BECAUSE

The endocrine system controls and excites growth in the body and affects our emotions and behaviors. Hormones secreted by the endocrine system can cause the body to react and become very active. Understanding functions such as these "adrenaline rushes" help us understand how and why body processes can affect our behavior.

The Endocrine Glands

GUIDING QUESTION *What is the function of the pituitary gland?*

The nervous system is one of two communication systems for sending information to and from the brain. The second is the **endocrine system**. The endocrine system sends chemical messages, called hormones. The **hormones** are produced in the endocrine glands and are distributed by the blood and other body fluids. Hormones circulate throughout the bloodstream but are properly received only at a specific site: the particular organ of the body that they influence. The endocrine glands are also called ductless glands because they release hormones directly into the bloodstream. In contrast, the duct glands release their contents through small holes, or ducts, onto the surface of the body or into the digestive system. Examples of duct glands are sweat glands, tear glands, and salivary glands.

Hormones have various effects on your behavior. They affect the growth of bodily structures such as muscles and bones, so they affect what you can do physically. Hormones affect your metabolic processes; that is, they can affect how much energy you have to perform actions. Certain hormones are secreted during stressful situations to prepare the body for action. Hormones also act in the brain to directly influence your moods and drives. Some hormonal effects take place before you are born. Essentially all the physical differences between boys and girls are caused by a hormone called testosterone.

Scientists have developed a synthetic steroid hormone that resembles testosterone. This drug can be **beneficial**, as it promotes muscle growth when it is taken as a drug. Steroids are used to treat weight loss caused by

Mike Kemp/age fotostock

some diseases. It is also used illegally by some athletes to enhance their physical performance. However, there are several endocrine glands throughout the body that produce hormones naturally.

Pituitary and Thyroid Glands

Directed by the hypothalamus, the **pituitary gland** acts as the master gland. Located near the midbrain and the hypothalamus, the pituitary gland secretes a large number of hormones, many of which control the output of hormones by other endocrine glands. The hypothalamus monitors the amount of hormones in the blood and sends out messages to correct imbalances. What do these hormone messages tell the body to do? They carry messages to organs involved in regulating and storing nutrients so that despite changes in conditions outside the body, cell metabolism can continue on an even course. They also control growth and reproduction, including ovulation and lactation (milk production) in females. The pituitary gland is about the size of a pea and weighs only half of a gram.

The *thyroid gland* is one of the largest endocrine glands in the human body. It is located in the neck and is separated into two lobes. The glands can be felt on either side of the neck below the jaw. The thyroid controls how quickly the body uses energy and makes proteins. It produces the hormone thyroxine. Thyroxine stimulates certain chemical reactions that are important for all tissues of the body. Too little thyroxine makes people feel lazy and lethargic—a condition known as hypothyroidism. Too much thyroxine may cause people to lose weight and sleep and to be overactive—a condition known as hyperthyroidism.

Adrenal Glands

The *adrenal glands* are located on top of the kidneys, one on each side of the body. They become active when a person is angry or frightened. Neural responses from the adrenal glands originate near the spinal column. Each adrenal gland consists of a medulla (the center of the gland), surrounded by a cortex. The adrenal medulla is responsible for producing epinephrine and norepinephrine (also called adrenaline and noradrenaline). When released into the bloodstream, these secretions cause the heartbeat and breathing to increase. They can heighten emotions, such as fear and anxiety. These and other changes help a person generate the extra energy he or she needs to handle a difficult situation. Most of the responses that our bodies have to stress, fear, anger, and other emotional reactions are controlled by the adrenal glands. The adrenal glands also regulate salt and water levels in the body and help regulate the body's metabolic processes. The adrenal cortex produces cortical steroids, which help regulate blood pressure, inflammation, and the body's immune response. They have an **impact** on the body's use of fats, proteins, and carbohydrates.

Sex Glands

There are two types of sex glands—*testes* in males and *ovaries* in females. Testes produce sperm and the male sex hormone *testosterone*. Even though they do not have testes, low levels of testosterone are also found in females. Ovaries produce eggs and the female hormones *estrogen* and *progesterone*, although, just as with the testosterone hormone in females, low levels of estrogen and progesterone are also found in males.

Testosterone is important in the physical development of males, especially in the prenatal period and in adolescence. In the prenatal period, testosterone helps decide the sex of a developing fetus. In adolescence, testosterone is important for the growth of muscle tissue and bones along with the growth of secondary male sexual characteristics. In adulthood, testosterone helps to keep muscle tissue and bones strong and to maintain an interest in sex.

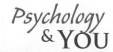

Psychology & YOU

Do You Do This?

Human ethology is the study of human behavior as it naturally occurs. Basketball fans know that Michael Jordan stuck out his tongue when he attempted a difficult shot. Similarly, it has been found that expert billiard players stick out their tongues more often when making hard shots than when attempting relatively easy shots. According to ethologists, a tongue display acts as a nonverbal sign that interaction is not desired. For humans, the tongue displays seem to indicate that the person does not want to be interrupted because of the need to concentrate in a difficult situation.

endocrine system a chemical communication system, using hormones, by which messages are sent through the bloodstream

hormones chemical substances that carry messages through the body in blood

beneficial having a helpful or useful effect

pituitary gland the center of control of the endocrine system that secretes a large number of hormones

impact to have a direct effect upon something

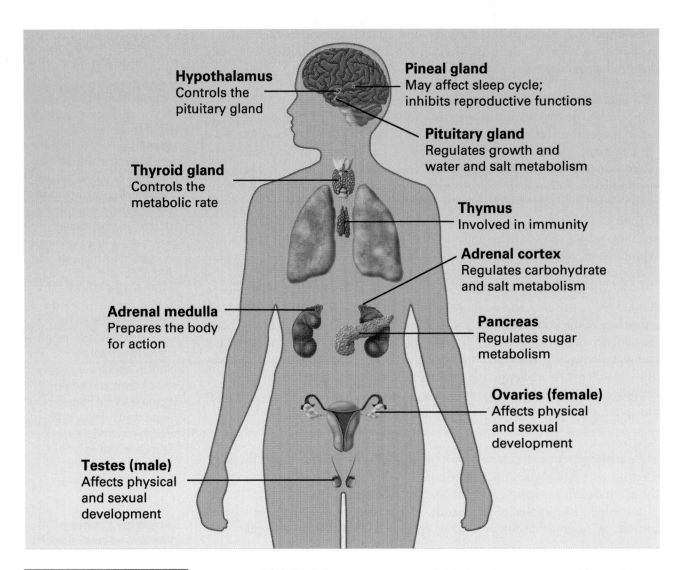

Hypothalamus
Controls the
pituitary gland

Pineal gland
May affect sleep cycle;
inhibits reproductive functions

Pituitary gland
Regulates growth and
water and salt metabolism

Thyroid gland
Controls the
metabolic rate

Thymus
Involved in immunity

Adrenal cortex
Regulates carbohydrate
and salt metabolism

Adrenal medulla
Prepares the body
for action

Pancreas
Regulates sugar
metabolism

Ovaries (female)
Affects physical
and sexual
development

Testes (male)
Affects physical
and sexual
development

DIAGRAM ⌃

**THE ENDOCRINE
SYSTEM**
The endocrine system, which
consists of ductless glands and the
hormones they produce, works
closely with the nervous system in
regulating body functions.

▶ **CRITICAL THINKING**

1. *Analyzing Visuals* What is the
   function of the adrenal glands?

2. *Gathering Information* Which
   part of the endocrine system
   controls metabolic rate?

After the age of 30 a man's testosterone levels gradually begin to decrease. Low levels of testosterone can lead to fatigue, weakness, depression, and low sex drive. Even when these symptoms are not present, men are encouraged to seek treatment because a low level of testosterone can often lead to a decrease in bone density, making bones more fragile and prone to breaking.

Estrogen and progesterone are important in the development of female sex characteristics. These two hormones also regulate the reproductive cycle of females. The levels of estrogen and progesterone vary throughout the menstrual cycle. These variances can cause premenstrual syndrome, also commonly known as PMS, in some women. PMS can include such symptoms as abdominal pain, headaches, fatigue, irritability, and depression.

The change of hormone levels during and after pregnancy can also lead to postpartum depression in a small percentage of women. This depression is characterized by trouble sleeping, anxiety, changes in appetite, or loss of concentration. More serious symptoms include thoughts of death or suicide, or negative feelings toward the baby. Women with postpartum depression should seek help from a doctor. The symptoms usually develop shortly after the birth of the child but can occur up to a year afterwards. Postpartum depression can be treated with medications.

☑ **READING PROGRESS CHECK**

Locating Where do endocrine glands release hormones in the body?

Hormones vs. Neurotransmitters

GUIDING QUESTION *What is the difference between a hormone and a neurotransmitter?*

Both hormones and neurotransmitters work to affect the nervous system. In fact, the same chemical can be used as both a hormone and a neurotransmitter. So what is the difference between a hormone and a neurotransmitter?

When a chemical is used as a neurotransmitter, it is released right beside the cell that it is to excite or inhibit. When a chemical is used as a hormone, it is released into the blood, which diffuses it throughout the body. For example, norepinephrine is a hormone when it is secreted into the blood by the adrenal glands. It is a neurotransmitter when it is released by the sympathetic motor neurons of the peripheral nervous system.

Hormones and neurotransmitters appear to have a common evolutionary origin. As multicellular organisms evolved, the system of communication among cells coordinated actions so that all cells of the organism acted as a unit. As organisms grew more complex, this communication system began to split into two more specialized communication systems: the nervous system, developed to send rapid and specific messages, and the other, involving the circulatory system, developed to send slow and widespread communication. In this system, the chemical messengers evolved into hormones. Whereas neural messages can be measured in thousandths of a second, hormonal messages may take minutes to reach their destination and weeks or months to have their total effect.

Hormones and neurotransmitters work together in our bodies, and can even compete with each other. For example, neurotransmitters may become out of balance due to stress, poor diet, or a genetic predisposition. This, in turn, causes hormonal imbalances. Mood swings, lack of energy, and even depression can result. Similarly, the hormones released by the thyroid may become imbalanced and affect the work of neurotransmitters in the body. Medications can be used to regulate the balance between hormones and neurotransmitters when the body is not functioning properly. Some medications use hormones such as estrogen or progesterone. The levels of hormones and neurotransmitters in our bodies control everything from our emotions to our physical growth and bodily functions.

In the event of a life-threatening or highly stressful situation, the adrenal glands produce adrenaline to give people the necessary energy to cope.

▶ **CRITICAL THINKING**

Drawing Conclusions How does adrenaline affect emotions?

✔ **READING PROGRESS CHECK**

Comparing and Contrasting How does the speed of neural messages differ from the speed of chemical messages?

LESSON 3 REVIEW

Reviewing Vocabulary

1. *Defining* What are three ways that the endocrine system affects behavior?

Using Your Notes

2. *Applying* Using the notes you took during this lesson, write a paragraph explaining the function of hormones that are produced by the glands of the endocrine system.

Answering the Guiding Questions

3. *Expressing* What is the function of the pituitary gland?

4. *Explaining* What is the difference between a hormone and a neurotransmitter?

Writing Activity

5. *Informative/Explanatory* Write a description of a medical situation in which a psychologist would examine the thyroid gland. Describe the situation from the perspective of a patient.

Reader's Dictionary (CCSS)

Childhood Trauma and Depression

pathophysiology functional changes that occur with a disease or syndrome

transient lasting only for a short time

Genetically Programmed to Be Nice?

maternal characteristic of a mother

prosocial acting for the benefit of others

endeavor a serious effort or attempt

Studies continue to demonstrate that personality, behavior, and development can be affected by many things, including genetics, hormones, and life events. The body can affect the mind, and vice versa. The studies in these two articles indicate that we can be influenced both by nature (genetics) and nurture (environmental factors).

Childhood Trauma and Depression

By APS Observer

PRIMARY SOURCE

Childhood is supposed to be a happy, carefree time, and for most of us, it is. But for over one million children a year in the United States alone, this period will be marred by trauma. A wide spectrum of later disorders and symptoms have been linked to early-life stress and abuse, including cardiovascular disease, fibromyalgia, fatigue, anxiety, and addiction. However, one of the most common consequences of having suffered trauma as a child is a higher risk in adulthood of developing depression, a psychiatric disorder that is debilitating, and in many cases, fatal.

At the APS 22nd Annual Convention, Emory University's Christine Heim presented a wealth of research documenting how childhood trauma can cause depression later in life. Although stress is something we believe we go "through" and survive relatively unscathed, it appears that stressful events, such as the death of a parent, physical abuse or sexual abuse, particularly experienced early in life, causes multiple changes in the central nervous system that result in physiological and behavioral changes. Early-life stress appears to radically alter neurobiological systems involved in the **pathophysiology** of depression.

On the basis of extensive endocrine, brain imaging, genetic, and behavioral analyses, Heim showed a clear link between childhood trauma, altered gene regulation, increased levels of stress hormones, and changes in brain structure. Changes resulting from stress included a smaller hippocampus, disruption of cortisol regulation and increased corticotrophin releasing factor. These effects add up to a shift in the body's fundamental stress-coping mechanisms, particularly the hypothalamic-pituitary-adrenal axis, causing behavioral changes.

In plain English, suffering stress early in life makes us more vulnerable to stress later in life. The evidence for this can be seen in multiple physiological and behavioral changes: in blood pressure, heart rate, and blood glucose levels, as well as disrupted sleep cycles, eating patterns, and fear conditioning. Far from being **transient**, stress experienced early in life has long-term and damaging effects on the entire body.

According to Heim, there is more than one type of depression. Specifically, depression that developed in relation to early life stress seems to have a distinct biological profile compared to depression that is not related to early-life stress. These groups of patients also do not respond to the same treatment, and Heim suggests that in order to successfully treat them, therapies can be tailored to restore the pathways involved in each subtype.

Genetically Programmed
to Be Nice?
by Rick Nauert, PhD

PRIMARY SOURCE

Emerging research suggests that some people may be genetically endowed to be nice. Investigators from the University at Buffalo and the University of California, Irvine, discovered the genetic association for a trait that many assume is a product of how we are raised.

"We aren't saying we've found the niceness gene," said researcher and psychologist Michael Poulin, PhD. "But we have found a gene that makes a contribution. What I find so interesting is the fact that it only makes a contribution in the presence of certain feelings people have about the world around them."

The study, published in the journal *Psychological Science*, examines the behavior of subjects who have versions of receptor genes for two hormones that, in laboratory and close relationship research, are associated with niceness.

Previous laboratory studies have linked the hormones oxytocin and vasopressin to the way we treat one another, said Poulin. Psychologists believe the hormones make us nicer people, at least in close relationships. Oxytocin promotes

maternal behavior, for example, and in the lab, subjects exposed to the hormone demonstrate greater sociability.

Poulin said the current study was an attempt to apply previous findings to social behaviors on a larger scale; to learn if these chemicals provoke in us other forms of **prosocial** behavior. Examples could be the urge to give to charity, or to more readily participate in such civic **endeavors** as paying taxes, reporting crime, giving blood or sitting on juries.

Scientists say that hormones work by binding to cells through receptors that come in different forms. In that regard, there are several genes that control the function of oxytocin and vasopressin receptors.

Subjects were surveyed as to their attitudes toward civic duty, other people and the world in general, and about their charitable activities.

Specifically, participants completed an Internet survey with questions about civic duty, such as whether people have a duty to report a crime or pay taxes; how they feel about the world, such as whether people are basically good or whether the world is more good than bad; and about their own charitable activities.

Of those surveyed, 711 subjects provided a sample of saliva for DNA analysis, which showed what form they had of the oxytocin and vasopressin receptors.

"The study found that these genes combined with people's perceptions of the world as a more or less threatening place to predict generosity," Poulin said. "Specifically, study participants who found the world threatening were less likely to help others— unless they had versions of the receptor genes that are generally associated with niceness," he said.

"These "nicer" versions of the genes," said Poulin, "allow you to overcome feelings of the world being threatening and help other people in spite of those fears.

"The fact that the genes predicted behavior only in combination with people's experiences and feelings about the world isn't surprising," Poulin said, "because most connections between DNA and social behavior are complex.

"So if one of your neighbors seems really generous, caring, civic-minded kind of person, while another seems more selfish, tight-fisted and not as interested in pitching in, their DNA may help explain why one of them is nicer than the other," he said.

Analyzing Primary Sources

1. **Identifying Bias** What is a possible source of bias in the second article?

2. **Drawing Conclusions** According to the first article, why should childhood history be probed before treating depression?

3. **Comparing and Contrasting** On a physiological level, how is the "niceness" trait different from adult-onset depression?

netw◉rks
There's More Online!

☑ **DIAGRAM** DNA and Genes

☑ **DIAGRAM** Punnett Square

☑ **IMAGE** Fraternal and Identical Twins

☑ **IMAGE** Environmental Influence

☑ **SELF-CHECK QUIZ**

LESSON 4

Heredity and Environment

ESSENTIAL QUESTION • *How do internal functions of the body affect behavior?*

Reading **HELP**DESK CCSS

Academic Vocabulary
• modify   • similar

Content Vocabulary
• heredity
• genes
• genotype
• phenotype
• inbred
• outbred
• identical twins
• fraternal twins

TAKING NOTES:

Key Ideas and Details

GATHERING INFORMATION Use a graphic organizer like the one below to find examples of nature and nurture.

Nature	Nurture

IT MATTERS BECAUSE

For decades, scientists have been trying to figure out how much of our behavior is the result of our genes and how much is a result of our environment. Some psychologists believe that genetics is like a flower, and the environment is like rain, soil, or fertilizer. Genes establish what you could be, and the environment defines the final product.

Nature versus Nurture

GUIDING QUESTIONS *What is heredity? How does heredity affect behavior?*

People often argue about whether human behavior is instinctive (due to heredity) or learned (due to environment). **Heredity** is the genetic transmission of characteristics from parents to their offspring. Do people learn to be good athletes, or are they born that way? Do people learn to do well in school, or are they born academically gifted? Many people assume that something learned can probably be changed, whereas something inborn will be difficult or impossible to change.

This issue, commonly called nature versus nurture, is not so simple. Nature refers to characteristics that a person inherits—his or her biological makeup. Nurture refers to environmental factors, such as education, family, culture, and individual experiences. Inherited factors and environmental conditions always act together in complicated ways. Asking whether heredity or environment is responsible for a person's behavior is like asking, "What makes a cake rise, baking powder or heat?" Obviously, an interaction of the two is responsible.

The argument over the nature versus nurture question has been going on for centuries, and it continues today. The British scientist Sir Francis Galton became one of the first to support the importance of nature in the modern era. In 1869 he published *Hereditary Genius*, a book in which he analyzed the families of over 1,000 eminent politicians, religious leaders, artists, and scholars. He found that success ran in families and concluded that heredity was the cause. Many psychologists, however, have emphasized the importance of the environment. The tone was set by John Watson, the founder of behaviorism, who wrote:

" Give me a dozen healthy infants, well-formed, and my own specified world to bring them up in and I'll guarantee to take any one at random and train him to become any type of specialist I might select—a doctor, lawyer, artist, merchant-chief, and, yes, even beggarman and thief, regardless of his talents, penchants, tendencies, abilities, vocations, and race of his ancestors. "

—*John B. Watson*, Behaviorism *(1924)*

heredity the genetic transmission of characteristics from parents to their offspring

Genotypes and Phenotypes

A large part of new research on heredity has focused on genes. **Genes** are the basic units of heredity. They are reproduced and passed along from parent to child. All the effects that genes have on behavior occur through their role in building and **modifying** the physical structures of the body. Those structures must interact with their environment to produce behavior.

In the normal structure of human DNA there are a total of 46 chromosomes, or 23 pairs. Twenty-two of these pairs are autosomes, which determine many of the traits an individual will have. One pair of chromosomes determines the sex of the individual while also carrying some sex-specific traits. The X chromosome is found in both males and females. The Y chromosome is found only in males. So a chromosomal pair of XX would belong to a woman, and an XY pair would belong to a man. There are variations among this normal structure, which cause abnormalities within the individual.

The sets of genes you have in your body are considered your **genotype**. They are the blueprint of a person's genetic information. At the time of reproduction or cell division, this inherited information is passed from one generation to the next. This genetic code indicates an infinite amount of information about the organism. It might indicate the possible traits a person can have in terms of hair color, gender, height, weight, or any number of characteristics, both physical and behavioral. A person's genotype may even make them predisposed to such conditions as heart disease, diabetes, Alzheimer's disease, epilepsy, or cancer.

genes the basic building blocks of heredity

modify to change something slightly

genotype the set of genes in an organism

⌄ DIAGRAM

DNA AND GENES
The molecules of DNA make up chromosomes that contain the codes for our biological makeup.

▶ **CRITICAL THINKING**

1. Assessing What are genes?

2. Analyzing Visuals Where are the instructions for development located in a cell?

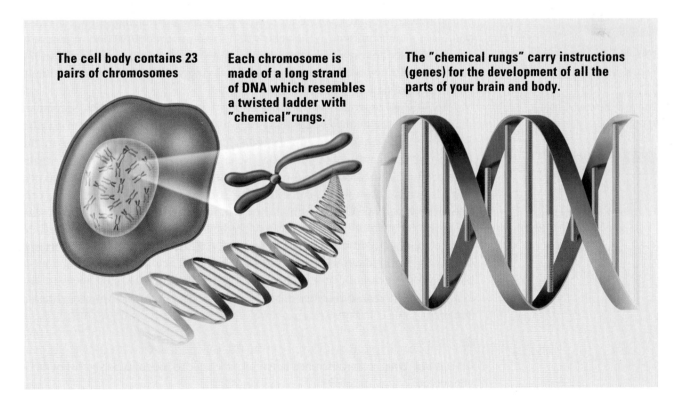

The cell body contains 23 pairs of chromosomes

Each chromosome is made of a long strand of DNA which resembles a twisted ladder with "chemical" rungs.

The "chemical rungs" carry instructions (genes) for the development of all the parts of your brain and body.

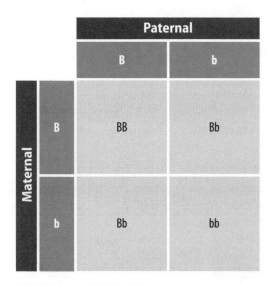

	Paternal	
	B	b
B	BB	Bb
b	Bb	bb

Maternal

PUNNETT SQUARE

Assign the letter to each box of the Punnett Square based on the corresponding gene from each parent. Dominant genes are listed first and mask recessive genes.

▶ **CRITICAL THINKING**

1. *Calculating* What is the likelihood of parents with a BB and bb combination having a blond child?

2. *Analyzing* Why can't two blond parents have a brown-haired offspring?

phenotype the expression of a particular trait in an organism

inbred descended from ancestors with similar genetics

outbred descended from ancestors with dissimilar genetics

The outward expression of those genes is a person's **phenotype**. A person's phenotype is expressed in his or her cells, tissues, organs, reflexes, behaviors, and anything observable in the living organism. A person may have a genotype that does not express itself as a phenotype except under certain environmental conditions. For example, a gene for diabetes may not be expressed as an observable phenotype unless diet and other environmental factors come into play in the person's life. Other genes, such as a person's gender or eye color, are expressed and observable immediately at birth and remain as the person ages.

Chromosomal Abnormalities

There are also chromosomal abnormalities that can spontaneously occur in offspring. For example, Down syndrome is a result of an extra chromosome on the 21st chromosomal pair. As a result, the individual has 47 chromosomes instead of 46. British physician John Langdon Down was the first to notice the symptoms in patients in 1866. The abnormality is characterized by cognitive disabilities and delayed physical growth, as well as characteristic facial structure and physical features. Approximately one in every 740 births results in Down syndrome. Offspring from older mothers tend to have a higher incidence of Down syndrome—from 1 in 100 to 1 in 30 births, as opposed to the incidence of 1 in 1,000 births from younger mothers. Other abnormalities, such as sickle-cell anemia, cystic fibrosis, albinism, and many other conditions are also the result of chromosomal inheritance.

In the early 1900s, biologist Reginald C. Punnett developed a method of predicting the likelihood of genotypes based on particular crossbreeding called a Punnett Square. With a Punnett Square, letters are assigned to certain attributes to indicate the dominant, or likely, trait and the recessive, or less likely, trait. For example, brown hair is a dominant trait indicated by a capital B. Blond hair is recessive, and indicated with a lowercase b. Each parent carries a genotype for hair type. A Punnett Square like the one shown in the diagram indicates the likelihood that those parents have an offspring with brown or blond hair. When a dominant gene is present in the genotype it masks the recessive one. When only recessive genes are present in the genotype, the recessive gene is reflected in the phenotype. So two brown-haired parents carrying a Bb genotype have a one in four chance of having a blond child.

An **inbred** organism is one that comes from two parents with similar or shared genetic makeup. An **outbred** organism is one that comes from parents with unrelated genetic makeup. Heredity can be a contributing factor in the development of certain characteristics. Scientists have found that inbred organisms produce more predictable results in their offspring. However, inbreeding may also create undesirable combinations, such as harmful recessive genes carried by both parents. Outbreeding brings a more varied gene selection but makes the characteristics of the offspring less predictable. Scientists have been able to witness this in a controlled environment by comparing the differences between inbred and outbred animals such as rats and mice. They found that inbred mice had more predictable features and characteristics similar to their parents, but exhibited an increased number of abnormalities. The outbred animals exhibited less predictable characteristics but fewer abnormalities.

☑ **READING PROGRESS CHECK**

Contrasting What is the difference between an individual's genotype and his or her phenotype?

Twin Studies

GUIDING QUESTION *What can be learned about nature and nurture from twin studies?*

One way to find out whether a trait is inherited is to study twins. **Identical twins** develop from a single fertilized egg and share the same genes. Because they develop from a single fertilized egg (a single *zygote*), identical twins are called *monozygotic*. **Fraternal twins** develop from two fertilized eggs and their genes are not more **similar** than those of brothers or sisters. That is, since fraternal twins are from separate eggs, like brothers or sisters from single births, they share only fifty percent of their genes. Having developed from two fertilized eggs, fraternal twins are called *dizygotic*.

Twin studies can tell us quite a bit about the impact of heredity and environment. Twins growing up in the same house share the same general environment, but identical twins also share the same genes. So, if identical twins who grow up together prove to be more alike on a specific trait than fraternal twins do, it probably means that heredity and genes are important for that trait.

In addition to twin studies, psychologists have found it helpful to study full siblings who are not twins. The genes of the individuals being compared would be similar because they came from the same parents, but they would not be the same as individuals in an identical twin study. The ages of the individuals would also be different. However, the environments that the children grew up in would be considered similar. Most siblings who grow up in the same household have the same general life experiences and interact with many of the same people. Comparisons between these individuals would show how much their environmental upbringing might affect their decision-making, their social skills, or their likes or dislikes.

Similarly, studies of adopted people also give psychologists clues about nature versus nurture. When studying an adopted sibling along with one that is an offspring of the parents, there may be clues about how much of an impact environment alone would have on a person's behavioral traits. Comparing two siblings who grew up in the same household but have no genetic similarities can indicate exactly how much impact experience has on an individual.

identical twins twins who come from one fertilized egg; twins having the same heredity

fraternal twins twins who come from two different eggs fertilized by two different sperm

similar alike but not exactly the same

Fraternal twins come from two eggs and share no more genetic similarities than other siblings. Identical twins come from a single egg and share their genetic code.

▶ **CRITICAL THINKING**

Assessing How would studies of identical and fraternal twins provide evidence in the nature–nurture debate?

Some people may have a predisposition for being good swimmers, but if they are not exposed to the correct environment to develop the skill, they may not realize their genetic potential.

▶ **CRITICAL THINKING**

Drawing Inferences How might a person's environment make them more or less aware of their genetically determined skills?

Psychologists at the University of Minnesota have been studying identical twins who were separated at birth and reared in different environments. One of the researchers, Thomas Bouchard, reports that despite very different social, cultural, and economic backgrounds, the twins shared many common behaviors. For example, in one set of twins (both named Jim), both had done well in math and poorly in spelling while in school, both worked as deputy sheriffs, vacationed in Florida, gave identical names to their children and pets, bit their fingernails, had identical smoking and drinking patterns, and liked mechanical drawing and carpentry. These similarities and others suggest that heredity may contribute to behaviors that we normally associate with experience.

Many researchers now believe that many of the differences among people can be explained by considering heredity as well as experience. Contrary to popular belief, the influence of genes on behavior does not mean that nothing can be done to change the behavior. Although it is true that it is difficult and some believe undesirable for scientists to attempt to identify and change the genetic code that may direct certain behaviors, it is possible to alter the environment in which the genes operate.

✔ **READING PROGRESS CHECK**

Explaining Why are scientists particularly interested in twins when studying heredity?

LESSON 4 REVIEW

Reviewing Vocabulary
1. **Defining** Explain the difference between fraternal twins and identical twins.

Using Your Notes
2. **Hypothesizing** Using the notes you took during this lesson, find an example of two characteristics, one that could be classified as a result of nature and one a result of nurture. Construct alternative explanations that could describe how the characteristic is actually a result of the opposite stimulus.

Answering the Guiding Questions
3. **Applying** What is heredity? How does heredity affect behavior?

4. **Identifying** What can be learned about nature and nurture from twin studies?

Writing Activity
5. **Argument** Research what evidence each side of the nature versus nurture argument uses to disprove the opposing viewpoint. Taking one side of the argument, write an opinion piece supporting your view and opposing the other.

174

Directions: On a separate sheet of paper, answer the questions below. Make sure you read carefully and answer all parts of the question.

Lesson Review

Lesson 1

1 *Describing* Explain how messages travel to and from the brain through the nervous system.

2 *Identifying* What part of the brain controls voluntary activities?

Lesson 2

3 *Applying* Describe four methods used to study the brain.

4 *Summarizing* Which part of the brain controls the movements of the right side of the body?

Lesson 3

5 *Expressing* How are messages of the endocrine system transmitted throughout the body?

6 *Specifying* Which gland in the body is the master control of hormone output by the endocrine system?

Lesson 4

7 *Expressing* One way to find out whether a trait is inherited is to compare the behavior of identical and fraternal twins. Explain how this works.

8 *Specifying* What chromosomal abnormality causes Down syndrome?

Research and Technology

9 *Researching* Brain plasticity is the capacity of the brain to change with learning. Just as physical exercise improves physical fitness, exercising one's brain results in better mental fitness. Research the topic of "brain fitness" and, as a class or within groups, use software to write and design a brain fitness activity for the Web. Track changes and review each other's work. If you can't post to the Web, present the "site" as a storyboard or as PowerPoint slides. Explain to the viewer what specific cognitive skill(s) or improvement the activity is meant to achieve and which area(s) of the brain will most likely be affected.

21st Century Skills

Creating and Using Graphs, Charts, Diagrams, and Tables Researchers have found that the brains of patients with Alzheimer's disease have a large number of destroyed neurons in the part of the brain that is crucial for making memories permanent. These patients have also exhibited a loss of the neurotransmitter acetylcholine, resulting in memory difficulties. Review the graph and then answer the questions that follow.

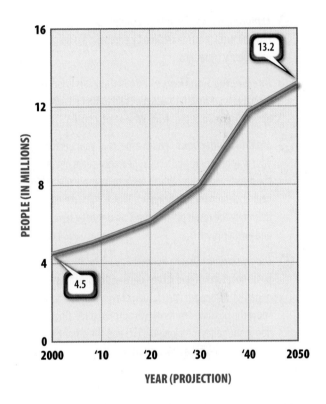

10 According to the graph, how many people in the United States suffer from Alzheimer's disease?

11 How would you describe the projected number of cases of Alzheimer's by the year 2050?

12 What impact might the researchers' findings and the information in the graph have on the direction researchers might take to find a cure for the disease?

Need Extra Help?

If You've Missed Question	1	2	3	4	5	6	7	8	9	10	11	12
Go to page	149	149	158	155	164	165	172	173	157	157	157	157

Directions: On a separate sheet of paper, answer the questions below. Make sure you read carefully and answer all parts of the question.

Critical Thinking Questions

13 *Analyzing* How would people's lives be different if the nervous system were not made of the somatic and the autonomic nervous systems? What if people had only a somatic nervous system?

14 *Synthesizing* Suppose a person suffers a stroke that causes damage to the frontal lobes. What aspects of the person's behavior would you expect to see change?

15 *Exploring Issues* Provide an example of how the physiological reaction created by adrenaline is helpful in emergency situations.

16 *Interpreting Significance* Do you think it is important for parents who wish to adopt a child to find out about the genetic makeup of the child? Why or why not?

17 *Making Connections* Which aspects of your personality, your way of acting, and your appearance seem obviously the result of heredity? Which seem to be more related to your environmental upbringing? Which characteristics are definitely the result of an interaction between heredity and environment?

18 *Diagramming* Draw a Punnett Square to show the possible results of two inbred mice with pure recessive genes for tail length (tt/tt). Then draw a Punnett Square to show the possible results of two outbred mice. One has dominant genes for a long tail (Tt) and the other has recessive genes for a short tail (tt).

College and Career Readiness

19 *Research and Methods* Contact a radiologist or the radiology department of a local hospital to find out more about the uses of CT scans, PET scans, and fMRIs. Find out under what circumstances each of the techniques would be used. Present your findings in a written report.

Exploring the Essential Questions

20 *Examining* Working with two or three classmates, prepare a video that can be used to teach younger children how the brain and the nervous system work. You might consider making the video humorous to more easily gain the attention of younger children. Arrange to have children in lower grades view the video. Evaluate its effectiveness.

21 *Applying* Find out about problems that occur as a result of the malfunctioning of parts of the endocrine system. Find out how such problems are treated and present your findings in an oral report.

DBQ Analyzing Primary Sources

Use the document below to answer the following questions.

PRIMARY SOURCE

"*In other words, each hemisphere [of the brain] seems to have its own separate and private sensations; its own perceptions; its own concepts; and its own impulses to act. . . . Following surgery, each hemisphere also has thereafter its own separate chain of memories that are rendered inaccessible to the recall processes of the other.*"

—*Roger Wolcott Sperry*

22 *Specifying* What evidence does Roger Wolcott Sperry give that shows that observing brain activity after split-brain surgery can help us understand behavior?

23 *Discussing* How might a discovery like the one described help the research processes of other scientists?

Psychology Journal Activity

24 *Informative/Explanatory* Review your entry in your Psychology Journal for this chapter. After learning about the nervous system, how would you explain the connection between mind and body? List some examples of how this connection appears in everyday life.

Need Extra Help?

If You've Missed Question	13	14	15	16	17	18	19	20	21	22	23	24
Go to page	149	154	167	172	170	172	161	148	164	156	156	146

Altered States of Consciousness

ESSENTIAL QUESTIONS • *How does the body communicate with the mind?* • *How can behavior affect the mind?*

Psychology Matters...

Though we know that consciousness depends on brain function, scientists have not yet come up with a detailed explanation of how this works. Nevertheless, they have determined that there are correlations between various states of consciousness and specific functions of the brain. For example, levels of alertness or responsiveness correlate with electrical activity in the brain, which is measurable. The brain waves of the person who is wide awake are very different from those of a person who is asleep.

◀ An altered state of consciousness, like a dream, changes mental processes. In some cases the results can stretch reality.

Shawn Van Daele/Flickr Select/Getty Images

CHAPTER 7

Lab Activity

Dream
Plans

THE QUESTION...

RESEARCH QUESTION Is it possible to successfully plan your dreams?

One night you dream about not doing your math homework. The next night you may not be aware that you dream at all. The night after that you dream about a dramatic car chase. What causes this? One factor that might shape our dreams is what we think about immediately before sleeping. Some mental activity might have predictable effects, such as reading a horror novel before falling asleep. Does predictability mean that we can plan the content of our dreams? Can we decide to find the solution to a difficult problem in our dreams? How much influence do our conscious thoughts have on our dreams? In this experiment, we'll attempt to find out.

Psychology Journal Activity

Think about your sleep patterns. Write about them in your Psychology Journal. Consider some of these points as you write: Do you think you have healthy sleep habits? If you have any sleep disruptions, what do you think might cause them?

FINDING THE ANSWER...

HYPOTHESIS If planned, the content of dreams can be controlled.

THE METHOD OF YOUR EXPERIMENT

MATERIALS   dream journals

PROCEDURE   Recruit eight participants. Ask each participant to keep a nightly dream journal for a period of five consecutive days. In their journal your participants will record three pieces of data: a brief recording of the events of their full day prior to sleep, a listing of what they plan to dream about, and a recording of any dream activity experienced. Instruct your participants to keep their dream journal near their sleeping area so they can quickly record any pertinent information. Also, instruct your participants to write as many details as possible about their planned dreams and actual dreams and to do so immediately before sleep and immediately after waking up.

DATA COLLECTION   Once the five days have passed, you will have several nights' data. Study your data to identify any patterns present between daily activities, dream plans, and actual dreams.

ANALYSIS & APPLICATION

1. Did your results support the hypothesis?

2. Did you see any correlation between dream plans and actual dreams? Did you see any correlation between a day's activities and actual dreams?

3. Why do you think it is important that journaling be the last activity before sleep?

netw⊕rks   ONLINE LAB RESOURCES

Online you will find:

- An **interactive lab experience**, allowing you to put principles from this chapter into practice in a digital psychology lab environment. This chapter's lab will include an experiment allowing you to explore issues fundamental to altered states of consciousness.

- A **Skills Handbook** that includes a guide for using the scientific method, creating experiments, and analyzing data.
- A **Notebook** where you can complete your Psychology Journal, and record and analyze data from your experiment.

Altered States of Consciousness **179**

networks

There's More Online!

☑ **DIAGRAM** Freud's Levels of Consciousness

☑ **DIAGRAM** Patterns of Sleep

☑ **IMAGE** Woman Dreaming

☑ **SELF-CHECK QUIZ**

Reading **HELP**DESK ⒸⒸⓈⓈ

Academic Vocabulary

• approximate • interpret

Content Vocabulary

• consciousness
• REM sleep
• circadian rhythm
• insomnia
• narcolepsy
• night terrors
• sleepwalking

TAKING NOTES:

Key Ideas and Details

ORGANIZING Use a graphic organizer like the one below to list the five sleep disorders discussed in this lesson.

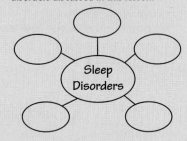

Sleep Disorders

LESSON 1

Sleep and Dreams

ESSENTIAL QUESTION • *How does the body communicate with the mind?*

Ⓒ IT MATTERS BECAUSE

Sleep is vital to mental health. If a person is deprived of sleep, he or she will have psychological symptoms. Most people think of sleep as a state of unconsciousness, punctuated by brief periods of dreaming. This is only partially correct. Sleep is a state of altered consciousness, characterized by certain patterns of brain activity and inactivity.

Why We Sleep

GUIDING QUESTION *Why is sleep difficult to study?*

What is consciousness? **Consciousness** is a state of awareness. When we discuss altered states of consciousness, we mean that people can have different levels of awareness. Consciousness can range from alertness to non-alertness. People who are fully aware with their attention focused on something are conscious. A person who is not completely aware is in a different level of consciousness—an altered state of consciousness. Sleep illustrates an altered state of consciousness.

Although sleep is a major part of human and animal behavior, it has been extremely difficult to study. A researcher cannot ask a sleeping person to report on the experience without first waking the person. The study of sleep was aided by the development of the electroencephalograph (EEG), a device that records the electrical activity of the brain.

We are not sure why people sleep. Sleep is characterized by unresponsiveness to the environment and usually limited physical mobility. Some psychologists believe that sleep is restorative. They believe that sleep is a time when the brain recovers from exhaustion and stress. Others believe it is a type of primitive hibernation: we sleep to conserve energy. Some psychologists suggest that sleep is an adaptive process—in earlier times sleep kept humans out of harm's way at night when they were most vulnerable to animals. Still others believe we sleep to clear our minds of useless information. As a variation of this theory, some people believe we sleep to dream.

☑ **READING PROGRESS CHECK**

Explaining Why do people sleep?

180

VikaValter/Vetta/Getty Images

Stages of Sleep

GUIDING QUESTION *How does REM sleep differ from the other sleep stages?*

As you begin to fall asleep, your body temperature and pulse rate decrease while your breathing becomes slow and even. Gradually, your eyes close and your brain briefly shows alpha waves on the EEG, which are associated with the absence of concentrated thought and with relaxation. Your body may twitch, your eyes roll, and brief visual images flash across your mind (although your eyelids are shut) as you enter Stage I sleep.

In Stage I sleep, the lightest level of sleep, your pulse slows a bit more and your muscles relax. During this stage, your breathing becomes uneven and your brainwaves grow irregular. If awakened during this stage, you would report that you were "just drifting." This phase lasts for up to 10 minutes and is marked by the presence of theta waves, which are lower in amplitude and frequency than alpha waves. At this point, your brainwaves occasionally shift from low-amplitude, high-frequency waves to high-amplitude, low-frequency waves—a pattern that indicates you have entered Stage II sleep. Your eyes roll slowly from side to side. Some 30 minutes later, you drift down into a deeper level of Stage III sleep, and large-amplitude delta waves begin to sweep your brain every second or so.

Stage IV is the deepest sleep. It is difficult to awaken a sleeper in this stage. Large, regular delta waves occurring more than 50 percent of the time indicate a state of deep sleep. Uncommon sleep events such as talking out loud, sleepwalking, and bed-wetting may occur in this stage. Deep sleep is important to your physical and psychological well-being. Perhaps this is why people who are able to sleep only a few hours at a time descend rapidly into Stage IV and remain there for most of their nap.

On average a person spends 75 percent of sleep time in Stages I through IV. In Stage IV, something curious happens to you: while your muscles are even more relaxed than before, your eyes begin to move rapidly. You have left Stage IV for **REM sleep**. Often, your face or fingers twitch and the large muscles in your arms and legs are paralyzed. Your brain now shows waves that closely resemble those of a person who is fully awake. For this reason, REM sleep is called active sleep. Stages I through IV are referred to as NREM (non-REM) or quiet sleep. NREM sleep is accompanied by the slower pattern of brain waves. It is during REM sleep that most dreaming normally takes place.

consciousness a state of awareness, including a person's feelings, sensations, ideas, and perceptions

REM sleep a stage of sleep characterized by rapid eye movements, a high level of brain activity, a deep relaxation of the muscles, and dreaming

∨ **DIAGRAM**

FREUD'S LEVELS OF CONSCIOUSNESS

Sigmund Freud identified three levels of consciousness. In his approach to consciousness, he claimed that preconscious ideas are not in your awareness now, but you are able to recall them with some effort. Unconscious ideas are hidden and mostly unretrievable.

▶ **CRITICAL THINKING**

1. *Analyzing Visuals* When would you use information from the preconscious level?

2. *Assessing* At which level of consciousness does Freud suggest we would keep a memory of which we are ashamed?

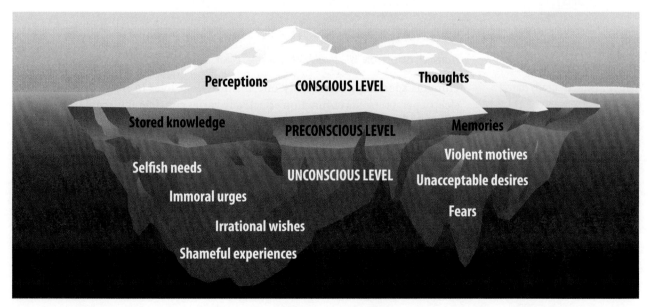

Perceptions   CONSCIOUS LEVEL   Thoughts

Stored knowledge   PRECONSCIOUS LEVEL   Memories

Selfish needs   UNCONSCIOUS LEVEL   Violent motives

Immoral urges   Unacceptable desires

Irrational wishes   Fears

Shameful experiences

The top diagram shows the passage of a sleeper through the various stages of sleep over a seven-hour period. The bottom diagram shows the patterns of electrical activity (EEGs) in the brain that correspond to the various stages of sleep. The EEG pattern shown for being awake is one that occurs when a person is resting quietly with eyes closed.

▶ CRITICAL THINKING

1. *Analyzing Visuals* How often during a night's sleep does a person reach Stage IV?

2. *Comparing* Which two sleep stages have the most similar EEG patterns?

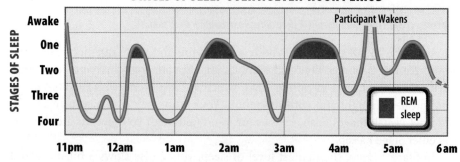

STAGES OF SLEEP OVER A SEVEN-HOUR PERIOD

STAGES OF SLEEP: Awake, One, Two, Three, Four

Participant Wakens

REM sleep

11pm 12am 1am 2am 3am 4am 5am 6am

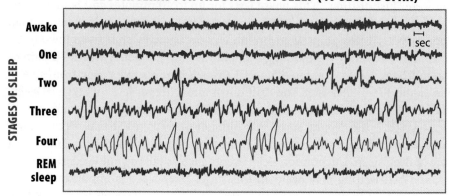

EEG PATTERNS FOR THE STAGES OF SLEEP (40-SECOND SPAN)

STAGES OF SLEEP: Awake, One, Two, Three, Four, REM sleep

1 sec

REM sleep lasts from about 15 minutes (early at night) to 45 minutes (late at night), after which you retrace the descent to Stage IV. You go through this cycle every 90 minutes or so. Each time the period of Stage IV sleep decreases and the length of REM sleep increases until you eventually wake up. Your brain never becomes totally inactive during sleep. REM sleep seems to serve psychological functions, such as building efficient learning and memory processes. Why the eyes move rapidly during this stage is the subject of debate and research.

☑ READING PROGRESS CHECK

Describing What is Stage IV sleep?

Quantity and Quality of Sleep

GUIDING QUESTION *Why should we be concerned about sleep disorders?*

approximate nearly correct or exact

Humans spend **approximately** one-third of their lives in sleep. The amount of sleep a person needs to function effectively varies considerably from individual to individual and from time to time within a person's life. Newborns spend an average of 16 hours a day sleeping, almost half of it in REM sleep. Sixteen-year-olds may spend as much as 10 to 11 hours asleep each night. Students in graduate school average 8 hours a night. Men and women who are 70 years old or older may need only 5 hours of sleep.

Though the amount of sleep needed can vary from person to person, a few factors of sleep seem to be constant. On average, adults spend about 25 percent of their time in REM sleep and the remaining 75 percent in NREM sleep. Although the amount of sleep a person needs may vary, from person to person, it does appear that everyone of us sleeps and that both types of sleep, NREM and REM, are important to normal functioning.

Circadian Rhythm

People seem to have an internal biological clock that regulates the sleep-wakefulness cycle. Blood pressure, heart rate, appetite, secretion of hormones and digestive enzymes, sensory sharpness, and elimination processes all follow circadian rhythms. A **circadian rhythm** is a biological clock that is genetically programmed to regulate physiological responses within a time period of 24 or 25 hours. Circadian rhythms operate even when normal day and night cues are removed. For example, we usually standardize our sleep patterns according to the light of day and dark of night; yet experimenters who have lived for months at a time in the depths of a cave have still maintained a rhythm to their behaviors. Without any environmental cues, people maintained their circadian rhythms on about a 24- to 25-hour cycle. Researchers have determined that humans have a circadian cycle of 24.18 hours.

Circadian rhythms do not control our sleep cycles; the environment and the 24-hour day control our cycles. Thus, when you miss sleep, this disruption becomes very apparent. Some travelers experience jet lag. This occurs when their internal circadian rhythms do not match the external clock time. For example, when you travel from New York to Moscow, your body is on a different time clock when you reach Moscow. You may feel tired and disoriented. It usually takes about one day for each hour of time change to reset your circadian clock.

Sleep Disorders

Sleep is an active state essential for mental and physical restoration. Sometimes, though, we may have problems with falling asleep or during sleep. These sleep disorders may interfere with our quality of life and personal health, as well as endanger public safety because of their role in industrial and traffic accidents.

Everyone has an occasional sleepless night. Some people have sleep problems like this all the time, rarely getting more than an hour or two of uninterrupted sleep a night. **Insomnia**—a prolonged and usually abnormal inability to obtain adequate sleep—has many causes and takes many forms. It may be caused by anxiety or depression. Overuse of alcohol or drugs can also cause insomnia.

The sleep disorder sleep apnea causes frequent interruptions of breathing during sleep. One of the most common symptoms is a specific kind of snoring that may occur hundreds of times during the night. Each episode lasts 10 to 15 seconds and ends suddenly, often with a physical movement of the entire body. A blockage of the breathing passages causes the snoring; the victim is in fact choking as the flow of air to the lungs stops. The episode ends when low levels of oxygen or high levels of carbon dioxide in the blood trigger breathing reflexes.

Sleep apnea affects more than 12 million Americans, occurring most often among older people. People suffering from this disorder may feel listless, sleepy, and irritable during the day. It is usually caused by a physical problem that blocks the airway, such as enlarged tonsils, repeated infections in the throat or middle ear, or obesity. These conditions may cause the muscles at the base of the tongue to relax and sag repeatedly.

Another disorder, **narcolepsy**, is characterized by a permanent and overwhelming feeling of sleepiness and fatigue. Other symptoms include unusual sleep and dream patterns, such as dreamlike hallucinations or a feeling of temporary paralysis. People with narcolepsy may have sleep attacks throughout the day. The sleep attacks are accompanied by brief periods of REM sleep. Victims of narcolepsy may have difficulties in the areas of work, leisure, and interpersonal relations and are prone to accidents because they have fallen asleep.

Frightening dreams, commonly known as nightmares, can occur during the dreaming phase of REM sleep. A nightmare may frighten the dreaming sleeper, who will often wake up with a very vivid memory of an overly terrifying dream.

More
ABOUT...

Freud on Dreams

Sigmund Freud was the first psychologist to study dreams thoroughly. He hypothesized that dreams express impulses and thoughts, often in highly symbolic form, that are unacceptable at the conscious level. Freud used the term *manifest content* to refer to the story line, images, and other perceptual aspects of dreams. Freud defined *latent content* as the hidden meaning of dreams that comes from the dreamer's unconscious wishes (Freud, 1965).

circadian rhythm the rhythm of activity and inactivity lasting approximately one day

insomnia the failure to get enough sleep at night in order to feel rested the next day

narcolepsy a condition characterized by suddenly falling asleep or feeling very sleepy during the day

Some researchers believe that when we sleep, electrical bursts occur that hit portions of the brain, firing off various memory circuits. Dreams are the result.

▶ **CRITICAL THINKING**

Comparing What are other explanations for dreaming?

night terrors sleep disruptions that occur during Stage IV of sleep, involving screaming, panic, or confusion

sleepwalking walking or carrying out behaviors while asleep

On the other hand, **night terrors** occur during Stage IV sleep (usually within an hour after going to bed). They may last from 5 to 20 minutes and involve screaming, sweating, confusion, and a rapid heart rate. The person may suddenly awaken or have a persistent fear that occurs at night. People usually have no memory of night terrors.

Sleepwalking is a disorder in which a person is partly, but not completely, awake. That person may walk, often clumsily, or do other things without any memory of doing so. Sleepwalking is a disorder associated with children, although some adults may sleepwalk. Most children who sleepwalk do not have emotional problems and will outgrow it. This disorder has been linked to stress, fatigue, and for adults, the use of sedative medicines. Sleepwalking may also be inherited. It is usually harmless; however, sleepwalkers may fall or otherwise injure themselves.

Sleep talking is a common sleep disruption. Most people talk in their sleep more than they realize because they do not remember talking during sleep. Sleep talking can occur in either REM or NREM sleep. It can happen once or many times during the night and can be a single word or a longer speech. Sometimes sleep talkers pause between sentences or phrases as if they are carrying on a conversation with someone else. You can even engage a sleep talker in a conversation. Like sleepwalking, sleep talking is harmless.

✅ **READING PROGRESS CHECK**

Assessing What symptoms do people who suffer from narcolepsy experience?

Dreams

GUIDING QUESTION *In which sleep stage does dreaming occur?*

Though not everyone remembers their dreams, everyone has them. Most people can recall only a few, if any, of their dreams, but people from cultures that value dreams usually do remember them. The first few dreams of the night are usually composed of vague thoughts left over from the day's activities. Later dreams become longer, more vivid, and more dramatic, especially dreams that take place during REM sleep. Because the amount of time spent in REM sleep increases during the night, the last dream is often the longest and the one that people remember upon waking. Even so, people can rarely recall more than the last 15 minutes of their dream after waking. Researchers have found that after being deprived of REM sleep, people increase the amount of time they spend in REM sleep, so it seems that a certain amount of dreaming each night is necessary.

The Content of Dreams

When people are awakened randomly during REM sleep and asked what they had just been dreaming the reports are usually commonplace rather than unreal. The dreams we remember outside of the lab and talk about "are more coherent . . . and generally more interesting" than those collected in systematic research. Often we incorporate our everyday activities into our dreams. Researchers who have recorded the contents of thousands of dreams have found that most occur in such commonplace settings as living rooms, cars, and streets and involve either strenuous recreational activities or passive events such as sitting and watching. Most emotions experienced in dreams are negative—anxiety, anger, sadness, and so on. Contrary to popular belief, dreams correspond to a realistic time scale.

Some dreams are negative enough to be considered nightmares. Nightmares often have such a frightening quality that we awaken in the middle of them. The sense of dread in nightmares may be related to the intensity of brain activity and to the stimulation of those parts of the brain responsible for emotional reactions. The emotional reaction of dread may then influence the content of the dream.

Dream Interpretation

Dream **interpretations** have been discovered dating back to 5000 B.C. Sigmund Freud believed that no matter how simple or mundane, dreams may contain clues to thoughts the dreamer is afraid to acknowledge in his or her waking hours. The Inuit people of North America, like Freud, believe that dreams contain hidden meanings. They believe that when dreaming, people enter the spiritual world where they interact with those who have passed away. These departed souls help the living reflect on some current or future event.

interpret to tell the meaning of

Some social scientists, however, are skeptical of dream interpretations. Nathaniel Kleitman, one of the pioneers who discovered REM sleep, wrote in 1960: "Dreaming may serve no function whatsoever." According to this view, the experience of a dream is simply an unimportant by-product of stimulating certain brain cells during sleep. Others argue that the common experience of feeling paralyzed in a dream simply means that brain cells that inhibit muscle activity were randomly stimulated. Another dream research theory proposes that dreaming allows people a chance to review and address some of the problems they faced during the day. One theorist, Francis Crick, believes that dreams are the brain's way of removing certain unneeded memories. In other words, dreams are a form of mental housecleaning. This mental housecleaning may be necessary because it is not useful to remember every single detail of your life.

Daydreaming requires a low level of awareness and involves fantasizing, or idle but directed thinking, while we are awake. Usually we daydream when we are in situations that require little attention or when we are bored. Daydreaming serves useful purposes such as reminding us of or preparing us for events in our future. Daydreaming may also improve our creativity by generating thought processes. Some psychologists believe that daydreaming allows us to control our emotions.

☑ **READING PROGRESS CHECK**

Contrasting How does daydreaming differ from dreaming?

LESSON 1 REVIEW

Reviewing Vocabulary
1. *Defining* What is a circadian rhythm?

Using Your Notes
2. *Describing* Using the notes you completed during this lesson, write a brief description of each sleep disorder.

Answering the Guiding Questions
3. *Explaining* Why is sleep difficult to study?

4. *Contrasting* How does REM sleep differ from the other sleep stages?

5. *Assessing* Why should we be concerned about sleep disorders?

6. *Identifying* In which sleep stage does dreaming occur?

Writing Activity
7. *Informative/Explanatory* For one week write a daily diary and a dream diary. Then analyze any correlations between your dreams and what you ate, how much you exercised, and other events.

Reader's Dictionary (CCSS)

mandate: a command, instruction, or assignment given by an authority

cortex: the outer part of an organ

lucid: being fully aware and having full use of one's faculties and abilities

mitigate: to make less severe

Can science fiction predict future science facts? In this article, author Oliver Chiang explores current research that may lead to brain and dream manipulation imagined in the popular film *Inception*. Neuroscientists are learning how to translate brain activity into the visual images seen by the participant, with future implications for the understanding of dreams and mind manipulation.

The
Science
of "Inception"
By Oliver Chiang

PRIMARY SOURCE

There's a scene from the film *Inception* in which the main character, played by Leonardo DiCaprio, has entered another character's mind through a dream and tells him, "I know how to find secrets from your mind—I know all the tricks!"

It's easy for DiCaprio's character to make this claim. After all, he's in a big-budget Hollywood movie. He can do anything he wants, given the right special effects. But can real-life technologies perform these kinds of mind-reading "tricks" too? While we can't use a device to recreate elaborate and shared dreamscapes yet, it may surprise you just how much existing technologies that read dreams and minds can do.

One of the researchers on the forefront of such technology is Jack Gallant, a neuroscientist at the University of California, Berkeley. Gallant has spent the past 15 years heading a neuroscience and psychology lab at Berkeley whose **mandate** is to tap into the mind to see what it sees. Gallant does this by showing people images and movies while taking a functional magnetic resonance imaging (fMRI) scan of their brains. He uses brain-pattern analysis and computer algorithms to analyze the fMRI scans and build a model of the subject's visual system. Using the model, Gallant can then have his subject watch a completely new movie and reproduce the images the subject has seen with very good accuracy. In other words, he can take the pictures right out of our heads.

Gallant says it should be possible to use the same technology to reproduce the images of the dreams from a person's brain. However, it would be difficult to verify the accuracy of those images, since only the dreamer ever "sees" them.

Another team of researchers in Japan has been tackling the dream-reading problem from a different direction. Advanced Telecommunications Research (ATR) Computational Neuroscience Laboratories also takes fMRI scans of what the subject sees. Instead of building a model of the visual system, ATR feeds fMRI scans into a computer, which "learns" how to associate changes in brain activity with different images. Lab scientists can reconstruct simple black-and-white images the subject is viewing by analyzing the blood flow in the brain's visual **cortex**. ATR says reconstructing dreams is harder because the brain signals during sleep may be "noisier," and is now researching how to get more meaningful information from a sleeper's brain.

"It is possible that brain signals during sleep measured by fMRI are too noisy," says Yukiyasu Kamitani,

some control over the dream. Some lucid dreamers can do so naturally, but others must learn it—and one device claims to help. Called NovaDreamer, the device is a sleep mask that detects when to give cues—flashing lights—to the dreamer to stimulate awareness, but not wake him. NovaDreamer was developed by Stephen LaBerge, a psychophysiologist who popularized the concept of lucid dreaming while teaching at Stanford University for 25 years.

While mind-reading technology pushes ahead, there are limitations. In *Inception*, DiCaprio's character is able to detect higher-order thoughts, like internal speech or decision-making, and even "steal" them. Gallant says that how the brain processes information on thoughts isn't understood well enough yet to "decode," or read, them. As such, scientists can't yet reproduce or capture an explicit thought like "I want to go skydiving" by peering into the mind alone.

And finally, like the title of the movie suggests, is it possible for "inception" to occur—to be able to plant a new idea into someone's mind? There is a way to currently inject very crude signals into the brain. A device called a brain pacemaker implanted in the brain stem can send electrical impulses to specific parts of the brain. It is similar to a pacemaker for the heart, and also has medical applications. The brain pacemaker is used in some patients to **mitigate** symptoms of diseases like Parkinson's with pulses that affect certain neurons. But the ability to plant an actual higher-order thought remains, at least for the time being, pure fiction.

"You have to have a way to manipulate specific neurons and synapses in specific ways—and that's really difficult and not going to happen anytime soon," says Gallant. "I think it's legitimate for some people to have some concerns about brain-reading technology being used for bad things, but nobody has to be worried about one of those bad things being writing stuff to the brain."

ATR's head of Neuroinformatics. "We are now trying to figure out what we can do to get meaningful information from brain signals during sleep."

> "Lab scientists can reconstruct simple black-and-white images the subject is viewing by analyzing the blood flow in the brain's visual cortex."

Brain-pattern analysis using fMRI is also being researched for other applications. John-Dylan Hanes, a senior researcher at the Max Planck Institute for Human Cognitive and Brain Sciences in Germany, can predict your actions before you take them. Specifically, he has been using fMRI scans to explore the relationship between brain activation patterns and real-life behavior. In one study involving free will, Hanes showed that he could analyze the scans to predict accurately whether subjects would press a button with their left or right hand seven seconds before they actually pressed it.

Another idea *Inception* director Christopher Nolan based his movie on was **lucid** dreaming, in which the sleeper is aware he is dreaming and can even exert

Analyzing the Reading

1. *Identifying* What are the two ways in which researchers have reconstructed images using fMRI?

2. *Using Context Clues* What does researcher Kamitani mean when he says the brain signals measured during sleep are too "noisy"?

3. *Making Connections* Why is it difficult to manipulate specific neurons and synapses, as Gallant states?

Reading **HELP**DESK

Academic Vocabulary

- **reveal**
- **constriction**

Content Vocabulary

- **hypnosis**
- **posthypnotic suggestion**
- **biofeedback**
- **meditation**

TAKING NOTES:

Key Ideas and Details

LISTING Use a table like the one below to list some explanations of hypnosis.

Explanations of Hypnosis		
1.	2.	3.

LESSON 2

Hypnosis, Biofeedback, and Meditation

ESSENTIAL QUESTION • *How does the body communicate with the mind?*

IT MATTERS BECAUSE

Surgery without anesthesia may sound unlikely, but such operations have been performed by hypnotizing the patient. Although hypnosis may conjure up images of a magician saying, "You are getting sleepy, very sleepy . . . ," researchers are learning more about this connection of mind and body. Therapists use hypnosis to help people quit smoking, lose weight, manage stress, overcome phobias, and diminish pain.

Hypnosis

GUIDING QUESTION *What type of relationship is needed between a hypnotist and a participant?*

Hypnosis is a form of altered consciousness in which people become highly suggestible to changes in behavior and thought. By allowing the hypnotist to guide and direct them, people can be made conscious of things they are usually unaware of and unaware of things they usually notice. Participants may recall in vivid detail incidents they had forgotten or feel no pain when pricked with a needle. It happens in this way: At all times, certain sensations and thoughts are filtered out of our awareness. For example, as you read this sentence, you were probably not aware of the position of your feet until your attention was called to it. By mentioning the position of your feet, your attention shifted to your feet—an area of your body that seconds before was outside your consciousness. Hypnosis shifts our perceptions in the same way.

Hypnosis does not put the participant to sleep. Rather, during a hypnotic trance participants remain awake but become highly receptive to certain internal and external stimuli. They are able to focus attention on one tiny aspect of reality and ignore all others. To induce a trance the hypnotist slowly persuades a participant to relax and to lose interest in other external distractions. This may take a few minutes or much longer depending on the purpose of the hypnosis, the method of induction used by the hypnotist, and the participant's past experiences with hypnosis.

In an environment of trust, a participant with a rich imagination can become susceptible to the hypnotist's suggestions. Psychologists using hypnosis stress that the relationship between hypnotist and participant should involve cooperation, not domination. The participant is not under the hypnotist's control but can be convinced to do things he or she would not normally do. The person is simply cooperating with the hypnotist. Together they try to solve a problem or to learn more about how the participant's mind works. Anyone can resist hypnosis by refusing to open his or her mind to the hypnotist. Furthermore, people under hypnosis cannot be induced to do things against their will. Mutual trust is important for hypnosis to be successful.

hypnosis a state of consciousness resulting from a narrowed focus of attention and characterized by heightened suggestibility

Theories of Hypnosis

Psychologists do not agree about the nature of hypnosis. Some, like Theodore Barber, argue that hypnosis is not a special state of consciousness but simply the result of suggestibility. If people are just given instructions and told to try their hardest, they will be able to do anything that hypnotized people can do.

Others, like Ernest Hilgard, believe that there is something special about the hypnotic state. People who are hypnotized are very suggestible; they go along with the hypnotist and do not initiate activities themselves; and they can more easily imagine and remember things. Hilgard believes that consciousness includes many different aspects that may become separated, or dissociated, during hypnosis. This view is called the *neodissociation theory*, which includes a "hidden observer"—a portion of the personality that watches and reports what happens to the hypnotized person.

Connecting **Psychology** to Economics

FLOW STATES

The idea of *flow states* was developed by psychologist Mihály Csíkszentmihályi, whose goal was to find out what made people most truly happy. According to the flow state theory, as humans become more complex, we strive to grow intellectually and emotionally so that we can respond to more challenges. When we experience personal and work-based opportunities for growth at just the right level, we experience meaningful moments he calls "flow." Flow is a deep and uniquely human motivation to excel, exceed, and triumph over limitation. We are happiest, and perform best, when we are in a state of flow.

Artists and musicians enter flow states when they are immersed in creative tasks. But anyone who takes on challenges and focuses on the task at hand can enter an anxiety-free flow state. When the task becomes completely absorbing, flow is achieved. Employers can foster flow in the workplace by providing a supportive environment, setting clear goals, providing immediate feedback, and creating a balance between opportunity and ability. They can find out what workers do well and make use of their unique skills as often as possible. Employees who find their work intrinsically rewarding are motivated to achieve.

▶ **CRITICAL THINKING**

1. Finding the Main Idea What is flow?

2. Making Connections How can employers help their workers find flow?

▲ Many musicians who appear deep in concentration have often entered a flow state.

Franz Anton Mesmer
(1734–1815)

Franz Anton Mesmer became the first person to study and practice hypnosis. Mesmer believed that the human body is filled with a magnetic fluid that can become misaligned, causing illness. Realignment would restore health. He first tried to treat his patients using magnets. Some of his patients reported dramatic results.

Later, Mesmer used his own hand, claiming that he discharged *animal magnetism*. Before treating his patients, he told them to expect certain reactions, and his patients responded as anticipated. This healing technique came to be called "mesmerism" or "hypnotism." Although Mesmer was denounced as a fraud, he paved the way for serious studies of hypnotic suggestions.

▶ **CRITICAL THINKING**

Interpreting Significance
What is the significance of Mesmer's experiments with animal magnetism?

reveal to make generally known

posthypnotic suggestion
a suggestion made during hypnosis that influences the participant's behavior afterward

Another explanation of hypnosis is based on the importance of suggestibility in the hypnotic induction. According to some theorists, hypnotized people behave as they do because they have accepted the role of a hypnotized subject. We expect that hypnotized individuals will forget certain things when told or will recall forgotten material, and we play the role. Whether hypnosis is a special state of consciousness or not, it does **reveal** that people often have potential abilities that they do not use. Continued study may help us understand where these abilities come from and how to use them better.

Uses of Hypnosis

Although people have often seen hypnosis as a part of an entertainment act, it has serious uses in medical and therapeutic settings. Hypnosis may be used to reduce pain. *Hypnotic analgesia* refers to a reduction of pain reported by patients after they had undergone hypnosis.

Hypnotists can suggest things for their participants to remember or forget when the trance is over. This is known as **posthypnotic suggestion**. For example, the hypnotist can suppress memory by suggesting that after the person is awakened, she will be unable to hear the word *psychology*. When she comes out of the trance, the participant may report that some people around her are speaking strangely. They seem to leave out some words occasionally, especially when they are talking about topics involving the taboo word *psychology*. The participant is not aware that part of her consciousness has been instructed to block out that word. Memory can also be aided or enhanced through posthypnotic suggestion. Posthypnotic suggestion has been found to be particularly helpful in changing unwanted behaviors, such as smoking or overeating.

Olympic athletes use self-hypnosis to achieve peak performance. Many coaches and trainers recognize the importance of mental rehearsal prior to competition. Steps that athletes use include relaxing; setting specific, measurable short-term goals; visualizing the peak performance; and designing a plan of action that the athlete mentally rehearses when preparing to compete.

Therapists use hypnosis to help clients reveal their problems or gain insight into their lives. For example, hypnotherapists use hypnosis to allow their patients to think of their problems in a new way. Hypnosis, though, is not for all patients. Some fear the loss of control associated with hypnosis. Therapists often combine hypnosis with other therapies to help patients work through their problems.

☑ **READING PROGRESS CHECK**

Explaining How do therapists use hypnosis?

Biofeedback and Meditation

GUIDING QUESTION *What are the benefits of biofeedback and meditation?*

Biofeedback is a technique in which a person learns to control his or her internal physiological processes with the help of feedback. For example, you can be hooked up to a biofeedback machine so that a light goes on every time your heart rate goes over 80. You could then learn to keep your heart rate below 80 by trying to keep the light off.

Biofeedback has been used to teach people to control a wide variety of physiological responses, including brain waves, heart rate, blood pressure, skin temperature, and sweat-gland activity. The basic principle of biofeedback is simple: Feedback makes learning possible. Biofeedback involves using machines to tell people about very subtle, moment-to-moment changes in the body. When people are connected to the machines, they can experiment with different thoughts and feelings while they watch how each affects their bodies. In time, people can learn to change their physiological processes.

Some of the best-documented biofeedback cures involve special training in muscular control. Tension headaches often seem to result from **constriction** of the frontalis muscle in the forehead. Thomas Budzynski and others used biofeedback to teach people to relax this specific muscle. The practice went on for several weeks, while other people were given similar treatments without biofeedback. Only the biofeedback group improved significantly. Biofeedback used without drugs seems to help many people.

When a person focuses his or her attention on an image or thought with the goal of clearing the mind and producing relaxation, or an inner peace, that person is meditating. **Meditation** has been practiced for thousands of years.

There are three major approaches to meditation. *Transcendental meditation* involves the mental repetition of a mantra, usually a Sanskrit phrase. The participant sits with eyes closed and meditates for 15 to 20 minutes twice a day. *Mindfulness meditation* was developed from a Buddhist tradition. This form of meditation focuses on the present moment. For example, the participant may move his or her focus through the body from the tips of the toes to the top of the head, while paying particular attention to areas that cause pain. *Breath meditation* is a concentration on one's respiration—the process of inhaling and exhaling.

Researchers generally agree that most people can benefit from the sort of systematic relaxation that meditation provides. Meditation may help people lower blood pressure, heart rate, and respiration rate. The issue is not clear-cut, however. The people who benefit from meditation continue to practice it. Thus, the reported benefits may come from a biased, self-selected sample of successful practitioners. Other data suggest that while meditating, some people may actually be sleeping. If so, the reported benefits of meditation may result simply from relaxation.

☑ READING PROGRESS CHECK

Summarizing How does meditation work?

Quick Lab

CAN YOU HYPNOTIZE YOURSELF?
Sometimes just thinking of an action can result in producing that action—if you can imagine that action clearly enough.

Procedure
1. Stretch your arms in front of you, making sure the palms are facing each other at the same height and about 2 inches apart.
2. Close your eyes. Imagine that your right arm is getting heavier and heavier, while your left arm is getting lighter and lighter.
3. To help yourself, imagine that your right hand is holding a strap wrapped around several heavy books, while your left hand is holding a string tied to a helium balloon.

Analysis
1. After about a minute, open your eyes and see how far your hands have actually moved. Are they 1 or 2 inches apart or several inches apart?
2. Using what you have learned about hypnosis, explain the results in a brief report.

biofeedback the process of learning to control bodily states with the help of machines monitoring the states to be controlled

constriction a narrowing of a channel or vessel, or a feeling of tightness or pressure

meditation the focusing of attention to clear one's mind and produce relaxation

---

LESSON 2 REVIEW

Reviewing Vocabulary
1. *Explaining* Explain how a person can alter his or her consciousness by using meditation.

Using Your Notes
2. *Applying* Using the notes you completed during this lesson, write a brief example illustrating each explanation of hypnotism.

Answering the Guiding Questions
3. *Describing* What type of relationship is needed between a hypnotist and a participant?

4. *Summarizing* What are the benefits of biofeedback and meditation?

Writing Activity
5. *Informative/Explanatory* Try this meditation technique: (1) Take a few moments and form your lips into a half smile; (2) Hold this half smile for at least 10 minutes as you go about your ordinary activities. Did you notice a shift in how you acted and responded to others? Did others respond to you differently? Write an analysis of your experiences.

Case Study

A Breath of Fresh Air

Period of Study: Late 1970s to early 1980s

Introduction: Approximately 20 million people in the United States suffer from asthma, a chronic respiratory condition characterized by hypersensitivity, inflammation, and obstruction or narrowing of the airways. An asthmatic person develops swollen airways lined with thick mucus. This causes the surrounding muscles to constrict, making it extremely difficult to breathe and sometimes leading to a life-threatening event. The occurrence of these symptoms is known as an asthmatic episode.

The causes of asthma are generally the results of allergic reactions, stress, endocrine changes, genetic makeup, and/or psychological traits. People with asthma suffer from both gasping and irritating interruptions of their daily routine. They must always be prepared to manage an oncoming episode.

Medication in the form of an oral inhaler has long been the common way to treat an asthmatic episode. Researchers, however, are investigating a connection between halting an asthmatic episode and the use of biofeedback, or gaining conscious control over an unconscious event.

Hypothesis: Through the use of biofeedback, or gaining conscious control over an unconscious event, an asthma sufferer can gain control and relieve the tightening of the muscles that constrict airways.

Method: Recent studies have attempted to find the relationship between changes in muscular tension and breathing patterns in both asthmatic and non-asthmatic individuals. Researchers instructed participants to use deep breathing exercises while hooked up to biofeedback monitors. This allowed the participants to learn to control their heart rates during breathing cycles. The goal of this experiment was to control the muscle reflex that constricts airways during an asthmatic episode. Other types of biofeedback experiments were performed as well, in which no biofeedback machine was used. Instead, the participant would perform the same type of breathing exercises in front of the mirror, thus monitoring muscle tension.

Results: Initial observation showed that the performance of these types of exercises might lead to a noticeable decrease in asthma symptoms. Participants took lower dosages of medication, sometimes eliminating the medication entirely. Emergency room visits by participants directly involving asthmatic episodes decreased significantly.

Overall, the benefits of biofeedback techniques to control asthma are apparent. A number of questions regarding biofeedback techniques and asthma, however, remain unanswered. One such question involves differing methods for researching long-term effects of these specific techniques. What impact do these techniques have on participants over a greater period of time? Because this research is relatively new, such questions may not be answered for years to come.

PRIMARY SOURCE

"The limitations [of biofeedback] are the skepticism of the patient and tolerance for investing the practice time to achieve results."

—Robert A. Anderson, "Asthma/Biofeedback and Relaxation," *Townsend Letter* (2008)

Analyzing the Case Study

1. *Explaining* What causes asthma?

2. *Describing* Describe how participants monitored their physiological processes in the experiments.

3. *Drawing Inferences* How did participants use biofeedback in the experiments? Why was it successful?

4. *Analyzing Primary Sources* Why might the true effectiveness of biofeedback in the treatment of asthma actually be greater than shown?

netw⊙rks

There's More Online!

- ☑ **IMAGE** Drug-Use Warning
- ☑ **CARTOON** Hallucinations
- ☑ **TABLE** Psychoactive Drugs
- ☑ **SELF-CHECK QUIZ**

Reading **HELP**DESK

Academic Vocabulary

- **augment** • **inhibit**

Content Vocabulary

- **psychoactive drugs**
- **hallucinations**
- **hallucinogens**

TAKING NOTES:

Key Ideas and Details

CLASSIFYING Use a graphic organizer like the one below to list three drugs. Then, below each one, indicate which class or type of drugs it belongs to.

LESSON 3

Drugs and Consciousness

ESSENTIAL QUESTION • *How can behavior affect the mind?*

IT MATTERS BECAUSE

After dropping briefly, between 2003 and 2005, marijuana use among eighth, tenth, and twelfth graders is rising. Among twelfth graders, daily use of marijuana has been at its highest point since the early 1980s. The National Institute on Drug Abuse (NIDA) warns parents that marijuana is a serious threat, which they must talk to their children about.

Drugs and Their Effects

GUIDING QUESTION *How do different drugs change a person's consciousness?*

Psychoactive drugs interact with the central nervous system to alter a person's mood, perception, and behavior. These drugs range from stimulants like the caffeine in coffee and cola drinks, to depressants like alcohol, to powerful hallucinogens like marijuana and LSD.

Like hormones, drugs are carried by the blood and taken up in target tissues in various parts of the body. Unlike hormones, though, drugs are taken into the body from the outside. People introduce drugs into their systems through routes that bring the drugs into contact with capillaries (the smallest blood vessels). From there, drugs are gradually absorbed into the blood. Then drug molecules act like neurotransmitters—they hook onto the dendrites of neurons and send out their own chemical messages. For example, alcohol molecules may cause a nerve cell not to fire. As more and more cells cease firing, the alcohol user becomes slower and may eventually lose consciousness. LSD molecules may cause circuits in different areas of the brain to start firing together instead of separately, resulting in hallucinations.

Marijuana

Marijuana, used as an intoxicant and hallucinogen among Eastern cultures for centuries, is a legally and morally acceptable substance in some societies. In the United States, the sale and possession of marijuana is against the law in most states. Before 1960, marijuana use in the United States was common only among members of certain subcultures. Marijuana use increased throughout the 1960s and most of the 1970s but then began to decline. In recent years, its usage has again seen an increase.

psychoactive drugs
chemicals that affect the nervous system and result in altered consciousness

augment to increase in number, size, or intensity

TABLE ⌄

PSYCHOACTIVE DRUGS
Psychoactive drugs influence how we sense and perceive things and modify our moods, feelings, emotions, and thoughts.

▶ **CRITICAL THINKING**

1. *Identifying Cause and Effect*
   What effects do depressants produce?

2. *Comparing* What similarities, if any, are there between the effects of marijuana and hallucinogens?

The active ingredient in marijuana is a complex molecule called tetrahydro-cannabinol (THC), which occurs naturally in the common weed *Cannabis sativa*, or Indian hemp. Marijuana is made by drying the plant; hashish is a gummy powder made from the resin exuded by the flowering tops of the female plant. Both marijuana and hashish are usually smoked, but they can also be cooked with food and eaten. Synthetic marijuana is sold under a number of names, including Spice and K2. It is made by lacing a blend of herbs and spices with cannabis-like chemicals. There have been numerous reports of synthetic marijuana causing heart attacks and other health risks.

The effects of marijuana vary somewhat from person to person and seem to depend on the setting in which the drug is taken and the user's past experience. In general, though, many marijuana users report that most sensory experiences seem greatly **augmented**—music sounds fuller, colors look brighter, smells are stronger, foods have more flavor, and other experiences are more intense than usual. Users may feel elated, the world may seem somehow more meaningful, and even the most ordinary events may take on great significance. Marijuana is not physically addictive, although people may become psychologically dependent on it.

As many users of marijuana have discovered, the drug can instill or heighten a variety of unpleasant experiences. If a person is frightened, unhappy, or depressed to begin with, the chances are good that taking the drug will blow the negative feelings out of proportion so that the user's world, temporarily at least, becomes very upsetting. Cases have been reported in which marijuana appears to have helped bring on psychological disturbances in people who were already unstable before they used it.

Despite the obvious need for careful research on marijuana, the first controlled scientific studies of its effects did not appear until the late 1960s, scarcely anticipating its surge in popularity. Studies suggest that marijuana use is more damaging to the lungs than cigarette use. Although there is no direct evidence that marijuana use causes lung cancer, the tar and other chemicals in marijuana smoke are drawn deep into the lungs and held 20 to 40 seconds, adding to the drug's potential for hindering lung function.

Marijuana also disrupts memory formation, making it difficult to carry out mental and physical tasks. Some researchers believe that long-term use can lead to dependence. Research also showed that adults using marijuana scored lower than equal-IQ nonusers on a twelfth-grade academic achievement test.

Drug Category	Effects on Behavior
Depressants Alcohol	Relaxants; relieve inhibitions; impair memory and judgment
Tranquilizers Barbiturates, benzodiazepines (Valium, Xanax)	Relieve anxiety; relax muscles; induce sleep
Opiates Morphine, heroin	Decrease pain; decrease attention to real world; unpleasant withdrawal effects as the drugs wear off
Stimulants Caffeine, amphetamines, cocaine	Increase energy, alertness
Mixed Stimulant-Depressants Nicotine	Stimulate brain activity, but most smokers say cigarettes relax them
Distortion of Experience Marijuana (THC)	Intensify sensory experiences; distorts perception of time; can relieve glaucoma, nausea; sometimes impairs learning, memory
Hallucinogens LSD, mescaline	Cause hallucinations, sensory distortions, and occasionally panic

During the 1970s and 1980s, several states began to fund research into the medicinal uses of marijuana. They have discovered several therapeutic uses of the drug in the treatment of patients with glaucoma, multiple sclerosis, and those undergoing chemotherapy. California legalized marijuana for medicinal use in 1996. Since then about a third of the states have followed suit, but the laws vary widely from state to state. Although numerous other states have proposed legislation to legalize some usage of the drug, it still remains against federal law to possess or sell marijuana.

Hallucinations and Hallucinogens

Hallucinations are perceptions that have no direct external cause. They involve seeing, hearing, smelling, tasting, or feeling things that do not exist. Hypnosis, meditation, certain drugs, withdrawal from a drug to which one has become addicted, and psychological breakdown may produce hallucinations. Hallucinations can also occur under normal conditions. People hallucinate when they are dreaming and when they are deprived of the opportunity to sleep. Periods of high emotion, concentration, or fatigue may also produce false sensations and perceptions. For example, truck drivers on long hauls have been known to swerve suddenly to avoid stalled cars that do not exist. Even daydreams involve mild hallucinations.

hallucinations
perceptions that have no direct external cause

Interestingly enough, it appears that hallucinations are very much alike from one person to the next. Soon after taking a drug that causes hallucinations, for example, people often see many geometric forms in a tunnel-like perspective. These forms float through their field of vision, combining with each other and duplicating themselves. While normal imagery is often reported as being in black and white, hallucinations are more likely to involve color.

One researcher traveled to Mexico's Sierra Madreto to study the reactions of Huichol Native Americans who take peyote. He found that their hallucinations were much like those of American college students who took similar drugs. He believes that these reactions are similar because of the way such drugs affect the brain: Portions of the brain that respond to incoming stimuli become disorganized, while the entire central nervous system is aroused.

So-called because their main effect is to produce hallucinations, **hallucinogens** are found in plants that grow throughout the world. They have been used for their effects on consciousness since earliest human history. These drugs are also called *psychedelics* because they result in an individual's loss of contact with reality. They can create a false body image and cause loss of self, dreamlike fantasies, and hallucinations.

hallucinogens drugs that often produce hallucinations

The best-known, most extensively studied, and most potent hallucinogen is LSD (lysergic acid diethylamide), or "acid." LSD is a synthetic substance. A dose of a few millionths of a gram has a noticeable effect; an average dose of 100 to 300 micrograms produces an experiential state that lasts from 6 to 14 hours. LSD is often dissolved into strips of paper or sugar cubes.

Under the influence of LSD, a person can experience any number of perceptions, often quite intense and rapidly changing. As with other potent hallucinogens, the person's expectations, mood, beliefs, and the circumstances under which he or she takes LSD can affect the experience. Perceptual hallucinations are very common with LSD. An individual's surroundings will shift and change. A wall, for example, may seem to pulsate or breathe. A person may experience a dissociation of the self into one being who observes and another who feels. Distortions of time are also common. As measured by the ability to perform simple tasks, LSD impairs thinking, even though users may feel they are thinking more clearly and logically than ever before. Intense panic reactions are the most common of LSD's unpleasant side effects.

Use of LSD peaked in the 1960s. The likelihood of recurring hallucinations, even months after taking LSD, and public fears of chromosome damage may have led to LSD's declining popularity. Between the 1960s and the early 1990s, researchers experimented with LSD in the treatment of neuroses, alcoholism, narcotic addiction, autism, and other disorders, as well as to reduce the suffering of cancer patients. Although most researchers concluded there was little clinical value in LSD, research into its use to treat alcoholism has revived in recent years.

Stimulants

Stimulants are drugs that achieve their effect by stimulating the brain and central nervous system. They increase alertness and wakefulness, elevate mood, increase speech and motor activity, and suppress appetite. Some stimulants are natural and others are synthetic. Probably the most familiar stimulant is caffeine, which occurs naturally in coffee, tea, kola nuts (which are used to flavor cola soft drinks), and cacao (from which we get chocolate). Caffeine stimulates the central nervous system, heart, blood vessels, and kidneys. Its positive effects include increased alertness, decreased fatigue, improved motor skills, and heightened sensory activity. However, it may cause irritability, nervousness, headaches, and insomnia.

Other natural stimulants include cocaine and nicotine. Both are extremely addictive. Cocaine comes from the leaves of the coca plant, which is native to South America. It acts as an anesthetic, but it also produces euphoria, or a feeling of well-being. It may be taken by mouth, sniffed, or smoked in the form of crack cocaine. Cocaine use may lead to severe personality disturbances, inability to sleep, psychotic reactions, and death.

Amphetamines are synthetic stimulants. The best-known of these is methamphetamine, also referred to as "meth" or "speed." Methamphetamine increases physical activity and suppresses appetite. Among the side effects are aggression, paranoia, agitation, chronic depression, convulsions, insomnia, violent behavior, schizophrenia, convulsions, and damage to internal organs.

CARTOON >

HALLUCINATIONS

In this cartoon, the man sitting on the bench has apparently become a little disturbed psychologically. His unconscious has produced a hallucinatory companion.

▶ **CRITICAL THINKING**

1. *Identifying Cause and Effect* What could have contributed to the man's hallucinations?

2. *Describing* How have people described their experiences after taking a drug that causes hallucinations?

The term *designer drugs* is sometimes used to refer to illegal synthetic drugs, including methamphetamine and Ecstasy. Many of these drugs became a part of youth subcultures. However, because these drugs are often very strong, overdoses are more likely to occur. Because they are made illegally, errors in drug formulas often occur, which can prove deadly.

Opiates

Opiates, usually called narcotics, include opium, morphine, and heroin. Opiates produce analgesia, or pain reduction; euphoria, which is sometimes described as a pleasurable state somewhere between awake and asleep; and constipation. Regular use of opiates can lead to physical addiction. An overdose of opiates results in a loss of control of breathing—the user then dies from respiratory failure.

Depressants

The most widely used and abused mind-altering substance in the United States is alcohol. The consumption of alcohol is encouraged by advertisements and by social expectations and traditions. The immediate effect of alcohol is a general loosening of inhibitions. Despite its seeming stimulating effect, alcohol is actually a depressant that serves to **inhibit** the brain's normal functions. When people drink, they often act without the social restraint or self-control they normally apply to their behavior.

The effects of alcohol use depend on the amount and frequency of use and the drinker's body weight. As the amount consumed increases within a specific time, the drinker's ability to function diminishes. The person experiences slurred speech, blurred vision, and impaired judgment and memory. Brain and liver damage and personality changes can result from prolonged heavy use of alcohol.

Several studies suggested that not all of the early effects of drinking are the result of the alcohol alone; some are social effects. People expect to feel a certain way when they drink. In one study, men who were led to believe they were drinking alcohol when they were, in fact, drinking tonic water became more aggressive. They also felt more sexually aroused and less socially anxious.

Barbiturates are drugs that act on certain parts of the brain, although they also tend to depress the functioning of all bodily tissues. Most of them produce a calming effect in small doses and sleep in larger doses. Prolonged use can lead to the development of tolerance, so that doses need to be increased in order to have the same or desired effect. Habitual users may become dependent and go through withdrawal if access to the drug is denied. An overdose can result in coma or death.

Abuse of barbiturates became widespread between the 1940s and the 1970s. Alcohol greatly increases their depressant effect. The use and abuse of barbiturates dropped considerably with the passage of the federal Comprehensive Drug Abuse Protection and Control Act of 1970. In routine medical practice, barbiturates have largely been replaced by another family of depressants, benzodiazepines (Valium, Xanax), for the treatment of insomnia and anxiety.

✔ READING PROGRESS CHECK

Describing What are the major effects of each type of psychoactive drug on the mind and body?

Many advertisements and programs aimed at kids, such as this one, warn of the dangers involved with drug use.

▶ **CRITICAL THINKING**

Gathering Information What is the general treatment for those who abuse drugs?

inhibit to discourage from spontaneous activity, especially through the operation of inner psychological or external social pressures

Altered States of Consciousness **197**

Drug Abuse and Treatment

GUIDING QUESTION *Why is the first step of drug treatment important?*

We might have been unaware of it, but most of us have taken a psychoactive drug at some time. For the majority of people this is usually something like the caffeine in soda, coffee, or tea. When does a person cross the line into drug abuse? Drug abusers regularly use illegal drugs or excessively use prescription drugs obtained legally. In some instances, they may abuse other substances, such as improperly using steroids or inhaling aerosols, adhesives, or household cleaners.

People use and abuse drugs for many reasons—to avoid boredom, to fit in with peers, to gain more self-confidence, to forget about problems, to relax, or simply to feel good. Despite the reason for using or abusing a drug, all of these reasons result in a drastic change of how people feel. All drug use—and abuse, too—involves a certain amount of risk.

There are many risks associated with drug abuse, including danger of death or injury by overdose or accident; irreparable damage to the mind; legal consequences (including incarceration); destructive behavior, which risks the property of self and others; danger of injuring others; and loss of income. The greatest risk associated with the abuse of psychoactive drugs, though, is loss of control.

Although addiction does not occur immediately, drug abuse can turn into addiction—an overwhelming and compulsive desire to obtain and use drugs. Treatment for drug abuse usually involves the following steps:

1. The drug abuser must admit that he or she has a problem.
2. The drug abuser must enter a treatment program and/or get therapy.
3. The drug abuser must remain drug-free. (Many drug addicts suffer a relapse; that is, they return to using drugs. Support groups can be a powerful force in preventing that occurrence.)

A number of organizations provide help for people with substance abuse problems and their families, including local hospitals and mental health facilities. Alcoholics Anonymous and Narcotics Anonymous are two of the best-known organizations. The Substance Abuse and Mental Health Services Administration, a branch of the U.S. Department of Health, maintains an online drug abuse and alcoholism treatment facility locator.

✅ READING PROGRESS CHECK

Defining What are the risks of drug abuse?

LESSON 3 REVIEW **CCSS**

Reviewing Vocabulary

1. ***Describing*** How do psychoactive drugs affect consciousness? Describe the effects of marijuana and LSD.

Using Your Notes

2. ***Identifying Cause and Effect*** Use the notes you completed during this lesson to list the effects of three drugs on consciousness.

Answering the Guiding Questions

3. ***Summarizing*** How do different drugs change a person's consciousness?

4. ***Speculating*** Why is the first step of drug treatment important?

Writing Activity

5. ***Argument*** Design and write an antidrug brochure. Keep in mind the reasons people choose to use and abuse drugs when creating your brochure.

Directions: On a separate sheet of paper, answer the questions below. Make sure you read carefully and answer all parts of the question.

Lesson Review

Lesson 1

1 *Specifying* What percentage of sleep time do adults usually spend in REM sleep?

2 *Identifying* What bodily functions follow circadian rhythms?

3 *Summarizing* Identify and describe five sleep disorders.

Lesson 2

4 *Explaining* Explain the phenomenon of posthypnotic suggestion.

5 *Listing* List some health problems that biofeedback can potentially help.

6 *Identifying* What benefits may be provided by meditation?

Lesson 3

7 *Identifying* What is the most widely used and abused mind-altering substance in the United States? How does it affect the user?

8 *Defining* What are psychoactive drugs?

9 *Listing* What are six possible risks associated with drug abuse?

Research and Technology

10 *Comparing and Contrasting* Meditation comes from a culture that defines quality of life differently from the way it is defined in traditional American culture. Use the Internet to conduct research on meditation in one of those cultures and report on the effectiveness of meditation techniques. Then compare and contrast the cultural definitions of quality of life in these cultures.

21st Century Skills

Interpreting a Chart Review the chart below, then answer the questions that follow.

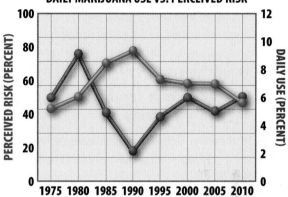

**U.S. 12TH GRADE STUDENTS
DAILY MARIJUANA USE VS. PERCEIVED RISK**

Source: University of Michigan, 2010 Monitoring the Future Study (Note: "Perceived Risk" refers to concern about the dangers of marijuana use.)

11 *Identifying* What was the approximate percentage of high school seniors using marijuana daily in 2009?

12 *Analyzing Visuals* In what year was marijuana use among high school seniors at its lowest? When was the perceived risk at its highest?

13 *Evaluate* Describe the relationship between perceived risk and daily marijuana use among high school seniors.

Exploring the Essential Questions

14 *Evaluating* Meditation as a means to relax is a classic example of the ways in which conscious behavior affects the mind. Search the Internet to find out about various meditation practices. Many Web sites provide techniques you can use to meditate. Try one or two of the techniques and report on their effectiveness to the class.

Need Extra Help?

If You've Missed Question	**1**	**2**	**3**	**4**	**5**	**6**	**7**	**8**	**9**	**10**	**11**	**12**	**13**	**14**
Go to page	182	183	183	190	190	191	197	193	198	191	193	193	193	191

Directions: On a separate sheet of paper, answer the questions below. Make sure you read carefully and answer all parts of the question.

Critical Thinking Questions

15 *Analyzing* Choose a behavior that you perform automatically and pay close attention to how you perform it. How does consciously thinking about the behavior affect your performance of it?

16 *Defending* Social scientists have varying ideas about the purpose and meaning of dreams. Review the various theories of social scientists presented in this chapter. Whose theory do you agree with the most? Why?

17 *Making Inferences* Do you think you could be hypnotized? Why or why not?

18 *Synthesizing* Have you ever hallucinated a sight or sound—perhaps when you were very tired or upset? What did you experience? Why do you suppose you created this particular hallucination?

19 *Drawing Conclusions* How does a person's culture influence his or her drug use?

College and Career Readiness

20 *Research Skills* Research places in your community where a substance abuser can go for help. You may wish to start by visiting the drug abuse and alcoholism treatment facility locator at http://findtreatment.samhsa.gov. Contact each local treatment facility or check its Web site to find out the types of services offered in each place. Create an informational pamphlet listing all the local treatment facilities, along with their addresses, telephone numbers, Web sites, and a brief description of the services they offer.

21 *Identifying Perspectives* Contact a hypnotherapist and a stage hypnotist. Ask both: Is hypnosis an altered state of consciousness? What is the difference between a person's usual waking state and a hypnotic state? Ask other questions to compare their views and uses of hypnosis. Report your findings to the class.

DBQ Analyzing Primary Sources

Use the document below to answer the following questions.

PRIMARY SOURCE

"As many as 18 million Americans have obstructive sleep apnea, according to the National Sleep Foundation. But researchers estimate that as many as 90 percent of them don't know they have it.

Sleep apnea causes people's airways to become blocked while they sleep, depriving them of the oxygen the body needs.

Many people with sleep apnea are chronic snorers. Their partners probably complain of loud snoring during the night, which may or may not be accompanied by gasping or choking sounds. People with sleep apnea are often startled awake many times during the night as the body becomes starved of oxygen. Often, though, people don't even realize that they've briefly woken up.

However, it's these numerous interruptions in sleep, though brief, that can cause severe daytime sleepiness. . . .

"Besides a lack of energy and the byproducts of too little sleep, sleep apnea can increase your risk of a car accident by as much as 15 times the normal risk," said Dr. Steven Park, an integrative sleep surgeon at Montefiore Medical Center in New York City. "It also puts you at greater risk of industrial accidents."

In addition, he said, sleep apnea increases people's risk for a host of other ailments, including type 2 diabetes, high blood pressure, heart disease, heart attack, stroke and early death.

"I've seen estimates that life expectancy is lowered by 20 years if you have untreated sleep apnea," Park said. "

—Serena Gordon, *Feeling Lackadaisical? Sleep Apnea May Be to Blame*

22 *Analyzing* According to the excerpt, how does sleep apnea affect the body in the short term and in the long term?

23 *Making Connections* Why might people with sleep apnea be at greater risk of car or industrial accidents?

Psychology Journal Activity

24 *Informative/Explanatory* Review your entry in your Psychology Journal for this chapter. Were your thoughts about sleep habits confirmed by what you learned in the chapter? How would you summarize the causes of common sleep disruptions?

Need Extra Help?

If You've Missed Question	**15**	**16**	**17**	**18**	**19**	**20**	**21**	**22**	**23**	**24**
Go to page	190	185	188	195	198	198	188	181	200	178

Sensation and Perception

ESSENTIAL QUESTION • *How does the mind react to changes?*

netw⊙rks

There's More Online about sensation and perception.

CHAPTER 8

LAB ACTIVITY
Testing Your Taste

Lesson 1
Sensation

Lesson 2
The Senses

Lesson 3
Perception

Psychology Matters...

Could the woman in the picture really be swinging from a chandelier suspended over a living room? Look around her and you see that she is actually standing on a flat painting on a city sidewalk. The painter uses techniques in his painting to fool our sense of sight. Psychologists examine the ways in which stimuli affect our senses and cause us to interpret the world around us in certain ways.

◀ This painting, created on a sidewalk by Joe Hill, uses *trompe l'oeil* techniques to distort our perception.

Steve Finn/Splash News/Corbis

201

Lab Activity

Testing Your Taste

THE QUESTION...

RESEARCH QUESTION Does the sense of taste occur on your tongue or in your nose?

Have you ever had a cold that made your food taste odd? Or maybe your food had almost no taste at all. Being sick can affect your sense of taste, but why? Unless your illness specifically involves your tongue, it remains fully functional. This being so, why can't you taste things properly? The answer lies in the connection between taste and smell.

How dependent is our sense of taste on our sense of smell? Does our sense of smell depend on our sense of taste? You will find out in the following experiment.

Psychology Journal Activity

Think about what you feel the first moment you taste something. Write about this in your Psychology Journal. Address the following questions: Does it feel like that moment is happening on your tongue or in your nose? Why might food manufacturers increase the aroma of their products? Do you think your senses are constant or do they change over time?

FINDING THE ANSWER...

HYPOTHESIS Our sense of taste is dependent on our sense of smell.

THE METHOD OF YOUR EXPERIMENT

MATERIALS   seedless grapes

PROCEDURE   Your first task will be to decide how to "turn off" a person's sense of smell while eating a grape. Gather all of the materials and information you need to make this decision. Make a list of the options and predict the consequences of each option. Once you have made a decision, assemble a group of four to five participants. Have all participants use your method to close off their sense of smell while eating two or three grapes. Record their sensations. How much did they taste? Next, have your participants eat two or three grapes without turning off their sense of smell. Record and compare their sensations.

DATA COLLECTION   After you have completed testing each participant, gather your findings into a single document. Summarize your data by comparing the sensations of eating the grapes with and without the sense of smell.

ANALYSIS & APPLICATION

1. Did your results support the hypothesis?

2. What other variables could you change in this experiment that might affect the results?

3. Provide two possible implications of your results.

networks   ONLINE LAB RESOURCES

Online you will find:

- An **interactive lab** experience, allowing you to put principles from this chapter into practice in a digital psychology lab environment. This chapter's lab will include an experiment allowing you to explore issues fundamental to sensation and perception.

- A **Skills Handbook** that includes a guide for using the scientific method, creating experiments, and analyzing data.

- A **Notebook** where you can complete your Psychology Journal and record and analyze data from your experiment.

netw⊙rks

There's More Online!

☑ **DIAGRAM** Fraser's Spiral

☑ **DIAGRAM** The Disappearing Circle

☑ **DIAGRAM** The Stroop Effect

☑ **SELF-CHECK QUIZ**

☑ **TABLE** The Human Senses

Reading **HELP**DESK

Academic Vocabulary

• perceive   • ratio

Content Vocabulary

• sensation
• perception
• psychophysics
• absolute threshold
• difference threshold
• signal-detection theory

TAKING NOTES:

Integration of Knowledge and Ideas

GATHERING INFORMATION

Complete the graphic organizer below with terms associated with sensation. Write a definition for each term.

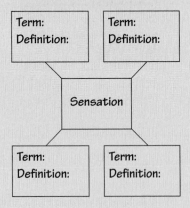

LESSON 1

Sensation

ESSENTIAL QUESTION • *How does the mind react to changes?*

IT MATTERS BECAUSE

Have you ever lost something and not realized how valuable it was until it was gone? Likewise, we often take our senses for granted. However, losing a sense, such as vision or hearing, makes us realize its value. Without our senses, we would not be able to interact with our world. By studying the senses, we can better appreciate them and understand how they work.

Understanding Sensation

GUIDING QUESTION *What is a stimulus?*

Helen Keller had been blind and deaf since she was nineteen months old. For the next four years, Helen was "wild and unruly." Then when she was six, Anne Sullivan, a teacher, entered her life. Using the sense of touch as the link between their two worlds, Anne tried again and again, by spelling words into Helen's hand, to help Helen grasp the connection between words and the things they stood for. "Suddenly I felt...a thrill of returning thought; and somehow the mystery of language was revealed to me," Helen recalled. From that day forward, Helen "saw" the world in a new way. She gradually learned new ways of responding to the events and physical changes occurring in her world.

Like Helen, we all respond to the physical changes that surround us. An alarm clock sounds; the flip of a switch fills a room with light; you stumble against a door; steam from a hot shower billows out into the bathroom, changing the temperature and clouding the mirror. Any aspect of or change in the environment to which an organism responds is called a *stimulus*. An alarm, an electric light, and an aching muscle are all stimuli for human beings.

A stimulus can be measured in many physical ways, including its size, duration, intensity, or wavelength. A **sensation** occurs anytime a stimulus activates one of your receptors. The sense organs detect physical changes in energy such as heat, light, sound, and physical pressure. The skin reacts to changes in heat and pressure, the eyes note changes in light, and the ears note changes in sound. Other sensory systems note the location and position of your body.

Science Source/Photo Researchers, Inc.

A sensation may be combined with other sensations and your past experience to yield a perception. A **perception** is the organization of sensory information into meaningful experiences. Optical illusions such as Fraser's Spiral may cause you to question the truth of your perceptions.

Psychologists are interested in the relationship between physical stimuli and sensory experiences. In vision, for example, the perception of color corresponds to the wavelength of the light, whereas brightness corresponds to the intensity of this stimulus.

What is the relationship between color and wavelength? How does changing a light's intensity affect your perception of its brightness? The psychological study of such questions is called **psychophysics**. The goal of psychophysics is to understand how stimuli from the world (such as frequency and intensity) affect the sensory experiences (such as pitch and loudness) produced by them.

sensation what occurs when a stimulus activates a receptor

perception the organization of sensory information into meaningful experiences

psychophysics the study of the relationships between sensory experiences and the physical stimuli that cause them

✓ **READING PROGRESS CHECK**

Identifying Cause and Effect How are sensations related to stimuli?

Threshold

GUIDING QUESTION *What does absolute threshold tell researchers about sensation?*

In order to establish laws about how people sense the external world, psychologists first try to determine how much of a stimulus is necessary for a person to sense it at all. How much energy is required for someone to hear a sound or to see a light? How much of a scent must be in the room before one can smell it? How much pressure must be applied to the skin before a person will feel it?

To answer such questions, a psychologist might set up the following experiment. First, a person (the participant) is placed in a dark room to dark-adapt. He is instructed to look at the wall and say "I see it" when he is able to detect a light. The psychologist then uses an extremely precise machine that can project a low intensity beam of light against the wall.

‹ **DIAGRAM**

FRASER'S SPIRAL
Fraser's spiral illustrates the difference between sensation and perception. Our perception of this figure is that of a spiral but it is actually an illusion. Trace a circle with your finger. You will always come back to your starting point.

▶ **CRITICAL THINKING**

1. *Making Inferences* How do we use sensation and perception together to understand our world?

2. *Making Connections* What did you learn about perception by studying this image?

Gustav Theodor Fechner started out as a young professor trying to demonstrate that every person, animal, and plant has both matter and soul. He failed. In the midst of a depression, he painted his room black and remained in it day and night. When he finally left the room, he walked through a garden, and the flowers looked brighter to him than they ever had before. On the morning of October 22, 1850, Fechner had an idea. He concluded that a systemic relationship between bodily and mental experiences could be demonstrated if a person were asked to report changes in sensations while a physical stimulus was varied. In testing these ideas, Fechner created the area of psychology known as psychophysics.

▶ **CRITICAL THINKING**

Interpreting Significance
Why was Fechner's conclusion important to the field of psychology?

absolute threshold the weakest amount of a stimulus that a person can detect half the time

The experimenter turns on the machine to its lowest light projection. The participant says nothing. The experimenter increases the projected light's brightness on each presentation until finally the participant responds, "I see it." Then the experimenter begins another series in the opposite direction. He starts with a visible but faint light and decreases its intensity on each trial until the light seems to disappear. Many trials are completed and averaged. This procedure detects the **absolute threshold**—the weakest amount of a stimulus required to produce a sensation. The absolute threshold is the level of stimulus that is detected 50 percent of the time.

The absolute thresholds for the five senses in humans are as follows: vision—seeing a candle flame 30 miles away on a clear night; hearing—hearing a watch ticking 20 feet away; taste—tasting 1 teaspoon of sugar dissolved in 2 gallons of water; smell—smelling 1 drop of perfume in a 3-room house; touch—feeling a bee's wing falling a distance of 1 centimeter onto your cheek.

While these thresholds may seem impressive, we respond to very little of the sensory world. We cannot see X rays or microwaves. Dogs can hear the sound of a dog whistle, while we cannot. Eagles' visual acuity is from 2.0 to 3.6 times better than that of humans. Grasshoppers are covered with hairs that let them sense minute amounts of air movement. Unlike humans, some animals have receptors that can sense magnetic fields. Migratory birds use this magnetic sense to help find their way south in the fall. Some animals, such as bats and porpoises, can hear sounds in much higher ranges than humans. They use this ability and a process called echolocation to determine the position of objects. In echolocation, the animal emits sound waves, which then bounce back to them. This "echo" allows the animal to determine not only an object's location, but also its size and shape.

☑ **READING PROGRESS CHECK**

Analyzing Why could establishing an absolute threshold for taste help a psychologist understand how people sense their world?

Measuring the Senses

GUIDING QUESTION *According to Weber's law, how much must a strong stimulus change for a person to notice the change?*

Another type of threshold is the **difference threshold**. The difference threshold refers to the minimum amount of difference a person can detect between two stimuli half the time. To return to our example of the person tested in a dark room, a psychologist would test for the difference threshold by gradually increasing the intensity of a visible light beam until the person says, "Yes, this is brighter than the light I just saw." With this technique, it is possible to identify the smallest increase in light intensity that is noticeable to the human eye.

Sensory Differences and Ratios

A related concept is the *just noticeable difference*, otherwise known as the *JND*. The JND refers to the smallest increase or decrease in the intensity of a stimulus that a person is able to detect half the time. A particular sensory experience depends more on *changes* in the stimulus than on the absolute size or amount of the stimulus.

For example, if you put a 3-pound package of food into an empty backpack, the **perceived** weight will be greatly increased. If you add the same amount to a backpack with a 100-pound weight in it, however, your perception of the weight will hardly increase at all. This is because the perception of the added weight reflects a proportional change. An addition of 3 pounds is not much change to an already heavy 100-pound load.

This idea is known as Weber's law: the larger or stronger a stimulus, the larger the change required for a person to notice that anything has happened to it. The **ratio** of the strength of the stimulus as compared to the size of the change always remains the same. By experimenting in this way with variations in sounds, temperatures, pressures, colors, tastes, and smells, psychologists are learning more about how each sense responds to change.

Some senses produce huge increases in sensation in response to small increases in energy. For instance, the pain of an electric shock can be increased more than eight times by doubling the voltage. On the other hand, the intensity of a light must be increased many times to double its perceived brightness. Some people are more sensitive to these changes than others. For example, people who can detect small differences in sensation work as food tasters, wine tasters, smell experts, perfume experts, and so on.

Sensory Adaption

Psychologists have focused on people's responses to changes in stimuli because they have found that the senses are tuned to change. Senses are most responsive to increases and decreases, and to new events rather than to ongoing, unchanging stimulation. We are able to respond to changes in our environment because our senses have an ability to adapt, or adjust themselves, to a constant level of stimulation. They get used to a new level and respond only to deviations from it.

A good example of this sensory adaptation is the increase in visual sensitivity that you experience after a short time in a darkened movie theater. At first you see only blackness, but after a while your eyes adapt to the new level, and you can see seats, faces, and so forth. Adaptation occurs for the other senses as well. Receptors in your skin adapt to the cold water when you go for a swim; disagreeable odors in a lab seem to disappear after a while; street noises cease to bother you after you have lived in a city for a time. Without sensory adaptation, you would feel the constant pressure of the clothes on your body, and other stimuli would seem to be bombarding all your senses at the same time.

Sensory adaptation allows us to notice differences in sensations and react to the challenges of different or changing stimuli. This principle is helpful when performing many activities, such as the work of police, security guards, and home inspectors. These people may notice minute changes and act appropriately.

difference threshold the smallest change in a physical stimulus that can be detected half the time

perceive to notice or be aware of

ratio relationship between two or more values

⌄ **TABLE**

THE HUMAN SENSES

The chart lists the fundamental features that make up the human sensory system.

▶ **CRITICAL THINKING**

1. *Making Connections* What is the vestibular sense?

2. *Identifying* What receptors are used in kinesthesis?

Sense	Stimulus	Sense Organ	Receptor	Sensation
Sight (Vision)	Light waves	Eye	Rods and cones of retina	Colors, patterns, textures, motion, depth in space
Hearing (Audition)	Sound waves	Ear	Hair cells located in inner ear	Noises, tones
Skin sensations (Somesthesis)	External contact	Skin	Nerve endings in skin	Touch, pain, warmth, cold
Smell (Olfaction)	Odoriferous substances	Nose	Hair cells of olfactory membrane	Odors (musky, flowery, burnt, minty)
Taste (Gustation)	Soluble substances	Tongue	Taste buds of tongue	Flavors (sweet, sour, salty, bitter)
Vestibular sense	Mechanical and gravitational forces	Inner ear	Hair cells of semicircular canals and vestibule	Spatial movement, gravitational pull
Kinesthesis	Body movement and position	Muscles, tendons, and joints	Nerve fibers in muscles, tendons, and joints	Movement and position of body parts

CAN YOU DETECT CHANGES IN STIMULI?
What would it take for you to notice a difference in the weight of your backpack?

Procedure
1. Fill your backpack with materials so that it weighs 10 pounds, and put it on your back.
2. Assemble a collection of objects that weigh about 4 ounces (113 g) each, such as apples or oranges.
3. Ask a friend to insert the objects one at a time while you are seated, with the weight of your backpack off your back. Be sure you cannot see which object is being placed in the pack.

Analysis
1. After each object is placed in the backpack, stand and report whether or not the backpack feels heavier.
2. Record the point at which you notice the difference in the weight of the backpack.
3. Use the concept of difference threshold to explain your results.

signal-detection theory
the summary of people's tendencies to make correct judgments in detecting the presence of stimuli

Signal-Detection Theory
There is no sharp boundary between stimuli that you can perceive and stimuli you cannot perceive. The **signal-detection theory** summarizes the relations between motivation, sensitivity, and decision-making in detecting the presence or absence of a stimulus. Detection thresholds involve recognizing some stimulus against a background of competing stimuli. A radar operator must be able to detect an airplane on a radar screen even when the plane's blip is faint and difficult to distinguish from blips caused by flocks of birds or bad weather, which can produce images that are like visual "noise." The radar operator's effective performance depends on being able to distinguish between the visual noise and the signals that indicate planes. The radar operator's judgment will be influenced by many factors, and studies show that different operators appear to have different sensitivities to blips. Moreover, a specific individual's apparent sensitivity seems to fluctuate, depending on the situation. For example, a radar operator may be able to ignore other stimuli as long as she is motivated to keep focused, just as you may be motivated to complete your reading assignment no matter what distractions you encounter.

In studying the difficulties faced by radar operators, psychologists have reformulated the concept of absolute threshold. Most importantly, the concept now takes into account the many factors that affect detection of minimal stimuli. As a result, signal-detection theory abandons the idea that there is a single true absolute threshold. Instead, it is based on the notion that the stimulus, here called a signal, must be detected in the presence of competing stimuli, which can interfere with detection of the signal in various ways.

DIAGRAM >

THE STROOP EFFECT
Some stimuli interfere with your ability to perform a task efficiently.

▶ **CRITICAL THINKING**

1. *Hypothesizing* Why was it more difficult to name the colors in *b*?

2. *Interpreting* How does your mind use preattentive processing when performing this activity?

Name the colors of the boxes in *a* as fast as you can. Then read the words in *b* as fast as you can. Finally, name the colors of the words in *b* as fast as you can. You probably proceeded more slowly when naming the colors in *b*.

a
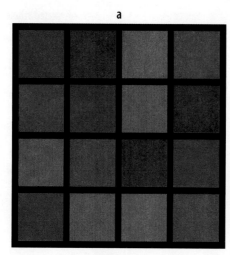

b
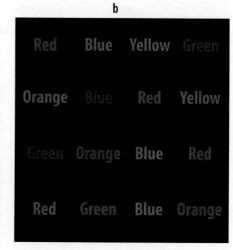

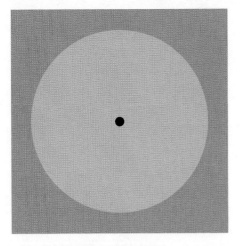
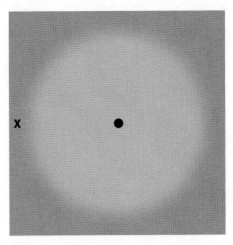

< DIAGRAM

THE DISAPPEARING CIRCLE
Sensation depends on change and contrast in the environment.

▶ **CRITICAL THINKING**

1. *Drawing Conclusions* What is the purpose of sensory adaptation?

2. *Speculating* Why will the circle reappear if you close and reopen your eye?

Hold your hand over one eye and stare at the dot in the middle of the circle on the left. You should have no trouble maintaining the image of the circle. If you do the same with the circle on the right, however, the image will fade. The gradual change from light to dark does not provide enough contrast to keep the visual receptors in your eye firing at a steady rate. The circle reappears only if you close and reopen your eye or you shift your gaze to the X.

Psychologists have identified two different types of processing stimuli, or signals. *Preattentive process* is a method for extracting information automatically and simultaneously when presented with stimuli. *Attentive process* is a procedure that considers only one part of the stimuli presented at a time. For example, when looking at illustrations of the Stroop effect, preattentive, or automatic, processing acts as an interference. The tendency is to read the word instead of saying the color of the ink. Apparently people find it almost impossible not to read color names that appear before their eyes, because the name interferes with the response of naming the ink color when the two are different. In summary, we notice some things automatically in spite of distracting information. However, it requires more careful attention to notice other, less distinct items. This difference, though, is one of degree—all tasks require attention, but some require more attention than others.

☑ **READING PROGRESS CHECK**

Constructing Arguments Why do you think the mind can process preattentive processing more quickly than attentive processing?

LESSON 1 REVIEW

Reviewing Vocabulary
1. *Explaining* How does signal-detection theory attempt to explain why there is no clear boundary between a stimulus you can perceive and one that you cannot perceive?

Using Your Notes
2. *Comparing and Contrasting* Review the notes that you completed during the lesson to list the similarities and differences between the terms *sensation* and *perception*.

Answering the Guiding Questions
3. *Defining* What is a stimulus?

4. *Assessing* What does absolute threshold tell researchers about sensation?

5. *Explaining* According to Weber's law, how much must a strong stimulus change for a person to notice the change?

Writing Activity
6. *Argument* Choose the sense that you think is personally most valuable to you. Write an essay in which you explain why this sense would cause you the most difficulty if you were to lose it.

netw⊙rks

There's More Online!

- ☑ **CHART** Decibel Levels
- ☑ **DIAGRAM** A Changing Flag
- ☑ **DIAGRAM** The Electromagnetic Spectrum
- ☑ **DIAGRAM** The Human Ear
- ☑ **DIAGRAM** The Human Eye
- ☑ **DIAGRAM** The Human Tongue
- ☑ **DIAGRAM** Testing for Color Deficiency
- ☑ **IMAGE** Vestibular System at Work

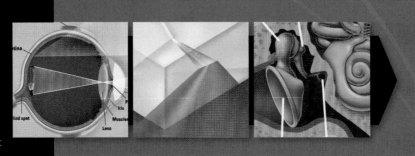

Reading **HELP**DESK (CCSS)

Academic Vocabulary

- visible
- accessibility

Content Vocabulary

- pupil
- lens
- retina
- optic nerve
- binocular fusion
- retinal disparity
- auditory nerve
- olfactory nerve
- somesthesis
- vestibular system
- kinesthesis

TAKING NOTES:

Key Ideas and Details

CATEGORIZING Complete the table below by listing each of the senses discussed in this lesson. In the right column, list the body parts that are associated with each sense.

Sense	Parts of the Body
vision	eyes, optic nerve, brain

210

LESSON 2

The Senses

ESSENTIAL QUESTION • *How does the mind react to changes?*

IT MATTERS BECAUSE

Our senses may seem very different from one another. The sense of smell, for example, might not seem at all like the sense of hearing. However, in each case, a specific type of sensory receptor is responding to a particular stimulus. Learning how these receptors function helps us understand the ways in which we interact with our surroundings.

Vision

GUIDING QUESTION *How do people see color?*

Try this experiment. Find a pitch black space such as a closet, a room so dark that you cannot see anything. Hold your hand in front of your face, although you cannot see it in the dark. Now, wave your hand from side to side. What do you see? You see your hand in motion.

How could you see your hand moving even though it was totally dark? You have just experienced kinesthesis—one of the senses. Although people are thought to have five senses, there are actually more. In addition to vision, hearing, taste, smell, and touch, there are several skin senses and two internal senses: *vestibular* and *kinesthetic*.

Each type of sensory receptor takes some sort of external stimulus—light, chemical molecules, sound waves, and pressure—and converts it into a chemical–electrical message that can be transmitted by the nervous system and interpreted by the brain. So far, we know the most about vision and hearing. The other senses have received less attention and are more mysterious in their functioning.

Vision is the most studied of all the senses, reflecting the high importance we place on our sense of sight. Vision provides us with a great deal of information about our environment—the sizes, shapes, and locations of objects, and their textures, colors, and distances.

How does vision occur? Light enters the eye through the **pupil** and reaches the **lens**, a flexible structure that focuses light on the **retina**. The retina contains two types of light-sensitive receptor cells, or photoreceptors: *rods* and *cones*. These cells are responsible for changing light energy into neuronal impulses, which then travel along the **optic nerve** to the brain, where they are routed to the occipital lobe.

Cones are photoreceptor cells in the retina that allow us to see color. Cones require relatively more light than rods before they begin to respond, and so cones work best in daylight. Since rods are photoreceptor cells that are sensitive to much lower levels of light than cones, they are the basis for night vision. There are many more rods in the human retina (75 to 150 million) than there are cones (6 to 7 million), but only cones are sensitive to color. Rods and cones can be compared to black-and-white and color film. Color film takes more light and thus works best in daylight, like our cones. Sensitive black-and-white film works not only in bright light but also in shadows, dim light, and other poor lighting conditions, just like our rods.

Scientists have developed different theories about why we see colors. One of them is the *trichromatic theory*. This theory hypothesizes that the eye contains three types of cones. Each type is especially sensitive to either the blue, green, or red regions of the electromagnetic spectrum. The three sets are typically referred to as S, M, and L because they are sensitive to either short, medium, or long wavelengths. According to this theory, color vision depends on how strongly each type of cone responds to a specific stimulus. (If all three types of cones are equally stimulated, the viewer perceives the stimulus as being white.) One strength of the trichromatic theory is that it is able to explain color deficiency, which is discussed later in this lesson.

Light

Light is a form of electromagnetic radiation. Other forms of electromagnetic radiation include radio waves, microwaves, infrared radiation, ultraviolet rays, X-rays, and gamma rays. All of these are known collectively as the electromagnetic spectrum. The electromagnetic spectrum is composed of waves of different length and frequency.

pupil the opening in the iris that regulates the amount of light entering the eye

lens a flexible, elastic, transparent structure in the eye that changes its shape to focus light on the retina

retina the innermost coating of the back of the eye, containing the light-sensitive receptor cells

∨ DIAGRAM

THE HUMAN EYE
This cross section of the human eye shows the passage of light. Note that the retina receives an inverted image.

▶ CRITICAL THINKING

1. *Analyzing* What is the main function of the rods and cones?

2. *Analyzing Visuals* What part does the lens play in transmitting an image to the brain?

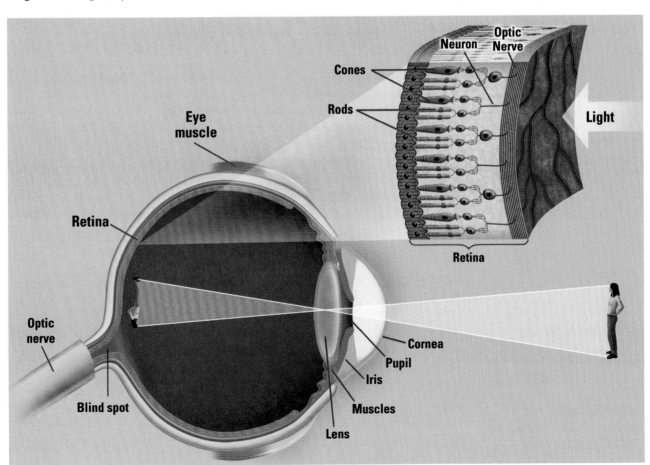

THE ELECTROMAGNETIC SPECTRUM

Light is the visible portion of the electromagnetic spectrum. When the wavelengths in white light are separated, the visual effect is an array of colors because different wavelengths are seen as different colors.

▶ **CRITICAL THINKING**

1. *Analyzing* Why are we able to see the wavelengths of the visible spectrum?

2. *Speculating* How have wavelengths outside the human visible range been used for human activities?

optic nerve the nerve that carries impulses from the retina to the brain

visible capable of being seen

binocular fusion the process of combining the images received from the two eyes into a single, fused image

retinal disparity the differences between the images stimulating each eye

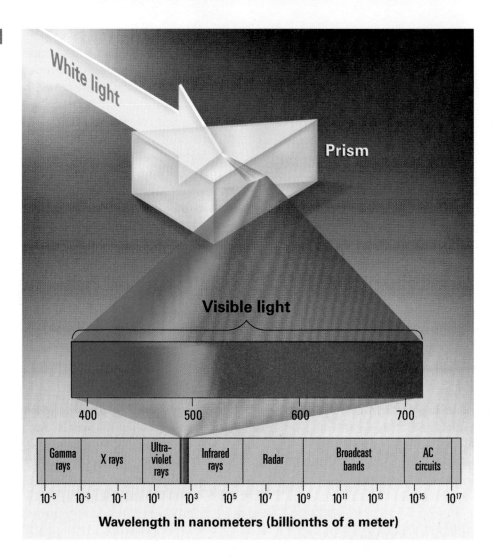

As you can see in the diagram of the electromagnetic spectrum, light that is visible to humans makes up only a small portion of the electromagnetic spectrum. Other animals can see light outside the human range. For example, bees can see ultraviolet light, which aids them in their search for pollen. Being able to see in the infrared range helps snakes in locating prey.

You can see the wavelengths of **visible** light with a prism. Passing light through a prism breaks it into a rainbow of colors. Each color is comprised of light of different wavelengths. While prisms transmit light, other objects absorb and reflect it. An object's color depends, in part, on the light that reaches our eyes. For example, a pea looks green because it reflects green light and absorbs other colors.

Binocular Fusion

Because we have two eyes, located about 2.5 inches (6.4 cm) apart, the visual system receives two images. Instead of seeing double, however, we see a single image—a composite of the views of two eyes. The combination of the two images into one is called **binocular fusion**. Not only does the visual system receive two images but there is also a difference between the images on the retinas. This difference is called **retinal disparity**. You can easily observe retinal disparity by bringing an object, such as an eraser, close to your eyes. Without moving it, look at the eraser first with one eye, then with the other. You will see a difference in the two images because of the different viewpoint each eye has. When you open both eyes, you will no longer see the difference but will instead see the object as solid and three-dimensional, if you have good binocular vision.

Retinal disparity is essential to your sense of depth perception. The brain interprets a large retinal disparity (a large difference between what the right eye and what the left eye are seeing) to mean that an object is nearby. The brain interprets a small retinal disparity (not much difference between the images the left and right eyes receive) to mean a distant object.

Some of us are born with perfectly shaped eyeballs. These people have almost perfect vision. The cornea and lenses in their eyes are able to properly focus light rays on the retina. However, many people have vision that is less than perfect. There are several ways that this can happen. In nearsightedness (myopia), the eye focuses the image slightly in front of the retina. You can see near objects clearly, but distant objects are blurry. This is usually caused by the eyeball being longer or the cornea more curved than normal. In farsightedness (hyperopia), the eye focuses the image slightly behind the retina. You can see distant objects clearly, but near objects are blurry. Farsightedness occurs if the eyeball is too short or the cornea is less curved than normal. The tendency to be nearsighted or farsighted is inherited. As people reach the age of about 40, the eye's lens becomes less flexible, making it harder to focus on close objects. This explains why people over 40 have more difficulty seeing close objects.

Eyeglasses and contact lenses are used to adjust the eye's focus so that a person can see more clearly. A permanent solution is LASIK, a process that uses a laser to reshape the cornea. This reshaping improves the eye's ability to focus light so that images are sharper. LASIK eye surgery can be used to correct both near- and farsightedness.

Color Deficiency

When some or all of a person's cones do not function properly, he or she is said to be color-deficient. The individual cannot differentiate between certain shades of color. However, color-deficient people do see some colors. The most common color deficiency involves the inability to tell the difference between shades of reds and greens. Blue-yellow color deficiency is rarer. It also is more severe because people with blue-yellow deficiency often have problems distinguishing reds and greens also.

In a normal eye, pigments in the cones recognize different colors and transmit this information to the brain over the optic nerve. As previously discussed, the trichromatic theory states that there are three types of cones, each having pigments that are sensitive to a different primary color: blue, green, or red. If the cones are lacking one or more of these pigments, the individual will have difficulties recognizing that color.

A small number of people are totally color-deficient. They depend on their rods, so to them the world looks something like black-and-white television programs. They see nothing but blacks, whites, and shades of gray.

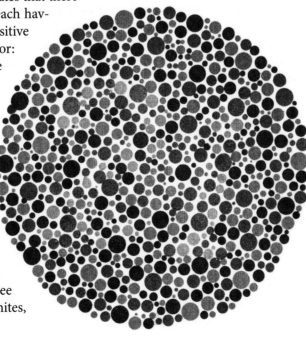

Steve Allen/Brand X Picture/Getty Images

Your Blind Spot

The point where the optic nerve exits the eye is called the blind spot. When light hits that point, the eye registers nothing because this area lacks photoreceptors—neurons that are sensitive to light. Find your blind spot by holding the diagram below about 3–4 inches (8–10 cm) away from your eyes.

Close your right eye and look at the cross with your left eye. At a comfortable reading distance, move the book backward and forward, keeping your eye focused on the cross. Notice that you can also see the dot. Focus on the cross, but be aware of the dot as you slowly bring the diagram toward your face. The dot will disappear and then reappear. Now close your left eye and look directly at the dot with your right eye. This time the cross will disappear and reappear as you bring the diagram toward your face. What has happened? When you hold the diagram so that the light from the dot falls on your blind spot, you cannot see the dot.

‹ DIAGRAM

TESTING FOR COLOR DEFICIENCY

Can you see numerals in the dot patterns that make up this figure? Those with normal vision will see a number, while those with red-green deficiency will see only random patches of color.

▶ CRITICAL THINKING

1. *Identifying Cause and Effect* What causes color deficiency?

2. *Evaluating* Could this test be used to check for a yellow-blue deficiency? Why or why not?

Sensation and Perception **213**

A CHANGING FLAG

Stare steadily at the lowest right-hand star for about 45 seconds. Then stare at the blank space to the left. You should see a negative afterimage of this figure. This occurs because the receptors for green, black, and yellow become fatigued or neuronal firing rates shift, allowing the complementary colors of each to predominate when you stare at a blank space.

▶ **CRITICAL THINKING**

1. *Hypothesizing* What happens when you shift your glance to a blank wall some distance away? Why?

2. *Drawing Conclusions* What does this test tell you about the receptors that detect color?

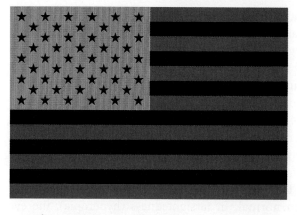

There is no cure for color deficiency. Most color-deficient people use cues to identify the correct colors. For example, on stop lights, red is at the top and green is at the bottom. Color-deficient individuals may learn to label items such as clothing so that they do not wear colors that clash.

About 8 percent of American men and less than 1 percent of American women are affected by color deficiency, which is a hereditary condition. The gene is carried in the genes of women who pass the genes on to their sons, who are born color-deficient.

Blindness

Total blindness refers to the inability to see any light. Many people who are referred to as being blind do have some vision—for example, they may see shadows or vague movement. Another term that is commonly used is "legally blind." This government-defined term establishes whether an individual is eligible for certain benefits and is restricted from activities such as driving.

Around the world, the leading cause of blindness is cataracts, which are caused by a clouding of the eyes' lenses. Fortunately, the cloudy lens can be replaced with an artificial one. By the age of 80, about half the individuals in the United States will have cataracts or will have had them surgically removed.

In glaucoma, the pressure within the eye rises to above normal levels. This increased pressure can damage the optic nerve, causing vision loss. Fortunately, glaucoma can be controlled by medication and surgical procedures. Annual eye exams include a test for glaucoma.

Macular degeneration, like cataracts, is primarily associated with aging. It is caused by a gradual deterioration of the cones in the retina. Vision is mainly lost in the central area of the eye—side (peripheral) and night vision often remain normal. Getting an adequate amount of nutrients, such as zinc, and wearing sunglasses when outside helps protect against macular degeneration.

Scientists have long been interested in whether other senses are heightened in blind people. Research shows that individuals who have been blind from birth use the visual area of their brains to strengthen senses such as touch and hearing. They also respond much more quickly to these stimuli than people with normal vision.

Historically, blind people have often felt excluded from the daily life of the sighted world. Today, **accessibility** laws and the growth in technology have increased this group's independence. Blind people use Braille, which consists of series of raised dots, to "read" with their fingertips. The growth of the Internet allows blind individuals to interact in ways that were not possible a generation ago. Organizations such as the National Federation of the Blind encourage online discussions and promote beneficial government legislation. Those who are blind or have low vision typically use screen-readers with synthetic speech to read aloud the contents of web pages. Some smart phones come with built-in speech software. These assistive devices help the blind access and share information.

accessibility capable of being easily used or seen

✓ **READING PROGRESS CHECK**

Making Predictions What would our vision be like if our eyes contained only rods and no cones?

Hearing

GUIDING QUESTION *How do people hear sound?*

Hearing, or *audition*, depends on vibrations of the air, called sound waves. Sound waves from the air pass through various small bones in the ear until they reach the inner ear, which contains tiny hair-like cells that move back and forth (much like a field of wheat waving in the wind). These hair cells change sound vibrations into neuronal signals that travel through the **auditory nerve** to the brain. Loudness of sound is determined by the amplitude, or height, of sound waves. The higher the amplitude, the louder the sound. This strength, or sound-pressure energy, is measured in *decibels*. The sounds humans hear range upward from 0 decibels, just below the softest sound the human ear can detect, to about 140 decibels, which is roughly as loud as a jet plane taking off. Any sound over 110 decibels can damage hearing, as can persistent sounds as low as 80 decibels. Any sound that is painful when you first hear it *will* damage your hearing if you are exposed to it often enough. Decibel levels of some common sounds are listed on the chart.

Pitch depends on sound-wave frequency, or the rate of the vibration of the medium through which the sound wave is transmitted. Low frequencies produce deep bass sounds, and high frequencies produce shrill squeaks. If you hear a sound composed of a combination of different frequencies, you can hear the separate pitches even though they occur simultaneously. For example, if you strike two keys of a piano at the same time, your ear can detect two distinct pitches.

Sources of sounds can be located when your ears work together. When a noise occurs on your right, for example, the sound wave comes to both ears, but it reaches your right ear a fraction of a second before it reaches the left. It is also slightly louder in the right ear. These differences tell you from which direction, left or right, the sound is coming.

The Pathway of Sound

The entire structure of the ear is designed to capture sound waves. The outer ear receives sound waves, and the earflap directs the sounds down a short tube called the auditory canal. The vibration of air (the sound wave) causes air in the auditory canal to vibrate, which in turn causes the eardrum to vibrate.

The middle ear is an air-filled cavity. Its main structures are three tiny bones—the hammer, anvil, and stirrup. These bones are linked to the eardrum at one end and to the cochlea at the other end. When sound waves cause the eardrum to vibrate, these bones vibrate and push against the cochlea.

The cochlea makes up the inner ear. The cochlea is a bony tube that contains fluids and neurons. The pressure against the cochlea makes the liquid inside the cochlea move. Tiny hairs inside the cochlea pick up the motion. These hairs are attached to sensory cells. The sensory cells turn the sound vibrations into neuronal impulses. The auditory nerve carries these impulses to the brain. This neuronal input goes to the hearing areas of the cerebral cortex of the brain.

auditory nerve the nerve that carries impulses from the inner ear to the brain, resulting in the perception of sound

DECIBEL LEVELS
The loudness of a sound (its amplitude) is measured in decibels. Each increase of 10 decibels makes a sound 10 times louder. A normal conversation at 3 feet measures about 60 decibels, which is 10,000 times louder than a whisper of 20 decibels. Sound becomes painful at 130 decibels.

▶ **CRITICAL THINKING**

1. *Analyzing Visuals* What is the measurement in decibels of a subway train?

2. *Comparing* How far from the threshold of severe pain is water at the foot of Niagara Falls?

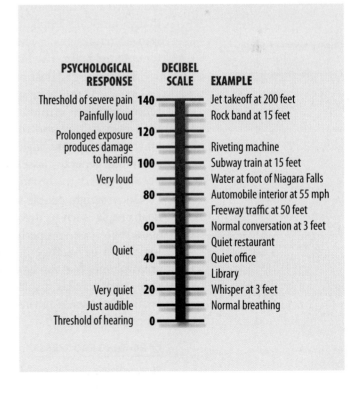

PSYCHOLOGICAL RESPONSE	DECIBEL SCALE	EXAMPLE
Threshold of severe pain	140	Jet takeoff at 200 feet
Painfully loud		Rock band at 15 feet
Prolonged exposure produces damage to hearing	120	Riveting machine
	100	Subway train at 15 feet
Very loud		Water at foot of Niagara Falls
	80	Automobile interior at 55 mph
		Freeway traffic at 50 feet
	60	Normal conversation at 3 feet
		Quiet restaurant
Quiet	40	Quiet office
		Library
Very quiet	20	Whisper at 3 feet
Just audible		Normal breathing
Threshold of hearing	0	

THE HUMAN EAR

The earflap funnels sound waves down the ear canal to the eardrum. The bones of the middle ear pick up the vibrations and transmit them to the inner ear.

▶ **CRITICAL THINKING**

1. *Making Connections* What is the function of the cochlea?

2. *Identifying Cause and Effect* How does the eardrum affect the cochlea?

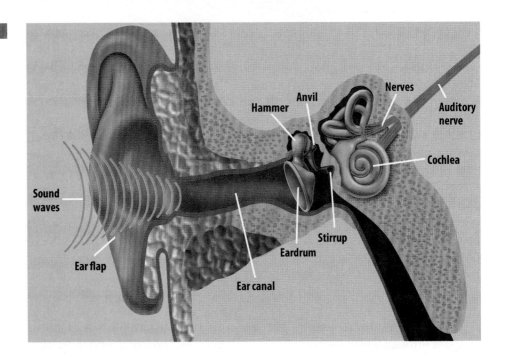

Deafness

There are two types of deafness. Conduction deafness occurs when anything hinders physical motion through the outer or middle ear or when the bones of the middle ear become rigid and cannot carry sounds inward. People with conduction deafness can usually be helped with a conventional hearing aid. A hearing aid picks up sound waves, changes them into magnified vibrations, and sends them to the inner ear.

Sensorineural deafness occurs from damage to the cochlea, the hair cells, or the auditory neurons. People with complete sensorineural deafness cannot be helped with a conventional hearing aid but may be helped with a special hearing aid called a cochlear implant. A cochlear implant is a miniature electronic device that is surgically implanted into the cochlea. The device changes sound waves into electrical signals. These signals are fed into the auditory nerve, which carries them to the brain. The brain then processes the sensory input.

The culture of deaf people has changed considerably over the last 200 years. In 1817 the first private schools for the deaf opened in the United States. In these schools children learned American Sign Language (ASL) and usually developed their own culture and society. Today, many deaf children go to public schools where they are provided with interpreters and special instruction along with attending general classes with their hearing classmates. This helps children become part of the broader culture at a younger age.

Increasingly, people with hearing disabilities are living independently. Many deaf people learn to drive, knowing that they must use visual clues in place of sound to respond properly to such things as emergency vehicles. The ever expanding use of technology has helped the hearing impaired integrate into society. Smartphones that can be used for e-mailing and texting, movie theaters that provide small screens displaying captions of dialogue, and handheld devices that translate spoken English into a video of sign language all make life easier and more pleasant.

☑ **READING PROGRESS CHECK**

Summarizing Briefly explain the different components of the ear and how they work together to produce hearing.

The Chemical Senses: Smell and Taste

GUIDING QUESTION *How do the senses of taste and smell work together?*

Smell and taste are called chemical senses because their receptors are sensitive to chemical molecules rather than to light energy or sound waves. Scientists call the sense of smell *olfaction* and the sense of taste *gustation*. Olfaction occurs when the appropriate gaseous molecules come into contact with your smell receptors in a special membrane in the upper part of your nasal passages. These receptors send messages about smells through the **olfactory nerve** to the brain. For you to taste something, appropriate liquid chemicals must stimulate receptors in the taste buds on your tongue. Taste information is relayed to the brain along with data about the texture and temperature of the substance in your mouth.

Studies show that four primary sensory experiences—sour, salty, bitter, and sweet—make up taste. The combining of taste, smell, and tactile sensations is known as *flavor*. Research suggests that a person can detect flavors anywhere on the tongue through the taste buds. Some people have greater taste sensitivities than others. So-called supertasters have two or more times the taste buds than nontasters, resulting in increased sensitivity to sweet, bitter, sour, and salty.

Much of what is referred to as taste is actually produced by the sense of smell. As people age, their sense of taste does not seem to decline. When older people complain that food does not taste as good as it once did, the reason usually is a loss of smell rather than a failing sense of taste. You have undoubtedly noticed that when your nose is blocked by a cold, foods usually taste bland.

Sensations of warmth, cold, and pressure also affect taste. Try to imagine eating cold chicken soup or drinking a hot soda. Now imagine the textural differences between a spoonful of pudding and a crunchy chocolate bar, and you will see how the texture and temperature of food influence taste.

The chemical senses of taste and smell give humans a great deal of pleasure. Walking into our favorite restaurant or smelling freshly washed clothes can offer us a sense of comfort. However, taste and smell seem less important to humans than to lower animals. For animals, taste and smell can be vital to survival. Insects often depend on smell to communicate with one another and to locate food. Taste and smell help animals recognize foods that are safe to eat. Wolves can smell prey up to 1.5 miles away, especially if the wind is blowing toward them. Rabbits have an extraordinary sense of smell. While humans have 40 million smell receptor cells, a rabbit has over a billion.

✔ **READING PROGRESS CHECK**

Contrasting How are the receptors used for smell and taste different from the receptors used for vision and hearing?

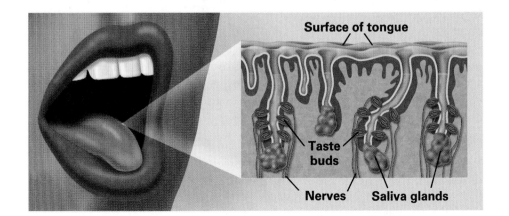

Surface of tongue

Taste buds

Nerves   Saliva glands

Orange Juice and Toothpaste

Have you ever brushed your teeth and then had orange juice for breakfast? How did the orange juice taste? Usually the orange juice will taste bitter. Our taste buds have membranes that contain fatlike phospholipids, while toothpastes contain a detergent that breaks down fat and grease. So the toothpaste first assaults the membranes with its detergents, leaving them raw. Then chemicals in the toothpaste, such as formaldehyde, chalk, and saccharin, cause a sour taste when they mix with the citric and ascorbic acids of orange juice. Try eating artichokes, then drinking water. What does the water taste like?

olfactory nerve the nerve that carries smell impulses from the nose to the brain

‹ DIAGRAM

THE HUMAN TONGUE
When you chew, chemicals of the food mix with saliva and run down into trenches in your tongue. Once there, taste buds react to chemicals dissolved in saliva.

▶ **CRITICAL THINKING**

1. *Making Connections* How does saliva help our sense of taste function?

2. *Speculating* Why do you think the taste buds are in trenches?

Balance and the Skin and Body Senses

GUIDING QUESTION *What purpose does pain serve?*

The term **somesthesis** is used when referring to the group of senses that includes balance, touch, and body positioning. These sensory receptors allow us to experience sensations such as dizziness and pain and to maintain a sense of how our bodies are positioned in relationship to our environment.

Balance

The body's sense of balance is regulated by the **vestibular system** inside the inner ear. Its prominent feature is the three *semicircular canals*. Hair cells project into the fluid within each of the canals. When you turn your head, these canals also move. Inertia causes the fluid in the canals to resist changes in motion, which bends receptor hair cells projecting into the fluid.

The stimuli for vestibular responses include movements such as spinning, falling, and tilting the body or head. Overstimulation of the vestibular sense by such movements can result in dizziness and motion sickness, as you probably have experienced by going on amusement-park rides. Although you are seldom directly aware of your sense of balance, in its absence you would be unable to stand or walk without stumbling or falling.

The Skin Senses

Receptors in the skin are responsible for providing the brain with at least four kinds of information about the environment: pressure, warmth, cold, and pain. Sensitivity to pressure varies from place to place in the skin. Some spots, such as your fingertips, are densely populated with receptors and are, therefore, highly sensitive. Other spots, such as the middle of your back or the back of your calf, contain relatively few receptors. Pressure sensations can serve as protection. For example, feeling the light pressure of an insect landing on your arm warns you of the danger of being stung.

Some skin receptors are particularly sensitive to hot or cold stimuli. To create a hot or cold sensation, a stimulus must have a temperature greater or less than the temperature of the skin in the sensing area. If you plunge your arm into a sink of warm water on a hot day, you will experience little or no sensation of its heat. If you put your arm in the same water on a cold day, however, the water will feel quite warm.

Many kinds of stimuli—scratches, punctures, pressure, heat, and cold—can produce pain. What they have in common is real or potential injury to bodily tissues. Pain makes it possible for you to prevent damage to your body; it is an emergency system that through your prior experience with pain demands immediate action.

Perceptions of Pain

Whereas other senses rely primarily on a single stimulus, pain results from many different stimuli. For example, intense pressure, bright lights, loud noises, intense heat, and so on can cause pain. There are two types of pain sensations—the sharp, localized pain you may feel immediately after an injury and the dull, generalized

A good vestibular system helps us navigate a three-dimensional world.

▶ **CRITICAL THINKING**

Analyzing How does the body react if the vestibular system is overstimulated?

somesthesis the group of senses that includes balance, touch, and body positioning

vestibular system three semicircular canals that provide the sense of balance, located in the inner ear and connected to the brain by a nerve

pain you may feel later. When you hit your thumb with a hammer, the pain is acute. Such pain has a clear source and lasts a short time. Chronic pain often lasts for months or years. Its source is not always easily recognized. For example, a person may suffer chronic back pain though no specific injury has occurred.

Have you ever stubbed your toe and then rubbed it to reduce the pain? According to the *gate control theory of pain*, we can lessen some pains by shifting our attention away from the pain. This creates a sort of competition between nonpain and pain impulses. A bottleneck, or gate, limits the number of impulses that can be transmitted. Thus, by increasing nonpainful impulses (rubbing your toe), you decrease the pain impulses, and the sensation of pain is dulled.

The gate control theory of pain could explain how athletes are able to complete a game even though they have injured themselves. Although a soccer player may know that she has bruised her side, she may not feel the pain fully until the game is over and she has calmed down, so the pain draws greater attention.

The Body Senses

The sense of movement and body position is **kinesthesis**. It cooperates with the vestibular and visual senses to maintain posture and balance. The sensation of kinesthesis comes from receptors in and near the muscles, tendons, and joints. When any movement occurs, these receptors immediately send messages to the brain. Without kinesthetic sensations being transmitted by the receptors, your movements would be jerky and uncoordinated. You could not walk without looking at your feet and complex physical activities, such as conducting surgery, piano playing, and acrobatics, would be impossible.

kinesthesis the sense of movement and body position

Because we rely so heavily on our senses, it is vital to do everything possible to keep them working properly. For example, wearing sunglasses when you are outdoors reduces the risk of macular degeneration. Annual eye exams are also an important way of protecting vision. These exams can detect vision problems such as nearsightedness. If not corrected, these problems can make it difficult for students to do well in school. Other conditions, such as diabetes and glaucoma, can also be detected during an eye exam. Wearing eye protection when playing sports such as racquetball is vital. Similarly, ear plugs or ear muffs should be worn when exposing the ears to loud noises like rock music or industrial equipment. Keeping our bodies, especially our brains, healthy by eating a well-balanced diet, exercising, and avoiding risky behaviors such as drug abuse improves the functioning of our senses.

☑ **READING PROGRESS CHECK**

Analyzing How does kinesthesis help when you are jogging or playing basketball?

LESSON 2 REVIEW

Reviewing Vocabulary
1. *Explaining* How do binocular fusion and retinal disparity help us observe our surroundings?

Using Your Notes
2. *Sequencing* Review the notes that you completed and choose one of the senses discussed in this lesson. In correct sequence, explain the purpose of each body part associated with that sense.

Answering the Guiding Questions
3. *Summarizing* How do people see color?

4. *Describing* How do people hear sound?

5. *Making Connections* How do the senses of taste and smell work together?

6. *Drawing Conclusions* What purpose does pain serve?

Writing Activity
7. *Informative/Explanatory* Imagine that you are walking up an uneven hill and suddenly start to lose your balance. Write an explanation of how your vision, vestibular senses, and kinesthesis could work together to keep you from falling.

acute: severe

indolence: laziness or sloth

retina: the sensory membrane that lines the eye and functions as the instrument of vision

cataract: a clouding of the lens of the eye

incessant: continuing without interruption

coherence: being unified or understandable

agnostic: loss of ability to recognize familiar objects

To See
and Not See
by Oliver Sacks

PRIMARY SOURCE

Virgil (nearly all the names in this account have been changed, and some identifying details have been disguised) was born on a small farm in Kentucky soon after the outbreak of the Second World War. He seemed normal enough as a baby, but (his mother thought) had poor eyesight even as a toddler, sometimes bumping into things, seemed not to see them. At the age of three, he became gravely ill with a triple illness—a meningitis or meningoencephalitis (inflammation of the brain and its membranes), polio, and cat-scratch fever. During this **acute** illness, he had convulsions, became virtually blind, paralyzed in the legs, partly paralyzed in his breathing, and, after ten days, fell into a coma. He remained in a coma for two weeks. When he emerged from it, he seemed, according to his mother, "a different person" and "sort of dull inside"; he showed a curious **indolence**, nonchalance, passivity, seemed nothing at all like the spunky, mischievous boy he had been.

How do we recognize an object we are seeing? The experience of Virgil, a 55-year-old man who regained his sight after being blind, raises questions about seeing and perception. Oliver Sacks, a physician, is known for writing case histories of neurological experiences. This account appeared in *The New Yorker* on May 10, 1993.

The strength in his legs came back over the next year, and his chest grew stronger, though never, perhaps, entirely normal. His vision also recovered significantly—but his **retinas** were now gravely damaged. Whether the retinal damage was caused wholly by his acute illness or perhaps partly by a congenital retinal degeneration was never clear.

In Virgil's sixth year, **cataracts** began to develop in both eyes, and it was evident that he was becoming functionally blind. That same year, he was sent to a school for the blind, and there he eventually learned to read Braille and to become adept with the use of a cane....

Virgil graduated from the school, and when he was twenty, decided to leave Kentucky, to seek training, work, and a life of his own in a city in Oklahoma. He trained as a massage therapist, and soon found employment at a Y.M.C.A. He was obviously good at his job, and highly esteemed, and the Y was happy to keep him on its permanent staff and to provide a small house for him across the road, where he lived with a friend, also employed at the Y. Virgil had many clients—it is fascinating to hear the tactile detail with which he can describe them—and seemed to take a real pleasure and pride in his job.... Life was limited, but stable in its way.

Then, in 1991, he met Amy.... [Amy] saw Virgil stuck (as she perceived it) in a vegetative, dull life.... Restoring his sight [through surgery], she must have felt, would, like marriage, stir him from his indolent

Steve Hamblin/Alamy

senses, and correlating these, one with the other, create a sight world from the start, a world of visual objects and concepts and meanings. When we open our eyes each morning, it is upon a world we have spent a lifetime learning to see. We are not given the world: we make our world through **incessant** experience, categorization, memory, reconnection. But when Virgil opened his eye, after being blind for forty-five years—having had little more than an infant's visual experience, and this long forgotten—there were no visual memories to support a perception, there was no world of experience and meaning awaiting him. He saw, but what he saw had no **coherence**. His retina and optic nerve were active, transmitting impulses, but his brain could make no sense of them; he was, as neurologists say, **agnostic**.

"There was light, there was movement, there was color, all mixed up, all meaningless, a blur."

Everyone, Virgil included, expected something simpler. A man opens his eyes, light enters, and falls on the retina: he sees. It is as simple as that, we imagine. And the surgeon's own experience, like that of most ophthalmologists, had been with the removal of cataracts from patients who had almost always lost their sight late in life—and such patients do indeed, if the surgery is successful, have a virtually immediate recovery of normal vision, for they have in no sense lost their ability to see. And so, though there had been a careful surgical discussion of the operation and of possible postsurgical complications, there was little discussion or preparation for the neurological and psychological difficulties that Virgil might encounter….

On the day he returned home after the bandages were removed, his house and its contents were unintelligible to him, and he had to be led up the garden path, led through the house, led into each room, and introduced to each chair.

bachelor existence and provide them both with a new life…. Virgil himself showed no preference in the matter; he seemed happy to go along with whatever they decided.

Finally, in mid-September, the day of the surgery came. Virgil's right eye had its cataract removed, and a new lens implant was inserted; then the eye was bandaged, as is customary, for twenty-four hours of recovery. The following day, the bandage was removed, and Virgil's eye was finally exposed, without cover, to the world. The moment of truth had come.

Or had it? The truth of the matter (as I pieced it together later), if less "miraculous" than Amy's journal suggested, was infinitely stranger. The dramatic moment stayed vacant, grew longer, sagged. No cry ("I can see!") burst from Virgil's lips. He seemed to be staring blankly, bewildered, without focusing, at the surgeon, who stood before him, still holding the bandages. Only when the surgeon spoke—saying "Well?"— did a look of recognition cross Virgil's face.

Virgil told me later that in this first moment he had no idea what he was seeing. There was light, there was movement, there was color, all mixed up, all meaningless, a blur. Then out of the blur came a voice that said, "Well?" Then, and only then, he said, did he finally realize that this chaos of light and shadow was a face—and, indeed, the face of his surgeon….

The rest of us, born sighted, can scarcely imagine such confusion. For we, born with a full complement of

Analyzing Primary Sources

1. *Identifying* How did Virgil become blind?

2. *Drawing Conclusions* Why didn't Virgil realize what he was seeing after his sight was regained?

3. *Analyzing Primary Sources* What psychological difficulties do you think Virgil encountered after regaining his sight?

netw⊚rks

There's More Online!

- ☑ **DIAGRAM** Gestalt Principles
- ☑ **DIAGRAM** Lines of Different Lengths?
- ☑ **DIAGRAM** The Necker Cube
- ☑ **DIAGRAM** Shape Constancy
- ☑ **DIAGRAM** What Is It?
- ☑ **IMAGE** Illusions of Height
- ☑ **SELF-CHECK QUIZ**

Reading **HELP**DESK (CCSS)

Academic Vocabulary

- overlap
- distort

Content Vocabulary

- Gestalt
- subliminal messages
- motion parallax
- constancy
- extrasensory perception (ESP)

TAKING NOTES:

Integration of Knowledge and Ideas

ACTIVITY For each of these Gestalt principles, describe its effect on perception.

Principle	→	Effect
Proximity	→	
Similarity	→	
Closure	→	
Continuity	→	

LESSON 3
Perception

ESSENTIAL QUESTION • *How does the mind react to changes?*

IT MATTERS BECAUSE

Recognizing how our senses function lets us understand the ways we interact with our environment. How we interpret sensory input helps us grasp why perceptions of the same event can vary widely. For example, two people involved in a car accident may perceive the event very differently. Psychologists study perception to learn more about how we analyze the external stimuli that are constantly flooding our brains.

Principles of Perceptual Organization

GUIDING QUESTION *How do the Gestalt principles of organization help explain perception?*

PRIMARY SOURCE

" *The frog's bug detector shows the rigidity of reflexive behavior. If you sever the frog's optic nerve, it will grow back together, and the bug detector will still work fine. If you sever the optic nerve and then rotate the frog's eye 180 degrees, the nerve will still heal and reestablish all the old connections; however, this time the results will not be so good. The bug detector does not know that everything has been rotated, so it miscomputes a bug's location. If the bug is high, the frog shoots its tongue low. If the bug is to the right, the tongue goes to the left. The frog never learns to compensate for the changed situation.* "

— *Edmund Blair Bolles,* A Second Way of Knowing: The Riddle of Human Perception *(1991)*

This excerpt shows how useful our powers of perception are. Perception goes beyond reflexive behavior—it allows us to confront changes in our environment. Perceptual thinking lets us adapt to change. People do not usually experience a mass of colors, noises, temperatures, and pressures. Rather, we see clearly defined cars and buildings, hear distinct voices and clear music, and feel thin pencils, wooden desks, and the warmth of physical contact.

We do not merely have sensory experiences; we perceive objects. The brain receives information from the senses and organizes and interprets it into meaningful experiences. This process is called *perception*. All of this happens unconsciously. From birth the majority of us receive sensations from the world around us involuntarily.

Gestalt Principles

Through the process of perception, the brain tries to comprehend the confusing environmental stimuli that bombard the senses. The brain makes sense of the world by creating structures out of bits of information. Each whole structure that is organized by the brain is called a **Gestalt**. Here, the whole is more than the sum of the parts. (*Gestalt* is a German word meaning "pattern" or "configuration.")

Gestalt psychologists have tried to identify the principles the brain uses in constructing perceptions. For example, we tend to see dots in patterns and groups. Principles that people use in organizing such patterns are *proximity, similarity, continuity, simplicity,* and *closure.* If the pattern's elements are close to one another or similar in appearance, they tend to be perceived as belonging to one another.

The Gestalt principles of organization help explain how we group our sensations and fill in gaps to make sense of our world. In music, for instance, you tend to hear notes occurring at the same time not as clusters of notes, but as chords—you hear melodies, not single notes. Similarity and continuity allow you to follow the sound of a particular voice or instrument even when many other sounds are occurring. Closure aids us in perceiving an object even though there may be gaps in what our senses pick up. The rule of simplicity states that we tend to perceive complex figures as divided into several simpler figures.

Figure-Ground Perception

One form of perceptual organization is the division of experience into figure and ground. Figure-ground perception is the ability to discriminate properly between a figure and its background. When you look at a three-dimensional object against the sky, you have no trouble distinguishing between the object and its background. Objects become the figure and stand out from the background. It is when something is two-dimensional that you may have trouble telling the figure from the ground. Nevertheless, such figure-ground perceptions give clues as to the nature of perception. That we can perceive a single pattern in more than one way demonstrates that we are not passive receivers of stimuli.

Figure and ground are important in hearing as well as in vision. When you follow one person's voice at a noisy meeting, that voice is a figure and all other sounds become ground. Similarly, when you listen to a piece of music, a familiar theme may leap out at you: the melody becomes the figure, and the rest of the music merely background.

Gestalt the experience that comes from organizing bits and pieces of information into meaningful wholes

GESTALT PRINCIPLES

PROXIMITY
When we see a number of similar objects, we tend to perceive them as groups or sets of those that are close to each other.

●● ●● ●● ●● ●● ●● ●●
[ab cd ef gh ij kl mn]

SIMILARITY
When similar and dissimilar objects are mingled, we see the similar objects as groups.

○○●●○○●●○○●●○○●●

CLOSURE
When we see a familiar pattern or shape with some missing parts, we fill in the gaps.

CONTINUITY
We tend to see continuous patterns, not disrupted ones.

B
C
A
D

SIMPLICITY
We see the simplest shapes possible.

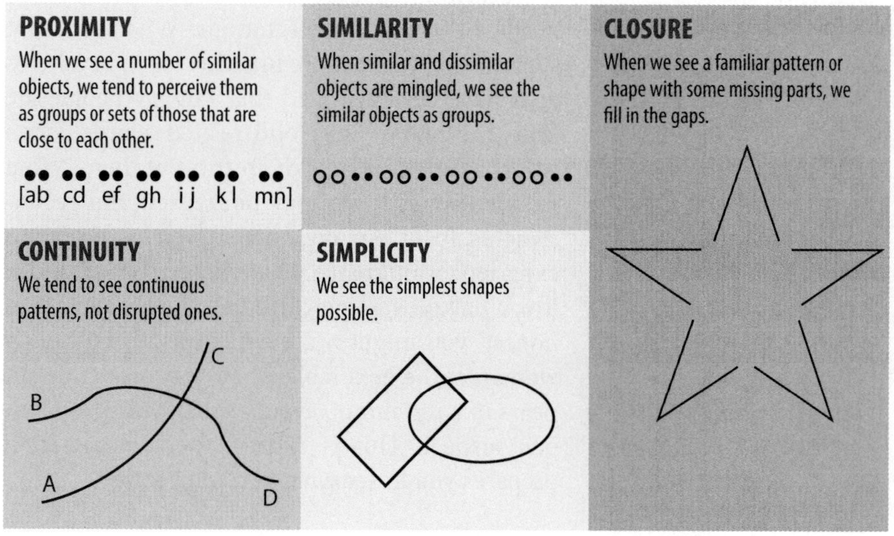

< DIAGRAM

GESTALT PRINCIPLES
Humans see patterns and groupings in their environment rather than disorganized arrays of bits and pieces.

▶ CRITICAL THINKING

1. *Analyzing* Why do we use the principles of organization illustrated here?

2. *Constructing Arguments* How is the principle of proximity used in the writing of textbooks such as this one?

Often we have perceptions that are not based entirely on current sensory information. When you hear barking as you approach your house, you assume it is your dog—not a cat or a rhinoceros or even another dog. When you take a seat in a dark theater, you assume it is solid and will hold your weight even though you cannot see what supports the seat. When you are driving in a car and see in the distance that the road climbs up a steep hill and then disappears over the top, you assume the road will continue over and down the hill, not come to an abrupt end just out of sight.

This phenomenon of filling in the gaps in what our senses tell us is known as *perceptual inference*. Perceptual inference is largely automatic and unconscious. We need only a few cues to inform us that a noise is our dog barking or that a seat is solid. Why? Because we have encountered these stimuli and objects in the past and know what to expect from them in the present. Perceptual inference, thus, often depends on experience. On the other hand, we are probably born with some of our ability to make perceptual inferences.

✔ READING PROGRESS CHECK

Making Connections Why are the Gestalt principles called "principles of perceptual organization"?

Learning to Perceive

GUIDING QUESTION *Why do wants and needs influence our perception?*

In large part, perceiving is something that people *learn* to do. For example, infants under one month will smile at a nodding object the size of a human face, whether or not it has eyes, a nose, or other human features. At about 20 weeks, however, a blank oval will not make most infants smile, but a drawing of a face will. The infant has learned to distinguish something that looks like a person from other objects. Infants 28 weeks and older are more likely to smile at a female than a male face. By 30 weeks, most infants smile more readily when they see a familiar face than when they see someone they do not know. It takes, however, 7 or 8 months for infants to learn to recognize different people.

Experiments with humans have also shown that active involvement in one's environment is important for accurate perception. People who have been blind from birth and have their sight restored by an operation have visual sensations, but initially they cannot tell the difference between a square and a circle or see that a red cube is like a blue cube. These visual associations must be learned.

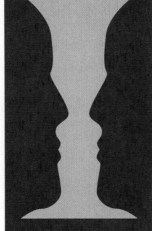

Learning to perceive is influenced by our needs, beliefs, and expectations. When we want something, we are more likely to see it. Psychologists have demonstrated that hungry people are faster at identifying food-related words when words are flashed quickly in front of them. What we identify as truth may be twisted and reconstructed to fit our own belief systems. Previous experiences influence what we see. For example, if you have always perceived all elderly women as honest, you might not even question the elderly woman at the next table when your wallet disappears in a restaurant, even if she is the most obvious suspect. This is called a perceptual set. It prepares you to see what you want to see.

Subliminal Advertising

In his 1957 book *The Hidden Persuaders,* Vance Packard divulged that advertisers were using a breakthrough in marketing techniques—subliminal advertising. The word *subliminal* comes from the Latin: *sub* ("below") and *limen* (threshold). This concept used **subliminal messages**, which are brief auditory or visual messages presented below the absolute threshold so that there is less than a 50 percent chance that they will be perceived.

One advertiser, James Vicary, falsely claimed that the words "Eat Popcorn" and "Drink Coke" had been flashed on a movie screen in a New Jersey theater on alternate nights for six weeks. According to Vicary, the flashes were very brief. Each image would appear for only 1/3000 of a second, and the images would appear once every five seconds. As the images appeared so briefly none of the moviegoers would have been able to notice them. Vicary claimed that sales during the experiment surprised even him, with popcorn sales rising 58 percent and Coke sales rising 18 percent.

The public response to Vicary's experiment was long, loud, and hysterical. Congressional representatives called for FCC regulations on subliminal advertisements, while several state legislatures passed laws banning them. Eventually, Vicary admitted that the data from the movie theater experiment were false. Despite this admission public furor over the potential for abuse of subliminal advertising remained strong. In 1974 the FCC went so far as to condemn subliminal advertising.

Subliminal Perception

The idea for subliminal ads was an outgrowth of a series of controversial studies on *subliminal perception*—the ability to notice stimuli that affect only the unconscious mind. Most of these earlier studies involved presenting verbal or visual material at intensities that were considered too low to be perceived. A more critical look at the studies revealed flaws. For the Coke and popcorn example, no attempt was made to assess or control factors that might have influenced the purchase of Coke or popcorn. For example, the temperature in the theater or the genre of movie that was being shown might have contributed to increased sales. Unfortunately, the study was not presented in enough detail to be evaluated by scientists.

Even if it is possible for people to perceive information at very low intensities, there is no clear evidence that these weak messages would be more influential than would conscious messages. Nevertheless, many people continue to believe that subliminal advertising is a very real and powerful thing.

✓ **READING PROGRESS CHECK**

Speculating What can influence the way we learn to perceive?

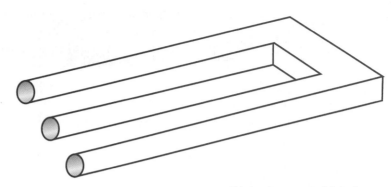

This drawing seems to defy basic geometric laws.

subliminal messages brief auditory or visual messages that are presented below the absolute threshold

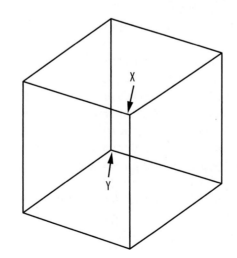

‹ DIAGRAM

THE NECKER CUBE
The Necker cube is an ambiguous figure. You can will yourself to see it as if you were looking down on it, with corner X closest to you, or as if you were looking up at it, with corner Y closest to you.

▶ **CRITICAL THINKING**

1. ***Making Predictions*** How might you make this cube less ambiguous by adding details?

2. ***Making Comparisons*** How is the Necker cube similar to the Pop-Out Features image?

ADAPTING THE ENVIRONMENT

Imagine that you lost one of your senses, such as hearing. How would you adapt to your environment so that you could continue to function independently? Some who suffer from hearing loss use specially trained dogs called hearing-ear dogs to help them adjust. Much like seeing-eye dogs who help the blind, hearing-ear dogs can help those suffering from hearing loss better navigate their surroundings, from helping them hear normal sounds like bells or alarms, to helping them navigate busy streets. Without full access to our senses, local geography can become dangerous. Hearing-ear dogs help those who have lost access to certain senses continue to live independently and safely.

▶ **CRITICAL THINKING**

1. *Drawing Conclusions* If you were to lose your sight what changes do you think you would need to make in your home to maintain your normal behaviors?

2. *Gathering Information* Conduct research on the Internet to learn more about how people with sensory deficiencies adapt their environments to meet their needs. Create a presentation to share your findings with your class.

▲ The hearing-ear dog seen here is learning to respond to a doorbell.

Types of Perception

GUIDING QUESTIONS *How do monocular and binocular depth cues differ?*

How we navigate the world depends on not only what we see but also how we interpret what we are seeing. Remember that the process of learning to perceive is influenced by our needs, beliefs, and expectations. We gradually acquire different ways to interpret the world around us, and different ways to interpret perceptual cues. This includes those moments when our perceptual cues might be distorted or illusory.

Depth Perception

Depth perception—the ability to recognize distances and three dimensionality—develops in infancy. Psychologists have placed infants on large tables and found that they are unlikely to crawl over the edge. From this observation, it is possible to infer that infants have depth perception.

People use many monocular depth cues to perceive distance and depth. *Monocular depth cues* are cues that can be used with a single eye. In the absence of any other cues, the size of an object—bigger is nearer—will be used. We use *relative height*—objects that appear farther away from another object are higher on your plane of view. When looking down a stretch of highway, the parallel lines appear to converge, providing a sense of distance. *Interposition*, or the **overlapping** of images, causes us to view the object we can see in its entirety to be closer than one whose outline is interrupted by another object. *Light and shadows* yield information about an object's shape and size. Brightly lit objects appear closer. *Texture-density gradient* means that the farther removed an object is, the less detail we can identify on that object.

QQQQQQQQ
QQQQQPQQ
QQOQQQQQ
QQQQQQQQ

DIAGRAM ∧

POP-OUT FEATURES

Reality is a jumble of sensations and details. The letter *P* probably pops out to you. The *Q*s may also pop out, but not as much as the *P*. You may not have noticed the *O*.

▶ **CRITICAL THINKING**

1. *Analyzing Visuals* Why does the *P* pop out?

2. *Problem-Solving* Why changes might you make to this image to make the *O* pop out?

Hans Gutknecht/ZUMA Press/Corbis

Another cue is **motion parallax**—the apparent movement of objects that occurs when you move your head from side to side or walk around. You can demonstrate motion parallax by looking at two objects in the same line of vision, one near you and the other some distance away. If you move your head back and forth, the near object will seem to move more than the far object. Motion parallax gives clues as to which objects are closer than others.

Linear perspective is based on the fact that parallel lines converge when stretched into the distance. When you look at a long stretch of road, it appears that the sides of the road converge on the horizon. A final related cue is *relative motion*. When you are riding in a car and look at distant hills, the objects in a nearby field seem to be moving in the opposite direction to your movement. Yet, when you look at an animal in a nearby field, the hills beyond the animal seem to be moving in the same direction you are.

Binocular depth cues depend upon the existence or movement of both eyes. For example, *convergence* is the process by which your eyes turn inward to look at nearby objects. Another cue is the information provided by retinal disparity, as discussed earlier in the chapter. Because each of your eyes occupies a different position, each eye receives a slightly different image. That difference is *retinal disparity*. The brain interprets a large retinal disparity to mean a close object and a small retinal disparity to mean a distant object.

Constancy

When we have learned to perceive certain objects in our environment, we tend to see them in the same way, regardless of changing conditions. You probably judge the whiteness of pages in a book you are reading to be fairly constant, even though it is likely that you have read the book under a wide range of lighting conditions. The light, angle of vision, distance, and, therefore, the image on the retina all change, but your perception of the object does not. Thus, despite changing physical conditions, people are able to perceive objects as the same by the processes of size, shape, brightness and color **constancy**.

An example of size constancy will illustrate how we have an automatic system for perceiving an object as being the same size whether it is far or near. A friend walking toward you does not seem to change into a giant even though the images inside your eyes become larger as she approaches. Her appearance stays the same size because even though the size of your visual image is increasing, you are

overlap to extend over and cover part of something else

motion parallax the apparent movement of stationary objects relative to one another that occurs when the observer changes position

constancy the tendency to perceive certain objects in the same way regardless of changing angle, distance, or lighting

ᐯ DIAGRAM

SHAPE CONSTANCY
We perceive the opening door as being rectangular in shape, although our view of the shape of it changes as it opens.

▶ **CRITICAL THINKING**

1. *Analyzing* Why are perceptual constancies important to our understanding of the world?

2. *Analyzing Visuals* Why is the outer edge of the third door from the left larger than the inner edge?

perceiving that distance is decreasing. The enlarging eye image and the distance information combine to produce a perception of an approaching object that stays the same size.

If information about distance is eliminated, your perception of the size of the object begins to correspond to the actual size of the eye image. For example, it is difficult for most people to estimate the size of an airplane in the sky. Pilots, however, can determine whether a flying plane is large and far away or small and close because they are experienced in estimating the sizes and distances of planes.

Through the wide middle range of brightness, and in a mix of many colors, reds are perceived as red, greens as green—color constancy. Similarly, across a wide range of light, from dawn's early light to dusk's fading light, the brightest shirt in a crowd will always be perceived the brightest—brightness constancy. With brightest light, colors fade to white; at dusk, they fade to gray or black.

Illusions

Illusions are incorrect perceptions. Illusions can be useful in teaching us how our sensory and perceptual systems work. Illusions are created when perceptual cues are **distorted** so that our brains cannot correctly interpret space, size, and depth cues. For example, look at the Lines of Different Lengths? diagram. Which lines in each set are longer? Measure the lengths of the pairs of lines with a ruler, then look again. Do the lines look as long now that you know they are the same? For most people, the answer is no.

A possible explanation of this type of illusion is that even though the patterns are two-dimensional, your brain treats them as three-dimensional. The top line in (A), for example, can be thought of as the far corner of a room; the bottom line is like the near corner. In (B) and (C), the converging lines create the illusion of distance so that the lower bar looks nearer and shorter than the upper bar.

Extrasensory Perception

Humanity is often fascinated by things that cannot be seen, easily explained, or even verified. **Extrasensory perception (ESP)**—receiving information about the world through channels other than the normal senses—is a hotly debated topic. Some people claim to have one or more of the four types of ESP. These include: (1) clairvoyance, or the perceiving of objects or information without any sensory input; (2) telepathy, or the reading someone else's mind or transferring thoughts;

---

distort to twist out of true meaning or proportion

extrasensory perception (ESP) an ability to gain information by some means other than the ordinary senses

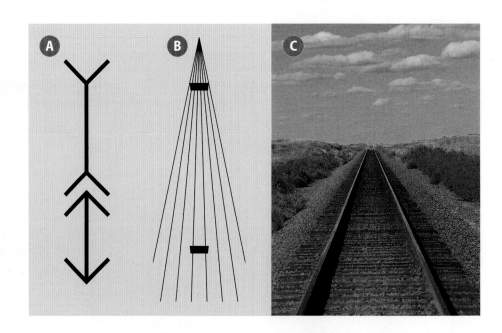

Stockdisc/Digital Vision

(3) psychokinesis, which involves moving objects through mental effort alone; and (4) precognition, also known as "fortune telling", or the ability to foretell events.

Many people are convinced that ESP exists because of an intense personal experience that cannot be scientifically validated. For instance, we may imagine the worst before travelling: our plane will crash or we will have a car accident. These events almost never happen, and we forget about our frightening premonitions. If the improbable should actually take place, however, our premonitions turn into compelling evidence for the existence of precognition. If we truly want to validate the existence of ESP, though, we must keep track of the frequency of its failures as well as its successes.

Scientists have been investigating ESP since the 1900s. (J.B. Rhine may remain the best known parapsychologist.) Many scientists do not accept the results of experiments supporting ESP because the findings are highly unstable. ESP experiments yield contradictory findings. Perhaps the most telling argument against ESP is that when strict controls are used in an experiment, there is little likelihood of demonstrating ESP. This is contrary to what one expects when trying to demonstrate a phenomenon using scientific methods.

Over the years, James Randi, who began his career as a magician known as "The Amazing Randi" has exposed as frauds many people who claim to have one or more of these types of ESP. After retiring as a magician at the age of 60 he began investigating claims into ESP and the paranormal. In 1996 he founded the James Randi Educational Foundation which serves to educate the public and the media on the dangers of accepting unproven claims or proof of ESP and the paranormal.

The two individuals appear to be the same height. In reality, however, the ceiling and the walls are slanted so that the back wall is both shorter and closer on the right than on the left.

▶ **CRITICAL THINKING**

Making Judgments What do you think makes this illusion work?

☑ **READING PROGRESS CHECK**

Describing What is the strongest argument against ESP?

LESSON 3 REVIEW

Reviewing Vocabulary
1. *Comparing* How is motion parallax related to constancy?

Using Your Notes
2. *Categorizing* Review the notes that you completed during this lesson to give examples of situations in which you might apply each of these Gestalt principles: proximity, similarity, closure, and continuity.

Answering the Guiding Questions
3. *Finding the Main Idea* How do the Gestalt principles of organization help explain perception?

4. *Analyzing Cause and Effect* Why do wants and needs influence our perception?

5. *Contrasting* How do monocular and binocular depth cues differ?

Writing Activity
6. *Informative/Explanatory* Consider the following question: You have suddenly lost all perceptual constancies—what specific problems do you encounter? Write a scene in the form of a play, narrative, or newspaper article that illustrates a problem you might encounter.

on research

Case Study

Seeing Is Believing

Period of Study: Late 1950s and early 1960s

Introduction: In the late 1950s and early 1960s, an anthropologist, C.M. Turnbull, traveled to the Ituri Forest in the present-day country of the Democratic Republic of the Congo (formerly Zaire) to study the life and culture of the BaMbuti Pygmies. Turnbull traveled from one village to another. A 22-year-old man named Kenge from a local Pygmy village accompanied and assisted him. Kenge had spent all of his life living in the dense forests surrounding his village.

PRIMARY SOURCE

❝*As we turned to get back in the car, Kenge looked over the plains and down to where a herd of about a hundred buffalo were grazing some miles away. He asked me what kind of insects they were, and I told him they were buffalo, twice as big as the forest buffalo known to him. He laughed loudly and told me not to tell such stupid stories...*

We got into the car and drove down to where the animals were grazing. He watched them getting larger and larger, and though he was as courageous as any Pygmy, he moved over and sat close to me and muttered that it was witchcraft...Finally when he realized that they were real buffalo he was no longer afraid, but what puzzled him still was why they had been so small, and whether they really had been small and had suddenly grown larger, or whether it had been some kind of trickery.❞

—Colin M. Turnbull, *"Some Observations Regarding the Experiences and Behavior of the BaMbuti Pygmies,"* American Journal of Psychology, *74, 304-308, (1961)*

Hypothesis: Because Kenge had been isolated by the forests all of his life, the sight of new images would appear complex and confusing. The thick forests blocked the local villagers' view of distant objects such as animals, mountains, and the sun and moon on the horizon. Because Kenge had never seen these things, his perceptual development (in this case, *size constancy*, or the ability to perceive a familiar object as being the same size regardless of its distance from you) was limited. He understood only what he could see directly in front of him. The information collected from Turnbull's experience with Kenge raised the question of whether perceptual understanding is a learned ability or biological mechanism: a question of nature versus nurture.

Method: The discovery of Kenge's perceptual limitations took place when Turnbull and Kenge came to a clearing on the eastern edge of the Ituri Forest. At that point Kenge and Turnbull enjoyed a clear view of the Ruwenzori Mountains. Confused by the sight of the mountains, Kenge asked Turnbull if the mountains were hills or clouds. Turnbull explained that they were hills but much larger than any Kenge had seen before. Kenge agreed to ride with Turnbull to the mountains for further inspection. A passing thunderstorm obstructed the travelers' view and did not clear until the two reached the mountains. When Kenge peered up at the enormous mountain range, he was amazed.

Results: Turnbull's accounts support the idea that human perception develops (at least in the case of size constancy) as we use the environment around us, or by nurture. However, some research with infants supports the nature side of perception. For example, individuals who were blind at birth and later gained their sight were able to perceive figure-ground relationships. Are we born with certain perceptual abilities and not others, or is perception something we learn? For Kenge, perceptual ability was a learned phenomenon. Certain perceptual skills may be necessary for our survival. In Kenge's case, he did not need a wide range of size constancy to survive in the dense jungle.

Analyzing the Case Study

1. *Identifying Perspectives* What is Turnbull's opinion on how we learn size constancy?

2. *Analyzing Primary Sources* Do you think the quote from Turnbull's writing supports his hypothesis as stated in this case study? Give specific reasons for your answer.

3. *Making Predictions* Do you think that Kenge could adjust to life in your city or town? Explain the difficulties he might encounter.

Directions: On a separate sheet of paper, answer the questions below. Make sure you read carefully and answer all parts of the question.

Lesson Review

Lesson 1

1 *Exploring Issues* How does psychophysics help us understand the ways in which we interact with our surroundings?

2 *Diagramming* Create a diagram that illustrates the ideas behind Weber's Law.

Lesson 2

3 *Explaining* What is the electromagnetic spectrum and why do we see only a portion of it?

4 *Sequencing* Create a flow chart of how each part of the eye works together to transmit an image to the brain.

5 *Making Connections* What sensation do you experience when you close your eyes and gently press on one of your eyeballs at the outer edge? How can you explain the visual experience in the absence of light rays?

Lesson 3

6 *Applying* Give a specific example of how the Gestalt principle of closure helps us when viewing objects around us. When might closure create problems?

7 *Exploring Issues* One of the objections to the use of subliminal advertising techniques is that they could be used to manipulate or influence large numbers of people without their knowing it. Do you think this is an important objection? Why or why not?

8 *Explaining* How could relative height cues help you perceive distance in a desert?

Critical Thinking Questions

9 *Analyzing* How do the concepts of absolute threshold and difference threshold apply to sensation?

10 *Speculating* Why is sensory adaptation necessary for our survival?

11 *Drawing Conclusions* What are binocular and monocular depth cues? How do they help us judge reality?

12 *Summarizing* Conduct research to learn about several theories associated with hearing. These might include the frequency theory, volley theory, and place theory. Write a brief summary of each.

21st Century Skills

Interpreting Graphs Study the graph below. Then answer the questions that follow.

SKIN SENSITIVITY

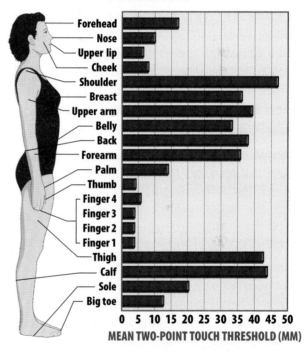

MEAN TWO-POINT TOUCH THRESHOLD (MM)

13 How do you explain that some parts of the body are more sensitive to touch than others?

14 Which three body parts are the least sensitive to touch?

15 How does the information in the graph help explain why people reading in Braille use their fingertips?

Need Extra Help?

If You've Missed Question	1	2	3	4	5	6	7	8	9	10	11	12	13	14	15
Go to page	205	207	212	211	218	223	225	226	206	207	212	215	218	218	218

Directions: On a separate sheet of paper, answer the questions below. Make sure you read carefully and answer all parts of the question.

DBQ Analyzing Primary Sources

Use the document below to answer the following questions.

PRIMARY SOURCE

Synesthesia, the condition in which the stimulation of one sense leads to consciously experiencing another sense, is of interest to researchers who are working to learn more about the interaction of sensory receptors and the brain.

❝*Simon Baron-Cohen, PhD, who studies synesthesia at the University of Cambridge, ... proposes that synesthesia results from a genetically driven overabundance of neural connections in the brain. Ordinarily, Baron-Cohen explains, different sensory functions are assigned to separate modules in the brain, with limited communication between them. In synesthesia, Baron-Cohen and his colleagues posit, the brain's architecture is different. Synesthetes' brains, they believe, are equipped with more connections between neurons, causing the usual modularity to break down and giving rise to synesthesia.*

Naropa University psychologist Peter Grossenbacher, PhD, believes that there's likely a genetic root to synesthesia, but Grossenbacher and his colleagues suspect a different brain mechanism. "We don't need to posit some abnormal architecture of connections in order to account for synesthesia," Grossenbacher argues. Instead, he proposes that in the brains of synesthetes, "feed-backward" connections that carry information from high-level multisensory areas of the brain back to single-sense areas are not properly inhibited (prevented.) Ordinarily, information processed in such multisensory areas is allowed to return only to its appropriate single-sense area. But in synesthetes' brains, Grossenbacher argues, that inhibition is disrupted somehow.❞

—Siri Carpenter, "Everyday Fantasia: The World of Synesthesia," *Monitor on Psychology*, March 2001

16 *Analyzing* What do psychologists hope to learn by studying synesthesia?

17 *Differentiating* How is Baron-Cohen's hypothesis different from that of Grossenbacher?

Exploring the Essential Questions

18 *Defending* Write an essay either supporting or opposing this statement: "The human mind is a passive recipient of stimuli." Use specific details from this chapter to support your position. In your essay, explain how the senses work with the mind in responding to stimuli and how the process of perception differs from that of sensation.

College and Career Readiness

19 *Problem Solving* Investigate how your community is helping those who have a specific sensory deficiency. For example, how do stoplights serve those who have color deficiencies? What about road signs, such as yield and directional signs? When you are done with your investigation, write a short report summarizing what you have learned.

Research and Technology

20 *Gathering Information* Conduct research on the Internet to determine how factors such as being vaccinated against diseases, a healthy diet, regular exercise, avoiding risky behaviors such as drug abuse, and protecting the ears against loud noises in the environment can lead to healthy sensory functioning throughout life. Create a presentation from your findings. In particular, characterize the major categories of psychoactive drugs and how they can affect the senses. Be sure to cover the effects of various drugs and toxins on the brain and neurotransmitters.

Psychology Journal Activity

21 *Informative/Explanatory* Review your entry in your Psychology Journal for this chapter. After learning key concepts in this chapter, including threshold, adaptation, and constancy of the senses, how would you change your journal entry? Explain why your initial ideas were or were not accurate.

Need Extra Help?

If You've Missed Question	**16**	**17**	**18**	**19**	**20**	**21**
Go to page	224	232	204	214	219	202

Learning: Principles and Applications

ESSENTIAL QUESTION • *How do our experiences change our behavior?*

Purestock/Getty Images

Psychology Matters...

How do people learn new things? Behavioral psychologists are applying their animal research results to further their understanding of human behavior. Behavioral psychologists recognize that humans learn with a purpose that animals do not have. Some psychologists focus their efforts on giving people resources to help them learn more effectively. This chapter will discuss the studies of behaviorists and their application to humans in general.

◀ Is learning a new skill a matter of simple conditioning? Or is there more to learning?

CHAPTER 9

Lab Activity

Sounds and Learning

THE QUESTION...

RESEARCH QUESTION Can you effect a preference for an image by creating an association between it and a sound?

There are many sounds we associate with either pleasant or unpleasant experiences. Think about an ice cream truck. It plays a song that lets every person, young and old, within earshot know a sweet frozen treat is just around the corner. Most come to associate the truck's song to ice cream, and ice cream is what they think of when they hear the song, even if it's not coming from the ice cream truck.

This is a type of learning that happens every day. Let's take a look at this in action by conducting an experiment in which we will attempt to effect the preferences of another person.

Psychology Journal Activity

Think about songs or sounds that trigger memories from your life. Write about this association in your Psychology Journal. Some things to consider as you write: Describe the occasion in which you learned this association. Why does that memory have an association with that song or sound? Does this sound or song produce an emotion as well?

FINDING THE ANSWER...

HYPOTHESIS Because pleasant sounds make people feel happy, people will prefer an image paired with a pleasant sound more than an image paired with an unpleasant sound.

THE METHOD OF YOUR EXPERIMENT

MATERIALS abstract images; mp3s or other sound files of pleasant sounds such as the ocean, light rainfall, or children's laughter, and unpleasant sounds such as an alarm, buzzer, or crash

PROCEDURE Using the Internet search engine of your choice, find at least four abstract images from the same artist or from a group of artists with a similar style. Ready your selected images for display by creating a digital or print slideshow. In a quiet room, present the images one at a time to your participant. As you show the first image, play one of your pleasant sound files. Then, switch to your second image and play one of your unpleasant sound files. Alternate pleasant and unpleasant sounds for the remainder of your images, using a different pleasant or unpleasant sound file for each image. Make certain both the pleasant and unpleasant sounds are played at the same volume.

DATA COLLECTION After you have presented all of the images to your participant, ask them which image is their favorite. Keep track of preferred images that are paired with a pleasant sound.

ANALYSIS & APPLICATION

1. Did your data support the hypothesis?

2. What conclusions can you draw about learning from this experiment?

3. How could you alter this experiment to test the hypothesis in a different way?

networks ONLINE LAB RESOURCES

Online you will find:

- An **interactive lab experience**, allowing you to put principles from this chapter into practice in a digital psychology lab environment. This chapter's lab will include an experiment allowing you to explore issues related to learning and to training animals.

- A **Skills Handbook** that includes a guide for using the scientific method, creating experiments, and analyzing data.
- A **Notebook** where you can complete your Psychology Journal and record and analyze data from your experiment.

LESSON 1

Classical Conditioning

Reading **HELP**DESK (CCSS)

Academic Vocabulary

- **process**
- **demonstrate**

Content Vocabulary

- **classical conditioning**
- **neutral stimulus**
- **unconditioned stimulus**
- **unconditioned response**
- **conditioned stimulus**
- **conditioned response**
- **generalization**
- **discrimination**
- **extinction**

TAKING NOTES:

Key Ideas and Details

SEQUENCING Use a graphic organizer like the one below to record the process of classical conditioning.

Classical Conditioning

ESSENTIAL QUESTION · *How do our experiences change our behavior?*

IT MATTERS BECAUSE

Have you ever heard the beginning of a catchy tune on a television commercial and found yourself singing along? The tune and the advertisement are so connected that you cannot hear the music without remembering the words. When you are shopping for the type of item advertised, the tune you remember will make that product feel familiar.

Pavlov's Dog

GUIDING QUESTION *What did Pavlov's discovery demonstrate?*

A memorable advertising jingle is an example of the way advertisers use psychological principles. Studies have shown that pairing a product with pleasant sensations, such as memorable music, motivates consumers to choose that product. Add a catchy jingle that carries the product's name and you may find yourself buying it without stopping to think.

This conscious or unconscious training of our behaviors is known as conditioning. Russian physiologist Ivan Pavlov was the first to document in great detail conditioning as we know it. Today, we call the types of conditioning documented by Pavlov classical conditioning. In **classical conditioning**, a person's or animal's old response to a prompt or stimulus becomes attached to a new prompt or stimulus. This can be done even if the second stimulus has little to no similarity to the first. Classical conditioning is an example of a relatively permanent change in a behavioral tendency that results from experience. This is one type of learning.

Pavlov's discovery of the principle of classical conditioning was accidental. Around the turn of the twentieth century, Pavlov had been studying the **process** of, or steps involved in, digestion. Pavlov wanted to understand how a dog's stomach prepares to digest food when something is placed in its mouth. Then he noticed that the mere sight or smell of food was enough to start a hungry dog salivating. Pavlov became fascinated with how the dog anticipated the food and how salivation occurred before the food was presented, and he decided to investigate.

Pavlov began his experiments by ringing a tuning fork and then immediately placing some meat powder on the dog's tongue. He chose the tuning fork because it was a **neutral stimulus**—that is, one that initially had nothing to do with the dog's salivating response to the meat. After only a few meal times that were paired with the tuning fork, the dog started salivating as soon as it heard the sound, even if the food was not placed in its mouth. Pavlov demonstrated that a neutral stimulus (tuning fork's ring) can cause a formerly unrelated response. This occurs if it is presented regularly just before the stimulus (food) that normally brings about that response (salivation).

Pavlov used the term *unconditioned* to refer to stimuli and to the automatic, involuntary responses they caused. Such responses include blushing, shivering, being startled, or salivating. In the experiment, food was the **unconditioned stimulus (US)**—an event that leads to a certain, predictable response usually without any previous training. Food normally causes salivation. A dog does not have to be taught to salivate when it smells meat. The salivation is an **unconditioned response (UR)**—a reaction that occurs naturally and automatically when the unconditioned stimulus is presented, in other words, a reflex.

Under normal conditions, the sound of a tuning fork would not cause salivation. The dog had to be taught, or conditioned, to associate this sound with food. An ordinarily neutral event that, after training, leads to a response such as salivation is termed a **conditioned stimulus (CS)**. The salivation it causes is a **conditioned response (CR)**. A conditioned response is learned. A wide variety of events may serve as conditioned stimuli for salivation—the sight of food, an experimenter entering the room, the sound of a tone, or a flash of light. A number of different reflex responses that occur automatically following an unconditioned stimulus (US) can be conditioned to occur following the correct conditioned stimulus (CS).

✓ READING PROGRESS CHECK

Summarizing Why did Pavlov's dog salivate at the sound of the tuning fork?

General Principles of Classical Conditioning

GUIDING QUESTION *When does extinction occur?*

The learning present in classical conditioning helps animals and humans adapt to the environment. It also helps humans and animals correct mistakes and avoid danger. Psychologists and researchers have investigated why and in what circumstances classical conditioning occurs. The basic principles they have established lead to a greater understanding of classical conditioning.

Acquisition

Acquisition of a classically conditioned response generally occurs gradually. With each pairing of the conditioned stimulus (CS) and the unconditioned stimulus (US), the conditioned response (CR)—or learned response—is strengthened. In Pavlov's experiment, the more frequently the tuning fork was paired with the food, the more often the tone brought about salivation—the conditioned response.

The timing of the association between the conditioned stimulus (the tone) and the unconditioned stimulus (food) also influences learning. Pavlov tried several different conditioning procedures in which he varied the time between presenting the conditioned stimulus and the unconditioned stimulus. He found that classical conditioning was most reliable and effective when the conditioned stimulus was presented just before the unconditioned stimulus. He found that presenting the conditioned stimulus (CS) about half a second before the unconditioned stimulus (US) would yield the strongest associations between the tuning fork and the meat. The sound predicted the meat powder for the dog, so it began to salivate in anticipation when the tuning fork sounded.

Ivan Petrovich Pavlov
(1849-1936)

Born in central Russia, Pavlov obtained a doctoral degree in science from the University of St. Petersburg. In 1897 he began his own research into digestion and blood circulation. Pavlov's original work actually began as a study of digestion, for which he won the Nobel Prize in 1904. Pavlov discovered that salivation and the action of the stomach were closely linked to reflexes in the autonomic nervous system. By studying conditioned reflexes, it became possible to examine human behavior objectively, instead of resorting to subjective methods.

Pavlov distrusted the new science of psychiatry. He did think, though, that conditioned reflexes could explain the behavior of psychotic people. He believed that those who withdrew from the world may associate all stimuli with possible injury or threat.

▶ CRITICAL THINKING

Identifying Cause and Effect
How did Pavlov connect his work with dogs to the understanding of psychotic people?

classical conditioning a learning procedure in which associations are made between a neutral stimulus and an unconditioned stimulus

process a series of actions or operations directed toward a specific end

neutral stimulus a stimulus that does not initially elicit any part of an unconditioned response

unconditioned stimulus (US) an event that elicits a certain predictable response typically without previous training

unconditioned response (UR) an organism's automatic (or natural) reaction to a stimulus

conditioned stimulus (CS) a once-neutral event that elicits a given response after a period of training in which it has been paired with an unconditioned stimulus

conditioned response (CR) the learned reaction to a conditioned stimulus

generalization responding similarly to a range of similar stimuli

discrimination the ability to respond differently to similar but distinct stimuli

extinction the gradual disappearance of a conditioned response when the conditioned stimulus is repeatedly presented without the unconditioned stimulus

Generalization and Discrimination

In the same set of experiments, Pavlov also explored the processes that are known as generalization and discrimination. **Generalization** occurs when an animal responds, or reacts, to a second stimulus similar to the original CS without prior training with the second stimulus. When Pavlov conditioned a dog to salivate at the sight of a circle (the CS), he found that the dog would salivate when it saw another geometric figure as well. However, the more closely the figure resembled the circle, such as an oval, the more the dog would salivate. The dog had generalized its response to include a similar stimulus. Pavlov was later able to do the opposite, teaching the dog to respond only to the circle by always pairing meat powder with the circle but never pairing it with the oval. In this way Pavlov had taught the dog **discrimination**—the ability to respond in different ways to different stimuli.

Generalization and discrimination are complementary processes and are part of your everyday life. Both may occur spontaneously in some situations, and both can be taught in others. For example, assume a friend has come to associate the sound of a dentist's drill (the conditioned stimulus) with a fearful reaction (the conditioned response). After several exposures to a dentist's drill, your friend may find that he or she has generalized this uncomfortable feeling to the sound of other, nondental drills. Later, your friend may learn to discriminate between the sound of a dentist's drill and other drills.

Extinction and Spontaneous Recovery

A classically conditioned response, like any other behavior, is subject to change. Pavlov discovered that if he stopped presenting food after the sound of the tuning fork, the sound gradually lost its effect on the dog. After he repeatedly struck the tuning fork without giving food, the dog no longer associated the sound with the arrival of food—the sound of the tuning fork no longer caused the salivation response. Pavlov called this effect **extinction** because the conditioned response had gradually died out. The conditioned response was no longer a reliable predictor of the arrival of food.

Even though a classically conditioned response may be extinguished, this does not mean that the conditioned response has been completely unlearned. If a rest period is given following extinction, the conditioned response may reappear when the conditioned stimulus is presented again but not followed by an unconditioned stimulus. This spontaneous recovery does not bring the conditioned response back to original strength, however. Pavlov's dogs produced much less saliva during spontaneous recovery than they did at the end of their original conditioning. Alternating lengthy rest periods and the tone without food caused more rapid loss of salivation each time and less recovery the next time the conditioned stimulus was presented.

A good example of extinction and spontaneous recovery can occur if you are involved in a car accident. Following the accident it may at first be difficult to drive again. You might even find it difficult to open the door and get into the car. As you approach the car, your hands begin to shake and your knees get shaky as well. Your heartbeat even increases as you get nearer. After a few days, opening the door and getting into the car do not bother you as much. Several months go by and the fear of the car and the accident have been extinguished. One day, several months later, as you begin to approach the car, your heart begins to race and your knees and hands begin to shake. You have had a spontaneous recovery of the fear reaction.

✔ **READING PROGRESS CHECK**

Identifying What are the general principles behind classical conditioning?

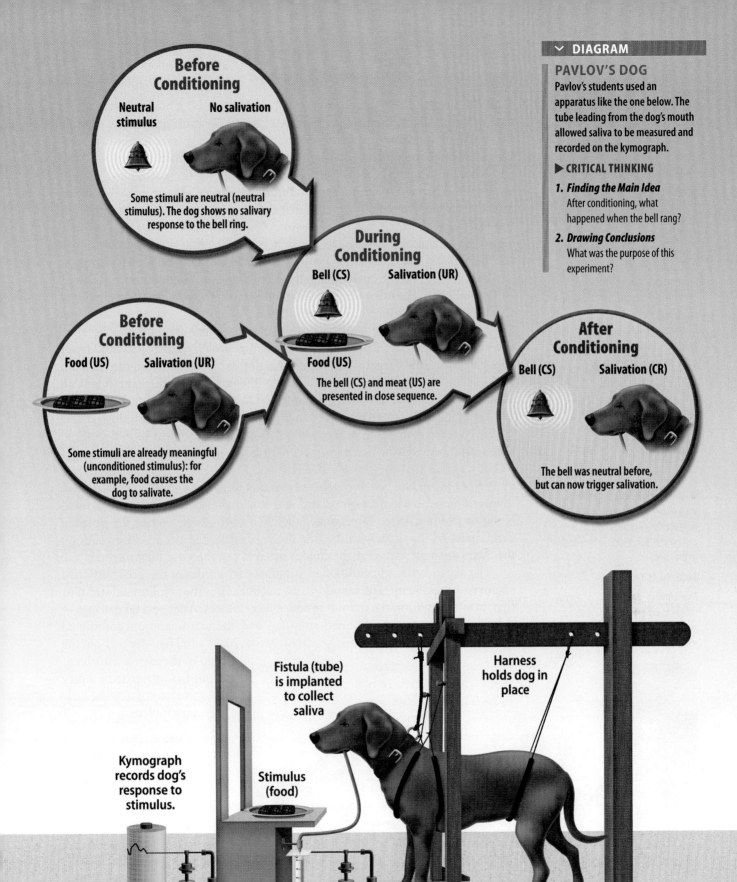

Classical Conditioning and Human Behavior

GUIDING QUESTION *How do people develop taste aversions?*

Have you ever noticed how movie directors use music in their movies? Did you ever hear a song and then think about either the movie it was from or the person you were with when you saw the movie? If so, you experienced classical conditioning. The music had become a "signal" that triggers memories and emotions. A conditioned emotion, such as fear, is a very difficult response to extinguish. It may trigger physical, cognitive, and emotional reactions.

John B. Watson and Rosalie Rayner used conditioning on a human infant in the case of Little Albert, the case study in this chapter. Watson questioned the role that conditioning played in the development of emotional responses in children. He and Rayner attempted to condition an 11-month-old infant named Albert to fear laboratory rats. At first Albert happily played with the rats. When Watson struck a steel bar with a hammer to produce a loud sound, Albert began to display a fear response. Eventually Albert showed fear each time he saw the rat even though the loud sound was not repeated. Although this demonstration is now viewed as unethical (because the researchers taught Little Albert to fear things that he previously had no fear of), it provided evidence that emotional responses can be classically conditioned in humans. In this case the unconditioned stimulus is the loud noise, the unconditioned response is fear, the conditioned stimulus is the rat, and the conditioned response is fear.

In a 2012 study, researchers have claimed to have identified the child in Watson and Rayner's study. This boy suffered from neurological problems and brain abnormalities. This suggests that Albert was not, as Watson and Rayner claimed, a normal child. However, this does not alter the outcome of the experiment, in which the subject was conditioned to respond to a specific stimulus.

Using the principle of classical conditioning in 1938, O. Hobart Mowrer and Mollie Mowrer discovered a practical solution to the problem of bed-wetting. One reason bed-wetting occurs is that children do not wake up during the night to body signals that they have a full bladder. The Mowrers developed a device known as the *bell and pad*. It consists of two metallic sheets perforated with small holes and wired to a battery-run alarm. The thin, metal sheets—wrapped in insulation or padding—are placed under the child's bed sheets. When the sleeping child moistens the sheet with the first drops of urine, the circuit closes, causing the alarm to go off and wake the child. The child can then use the bathroom.

The alarm is the unconditioned stimulus that produces the unconditioned response of waking up. The sensation of a full bladder is the conditioned stimulus that, before conditioning, did not produce wakefulness. After several pairings of the full bladder, the conditioned stimulus, and the alarm, the unconditioned stimulus, the child is able to awaken to the sensation of a full bladder without the help of the alarm. This technique has proven to be a very effective way of treating bed-wetting problems.

Taste Aversions

Suppose you go to a fancy restaurant. You decide to try an appetizer you have never eaten, for instance, snails. Then suppose that, after dinner, you go to a concert and become violently ill. You will probably develop a taste aversion; you may never be able to look at another snail without feeling at least a little nauseated.

Watson and Rayner's experiments with Albert were controversial because they did not attempt to correct the fear response they created in the child.

▶ **CRITICAL THINKING**

Speculating Why did the researchers design an experiment that created a negative response, rather than a positive response?

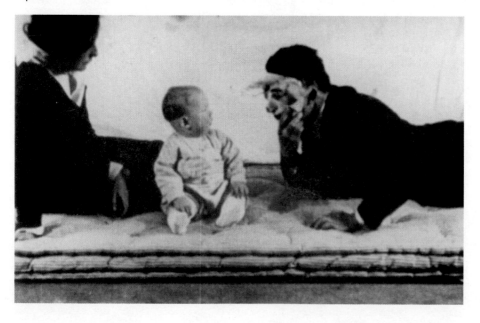

Conditioned Stimulus	Conditioned Response	Unconditioned Stimulus	Unconditioned Response
Dentist/ sound of drill	Tension	Drill	Tension
Product (soda pop)	Favorable feeling	Catchy jingle or slogan	Favorable feeling
Flashing police car lights	Distress	Speeding ticket	Distress

◀ TABLE

EXAMPLES OF COMMON CONDITIONED RESPONSES

If you have pets and feed them canned food, what happens when you use the can opener? You may notice that your pets may come running even when you are opening a can of peas.

▶ **CRITICAL THINKING**

1. *Interpreting* Why do you feel distress at the mere sight of flashing police lights?

2. *Theorizing* If you became sick after eating your favorite candy and a less favorite candy, to which would you most likely develop an aversion? Why?

Your nausea reaction to snails is another example of classical conditioning. What makes this type of conditioning interesting to learning theorists is that when people or other animals become ill, they seem to decide, "It must have been something I ate," even if they have not eaten for several hours. It is unlikely that the concert hall in which you were sick will become the conditioned stimulus, nor will other stimuli from the restaurant—the wallpaper pattern or the type of china used. What is more, psychologists can even predict which part of your meal will be the CS—you will probably blame a new food. Thus, if you get sick after a meal of salad, steak, and snails, you will probably learn to hate snails, even if they are really not the cause of your illness.

John Garcia and R.A. Koelling first **demonstrated** this phenomenon with rats. The animals were placed in a cage with a tube containing flavored water. Whenever a rat took a drink, lights flashed and clicks sounded. Then, some of the rats were given an electric shock after they drank. All these rats showed traditional classical conditioning—the lights and the sounds became conditioned stimuli, and the rats tried to avoid them in order to avoid a shock. The other rats were not shocked but were injected with a drug that made them sick after they drank and the lights and sounds occurred. These rats developed an aversion not to the lights or the sounds but only to the taste of the flavored water.

This special relationship between food and illness was used in a study that made coyotes avoid sheep by giving them a drug to make them sick when they ate sheep. This application is important because sheep farmers in the western United States would like to eliminate the coyotes that threaten their flocks, while naturalists are opposed to killing the coyotes. If coyotes could be trained to hate the taste of sheep, they would rely on other food sources and thus learn to coexist peacefully with sheep.

In summary, classical conditioning helps animals and humans predict what is going to happen. It provides information that may be helpful to their survival. Learning associated with classical conditioning may aid animals in finding food or help humans avoid pain or injury. Avoiding foods that cause sickness helps animals and humans. For example, parents may condition an infant to avoid a danger such as electrical outlets by shouting "NO!" and startling the infant each time he approaches an outlet. The infant fears the shouts of the parents, and eventually the infant fears the outlet even when the parents are not there.

demonstrate to show something clearly by giving evidence

CLASSICAL CONDITIONING VS. OPERANT CONDITIONING

All conditioning involves establishing relationships between two events. The two forms of conditioning, though, use very different procedures to reach their goals.

▶ **CRITICAL THINKING**

1. *Synthesizing* Apply the three steps (stimulus, response, and environment) to the development of a taste aversion.

2. *Identifying Central Issues* What role does the learner's environment play in each type of conditioning?

Classical Conditioning	Operant Conditioning
1. The response triggered by the stimulus is an involuntary reponse.	1. The voluntary response causes a reinforcing stimulus
2. Always a specific stimulus (US) that elicits a certain response	2. No identifiable stimulus; learner must first respond, then behavior is reinforced
3. US does not depend upon learner's response	3. Reinforcement depends upon learner's response behavior
4. Environment elicits response from learner	4. Learner actively operates on its environment

Behaviorism

Classical conditioning is an example of a behaviorist theory. Behaviorism is the attempt to understand behavior and mental states in terms of relationships between observable stimuli and observable responses. Behaviorists are psychologists who study only those behaviors that they can observe and measure. Behaviorists are not concerned with unobservable mental processes. They emphasize actions instead of thoughts. According to behaviorists, a person's environment is what determines how they will behave. Due to their emphasis on behavior, behaviorists define psychology as the scientific study of behavior, not the study of behavior and mental processes. Opponents of behaviorism disagree with this approach because it does not account for a person's feelings, their thoughts, or their will when it comes to their responses.

We will discuss another behaviorist learning theory, operant conditioning, in the next lesson. Classical conditioning is a process by which a stimulus that previously did not elicit a response comes to elicit a response after it is paired with a stimulus that naturally elicits a response. In contrast, operant conditioning is a process by which the consequences of a response affect the likelihood that the response will occur again.

☑ **READING PROGRESS CHECK**

Explaining Give an example of classical conditioning in everyday life.

LESSON 1 REVIEW

Reviewing Vocabulary

1. *Identifying* What is the difference between a neutral stimulus and an unconditioned stimulus?

2. *Understanding Relationships* How are generalization and discrimination related to classical conditioning?

Using Your Notes

3. *Describing* Use the notes you have taken throughout the lesson to describe the process of classical conditioning.

Answering the Guiding Questions

4. *Explaining* Under what conditions might a conditioned response become extinct?

5. *Summarizing* How do people develop taste aversions?

Writing Activity

6. *Informative/Explanatory* You have a friend who inhales noisily when standing next to you and then puffs air into your eye. You discover that you now blink when you hear your friend inhale. Write a description of this process, identifying and describing the neutral stimulus, the US, UR, CS, and CR in your behavior.

Case Study

CCSS

The Case of Little Albert

Winter, 1919–1920

Introduction: Through research with an infant, John B. Watson and Rosalie Rayner concluded that there are only a few instinctive reflexes and innate emotions in human infants. Using one of those innate emotions, fear of loud sounds, Watson and Rayner made discoveries about the conditioning of human behavior and emotional reactions.

Hypothesis: Most human behaviors and emotional reactions are built up of conditioned responses. (When an emotionally exciting object stimulates the subject simultaneously with an object not emotionally exciting, the latter object may in time arouse the same emotional reaction as the former object.)

Method: Watson and Rayner presented Albert, a 9-month-old boy, with many objects, including a rat, blocks, a rabbit, a dog, a monkey, masks with and without hair, cotton, wool, and burning newspapers. Albert showed no fear of any of these objects—they were all neutral stimuli for the fear response.

When Albert was 11 months old, Watson and Rayner conditioned him to fear rats. They began by placing a furry white rat in front of him. Each time Albert reached out to touch it, one of Watson's assistants would strike a metal bar with a hammer behind Albert. The first time the metal bar was struck, Albert fell forward and buried his head in a pillow. The next time he reached for the rat and the bar was struck, Albert began to whimper. The noise, the unconditioned stimulus, brought about a naturally unconditioned response, fear. After only a few such pairings, the rat became a conditioned stimulus that elicited a conditioned response, fear.

Five days after Watson and Rayner conditioned Albert to fear rats, they presented him with blocks, a rabbit, a rat, and a dog, each alone. They also showed him a number of other stimuli, including a Santa Claus mask. Albert reacted fearfully to all but the blocks. His conditioned fear response generalized to include the rabbit and all of the white furry objects he was shown, but not to any dissimilar toys.

Results: One of the most frequent criticisms of the experiment was that Watson and Rayner taught a child to be fearful. In their published findings, Watson and Rayner dismissed this concern.

PRIMARY SOURCE

❝ *At first there was considerable hesitation upon our part in making the attempt to set up fear reactions experimentally. A certain responsibility attaches to such a procedure. We decided finally to make the attempt, comforting ourselves by the reflection that such attachments would arise anyway as soon as the child left the sheltered environment of the nursery for the rough and tumble of the home. We did not begin this work until Albert was eleven months, three days of age.* ❞

—*"Conditioned Emotional Reactions," by John B. Watson and Rosalie Rayner*

The researchers also made no attempt to extinguish Albert's conditioned fears. The Little Albert study cannot be repeated today because of the ethical standards of the APA. One of Watson's students, Mary Cover Jones, developed an extinction procedure called counterconditioning to reduce people's existing fears. Jones helped Peter, a boy who was fearful of rabbits, eliminate his fear by pairing the feared object (the rabbit) with pleasant experiences, such as eating ice cream or receiving special attention.

Analyzing the Case Study

1. ***Interpreting*** Did the results of Watson and Rayner's experiment support their hypothesis? Explain.

2. ***Making Connections*** How did Albert's response become generalized?

3. ***Drawing Conclusions*** How were the principles of classical conditioning used to reduce Peter's fear of rabbits?

4. ***Analyzing Ethical Issues*** What defense did Watson and Rayner give for their decision to experiment on Albert? Do you consider their justification valid?

PHOTO: (l)Index Stock Photography Inc./Photodisc/Getty Images; (r)By Eric Lorentzen-Newberg/Flickr Open/Getty Images; TEXT: John B. Watson and Rosalie Rayner Conditioned emotional reactions. Journal of Experimental Psychology: General, Vol. 3, No. 1 (Feb. 1920)

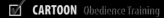

Reading **HELP**DESK

Academic Vocabulary
• affect   • obtain

Content Vocabulary
• operant conditioning
• reinforcement
• secondary reinforcer
• primary reinforcer
• shaping
• response chain
• aversive control
• negative reinforcement
• escape conditioning
• avoidance conditioning

TAKING NOTES:
Integration of Knowledge and Ideas

IDENTIFYING Use a graphic organizer like the one below to list reinforcers and methods that impact behavior.

Behaviors

Operant Conditioning

ESSENTIAL QUESTION • *How do our experiences change our behavior?*

IT MATTERS BECAUSE
Our actions have consequences. Sometimes these consequences make us more likely to repeat a certain behavior. Other consequences may make us more likely to avoid a certain behavior. Both sets of actions and consequences are operant conditioning. Operant conditioning occurs when the consequences that follow a behavior increase or decrease the likelihood of that behavior occurring again.

Reinforcement

GUIDING QUESTION *What are the central features of operant conditioning?*

Suppose your dog is wandering around the neighborhood, sniffing trees, checking garbage cans, looking for a squirrel to chase. A kind neighbor sees your dog and tosses a bone out the kitchen door to it. The next day, the dog is likely to stop at the same door on its rounds, and maybe even go to the door directly. When your dog shows up again your neighbor produces another bone, and the same thing happens the next day. Your dog now visits your neighbor on a daily basis.

This story is an example of **operant conditioning**—that is, learning from the consequences of behavior. The term *operant* is used because the subject, the wandering dog in our example, operates on or causes some change in the environment. This produces a result that influences whether the subject will operate or respond in the same way in the future. Depending on the effect of the operant behaviors, the learner will repeat or eliminate these behaviors to get rewards or avoid punishment.

How does operant conditioning differ from classical conditioning? One difference lies in how the researcher conducts the experiment. In classical conditioning, the researcher presents the conditioned and unconditioned stimuli independent of the participant's behavior. The unconditioned response is drawn out of the participant. Reactions to the conditioned stimulus are then observed by the researcher. In operant conditioning, the participant must engage in a behavior in order for the programmed outcome to occur. In other words, the study of operant conditioning is a study of how voluntary behavior is **affected**, or influenced, by its consequences.

Positive and Negative Reinforcement

Burrhus Frederic (B.F.) Skinner has been the psychologist most closely associated with operant conditioning. He believed that most behavior is influenced by a person's history of rewards and punishments. Skinner trained (or shaped) rats to respond to lights and sounds in a special enclosure called a Skinner box. To conduct this experiment, a rat is placed inside the box. The rat must learn how to solve the problem of how to get food to appear in the cup, which can be done by pressing a bar on the cage wall. The rat first explores the box. When the rat moves toward the bar, the experimenter drops food into the cup. The food is important to the hungry rat. After the rat begins to approach the cup for food consistently, the experimenter begins to drop food into the cup only if the rat presses the bar. Eventually, when the rat is hungry it will press the bar to get food.

The food that appears in the cup is a reinforcer in this particular demonstration. **Reinforcement** can be defined as a stimulus or an event that increases the likelihood that the preceding behavior will be repeated. Whether or not a particular stimulus is a reinforcement depends on the effect the stimulus has on the learner. Examples of reinforcers that people usually respond to are social approval, money, and extra privileges.

Suppose you want to teach a dog to shake hands. One way would be to give the animal a treat every time it lifts its paw up to you. The treat is called a *positive reinforcer*. In this example, the dog will eventually learn to shake hands in order to get the reward. Your dog will stop shaking hands when you forget to reward it for the trick. Extinction will occur because the reinforcement is withheld, but it will take a period of time. Remember, in classical conditioning, extinction is the disappearance of a conditioned response when an unconditioned stimulus no longer follows a conditioned stimulus. In fact, for a while after you stop rewarding the dog, it will probably become impatient, bark, and paw even more insistently than it did before to get you to provide the reward. However, the dog will give up shaking hands. Later the dog will try to shake hands again, indicating that spontaneous recovery has occurred.

Whereas positive reinforcement occurs when something desirable is *added* after an action, negative reinforcement occurs when something undesirable is *removed,* or stopped, after an action. For instance, there are automobiles that when driven produce an unpleasant dinging sound if the driver has left her seat belt unbuckled. When the driver buckles her seat belt, the dinging sound goes away. She has to perform the action of buckling her seat belt to receive the desired result of the removal of the dinging sound. This is negative reinforcement.

operant conditioning learning in which a certain action is reinforced or punished, resulting in corresponding increases or decreases in occurrence

affected influenced or changed by a set of consequences

reinforcement stimulus or event that follows a response and increases the likelihood that the response will be repeated

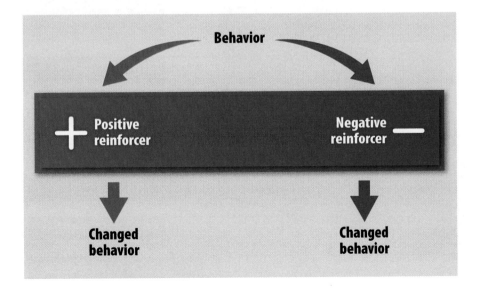

‹ DIAGRAM

OPERANT CONDITIONING
A change in behavior is often the result of both positive and negative reinforcement.

▶ **CRITICAL THINKING**

1. *Analyzing Visuals* According to the diagram, what must happen for behavior to change?

2. *Differentiating* How is operant conditioning different from classical conditioning?

Primary and Secondary Reinforcers

Reinforcers come in many varieties. Some reinforcers are primary and some are secondary. A **primary reinforcer** is one that satisfies a biological need such as hunger, thirst, or sleep. Food and water are examples of primary reinforcers. A **secondary reinforcer** is one that has been paired with a primary reinforcer and through classical conditioning has acquired value and the ability to reinforce. With conditioning, almost any stimulus can acquire value and become a secondary reinforcer, such as a warm bed or spoken praise.

An experimenter named Wolfe demonstrated this in 1936 with chimpanzees. Poker chips have no value for chimps—they are not edible and they are not very much fun to play with. This experimenter, however, used operant and classical conditioning to teach chimps to value poker chips as much as humans value money. He provided the animals with a "Chimp-O-Mat" that dispensed peanuts or bananas, which are primary reinforcers to chimpanzees. To **obtain** food, the chimps had to pull down on a heavily weighted bar to obtain poker chips, and then insert the chips in a slot in the machine. With repetition, the poker chips became conditioned, or secondary reinforcers. Their value was evident from the fact that the chimpanzees would work for the pokers chips, save them, and sometimes try to steal them from one another.

Money is the best example of a secondary reinforcer in human society. You have learned that getting money is associated with buying food or other material things. A dollar bill in and of itself is not a reinforcer; being able to purchase food, water, and other primary reinforcers with the dollar is what gives it its value or reinforcement to humans. Other examples of secondary reinforcers would include praise, status, and prestige. Most likely you have been the recipient of a secondary reinforcer because of your efforts at school. For example, you have to write a paper for your history class. You work several hours researching information on a specific event and then carefully write, edit, and proofread your paper. As a result, you receive an A+ on the paper. The final grade is an example of a secondary reinforcer. All of these items are associated with a primary reinforcer and have acquired value, so they reinforce certain types of behavior when they are earned.

---

primary reinforcer
stimulus that is naturally rewarding, such as food or water

secondary reinforcer
stimulus such as money that becomes rewarding through its link with a primary reinforcer

obtain to get possession of something, especially by making an effort or having the necessary qualifications

---

DIAGRAM ⌄

SKINNER BOX

The Skinner box is a basic apparatus used to test theories of operant conditioning. When the rat presses the bar located on the side of the box, food is delivered to the cup.

▶ **CRITICAL THINKING**

1. *Sequencing* How does the researcher teach the rat to press the lever?

2. *Identifying Cause and Effect* How does the rat display that learning has occurred?

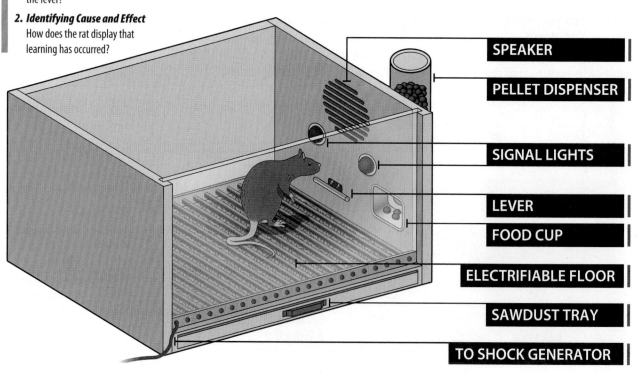

SPEAKER

PELLET DISPENSER

SIGNAL LIGHTS

LEVER

FOOD CUP

ELECTRIFIABLE FLOOR

SAWDUST TRAY

TO SHOCK GENERATOR

Schedules of Reinforcement

One important factor in operant conditioning is the timing and frequency of reinforcement. Behavior that is reinforced every time it occurs is said to be on a *continuous schedule* of reinforcement. You might suppose that behavior would best be maintained by reinforcing every response. However, when positive reinforcement occurs only intermittently, or on a *partial schedule*, the responses are generally more stable and last longer once they are learned. A person or animal that is continuously reinforced for a behavior tends to maintain that behavior only when the reinforcement is given. If the reinforcement stops, the behavior quickly undergoes extinction. For example, a rat learns to press a bar most rapidly when it receives food each time it does so. When the rat stops receiving food each time it presses the bar, however, it quickly stops its bar-pressing.

Behaviors that are acquired on partial schedules of reinforcement are established more slowly but are more persistent. For example, a rat that is only sometimes rewarded with food for pressing a bar will continue to press even though no food appears. Rats and humans that are reinforced on partial schedules of reinforcement cannot always predict when the next reinforcement will occur, so they learn to be persistent. Skinner discovered the strength of partial reinforcement when his apparatus kept breaking down. Skinner found that the rats kept responding even though they were reinforced randomly. In fact, the rats responded with even greater endurance.

Although intermittent reinforcement may be arranged in a number of ways, four basic methods, or schedules, have been studied in the laboratory. Schedules of partial reinforcement may be based either on the *number* of correct responses that the animal makes between reinforcements (*ratio* schedule) or on the *amount of time* that elapses before reinforcement is given (*interval* schedule). In either case, reinforcement may appear on a *fixed*, or predictable, schedule or on a *variable*, or unpredictable, schedule. The four basic schedules result from the combination of these four possibilities. People and animals respond differently to each.

In a *fixed-ratio schedule*, reinforcement depends on a specified quantity of responses, such as rewarding every fourth response. The student who receives a good grade after completing a specified amount of work and the typist who is paid by the number of pages completed are on fixed-ratio schedules. People tend to work hard on fixed-ratio schedules. Another example would be dentists who get paid $150 for *each* cavity repaired or filled.

A *variable-ratio schedule* does not require that a fixed or set number of responses be made for each reinforcement, as in the fixed-ratio schedule. Rather, the number of responses needed for a reinforcement changes from one reinforcer to the next. Slot machines are a good example of a variable-ratio schedule. They are set to pay off after a varying number of attempts at pulling the handle. Generally, animals on variable-ratio schedules of reinforcement tend to respond at a steady, high rate. Since the reinforcement is unpredictable, there is typically no pause after a reward because a reward might occur on the very next response.

Quick Lab

WHAT REINFORCEMENT SCHEDULES OPERATE IN YOUR CLASSROOM?

Do you think that students would do schoolwork if there were no grading system? What reinforcements would operate if grades were abolished?

Procedure

1. Identify the types of reinforcers that operate in your classroom.
2. Make a chart that lists the type of reinforcer (primary, secondary, positive, negative) and the classroom behavior it usually elicits.
3. Devise a system for your classroom that could replace the existing reinforcers with new ones (and achieve the same results).

Analysis

1. Describe how the new reinforcers operate.
2. Indicate what responses the new reinforcers are supposed to elicit.

Door-to-door salespeople and individuals who do telephone surveys are also operating on variable-ratio schedules since they never know how many doorbells they will have to ring or how many calls they will have to make before they make a sale or find someone who will answer the survey.

On a *fixed-interval schedule*, the first correct response after a specified amount of time is reinforced. The time interval is always the same. Once animals gain experience with a fixed-interval reinforcement schedule, they adjust their response rates. Since no reinforcement occurs for a period of time no matter what their behavior, they learn to stop responding immediately after reinforcement is given and then begin to respond again toward the end of the interval. The result is regular, recurring periods of inactivity followed by short bursts of responding, producing a "scalloped" response curve. Tests are often given on a fixed-interval schedule. It is likely that you will study feverishly the day before a test but study much less immediately afterwards.

On a *variable-interval schedule*, the time at which the reinforcement is given changes. If a teacher announced at the beginning of the year that your grade will include random quizzes given throughout the year on material that was covered the day before, what would you do if you wanted to get an A in that class? You would do a quick nightly review of what you covered in class that day in case there was a quiz the next day. The reinforcer is gained the first time you are given a pop quiz, but you do not know when that is going to occur. The usual response rate on a variable-interval schedule is slow, but steady—slower than on any other schedule of partial reinforcement. In fact, your eagerness to score well on the quizzes probably will determine roughly how often you review your notes for that class each day.

In summary, ratio schedules are based on numbers of responses, while interval schedules are based on time. Responses are more resistant to extinction when reinforced on a variable rather than on a fixed schedule. To be most effective, however, the reinforcement must be consistent for the same type of behavior, although it may not occur each time the behavior does. The complexity of our behavior means that most reinforcers in human relationships are on a variable schedule. How people will react cannot always be predicted.

☑ **READING PROGRESS CHECK**

Analyzing How are different types of reinforcers used to change behavior?

Fixed schedules

Ratio	**Interval**
Fixed Ratio (reinforcement after a fixed number of responses) • being paid for every 10 pizzas made • being ejected from a basketball game after five fouls	**Fixed Interval** (reinforcement of first response after a fixed amount of time has passed) • cramming for an exam • picking up your check from your part-time job
Variable Ratio (reinforcement after varying number of responses) • playing a slot machine • sales commissions	**Variable Interval** (reinforcement of first response after varying amounts of time) • surprise (pop) quizzes in class • checking your favorite blog for an update

Variable schedules

Clicker training is a common form of shaping. The trainer waits for the dog to perform the desired action on its own. The instant it performs, the trainer hits the clicker (an audio signal) and the dog gets the treat. The clicker acts as an acoustical marker to tell the dog, "That's what I'm reinforcing."

▶ **CRITICAL THINKING**

Predicting Consequences How might you use shaping to teach a dog to "shake hands"?

Shaping and Chaining

GUIDING QUESTION *How do we learn complex processes?*

Operant conditioning is not limited to simple behaviors. When you acquire a complex skill such as knitting, photography, playing basketball, or talking persuasively, you learn more than just a single new stimulus-response relationship. You learn a large number of them, and you learn how to put them together into a large, flowing unit. In learning complex processes such as these, you are engaging in both shaping and chaining.

Shaping

Shaping is a process in which reinforcement is used to sculpt new responses out of old ones. An experimenter can use this method to teach a rat to do something it has never done before and would never do if left to itself. He or she can shape it, for example, to raise a miniature flag. The rat is physically capable of standing on its hind legs and using its mouth to pull a miniature flag-raising cord, but at present it does not do so. The rat probably will not perform this by accident, so the experimenter begins by rewarding any action similar to the wanted responses, using reinforcement, such as food pellets, to produce closer and closer approximations of the desired behavior.

Imagine the rat roaming around on a table with the flag apparatus in the middle. The rat inspects everything and finally sniffs at the flagpole. The experimenter immediately reinforces this response by giving the rat a food pellet each time it comes to the pole. Now the rat frequently sniffs the flagpole, hoping to get another pellet, but the experimenter waits until the rat lifts a paw before he gives it another reward. Now the experimenter waits until the rat stands on its hind legs before giving another reward. This process continues with the experimenter reinforcing close responses and then waiting for even closer ones.

Eventually, the experimenter has the rat on its hind legs nibbling at the cord. Suddenly the rat seizes the cord in its teeth and yanks it. Immediately the rat is rewarded, and it begins pulling rapidly on the cord. A new response has been shaped. Shaping is used to teach animals tricks. For example, when a television character points her finger to the ground and her dog immediately lies down, shaping was involved in the dog's behavior. If shaping is done properly, almost any animal can learn some unusual tricks.

shaping technique in which the desired behavior is "molded" by first rewarding any act similar to that behavior and then requiring ever-closer approximations to the desired behavior before giving the reward

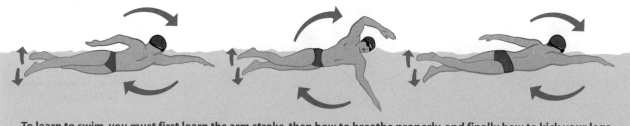

To learn to swim, you must first learn the arm stroke, then how to breathe properly, and finally how to kick your legs.

DIAGRAM ∧

SWIMMING: A RESPONSE CHAIN

To learn to swim, you must first learn the arm stroke, then how to breathe properly, and finally how to kick your legs.

▶ **CRITICAL THINKING**

1. *Comparing* What similar response chains can you describe that you would have to develop to learn other skills?

2. *Identifying Central Issues* How does chaining allow us to learn complex processes?

response chain learned reactions that follow one another in sequence, each reaction producing the signal for the next

aversive control process of influencing behavior by means of unpleasant stimuli

negative reinforcement increasing the strength of a given response by removing or preventing a painful stimulus when the response occurs

escape conditioning training of an organism to remove or terminate an unpleasant stimulus

Combining Responses: Chaining

In order to learn a skill, a person must be able to put various new responses together. Responses that follow one another in a sequence are combined into **response chains**. Each response is the signal for the next one.

In learning, chains of responses are organized into larger *response patterns*. For example, the complex skill of swimming has three major chains that are combined to make up the whole swimming pattern—an arm-stroking chain, a breathing chain, and a leg-kicking chain. After much practice, you no longer have to think about the different steps involved. The behavior takes on a rhythm of its own: the chains of responses flow naturally as soon as you dive into the water.

It is usually necessary to learn simple responses before mastering a complex pattern. Before a person can learn to perform a particular skill, he or she must learn all the lower skills that make the larger skill possible. A woodcarver does not produce a masterpiece the first time he picks up a carving tool. He first learns which tools to use for each purpose and how to hold his tools. He works from simple to complex designs. Only after much practice is he able to carve an intricate and ornate masterpiece.

☑ **READING PROGRESS CHECK**

Analyzing How can skills be taught using operant conditioning over time?

Aversive Control

GUIDING QUESTION *How can unpleasant stimuli affect our behavior?*

Reinforcement refers to anything that increases the frequency of an immediately preceding behavior. Aversive, or unpleasant, consequences influence much of our everyday behavior. **Aversive control** refers to this type of conditioning or learning. There are two ways in which unpleasant events can affect behavior—as negative reinforcers or as punishers.

Negative Reinforcement

In **negative reinforcement**, a painful or unpleasant stimuli is reduced or removed. The removal of unpleasant consequences increases the frequency of a behavior. It may help you to understand negative reinforcement if you remember that it *follows* and *negates*, or takes away, an aversive stimulus. B.F. Skinner provided this example: If walking with a stone in your shoe causes you to limp, removing the stone (negating it) allows you to walk without pain. Other examples of negative reinforcers are fear reduction and experiencing disapproval of unwelcome behavior.

Two uses of negative reinforcement that psychologists have studied in detail are *escape conditioning* and *avoidance conditioning*. In **escape conditioning**, a person's behavior causes an unpleasant event to stop. Consider the case of a child who hates liver and is served it for dinner. She whines about the food and gags

250

while eating it. At this point, her father removes the liver. The whining and gagging behavior has been thus negatively reinforced, and the child is likely to whine and gag in the future when given an unpleasant meal. This kind of learning is called escape conditioning because the behavior of the child allowed her to escape the dreaded liver meal.

In **avoidance conditioning**, the person's behavior has the effect of preventing an unpleasant situation from happening. In our example, if the child starts whining and gagging when the father removes the liver from the refrigerator to cook it, he may decide to put it back and fix something else. We would identify the situation as avoidance conditioning; the child avoided the unpleasant consequences by whining early enough. The reinforcer here is the reduction of the child's disgust—not having to eat liver.

You may have begun your day with the negative reinforcement of an alarm clock. The unpleasant sound of the alarm does not end until you wake up enough to shut it off. Shutting off the alarm clock is an example of escape conditioning. Learning to wake up just before the alarm sounds is avoidance conditioning.

Aversive conditioning is also used to treat some forms of addictions. An unpleasant stimulus is applied while a person is participating in the behavior being targeted. A person being treated for a tobacco or alcohol addiction would be given, while smoking or drinking, a medicine that produces nausea. The addictive behavior becomes associated with the unpleasant stimulus, encouraging the person to avoid the addictive behavior.

avoidance conditioning
training of an organism to respond so as to prevent the occurrence of an unpleasant stimulus

Connecting Psychology to History

THORNDIKE AND THE LAW OF EFFECT

As you have read, behaviorism is a method to understand actions in terms of the stimuli that produce them. Classical conditioning uses a stimulus to produce a desired response. Operant conditioning uses consequences of responses to produce desired behavior.

Edward Thorndike (1874–1949) was a pioneer in the study of behavior. As an educator, he wanted to understand how people learned. He tested his ideas with chickens and cats to observe trial-and-error learning. Thorndike placed cats in a "puzzle box" and placed fish outside the box. By watching the behavior of cats learning to escape from a "puzzle box," Thorndike determined that behaviors which produced satisfaction (here escape from the box and being fed the fish) were "stamped in" and more readily repeated. Responses leading to failure, or dissatisfaction, were "stamped out," or less likely to be repeated. This led Thorndike to formulate the Law of Effect, one of the two laws of learning he proposed from his study. The Law of Effect says that behaviors leading to satisfactory outcomes are likely to be repeated while behaviors leading to unsatisfactory outcomes are less likely to be repeated.

The Law of Exercise, his second law of learning, states that associations which are practiced are "stamped in" while others are extinguished. These two laws of learning set out the principle that behavior is associated with reward and punishment. Thorndike's work laid the groundwork for the field of operant conditioning.

▲ Edward Thorndike's work helped lay the foundation for educational psychology.

▶ **CRITICAL THINKING**

1. *Interpreting Significance* How is the Law of Effect important to understanding the way people learn?

2. *Making Connections* How is the Law of Effect similar to trial-and-error?

CARTOON ^

OBEDIENCE TRAINING
Aversive control pairs a painful response with a neutral stimulus in order to change behavior.

▶ CRITICAL THINKING

1. *Identifying Perspectives*
What type of conditioning has the owner been subjected to?

2. *Explaining* How could the dog use avoidance conditioning on its owner?

Punishment

The most obvious form of aversive control is punishment. In punishment, an unpleasant consequence occurs and decreases the frequency of the behavior that produced it. Negative reinforcement and punishment operate in opposite ways. In negative reinforcement, escape or avoidance behavior is *repeated* and increases in frequency. In punishment, behavior that is punished decreases or is *not repeated*. If you want to stop a dog from pawing at you when it wants attention, you should loudly say, "NO!" and reprimand it when it paws at you. Such actions are called *punishers*. They are intended to reduce the frequency of the dog pawing at you.

As with reinforcers, the events or actions that serve as punishers depend on their effect on the learner. For example, if a young child in a large family seeks extra attention from her parents, that child may misbehave. In response the parents punish the child by reprimanding her. The reprimands are meant to be punishers. They, however, may actually serve as reinforcers for the child because she is getting the attention she is seeking from her parents. Perhaps a more appropriate punisher would be to send her to her room or to another place in the house every time she misbehaved. In this way, she would not get the attention she was seeking. This unpleasant stimulus would discourage the child from repeating the behavior.

Remember that the goal of negative reinforcement is to increase the occurrence of behavior that ends an unpleasant stimulus. The goal of punishment is to decrease the occurrence of a particular behavior. Reinforcement can be either positive or negative. Punishment can be positive and negative also. Negative reinforcement occurs when something desirable is taken away. In the case of the child who sought attention, the reprimands were a form of positive punishment. Sending her to her room or to an equally "lonely" place would have been negative punishment since it took away something she wanted—attention. Parents of a student who fails to complete his homework may find that they can use negative punishment by requiring their son to finish his homework before he is allowed to hang out with his friends, watch TV, play video games, or take part in any other desirable activity. Until his work is completed, he cannot participate in the activities he enjoys most. Doing the homework is an unpleasant situation, but the activities he is missing are a stronger negative situation and one that he would be willing to avoid.

Disadvantages of Punishment

Psychologists have found several disadvantages in using aversive stimuli (punishment) to change behavior. For one thing, aversive stimuli can produce unwanted side effects such as rage, aggression, and fear. Then, instead of having to change only one problem behavior, additional behaviors may need to change. For example, children whose parents rely on spanking to control disobedience may also have to deal with the problem of their children's increased aggressiveness toward other children. The child may become confused because the spanking itself, or use of a physical action, may seem like an acceptable behavior in her or others.

A second problem with punishment is that people learn to avoid the person delivering the aversive consequences. Children learn to stay away from their parents or teachers who often punish them. Children may also learn to act one way around their parents or teachers to avoid the punishment, while they continue the same behavior when they are around their peers. One consequence of this is that parents and teachers have less opportunity to correct the children's inappropriate behavior because they will not be near them when they are acting in this way. Also, punishment is likely to merely suppress, but not eliminate, the behavior. The punished behavior is likely to occur at some other time or in some other place. The child may have learned something from the punishment, but it was not the lesson the parent or teacher intended.

Punishment alone does not teach appropriate and acceptable behavior. It must be accompanied by modeling of the desired behaviors. Without positive coaching and modeling, the child may never learn the correct behavior or understand what the parents think is the acceptable behavior in a given situation. Punishment is even less likely to be effective if a child sees a parent or other trusted adult performing the same behavior for which he or she has been punished.

Punishment is a form of aversive control that seeks to reduce a specific behavior.

▶ **CRITICAL THINKING**

Predicting Consequences What additional problem behaviors may a young child exhibit after receiving punishment?

☑ **READING PROGRESS CHECK**

Classifying What is the difference between negative reinforcement and punishment?

KidStock/Blend Images/Getty Images

LESSON 2 REVIEW

Reviewing Vocabulary

1. ***Summarizing*** How do the four schedules of partial reinforcement work?

2. ***Identifying*** What is the difference between escape conditioning and avoidance conditioning?

Using Your Notes

3. ***Interpreting*** Use the notes from your graphic organizer to explain the relationship between the various reinforcers and behavior.

Answering the Guiding Questions

4. ***Identifying*** What are the central features of operant conditioning?

5. ***Describing*** How do we learn complex processes?

6. ***Specifying*** How can unpleasant stimuli affect our behavior?

Writing Activity

7. ***Informative/Explanatory*** Using principles of operant conditioning, write a description of the process you would use to teach a puppy a new trick.

Learning: Principles and Applications **253**

Analyzing
Readings in Psychology

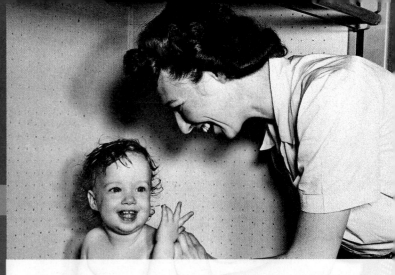

PHOTO: Bettmann/Corbis; TEXT: Republished with permission of ASSOCIATION FOR PSYCHOLOGICAL SCIENCE from B.F. Skinner: Scientist, Celebrity, Social Visionary by Alexandra Rutherford, APS observer Vol. 25, No. 3, March 2012; permission conveyed through Copyright Clearance Center, Inc. APS observer by AMERICAN PSYCHOLOGICAL SOCIETY Copyright 2012 Reproduced with permission of ASSOCIATION FOR PSYCHOLOGICAL SCIENCE in the format Republish in "other" book via Copyright Clearance Center.

Reader's Dictionary

polarizing controversial, dividing people into groups

trajectory the path along which something travels

notoriety condition of being famous for something negative

authoritatively with impressive knowledge of a subject

unwarranted not necessary or appropriate

ascendant becoming more powerful

affiliated closely connected

utopian an imaginary place where social conditions, laws, and government are perfect

B.F. Skinner is one of the most famous, or to some most infamous, psychological theorists. Skinnerian conditioning was at first hailed as a way of perfecting imperfect people. Later it came to be derided as social engineering. The truth likely falls somewhere in between. In this excerpt, Skinner's work and its lasting influence and usefulness are examined.

B.F. Skinner:
Scientist, Celebrity, Social Visionary

Alexandra Rutherford

PRIMARY SOURCE

Burrhus Frederic Skinner once famously stated, "If I am right about human behavior, I have written the autobiography of a nonperson." This attention-grabbing remark, made in 1983 after he had completed the *third* volume of his autobiography, captures why Skinner has been such a **polarizing** figure: We tend to be interested in *people*. Moreover, we tend to *experience* ourselves as people, not as loci of genes, environmental stimuli, and complex reinforcement histories. The two *Psychology Today* interviews with Skinner, the first by Mary Harrington Hall in 1967 and the second by Elizabeth Hall in 1972, actually reveal much about Skinner as a person and as a deeply impassioned scientist-turned-social-visionary. For as careful and rigorous a scientist as Skinner was, it was his social vision that made him, at least for a brief moment, a celebrity.

Published just five years apart, these two interviews capture an important slice of Skinner's career **trajectory**. When he was first interviewed in 1967, it was already eight years after Noam Chomsky's review of Skinner's *Verbal Behavior* had supposedly dealt a death-blow to behaviorism, and Skinner remarked casually that he might have another five good years left (he was actually productive right up to his death in 1990). In the late 1960s, behavior modification was spreading like wildfire in classrooms, hospitals, and prisons. Skinner made a reference in both interviews to a program he was particularly excited about, a program at the National Training School for Boys (which was a juvenile correctional facility in the mid-1960s) that employed a token economy to help inmates reach educational goals. By the time Skinner was interviewed in 1972, he had published *Beyond Freedom and Dignity* (*BFD*) and was widely characterized as a fascist.

By the time of the 1972 interview, *BFD* had reached the top of the *New York Times* bestseller list. The second interview was conducted "in the aftermath" of this new-found **notoriety**. It reflects Skinner's fervent desire to see behavioral technology taken up to solve social problems. As Skinner put it, "I think we're making a mess of things, and all our problems have to do with behavior." This belief in using behavioral technology to design suitable cultures led Skinner to write *BFD*. The trick, according to him, was to convince people that we *need* to design cultures using effective methods, given our behaviors are already being

254

manipulated anyway. Of particular concern to him, in the interview and in his book, was the threat of nuclear war. The Cold War was a consistent backdrop to Skinner's scientific career and no doubt influenced much of his thinking about the need for behavioral technology.

Skinner's particular technological bent, however, was evident very early in his upbringing. As a young boy, he grew tired of being scolded for leaving his pajamas on the bedroom floor, so he invented a gadget that would remind him to pick them up before leaving his room. Designing gadgets to make life easier was a consistent theme both at home and at work. His first professional "gadget" was a pigeon-guided missile system designed for use in WWII, although it never got past the prototype stage. His next invention, which he discussed in the 1967 interview, was the baby tender, also called the aircrib and—infamously—the baby box. Skinner and his wife Yvonne used the tender with their second daughter, Deborah.

A gadget in which Skinner did take a serious professional interest was the teaching machine, or, more properly, programmed instruction. In the 1967 interview, he stated **authoritatively** and optimistically, "I have no doubt at all that programmed instruction based on operant principles will take over education." Skinner's optimism was not **unwarranted** at the time. In the early 1960s, programmed instruction was touted widely as one of the most promising, indeed revolutionary, of the educational technologies being developed in the then-**ascendant** educational technology

movement. In 1961, a writer for *Science Digest* wrote, "A few months ago, thousands of school children from coast to coast were quietly subjected to what may turn out to be the greatest educational revolution in history. They began the first large-scale experiment in learning, not from human teachers, but from teaching machines." By 1972, however, the enthusiasm for the machines had diminished. Reflecting his increasing pessimism about the state of education (and the world) that had catalyzed *BFD*, Skinner said, "I'm concerned with improving education. Programmed instruction could make a great difference. Industry, which appreciates a good thing, uses it extensively. Yet it is only beginning to be used on a reasonable scale in grade schools and high schools." Indeed, the "takeover" of education that Skinner envisioned never came to pass.

With 40 years of hindsight, what is Skinner's place in history? Mary Harrington Hall, in the preface to her 1967 interview, suggests that "when history makes its judgment, he may well be known as the major contributor to psychology in this century." It is safe to say that Hall's rather cautious prediction has been borne out. In contemporary surveys of disciplinary eminence, Skinner's name always rises to the top of the list. Over a career that spanned more than 60 years, he published over 20 books. His science of behavior became the foundation for the contemporary discipline of behavior analysis, whose professional organization, the Association for Behavior Analysis International, currently has over 5,000 members in the United States and 13,000 members in **affiliated** chapters around the world. Numerous behavior analytic journals carry on the Skinnerian tradition. You can even become a certified Skinnerian — a board-certified behavior analyst.

For all of these reasons, Skinner is a notable figure in the history of psychological science. But it is clear that Skinner's historical significance transcends simple disciplinary eminence. I would propose that for all of his contributions to psychology, Skinner should perhaps more appropriately be placed in the long line of **utopian** thinkers who have tried to imagine what a better world would look like. In Skinner's case, he also offered some tools to build it. Too bad he just couldn't convince enough of us to take them up.

Analyzing Primary Sources

1. *Analyzing* Why did B.F. Skinner believe that behavioral technology could solve social problems?

2. *Hypothesizing* Why do you think public reaction to the aircrib was so negative?

3. *Making Connections* In what ways has Skinner's vision of computer-assisted instruction (CAI) been realized in education today?

There's More Online!

 CHART How Social Learning Works Circle

 GRAPHIC ORGANIZER

 SELF-CHECK QUIZ

Reading **HELP**DESK ⓒⓒⓢⓢ

Academic Vocabulary
• **involve**   • **alleviate**

Content Vocabulary
• social learning
• cognitive learning
• cognitive map
• latent learning
• learned helplessness
• modeling
• token economy

TAKING NOTES:
Key Ideas and Details

IDENTIFYING Use a graphic organizer like the one below to identify the aspects of social learning covered in the lesson.

Cognitive Learning	
Modeling	
Behavior Modification	

LESSON 3
Social Learning

ESSENTIAL QUESTION • *How do our experiences change our behavior?*

IT MATTERS BECAUSE

Have you ever seen a youth sporting event in which the parents are deeply involved? Sometimes it is the parents who do the most arguing with the coach, the referees, and with one another over the plays and the calls. Have you wondered what sort of sportsmanship the children are learning as they watch these adults? Understanding how we learn helps us understand how experiences change our behavior.

Cognitive Learning

GUIDING QUESTION *What is the principle behind cognitive learning?*

Where does aggression come from? Do children develop aggressive habits on their own, or do they learn such behaviors from the adults around them? Albert Bandura performed a study in 1961 to demonstrate that the children learned aggressive behaviors simply by watching a model perform these behaviors. The study illustrated the third type of learning, called social learning. Social learning theorists view learning as purposeful. They theorize that learning goes beyond mechanical responses to stimuli or reinforcement.

The two types of social learning are cognitive learning and modeling. Cognitive learning focuses on how information is obtained, processed, and organized. Such learning is concerned with the mental processes involved in learning. We will begin with a discussion of cognitive learning and some of its different types. Latent learning and learned helplessness are examples of cognitive learning.

Latent Learning and Cognitive Maps

As you discovered in Lesson 1, classical conditioning is learning which results from stimulus and response. A process which previously did not elicit a response is made to elicit a response by pairing it with a stimulus that naturally elicits the desired response. Behaviorists like Skinner studied operant conditioning, in which learning results from consequences, both positive and negative, of behavior.

Both classical conditioning and operant conditioning seek to explain learning through behavior that can be observed. Before John Watson tested his learning theories on Little Albert, other psychologists were researching the importance of cognition in learning. Based on his observations of chimpanzees, Wolfgang Köhler suggested that animals had the ability to assess a situation and arrive at a solution through basic understanding, or insight, rather than through trial and error. He observed chimpanzees finding ways to reach food beyond their grasp that seemed to consider the problem and used insight in order to solve it.

In the 1920s and early 1930s, the American behavioral psychologist Edward Tolman demonstrated that learning can occur without outward signs of learning. Unlike classical conditioning and operant conditioning, this type of learning occurs without reinforcement. Tolman argued that it also **involved** mental processes. To demonstrate, Tolman would place a rat in a maze and allow it to explore the maze without giving the rat any reinforcement, such as food. Then he would place food at the end of the maze and record which path the rat took to reach the food. The rat quickly learned to take the shortest route to the food.

Tolman's next step was to block the shortest path to the food. Once this was done, the rat would then follow the next shortest path to the food. Tolman believed that the rat had developed a **cognitive map** of the maze. A cognitive map is a mental picture of a place, such as the maze. The rats had developed a cognitive map of the maze when they were allowed to explore the maze on their own, which helped them find the paths to the food.

Tolman called the type of learning demonstrated by the rat **latent learning**. Latent learning is not demonstrated by an immediately observable change in behavior at the time of the learning. Although the learning typically occurs, or happens, in the absence of a reinforcer, it may not be demonstrated until a reinforcer appears. For example, have you ever had to locate a building or street in a section of your city or town that you were unfamiliar with? You may have been through that section of town before and remembered details such as an unusual sign or large parking lot. Remembering these details may have helped you find the building or street you were looking for. You had learned some details without intending to do so.

Another researcher, Harry Harlow, studied latent learning with monkeys. He presented monkeys with a complex hinge that required several steps in order to get it to open. The monkeys learned to remove the various pins and bolts without receiving any reward. They seemed to enjoy the task for its own sake. Some birds learn the positions of stars while still in the nest, long before they need this information for migration.

social learning process of altering behavior by observing and imitating the behavior of others

cognitive learning form of altering behavior that involves mental processes and may result from observation or imitation

involve to contain or include something as a necessary element

cognitive map a mental picture of spatial relationships or relationships between events

latent learning alteration of a behavioral tendency that is not demonstrated by an immediate, observable change in behavior

Examples of How Learned Helplessness Develops

- Parents punish children constantly for any and all offenses.
- You are overly critical of all your friends' actions.
- A student is placed in an advanced math course without proper preparation (taking and passing the basic math course first).

Common Factors of Learned Helplessness Situations

- Subjects believe they have no control over their own environment.
- Success seems a matter of luck, rather than skill.
- Subjects watch others who seem to easily succeed.

Elements That Make Learned Helplessness Persist in Some Students

- Students believe that failing is a permanent condition—they failed once, and will continue to fail. Failure is a permanent condition.
- Students believe that failure in one subject means that they will fail in all subjects. Failure is global.
- Students believe that the failure is the result of their own weaknesses.

< TABLE

LEARNED HELPLESSNESS
What happens when it is impossible for a learner to have an effect on the environment? What happens when a learner is punished and cannot escape the punishment? The learner may give up trying to learn.

▶ CRITICAL THINKING

1. *Drawing Conclusions* How can learned helplessness cause depression?

2. *Problem-Solving* In the math class example of how learned helplessness develops, what steps can the student take to avoid learned helplessness?

Surveys show that the average elementary school child spends more than 40 hours a week playing video games. Does playing violent video games affect the players?

Many researchers believe that watching violence desensitizes the brain and leads to increased aggression.

In a 2011 study, participants played a video game for 25 minutes. Some games were violent, others were not. Then researchers measured brain activity as participants viewed photos of violent and neutral subjects. Then the participants played a game in which they set the level of noise inflicted on their opponent, which was used to measure aggression.

Participants who played a violent game during the experiment but did not usually play them showed a lower response to the violent photos. In addition, the lower the response to the violent photos, the more aggressive participants were in setting a loud noise. Researchers believe this shows that their brains had become desensitized during the violent video game.

learned helplessness
condition in which repeated attempts to control a situation fail, resulting in the belief that the situation is uncontrollable

Latent learning also impacts conditioned learning. A rat can be conditioned to find the food, or reward, in its maze. As Tolman demonstrated, through latent learning the rat knows various paths to its food and chooses the next shortest route when the shortest one is blocked. However, if two or more paths are equally distant from the food, the rats vary their route. A radial maze has eight paths leading out of a central location. Rats placed in a radial maze in which food has been placed at the end of each path explore each path and collect all the food rather than simply expecting food at the end of the first path where it was found. In fact, they will not take a path they have already explored. The rats seemed to be able to keep track of the routes already taken and avoid taking them again.

Learned Helplessness

Psychologists have shown that general learning strategies can affect a person's relationship to the environment. For example, if a person has numerous experiences in which his or her actions have no effect, he or she may learn a general strategy of helplessness or laziness. They see no evidence that their efforts produce results, so they simply stop trying.

In the first stage of one study, a group of college students was able to turn off an unpleasant loud noise, while another group had no control over the noise. Later, the students were placed in a situation in which they merely had to move a lever to stop a similar noise. Only those students who had control over the noise in the first instance learned to turn off the noise. The students who had not been able to turn off the first noise made no effort to try and turn off the second noise.

It is not hard to see how these results can apply to everyday situations. In order to be able to try hard and to be full of energy, people must learn that their actions do make a difference. If rewards come without any effort, a person never learns to work. This is called learned laziness. A student who earns an A in one class without studying may have trouble disciplining himself to study for a different class. If pain comes no matter how hard one tries, a person gives up. If a student routinely earns Ds in a class despite hours of studying, he may decide that studying is useless and stop trying altogether. This occurrence is called **learned helplessness**.

Martin Seligman believes that learned helplessness is one major cause of depression. He reasons that when people are unable to control events in their lives, they generally respond in one of the following ways. First, they may be less motivated to act and thus stop trying altogether. Second, they may experience a lowered sense of self-esteem and think negatively about themselves. Third, they may feel depressed.

Seligman also identified three important elements of learned helplessness: *stability*, *globality*, and *internality*. Stability refers to the person's belief that the state of helplessness results from a permanent characteristic. For example, a student who fails a math test can decide that the problem is either temporary ("I did poorly on this math test because I was sick") or *stable* ("I never have done well on math tests and never will"). Similarly, the person can decide that the problem is either specific ("I'm no good at math tests") or *global* ("I'm just dumb"). Both stability and globality focus on the student—on *internal* reasons for failure. The student could have decided that the problem was external ("This was a bad math test") instead of internal. People who attribute an undesirable outcome to their own inadequacies will probably experience depression along with guilt, low self-esteem, and self-blame behavior reflecting the belief that "nothing I do matters."

☑ READING PROGRESS CHECK

Analyzing In what ways do humans use information obtained from latent learning in daily life?

Modeling

GUIDING QUESTION *What does the Bobo doll exercise demonstrate about modeling?*

The second type of social learning is **modeling**. When you go to a concert for the first time, you may be very hesitant about where to go, when to enter, when to clap, when to stand or sit down, how to get a better seat after the first intermission, and so on. So you observe others at the concert, follow their lead, and soon you have it all figured out. Through observation and imitation, you have learned what to do.

Modeling is the general term for this kind of learning. It includes three different types of effects. In the simplest case— the first type of modeling—witnessing the behavior of others simply increases the chances that we will follow their lead and do the same thing. You could think of this as *mimicry*. We clap when others do, look up at a building if everyone else is looking there, and copy the fashion styles and verbal expressions of our peers. No learning occurs in this case, in the respect of acquiring new responses. We simply perform old responses that we otherwise might not be using at the time.

The second type of modeling is usually called *observational learning*, or imitation. In this sort of learning an observer watches someone perform a behavior and is later able to reproduce it closely, though the observer was unable to do this before he or she observed the actions of the model. An example is watching someone else do an unfamiliar dance step and afterward being able to do the dance step yourself.

Have you ever noticed that some children seem to behave in a manner similar to their parents? Albert Bandura suggested that we watch models perform and then imitate the models' behavior. Bandura and his colleagues demonstrated observational learning by using a Bobo doll. The experimenters found that children were more likely to act aggressively after they had observed aggressive behavior in which the models were rewarded or at least not punished.

Individual differences in personality may help to explain why people act differently when shown the same movie containing violent material. The American Psychological Association (APA) Commission on Violence and Youth reported in 1993 that personal qualities do play a role in how we respond. One child may learn that violence is right and another child may view violence as pitiful. Others have found that more aggressive children seek out violent television and are also more affected by it.

A third type of modeling involves *disinhibition*. When an observer watches someone else engage in a threatening activity without being punished, the observer may find it easier to engage in that behavior later. Desensitization is a form of disinhibition. It can be either positive or negative depending on how it is used. When someone becomes less and less impacted by violence through multiple exposures, it can make a person more accepting of violence. On the other hand, someone with a snake phobia may watch another person handling snakes. Such observation may help **alleviate** the phobia. This procedure is used in clinical work as we will see in the chapter on therapies.

In the Bobo doll experiments, children watched films in which a woman sat on, punched, and threw the doll, which was a popular toy in the 1960s. Pictured is a typical response when allowed to interact with the doll.

▶ **CRITICAL THINKING**

Analyzing Visuals Describe the type of modeling the boy is employing in this photograph.

modeling learning by imitating others; copying behavior

alleviate to ease or lessen pain or hardship

✔ **READING PROGRESS CHECK**

Interpreting Significance How did Bandura demonstrate molding with children?

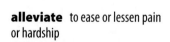

Mirrorpix/Newscom

Behavior Modification

GUIDING QUESTION *What is the first step in behavior modification?*

The term *behavior modification* often appears in articles describing research on changing people's behavior through drugs, "mind control," or even brain surgery. However, it is none of these things. Behavior modification refers to the systematic application of learning principles (classical conditioning, operant conditioning, and social learning) to change people's actions and feelings. Behavior modification involves a series of well-defined steps that are designed to change behavior. The success of each step is carefully evaluated to find the best solution for a given situation.

The behavior modifier usually begins by defining a problem in concrete terms. For example, Johnnie's mother might complain that her son is messy. If she used behavior modification to reform the child, she would first have to define "messy" in objective terms. For example, he does not make his bed in the morning, he drops his coat on the couch when he comes inside, and so on. She would not worry about where his bad habits come from. Rather, she would work out a system of rewards and punishments aimed at getting Johnnie to make his bed, hang up his coat, and do other straightening-up tasks.

Modeling, operant conditioning, and classical conditioning principles have been used in behavior modification. Classical conditioning principles are particularly useful in helping people to overcome fears. Modeling is often used to teach desired behaviors. In addition, as you will see in the following examples, operant conditioning principles have also been applied to everyday problems.

Computer-Assisted Instruction

Some instructors teach their students by a conversational method very similar to what computer-assisted instruction (CAI) is using today. CAI is a refinement of the concept of programmed instruction that was introduced by S.L. Pressey in 1933 and refined by B.F. Skinner in the 1950s.

The essential concept of programmed instruction is based on operant conditioning. The material to be learned is broken down into simpler units called frames. Each time a student shows that she or he has learned the information in a frame, the student is given positive reinforcement in the form of new information, choices, or point rewards similar to those used in video games. Each question, or prompt, builds on information already mastered. The computer retains (as does the student) exactly what the learner understands on the basis of the student's answers to questions.

Several principles of learning are being applied in CAI. The student is learning complex material through a response chain. She or he is reinforced constantly. Knowledge is being shaped in a systematic and predictable way. The student is able to have a dialogue with the instructor on every point, which is often impossible for a class of students in a conventional setting.

Token Economics

Psychologists tried an experiment with a group of troubled boys in Washington, D.C. In fact, the boys had been labeled "uneducable" and placed in the National Training School. The experimenters used

---

token economy conditioning in which desirable behavior is reinforced with valueless objects, which can be accumulated and exchanged for valued rewards

CHART ∨

HOW SOCIAL LEARNING WORKS CIRCLE

Social learning theorists argue that much learning results from observing the behavior of others and from imagining the consequences of our own behavior.

▶ **CRITICAL THINKING**

1. *Analyzing Visuals* What role does the environment play in social learning?

2. *Interpreting* How do beliefs and values play a role in social learning?

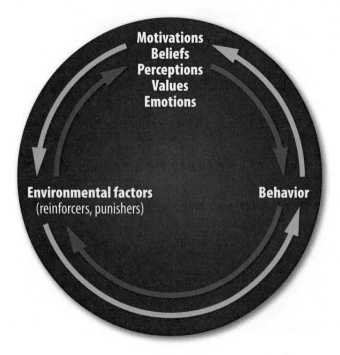

Motivations
Beliefs
Perceptions
Values
Emotions

Environmental factors
(reinforcers, punishers)

Behavior

what is known as a **token economy** to motivate the boys. The youngsters received points—or secondary reinforcers— for good grades on tests. They could cash in these points for such rewards as snacks or lounge privileges. A majority of the students showed a significant increase in IQ scores. The boys continued to improve in the months that followed, showing that they were, indeed, educable. Similarly, behavioral programs to reduce prison violence reduce post-prison violence in the community.

In token economies people are systematically paid to act appropriately. In the real world, behaviorists argue, the rewards are just as real but less systematic. In overcrowded classrooms, for example, the only way some students can get attention is by acting out. Overworked teachers may not have time to respond to students who are not causing trouble. Since attention from the teacher is reinforcing for these students, they are rewarded for undesirable behavior. By systematically rewarding only desirable behavior, token economies have also been effective in improving conditions in prisons, mental hospitals, and halfway houses.

Self-Control

One of the most important features in behavior modification is an emphasis on asking people to set up personal systems of rewards and punishments to shape their own thoughts and actions—this is a self-control program. As in any application of behavior modification, the first step in self-control is to define the problem. People who smoke too much would be encouraged to actually count how many cigarettes they smoked every hour of the day and note what kinds of situations led them to smoke. (After a meal? When talking to friends? Driving to work?) Similarly, people who have a very poor opinion of themselves would have to define the problem of low self-esteem more concretely. They might begin by counting the number of self-deprecating remarks they make and thoughts they have. Researchers have found that just keeping track of behavior in this way often leads a person to start changing it.

The next step may be to set up a behavioral contract. A behavioral contract simply involves choosing a reinforcer (buying a new shirt, watching a favorite TV program, going to a new restaurant) and making it depend on some less desirable but necessary act such as getting to work on time or washing the kitchen floor.

Psychology & YOU

How You Form Bad Habits

Do you procrastinate? For example, have you ever found yourself cramming for an important test the night before? Operant conditioning probably played a role in your bad habit of procrastination. You selected immediate positive reinforcement and delayed punishment. That is, you opted to spend your time doing something else, such as watching TV, instead of studying.

Procrastination provided the immediate reinforcement of giving you more leisure time. The punishment, lower grades or lack of sleep the day before the test, was delayed. Many bad habits are formed when people follow this pattern of immediate reinforcement and delayed punishment.

SQ4R METHOD

Survey the chapter. Read the headings. Read any summaries. Your goal is to get a general understanding of the chapter.
Question the material. Formulate questions about the material as if you were the instructor writing the test.
Read carefully and try to answer the questions you formulated. If you become distracted or tired, stop reading. Pick it up later.
Write down the answers to your questions. Sum up the information in your own words.
Recite to yourself what you have read. Recall main headings and ideas. Be sure to put the material into your own words.
Answer questions aloud.
Review the material. Summarize the main points in the chapter. Answer the questions you have formulated.

PQ4R METHOD

Preview the chapter by surveying general topics to be studied.
Question yourself by transforming headings into questions.
Read the section or chapter carefully while trying to answer the questions you created.
Reflect on the text as you are reading to try and understand it, think of examples, and relate to information about the topic that you already know.
Recite the information by answering your own questions aloud.
Review the material by recalling and summarizing main points.

< TABLE

IMPROVING STUDY HABITS
Studying effectively is an active process. The SQ4R and PQ4R methods are active methods of studying. You can also improve your motivation and study habits using successive approximations (reading one more page each time you sit down to study) and positive reinforcements (rewarding yourself for productive studying).

▶ **CRITICAL THINKING**

1. ***Making Decisions*** How can you improve your own study habits?

2. ***Identifying Cause and Effect*** Why do different people need different rewards as positive reinforcements in improving their study habits?

Some students find study groups an effective way to prepare for tests.

▶ **CRITICAL THINKING**

Identifying What qualities would or do you look for in a study partner?

One soda lover who had trouble studying decided that she would allow herself a soda only after she studied for half an hour. Her soda addiction remained strong, but her study time increased dramatically under this system.

Improving Your Study Habits

In one program to help students improve their study habits, a group of student volunteers were told to set a time when they would go to a small room they had not used before in the library. They were then to work only as long as they remained interested. As soon as they found themselves fidgeting, daydreaming, or becoming bored, they were to read one more page before they left.

The next day they repeated the procedure, adding a second page to the amount they read between the time they decided to leave and the time they actually left the library. The third day they added a third page, and so on. Students who followed this procedure found that in time they were able to study more efficiently and for longer periods.

Why did this procedure work? Requiring students to leave as soon as they felt distracted helped reduce the negative emotions associated with studying. Studying in a new place removed the conditioned aversive stimulus. Thus, aversive responses were not conditioned to the subject matter or the room, as they are when students force themselves to work. The procedure also made use of successive approximations. The students began by reading just one more page after they became bored and only gradually increased the assignment. In conclusion, it is important to note that classical and operant conditioning and social learning do not operate independently in our lives. All three forms of learning interact in a complex way to determine what and how we learn.

Not all learning is passive—the simple result of responses to stimuli. We can take an active role in learning by setting specific, measurable goals. Goals make us more efficient and effective learners. To achieve the greatest benefit, establish goals that are challenging, yet achievable with a reasonable effort.

☑ **READING PROGRESS CHECK**

Analyzing Why does one begin behavior modification by defining a problem in concrete terms?

Echo/Cultura/Getty Images

LESSON 3 REVIEW (CCSS)

Reviewing Vocabulary
1. *Explaining* How is a token economy an example of behavior modification?

Using Your Notes
2. *Applying* Use your notes from your graphic organizer to apply behavior modification to overcoming learned helplessness.

Answering the Guiding Questions
3. *Explaining* What is the principle behind cognitive learning?

4. *Applying* What principles of modeling should parents consider when rewarding and punishing their children? Provide reasons for your answer.

5. *Stating* What is the first step in behavior modification?

Writing Activity
6. *Informative/Explanatory* Write out a behavior modification plan (example: stopping your friend from knuckle cracking) that includes a specific application of learning principles.

Directions: On a separate sheet of paper, answer the questions below. Make sure you read carefully and answer all parts of the question.

Lesson Review

Lesson 1

1 *Sequencing* Describe the process of acquisition in classical conditioning using the terms US, UR, CS, and CR.

2 *Making Connections* Explain how generalization and discrimination of stimuli are complementary processes in classical conditioning.

3 *Analyzing* Businesses often make use of conditioning techniques in their commercials. Think of specific examples of such advertising. Describe how the principles of conditioning are used in those advertisements.

Lesson 2

4 *Contrasting* What are the key differences between classical conditioning and operant conditioning?

5 *Identifying* What are the four partial schedules of reinforcement and how do they differ?

6 *Explaining* Describe the Law of Effect.

Lesson 3

7 *Identifying Central Issues* How does the concept of latent learning demonstrate cognitive learning principles?

8 *Drawing Conclusions* What types of environments might contribute to learned helplessness?

9 *Contrasting* How does observational learning differ from disinhibition? Give classroom examples.

21ˢᵗ Century Skills

Using Charts Review the chart of O. Hobart Mowrer's experiment to stop bed-wetting. Then answer the questions that follow.

Mowrer's Experiment	Stimulus	Response
Before Conditioning	Full bladder (neutral stimulus); alarm (US)	No awakening; Awakening (UR)
During Conditioning	Full bladder (CS) paired with an alarm (US)	Awakening (UR)
After Conditioning	Full bladder (US)	Awakening (CR)

10 *Understanding Relationships Among Events* What happened in the above experiment? What things were paired to lead to awakening?

11 *Problem Solving* Explain how the CS, US, CR, and UR relate to the end result (awakening).

12 *Drawing Conclusions* Will the newly conditioned behavior be subject to extinction?

Exploring the Essential Question

13 *Simulating* Select some particular task you find unpleasant. Make a playlist of some of your favorite songs and listen to it whenever you begin working on this task. Do this for two weeks and then analyze your reactions. Have your feelings toward the music become associated with the task? Do you find it easier to work and complete the task? Write a report that explains your findings in light of what you know about conditioning techniques.

Need Extra Help?

If You've Missed Question	1	2	3	4	5	6	7	8	9	10	11	12	13
Go to page	237	238	236	244	247	251	256	258	259	240	237	238	237

Directions: On a separate sheet of paper, answer the questions below. Make sure you read carefully and answer all parts of the question.

Critical Thinking Questions

14 *Synthesizing* How might a therapist help cigarette smokers quit smoking using classical conditioning techniques? Using operant conditioning techniques? Using social learning techniques?

15 *Debating* Is punishment an effective learning tool? Debate the advantages and disadvantages of using punishment as a technique to reinforce behavior.

16 *Identifying Cause and Effect* Which of the schedules of reinforcement do your instructors generally use in conducting their classes? How would your classes be different if they used the other schedules?

College and Career Readiness

17 *Research and Methods* Go to a public place where you can watch parents and children interacting. Watch a parent-child interaction long enough to identify an aversive stimulus the parent or child may be using to control behavior. What particular behavior of the child is the parent attempting to change? What particular behavior of the parent is the child attempting to change? Are they successful? Collect your observations and conclusions in a report.

Research and Technology

18 *Evaluating* Use the Internet to locate the Web site of a self-help or support group at which self-control and other self-improvement techniques are taught. You should look for the following stages and techniques: definition of the problem, establishment of behavioral contracts, and application of reinforcers in a program of successive approximations. Evaluate the site and summarize your findings in a brief report.

DBQ Analyzing Primary Sources

Use the document to answer the following questions.

PRIMARY SOURCE

"One depressed woman would not eat and was in danger of dying of starvation, but she seemed to enjoy visitors and the TV set, radio, books and magazines, and flowers in her room. The therapists moved her into a room devoid of all these comforts, and put a light meal in front of her; if she ate anything at all, one of the comforts was temporarily restored. The therapists gradually withheld the rewards unless she ate more and more. Her eating improved, she gained weight, and within two months she was released from the hospital. A follow-up eighteen months later found her leading a normal life."

-from *The Story of Psychology* by Morton Hunt, 1993

19 *Identifying* What type of learning is being applied in the woman's treatment?

20 *Theorizing* What are some other situations where this type of treatment could change behavior?

Psychology Journal Activity

21 *Informative/Explanatory* Reread the journal entry in which you described your attempts to teach a skill or task. Did you use classical conditioning, operant conditioning, or social learning techniques? Make a new entry, describing and identifying your learning techniques. Explain why your teaching strategy was successful or unsuccessful.

Need Extra Help?

If You've Missed Question	14	15	16	17	18	19	20	21
Go to page	237	252	247	250	260	244	244	234

Memory and Thought

ESSENTIAL QUESTION • *How does the passage of time affect the brain?*

Psychology Matters...

Your brain holds and processes an impressive amount of information. This information forms the basis of your memories, which play a significant role in making you who you are. Psychologists continue to study the brain to learn more about how it captures the endless details that you encounter every second of the day—things like sounds, smells, faces, images, directions, and names. In this chapter, you will learn how your brain processes, stores, and retrieves information.

◀ The brain holds a lifetime of memories, enabling our storage and retrieval of memories of recent events as well as our earliest childhood experiences.

Paul Viant/Taxi/Getty Images

265

Lab Activity

You Might Not

Remember, But . . .

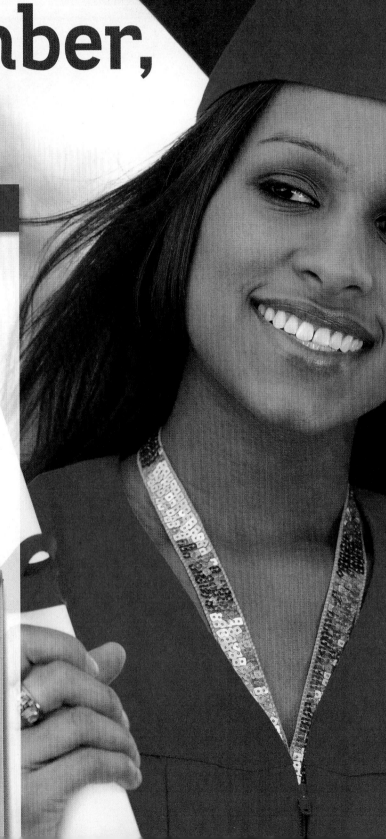

THE QUESTION...

RESEARCH QUESTION How vulnerable is memory to distortion?

Have you ever experienced a special moment that you hoped would live on as a great memory? Perhaps crossing the stage to collect your diploma or catching a beautiful sunset at the end of a great day made you say to yourself, "I'm going to remember this for the rest of my life." Will you? Much about the process of forming memories remains a mystery. Laboratory psychologists have yet to fully understand the process. However, there is much that we *do* know, including how essential memory is to thought.

The formation of memories is a complex process. Let's make use of its twists and turns in the following experiment.

Psychology Journal Activity

Think about the relationship between studying and memory. Write about this in your Psychology Journal. Consider these issues: Have you seen evidence that the more you study the more you remember? Have you seen evidence that deep thinking on a subject leads to stronger memories than skimming the material?

FINDING THE ANSWER...

HYPOTHESIS Memory can be distorted by simple suggestion.

THE METHOD OF YOUR EXPERIMENT

MATERIALS two detailed images, descriptions of both images

PROCEDURE Use the Internet to find a highly detailed image, such as an urban scene with buildings, signs, cars, and people. Print out two copies of the image. Create a short description of the image, including as many of the details as possible. Then, in a separate document, create another description that includes several purposefully inaccurate details about the image. Recruit six participants. To administer the experiment, show the image to each person for 15 seconds. Then, have three participants read the accurate description, and the other three read the inaccurate one. After three days, bring your participants together and have them write ten details they remember about what was contained in the photo.

DATA COLLECTION Count the number of inaccurate details reported in each test. Indicate on each test whether that participant had read the accurate or inaccurate description. Study your results to see if there is a relationship between the misleading description and the subjects' memories of the details in the image.

ANALYSIS & APPLICATION

1. Did your results support the hypothesis?

2. How could this experiment have been improved to yield better data?

3. What does this experiment tell you about how memories are formed? What are some other ways that the memory process could be disrupted?

networks ONLINE LAB RESOURCES

Online you will find:

- An **interactive lab experience**, allowing you to put principles from this chapter into practice in a digital psychology lab environment. This chapter's lab will include an experiment allowing you to explore issues fundamental to memories and thought.

- A **Skills Handbook** that includes a guide for using the scientific method, creating experiments, and analyzing data

- A **Notebook** where you can complete your Psychology Journal, and record and analyze data from your experiment

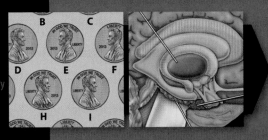

networks

There's More Online!

- ☑ **CHART** Three Systems of Memory
- ☑ **DIAGRAM** Memory Centers in the Brain
- ☑ **DIAGRAM** Processes of Memory
- ☑ **DIAGRAM** Spot the Real Penny
- ☑ **SELF-CHECK QUIZ**
- ☑ **TABLE** Stages of Memory

LESSON 1
Taking In and Storing Information

ESSENTIAL QUESTION • *How does the passage of time affect the brain?*

Reading HELPDESK (CCSS)

Academic Vocabulary
- series
- precede

Content Vocabulary
- encoding
- storage
- retrieval
- sensory memory
- short-term memory
- maintenance rehearsal
- chunking
- semantic memory
- episodic memory
- declarative memory
- procedural memory

TAKING NOTES:

Key Ideas and Details

DIFFERENTIATING In a diagram similar to the one below, identify the stages of memory. Describe the functions and limits of each stage.

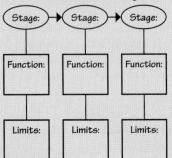

IT MATTERS BECAUSE

Consider all the material packed into your memory: your locker combination, the lyrics to all your favorite songs, your best friend in first grade, and so on. What kind of incredible filing system allows you to instantly recover a line from your favorite movie? This is the power of memory, which captures and stores endless amounts of information.

Processes and Stages of Memory

GUIDING QUESTION *How does information transition from short- to long-term memory?*

Memory is the input, storage, and retrieval of what has been learned or experienced. Who sings your favorite song? Who were your closest friends in eighth grade? To recall this information, your brain must first encode and store it.

The first memory process is **encoding**—the transforming of information so that the nervous system can process it. You use your senses—hearing, sight, touch, taste, and smell—to encode memories. You use *acoustic codes* when you try to remember something by saying it out loud or to yourself. For example, in trying to remember the notes that make up the spaces in the treble clef of a musical measure, you would repeat the letters "F," "A," "C," and "E." When you attempt to keep a mental picture of the letters, you are using *visual codes*. Another way you might try to remember the notes is by using *semantic codes*. In this way, you try to remember the letters by making sense of them. For example, if you wanted to remember the letters "F," "A," "C," "E," you might remember the word *face*. This way you only have to remember the word rather than the individual letters.

After information is encoded, it goes through the second memory process, **storage**. This is the process by which information is maintained over time. How much information is stored depends on how much effort was put into encoding the information and its importance. Information can be stored for a few seconds or for much longer.

The third memory process, **retrieval**, occurs when information is brought to mind from storage. The ease with which information can be retrieved depends on how efficiently it was encoded and stored, as well as on other factors, such as genetic background and our past experiences.

Sensory Memory

Once the senses encode a memory in the brain, the brain must hold on to the input and store it for future reference. One model distinguishes three stages of memory—sensory, short-term, and long-term—each of which has a different function and time span.

In **sensory memory**, the senses of sight, hearing, and touch are able to hold an input for a fraction of a second before it disappears. For example, when you watch a movie, you do not notice the gaps that actually exist between frames. The actions seem smooth because each frame is held in your sensory storage until the next frame arrives. In 1960, researcher George Sperling demonstrated this phenomenon in an ingenious experiment. He used a tachistoscope, a device that presents a picture for a very brief time, to present a group of letters and numbers to people for a twentieth of a second. For instance, take a look at the image below:

8	1	V	F
X	L	5	3
B	7	W	4

Previous studies had shown that if you present a stimulus like this to people, they will usually be able to tell you four or five of the items. Sperling believed that the stimulus created a visual image of the letters and that only a few could be read back before the image faded. Psychologists refer to this visual sensory memory as *iconic memory*. You can think of this in terms of your brain taking a quick mental picture of an object or image. Iconic memories hold visual information for up to a second.

Sperling told the participants in his experiment that after he flashed the letters on the tachistoscope screen, he would present a tone. Upon hearing a high tone, the participants were to tell him the top row. Upon hearing a medium tone, they were to tell him the middle row. Finally, with a low tone they were to tell him the bottom row. Participants found that they were able to remember a great deal. They could recall about 75 percent of any one row if asked to do so immediately.

encoding the transforming of information so the nervous system can process it

storage the process by which information is maintained over a period of time

retrieval the process of obtaining information that has been stored in memory

sensory memory very brief memory storage immediately following initial stimulation of a receptor

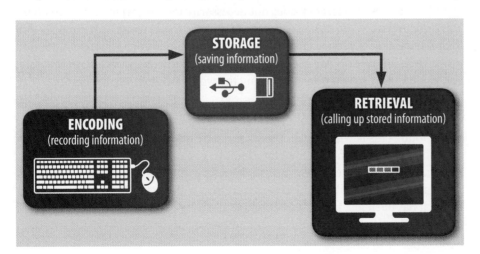

‹ DIAGRAM

PROCESSES OF MEMORY

Memory involves three processes. Each process is as important as the others. If one process fails, memory fails.

▶ CRITICAL THINKING

1. *Differentiating* What does the first process of memory involve?
2. *Analyzing Visuals* What does this model suggest is the nature of memory?

STAGES OF MEMORY
Psychologists often compare human memory to a computer, though our storage is not so large and our recall is less than perfect. Beyond our working years human memory seems to grow more limited. We retain less and recall many later-life experiences with both greater difficulty and usually less accuracy.

▶ **CRITICAL THINKING**

1. *Contrasting* How do the capacities of sensory memory and short-term memory differ?

2. *Differentiating* Give another example of short-term memory.

	Sensory memory	Short-term memory	Long-term memory
Capacity	Virtually everything you see or hear at one instant	About 7 items in healthy adults	Vast; uncountable
Duration	Fraction of a second	Less than 20 seconds if not rehearsed	Perhaps a lifetime
Example	You see something for an instant, and then someone asks you to recall one detail	You look up a telephone number and rehearse it long enough to dial it	You remember the house where you lived when you were 7 years old

Sperling proved that the participant retains a brief image of the whole picture so that he or she can still read off the items in the correct row after the picture has left the screen. Psychologists refer to auditory sensory memory as *echoic memory*, a type of sensory memory that holds auditory information for 1 or 2 seconds.

Sensory memory serves three functions. First, it prevents you from being overwhelmed. Every second of every day, you are bombarded with various incoming stimuli. If you had to pay attention to all of these stimuli—what you are immediately seeing, hearing, smelling, and feeling—you would be easily overwhelmed. Since the information in sensory memory is short-lived, anything that you do not pay attention to vanishes in seconds.

Second, sensory memory gives you some time to make a decision. The information in sensory memory is there for only a few seconds. It is present just long enough for you to decide whether it is worth paying attention to or not. If you choose to pay attention, the information is automatically transferred to short-term memory.

Finally, sensory memory allows for continuity and stability in your world. For instance, iconic memory makes images in your world smooth and continuous, whereas echoic memory lets you play back auditory information, giving you time to recognize sounds as words. The information held momentarily by the senses has not yet been narrowed down or analyzed. It is short-lived, temporary, and fragile. However, by the time information gets to the next stage—short-term memory—it has been analyzed, identified, and simplified so that it can be stored and handled for a longer time.

Short-Term Memory

The things you have in your conscious mind at any one moment are being held in **short-term memory**. The operations of short-term memory can be likened to the operations of random access memory in a computer—the information that is entered is only temporary until it is saved to the hard drive, or long-term memory. Our short-term memory does not necessarily involve paying close attention. You have probably had the experience of listening to someone only partially and then having that person accuse you of not paying attention. You deny it, and to prove your innocence, you repeat, word for word, the last words he or she said. You can do this because you are holding the words in short-term memory.

Maintenance Rehearsal To keep information in short-term memory for more than a few seconds, you usually have to repeat the information to yourself or out loud. This is what psychologists mean by **maintenance rehearsal**. When you look up a telephone number, for example, you can remember the seven digits long enough to dial them if you repeat them several times. If you are distracted or make a mistake in dialing, the chances are you will have to look up the number again. It has been lost from short-term memory. By using maintenance rehearsal, repeating the telephone number over and over again, you can keep the information longer in short-term memory.

short-term memory
memory that is limited in capacity to about seven items and in duration by the subject's active rehearsal

maintenance rehearsal
a system for remembering that involves repeating information to oneself without attempting to find meaning in it

Psychologists have measured short-term memory by seeing how long a participant can retain a piece of information without rehearsal. The experimenter shows the participant three letters, such as CPQ, followed by three numerals, such as 798, one second later. To prevent rehearsal, the participant has been instructed to start counting backward by threes and reporting the result in time with a time keeping device, like a metronome, striking once per second. If the participant performs this task for only a short time, she or he will usually remember the letters. If kept from rehearsing for 18 seconds, however, recall will be no better than a random guess; the information is forgotten. Short-term memory lasts a bit less than 20 seconds without rehearsal.

Chunking Short-term memory is limited not only in its duration but also in its capacity. It can hold only about seven unrelated items at one time. Suppose, for example, someone quickly reels off a long **series** of numbers to you in conversation. You will be able to keep only about seven (plus or minus two) of them in your immediate memory. Beyond that number, confusion about the remaining numbers in the series will set in. The same limit is there if the unrelated items are a random set of words. We may not notice this limit to our capacity because we usually do not have to store so many unrelated items in our immediate memory. Either the items are related, as when we listen to someone speak, or they are rehearsed and placed in long-term memory.

The most interesting aspect of this limit is that it involves about seven items, on average, of any kind. Each item may consist of a collection of many other items, but if they are all packaged into one chunk, then there is still only one item. Thus we can remember about seven unrelated sets of initials, such as COMSAT, HIV, DVR, or the initials of our favorite radio stations, even though we could not remember all the letters separately. This is referred to as **chunking** because we have connected, or chunked, these letters together. In other words, the letters HIV become one item, not three individual items.

One of the tricks of memorizing a lot of information quickly is to chunk together the items as fast as they come in. If we connect items in groups, we have fewer to remember. For example, we remember new phone numbers in two or three chunks (253-6794 or 253-67-94) rather than as a string of seven digits (2-5-3-6-7-9-4). We use chunking to remember visual as well as verbal inputs. We remember shape and appearance as much or easier than we remember the actual pieces of information.

Even with chunking, storage in short-term memory is only temporary. Information is available, generally, for less than 20 seconds and no more than 30 seconds, assuming no rehearsal has occurred. After that, it is stored in long-term memory, or it is lost. Short-term memory contains information that is of possible interest. Information worth holding on to must be rehearsed with the intent to learn in order to transfer it to long-term memory. Rehearsal without intent to learn yields no transfer, no memory.

series a number of related or similar things arranged in a sequence

chunking the process of grouping items to make them easier to remember

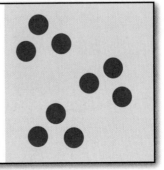

Glance quickly at the left figure in this pair, then look away. How many dots did you see? Now do the same with the right figure. You were probably surer and more accurate in your answer for the right figure.

< DIAGRAM

USING SHORT-TERM MEMORY
One of the ways to memorize information quickly is to organize it by number, shape, or appearance.

▶ CRITICAL THINKING

1. **Analyzing** Why were you surer and more accurate in your answer for the right figure?

2. **Interpreting** How many chunks does the right figure show?

The Primacy-Recency Effect The *primacy-recency* effect refers to the fact that we are better able to recall information presented at the beginning and end of a list. Suppose you read a 15-item grocery list and then immediately wrote down as many items as you could remember. You would most likely remember the first few items in the list because you had more time to rehearse them. This is the *primacy effect*. You may have also recalled the last four or five items in the list because they were still accessible in short-term memory. This is the *recency effect*. However, you may have forgotten the middle items in the list. When trying to remember the middle items in a list, your attention is split between trying to remember previous items and trying to rehearse new ones.

Working Memory *Working memory* is essential for thinking and problem solving. It includes two components: short-term memory and executive attention. The short-term memory component consists of the limited information that humans can keep in mind at one time. The executive attention component is a regulatory process that determines the type and amount of information that short-term memory can access. Working memory has been described as a mental scratch pad on which relevant bits of information are stored. When it is no longer needed, that information is erased or replaced by more pertinent information. There may be differences in the ways we process working short-term visual and spatial memories from the ways we process working short-term verbal memories. Research has focused primarily on short-term verbal memory.

Long-Term Memory

Long-term memory refers to the storage of information over extended periods of time. Information is not stored like a piece of paper in a filing cabinet; it is stored according to categories or features. You reconstruct what you must recall when you need it. When you say a friend has a good memory, you probably mean he or she can recall a wide variety of information accurately. The capacity of long-term memory appears to be limitless. Long-term memory contains representations of countless facts, experiences, and sensations. You may not have thought of your childhood home for years, but you can probably still visualize it.

Long-term memory involves all the processes we have been describing. Suppose you go to see a play. As the actors say their lines, the sounds flow through your sensory storage. These words accumulate in short-term memory and form meaningful phrases and sentences.

You attend to the action and changing scenery in much the same way. Together, they form chunks in your memory. An hour or two later, you will have forgotten all but the most striking lines, but you have stored the meaning of the lines and actions in your long-term memory. The next day, you may be able to give a scene-by-scene description of the play to someone else who did not see it.

Maintenance rehearsal

Sensory input → **SENSORY MEMORY** → Attention → **SHORT-TERM (WORKING) MEMORY** → Encoding → **LONG-TERM MEMORY**

Retrieval

Unattended information is quickly lost

Unrehearsed information is quickly lost

Some information may be lost over time

Throughout this process, the least important information is dropped and only the essentials are retained. A month or two later, without much rehearsal, you may remember only a brief outline of the plot and perhaps a few particularly impressive moments. In time you may not remember much of anything about the play. Other, more recently stored items block your access to earlier memories, or may even replace them. Yet if you see the play again, you will probably remember the key elements of the plot, recognize the lines of the play, and anticipate the actions. Although it has become less accessible, the different elements of the play are still stored in long-term memory.

For almost a century, the study of memory focused on how long information was stored for usage. Then a Canadian psychologist, Endel Tulving, proposed that we have two types of memory. The first, semantic memory, is our knowledge of language, including its rules, words, and meanings. We share that knowledge with other speakers of our language. The second, episodic memory, is our memory of our own life, such as when you woke up this morning. Stored here are personal things where time of occurrence is important. Everyone's episodic memory is unique.

Tulving was merely giving names to types of memory that had already been recognized by others:

> ❝The 1972 distinction between episodic and semantic memory was not at all original. Many philosophers as well as students of memory pathology had expressed similar ideas all along. I suspect that my paper turned out to be popular partly because, like the character in Moliere's play who discovers that he has been speaking prose all his life without knowing it, mainstream students of memory were pleased to find out what it was that they had been studying.❞
>
> —Endel Tulving
> This Week's Citation Classic® CC/Number 48 (1987)

L.R. Squire has proposed a related model of memory. Declarative memory involves both episodic and semantic memory. This is information you call forth consciously and use as you need it. Procedural memory does not require conscious recollection to have past learning or experiences impact our performance. One form of procedural memory involves *skills*, learned as we mature—including both complex skills such as swimming or driving a car and simple skills such as tying a tie. As we gain a skill, we gradually lose the ability to describe what we are doing. Other types of procedural memory, such as fear of bugs, include habits and things learned through classical conditioning.

✅ **READING PROGRESS CHECK**

Differentiating What is the difference between iconic and echoic memory?

Memory and the Brain

GUIDING QUESTION *Where in the brain does the process of memory begin?*

Over the years, philosophers and psychologists have used many different metaphors to help explain how memory works. Most of these assumed that memories are stored in specific locations in the brain. The metaphors changed as technology changed. Aristotle compared these locations to a wax tablet, and John Locke compared them to a cabinet. In the 1950s, memory was compared to a telephone exchange system, and today it is most often compared to a computer. Models of memory focused on a dual-storage system, with both short-term storage and long-term storage.

∧ **DIAGRAM**

SPOT THE REAL PENNY

Which is the genuine penny among the fakes? (Look at a penny or ask your teacher for the correct answer.) Even though you live in the United States and probably see hundreds of pennies a week, it is difficult to identify the real one. Mere repetition, such as seeing something over and over again, does not guarantee a strong memory.

▶ **CRITICAL THINKING**

1. ***Analyzing*** What could you do to remember exactly how a penny looks?

2. ***Drawing Inferences*** Suppose you learned the history of each element on a penny. How could this help you remember what a penny looks like?

semantic memory
knowledge of language, including its rules, words, and meanings

episodic memory
chronological retention of the events of one's life

declarative memory stored knowledge that can be called forth consciously as needed

procedural memory
permanent storage of learned skills that does not require conscious recollection

The Study of Memory and the Brain

Modern studies of memory have their beginnings in 1885, when German psychologist Hermann Ebbinghaus published a paper entitled *Memory*. Using himself as the only subject, he gathered experimental data for over a year. Ebbinghaus then duplicated the entire procedure during another year before publishing. He came up with the idea of using 2,300 nonsense syllables (consonant-vowel-consonant combinations) with which to measure the amount of material that could be retained. He had to develop methods of controlling the degree of learning and measuring the amount of retention. He used mathematics to calculate the statistical significance of his findings. His innovations in methodology, as well as his findings on memory, have stood the test of time.

Ebbinghaus was the first to discover the shape of the learning curve; the length of time it takes to memorize nonsense syllables increases sharply as the number of syllables increases. He discovered that distributing learning over time is more effective than trying to "cram" information in a single session. He also found that continuing to practice material even after it has been learned has the effect of improving retention.

Five years later, American philosopher and psychologist William James published *The Principles of Psychology,* which is considered to be the first important complete psychology text. James believed that memory was essential to survival, but that there was no need to retain every bit of information, which would overload the brain with useless information. He divided all memory into two types, which he called primary and secondary memory, or "memory proper."

According to James, primary memory is short-lived. It allows us to experience consciousness and handle immediate concerns, such as problem solving. Secondary memory is used to manage the relatively permanent information stored in the brain. In the 1950s and 1960s, primary memory came to be known as short-term memory, and secondary memory as long-term memory.

DIAGRAM >

MEMORY CENTERS IN THE BRAIN
Researchers have identified the parts of the brain that are involved in memory.

▶ **CRITICAL THINKING**

1. *Analyzing Visuals* What parts of the brain are involved in remembering the date of a special event?

2. *Making Inferences* How might injury to the hippocampus affect a person's memory?

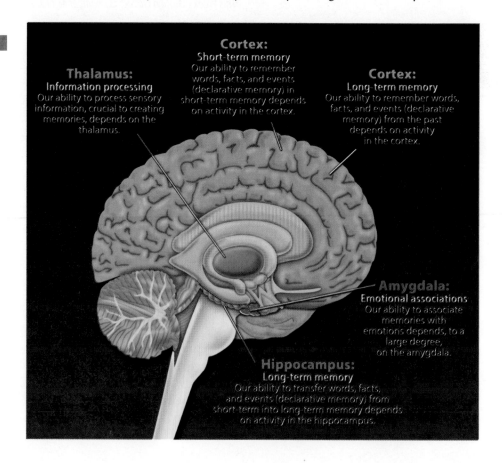

Thalamus:
Information processing
Our ability to process sensory information, crucial to creating memories, depends on the thalamus.

Cortex:
Short-term memory
Our ability to remember words, facts, and events (declarative memory) in short-term memory depends on activity in the cortex.

Cortex:
Long-term memory
Our ability to remember words, facts, and events (declarative memory) from the past depends on activity in the cortex.

Amygdala:
Emotional associations
Our ability to associate memories with emotions depends, to a large degree, on the amygdala.

Hippocampus:
Long-term memory
Our ability to transfer words, facts, and events (declarative memory) from short-term into long-term memory depends on activity in the hippocampus.

MODELS OF MEMORY

Starting in the 1960s and 1970s, memory research focused on differences between short-term and long-term memory and among types of long-term memory. In 1968, Richard Atkinson and Richard Shiffrin proposed that memories pass from sensory to short-term to long-term stores. They viewed each stage as a separate store, or compartment, of memory. This is the *multi-store model* described in this lesson. In the early 1970s, Alan Baddeley and Graham Hitch reconceptualized short-term memory as working memory. They saw working memory as a separate system from long-term memory. In 1972 Endel Tulving distinguished between the types of long-term memory: episodic and semantic.

Fergus Craik and Robert Lockhart, also in 1972, envisioned mental processing as a continuum from shallow to deep. Their *levels of processing model* proposed that the strength of memory depends on the depth with which incoming information is analyzed and encoded. *Shallow* or *surface processing* takes in information based on sensory features. This results in fragile memory that fades quickly. *Deep* or *elaborate processing* analyzes information based on semantic and conceptual features, creating more enduring memories. Instead of maintenance rehearsal, which is simple repetition, *elaborative rehearsal* involves thinking about the meaning in an active, purposeful way. Strategies include paraphrasing, applying, providing examples, and relating the concept to other concepts you already know. For example, suppose you want to remember the term "cortex." You could look up its meaning, study its parts, think about what it does, and relate it to other parts of the brain that you have studied previously.

Researchers today are using neuroimaging technology to relate brain activity to memory processes. Many recent studies are looking at how memory systems interact with each other.

Levels of Processing

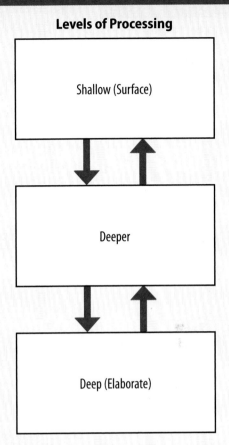

▶ **CRITICAL THINKING**

1. *Applying* How would you learn the term "memory" based on shallow processing?

2. *Applying* How would you learn the term "memory" based on deep processing?

Physiological Changes

What happens in the brain when something is stored in long-term memory? The answers are highly controversial. There is growing evidence that physiological changes occur in the brain, but psychologists are only beginning to identify how and where memories are stored.

What physiological changes occur when we learn something? Some psychologists theorize a change in the neuronal structure of nerves occurs. Others contend that learning is based on molecular or chemical changes in the brain. The evidence is more and more clear that both sides are correct. What changes occur depend on the level at which you are examining the changes learning creates.

Where does learning occur? Different areas of the brain are responsible for different kinds of memories. There is growing evidence that formation of procedural memories involves activity in an area of the brain called the *striatum*, deep in the front part of our cortex. Declarative memories result from activity in the hippocampus and the amygdala.

Memory problems can sometimes take a surprising twist. One example is the peculiar condition known as *prosopagnosia* (pro · so · pahg · NO · shia), in which the patient is unable to recognize familiar faces—even his or her own face. People who have this condition can still perceive other aspects of faces, however, such as whether a person's expression is happy or sad. This memory problem usually results from a stroke or head injury.

precede to come before in time, order, or rank

It is not clear yet how individual nerve cells—called neurons—establish connections with one another when learning occurs. It is clear that a very complex chemical process **precedes** the formation of new connections between neurons. Some have credited increases in calcium. Others talk of decreased potassium flow. Processes as diverse as increased protein synthesis, heightened levels of glucose, and other biochemical processes are involved. Exactly how it all fits together remains an active area of research.

As people age, their ability to retrieve memories changes, in large part due to physiological changes in the brain. A younger person's frontal lobes are adept at focusing on important information and screening out less important events. An older person may find it more difficult to multi-task as the lobes are not as agile, finding it more difficult to discriminate between environmental stimuli and admit only those that are important.

Searching for the Engram

Over the years, there have been various theories concerning where in the brain memories are located or stored. Since the 1920s, scientists have looked for a chemical code that produces an actual physical change, or memory trace, in the nervous system. They call the hypothetical means by which memory traces are stored the *engram*.

American psychologist Karl S. Lashley spent three decades searching for the engram. He conducted experiments in which he removed tissue from the cortex of rats' brains in an attempt to locate the physiological seat of memory. Rats were trained to run a maze. Their ability to remember what they had been trained to do was observed and measured after tissue had been removed from different locations on the cortex. While the amount of tissue removed affected rats' memories, the location from which it was removed did not appear to have any effect. Lashley concluded that memories are not stored in a specific location but distributed throughout the cortex. His failure to find the engram may have been a result of his choice of memory task or his choice of the brain region to study. Nonetheless, his work demolished previous theories on brain function and learning, including a theory that the brain functioned like a type of switchboard.

Other experimental psychologists have posited that the engram may be located in the cerebellum or the hippocampus, or even in our RNA. Various experiments have been conducted on a number of animal species, but the search for the engram continues. Its existence remains hypothetical.

☑ READING PROGRESS CHECK

Specifying What kinds of physiological changes occur when we learn something?

LESSON 1 REVIEW

Reviewing Vocabulary
1. *Describing* List and describe the processes of memory.

Using Your Notes
2. *Differentiating* Review the notes that you completed during the lesson to write a paragraph that differentiates among the three stages of memory.

Answering the Guiding Questions
3. *Finding the Main Idea* How does information transition from short- to long-term memory?

4. *Identifying* Where in the brain does the process of memory begin?

Writing Activity
5. *Informative/Explanatory* Write a skit that illustrates how you would perform activities such as swimming or bicycle riding if you did not have procedural memory. Share your skit.

FOCUS
on research

Case Study

The Case of H.M.

Period of Study: 1953

Introduction: In 1953 a man named Henry, who was known by the initials H.M., underwent major surgery in an effort to cease or minimize the occurrence of severe epileptic seizures. The seizures impacted his ability to hold a job. The doctors chose to remove the hippocampus. Knowledge regarding the function of the hippocampus, however, was limited at that time.

The surgery proved quite effective in decreasing the frequency and severity of the seizures. In fact, preliminary tests showed that H.M.'s IQ had risen slightly because he now could better concentrate on tasks. Doctors detected an unforeseen and devastating result of the surgery—H.M. had lost the ability to store new long-term memories. Although he could remember events that occurred before the operation, H.M. could no longer retain information about events occurring after the surgery. If he saw a new face or learned a new fact, he would forget it just minutes later. Amazingly, he could still read, carry on conversations, and solve problems. He could recall information he learned five to ten seconds beforehand, but H.M.'s brain could not transfer that recently experienced information into long-term memory.

PRIMARY SOURCE

❝*Dr. MILNER: Could you tell me what you had for lunch today?*
H.M.: I don't know, to tell you the truth. . . .
Dr. MILNER: What happened in 1929?
H.M.: The stock market crashed.
Dr. MILNER: It sure did.❞

—*Dr. Suzanne Corkin*

Hypothesis: The case of H.M. sparked many theories about the functions of the hippocampus region of the brain. One theory proposed that the transfer of short-term memory into long-term memory was fixed in the hippocampus region. H.M.'s memories before the operation remained mostly intact, but after the operation, there was no hippocampal region to which to transfer new memories—new information had nowhere to go and so could not be recalled later.

Method: Doctors tested H.M. by presenting him with information, distracting him momentarily, and then asking him to recall the first discussion.

Results: H.M. was unable to learn sequences of digits beyond the usual short-term span of seven digits. Likewise, he could not recognize images of people shown and described to him just a short time earlier.

Interestingly, H.M. demonstrated that he could learn difficult motor skills such as learning to use a walker. Although H.M. clearly demonstrated skill in completing these activities, he reported never to have learned the activities. This implied that H.M. could learn new motor abilities even though he could not retain new long-term memories. The most apparent source of H.M.'s problem was a disruption in transferring short-term memory to long-term memory. This indicated that the hippocampal region is not involved with storing long-term memory, because recollection of presurgery events was intact. Thus, the hippocampus region of the brain *may be* the component involved in this memory transferring process but *definitely is* a pathway through which this information travels.

H.M. lived the rest of his life with the frustration of not remembering the current year, his age, or where he lived. Initially cared for by relatives, he spent the last 28 years of his life in a nursing home and had to be accompanied by someone everywhere he wanted to go. He needed constant reminders of what he was doing. He could not remember anything following the year 1953—the year of his surgery. Sadly, H.M. was literally "frozen in time."

Analyzing the Case Study

1. *Identifying Central Issues* What type of surgery did H.M. have? Why?

2. *Interpreting* What does the excerpt tell you about H.M.'s memory?

3. *Making Inferences* If a virus destroyed your hippocampus, what effect would it have on your performance in school?

Memory and Thought **277**

PHOTO: (l) Jeffrey Coolidge/The Image Bank/Getty Images; (r)Taxi/Getty Images; TEXT: Excerpt from interview with Henry Molaison, conducted by Suzanne Corkin. Copyright © 1992 by Suzanne Corkin, used by permission of The Wylie Agency LLC.

Reader's Dictionary

exertion: physical or mental effort

prowess: skill or expertise in an activity or field

stark: severe or bare in appearance or outline

deceptive: misleading

perpetrator: someone who commits wrongdoing

Are police officers, witnesses, and victims of crime always reliable sources? In this article, we explore the impact of physical exertion on the ability to remember details of an incident or surrounding environment. Studies have shown that using physical energy in a stressful, combative situation may decrease one's ability to remember details of the encounter. These findings have implications for law enforcement and the legal system.

Just 60 Seconds of Combat Impairs Memory

Association for Psychological Science press release

PRIMARY SOURCE

Just 60 seconds of all-out physical **exertion** in a threatening situation can seriously damage the memories of those involved for many details of the incident, according to a new study of police officers.

Police officers, witnesses and victims of crime suffer loss of memory, recognition and awareness of their environment if they have had to use bursts of physical energy in a combative encounter, according to scientists.

Researchers, led by Dr Lorraine Hope of the University of Portsmouth, found that less than 60 seconds of all-out exertion, as might happen when an officer is forced to chase-down a fleeing suspect or engage in a physical battle with a resistant criminal, can seriously impair their ability to remember details of the incident—or even identify the person who was involved.

Even officers in top condition are not immune to the rapid drain of physical **prowess** and cognitive faculties resulting from sustained hand-to-hand combat.

The findings, published in *Psychological Science,* a journal of the Association for Psychological Science, are a **stark** warning to police officers, police chiefs and the courts, according to Dr Hope, a Reader in applied cognitive psychology of the university's Department of Psychology.

She said: "Police officers are often expected to remember in detail who said what and how many blows were received or given in the midst of physical struggle or shortly afterwards. The results of our tests indicate it may be very difficult for them to do this.

"As exhaustion takes over, cognitive resources tend to diminish. The ability to fully shift attention is inhibited, so even potentially relevant information might not be attended to. Ultimately, memory is determined by what we can process and attend to.

"The legal system puts a great deal of emphasis on witness accounts, particularly those of professional witnesses like police officers. Investigators and courts need to understand that an officer who cannot provide details about an encounter where physical exertion has played a role is not necessarily being **deceptive** or uncooperative. An officer's memory errors or omissions after an intense physical struggle should not unjustly affect his or her credibility."

The research, conducted on police officers in Winnipeg, Canada was coordinated and funded by the Force Science Institute. The research team in Canada included Dr Lorraine Hope (University of Portsmouth), Dr Bill Lewinski (Force Science Institute) and specialists from the Metropolitan Police in the UK.

Researchers recruited 52 officer volunteers (42 males, 10 females), with an average of eight years on the job. All officers were fit and healthy and engaged in regular exercise.

During an initial briefing, the officers were given background information about a recent spate of armed robberies in the city. The briefing included details of how the robberies were conducted and witness descriptions of the **perpetrators**. Half of the officers then engaged in a full-force physical attack on a 300lb hanging water bag and the others (a control group) were assigned as observers. Officers selected their own "assault movements" on the bag attack—punches, kicks, and/or palm, elbow, and knee strikes—and were verbally encouraged by a trainer during the task. They continued the assault on the bag until they no longer had strength to keep going or until they were breathless and struggling to continue.

The next part of the test required the officers to approach a trailer that a "known criminal" was suspected of occupying. On entering the trailer, the officers found themselves in a realistic living area where a number of weapons, including an M16 carbine, a revolver, a sawn-off shotgun and a large kitchen knife were visible. After a short delay, the "target individual" emerged from another room and shouted aggressively at the officer to get out of his property. The individual was not armed, but several of the weapons were within easy reach.

Dr Hope found those who had been asked to exert themselves physically remembered less about the target individual and made more recall errors compared to the control group of observers. The officers who had been exerted also recalled less about the initial briefing information and what they did report was less accurate. Officers who had been exerted also reported less about an individual they encountered incidentally while en route to the trailer. While more than 90 per cent of non-exerted observers were able to recall at least one descriptive item about him, barely one-third of exerted officers remembered seeing him at all.

Everyone remembered seeing the angry suspect in the trailer, but non-exerted observers provided a significantly more detailed description of him and made half as many errors in recall as those who were exhausted. These observers were also twice as likely to correctly identify the suspect from a line-up.

However, another striking aspect of the findings showed that exerted officers were able to register threat cues in the environment to the same degree as non-exerted officers.

These new findings reveal that although exerted officers were able to pay attention to the threatening aspects of the scene, their ability to then process other aspects of the interaction was affected. As a result of this, some information may only have been processed weakly or not at all—resulting in an impaired memory for many details of the encounter.

Analyzing Primary Sources

1. *Paraphrasing* Why does memory for detail decrease when one is physically exerted?

2. *Applying* Why would a police offer be able to remember the type of gun pointed at him during an altercation, but not the color of the perpetrator's coat?

3. *Drawing Conclusions* What implications do these study findings have for the legal system?

Reading **HELP**DESK (CCSS)

Academic Vocabulary

• **index** • **mental**

Content Vocabulary

• **recognition**
• **recall**
• **reconstructive processes**
• **confabulation**
• **schemas**
• **eidetic memory**
• **decay**
• **interference**
• **elaborative rehearsal**

TAKING NOTES:

Key Ideas and Details

DIAGRAMMING In a diagram similar to the one below, identify five techniques that you can use to improve your memory.

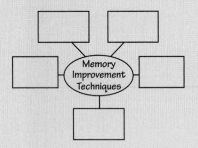

LESSON 2

Retrieving Information

ESSENTIAL QUESTION • *How does the passage of time affect the brain?*

IT MATTERS BECAUSE

The brain has a tremendous capacity for storing and retrieving information. Have you ever wondered why you remember some things more easily or vividly than others, or why something you haven't thought about for years is so easy to recall? In this lesson, you will learn how your brain recalls memories, why you sometimes forget, and how you can improve your memory.

Recognition, Recall, and Relearning

GUIDING QUESTION *Why is eyewitness testimony prone to distortion?*

The problem of memory is to store many thousands of items in such a way that you can find the particular item you need when you need it. The solution to retrieval is organization. Because human memory is extraordinarily efficient, it must be extremely well organized. Psychologists do not yet know how it is organized, but they are studying the processes of retrieval for clues.

Human memory is organized in such a way as to make recognition quite easy—people can say with great accuracy whether or not something is familiar to them. If someone asked you to recall the name of your first-grade teacher, for example, you might not remember it. Chances are, however, that you would recognize that same teacher's name if you heard it. Similarly, a multiple-choice test may bring out knowledge that a student might not be able to show on an essay test. The ability to recognize suggests that much more information is stored in memory than one might think.

The process of **recognition** provides insight into how information is stored in memory. We can recognize the sound of a particular musical instrument (say, a piano) no matter what tune is being played on it. We can also recognize a tune no matter what instrument is playing it. This pattern of recognition indicates that a single item of information may be indexed under several headings so that it can be reached in many ways. A person's features, for instance, may be linked to a large number of categories. The more categories the features are filed in, the more easily they can be retrieved, and the more likely you are to recognize someone.

Recall

More remarkable than the ability to recognize information is the ability to recall it. **Recall** is the active reconstruction of information. Just think about the amount of recall involved in a simple conversation. Each person uses hundreds of words involving all kinds of information, even though each word and bit of information must be retrieved separately from the storehouse of memory.

Recall involves more than searching for and finding pieces of information, however. It involves a person's knowledge, attitudes, and expectations. The brain is not like a video recorder that plays back episodes intact. Remembering is an active process guided by experience, knowledge, and cues we receive from the environment. Recall is influenced by **reconstructive processes**. Our memories may be altered or distorted, depending on our experiences, attitudes, and inferences from other information. One type of mistake is called **confabulation**, which is when a person "remembers" information that was never stored in memory. If our reconstruction of an event is incomplete, we fill in the gaps by making up what is missing. Sometimes we may be wrong without realizing it.

Occasionally our memories are reconstructed in terms of our **schemas**. These are conceptual frameworks we use to make sense of the world. They are sets of expectations about something that is based on our past experiences. Elizabeth Loftus and J.C. Palmer conducted a classic study on the roles that schemas play in memory reconstruction.

Participants in this study watched a film of a two-car accident. They were then asked to fill out a questionnaire about the accident. One of the questions had four different versions. Some participants were asked, "About how fast were the two cars going when they *contacted* each other?" In the other versions of the questions, the words *hit, bumped,* or *smashed* were substituted for the word *contacted*. Participants given the question with the word *contacted* recalled a speed of 32 mph. Those given the word *hit* recalled a speed of 34 mph, those given the word *bumped* recalled 38 mph, and those given the word *smashed* recalled speeds of 41 mph. Therefore, the schemas people used—whether the cars contacted, hit, bumped, or smashed—affected the way they reconstructed the crash.

recognition memory retrieval in which a person identifies an object, idea, or situation as one he or she has or has not experienced before

recall memory retrieval in which a person reconstructs previously learned material

reconstructive processes the alteration of a recalled memory that may be simplified, enriched, or distorted, depending on an individual's experiences, attitudes, or inferences

confabulation the act of filling in memory gaps

schemas conceptual frameworks a person uses to make sense of the world

We can recognize the same person in different contexts, such as face-to-face or in a picture.

▶ **CRITICAL THINKING**

Drawing Inferences What does the phenomenon of recognition suggest about how information is stored in memory?

Elizabeth Loftus
(1944–)

Elizabeth Loftus has spent much of her life gathering evidence that memory is extremely fragile and not always accurate. She has shown that eyewitness testimony is often unreliable and that false memories can be triggered merely by suggestion.

Loftus' work is controversial because it raises doubts about the validity of repressed memories of repeated trauma, such as that of childhood abuse. Loftus testified in the case of George Franklin. Franklin was sent to jail for murder after his daughter Eileen recalled, 20 years later, that her father had killed her friend. Eileen had recounted the details of the murder to the police in amazing detail. Eileen's memory of the event, though, had changed to match media descriptions of it. Loftus noted that memory changes over time, and as time passes, memories distort. She believes Eileen may have unconsciously created the memory as a result of childhood abuse she suffered at the hands of her father.

▶ **CRITICAL THINKING**

Drawing Conclusions Based on this account, do you think Eileen believed her testimony or was intentionally lying? Explain.

Ask your parents where they were on September 11, 2001, when they found out that terrorists had attacked New York's World Trade Center. They will most likely remember it in vivid detail. Similarly, people who were alive at the time have vivid memories of hearing about the bombing of Pearl Harbor or the assassinations of President John F. Kennedy or Martin Luther King. This ability is called *flashbulb memory*. This type of memory usually involves events that are shocking or emotional. Scientists have concluded that flashbulb memories involve special kinds of encoding that occur when events are extreme and/or personal. Studies have revealed that the details of people's flashbulb memories are not always accurate, although people generally perceive them as accurate. Each generation has its flashbulb memories. The flashbulb memories your generation shares will differ from those of your parents' generation.

About 5 percent of all children do not seem to reconstruct memories actively. They have an **eidetic memory**, a form of photographic memory shared by few adults. Children with eidetic memory can recall very specific details from a picture, a page, or a scene briefly viewed. Photographic memory in adults is extremely rare. It involves the ability to form sharp visual images after examining a picture or page for a short time and then recalling the entire image later.

State-Dependent Learning

Have you ever become upset at someone and, while doing so, remembered many past instances of when you were upset at the same person? This is an example of state-dependent learning. *State-dependent learning* occurs when you recall information easily when you are in the same physiological or emotional state or setting as you were when you originally encoded the information. This is why some people advise you to study for a test in the same classroom or setting in which you will take the test. Being in a certain physiological or emotional state serves as a cue to help you more easily recall stored information.

One situation in which recognition is extremely important is in the courtroom. It is very convincing to a judge or jury when an eyewitness points to someone in the room and says, "He's the one who did it."

Elizabeth Loftus has shown that even after it had been proven that the eyesight of a witness was too poor for her to have seen a robber's face from where she stood at the scene of a robbery, the jury was still swayed by her testimony. Lawyers cite many cases of people falsely accused by eyewitnesses whose testimonies later proved to be inaccurate.

A person's memory of an event can be distorted in the process of remembering it. Shocking events, such as those involving violence, can disrupt our ability to form a strong memory. Without a strong, clear memory of the event, the eyewitness is more likely to incorporate after-the-fact information into the recall. Jurors should remember that the eye is not a camera, and recall is not like videotape.

Relearning

While recognition and recall are measures of declarative memory, relearning is a measure of both declarative and procedural memory. Suppose you learned a poem as a child but have not rehearsed it in years. If you can relearn the poem with fewer recitations than someone with ability similar to yours, you are benefiting from your earlier learning. Psychologists measure relearning in terms of savings. If it originally takes ten attempts before something is remembered completely, but after five relearning trials only takes five attempts, then five trials have been saved. Relearning previously acquired knowledge can thus enhance future learning.

✓ **READING PROGRESS CHECK**

Explaining Why might a multiple choice test be easier than an essay test?

Forgetting

GUIDING QUESTION *Why do people forget?*

Everyone experiences a failure of memory from time to time. You are sure you have seen that person before but cannot remember exactly where. You have the word on the tip of your tongue, but. . . . When information that once entered long-term memory is unable to be retrieved, it is said to be forgotten. Forgetting may involve decay, interference, or repression.

Some inputs may fade, or **decay**, over time. Items quickly decay in sensory storage and short-term memory, as indicated earlier. It is not certain, however, whether long-term memories ever decay. We know that a head injury or electrical stimulation of certain parts of the brain can cause loss of memory. The memories lost, however, are the most recent ones; older memories seem to remain. The fact that apparently forgotten information can be recovered through meditation, hypnosis, or brain stimulation suggests that at least some memories never decay. Rather, interference or repression causes people to lose track of them.

Interference

Interference refers to a memory being blocked or erased by previous or subsequent memories. This blocking is of two kinds: proactive and retroactive. In *proactive interference* an earlier memory blocks you from remembering later information. In *retroactive interference* a later memory or new information blocks you from remembering information learned earlier. Suppose you move to a new home. You now have to remember a new address and phone number. At first you may have trouble remembering them because the memory of your old address and phone number gets in the way (proactive interference). Later, you know the new information but have trouble remembering the old data (retroactive interference). It is important to note that proactive interference does not lead to retroactive interference; the two are separate concepts.

It may be that in some cases, interference does erase some memories permanently. In other cases, the old data have not been lost. The information is in your memory somewhere, if only you could retrieve it. According to Sigmund Freud, sometimes blocking is no accident. A person may subconsciously block memories of an embarrassing or frightening experience. This kind of forgetting is called *repression*. The material still exists in the person's memory, but it has been made inaccessible because it is so disturbing, according to Freud.

Amnesia

Some also forget information due to amnesia. *Amnesia* is a loss of memory that may occur after a head injury or as a result of brain damage. Amnesia may also be the result of drug use or severe psychological stress. *Infant amnesia* is the relative lack of memories from early in life. For example, why is it that we do not seem to remember much from when we were 2 or 3 years old? Although some children do form lasting memories, most memories from early childhood seem to fade away.

Psychologists have proposed several theories to explain infant amnesia. Freud thought that infant memories are repressed because of the emotional traumas of infancy. Others believe that because infants do not yet understand language, their memories are nonverbal, whereas later memories are verbal (once language is learned). Still others claim that the hippocampus may not be mature enough in infancy to spark memories or that infants have not yet developed a sense of self to experience memories.

☑ **READING PROGRESS CHECK**

Identifying What are three processes involved in forgetting?

eidetic memory the ability to remember with great accuracy visual information on the basis of short-term exposure

decay fading away of memory over time

interference blockage of a memory by previous or subsequent memories or loss of a retrieval cue

At one time or another we have all had to memorize items—a list of facts, telephone numbers, or a dialogue in a play. Are there ways to improve these memorization tasks?

Procedure

1. Give several friends and classmates the following list of numbers to memorize: 6, 9, 8, 11, 10, 13, 12, 15, 14, 17, 16, etc.
2. Tell some people to simply memorize the number sequence.
3. Tell others that there is an organizational principle behind the number sequence (which they are to discover) and to memorize the numbers with the aid of this principle. (The principle here is "plus 3, minus 1.")

Analysis

1. Which group was better at remembering the number sequence?
2. Why do you think this is so? Write a brief analysis.

elaborative rehearsal the linking of new information to material that is already known

index to enter into a sequential arrangement of material

Improving Memory

GUIDING QUESTION *What are the benefits of rehearsal?*

Scientists have identified three phases in the "life" of long-term memory: acquisition, storage, and retrieval. Information must first be acquired, or learned. Once you have acquired a piece of new information, your brain must process it and place it in storage. Finally, it must be possible to retrieve that memory at a later time if it is to have any value. Researchers have learned a great deal about the methods our brains use to acquire, store, and retrieve memories for long-term use. Techniques for improving your memory are based on the efficient organization of the things you learn and on chunking information into easily handled packages, or chunks.

Meaningfulness and Association

As we discussed earlier, using repetition, or maintenance rehearsal, can help you remember for a short period of time. In this method, words are merely repeated with no attempt to find meaning. A more efficient way of remembering new information involves **elaborative rehearsal**. In this method, you relate the new information to what you already know. The more meaningful something is, the easier it will be to remember. For example, you would be more likely to remember the six letters DFIRNE if they were arranged to form the word FRIEND.

Similarly, you remember things more vividly if you associate them with things already stored in memory or with a strong emotional experience. The more categories a memory is **indexed** under, the more accessible it is. If an input is analyzed and indexed under many categories, each association can serve as a trigger for the memory. If you associate the new information with strong sensory experiences and a variety of other memories, any of these stimuli can trigger the memory. The more senses and experiences you use when trying to memorize something, the more likely it is that you will be able to retrieve it—a key to improving memory.

For similar reasons, a good way to protect a memory from interference is to overlearn it—to keep rehearsing it even after you think you know it well. Another way to prevent interference while learning new material is to avoid studying similar material together. Instead of studying history right after political science, study biology in between.

Your memory will also improve by spacing out your learning. It is more effective to study a few times over a long period of time rather than trying to absorb large amounts of information at one sitting. *Distributed practice*, or spreading out learning over time, results in stronger memories that are easier to retrieve. This is the *spacing effect*.

In addition, how you originally learn or remember something influences how readily you recall that information later. If a bit of information is associated with a highly emotional event or if you learned this bit of information in the absence of interference, you will more easily recall that information because of the strength of that memory.

Mnemonic Devices

Techniques for using associations to memorize information are called mnemonic devices. The ancient Greeks memorized speeches by mentally walking around their homes or neighborhoods and associating each line of a speech with a different spot—called the Method of Loci. Once they made the associations, they could recall the speech by mentally retracing their steps and picking up each line. The rhyme we use to recall the number of days in each month ("Thirty days has September") is a mnemonic device. In the phrase "Every Good Boy Does Fine," the first letters of the words are the same as the names of the musical notes on the lines of a staff (E, G, B, D, and F).

Another useful mnemonic device is to form **mental** pictures. Suppose you have trouble remembering the authors and titles of books or which artists belong to which schools of painting. To plant the fact in your mind that John Updike wrote *Rabbit, Run,* you might picture a RABBIT RUNning UP a DIKE. To remember that Picasso was a Cubist, picture someone attacking a giant CUBE with a PICKAX, which sounds like Picasso. Mnemonic devices are not magical. Indeed, they involve extra work—making up words, stories, and so on. The very effort of trying to do this, however, may help you remember things.

mental of or relating to the mind

Additional Strategies for Remembering What You Study

Memory aids, or little things people do to help improve their ability to remember things, have probably existed since the beginning of time. Tying a string around your finger or writing notes on your hand are two time-honored methods of aiding stimulus recall, or at least reminding you that you have something you should recall. These methods are simple, and have a limited application. What about techniques that can hep you with the more complex tasks of your daily life? Consider the follow techniques to help you remember what you study.

As you study, organize large blocks of information in a way that is meaningful for you. Since we can usually remember only five to nine items at a time, try to organize the information you need to remember into groups of no more than seven items. When you group information, do it in a way that has personal meaning for you. As you do so, try to put the information in sequence, for instance, by alphabetizing it or placing it in chronological order. See if you can come up with a mnemonic device to help you remember the information. For example, take the first letter or syllable of each item and try to make a word.

A mnemonic device is a technique that aids learning. The acronym HOMES helps to remember the names of the Great Lakes: **H**(uron), **O**(ntario), **M**(ichigan), **E**(rie), and **S**(uperior).

▶ CRITICAL THINKING

Interpreting How does this mnemonic device make the information in this photograph easier to remember?

On the Tip of Your Tongue

Have you ever tried to remember something but could not quite do so, saying, "I know it; it's on the tip of my tongue"? What you experienced is called the tip-of-the-tongue phenomenon. Later, in a different situation, the information you were looking for earlier comes to you. Why does this happen? In certain cases, maybe you encoded the information in your memory with insufficient retrieval cues and just cannot find an association to retrieve the memory. In other cases, the information may be blocked through interference. When you think about other things, the information pops back into your memory.

One effective aid to memory is to capture the essence of a lecture. This doesn't mean to record it word-for-word, but to create a summary of its contents. Note-taking, brief, but complete, should summarize the key points, new vocabulary, and any diagrams or tables not included or modified in your text. Go over your notes as soon as possible after class and fill in additional facts and examples. If you have trouble understanding anything that was said, clarify it with a classmate or your teacher. It is crucial, too, that you take your own notes during lecture. Copying class notes from a friend limits the effectiveness of those notes.

Note taking alone is not enough. Students who review their notes do better than those who do not. Reviewing your notes within one or two days helps you cut down on the amount of information that you will have to relearn before a quiz or test. When you review, your notes will help you find what is most important in your textbook. Summarizing your notes in your own words can also help you better understand and remember. Practicing and rehearsing things after you've learned them is called "overlearning." Overlearning is a great help with mastery.

Other Methods of Improving Memory

A number of "smart drugs"—that is, drugs that are designed to enhance memory—have been introduced recently. As tempting as it might be to dream of a pill to improve memory, there's really no demonstrated effective replacement for regular meals, proper drinks, and a reasonable amount of rest. There is very little evidence that pills targeted at improving learning and memory will replace the effort such effects require.

Ginkgo biloba has been used for thousands of years as a medicinal herb. There is evidence that it may enhance memory in healthy people. Vitamin B12 is essential in maintaining healthy nerve cells. That the vitamin is found in animal products, such as fish, meat, eggs, and milk, means that strict vegetarians may develop a B12 deficiency, which has been found to cause memory loss. However, there is no evidence that taking a vitamin supplement enhances memory in people who get enough B12 in their normal diet.

It is important to remember that there is no quick or easy method to improving memory. No pill or dietary supplement can take the place of diligence and studying. It may seem like simple advice, but paying attention and keeping your mind focused on the task at hand is crucial to later recall of information. Also, you should remember that your memory is a function of your body and benefits when you take proper care of yourself. A healthy diet and plenty of rest are vitally important to a fully functioning memory.

☑ **READING PROGRESS CHECK**

Specifying What are some common mnemonic devices?

LESSON 2 REVIEW

Reviewing Vocabulary
1. *Differentiating* What is the difference between proactive and retroactive interference? Between maintenance and elaborative rehearsal?

Using Your Notes
2. *Explaining* Use your notes to list and briefly describe five techniques you can use to improve your memory.

Answering the Guiding Questions
3. *Analyzing* Why is eyewitness testimony prone to distortion?

4. *Identifying Cause and Effect* Why do people forget?

5. *Finding the Main Idea* What are the benefits of rehearsal?

Writing Activity
6. *Informative/Explanatory* Write about a mnemonic device you could use to help you remember something.

Directions: On a separate sheet of paper, answer the questions below. Make sure you read carefully and answer all parts of the question.

Lesson Review

Lesson 1

1 **Describing** What is the purpose of maintenance rehearsal? How does the process work?

2 **Explaining** How does chunking aid short-term memory?

3 **Specifying** What physiological changes occur in the brain when you learn something?

Lesson 2

4 **Explaining** Explain how memories are recalled.

5 **Applying** What is state-dependent learning? How does it relate to studying and taking exams?

6 **Describing** How does confabulation occur?

Critical Thinking Questions

7 **Comparing and Contrasting** In what ways is your memory like a computer? In what ways is it different? Explain your responses.

8 **Synthesizing Information** Try to remember what you did on your last birthday. As you probe your memory, list the mental steps you are going through. What processes do you use to remember?

9 **Making Inferences** As a juror, what concerns might you have when hearing eyewitness testimony? Why?

10 **Assessing** If you were a teacher, why would it be important for you to help make learning meaningful for your students? How would you go about it?

11 **Speculating** Why might a soldier forget a battle memory?

21st Century Skills

Using Graphs The graph below shows the results of an experiment that tested the ability of high school graduates to remember names and faces of classmates. In a recognition test, participants were asked to match yearbook pictures of classmates with their names. In a recall test, participants were shown yearbook pictures and asked to recall the names. Review the graph below and answer the questions that follow.

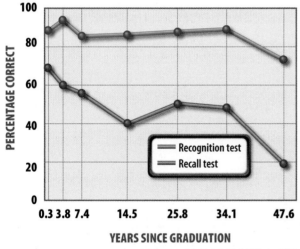

YEARS SINCE GRADUATION

Source: Bahrick, Bahrick, & Wittinger, 1974.

12 **Analyzing Visuals** Which group of participants was most able to recall the names of their classmates?

13 **Analyzing Visuals** What percentage of participants recalled the names of their classmates 34 years after graduation? 48 years after graduation?

14 **Identifying Cause and Effect** What effect does time have on retrieving information when recall is used? When recognition is used?

15 **Speculating** When you remember past events and people, how accurate do you think your memory is? Explain.

Need Extra Help?

If You've Missed Question	**1**	**2**	**3**	**4**	**5**	**6**	**7**	**8**	**9**	**10**	**11**	**12**	**13**	**14**	**15**
Go to page	270	271	275	281	282	281	269	281	282	284	283	281	281	280	282

Directions: On a separate sheet of paper, answer the questions below. Make sure you read carefully and answer all parts of the question.

College and Career Readiness

16 *Understanding Relationships Among Events* Interview four people from your grandparents' generation and four from your parents' generation. Explain what a flashbulb memory is. Then ask them to identify and describe a flashbulb memory from their experience. Write a brief description of the similarities and differences in the memories within each generation. How do you think these flashbulb memories affected the people of that generation?

Research and Technology

17 *Exploring Issues* Search the Internet for Web sites that provide information to help you improve your memory. Several Web sites provide strategies and techniques to help you remember a variety of facts, such as mathematical formulas. Explore and evaluate these sites, try out several memory-improving strategies for yourself, and determine which strategies you found to be the most effective. Classify these strategies according to the *level of processing* theory of memory. Which strategies relied on shallow processing? Which strategies relied on deep processing? Create a report of your findings and share it with your class.

Exploring the Essential Question

18 *Analyzing* With a partner, research techniques advertisers use to move the memory of their product from sensory to short-term to long-term memory. Assess how advertisers adjust their techniques when advertisements have run for a period of time. Create an electronic slide show of your findings. Include advertisements that illustrate different techniques.

DBQ Analyzing Primary Sources

Use the document below to answer the following questions.

PRIMARY SOURCE

" *My experiments reveal how memories can be changed by things that we are told. Facts, ideas, suggestions and other forms of post-event information can modify our memories. The legal field, so reliant on memories, has been a significant application of the memory research.* "

—Elizabeth Loftus, July 2005

19 *Interpreting* According to Dr. Loftus, what is the nature of memory?

20 *Drawing Inferences* How might the legal field apply Dr. Loftus's findings?

Psychology Journal Activity

21 *Interpretative/Explanatory* Review your entry in your Psychology Journal for this chapter. Having learned about encoding and the various steps of forming memories, were you correct about your own experience of forming memories? Why will intense studying lead to stronger memories than skimming the material?

Need Extra Help?

If You've Missed Question	**16**	**17**	**18**	**19**	**20**	**21**
Go to page	282	284	269	282	282	266

Thinking and Language

ESSENTIAL QUESTIONS • *How does the brain solve problems?* • *How does the brain learn new skills?*

Lab Activity
Problems and Solutions

Lesson 1
Thinking and Problem Solving

Lesson 2
Language

Psychology Matters...

Thinking and language are closely intertwined. Most of our thought processes involve language, and the variations in languages appear to color the way we think about things, make decisions, solve problems, and communicate with those around us. To solve the problems encountered on a daily basis we must have a firm grasp of the complexities of both thought and language.

◄ This scientist must have full mastery of both thought and language in order to perform well at his job.

Chris Sattlberger/Cultura/Getty Images

Lab Activity

Problems
and
Solutions

THE QUESTION...

RESEARCH QUESTION What is the best way to solve a difficult problem?

Working with a team of people is one approach to problem solving. If you have ever been involved in a group project, you know the effort it takes to coordinate everyone's role in completing the project. When done correctly, this approach can give you different points of view on to how to develop and complete the project. But does the group approach also work with problem solving? Does it create worthwhile solutions? Is it really the best method for solving problems?

The way to find if something is true or not is to conduct an experiment. The experiment for this lab explores two different methods of problem solving.

Psychology Journal Activity **CCSS**

Think about how you solve problems. Write about this in your Psychology Journal. Consider the following questions: Do you feel that solutions come to you naturally or do you feel like it is hard work? What role do flexibility and creativity play in problem solving?

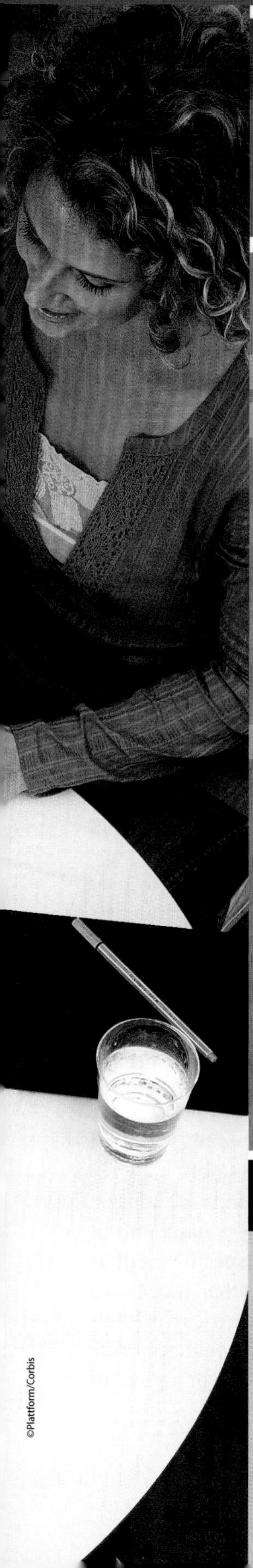

FINDING THE ANSWER...

HYPOTHESIS   As a problem-solving method, working with a group is more effective than working individually.

THE METHOD OF YOUR EXPERIMENT

MATERIALS   four sheets of paper, pens, two rooms

PROCEDURE   Write the following problem on four slips of paper: *Four people come to a river at night. There is a narrow bridge that can only hold two people. They have one flashlight and it must be used when crossing the bridge because it is so dark. Person A can cross the bridge in 1 minute, B in 2 minutes, C in 5 minutes, and D in 8 minutes. When two people cross the bridge together, they must go at the rate of the slower person. Can they all get across the bridge in 15 minutes or less?* Recruit six participants, divide them evenly, and put the two groups in different rooms. Give one slip of paper to the first group and tell the participants to work together to solve the problem. Give the other three participants the problem and tell them to work individually to solve the problem. Participants have 10 minutes to solve the problem and write the answer.

DATA COLLECTION   Determine who came up with the correct answer (*A and B cross in 2 minutes; A returns in 1 minute; C and D cross in 8 minutes; B returns in 2 minutes; A and B cross in 2 minutes*). Was it the group or an individual? Gather as a class to compare your results.

ANALYSIS & APPLICATION

1. Did your results support the hypothesis?

2. Did your subjects in the group solve the problem more quickly than your individuals? Explain why one might want a larger number of participants for solving a problem.

3. Why might working alone be less effective than working in a group to solve a problem?

netw⊙rks   ONLINE LAB RESOURCES

Online you will find:

- An **interactive lab experience**, allowing you to put principles from this chapter into practice in a digital psychology lab environment. This chapter's lab will include an experiment related to thinking and language.

- A **Skills Handbook** that includes a guide for using the scientific method, creating experiments, and analyzing data.

- A **Notebook** where you can complete your Psychology Journal and record and analyze data from your experiment.

©Plattform/Corbis

netw⊙rks

There's More Online!

☑ **DIAGRAM** Connecting the Dots

☑ **DIAGRAM** Decision Trees

☑ **DIAGRAM** Overcoming Functional Fixedness

☑ **DIAGRAM** Overcoming Wrong Assumptions

☑ **DIAGRAM** Using Imagery

☑ **SELF-CHECK QUIZ**

Reading **HELP**DESK (CCSS)

Academic Vocabulary

• approach   • flexibility

Content Vocabulary

• image
• symbol
• rule
• metacognition
• algorithm
• heuristic
• mental set
• functional fixedness

TAKING NOTES:

Key Ideas and Details

LISTING Use a graphic organizer like the one below to list the characteristics of creative thinking.

Characteristics of Creative Thinking

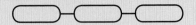

LESSON 1

Thinking and Problem Solving

ESSENTIAL QUESTIONS • *How does the brain solve problems?* • *How does the brain learn new skills?*

IT MATTERS BECAUSE

If storage and retrieval were the only processes we used to handle information, human beings would be little more than glorified recording devices. Yet we are capable of doing things with information that make the most complex computers seem simple by comparison. These processes—thinking and problem solving—are most impressive when they show originality or creativity.

Thinking

GUIDING QUESTION *What are the building blocks of mental activity?*

We may view *thinking* as changing and reorganizing the information stored in memory to create new or transformed information. Our thinking may be triggered by either internal or external stimuli. By thinking, humans are able to put together any combination of words from memory and create sentences never devised before, such as this one. Words play such an important part in most of our thinking that some psychologists have defined thinking as the stringing together of linguistic elements.

The psychology of thinking focuses on the kinds of activity typically associated with inventors and mathematicians. Psychologists do not agree on a single approach to thinking. Some see thinking as a cognitive process, involving the way we view and relate to the world. Others approach it as internal problem-solving behavior. In this lesson, you will learn about different kinds of thinking.

Units of Thought

The processes of thought depend on several devices, or units of thought: images, symbols, concepts, prototypes, and rules. One very basic unit of thought is an **image**, a visual, mental representation of a specific event or object. The representation is not usually an exact copy; rather, it contains only the highlights of the original. For example, if an adult tries to visualize a grandmother who died when he was seven, he would probably remember only a few details—perhaps the color of her hair or a piece of jewelry she wore—without a portrait or photo.

Imaging is an effective way to think about concepts. In one study, two researchers presented participants with 1,600 pairs of geometric images. The researchers then asked the participants to determine if the objects in each pair were identical or different. The researchers discovered that the participants completed the task by rotating an image of one of the objects in their minds in an effort to see both patterns from the same perspective. Another abstract unit of thought is a **symbol**, a sound, object, or design that represents an object or quality. The most common symbols in thinking are words; every word is a symbol that stands for something other than itself. An image represents a specific sight or sound, but a symbol may have a number of meanings. That symbols differ from the things they represent enables us to think about things that are not present, to consider the past and future, and to imagine things and situations that never will be or never were. Numerals, letters, punctuation marks, and icons are all familiar symbols of ideas that have no concrete existence.

When a symbol is used as a label for a class of objects or events with at least one common attribute—or for the attribute itself—it is called a *concept*. *Animals*, *music*, *liquid*, and *beautiful people* are examples of concepts based on the common attributes of the objects and experiences belonging to each category. Thus the concept *animal* separates a group of organisms from such things as automobiles, carrots, and Roquefort cheese. Concepts enable us to chunk large amounts of information. We do not have to treat every new piece of information as unique, since we already know something about the class of objects or experiences to which the new item belongs.

When we think of a concept, we often think of a representative example of it. When you think of a vehicle, for example, you might picture a car or a truck. This representation is called a *prototype*. The prototype you picture may not be an example that you have actually experienced. Most often it simply is an example that has most of the characteristics of the particular concept.

A more complex unit of thought is a **rule**, a statement of a relation between concepts. The following are examples of rules: a person cannot be in two places at the same time; mass remains constant despite changes in appearance. Rules are particularly important in problem solving.

Images, symbols, concepts, prototypes, and rules are the building blocks of mental activity. They provide an economical and efficient way for people to represent reality, to manipulate and reorganize it, and to devise new ways of acting. For example, a person can think about pursuing several different careers, weigh the pros and cons of each career, and then decide which one to pursue without having to try every one of them.

Rather than considering thinking a verbal process (that is, one involving words), scientists who are cognitivists view thinking as made up of unique processes. They believe that the way "cognitive" elements are organized is of supreme importance. They see inferences, applications of rules, and other components of thinking at work in even the most basic kinds of learned behavior.

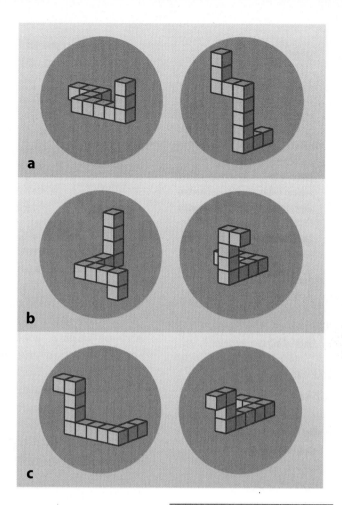

a

b

c

^ DIAGRAM

USING IMAGERY
Mentally rotate the patterns paired above to make them match. Do the drawings in each pair represent the same object, or are they different? (Check which pairs match with your teacher.)

▶ **CRITICAL THINKING**

1. *Explaining* How do we use images when we are thinking about something?

2. *Analyzing* How do concepts help us process information?

image a visual, mental representation of an event or object

symbol an abstract unit of thought that represents an object or quality; anything that stands for or represents something else

rule a statement of relation between concepts

Thinking and Language **293**

DIRECTED VS. UNDIRECTED THINKING

This problem was devised by psychologist Edward de Bono, who believes that conventional directed thinking is insufficient for solving new and unusual problems. His approach to problem solving requires use of undirected thinking to generate new ways of looking at the problem situation. The solution appears on the final page of this lesson.

▶ **CRITICAL THINKING**

1. *Explaining* When are people most likely to engage in undirected thinking?

2. *Making Connections* How is metacognition related to directed thinking?

approach a way of thinking about something

flexibility able to change to meet new conditions or situations

---

An old money-lender offered to cancel a merchant's debt and keep him from going to prison if the merchant would give the money-lender his lovely daughter. Horrified yet desperate, the merchant and his daughter agreed to let Providence decide.

The money-lender said he would put a black pebble and a white pebble in a bag and the girl would draw one. The white pebble would cancel the debt and leave her free. The black one would make her the money-lender's, although the debt would be canceled. If she refused to pick, her father would go to prison.

From the pebble-strewn path they were standing on, the money-lender picked two pebbles and quickly put them in the bag, but the girl saw that he had picked up two black ones. What would you have done if you were the girl?

Kinds of Thinking

People think in many different ways. There have been a number of attempts to categorize the ways people think, but no one system has prevailed. One **approach** is to divide them into reasoning and problem solving. Another is to divide them into directed thinking and undirected thinking.

Reasoning brings together the results of two or more learning experiences to arrive at a desired goal. There are two major types of reasoning: deductive reasoning, or deduction, and inductive reasoning, or induction. *Deduction* takes a "top-down" approach, working from the more general to the more specific. In other words, it is schema-driven. Here is an example of deduction: *All mammals have DNA. Sheep are mammals. Therefore, sheep have DNA.*

Induction, on the other hand, takes a "bottom-up" approach, working from the specific to broader generalizations. Here is an example of induction: *Sheep are mammals and they have DNA. Pigs are mammals and they have DNA. Horses are mammals and they have DNA. Therefore, all mammals have DNA.* Good inductive reasoning leads to a conclusion that is probable, or likely to be true, but may require further investigation.

Directed thinking is a systematic and logical attempt to reach a specific goal or answer, such as the solution to a math problem, through reasoning. This kind of thinking depends on symbols, concepts, and rules. Directed thinking is deliberate and purposeful. It is through directed thinking that we solve problems; formulate and follow rules; and set, work toward, and achieve goals.

Problem solving involves two main types of thinking—divergent and convergent thinking. *Divergent thinking* consists of trying to come up with a variety of possible alternative solutions to a problem. *Convergent thinking* consists of trying to narrow down many possibilities to find the one best answer to a problem. An essay test would normally involve divergent thinking, while a multiple-choice test is an example of convergent thinking. Divergent thinking is sometimes referred to as *creative thinking* since it calls for **flexibility** and inventiveness.

In contrast to direct thinking, another type of thinking, called *undirected* (or *nondirected*) *thinking*, consists of a free flow of thoughts with no particular plan and depends more on images. Undirected thinking is usually rich with imagery and feelings such as daydreams, fantasies, and reveries. People often engage in undirected thought when they are relaxing or escaping from boredom or worry. This kind of thinking may provide unexpected insights into one's goals and beliefs. Scientists and artists say that some of their best ideas emerge from drifting thoughts that occur when they have set aside a problem for the moment.

One simple form of realistic thinking (that is, thinking concerned with the "outside" world) allows people to distinguish distinct objects or pieces of information. The outcome of this process is a *judgment*, and the process can be referred to as decision making. A number of factors affect people's ability to make good judgments. Generally, the more information we have available, the more sound our judgments will be. One of the symptoms of Alzheimer's disease, or dementia, is progressive difficulty in making sound judgments.

Yet another type of thinking is **metacognition**, which is the ability to control our cognitive processes. It is often defined as "thinking about thinking." You are using metacognition whenever you think of the accuracy or validity of your thoughts, decisions, and judgments. When you tackle an algebra problem and cannot solve it, thinking about your strategy may cause you to change to another strategy. Other types of activities related to metacognition include monitoring your understanding and measuring your progress toward the completion of a task. Metacognition plays an important part in successful learning.

metacognition the awareness of or thinking about one's own cognitive processes

Decision Making

Every day, we are called upon to make decisions. Some of them, such as what to wear or what to have for lunch, are routine. Others, such as where to locate a store or whether to discontinue a product line, are more complicated. When a decision is a step in the problem-solving process, it is especially important to make the right decisions.

Normally, the decision-making process is so automatic that we aren't even aware of the process, at least not until our decisions have unforeseen outcomes. Then we may ask ourselves why we decided to go with that particular option.

Connecting Psychology to Civics

TOP-DOWN AND BOTTOM-UP PROCESSING

The terms *top-down* and *bottom-up* originated with computerized information processing and are similar in meaning to *analysis* and *synthesis*. Both business and government have borrowed the two terms to refer to styles of policy making, or broad scale decision making. In top-down policy making, the government or organization initiates, or starts, the process. In bottom-up policy making, groups advocating for a policy take the initiative.

In governmental policy making, the top-down approach uses vision statements and issues of national priority as set by government leaders. Supporters of this approach view those who create policy as authorities and focus their attention on matters that can be controlled at the national level. The bottom-up approach to policy making emphasizes the group or groups that will be affected by a policy. Under this approach, grassroots groups can initiate policies.

Most theorists believe that there is a relationship between the two approaches. The best policies will not work if the people who are responsible for putting them into action are unwilling or unable to do so. The capabilities and commitment of mid-level departments or organizations can strongly affect a policy's success or failure.

A participatory approach to designing policy involves including those individuals or groups who are affected by the policy in the decision-making process. Their participation may be in the design, monitoring, evaluation, or reform of the policy. There can either be a top-down push for inclusion initiated by the government or organization, or a bottom-up push initiated by groups trying to influence a policy.

▲ Most decisions made by governments are top-down decisions.

▶ **CRITICAL THINKING**

1. *Identifying Cause and Effect* What effect would different types of policy making have on individual personality development?

2. *Making Connections* Have you ever been subject to a top-down decision? What was the resulting impact on your personal development?

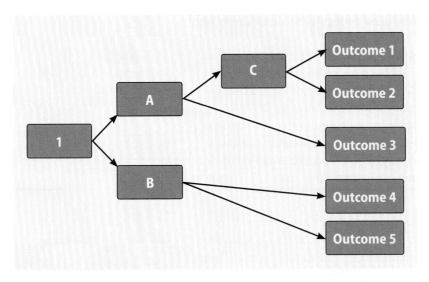

A "gut decision" is one we make by intuition. It may be influenced by our emotions, memories, or biases.

Finding the best way of making a decision is important. A number of strategies and tools have been devised to help people with the process. Setting deadlines can help people who are procrastinators. Creating lists, such as lists of priorities or pros and cons, can help people organize and see the available options.

Making good decisions is not just important for individuals. It is also one of the most important management skills for the leaders of companies and businesses. Spreadsheets can help provide "what-if" scenarios. An impact analysis can help identify the unexpected consequences of a decision. One popular tool is the decision tree. The decision tree is a diagram showing various courses of action, any factors that may cause uncertainty, and various possible outcomes for all those actions and factors. A decision tree is particularly helpful in making decisions involving many stages or alternatives.

Obstacles to Decision Making

The decision-making process can itself become a problem. People often have difficulty making decisions for a number of reasons. Sometimes they simply avoid making decisions altogether; other times they just procrastinate, or put them off until later. There are other obstacles, as well. People may fear failure, they may not completely understand the choices that need to be made, or they may not take the correct approach.

✔ **READING PROGRESS CHECK**

Contrasting What is the difference between a symbol and a concept? An image and a prototype?

Problem Solving

GUIDING QUESTION *How can problem solving strategies become obstacles?*

One of the main functions of directed thinking is to solve problems—to bridge the gap mentally between a present situation and a desired goal. The gap may be between hunger and food, a column of figures and a total, a lack of money and bills to pay, or cancer and a cure. In all these examples, getting from the problem to the solution requires some directed thinking.

Strategies

Problem solving depends on the use of strategies, or specific methods for approaching problems. There are usually several steps to solving a problem. Each step involves making decisions. The first step is to define the problem. The second step is to come up with alternatives, or possible solutions to the problem. One way of doing this is to brainstorm; that is, to just throw out any ideas that come to mind, no matter how ridiculous they may seem. The next step is to evaluate the alternatives and select the best one. Finally, it is time to put the solution to the problem into action.

When dealing with complex problems, one strategy is to break down the problem into a number of smaller, more easily solved subgoals. *Subgoals* are intermediate steps toward a solution. For example, it is the end of the semester and your schedule is crazy. You solve the problem by breaking it down into small pieces: studying for the science exam, finishing that overdue paper, canceling your movie date, scheduling regular study breaks to maintain what is left of your sanity, and so forth. For some problems, you may work backward from the goal you have set. Mystery writers often use this method: They decide how to end the story ("who did it") and then devise a plot leading to this conclusion.

Another problem may require you to examine various ways of reaching a desired goal. Suppose a woman needs to be in Chicago by 11 A.M. on July 7 for a business conference. She checks train departures and arrivals, airline schedules, and car-rental companies. The only train to Chicago that morning arrives at 5 A.M. (too early), and the first plane arrives at 11:30 A.M. (too late). So she decides to rent a car and drive.

There is evidence that experts and novices think and solve problems in different ways. To determine which strategy to use, most of us analyze the problem to see if it resembles a situation we have experienced in the past. A strategy that worked in the past is likely to work again. We tend to do things the way we have always done them before, and we often shy away from new situations that call for us to use new strategies. The more unusual the problem, the more difficult it is to devise a strategy for dealing with it. Two methods for solving problems are algorithms and heuristics.

An **algorithm** is a fixed set of procedures that, if followed correctly, will lead to a solution. Mathematical and scientific formulas are algorithms. For example, to find the product of 345 and 23, we multiply the numbers according to the rules of multiplication to get a correct answer of 7,935. To play chess or checkers, we follow algorithms, or a fixed set of rules.

While algorithms can be useful in finding solutions to problems, they are a time-consuming method. People often use shortcuts to solve problems, and these shortcuts are called heuristics. **Heuristics** are experimental strategies, or rules of thumb, that simplify a problem, allowing one to solve problems quickly and easily. For example, when watching the *Wheel of Fortune* game show, you might use what you already know about prefixes, suffixes, and roots of words to fill in the missing letters of a word or phrase. If a friend comes to you with a problem, your advice might include what has worked for you in the past.

Although heuristics allow us to make quick decisions, they can result in bad decisions. When we make decisions using shortcuts, we sometimes ignore pertinent information.

algorithm a step-by-step procedure for solving a problem

heuristic a rule-of-thumb problem-solving strategy

TABLE ⌄

TYPES OF HEURISTICS
Heuristics are mental shortcuts. Although they are not rules that always provide the correct answers, they are strategies that experience has taught us to apply.

▶ **CRITICAL THINKING**

1. *Defining* What is the representative heuristic?

2. *Making Predictions* The weather has been unusually hot and dry for the past six months. If you were asked to predict what the probability was that it would be hot and dry for the next year, what would you say? What heuristic might you use in making your prediction?

Availability Heuristic	We rely on information that is more prominent or easily recalled and overlook information that is available but less prominent.	**Example:** In the news, we see people winning the lottery all the time and overestimate our chances at winning it also.
Representativeness Heuristic	We tend to assume that if an item is similar to members of a particular category, it is probably a member of that category, too.	**Example:** A person flips a coin 10 times and it has landed on tails every time. The odds are it will land on heads this time. (The odds are 50–50, as they are for each coin toss.)
Anchoring Heuristic	We make decisions based on certain ideas, or standards, that are important to us. We place a mental "anchor" on a piece of information, which is our starting point. We will then adjust away from that anchor until we reach a decision that seems acceptable to us.	**Example:** A couple is selling their house. They do not want to sell it for less than $200,000. Another couple wants to purchase the house, but will not pay more than $210,000 for it. The final sale of the house is negotiated at $205,000, which satisfies both the buyers and sellers.

How would you go about solving this problem? A man and his two sons want to get across a river. The boat they have available can hold a maximum of only 200 pounds. The father weighs 200 pounds and the sons weigh 100 pounds each. How can all three people cross the river? (The solution appears on the final page of this lesson.)

mental set a habitual strategy or pattern of problem solving

functional fixedness the inability to imagine new uses for familiar objects

DIAGRAM ∨

CONNECTING THE DOTS

Connect all nine dots shown below by drawing four straight lines without lifting your pencil from the paper or retracing any lines. The solution appears on the final page of this lesson.

▶ **CRITICAL THINKING**

1. *Describing* How would you describe your original strategy, or mental set, for solving this problem?

2. *Explaining* How does following a mental set sometimes interfere with problem solving?

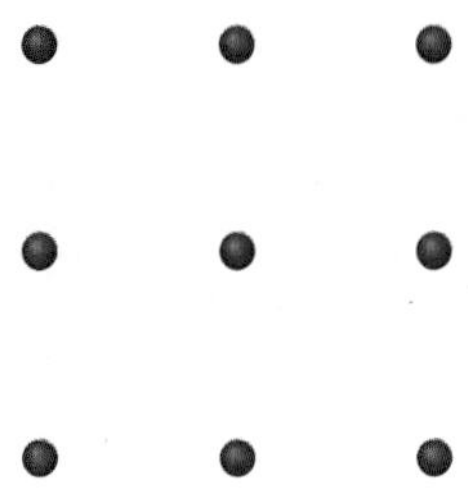

Obstacles to Problem Solving

There are times when certain useful strategies become cemented into the problem-solving process. When a particular strategy becomes a habit, it is called a **mental set**—you are set to treat problems in a certain way. For example, a chess player may always attempt to gain or maintain control the four center squares of the chessboard. Whenever her opponent attacks, she responds by looking for ways to regain control of those four squares. She has a set for these strategies. If this set helps her win, fine. Sometimes, however, a set interferes with problem solving, and then it is called rigidity.

One type of rigidity that can interfere with your ability to problem solve is **functional fixedness**—the inability to imagine new uses for familiar objects. In experiments on functional fixedness, people are asked to solve a problem that requires them to use a familiar object in an unfamiliar way. Because they are set to use the object in the usual way, people tend to pay attention only to the features of the object that relate to its everyday use. They respond in a rigid way. Another type of rigidity occurs when a person makes a wrong assumption about a problem. In the *Overcoming Wrong Assumptions* feature in this lesson, for example, the problem is to arrange the six matches into four equilateral triangles. Most people have trouble solving this puzzle because they falsely assume that they must stay within a two-dimensional figure. A third kind of rigidity is when people look for direct methods of solving problems and do not see solutions that require several intermediate steps.

Rigidity can be overcome if the person realizes that his or her strategy is not working and looks for other, more innovative ways to approach the problem. The more familiar the situation, the more difficult this will be. Rigidity is less likely to occur with unusual problems. Many individuals are trained, through formal education, to think of only one way to do things. Rigidity can be overcome by thinking about—or being taught to think about—and analyzing situations from many different perspectives.

Using Computers to Solve Problems

IBM's Watson computer, which defeated the world's best players on *Jeopardy!*, is good for more than winning game shows. Memorial Sloan-Kettering Cancer Center is using the computer in the war on cancer. Watson is being fed textbooks, medical journals, and medical records. After testing it with various cancer scenarios, researchers hope to put it to work helping to diagnose and treat cancer more quickly and accurately. "Unlike my medical students," said the head of breast cancer programs at Sloan-Kettering, "Watson doesn't forget anything."

Because of the way computers work—everything they do must first be programmed by a human—computers use algorithms to solve problems. Humans also use algorithms to solve problems but because it can be time consuming to use algorithms, we often resort to heuristics. Watson, however, can perform algorithms with blazing speed, so it has no need for heuristics.

Sometimes, however, computers are unable to solve problems without human assistance. An online game called Foldit combines thousands of human gamers with computers to solve puzzles. The game is made up of several puzzles requiring players to manipulate, or fold, three-dimensional graphics of protein structures to get them into the correct shape. Players are awarded points based on the quality of their folds. They are then scored on how closely the new shape reflects what would be expected in nature. Researchers have determined that humans are better than computers at predicting protein shapes.

☑ **READING PROGRESS CHECK**

Describing Describe two obstacles to problem solving.

Creative Thinking

GUIDING QUESTION *How do flexibility and recombination lead to insight?*

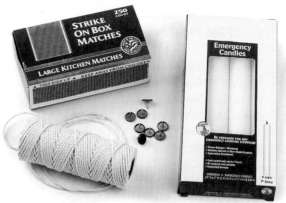

The ability to use information in such a way that the result is somehow new, original, and meaningful is *creativity*. All problem solving requires some creativity. Certain ways of solving problems, however, are simply more brilliant or beautiful or efficient than others. Psychologists do not know exactly why some people are able to think more creatively than others, although they have identified some of the characteristics of creative thinking, including flexibility and the ability to recombine elements to achieve insight.

Creative thinking may be viewed as a process involving several steps or phases. In one theory, the first phase is preparation, which is devoted to gathering information. The second phase, incubation, consists of defining the problem and processing information, either consciously or unconsciously, to seek a solution. In the third phase, illumination, pieces fall into place. In the fourth phase, verification, the thinker evaluates the results and makes any necessary adjustments to it.

Flexibility

The ability to overcome rigidity is *flexibility*. Psychologists have devised a number of ingenious tests to measure flexibility. In one test, psychologists ask people how many uses they can imagine for a single object, such as a brick or a paper clip. The more uses a person can devise, the more flexible he or she is said to be. Whether such tests actually measure creativity is debatable. Nevertheless, it is obvious that inflexible, rigid thinking leads to unoriginal solutions or no solutions at all.

Recombination

When the elements of a problem are familiar but the required solution is not, it may be achieved by *recombination*, a new mental arrangement of the elements. In football and basketball, for example, there are no new moves—only recombinations of old ones. Such recombination seems to be a vital part of creativity. Many creative people say that no truly great poem, no original invention, has ever been produced by someone who has not spent years studying his or her subject. The creative person is able to take the information that he or she and others have compiled and put it together in a totally new way.

The reknowned philosopher and mathematician Sir Isaac Newton, who discovered the laws of motion, once said, "If I have seen further, it is by standing on the shoulders of giants." In other words, he did not create his innovations alone and from nothing. He made his discoveries only by recombining the discoveries of the great scientists who had preceded him so that he uncovered new and more far-reaching truths.

Insight

The sudden emergence of a solution by the recombination of elements is called *insight*. Insight usually occurs when problems have proved to be resistant to all other problem-solving efforts and strategies. The scientist, artist—or, in fact, anyone—can reach a point of high frustration and temporarily abandon a task. Yet the recombination process seems to continue on an unconscious level. When the person is absorbed in some other activity and not thinking about the problem, the answer seems to appear out of nowhere. This sudden insight has appropriately been called the "aha" experience.

∧ **DIAGRAM**

OVERCOMING FUNCTIONAL FIXEDNESS

Given the materials pictured here, how would you go about mounting a candle vertically on a wooden wall in such a way that it can be lit? The solution appears on the final page of the lesson.

▶ **CRITICAL THINKING**

1. Speculating How might functional fixedness make it difficult to solve this problem?

2. Describing Describe a situation when you had to overcome functional fixedness in order to solve a problem.

∨ **DIAGRAM**

OVERCOMING WRONG ASSUMPTIONS

Arrange these six matches so that they form four equilateral triangles. The solution appears on the final page of the lesson.

▶ **CRITICAL THINKING**

1. Identifying What was your original assumption when you were trying to solve this problem?

2. Listing What are two characteristics of creative thinking?

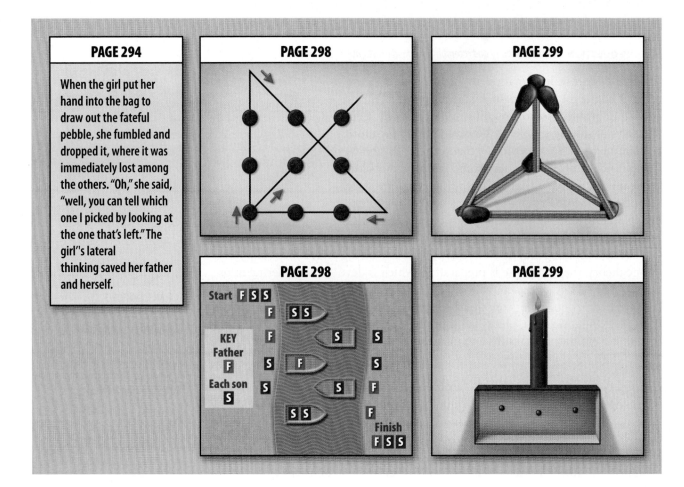

PAGE 294

When the girl put her hand into the bag to draw out the fateful pebble, she fumbled and dropped it, where it was immediately lost among the others. "Oh," she said, "well, you can tell which one I picked by looking at the one that's left." The girl"s lateral thinking saved her father and herself.

PAGE 298

PAGE 299

PAGE 298

Start **F** **S** **S**

KEY
Father
F

Each son
S

Finish
F **S** **S**

PAGE 299

Here are the answers to problems within this lesson.

▶ **CRITICAL THINKING**

1. *Analyzing* If you solved the questions correctly, how did you find your answers?

2. *Analyzing* If you did not find the correct answers, what obstacles prevented you from doing so?

Certain animals appear to experience this same cycle of frustration, temporary diversion (during which time the problem incubates), and then sudden insight. For example, Wolfgang Köhler placed a chimpanzee in a cage and hung a cluster of bananas just out of its reach. In the cage were several wooden boxes. At first the chimpanzee tried various unsuccessful ways of getting at the fruit. Finally it sat down, apparently giving up, and simply stared straight ahead for a while. Then suddenly it jumped up, piled three boxes on top of one another, climbed to the top of the pile, and grabbed the bananas.

✓ **READING PROGRESS CHECK**

Defining What is creativity?

LESSON 1 REVIEW

Reviewing Vocabulary

1. *Contrasting* What is the difference between algorithms and heuristics?

Using Your Notes

2. *Describing* Review the notes that you completed during the lesson to describe the characteristics of creative thinking.

Answering the Guiding Questions

3. *Listing* What are the building blocks of mental activity?

4. *Listing* How can problem-solving strategies become obstacles?

5. *Explaining* How do flexibility and recombination lead to insight?

Writing Activity

6. *Informative/Explanatory* Think of a situation affecting your community or school. Provide a written description of problem-solving techniques you would use to solve this problem. Compare your chosen problem and planned strategy with those of your classmates.

Case Study

Checkmate

Period of Study: 1997

Introduction: On May 11, 1997, the final match of a rematch took place in the contemplative game of chess. The champion of the previous match, which had taken place a year earlier, was Garry Kasparov, a former scientist. Many consider Kasparov to be the best chess player to have ever lived. Kasparov's opponent was Deep Blue, a computer.

Hypothesis: The idea of a human competing against a machine fascinated experts in a wide range of scientific studies. Most of these experts had the highest confidence in Kasparov's chances to defeat the computer for the second time. Psychologists believed that a computer preprogrammed with information of any kind would prove to be no match for the thought capacity and perceptions of the human mind. Even though Deep Blue was programmed to play the game of chess with perfection, a nonfeeling and nonthinking machine could not defeat the ability of the human mind to think abstractly. A machine could also not match the human mind's feelings of determination and desire to win the game.

Method: As we know, computers are not thinkers—they can only do what humans have programmed them to do. Deep Blue, however, has amazing capacities. It can consider 300 million possible chess moves per second. With each of these 300 million possibilities, Deep Blue is programmed to assess the situation these moves will put it in. The human brain can evaluate only a very small fraction of moves compared to what Deep Blue can process. The Deep Blue that was defeated by Kasparov the previous year was an earlier version of the 1997 model. A victory for Deep Blue could mean computers would not have to operate like a human brain to surpass it.

For his rematch with Deep Blue, Kasparov planned to copy his strategy from the previous year. This would involve using the early match (in a series of matches) to inspect the mighty computer for weaknesses and then to exploit those weaknesses.

Results: Deep Blue, the computer, defeated Kasparov. Experts explained that Kasparov's defeat was the result of comparing Deep Blue too much to the version he had played against the year before. The new and improved Deep Blue seemed to use moves that were very human-like. For every seemingly well-conceived move Kasparov made, the computer countered in devastating ways.

The time-consuming chess game robbed Kasparov of much of his concentration, whereas Deep Blue displayed no fatigue, frustration, or other human weaknesses. Now that psychologists know a human's mental capacity can be outmatched by a computer's programming, what assumptions can they make? Can a machine really prove to be more intelligent than the person who creates it? Do the physical limitations or the emotions of humans prevent us from using our mental capabilities to their fullest? These questions and others like them may not be answered for years to come. This situation is new, and further testing in this area is needed to assess the issues accurately.

PRIMARY SOURCE

> *The mind has an amazing ability to integrate ambiguous information across the senses, and it can effortlessly create the categories of time, space, object, and interrelationship from the sensory data. …There are no computers that can even remotely approach the remarkable feats the mind performs.*
>
> —*Dharmendra Modha (IBM), quoted in "IBM 'Cat Brain' Project," Anuradha Menon, http://thefutureofthings.com*

Analyzing the Case Study

1. ***Analyzing*** What advantages did each opponent bring to the contest?

2. ***Explaining*** Why were psychologists interested in the rematch between these two opponents?

3. ***Comparing*** Does Modha's quote contradict the results of this case? Why or why not?

Analyzing
Readings in Psychology

Reader's Dictionary

adept: very skilled or efficient at something

compulsive: related to, caused by, or suggestive of a psychological obsession

behemoth: something enormous

neurobiology: the study of anatomy, physiology, and pathology of the nervous system

neurotransmitter: a substance that transmits nerve impulses across a synapse

Concerns over the negative effects of violent videogames, and excessive gaming in general, have prompted many studies. However, until recently, there was little focus on the positive effects videogames have on the brain and related abilities. In this article, some of the positive effects and the implications are discussed.

When
Gaming
Is Good for You

By Robert Lee Hotz

PRIMARY SOURCE

Videogames can change a person's brain and, as researchers are finding, often that change is for the better. A growing body of university research suggests that gaming improves creativity, decision-making and perception. The specific benefits are wide ranging, from improved hand-eye coordination in surgeons to vision changes that boost night driving ability.

People who played action-based video and computer games made decisions 25% faster than others without sacrificing accuracy, according to a study. Indeed, the most **adept** gamers can make choices and act on them up to six times a second—four times faster than most people, other researchers found. Moreover, practiced game players can pay attention to more than six things at once without getting confused, compared with the four that someone can normally keep in mind, said University of Rochester researchers. The studies were conducted independently of the companies that sell video and computer games.

Scientists also found that women—who make up about 42% of computer and videogame players—were better able to mentally manipulate 3D objects, a skill at which men are generally more adept. Most studies looked at adults rather than children.

Electronic gameplay has its downside. Brain scans show that violent videogames can alter brain function in healthy young men after just a week of play, depressing activity among regions associated with emotional control, researchers at Indiana University recently reported. Other studies have found an association between **compulsive** gaming and being overweight, introverted and prone to depression. The studies didn't compare the benefits of gaming with such downsides.

The violent action games that often worry parents most had the strongest beneficial effect on the brain. "These are not the games you would think are mind-enhancing," said cognitive neuroscientist Daphne Bavelier, who studies the effect of action games at Switzerland's University of Geneva and the University of Rochester in New York.

Computer gaming has become a $25 billion-a year entertainment business **behemoth** since the first coin-operated commercial videogames hit the market 41 years ago. In 2010, gaming companies sold 257 million video and computer games, according to figures compiled by the industry's trade group, the Entertainment Software Association.

For scientists, the industry unintentionally launched a mass experiment in the **neurobiology** of learning.

PHOTO: Robert Daly/OJO Images/Getty Images; TEXT: Republished with permission of DOW JONES & COMPANY, INC. from When Gaming Is Good for You by Robert Lee Hotz, The Wall Street Journal, March 6, 2012, page D1; U.S. edition; permission conveyed through Copyright Clearance Center, Inc. Wall Street Journal Copyright 2012 by DOW JONES & COMPANY, INC., Reproduced with permission of DOW JONES & COMPANY, INC. in the format Republish in a textbook via Copyright Clearance Center.

Millions of people have immersed themselves in the interactive reward conditioning of electronic game play, from Tetris, Angry Birds, and Farmville, to shooter games and multiplayer, role-playing fantasies such as League of Legend, which has been played 1 billion times or so in the two years since it was introduced.

"Videogames change your brain," said University of Wisconsin psychologist C. Shawn Green, who studies how electronic games affect abilities. So does learning to read, playing the piano, or navigating the streets of London, which have all been shown to change the brain's physical structure. The powerful combination of concentration and rewarding surges of **neurotransmitters** like dopamine strengthen neural circuits in much the same the way that exercise builds muscles. But "games definitely hit the reward system in a way that not all activities do," he said.

"There has been a lot of attention wasted in figuring out whether these things turn us into killing machines," said computational analyst Joshua Lewis at the University of California in San Diego, who studied 2,000 computer game players. "Not enough attention has been paid to the unique and interesting features that videogames have outside of the violence."

Broadly speaking, today's average gamer is 34 years old and has been playing electronic games for 12 years, often up to 18 hours a week. By one analyst's calculation, the 11 million or so registered users of the online role-playing fantasy World of Warcraft collectively have spent as much time playing the game since its introduction in 2004 as humanity spent evolving as a species—about 50 billion hours of game time, which adds up to about 5.9 million years.

With people playing so many hundreds, if not thousands, of different games, though, university researchers have been hard-pressed to pinpoint the lasting effects on cognition and behavior.

The vast majority of the research did not directly compare gaming with hours of other intense, mental activities such as solving math equations. Almost any computer game appears to boost a child's creativity, researchers at Michigan State University's Children and Technology Project reported in November.

A three-year study of 491 middle school students found that the more children played computer games the higher their scores on a standardized test of creativity—regardless of race, gender, or the kind of game played. The researchers ranked students on a widely used measure called the Torrance Test of Creativity, which involves such tasks as drawing an "interesting and exciting" picture from a curved shape on a sheet of paper, giving the picture a title, and then writing a story about it. The results were ranked by seven researchers for originality, length, and complexity on a standardized three-point scale for each factor, along with detailed questionnaires.

In contrast, using cellphones, the Internet, or computers for other purposes had no effect on creativity, they said. "Much to my surprise, it didn't matter whether you were playing aggressive games or sport games, not a bit," said psychologist Linda Jackson, who led the federally funded study of 491 boys and girls at 20 Michigan schools.

Even so, researchers have yet to create educational software as engaging as most action games. Without such intense involvement, neural circuits won't change, they believe. "It happens that all the games that have the good learning effect happen to be violent. We don't know whether the violence is important or not," said Dr. Bavelier. "We hope not."

Until recently, most researchers studied the effects of gaming on small groups of volunteers, who learned to play under laboratory conditions. Some scientists now are turning the commercial games themselves into laboratories of learning.

Analyzing Primary Sources

1. *Finding the Main Idea* How do researchers view video games as a result of this research?

2. *Analyzing* What are some advantages to playing video games?

3. *Drawing Conclusions* Why might video games increase creativity while the use of cell phones, the Internet, or computers do not?

Jamaway/Alamy

Reading **HELP**DESK (CCSS)

Academic Vocabulary

• factor   • contribute

Content Vocabulary

• language
• phoneme
• morpheme
• syntax
• semantics

TAKING NOTES:

Craft and Structure

VISUALIZING Use a flowchart similar to the one below to list the stages of language development.

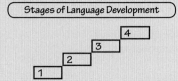

Stages of Language Development

1 2 3 4

LESSON 2

Language

ESSENTIAL QUESTIONS • *How does the brain solve problems?* • *How does the brain learn new skills?*

IT MATTERS BECAUSE

Of all the things we do, nothing seems as complex and as important as understanding and speaking a language. We must learn thousands of words and a limited number of rules of grammar to make sense of those words to communicate and share ideas. Of all the animals, only humans appear to have this ability to put words together grammatically in order to communicate with one another.

The Structure of Language

GUIDING QUESTION *What are the three elements of language?*

Do you ever talk to yourself? Some people talk to themselves when they are thinking or solving a problem. When we are talking or thinking, we are using language. What is **language**? Language is a system of communication that involves using rules to make and combine symbols in ways that produce meaningful words and sentences. The scientific study of language is known as *linguistics*.

Language functions in many different ways. Its most familiar function is informative: it lets us communicate facts and ideas. It allows us to tell each other about the past, present, and future. We solve problems and make decisions based on learning that has been transmitted through language. We also use language to express emotion and to tell the stories that make up our literature.

Language consists of three elements: phonemes (units of sound), morphemes (units of meaning), and syntax (units of organization). The study of meaning, or semantics, is the most complex aspect of language.

The smallest units of sound in human languages are **phonemes**. Phonemes can be represented by a single letter (such as consonants like *t* or vowels like *e*) or a combination of letters, such as *sh*. Some linguists also include differences of pitch, stress (or accent), and rhythm.

We can produce about 100 different recognizable sounds, but not all sounds are used in all languages. For instance, the English language uses about 43 sounds. Some languages use as few as 15 sounds and others use as many as 85 sounds.

Phonemes
(units of sound):

FEARLESSNESS

Morphemes
(units of meaning):

< DIAGRAM

PHONEMES AND MORPHEMES

The word *fearlessness* has nine phonemes and three morphemes.

▶ **CRITICAL THINKING**

1. *Contrasting* What is the difference between phonemes and morphemes?

2. *Conjecturing* What is the purpose of the three brackets above the word?

A **morpheme** is the smallest unit of meaning. It is made up of one or more phonemes. Morphemes can be a word, a letter (*s*), a prefix (*un-* in *uncertain*), or a suffix (*-ly* in *slowly*). For example, the words *book, love,* and *reason* are single morphemes, while *loves, relearn,* and *walked* have two morphemes (*love* and *-s, re-* and *learn, walk* and *-ed*).

Syntax refers to rules for combining words into meaningful phrases or sentences to express thoughts that can be understood by others. For example, the following string of words probably does not make sense: "Boy small bike large rode." In English we follow grammatical rules, such as placing adjectives in front of nouns. If you applied these rules to the sentence above, it could read: "The small boy rode a large bike." Every language has these rules, although the rules differ from language to language.

The fact that the rules of syntax differ from one language to another causes major problems to people learning a second language. Language learners tend to base their acquisition of a second language on principles that are common to all languages as well as the rules of each language. For example, both Spanish and English use adjectives. However, in English, adjectives come before nouns, while in Spanish they follow nouns. At first, learners will typically try to use the syntax of their first language. They must learn how to put words together to form phrases and sentences. They do this by studying the new language's grammar. As they internalize these rules, it becomes part of their mental grammar.

The study of meaning or extracting meaning from morphemes, words, sentences, and context is **semantics**. The same word can have different meanings. Consider the following sentences: "A mind is a terrible thing to waste." "Do you mind if I sit next to you?" The word *mind* is understood differently in the two sentences. How did you know what the word *mind* meant in each sentence? From your knowledge of semantics, you knew that in the first sentence *mind* was a noun, while in the second sentence it was a verb. Your knowledge of a word's meaning depends partly on context.

language the expression of ideas through symbols and sounds that are arranged according to rules

phoneme an individual sound that is a basic structural element of language

morpheme the smallest unit of meaning in a given language

syntax language rules that govern how words can be combined to form meaningful phrases and sentences

semantics the study of meaning in language

✔ READING PROGRESS CHECK

Defining What is semantics?

Language Development

GUIDING QUESTION *What is the nature-versus-nurture debate concerning language development?*

Researchers first identified the regions of the brain associated with language by studying people who developed speech problems after sustaining brain injuries. They were able to pinpoint two parts of the brain, Broca's area and Wernicke's area, vital to understanding speech and writing. With the development of scanning methods such as magnetic resonance imaging, researchers can examine the brains of healthy, conscious people to find out which areas of the brain are active.

Noam Chomsky (1928–)

Avram Noam Chomsky conceived *generative-transformational grammar* to describe the rules that govern all possible sentence formations in any language. Chomsky claims that each of us is born with brain structures that make it relatively easy to learn the rules of language. Chomsky called those innate brain structures the *language-acquisition device,* or *LAD.* LAD mechanisms guide a person's learning of the unique rules of his or her native language.

Chomsky adopted what he called a "mentalistic" theory of language that differentiated between linguistic competence—how well a person knows the rules and structure of a language—and performance—how effectively that person actually uses language. According to this theory, linguists should concern themselves with a person's linguistic competence rather than performance.

▶ **CRITICAL THINKING**

Describing How might Chomsky's findings account for the fact that children appear to go through the same stages of language development no matter what language they are acquiring?

They can use other types of imaging to see how regions of the brain are connected. As a result of recent research, we now know that speech requires at least five regions of the brain.

The psychology of language is known as *psycholinguistics*. It brings together aspects of linguistics and psychology to study the factors that allow humans to acquire, use, and understand language. Developmental psycholinguistics is the branch that studies children's ability to learn language.

For many years a debate over exactly how children learn language raged. B.F. Skinner believed that children learned language as a result of operant conditioning. When children utter sounds that are similar to adult speech patterns, their behavior is reinforced through smiles and extra attention; therefore, children repeat those sounds. Eventually children learn to produce speech.

Critics state that children understand language before they speak—and before they receive any reinforcement. They also believe that children learn the rules of language before they receive any feedback on speaking correctly.

Some psychologists argue that children learn language through observation, exploration, and imitation. These social learning advocates point out that children use language to get attention, ask for help, or to gain other forms of social contact. Parents can stimulate language acquisition by responding to and encouraging language development. These psychologists believe that both innate and environmental **factors** play a part in how a child learns language.

Although Noam Chomsky believed that reinforcement and imitation do **contribute** to language development, he did not believe that all the complex rules of language could be learned that way. Chomsky theorized that infants possess an innate capacity for language; that is, children inherit a mental program that enables them to learn grammar. This theory is supported by the fact that children acquire language skills more quickly than other abilities.

How Language Develops

If Chomsky is right, then we would expect that all children go through similar stages of language development, no matter what culture or language group they belong to. Infants, in fact, do go through four stages of language development.

Beginning at birth, infants can cry and produce other sounds indicating distress. Around 2 months of age, infants begin to *coo*. Cooing refers to long, drawn-out sounds such as *oooh* or *eeeh*. At around 4 months of age, infants reach the first stage of language development and begin to *babble*. Babbling includes sounds found in all languages, such as *dadada* and *bababa*. When babbling, infants learn to control their vocal cords and to make, change, repeat, and imitate the sounds of their parents. At around 9 months of age, infants refine their babbling to increasingly include sounds that are part of their native language. Children who can hear babble orally. Deaf children babble by using hand signals. They repeat the same hand signals over and over again.

At around 12 months of age, infants begin to utter single words. They use these words to describe familiar objects and people, such as *da-da* or *doggie*. At this stage, children use single words to describe longer thoughts. For example, a child may say "da" to mean "Where is my father?" or "I want my father."

Toward the end of their second year, children place two words together to express an idea. Children may say "Milk gone" to indicate that the milk has spilled or "Me play" to mean "I want to play." This stage indicates that the child is beginning to learn the rules of grammar. The child's vocabulary has expanded to about 50 to 100 words and continues to expand rapidly.

By age 2 to 3, children form sentences of several words. These first sentences follow a pattern called *telegraphic speech*. In this telegraphic speaking pattern, the child leaves out articles such as *the*, prepositions such as *with*, and parts of verbs.

For example, a child may say, "I go park," to mean, "I am going to the park." By age 5, language development is largely complete, although vocabulary and sentence complexity continue to develop.

All children are born with the ability to learn any language. For babies born to bilingual mothers, studies show that they are able to register differences between the two languages while they are still infants. Psychologists have also studied how infants use different kinds of perception in order to learn languages and, if they are in a bilingual environment, to keep the two languages separate.

Children are able to infer grammatical rules from the speech they hear. They can then use those rules to put together sentences they have never heard before. This learning is reinforced when parents encourage their children to talk and then correct their mistakes. Language learning at school is mainly concerned with reading and writing, formal grammar, and, in some instances, the "correct" way of speaking. All of this assumes that children already have a working knowledge of their first (or native) language, including vocabulary and the basic structure.

Research has shown that children go through the same stages of language development no matter which language they are acquiring. It is estimated that two-thirds of the world's children grow up speaking two languages and learn them as quickly as other children learn one. In fact, there does not appear to be any limit to the number of languages young children can learn.

Do Animals Learn Language?

Animals communicate with one another. We have all heard dogs bark or growl at each other. Do animals, though, learn language? Language involves more than just communicating. It involves rules of grammar and combining words or phrases into meaningful sentences. Although animals do not possess the ability to use grammatical rules, they have been taught to communicate with humans.

Psychologists believe that chimpanzees possess some of the same developmental skills as do 2-year-old humans. Like 2-year-olds, chimpanzees will look for a toy or a bit of food that has disappeared from sight. They can remember the existence of that missing toy or bit of food. Can they be taught to "talk" about it?

factor something that contributes to producing a result; an ingredient

contribute to give or supply along with others

Frans Lanting/Corbis

Dr. Sue Savage Rumbaugh works on language skills with a female Bonobo chimpanzee using a lexigram, or symbol, keyboard.

▶ **CRITICAL THINKING**

Contrasting What has research discovered about a chimpanzee's use of language versus a human's use of language?

Bilingualism is the ability to speak and understand two languages. How do bilingual people, though, keep the two languages separate? They do not. Try this experiment. Say the visible color of the following words aloud.

YELLOW GREEN RED BLUE
VERDE AZUL AMARILLO ROJO

If you speak only English, you probably had a little trouble with the first four words and less trouble with the last four. If you also speak Spanish, however, you knew that *verde, azul, amarillo,* and *rojo* are the Spanish words for *green, blue, yellow,* and *red.* You had difficulty with all the items.

Although it takes children longer to master two languages rather than just one, as bilinguals they are able to express their thoughts in a wide variety of ways. Bilingual children also learn early that there are different ways of expressing the same idea.

Allen and Beatrice Gardner raised a baby chimpanzee named Washoe in their home and, since chimpanzees are good with their hands, taught her to use American Sign Language. At 3½ years of age, Washoe knew at least 87 signs for words like *food, dog,* and *toothbrush.* By age 5, Washoe used more than 160 signs.

Several chimpanzees have been taught to converse in other ways. Chimpanzees have been trained on special typewriters connected to computers. One chimpanzee, Panzee, used a special computer keyboard with symbols to communicate with humans. The chimpanzees use only aspects of the human language. Chimpanzees use words as symbols but do not apply grammatical rules. The ability to arrange symbols in new combinations to produce new meanings is especially well developed in the human brain. The rules for such organization of symbols are called *grammar.* Grammatical rules are what make the sentence "the rhinoceros roared at the boy" mean the same thing as "the boy was roared at by the rhinoceros." It may be in our ability to use such grammatical rules that we surpass the simpler language of the chimpanzee.

Opinions vary on the ability of animals to use language. Noam Chomsky believes that only humans have the innate ability to use language. Because of this, children are able to learn language effortlessly. Steven Pinker believes that animals simply learn to mimic language use because they will be rewarded for it. Based on her experience with bonobo chimpanzees, Sue Savage-Rumbaugh strongly believes in the ability of animals to use language. Critics say that chimpanzees can respond to commands does not amount to true language use.

Gender and Cultural Differences

There is an intersection of linguistics with anthropology and sociology as well as with psychology. *Anthropological linguistics* studies the relationship between language and culture. *Sociolinguistics* studies language as an instrument of socialization.

People use language to communicate their culture and express their ideas. Do people who speak different languages actually think differently from one another? Benjamin Whorf argued that language affects our basic perceptions of the physical world. Whorf used the term *linguistic relativity* to refer to the idea that language influences thoughts. For instance, consider the word *snow.* Whorf estimated that the Inuit have many words for snow (including separate words for damp snow, falling snow, and melting snow) because their survival depends upon traveling and living in snow. According to Whorf's theory, different terms for snow help the Inuit see the different types of snow as different. On the other hand, Whorf claimed that Americans have one word for snow. Critics have pointed out that Americans actually have many words for snow. Whorf's theory of linguistic relativity still claims supporters, but it is difficult to separate culture from language when studying the use of language and the perceptions it influences.

Recent research has shown that language affects the way people perceive space and time. In about a third of the world's languages, people use references to absolute, or cardinal, directions (such as *east* and *west*) rather than relative terms like *right* and *left.* Researchers have found that speakers of those languages are more capable of staying oriented and keeping track of where they are, even when they are not familiar with their surroundings, than people who use relative terms.

Human relationships are also colored by language. In English, only near relatives, such as siblings, parents and grandparents, and aunts and uncles, are normally differentiated by sex. Cousins are not. In other languages, such as Malay, the main distinction is by age, so the term used to refer to an older sibling is different from the term used to refer to a younger sibling. Some Native American languages have words that distinguish between the sister of a man and the sister of a woman.

LANGUAGE AND GENDER

Unlike English, many other languages assign gender to all objects, not just people or animals. There are a few instances, however, when English speakers do use gender terms to refer to inanimate objects. For example, in casual speech, someone may refer to a ship as "she" or "her" rather than "it."

▶ **CRITICAL THINKING**

1. *Naming* Can you think of any other inanimate objects to which English speakers casually assign a gender?

2. *Identifying* List some additional gender-specific terms for which gender-neutral versions have been created.

Languages also influence the way we understand how things happen. Speakers of English tend to say things like "Mary broke the window." Speakers of Spanish or Japanese would be more likely to say, "The window broke." Such linguistic differences have a huge effect on how the speakers view these events. These differences can have an effect on such things as eyewitness reports and how much they blame and punish others.

If people change the way they talk, that changes the way they think. When people learn a new language, they also learn a new way of viewing the world. Even when they switch from one language to another, bilingual people automatically start to think differently as well. Not only does our language reflect the way we talk, it shapes the way we think.

Many languages have grammatical gender. That is, parts of speech—usually nouns, or words that name things—are assigned gender. Other words, such as the adjectives that describe those nouns, vary in form to reflect the gender of the noun they modify. French, Spanish, and Italian have two genders, masculine and feminine. German and Russian also have a third gender, neuter. In French and Spanish, for example, the words for *table* (*table* and *mesa*) are feminine, whereas the words for book (*livre* and *libro*) are masculine.

In English, gender is normally used only when referring to natural gender or sex. We use *he* and *him* to refer to males, *she* and *her* to refer to females, and *it* to refer to inanimate objects. The plural forms of these pronouns, *they* and *them*, do not indicate gender. Nor does the English word *friend* indicate the sex of the friend, whereas in other languages, such as Spanish, the sex of the friend would be apparent—either *amiga* (female) or *amigo* (male).

On the surface, these magazines and newspapers look very much like English-language periodicals.

▶ **CRITICAL THINKING**

Explaining How do different languages affect the way that people relate to the world around them?

Does the English language express a particular value system? Some people argue that certain words in the language create gender stereotypes. For example, a chairman of the board may be a man or a woman, but the word "chairman" creates a male stereotype. The use of pronouns reflects and also affects our thinking. For example, people used to think of certain occupations as gender-specific. Nurses, administrative assistants, and schoolteachers were often referred to as *she,* while doctors, engineers, and presidents were often referred to as *he.* Now, if we didn't know which pronoun was accurate, we would say *he or she.* In recent decades, there has also been a trend away from gender-specific terminology. For example, instead of a *fireman,* we now refer to a *firefighter.* Instead of committee *chairman*, we now refer to the committee *chairperson* (or just committee *chair.*) Many organizations have instituted guidelines for the use of nonsexist language.

☑ **READING PROGRESS CHECK**

Explaining How do scientists believe humans differ from animals in our use of language?

LESSON 2 REVIEW

Reviewing Vocabulary

1. *Analyzing* How many phonemes are in the word "thoughtfully"? How many morphemes?

Using Your Notes

2. *Applying* Review the notes that you completed during the lesson to provide an example for each stage of language development.

Answering the Guiding Questions

3. *Listing* What are the three elements of language?

4. *Explaining* What is the nature-versus-nurture debate concerning language development?

Writing Activity

5. *Informative/Explanatory* Consult one or more guides to nonsexist language. Then write guidelines to help students use nonsexist language in the classroom.

Directions: On a separate sheet of paper, answer the questions below. Make sure you read carefully and answer all parts of the question.

Lesson Review

Lesson 1

❶ Defining Define the five units of thought. Then list the five units of thought in order of increasing complexity.

❷ Describing What is creativity? What are the three characteristics of creative thinking? Give an example of one of the three characteristics.

❸ Explaining What are three strategies people often use to solve problems? Explain how you have used one of these strategies to solve a problem.

Lesson 2

❹ Identifying Identify and explain the structures of language.

❺ Contrasting How did B.F. Skinner and Noam Chomsky differ in their ideas about how children learn language?

❻ Discussing How might we express gender values in our use of language?

Exploring the Essential Question

❼ Speculating Summarize the process of language acquisition. At approximately what age do you think people would be most receptive to learning a second language? What kinds of thinking might they use to help them learn?

Research and Technology

❽ Comparing and Contrasting Use the Internet to explore recent scientific studies of language acquisition in humans and nonhuman animals. Compare and contrast basic research with applied psychological research in the field.

21st Century Skills

Using Graphs Review the graph below and then answer the questions that follow.

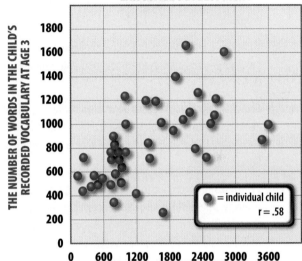

PARENT INVOLVEMENT IN LANGUAGE DEVELOPMENT

THE NUMBER OF WORDS IN THE CHILD'S RECORDED VOCABULARY AT AGE 3

● = individual child
r = .58

THE AVERAGE NUMBER OF WORDS SAID PER HOUR BY THE PARENT TO THE CHILD BEFORE THE CHILD WAS 3 YEARS OLD

❾ Analyzing Visuals What does the graph illustrate?

❿ Drawing Conclusions What conclusion can you draw about the relationship of the number of words that a parent says to a child and the size of the child's vocabulary?

⓫ Making Connections What theory of language development does the information in this graph best support?

Need Extra Help?

If You've Missed Question	❶	❷	❸	❹	❺	❻	❼	❽	❾	❿	⓫
Go to page	294	299	296	304	306	308	307	307	306	306	305

Directions: On a separate sheet of paper, answer the questions below. Make sure you read carefully and answer all parts of the question.

Critical Thinking Questions

12 *Analyzing* Do you think using algorithms rather than heuristics is always the best way to solve problems? Why or why not?

13 *Speculating* What kind of thinking—directed or undirected—do you think is required for creativity? Why do you think so?

14 *Comparing and Contrasting* What similarities are there between decision making and problem solving? How are they different?

15 *Drawing Conclusions* Based on what you have learned about language development, do you think all students in elementary school should be taught a foreign language? Why or why not?

16 *Synthesizing* According to the theory of linguistic relativity, a person's language influences his or her thoughts. Do you believe that bilingual people have more complex thought processes than people who speak only one language? Explain your answer.

College and Career Readiness

17 *Decision Making* To help plan for your future, create a decision tree exploring various options any high school student could consider, including dropping out of high school and going to work, graduating and going directly to work without continuing your education, continuing your education at a community college or trade school, continuing your education at a state university, and continuing your education at a private college. Conduct research to determine the probable outcomes of each action, including the expense of continuing an education at each type of institution and the probable lifetime income differences. Based on your research, which decision appears to be the best one for you?

DBQ Analyzing Primary Sources

Use the document below to answer the following questions.

PRIMARY SOURCE

"*Human languages, in all their exquisite diversity, complexity and sophistication are some of our species' most impressive achievements. Each language provides its own cognitive toolkit, and encapsulates the knowledge and worldview developed over thousands of years within a culture. While language is a central part of cognition, there is nothing magical about how language shapes thought. Languages shape our thinking in the same ways that going to medical school or learning to fly a plane also build expertise and transform what we can do. Different languages encourage different kinds of cognitive expertise in their speakers, and as a result, speakers of different languages end up thinking differently.*"

—Lera Boroditsky, "Language: The Proposer's Opening Remarks,"
The Economist *(December 13, 2010)*

18 *Interpreting* Based on this paragraph, what is the author's belief about the effect of languages on their speakers?

19 *Analyzing* Based on this excerpt, what is the connection between language and thought?

Psychology Journal Activity

20 *Informative/Explanatory* Review your entry in your Psychology Journal for this chapter. Having learned about the process of thinking and problem solving, how would you summarize the mental steps one takes in solving a difficult problem?

Need Extra Help?

If You've Missed Question	12	13	14	15	16	17	18	19	20
Go to page	297	294	295	306	308	296	305	292	290

Motivation and Emotion

ESSENTIAL QUESTION • *What motivates behavior?*

Jon Feingersh/Stone/Getty Images

Psychology Matters...

Motivation and emotion get to the underlying "why" of our behaviors. Our motivations are the physical and mental factors that cause us to act in a specific way when stimulated. Emotion involves our subjective feelings, physical arousal, and external expressions in response to situations and events. Both come together in the achievement of goals or as the result of failures.

◄ Many people spend years in pursuit of lofty goals and wishful desires. How do our motivations and emotions help us to succeed?

Marshmallows and Motivation

THE QUESTION...

RESEARCH QUESTION Is self-control the key to success in school?

In 1972 psychologist Walter Mischel tested the self-control of young children using a sweet treat—marshmallows. He would give a child one marshmallow and leave the room, promising a second if the child waited to eat the first. Some showed high self-control by waiting for his return, while others chomped it down quickly. Later in childhood, those children who had shown high levels of self-control were more likely to be successful in school than their peers. The experiment drew a connection between delayed gratification in young children and later academic performance.

An important step in the practice of science is replicating an experiment to confirm its results. Let's conduct a variation of the marshmallow experiment and see if the results are similar.

Psychology Journal Activity

Think about what motivates you throughout your day and write about it in your Psychology Journal. Consider the following issues: Are you motivated by factors such as food, comfort, or social acceptance? Do you consider some of your motivations to be distractions from what you "should" be doing?

FINDING THE ANSWER...

HYPOTHESIS Students who exhibit greater amounts of self-control will prove to study more than those who exhibit lesser amounts.

THE METHOD OF YOUR EXPERIMENT

MATERIALS clean room devoid of distractions, large marshmallows, napkins, table

PROCEDURE Recruit five participants. In each part of the experiment, you will test the participants individually. First, bring a participant into the room with a table. Place a single marshmallow (you may choose to use another snack, such as bananas) on a napkin on the table. Tell the participant that he or she can eat it at any time; however, if the participant waits 15 minutes, he or she will get a second marshmallow. Then, leave the room. Return after 15 minutes. If the participant has not eaten the marshmallow, give him or her another. In Part 2 of the experiment, have the participant recall information from the previous 5 days. Ask: What did you eat for dinner? How many hours did you sleep? How many hours did you study? Record all the answers, though only the answer to the number of hours you studied will be used. Complete Parts 1 and 2 with each of the participants.

DATA COLLECTION Assemble your data into a 3-column table. The columns will be the subject's name, the results of the marshmallow test, and the hours he or she studied over the course of five nights.

ANALYSIS & APPLICATION

1. Did your results support the hypothesis?

2. How could the choice of using only marshmallows lead to inaccurate results? How could the experiment be improved?

3. Why do you think high levels of self-control in children could lead to success in school?

networks   ONLINE LAB RESOURCES

Online you will find:

- An **interactive lab experience**, allowing you to put principles from this chapter into practice in a digital psychology lab environment. This chapter's lab will include an experiment that explores issues fundamental to motivation and emotion.

- A **Skills Handbook** that includes a guide for using the scientific method, creating experiments, and analyzing data.
- A **Notebook** where you can complete your Psychology Journal and record and analyze your experimental data.

Motivation and Emotion **315**

Amy Strycula/Flickr/Getty Images

LESSON 1
Theories of Motivation

Reading **HELP**DESK (CCSS)

Academic Vocabulary

• conclude   • motive

Content Vocabulary

• motivation
• instincts
• drive
• homeostasis
• incentive
• extrinsic motivation
• intrinsic motivation

TAKING NOTES:

Integration of Knowledge and Ideas

LABELING Use a graphic organizer similar to the one below to list the human instincts identified by William James in 1890.

HUMAN INSTINCTS

ESSENTIAL QUESTION • *What motivates behavior?*

IT MATTERS BECAUSE

People are motivated to do things for very different reasons. One person might want to play football to gain the respect of his friends while another might want to play for the feeling of personal accomplishment. Even though motivations and goals may differ, the thought processes and instincts are often the same. When we understand what motivates us, we can better understand how our minds work.

Instinct and Drive-Reduction Theories

GUIDING QUESTION *What is the difference between a need and a drive?*

When we think about people who have accomplished great things, we might wonder how they reached their goals. What motivates people to do things such as learn to speak another language or ride a hot air balloon? What makes some people draw pictures and others write poems? Although all psychology is concerned with what people do and how they do it, research on motivation and emotion focuses on the underlying questions about why we behave the way we do.

Motivation includes the various psychological and physiological factors that cause us to act a certain way at a certain time. You might see one person studying all weekend while her friends relax and hang out. Knowing that the person wants to go to law school might help you to **conclude** that she is motivated by her desire to get good grades. You might see another person after classes working at a job he does not like. But understanding that he wants to buy a car might help you to conclude that he is motivated to earn money for the car.

Different aspects of your environment motivate you to do different things. Your most basic motivations lead you to survive and meet your need to stay safe or to obtain food, water, or shelter. These are instinctive motivations that you do not think much about. Other motivations may help you meet long-term or short-term desires in your life. Psychologists explain motivation and why we experience it in different ways through instinct, drive-reduction, incentive, and cognitive theories of motivation.

Instinct Theory

Movies and books often have the **motives** or emotions of the characters as their central theme. On the street, you hear words like *anger, fear, pain, starving*, and hundreds of others describing people's motives and emotions. Conceptions of motivation in psychology are in many ways similar to those expressed in everyday language. Because motivation cannot be observed directly they must be inferred from goal-directed behaviors. Human behavior is energized by many motives that may originate from outside of us or inside of us.

In the 1900s, psychologist William McDougall proposed that humans were motivated by a variety of instincts. **Instincts** are natural or inherited tendencies of an organism to make a specific response to certain environmental stimuli without involving reason. Instincts occur in almost the same way among all members of a species. For example, salmon respond to instinctive urges to swim thousands of miles through ocean waters and up rivers to reach the exact spot in a gravel bed where they were spawned years earlier. In the late 1800s, psychologist William James proposed that humans have instincts such as cleanliness, curiosity, parental love, sociability, and sympathy.

Eventually, though, psychologists realized a flaw in the instinct theory. Instincts do not explain behavior; they simply label behavior. Today, instinctive behaviors, now called fixed action patterns, are still studied by psychologists and researchers. In order to explain motivation, however, they have turned to other theories.

Drive-Reduction Theory

Something that motivates us moves us to action. The thing that motivates us starts with a need that leads to a drive. A need results from a lack of something desirable or useful. We have both physiological and psychological needs. We need oxygen and food to survive. These are physiological needs. We may also need self-esteem or social approval. These are psychological needs. Our psychological needs are learned through experience and failing to fulfill some of them is not life-threatening.

A need produces a drive. A **drive** is an internal condition that can change over time and orients an individual toward a specific goal or goals. We have different drives with different goals. For example, hunger drives us to eat, curiosity drives us to find something out, and fatigue drives us to rest.

Drive-reduction theory emerged from the work of experimental psychologist Clark Hull, who traced motivation back to basic physiological needs. According to Hull, when an organism is deprived of something it needs or wants, such as food or water, it becomes tense and agitated. To relieve this tension, it engages in targeted behavior to reduce needs. Thus biological needs *drive* an organism to act, and the organism strives to maintain homeostasis. **Homeostasis** is the tendency of the body to return to or maintain a balanced state.

motivation an internal state that activates behavior and directs it toward a goal

conclude to decide or believe something as a result of what you have heard or seen

motive a reason for doing something

instincts innate tendencies that determine behavior

drive a state of tension produced by a need that motivates an organism toward a goal

homeostasis the tendency of all organisms to correct imbalances and deviations from their normal state

Psychologists now generally focus on theories other than instinct to explain human motivation.

▶ **CRITICAL THINKING**

Assessing What motivations are at play in the image below?

John Warden/Stone/Getty Images

If a behavior reduces a drive, the organism will begin to acquire a habit. That is, when the drive is again felt, the organism will tend first to try the same behavioral response. Habits channel drives in certain directions. In short, drive-reduction theory states that physiological needs drive an organism to act in either random or habitual ways. This drive continues until the organism's needs are satisfied and it returns to an optimal state.

Hull suggested that all human motives—from the desire to acquire property to striving for excellence and seeking affection or amusement—are extensions of basic biological needs. For example, people develop the need for social approval because as infants they were fed and cared for by a smiling mother or father. Gradually, through conditioning and generalization, the need for approval becomes important in and of itself. So, according to Hull, approval becomes a learned drive.

The results of subsequent experiments suggested, however, that Hull had overlooked some of the more important factors in human—and animal—motivation. According to drive-reduction theory, infants become attached to their mothers because mothers usually relieve such drives as hunger and thirst. Harry Harlow and other researchers doubted that this was the only, or even the main, source of an infant's love for its mother.

Cloth and Wire Mothers

Harlow took baby monkeys away from their mothers and put them alone in cages with two surrogate, or substitute, mothers made mostly of wire. One of the wire mothers was equipped with a bottle. If the drive-reduction theory were correct, the monkeys would become attached to this figure because it was their only source of food. The other wire mother was covered with soft cloth but could not provide food to relieve hunger. In test after test, the baby monkeys preferred to cling to the cloth mother, particularly when strange, frightening objects were put into their cages.

Some drive theorists overlooked the fact that some experiences, such as hugging something or someone soft, are inherently pleasurable. Although these experiences do not seem to reduce biological drives, they serve as incentives or goals for behavior. Also, sometimes we engage in activities that increase the tension we experience. For example, although you do not seek out anxiety, you may enjoy riding roller coasters or watching scary movies. These activities momentarily increase your anxiety and disrupt your homeostasis. Many psychologists conclude that the general theory of motivation that Hull suggested left many additional factors unexplained. Consequently, there are many types of behavior that cannot be explained through deprivation.

☑ **READING PROGRESS CHECK**

Interpreting Significance According to the drive-reduction theory, why might someone develop a habit?

The monkeys in Harlow's study spent most of their time with the cloth mother even though they fed from the wire mother.

▶ **CRITICAL THINKING**

Drawing Inferences What does this result indicate about motivation?

Incentive and Cognitive Theory

GUIDING QUESTION *How do incentives direct behavior?*

The drive-reduction theory of motivation emphasizes the internal states of the organism; however, the incentive theory stresses the role of the environment in motivating behavior. Whereas a drive is something inside of us that causes us to act, our actions are directed toward a goal, or incentive. An **incentive** is the object we seek or the result we are trying to achieve through our motivated behavior. Incentives are also known as reinforcers, goals, and rewards. While drives push us to reduce needs, incentives pull us to obtain them. For example, hunger may cause us to walk to the cafeteria, but the incentive for our action is the sandwich we intend to eat. Sometimes a drive can be so strong that we do not care if the incentive is weak. For example, if we have a strong hunger drive, we may accept a weak incentive, like a sandwich from the cafeteria even though we know that the cafeteria's sandwiches are not that tasty. However, if our drive is weak, our incentive must be strong. For instance, you may be slightly hungry but really like peanut butter sandwiches, so you will eat one.

People are motivated to obtain positive incentives and to avoid negative incentives. For example, the incentive of food may draw you to the refrigerator. The motivations we have discussed thus far have been largely biological. Some motivations are different and are dependent on things outside of the individual. This type of motivation, or cognitive expectation, also guides human behavior.

Cognitive psychologists seek to explain motivation by looking at forces inside and outside of us that energize us to move. They propose that we act in particular ways at particular times as a result of extrinsic and intrinsic motivations. **Extrinsic motivation** refers to engaging in activities to reduce biological needs or obtain incentives or external rewards. **Intrinsic motivation** refers to engaging in activities because those activities are personally rewarding or because engaging in them fulfills our beliefs or expectations. For example, if you spend hours and hours playing basketball because you wish to excel at the sport, you are responding to intrinsic motivation. If you spend hours playing basketball because your parents want you to excel at the sport, you are responding to extrinsic motivation. Finally, if you play basketball just for the fun of it, you are playing because of intrinsic motivation.

Extrinsic and intrinsic motivations are not mutually exclusive. Meaning, in many instances, you engage in an activity because of both extrinsic and intrinsic motivations. For example, you may go out to dinner with your friends because you need to satisfy your hunger, which is an extrinsic motivation. You also may go out to dinner with your friends because you enjoy the taste of the restaurant's food and you wish to socialize with your friends, both of which are intrinsic motivations.

Quick Lab

HOW DO ADVERTISEMENTS "MOTIVATE" PEOPLE TO BUY PRODUCTS?

Advertisers use a variety of techniques to appeal to consumers. Do any of these techniques appeal to human motivations?

Procedure
1. Find examples of various advertisements in magazines.
2. Record the kinds of items being advertised.
3. Focus on the way the advertisers promote the items.
4. Think about how the advertisers appeal to consumers to buy the product.

Analysis
1. Apply the method used to advertise the product to one of the theories of motivation discussed in the chapter.
2. How do the advertisements appeal to human motives? Present your analysis in a written report.

incentive an external stimulus, reinforcer, or reward that motivates behavior

extrinsic motivation engaging in activities that either reduce biological needs or help us obtain external incentives

intrinsic motivation engaging in activities because they are personally rewarding or because they fulfill our beliefs and expectations

Eating and socializing with friends may satisfy both an extrinsic motivation (hunger) and intrinsic motivations (enjoyment of the food and the company).

▶ **CRITICAL THINKING**

Contrasting Which motivation causes us to seek out friends?

Fuse/Getty Images

If you are motivated by both intrinsic and extrinsic motivations, do you perform more effectively or persistently at a task? Psychologists have proposed the *overjustification effect*: When people are given more extrinsic motivation than necessary to perform a task, their intrinsic motivation declines. Say, for example, you enjoy reading books. According to the overjustification effect, if someone started paying you to read books, you would enjoy reading books less. You might ask yourself, "Why am I doing this?" and answer, "It's not because I enjoy reading books; it's because I'm getting paid to do it." If you are suddenly paid less, you may start reading less. If you are no longer being paid to read books, you might lose all interest in the task.

✔ **READING PROGRESS CHECK**

Differentiating How are incentives different from drives?

LESSON 1 REVIEW

Reviewing Vocabulary
1. *Contrasting* What is the difference between extrinsic and intrinsic motivation?

Using Your Notes
2. *Explaining* Give an example of a human instinct as proposed by William James that you identified in the notes you completed for this lesson. Why do modern psychologists feel that instincts are not enough to explain motivation adequately?

Answering the Guiding Questions
3. *Contrasting* What is the difference between a need and a drive?

4. *Analyzing* How do incentives direct behavior?

Writing Activity
5. *Informative/Explanatory* When you are motivated, you are energized to engage in an activity, focus your energies toward reaching a goal, and feel strongly about achieving your goal. Use the criteria above to write a description of two activities or behaviors you engaged in today related to motivation.

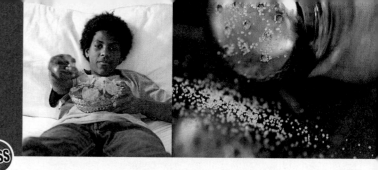

Case Study

CCSS

A Balance for Living

Period of Study: 1940

Introduction: When you are driving a car for a long time, eventually the gas tank will need refueling. Today, a car's computer system can tell when almost anything needs attention, from changing the oil to closing a door. It is important that we respond to these signals. The same can be said for human beings; we require maintenance for operating properly as well.

Like modern cars, humans also have a built-in computer: the brain. The human body must keep in balance all of the particles and liquids that help maintain our organ systems and, together, keep us alive and well. This collective action is known as homeostasis. *Homeostasis* refers to a person's behavior and the corresponding actual physical need. For example, when a person is hungry, he eats. When he has completed a strenuous physical activity and becomes thirsty, he drinks.

In 1940 a one-year-old boy, referred to as D.W., revealed an odd craving for salt. His favorite foods included any items in which a major ingredient was salt. Also, to the shock of his parents, D.W. would pour salt from the shaker directly into his mouth. When his parents denied him access to these salted edibles, D.W. would cry and throw tantrums until his parents gave in.

Hypothesis: At this time, doctors were not aware of any physiological need for a person, especially at this young age, to consume as much salt as D.W. demanded. The only possible explanation was that the young child just liked the taste of salt. The case of D.W. would eventually result in a number of both physiological and psychological hypotheses.

PRIMARY SOURCE

" *At eighteen months he was just starting to say a few words, and salt was among the first ones. We had found that practically everything he liked real well was salty, such as crackers, pretzels, potato chips, olives, pickles, fresh fish, salt mackerel, crisp bacon and most foods and vegetables if I added more salt.* "

—*from a letter written by D. W.'s parents to his doctor,*
A Great Craving for Salt, 1940

Method: When he was three and a half years old, D.W.'s parents placed him in a hospital setting where he could be checked by doctors because they believed there was more to this unusual situation than just a child's pleasure in tasting salt. The doctors planned to begin general physiological testing to check for chemical deficiencies, disease, or even mental disabilities. During this time—about two days—D.W. became excessively aggravated and enraged. His hospital diet did not include the sufficient amount of salt that D.W. had craved his whole life. Unfortunately, D.W. died only a short time after he entered the hospital and before the scheduled tests could be completed.

Results: An autopsy on D.W. revealed that his adrenal glands did not adequately supply his body with the amount of salt it needed. Although he was very young, D.W.'s body relayed to his brain that he needed to consume more salt to balance out his body systems. It is safe to believe that a child at that age could not understand what salt is or how it operates within the human body, yet somehow young D.W. knew that he did indeed need to have salt and he knew where to get it. This example demonstrates the important role homeostasis plays within the human body and the effect it has on the mind and behavior of a person to maintain various physiological balances.

Analyzing the Case Study

1. **Explaining** What is homeostasis? How does it affect behavior?

2. **Identifying** Why did D.W. crave salt?

3. **Making Connections** Recall a time when you experienced your own body's homeostasis in action. Describe the episode. How did you know what you needed?

4. **Analyzing Primary Sources** Review the quote from the letter written by D. W.'s parents. In what way did D. W.'s behaviors support the results found in this case study?

netw⦿rks

There's More Online!

☑ **CARTOON** Fear of Failure

☑ **DIAGRAM** Maslow's Hierarchy

☑ **GRAPH** Overweight Americans

☑ **GRAPHIC ORGANIZER**

☑ **SELF-CHECK QUIZ**

Reading **HELP**DESK

Academic Vocabulary

- dominate
- scheme

Content Vocabulary

- **lateral hypothalamus (LH)**
- **ventromedial hypothalamus (VMH)**
- **fundamental needs**
- **psychological needs**
- **self-actualization needs**

TAKING NOTES:

Integration of Knowledge and Ideas

FINDING THE MAIN IDEA Use a graphic organizer similar to the one below to list four motives associated with hunger.

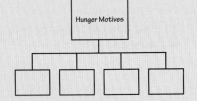

LESSON 2

Biological and Social Motives

ESSENTIAL QUESTION · *What motivates behavior?*

IT MATTERS BECAUSE

Much of life is spent trying to satisfy biological and social needs. Biological needs are physiological requirements that we must fulfill to survive, whereas social needs are those that are learned through experience. Our behaviors are a result of both biological and physiological reactions. Understanding what motivates our bodies and minds to meet our needs and achieve our goals will help us to better understand our own and others' behavior.

Biological Motives

GUIDING QUESTION *What are the different motivations people have to eat?*

Some behavior is determined by the internal, or physiological, state of the organism. Like other animals, human beings have certain survival needs. Our biological needs are critical to our survival and physical well-being. The nervous system is constructed in such a way that mild to heavy variations in blood sugar, water, oxygen, salt, or essential vitamins lead to changes in behavior designed to return the body to a condition of chemical balance. The first part of this section discusses the role of such physiological factors in motivating behavior.

All organisms, including humans, have built-in regulating systems that work to maintain such internal processes as body temperature, the level of sugar in the blood, and the production of hormones. For example, when the level of thyroxine in the bloodstream is low, the pituitary gland secretes a thyroid-stimulating hormone, causing the thyroid gland to secrete more thyroxine. When the thyroxine level is high, the pituitary gland stops producing this hormone. Similarly, when your body temperature drops below a certain point, you start to shiver, certain blood vessels constrict, and blood is redirected to the surface for heat.

All these activities reduce heat loss and bring body temperature back to the correct level. If your body heat rises above a certain point, you start to sweat, other blood vessels dilate, and evaporation cools you. The tendency of all organisms to correct imbalances and deviations from their normal state is known as homeostasis. The drives that motivate behavior are homeostatic—such as hunger and thirst.

Hunger

What motivates you to seek food? Often you eat because of the sight and smell of food. Other times you eat out of habit because you always have lunch at 12:30 or to be sociable because a friend invites you out for a snack. Yet suppose you are working frantically to finish a term paper. You do not have any food, so you ignore the fact that it is dinnertime and you keep working. At some point your body will increase its demand for food. You may feel an aching sensation in your stomach. What produces this sensation? What makes you feel hungry?

Your body requires food to grow, to repair itself, and to store reserves. To what is it responding? If the portion of the hypothalamus called the **lateral hypo-thalamus (LH)** is stimulated with electrodes, a laboratory animal will begin eating even if it has just finished a large meal. Conversely, if the LH is removed surgically, an animal will stop eating and eventually die of starvation if it is not fed artificially. Thus the LH provides the signals that stimulate eating.

If a different portion of the hypothalamus called the **ventromedial hypo-thalamus (VMH)** is stimulated, an animal will slow down or stop eating altogether even if it has been kept from food for a long period. If the VMH is removed, however, the animal will eat and overeat until it becomes so obese it can hardly move. This indicates that the VMH provides the signals that cause you to stop eating. In addition, the hypothalamus responds to temperature—the LH signal is more active in cold temperatures, while the VMH signal is more active in warm temperatures.

Other factors also influence your hunger. The *glucostatic theory* suggests that the hypothalamus monitors the amount of glucose, or ready energy, available in the blood. As the level of blood glucose entering cells drops, the LH fires to stimulate you to eat. At the same time, the pancreas releases *insulin* to convert the incoming calories into energy—whether to be consumed by active cells or converted into stored energy in the form of fat for use later. Your blood glucose level drops after your meal. The pancreas now secretes *glucagon*, which helps convert the stored energy back into useful energy.

Another factor affecting eating is your *set-point*, or the point around which your day-to-day weight tends to fluctuate. Although your daily calorie intake and expenditure of energy vary, your body maintains a very stable weight over the long run. Thus, the hypothalamus interprets at least three kinds of information—the amount of glucose entering the cells of your body, your set-point, and your body temperature. These determine whether or not the hypothalamus will contribute the signals that make you feel hungry and cause you to eat.

Other Hunger Factors

Besides our individual set-points—the weight that our bodies strive to maintain throughout our lives—other genetic factors affect our weight. With a higher set-point we can store more fat. When we add weight, we add fat cells. When we lose weight, each fat cell gives up a little stored fat, emitting signals for more.

Genetics are also at play in how, when, and what we choose to eat. Each of us has inherited different rates of metabolism from our parents. Your rate of metabolism reflects how efficiently your body breaks down food into energy and how quickly your body burns off stored calories.

lateral hypothalamus (LH) the part of the hypothalamus that produces hunger signals

ventromedial hypothalamus (VMH) the part of the hypothalamus that can cause one to stop eating

> ∨ **TABLE**
>
> ### SOME BIOLOGICAL AND SOCIAL NEEDS
>
> Whereas biological needs are physiological requirements critical to our survival, we acquire social needs through experience and learning.
>
> ▶ **CRITICAL THINKING**
>
> 1. *Drawing Conclusions* Which needs do you think we try to satisfy first?
> 2. *Analyzing* What is another social need that might be added to the list?

Some Biological Needs

- Food
- Water
- Oxygen
- Sleep
- Avoidance of Pain

Some Social Needs

- Need to excel
- Need for social bonds
- Need to nourish and protect others
- Need to influence and control others
- Need for orderliness
- Need for fun and relaxation

Blend Images/SuperStock

You may eat the same number of calories as your friend, but if you have a lower metabolic rate than your friend, you burn fewer calories and are more likely to store excess food as fat. As you lose weight the efficiency of your digestive system increases, storing more calories out of each bite. Researchers have found weight-regulating genes that play a role in metabolism. One gene increases neuropeptide Y, a brain chemical that leads to increased eating. Another gene increases a person's metabolism.

Obesity

There is a growing body of evidence that a person's weight is controlled by biological factors. There appears to be a genetic component that may predispose some people to obesity. Factors that indicate whether someone is overweight or obese are determined by body mass index (BMI), a measure based on height and weight. Using the BMI measure, about 68 percent of American adults are overweight and about 34 percent are obese.

Stanley Schachter and his colleagues at Columbia University conducted a number of studies that show that obese people respond to external cues, eating not because they are hungry, but because they see something good to eat or a clock tells them it is time to eat. To prove this, Schachter first set up a staged taste test in which people were asked to rate five kinds of crackers. The goal was to see how many crackers people at a normal body weight would eat in comparison to how many crackers overweight people would eat. Each person, instructed to skip lunch, came hungry. Some were told the taste test required a full stomach, and they were given as many roast beef sandwiches as they wanted. The rest stayed hungry.

Schachter had predicted that normal-weight people would eat because they were hungry, while obese people would eat whether they were hungry or not. This was true. People of normal weight ate more crackers than overweight people did when both groups were hungry and fewer crackers after they had eaten the roast beef. In another study, Schachter put out a bowl of almonds that people could eat while they sat in a waiting room. Overweight people ate the nuts only when they did not have to take the shells off. Thus, again they ate simply because the food was there. People of normal weight were equally likely to try a few nuts whether they were shelled or not.

In summary, Schachter argued that overweight people respond to external cues (for example, the smell of fresh-baked cookies, or the clock saying it is mealtime), while normal-weight people respond to internal cues, such as the stomach signals of hunger. His work shows that even physiological needs like hunger are influenced by complex factors beyond basic biological cues.

Other factors, such as an insufficient level of physical exercise, also contribute to obesity. Increasing your level of physical exercise can lead to weight loss, just as too little exercise in proportion to the food you eat leads to a gain in weight. Anxiety and depression disorders might contribute to, but do not cause, overeating and obesity. These disorders occur just as frequently among people of normal weight as among those who are overweight or obese.

An obese mouse with a damaged ventromedial hypothalamus will overeat until it weighs many times more than a normal mouse at the same age weighs.

▶ **CRITICAL THINKING**

Identifying Cause and Effect How does the hypothalamus help determine whether or not you will eat?

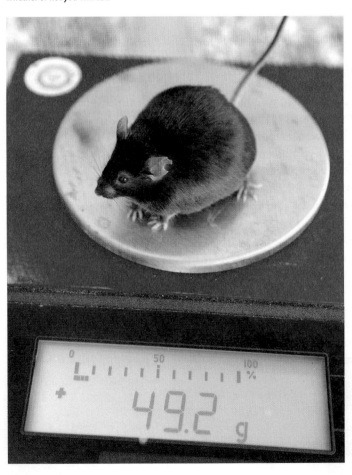

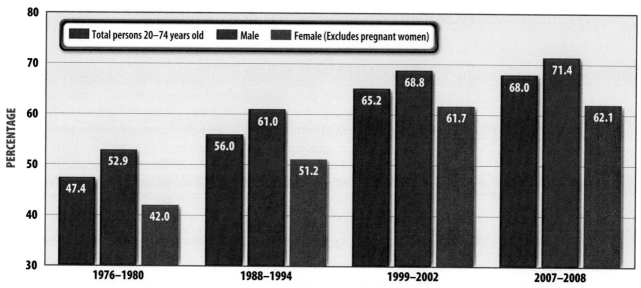

Source: Centers for Disease Control and Prevention, *Health, United States, 2010.*

Psychosocial Hunger Factors

Besides biological motives, other factors may be at work when you feel hungry or eat. These factors are sometimes called *psychosocial hunger factors.* These are external cues that can affect eating, such as where, when, what, and how much we eat. For example, imagine that you and some friends are at the food court of a shopping mall. External cues such as the smell and appearance of the food make your mouth water, and you decide you are hungry. When other people are eating, we tend to eat more, and you find yourself ordering more than you would have if you had been on your own. You might have been content with a fresh-baked pretzel, but your friends convince you to share a large pizza and ice cream sundaes.

On the other hand, you might ignore your hunger pangs and choose not to eat because of social pressures, such as trying to look like the thin models in magazines or because your friends say they are not hungry and do not want to stop to eat. Once you are alone, you might then gorge on food until you are painfully full. Psychosocial factors have a large impact on our eating habits and sometimes contribute to eating disorders, such as binge eating or self-starvation.

Sometimes when we are bored or stressed, we eat more. For instance, you might find yourself rummaging through the refrigerator for a snack just because you are avoiding studying or because someone insulted you and your feelings are hurt. You might eat a tub of popcorn when watching a movie just because that is what you always do, or you may eat a super-sized fast-food meal just because it seems like a better value. Current thinking holds that environmental factors such as habit and convenience often override hormonal and neural control of eating.

One study made a connection between eating and stress. The study found that when rats were given the physical stressor of a pinch to their tails they reacted by eating more afterwards. The rats that were pinched twice a day gained more weight than those that were not pinched. The study has been repeated using different types of stressors. In this study 24 rats, 16 with prior experience in tail pinching studies, were subjects. When presented with the stressor of a noise the rats with experience in tail pinching studies would eat. Those without prior experience did not. The study concluded that if a rat turned to eating in the face of one stressor, it would use this coping mechanism in the face of another as well.

☑ **READING PROGRESS CHECK**

Analyzing What kinds of external cues might signal an overweight person to eat?

△ **GRAPH**

PERCENTAGE OF OVERWEIGHT AMERICANS
Overweight people face increased risk for heart disease, stroke, high blood pressure, clogged arteries, adult-onset diabetes, and the risk of an early death.

▶ **CRITICAL THINKING**

1. ***Analyzing Visuals*** Some studies indicate that the percentage of overweight Americans has remained about the same since 2008. What has been the trend since the mid-1970s?

2. ***Evaluating*** Why is it important that psychologists study eating behaviors?

Social Motives and the Need for Achievement

GUIDING QUESTION *What is the motive to avoid success?*

Just as we spend much of our time meeting our own physical needs, our social needs, such as the need for achievement, also greatly influence our lives and motivate us to behave in various ways. Why is it, though, that some people seem more motivated than others when it comes to achieving something, such as a win in basketball or success at a job? Many psychologists have concentrated their research on social motives for behavior rather than on the intrinsic, biological motives we have been discussing. Social motives are learned from our interactions with other people.

Measuring the Need for Achievement

The achievement motive concerns the desire to set challenging goals and to persist in trying to reach those goals despite obstacles, frustrations, and setbacks. One reason the achievement motive has been so well researched is that David McClelland became interested in finding some quantitative way of measuring social motives. His main tool for measuring achievement motivation was the Thematic Apperception Test (TAT). This test consists of a series of pictures. Participants are told to make up a story that describes what is happening in each picture. At this point, it is only important to know that there are no right or wrong answers. Since the test questions are ambiguous, the answers must be created from the participant's own beliefs, motives, and attitudes. Each story is coded for certain kinds of themes. Coding has been refined to the extent that trained coders agree about 90 percent of the time. These themes are scored according to their relevance to various types of needs, such as achievement, that is, setting goals, competing, and overcoming obstacles.

Based on these tests, McClelland developed a scoring system for the TAT. For example, a story would be scored high in achievement imagery if its main characters were concerned with standards of excellence, high levels of performance, unique accomplishments (such as inventions and awards), or the pursuit of long-term careers or goals. Participants register a high need for achievement if they display persistence on tasks or the ability to perform better on tasks, set challenging but realistic goals, compete with others to win, and are attracted to challenging tasks or careers.

People who scored high and low in achievement on the TAT were compared in a variety of situations. McClelland followed up on the careers of some students at Wesleyan University who had been tested with the TAT in 1947. He wanted to see which students had chosen entrepreneurial work—that is, work in which they had to initiate projects on their own. He found that 11 years after graduation, 83 percent of the entrepreneurs (business managers, insurance salespeople, real estate investors, consultants, and so on) had scored high in achievement, but only 21 percent of the non-entrepreneurs had scored that high.

McClelland did not believe we should all train ourselves to be high achievers. In fact, he said that such people are not always the most interesting and they are usually not artistically sensitive. They would also be less likely to value intimacy in a relationship. Studies have shown that high achievers prefer to be associated with experts who will help them achieve, instead of with more friendly people.

McClelland's TAT is not without its critics. They have claimed that using TAT is not a reliable method of testing the need for achievement. They assert that TAT stories are difficult to score because different test-scorers may assign different importance to particular responses.

Fear of Failure

While some people are motivated by a need for achievement, others may be motivated by a fear of failure. A person displays a fear of failure, for example, when he stops taking guitar lessons because improvement seems too difficult, or she decides not to try out for the softball team because she probably cannot make it anyway. How does the fear of failure differ from the need for achievement? People display fear of failure when they choose easy tasks offering assured success or impossible tasks with no chance of success.

For example, let us say that you have your choice of three puzzles to solve. The first puzzle is extremely easy, and you know that you can solve it. The second puzzle is more difficult, but it can be solved with effort. The third puzzle is extremely difficult, and you are certain it is impossible to solve. People with a strong need for achievement tend to choose the puzzle that is difficult but not impossible. People who choose the extremely easy puzzle, however, display a fear of failure. Choosing the extremely difficult puzzle also shows a fear of failure because the person can blame failure on the difficulty of the task.

People who are motivated by the fear of failure often find excuses to explain their poor performances. They do this to maintain a good self-image. For example, a sprinter may explain her slow time in the race as a result of missed sleep. If you receive a poor grade on a test, you may claim that the test was biased. Although creating these types of excuses helps us maintain positive feelings about ourselves, it may also prevent us from taking responsibility for our own actions.

Fear of Success

In the late 1960s, researcher Matina Horner asked 89 men to write a story beginning with the line, "After first term finals, John finds himself at the top of his medical school class." Substituting the name Anne for John in the opening line, she also asked 90 women to write a story. Ninety percent of the men wrote success stories. However, more than 65 percent of the women predicted doom for Anne.

On the basis of this study, Horner identified another dimension of achievement motivation—the *fear of success*. Some people (like the females in Horner's study) are (or were) raised with the idea that being successful in all but a few careers is odd and unlikely. Thus, a woman who is a success in medicine, law, and other traditionally male occupations must be a failure as a woman. It might have been acceptable for Anne to pass her exams, but the fact that she did better than all the men in her class made the female participants anxious.

∧ CARTOON

FEAR OF FAILURE
The way a person is motivated to achieve at a task relates to the person's view of success and achievement in that task.

▶ **CRITICAL THINKING**

1. **Drawing Conclusions** How might this person demonstrate the fear of failure?

2. **Assessings** Disregarding his apparent fear at the finish line, how has the runner demonstrated a need for achievement?

Horner discovered that bright women, who had a very real chance of strong achievements in their chosen fields, exhibited a stronger fear of success than did women who were average or slightly above average. Expecting success made them more likely to avoid it, despite the obvious advantages of a rewarding career. This seemed to confirm Horner's belief that success involves deep conflicts for some people.

Other researchers then set out to verify Horner's findings. They quickly found that the picture was more complicated than Horner's study suggested. For one thing, it is very difficult to define success. Being a stay-at-home mother might be quite satisfying for one woman but a sign of failure for someone who would have preferred a career outside the home. Also, it is often difficult to tell whether a person who does not try something is more afraid of success or failure.

In the late 1960s, when Horner's study was conducted, medical school was still **dominated** by males. Likewise, nursing school was dominated by females. What if females write about males and vice versa? For instance, what if females or males write about males' success in a female-dominated occupation? Then we find both men and women write stories reflecting Horner's fear of success. Later, researchers analyzed 64 studies bearing on the issue that Horner had raised. Measured on a mean rate, 45 percent of the men expressed a fear of success, while 49 percent of the women did—a small difference. So, fear of success is found in both men and women.

Other Theories

J.W. Atkinson developed an *expectancy-value* theory to explain goal-directed behavior. *Expectancy* is your estimated likelihood of success, and *value* is simply what the goal is worth to you. Others have argued instead for a *competency*

dominate to rule over or to stand out above all others

CHART >

YOUR PERFORMANCE
The Yerkes-Dodson law says that your performance on a task is an interaction between the level of physiological arousal and the difficulty of the task. So on difficult tasks, you do better if your arousal level is low.

▶ **CRITICAL THINKING**

1. *Analyzing Visuals* According to the Yerkes-Dodson law, what level of arousal would help you do well on an exam?

2. *Gathering Information* In order to do well on most tasks, what kind of arousal is optimal?

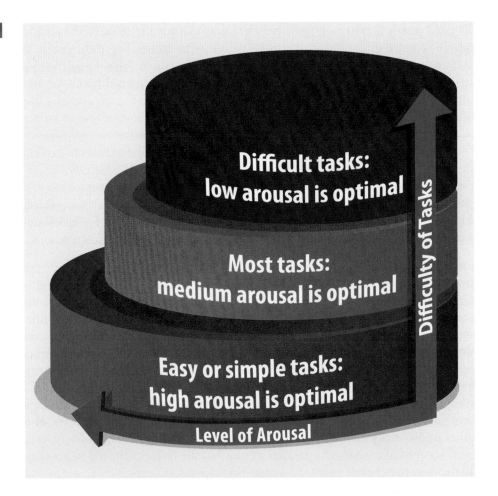

Difficult tasks:
low arousal is optimal

Most tasks:
medium arousal is optimal

Easy or simple tasks:
high arousal is optimal

Level of Arousal

Difficulty of Tasks

Meg Takamura/Getty Images

Children with a high need for achievement are more likely to position themselves an average distance from the goal rather than at an easy or difficult distance.

▶ **CRITICAL THINKING**

Analyzing Visuals Does the child pictured here exhibit a high need for achievement? Explain.

theory. Too easy a task or too difficult a task means we do not learn anything about how competent we are. So, to prove and improve our competency, we choose moderately difficult tasks where both successes and failures may prove to be instructive.

For example, in one experiment in a ring toss game, children could choose to stand 1 to 15 feet away from the stake onto which they tried to toss rings as a group watched. Those with a high need for achievement were up to 10 times more likely to choose an intermediate distance from the stakes than to choose ridiculously easy or impossibly difficult distances.

☑ **READING PROGRESS CHECK**

Analyzing What factors influence why people who are motivated by the fear of failure do not perform as well as people who are motivated by the need for achievement?

Maslow's Hierarchy of Needs

GUIDING QUESTION *Why do fundamental needs form the foundation of Maslow's hierarchy?*

Abraham Maslow, one of the pioneers of humanistic psychology, believed that *all* human beings need to feel competent, to win approval and recognition, and to sense that they have achieved something. He placed achievement motivation in the context of a hierarchy of needs all people share. Maslow proposed that after we satisfy needs at the bottom of the triangle, we advance up to the next level and seek to satisfy the needs at that level. If we are at a higher level and our basic needs are not satisfied, we will drop down Maslow's hierarchy to deal with basic needs.

Maslow's **scheme** incorporates all the factors we have discussed so far in this chapter and goes a step further. He begins with biological drives, including the need for physical safety and security. He asserted that people have to satisfy these **fundamental needs** to live. If people are hungry, most of their activities will be motivated by the drive to acquire food, and their functioning on a higher level will be hindered.

scheme a system for organizing or arranging things

fundamental needs biological drives that must be satisfied to maintain life

DIAGRAM ∨

MASLOW'S HIERARCHY OF NEEDS

According to Maslow, only after satisfying the lower level of needs is a person free to progress to the ultimate need, self-actualization.

▶ **CRITICAL THINKING**

1. *Analyzing Visuals* Into what category in the hierarchy do biological needs fall?

2. *Categorizing* According to Maslow's theory, what is the next level of need that must be satisfied by someone who is hungry and homeless before reaching self-actualization?

The second level in Maslow's hierarchy consists of **psychological needs**: The need to belong and to give and receive love, and the need to acquire esteem through competence and achievement. Maslow suggested that these needs function in much the same way that biological needs do and that they can be filled only by an outside source. A lack of love or esteem makes people anxious and tense, which motivates behavior to meet those needs. For example, a frightened child may seek the security of a loving caregiver. A young person may feel the need to explore her sexual orientation or gender identity in order to understand her need for love and belonging. An adult may strive to develop expertise and make a contribution to society in order to meet his need for esteem.

Maslow suggested that a need that is met loses some of its motivating force. On the other hand, if a need goes unmet, it may have an adverse effect on the individual. There is a driven quality to the behavior of those whose basic psychological needs have not been met. They may experiment in different behaviors to determine which, if any, will ease their tensions and meet their needs.

Self-actualization needs are at the top of Maslow's hierarchy. These may include the pursuit of knowledge and beauty or whatever else is required for the realization of one's unique potential. Maslow believed that although relatively few people reach this level, we all have these needs. To be creative in the way we conduct our lives and use our talents, we must first satisfy our fundamental and psychological needs. The satisfaction of these needs motivates us to seek self-actualization. Maslow thus added to motivation theory the idea that some needs take precedence over others and the suggestion that achieving one level of satisfaction releases new needs and motivations.

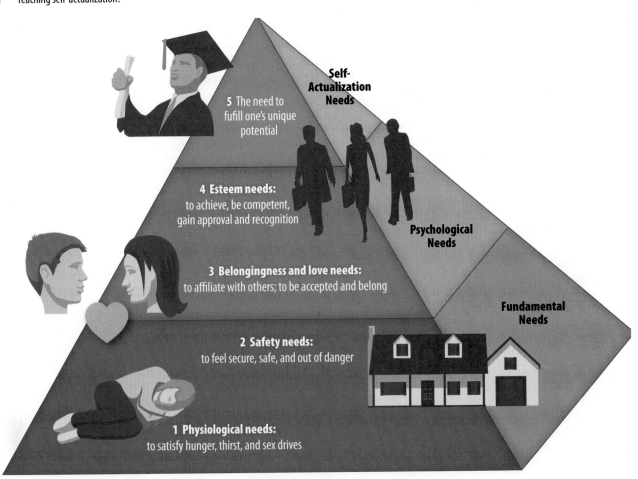

Self-Actualization Needs

5 The need to fufill one's unique potential

4 Esteem needs: to achieve, be competent, gain approval and recognition

Psychological Needs

3 Belongingness and love needs: to affiliate with others; to be accepted and belong

Fundamental Needs

2 Safety needs: to feel secure, safe, and out of danger

1 Physiological needs: to satisfy hunger, thirst, and sex drives

Other research does not support Maslow's conclusion that one need must be satisfied before another can be. Christopher Columbus, for example, may have achieved self-actualization, but he certainly put his (and many others') need for safety at risk in opting to seek a new route to China. Would we not conclude that his need for esteem was dominant in his search? Also, some people do not seem interested in fulfilling higher needs, such as achievement, although their lower, biological needs or safety needs have been met.

These researchers are suggesting that perhaps Maslow identified types of needs that may operate in all of us, but there is no particular order in which the needs must be satisfied. Any one need may dominate at a particular time, even as the organism is seeking to respond to others among his or her dominant needs. A need may be dominant in any of us at a particular moment, without necessarily meaning the other needs are not present and influencing our behavior at some level.

☑ READING PROGRESS CHECK

Classifying According to Maslow's hierarchy of needs, what is needed in order to achieve self-actualization?

Maslow proposed that we must satisfy our fundamental and psychological needs before we pursue and realize self-actualization.

▶ **CRITICAL THINKING**

Speculating Can you determine which level of Maslow's hierarchy of needs has been fulfilled by one or more of the people in this photo? Explain.

LESSON 2 REVIEW

Reviewing Vocabulary

1. *Explaining* Describe how fundamental, psychological, and self-actualization needs differ.

Using Your Notes

2. *Applying* Using your notes from the graphic organizer that you created at the beginning of this lesson, explain why physiological needs make people more overweight than psychological needs.

Answering the Guiding Questions

3. *Describing* What are the different motivations people have to eat?

4. *Identifying* What is the motive to avoid success?

5. *Explaining* Why do fundamental needs form the foundation of Maslow's hierarchy?

Writing Activity

6. *Informative/Explanatory* Review Maslow's hierarchy of needs and analyze your life according to Maslow's scheme. Which groups of needs are frequently met? Write an essay about the ways in which your needs—both fulfilled and unfulfilled—affect your thoughts and behaviors.

Motivation and Emotion **331**

Analyzing
Readings in Psychology

Reader's Dictionary (CCSS)

epidemic: affecting a large number of people
alleviate: to make more bearable
novel: new or unusual

The prevalence of obesity in the United States has often been called an "epidemic." Changes in the food landscape may be the primary culprit, although changes in attitudes regarding food may also be to blame. In this article, the author examines the things that psychologists can do to promote healthier eating habits that, ultimately, will result in healthier people.

Eating into the Nation's

Obesity
Epidemic
By Ann Conkle

PRIMARY SOURCE

"What product does the slogan 'Melts in your mouth, not in your hand' belong to?" Kelly Brownell challenged his listeners. They chuckled and shouted in unison "M&Ms." The audience hadn't expected a pop quiz when coming to hear Brownell's invited address, "Changing the American Diet: Real Change Requires Real Change," at the APS 18th Annual Convention. Next came "They're Grrreat!," "I'm lovin' it," "Break me off a piece of that …," and finally "I go cuckoo for …" Of course, the audience knew every one. But they couldn't answer one question, what departments create the federal government's nutrition guidelines and, most importantly, what are they? "Well," answered Brownell, an APS Fellow from Yale University, "The real question is who has done your nutrition education? And most startlingly, who will do the nutrition education of your children? There's no question that the answer is the food industry."

With that, Brownell, who is among this year's Time 100, a list of people whose actions and ideas influence the world, began his introduction into the reality of nutrition in America. As the quiz shows, "little effort goes in on the government's part to show people how to eat in a healthy way." Meanwhile the food industry bombards us with messages about cheap, tasty processed foods, which are, of course, high in sugars and fats. People are broadly trained that fruits and vegetables are good for them, but many Americans also believe sugary cereals are part of a nutritious breakfast and any drink with fruit in its name is healthy.

Over the last few decades, America has experienced an "absolutely startling increase [in obesity]. Pandemic or epidemic is not overstating the situation." Some see this as a failure of personal responsibility, but evidence suggests that something larger in the environment is spurring this trend. There is no evidence to suggest that we are less responsible eaters than our grandparents. Studies of developing nations show that when packaged foods such as soft drinks and snack foods replace traditional diets, obesity increases. The obesity **epidemic** could feasibly have a genetic or biological basis, but then why has it happened so quickly and recently when the gene pool has not changed? Recent studies about the economy of food give some insight into the food landscape. Five factors influence food choice: accessibility, convenience, taste, promotion and cost. Unhealthy foods win out on all five. They are more accessible, more convenient, tastier, more heavily promoted and cheaper. No wonder we all eat so badly.

PHOTO: Westend61/SuperStock ; TEXT: Republished with permission of ASSOCIATION FOR PSYCHOLOGICAL SCIENCE from Eating into the Nation's Obesity Epidemic by Ann Conkle, APS observer Vol. 19, No. 8, August 2006; permission conveyed through Copyright Clearance Center, Inc. APS observer by AMERICAN PSYCHOLOGICAL SOCIETY Copyright 2006 Reproduced with permission of ASSOCIATION FOR PSYCHOLOGICAL SCIENCE in the format Republish in 'other' book via Copyright Clearance Center.

Tom Cockrem/Photolibrary/Getty Images

What Psychological Scientists Can Do

So, what roles can psychology play to **alleviate** this crisis? Many people jump to say that psychology could help with clinical interventions of the already obese, but sadly, the only treatment with impressive results for obesity is surgery, which is too costly and invasive to be a viable solution for treating the vast number of obese people in America today. Clinical treatments also ignore the larger public health issue. According to Brownell, treating obesity without looking at the broader health issues would be like treating lung cancer without addressing the fact that smoking causes lung cancer. "For every case we successfully treat," said Brownell, "thousands more are created because of the environment." According to him, a social movement against unhealthy eating, similar to the movement against tobacco, is the only way to improve the way America eats.

To be effective, psychologists must change their thinking and make **novel** connections with people outside their field. Researchers should also realize that they may have more influence than politicians because they are not caught in political messiness (some would say quagmire) between the government, the food industry, subsidies and giant agribusiness.

Brownell outlined several key research questions that psychologists will be instrumental in answering. In a broad sense, psychologists can investigate the behavioral economics of food—why do people make the eating decisions that they do? Psychologists should investigate attitudes about food supply and processing.

Over the last several decades, there was an increasing distance from food sources to our tables. Food moved from coming from the ground or an animal to coming from the supermarket or vending machine and is now often filled with ingredients whose names we can't pronounce and whose chemical effects are not completely understood. How does this affect consumption and health? In addition, Americans seem to have an ingrained "more for less is good" value when it comes to food, as has been dramatically exploited by the "supersize it" marketing campaigns at fast food restaurants and ballooning portion sizes (Super Big Gulp, anyone?). The quest for value clearly affects what and how much we eat.

A related issue is marketing. How does promotion affect food choice, particularly among children? As shown by the quiz at the beginning of the talk, food marketing is highly effective. We all know the jingles and take them with us all the way to the supermarket aisle. Brownell asks whether we can equate the food industry's kid friendly advertising (Ronald McDonald, Tony the Tiger, Toucan Sam, and others) to the cigarette industries' now infamous advertising campaigns aimed at children. This advertising could have life-long impacts on food choice.

Finally, can food be addictive? Clearly, most severely obese individuals have a toxic relationship with food. What causes the cravings and the inability to stop when one has gone from nourishing her or his body to killing it? How can this cycle be stopped? What about food enhanced with sweeteners? High fructose corn syrup may be metabolized differently than other foods, creating unforeseen effects on bodies as well as minds. Addiction research could change the whole political landscape by changing how we think about eating as a simple choice.

Brownell offered a challenge to the audience and the broader public with five action steps: foster a social movement for nutrition, emphasize strategic science, target frequent contributors to obesity (starting with soft drinks), transform the economics of food, and pressure politicians to change the way Americans are educated about nutrition. Maybe then we would know the answers to all the questions in Brownell's pop quiz.

Analyzing Primary Sources

1. *Identifying* Why are unhealthy foods often chosen over healthier alternatives?

2. *Making Connections* What is a possible biological explanation for the increase in obesity?

3. *Interpreting* The author states that psychologists may have to study "behavioral economics" rather than intervening in cases of clinical obesity. Why?

netw⊙rks

There's More Online!

☑ **CHART** Range of Emotions

☑ **GRAPHIC ORGANIZER**

☑ **SELF-CHECK QUIZ**

☑ **TABLE** Theories of Emotion

LESSON 3
Emotions

Reading **HELP**DESK **CCSS**

Academic Vocabulary
- **pursue**   - **neutral**

Content Vocabulary
- **emotion**

TAKING NOTES:
Integration of Knowledge and Ideas

ORGANIZING Use a graphic organizer like the one below to describe how the opponent-process theory works.

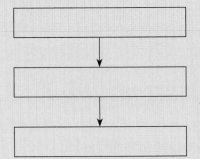

ESSENTIAL QUESTION • *What motivates behavior?*

IT MATTERS BECAUSE

Our emotions guide our behaviors. Whether we are feeling happy about being with a friend, angry about losing a soccer game, or frightened about coming face to face with an angry dog, the body reacts with appropriate emotions. All emotions consist of three parts—the physical, cognitive, and behavioral aspects. Theories of emotion propose that emotions result from physical changes and/or mental processes.

Expressing Emotions

GUIDING QUESTION *What are the three parts of emotion?*

What drives a world-class soccer player to perfect her game? Why does she try so hard? How does she feel when she scores the winning goal? Is she tired, thirsty, excited, nervous, or happy? It is difficult to draw a clear line between motives and emotions. When a person needs food, the stomach contracts, the level of sugar in the blood drops, neural and endocrine systems are thrown slightly off balance, and taste buds become more sensitive. When a person is frightened, heart and breathing rates quicken, energy level rises, senses mobilize, and blood rushes away from the stomach to the brain and to the heart and other muscles. Of course, a poet might diagnose a pounding heart, loss of appetite, and heightened awareness of the moonlight and scented breezes as love. Why, if all three involve identifiable physiological changes, do we call hunger a biological drive, and fear and love emotions?

How we label these processes depends on whether we are describing the source of our behavior or the feelings associated with our behavior. When we want to emphasize the needs, desires, and mental calculations that lead to goal-directed behavior, we use the word *drive* or *motivation*. When we want to stress the feelings associated with these decisions and activities, we use the word *emotion* or *affect*.

Clearly, the two are intertwined. We frequently explain our motives in terms of emotions. Why did you walk out of the meeting? I was angry. Why do you go to so many parties? I enjoy meeting new people and love to dance. Why did you lend your notes to someone you do not particularly like? I felt guilty about talking behind his back.

334

Ashley Cooper/Corbis

Defining Emotion

As these examples demonstrate, emotions push and pull us in different directions. Sometimes emotions function like biological drives—our feelings energize us and make us **pursue** a goal. Which goal we pursue may be determined by our social learning experiences. Other times we do things because we think they will make us feel good, and the anticipated emotions that will result from these behaviors become the incentive for our actions. Finally, emotions help us make decisions and communicate what is going on inside of us. As a result, others respond to our emotions and treat us accordingly.

Many psychologists talk about our *emotional intelligence*. This is the ability to perceive, imagine, and understand emotions and to use that information in decision making. We often need to make complicated decisions at work, in school, and with family and friends. The wrong decision can get us in trouble. Our emotional intelligence helps us gauge the situation and determine an appropriate action. For example, suppose you were talking with friends and wanted to tell a joke. Will your friends enjoy the joke, or will they think it is offensive? Judging the emotions involved in this social situation is a sign of your emotional intelligence.

An **emotion** is a subjective feeling provoked by real or imagined objects or events that have high significance to the individual. Emotions result from four occurrences. First, you must interpret some stimulus. Second, you have a subjective feeling, such as anger or happiness. Third, you experience physiological responses, such as an increased heart rate. Fourth, you display an observable behavior, such as smiling or crying. For example, if you are out walking and happen upon a growling, slobbering dog in your path, your breathing quickens and your muscles tense. You feel fear and freeze in your tracks, or maybe you shout out in alarm. If someone were to see this happening to you, they would most likely be able to interpret what you were feeling by the expression on your face.

All emotions have three parts: physical, behavioral, and cognitive. The physical aspect has to do with how the emotion affects the physical arousal of an individual. This level of arousal directs the body how to respond to the experienced emotion. The behavioral part is the outward expression of the emotion, such as body language, hand gestures, and the tone of a person's voice. The cognitive aspect concerns how we think about or interpret a situation, which affects our emotions. For example, if someone says hello, we interpret that person as being friendly, hostile, or mocking, which in turn affects our emotional response.

pursue to follow or seek

emotion a set of complex reactions to stimuli involving subjective feelings, physiological arousal, and observable behavior

---

⌄ CHART

RANGE OF EMOTIONS
Emotions are subjective feelings. Consequently, psychologists debate how many emotions exist and their specific individual impact.

▶ **CRITICAL THINKING**

1. ***Comparing*** How can you explain "avoidance behavior" and "approach behavior" indicated in this chart?

2. ***Analyzing Visuals*** What kind of behaviors are hatred and contempt, according to the chart?

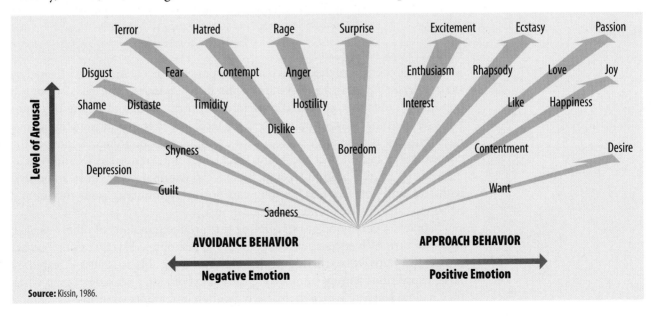

Source: Kissin, 1986.

THREATENING ELEMENTS

When people from various cultures were asked to identify the threatening shapes in each pair, they consistently selected the triangular and diagonal elements.

▶ **CRITICAL THINKING**

1. *Evaluating* Which elements would you use to make a scary mask? Why?

2. *Analyzing Visuals* Which elements look like they belong on a happy face? Explain.

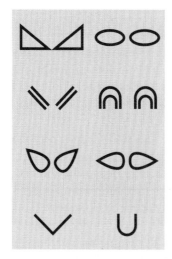

Identifying Emotions

In *The Expression of the Emotions in Man and Animals*, published in 1872, Charles Darwin argued that all people express certain basic feelings in the same ways. Without knowing a person's language, you can tell whether he or she is amused or infuriated just by looking at that person's face. In 1972, one group of researchers selected a group of photographs they thought depicted surprise, anger, sadness, and happiness. They then showed the photographs to people from five different cultures and asked them to say what they believed the person in each photograph was feeling. The overwhelming majority of the participants identified the emotions as the researchers expected they would. Was this simply because they were familiar with Americans, or at least American media, and so learned how to read their facial expressions? Apparently not. A second study was conducted in a remote part of New Guinea with people who had relatively little contact with outsiders and virtually no exposure to mass media. They, too, were able to identify the emotions being expressed.

These studies imply that certain basic facial expressions are *innate*—that is, part of our biological inheritance. Observations of children who were born without sight and hearing lend support to this view. These youngsters could not have learned how to communicate feelings by observing other people. Still, they laugh like other children when they are happy, pout and frown to express resentment, and clench their fists and teeth in anger.

Psychologist Carroll Izard and his colleagues developed a coding system for assessing emotional states in people. By noticing changes in different parts of the face, such as the eyebrows, eyes, and mouth, they have been able to identify 10 different emotional states. For example, anger is indicated when a person's eyebrows are sharply lowered and drawn together, and the eyes narrowed or squinted. A smile that indicates enjoyment involves not only a pulling up at the corners of the lips, but contraction of the muscles around the eyes. Another psychologist, James A. Russell, studied the impact of emotions on facial structures in 11 cross-cultural studies. He concluded that there are universally recognized facial expressions of emotions, including happiness, surprise, fear, anger, disgust, and sadness.

Facial Feedback Theory

Many researchers have theorized that our experience of an emotion is affected by the feedback our brains receive from our facial muscles. The facial feedback hypothesis holds that our facial expressions contribute to and define the emotions we feel. That is, your brain interprets feedback from the movement of your facial muscles as different emotions. For example, you see a dark shadow in the corner of your bedroom at night. You react by raising your eyebrows and widening your eyes. Your brain interprets these facial expressions as those associated with fear, and you feel fear. Smiling can positively influence your mood, and frowning can negatively influence your mood.

People are very good at interpreting the facial expressions of others as well, which in turn influences their own emotional responses. Psychologists Vanessa LoBue and Judy DeLoache found that children were able to detect threatening facial expressions among a group of different expressions. Moreover, even when they had no learned fear of them, both children and adults were able to identify snakes more quickly than other objects in a group of different stimuli. This evidence suggests that humans may have evolved the ability to visually interpret threats in their environment, which results in a fearful reaction to snakes and aggressive expressions, to avoid potentially dangerous situations. Critics of the facial feedback theory contend that although your facial expressions may influence your emotions, they do not cause your emotions. People whose facial muscles are paralyzed can experience emotions even though their facial muscles do not move.

Learning and Emotion

Learning is an important factor in emotional expression. James Averill believes that many of our everyday emotional reactions are the result of social expectations and consequences. He believes that emotions are responses of the whole person and that we cannot separate an individual's physical or biological experience of emotions from that person's thoughts or actions associated with those emotions.

We learn to express and experience emotions in the company of other people, and we learn that emotions can serve different social functions. Parents, for example, modify their children's emotions by responding angrily to some outbursts, by being sympathetic to others, and on occasion by ignoring their youngsters. In this way, children are taught—either directly or indirectly—which emotions are appropriate in certain circumstances. There are many cultural differences in how the display of emotion serves social functions. For instance, people from Japan are more likely than people from the U.S. to mask fear, disgust, or distress by presenting a smile. So, even as we learn how to express emotions at the appropriate times depending on social cues, we learn to repress or mask emotional expressions at other times. In effect, we learn an emotional culture.

Learning also explains the differences we find among cultures once we go beyond such basic expressions as laughing or crying. Children will imitate the expressions used by their parents or caregivers. Thus, emotions are universal, but the expression of them is learned. What these findings suggest is that all of us are born with the capacity for emotion and with certain basic forms of expression, but when, where, how, and to whom we express different feelings depend in large part on learning.

☑ **READING PROGRESS CHECK**

Making Decisions What emotion do you think a frown expresses in all cultures?

Physiological Theories

GUIDING QUESTION *How do the two physiological theories differ?*

Analyzing facial expressions helps us to describe emotions, but it does not tell us where emotions come from. Some psychologists believe emotions derive from physical changes, while others believe that emotions result from mental processes. Trying to figure out the cognitive, behavioral, and physical parts of emotions has led to several theories of emotions.

In *Principles of Psychology*, a classic work published in 1890, William James attempted to summarize the best available literature on human behavior, motivations, and feelings. When it came to drawing up a catalog of human emotions, James gave up; he felt there were too many subtle variations. Yet he was struck by the fact that nearly every description of emotions he read emphasized bodily changes. We associate feelings with sudden increases or decreases in energy, muscle tension and relaxation, and sensations in the pits of our stomachs.

Paul Ekman
(1934–)

Paul Ekman claims that human faces express emotion in a universal way: that, worldwide, we evolved with facial expressions that portray the same basic emotions. Ekman once thought that facial expressions were learned and differed depending on culture. Then, he traveled to Papua New Guinea and studied an isolated group called *Fores*. He found that they grinned when they were happy and scowled when angry, just like we do.

Since then, Ekman has developed the Facial Action Coding System (FACS), which organizes facial expressions into 46 separate movements, such as blinking, raising our brows, and pursing our lips. He used FACS to identify the facial characteristics of seven emotions: anger, fear, contempt, disgust, sadness, surprise, and happiness.

Most are able to accurately interpret another's expressions. Ekman claims that few of us (10 to 20 percent) can actually hide our true emotions—our facial movements give us away.

▶ **CRITICAL THINKING**

Making Connections What gives us away when we try to hide our emotions?

During surgery to remove a brain tumor, "Elliot" suffered damage to his prefrontal cortex. After the surgery, Elliot reported feeling almost no emotions. He described his brain surgery and the following deterioration of his life with calm detachment. Along with the loss of emotions, though, Elliot lost his ability to make decisions. When given information, he could discuss probable outcomes of each decision he might make, but he could not actually make the decision. If he forced himself to make a decision, he soon abandoned his decision. As a result, Elliot could not maintain normal relationships with friends. This points to the fact that our emotions play a large role in our decision-making.

The James–Lange Theory

After much thought, James concluded we use the word *emotion* to describe visceral, or gut, reactions to things that take place around us. In other words, James believed that emotions are the perception of certain internal bodily changes.

PRIMARY SOURCE

My theory . . . is that the bodily changes follow directly the perception of the exciting fact, and that our feeling of the same changes as they occur IS the emotion. Commonsense says, we lose our fortune, are sorry and weep; we meet a bear, are frightened and run; we are insulted by a rival, are angry and strike. . . . [T]he more rational statement is that we feel sorry because we cry, angry because we strike, afraid because we tremble. . . . Without the bodily states following on the perception, the latter would be . . . pale, colorless, destitute of emotional warmth.

—William James, Principles of Psychology (1890)

Whereas other psychologists had assumed that emotions trigger bodily changes, James argued that bodily reactions form the basis of labeling and experiencing emotions. Because Carl Lange came to the same conclusion at about the same time, this position is known as the *James–Lange theory*.

Carroll Izard's theory of emotions bears a striking resemblance to the James–Lange theory. He believed that our conscious experience of emotion results from the sensory feedback we receive from the muscles in our faces. You can check this out by noticing the difference in your emotional experience when you smile for two minutes as opposed to when you frown for two minutes. According to Izard's view, if you continue to frown, you will experience an unpleasant emotion. Thus, we react to our physiological state and label it as sadness.

Criticisms of the James–Lange Theory

Walter Cannon and other critics of the James–Lange theory argued that different emotions such as anger, sadness, or fear are not necessarily associated with different physiological reactions. For example, anger and fear may cause the same bodily reactions. Therefore, James had it backwards—you do not run from trouble and then feel fear; you feel fear first and then run. Critics also argued that the James–Lange theory leaves out the influence of cognition on emotion; some complex emotions such as jealousy and love require much interpretation and thought.

In light of such criticisms, Cannon and other critics proposed that emotions *accompany* physiological responses—they are not *caused* by them. Further, although physiological changes do not cause emotions, they may increase the intensity of the emotions that we feel. For instance, when we feel anger and our hearts race, that anger may be heightened by the way our body reacts to it.

The Cannon–Bard Theory

In 1927 Cannon published a summary of the evidence against the James–Lange theory. Cannon argued that the brain, specifically the thalamus, is the seat of emotion—an idea Philip Bard expanded and refined. According to the *Cannon–Bard theory*, certain experiences activate the thalamus, which sends messages to the cortex and to other body organs. This theory states that the brain sends two reactions—arousal and experience of emotion, but one does not cause the other. Thus, when using the word *emotion*, we refer to the simultaneous burst of activity in the brain and gut reactions. In Cannon's words, "The peculiar quality of emotion is added to simple sensation when the thalamic processes are aroused."

Later, more sophisticated experiments showed that the thalamus is not involved in emotional experience, but the hypothalamus is. Cannon also emphasized the importance of physiological arousal in many different emotions. He was the first to describe the fight-or-flight reaction of the sympathetic nervous system that prepares us for an emergency.

Physiological Arousal and Lie Detection

Some of the signs of physiological arousal are measured in one of the most famous applications of psychological knowledge—lie detection. Throughout time, people have tried to find a way to detect when others are lying. Lie detector tests are frequently used in criminal investigations. The polygraph is an instrument that records the arousal of the sympathetic nervous system, including blood pressure, electrodermal response (sweating), heart rate, and breathing rate, of a witness or suspect on trial. The polygraph works under the assumption that people feel nervous when they lie, so their physiological reactions will give them away. However, many innocent people become nervous when questioned and so appear to be lying. Factors such as tense muscles, drug use, and previous experience with a polygraph test can reduce the accuracy rate of the results.

The Guilty Knowledge test is a modified version of the polygraph test. The examiner asks questions that could be threatening only to someone who knows the unpublicized facts of the crime. For example, instead of asking, "Did you rob the gas station?" the person is asked, "Was the gas station robbed at 6:00 p.m.? At midnight? With a gun? With a knife?" People who display heightened arousal in response to the correct answers are presumed guilty. This test identifies guilty people more accurately.

✔ READING PROGRESS CHECK

Comparing How does the Cannon–Bard theory differ from the James–Lange theory?

Cognitive Theories

GUIDING QUESTION *What role does the environment play in the emotions you experience?*

Cognitive theorists believe that bodily changes and thinking work together to produce emotions. For cognitive theorists, physiological arousal is only half of the story. What you feel depends on how you interpret your symptoms. This, in turn, depends on labeling the physical arousal with an emotion to interpret your internal state. This emphasis on cognitive factors—that our thoughts play an important role in our feelings—is the premise of more recent theoretical approaches to emotion. Cognitive theorists design their research and experiments to focus on how a person's environment, beliefs, expectations, and need for order and understanding contribute to that person's emotional responses.

The Schachter–Singer Experiment

Stanley Schachter and Jerome Singer designed an experiment to explore the cognitive theory. They told all their participants they were testing the effects of a vitamin on eyesight. In reality, most received an adrenaline injection. The *informed* group was told that the injection would make their hearts race and their bodies tremble. This was the true effect. The *misinformed* group was told that the injection would calm them. An *uninformed* group was not told anything about how their bodies would react to the shot. A *control* group received a **neutral** injection that did not produce any symptoms. Like the third group, these participants were not given any information about possible side effects.

After the injection, each participant was taken to a room to wait for the test. There they found another person who was in truth part of the experiment. The participants thought the accomplice had had the same injections. Everyone completed the same questionnaire. As this happened, the accomplice began the second independent variable. For half the participants he became very happy, eventually shooting the questionnaire into the trash. For the other participants he became very angry, eventually throwing away the wadded-up questionnaire.

neutral impartial; not belonging to one side or another

Participants from the first group, who had been told how the injection would affect them, watched the accomplice with mild amusement. So did participants who had received the neutral injection. However, those from the second and third groups, who either had an incorrect idea or no idea about the side effects, joined in with the accomplice. If he was euphoric, so were they; if he was angry, they became angry.

What does this experiment demonstrate? Internal components of emotion, such as those produced by adrenaline, affect a person differently, depending on his or her interpretation or perception of the social situation. When people cannot explain their physical reactions, they take cues from their environment. The accomplice provided cues. Yet when people knew that their hearts were beating faster because of the shot, they did not feel particularly happy or angry. The experiment also shows that internal changes are important—otherwise the participants from the neutral group would have acted in the same way as those from the misinformed groups. Perception and arousal *interact* to create emotions.

Critics of this theory point out that you do not need to first experience physiological arousal to feel an emotion. Sometimes you feel an emotion first, and then your body reacts. For example, you may let your brother use your computer. Later, when your brother is finished and you return to use your computer only to find that all of your files have been destroyed, you get angry. Only then does

Connecting Psychology to Geography

EMOTION AND CULTURE

Within each culture around the world, there are different traditions and different expectations of its people. For example, in most Western cultures it is acceptable for women to wear fitted clothing that reveals the outline of their bodies. In contrast, in some Middle Eastern countries it is a cultural tradition for women to be covered up, including their faces. In the U.S., individualism is highly valued and people are likely to give priority to their own personal goals over those of the group. In other cultures, individual goals are less important than collective ones, whether those of the family, region, or nation.

When someone moves away from his culture and is faced with the norms and traditions of another culture, he may find himself emotionally unprepared for the changes. This could be a positive experience, but it could also be an experience of culture shock for some. A traveler may feel lost or alone in a culture very different from the one she grew up in. In the U.S., home to multiple cultural groups, just visiting another part of the country or a different neighborhood in a large city can make one feel like a stranger in a strange land.

Tourists visiting another country may experience emotional reactions—positive and negative—when seeing how others live or learning of that culture's history. If you've traveled far from home, you certainly experienced a range of emotions. An interesting method one can use to see how people from around the world share similar reactions is to visit an international airport and watch how a newcomer's facial expressions convey their emotional responses to their new environment.

▲ The stimulus of sharing in another culture's traditions can result in a positive emotional experience.

▶ CRITICAL THINKING

1. *Analyzing Visuals* What can you interpret from the expression on the tourist's face?

2. *Identifying Perspectives* Have you ever visited with or lived with people from another culture? If so, what was the experience like? If not, how do you imagine you would react?

your body react with anger. Critics also say that you use processes other than environmental cues to interpret your emotions. Your thoughts play a large role in appraising your emotions.

Cognitive Appraisal Theory

Imagine you are approached by someone in a dimly lit parking lot. If the person appears to be a stranger, you might begin to feel nervous or even scared. If the person turns out to be an old friend of yours, your relief at being safe might turn to pleasure at the sight of your friend. If the person ends up being someone you want to avoid, your relief might quickly transform into annoyance. This example illustrates Richard Lazarus's cognitive appraisal theory of emotion. This theory asserts that your cognitive appraisal, or interpretation, of a situation or stimulus is the most important aspect of an emotional experience. The same situation in that dimly lit lot might elicit a variety of different emotions in different people. Thus, emotions result from our appraisal of events and experiences to which we have assigned personal meaning.

The cognitive appraisal theory and the Schachter–Singer experiment, at first glance, might appear to be very similar. Both theories emphasize cognitive appraisal. The Schachter–Singer theory, however, proposes that two factors influence an emotional reaction: physiological arousal *plus* a cognitive interpretation. In contrast, appraisal theorists assert that it is the cognitive appraisal alone that results in an emotional response.

Critics of the appraisal theory argue that emotional reactions are instantaneous, bypassing conscious consideration—we feel first and think later. Certainly, scientists have demonstrated that our brains can respond to threats with an instinctive emotional response that does not involve our thought processes. Emotion researchers now recognize that there are multiple ways by which emotions are triggered. The more complex the stimuli, such as social and personal relationships, the more cognitive appraisal must be involved in generating a response. The more complex the emotional response, such as mixed emotions, the more conscious appraisal is likely involved.

Opponent–Process Theory

Physiological processes clearly are controlled by homeostatic mechanisms that usually keep the body within certain narrow limits. Emotions can be as disabling as a salt imbalance to normal activity. Why would the body not develop a homeostatic mechanism to control the effects of extreme emotions? The body has sympathetic and parasympathetic systems. The sympathetic system energizes the body for activity, while the parasympathetic system calms and relaxes the body. The opponent-process theory states that these two systems act in concert to regulate and manipulate our emotions.

In 1974, psychologists Richard Solomon and John Corbit proposed the opponent-process theory. Their work resulted in a homeostatic theory of emotional reactions based on principles of classical conditioning. They proposed that the removal of a stimulus that excites one emotion causes a swing to an opposite emotion. If the external, emotion-arousing event is labeled State A, the internal force is labeled State B.

James–Lange Theory

1. You experience physiological changes.
2. Your brain interprets the physiological changes.
3. You feel a specific emotion.
4. You demonstrate observable behavior.

Facial Feedback Theory

1. The muscles in your face move to form an expression.
2. Your brain interprets the muscle movement.
3. You feel an emotion.
4. You demonstrate observable behavior.

Cannon–Bard Theory

1. Your experience activates the hypothalamus.
2. This produces messages to the cerebral cortex and your body organs. The reacting organs activate sensory signals.
3. Sensory signals combine with cortical message, yielding emotion.

Schachter–Singer Experiment

1. You experience physiological arousal.
2. You interpret (cognitively) environmental cues.
3. You feel an emotion.
4. You demonstrate observable behavior.

▲ TABLE

THEORIES OF EMOTION

These theories of emotion differ depending on the relationship of physiological change and cognitive interpretation of emotion.

▶ CRITICAL THINKING

1. *Identifying Cause and Effect* What causes the emotion in each theory?

2. *Sequencing* What is the *last* thing to happen in each theory?

Suppose you meet someone on the first day of school, and from the start you like each other. You have several classes together and later you enjoy spending time with one another at lunch. An afternoon doing homework assignments together made them easy. Then, later that same day, your friend tells you that his or her family is moving away. You are unhappy . . . but let us face it, the next day you are back out looking for another special person, because little classical conditioning has occurred. To put it simply, too little time has passed. The opponent-process theory would indicate that you were subjected to State A with this person, which aroused your emotions, but because you spent so little time together, no State B had developed.

Now let us put a different slant on the ending. Your friend did not move away. You enjoy a close relationship and a long, healthy life together as the best of friends. One morning, late in your life, your friend dies. Your years together had produced a strong countering State B, which kept your emotions near neutral and allowed you to get on with your daily activities. Yet now that your friend is gone, you are left with only the depressing effects of the remaining classically conditioned State B.

The significance of this theory is that if the State A event is a terrifying one, such as your first parachute jump, it still predicts what will happen. Novice parachutists are terrified coming out of a plane but are wildly delighted when they return to the ground. They are subject to a brief, happy rebound. To experienced parachutists, the jump is eventually only a bit stressful due to the positive, classically conditioned State B. They usually jump for the long-term satisfaction that is generated—again, due to the long-lasting, positive counter reaction to the now-absent State A—once the jump itself is completed.

In fact, other researchers studying emotion believe that emotion may play an important role in our survival as human beings and in our ability to achieve goals. Emotion, they theorize, is so important to our survival because it spurs us to action. Emotions and the physical changes they cause are complexly intertwined. It will likely be many years before we fully understand their interactive impact on human behavior.

✔ **READING PROGRESS CHECK**

Identifying Cause and Effect According to the opponent–process theory, what happens when the stimulus for one emotion is removed?

LESSON 3 REVIEW

Reviewing Vocabulary
1. *Explaining* What does it mean when psychologists say that certain facial expressions are *innate*?

Using Your Notes
2. *Identifying Cause and Effect* Using the notes you took during this lesson about the opponent-process theory, describe what happens when an experience is repeated many times.

Answering the Guiding Questions
3. *Differentiating* What are the three parts of emotion?

4. *Contrasting* How do the two physiological theories differ?

5. *Analyzing* What role does the environment play in the emotions you experience?

Writing Activity
6. *Informative/Explanatory* Write about a time when you were able to change the way you felt by doing something. For example, you may have deliberately worked yourself up into a rage or done something fun to put yourself in a better mood. Relate those personal experiences to the various theories of emotion.

Directions: On a separate sheet of paper, answer the questions below. Make sure you read carefully and answer all parts of the question.

Lesson Review

Lesson 1

1 *Identifying* Which theory of motivation suggests that all human motives are extensions of basic biological needs?

2 *Describing* Explain the difference between extrinsic motivation and intrinsic motivation.

Lesson 2

3 *Expressing* How does McClelland measure a person's need for achievement?

4 *Summarizing* Describe the five levels of needs in Maslow's hierarchy.

Lesson 3

5 *Explaining* Why are facial expressions a good way to tell what someone's emotions are?

6 *Specifying* What are the basic principles of the Cannon–Bard theory of emotions?

Research and Technology

7 *Researching* Use the Internet to find the latest research about motivation. Summarize your findings in a short paper, comparing the latest research results with the theories discussed in the chapter.

21ˢᵗ Century Skills

Creating and Using Graphs, Charts, Diagrams, and Tables In an experiment run by Paul Ekman, actors were hired to assume specific facial expressions that mirrored universal emotions. The researchers then measured several physiological responses of the actors. Review the information in the chart and then answer the questions that follow.

8 *Acquiring Information* What emotions did the study address? What physiological changes were measured?

9 *Identifying Cause and Effect* Which emotional expression seemed to have the greatest effect on physiology? The least effect?

10 *Hypothesizing* Why do you think that certain emotional expressions cause greater physiological changes than other emotional expressions?

Changes in Heart Rate and Skin Temperature for Six Emotions		
Emotional Expression	Change in Heart Rate (beats/min.)	Change in Skin Temperature (degrees C)
Anger	+8.0	+.16
Fear	+8.0	−.01
Distress	+6.5	+.01
Joy	+2.0	+.03
Surprise	+1.8	−.01
Disgust	−0.3	−.03

Source: *Ekman, Levenson, & Friesen, 1983.*

Need Extra Help?

If You've Missed Question	**1**	**2**	**3**	**4**	**5**	**6**	**7**	**8**	**9**	**10**
Go to page	317	319	326	329	336	338	337	337	337	336

Directions: On a separate sheet of paper, answer the questions below. Make sure you read carefully and answer all parts of the question.

Exploring the Essential Question

11 **Applying**   With a partner or as a group, select 10 emotions to express with facial expressions. What emotions are harder to convey than others? Are there consistent differences in interpretation between individuals? How important do you think context (the social situation in which the facial expression occurs) is in perceiving other people's emotions? Summarize your group interaction.

Critical Thinking Questions

12 **Evaluating**   Choose one of the following theories of motivation: the drive-reduction theory, the incentive theory, or the cognitive theory. Review each theory's explanation of motivation as it relates to hunger and appetite. What are the limitations of each theory?

13 **Synthesizing**   Try going without bread in your meals for several days this week. Do you find that you are beginning to think about bread more often? Are you becoming more aware of advertisements for bread? Compare your experience with the description of drive-reduction behavior in this chapter.

14 **Differentiating**   Which theory of motivation would best explain why some people engage in high-risk activities, such as skydiving or mountain climbing?

15 **Making Decisions**   Cognitive psychologists believe that people behave in particular ways because of extrinsic motivation or intrinsic motivation. Which of the two do you think is the stronger motivator? Why do you think so?

16 **Identifying Bias**   Using what you have learned about emotions in the chapter, respond to the following statement: Men feel fewer emotions than women.

DBQ Analyzing Primary Sources

Use the document below to answer the following questions.

PRIMARY SOURCE

❝*The face is the primary site for the display of emotions. Together with the voice, it may tell the listener how the speaker feels about what is being said . . .*❞

—Paul Ekman

17 **Interpreting**   What might you conclude if someone's facial expression does not match the tone in the person's voice?

18 **Drawing Conclusions**   Does facial expression always work as a means of finding out what a person is feeling or thinking? Why or why not?

College and Career Readiness

19 **Clear Communication**   Contact a hospital, school, or local psychiatrist's office to set up an interview with a psychologist. Make a list of questions you would like to ask about emotions, the ways in which people deal with their emotions, and the problems that come up as a result of the way they express their emotions. Conduct the interview and write a summary of your findings.

Psychology Journal Activity

20 **Informative/Explanatory**   Review your entry in your Psychology Journal for this chapter. After reading about motivation in this chapter, do you think you accurately described your daily motivations? How would you change or add to your answer about what motivates you?

TEXT: From TELLING LIES: CLUES TO DECEIT IN THE MARKETPLACE, POLITICS, AND MARRIAGE by Paul Ekman. Copyright © 2001, 1992, 1985 by Paul Ekman. Used by permission of W. W. Norton & Company, Inc.

Need Extra Help?

If You've Missed Question	11	12	13	14	15	16	17	18	19	20
Go to page	336	317	317	316	319	334	337	337	339	314

Psychological Testing

ESSENTIAL QUESTION • *How do psychologists gather information?*

netw⊙rks

There's More Online about psychological testing.

CHAPTER 13

Psychology Matters...

Psychological testing is designed to assess your interests, your achievements (such as final exams), and your aptitude or ability in a subject. The two biggest areas of testing are intelligence and personality. As psychologists gather this data, the crucial issues concern the reliability and validity of each test.

◀ Psychologists and other professionals use test results to predict future behavior.

Do Tests Work?

THE QUESTION...

RESEARCH QUESTION Are tests a reliable method for studying human behavior?

Every field has its own sets of measuring tools and units, and professionals in every field must know the uses, benefits, and limitations of their tests and the measurements they take. A math teacher selects a test to determine what students have learned in class. A medical laboratory tests blood to assess a patient's health. A food marketer collects taste-testers' responses to measure a product's appeal. How do they know whether a test is measuring what it purports to measure? How can a researcher determine whether test results are accurate?

In this experiment, we will test a test by administering it multiple times to the same participants and judging the results.

Psychology Journal Activity

Do you consider yourself a good test taker? Write about this in your Psychology Journal. Consider the following questions: Have you ever taken a personality test? If so, do you think the test result accurately revealed your personality type? If you have not taken one, do you think your personality can be accurately tested and scored? Explain.

FINDING THE ANSWER...

HYPOTHESIS A test can measure consistent behavior.

THE METHOD OF YOUR EXPERIMENT

MATERIALS paper and pens/pencils

PROCEDURE Pick a behavioral topic, such as the way in which an individual reacts to stress, makes a decision, or responds to some other stimulus. Write a test with 20 statements by an individual regarding that behavior. (For example, decision-making test statements might include: *I need to be pushed into making a decision. I like to make decisions quickly. I do not question my own decisions.*) Each entry requires a set response, such as "True" or "False," or a scaled response, such as 1 to 5, "Always–Never." Jumble the order of the first test to make a second and third test; make 10 copies of each version. Recruit 10 participants and tell each of them that you will administer a different version of the test to them three different times during the week.

DATA COLLECTION Score the three test versions each participant provided. Note how consistent or inconsistent the answers were for each participant across the test series. Compare your results with those obtained by your classmates.

ANALYSIS & APPLICATION

1. Did your results support the hypothesis?

2. Regarding your sample test results, what factors might influence the results of any test?

3. What can a test maker do to ensure that the test is measuring what it is intended to measure?

netw🌐rks   ONLINE LAB RESOURCES

Online you will find:

- An **interactive lab experience**, allowing you to put principles from this chapter into practice in a digital psychology lab environment. This chapter's lab will include an experiment allowing you to explore issues related to consistency in psychological testing.

- A **Skills Handbook** that includes a guide for using the scientific method, creating experiments, and analyzing data.
- A **Notebook** where you can complete your Psychology Journal and record and analyze your experiment data.

Radius/SuperStock

Reading HELPDESK

Academic Vocabulary
- **assume**
- **summary**

Content Vocabulary
- **reliability**
- **validity**
- **standardization**
- **percentile system**
- **norms**

TAKING NOTES:
Key Ideas and Details

FINDING THE MAIN IDEA Use a graphic organizer similar to the one below to identify and define the key characteristics of psychological testing.

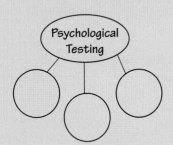

Psychological Testing

LESSON 1

Characteristics of Psychological Tests

ESSENTIAL QUESTION • *How do psychologists gather information?*

IT MATTERS BECAUSE

Tests. You have been taking them forever. In fact, you may feel as if you have been filling in "bubbles" on optical-scan test cards since the first time you held a pencil. Since the test results are used to determine access to college, it is important to assess the tests' accuracy. How well do they measure your knowledge, intelligence, and abilities?

Test Reliability and Validity

GUIDING QUESTION *What two qualities do useful tests exhibit?*

All psychological tests share one goal that makes them both interesting and practical—they all try to find out a great deal about a person in a short time. Tests can be useful in predicting a person's success in a particular career; in assessing an individual's desires, interests, and attitudes; and in revealing psychological problems. Standardized tests can provide comparable data about many individuals or show how one individual compares to others. Psychologists can use some tests to help people understand things about themselves more clearly. However, using tests to predict behavior can be controversial.

Tests are merely tools for measuring and predicting human behavior. We cannot think of test results, such as IQ scores, as ends in themselves. The justification for using a test to verify decisions about a person's future is that a decision based on test scores is more fair and accurate than decisions based on other available criteria. The fairness and usefulness of a test depends on its reliability, validity, and standardization.

Reliability

The term **reliability** refers to a test's consistent ability to yield the same result under a variety of similar circumstances. There are three ways to determine a test's reliability. In the first measure of reliability, people who take a test several times within a short time span should score approximately the same as the first time they took the test. Suppose, for example, that you take a mechanical aptitude test three times in six months. You score 65 in January, a perfect score of 90 in March, and 70 in June.

(l)Todd Warnock/Lifesize/Getty Images; (r)Chris Ryan/OJO Images/Getty Images

The test is unreliable because it does not produce a measurement that is stable over time. The scores vary too much. This is assessing the measure's *test–retest* reliability.

In the second measure of reliability, a test yields the same results when scored at different times by different people. If both your teacher and another teacher critique an essay test that you have taken, and one gives you a B while the other gives you a D, then you have reason to complain about the test's reliability. The score you receive depends more on the grader than on you. This is called *inter-scorer* reliability. If the same teacher grades papers at different times, he or she may score the same essay differently. This is *scorer* reliability. On a reliable test, your score would be the same no matter who graded it and when it was graded.

One final way of determining a test's reliability is to randomly divide the test items in half and score each half separately. The two scores should be approximately the same. This is called *split-half* reliability. If a test is designed to measure one quality in a person—for example, reading comprehension or mathematical ability—the test results on each randomly selected half should agree with one another, reflecting the consistent performance of the test taker.

In checking tests for reliability, psychologists try to prevent irrelevant variables from influencing a person's score. All kinds of matters can interfere with a test. No test can screen out all interferences, but a highly reliable test can eliminate a good part of them.

Diversity in Psychology

BALANCE AND FAIRNESS IN TESTING

The sheer variety in theories about intelligence demonstrates that we do not have a precise, authoritative definition of it. Therefore, we have no perfect way to measure it. Furthermore, when tests are devised to measure ability or achievement, there is disagreement over how the tests should be constructed and how to interpret the data.

In the mid-20th century, standardized tests became an important feature of the American educational system. Test scores indicated gaps between social classes, regions of the country, and ethnic or racial groups. Many people believed unequal educational systems in different areas caused the differences in test results, but researchers offered three other possible explanations: individuals scoring well were genetically superior; group differences were the result of faulty tests; and higher scores were the result of a superior environment.

In recognition of the cultural diversity within the United States, the American Psychological Association has adopted guidelines on multicultural education, training, research, practice, and organizational change. These guidelines recognize that psychologists can provide leadership in combating the damaging effects of racism, prejudice, and oppression based on stereotyping and discrimination.

Achievement gaps do not just occur in testing; they appear in other forms, such as dropout rates and participation in remedial programs. To a certain extent, these differences may be a result of self-fulfilling prophecies: those who expect to succeed are more likely to do so than those who expect to fail.

▲ Preparing for success leads to higher achievement.

▶ **CRITICAL THINKING**

1. *Drawing Conclusions* What impact does the environment in which a child develops have on his or her measured intelligence?

2. *Speculating* Is it possible to separate the testing of someone's intelligence from the environment in which they are raised? How does this issue impact the fairness of psychological testing?

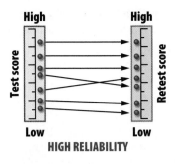

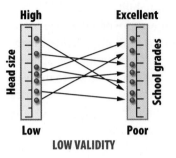

HIGH RELIABILITY

HIGH VALIDITY

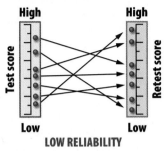

LOW RELIABILITY

LOW VALIDITY

DIAGRAM ∧

JUDGING RELIABILITY AND VALIDITY

The two sets of test scores in the top left diagram correspond very closely—meaning the test is reliable. In the diagrams on the right, the test comparing IQ scores with grades has high validity, whereas the test comparing head size with grades does not.

▶ **CRITICAL THINKING**

1. *Analyzing Visuals* Why does the test in the lower left diagram have a low measure of reliability?

2. *Drawing Conclusions* Use the bottom right diagram to explain why head size is or is not a valid test for predicting good grades.

validity the ability of a test to measure what it is intended to measure

assume to think or accept that something is true but without having proof of it

standardization the administering and scoring of tests in the same way every time; establishing the average score made by a large group of people

Validity

A test can be reliable but yet not valid. **Validity** is the ability of a test to measure what it is intended to measure. A history test does not measure engineering ability, nor does a grammar test measure ability in math.

Determining the validity of a test is more complex than assessing its reliability. One of the chief methods for measuring validity is to find out how well a test predicts performance—its *predictive* validity. For example, a group of psychologists designs a test to measure management ability. They ask questions about management systems, attitudes toward employees, and other relevant information. Will the people who score high on this test really make good managers?

Suppose the test makers decide that a good way to check the validity of the test is to find out how much a manager's staff improves in productivity in one year. If the staff of those equally skilled managers who scored high on the test improve more than the staff of those managers who scored low on the test, the test is considered valid. Corporations may then adopt it as one tool to use in deciding whom to hire as managers, **assuming** the test has been demonstrated as acceptable, reliable, and valid.

What if managers who are good at raising productivity are poor at decision making? It may be that this test measures talent for improving productivity, not general management ability. This is the kind of difficulty psychologists encounter in trying to assess the validity of a test. As the example shows, nothing can be said about a test's validity unless the purpose of the test can be completely specified.

☑ **READING PROGRESS CHECK**

Finding the Main Idea How can you judge the fairness and usefulness of a test?

Standardization

GUIDING QUESTION *Why should raw test scores be turned into percentile scores?*

Tests must be standardized. **Standardization** refers to two things. First, standardized tests must be administered and scored the same way every time. Test administrators are trained to follow the same procedures and to ask the same questions the same way. If test administrators give instructions in an inconsistent manner or provide hints, errors in assessing the test taker would result. Second, standardization refers to establishing the norm, or average score, made by a large group of people.

Once a test result is obtained, the examiner must translate the score into something useful. Suppose a child answers 32 of 50 questions on a vocabulary test correctly. If the test is reliable and valid, the score predicts that the child will understand a certain percentage of the words in a book at the reading level being tested. Yet a raw score does not tell us where the child stands in relation to other children at his or her age and grade level. If most children answered 45 or more questions correctly, 32 is a low score. If most answered only 20 questions correctly, however, 32 is a high score.

PERCENTILE SCORES

RELATIVE FREQUENCY →

1st 5th 10th 20th 40th 60th 80th 90th 95th 99th

0   5   10   15   20   25   30   35   40   45   50

TEST SCORES

When psychologists design a test to be used in a variety of settings, they usually transform raw test scores into a **percentile system**. Actual test scores are placed in order from highest to lowest. Each score is then assigned a percentile according to the percentage of scores that fall at or below its point on the scale. For example, if half the children in the above example scored 32 or below, then a score of 32 is at the 50th percentile. In the example given in the graph Establishing Percentiles, a score of 32 puts the child in the 75th percentile, because only 25 percent of the children tested achieved a higher score.

In order to make such comparisons, the test is given first to a large representative sample of the group to be measured. Percentiles are then established on the basis of the scores achieved by this group. These percentiles are called the test's **norms**. Most of the intelligence, aptitude, and personality tests you will encounter have been provided with norms in this way. Norms refer to what has been demonstrated to be a widespread, usual, or typical behavior pattern for members of a group, often considered to be "average" behavior.

In **summary**, anyone taking a published, nationally distributed test can be assured the test results achieved are an accurate assessment of the test taker's abilities at the time of the test. However, there are several factors which could reduce any test's accuracy. Some are biological, such as the test taker being tired or exhausted from lack of sleep, or the test taker being overly hungry or thirsty. Some could be attributed to the testing conditions themselves, or the prior experience of the person being tested.

☑ **READING PROGRESS CHECK**

Stating What does it mean if a test is standardized? Why do we standardize tests?

‹ GRAPH

ESTABLISHING PERCENTILES

The range of possible raw scores on a test is shown in relation to an idealized curve that indicates the proportion of people who achieved each score. The vertical lines indicate percentiles, or proportions of the curve below certain points. Thus, the line indicated as the 1st percentile is the line below which only 1 percent of the curve lies.

▶ **CRITICAL THINKING**

1. *Identifying* How do psychologists establish a scale for comparing test results?

2. *Explaining* Explain how a raw score of 35 relates to the other scores in terms of percentiles.

percentile system ranking of test scores that indicates the ratio of scores lower and higher than a given score

norms standard of comparison for test results developed by giving the test to large, well-defined groups of people

summary a shortened version of something that has already been said or written, containing only the main points

---

LESSON 1 REVIEW

Reviewing Vocabulary

1. *Explaining* What is meant when we ask about the reliability or validity of a test?

Using Your Notes

2. *Making Connections* Use the notes you have completed throughout the lesson to explain the relationship of reliability, validity, and standardization to psychological testing.

Answering the Guiding Questions

3. *Comparing* What two qualities do useful tests exhibit?

4. *Drawing Conclusions* Why should raw test scores be turned into percentile scores?

Writing Activity

5. *Informative/Explanatory* Ask a teacher for an anonymous listing of all the scores on a recent test. Establish the percentiles for the test scores. Describe your method in a short paragraph.

PHOTO: Comstock/PictureQuest; TEXT: Republished with permission of DOW JONES & COMPANY, INC. from As Brain Changes, So Can IQ by Robert Lee Hotz, The Wall Street Journal, October 20, 2011; permission conveyed through Copyright Clearance Center, Inc. Wall Street Journal Copyright 2011 by DOW JONES & COMPANY, INC., Reproduced with permission of DOW JONES & COMPANY, INC. in the format Republish in a textbook via Copyright Clearance Center.

Reader's Dictionary

malleable: able to be changed or influenced

plausibly: credibly; easy to believe

flux: continuous change

The "intelligence quotient," or IQ, was long believed to be a constant, something that did not change significantly over the course of one's lifetime. Recently, psychologists and researchers have discovered that IQ can, in fact, change due to many factors. This article outlines research in this area and implications for the future.

As Brain Changes,
So Can IQ:

Study Finds Teens' Intellects May Be More Malleable Than Previously Thought

by Robert Lee Hotz

PRIMARY SOURCE

"A teenager's IQ can rise or fall as many as 20 points in just a few years," a brain-scanning team found in a study published Wednesday that suggests a young person's intelligence measure isn't as fixed as once thought.

The researchers also found that shifts in IQ scores corresponded to small physical changes in brain areas related to intellectual skills, though they weren't able to show a clear cause and effect.

"If the finding is true, it could signal environmental factors that are changing the brain and intelligence over a relatively short period," said psychologist Robert Plomin at Kings College in London, who studies the genetics of intelligence and wasn't involved in the research. "That is quite astounding."

Long at the center of debates over how intelligence can be measured, an IQ score—the initials stand for "intelligence quotient"—typically gauges mental capacity through a battery of standardized tests of language skill, spatial ability, arithmetic, memory and reasoning. A score of 100 is considered average. Barring injury, that intellectual capacity remains constant throughout life, most experts believe.

But the new findings by researchers at University College London, reported online in Nature, suggest that IQ, often used to predict school performance and job prospects, may be more **malleable** than previously believed—and more susceptible to outside influences, such as tutoring or neglect.

"A change in 20 points is a huge difference," said the team's senior researcher, Cathy Price, at the university's Wellcome Trust Centre for Neuroimaging. Indeed, it can mean the difference between being rated average and being labeled gifted—or, conversely, being categorized as substandard.

To better understand intelligence, Dr. Price and her colleagues studied 33 healthy British teenagers whose IQ scores initially ranged from 80 to 140. They tested the volunteers on standardized intelligence exams in 2004 and again in 2008, to encompass the peak years of their adolescence, while monitoring subtle changes in brain structure using functional magnetic resonance imaging.

By analyzing verbal and nonverbal IQ performance separately, the researchers discovered that these fundamental facets of intelligence could change markedly, even in cases when an overall composite IQ score remained relatively constant.

©Ocean/Corbis

with disuse. Expert musicians, circus jugglers and London cab drivers studying maps—even Colombian guerillas learning to read—have all shown brain changes linked to practice, several brain imaging studies have reported. But until now, researchers had considered general intelligence too basic to be affected by such relatively small neural adjustments. Dr. Price and her colleagues don't know what caused the changes in both the brain and the scores they documented, but speculated they could be a result of learning experiences.

Several brain specialists said the changes could just as **plausibly** reflect the pace of normal growth, and shifts in scores could be due to inconsistent test performance.

The varying IQ scores could also indicate the test itself is flawed. "It could be a real index of how intelligence varies or it could suggest our measures of intelligence are so variable," said neuroimaging pioneer B.J. Casey at Cornell University's Weill Medical College, who wasn't involved in the study.

The size of the study was too small to warrant broad conclusions about adolescence and learning, a time when the brain is normally in **flux**, experts said. Studies seeking the genetic origins of intelligence, for example, have encompassed thousands of test subjects across decades yet have been unable to conclusively identify the genes that shape intelligence, said Dr. Plomin, the Kings College psychologist.

Other experts were confident the IQ variations were evidence of the neural impact of experience, for better or worse.

"An important aspect of the results is that cognitive abilities can increase or decrease," said Oklahoma State University psychometrician Robert Sternberg, a past president of the American Psychological Association who wasn't part of the study.

"Those who are mentally active will likely benefit. The couch potatoes among us who do not exercise themselves intellectually will pay a price."

"One fifth of them jumped one way or the other," Dr. Price said. One teenager's verbal IQ score rose to 138 at age 17 from 120 at age 13, while her nonverbal IQ dropped to a below-average score of 85 from 103. Another's verbal IQ soared to 127 from 104 in four years, while his nonverbal performance stayed the same.

"Expert musicians, circus jugglers and London cab drivers studying maps—even Colombian guerillas learning to read—have all shown brain changes linked to practice, several brain imaging studies have reported."

The rise or fall in verbal IQ scores appeared to be connected to changes in an area of the brain associated with speech, whereas shifts in nonverbal IQ related to an area involved in motor control and hand movements.

In recent years, scientists have determined that experience can readily alter the brain, as networks of neural synapses bloom in response to activity or wither

Analyzing Primary Sources

1. **Assessing** Why did the researchers study verbal and nonverbal IQ separately?

2. **Identifying Cause and Effect** Which area of the brain is involved when verbal IQ shifts upward?

3. **Making Generalizations** What is theorized to be the cause of increases in IQ score?

4. **Making Connections** Why would researchers expect to see the most drastic changes in IQ in teenagers?

5. **Drawing Conclusions** According to Robert Sternberg, what can one do to make a positive impact on one's cognitive abilities?

networks
There's More Online!

- ☑ **DIAGRAM** Wechsler Tests: Block Design
- ☑ **DIAGRAM** Wechsler Tests: Picture Arrangement
- ☑ **DIAGRAM** Wechsler Tests: Picture Completion
- ☑ **SELF-CHECK QUIZ**
- ☑ **TABLE** Dove Counterbalance Intelligence Test

Reading **HELP**DESK CCSS

Academic Vocabulary

- revise
- culture

Content Vocabulary

- two-factor theory
- triarchic theory
- emotional intelligence
- intelligence quotient (IQ)
- heritability
- cultural bias

TAKING NOTES:
Key Ideas and Details

GATHERING INFORMATION Use a graphic organizer like the one below to identify the various theories about the components of intelligence.

INTELLIGENCE

Theory of	Components of
1.	
2.	
3.	
4.	
5.	

ESSENTIAL QUESTION · *How do psychologists gather information?*

IT MATTERS BECAUSE

Have you ever wondered about your IQ? You may wonder what it is and how it relates to the IQs of your peers. You may also have wondered whether your IQ is a true measure of who you are and what you can accomplish. Is your IQ something you were born with or is it a result of your culture, your environment?

Views of Intelligence

GUIDING QUESTION *Why is intelligence not solely defined by academic ability?*

Members of the Trukese, a small tribe in the South Pacific, have amazing navigational skills. Although they are unable to explain how they do it, they can sail a hundred miles in open ocean waters and locate an island so small it could be easily missed. They navigate accurately without using any of the tools that western sailors consider indispensable: a compass, a chronometer, or a sextant. Even when prevailing winds require an indirect route, Trukese sailors find their goal. These Trukese navigation abilities point out the difficulty in coming to grips with what is meant by intelligence. Some might say that the inability of the Trukese to explain their sailing techniques is a sign of unintelligent behavior. It is hard to accuse the Trukese of being unintelligent, though. They sail successfully through the open ocean waters every day.

Psychologists do not agree on the meaning of the word *intelligence*. Most believe that intelligence is the ability to acquire new ideas and new behavior and to adapt to new situations. Others believe that intelligence is what allows you to do well on intelligence tests and in school. Two artificial intelligence researchers, Shane Legg and Marcus Hutter, recently compiled a list of more than 70 definitions of intelligence before coming up with a new definition of their own: "Intelligence measures an agent's ability to achieve goals in a wide range of environments." This definition takes into account the ability to learn and adapt, or to understand, which allows an agent to succeed in a variety of environments. The concept, however, continues to be difficult to pin down. Over the years, psychologists have presented several different views of intelligence.

Two-Factor Theory of Intelligence

British psychologist Charles Spearman proposed his **two-factor theory** of intelligence in 1904. According to Spearman's theory, two factors contribute to a person's intelligence. The first factor, *g*, represents a person's general intelligence. This involves a person's ability to perform complex mental work, such as problem solving. A second factor, *s*, represents a person's specific mental abilities, such as verbal or math skills. Spearman believed that every individual had a certain level of general intelligence.

Critics argue that *g* does not measure many other kinds of mental abilities such as motor, musical, or creative abilities. These critics argue that intelligence cannot be reduced to just *g* and expressed by a single IQ score.

two-factor theory proposes that a person's intelligence is composed of a general ability level and specific mental abilities

Thurstone's Theory of Intelligence

A major opponent of Spearman's theory was L. L. Thurstone. After testing a large number of people on more than 50 different ability tests, Thurstone concluded that there was no evidence for the general intelligence that Spearman had identified. Instead, Thurstone proposed that intelligence is composed of seven primary mental abilities. He believed that a person's intelligence needed to be a measurement of all seven mental abilities and not just a measurement of one factor.

When Thurstone tested his theory on a group of children, however, he was unable to find evidence to substantiate his thesis of seven separate primary abilities. In fact, he found evidence supporting the existence of *g*. The final version of his theory was a compromise that included both a general factor and the seven primary abilities, laying the groundwork for future research into theories of multiple intelligences.

Gardner's Theory of Multiple Intelligences

Psychologist Howard Gardner rejected the traditional idea of intelligence as primarily the ability to think logically. He believes this view is inadequate because it omits many important skills. Gardner argues for a broader perspective that includes several types of intelligence, the first two of which are familiar: verbal ability and logical-mathematical reasoning skills. He also includes spatial ability, or the ability to visualize an environment; musical ability, or the ability to perceive pitch and create rhythm; and body-kinesthetic ability, or the skill of controlling movement and handling objects required for tasks from surgery to athletics.

Mental Ability	Main Ideas
Verbal comprehension	ability to understand the meaning of words, concepts, and ideas
Numerical ability	ability to use numbers quickly to compute answers to problems
Spatial relations	ability to visualize and manipulate patterns and forms in space
Perceptual speed	ability to grasp perceptual details quickly and accurately and to determine similarities and differences between stimuli
Word fluency	ability to use words quickly and fluently in performing such tasks as rhyming, solving anagrams, and doing crossword puzzles
Memory	ability to recall information such as lists of words, mathematical formulas, and definitions
Inductive reasoning	ability to derive general rules and principles from presented information

◀ CHART

THURSTONE'S SEVEN PRIMARY MENTAL ABILITIES
Initially, Thurstone's theory of intelligence did not include the idea of a general intelligence.

▶ CRITICAL THINKING

1. *Comparing* How does Thurstone's theory compare to Gardner's theory?

2. *Interpreting* Which two of Thurstone's primary mental abilities are your strongest? Why?

Howard Gardner
(1943–)

Howard Gardner was born in Pennsylvania to parents who were refugees from Nazi Germany. He was educated at Harvard University as a psychologist and neuropsychologist. He conducted extensive studies of typical and gifted children and adults who had suffered brain damage. This research convinced him that humans possess eight different intellectual capacities, or intelligences. He argues that the biological organization of the brain affects one's strength in each of the eight areas. He proposed his theory of multiple intelligences in 1983 in the book *Frames of Mind*.

Gardner is involved in Project Zero, a research group at the Harvard Graduate School of Education, which designs "performance-based assessments, education for understanding, and the use of multiple intelligences to achieve more personalized curriculum, instruction, and assessment."

▶ **CRITICAL THINKING**

Drawing Conclusions How does Project Zero build on Gardner's multiple intelligence theory?

He then includes interpersonal skills, involving understanding the feelings of others, and intrapersonal skills, or knowledge of oneself. Gardner has later added an eighth type of intelligence—naturalist intelligence. Naturalist intelligence is a person's ability to identify and classify patterns in nature. Gardner has considered, but seems less certain about, a ninth intelligence, which concerns the experience of existence.

Many parents and teachers have embraced Howard Gardner's idea of multiple intelligences. In the classroom, teachers usually implement Gardner's theory by attacking a concept from many different perspectives or viewpoints. For example, to teach kids about the oceans, teachers have them write about cleaning a fish, draw a sea creature, role-play a sea creature, use diagrams to compare and contrast ships, and so forth.

Critics have voiced doubt that the multiple intelligences theory should be implemented in the classroom. They argue that although Gardner's theory has helped teachers appreciate the many talents of students, the theory is weak. The danger lies in wasting precious school time. Although a teacher may tap into a child's strongest intelligence by using various instructional approaches, that child must still rely on verbal and math skills to succeed in higher education and a career. Gardner's theory has yet to be stringently tested. Gardner himself claims, "We are not yet certain of the goodness of the idea of multiple intelligences."

Critics of Gardner's theory argue that some of what Gardner called "intelligence" are really skills. For instance, someone with exceptional musical abilities or body-kinesthetic abilities is really just talented. These critics claim that intelligence and talent (or skill) are two different things.

Sternberg's Theory of Intelligence

Robert Sternberg proposed another theory of intelligence. He suggested a **triarchic theory**, or three-part theory, of intelligence. Sternberg proposed that intelligence can be divided into three ways of processing information. The first way is using *analytical* thinking skills, or the ability to solve problems. These kinds of skills are the ones that are traditionally measured on intelligence tests. The second way is applying *creative* thinking to solving problems and dealing with new situations. The third is using *practical* thinking skills to help adjust to and cope with one's environment. Sternberg's ideas stress the point that traditional intelligence tests do not measure and assess intelligences found in everyday life. Like Gardner's theory, though, Sternberg's theory makes it difficult to measure intelligence, at least with traditional types of measurements.

Emotional Intelligence

Another type of intelligence is called **emotional intelligence**. It is related to Gardner's concepts of interpersonal and intrapersonal intelligences and has been discussed in the popular press. Emotional intelligence has four major aspects:

- The ability to perceive and express emotions accurately and appropriately
- The ability to use emotions while thinking
- The ability to understand emotions and use the knowledge effectively
- The ability to regulate one's emotions to promote personal growth

This view of intelligence has intrigued many psychologists. Major proponents of this view have linked emotional intelligence to success in the workplace. Some psychologists, however, argue that emotional intelligence is simply a measurement of extraversion.

☑ **READING PROGRESS CHECK**

Analyzing How did Thurstone's definition of intelligence differ from Spearman's?

Intelligence	Description	Example
Linguistic/Verbal	ability to utilize language	skilled at learning, using, and understanding languages
Logical-Mathematical	ability to process and compute logical problems and equations	skilled at solving algebra problems
Spatial	ability to comprehend shapes and images in three dimensions	skilled at putting puzzles together or molding sculptures
Musical	ability to perform and compose music	skilled at performing and comprehending music
Body-Kinesthetic	ability to perceive and control movement, balance, agility, grace	sense of how one's body should act and react in a physically demanding situation
Interpersonal	ability to interact with and understand others and to interpret their behavior	skilled at gauging others' moods and motivations
Intrapersonal	ability to understand and sense oneself	skilled at using self-esteem, self-enhancement, and strength of character to solve internal problems
Naturalist	ability to identify and classify patterns and relationships in natural surroundings	skilled at distinguishing differences among large numbers of similar objects

< CHART

GARDNER'S MULTIPLE INTELLIGENCES
Gardner proposed that each person has numerous and unrelated intelligences. He points out that a person can be outstanding in some intelligences and not in others.

▶ CRITICAL THINKING

1. *Contrasting* What is the difference between interpersonal and intrapersonal intelligence?

2. *Comparing* Compare Gardner's interpersonal and intrapersonal intelligence to emotional intelligence.

triarchic theory proposes that a person's intelligence involves analytical, creative, and practical thinking skills

emotional intelligence interpersonal and intrapersonal abilities needed to understand and use knowledge of emotions effectively

The Development of Intelligence Tests

GUIDING QUESTION *How do the Stanford-Binet and Wechsler tests differ?*

Among the most widely used and widely disputed tests in the United States and Canada today are those that are designed to measure intelligence in terms of an IQ score. Alfred Binet, a French psychologist, worked with Theodore Simon to develop a useful intelligence test. In 1904 Binet was asked by the Paris school authorities to devise a means of picking out "slow learners" so they could be placed in special classes from which they might better profit. Binet was unable to define intelligence, but he believed it was complex. He thought it was reflected in the things children do—making common-sense judgments, telling the meanings of words, and solving problems and puzzles. Binet also assumed that whatever intelligence was, it increased with age. That is, older children had more intelligence than younger children. Therefore, in selecting items for his test, he included only items on which older children did better than younger children.

By asking the same questions of many children, Binet determined the average age at which a particular question could be answered. For example, he discovered that certain questions could be answered by most 12-year-olds but not by most 11-year-olds. If a child of 11, or even 9, could answer these questions, he or she was said to have a mental age of 12. If a child of 12 could answer the 9-year-old-level questions but not the questions for 10-year-olds and 11-year-olds, he or she was said to have a mental age of 9. Thus a slow learner was one who had a mental age that was less than his or her chronological age.

The Stanford-Binet Intelligence Scale

Binet's intelligence test has been **revised** many times since he developed it. The Binet test currently used in the United States is a revision created at Vanderbilt University—the Stanford-Binet Intelligence Scale. The Stanford-Binet, like the original test, groups test items by age level. Used to test school-aged children and young adults, the test can also be used to test participants from age 3 to 85+.

revise to change or update something to make it more accurate or realistic

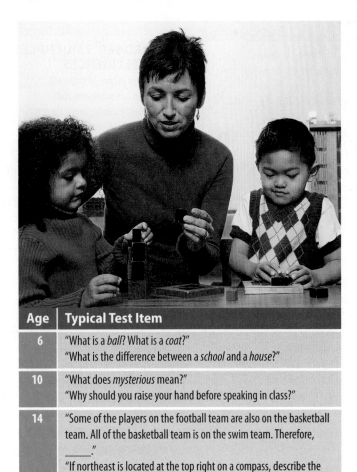

Age	Typical Test Item
6	"What is a *ball*? What is a *coat*?" "What is the difference between a *school* and a *house*?"
10	"What does *mysterious* mean?" "Why should you raise your hand before speaking in class?"
14	"Some of the players on the football team are also on the basketball team. All of the basketball team is on the swim team. Therefore, _____." "If northeast is located at the top right on a compass, describe the compass location of southwest."

Source: Modified from Nietzel and Bernstein, 1987.

CHART ⌃

TYPICAL ITEMS ON THE STANFORD-BINET TEST

An examiner has built a tower of blocks (top) and has told the child, "You make one like this."

▶ **CRITICAL THINKING**

1. *Analyzing* Why is age important in administering and scoring the Stanford-Binet test?

2. *Assessing* In what ways do the test questions require cultural understanding as well as cause-and-effect knowledge?

intelligence quotient (IQ)
standardized measure of intelligence based on a scale in which 100 is average

The test includes tasks from defining words to explaining events in daily life. Participants are tested one at a time. Examiners must carry out standardized instructions while putting the person at ease, getting him to pay attention, and encouraging him to try as hard as he can.

The IQ, or **intelligence quotient**, was originally computed by dividing a child's mental age (the average age of those who also received the same score as that child) by chronological (actual) age and multiplying by 100.

$$IQ = \frac{\text{Mental Age}}{\text{Chronological Age}} \times 100$$

So an 8-year-old child who scored at the mental age of 8 would have an IQ of 100. Although the basic principles behind the calculation of IQ remain, scores are figured in a slightly different manner today. Researchers assign a score of 100 to the average performance at any given age. Then, IQ values are assigned to all the other test scores for this age group. If you have an IQ of 100, for example, this means that 50 percent of the test takers who are your age performed worse than you. In addition, test scores for several abilities are now reported instead of one general score, but the test is no longer widely used.

The Wechsler Tests

Three frequently used intelligence tests are the revised versions of the Wechsler Adult Intelligence Scale, or WAIS-IV for adults aged 16 to 90; the Wechsler Intelligence Scale for Children, or WISC-IV for children 6 through 16 years old; and the Wechsler Preschool and Primary Scale of Intelligence, or WPPSI-IV, for children 2.5 to 7.5 years old. The WISC identifies cognitive strengths and weaknesses in children, especially in assessing learning disabilities, attention disorders, and giftedness. The WPPSI can be used as an assessment of general intellectual functioning and to identify intellectual giftedness or cognitive delays in young children.

In addition to yielding one overall score, the Wechsler tests yield percentile scores in several areas—vocabulary, information, arithmetic, visual puzzles, and so on. These ratings are used to compute separate IQ scores for verbal and performance (non-verbal) abilities. This type of scoring provides a more detailed picture of the individual's strengths and weaknesses than a single score does.

The Otis-Lennon School Ability Test

Because it is easier and less expensive to use than other IQ tests, the Otis-Lennon School Ability Test (OLSAT) is often used by schools. This test was originally developed for the U.S. Army as an alternative to the Stanford-Binet test. It seeks to measure the cognitive abilities that are related to a student's ability to learn and succeed in school. It does this by assessing a student's verbal, nonverbal, and quantitative abilities.

☑ **READING PROGRESS CHECK**

Evaluating Why are the Wechsler tests more useful for adults than the Stanford-Binet test?

SOMOS/SuperStock

IQ Scores: Uses, Meaning, and Controversy

GUIDING QUESTION *How can cultural bias affect test results?*

In general, the norms for intelligence tests are established in such a way that most people score near 100. This means that about 95 percent of people score between 70 and 130. Only a little more than 2 percent score at or above 130. These people are in at least the 97th percentile. Those who score below 70 have traditionally been classified as developmentally disabled. More specific categories include mildly disabled, but educable (55–69); moderately disabled, but trainable (40–54); severely disabled (25–39); and profoundly disabled (below 25).

What do these scores mean? What do the tests measure? IQ scores seem to be most useful when related to school achievement; they are quite accurate in predicting which people will do well in schools, colleges, and universities. Critics of IQ testing do not question this predictive ability. They do wonder, however, whether such tests actually measure intelligence, a point of controversy. As stated earlier, most psychologists agree that intelligence is the ability to acquire new ideas and new behavior and to adapt to new situations. Is success in school or the ability to take a test a real indication of such ability? Generally, IQ tests measure the ability to solve certain types of problems. Yet, as researchers as far back as 1962 have pointed out, IQ tests do not directly measure the ability to pose those problems or to question the validity of problems posed by others.

The question of cultural bias in intelligence tests has also been controversial. Much of the debate about IQ testing centers around the following issues: Do genetic differences or environmental inequalities cause two people to receive different scores on intelligence tests?

Nature versus Nurture

To determine whether intelligence test scores are affected by genetic differences or environmental inequalities, researchers have studied the test results of people who are genetically related to one another in varying degrees of kinship.

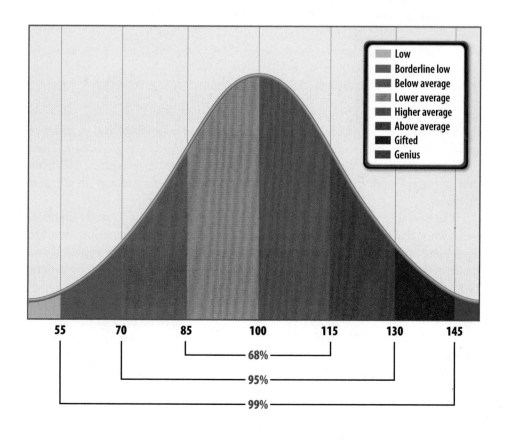

Low
Borderline low
Below average
Lower average
Higher average
Above average
Gifted
Genius

55   70   85   100   115   130   145

68%
95%
99%

GRAPH

DISTRIBUTION OF IQ SCORES

This normal curve displays intelligence as measured by the Stanford-Binet and Wechsler tests. The mean IQ score is 100; the standard deviation is 15.

▶ **CRITICAL THINKING**

1. *Analyzing Visuals* What percentage of people score at least 145 on IQ tests?

2. *Identifying* Where do the people identified as moderately, severely, and profoundly disabled fit on this curve?

VERBAL SCALE

EXAMPLE

Information
What day of the year is Independence Day?

Arithmetic
If eggs cost $.60 a dozen, what does one egg cost?

Vocabulary
Tell me the meaning of *scoff*.

Similarities
In what way are hats and shoes alike?

Digit Span
Listen carefully, and when I am through, say the numbers right after me.
7 5 1 8 2 9

PERFORMANCE SCALE

EXAMPLE

Picture Completion
What part is missing from this picture? ➡️

Picture Arrangement
Arrange the panels to make a meaningful story.

Block Design
Put the blocks together to make this picture.

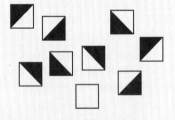 

▶ **DIAGRAM** ∧

SAMPLE ITEMS ON THE WECHSLER TESTS
These test items are similar to those included in the various Wechsler intelligence scales. (Not all test items and scales are included here.)

▶ **CRITICAL THINKING**

1. *Comparing* How do the Wechsler tests compare to the Stanford-Binet Intelligence test?

2. *Contrasting* How are the thinking skills required for the verbal scale different from the thinking skills required for the performance scale?

For intelligence, researchers have found a high degree of **heritability**—a measure of the degree to which a characteristic is related to inherited genetic factors. Their findings indicate that as the degree of genetic relationship increases, say, from that of parent and child to that of identical twins, the similarity in IQ also increases.

The best way to study the effects of nature and nurture is to study identical twins who have been separated at birth and raised in different environments. Dr. Tom Bouchard has studied more than 100 sets of twins who were separated and raised apart from one another. Bouchard concluded that IQ is affected by genetic factors—a conclusion supported by the discovery of a specific gene for human intelligence. Bouchard believes 70 percent of IQ variance can be attributed to heredity, but others have found the hereditary estimate to be only 52 percent.

Other studies have found that there is no significant relation between the intelligence of adopted children and biological children of the same family, even though they grew up in the same environment. This strengthens the idea that heredity has a greater influence than environment on intelligence.

Regarding environment, studies show that brothers and/or sisters raised in the same environment are more likely to have similar IQs than siblings raised apart. When infants from disadvantaged families (low parental IQ or little parental education and low incomes) receive enriched educational day care there are large gains in IQ. Environment, therefore, does impact IQs.

Some researchers study the effects of the environment on IQ factors by focusing on preschool programs, such as Head Start, that expose economically disadvantaged youths to enriching experiences. Some studies show that quality preschool programs help raise IQs initially, but the increase begins to fade after some years. Participating children, however, are less likely to be in special education classes, less likely to be held back, and more likely to graduate from high school than are children without such preschool experiences. One study showed that each year of school missed may drop a person's IQ as much as 5 points. The richness of the home environment, the quality of food, and the number of brothers and sisters in the family all affect IQ.

Both heredity and environment have an impact on intelligence. Advances in behavioral genetics research continue to refine results on the contributions that heredity and experience have on IQ. It remains clear that these two factors are both contributing and interact in their effects.

The Flynn Effect

The nature versus nurture debate took an interesting twist with the work of James R. Flynn, who discovered that, since 1918, IQ scores in the United States have risen nearly 25 points. Scores in Britain have jumped slightly more than that just since 1942. This trend has been seen in other developed nations as well. The IQ improvement is particularly apparent on the puzzle-and-maze portion of IQ tests—those portions that are least likely to be culturally linked.

The increase in IQ was not noticed at first because the IQ tests themselves are updated regularly. Test manufacturers maintain the norms by resetting the average score to 100. The result is that a person taking a test today that was written 30 years ago would score higher than on a current edition of the same test.

This rise in IQ scores cannot be genetic since the changes have occurred over the course of a generation. Yet the environment in which today's children are growing has not significantly altered either. Researchers have proposed a number of explanations for this. One theory is that more children today receive an education. This education provides earlier exposure to the type of thinking required to do well on IQ tests. Others suggest that better nutrition, both before and after birth, is the key. Still other researchers suggest that an abundance of reading material and electronic technology has led to more familiarity with the puzzle-and-maze type of questions.

Flynn himself has proposed that environment plays a special role in this development. Compare it to sports. As a particular sport, such as basketball or soccer, becomes popular, more people practice and participate in it. The skills become refined and, over time, the expected skill level to qualify for the team rises. A star player of 1945 might not make the team if competing against a genetically equal youth of today who has been practicing the sport since preschool days. So, too, with IQ tests. Genetics can be enhanced by environment.

Cultural Bias

A major criticism of intelligence tests is that they have a cultural bias—that is, that the wording used in questions may be more familiar to people of one social group than to another group. For example, on one intelligence test the correct response to the question, "What would you do if you were sent to buy a loaf of bread and the grocer said he did not have any more?" was "try another store."

More ABOUT...

Family Size and IQ

The classic study of family size and IQ was conducted in the Netherlands. It was based on the military examinations of more than 386,000 Dutch people. Researchers found that the brightest children came from the smallest families and had few, if any, brothers and sisters when they were born. Thus, the first-born child in a family of two was usually brighter than the last child in a family of 10. The differences in IQ, however, from one birth-order position to another averaged only about one-quarter point.

The effects of family size on intelligence may be explained by the impact of a houseful of children on the home environment. Larger families increase the amount of time a child spends with other children and decrease the amount of parental attention he or she receives. When this happens, studies have shown that the development of intelligence may suffer, but interpersonal skills may improve.

heritability the degree to which a characteristic is related to inherited genetic factors

cultural bias an aspect of an intelligence test in which the wording used in questions may be more familiar to people of one social group than to another group

Can we say that you do well in school because you have a high IQ? Consider this: a baseball player has a low batting average. A fan explains that the player does not get a lot of hits because he has a low batting average. Is this statement true? No, that baseball player has a low batting average because he does not get a lot of hits. In the same way, we cannot say that a student does poorly in school because he has a low IQ score. IQ tests measure the same skills that schoolwork requires. An IQ score measures performance; it does not explain it.

culture the beliefs, customs, practices, and social behavior of a particular nation or people

A significant proportion of minority students, however, responded that they would go home. When questioned about the answer, many explained that there was no other store in their neighborhood.

Studies of IQ tests show that socioeconomic and ethnic background is a factor in the scores. While IQ scores are lower among children of lower income classes, they tend to be higher among children from middle- and upper-class homes. Some ethnic groups, particularly African Americans and Latinos, tend to score lower than their European American counterparts.

Controversy surrounds the way in which these facts are interpreted. Psychologists may interpret the data according to their personal beliefs and ideas. A psychologist who believes that IQ is genetic and unchangeable might argue that lower IQ scores prove the existence of racial differences in intelligence. Some have, in the past, used this theory to argue that African Americans, Latinos, or women are genetically less intelligent than other groups. This is a rather simplistic explanation of test performance that ignores the role of environment, such as a student's poor educational experiences and learning opportunities.

Psychologists who fall on the nurture side of the debate would be more likely to argue that IQ discrepancies result from social and economic differences. They would argue that children from low-income families score lower because their parents lack the time and money to provide the interaction, training, and educational benefits that more affluent families can provide.

Finally, some psychologists argue that the tests themselves are flawed. Because they are written by and for European Americans, they are inherently biased toward that group and against people of other cultural backgrounds. Test questions and terms that might make perfect sense to European Americans might prove unintelligible and baffling to other cultural groups. The tests, then, have a cultural bias.

Psychologists admit that some tests have been biased because they assess accumulated knowledge, which is dependent on a child's environment and opportunities in that environment. As a consequence, efforts have been made to make the tests less biased. The Dove Counterbalance Intelligence Test is an example of such a test. However, it is unlikely that a test will ever be developed that will be completely free of cultural bias. All tests are based on the assumptions of a particular **culture**, or societal group.

Other standardized tests also exhibit cultural bias. For example, the Scholastic Aptitude Test (SAT) has been criticized for the advantage it gives wealthy whites. The critical reading and writing sections of the test deal with topics that whites are more likely to be exposed to than nonwhites. The verbal section favors white students by using language that whites may be more familiar with than nonwhite students might be. Results vary according to students' socioeconomic status, culture, primary language, and test-taking experience, as well. Discrepancies are not just linked to economic status. Scores by minority students of equal economic status lag behind those of white students.

Recently, the reading, math, and writing scores of high school students taking the SAT have dropped to the lowest level on record. This drop has been attributed by some to the growing number of minority students taking the test. More than one-third of all test takers were the first in their families to try to go to college. Others attribute the drop to curriculum issues within the educational system.

Interestingly, average scores of East Asians are higher than those of whites, both in the United States and around the world, in spite of the fact that IQ tests were developed by European Americans. Cultural and racial IQ differences among Asian American and African American children raised by white adoptive parents correspond to the differences in those raised by their biological parents.

1. "T-Bone Walker" got famous for playing what?
   a. Trombone   d. Guitar
   b. Piano   e. "Hambone"
   c. "T-Flute"

2. Who did "Stagger Lee" kill (in the famous blues legend)?
   a. His mother   d. His girlfriend
   b. Frankie   e. Billy
   c. Johnny

3. If you throw the dice and "7" is showing on top, what is facing down?
   a. "seven"   d. "little Joes"
   b. "snake eyes"   e. "eleven"
   c. "boxcars"

4. "You've got to get up early in the morning if you want to _____."
   a. catch the worms   c. try to fool me
   b. be healthy,   d. fare well
      wealthy, and wise   e. be the first one on the street

5. Many people say that "Juneteenth" (June 19) should be made a legal holiday because this was the day when _____.
   a. the slaves were freed in the USA   d. the slaves were freed in California
   b. the slaves were freed in Texas   e. Martin Luther King was born
   c. the slaves were freed in Jamaica   f. Booker T. Washington died

< **TABLE**

THE DOVE COUNTERBALANCE INTELLIGENCE TEST

In the 1960s, psychologist Adrian Dove developed the Counterbalance Intelligence Test to stress that cultural background can influence performance on an intelligence test.

▶ **CRITICAL THINKING**

1. *Specifying* What characteristics would a test without cultural bias have?

2. *Identifying Bias* For what cultural group is this test designed?

Gender Bias

There are also gaps between the sexes in some test scores. Males outscore females by about 40 points on the combined verbal and math portions of the SAT, even though female students actually outperform males in the real world of high school and college.

This discrepancy has led researchers to believe that males' and females' brains are "wired" differently. A study conducted by the Educational Testing Service and the College Board determined that the multiple-choice format used in most standardized tests is biased against females. The gender gap disappears with short-answer, essay, and other types of questions using constructed responses.

☑ **READING PROGRESS CHECK**

Identifying What happens when the wording used in test questions is more familiar to people of one social group than to another group?

LESSON 2 REVIEW

Reviewing Vocabulary

1. *Explaining* What are the two-factor and triarchic theories of intelligence?

Using Your Notes

2. *Finding the Main Idea* Use the notes you took while reading this lesson to write a paragraph identifying and summarizing the various views on intelligence.

Answering the Guiding Questions

3. *Differentiating* Why is intelligence not solely defined by academic ability?

4. *Contrasting* How do the Stanford-Binet and Wechsler tests differ?

Writing Activity

5. *Informative/Explanatory* Develop a list of criteria that you think are essential in determining intelligence. Compare your list with your classmates' lists and together create a class list. In a brief paragraph, categorize the items on your class list.

Case Study

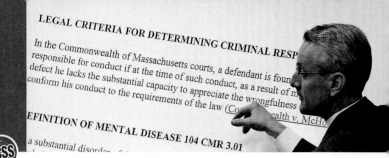

LEGAL CRITERIA FOR DETERMINING CRIMINAL RESP...
In the Commonwealth of Massachusetts courts, a defendant is foun...
responsible for conduct if at the time of such conduct, as a result of m...
defect he lacks the substantial capacity to appreciate the wrongfulness...
conform his conduct to the requirements of the law (Co...ealth v. McHo...

EFINITION OF MENTAL DISEASE 104 CMR 3.01
a substantial disord...

WAIS-R: Is It Reliable?

Period of Study: Unavailable

Introduction: It is common for psychologists to be called in on a court case to assess the competency and ability of certain individuals to play key roles in the case. Psychologists frequently use tests measuring intelligence levels in order to determine the ability of an individual to take part in a legal proceeding. In these instances, the validity of the tests used is assumed. However, reliability is equally critical. Psychological tests can be administered to an individual to gain certain results. If these results are not consistent with a repeat testing, the original results are meaningless.

The American Psychiatric Association's (APA) Council on Psychiatry and Law has developed policies for professionals involved in the assessment of intellectual functioning for court cases. In creating its policies, the APA Council embraced the approach outlined in a Virginia statute for applying clinical expertise to those court cases that require the reliable determination of mental disability. Based on that law, testimony from psychiatrists and psychologists, experts in such assessments, must include the results of at least one standardized test accepted by the field of mental health professionals.

PRIMARY SOURCE

❝*Testing of intellectual functioning should be carried out in conformity with accepted professional practice by a person skilled in the administration, scoring, and interpretation of such tests, and, whenever indicated, the assessment should include information from multiple sources.*❞

—Source: *Richard J. Bonnie, LLB*

In a trial involving the alleged statutory rape of a 22-year-old woman, psychological testing was crucial. Although the victim was of legal age, prosecutors filed charges of force or threatening of force to commit a sexual act, stating that the alleged victim was incapable of giving meaningful consent because of a mental disability. Prosecutors called in a psychologist to perform testing on the victim using the Wechsler-Adult Intelligence Scale-Revised test, or WAIS-R. This specific intelligence test is highly useful for measuring conditions of mental disability in individuals.

The results of the first test indicated the woman had an IQ below 70, demonstrating significant, but not clear, signs of possible mental disability. The defense attorney demanded a repeat test be performed.

Hypothesis: The prosecuting team knew the WAIS-R clearly measured what it is supposed to measure; thus, they wanted to see consistent results. The defending team, however, wanted to see inconsistencies in the test scores of the woman in the hopes the defendant would be set free. Because the WAIS-R holds much prestige within the psychological field, it seemed likely that results would be consistent.

Method: The psychologist who administered the WAIS-R informed the court that the odds were against a substantial rise in the IQ of the woman. The psychologist, however, also informed the court that pressure and stress surrounding the trial could have played a major impact on how the woman scored on the first test. With this second scenario weighing heavily on the minds of the prosecution, the psychologist presented the woman with the WAIS-R once again.

Results: On the second WAIS-R test, the woman scored only one point higher. The psychological test proved reliable. Validity and reliability proved important in deciding the fate of a man accused in a court of law; he was found guilty of rape and sentenced to 15 years in prison.

Analyzing the Case Study

1. **Assessing** Why was the WAIS-R used in this instance?

2. **Analyzing** Why did the defense team on this case want the alleged victim to retake the test?

3. **Evaluating** What might significantly different results on the WAIS-R have meant in this case?

4. **Synthesizing** How were the APA Council policies satisfied in this case? Would a retest qualify as "information from multiple sources"? Why or why not?

LESSON 3

Measuring Achievement, Abilities, and Interests

Reading **HELP**DESK **CCSS**

Academic Vocabulary
• fundamental   • correspond

Content Vocabulary
• aptitude test
• achievement test
• interest inventory

TAKING NOTES:
Key Ideas and Details

IDENTIFYING Use a graphic organizer like the one below to identify why someone would take an aptitude test, achievement test, or an interest inventory.

	Why would someone take this test?
Aptitude test	
Achievement test	
Interest inventory	

ESSENTIAL QUESTION • *How do psychologists gather information?*

IT MATTERS BECAUSE

What do you want to be when you grow up? As a child, you may have answered that you would like to be a firefighter, a police officer, a nurse, or a doctor. Now that you are in high school, your answer to that question matters more. It will shape your future. How do you know what you want to do?

Aptitude and Achievement Tests

GUIDING QUESTION *Why is the SAT considered an aptitude test?*

What subject fascinates you? What career should you choose? What are your interests and aptitudes? Which subject most motivates you to learn more? Intelligence tests are designed to measure a person's overall ability to solve problems that involve symbols such as words, numbers, and pictures. Psychologists have developed other tests to assess special abilities and experiences. These include aptitude tests, achievement tests, and interest inventories.

Aptitude tests attempt to discover a person's talents and to predict how well he or she will be able to learn a new skill. They are assessed primarily in terms of their *predictive validity*. Some of these assess career aptitude, while others are designed to assess thinking and reasoning skills. There are also aptitude tests geared to specific disciplines such as music, language, art, and mathematics. For instance, a music aptitude test would test understanding of music theory and might involve the ability to distinguish pitch, tone, and intervals. An aptitude test designed to assess your verbal ability—how well you communicate—might include spelling, grammar, and analogies. If designed to test your ability to use numbers, you will likely solve basic arithmetic problems and interpret charts and graphs. Some aptitude tests assess abstract reasoning—your ability to identify the underlying logic of a pattern and then determine the solution—to determine whether you learn new things quickly, while others assess one's spatial ability and require that you manipulate or visualize three-dimensional objects presented as two-dimensional pictures.

aptitude test estimates the probability that a person will be successful in learning a specific new skill

achievement test measures how much a person has learned in a given subject or area

CARTOON ⌄

TESTING ACRONYMS

You take tests to show what you have learned in high school and to predict how well you will do in college or in a particular career.

▶ **CRITICAL THINKING**

1. *Identifying Point of View* In what way does the friend's answer identify his opinion?

2. *Drawing Conclusions* Why are these tests so widely used?

The Scholastic Aptitude Test, more commonly known as the SAT, and the American College Test (ACT) are general aptitude tests. These tests were designed to predict a student's success in college. The best predictor of how a student will do in college should be how he or she did in high school. However, since grading standards differ among high schools, a combination of high school grades and the SAT is a fairly good predictor of student success in college.

Aptitude tests can also help determine whether a person is well suited to a particular career. The Law School Admissions Test (LSAT) is required for admission to most law schools. The LSAT helps predict how well a student will do in law school based on his or her aptitude for logical reasoning, analytical reasoning, reading comprehension, and writing. The Medical College Admission Test (MCAT) is required for admission to most medical schools. Admissions officers use the test results as a predictor of the candidate's success in medical school. The exam is designed to test the skills medical school students will use when they get there, including aptitude for and knowledge of the concepts and principles of the physical and biological sciences, verbal reasoning, problem solving, critical thinking, and writing.

Whereas aptitude tests are designed to predict how well a person will be able to learn a new skill, **achievement tests** are designed to measure how much a person has already learned in a particular area. Such tests not only enable an instructor to assess a student's knowledge, but they also help students assess their progress for themselves. Such tests are validated in terms of their *content validity*, or how well they measure students' mastery of a set of knowledge.

Computers are often used to administer achievement tests. One method is called *adaptive testing*. In a standard test, everyone gets the same questions in the same order. With adaptive testing, however, the computer changes the question difficulty as it adapts the test to your performance. If you answer several problems correctly, the computer challenges you with harder problems. If you miss a question, the computer follows it with an easier problem. This process enables the

computer to identify your ability by finding the difficulty level at which you answer most, but not all, of the problems correctly. Adaptive testing is more accurate than standard testing, especially when test takers are either very high or very low in ability.

Computers can also adapt tests to include more problems in areas where your answers are frequently wrong. This procedure is called *adaptive instruction*. By increasing the questions posed on topics you are missing, the computer reinforces more careful studying in areas least understood.

The distinction between achievement and aptitude tests has become somewhat blurred. What psychologists had thought were tests of aptitude—defined as *innate* ability or talent—turned out to measure experience as well, so that in part they were achievement tests. On the other hand, achievement tests often turned out to be the best predictors of many kinds of occupational abilities, so that they were in some sense aptitude tests. Because of this overlap, the distinction between the two types of tests rests more on purpose and validation than on content. If a test is used to predict future ability, it is considered an aptitude test; if it is used to assess what a person already knows, it is an achievement test.

☑ **READING PROGRESS CHECK**

Identifying What is the purpose of an aptitude test?

Interest Inventories

GUIDING QUESTION *What is the essential purpose of an inventory?*

The instruments for measuring interests are **fundamentally** different from the instruments for measuring abilities. Answers to questions on an intelligence test indicate whether a person can, in fact, do certain kinds of thinking and solve certain kinds of problems. There are right and wrong answers. The answers to questions on an interest or a personality test, however, are not scored as right or wrong. The question in this type of testing is not, "How much can you do?" or "How much do you know?" but, "What are you like?" or "What do you like?"

The essential purpose of an **interest inventory** is to determine a person's preferences, attitudes, and interests. One of the most thoroughly researched and widely used interest inventory, the Strong Interest Inventory (SII), was created in 1927 to help people who were leaving military service make educational and career plans by measuring their interests in a broad range of occupations, leisure activities, and educational subjects. The SII continues to be used in educational settings, public institutions, and private organizations.

Most interest inventories compare a person's responses to the responses given by people in clearly defined groups, such as professions or occupations. The more a person's interest patterns **correspond** to those of people in a particular occupation, the more likely he or she is to enjoy and succeed in that profession.

Quick Lab

DO INTEREST INVENTORIES HELP DETERMINE A CAREER?
Interest inventories are used as predictors of how likely an individual completing the inventory will enjoy and succeed in a profession.

Procedure
1. Choose a profession that you might be interested in pursuing and find information about its requirements and responsibilities.
2. Develop a series of questions that would address and assess a person's interest in the particular profession.
3. Administer the inventory to classmates.

Analysis
1. Determine whether the responses indicate an interest in the profession you chose. Then ask those who took the inventory if a career in the profession you chose is something they might enjoy.
2. How would you evaluate your inventory in terms of its predictive value?

---

fundamental central; forming the necessary basis of something

interest inventory
measures a person's preferences and attitudes in a wide variety of activities to identify areas of likely success

correspond to be similar or equivalent to something

THE KCS

Shown are items from the *Kuder® Career Search with Person Match* (KCS), Kuder's interest assessment. The individual taking the assessment selects a first, second, and third choice from possible activities that are listed in groups of three. This assessment can be taken in Kuder Navigator, for middle and high school students, and Kuder Journey, for college students and adults.

▶ **CRITICAL THINKING**

1. *Interpreting* What is the *Kuder® Career Search* designed to measure?

2. *Posing Questions* Write your own interest inventory question following the system used with the *Kuder Career Search* test. What will you learn about the test taker through the options you provide?

	1st	2nd	3rd
Take apart a radio to see how it works	☐	☐	☐
Run for election to a city or county office	☐	☐	☐
Take a photography class	☐	☐	☐
Visit a famous art museum	☐	☐	☐
Explain why there are waves in the ocean	☐	☐	☐
Measure a kitchen floor for the amount of material needed to cover it	☐	☐	☐
Help a friend plan a budget	☐	☐	☐
Plant a tree in your yard	☐	☐	☐
Prepare advertising for a new product	☐	☐	☐
Look up addresses of people in the phone book	☐	☐	☐
Use a formula to solve a math problem	☐	☐	☐
Take a pottery class	☐	☐	☐

For example, when constructing the widely used Campbell Interest and Skill Survey, psychologists compared the responses of people who are successfully employed in different occupations to the responses of people in general. Suppose most engineers said they liked the idea of becoming astronomers but would not be interested in a coaching job, whereas people in general were evenly divided on these (and other) questions. A person who responded as the engineers did would rank high on the scale of interest in engineering. The *Kuder® Career Search with Person Match* is based on the same principle.

The purpose of these measures is to help people find the career that is right for them. It is important to note that although interest inventories can be of great value to people who are undecided about the career path they should take, they provide only one source of information. Along with interests, a student's abilities should be taken into account. A person should not make an important decision, such as that of career, on the basis of a single test or inventory.

☑ **READING PROGRESS CHECK**

Explaining How does an interest inventory work?

TEXT: *Kuder® Career Search with Person Match*, copyright © Kuder, Inc., www.kuder.com

---

LESSON 3 REVIEW

Reviewing Vocabulary

1. *Describing* Write a short paragraph explaining what aptitude, achievement tests, and interest inventories are designed to measure.

Using Your Notes

2. *Identifying Central Issues* Use your notes to identify why an individual might take an aptitude test, an achievement test, or an interest inventory.

Answering the Guiding Questions

3. *Evaluating* Why is the SAT considered an aptitude test?

4. *Finding the Main Idea* What is the essential purpose of an interest inventory?

Writing Activity

5. *Informative/Explanatory* Choose a favorite sport or hobby. Devise a short aptitude test that you think would help predict how well an individual would be able to learn the skills needed for the sport or hobby you chose. Explain your thinking in a paragraph.

networks

There's More Online!

☑ **CHART** Approaches to Reducing Test Anxiety

☑ **SELF-CHECK QUIZ**

Reading **HELP**DESK CCSS

Academic Vocabulary
• flexible   • emerge

Content Vocabulary
• personality test
• objective test
• projective test

TAKING NOTES:
Integration of Knowledge and Ideas

IDENTIFYING Use a graphic organizer like the one below to define and identify the five types of personality tests.

Objective Tests	Projective Tests
Definition:	Definition:
1.	1.
2.	2.
3.	

LESSON 4

Personality Testing

ESSENTIAL QUESTION • *How do psychologists gather information?*

IT MATTERS BECAUSE

Have you ever wondered why you are more outgoing or introverted than other members of your family? You may describe yourself as driven, analytical, expressive, or amiable. The Greek physician Hippocrates proposed four possible personality types. A person was cheerful (sanguine), brooding (melancholy), easily angered (choleric), or mellow (phlegmatic) because of the fluids, or humors, in his or her body.

Objective Personality Tests

GUIDING QUESTION *What is the goal of an objective personality test?*

Personality. It is what makes you who you are. It is a person's consistent, unique, and enduring characteristics. The adjectives *sanguine, melancholy, choleric,* or *phlegmatic* used by the Greeks survive today in the words we use to describe different personality types. The explanations for what causes personality differences, though, have changed dramatically. Psychologists and psychiatrists use **personality tests** as tools to assess an individual's characteristics, to identify various problems and psychological disorders, and to predict how a person might behave in the future. Some of these tests are objective tests, while others are more open-ended projective tests.

Some of the most widely used personality tests are based on simple pencil-and-paper responses. **Objective tests** are usually constructed in a limited- or forced-choice format; that is, a person must select one of a small number of possible responses, and a specific scoring key is created.

The MMPI

One of the most widely used tests for general personality assessment is the Minnesota Multiphasic Personality Inventory (MMPI). (The MMPI was revised, updated, and published in 1990. The new version is called MMPI-2.) Like other personality tests, the MMPI-2 has no right or wrong answers. The test consists of 567 statements to which a person can respond *true, false,* or *cannot say.* Some examples of test statements are: I like tall women; I wake up tired most mornings; I am envied by most people; and I often feel a tingling in my fingers.

(l)Science and Society/SuperStock ; (r)Spencer Grant/PhotoEdit

Psychological Testing **369**

MMPI-2 SCALES

The MMPI is a true–false self-questionnaire that is designed to assess major patterns of personality and emotional disorders. Clinical scales identify that a test taker has answered certain questions on the test in a specific manner. Validity scales assess whether the test taker was lying or faking answers.

▶ **CRITICAL THINKING**

1. *Evaluating* Why is the MMPI considered an objective test?

2. *Drawing Conclusions* Explain how the items on the validity scales are identified.

The items on the MMPI-2 reveal habits, fears, delusions, sexual attitudes, and symptoms of psychological disorders. Psychologists originally developed the test to help diagnose psychiatric disorders. Although the statements that relate to a given characteristic (such as depression) are scattered throughout the test, the answers can be pulled out and organized into a single depression scale or scoring key. There are 10 such clinical scales to the MMPI. In scoring the MMPI, a psychologist looks for patterns of responses, not a high or low score on one or all of the scales. This is because the test items do not, by themselves, identify personality types; the pattern of scale scores does so.

In creating the original MMPI, the test makers did not try to think up statements that would identify depression, anxiety, and so forth. Rather, they invented a wide range of statements about all sorts of topics and gave the test to groups of people already known to be well-adjusted, depressed, anxious, and so on. They retained for the test those questions that discriminated among these groups—questions, for example, that people suffering from depression almost always answered differently from other groups. As a result, many of the items on the test may cause critics to question the test's face validity. For example, if you answer *false* to "I attend religious services frequently," or "occasionally I tease animals," you will score one point on the depression scale. This and other items like it were

Clinical Scales	High scores indicate that the test taker:
Hs–Hypochondriasis	expresses stress in physical terms
D–Depression	experiences depression and hopelessness
Hy–Conversion Hysteria	expresses emotion without insight
Pd–Psychopathic Deviate	is maladaptive and fights authority
Mf–Masculinity-Feminity	rejects, confuses, or questions traditional gender roles
Pa–Paranoia	has a tendency to misinterpret others' motives
Pt–Psychasthenia	worries obsessively
Sc–Schizophrenia	has a situational problem, not necessarily schizophrenia
Ma–Hypomania	has too much energy and is unable to get anything done
Si–Social Introversion	is withdrawn

Sample of Validity Scales (all Validity Scales are not included in the list below)	
?–CNS–(Cannot Say)	Corresponds with the number of items left unanswered
L–Lie	Some individuals fail to mark items truthfully and describe someone whom they envision as having a perfect personality
F–Infrequency	Some individuals are unwilling to cooperate with the test instructions and mark items in a random manner; others exaggerate their difficulties to get special attention
K–Correction	Some individuals deny certain characteristics about themselves and their families and so slant their answers to hide something

included simply because more depressed people than nondepressed people answer *false* to this item. One of the ways in which the MMPI-2 identifies individuals who give inaccurate responses is that an untrue response to one statement may be caught by the rephrasing of the same question at a later point.

The subject of thousands of studies, the MMPI has been one of the most frequently used psychological tests. The MMPI-2 includes revisions aimed at modernizing the language, removing sexist terms or phrases, and adding items reflecting current issues such as Type A personalities, alcohol abuse, drug abuse, eating disorders, and suicide.

The test can also differentiate common demeanors such as introversion-extraversion and assertiveness. Most psychologists believe that scores on the MMPI-2 should be supplemented and confirmed with interviews and observation for proper diagnosis. The MMPI-2 test is best for diagnosing extreme cases of psychological disorders.

The CPI

The California Psychological Inventory (CPI) is similar to the MMPI but is developed for more general use. Even though it uses some of the same questions, it does not have any of the questions that reveal psychiatric illnesses. It measures traits such as responsibility, self-control, and tolerance. The CPI is used to predict things like adjustment to stress, leadership, and job success.

Although it is known to be fairly valid and reliable, the CPI can prove faulty. The test results may point out that the individual has a problem when that individual really does not. Like all personality tests, the CPI is useful for general screening and in locating individuals who may need help. If an individual's scores indicate that a problem exists, though, the test should be followed by one-on-one discussion with a counselor or psychologist for further investigation.

The Myers-Briggs Test

Another popular personality test is the Myers-Briggs Type Indicator (MBTI). The test focuses on how a person takes in information, makes decisions, and approaches day-to-day tasks. This test characterizes personality on four different scales—introversion vs. extraversion, intuition vs. sensing, feeling vs. thinking, and judging vs. perceiving. An introvert prefers the inner world (ideas and images), whereas an extravert prefers engaging in activities involving the outer world (people and things). Sensing and intuition refer to the contrast between using senses primarily in a practical way ("seeing is believing") or paying more attention to impressions or patterns. When responding to events and people, thinking involves a more logical approach, whereas feeling involves using a personal, values-oriented approach. Finally, those who are oriented to judging tend to have a more organized and structured manner and lifestyle, while those who are oriented toward perceiving tend to be more **flexible**.

The creators of the MBTI believe that each person's personality is a combination of these characteristics. Your personality type influences your communication style, how you carry out relationships, your work style, as well as other lifestyle choices. The purpose of the test is to offer test takers an evaluation of their personalities so that they may better understand how they relate to others and how others relate to them. Businesses may use this test to make better decisions about whom to hire and promote. Students can use this test to optimize the match between their learning style and the teaching styles of their instructors.

☑ **READING PROGRESS CHECK**

Expressing What is the purpose of the MMPI?

— *More* —

ABOUT...

The Validity of Horoscopes

How can astrologers and horoscopes accurately describe you and your life? Horoscope writers and astrologers actually describe your personality traits in such a way that they apply to almost everyone. They use what is called the Barnum principle. Named after circus owner P. T. Barnum, it is a method of naming general traits, not specific traits. This means horoscopes lack validity, an essential factor in any good personality test. Because horoscopes are aimed at applying to everyone, they do not measure what they are supposed to measure—individual personality traits.

personality test assesses an individual's characteristics and identifies problems

objective test a limited- or forced-choice test in which a person must select one of several answers

flexible able to change or be changed according to circumstances

Projective Personality Tests

GUIDING QUESTION *What is the goal of a projective personality test?*

Unlike objective tests, **projective tests** encourage test takers to respond freely, giving their own interpretations of various test stimuli. These tests are open-ended examinations that invite people to tell stories about pictures, diagrams, or objects. Children might be asked to draw pictures and then describe what they've drawn.

The idea is that the test material has no established meaning, so the story a person tells must say something about his or her needs, wishes, fears, and other aspects of personality. In other words, the test taker will project his or her feelings, perspectives, and attitudes onto the test items.

The Rorschach Inkblot Test

Perhaps the best-known and most widely discussed projective measure is the Rorschach inkblot test, developed by Swiss psychiatrist Hermann Rorschach in 1921. Rorschach created 10 cards with inkblot designs and a system for interpreting responses. After 10 years of researching responses to thousands of inkblots, he chose 10 specific ones that elicited emotional responses in people. Five of the blots are black and gray on a white background; two have red splotches plus black and gray; and three cards have a mixture of different colors.

To administer the test, a psychologist hands the inkblots one by one to the test taker, asking the person to say what he or she sees. The person might say that a certain area represents an airplane or an animal's head. In a second round, the psychologist asks certain general questions in an attempt to discover what aspects of the inkblot determined the person's response. There are no right or wrong answers. The psychologist keeps a record of things the test taker does, such as what he says he reports seeing, where and how he holds the cards, and the length of time he pauses before answering.

In interpreting a person's responses to the inkblots on the Rorschach test, as much attention may be paid to the style of the responses as to their content.

▶ **CRITICAL THINKING**

Describing What are projective tests?

Science and Society/SuperStock

The theory underlying the test is that anything that someone does or says will reveal an aspect of that person's personality. There are several systems for scoring Rorschach responses. Some are very specific; for example, according to one system, a person who mentions human movement more often than color in the ink blots is probably introverted, while an extrovert will mention color more than movement. Other systems are far more intuitive—for example, noting whether the test taker is open or hostile.

Many researchers have criticized the Rorschach, charging that the scoring systems are neither reliable nor valid and that the results often depend on the psychologist's expectations. The test, though, continues to be used by therapists as an introduction to therapy.

The TAT

The second most widely used projective measure was developed by Henry Murray in 1943. The Thematic Apperception Test (TAT) consists of a series of 20 cards containing pictures of vague but suggestive situations. The individual is asked to tell a story about the picture, indicating how the situation shown on the card developed, what the characters are thinking and feeling, and how it will end. The TAT is used to urge clients to speak freely about their problems.

As with the Rorschach, there are many different scoring systems for the TAT. The interpreter usually focuses on the consistent emotions, issues, or themes that **emerge** from the story the client relates about the situations, emotional states, or needs of the main characters in the cards: Are they aggressive? Do they seem to have needs for achievement, love, or sex? Are they being attacked or criticized by another person, or are they receiving affection and comfort? The responses are used to assess the healthy and unhealthy functioning of the individual taking the test, including areas of motivation and personality characteristics.

emerge to become known or apparent

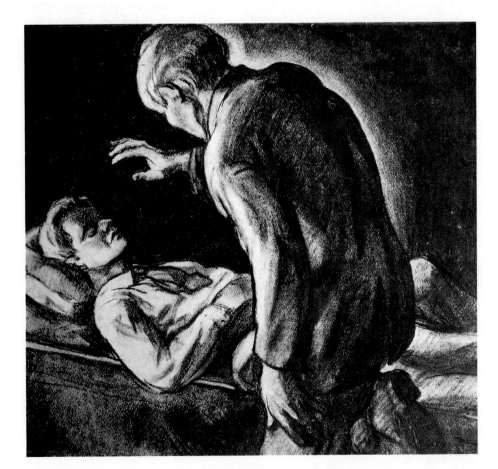

A person taking the TAT would be shown a picture such as this one and asked to make up a story about it.

▶ **CRITICAL THINKING**

Explaining What does the TAT assess?

Many people worry about taking any kind of test. When someone comes to a psychologist complaining of test anxiety, the psychologist may approach the problem in a variety of ways, depending on his or her theoretical orientation.

▶ **CRITICAL THINKING**

1. *Interpreting* How would a behaviorist attempt to reduce testing anxiety?

2. *Contrasting* How does the humanistic approach differ from the behavioral approach?

Approach	Solution
Biological (focus on physiological arousal, i.e. sweaty palms)	Reduce anxiety through stress-reducing activities
Cognitive (focus on thinking/ excessive worrying)	Channel worry into studying
Behavioral (focus on actual behaviors)	Increase study time by selecting a good place to study, rewarding yourself for studying, keeping a record of your study time, establishing priorities, specifying time for specific tasks
Psychoanalytic (focus on personality problems that underlie bad study habits)	Work to change personality characteristics, such as procrastination
Humanistic (focus on conscious beliefs and perceptions)	Teachers work with students so that students develop feelings of competence and reach their full potential
Sociocultural (focus on influence of culture and ethnicity)	Students from different cultures have different values and resources; work to understand differences and similarities

Source: Adapted from Plotnik, 2005.

Unlike other personality tests, projective tests are derived from the psychoanalytic perspective and images and stories are purported to reflect an individual's unconscious urges and desires. Test results are subject to the interpretation of the clinician and coding systems are used to minimize varying interpretations.

It is important to note that a personality test, as with an aptitude, achievement, interest, or intelligence test, is just one of the tools that a psychologist can use to evaluate a person's psychological state. A conscientious psychologist should pair testing with other evidence gained through interviews and observation before drawing any conclusions or making any diagnoses.

✓ **READING PROGRESS CHECK**

Identifying What is the underlying theory in the Rorschach test?

LESSON 4 REVIEW

Reviewing Vocabulary

1. *Contrasting* What is the difference between objective and projective tests?

2. *Describing* What is the purpose of a personality test?

Using Your Notes

3. *Comparing and Contrasting* Use your notes to compare and contrast the five types of personality tests.

Answering the Guiding Questions

4. *Explaining* What is the goal of an objective personality test?

5. *Summarizing* What is the goal of a projective personality test?

Writing Activity

6. *Informative/Explanatory* Choose two personality traits. Develop several test questions that you think would assess these traits. Explain your thinking in a short paragraph. Discuss and evaluate your questions with your classmates.

Directions: On a separate sheet of paper, answer the questions below. Make sure you read carefully and answer all parts of the question.

Lesson Review

Lesson 1

1 *Explaining* What does it mean if a test is standardized? Why do we standardize tests?

2 *Assessing* Would an intelligence test be a valid test for measuring a person's knowledge of a foreign language? Explain.

Lesson 2

3 *Describing* Describe Gardner's theory of multiple intelligence. Why do proponents of this theory support its use in the classroom?

4 *Exploring Issues* Explain the nature-versus-nurture debate. Which theories of intelligence fall into the nature-versus-nurture camp? Which do you think has the greatest effect on intelligence, nature or nurture? Explain.

5 *Identifying Bias* Look back at the sample items from the Stanford-Binet Test and the Wechsler Tests to identify one question which you feel is culturally biased. Why?

Lesson 3

6 *Contrasting* What is the difference between the content validity and predictive validity of a test?

7 *Explaining* How do tests like the SAT, LSAT, and MCAT measure aptitude?

Lesson 4

8 *Contrasting* What are the two basic types of personality tests? What are some of the differences between the two types? Give an example of each test.

9 *Differentiating* How does the CPI differ from the MMPI? How does the CPI differ from the Myers-Briggs test?

21st Century Skills

Identifying Perspectives *Read the cartoon below. Then answer the questions that follow.*

"All right, which one of you heard the break-in?"

10 Which person shown in the cartoon is assumed to have heard the break-in? Explain.

11 What assumptions are being made by the cartoonist?

Exploring the Essential Question

12 *Making Connections* Summarize the relationship between reliability and validity. Can a test be reliable without being valid? Can it be valid without being reliable? Provide examples to support your statements. Why do psychologists need special guidelines to gather information from diverse populations?

Need Extra Help?

If You've Missed Question	**1**	**2**	**3**	**4**	**5**	**6**	**7**	**8**	**9**	**10**	**11**	**12**
Go to page	350	350	355	359	358	365	366	369	369	355	355	348

Directions: On a separate sheet of paper, answer the questions below. Make sure you read carefully and answer all parts of the question.

Critical Thinking Questions

13 *Comparing and Contrasting* What is the purpose of and difference between Intelligence Quotient (IQ) tests, achievement tests, and aptitude tests?

14 *Synthesizing* If you were asked to rate people on an intelligence scale of your own making, what criteria would you use and how would you make your decisions? What roles would memory, creativity, and emotional maturity play in your scale?

15 *Evaluating* Only a few tests have been used to predict how happy people will be with their lives or how successful they will be in their careers. Explain why you think this may be the case.

16 *Drawing Conclusions* How accurate do you think the scoring for projective tests is? Can the scoring for these kinds of tests be standardized? Explain.

17 *Evaluating* Do you think personality tests should be used by employers to make decisions about hiring employees? Explain.

College and Career Readiness

18 *Identifying Perspectives* Devise your own version of a Dove Counterbalance test from the point of view of the culture with which you and your family identify. Use slang, movies, musical lyrics, and other ideas that are known and understood within your culture. Create at least five questions that reflect your culture yet assess intelligence. How do your questions reflect your point of view? Have you developed questions which others would agree are free of cultural bias?

Research and Technology

19 *Researching* In recent years, take-at-home computerized IQ tests have become increasingly popular. Search the Internet to find examples of these kinds of tests. Also, find out about intelligence tests offered on CD-ROMs that parents can administer to their children. Evaluate the pros and cons of using these kinds of intelligence tests.

20 *Speculating* To investigate the possibility of a correlation between genius and birth order, create a spreadsheet with data you found for at least 10 people famed for their intelligence and the birth order of each. Convert your data into a chart. Explain your results.

DBQ Analyzing Primary Sources

Use the document to answer the following questions.

PRIMARY SOURCE

"*The question of whether there are innate differences in intelligence between black and white goes back more than a thousand years, to the time when the Moors [who were from North Africa] invaded Europe. The Moors speculated that Europeans might be congenitally incapable of abstract thought.*"

—*Richard E. Nesbitt* Intelligence and How to Get It: Why Schools and Culture Count (2009)

21 *Synthesizing* Do a quick search of the Moors and their occupation of Spain. How could the Moors have used the idea of nature versus nurture, along with intelligence testing, to justify their invasion and subjugation of Spain?

Psychology Journal Activity

22 *Informative/Explanatory* Review your entry in your Psychology Journal for this chapter. After reading about different psychological tests in this chapter, do you have more faith or less faith in their ability to accurately test your personality? Explain by using details from the chapter.

Need Extra Help?

If You've Missed Question	**13**	**14**	**15**	**16**	**17**	**18**	**19**	**20**	**21**	**22**
Go to page	357	357	367	372	369	362	357	361	361	346

Theories of Personality

ESSENTIAL QUESTIONS • *How is behavior influenced by environment?* • *How does experience influence personality?*

Psychology Matters...

What is "personality"? We are all interested in the reasons for our individuality. Psychological theorists have utilized different perspectives to answer the questions of what personality is, where it comes from, how it forms, and how it evolves.

◄ The way a person acts in different social settings tells a lot about their personality.

Ryan McVay/Stone+/Getty Images

Lab Activity

Testing Personality

THE QUESTION...

RESEARCH QUESTION Is personality determined by birth order?

People often look for similarities among their peers that might explain different personality types. When you hear someone say, "She's so in control, she must be a firstborn" or "He must be the baby in the family," you are hearing the birth order explanation. Some psychologists believe sibling birth order is a major factor in shaping personality in some cultures. Belief in the significance of birth order is open to investigation.

In this experiment, we will use the scientific method to evaluate one common belief about birth order by constructing a comparison of birth order to personality type.

Psychology Journal Activity CCSS

Do you think you were born with your personality or did it develop over time? Write about this in your Psychology Journal. Consider the following issues: Do you see similarities between your personality and that of family members? Has your environment played a role in your development? Has your personality changed over the years? If so, how?

FINDING THE ANSWER...

HYPOTHESIS In a group of siblings the oldest sibling is the most responsible one.

THE METHOD OF YOUR EXPERIMENT

MATERIALS paper, pens, personality assessments, quiet room

PROCEDURE Using a library or the Internet, acquire printed copies of a short personality assessment. You can use tests such as the TIPI (Ten Item Personality Measure) or similar short personality assessments you find during your search. Also prepare a short questionnaire that collects the following information: number of siblings, ages of siblings, and participant's age and place in sibling birth order. Administer the personality assessment and questionnaire to 10 to 15 individuals. Remember to assure your participants that their results will remain confidential.

DATA COLLECTION Score the tests and note the results that are related to seriousness and conscientiousness, or carefulness. Compare each participant's test results with the participant's place in birth order. Look for a relationship between oldest children and conscientiousness.

ANALYSIS & APPLICATION

1. Did your results support the hypothesis?

2. Prior to starting the experiment how could the procedures have been altered to produce different results?

3. Why do you think people want to see patterns in personality and behavior?

netw⊙rks ONLINE LAB RESOURCES

Online you will find:

- An **interactive lab experience**, allowing you to put principles from this chapter into practice in a digital psychology lab environment. This chapter's lab will include an experiment that explores issues fundamental to personality.

- A **Skills Handbook** that includes a guide for using the scientific method, creating experiments, and analyzing data.
- A **Notebook** where you can complete your Psychology Journal and record and analyze data from your experiment.

Garry Wade/Taxi/Getty Images

LESSON 1

Purposes of Personality Theories

Reading **HELP**DESK

Academic Vocabulary

• **aspect** • **conflict**

Content Vocabulary

• **personality**

TAKING NOTES:
Key Ideas and Details

Identifying Perspectives Use a graphic organizer like the one below to explain the focus of each personality theory.

Theory	Focus
Psychoanalytic	
Behaviorist	
Social Learning	
Cognitivist	
Humanist	
Trait	
Sociocultural	

ESSENTIAL QUESTIONS • *How is behavior influenced by environment?*
• *How does experience influence personality?*

IT MATTERS BECAUSE

A study of human behavior can teach us many things about personality. We can learn how people deal with conflicts and problems in their lives, and how personalities contribute to work styles and personal relationships. Personality theorists have taught us a lot about organizing the many characteristics that people display every day.

The Purpose of Personality Theory

GUIDING QUESTION *How might psychologists explain differences in personality?*

We know that different people may react differently to the same situation. One person may feel saddened and inadequate upon learning that he or she failed a test in school, while another person may not be bothered by the score. Why do people act so differently in similar situations? There is something inside people that makes them think, feel, and act differently, and that something inside is what we mean by *personality*.

When psychologists talk about the **aspects**, or features, of personality, most agree that **personality** consists of the consistent, enduring, and unique characteristics of a person. For instance, maybe you have taken an informal test that attempts to measure your different characteristics and that tells you the personality type that fits you best. More formally, many psychologists have developed theories that attempt to quantify and explain differences in personality.

The first purpose of personality theories is to provide a way of organizing the many characteristics psychologists and you know about yourself and other people. You know people may be outgoing or shy, bossy or meek, quick-tempered or calm, witty or dull, fun-loving or gloomy, industrious or lazy. These words describe general ways of behaving that characterize an individual. Some personality theorists try to determine whether certain traits go together, why a person has some traits and not others, and why a person might exhibit different traits in different situations. There is a good deal of disagreement among these theorists as to which traits are significant. Nevertheless, all theorists look to discover patterns in the ways people behave.

A second purpose of any personality theory is to explain the differences among individuals. In so doing, theorists probe beneath the surface. Some theorists might explain different behaviors in terms of motives. Others might try to find out how motives were established in the first place. Still other theorists might seek less obvious causes for individual differences, arguing, for example, that the roots of these differences could be traced back to childhood **conflicts**.

A third goal of personality theory is to explain how people conduct their lives. It is no accident that most personality theorists began as psychotherapists. In working with people who had difficulty coping with everyday problems, psychotherapists inevitably developed ideas about what it takes to live a relatively happy, untroubled life. Personality theorists try to explain why problems arise and why they are more difficult for some people to manage than for others.

In addition, the fourth purpose of personality theories is to determine how life can be improved. It seems obvious that some people are dissatisfied with themselves, their parents, their husbands, wives, or children, or their home lives. People resign themselves to unrewarding jobs, and there is a widespread feeling that much is wrong with society and the world. Almost everyone recognizes that we need to grow and change, both individually and collectively. But what are the proper goals of growth and change? How can we cope with the inevitable conflicts of life?

Psychologists interested in personality attempt to answer these questions with systematic theories about human behavior. These theories are used to guide research. Research, in turn, can test how well a theory explains behavior. Thus, formal personality theories are attempts to make ideas about why people act in certain ways more scientific by stating them precisely and testing them systematically.

☑ **READING PROGRESS CHECK**

Synthesizing How can learning about personality theory help people to improve their lives?

aspect a part or feature of something

personality the consistent, enduring, and unique characteristics of a person

conflict a clash of opposing wishes or needs

Psychologists who study personality explore the elements that make one person think, feel, and act differently from another.

▶ **CRITICAL THINKING**

Analyzing Why might a theorist be interested in finding out why some people are more outgoing or social than others?

Sandra Eckhardt/Stock4B/Getty Images

Major Schools of Personality Theory

GUIDING QUESTION *Why are there many different theories of personality?*

Psychology is a young discipline, and the development and testing of personality theories are still gaining sophistication. There are now many conflicting theories of personality, each with positive and negative aspects. Discussing both sides of various theories helps invigorate the discussion about personality. In this chapter, we will describe major schools of thought among personality theorists.

Psychoanalytic theories, developed by Sigmund Freud and his followers, emphasize the importance of motives hidden in the unconscious. They believe that it is the conflict between different parts of our unconscious mind that motivate our behaviors, drives, and desires. Psychoanalytic theorists have developed the view that there are three distinct parts of our personality as well as five distinct stages of our psychosexual development. In addition to Freud, some of the major psychoanalytic theorists were Carl Jung, Alfred Adler, Karen Horney, Erik Erikson, and Margaret Mahler.

B.F. Skinner and the behaviorists focus on observable behaviors and the situations in which those behaviors occur. A behaviorist is especially interested in the way rewards and punishments shape our actions. They believe that personality is influenced by the situational and environmental variables experienced by a person, not by internal, individual variables. For instance, parental approval and social custom cause us to want certain things and not want others, which in turn shape our behavior.

Like the behaviorists, social learning theorists, such as Albert Bandura, examine the impact of observational learning on personality. And like behaviorists, they focus on how the situations that a person is in contribute to who that person becomes. Unlike behaviorists, however, social learning theorists assert that personal variables, such as knowledge, expectations, and emotions, are as important as observable behavior in understanding personality.

Cognitive theorists focus on how our thoughts, perceptions, and feelings shape our personalities. It was Jean Piaget's observations of the cognitive stages of development in children that helped psychologists understand how children begin to learn, think, and reason on their own. To a cognitive theorist, the development of abstract thought and the ability to assimilate into one's environment are significant contributors to one's personality.

CARTOON ⌄

PERSONALITY CHARACTERISTICS

In psychology, personality refers to the essential characteristics of a person. Cartoons can make fun of human personality characteristics by giving them to an animal.

▶ **CRITICAL THINKING**

1. *Interpreting* What factors do you think are influencing the personality of the dog in this cartoon?

2. *Analyzing Visuals*
   Why is the man surprised by the woman's statements?

HE'S PRETTY INTROSPECTIVE. SOME DAYS HE POUTS, OTHER DAYS, HE'S PRETTY TALKATIVE ABOUT HIS FEELINGS.

Humanistic theorists, like Abraham Maslow and Carl Rogers, stress that a person is an active participant in his or her own growth, and that free will and the choices one makes shape a person's personality. Humanists feel that people are born with the drive to become what they are capable of being, and that people are free to reach these goals once their basic needs for survival are met. The humanistic theory of personality explains that humans can develop their unique potential even within a hostile environment.

Trait theorists, like Gordon Allport, Hans Eysenck, and Raymond Cattell, emphasize the importance of stable internal characteristics, or traits, and how those traits influence the way we behave across most situations. Trait theory dates all the way back to Hippocrates, who isolated four basic personality traits. These ideas were developed further by Allport, Eysenck, and Cattell, and today trait theory consists of a five-factor model of personality upon which human behavior and personality can be analyzed—openness to experience, conscientiousness, extroversion, agreeableness, and neuroticism. The acronym OCEAN is a handy mnemonic for these five factors.

A sociocultural perspective on personality has been explored more recently by modern psychologists. This perspective considers the roles of a person's ethnicity, culture, socioeconomic status, and gender in the development of their personality. This approach suggests that the society you grow up in plays a role in the formation of your behaviors and your concept of yourself.

Each of the theories we will discuss has a different image of human nature. Some psychologists also suggest a biological component to personality and the way it is expressed. All personality theories seek to understand what makes people different and what makes them similar.

Theorists vary in their thinking about what shapes our personality: hidden motives, rewards/punishments, learning, feelings, our potential, our basic traits, or perhaps our society.

▶ **CRITICAL THINKING**

Making Connections How have the different environments you've been in this past week affected your personality?

☑ **READING PROGRESS CHECK**

Differentiating How are the theories of Sigmund Freud different from the theories of B.F. Skinner?

LESSON 1 REVIEW

Reviewing Vocabulary

1. *Making Connections* Write your own definition of *personality*. How does your definition compare to the textbook's definition?

2. *Identifying* How do humanistic theorists, such as Maslow, view human biological needs?

Using Your Notes

3. *Analyzing* Review the notes that you completed during the lesson. Choose one of the personality theories and give an example of its view on human behavior.

Answering the Guiding Questions

4. *Explaining* How might psychologists explain differences in personality?

5. *Speculating* Why are there many different theories of personality?

Writing Activity

6. *Informative/Explanatory* Work with a small group of students and take turns recalling some early memories. Write down those memories, considering the following question: Do these early memories relate to your present personality?

netw⊙rks

There's More Online!

☑ **CARTOON** Freudian Slips

☑ **DIAGRAM** Freud's Model

☑ **GRAPHIC ORGANIZER**

☑ **IMAGE** Displacement

☑ **IMAGE** Projection

☑ **IMAGE** Repression

☑ **SELF-CHECK QUIZ**

LESSON 2

Psychoanalytic Theories

ESSENTIAL QUESTIONS • *How is experience influenced by environment?* • *How does experience influence personality?*

Academic Vocabulary

• energy • primary

Content Vocabulary

• unconscious
• id
• ego
• superego
• defense mechanisms
• collective unconscious
• archetype
• inferiority complex

TAKING NOTES:

Key Ideas and Details

Identifying Perspectives Use a graphic organizer like the one below to describe the basic views of each psychoanalyst.

Carl Jung	
Alfred Adler	
Sigmund Freud	

IT MATTERS BECAUSE

Personality theorists such as Sigmund Freud, Carl Jung, and Alfred Adler have come up with ideas about our personalities and what makes us do things. Freud believed that even our mistakes are not mistakes at all, but a way for our innermost feelings to slip out. Considering different personality theories will help us to broaden our understanding of human behavior and why people's personalities are related to their experiences.

Sigmund Freud and the Unconscious

GUIDING QUESTION *What is the function of the unconscious in Freud's theory?*

Have you ever made a mistake, or a slip, while speaking and said something that you did not mean? Everyone has made a remark that hurt a friend and has later asked himself, "Why did I say that? I didn't mean it." Yet, when he thinks about it, he may realize that he was angry at his friend and wanted to get back at him.

It was Sigmund Freud who first suggested that the little slips that people make, the things they mishear, and the odd misunderstandings they have are not really mistakes at all. Freud believed there was something behind these mistakes, even though people claimed they were just accidental and quickly corrected themselves. Similarly, when he listened to people describe their dreams, he believed the dreams had some unconscious meaning, even though the people who dreamed them did not know what they meant.

Freud was a neurologist who practiced in Vienna in the late 1800s and early 1900s. Although he specialized in nervous disorders, many people talked to him about their private lives, conflicts, fears, and desires. He concluded that the most powerful influences on human personality are things outside our conscious awareness with no physiological basis.

Freud was the first modern psychologist to suggest that every personality has a large and significant **unconscious** component. For Freud, experiences include feelings and thoughts as well as actual events. Freud believed that many of our experiences, particularly the painful episodes of childhood, are not forgotten but are stored in the unconscious.

Although we may not consciously recall these experiences, they continue to influence our behavior. Freud believed that unconscious motives and the feelings people experience as children have an enormous impact on adult personality and behavior. Between the unconscious and the conscious is the *preconscious*—thoughts that can be recalled with relatively little effort. These thoughts consist of information just below the surface of awareness. Preconscious thoughts may include memories of recent events, recollections of friends, and simple facts—anything we can recall. The *nonconscious* includes information that is not a part of consciousness or memory. The back and forth communication between the conscious and nonconscious minds make up a portion of our personalities, according to Freud.

unconscious the part of the mind that contains material of which we are unaware but that strongly influences conscious processes and behaviors

✅ **READING PROGRESS CHECK**

Assessing According to Freud, what is significant about painful experiences from childhood?

The Id, Ego, and Superego

GUIDING QUESTION *What functions do the id, ego, and superego perform?*

Freud explained human personality by saying that it was a kind of **energy** system, like a steam engine. The energy in personality comes from two kinds of powerful instincts—the life instincts and the death instincts. Freud theorized that all of life moves toward death and that the desire for a final end shows up in human personality as destructiveness and aggression. *Life* instincts, however, were more important in Freud's theory and he saw them primarily as erotic or pleasure-seeking urges. By 1923, Freud had described what became known as the structural concepts of the personality: id, ego, and superego. Freud introduced them as a model of how the mind works. In other words, the id, ego, and superego are not actual parts of the brain; instead, they explain how the mind functions and how the instinctual energies are organized and regulated.

energy power or strength required to maintain activity

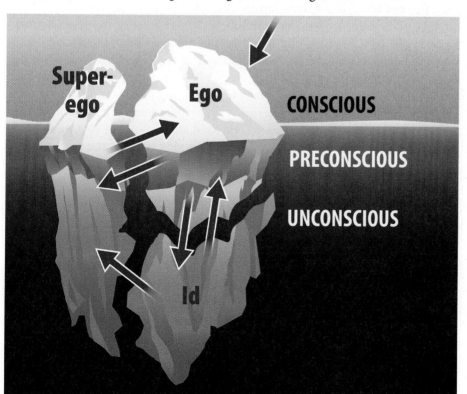

❮ DIAGRAM

FREUD'S MODEL
The ego tries to balance the demands of the id and the superego and the realities of the world. These interactions and conflicts are represented by arrows in the figure.

▶ **CRITICAL THINKING**

1. *Analyzing Visuals* Which of these components is the source of guilt feelings?

2. *Contrasting* How is the id treated differently in the diagram from the ego and the superego?

FREUDIAN SLIPS

Freudian slips are mistakes or slips of the tongue that we make in everyday speech. Freud believed that these slips reflect our unconscious thoughts or wishes.

▶ **CRITICAL THINKING**

1. *Analyzing* What is the Freudian slip that this speaker makes?

2. *Drawing Inferences* How might other personality theorists explain the comment?

"And here we can clearly see the past year's highs and nose."

id the part of the unconscious personality that contains our needs, drives, instincts, and repressed material

ego the part of the personality that is in touch with reality and strives to meet the demands of the id and the superego in socially acceptable ways

superego the part of the personality that is the source of conscience and counteracts the socially undesirable impulses of the id

primary of principle or chief importance

In Freud's theory, the **id** is the reservoir or container of the instinctual and biological urges. At birth, all your energy is invested in the id, responding unconsciously to inborn instinctive urges for food and water. The id is the lustful, impulsive, fun, or drive-ridden part of the unconscious. The demand of Sesame Street's Cookie Monster—"Me want cookie!"—is pure id. It operates in terms of what Freud called the *pleasure principle*, seeking immediate gratification of desires, regardless of the consequences. Doing something that may hurt someone's feelings, lying, and having fun are examples of the id's influence.

The personality process that is mostly conscious is called the **ego**. Gradually forming during the second and third years of life and driven by psychic energy borrowed from the id, the ego is the rational, sensible personality process that operates in terms of Freud's *reality principle*. If, for example, a person is hungry, the id might drive her to seek immediate satisfaction by dreaming of food or by eating all the available food at once instead of keeping some of it for later. The ego would recognize that the body needs real food and that it will continue to need food. It would use the id's energy to urge preserving some of the food available now and looking for ways of finding more.

Suppose you thought of stealing the desired food from someone else. The **superego**, which represents the learning and incorporation of your **primary** caretaker's ideals, is the part of the personality that would stop you. The id represents what the person wants to do, the ego plans what she can do, and the superego advocates what she should do. It is the moral part of the personality, the source of conscience and of high ideals, that can be said to operate in terms of a *moral principle*. The superego can also create conflicts and problems. It is sometimes overly harsh, like a very strict parent. Hence, it is the source of guilt feelings, which come from deviations from what it defines as right—better known as the conscience, or internalized values of the parents. The superego is responsible for our socially responsible behavior. If it is the id that contains our base instinct and drives, and directs our desires for pleasure, it is the superego that drives us toward equally irrational good behavior without considering any costs.

The id and the superego frequently come into conflict with each other. Because neither is concerned with reality, they may both come into conflict with the outside world as well. Freud saw the ego as the part of the person that must satisfy the demands of the id without offending the superego. If the id is not satisfied, the person feels an intolerable tension of longing or anger or desire. If the superego is not obeyed, the person feels guilty and inferior. If outside reality is ignored, the person suffers such outcomes as starvation or dislike by other people.

☑ READING PROGRESS CHECK

Identifying Cause and Effect According to Freud's theories, how can a human keep from acting on every desire of the id?

Defense Mechanisms

GUIDING QUESTION *Why did Freud believe people create defense mechanisms?*

The ego's job is so difficult that all people unconsciously resort to psychological defenses. Rather than face intense frustration, conflict, or feelings of unworthiness, people deceive themselves into believing nothing is wrong. If the demands of the id and the ego cannot be resolved, it may be necessary to distort reality. Freud called these techniques **defense mechanisms** because they defend the ego from experiencing anxiety about failing in its tasks. Freud believed that these defense mechanisms stem from the unconscious part of the ego. They ordinarily become conscious to the individual only during a form of psychotherapy called psychoanalysis—and then only with great difficulty.

defense mechanisms
certain specific means by which the ego unconsciously protects itself against unpleasant impulses or circumstances

To some degree, defense mechanisms are necessary for psychological well-being. They relieve intolerable confusion and stress. They help people weather intense emotional crises. They also give individuals time to work out seemingly unsolvable problems by blocking the effects of conflicting internal emotional pressures. However, if a person resorts to defense mechanisms all of the time, he will avoid facing and solving his problems realistically. A few of the defense mechanisms Freud identified are discussed below.

Rationalization If you explained your poor performance on your last math test by saying, "The test questions were bad; they didn't make sense," rather than admitting that you did not study for the test, you practiced *rationalization*. Rationalization involves making up acceptable excuses for behaviors that cause us to feel anxious.

Repression When a person has painful memories and unacceptable thoughts and motives that cause the ego too much anxiety, she may push those thoughts or urges out of consciousness down into the unconscious. This process is called *repression*. The person simply pushes the disturbing thoughts and memories out of awareness without ever realizing it. For example, a person who is afraid of dentists forgets he has a 3 P.M. appointment until he suddenly remembers it at 6 P.M., when the dentist is closed for the day.

Denial You are in *denial* if you refuse to accept the reality of something that makes you anxious. For example, it is a stormy and frightening night, and the local television and radio announcers are advising people to take cover and observe the tornado warnings in effect. David does not believe that his town will get hit (he is in denial) and is severely injured after failing to heed the warnings. Alcoholics and drug users are in denial when they say, "I can stop whenever I want." People may also exhibit denial when they hear bad news about their own health or the health of a loved one.

Projection a person convinces himself that impulses coming from within himself are coming from another person. (He is jealous of his girlfriend but claims that she is the one who is jealous.)

Displacement a person transfers positive or negative feelings away from the real cause of those feelings

Repression a person pushes painful memories or anxiety out of his consciousness; a person denies or forgets what is disturbing him

According to Freud, a person unconsciously protects his or her ego from the anxiety of failure by defense mechanisms, such as self-deception.

▶ **CRITICAL THINKING**

Drawing Conclusions In what ways are defense mechanisms helpful?

Projection Another way the ego avoids anxiety is to believe that impulses coming from within are really coming from other people. For example, a boy who is extremely jealous of his girlfriend but does not want to admit to himself that he is threatened by her independence may claim, "I'm not jealous—she's the one who's always asking where I've been, who that girl was I was talking to. She's the one who's jealous." This mechanism is called *projection* because inner feelings are thrown, or projected, outside the self and assigned to others. If a person thinks, for example, that others dislike him when in reality he dislikes himself, he is said to be projecting. This is a common mechanism, which you may have used yourself from time to time.

Reaction Formation *Reaction formation* involves replacing an unacceptable feeling or urge with an opposite one. For example, a divorced father may resent having his child for the weekend. Unconsciously, he believes it is terribly wrong for a father to react that way, so he showers the child with expressions of love, toys, and exciting trips. A woman who finds her powerful ambitions unacceptable may play the role of a weak, helpless, passive female who wants nothing more than to please the men in her life—unconsciously covering up her true feelings. Have you ever put on a front and acted confident when you were really scared?

Regression *Regression* means going back to an earlier and less mature pattern of behavior. When a person is under severe pressure, he may start acting in ways that helped him in the past. For example, he may throw a temper tantrum, make faces, cry loudly, or revert to eating and sleeping all the time the way he did as a small child. If you have ever been tempted to stick out your lower lip and pout when you know that you should really accept that you cannot have your own way, you have experienced regression.

Displacement *Displacement* occurs when you cannot take out your anger on the source of your frustrations, so you displace it or take it out on a less powerful person. For example, if you wanted to hit your father but were afraid to, you might hit your little brother instead. Your poor brother gets hit partly because he reminds you of your father and partly because he is not as likely to hit back.

Sublimation *Sublimation* refers to redirecting a forbidden desire into a socially acceptable desire. For example, you may be so frustrated by your friend's arrogant attitude that you work extra hard at soccer practice, pushing yourself to your physical limits. You have channeled your aggressive feelings into a productive physical activity.

✔ **READING PROGRESS CHECK**

Analyzing Under what kinds of conditions might someone display regression or displacement?

The First Psychoanalysts

GUIDING QUESTION *How did the psychoanalysts who followed Freud build on his theories?*

When we think of the contributions of psychoanalysts, Sigmund Freud comes to mind almost immediately. He was the first to practice a *psychodynamic approach* to personality—emphasizing the interaction of various conscious and unconscious motives—which contributed many of the ideas common to psychoanalytic theory and therapy practices today.

Evaluating Freud's Contribution

The recognition of the tremendous forces that exist in human personality and the difficulty of controlling and handling them were Freud's great contributions to understanding human life. Considering the structures of the id, ego, and superego and the parts they play in the human mind made it easier for psychoanalysts to understand why human life contains so much conflict. It is a matter, Freud thought, of a savage individual coming to terms with the rules of society. The id is the savage part, and the superego is the representative of society. In a healthy person, the ego (the "I") is strong enough to handle the struggle between the id and the superego.

Freud was the first psychologist to explain the development of personality and to claim that infancy and childhood are critical times for forming a person's basic character. In his theory of psychosexual development, Freud reasoned that a child goes through five stages of development—oral, anal, phallic, latent, and genital. Conflicts arise in each of the stages. Freud claimed that a child's personality largely develops in the first five years, during which the child goes through the first three stages of development. That child's personality becomes the result of how the child deals with the conflicts that arose in each stage of development. Freud believed that personality is well formed by the time the child enters school and that its growth consists of elaborating this basic structure.

Freud was also the first person to propose a unified theory to understand and explain human behavior. Freud's psychodynamic approach to personality is based on the idea that human functioning results from the interaction of the drives and forces within a person, and between the different structures of the personality. That is, every behavior one engages in, including mistakes, can be analyzed within the structures of the id, ego, and superego. No other theory has been more complete, complex, or controversial. Some psychologists treat Freud's writings as a sacred text; others accused Freud of being unscientific by proposing a theory too complex to be tested. Freud's theories continue to be debated. Although not widely practiced now, psychoanalysis was the predecessor of all later personality theories, which were either extensions of Freud's work or reactions against it. A number of Freud's followers developed important psychodynamic approaches and psychoanalytic theories of their own.

More
ABOUT...

Birth Order

Are you either the oldest child in the family or the youngest? Does this affect your personality? A 1996 study by Frank Sulloway on birth-order effects on personalities came up with the following characteristics:

- Firstborns are interested in preserving the status quo; later-borns are more open to new experiences and ideas.

- Firstborns are usually more responsible, achievement-oriented, and organized than those born later.

- Later-borns are usually more agreeable than firstborns.

- Firstborns are more jealous and fearful than later-borns.

- Firstborns have more assertive and dominant personalities but may not be as sociable as later-borns.

It is important to note that Sulloway's research focused on middle- to upper-class people in Western cultures and therefore may not apply to other classes or cultures. Sulloway's research also is generalized, meaning it may not apply to every individual or every family.

According to Jung's theory, Superman can be considered an archetype of a hero and of goodness.

▶ CRITICAL THINKING

Defending Why is Superman considered an archetype?

collective unconscious
the part of the mind that contains inherited instincts, urges, and memories common to all people

archetype an inherited idea, based on the experiences of one's ancestors, which shapes one's perception of the world

inferiority complex a pattern of avoiding feelings of inadequacy rather than trying to overcome their source

Carl Jung

At one time, Carl Jung (1875–1961) was Freud's closest associate. When Freud and Jung started to argue about psychoanalytic theory, though, their personal relationship became strained. They stopped speaking to each other entirely a mere seven years after they met.

Jung disagreed with Freud on two major points. First, he took a more positive view of human nature, believing that people try to develop their potential as well as handle their instinctual urges. Second, he distinguished between the personal unconscious, which was similar to Freud's idea of the unconscious, and what Jung called the **collective unconscious**, which is a storehouse of instincts, urges, and memories of the entire human species throughout history. He called these inherited, universal ideas **archetypes**. The same archetypes are present in every person. They reflect the common experiences of humanity regarding mothers, fathers, nature, war, and so on.

Jung went on to identify the archetypes by studying dreams and visions, paintings, poetry, folk stories, myths, and religions. He found that the same themes—the archetypes—appear again and again. He found that many cultures share certain myths, dreams, religious beliefs, and symbols separated by time. For example, the story of Jack and the Beanstalk is essentially the same as the story of David and Goliath. Both tell how a small, weak, good person triumphs over a big, strong, bad person. Jung believed such stories are common and easy to understand because the situations they describe have occurred over and over again in human history and have been stored as archetypes in the unconscious of every human being. Jung argued that these archetypes influence our thoughts and feelings and help us build the foundation of our personalities. For example, one archetype is our sense of self. Our sense of self gives us direction and provides a sense of completeness. We use the concepts in our personal unconscious and collective unconscious to develop our personalities. We fit our personalities to these concepts. In the process of fitting our personalities to these beliefs, we may hide our real feelings and our real personalities, though.

Alfred Adler

Like Jung, Alfred Adler (1870–1937) was an associate of Freud who left his teacher in the early part of the twentieth century to develop his own approach to personality theory. Adler believed that the driving force in people's lives is a desire to overcome their feelings of inferiority. Classic examples are Demosthenes, who overcame a speech impediment by practicing speaking with pebbles in his mouth and became the greatest orator of ancient Greece; Napoleon, a short man who conquered Europe in the early 1800s; and Glenn Cunningham, an Olympic runner who lost his toes in a fire as a child and had to plead with doctors who wanted to amputate his legs because they thought he would never be able to walk again.

Everyone struggles with inferiority, said Adler. He describes a person who continually tries to compensate for his weakness and avoid feelings of inadequacy as having an **inferiority complex**. Children first feel inferior because they are so little and so dependent on adults. Gradually they learn to do the things that older people can do. The satisfaction that comes from such simple acts as walking or learning to use a spoon sets up a pattern of overcoming inadequacies, a pattern that persists throughout life. Adler called these patterns *lifestyles*.

Adler believed that the way parents treat their children influences the styles of life they choose. Over pampering, in which the parents attempt to satisfy the child's every whim, tends to produce a self-absorbed and self-centered person.

The self-centered person has little regard for others and expects everyone else to do what he or she wants. On the other hand, the child who is neglected by his or her parents may seek revenge by becoming an angry, hostile person. Both the pampered and the neglected child tend to grow into adults who lack confidence in their ability to meet the demands of life. Ideally, said Adler, a child should learn self-reliance and courage from the father and generosity and a feeling for others from the mother. Adler believed that all humans are motivated by social urges and that each person is a social being with a unique personality.

Other Theorists

Although Jung and Adler were the first figures to break with Freud, many others have followed. Most of these theorists believed there was something more driving the human personality than just the messages from the unconscious mind. While they understood the importance of Freud's work, they were not able to accept it fully. Each of the theorists who broke with Freud's thinking contributed his or her own thinking to the understanding of personality.

Erich Fromm's (1900–1980) theory centered around the need to belong and the loneliness that freedom can bring. Fromm believed that it was human nature to try to escape from the feelings of isolation that freedom can bring us. As a result, we are driven to belong to groups, conform to the ideas of others, form family circles, and even take part in self-destructive behavior.

Karen Horney (1885–1952) stressed the importance of basic anxiety, which a child feels due to helplessness, and basic hostility, a feeling of resentment towards one's parents that generally accompanies this anxiety. She disagreed with Freud on several basic beliefs. Horney believed that a child raised in an atmosphere of love and security could avoid Freud's psychosexual parent-child conflict.

Adler believed self-reliant children would become happier and more successful adults. He felt that giving in to children too often could lead to outbursts, selfishness, and insensitivity later in life.

▶ CRITICAL THINKING

Analyzing How would a child's self-esteem be affected by an overprotective parent?

(l)Image Source/Getty Images; (r)i love images/Cultura/Getty Images

According to Karen Horney, when a child feels helpless it becomes anxious. The child then directs hostility toward the caregivers who were responsible for those feelings of helplessness.

▶ CRITICAL THINKING

Speculating What emotions do you think this child is expressing?

VStock/Alamy

Horney suggested that a person's social surroundings and environmental upbringing contribute to that person's personality. This approach is similar to the socio-economic and cultural perspectives that have been made popular by recent theorists.

Erik Erikson (1902–1994) accepted Freud's basic theory, but he outlined eight psychosocial stages that every person goes through from birth to old age and that describe the importance of interacting with other people. His theories describe the development of complex parts of our personalities, such as trust and mistrust of others, shame, self control, guilt, and feelings of inferiority. Erickson's studies showed that these feelings develop at quite a young age and can affect the development of personality. These and other neo-Freudians have helped keep psychoanalytic theory alive and debated.

The work of these theorists has shown that personality can be a complex issue. Even views of the unconscious self can be thought of from different perspectives. Cultural perspectives may also play into the thoughts of the unconscious mind. The way we are raised and the cultural and socioeconomic experiences we have may affect our unconscious. How do you think individualistic and collectivistic cultural perspectives relate to personality?

✓ READING PROGRESS CHECK

Drawing Conclusions Why do Alfred Adler's theories of personality rely heavily on people's feelings about themselves?

LESSON 2 REVIEW

Reviewing Vocabulary

1. *Summarizing* Explain how the id, ego, and superego work together in a person.

Using Your Notes

2. *Comparing* Review the notes that you completed during this lesson to explain what Jung, Adler, and Freud have in common in their theories of personality.

Answering the Guiding Questions

3. *Explaining* What is the function of the unconscious in Freud's theory?

4. *Discussing* What functions do the id, ego, and superego perform?

5. *Analyzing* Why did Freud believe people create defense mechanisms?

6. *Making Connections* How did the psychoanalysts who followed Freud build on his theories?

Writing Activity

7. *Informative/Explanatory* Create a cartoon that illustrates the use of one of the defense mechanisms discussed in this section. Explain how your cartoon illustrates the defense mechanism in a brief paragraph.

Academic Vocabulary

• hence   • complex

Content Vocabulary

• **behaviorism**
• **contingencies of reinforcement**

TAKING NOTES:

Integration of Knowledge and Ideas

Comparing and Contrasting Use a graphic organizer like the one below to compare and contrast behaviorism and social cognition.

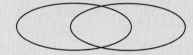

LESSON 3
Learning Theories

ESSENTIAL QUESTIONS • *How is behavior influenced by environment?*
• *How does experience influence personality?*

IT MATTERS BECAUSE

Different situations can affect behavior. Some people might feel that circumstances make them feel oppressed or angry, depressed or sad. In these situations, are we learning from our environment? Is our environment shaping our personality? There are different theories about how and why we learn. Understanding these theories can help us understand how our experiences shape our personality.

B.F. Skinner: Behaviorism

GUIDING QUESTION *How do behaviorists study personality?*

Psychologists have found that when people are oppressed or living in an oppressive environment, they begin to give up hope. Their behaviors become depressive and they no longer feel that they have control over their environment. How do feelings of oppression, hopelessness, depression, and lack of control affect people and their personalities? Behaviorists look to the environment to see what is reinforcing people's behavior and how their environment is affecting their ability to learn and express themselves.

American psychology has long been dominated by the study of human and animal learning. John Watson believed that the proper subject matter of psychology ought to be observable behavior and not the subjective unconsciousness. He believed that if something could not be seen, then it could not be studied. His beliefs led to the study of behavior and what is called **behaviorism**. Behaviorists believe that as individuals acquire different learning experiences, they acquire different behaviors and, **hence**, different personalities.

Although his behaviorism was not proposed as a theory of personality, B.F. Skinner had a major impact on personality theory. Skinner saw no need for a general concept of personality structure. He focused instead on precisely what causes a person to act in a specific way. It is a very pragmatic approach, one that is less concerned with understanding behavior than with predicting it and controlling it. He was interested in how aspects of one's personality are learned.

The Behaviorist Approach

Consider the case of Ruben, a college sophomore who has been rather depressed lately. Sigmund Freud would likely seek the roots of Ruben's unhappiness in events in his childhood. Skinner's approach is more direct. First, Skinner would reject the vague label *depressed*. Instead, he would ask exactly how Ruben behaves. The answer may be that Ruben spends most of the day in his room, cuts all his classes, rarely smiles or laughs, and makes little effort to talk to anyone.

Skinner would try to uncover the **contingencies of reinforcement**. What conditions are reinforcing these behaviors? What rewards does Ruben receive for never leaving his room? One hypothesis is that Ruben's girlfriend Brandi has unintentionally reinforced this behavior by spending a lot of time with him, trying to cheer him up. Perhaps she did not pay enough attention to Ruben before he was depressed. Note that Skinner's approach immediately suggests a hypothesis that can be proved true or false. If paying attention to Ruben encourages his depression, then ignoring him should decrease the likelihood of this behavior. Brandi, therefore, might try ignoring Ruben for a few days. If he then starts leaving his room, which she should reinforce, she has discovered the contingencies of reinforcement that govern Ruben's behavior. If he does not leave his room, she will know that the hypothesis is wrong, and she can try something else. Perhaps Ruben is glued to the television in his room all day and has become a game show addict. Take away the television, and you will find out whether that is the reinforcer.

At first, behaviorism may seem to imply that Ruben is somehow faking his depression so that he can watch game shows or see more of his girlfriend. Skinner does not make this assumption. Ruben may be entirely unaware of the rewards that are shaping his behavior. In any case, Ruben's feelings are beside the point. What matters is not what is going on inside Ruben's head but how he is behaving. The point is to specify his behavior and then find out what causes (reinforces) it.

Skinner devised a box to test the observable behavior of rats.

▶ **CRITICAL THINKING**

Analyzing According to Skinner, what motivates behavior?

Behaviorism Today

Skinner's approach has become very popular among psychologists, partly because it is so action-oriented. Followers of Skinner's work have applied the techniques to a wide range of behaviors, from teaching pigeons to play table tennis to teaching severely mentally challenged people to dress themselves and take part in simple activities once believed beyond their abilities.

Other human behavior, too, can be changed using rewards and punishments. The success of behaviorists with most people has been limited, however, partly because our reinforcers are so **complex**. To behaviorists, behavior in general is a combination of specific behaviors that have been reinforced, or learned. To change behavior, you change the reinforcer. Therapies have also been devised to help people with specific behavioral problems, such as phobias and obsessive-compulsive behavior.

A phobia is a debilitating fear that would keep someone from functioning normally. Someone with a phobia of small places, for instance, may panic at the thought of using an elevator. The panic may cause a racing heartbeat, sweating, or trembling in the patient. Behavioral therapy seeks to slowly help overcome the phobia, perhaps first by introducing the patient to pictures of elevators or small places until the patient feels comfortable. The therapist and patient may then encounter the phobia together in real life, slowly and repeatedly until the patient realizes there is no threat of danger from encountering the experience. The treatment is practical and may involve rewards for hitting milestones in treatment.

With obsessive-compulsive disorder, the patient displays a repetitive and compulsive behavior that may interfere with the person's life and ability to function. Obsessive hand washing or checking that doors are locked are common examples of this disorder. The behaviorist assumes that these behaviors are rooted in some kind of fear, so the treatment seeks to address the fears with behavioral therapy, slowly exposing the patient to the fear until it is overcome.

✔ READING PROGRESS CHECK

Drawing Conclusions According to Skinner's theories, why does someone learn a new skill?

Albert Bandura: Social Cognitive Theory

GUIDING QUESTION *What is social cognitive theory?*

Skinner emphasized reinforcement in his description of how personalities develop. Albert Bandura and his colleague Richard Walters, however, argued that personality is acquired not only by direct reinforcement of behavior but also by observational learning, or imitation. As you remember, in *observational learning* an individual acquires a new behavior by watching other people's actions. For example, to teach a child how to hit a baseball with a bat, you could hand the child the bat and ball and reinforce every time he used the bat and ball correctly. However, you would probably demonstrate the correct way to hold the bat and swing at the ball instead because this way the child would acquire the behavior more quickly. Bandura and Walters believed that much of a young child's individual behavior and personality is acquired by exposure to specific everyday models.

In Bandura's view, people direct their own behavior by their choice of models. In part, when your parents object to the company you keep, they are trying to change the models you use. The most effective models are those who are the most similar to and most admired by the observer. Thus, you are more likely to learn new behaviors from friends of your choosing than from friends your parents choose for you.

Psychology & YOU

What Is Your Locus of Control?

Julian Rotter wrote the first book describing the social cognitive approach to personality. Rotter argued that a person's behavior depends not only on objective, situational factors but also on that person's subjective beliefs. Our *locus of control* refers to our beliefs about how much control we have over certain situations. If you believe that you do have control over situations, you have an *internal* locus of control. If you think that your fate is determined by forces beyond your control, you have an *external* locus of control. People with an internal locus of control are, on average, less anxious and more content with life than those with an external locus of control.

To find a person's locus of control, a psychologist might ask the person which among the following he or she believes:

1. In the long run, people get what they deserve.

2. Most tests are fair if a student is prepared.

3. Many times, tests are so unfair that studying is wasted energy.

4. It is better to make decisions and take action than to trust fate.

complex complicated

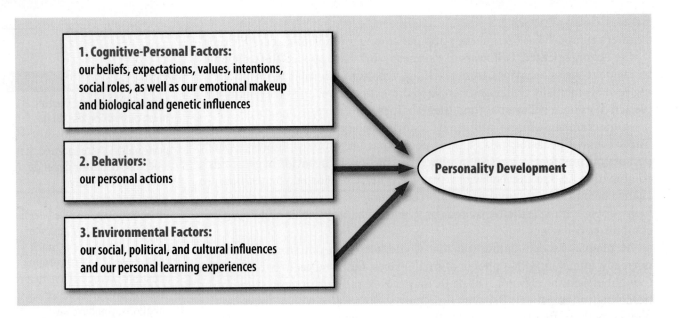

1. **Cognitive-Personal Factors:** our beliefs, expectations, values, intentions, social roles, as well as our emotional makeup and biological and genetic influences

2. **Behaviors:** our personal actions

3. **Environmental Factors:** our social, political, and cultural influences and our personal learning experiences

Personality Development

BANDURA'S SOCIAL COGNITIVE THEORY
According to Bandura's theory, a person's personality is shaped by an interaction among three forces—cognitive factors, behaviors, and environmental factors.

▶ **CRITICAL THINKING**

1. *Analyzing Visuals* Under which category in Bandura's theory does a person take part in going to school?

2. *Analyzing* If a person joins a baseball team, what part of Bandura's theory is being explored?

Bandura has made significant contributions to the development of behavioral theories of personality. His social cognitive theory recognizes the interaction called *reciprocal determinism* that occurs among the observing individual, the behavior of that individual, and the environment in which the behavior occurs. One important concept that governs our behavior is our view of our ability to succeed, which Bandura called *self-efficacy*. You decide whether to go on a date by assessing the environment—the weather, your parents' current state of mind, your potential date's recent behaviors—the effects of your own past behavior, and your long-term past successes and failures. This leads to the development of an expectancy of success. As the behavior unfolds, you also develop *outcome expectations*. As long as they remain positive, you will keep trying.

Whereas psychoanalytic theories emphasize the influence of childhood experiences, irrational thoughts, and unconscious forces, the advantage of learning theories of personality is that they focus on concrete actions that can be tested and measured. However, critics argue that the learning theories do not explain personality, nor do they give enough attention to the influence of genetic factors, emotions, and childhood experiences on personality.

☑ **READING PROGRESS CHECK**

Evaluating What factors contribute to a person's self-efficacy?

LESSON 3 REVIEW

Reviewing Vocabulary
1. *Determining Importance* According to behaviorism, what is the proper subject matter of psychology? How does this relate to the study of personality?

Using Your Notes
2. *Contrasting* Use your notes to determine how a behaviorist would explain why someone might go on a date even though the person is nervous about it. Then explain how a social cognitive theorist would explain this situation differently.

Answering the Guiding Questions
3. *Identifying* How do behaviorists study personality?

4. *Summarizing* What is social cognitive theory?

Writing Activity
5. *Argument* Choose a behavior of a younger sibling or of a friend that you would like to see change. Suggest a way to do so, using reinforcers to change the particular behavior. Use detailed, descriptive language when explaining the reinforcers.

netw⊙rks
There's More Online!

- ☑ **GRAPHIC ORGANIZER**
- ☑ **SELF-CHECK QUIZ**

Humanistic, Cognitive, and Sociocultural Theories

(l)Bettmann/Corbis; (c)Nancy Ney/Getty Images; (cr)Steve Debenport/the Agency Collection/Getty Images; (r)Ronnie Kaufman/Blend Images LLC

Reading **HELP**DESK

Academic Vocabulary

- accurate
- previous

Content Vocabulary

- humanistic psychology
- self-actualization
- self
- positive regard
- conditions of worth
- unconditional positive regard
- fully functioning

TAKING NOTES:

Integration of Knowledge and Ideas

Sequencing Use a graphic organizer like the one below to discuss the steps to becoming fully functioning, according to Rogers's theory.

Fully Functioning Individual

ESSENTIAL QUESTIONS • *How is experience influenced by environment?* • *How does experience influence personality?*

IT MATTERS BECAUSE

People have the ability to accomplish great things when they put their minds to it. Not all personality theorists think that a person's actions are the result of a previous action or experience. Humanistic, cognitive, and sociocultural theories of personality stress the positive aspect of human nature. The experiences an individual has can contribute to a happier life, higher accomplishment, and greater fulfillment.

Humanistic Psychology

GUIDING QUESTION *What does humanistic psychology emphasize?*

Did you ever think that you could do something to change the world? Doing something important takes determination and hard work. You have to believe in yourself. For example, baseball player Jackie Robinson believed in himself and changed the world. In 1947 life in America was one of segregation. There were separate schools for African Americans and whites, separate restaurants, separate hotels, separate drinking fountains, and even separate baseball leagues—that is, until Jackie Robinson began playing for the Brooklyn Dodgers. Robinson played the game passionately and, despite colossal obstacles, changed the face of baseball. His experience shows the impact that believing in one's own abilities can have on personal success. The idea that individuals' perceptions of themselves can become their reality is part of the humanistic and cognitive theories of personality.

In the humanist view, people have the freedom and will to change their behaviors. In other words, because humans can think and control their urges they are uniquely qualified to achieve their goals. To a humanist, our environment is less important to shaping our personality than our self-concept.

Humanistic psychology may be viewed as a rebellion against the rather negative, pessimistic view of human nature that dominated psychoanalytical and behaviorist personality theory in the early 1900s.

Theories of Personality **397**

humanistic psychology
a school of psychology that emphasizes personal growth and the achievement of maximum potential by each unique individual

self-actualization the humanist term for realizing one's unique potential

accurate correct or exact in its details

Jackie Robinson was the first African American to play in the major leagues and become a baseball hero to millions.

▶ **CRITICAL THINKING**

Analyzing How does Jackie Robinson's life reflect the humanist ideal of self-actualization?

Psychoanalysts emphasized the struggle to control primitive, instinctual urges on the one hand and to come to terms with the demands of the superego, or conscience, on the other. The behaviorists, too, saw human behavior in mechanistic terms: our actions are shaped by rewards and punishments. Humanistic psychologists object to both approaches on the grounds that they demean human beings—Freud by emphasizing irrational and destructive instincts, Skinner by emphasizing only external causes of behavior. In contrast, the humanists stress our ability to create and live by personal standards and perceptions.

Humanistic psychology is founded on the belief that all human beings strive for **self-actualization**—that is, the realization of our potentialities as unique human beings. Self-actualization involves an openness to a wide range of experiences, an awareness of and respect for one's own and other people's uniqueness, an acceptance of the responsibilities of freedom and commitment, a desire to become more *authentic* or true to oneself, and an ability to grow.

Abraham Maslow: Growth and Self-Actualization

Abraham Maslow (1908–1970) became one of the guiding spirits of the humanistic movement in psychology. He deliberately set out to create what he called "a third force in psychology" as an alternative to psychoanalysis and behaviorism. Maslow tried to base his theory of personality on studies of healthy, creative, self-actualizing people who fully utilize their talents and potential rather than on studies of disturbed individuals.

When Maslow decided to study the most productive individuals he could find—in history as well as in his social and professional circles—he broke new ground. Psychotherapists developed the theories of personality discussed earlier after years of working with people who could not cope with everyday frustrations and conflicts. In contrast, Maslow was curious about people who not only coped with everyday problems effectively but who also created exceptional lives for themselves, people like Abraham Lincoln, Albert Einstein, and Eleanor Roosevelt.

Maslow found that although these people sometimes had great emotional difficulties, they adjusted in ways that allowed them to become highly productive. Maslow also found that self-actualized individuals share a number of traits. First, they perceive reality in an **accurate** way, unlike most people who, because of prejudices and wishful thinking, perceive it rather inaccurately. Self-actualized people also accept themselves, other people, and their environments more readily than most people do. Without realizing it, most of us project our hopes and fears onto the world around us. We deny our own shortcomings and try to rationalize or change things we do not like about ourselves. Self-actualized individuals accept themselves as they are. Because they are secure in themselves, self-actualized individuals are more problem-centered than self-centered. They are able to focus on tasks in a way that people concerned about maintaining and protecting their self-image cannot. They are more likely to base decisions on

Bettmann/Corbis

< TABLE

CHARACTERISTICS OF SELF-ACTUALIZED PEOPLE

Maslow proposed the concept of a self-actualized personality, which identifies a person with high productivity and enjoyment of life.

▶ CRITICAL THINKING

1. *Analyzing* Do you think any person can develop a self-actualized personality, regardless of his or her social or economic status? Explain.

2. *Making Connections* Why might a hostile sense of humor be a characteristic that a non-self-actualized person displays?

Characteristics of Self-Actualized People

They are realistically oriented.

They accept themselves, other people, and the natural world for what they are.

They have a great deal of spontaneity.

They are problem-centered rather than self-centered.

They have an air of detachment and a need for privacy.

They are autonomous and independent.

Their appreciation of people and things is fresh rather than stereotyped.

Most of them have had profound mystical or spiritual experiences, although not necessarily religious in character.

They identify with humanity.

Their intimate relationships with a few specially loved people tend to be profound and deeply emotional rather than superficial.

Their values and attitudes are democratic.

They do not confuse means with ends.

Their sense of humor is philosophical rather than hostile.

They have a great fund of creativeness.

They resist conformity to the culture.

They transcend the environment rather than just coping with it.

Source: Abraham Maslow, *Motivation and Personality*, New York: Harper & Row, 1970.

ethical principles rather than on calculations of the possible costs or benefits to themselves. They have a strong sense of identity with other human beings, and they have a strong sense of humor but laugh with people, not at them.

Maslow also found that self-actualized people are exceptionally spontaneous. They do not try to be anything other than themselves, and they know themselves well enough to maintain their integrity in the face of opposition, unpopularity, and rejection. They are autonomous. They value privacy and frequently seek out solitude. This is not to say that they are detached or aloof; rather than trying to be popular, they focus on deep, loving relationships with the few people to whom they are truly close.

Finally, the people Maslow studied had a rare ability to appreciate even the simplest things. They approached their lives with a sense of discovery that made each day a new day. They rarely felt bored or uninterested. Given to moments of intense joy and satisfaction, or peak experiences, they enjoyed life itself. Maslow believed this to be both a cause and an effect of their creativity and originality.

Nancy Ney/Getty Images

Maslow believed that to become self-actualized, a person must first satisfy his or her basic, primary needs—for food and shelter, physical safety, love and belonging, and self-esteem. Of course, to some extent the ability to satisfy these needs is often beyond our control. Still, no amount of wealth, talent, or beauty can totally shield someone from frustration and disappointment. All people have to adjust to maintain themselves and to grow. Many psychologists have criticized Maslow's work. His claim that human nature is good, for example, has been called an intrusion of subjective values into what should be a neutral science. The levels of specific needs, such as physical contact comfort, have not been defined. His study of self-actualized people has been criticized because the sample was chosen on the basis of Maslow's own subjective criteria. How can one identify self-actualized people without knowing the characteristics of such people? But then, if one knows these characteristics to begin with, what sense does it make to list them as if they were the results of an empirical study?

Carl Rogers: Self Theory

Carl Rogers (1902–1987) called the people he counseled "clients," not "patients." The word *patient* implies illness, a negative label that Rogers rejected. As a therapist, Rogers was primarily concerned with the path to self-actualization, or "full functioning," as he called it. Rogers believed that many people suffer from a conflict between what they value in themselves and what they believe other people value in them. There are two sides or parts to every person. Rogers believed that each person is constantly struggling to become more and more complete and perfect. Anything that furthers this end is good—the person wants to become everything he or she can possibly be. Different people have different potentialities, but every person wants to realize these potentialities, to make them real, whatever they are. Whatever you can do, you want to do—and do as well as possible. This optimism about human nature is the essence of humanism.

Each individual also has what Rogers called a **self**. The self is essentially your image of who you are and what you value—in yourself, in other people, in life in general. The self is something you acquire gradually over the years by observing how other people react to you. You want approval or **positive regard**. You ask yourself, "How does she see me?" If the answer is "She loves me. She likes what I am and what I do," then you begin to develop positive regard for yourself.

Yet often this does not happen. In other words, she places conditions on her love: *If* you do what she wants, she likes you. Young and impressionable, you accept these verdicts and incorporate **conditions of worth** into yourself. You begin to see yourself as good and worthy only if you act in certain ways. You have learned from your parents and from other people who are significant to you that unless you meet certain conditions, you will not be loved.

Rogers's work as a therapist convinced him that people cope with conditions of worth by rejecting or denying parts of their person that do not fit their self-concept. For example, if your mother grew cold and distant whenever you became angry, you learned to

self one's experience or image of oneself, developed through interaction with others

positive regard viewing oneself in a favorable light due to supportive feedback received from interaction with other

conditions of worth the conditions a person must meet in order to regard himself or herself positively

Rogers proposed that people should relate to one another with unconditional positive regard.

▶ **CRITICAL THINKING**

Analyzing What is unconditional positive regard?

400

Steve Debenport/the Agency Collection/Getty Images

deny yourself the right to express or perhaps even feel anger. In effect, you are cutting off a part of your whole being; you are allowing yourself to experience and express only part of what you are.

The greater the gap between the self and the person, the more limited and defensive a person becomes. Rogers believed the cure for this situation—and the way to prevent it from ever developing—is **unconditional positive regard**. If significant others (parents, friends, a mate) convey the feeling that they value you for what you are in your entirety, you will gradually learn to grant yourself the same unconditional positive regard. The need to limit yourself declines or never develops in the first place. You will be able to accept your person and become open to *all* your feelings, thoughts, and experiences—and hence to other people. This is what Rogers meant by **fully functioning**. The person and the self are one. The individual is free to develop all of his or her potentialities. Like Maslow and other humanistic psychologists, Rogers believed that self-regard and regard for others go together and that the human potential for good and self-fulfillment outweighs the potential for evil and despair.

Humanistic approaches to personality emphasize that life is a conscious experience—that is, we freely choose how we spend our lives. Our conscious experience, though, is private and subjective. Critics argue that the humanistic theories cannot be tested. These theories describe behavior rather than explain it. Humanists themselves argue that each individual is unique, and therefore their theories cannot predict behavior.

✔ **READING PROGRESS CHECK**

Analyzing According to Carl Rogers, why aren't people born with a positive regard?

Cognitive Theory

GUIDING QUESTION *How does personal construct theory explain personality?*

Cognitive theory is based on analysis of our own perceptions, thoughts, and feelings. In other words, the cognitive theory of development attempts to explain human behavior by explaining the human thought process. Most of the theorists involved in cognitive theory focus on the logical thought processes that humans go through to make decisions.

George Kelly: Personal Construct Theory

One of the most famous theorists in cognitive development, George Kelly (1905–1967), developed the idea of *personal construct theory* in 1955. The theory is based on an analysis of our perception of ourselves and our environment. In Kelly's view, our personality consists of our thoughts about ourselves, including our biases, errors, mistakes, and false conclusions. The idea of the personal construct theory is to be able to categorize and order our actions and reactions to events and to be able to predict our behavior to upcoming events based on how we have reacted in the past. Our constructs, in his theory, are the ideas or theories that we base our actions on—not theories based on any actual evidence. The theory is mainly used to study individual behavior, families, and social groups, but it is also used to study business and marketing structures and educational groups. The constructs are meant to be a way for us to label our own values and sense of ourselves.

Kelly's fundamental idea is that our "processes are psychologically channelized by the ways in which (each of us) anticipates events." He thought these processes were channeled by the pathways of our potential responses, which limit our response options. We then create our own meaning for our version of reality.

Our individuality comes from the unique manner in which we organize our personal constructs—our schemas—our mental representations of people, events, and concepts.

According to the personal construct theory, for example, we exhibit personal constructs when deciding on the best place to work. We rate the job on the things that are important to us—pay rate, distance from home, work climate, job responsibilities. Each of these things are classified on a scale that will help us to use our thoughts and experiences to help us make a decision about whether to take the job and what we might like about the job.

Kelly also developed the *repertory grid*. The grid can be used as an interview tool by which psychologists can begin to understand a person's thought processes and constructs. The grid consists of six to twelve different examples that represent a wide range of approaches and constructs. Then, the participant independently identifies how some of the examples on the list may be different from others. The participant then uses the grid to rate and analyze the constructs. All of this information gives the interviewer a lot of information about the way the participant

Connecting Psychology to Geography

CULTURE AND PERSONALITY

The personality theories presented in this chapter do not apply evenly to everyone. The observations on which these theories are based center primarily on studies of people in North America and Western Europe. Those studied, then, represent only a minority of the humans on Earth. People who live elsewhere or who have been brought up in a non-Western cultural environment may look at themselves differently. For instance, a person raised in a non-Western cultural environment may not place a strong emphasis on her individual identity. She may not view herself as a separate entity from her family or community. She may avoid any form of conflict. The meanings she assigns to behaviors may be very different from the Western point of view.

Concepts such as internal locus of control, self-efficacy, and optimism may have different meanings depending on one's culture. In one study of Asian American college students whose home life had exposed them to traditional Asian cultures, for example, those who expressed pessimism about their abilities performed better at solving problems than those who expressed optimism. In studies of white American college students, just the opposite results were obtained— an optimistic belief in one's abilities correlated positively with problem-solving skills.

Geography can affect personality development and the values of individual people in a variety of ways. For example, areas of Afghanistan are extremely rugged and mountainous. Because of this, local groups have little contact with outside cultures. Difficulties in surviving and isolation cause the culture to place a high value on loyalty to the social group. All these concepts are part of sociocultural theory, which takes cultural commonalities into consideration as a way to explain why people act the way they do.

▲ Members of an Asian American family may place low emphasis on individual identity.

▶ CRITICAL THINKING

1. Analyzing Examine a video of proceedings at the United Nations. How do you think a psychologist would compare and contrast the behaviors of diplomats from different countries?

2. Making Generalizations How do you think your geographic location may have influenced your personality, goals, and values?

feels about the subject. As long as the interviewer does not try to lead the subject in identifying or analyzing important constructs, a repertory grid can be a good method for identifying the cognitive processes of a participant.

Kelly's grid technique is still adapted and used today. Although it was designed for use by people with full verbal abilities, doctors and therapists have been using a similar grid to communicate problems and progress of stroke victims. These patients do not always have full verbal abilities after their stroke, so the grid is a good way for therapists to pinpoint areas that need to be addressed and worked on. For example, the patient might be asked to consider three different constructs—themselves before the illness, themselves now, and the self they would like to be upon full recovery. The criteria that can be used to rate and analyze the constructs might be *very good to very bad*, *happy to sad*, *good movement to immobile*, or *angry to not angry*. While physical therapy may be able to help doctors assess a patient's physical progress, Kelly's grid is necessary for communicating ideas and feelings that might otherwise be lost or ignored as part of the patient's therapy.

Aaron T. Beck: Flawed Thought Processes

Expanding on Kelly's work, psychiatrist Aaron T. Beck (1921–) noted his clients' tendency to think negatively—anticipating the worst—and maintain irrational thought processes. Beck developed a theory that would concentrate on turning negative thoughts into constructive ones by challenging clients' fundamentally flawed thought processes. Beck's intent was to help the client develop ways to explain his or her problems as related to the environment rather than automatically assuming they were personality flaws. Finally, a rational analysis would be conducted to develop new, different strategies for the experiences that had yielded a **previous** negative conclusion from flawed thinking. Beck theorized that people's core beliefs are formed over a lifetime of experiences.

previous existing or occurring before something else

Martin Seligman: Helplessness and Happiness

Martin Seligman (1942–) is an American cognitive psychologist whose research helped to coin the term "learned helplessness." In his 1967 study with Steve Maier, it was discovered that dogs could be conditioned, or taught, to be helpless in their situation and lose their desire to overcome a bad situation. In a case where the dogs were given a shock, they started out trying to escape the inescapable situation. Over time, they began to become helpless in their situation, even when finally provided a way to escape. This learned helplessness, it was found, applied to human behavior also. People who are in less than desirable life situations may learn to become helpless in their situation and give up trying to better themselves.

Seligman's later work focused on positive psychology. His work criticized that others focused on mental illness and abnormal psychology, and his work began to study the psychology of happiness. In his studies, however, he noticed limitations that people put on their own happiness. He wondered why billionaires seek even more money than they already have, and why people who enjoy sports play them with such seriousness and dedication as to cut down on their happiness. He discovered that people not only want to be happy, they want to flourish, or have a good sense of well-being. They believe that this is linked to people's need to succeed and to reach an overall sense of happiness. People's cognitive processes contribute to their actions and help explain why they react in certain ways.

Seymour Epstein: Cognitive-Experiential Self-Theory

Another cognitive theory was developed by Seymour Epstein. The *cognitive-experiential self-theory* states that people operate based upon two separate systems for processing information. First, the analytical-rational thought process is slow and logical. It is related to the deeper analytical thoughts that we have.

Carl Rogers
(1902–1987)

Carl Rogers is best known for his role in the development of counseling. Rogers believed that therapy should focus on present problems—psychologists should not dwell on the past and the causes of present problems. Rogers believed that people are basically good and can solve their own problems once they realize that they can. Rogers started out by rejecting two principles. He realized that psychoanalysts focused on investigating the causes of a patient's problems. Rogers rejected this, creating his client-centered approach. Rogers used his approach to help clients better understand their subjective experiences and then work to change their own subjective views of themselves, the world, and other people. Rogers was also a teacher. He advocated one-on-one approaches to teaching. He saw the role of the teacher as one who creates an environment for engagement; that is, the teacher inspires an exploratory atmosphere in which students seek answers to problems.

▶ **CRITICAL THINKING**

Identifying Central Issues
Why did Rogers reject the psychoanalytic approach?

On the other hand, the intuitive-experiential thought process is faster, based on emotions, and uses little thought processes. It is the balance between these two thought systems that helps us think and function throughout the day. There is some interaction between the two systems. If the intuitive-experiential part of our thought processes directs our behavior in an inappropriate way, for example, it is our analytical-rational thought process that can catch the behavior and correct it or rationalize it. Also, it is the analytical-rational thought process that can help us to understand emotionally significant events that we experience through our intuitive-experiential thought process.

Similar to Freud's concepts of the id, ego, and superego, the rational system represents our conscious thoughts while the experiential system represents our preconscious thoughts. However, as a cognitive approach to our thought processes, the cognitive-experiential self-theory is able to explain our broader human concerns, such as spirituality, politics, responses to advertising, and the desires and needs to succeed in life. It is believed that the analytical-rational side of our thinking can provide insight into these richer experiences in life.

The approach even gives us a way to understand more about other cognitive approaches to psychology. For example, the intuitive-experiential thought process is instrumental in our learning about our cultural background, and the analytical-rational side makes it possible for us to think about what our cultural background really means in our lives. This cognitive approach to studying personality can look for similarities and differences among people with similar thought processes.

Some aspects of cognitive theory are moving closer to traditional behavioral theories of personality. Behaviorial theorists are primarily concerned with observing a person's behavior, which can be objectively and scientifically measured, as opposed to studying a person's internal processes, such as thoughts and emotions. To a behaviorist, all behavior is a result of stimulus and response, no matter how complex. However, the modern cognitive theories, in contrast to behavioral theory, maintain a more positive, optimistic view of our personality.

☑ **READING PROGRESS CHECK**

Differentiating According to the personal construct theory, how can negative feelings contribute to our perception of ourselves?

Sociocultural Theory

GUIDING QUESTION *How does culture influence personality?*

Humanistic and cognitive theories are not the only approaches to personality. Some psychologists feel that a person's ethnicity, gender, age, sexual orientation, socioeconomic status, culture, and even their genetic makeup contribute to their personality. The *sociocultural* personality theory considers the entire environment in which a person lives and reacts. For example, in some cultures, the acceptable conversational distance between people is closer than in others. In North American or Western European cultures, the amount of personal space a person expects to have is greater than that in some Asian cultures. Does that mean that a person's personality and comfort level among other people is dictated by his or her culture or by other factors within his or her own experience?

Psychoanalytic theorists would say that it is repressed feelings from childhood that might make someone uncomfortable standing and conversing in such close proximity to another person. Psychoanalysts would focus on what that other person represents. The sociocultural theory would attribute the discomfort to deep cultural roots and expectations within the society that were learned throughout a person's lifetime. In other words, people learn collective behaviors that transcend their culture instead of being affected only by individual experiences to shape their lives.

In addition, the sociocultural approach suggests that people adapt their behaviors to the cultures they are in. A person who moves to another culture can learn to become more like the people of that culture, adopting their cultural preferences, and affecting his or her own sense of self.

It is our society and our culture, according to sociocultural theorists, that dictates our personalities and our feelings about our personalities. Governing the behavior, values, beliefs, and attitudes of members of a society, generation to generation, our culture affects much of our behavior and attitudes. Violation of our cultural standards creates strong emotional reactions. A person who behaves in a way that goes against social norms, for instance, might be treated harshly or ostracized from society.

Gender roles and expected/accepted behavior may have, across time or cultures, influenced the personality displayed by women and men. For example, it is a rather recent trend for an American man to be complimented for his sensitivity or passivity, or for an American woman to be rewarded for her aggressive or competitive nature. The ideas we hold about a woman's role in business, politics, sports, and home life are most certainly a result of our cultural upbringing and expectations. A woman's view of herself is dictated by her culture's view of women and their traditional roles in society. Similarly, the way a man views himself and his role in society is a reflection of his culture's view of what is expected of him.

Critics of the sociocultural theory believe that it minimizes the importance of a person's individual characteristics and instead focuses too much on external factors that are beyond a person's control. Other critics contend that the base assumptions about different cultures are not accurate and can become stereotypical. For example, the theory states that people from more dominant cultures have a more positive sense of self, since they are more likely to share the same expectations of personal achievement as the majority of the people in power. This may not always be the case, but sociocultural theories make assumptions about a person's cultural surroundings as a way to explain personality traits. For instance, that a person from "Region X" acts a certain way, while a person from "Region Z" acts another way. Critics argue that there is as much variability in personality within cultures as across them.

☑ **READING PROGRESS CHECK**

Analyzing How might a sociocultural approach explain why someone is shy?

LESSON 4 REVIEW

Reviewing Vocabulary
1. *Explaining* What is self-actualization? How does one achieve it?

Using Your Notes
2. *Synthesizing* Think of the steps needed to take to become fully functioning. Why do you think some people have trouble becoming fully functioning based on Rogers's theory?

Answering the Guiding Questions
3. *Differentiating* What is emphasized by humanistic psychology?

4. *Analyzing* How does personal construct theory explain personality?

5. *Making Connections* How does culture influence personality?

Writing Activity
6. *Informative/Explanatory* Think of a close friend, family member, or one of your heroes. Using what you've learned about the traits of self-actualized individuals, evaluate which traits he or she shares.

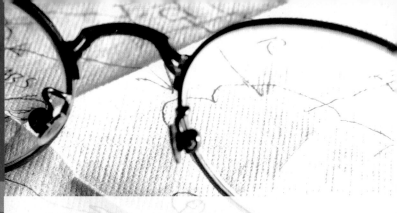

Reader's Dictionary

philanderer: one who has many love affairs

squandered: to lose an advantage or opportunity through negligence or inaction

entrenched: to establish solidly

enigma: a mystery

Psychologist Gordon Allport presents the letters of Jenny Gove Masterson (and others) as an intense case study of personality. Jenny's letters trace a life of frustration and defeat. Between the ages of 58 and 70, Jenny wrote a series of 301 letters to Glenn and Isabel, two young friends. The letters dramatically illustrate her relationship with her son Ross. Jenny tells of her interests, hates, fears, and conflicts. These letters have led many psychologists and students to seek to explain Jenny's behavior and her personality.

Letters
from Jenny
edited and interpreted
by Gordon W. Allport

PRIMARY SOURCE

Friday, April 19/29

Dear Glenn:

I'm afraid that I am quite a nuisance in shoving my affairs on Isabel and you, but when you remember the compact we made that time I was in Chicago, and all your care over me since, you will pardon. You are my only confidant.

My motive in telling you all this is not to gossip, or backbite, but because I know that when *I* drop out Ross will lie to you and make it appear that things were quite different with us. . . .

The chances are that Ross and I are again near the parting of the ways. He has never cared anything at all for me since he adopted, and was adopted by, the old **philanderer**. It is as well for him to try his luck again in matrimony—he can then take his other wife to visit his "Beloved Mother" his "B.M." as he did the first one, and they can all be happy together.

I have truly a noble son—an honor to his College, his friends, his family. And all for what? Can it be possible all this is merely for the sake of co-habiting with a woman who sells her body to the highest bidder?

Oh! If he would only settle down for 2 or 3 years and get a footing in business and not always belong to the "floating" population. He is not so very old yet altho' he has **squandered** 10 precious years. What in the world is the matter, Glenn dear?

I am not a charming person—not beautiful—not clever, but what of that? I carried him in my body for 9 mos. was good to him for many years (you know that) altho' he says I wasn't—that it was all *selfishness* on my part—but even granting all that to be so—I am still *his* Mother. Oh! what is it that's so wrong?

Be patient with me—I try you sadly—but I'm *alone*, and it's awful to be in the dark, and be alone. I sincerely hope you are all well.

Jenny

P.S. *Do not* write to Ross about me. You would mean all right, of course, but Ross would be very angry, and resent it dreadfully. He says you don't "live"—don't know what "life" is—sometimes I think he is a little "off", and might kill me—he resents your having helped me, and my gratitude to Isabel and you.

406

Mikael Andersson/Nordic Photos/Getty Images

From Isabel
[27 years after Jenny's death]

Dear Mr. Editor:

It is now twenty-seven years since Jenny Masterson died. You have asked me to re-read her Letters addressed to Glenn and myself, and in this perspective to make comments and interpretations concerning her tortured life.

Her Letters bring back many memories, but even in the perspective of years I cannot pretend to discover the key to her nature. Our relationship to her was essentially "neutral." We took pains not to become too deeply involved, but we always answered her communications and tried to help her in emergencies.

"to me the enigma is how she came to be such a problem to herself as well as to others"

Her behavior, like the Letters, was intense, dramatic, and sometimes "hard to take." But to us her nature posed a challenge to understanding. What made her so intense, so vivid, so difficult? Even now her communications arouse in me a sense of the **enigma** of her personality as well as sympathy for her predicament. . . .

So we know that early in her life Jenny showed some of the factors evident in the Letters: her aloneness, her intense individuality and dramatization, her temper and tendency to quarrel. She was a puzzle to her family, and socially a problem long before we knew her. But to me the enigma is *how* she came to be such a problem to herself as well as to others. . . .

This self-defeating formula was with her from early years. At the age of 70 she is "the same only more so." . . .

Excerpts from two letters
written by Ross to Glenn:

April 21, 1929

Your last letter was the one about Mother. I appreciate your interest and your desire to help me that I might help her. And yet, in a word, your letter merely emphasized my own feeling of frustration and futility. I'm afraid there is little one can do, or that I can do, to be a comfort and service of any real or lasting pleasure.

Mother has **entrenched** herself behind truths, half-truths, and utter fabrications concerning my limitations as the ideal son, and there is no dislodging her. No amount of even demonstrating my presence will change her constant reiteration that I am entirely bad and have cast her off in her old age. . . . Day and night, Mother recites her own good deeds to her family, her friends, her husband, her son, and how each in turn failed to pay her back. . . .

July 6, 1929

. . .I am sorry not to have something cheerful to say about Mother and me. Our lives seem constant problems —so constant that I am lost in their maze and see neither right nor wrong nor any solution.

. . .Meantime I can discuss nothing with Mother who will not talk—nor go anywhere with me. Every attempt boils down to a horrible scene. . .

Analyzing Primary Sources

1. *Making Inferences* What personality traits does Jenny display?

2. *Drawing Inferences* How does Ross view his mother?

3. *Analyzing Primary Sources* Isabel writes that Jenny's personality did not change as she aged, but became more difficult. Do you think that it is possible for a person to change his or her personality? Explain.

netw⊚rks

There's More Online!

- ☑ **CARTOON** Personality Traits
- ☑ **DIAGRAM** Eysenck's Personality Table
- ☑ **GRAPHIC ORGANIZER**
- ☑ **SELF-CHECK QUIZ**
- ☑ **TABLE** Theories of Personality

Reading **HELP**DESK ⓒⒸⓈⓈ

Academic Vocabulary

- core
- data

Content Vocabulary

- trait
- cardinal trait
- factor analysis
- surface trait
- source trait

TAKING NOTES:

Key Ideas and Details

Gathering Information Use a graphic organizer like the one below to list the traits that make up each of Eysenck's three dimensions of personality.

Eysenck's Dimensions of Personality

408

LESSON 5

Trait Theories

ESSENTIAL QUESTIONS · *How is behavior influenced by environment?*
· *How does experience influence personality?*

IT MATTERS BECAUSE

We describe people according to their personality traits. We may describe someone as even-tempered, friendly, or helpful and patient. We might describe someone else as arrogant, self-centered, or impatient. Understanding these traits helps us to understand human personality. Many theorists have attempted to explain human personality based on these traits and how they relate to human behavior in general.

Defining Trait Theories of Personality

GUIDING QUESTION *How does trait theory differ from the psychoanalytic theory of personality?*

Terms such as *nice, smart,* and *arrogant* refer to personality traits. Some theorists have argued that studying such traits in detail is the best approach to solving the puzzle of human behavior. A **trait** is "any relatively enduring way in which one individual differs from another." A trait, then, is a predisposition to respond in a certain way in many different kinds of situations—in a dentist's office, at a party, or in a classroom. More than any other personality theorists, trait theorists emphasize and try to explain the consistency of a normal, healthy individual's behavior in different situations.

Trait theorists generally make two basic assumptions about these underlying sources of consistency. First, every trait is universal: it applies to all people. For example, everyone can be classified as more or less dependent. Second, these descriptions can be quantified. We might, for example, establish a scale in which an extremely independent person scores 1, while a very dependent person scores 10.

Thus, every trait can be used to describe people. Aggressiveness, for example, is measured on a continuum; a few people are extremely aggressive or extremely unaggressive, and most of us fall somewhere in the middle. We understand people by specifying their traits, and we use traits to predict people's future behavior.

Trait theorists go beyond this level of analysis to look for the underlying sources of consistency in human behavior. They try to find the best way to describe the fundamental qualities of any given person's behavior.

Jacobs Stock Photography/Photographer's Choice RF/Getty Images

How can they best describe a person's behavior? Is he friendly, or socially aggressive, or interested in people, or self-confident, or something else? What underlying trait best explains his behavior?

trait a tendency to react to a situation in a way that remains stable over time

Digging Deeper

Most (but not all) trait theorists believe that a few basic traits are central for all people. A trait such as self-confidence, for example, might explain more superficial characteristics like social aggressiveness and dependency. In other words, a person who lacked the basic trait of self-confidence would be considered dependent or a person who possessed too much self-confidence would be considered socially aggressive. Psychologists who accept this approach set out on their theoretical search for basic traits with very few assumptions.

Trait theorist Gordon Allport came up with three ways to categorize human personality traits. The cardinal traits, his theory explained, are the ones that people use to describe your overall personality. Cardinal traits are the ones that dominate a person's personality to the extent that the person becomes known for that trait. For example, fictional character Ebenezer Scrooge is famous for the cardinal trait of stinginess. American Revolution general Benedict Arnold is famous for his traitorousness. Allport explained central traits as those that are less dominant but useful in describing a person's typical qualities, such as shyness, intelligence, or honesty. A secondary trait will appear only during certain situations. You may be an outgoing person with a secondary trait of being shy in groups or talking nervously in front of crowds.

A Break from Freud

The starting point for trait theory is very different from the starting point of other personality theorists. Freud, for example, began with a well-defined theory of instincts. When he observed that some people were stingy, he set out to explain this in terms of his theory. Trait theorists do not start by trying to understand stinginess. Rather, they try to determine whether stinginess is a trait. That is, they try to find out whether people who are stingy in one type of situation are also stingy in others. Then they might ask whether stinginess represents a more basic trait like possessiveness: Is the stingy person also very possessive in relationships? Thus, the primary question for a trait theorist is, "What behaviors go together?"

When trait theorists understand why people exhibit certain behaviors, they can then seek to understand what forms the personality. But this attempt to understand personality is not easy. What makes one person act stingy, greedy, or kind may not be what drives another person to display the same traits. Understanding cultural and social influences will help theorists to further define personality types. Intimate experiences and social or cultural upbringing may form people's personalities in even more complex ways than have yet been studied.

✔ **READING PROGRESS CHECK**

Assessing What do trait theorists do to explain why a person might have a particular personality trait?

"And this is him in a *bad* mood."

PERSONALITY TRAITS
This cartoon highlights personality traits. Often we describe a person's personality in terms of traits.

▶ **CRITICAL THINKING**

1. *Analyzing* Which personality traits does this cartoon emphasize?

2. *Making Connections* Thinking of these traits as a continuum, what might be the extreme ends for these traits?

Trait Theories and Theorists

GUIDING QUESTION *How do trait theories attempt to explain personality?*

There are many theorists who have attempted to explain why some people are outgoing and social while others are shy and reserved. Different trait theories take different approaches to understanding personality and the traits that people have. Some of the leading psychologists disagree on how humans develop their personalities and at what time in their lives this happens.

Gordon Allport: Identifying Traits

Gordon W. Allport (1897–1967) was an influential psychologist in his day. A trait, Allport said, makes a wide variety of situations "functionally equivalent"; that is, a person's traits will be consistent in different situations. Allport, along with H.S. Odbert, probed an English dictionary, searching for words that described personality traits. They found almost 18,000 such words. They then narrowed the list by grouping synonyms and keeping just one word for each cluster of synonyms. Assuming any important personality trait is reflected in language, if Allport's team found words such as *honesty* and *dishonesty*, each was assigned to a separate cluster with similar contrasting words. Allport defined common traits as those that apply to everyone and individual traits as those that apply more to a specific person.

cardinal trait a characteristic or feature that is so pervasive the person is almost identified with it

Allport described three kinds of individual traits. A **cardinal trait** is one that is so pervasive that the person is almost identified with that trait. An example would be Scrooge, who is identified as stingy and coldhearted in Charles Dickens's tale *A Christmas Carol*. A *central trait* makes us predictable (she's assertive; he's a flirt) in most situations. *Secondary traits*, such as our preferences in food and music, are least important to Allport and have a less consistent influence on us.

TABLE >

CATTELL'S SIXTEEN SOURCE TRAITS

Cattell used his sixteen source traits to develop a personality questionnaire, which was used to measure the traits in an individual. Each trait is listed as a pair of opposites on a continuum.

▶ **CRITICAL THINKING**

1. *Interpreting Significance* What did Cattell believe measuring the source traits could predict?

2. *Analyzing* How would someone be described who has the opposite traits of someone who is submissive and timid?

Cattell's Sixteen Source Traits		
Reserved	⟷	Outgoing
Less intelligent	⟷	More intelligent
Affected by feelings	⟷	Emotionally stable
Submissive	⟷	Dominant
Serious	⟷	Happy-go-lucky
Expedient	⟷	Conscientious
Timid	⟷	Venturesome
Tough-minded	⟷	Sensitive
Trusting	⟷	Suspicious
Practical	⟷	Imaginative
Forthright	⟷	Shrewd
Self-assured	⟷	Apprehensive
Conservative	⟷	Experimenting
Group-dependent	⟷	Self-sufficient
Uncontrolled	⟷	Controlled
Relaxed	⟷	Tense

An example of an individual trait is found in Allport's book *Letters from Jenny*, which consists of hundreds of letters that a woman whom Allport calls Jenny Masterson wrote to a friend. Jenny reveals herself in these letters, which she wrote between the ages of 58 and 70, as a complex and fiercely independent woman. In his preface to the book, Allport wrote:

PRIMARY SOURCE

❝ [The] fascination of the Letters lies in their challenge to the reader (whether psychologist or layman) to "explain" Jenny—if he can. Why does an intelligent lady behave so persistently in a self-defeating manner? ❞

Allport's own attempt to understand Jenny began with a search for the underlying traits that would explain the consistency of her behavior.

Raymond Cattell: Sixteen Trait Theory

More recent theorists have concentrated on what Allport called *common traits*, which they try to quantify in a precise, scientific manner. Their primary tool in this task has been **factor analysis**, a sophisticated mathematical technique that describes the extent to which personality variables are related.

Using Allport's list of some 18,000 words that describe personality traits, Raymond Cattell (1905–1998) proposed that approximately 46 of those words are descriptions of what he called **surface traits**—the personality characteristics easily seen by other people. Using further factor analyses, Cattell found that certain surface traits seem to occur in clusters. He hypothesized that there must be underlying factors that account for those clusters. Cattell's analyses into what those clusters had in common resulted in 16 **source traits**—stable characteristics or tendencies that he considered to be at the **core** of personality. Cattell believed that by measuring these traits, psychologists could better describe, explain, and predict people's behavior in certain situations.

Hans Eysenck: Dimensions of Personality

Using factor analysis of personality **data**, Hans Eysenck (1916–1997), an English psychologist, concluded that there are two basic dimensions of personality. The first dimension, *stability versus instability*, refers to the degree to which people have control over their feelings. At the emotionally stable end of the personality spectrum is a person who is easygoing, relaxed, well-adjusted, and even-tempered. At the anxiety-dominated end of the spectrum is the moody, anxious, and restless person.

Eysenck's second dimension was actually identified years earlier by Carl Jung as *extraversion versus introversion*. Extraverts are sociable, outgoing, active, lively people. They enjoy parties and seek excitement. On the other end of the dimension are introverts, who are more thoughtful, reserved, passive, unsociable, and quiet. Eysenck believed that these personality differences originate in the central nervous system and are determined by heredity. He maintained that differences in excitatory or inhibitory cortical processes in the brain resulted in different responses to stimuli for extraverts and introverts. The brains of introverts, according to Eysenck, react quickly and strongly to stimuli. Therefore, they cannot tolerate excessive stimulation, so they avoid it. Extraverts, on the other hand, react slowly to stimuli, so they tolerate high levels of stimulation.

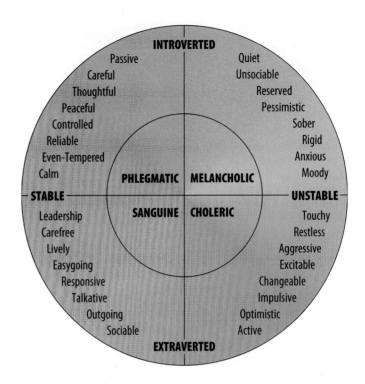

∧ DIAGRAM

EYSENCK'S PERSONALITY TABLE

Eysenck hypothesized that introverted people share a number of traits, while extraverted people share the opposite traits. Eysenck's theory is similar to Galen's ancient theory for four temperaments.

▶ CRITICAL THINKING

1. **Analyzing** What traits would an extraverted and stable (sanguine) person exhibit?

2. **Analyzing Visuals** How would Eysenck's table describe a person who is pessimistic and rigid?

factor analysis a complex statistical technique used to identify the underlying reasons variables are correlated

surface trait a stable characteristic that can be observed in certain situations

source trait a stable characteristic that can be considered to be at the core of personality

THEORIES OF PERSONALITY

Theories of personality are used to organize personality characteristics, explain differences among individuals, explore how people conduct their lives, and determine how life can be improved.

▶ **CRITICAL THINKING**

1. ***Analyzing*** Which type of theorist would be most interested in knowing how your childhood experiences affect your thoughts and actions?

2. ***Contrasting*** How is a behaviorist different from a cognitive theorist?

core base or central part of something

data facts and statistics collected for study

Theory	Main Ideas
Behaviorist Theories	focus on the way rewards and punishment shape our actions
Social Learning Theories	cognitive-personal factors, our behaviors, and environmental factors interact to shape our personalities
Psychoanalytic Theories	emphasize the importance of early childhood experiences, repressed thoughts, and conflict between conscious and unconscious forces
Cognitive Theories	our analysis of our own perceptions, thoughts, and feelings shape our personalities
Humanistic Theories	emphasize our capacity for personal growth, development of our full potential, and freedom to make choices
Trait Theories	focus on identifying, measuring, and classifying similarities and differences in personality characteristics or traits

Years after he identified the first two dimensions, Eysenck added a third, *psychoticism*. At one end of this dimension are self-centered, hostile, and aggressive people, who act without much thought. Individuals at the other end of this dimension have what Freud might label high superego. They tend to be socially sensitive, high on caring and empathy, and easy people with whom to work.

☑ **READING PROGRESS CHECK**

Making Decisions How has research on personality built upon the theories developed by Gordon Allport?

The Robust Five

GUIDING QUESTION *What are the main criticisms of trait theories?*

Over the years, trait theorists have devised a number of ways to measure personality. Each involves a different number of traits or factors. Trait psychologists have shown that five traits appear repeatedly in different research studies. Often called the "five robust factors," or "the big five," they are:

- *Extraversion*, which is associated with warmth, talkativeness, and being energetic. The opposite of this is introversion, meaning being quiet or reserved.
- *Agreeableness*, which involves being sympathetic to others, kind, and trusting; the opposite is cruel and non-trusting.
- *Conscientiousness*, which identifies individuals who are dutiful, dedicated to completing tasks, organized, and responsible.
- *Openness to experience*, which describes people who are open-minded and willing to try intellectual experiences, new ideas, or creative experiences.
- *Emotional stability*, which identifies individuals who experience things relatively easily and without getting upset. The opposite is neuroticism—a tendency to experience unpleasant emotions a great deal of the time.

Think of each robust five trait as a continuum. Each trait has many related traits. For example, conscientiousness at one end includes being responsible and dependable. The opposite end, though, involves impulsiveness or carelessness. Trait theorists assume traits are relatively fixed, or unchanging. The advantage of trait theories is that by identifying a person's personality traits, that person's behavior can be predicted. However, critics argue that trait theories describe personality rather than explain it.

Trait theorists cannot explain or predict behaviors across different situations. For example, a person may be quiet and reserved in class but outgoing and wild at a party. Why? Critics of trait theories propose that personality is an interaction between a person's traits and the effects of being in a particular situation. For example, whereas most theories of personality consider the person as an individual, some psychologists regard personality as a function of a person's social environment. One of the first of these thinkers was Harry Stack Sullivan (1892–1949).

Sullivan's ideas have been organized into a two-dimensional model. One dimension is power, which ranges from dominance at one end of the scale to submissiveness at the other. The second dimension is friendliness, which ranges from friendliness to hostility. Most behaviors can be described as a combination of these two dimensions. For example, helpfulness combines dominance and friendliness, while trust combines submissiveness and friendliness.

Researchers also noticed that a person's actions tend to elicit specific responses from other people. A behavior and its most likely response are said to be complementary. For example, most people will respond to a request for help (trusting) by offering advice (helping), regardless of how helpful they are as individuals. Thus, many behaviors result not simply from a person's personality but also from that person's social environment.

☑ **READING PROGRESS CHECK**

Making Decisions Do you think measuring personality traits on a continuum scale is a good way to measure personality? Explain.

Quick Lab

DO WE SEE OURSELVES AS OTHERS SEE US?

Some personality theorists talk about extraversion versus introversion as being a basic part of personality. Do people exhibit these traits in all situations? Are these traits easily identified?

Procedure

1. Choose five people (family members, friends, or acquaintances) and observe their behavior in several situations.
2. Record your observations by classifying each person as extraverted, introverted, or a combination of both.
3. Ask the five people whether they would consider themselves extraverted or introverted, and then record their responses.

Analysis

1. What do your results tell you about extraversion and introversion as personality traits? Are people extraverted or introverted in all situations all the time?
2. What do your results tell you about people's own perceptions of their personality versus the perceptions of others? What might account for any differences?

Reviewing Vocabulary

1. ***Identifying*** What is the difference between cardinal and central traits? Between surface and source traits?

Using Your Notes

2. ***Discussing*** Use your notes to explain Eysenck's theory of extraversion versus introversion and give an example of each kind of personality.

Answering the Guiding Questions

3. ***Contrasting*** How does trait theory differ from the psychoanalytic theory of personality?

4. ***Summarizing*** How do trait theories attempt to explain personality?

5. ***Identifying Central Issues*** What are the main criticisms of trait theories?

Writing Activity

6. ***Informative/Explanatory*** Choose a character in a movie or television show seen recently. Write a description of the character in terms of the personality traits theory proposed by one of the theorists discussed. Specify the reasons you selected that trait theory over other trait theories listed in the lesson.

Case Study

Personality Disorder

Period of Study: 1967

Introduction: An actor and radio disc jockey, Dan was highly successful in his professional roles, which required an entertaining and extremely outspoken personality. Although Dan had to maintain these personality traits at work, sometimes traces of those traits leaked out into his private life. In one situation while Dan and a friend dined at a restaurant, Dan explicitly and loudly complained about the condition of the food. In actuality, according to Dan's friend, the food was fine—there was no valid reason for Dan's public display.

Dan's friend, psychologist Elton McNeil, described Dan's reactions as inappropriate. When McNeil asked Dan why he had acted that way, Dan said he did it because "he wanted to show how gutless the rest of the world is." Concerned by his friend's statements, McNeil asked Dan if he felt guilty at all about treating his fellow human beings that way. Dan's answer was, "Who cares?"

Hypothesis: For those of us who are familiar with actors and radio disc jockeys, we know that their jobs require straightforward and sometimes confrontational behavior. An excess of these traits, though, can prove to be too much for healthy functioning in life.

Method: McNeil encouraged his friend to take part in some sort of counseling or therapy. Dan agreed. During the therapy sessions which followed, Dan disclosed some of his thoughts and memories to his therapist. One of his earliest memories involved the time in his youth when he recognized that he was a little different from others. In high school Dan's best friend was diagnosed with leukemia and soon after died. Dan remembered going to the funeral and, unlike the many mourners there, realized he didn't feel any emotion for his lost friend or for his family. Dan acknowledged to his therapist that after the funeral, when contemplating the loss of his parents and siblings, that he would not miss them or feel for them were they to die. It wasn't that he disliked them, but more that he did not have any emotions for them at all.

Results: This description detailing the absence of emotion clearly indicated the possibility of a personality disorder. The *Diagnostic and Statistical Manual of Mental Disorders, Fourth Edition (DSM-IV)* defines a personality disorder as an enduring pattern of inner experience and behavior that differs significantly from the individual's culture, is extensive and inflexible, has an onset in adolescence or early adulthood, is stable over time, and leads to distress or impairment. An individual with a personality disorder is often capable of functioning normally in society, including holding a job, maintaining some personal relationships, and, on some occasions, showing signs of emotions.

PRIMARY SOURCE

" *For persons with a personality disorder, personality traits are patterns of thinking, reacting, and behaving that remain relatively consistent and stable over time. Persons with a personality disorder display more rigid and maladaptive thinking and reacting behaviors that often disrupt their personal, professional, and social lives.* "

—From the article *Personality Disorders* by Johns Hopkins Medicine

Dan's unusual behavior may have gone unnoticed for so long because his occupations required a person to behave a certain way. In Dan's case, his role was his personality.

Analyzing the Case Study

1. *Explaining* Why did McNeil encourage Dan to enter therapy?

2. *Making Connections* Read the excerpt from the Johns Hopkins Medicine. Based on this excerpt and the descriptions of Dan's behavior in the case study, what characteristics of personality disorder does Dan exhibit?

3. *Making Generalizations* Does everyone's personality change depending on the role they are playing (for instance, as a student, friend, son, or daughter)? Explain.

Jacobs Stock Photography/Photographer's Choice RF/Getty Images

Directions: On a separate sheet of paper, answer the questions below. Make sure you read carefully and answer all parts of the question.

Lesson Review

Lesson 1

1 *Summarizing* What is personality?

2 *Describing* What are the major schools of personality, and how do they differ?

Lesson 2

3 *Explaining* What technique might you be using if you think a teacher is angry at you because he or she gave a difficult test, when in reality the teacher is not angry?

4 *Summarizing* What is the difference between personal unconscious and collective unconscious? How do both affect our personalities?

Lesson 3

5 *Expressing* How did Bandura and Walters believe personality is acquired?

6 *Examining* Why do you think people have different personalities? How would behaviorists explain the differences?

Lesson 4

7 *Explaining* According to Rogers, what situation creates a gap between the person and the self?

8 *Specifying* How do conditions of worth influence your personality, according to Rogers?

Lesson 5

9 *Identifying* List the "five robust factors" of personality.

10 *Explaining* What is the importance of common traits in Cattell's theory? What are Cattell's source traits?

21ˢᵗ Century Skills

Identifying Cause and Effect Review the cartoon, then answer the questions that follow.

11 What aspect of Freud's psychoanalytic theory of personality is reflected in the cartoon?

12 How might a behaviorist explain the man's behavior?

13 How might a humanist psychologist, such as Carl Rogers, explain the man's behavior?

14 How might a trait theorist describe the man's behavior?

Need Extra Help?

If You've Missed Question	**1**	**2**	**3**	**4**	**5**	**6**	**7**	**8**	**9**	**10**	**11**	**12**	**13**	**14**
Go to page	380	382	387	390	395	393	401	400	412	411	387	394	400	410

Directions: On a separate sheet of paper, answer the questions below. Make sure you read carefully and answer all parts of the question.

College and Career Readiness

15 *Clear Communication* Describe the theory of personality that is most appealing to you. Which seems to make the most sense? Why?

Research and Technology

16 *Evaluating* There are various personality tests available on the Internet. Locate the Web sites of these tests. Report on the aspects of personality that these tests address and evaluate how well they do so. Share the Web addresses you found with the class.

Critical Thinking Questions

17 *Synthesizing* Imagine that you have a friend who is failing several subjects in school, does little homework, and fails to study for tests. Based on your knowledge of personality theories, how would Skinner explain your friend's behavior? How would Bandura explain the behavior?

18 *Differentiating* What would life be like if people had only an id? An ego? A superego?

19 *Analyzing* Recall *Freudian slips* you have seen or heard. Write them down and try to determine the reasons for each slip.

20 *Evaluating* List the qualities and traits that you think comprise the self-actualized person.

21 *Defending* Some opponents of the humanistic theory of personality have criticized it for promoting the "me first" approach to living. They believe that the theory encourages selfishness. Do you agree with these critics? Why or why not?

DBQ Analyzing Primary Sources

Use the document below to answer the following questions.

PRIMARY SOURCE

" [T]he client knows what hurts, what directions to go, what problems are crucial, what experiences have been buried. "

—*Carl Rogers, On Becoming a Person*

22 *Interpreting* How does the quotation from Carl Rogers show evidence of how he feels about the relationship between the client and his or her counselor?

23 *Drawing Conclusions* How is Rogers' viewpoint different from that of a psychoanalyst such as Freud?

Exploring the Essential Question

24 *Synthesizing* Create a collage that depicts your personality, using original artwork, photos, and pictures and words from magazines and newspapers. In your collage, show how factors in your environment, such as your parents, school, and the climate in which you live, have affected your behavior. Also show experiences in life that have influenced your personality.

Psychology Journal Activity

25 *Informative/Explanatory* Review your entry in your Psychology Journal for this chapter. After reading in this chapter about the many factors that shape personality, how would you answer the same question: Do you think you were born with your personality or do you think it developed over time? Support your answer with details from the specific theories mentioned in the chapter.

Need Extra Help?

If You've Missed Question	**15**	**16**	**17**	**18**	**19**	**20**	**21**	**22**	**23**	**24**	**25**
Go to page	380	380	393	385	386	399	398	400	400	380	378

Stress and Health

ESSENTIAL QUESTION • *How does stress influence behavior?*

network❂rks
There's More Online about stress and health.

CHAPTER 15

Psychology Matters...

Stress is a factor in everyone's life. Whether you are a student, a parent, or a person trying to get a job done, life's stressors can cause emotional and physical trouble. Stress results from our perceptions of the demands placed upon us and how we evaluate the situations we encounter. Studying the way individuals deal with stressful situations can teach psychologists a great deal about how the mind and body work together.

◄ For many high school students, the pressure to get good grades is a significant life stressor.

Randy Faris/Corbis

417

Lab Activity

Stressed Out

THE QUESTION...

RESEARCH QUESTION What causes the most stress in daily life?

If you were asked to list the things that cause you stress on a normal day and rank them from least to worst, what would your list look like? Do things outside you—problems caused by people or events in your world—cause you the worst stress? Or do your own personal concerns—such as wanting to be liked or being afraid of embarrassment—cause the greatest stress level?

Analyzing the actual causes of stress can be difficult. However, finding out what the greatest causes of stress are in daily life is the first step in minimizing the effects of negative stress on our lives. In this lab, we will investigate whether self-esteem issues cause more negative stress than other daily events.

Psychology Journal Activity

How do you cope with stress in your daily life? Write about this in your Psychology Journal. Consider the following issues as you write: How does stress impact you on a daily basis? What do you do to minimize the effects of stress?

FINDING THE ANSWER...

HYPOTHESIS Concerns about self-esteem issues cause more stress than other problems in typical daily life.

THE METHOD OF YOUR EXPERIMENT

MATERIALS 10 sheets of paper, stress questionnaire

PROCEDURE Create a questionnaire to investigate your peers' feelings about stress. Your questionnaire will have six questions—three about stressful situations related to self-esteem concerns and three about stressful situations related to other kinds of problems. You will ask your participants to rate these situations according to how stressful they are, using a scale of 1 to 10, with 1 meaning "not very stressful," and 10 meaning "extremely stressful." The three self-esteem concerns you will include are: wanting to be liked, wanting to be attractive, and wanting to avoid embarrassment. The three problem/pressure situations you will include are: taking a driver's test, having your car break down, and getting the flu. Read the questions aloud to yourself beforehand to make sure they are clear and concise. Administer your questionnaire to ten participants. Take care to protect your participants' anonymity, destroying all data sheets once the responses are recorded without the participants' names.

DATA COLLECTION Gather your data for each question and calculate an average score. Use a spreadsheet to create a bar graph ranking the causes of stress in order from lowest score to highest. Compare your results with those of your classmates.

ANALYSIS & APPLICATION

1. Did your results support the hypothesis?

2. How did you turn qualitative data into quantitative data?

3. Why do you think stress related to self-esteem can be more intense than stress from other events?

networks ONLINE LAB RESOURCES

Online you will find:

- An **interactive lab experience,** allowing you to put principles from this chapter into practice in a digital psychology lab environment. This chapter's lab will include an experiment allowing you to explore issues fundamental to stress and health.

- A **Skills Handbook** that includes a guide for using the scientific method, creating experiments, and analyzing data.
- A **Notebook** where you can complete your Psychology Journal and record and analyze data from your experiment.

Owen Franken/Corbis

netw⊙rks

There's More Online!

☑ **CARTOON** Stress Appraisals

☑ **GRAPHIC ORGANIZER**

☑ **TABLE** Types of Conflict Situations

☑ **SELF-CHECK QUIZ**

Reading HELPDESK

Academic Vocabulary

- **violate**
- **conduct**

Content Vocabulary

- **stress**
- **stressor**
- **stress reaction**
- **distress**
- **eustress**
- **conflict situation**

TAKING NOTES:

Key Ideas and Details

IDENTIFYING Use a graphic organizer like the one below to identify different conflict situations and provide an example of each situation.

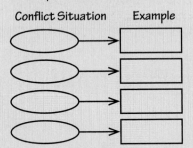

LESSON 1
Sources of Stress

ESSENTIAL QUESTION • How does stress influence behavior?

IT MATTERS BECAUSE

Stress can come in many forms in our daily lives. When situations do not go our way, unexpected things happen, or we have expectations placed on us that we are not sure we can live up to, we may feel stress. Stress is not only caused by major events. Minor irritations can also cause stress. Every day we have to make choices among different options that are presented to us, which can all create stress.

The Components of Stress

GUIDING QUESTION *What is the difference between primary and secondary appraisals?*

Brandon, an ambitious high school junior, fails his final exam in French; he is terrified that his chances of getting into college have been jeopardized, and a day or two later he develops an unsightly rash. Juanita, Brandon's classmate, learns that her parents cannot afford to pay her tuition for her first year of college; her friends wonder why she has suddenly become so bad-tempered. Angela gets her first leading role in a high school play; while running to call her boyfriend, she realizes that she cannot remember his phone number.

Brandon, Juanita, and Angela all have one thing in common: they are experiencing stress, which can have a variety of effects. When Brandon is terrified because of his failure, he experiences emotional stress. He also has a physical reaction when he develops the rash. Angela suddenly forgets her boyfriend's phone number because the stress, even though it is positive, has affected her thought processes.

What exactly is stress? Whether we defined it as stress or not it is something we all have experienced. There are many definitions, and even researchers in the field use the term in several ways. To some psychologists, stress is an *event* or *situation* that produces tension or worry. Others describe it as an individual's physical or psychological *response* to such an event or situation. Still other researchers regard stress as a person's *perception* of the event or situation. A slight variation on each of these ideas is the definition that will be used in this chapter. **Stress** is the anxious or threatening feeling resulting from our appraisal of a situation and our reaction to demands placed upon us.

(l)MBI/Alamy, (c)Lisette Le Bon/SuperStock, (r)moodboard/Corbis

To refer to the stress-producing event or situation, we shall use the term **stressor**. It is important to note that an event that is a stressor for one person may not be for another. For example, traveling in an airplane may be a stressor for someone who has never flown but not for a flight attendant. Stress, then, will be used to refer to a person's reactions—whether perceptual, cognitive, physical, or emotional—to a stressor. To discuss the body's observable response to a stressor, we shall use the term **stress reaction**.

Many people think of stress only as a condition to be avoided. Canadian researcher Hans Selye (1907–1982), however, distinguished between two different types of stress. Negative stress, or **distress**, stems from acute anxiety or pressure and can take a harsh toll on the mind and body. Positive stress, or **eustress**, results from the strivings and challenges that are the spice of life.

Stress is a normal, even essential, part of life that goes hand in hand with working toward any goal or facing any challenge. In fact, as athletes gearing up for a game or students cramming for an exam can testify, stress can spur us on to greater effectiveness and achievement in some situations. In addition, whether we like it or not, we cannot escape stress. "Complete freedom from stress," notes one psychologist, "is death." We can, however, learn to cope with stress so that it makes our lives interesting without overwhelming us.

There is another component of stress that can influence how it affects people's lives. Psychologist Richard Lazarus believed that how a person registers and evaluates an event is what makes the difference. In fact, Lazarus sometimes quoted Shakespeare: "For there is nothing either good or bad, but thinking makes it so." Lazarus was saying that it is our response to a situation, not the situation itself, that determines whether we will experience stress. This is called the cognitive model of stress. Stress, therefore, is not necessarily a result of how large or serious our problems are, but rather whether we think we are capable of handling them. For example, you may feel nervous and tense before taking an important exam. However, once you see the exam and realize you are well prepared, you relax. While you still may be under some stress, it has greatly lessened.

stress a person's reaction to his or her inability to cope with a certain tense event or situation

stressor a stress-producing event or situation

stress reaction the body's response to a stressor

distress stress that stems from acute anxiety or pressure

eustress positive stress, which results from motivating strivings and challenges

Most of us have experienced a headache, upset stomach, muscle tension, or sleeplessness as a result of feeling stressed.

▶ **CRITICAL THINKING**

Explaining What causes stress?

MBI/Alamy

Stress and Health **421**

Approach-Approach	Avoidance-Avoidance	Approach-Avoidance	Double Approach-Avoidance
You must choose between two attractive options.	You must choose between two disagreeable options.	You find yourself in a situation that has both enjoyable and disagreeable consequences.	You must choose between multiple options, each of which has pleasurable and disagreeable aspects.
Do I want to go to the concert or ballgame on Saturday?	Should I stay up all night studying for my physics final or math final?	Should I ask him to go to the party with me? (He may say yes, or he may say no.)	Should I wait for my girlfriend to call me, or should I just go out with my friends?

TABLE ⌃

TYPES OF CONFLICT SITUATIONS

Conflict situations cause stress because you must give up something you want to get or face something you wish to avoid.

▶ **CRITICAL THINKING**

1. *Contrasting* How is the double approach-avoidance conflict different from the approach-avoidance conflict?

2. *Analyzing* Why would an approach-approach conflict be just as difficult as an avoidance-avoidance conflict?

conflict situation when a person must choose between two or more options that tend to result from opposing motives

Conflict Situations

In our daily lives, we often have to evaluate situations and then make difficult decisions between two or more options—for example, going to a movie with friends or staying home to study for tomorrow's exam. These alternatives tend to result from conflicting motives—say, the desire to socialize versus the desire to do well in school—and they are major sources of stress. These choices create **conflict situations**, and they fall into four broad categories: *Approach-Approach, Avoidance-Avoidance, Approach-Avoidance, Double Approach-Avoidance.*

In an *approach-approach conflict,* the individual must choose between *two attractive alternatives.* For example, a high school senior has been accepted at two excellent colleges, and he must decide which one to attend. Such a "conflict" is generally easy to resolve. The student in this situation will find some reason to attend one college rather than the other—perhaps one college is located in a better climate or has more courses in his intended major field. An approach-approach conflict is a conflict in name only. It does not produce a great deal of stress because both choices are satisfying.

An *avoidance-avoidance conflict* occurs when an individual confronts *two unattractive alternatives.* Consider the case of a college graduate who is unable to find a job after many months of searching. She is finally offered a position that is not in her field of education, does not pay very well, and offers her no future. Should she accept the position, or should she continue to look for something better? Either course of action will be frustrating to her, and there is usually a high level of indecision and stress. The young woman in this example may decide that one option is the "lesser of two evils," or she may try to escape the decision—for instance, by registering with a temporary-employment agency until she finds a more satisfactory job.

An individual who wants to do something but has fears or doubts or is repulsed by it at the same time is experiencing an *approach-avoidance conflict.* For example, a man wants to ask for a raise, but he is afraid he will be fired if he does. In cases like this, the degree of stress depends on the intensity of the desire or of the perceived threat. Resolution of this type of conflict often is very difficult and depends generally on the person's finding added reasons to choose one alternative over the other. The man in this example may learn that his boss thinks his work has been excellent; therefore, he feels there is little risk of being fired if he asks for more money.

Probably the most common conflict situation is a *double approach-avoidance conflict* in which the individual must choose between *two or more alternatives, each of which has attractive and unattractive aspects.* To use a simple illustration, a young woman working in Chicago cannot decide whether to spend her vacation in Paris or at her parents' home in North Carolina. She has never been to Paris, but the airfare and hotel bills will be more than she can really afford. Visiting her parents will be inexpensive and relaxing but not very exciting. As in an approach-avoidance conflict, the degree of stress generated depends on the intensity of the attractions and repulsions.

Appraising a Situation

Why is it that some people view a situation, such as looking for a parking space, as stressful while others do not? The level of stress you feel depends on how you appraise the situation. There are two basic types of appraisals: primary and secondary.

Primary appraisal refers to our immediate evaluation of a situation. For instance, can we meet the demands of this situation? Does this situation present us with more challenges than we think we can handle? There are three ways you can appraise a situation—as irrelevant, positive, or negative. For example, if your teacher suddenly announces a pop quiz, you may feel okay about the situation. You think you know the material, and your teacher does not give difficult quizzes. You may look forward to pop quizzes and feel positive about the situation because you know the material on the quiz and are assured of a good grade. You may also evaluate the situation as a negative one—you have not looked at your notes in days. In this last example, you feel stressed.

Secondary appraisal occurs when we evaluate the different options for coping. In addition, we must consider our available resources. We then make a decision on how to deal with the potentially stressful situation. Secondary appraisals are slower and more deliberate than primary appraisals.

At this point, we may decide who should be held accountable for the situation. If the stress is negative, who should be blamed? If it is positive, who should be given the credit? In addition, we may see the situation as simply happening by chance. The way that we see who or what should be held accountable helps guide us in what emotions we should experience. For example, if we are involved in a minor car accident, our first reaction might be extreme stress. However, once it is clear the other driver is at fault, our stress will probably lessen. Another part of secondary appraisal is based on whether we expect the situation to change for the better or for the worse. This is referred to as future expectancy. Future expectancy influences what emotions we experience and the coping strategies we use. For example, if the other driver immediately admits that he or she is at fault, we will probably experience less stress than if he or she adamantly denies any responsibility.

✔ READING PROGRESS CHECK

Making Connections When appraising a situation in which you are late for school, what would you consider before deciding how stressed you feel about it?

∨ **CARTOON**

STRESS APPRAISALS

People appraise situations differently. Some see a particular situation as stressful while others handle it with relative ease.

▶ **CRITICAL THINKING**

1. *Analyzing Visuals* What is each teen's primary appraisal of the situation in the cartoon?

2. *Evaluating* What are the benefits of making a secondary appraisal of a situation?

Environmental Stressors

GUIDING QUESTION *How do life changes result in stressors?*

Environmental conditions such as noise may cause stress on the job, and these factors can have similar effects on the public at large. In fact, surveys have shown that Americans regard noise as one of the foremost irritants in their lives. Noise is particularly aggravating when it is loud, irregular, or uncontrollable. Constant exposure to unpleasant noise levels can lead to hearing loss and can interfere with learning. One study found that third and fourth graders in the flight path of a major airport showed significant increases in blood pressure and stress hormones, such as cortisol, compared to those who were not exposed to the noise. People exposed to excessive noise at work have reported more headaches, nausea, and moodiness than others.

Noise is not the only environmental stressor that tends to irritate people. Odors may also trigger stress in people. Studies have revealed that tobacco smoke odors and industrial odors such as factory smoke, industrial glues, and chemical smells can be an irritant to some subjects, although some people tend to cope with the stressors better than others. Stressors may also be triggered by temperature. Environments that are too hot or too cold increase demands on the body. Elevated humidity and lack of air movement can also have an effect on the body's ability to cope, increasing the level of psychological discomfort at the same time that physical discomfort grows.

Rank	Life Event	Mean Value	Rank	Life Event	Mean Value
1	Death of spouse	100	23	Son or daughter leaving home	29
2	Divorce	73	24	Trouble with in-laws	29
3	Marital separation	65	25	Outstanding personal achievement	28
4	Jail term	63	26	Spouse begins or stops work	26
5	Death of close family member	63	27	Begin or end school	26
6	Personal injury or illness	53	28	Change in living conditions	25
7	Marriage	50	29	Revision of personal habits	24
8	Fired at work	47	30	Trouble with boss	23
9	Marital reconciliation	45	31	Change in work hours or conditions	20
10	Retirement	45	32	Change in residence	20
11	Change in health of family member	44	33	Change in schools	20
12	Pregnancy	40	34	Change in recreation	19
13	Sex difficulties	39	35	Change in church activities	19
14	Gain of new family member	39	36	Change in social activities	18
15	Business readjustment	39	37	Mortgage or loans less than $10,000	17
16	Change in financial state	38	38	Change in sleeping habits	16
17	Death of close friend	37	39	Change in number of family get-togethers	15
18	Change to different line of work	36	40	Change in eating habits	15
19	Change in number of arguments with spouse	35	41	Vacation	14
20	Mortgage over $10,000	31	42	Christmas	12
21	Foreclosure of mortgage or loan	30	43	Minor violations of the law	12
22	Change in responsibilities at work	29			

It was long assumed that crowding was an environmental stressor. Indeed, most people dislike certain high-density situations and can feel stress when other people get too close. Studies on crowding have found a relationship between high-rise apartments with many crowded people and aggression. Crowding itself, however, is not the problem. The problems occur not when you are crowded but when you *feel* crowded. For instance, a crowded subway car could make one person feel crowded or even claustrophobic, while another person in the same subway car could fall asleep.

Some crowding situations bring about a similar reaction in most people. In a 1975 study psychologist Jonathan Freedman concluded that the effects of crowding depend on the situation. If the situation is pleasant, crowding makes people feel better; if the situation is unpleasant, crowding makes them feel worse. In other words, being packed together *intensifies* people's reactions, but it does not *create* them.

One situation in which crowding is of great concern is in prisons. Research shows that inmates in overcrowded prisons have higher levels of stress and that the rate of both violent and nonviolent deaths is higher there than in less crowded prisons. A long-term Japanese study showed a direct relationship among overcrowding, prisoners **violating** rules, and violent behavior. Overcrowding makes the job of the prison staff more difficult and puts them at greater risk for harm. The extreme loss of privacy is also a major factor in stress levels for the prisoners. For example, research shows that prisoners typically have less stress if they are in a private cell, even if this means that they have less physical space than in a larger shared cell.

violate to go against or refuse to obey a rule, law, or agreement

Life Changes and Stress

Our lives are full of major life changes and events such as marriage, divorce, a serious illness, a new job, moving away, and deaths in the family. All of these events are important sources of stress. Common to most of these events is the separation of an individual from familiar friends, relations, or colleagues. Positive events can bring about stress just as much as those that are negative. Marriage, while considered a positive change, may involve breaking free from many long-standing ties.

Many stress researchers have concentrated on these life changes to determine how much stress they are likely to cause. Two of the foremost researchers into the effect of life changes are Thomas H. Holmes and Richard H. Rahe, who developed a scale to measure the effects of 43 common events, ranging from the death of a spouse to going on a vacation. Holmes and Rahe asked a cross section of the population to rate each of these events on a scale of 1 to 100, with marriage assigned a value of 50, on the basis of how much adjustment the event required. The figures they obtained form the basis of their Social Readjustment Rating Scale (SRRS). Note that the SRRS was created in 1967 using male adults. Also note that one life change can trigger others, greatly increasing the level of stress.

Quick Lab

WHAT STRESSES TEENAGERS?

The SRRS lists events considered stressful for adults. Assume your job is to develop a similar scale for teenagers. In what ways would your scale be different?

Procedure

1. First, develop a list of life events that you deem stressful to teenagers and rank them from 1 to 20, with 20 being the most stressful. Assign each event a value based on how much adjustment the event requires.
2. Provide a copy of your list to several friends and ask them to circle the events that they have experienced in the past year.
3. Ask each person to indicate any illnesses they have had in the past year.

Analysis

1. For each person, add up the values for the events they have circled. Note the illnesses they recorded.
2. Does your rating scale show any relationship between stressful events that teenagers face and illnesses they experience? Explain.

---

conduct a person's behavior in a particular place or situation

Daily stressors such as minor arguments or dealing with financial problems are called hassles.

▶ **CRITICAL THINKING**

Making Connections Describe one hassle and one uplift you have experienced in the last week.

Marriage, for example, may be accompanied by a change in financial status, a change in living conditions, and a change in residence—collectively much more stressful than any one source listed on the scale.

Rahe administered this scale to thousands of naval officers and enlisted men and found that the higher a man's score, the more likely he was to become physically ill. Men with scores below 150 tended to remain healthy, while about 70 percent of those with scores over 300 became sick. There are problems, however. Some of the items on the SRRS may result from illness, rather than cause it. For example, for air traffic controllers, higher traffic volume and lower visual clarity lead to increased mood and health complaints. Several studies suggest there is only a small relationship between stressful life events and illness. The scale also fails to measure stress caused by ongoing situations such as racism, poverty, and ignored daily problems.

Since the SRRS scale was originally established, it has been revised and used to test the stress levels of women as well as men. One study rated the stress levels of female graduate students in an online graduate program. The study revealed that female graduate students have a considerable amount of stress related to their families and finances as well as their health and pressures to succeed. The study found significant stress levels in nearly all of the students, but revealed that demographic data also played a part. Female students with the highest stress levels were single, African American, and older. According to the study, family, social, and career pressures contributed to the need of the women to pursue a higher degree and to succeed in their efforts.

The scale has also been adapted to measure stress levels for students (teenagers and college-aged young adults). While stress levels in different groups of college students vary, research shows that most new students experience stress as a result of a number of factors. Being away from families and living in close quarters can be new experiences. Students may find the coursework more challenging than they anticipated. They often worry about money and some students must juggle a job along with their studies. Social activities may make it hard to get enough sleep. Meals may not be well balanced and may be eaten on the go. Students also must be responsible for their own **conduct**, such as attending classes and completing their homework or assignments without having their parents around to monitor them. As with many situations in life, it is the combination of many changes occurring at the same time that leads to stress.

426

(l)Lisette Le Bon/SuperStock, (r)/moodboard/Corbis

During day-to-day living, we encounter common stressors such as:	
• Household duties (cleaning, cooking, shopping) • Concerns about health • Time pressures (not enough time to get something done) • Environmental hassles (noise, pollution, crime)	• Financial hassles (paying bills, saving for the future) • Worries about our jobs • Concerns about our futures • Inner stressors (feelings of low self-esteem or loneliness)

Source: Lazarus et al, 1985.

Hassles

In addition to the impact that major stressful events such as a divorce or a death in the family can have, psychologists have studied the effects that relatively minor, day-to-day stressors have on health. These more common stressors are called *hassles*. Examples of hassles include losing your car keys, being caught in a crowded elevator, getting in a minor argument with someone in your family, or being late for work or school because you were stuck in traffic. Research has found a connection between these daily problems and health issues. It may be that these common stressors gradually weaken the body's defense system, making it harder to fight off potential health problems.

It has also been suggested that small, positive events, called *uplifts*, can protect against stress. Uplifts are things that make a person feel good, such as winning a tough chess match, going out to lunch with a good friend, or doing well on a semester exam. Some psychologists claim that uplifts can have the opposite effect of hassles; they can reduce stress and protect a person's health.

Every one of us faces many daily stresses—traffic, arguments, car trouble, and so on. The primary effects of stress might be caused by the impact of little things that just constantly seem to bother us. Seventy-five married couples recorded their everyday stressors, and it turned out that those with more of the common stressors had significantly more health problems, such as sore throats and headaches, which they experienced later.

☑ **READING PROGRESS CHECK**

Summarizing What effect can everyday stressors have on health problems?

LESSON 1 REVIEW

Reviewing Vocabulary
1. *Contrasting* What is the difference between eustress and distress? Should stress always be avoided? Explain.

Using Your Notes
2. *Applying* Use your notes to describe the different conflict situations. Provide an example of a double approach-avoidance conflict regarding school.

Answering the Guiding Questions
3. *Differentiating* What is the difference between a primary and secondary appraisal?

4. *Analyzing* How do life changes result in stressors?

Writing Activity
5. *Informative/Explanatory* Think of a time when you were bothered by environmental stressors such as noise, odor, heat, cold, or crowding. Write a short narrative that describes the stressors and the way that you coped with, or attempted to cope with, these stressors. Explain how the stressors affected you. Identify which, if any, of these stressors might have affected someone from another culture differently.

Reading **HELP**DESK (CCSS)

Academic Vocabulary

• **link**   • **exhibit**

Content Vocabulary

• social support

TAKING NOTES:
Craft and Structure

DESCRIBING Use a graphic organizer like the one below to identify and describe the stages of the general adaptation syndrome.

General Adaptation Syndrome

LESSON 2

Reactions to Stress

ESSENTIAL QUESTION • *How does stress influence behavior?*

IT MATTERS BECAUSE
People react differently to life's stressors. These reactions may be beneficial or harmful to the body and the mind. Sometimes people have trouble getting over life's difficulties. They may feel anger, anxiety, or fear. Knowing how to deal with stress can help people cope and react to stress in a more positive way.

Responding to Stress

GUIDING QUESTION *What is the fight-or-flight response?*

A person who encounters a stressor that is intense or prolonged will react to it. There are a wide variety of stress reactions, and their effects range from beneficial to harmful. For example, someone who does not do well in school may react in a negative way—acting out, pouting, or feeling bad. Eventually that person may find an academic subject in which to excel. Should this happen the person's reactions to stressors in school may have changed from negative to positive and the person will more likely succeed.

Many of the physiological responses to stress are inborn methods that probably evolved to cope with stress effectively. In addition, many responses to stress are automatic. Just as the body reacts to a cut by producing new tissue, it has methods to heal the wounds of stress—crying, for example.

Coping mechanisms that worked for our remote ancestors are not necessarily successful in our modern technological society. Human beings are often slow to give up anything that is well established. We are more likely to depend solely on these ancient stress responses than to make conscious attempts to modify them or adopt others that we now know are more appropriate to our modern lifestyle.

The ways in which different people react to stress vary considerably; each person's response is the product of many factors. Stress reactions may be physical, psychological, or behavioral, but these categories are not clear-cut. The human body is a *holistic*, or fully integrated, organism, and a negative effect in one area can affect others. Our physical well-being affects how we think and behave. For example, poor mental health can trigger physical illness or psychological illness. Research from the

Centers for Disease Control and Prevention (CDC) indicates that there is a strong correlation between mental and physical illnesses. For example, psychological disorders such as depression and anxiety are strongly associated with illnesses like cardiac disease, the common cold, and asthma. Chronic stress increases the likelihood of all these conditions.

Regardless of the stressor, the body reacts with immediate arousal. The adrenal glands are stimulated to produce: (a) hormones that increase the amount of blood sugar for extra energy; and (b) adrenaline, which causes rapid heartbeat and breathing and enables the body to use energy more quickly. These responses are designed to prepare a person for self-defense and are often called the *fight-or-flight response*. Wild animals experience the fight-or-flight response in reaction to attacks. This response is needed for survival. Although you do not need to fight wild animals, the fight-or-flight response prepares you in the same way to face potentially dangerous situations. However, if stress persists for a long time, the body's resources are used up. The person becomes exhausted and, in extreme cases, dies.

General Adaptation Syndrome

Hans Selye identified three stages in the body's stress reaction: alarm, resistance, and exhaustion. Selye called these short-term and long-term reactions to stressors the *general adaptation syndrome*. In the *alarm* stage, the body reacts to a stressor by mobilizing its fight-or-flight defenses. The heartbeat and breathing quicken, muscles tense, the pupils dilate, and hormones that sustain these reactions are secreted. The person becomes exceptionally alert and sensitive to stimuli in the environment and tries to keep a firm grip on his or her emotions. For example, a hiker who confronts a rattlesnake on a mountain trail freezes in his tracks, is suddenly aware of every sound around him, and tries not to panic. If the alarm reaction is insufficient to deal with the stressor, the person may develop symptoms such as anxiety.

When an animal senses possible danger, its nervous system directs great sources of blood to its muscles and brain, preparing the creature for rapid action. You react the same way.

▶ **CRITICAL THINKING**

Analyzing How is stress necessary for survival?

Imagine that you are excited about going to a friend's party, but when you walk into the house, you suddenly start to feel different. Your heart begins to race, you start to sweat, it becomes harder to breath, and your hands start to tingle. In short, you feel like you are "losing control." You could very well be experiencing a panic attack, a sudden feeling of terror or fear that can strike without warning. People who experience panic attacks may have such overwhelming feelings of panic that they believe they are having a heart attack, going crazy, or could even die.

While there is no real danger during a panic attack, the strong physical reactions are very real. Panic attacks are a type of anxiety disorder that affect approximately 3 percent of the adult U.S. population and around 2 percent of the teenage U.S. population. No one knows exactly why some people experience panic disorder while others do not. It could be related to a significant life event. However, it is known that panic disorder sometimes runs in families.

So what should you do if you experience a panic attack? First, in the moment of an attack, start by telling yourself to calm down and focus on breathing deeply. If the attacks persist, recognize that something is wrong and make an appointment to talk to a doctor about what you are experiencing. Depending on your symptoms, your doctor may prescribe psychotherapy, medication, or both to help you deal with the attacks.

In the *resistance* stage, the person often finds means to cope with the stressor and to ward off, superficially at least, adverse reactions. Blood pressure remains high and the body continues to secrete stress-fighting hormones. If this stress response continues, the body is thrown off-balance. The person is likely to have problems concentrating and may become irritable. Thus an isolated high-mountain hiker, caught off guard by a sudden blizzard, can use his knowledge of the mountains to shelter himself. When his food runs out, though, all of his activities gradually deplete his internal reserves. At this stage, the person may suffer psychosomatic symptoms, which result from strain that he pretends is nonexistent. Psychosomatic symptoms are real, physical symptoms that are caused by stress or tension.

If exposure to the stressor continues, the individual reaches the stage of *exhaustion*. At this point, the adrenal and other glands involved in the fight-or-flight response have been taxed to their limits and become unable to secrete hormones. The individual may reach the breaking point. He or she becomes exhausted and disoriented and may develop delusions—of persecution, for example—in an effort to retain some type of coping strategy. The military is aware of this type of exhaustion in soldiers who have been exposed to prolonged periods of combat. Both visual and auditory hallucinations can continue to occur, even longer after the individual has left the military.

The problem is that the very responses that were good for immediate resistance to stress, such as reducing digestion and boosting blood pressure, are detrimental in the long run. Some investigators have found that assembly-line workers in repetitive jobs over which they exercise very little control are likely to show the effects of stress. It is not surprising that the corporate executives running the company, who can control their own destiny to some degree, are less likely to show such stress. Farmers with high control over their work show very low susceptibility to chronic heart disease.

Emotional and Cognitive Responses

Short-term psychological stress reactions may be either emotional or cognitive. The most common response to a sudden and powerful stressor is anxiety, which is a feeling of an imminent but unclear threat. An employee whose boss passes by in the hall without saying hello may develop anxiety about her future on the job. Short-term feelings of extreme anxiety can occur if a person feels trapped in a situation he or she cannot control. For example, in medicine, magnetic resonance imaging (MRI) machines are used to obtain body images that aid in diagnosing medical conditions. The individual typically must lie quietly inside a metal chamber. In some people, this triggers feelings of claustrophobia, which is an irrational fear of being trapped in closed places. They panic and their blood pressure and heart rate spike dramatically. To counteract this situation, more open, less tube-like MRI equipment has been developed in recent years.

Another common reaction is anger, which is likely to result from frustration. A student who does not make the lacrosse team may fly into a rage over a completely unrelated, minor incident such as the sound failing in one of his MP3 player's earbuds. Fear is usually the reaction when a stressor involves real danger—a fire, for example. Fear directs the individual to withdraw or flee, but in severe cases he or she may panic and be unable to act. Common examples of short-term emotional stress reactions are overreacting to minor irritations, getting no joy from daily pleasures, and doubting one's own abilities, while feeling tense, short-tempered, and more anxious.

Cognitive reactions to stress include difficulty in concentrating or thinking clearly, recurring thoughts, confusion, and poor decision making. A student who must give an oral presentation may worry about the upcoming ordeal but find himself unable to prepare for it. A college student drives to her hometown to surprise her parents in person with the news that she has been admitted to graduate school, but when she gets to town, she cannot remember how to find the house she grew up in. Another type of cognitive stress reaction is unjustified suspicion or distrust of others.

Continued frustration can lead to burnout. People feel *burned out* when they feel they are incapable of doing their job well. They may feel physically worn out and emotionally exhausted from giving too much time or energy to a project while not receiving sufficient gratification. Prolonged stress, such as burnout, in combination with other factors, adversely affects mental health. It does not necessarily cause mental illness, but it may contribute to the severity of mental illness. There is an increased likelihood of developing a psychological disorder following a major life change, for example. Among those who attempt suicide and those with depression or anxiety-based disorders, there seems to be quite a definite **link** between stress and subsequent symptoms.

A psychological disorder called *post-traumatic stress disorder* is a condition in which a person who has experienced a traumatic event feels severe and long-lasting aftereffects. This disorder is common among veterans of military combat and survivors of acts of terrorism, natural disasters such as floods and tornadoes, other catastrophes such as plane crashes, and acts of human aggression such as rape and assault. The event that triggers the disorder overwhelms a person's normal sense of reality and ability to cope. The high stress levels associated with this disorder could result in a range of psychosomatic symptoms, such as insomnia, high blood pressure, chest pain, and stomach problems.

☑ **READING PROGRESS CHECK**

Summarizing How does the fight-or-flight response help people to deal with stressors in their lives?

Behavioral and Physical Reactions

GUIDING QUESTION *How does stress affect people physically?*

When we are under stress, our bodies respond in a variety of ways. Have you ever been under so much stress you were not able to sit still? Or alternately, maybe you slept more than usual just to avoid dealing with the situation. Both of these are examples of behavioral reactions. Our bodies also can have physical reactions to stress. If you have ever had an upset stomach before a big game or your performance in a play, you know about this kind of reaction. It is so common there is even an expression for it—having "butterflies" in your stomach.

Behavioral Reactions

There are many short-term behavioral changes that result from stress. A person may develop nervous habits (pacing, for example), gulp meals, or feel tired for no reason. That person may develop a shaky voice, tremors, strained expressions, or a hunched posture. He or she may temporarily lose interest in eating, grooming, and bathing. Some people react to stress by behaving aggressively toward their family members or strangers.

Some behavioral reactions are positive, however. During a natural disaster, some people will risk their lives to save or help others. Such stressors often create attitudes of cooperation that override individual differences and disagreements. During the stress of combat, well-trained soldiers can draw on the strength of their comrades to react in positive ways that can save the lives of both themselves and those around them.

Deepak Chopra
(1946–)

Dr. Deepak Chopra is a major figure in the trend of holistic healing. *Holistic healing* refers to the idea that a person's mind and body are not independent matters; they function together as a unit. Chopra blends Western medicine with the techniques of an ancient health care called Ayurveda. He believes that healing is a process that involves integrating the mind and the body, which is a basic idea behind Ayurveda.

Chopra argues that what we think and feel can actually change our biology. He believes that by finding an inner peace and by relieving the stress of living, we can become healthy in mind and body.

Chopra is a fellow of the American College of Physicians and a member of the American Association of Clinical Endocrinologists. He is a popular writer and adviser because he helps many people get past the problems of daily existence and find pleasure in life.

▶ **CRITICAL THINKING**

Finding the Main Idea What does Chopra believe about the healing process?

link a connection between two or more things

Although some people can endure great amounts of stress without marked behavioral responses, others cannot. Severe stress can lead to the development of escapist reactions and behaviors—alcoholism, drug addiction, chronic unemployment, and attempted suicide, for example. An inability to cope with stress can also contribute to aggressive personality formation, delinquency, and criminal behavior.

Research has shown that individuals who have greater coping skills are less likely to return to their negative behaviors in times of stress. For example, recovering alcoholics who experience psychological stress are likely to return to drinking. The more severe the person views the stress, the greater the likelihood drinking will start again. Individuals find it difficult to overcome a deep-seated coping strategy, even when it has severe negative consequences.

Physical Reactions

Why do daily hassles and major life changes sometimes make people ill? Your thoughts and emotions can produce physiological changes in your body. For example, some people develop *psychosomatic symptoms* as a result of stress. As mentioned earlier, psychosomatic symptoms are real, physical symptoms caused by stress or tension such as headaches, stomachaches, and muscle pains.

The physiological fight-or-flight response—accelerated heart rate and so on—is the body's immediate reaction to stress. This response, geared to prepare human beings to fight or run from an enemy such as a savage animal or band of warriors, was probably useful earlier in human history. We cannot deal with most modern stressors in this manner, and physical responses to stress are now generally inappropriate. In fact, prolonged physical arousal from almost any stress can cause health problems, including difficulty breathing, insomnia, migraines, urinary and bowel irregularities, muscle aches, sweating, and dryness of mouth.

Stress is certainly one cause of illness. We have already discussed the study that linked low scores on the Holmes-Rahe scale to reports of good health for the following year, while high scores were linked with illness in the following year. Emotional stress is related to such illnesses as peptic ulcers, hypertension, certain kinds of arthritis, asthma, and heart disease. Those who work in high-stress occupations may pay a high price. Air-traffic controllers, for example, juggle hundreds of lives where a minor error can mean mass death. They are said to suffer from the

Our reactions to various events depend on our personalities and on the severity of the event itself. The person who was in the car accident is facing a different level and kind of stress than someone who is waiting with a person coping with a terminal illness or waiting for a job interview.

▶ **CRITICAL THINKING**

Identifying Cause and Effect What happens during the resistance stage of stress?

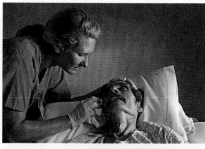

1.	You appraise a situation as physically or psychologically threatening.

2.	Your thoughts activate the hypothalamus (in the brain). The hypothalamus stimulates the pituitary gland to secrete ACTH (adrenocorticotopic hormone)—a stress-fighting hormone. The hypothalamus also activates the sympathetic division of the autonomic nervous system.

3.	The sympathetic nervous system stimulates a variety of physical responses to prepare the body for the stressful situation—this is the fight-or-flight response. (The parasympathetic nervous system later returns the body to its normal state.)

Fight-or-Flight Response:

- heart rate increases
- blood pressure increases
- respiration becomes rapid and shallow
- liver releases stores of glycogen, raising blood sugar level
- digestive system shuts down and blood reroutes to muscles
- pupils dilate
- hair stands up on end
- excitatory hormones are secreted (epinephrine and norepinephrine)
- muscles tense

< CHART

THE FIGHT-OR-FLIGHT RESPONSE

Our fight-or-flight response is triggered by potentially dangerous or stressful situations, such as a scare in the middle of the night or giving a speech in public. As soon as you feel threatened, your body prepares itself for action.

▶ CRITICAL THINKING

1. *Identifying Cause and Effect* Why do our pupils dilate during the fight-or-flight reaction? Why do our muscles tense?

2. *Analyzing Visuals* What part of your brain is activated when a situation is deemed to be physically or psychologically threatening?

highest incidence of peptic ulcers of any professional group. Further, air-traffic controllers at busy, high-stress airports have more ulcers than those at low-stress airports. Repeated instances of stress can weaken the body and its natural defenses, and as a result illness may follow.

Stress can be at least partly responsible for almost *any* disease, as shown by the scope of illness associated with high Holmes-Rahe scores. Stress can contribute to disease in several ways. Sometimes it can be the direct cause of illness. A migraine headache, for example, is usually a physical reaction to stress. Stress may also contribute indirectly to illness. It reduces our resistance to infectious disease by weakening the immune defense system. The immune system is your body's natural defense system against infection, and a gradual weakening of it through stress can have drastic consequences.

Consider a cold you may have caught right in the middle of final exams week. Why did this happen? When you experience stressful situations for a long period of time, it decreases your immune system's ability to cope. Your body is constantly exposed to millions of pathogens (disease-causing bacteria or viruses). When these pathogens enter your body, they attack your cells and use them to grow and multiply. The end result is an infection. Most of the time your body manages to stay free of infection because of the immune system. However, recall the third stage of Selye's general adaptation syndrome—exhaustion. When your body is continually involved in the fight-or-flight response, you become exhausted, and the immune system is suppressed. Your body becomes more susceptible to the diseases and infections caused by the pathogens that continually assault it.

☑ READING PROGRESS CHECK

Summarizing How can stress affect the body's behavior?

Factors Influencing Reactions to Stress

GUIDING QUESTION *How do different personality types respond to stressors differently?*

Imagine two assistant managers who work at two different stores. Both of the existing store managers suddenly leave their jobs and the assistant managers, both equally trained, unexpectedly find themselves promoted to store managers. The first one, Serena, sees this as the opportunity of a lifetime. She is optimistic she will succeed, has been well trained, and feels she has the support of the store's employees. She looks forward to this new challenge. The second one, Jared, feels pressured to prove himself. He is pessimistic because he does not believe that he has had enough training or experience. Jared is afraid the employees will compare him unfavorably with their previous manager. He thinks that he will fail publicly in this new challenge. Both Serena and Jared are confronted with similar stresses but have entirely different reactions. People's reactions to stress vary considerably. These reactions help people meet challenges in life, but they may also determine the type of stress one feels.

Personality Differences

exhibit to demonstrate or show clearly

In some cases, an individual's personality may make him or her more vulnerable to stress. Some psychologists have suggested that people who **exhibit** a behavior pattern they call Type A are very likely to have coronary artery disease, often followed by heart attacks, in their thirties and forties. According to one study, those who do not have this pattern (Type B people) almost never have heart attacks before the age of 70.

Whereas Type B people are generally relaxed, patient, and do not become angry easily, the Type A person's body is in a chronic state of stress with an almost constant flow of adrenaline into the bloodstream. This adrenaline apparently interacts with cholesterol or other chemical agents to block the coronary arteries that lead to the heart. It may be that high levels of adrenaline prevent the normal chemical breakdown of cholesterol in the blood.

Type A people are always prepared for fight or flight. They have a great deal of free-floating hostility, or anger that has no real focus. They are extremely irritable, and one thing that irritates Type A people the most is delay of any kind. They become impatient waiting in line, tend to move and eat rapidly, often try to do two or three things at once (such as reading while eating), and feel guilty when they are not actively doing something. They are also extremely competitive. In short, Type A people are always struggling—with time, other people, or both. Note that this describes an extreme version of the Type A personality. Most people respond to the world with Type A behavior at different times, but they are not in a constant state of stress. It is important to note that psychologists disagree about both the definition of Type A personality and its relation to heart disease.

In the 1950s two cardiologists, Dr. Meyer Friedman and Dr. Ray H. Rosenman, first came up with the concept of a Type A personality. They also studied how this personality type might be linked to an increased risk of coronary heart disease. At that time Freidman and Rosenman found themselves spending a great deal of money reupholstering chairs in their office waiting room. It turned out the upholstery on the front of the chairs was being worn out and literally "torn to shreds." When the upholsterer examined the chairs, he said he had never before seen this kind of damage. Chairs in the waiting rooms of other physicians, such as podiatrists and urologists, did not get destroyed like this—only the cardiologists. They discovered that the patients were sitting on the edges of their chairs, "fidgeting and clawing away." Friedman originally ignored what the upholsterer had pointed out, but four years later, when he was conducting research on the causes of heart disease, he remembered what the upholsterer had said. At that point Dr. Friedman began to recognize the link between the inability of this group of people to relax and their increased risk of coronary artery disease. From this experience, Doctors Friedman and Rosenman first proposed the concept of the Type A personality.

Another personality trait that can affect the strength of a stress reaction is emotional expressiveness. Some research suggests that people who neither express nor admit to strong feelings of despair, depression, and anger are more likely to develop cancer than those who can give vent to their emotions. Some investigators have proposed a cancer-prone behavior pattern. People who deny their negative emotions tend to express feelings less freely, show a high tendency toward social conformity, and have a greater risk of getting cancer. Negative life events, such as those measured by the Social Readjustment Rating Scale, do seem to be related to an increased likelihood of cancer in later life.

Some people react to stress by continually dwelling on negative feelings or repeatedly telling themselves "I feel terrible" or "I never do anything right." In the field of psychology, constant dwelling on such thoughts is called *rumination*. Psychology professor Susan Nolen-Hoeksema has conducted research on rumination that shows people who ruminate have a higher than normal incidence of depression and anxiety disorders. For example, one of Nolen-Hoeksema's studies showed that in people who had lost a loved one, those who reported dwelling on the loss had more symptoms of depression than those who did not.

Spirituality

Studies have shown that people with strong spiritual beliefs often have less stress than others. Spirituality can be defined in many ways. Some people think it means believing in a power greater than themselves. Some find comfort in religious observance, prayer, or meditation. Others think it refers to having a sense of purpose in life, an idea that life has meaning. Releasing responsibility for uncontrollable events in life is a great stress reliever. Recognizing that there is more to life than just the here and now relieves stress in some people.

Psychology & YOU

Road Rage

You may have witnessed road rage, or the inability to handle frustrations while driving. Road rage involves a desire to retaliate and punish another driver. It may result in criminal behavior, such as violence or threatened violence. Some psychological studies have shown that road rage reflects a driver's anger and lack of self-control. In one six-year period, at least 218 people were killed and 12,610 injured as a result of road rage.

What should you do to avoid road rage?

• Do not retaliate against another driver.

• Before reacting, consider if this episode is worth risking your life.

• Be polite and courteous, even when others are not.

• If you are harassed and followed by another driver, go to the nearest police station.

• Slow down, be calm, and drive safely.

Who has higher stress levels—men or women? Women in the United States are more likely than men to live in poverty, to experience discrimination, and to be sexually or physically abused. Also, some psychologists argue that the traditional roles of women as primary caretakers and wives place them in positions in which anxiety and depression are more likely. For example, mothers are often made to feel responsible for events they have little control over, such as the illness of a child. Taking a job outside the home often reduces psychological stress for women. Studies show that the stress and anxiety experienced by the different genders is more equalized when women take jobs outside the home.

Another way spiritual beliefs reduce stress is by decreasing negative behaviors. The Seventh Day Adventists, for example, are not supposed to smoke tobacco or drink alcohol. Research has shown that Seventh Day Adventist men in the Netherlands live 8.9 years longer than the national average. Many spiritual disciplines encourage forgiveness, which can help people to live in the present and not dwell on past hurts. In addition, religious groups often provide strong social support. For example, they may help families going through serious health problems by providing transportation to doctors' appointments, meals, counseling, or child care. Religious leaders may offer counseling from a spiritual perspective to people experiencing stress over various life changes such as divorce or death. These varied factors show how spirituality can reduce stress and improve a person's overall health.

Perceived Control Over Stressors

The accepted view today is that physical disorders are more likely when we do not have control over stressors. Most evidence to support this theory comes from experiments on animals. J.M. Weiss, for example, gave two groups of rats identical electric shocks. In one group, a rat could avoid the shock by touching its nose to a panel, while the other group had no control over the shocks. The group that could regulate the shocks developed far fewer ulcers than those that could not. Subsequent experiments showed that feedback is also an important factor. Animals that responded to avoid shock and then heard a tone to signal that they had done the right thing suffered fewer ulcers than those that responded to avoid the shock but were given no feedback. Weiss found that lack of feedback could harm human beings as well. His research showed that people develop ulcers when they have to make large numbers of responses but receive no feedback about their effectiveness.

So, in general, people prefer to have predictable stress over unpredictable stress. For example, when you know that a teacher has certain preferences in grading an essay, it makes writing the paper a little easier. If you do not have any idea how the teacher plans to grade the essay, the writing is much harder. In one study, psychologists exposed people to predictable and unpredictable noise, concluding that people may prefer predictable noise because it allows them to prepare and thus cope better.

We previously discussed that many people feel stressed when they are having magnetic resonance imaging (MRI) tests. To a large degree, this stress is caused by a feeling of a loss of control—the patients feel that they are "trapped" inside the MRI machine. To help deal with this stress, the patients may be given a "panic" button. This helps many people relax because they are empowered with the knowledge that if they press the button, they will be removed immediately from the machine, thereby regaining control. Our physical and psychological well-being is profoundly influenced by the degree to which we feel a sense of control over our lives.

There are different methods that we can use to control stress. One way is behavioral control. For example, if you find a certain person annoying, you might avoid being around that individual. A second method is cognitive control—if you cannot change the situation, you can at least change your way of thinking about it. Imagine that you go to your garage only to discover your car tire is flat. You can be annoyed and start feeling stressed or you can think of this as an opportunity to learn how to fix a flat tire. Another method of controlling stress is emotional control. Perhaps you did poorly on a test. Avoiding stress by refusing to dwell on this incident shows emotional control. For most people, emotional control is probably the most difficult method of controlling stress, but we can get better at it with practice.

Social Support and Treatment

Much research has pointed to the importance of social support in helping people work to decrease the effects of stressful situations. Social support and a social support network can buffer an individual from the effects of stress and help them cope. Family, friends, colleagues, coworkers, therapeutic groups, or organizations can be instrumental in providing an overly stressed individual with a caring, stress-reducing support network.

One researcher named Sidney Cobb has defined **social support** as information that leads someone to believe that he or she is cared for, loved, respected, and part of a network of communication and mutual obligation. He has found that social support can reduce both the likelihood and the severity of stress-related diseases—a finding often replicated. Social support benefits have been documented for cancer, crowding, military combat, natural disasters, and AIDS.

Social groups seem to offer at least four kinds of support. First, *emotional* support involves concerned listening, which forms a basis for offering affection and concern and bolstering the stressed person's self-confidence. Second, *appraisal* support is interactive. The listener feeds back information and probing questions to the stressed person as an aid in sorting out, understanding, and planning to deal with the sources of the stress. *Informational* support emerges from appraisal support. Here the stressed person responds to what he or she has learned and evaluates the manner in which he or she is dealing with stressors. Finally, *instrumental* support represents active, positive support in the form of direct help such as money or living quarters.

Yet there is evidence that some friends, despite the best intentions, may be more of a strain than a help in a crisis. Some may prove to be sources of pessimism or discord. Some sources of social support, however, can be especially helpful. Studies of male blue-collar workers have reported that social support from wives and supervisors counteracted the health consequences of stress more effectively than did support from coworkers, friends, or relatives.

social support information that leads someone to believe that he or she is cared for, loved, respected, and part of a network of communication and mutual obligation

☑ **READING PROGRESS CHECK**

Inferring How might someone with a Type A personality perceive stressors differently from other people?

LESSON 2 REVIEW

Reviewing Vocabulary
1. *Explaining* How does social support reduce stress?

Using Your Notes
2. *Sequencing* Use your notes to describe the steps that an individual's body goes through at each stage of the general adaptation syndrome.

Answering the Guiding Questions
3. *Identifying* What is the fight-or-flight response?

4. *Summarizing* How does stress affect people physically?

5. *Explaining* How do different personality types respond to stressors differently?

Writing Activity
6. *Informative/Explanatory* Measure a friend's heart rate. Then have the person think of a scary situation. Did their heart rate increase? Choose another person and measure their heart rate. Have the person think of a peaceful, calming situation. Did their heart rate decrease? Write a summary of your findings.

Reader's Dictionary ⒸⒸⓈⓈ

attuned: to be aware of or receptive to

perceive: to regard as being such

gerontology: the study of aging

kinesiology: the study of the mechanics of body movements

inoculation: precaution, as in a vaccination

In our busy world with its high expectations and focus on multitasking, it's not difficult to imagine why stress is on the rise. However, the amount of stress and the way we deal with it may depend on our gender; men report and handle stress differently than women. Researchers are finding that such differences may have implications for both mental and physical health.

Stress
Divides the Genders

By Sharon Jayson

PRIMARY SOURCE

Stressed women know it, live it and spend time trying to do something about it. Stressed men, not so much. That may well be the perception—that women are more aware of feelings than men—and in the wake of new survey results released this week, numbers support the stereotype.

The American Psychological Association's annual Stress in America survey finds that women historically have reported higher levels of stress than men and did so again in 2011. Over the past year, on a 1-10 scale of little-to-no stress to a great deal of stress, women report stress at a level of 5.4 and men at 4.8. But the gender divide is more pronounced when it comes to dealing with the stress or even wanting to own up to it.

"I honestly think women are more **attuned** to it," says Pat Chang, 66, of Indianapolis, who was among those surveyed. "I don't think they really feel it more, but men bottle things up more and are less likely to express their real feelings."

Stress happens when people **perceive** that the demands they face—work, school or relationships—exceed their ability to cope, say experts with the psychological association. At times, some stress can be beneficial because it produces a boost that can fuel the drive and energy to get through tough situations, such as exams or work deadlines.

But an extreme amount of stress can be harmful to health. In addition to the emotional toll, untreated chronic stress can result in anxiety, insomnia, muscle pain, high blood pressure and a weakened immune system. Research shows that stress can contribute to the development of major illnesses, such as heart disease, depression and obesity.

Men report being less concerned about managing stress and are more likely to say they are doing enough about it, while women think it's more important to manage stress and believe they aren't doing a good job of it, the survey finds.

"Men don't place as much value on stress management as women. They don't feel it impacts their health as much as women," says clinical psychologist Norman Anderson, the APA's chief executive officer. "Consequently, they're not doing the things to help them manage it as well."

"We know from many, many studies that social support is very, very beneficial for health, cardiovascular health and longevity," says Mara Mather, a professor of **gerontology** and psychology at the University of

Southern California in Los Angeles who studies stress and health. "It could be that under stress, women engage in strategies that are more beneficial for health than men do."

"Stressed women know it, live it and spend time trying to do something about it. Stressed men, not so much."

Anderson says women have been found to be more comfortable reporting stress. But he also says it's possible that women just have more stress in their lives. "In terms of certain societal issues—gender discrimination, sexual abuse, traumas—women experience them to a greater degree," he says. "It may be true women are experiencing more stressful events and more of the things that lead to stress."

More women than men use stress-busting strategies such as reading, exercising or being with friends and family.

Exercise is a stress reducer, says John Bartholomew, a professor of **kinesiology** and health education at the University of Texas-Austin. "The data are quite clear that almost any type of exercise will be sufficient to reduce feelings of anxiety and tension," he says. "Every form of physical activity has been demonstrated to produce a reduction in feelings of anxiety and negative moods."

What's new is that his research has found exercise also can reduce future stress. "The data suggest that people who exercise in the morning, for example, will have less of an increase in blood pressure and less of a feeling of stress if they are in a traffic jam on their way to work," Bartholomew says.

But to get what he calls an "**inoculation** effect" for later stress, the activity has to be either "high-intensity" or "long-duration," such as a hard run for 20 minutes or a 45-minute walk. That, he says, will have an effect for up to two hours.

His research also finds that "people who are dedicated exercisers exercise more under stress and those who are more infrequent exercisers exercise even less when they're experiencing stress."

Chang says she walks three times a week, does volunteer work and tries to focus on the positive. Her hobbies include photography, weaving and gardening. "I'm out in the yard even in the winter," she says.

Despite the gender differences in stress management, the survey found that both sexes report being generally satisfied with their lives and almost equal levels of life satisfaction. They also report similar concern over their financial outlook; only 45% of men and 44% of women say they're satisfied with their financial security.

Howard Hemsley, 73, who also took the survey, says he hasn't saved enough for retirement. "The reason I'm driving a cab is because I was unable to find employment after having been laid off almost three years ago."

Hemsley, a former legal word processor at a law firm, drives 12-hour shifts in Manhattan. He tries to think positively to cope with stress. "I listen to music and read," he says. "Before I started driving, I went to the gym two or three times a week, but I had to cancel the gym membership."

Despite the stress, Chang says, people just have to "keep going. Some things we can help, and some we can't."

Analyzing Primary Sources

1. *Identifying Central Issues* What are some possible reasons for the higher reporting of stress in women?

2. *Identifying Cause and Effect* Why might men experience more stress-related illnesses than women?

3. *Analyzing* What correlations have researchers found between stress and exercise? Explain your answer.

netw⊙rks

There's More Online!

☑ **GRAPHIC ORGANIZER**

☑ **TABLE** Types of Coping Strategies

☑ **SELF-CHECK QUIZ**

Reading **HELP**DESK

Academic Vocabulary

• thereby • device

Content Vocabulary

• cognitive appraisal
• intellectualization
• progressive relaxation
• biofeedback

TAKING NOTES:

Integration of Knowledge and Ideas

IDENTIFYING Use a graphic organizer like the one below to list active coping strategies for dealing with stress.

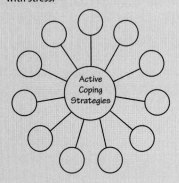

Active Coping Strategies

440

LESSON 3

Coping with Stress

ESSENTIAL QUESTION • *How does stress influence behavior?*

IT MATTERS BECAUSE

One person may view going away to college as a scary and stressful situation, while another may view it as an exciting opportunity that will be a lot of fun. While going to college is a life stressor for both individuals, they are each coping with the stress in a different way. People cope with the stresses in their lives by employing defensive or active coping strategies.

Defensive Coping Strategies

GUIDING QUESTION *How do defensive coping strategies fail to deal with legitimate stressors?*

Stress can smother your enjoyment of life and make you miserable. If you focus on the positive, however—the delightful blooming roses in a garden—the weeds that are also there need not be a source of stress but instead may be merely obstacles to overcome. Coping with stress is an attempt to gain control over a part of one's life. It is an attempt to master, control, reduce, and tolerate the stressors in one's life. People cope with stress in many ways. There is not just one way that is best for all people in all situations. People also have individualized coping styles. People know what works best for them. They have come to rely on what has worked in the past. What is your way of handling difficult situations?

Before beginning to cope with a stressful situation, we must first appraise it. As we discussed in Lesson 1, there are two basic appraisal methods: primary appraisal and secondary appraisal. Primary appraisal involves immediately assessing the situation. This assessment process includes determining whether we have the ability and necessary resources to meet the stressful situation. We also appraise the situation as being irrelevant, positive, or negative. Secondary appraisal comes later and is when we decide on the exact coping strategies to use. Secondary appraisal is slower and requires more thought than primary appraisal. Both of these appraisal methods work together to help us respond to stress.

Coping strategies may not always be healthy ways to adapt. Sometimes when we are under stress, we act in ways that are not in our best interests. There are methods that people use that hurt or harm others. These are known as dysfunctional ways of coping.

(l)Andersen Ross/Digital Vision/Getty Images, (r)Purestock/SuperStock

Our interpretation or evaluation of an event—a process psychologists call **cognitive appraisal**—helps determine its stress impact. For example, suppose you have a huge exam scheduled for next week. The way you appraise—or evaluate—the situation will determine the level of stress you feel. If you appraise the situation as a challenge that you can meet, you have positive feelings and your stress level is reduced. If you think of the situation as a threat, however, your negative feelings will increase your stress level. Drugs can affect cognitive appraisal. For example, drinking may help convince a man who has been fired that his troubles are not serious or that he will enjoy unemployment or that getting drunk is the best solution for the time being.

We can also try to influence our cognitive appraisals by means of defensive coping strategies, and stress reactions are more likely to occur when these strategies fail. Common defense mechanisms are denial, in which a person decides that the event is not really a stressor, and **intellectualization**, in which the person watches and analyzes the situation from an emotionally detached standpoint.

Both denial and intellectualization can prevent physical reactions to stress. In one study, three groups of participants viewed a film that showed gruesome accidents at a sawmill. One group was told that the injuries were not real but were staged by the actors (denial). A second group was advised that they were seeing an educational film about the importance of safety measures (intellectualization). The third group was told nothing. The levels of physical reaction were lower in the first two groups than in the third. Thus, if a person does not evaluate an event or situation as stressful, a stress reaction will not occur. Yet that is really failing to deal with what could be a legitimate stressor.

cognitive appraisal
the interpretation of an event that helps determine its stress impact

intellectualization a coping mechanism in which the person analyzes a situation from an emotionally detached viewpoint

✓ **READING PROGRESS CHECK**

Contrasting How is a defensive coping strategy different from an active coping strategy?

Connecting Psychology to Economics

MONEY AND STRESS

Are you a big spender, or are you a saver? Each person's individual values and beliefs influence his or her economic decisions. That means that even people with the means to buy things they want may not do so because of the pressures and stressors of money. People need money to plan for their future and to pay bills such as rent, mortgage, car payments, heat, electricity, phone service, food, and countless other expenses. Many people fear that they may not be able to meet these financial demands and that they will put their families or themselves at risk. To cope with these fears and to help them meet their financial goals, many people create budgets to help them organize their finances and live within their means. Overspending can be a large source of stress for many families. Creating and following a budget is a positive, healthy way to cope with those stresses. The economic stresses that families face make it easy to understand why getting a new job or losing a job is also a significant life stressor.

▶ **CRITICAL THINKING**

1. Evaluating How can buying a new home become a stressor on a family?

2. Analyzing How can a budget provide a way to manage stress?

▲ Paying bills is a stressor for almost everyone.

Active Coping Strategies

GUIDING QUESTION *How do active coping strategies work to moderate levels of stress?*

The attitude we have when we encounter a stressful situation makes a great deal of difference in our ability to cope with it. By appraising a situation as a challenge and not a threat, we can adopt an active coping strategy for dealing with stress and approach the situation in an upbeat, hands-on fashion. Active coping strategies involve changing our environment or modifying a situation to remove stressors or reduce the level of stress. With practice, we learn which strategies work best in specific situations. Often it is the most effective to use a combination of coping strategies.

Mental Strategies

Mental strategies entail using our intellectual capabilities to handle stressful situations. For example, you might find it stressful to be required to give a speech in history class on the same day that you must take an American literature exam. To cope with this stress, you ask your history teacher if you can change your speech to a different day. You have used problem solving, a type of mental strategy, to resolve the stress.

Hardiness Some people acquire personality traits that are, in effect, active coping strategies. *Hardiness* refers to the combined personality traits of control, commitment, and challenge that help us reduce the stress that we feel. *Control* involves feeling that we have the ability to affect the outcome of the situation. *Commitment* refers to establishing and pursuing our goals, while *challenge* means that we actively confront and solve problems instead of feeling threatened and powerless because of them. For instance, you may demonstrate hardiness if, when you are confronted with the assignment of giving a speech in public, you approach the assignment as a positive experience (challenge), believe that you can prepare and give a good speech (control), and then prepare for and practice your speech before delivering it in public (commitment).

TABLE >

TYPES OF COPING STRATEGIES
The two major ways that people deal with stress are by either focusing on it and trying to reduce it or ignoring the stress completely.

▶ CRITICAL THINKING

1. *Interpreting* Which of the strategies listed here involve an active attempt to reduce stress?

2. *Synthesizing* Why might an individual use behavioral disengagement as a coping strategy?

Coping Strategy	Example
Active coping	I take additional action to try to get rid of the problem.
Planning	I come up with a strategy about what to do.
Suppression of competing activities	I put aside other activities to concentrate on this.
Restraint coping	I force myself to wait for the right time to do something.
Seeking social support	I talk to someone about how I feel.
Positive reinterpretation and growth	I look for the good in what is happening.
Acceptance	I learn to live with it.
Turning to religion	I seek spiritual help.
Venting of emotions	I get upset and let my emotions out.
Denial	I refuse to believe that it has happened.
Behavioral disengagement	I give up the attempt to get what I want.
Mental disengagement	I turn to work or other substitute activities to take my mind off things.
Alcohol-drug disengagement	I drink alcohol or take drugs to think about it less.

Controlling Stressful Situations There are several ways in which we can control our exposure to stressful events and **thereby** reduce the levels of stress we are experiencing. As noted earlier, escape or withdrawal, when possible, can be an effective coping strategy. A young woman who is not enjoying herself at a party, for example, can leave. When avoiding an event is not practical, controlling its timing may be helpful; you can try to space out stress-producing events. A couple who is planning to have a baby in the summer, for instance, may postpone looking for a new house.

Problem Solving Sometimes neither avoiding nor spacing events is possible. A high school senior may face a deadline for a college application and an important exam on the same day. In cases like this, problem solving or confronting the matter head-on can be the best way to cope. Regarding frustrations or conflicts as problems to be solved means the situation becomes a positive challenge rather than a negative setback. Problem solving involves a rational analysis of the situation that will lead to an appropriate decision. The student in our example may map out the remaining days and allocate specific times to work on the application and other times to study for the test. He may also decide that he can gain more time for these activities by skipping band practice or postponing a date. Problem solving is a very healthy strategy that tends to develop flexibility and to sharpen insights and attention to detail.

Explanatory Style Martin Seligman describes two very different styles of thinking. The *optimist* typically puts the best face on any set of events. Following a loss, an optimistic quarterback will suggest, "What's done is done. Start thinking about next week!" The *pessimist* always sees the dark side. After becoming ill and missing the senior prom, the pessimist will say, "This always happens to me! I never get to. . . ." Seligman studied baseball players, grouping them as optimists or pessimists from their quotes in the sports pages. He found that the optimists were much more likely to live longer.

Humor Stress management experts often advise clients to try to maintain a sense of humor during difficult situations. Laughing actually releases the tension of pent-up feelings and can help you keep a proper perspective of the situation. In fact, people often resort to humor in very stressful situations. For example, a person may break out in hysterical laughter during the trying times following the death of a loved one. This laughter helps the individual deal with the intense emotional pain of a loss.

Physical and Social Strategies

Physical and social strategies use techniques such as mediation and outside resources, such as crisis prevention centers, to help in coping. If you listen to music to relax after a hectic afternoon at your part-time job, you are using a physical coping strategy. When you talk with your guidance counselor about a stressful situation at school, you are using professional help, which is a social strategy.

Relaxation Many techniques of relaxation have been developed especially to cope with stress. More than half a century ago, Dr. Edmond Jacobson devised a method called **progressive relaxation** to reduce muscle tension. This involves lying down and then tensing and relaxing each major muscle group in turn. Jacobson later added mental relaxation exercises in which a person conjures up images and then lets them go. This is known as meditation and is a relaxation technique that has been shown to counteract both physical and psychological responses to stress. Those with a large amount of experience in meditation quickly reach an alpha-wave mental state related to that of Stage I sleep and are able to resume their activities feeling refreshed.

thereby by or as a result of the situation or action mentioned

progressive relaxation lying down comfortably and tensing and releasing the tension in each major muscle group in turn

biofeedback the process of learning to control bodily states by monitoring the states to be controlled

device something made or adapted for a particular purpose

Biofeedback As explained in a previous chapter, **biofeedback** is a technique for bringing specific body processes, such as blood pressure and muscle tension, under a person's conscious control. The participant is hooked up to an electronic **device** that measures the process he or she wants to regulate and plays that process back in the form of either sounds or visual patterns. This feedback enables many, although not all, people to learn to control various bodily responses. Biofeedback has been used most successfully to train tense people to relax and can be used to manage pain.

Exercise Physical exercise is another constructive way to reduce stress. It stimulates and provides an outlet for physical arousal, and it may burn off stress hormones. Rigorous exercise also increases production of the neurotransmitters called endorphins that bring a sense of power and strength. Continuous rhythmic exercise—running or swimming, for example—is not only effective against stress but also ideal for respiratory and cardiovascular fitness. David Holmes and colleagues have performed experiments that indicate aerobic exercise reduces cardiovascular response and arousal following both stressful life events and immediate stress.

Support Groups and Professional Help We have discussed the positive role that social support plays in reducing stress. Groups that operate beyond ordinary personal networks, including Alcoholics Anonymous, Weight Watchers, and crisis prevention centers, can help people with specific stress-related problems. Professionals such as psychologists, doctors, social workers, and ministers can also be consulted.

Training A new, unfamiliar, or dangerous situation can be stressful because we are unsure we can deal with it. Training to prepare for such a situation can ease the stress. For instance, a person who is nervous about going to hit balls at the batting cages with friends who are excellent hitters might practice first. Exposure to moderate stressors in a relatively safe but challenging environment allows a person to gain experience and confidence in coping.

TABLE ›

IRRATIONAL ASSUMPTIONS THAT CAN CAUSE STRESS
Some people hold self-defeating, irrational beliefs that cause stress and prevent them from adequately adjusting to life's challenges.

▶ **CRITICAL THINKING**

1. **Evaluating** How might recognizing your irrational assumptions help you better cope with stress?

2. **Speculating** How might irrational assumptions prevent people from doing what they want in life?

Irrational Assumptions	Constructive Alternative
1. Everyone must approve of what I do.	I should concentrate on my own self-respect.
2. I must do everything to perfection.	I am imperfect; I have limitations, and that's okay.
3. Things must be the way I want them to be.	There are some situations that I cannot control. It's better to concentrate on matters that I can control.
4. Unhappiness is inevitable.	Unhappiness is the result of how I look at things.
5. I need someone stronger than I am to rely on.	I must rely on myself and act independently when necessary.
6. The world should be fair and just.	Although I can try to be fair and just in my behavior, sometimes the world is not fair.
7. I should worry about dangerous and fearsome things.	I realize that I can face what I consider fearful and try to render it nondangerous.
8. There's always a perfect solution out there that I should find.	Life is filled with probability and chance. I can enjoy life even though sometimes no perfect solution to a problem exists.
9. I should not question authority or social beliefs.	It's better to evaluate situations and beliefs for myself.
10. It's better to avoid difficult and stressful situations.	There is no "easy way out"; I need to face my problems and work on solutions.

Source: Ellis, 1986

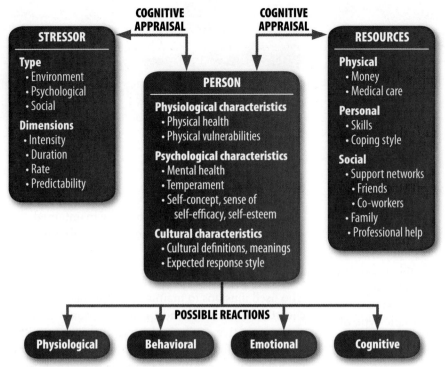

STRESSOR

Type
- Environment
- Psychological
- Social

Dimensions
- Intensity
- Duration
- Rate
- Predictability

COGNITIVE APPRAISAL

PERSON

Physiological characteristics
- Physical health
- Physical vulnerabilities

Psychological characteristics
- Mental health
- Temperament
- Self-concept, sense of self-efficacy, self-esteem

Cultural characteristics
- Cultural definitions, meanings
- Expected response style

COGNITIVE APPRAISAL

RESOURCES

Physical
- Money
- Medical care

Personal
- Skills
- Coping style

Social
- Support networks
  - Friends
  - Co-workers
- Family
- Professional help

POSSIBLE REACTIONS

Physiological | Behavioral | Emotional | Cognitive

Source: Adapted from Gerrig and Zimbardo, 2005

Improving Interpersonal Skills Much of the stress we undergo results from interpersonal relationships. Developing skills in working with others, including our family, friends, fellow students, teachers, and coworkers, is thus one of the best ways to manage stress. In addition to helping us form closer bonds and friendships, there are several advantages to being able to interact well with others. Working well with others provides an increase in self-confidence and in self-esteem, reduces our exposure to prolonged loneliness or interpersonal conflict, and results in the development of social support systems that can aid us during stressful times.

✓ READING PROGRESS CHECK

Determining Importance Why would people benefit from adopting active coping strategies in their lives?

LESSON 3 REVIEW

Reviewing Vocabulary
1. **Explaining** How does your cognitive appraisal of an event determine your stress level?

Using Your Notes
2. **Identifying** Use your notes to identify active coping strategies for dealing with stress. What is an example of using an active coping strategy for someone who feels stress and pressure about going away to college?

Answering the Guiding Questions
3. **Expressing** How do defensive coping strategies fail to deal with legitimate stressors?

4. **Identifying** How do active coping strategies work to moderate levels of stress?

Writing Activity
5. **Informative/Explanatory** Think of a stressful situation that you have recently experienced. How did you cope with it? Describe and analyze your coping mechanism as a psychologist might in a brief report.

Case Study

The Illusion of Stress

Period of Study: 1983, 1988

Introduction: In psychology, the term *illusions* is usually considered to be related to a psychosis, or a major psychological disorder in which a person's ability to think, respond emotionally, remember, communicate, or interpret reality is noticeably impaired. Although everyone experiences some perceptual illusions, those diagnosed with a schizophrenic-type disorder often experience bizarre illusions, hallucinations, or delusions. However, Shelley Taylor in 1983 and Taylor with Jonathon Brown in 1988 discovered that illusions might actually promote healthy living. These illusions are voluntary, unlike those associated with schizophrenia. Individuals use illusions to maintain optimistic, hopeful outlooks on situations that otherwise could cause an unhealthy amount of stress. Illusions such as these work for cancer sufferers, AIDS patients, individuals with physical injuries or mental disabilities, and people suffering from other serious illnesses.

Hypothesis: Taylor described illusions as beliefs that were based on "an overly optimistic view of the facts or that had no factual basis at all." Her hypothesis stated that women suffering from breast cancer who had illusions, by her definition, would cope better with stress from disfiguring surgeries, painful treatments, and the possibilities of death than would the same women who did not have these illusions. The women who would have illusions would benefit from placing themselves in hopeful situations. In addition to studying women with breast cancer, Taylor and Brown researched the illusion hypothesis further by expanding the population studied in 1988.

Method: Taylor conducted a two-year study on women diagnosed with breast cancer. Five years later, Taylor and Brown conducted their research. Both studies consisted of a control group who did not use optimistic illusions and an experimental group of those individuals who did. Once Taylor and Brown established the two groups, they assessed the emotions the participants displayed concerning their conditions,

expectations for the future, how they maintained social relationships during their illnesses, and other measures focusing on self-esteem.

Results: Taylor and Brown found that the participants who used illusions to maintain an optimistic view were cheerful; had more friends; and were usually more persistent, creative, and productive than those without such positive illusions. The positive outlooks these people held created confidence and the motivation to pursue their interests. Thus, according to Taylor and Brown's findings, the use of illusions can reduce the occurrence of stress in situations that may otherwise be extremely stressful. In a later interview, Taylor said,

PRIMARY SOURCE

" We've been able to show things like people who are optimistic and feel good about themselves confront stressful situations with lower biological responses to stress. "

—*Shelley E. Taylor*

Extreme caution, though, should be taken when a person uses illusions. As mentioned earlier, illusions are often associated with psychological disorders. Not everyone can separate reality from fantasy. Some people who may use illusions by Taylor's definition could become fixed in their fantasies and lose the capability of returning to the real world. The use of illusions to reduce or eliminate stress not only requires a vivid imagination but also a strong mind.

Analyzing the Case Study

1. *Explaining* How is the use of illusions related to stress?

2. *Identifying* How did Taylor and Brown test their hypothesis?

3. *Applying* When do you think the use of illusions crosses the line from healthy to unhealthy living?

4. *Analyzing* How does the quote from Taylor demonstrate the importance of having a positive outlook on life?

Chris Clinton/Stone/Getty Images

Directions: On a separate sheet of paper, answer the questions below. Make sure you read carefully and answer all parts of the question.

Lesson Review

Lesson 1

1 *Describing* What is probably the most common conflict situation, and in what ways can this conflict be resolved?

2 *Identifying* What words do psychologists use to refer to negative stress and positive stress?

Lesson 2

3 *Discussing* Identify and explain the four kinds of support that social groups offer for reducing stress.

4 *Specifying* How can stress impact you physically? How does stress affect the immune system?

Lesson 3

5 *Describing* How do people use denial and intellectualization to cope with stress?

6 *Summarizing* What are two relaxation techniques that can be used for coping with stress? How do they work?

Exploring the Essential Question

7 *Applying* Work with a partner to create a skit that illustrates each of the four conflict situations: approach-approach, avoidance-avoidance, approach-avoidance, and double approach-avoidance. Present your skit to the class and have your classmates identify the conflict situation you are demonstrating.

8 *Examining* Find recent magazine articles about the latest research into the connection between stress and illness. Find out how stress contributes to the development of certain diseases. Report your findings in an oral report.

College and Career Readiness

9 *Research and Methods* Find out about various support groups and professional help available in your community (for illnesses, and so on). You might look through your local phone book, contact a local hospital, or contact your local government offices for information. Identify the groups and help that are available, and explain how they can help an individual cope with stress. Present your findings in an informational pamphlet.

21st Century Skills

Using a Graph Review the graph of the phases of Selye's general adaptation syndrome, then answer the questions.

PHASES OF SELYE'S GENERAL ADAPTATIONS SYNDROME

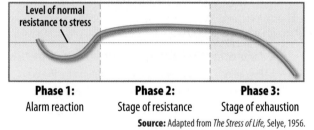

Level of normal resistance to stress

| Phase 1: | Phase 2: | Phase 3: |
| Alarm reaction | Stage of resistance | Stage of exhaustion |

Source: Adapted from *The Stress of Life*, Selye, 1956.

10 *Identifying* What are the three phases of the general adaptation syndrome?

11 *Drawing Conclusions* In what phase might a person become most vulnerable to catching a cold? Why?

12 *Making Connections* From the information contained in this graph, explain why people with stressful occupations might be prone to developing serious illnesses.

Need Extra Help?

If You've Missed Question	**1**	**2**	**3**	**4**	**5**	**6**	**7**	**8**	**9**	**10**	**11**	**12**
Go to page	422	421	437	432	441	443	422	432	437	429	433	432

Directions: On a separate sheet of paper, answer the questions below. Make sure you read carefully and answer all parts of the question.

Critical Thinking Questions

13 *Analyzing* As you have learned, some psychologists believe that stress is an event that produces worry. Others believe that stress is an individual's response to such an event. Still others believe stress is an individual's perception of the event. Which definition of stress do you agree with? Why?

14 *Evaluating* Do you think all individuals are equally susceptible to stress-related illnesses? Are some people better able to cope with stress than others? What does this say about stress as a *cause* of illness? Explain.

15 *Differentiating* Two kinds of coping strategies are defensive coping strategies and active coping strategies. What is the difference between these coping strategies? Which of the two do you think is more effective in helping an individual cope with stress? Why do you think so?

16 *Drawing Conclusions* Describe two recent stressful situations you experienced and how you responded. Include any physical or behavioral reactions you had. Were your responses typical for you? Why or why not? How would you characterize your personality type based on these responses? Explain your reasoning.

17 *Hypothesizing* Describe a situation in which you would need to use a behavioral response in order to protect yourself or other people. Why would this response be necessary for your survival or the survival of others involved in the situation?

DBQ Analyzing Primary Sources

Use the quote below from an interview with Deepak Chopra to answer the following questions. Chopra was responding to a question regarding the way meditation lowers biological age.

PRIMARY SOURCE

"*By quieting the mind which then quiets the body and the less turbulent the body is, the more the self-repair, healing mechanisms get amplified.*"

—Deepak Chopra

18 *Analyzing* According to Deepak Chopra's view on how to handle stress, how do you think someone should act before a big test at school to help deal with the stress?

19 *Discussing* How do stressors of the mind affect the body?

Research and Technology

20 *Researching* The Internet provides many Web sites regarding teen stress. Find several of these sites. What kinds of information do they provide? What kind of help do they describe for dealing with teen stress? Create a comprehensive report with your findings. Include a section of strategies and techniques for how to handle stress in various situations that teens encounter. Be sure to provide the addresses of the Web sites you found in your report.

Psychology Journal Activity

21 *Informative/Explanatory* Review your entry in your Psychology Journal for this chapter. Summarize the ways that people are affected by stress, including both behavior and physical reactions. Which of these reactions were more prominent in your journal entry?

Need Extra Help?

If You've Missed Question	13	14	15	16	17	18	19	20	21
Go to page	420	432	440	434	431	431	432	440	418

Psychological Disorders

ESSENTIAL QUESTION • *What happens when psychological processes break down?*

Psychology Matters...

Families in which one member has a psychological disorder face special problems. Members of these families often have to try to cope with instability or unpredictability. Children may have to take care of the physical and emotional needs of their siblings or a parent. As a result, they may be unable to think of their own needs.

◀ Psychological disorders affect the whole family.

Ron Chapple/Taxi/Getty Images

Lab Activity

Addicted to
Social Media

THE QUESTION...

RESEARCH QUESTION Can people use social media to excess?

You're taking a walk with your friend and trying to tell him a story. He's ignoring you, however, his eyes glued to the social media site on his device. As you reach a street corner, you have to grab his jacket to keep him from walking out into the street. He's been posting online every night instead of studying and he's been flunking quizzes. Social media seems to be the only thing to which he can pay attention.

In this experiment, we will examine how people use social media and the way it has changed people's lives. At this point, feel free to power down your cell phone and get out some paper (you know, the flat white stuff that you can write on).

Psychology Journal Activity

Do you or someone you know use social media sites excessively? Write about this in your Psychology Journal. Consider the following questions: What's the difference between "excessive" use and very frequent use? What do you think might determine how much is too much for any particular activity?

FINDING THE ANSWER...

HYPOTHESIS Overuse of social media will have a negative effect on one's normal routines and activities.

THE METHOD OF YOUR EXPERIMENT

MATERIALS paper

PROCEDURE Gather no fewer than 10 participants. All of your participants should have experience using social media. Develop a series of questions to use in asking your participants how many hours they spend doing the following on a daily basis: using social media sites, doing homework, eating, sleeping, exercising or playing sports, playing video games or watching TV, shopping, engaging in a hobby, working at a job, and socializing in person. Ask how many hours they estimate that they spent on these activities before they discovered social media. Also, ask participants if they think the use of social media sites has affected any of their daily activities in a negative way. Finally, ask your subjects how they would feel if they went without using these sites for one week; ask them to be specific.

DATA COLLECTION Look for patterns in your data. For example, an increase in the use of social media might be connected to a decrease in time spent on a particular activity. Also look for patterns in the way subjects described how they would feel if they went without using social media for a week.

ANALYSIS & APPLICATION

1. Did your results support the hypothesis?

2. Were there patterns in how subjects described the way they would feel if they went without using social media for a week? If so, what were some of the common responses?

3. Why is it necessary to ask the subject about his or her daily activities in order to learn about social media use? Why must the survey include more than a simple question about how one reacts to social media?

net**w**rks   ONLINE LAB RESOURCES

Online you will find:

- An **interactive lab experience**, allowing you to put principles from this chapter into practice in a digital psychology lab environment. This chapter's lab will include an experiment allowing you to explore issues fundamental to psychological disorders.

- A **Skills Handbook** that includes a guide for using the scientific method, creating experiments, and analyzing data.
- A **Notebook** where you can complete your Psychology Journal and record and analyze your experiment data.

Reading **HELP**DESK **CCSS**

Academic Vocabulary
- **label**   - **comprehensive**

Content Vocabulary
- **DSM-5**

TAKING NOTES:
Key Ideas and Details

IDENTIFYING As you read the chapter, create a graphic organizer for the major types of abnormal behavior described. Look for the causes of each abnormal behavior and categorize them along with the name of the disorder.

Abnormal Behavior	
Type	Cause

LESSON 1

Defining Psychological Disorders

ESSENTIAL QUESTION · *What happens when psychological processes break down?*

IT MATTERS BECAUSE

It is often difficult to draw a line between normal and abnormal behavior. Behavior that some people consider normal may seem abnormal to others. For instance, some people believe that having visions and hearing voices are important parts of a religious experience. Other people believe these behaviors are symptoms of a psychological disorder.

Identifying Psychological Disorders

GUIDING QUESTION *Why is the deviance approach not a useful standard on its own?*

What is normal? There is a concern among some mental health professionals that normal emotions and personality traits are being mislabeled. Sadness is **labeled** as depression. Shyness has turned into social phobia. Youthful enthusiasm is called an attention deficit. One critic mourns, "We've narrowed healthy behavior so dramatically that our quirks and eccentricities—the normal emotional range of adolescence and adulthood—have become problems we fear and expect drugs to fix."

Just because a person is "different" does not necessarily mean that he or she is suffering from a mental illness. Indeed, going along with the crowd may at times be self-destructive. Most readers—and most psychologists—would agree that teen cocaine users have a problem, even if they try to justify it by saying everyone in their social circle uses it, too.

Despite this, some self-destructive behavior is, in fact, a symptom of mental illness, especially if it is severe and persists over time. Other symptoms include hallucinations, persistent odd beliefs, moods that do not seem to be appropriate to the circumstances, inability to get along with others, a persistent lack of self-worth, inability to maintain a job, inability to follow basic instructions, lack of empathy, and inability to take care of one's own needs. It is estimated that 26.2 percent of all adults experience episodes of mental disorder each year, though not all seek treatment.

How do psychologists distinguish the normal from the abnormal? There are a number of ways to define abnormality, none of which is entirely satisfactory. We will look at the most popular ways of drawing the line between normal and abnormal in terms of deviance, adjustment, and psychological health. Then we will look at the application of these principles in legal definitions of abnormality. Finally, we will consider the criticism that in all these models people are arbitrarily labeled mentally ill.

label to describe or identify with a word or phrase

Deviation from Normality

One approach to defining abnormality is to say that whatever most people do is normal. Abnormality, then, is any deviation from the average or from the majority. It is normal to bathe periodically, to express grief at the death of a loved one, and to wear warm clothes when going out in the cold, because most people do so. Because very few people take ten showers a day, laugh when a loved one dies, or wear bathing suits in the snow, those who do so may be considered abnormal.

The deviance approach, however, as commonly used as it is, has serious limitations. If most people cheat on their income-tax returns, are honest taxpayers abnormal? If most people are noncreative, was Shakespeare abnormal? Different cultural norms must also be taken into consideration. Because the majority is not always right or best, the deviance approach to defining abnormality is not by itself a useful standard.

Adjustment

Another way to distinguish normal from abnormal people is to say that normal people are able to get along in the world—physically, emotionally, and socially. They can feed and clothe themselves, work, find friends, and live by the rules of society. By this definition, abnormal people are the ones who fail to *adjust*. They may be so unhappy that they refuse to eat or so lethargic that they cannot hold a job. They may experience so much anxiety in relationships with others that they end up avoiding people, living in a lonely world of their own. However, not all people with psychological disorders are violent, destructive, or isolated. Sometimes, a person's behavior may only seem normal. Also, behavior that is socially acceptable in one society may not be acceptable in another. Again, the cultural context of a behavior must also be taken into consideration.

This person is obviously sad, but is he so unhappy he is unable to function normally? If a psychological problem is severe enough to disrupt everyday life, a mental illness may be present.

▶ **CRITICAL THINKING**

Speculating Why is adjustment an important way to distinguish normal behavior from abnormal behavior?

Sometimes a lack of knowledge leads to nonsensical explanations for psychological phenomena. For example, the term *hysteria* comes from the Greek word for "uterus." The ancient Greeks diagnosed women with mental disorders by using a theory that the womb somehow moved around the body, occupying different positions. This "wandering of the uterus" theory led to characterizing any highly emotional behavior as hysteria. In the Middle Ages, the wandering uterus theory was used to explain demonic possession and led to persecutions of some women for witchcraft.

What we consider normal and abnormal behavior depends on the context of the behavior. Here two men in Michoacán State, Mexico, display cultural dance masks.

▶ **CRITICAL THINKING**

Understanding Perspectives
Why must you consider the cultural context of a behavior when determining whether the behavior is abnormal?

comprehensive covering completely

DSM-5 current version of the American Psychiatric Association's *Diagnostic and Statistical Manual of Mental Disorders*

454

Psychological Health

The terms *mental illness* and *mental health* imply that psychological disturbance or abnormality is like a physical sickness—such as the flu or tuberculosis. Many psychologists do not agree with this, but some do think that mental and physical functioning are alike in one way—there is an ideal way for people to function. Some psychologists believe that the normal healthy person is functioning ideally or striving toward ideal functioning. Personality theorists such as Carl Jung and Abraham Maslow have described this striving process, which is often called *self-actualization*. According to this line of thinking, to be normal or healthy involves full acceptance and expression of one's own individuality and humanness.

One problem with this approach to defining abnormality is that it is difficult to determine whether or not a person is doing a good job of actualizing himself or herself. How can you tell when a person is doing his or her best? What are the signs that he or she is losing the struggle? Answers to such questions often are arbitrary. That definitions of abnormality are somewhat arbitrary has led some theorists to conclude that labeling a person as mentally ill simply because his or her behavior is unusual or odd is not only a mistake, but cruel and irresponsible as well. The foremost spokesperson of this point of view is American psychiatrist Thomas Szasz.

Szasz argued that most of the people whom we call mentally ill are not ill at all. They simply have "problems in living" that cause serious conflicts with the world around them. Yet instead of dealing with the patients' conflicts as things that deserve attention and respect, psychiatrists simply label them as sick and shunt them off to hospitals. Society's norms remain unchallenged, and psychiatrists remain in a comfortable position of authority. The ones who lose are the patients, who by being labeled abnormal are deprived both of responsibility for their behavior and of their dignity as human beings. As a result, Szasz claimed, the patients' problems intensify. Szasz's position, however, is a minority stand. Most psychologists and psychiatrists would agree that a person who claims to be God or Napoleon is truly abnormal and disturbed.

David Hiser/Stone/Getty Images

The fact that it is difficult to define abnormality does not mean that such a thing does not exist. What it does mean is that we should be very cautious about judging a person to be mentally ill just because he or she acts in a way that we cannot understand. It should also be kept in mind that mild psychological disorders are common. It is only when a psychological problem becomes severe enough to disrupt everyday life that it is thought of as an abnormality or illness.

☑ **READING PROGRESS CHECK**

Describing How do psychologists distinguish the normal from the abnormal?

The Problem of Classification

GUIDING QUESTION *How are mental disorders categorized?*

For years psychiatrists have been trying to devise a logical and useful method for classifying emotional disorders. This task is difficult, because psychological problems do not lend themselves to the same sort of categorization that physical illnesses do. The causes and symptoms of psychological disturbances and breakdowns and the cures for those breakdowns are rarely obvious or clear-cut.

All major classification schemes have accepted the medical model, which describes abnormal behavior in the same manner as any physical illness. The physician diagnoses a specific disease when a person has certain symptoms.

In 1952 the American Psychiatric Association agreed upon a system for classifying abnormal symptoms, which it published in the *Diagnostic and Statistical Manual of Mental Disorders*, or DSM. This book has been revised several times, first as the DSM-II (1968), DSM-III (1980), and DSM-III-Revised (1987). The DSM-IV, a **comprehensive** revision, was published in 1994 and the DSM-IV-TR, a minor text revision, in 2000. Roman numerals were no longer used in the title of the newest version, the **DSM-5**, published in 2013.

A major change occurred in the shifts from DSM-II to DSM-III-R. Before 1980, the two most commonly used diagnostic distinctions were *neurosis* and *psychosis*. Although these terms have been replaced by more specific ones, they still are used by many psychologists. However, the conditions originally identified under neurosis and psychosis were expanded into more detailed categories, including anxiety disorders, somatoform disorders, dissociative disorders, mood disorders, and schizophrenia. DSM-IV built on these classifications.

The goal in developing DSM-5 was to create a manual based on evidence to improve clinical diagnosis. The total number of diagnoses did not increase, although the classification of disorders has been improved. Most diagnoses from the DSM-IV have not changed. However, disorder groups are now organized along a developmental continuum, from childhood through adolescence, adulthood, and later life and are sequenced by relationship to one another, allowing the practitioner to see relationships between specific disorders.

Categorization of Mental Illness

Within each diagnostic category of the DSM, the following descriptions are included:

1. *essential features*—characteristics that define the disorder;
2. *associated features*—additional features that are usually present;
3. information on *differential diagnosis*—that is, how to distinguish this disorder from other disorders with which it might be confused; and
4. *diagnostic criteria*—a list of symptoms, taken from the lists of essential and associated features, that must be present for the patient to be given a particular diagnostic label.

Profiles in
Psychology

Abraham Maslow
(1908–1970)
One of the founders of humanistic psychology, Abraham Maslow upset behaviorists by contradicting their theories that individuals learn new behaviors by responding to environmental stimuli that reward or punish their behaviors. Maslow emphasized that each individual has freedom in directing his or her own future. Maslow believed that individuals could achieve personal growth and self-fulfillment.

Maslow developed a theory of motivation that describes an individual's hierarchy of needs. As described earlier, individuals progress from filling basic, biological needs to the highest social needs of what Maslow called self-actualization—the fulfillment of one's greatest human potential. Individuals organize their lives around these needs, trying to fulfill the needs at each level. If needs are not fulfilled at any level, conflict results. Attention to these needs, then, is a method to resolve psychological conflict.

▶ **CRITICAL THINKING**

Defining Define Maslow's idea of self-actualization.

When John Hinckley was tried for shooting President Ronald Reagan in 1981, he was found "not guilty by reason of insanity." This raised public concerns about the legal definition of sanity.

In this case, not guilty did not mean that Hinckley did not commit the crime; it meant that he could not tell right from wrong or could not control his behavior because of a psychological disorder. Therefore, he could not be held criminally responsible for his behavior.

The terms *sane* and *insane* are legal terms. Psychological research has identified so many disorders of varying degrees that *insane* is too simplistic a term for a person with a psychological disorder. In fact, many people with psychological disorders are classified as sane under current legal standards.

People found not guilty by reason of insanity are not simply released; they are confined for treatment in special hospitals. Studies show that people found not guilty by reason of insanity are held for at least as long as people found guilty and sent to prison for similar crimes. After the Hinckley insanity defense, many states created review boards to oversee the treatment provided to those who have been found not guilty by reason of insanity.

Precise diagnostic criteria reduce the chances that the same patient will be classified as schizophrenic by one doctor and manic depressive by another. Because researchers often rely on diagnostic labels to study underlying factors that may cause disorders, it is especially important for their work that patients with similar symptoms be classified in the same diagnostic category.

The Axes

The DSM recognizes the complexity of classifying people on the basis of mental disorders. Often a person may exhibit more than one disorder or may be experiencing other stresses that complicate the diagnosis. In early classification systems, it was difficult to give a patient more than one label. The DSM-III-R and the DSM-IV overcame this problem by using five major dimensions, or *axes*, to describe a person's mental functioning. Each axis reflects a different aspect of a patient's case.

Axis I is used to classify current symptoms into explicitly defined categories. These categories range from disorders that are usually first evident in infancy, childhood, or adolescence (such as conduct disorders) to substance-use disorders (such as alcoholism) to schizophrenia.

Axis II is used to describe developmental disorders and chronic personality disorders or maladaptive traits such as compulsiveness, over-dependency, or aggressiveness. Axis II is also used to describe specific developmental disorders for children, adolescents, and, in some cases, adults. Examples of developmental problems that would be classified under Axis II are language disorders, reading or writing difficulties, mental retardation, autism, and speech problems.

It is possible for an individual to have a disorder on both Axis I and Axis II. For example, an adult may have a major depression noted on Axis I and a compulsive personality disorder noted on Axis II. A child may have a conduct disorder noted on Axis I and a developmental language disorder on Axis II. In other cases, a person may be seeking treatment primarily for a condition noted on Axis I or Axis II only. The use of both Axes I and II permits multiple diagnoses and allows the clinician flexibility in making provisional diagnoses when there is not enough information available to make a firm diagnosis.

Axis III is used to describe physical disorders or general medical conditions that are potentially relevant to understanding or caring for the person. In some cases, a physical disorder such as brain damage or a chemical imbalance may be causing the syndrome diagnosed on either Axis I or II.

Axis IV is a measurement of the current stress level at which the person is functioning. The rating of stressors (such as death of a spouse or loss of a job) is based on what the person has experienced within the past year. The prognosis may be better for a disorder that develops following a severe stressor than for one that develops after no stressor or a minimal stressor.

Axis V is used to describe the highest level of adaptive functioning present within the past year. Adaptive functioning refers to three major areas: *social relations*, occupational functioning, and the person's use of leisure time. Social relations refer to the quality of a person's relationships with family and friends. *Occupational functioning* involves functioning as a worker, student, or homemaker and the quality of the work accomplished. *Use of leisure time* includes recreational activities or hobbies and the degree of involvement and pleasure a person has in them.

This five-part diagnosis may be of the most help to researchers trying to discover connections among psychological disorders and other factors such as stress and physical illness. Although it is helpful, the DSM labels a person, which may have negative influences in the long run. When the label of a mental disorder is applied, it can reduce that person's sense of responsibility for his or her own actions.

It also affects how others, including mental health professionals, regard that person. Experiments have demonstrated that labels affect how others view someone. In one experiment, grade-school boys behaved in a more critical manner toward other boys if they had been led to believe that those other boys had a psychological disorder, such as attention deficit disorder. It is important to note that many people develop a disorder listed in the DSM-IV at some point in their life. Of course, many of these incidences are temporary. In effect, many people who qualify for a disorder as diagnosed according to the DSM-IV are not very different from anyone else.

DSM-5

The publication of the current edition of *Diagnostic and Statistical Manual of Mental Disorders*, or DSM-5, was a major event in the field of mental health. Among other changes, DSM-5 includes new categories for learning disorders, behavioral addictions such as gambling, improved criteria for gender and eating disorders, and suicide scales for adolescents and adults to help clinicians identify those who are most at risk.

DSM-5 attempts to address the ways in which a person's gender, race, and ethnicity may affect the diagnosis of mental illness. It includes a Cultural Formation Interview (CFI) that helps take into consideration a patient's cultural background. In this case, the word *culture* refers to the values, orientations, and assumptions that individuals possess as members of diverse social groups.

Disorders usually first diagnosed in infancy, childhood, or adolescence	Includes disorders typically arising before adolescence, including attention deficit disorders, mental retardation, and stuttering
Delirium, dementia, and other cognitive disorders	Includes disorders of perceptual, memory, and thought distortion that stem from damage to the brain, such as Alzheimer's disease
Substance-related disorders	Includes maladaptive use of alcohol and drugs
Schizophrenia and other psychotic disorders	Characterizes types of schizophrenia and psychotic disorders by symptoms
Mood disorders	Includes disorders characterized by emotional disturbance, such as depression and bipolar disorder
Anxiety disorders	Includes disorders characterized by signs of anxiety, such as panic disorders and phobias
Somatoform disorders	Includes disorders characterized by somatic symptoms that resemble physical illnesses, such as conversion disorder and hypochondriasis
Dissociative disorders	Includes disorders that are characterized by sudden and temporary changes in memory, consciousness, identity, and behavior, such as dissociative identity disorder
Sexual and gender-identity disorders	Includes preferences for unusual acts to achieve sexual arousal and sexual dysfunctions
Eating disorders	Includes disorders such as anorexia nervosa and bulimia nervosa
Sleep disorders	Includes disorders associated with sleep, such as insomnia and sleepwalking
Impulse control disorders	Includes disorders characterized by a tendency to act on impulses that others usually inhibit, such as to gamble excessively or steal

Source: DSM-IV, American Psychiatric Association, 1994.

< TABLE

PSYCHOLOGICAL DISORDERS OF AXIS I

Individual psychological disorders are diagnosed on five axes in the DSM-IV. Axis I classifies symptoms into categories.

▶ CRITICAL THINKING

1. *Describing* What are impulse control disorders?

2. *Contrasting* How do mood disorders differ from anxiety disorders?

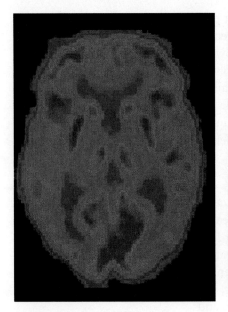 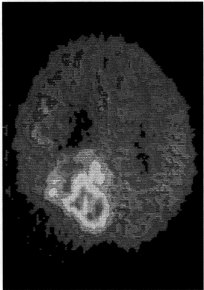 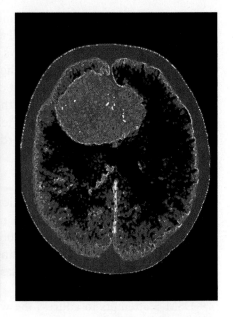

The biological roots of abnormal behavior include genetic factors and occurrences that can lead to abnormal brain development. From left to right, these PET scans show a normal human brain, a brain tumor, and a brain aneurysm.

▶ **CRITICAL THINKING**

Identifying Which axis of the DSM describes the medical conditions of psychological disorders?

These diverse cultural groups include ethnic groups, the military, and faith communities. The word *culture* also refers here to any other socioenvironmental aspects in a person's background that may affect his or her perspective.

The CFI examines four major domains. It examines the illness from the patient's worldview. It helps to provide the clinician with a holistic view of the patient's cultural background, examining the causes and support from the patient's perspective. The third domain looks at the cultural factors that have been most helpful and least helpful. The fourth domain explores the way the patient views his or her relationship with the clinician, preferences for treatment, and potential barriers to treatment. Additional modules can be used for populations with special needs, such as children and adolescents, the elderly, immigrants, and refugees.

☑ **READING PROGRESS CHECK**

Summarizing What are the advantages and disadvantages of categorizing and labeling people by their mental disorders?

LESSON 1 REVIEW

Reviewing Vocabulary
1. *Defining* What is the DSM? How do psychologists use it?

Using Your Notes
2. *Describing* Use the notes you completed during the lesson to describe the three approaches psychologists use to identify psychological disorders.

Answering the Guiding Questions
3. *Explaining* Why is the deviance approach not a useful standard on its own?

4. *Describing* How are mental disorders categorized?

Writing Activity
5. *Informative/Explanatory* Write a brief essay discussing popular misconceptions about mental disorders.

netw●rks

There's More Online!

☑ GRAPHIC ORGANIZER

☑ SELF-CHECK QUIZ

Reading HELPDESK (CCSS)

Academic Vocabulary
- **stress**
- **display**

Content Vocabulary
- **anxiety**
- **phobia**
- **panic disorder**
- **post-traumatic stress disorder**

TAKING NOTES:
Key Ideas and Details

GATHERING INFORMATION Use a graphic organizer like the one below to list five general symptoms of an anxiety disorder.

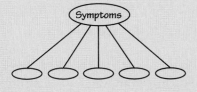

LESSON 2
Anxiety Disorders

ESSENTIAL QUESTION • *What happens when psychological processes break down?*

IT MATTERS BECAUSE
Anxiety disorders are the most common type of mental disorders in the United States, affecting 40 million Americans annually. People suffering from anxiety disorders feel anxiety but not just normal anxiety. They suffer from anxiety that is out of proportion to the situation provoking it. This intense anxiety may interfere with normal functioning in everyday life.

Generalized Anxiety Disorder

GUIDING QUESTION *What is the difference between fear and anxiety?*

Anxiety is a generalized apprehension—a vague feeling that one is in danger. This anxiety potentially could blossom into full-fledged panic attacks, which may include choking sensations, chest pain, dizziness, trembling, and hot flashes. Unlike fear, which is a reaction to real and identifiable threats, anxiety is a reaction to vague or imagined dangers.

Everyone experiences anxiety at times. Many people feel nervous when faced before taking tests, when making important decisions, or when facing a problem at work. These are normal human emotions. Once in a while, everyone feels nervous for reasons he or she cannot explain, but a severely anxious person almost always feels this way. Anxiety becomes a disorder when it lasts for six months or longer, and causes such distress that it interferes with a person's ability to lead a normal life.

People with anxiety disorders share certain characteristics, including feelings of anxiety and personal inadequacy and an avoidance of dealing with problems. They often have unrealistic images of themselves. People who are deeply anxious seem unable to free themselves of recurring worries and fears. Their emotional problems may be expressed in constant worrying, sudden mood swings, or a variety of physical symptoms (for example, headaches, sweating, muscle tightness, weakness, and fatigue). Symptoms vary from one anxiety disorder to another, but general symptoms include the following: feelings of panic or fear, obsessive thoughts, an inability to stay calm, trouble sleeping, shortness of breath, palpitations, dry mouth, and dizziness.

Many situations may cause temporary anxiety or tension. Anxiety becomes a problem only when it interferes with your ability to cope with everyday life.

▶ **CRITICAL THINKING**

Describing What are some characteristics of people who suffer from anxiety disorders?

anxiety a vague, generalized apprehension or feeling that one is in danger

Characteristics of Generalized Anxiety Disorder

Some people experience a continuous, generalized anxiety. Fearing unknown and unforeseen circumstances, they are unable to make decisions or enjoy life. They may become so preoccupied with their internal problems that they neglect their social relationships and often have difficulty forming stable and satisfying relationships with others. Generalized anxiety disorder (GAD), which is characterized by a pattern of constant and excessive worry about different activities and events, is a common condition. People who experience generalized anxiety often have trouble dealing with their family and friends and fulfilling their responsibilities, and this adds to their anxiety. They are trapped in a vicious cycle: the more they worry about things, the more difficulty they have; the more difficulty they have, the more they worry. Even though their behavior may be self-defeating and ineffective in solving problems, those driven by anxiety often refuse to give up their behaviors in favor of more effective ways of dealing with anxiety.

Often the experience of generalized anxiety is accompanied by physical symptoms such as muscular tension, shakiness, headaches, irritability, sweating, lightheadedness, an inability to relax, restlessness, shortness of breath, and a strained face. Difficulty swallowing, poor appetite, indigestion, diarrhea, and frequent urination are also common. Because anxious people are in a constant state of apprehension, they may have difficulty sleeping or, once asleep, may wake up suddenly in the night. As a result, they may feel tired all day and have difficulty concentrating.

Anyone can develop this disorder, even children and adolescents. Most people who have trouble with GAD report having "always" felt this way, for as long as they can remember. Why are some people so anxious? Some theorists stress the role of learning in producing anxiety. If a man feels very anxious about going on a date, for example, even the thought of going on another date may make him nervous. As a result, he learns to avoid having any dates because it causes him so much anxiety and therefore he never has a chance to unlearn that anxiety. His anxiety may then generalize to other situations and become an even worse problem.

Other research suggests that anxiety disorders may be partly inherited. Environmental factors, such as unpredictable traumatic experiences in childhood, may also predispose someone to developing an anxiety disorder. Such a disorder usually occurs following a major life change, such as getting or losing a job, losing a loved one, or having a baby. The uncertainties of modern life also may help explain the high incidence of generalized anxiety.

☑ **READING PROGRESS CHECK**

Explaining What is anxiety? When is it normal? Abnormal?

Specific Anxiety Disorders

GUIDING QUESTION *How is a phobia deeper than simple fear?*

Anxiety is one of the most prevalent psychiatric disorders in the general population. Some of the specific anxiety disorders discussed in the DSM-IV include phobic disorder, social anxiety disorder (which is sometimes referred to as social phobia), panic disorder, obsessive-compulsive disorder, and post-traumatic **stress** disorder (PTSD). As with generalized anxiety disorder, those with a specific anxiety disorder report symptoms of uncontrollable anxiety, physical and mental distress, sleep disturbances, concentration problems, and trouble functioning in their social or professional lives.

stress a physical, chemical, or emotional factor that causes physical or mental tension and may be a factor in causing disease

Phobic Disorder

When severe anxiety is focused on a particular object, animal, activity, or situation that seems out of proportion to the real dangers involved, it is called a phobic disorder, or **phobia**. Phobias may be classified as specific phobias, social phobias, and agoraphobia. A *specific phobia* can focus on almost anything, including high places (acrophobia), enclosed spaces (claustrophobia), and loud noises (phonophobia). Victims of *social phobias* fear that they will embarrass themselves in a public place or a social setting. Perhaps the most common specific fear is of speaking in public (glossophobia), but others include eating in public, using public restrooms, meeting strangers, and going on a first date.

phobia an intense and irrational fear of a particular object or situation

Phobic individuals develop elaborate plans to avoid the situations they fear. For example, people suffering from *agoraphobia*, an extreme fear of being in a public place, may stop going to movies or shopping in large, busy stores. Some reach the point where they will not leave their houses at all because that is the only place they feel safe.

Phobias range in intensity from mild to extremely severe. Most people deal with their phobias by avoiding the things that frightens them. Thus, the phobias are learned and maintained by the reinforcing effects of repeated avoidance.

Acarophobia: fear of itching or the insects that cause itching
Acrophobia: fear of heights
Aerophobia: fear of flying
Agoraphobia: fear of open spaces
Atelophobia: fear of imperfection
Autophobia: fear of being alone
Catagelophobia: fear of being ridiculed
Claustrophobia: fear of closed spaces
Entomophobia: fear of insects
Felinophobia: fear of cats
Heliophobia: fear of the sun
Hemophobia: fear of blood
Hydrophobia: fear of water
Logizomechanophobia: fear of computers
Lygophobia: fear of darkness
Nosocomephobia: fear of hospitals
Verminophobia: fear of germs
Zoophobia: fear of animals

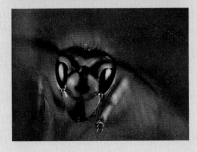

◄ DIAGRAM

PHOBIAS
Some people's lives are consumed by inappropriate fears. These fears interfere with normal, everyday life. These people are suffering from a phobia.

▶ CRITICAL THINKING

1. *Identifying* What is the fear of flying called?

2. *Researching* Find five other phobias not mentioned here and list them along with descriptions.

Although most people do not experience severe phobias, many do experience mild fears. Find out what fears your classmates experience or have experienced.

Procedure

1. Prepare a list identifying some objects, animals, activities, or situations that are feared.
2. Distribute the list among your friends, classmates, and the adults you know.
3. Direct them to check the items on the list that identify a fear that they have; encourage them to write a fear they have that does not appear on the list.
4. Tally the responses.

Analysis

1. Record the results in a chart or graph, differentiating responses of the teenagers from those of the adults.
2. Determine the most common fears. What reasons can you provide for the similarities or the differences between the two groups?

panic disorder an extreme anxiety that manifests itself in the form of panic attacks

Avoidance reduces anxiety but not the phobia. One form of treatment for phobias involves providing the phobic person with opportunities to experience the feared object under conditions in which he or she feels safe.

Panic Disorder

Another kind of anxiety disorder is **panic disorder**. (*Panic* is a feeling of sudden, helpless terror, such as the overwhelming fright one might experience when cornered by a predator.) During a panic attack, a victim experiences sudden and unexplainable feelings of intense anxiety, leading the individual to fear the approach of impending doom or even to fear that he or she is about to die. Although symptoms of panic disorder differ from individual to individual, they may include a sense of smothering, choking, or difficulty breathing; faintness or dizziness; nausea; and chest pains. Although panic attacks sometimes last for an hour or more, they usually last just a few minutes and occur without warning.

Panic disorder may be inherited, in part. However, the panic victim usually experiences the first attack shortly after a stressful event. The disorder may also be the result of interpreting physiological arousal, such as an increased heart rate, as disastrous.

Obsessive-Compulsive Disorder

A person suffering from acute anxiety may think the same thoughts over and over. Such an uncontrollable pattern of thoughts is called *obsession*. A person also may repeatedly perform coping behaviors, called *compulsions*. A person with an anxiety-based disorder may experience both these agonies together—a condition called *obsessive-compulsive disorder*.

A compulsive person may feel compelled to wash his hands 20 or 30 times a day or to avoid stepping on cracks in the sidewalk when he goes out. An obsessive person may be unable to rid herself of unpleasant thoughts about death or of a recurring impulse to make obscene remarks in public. The obsessive-compulsive person may wash her hands continually *and* torment herself with thoughts of obscene behavior.

Everyone has obsessions and compulsions. Love might be described as an obsession, as might a hobby that occupies most of a person's spare time. Striving to do something perfectly is often considered to be a compulsion. If the person who is deeply engrossed in a hobby or who aims for perfection enjoys this intense absorption and can still function effectively, he or she usually is not considered disabled by anxiety. Psychologists consider it a problem only when such thoughts and activities interfere with what a person wants and needs to do. Someone who spends so much time double-checking every detail of her work that she can never finish a job is considered more anxious than conscientious.

Why do people develop obsessions and compulsions? Perhaps it is because they serve as diversions from a person's real fears and their origins and thus may reduce anxiety somewhat. In addition, compulsions provide a disturbed person with the evidence that she is doing something well, even if it is only avoiding the cracks on a sidewalk. Obsessive-compulsive disorder does run in families, so there may be a genetic basis. Although most people with obsessive-compulsive disorder realize that their thoughts and actions are irrational, they feel unable to stop them.

Post-Traumatic Stress Disorder

People who experience severe and long-lasting psychological effects after a traumatic event may be diagnosed with **post-traumatic stress disorder**. A significant percentage of military combat veterans suffer from this disorder. The disorder also frequently occurs among survivors of other overwhelmingly traumatic events such as natural disasters, physical catastrophes, or acts of human aggression. The event that triggers the disorder affects the victim's perception of reality and ability to cope. The disorder may begin immediately after the occurrence of the traumatic event or it may develop later. Typical symptoms include involuntary flashbacks or recurring nightmares during which the victim reexperiences the ordeal, often followed by insomnia and feelings of guilt.

Post-traumatic stress disorder can be extremely long-lasting. Studies show that survivors of Nazi concentration camps and soldiers returning from war may **display** symptoms decades after the traumatic events they experienced. Not everyone who experiences a traumatic event, though, develops post-traumatic stress disorder. People who are exposed repeatedly or over a long period of time to distressing conditions are more likely to develop the disorder. Social support may protect a victim of trauma from the psychological aftereffects.

The National Center for PTSD conducts research and education programs focusing on PTSD and other psychological and medical consequences of traumatic stress. Originally considered an exclusive problem of Vietnam veterans, PTSD is now recognized as a major public health problem due to the high incidence of assault, rape, child abuse, disaster, and other traumatic events in the civilian sector. It has been estimated that PTSD affects more than 10 million Americans at some point in their lives.

☑ **READING PROGRESS CHECK**

Describing What is a panic attack?

Estimates suggest that about 18 percent of the American soldiers who fought in the Iraq War will develop post-traumatic stress disorder.

▶ CRITICAL THINKING

Speculating How might war cause someone to develop this disorder?

post-traumatic stress disorder disorder in which victims of traumatic events experience the original event in the form of dreams or flashbacks

display to exhibit

Department of Defense photo by Airman 1st Class Kurt Gibbons III - U.S. Air Force

LESSON 2 REVIEW (CCSS)

Reviewing Vocabulary

1. *Explaining* Explain how excessive anxiety may lead to phobias or panic disorders.

Using Your Notes

2. *Describing* Use the notes you completed during the lesson to briefly describe each of the five general symptoms of an anxiety disorder.

Answering the Guiding Questions

3. *Contrasting* What is the difference between fear and anxiety?

4. *Comparing* How is a phobia deeper than simple fear?

Writing Activity

5. *Informative/Explanatory* Interview a doctor or nurse who deals with war veterans (such as at your local vets center). Ask the professional to list the symptoms of post-traumatic stress disorder. Summarize your findings.

Psychological Disorders **463**

PHOTO: Paul Hawkert/Alamy; TEXT: Republished with permission of Association for Psychological Science, from psychologicalscience.org, *Embattled Childhood: The Real Trauma of PTSD* by Wray Herbert, published June 13, 2012, © 2012 Association for Psychological Science; permission conveyed through Copyright Clearance Center, Inc.; Association for Psychological science (APS) by Association for Psychological Science Copyright 2012 Reproduced with permission of ASSOCIATION FOR PSYCHOLOGICAL SCIENCE in the format republish in "other" book via Copyright Clearance Center.

Reader's Dictionary   (CCSS)

arid: having little or no rain; too dry or barren to support vegetation

tedium: the state of being tiresome or monotonous

unscathed: without suffering any injury, damage, or harm

impervious: unable to be affected by

ameliorate: make (something bad or unsatisfactory) better

What causes Post Traumatic Stress Disorder (PTSD), and is it possible to predict which individuals might be more susceptible to the disorder? In this study, Danish and American psychologists studied soldiers not just after a combat experience, but before as well, to determine if there were patterns in the incidence of PTSD. Their findings shed some new light on the disorder.

Embattled Childhood:
The Real Trauma in PTSD

By Wray Herbert

PRIMARY SOURCE

In 2009, a regiment of Danish soldiers, the Guard Hussars, was deployed for a six-month tour in Afghanistan's **arid** Helmand Province, a Taliban stronghold. They were stationed along with British soldiers—270 in all—at a forward operating base called Armadillo. Although none of the Guard Hussars was killed during the tour of duty, they nevertheless experienced many horrors of battle. A commander was seriously injured by a roadside bomb, and a night patrol ended in a firefight that killed and dismembered several Taliban combatants.

The Guard Hussars' war experience is graphically depicted in the award-winning documentary film *Armadillo,* which follows the young soldiers from their emotional farewells in Denmark through their six months in combat and, finally, back to joyous homecomings and family reunions. The film is a study of the inner lives of young men as they experience the excitement and camaraderie, the **tedium** and—mostly—the terror and trauma of war.

Coincidentally, these same soldiers were also the subject of another, very different kind of study. At the same time that the film was being shot, the soldiers were part of a larger group of Danish soldiers who were being scientifically observed and tested for emerging symptoms of Post Traumatic Stress Disorder, or PTSD. A large team of Danish and American psychological scientists, headed up by Dorthe Berntsen of Aarhus University, wanted to do what had never been done before in the field of PTSD research: Instead of studying soldiers who were already suffering from PTSD, they decided to assess young recruits before they were sent off to war, while they were still relatively **unscathed**; then to follow them during the war experience; and finally to follow them back home and through several months of readjustment. In this way, the scientists hoped to see why some soldiers develop PTSD, and others do not, and how the symptoms of the disorder progress.

So, as in the film, the scientists first encountered the soldiers at home in Denmark, where they were readying for deployment to Afghanistan. Psychologists met with the soldiers five or six weeks before they were scheduled to leave, and administered a battery of psychological tests. These included a PTSD inventory, a test for depression, and a questionnaire about

©Bryan Denton/Corbis

traumatic life events, including childhood experiences of family violence, physical punishment, and spousal abuse. Additional tests were administered during the soldiers' service in Helmand Province, related to the direct experience of war: perceptions of war zone stress, actual life-threatening war experiences, battlefield wounds, and the experience of actually killing an enemy. The scientists continued to assess the soldiers when they were sent home—a couple weeks after their return, at three months, and finally at least seven months following their return from war.

The study revealed some surprising findings. The current and widely held view of PTSD is that exposure to combat and other war atrocities is the main cause of the disorder—and that more exposure to trauma boosts the likelihood of experiencing the disorder. Moreover, it's believed that for those who develop PTSD, the typical pattern is for symptoms to emerge soon after a particularly traumatic experience and to persist over time. For unknown reasons, some soldiers appear resilient in the face of war trauma, never developing symptoms or rapidly recovering.

This is not what these scientists found. Indeed, the consensus view of the disorder may be fundamentally wrong in at least two ways. As reported in a forthcoming issue of the journal *Psychological Science*, PTSD does not appear to be triggered by a traumatic battle experience, nor does there appear to be any typical trajectory for PTSD symptoms.

What Berntsen and colleagues found instead is wide variation in both causes and development of PTSD. The vast majority of Danish soldiers were resilient—recovering quickly from mild symptoms—or altogether **impervious** to psychological harm. The rest fell into distinct and unexpected patterns of PTSD: Some showed no symptoms before deployment or even during their tour of duty, but symptoms spiked after they returned home. Symptoms did not appear to follow any specific traumatic event, but by seven months

after returning from war, stress symptoms had worsened to the point where the soldiers were diagnosed with PTSD.

Even more interesting were the remaining soldiers, about 13 percent of the soldiers in the study, who actually showed temporary improvement in symptoms during deployment. That is, they had significant stress symptoms after signing up for service, but before deploying—symptoms that eased in the first months or war, only to spike again later, when they were safely at home. This pattern of symptoms has never been observed before, and it's puzzling: Why would shipping off to a dangerous and unfamiliar war zone **ameliorate** stress symptoms?

The scientists have a theory, and it has to do with the root causes of PTSD, previously undocumented. All the Danish soldiers who developed PTSD were much more likely (compared to resilient soldiers) to have suffered emotional problems and traumatic events prior to deployment. In fact, it wasn't traumatic war experiences that predicted the onset of PTSD, but rather childhood experiences of violence, especially punishment severe enough to cause bruises, cuts, burns, and broken bones. PTSD sufferers were also more likely to have witnessed family violence, and to have experienced physical attacks, stalking or death threats by a spouse. They were also more likely to have past experiences that they could not, or would not, talk about.

These previously overlooked PTSD sufferers were also much less educated than the resilient soldiers. This disadvantage, combined with their pronounced mental health problems before going to war, suggests that they may in reality have been escaping a different war zone: the family. In other words, they only showed improvement as soldiers because they were in such poor psychological condition in civilian life. Army life—even combat—offered them more in the way of social support and life satisfaction than they had ever had at home. These soldiers were probably benefiting emotionally from being valued as individuals for the first time ever, and from their first authentic camaraderie—mental health benefits that diminished when they once again returned to civilian life.

Analyzing Primary Sources

1. **Explaining** How is the study detailed in this article different from previous studies on PTSD?

2. **Paraphrasing** Why are soldiers with past negative experience with family and home life theorized to be more likely to develop PTSD?

3. **Speculating** What might this study's findings and subsequent theory mean for the selection of and support for soldiers?

LESSON 3
Somatoform and Dissociative Disorders

Reading **HELP**DESK ⓒⒸⓈⓈ

Academic Vocabulary
• **challenge** • **ultimate**

Content Vocabulary
• somatoform disorder
• conversion disorder
• dissociative disorder
• dissociative amnesia
• dissociative fugue
• dissociative identity disorder

TAKING NOTES:
Key Ideas and Details

GATHERING INFORMATION Use a graphic organizer like the one below to list dissociative disorders.

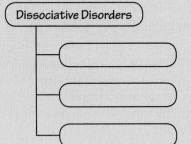

ESSENTIAL QUESTION • *What happens when psychological processes break down?*

IT MATTERS BECAUSE

A few years ago, fake "science" Web sites predicted that the world as we know it would be destroyed on December 21, 2012. This rumor was supported by reports that the ancient Maya calendar ends in 2012. The distributors of the movie 2012 played up the end-of-the-world scare while promoting their disaster film, encouraging people to imagine a final cataclysm and to "Vote for the Leader of the Post-2012 World."

Somatoform Disorders

GUIDING QUESTION *What is the relationship between anxiety and somatoform disorders?*

The Internet is a very powerful medium. Once information has been posted on it, it can quickly "go viral." Many people believe that, if they see something on the Internet, then it must be true. As a result of the end-of-the-world rumors spread on the Internet, some people reported that their children were so frightened that they were refusing to eat. Two teenagers told a NASA scientist that they were thinking of ending their lives because they did not want to see the world end.

Anxiety can create a wide variety of physical symptoms for which no physical cause is clearly evident. This phenomenon is known as *somatization*, or hysteria. The term *hysteria* was more commonly used in Sigmund Freud's time to refer to unexplainable fainting, paralysis, or deafness. Today the term **somatoform disorder** is preferred for disorders arising from somatization. Two of the major types of somatoform disorders that psychologists identify are *conversion disorders* and *hypochondriasis*.

Somatoform disorders are characterized by physical symptoms, such as loss of functioning, pain, or preoccupation about a disease in some part of the body with no apparent physical reason, which are brought about by psychological distress. Psychologists generally treat a somatoform disorder by helping the person change the errors in their thinking or by **challenging** the individual and attempting to force him out of the symptoms.

David Longstreath/AP Images

Conversion Disorders

A **conversion disorder** is the conversion of emotional difficulties into the loss of a specific physiological function. While the loss of functioning is real, no actual physical damage is present. Many people occasionally experience mild conversion disorders, such as when someone is so frightened he or she cannot move, but a conversion disorder is not simply a brief loss of functioning due to fright. It is a condition that persists.

A conversion disorder results in a real and prolonged handicap; the person literally cannot feel anything in his left hand, move his legs, see, hear, or exercise some other physical function. A man might wake up one morning and find himself paralyzed from the waist down. The normal reaction to this would be panic. However, he might accept the loss of function with inappropriate calm, called *la belle indifférence* (lah BEL an • dee • fay • RAHNZ). This calmness is one sign that a person is suffering from a psychological rather than a physiological problem.

Most psychologists believe that people suffering from conversion disorders unconsciously invent physical symptoms to gain freedom from unbearable conflict. For example, a woman who lives in terror of blurting out things that she does not want to say may lose the power of speech. This resolves the conflict about speaking. Conversion disorders are comparatively rare.

Hypochondriasis

Conversion disorders must be distinguished from *hypochondriasis*, in which a person who is in good health becomes preoccupied with imaginary ailments. The hypochondriac spends a lot of time looking for signs of serious illness and often misinterprets minor aches, pains, bruises, or bumps as early signs of a fatal illness. For instance, a person suffering hypochondriasis will think his headache indicates that he has a brain tumor or something equally serious. Despite negative results from medical tests and physical evaluations, the hypochondriac will typically continue to believe that a disease or malfunction exists and may switch practitioners, believing each doctor has failed to find the underlying disorder.

somatoform disorder a condition in which there is no apparent physical cause

challenge to confront; to question formally

conversion disorder changing emotional difficulties into a loss of a specific voluntary body function

< CARTOON

AVOIDING HAPPINESS
Some people may accuse those suffering from hypochondriasis of faking their illness (and preventing their own happiness). These people, though, do not fake their symptoms; they unrealistically interpret normal aches and pains as symptoms of more serious illnesses.

▶ **CRITICAL THINKING**

1. *Analyzing Visuals* How does the man in the cartoon demonstrate hypochondriasis?

2. *Explaining* What is believed to be the cause of hypochondriasis?

As they become increasingly concerned with their health, a hypochondriac's work performance and personal relationships often suffer. The illness can be chronic and lifelong.

The onset of hypochondriasis is mainly during young adulthood and it is equally common in men and women. According to psychoanalytic theory, hypochondriasis, like conversion, occurs when an individual represses emotions and then expresses them symbolically in physical symptoms.

☑ **READING PROGRESS CHECK**

Contrasting What is the difference between a conversion disorder and hypochondriasis?

Dissociative Disorders

GUIDING QUESTION *What is a common element of all dissociative disorders?*

You have probably had the experience of being lost in a daydream and failing to notice your friend calling your name. This is a normal dissociative experience. A **dissociative disorder** involves a more significant breakdown in a person's normal conscious experience, such as a loss of memory or identity. These psychological phenomena fascinate many people, so we hear a good deal about amnesia and multiple personalities. Actually, they are very rare.

Memory loss that has no biological explanation, or **dissociative amnesia**, may be an attempt to escape from problems by blotting them out completely. Amnesiacs remember how to speak and usually retain a fund of general knowledge, but they may not know who they are, where they live and work, or who their family is. This amnesia should be distinguished from other losses of memory that result from physical brain damage, normal forgetting, or drug abuse. Dissociative amnesia most often results from a traumatic event, such as witnessing a terrible accident.

In **dissociative fugue**, another type of dissociative reaction, amnesia is coupled with active flight to a different environment. For example, a woman may suddenly disappear and wake up three days later in a restaurant 200 miles from home. If she is not treated, she may actually establish a new identity—assume a new name, marry, take a job, and so forth—in a new place. She may repress all knowledge of a previous life. A fugue state may last for days or for decades. However long it lasts, the individual, when she comes out of it, will have no memory of what happened in the interim. Fugue, then, is a sort of traveling amnesia, and it probably serves the same psychological function as dissociative amnesia—escape from unbearable conflict or anxiety.

In **dissociative identity disorder** (previously known as multiple personality disorder), a third type of dissociative disorder, someone seems to have two or more distinct identities, each with its own way of thinking and behaving. These different personality states may take control at different times.

Eve White, a young woman who sought psychiatric treatment for severe headaches and blackouts, has become a famous example. Eve White was a conscientious, self-controlled, rather shy person. However, during one of her therapy sessions, her expression—and her personality—suddenly changed. Eve Black, as she now called herself, was childlike, fun-loving, and irresponsible—the opposite of the woman who originally walked into the psychiatrist's office. Eve Black was conscious of Eve White's existence but considered her a separate person. Eve White did not know about Eve Black, however, and neither was she conscious of Jane, a third personality that emerged during the course of therapy. (This case served as the basis for the film *The Three Faces of Eve*.) Some psychologists believe

dissociative disorder a disorder in which a person experiences alterations in memory, identity, or consciousness

dissociative amnesia the inability to recall important personal events or information; is usually associated with stressful events

dissociative fugue a dissociative disorder in which a person suddenly and unexpectedly travels away from home or work and is unable to recall the past

dissociative identity disorder a person exhibits two or more personality states, each with its own patterns of thinking and behaving

Chris Sizemore (Eve) was able to overcome her disorder through therapy. This photograph symbolizes the personalities present within her when she began therapy.

▶ CRITICAL THINKING

Explaining What causes dissociative identity disorder?

that this dividing up of the personality is the result of the individual's effort to escape from a part of the self that he or she fears. The secret self then emerges in the form of a separate personality. Dissociative identity disorder is extremely rare.

Eve's real name is Chris Costner Sizemore, and she published a book, *I'm Eve*, many years later, explaining that Eve **ultimately** had 22 separate personalities. Her case is often confused with "Sybil," a woman whose 16 personalities were also described in a book and a film. While cases like "Eve" and "Sybil" are fascinating, they are extremely rare and very controversial. A book was published in 2011 that claimed that "Sybil" was a fraud, and that she had admitted in a letter to her therapist before her story was published that she had invented the multiple personalities to gain attention.

ultimate in the end; finally

People diagnosed with this disorder usually suffered severe physical, psychological, or sexual abuse during childhood. Individuals with dissociative disorders have learned to dissociate themselves from such stressful events by selectively forgetting them, thereby reducing the anxiety they feel.

☑ READING PROGRESS CHECK

Contrasting How is dissociative amnesia different from dissociative fugue?

LESSON 3 REVIEW

Reviewing Vocabulary
1. *Explaining* Besides anxiety, how might you realize that you are suffering from either a somatoform or a dissociative disorder?

Using Your Notes
2. *Describing* Use the notes you completed during the lesson to briefly describe the dissociative disorders you listed.

Answering the Guiding Questions
3. *Speculating* What is the relationship between anxiety and somatoform disorders?

4. *Identifying* What is a common element of all dissociative disorders?

Writing Activity
5. *Informative/Explanatory* As a class or in groups, arrange an appointment with a clinical psychologist, nurse, physician, or counseling psychologist. Question this person regarding the most common psychological problems young people face. Write a brief report of your findings to present to the class.

Case Study

Munchausen's Syndrome

Period of Study: 1994

Introduction: In 1994 a physician consulted psychiatrist Berney Goodman regarding the condition of a patient who seemingly had a rare bowel condition—the patient vomited every time she ate. Together they diagnosed the patient with bowel paralysis. Goodman wanted to examine the patient himself. From the start, the patient refused to cooperate with Goodman. Goodman discovered that the patient had low blood pressure. This, however, was not consistent with the diagnosis of bowel paralysis.

Hypothesis: Goodman suspected that the patient suffered from *Munchausen's Syndrome*. Those who suffer from the ailment have developed great sensitivity to emotional pain and will use any methods possible to avoid feeling it. These methods are quite extreme and often deadly. The sufferers often attempt to hospitalize themselves with self-defined or self-induced symptoms. Their ultimate goal is to have the physician take extraordinary measures to save their life.

Method: After further investigation, Goodman discovered that the patient was secretly taking diuretics to produce the symptoms associated with bowel paralysis. His suspicions had been correct. A Munchausen's patient might complain of a variety of symptoms. A physician, though, has trouble finding these symptoms when examining the patient. Patients have added sugar to samples of urine to suggest diabetes. They have visited dermatologists with rashes or sores that they have caused with sandpaper, chemical irritants, or excessive heat.

Munchausen's patients also imitate psychiatric disorders. They may induce delusions and hallucinations by taking psychoactive drugs. They may try to influence the physician to perform thorough medical investigations. Munchausen's patients have a tendency to hide their methods poorly. They may even allow themselves to be observed during their symptom-causing routines. These scenarios result in most diagnoses.

Results: Describing how Munchausen's Syndrome sufferers behave is much easier than explaining why. Some investigatory leads suggest that either all-caring or all-rejecting parental relationships are experienced and then re-created by the patient. They seem to invite their physicians into an all-nurturing relationship, and at other times they despise their physicians and create an all-rejecting relationship.

The difficulty in discovering and diagnosing Munchausen's Syndrome led to the absence of a clear-cut definition in the DSM-IV. Because of this, it is extremely difficult to treat those who are affected, prior to an accurate diagnosis.

PRIMARY SOURCE

" *[W]e all experience occurrences of somatization, whether or not we are aware of them. For the most part, these are related to stress and are normal. We usually identify the physical feelings as stress induced and may say, 'I had such a bad day at the office, my stomach is still tied up in knots,' or 'I'm tense—I feel it in my neck.' These sensations are usually relieved by . . . a hot bath, a good dinner, exercise, or a good night's sleep.* "

—Dr. Berney Goodman, *When the Body Speaks Its Mind* (1994)

Analyzing the Case Study

1. *Defining* What is Munchausen's Syndrome?

2. *Speculating* What are some possible causes of Munchausen's Syndrome?

3. *Contrasting* How does Munchausen's Syndrome differ from the type of ordinary occurrences of somatization that we all experience, according to the quote?

4. *Making Connections* Why might a physician or psychologist suspect that someone is suffering from Munchausen's Syndrome?

5. *Analyzing Cause and Effect* What is the danger of a physician or psychologist misdiagnosing this disorder?

Reading **HELP**DESK CCSS

Academic Vocabulary

• somewhat • decline

Content Vocabulary

• schizophrenia
• delusions
• hallucinations
• major depressive disorder
• bipolar disorder

TAKING NOTES:

Key Ideas and Details

FINDING THE MAIN IDEA Use a graphic organizer similar to the one below to identify types of schizophrenia.

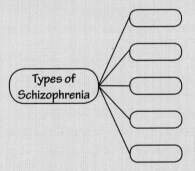

Types of Schizophrenia

LESSON 4

Schizophrenia and Other Disorders

ESSENTIAL QUESTION • *What happens when psychological processes break down?*

IT MATTERS BECAUSE

Schizophrenia is often misunderstood. The term schizophrenia *comes from Greek for "split personality." However, schizophrenia does not refer to dissociative identity disorder. Instead, it involves a split between the intellectual and emotional parts of a single personality. People with schizophrenia experience a variety of problems that make it hard for them to function at home, at work, and in social situations.*

Defining Schizophrenia

GUIDING QUESTION *How is schizophrenia a split between the emotional and intellectual parts of a person?*

We can understand depression, and most of us have experienced anxiety. In addition, we can appreciate how people with these problems strive to overcome them as best they can. An individual with schizophrenia, however, who withdraws from normal life and whose distorted perceptions and behavior reach an irrational, fantastic, fear-laden, unimaginable level, does so in ways that are difficult to understand. Yet, psychologists are making progress in furthering our understanding of schizophrenia—the most complex and severe psychological problem we encounter.

What Is Schizophrenia?

While the disorders discussed thus far are primarily problems of emotion, schizophrenia is a problem of cognition also involving emotion, perception, and motor functions. Schizophrenia affects about 1 percent of people worldwide, including 2.4 million Americans, but the odds increase if schizophrenia is already in the family. What distinguishes this disorder from other types of psychological disturbance? Schizophrenia involves confused and disordered thoughts and perceptions. With schizophrenia, a person's thought processes are **somewhat** disturbed, and the person has lost contact with reality to a considerable extent. One expert noted that someone with depression or severe anxiety problems dreams in an unreal way about life, while a person with schizophrenia lives life as an unreal dream.

A male patient diagnosed with schizophrenia with paranoid tendencies created this painting. It displays the symbolism of watchful eyes, grasping hands, and the self as subject matter.

▶ **CRITICAL THINKING**

Classifying How is the paranoid type of schizophrenia characterized?

schizophrenia a group of disorders characterized by confused and disconnected thoughts, emotions, and perceptions

somewhat slightly, to some extent

Schizophrenia is not a single problem; it has no single cause or cure. Rather, it is a collection of symptoms that indicates an individual has serious difficulty trying to meet the demands of life.

People with schizophrenia often have difficulty using language to communicate. They seem to go from one phrase to another by random association. Confused language may result because schizophrenia affects the working memory, which is used to form sentences. A person with schizophrenia will not remember the beginning of a sentence and thus finishes it with an unrelated thought.

Suppose a psychiatrist is interviewing a patient who has just been admitted to a hospital. The individual demonstrates a wide assortment of symptoms. He is intensely excited, expresses extreme hostility toward members of his family, and at the same time claims that he loves them, showing conflicting feelings. One minute he is extremely aggressive, questioning the psychiatrist's motives and even threatening her. The next minute he withdraws and acts as if he does not hear anything she says. Then he begins talking again. "Naturally," he says, "I am growing my father's hair." Although all of the person's other behavior indicates psychological problems, this last statement would be the diagnostic bell ringer. It reveals that the man is living in a private, disordered reality.

delusions false beliefs that a person maintains in the face of contrary evidence

hallucinations perceptions that have no direct external cause

decline to drop or become less in amount

Many individuals with schizophrenia experience **delusions**—false beliefs maintained in the face of contrary evidence—and **hallucinations**—perceptions in the absence of corresponding sensation. For example, a person with schizophrenia may perceive a voice when, in fact, there is no sound present. A person with schizophrenia may show a number of other symptoms as well. One is *incoherence*, or a marked **decline** in thought processes. The language of someone with schizophrenia may be sped up; sometimes, it is described as "word

Louise Williams/Photo Researchers, Inc.

salad"—lots of words thrown together. Another symptom is *disturbance of affect*, or emotions that are inappropriate for the circumstances. Some individuals may show a lack of emotion in their tone of voice and do not respond with any emotion to what is happening around them. This is known as a flat affect. Others may respond to situations with an emotional tone or outward display that does not match the situation. For example, the individual may laugh uncontrollably when they learn of something tragic that has happened. This is known as an inappropriate affect.

In addition, an individual with schizophrenia may display severe *deterioration in normal movement*, which may occur as slowed movement, non-movement, or as highly agitated behavior. Another symptom is a marked *decline in previous levels of functioning;* for example, a sharp drop off in productivity at work. Yet another symptom is *diverted attention*, perhaps brought about by cognitive flooding, as if the person is unable to focus his or her attention.

Types of Schizophrenia

Psychologists classify schizophrenia into several subtypes. One, the *paranoid type*, involves hallucinations and delusions, including *grandeur*: "I am the savior of my people"; or *persecution*: "Someone is always watching me." People with the *catatonic type* may remain motionless for long periods, exhibiting a waxy flexibility in which limbs in unusual positions may take a long time to return to a resting, relaxed position—exactly as if melting a wax statue. Symptoms of the *disorganized type* include incoherent language, inappropriate emotions, giggling for no apparent reason, generally disorganized motor behavior, and hallucinations and delusions. Another form of schizophrenia is the *remission type*. This diagnostic label is applied to anyone whose symptoms are completely gone or still exist but are not severe enough to have earned a diagnosis of schizophrenia in the first place. The expectation is that symptoms will return, so the schizophrenia is simply viewed as in remission. It is sometimes difficult to differentiate between types of schizophrenia because some symptoms are shared by all types. The *undifferentiated type* encompasses the basic symptoms of schizophrenia, such as deterioration of daily functioning, hallucinations, delusions, inappropriate emotions, and thought disorders.

Schizophrenia is a very complex condition, and treatment is long-term and usually requires hospitalization. Long-term institutionalization sometimes leads to a patient who is *burned out*—one who is unlikely to function normally in society.

Schizophrenia may go into remission, in which the symptoms disappear and the person seems quite normal, but according to the DSM-IV, adjustment tends to deteriorate between successive episodes of the reappearance of symptoms. Although recovery from schizophrenia is possible, no real cure exists, and an individual diagnosed with schizophrenia may never escape from the condition.

✔ **READING PROGRESS CHECK**

Describing How does a schizophrenic person perceive reality?

A person suffering from the catatonic type of schizophrenia can hold an unusual position for long periods of time.

▶ **CRITICAL THINKING**

Stating Is schizophrenia curable? Explain your answer.

Women are nearly twice as likely as men to experience major depression. Why? One possibility is that hormonal changes contribute to depression, although hormonal fluctuations alone don't cause depression. Other biological factors, such as inherited traits and personal experiences, are also implicated. Cultural stressors, such as poverty and abuse, may also play a role in the higher rate of depression in women. Then, too, women are more likely than men to report their depression and seek help. Men often attempt to distract themselves when experiencing depression rather than seeking help.

Causes of Schizophrenia

GUIDING QUESTION *What is the diathesis-stress hypothesis?*

What is the actual cause of schizophrenia? There are many theories, and just as certainly, there is disagreement among practitioners. In all likelihood, the ultimate cause is an interaction of environmental, genetic, and biochemical factors.

Biological Influences

Genetics is almost certainly involved in causing schizophrenia. Scientists have known for a long time that schizophrenia tends to run in families. One psychologist summarized the results of more than 35 studies conducted in Western Europe from 1920 to 1987. As confirmed by others, he found that there is a 1 percent likelihood that anyone in the general population will develop schizophrenia. These odds, however, increase to 10 percent if schizophrenia is already in the family. People who have a family history of the illness have a greater likelihood of developing it than the general population. Yet, even among identical twins, if one twin develops schizophrenia, only 48 percent of the twin's siblings will develop it. Schizophrenia is likely caused by a combination of genetic, epigenetic (factors that affect a cell but not its DNA), and environmental factors.

Researchers have studied children born into families where either parent or a parent's sibling was diagnosed with schizophrenia. Across several studies, if one or more siblings are diagnosed with schizophrenia, other children in the family will later be diagnosed with the condition less than 2 percent of the time. That probability rises to 5.5 percent if a parent or sibling is diagnosed. Even where both parents were later diagnosed as having schizophrenia, about 50 percent of the children show no signs of schizophrenia. In summary, psychologists cannot specify the exact contribution hereditary factors make to schizophrenia.

Biochemistry and Physiology

The proper working of the brain depends on the presence of the right amounts of many chemicals, from oxygen to proteins. Some psychologists believe that psychosis is due largely to chemical imbalances in the brain. According to some theorists, occasionally people are born with a nervous system that gets aroused very easily and takes a long time to return to normal.

Chemical problems may also be involved in the occurrence of schizophrenia. A number of researchers believe the basic problem in schizophrenia is that too much or too little of certain chemicals has upset the brain's mechanisms for processing information, perhaps interfering with normal synaptic transmission. The *dopamine hypothesis* suggests an excess of dopamine at selected synapses is related to a diagnosis of schizophrenia. One psychologist notes that correlational studies are not enough to demonstrate a direct role for dopamine in schizophrenia.

It seems likely that chemicals play a role, but it is hard to tell whether these chemicals are the cause of schizophrenia or the result of it. Symptoms of schizophrenia may even be caused by the fact that people with schizophrenia tend to live in hospitals, where they get little exercise, eat institutional food, and are usually given daily doses of tranquilizers. Living under such conditions, anyone might develop chemical imbalances and abnormal behavior.

The use of brain imaging technology has led to the discovery that the brains of people with schizophrenia often show signs of deteriorated tissue. The results of a study about pregnancy complications as a risk factor for schizophrenia suggest that people who at some time developed the disorder were more likely to have had mothers who had experienced difficult pregnancies and complications while giving birth to them. Maternal obesity, infection during the second

In 1930 four identical girls were born. By high school, people had labeled the Genain quadruplets as somehow different. By the time they were young adults, all four were diagnosed with schizophrenia.

▶ **CRITICAL THINKING**

Inferring From this case, what can psychologists infer about the causes of schizophrenia?

trimester of pregnancy, and oxygen deprivation to the fetus are correlated with children developing schizophrenia. The exact role of the environment in fostering schizophrenia is unclear, but it is involved.

Family and Interactions

From Freud onward, it has been tempting to blame the family situation in childhood for problems that develop during adulthood. Paul Meehl suggested that bad experiences during childhood are not enough, in and of themselves, to lead to schizophrenia; being part of a *pathogenic*, or unhealthful, family may contribute to problems in the adult years. Studies show that families of individuals who later develop schizophrenia are often on the verge of falling apart. Another frequent finding is that family members organize themselves around—or in spite of—the very unusual, demanding, or maladaptive behavior of one member of the family. Communication, too, often seems disorganized in the early family life of people who later develop schizophrenia.

Stressors

Which of these theories is correct? At this point, psychologists do not know. It may be that each is partially true. Perhaps people who inherit a tendency toward psychological disorders react more strongly to stressful situations than others would. The *diathesis-stress hypothesis* states that an individual may have inherited a predisposition toward schizophrenia. For schizophrenia to develop, however, that person must be exposed to an environment with certain stressors, such as bad family experiences, before the schizophrenia will develop. Explaining the causes of schizophrenia is perhaps the most complex research problem psychologists face.

✓ READING PROGRESS CHECK

Explaining How does the diathesis-stress hypothesis explain the development of schizophrenia?

Developmental Disorders

GUIDING QUESTION *How are autism and Asperger's syndrome similar?*

Pervasive development disorders are a group of disorders marked by delayed development of socialization and communication skills. These disorders, shortened to PDDs, are sometimes referred to as autism spectrum disorders, or ASDs. Symptoms for PDDs usually appear by the age of three, although they may appear as early as infancy. Besides problems with language and relating to other people, symptoms may include repetitive patterns of behavior, unusual styles or habits in play, and difficulty in dealing with changes in a daily routine or in one's immediate surroundings.

These disorders include classic autism and Asperger's syndrome, as well as several more rare disorders. In spite of the word *pervasive* (which means to be spread widely or throughout) in the name, not all children with PDDs have problems in all areas of their life or in their development. Children with PDDs vary greatly in their abilities and in their intelligence. Most children with PDDs function very well in some areas.

Not all doctors agree on the usage of the term PDD. Some use the label generally when hesitant to diagnose very young children with a specific type of PDD, such as autism. It is important to remember that PDD refers to a category of disorders and is not itself a diagnosis.

Connecting Psychology to History

A CHANGING UNDERSTANDING OF SCHIZOPHRENIA

Documents describing schizophrenia date back thousands of years. For centuries, it was believed that people with schizophrenia were possessed, either by the devil or an evil spirit. They were exorcised, tortured, and burnt at the stake. Even after schizophrenia was recognized as an illness, the practice of treating people by bloodletting—intentionally cutting the patient to release "excess" blood—often resulted in the patient's death.

▲ This painting from the 1700s depicts Bedlam, one of the earliest mental hospitals in the U.K. It became notorious for poor treatment of its patients.

In his 1887 classification of mental disorders, German physician Emile Kraepelin called the disorder *dementia praecox* ("early dementia"). Swiss psychiatrist Eugen Bleuler changed the name to *schizophrenia* in 1908 to describe the fragmented thinking of people with the disorder. Both Kraepelin and Bleuler subdivided schizophrenia into categories.

Treatment remained harsh well into the twentieth century. People with schizophrenia were restrained and locked away in "insane asylums," where they were subject to abuse and sometimes made a public spectacle. Other treatments included lobotomies, in which part of the brain is surgically removed, and electroconvulsive therapy. The first antipsychotic medication, Thorazine, was introduced in the early 1950s. Since that time, antipsychotic medications have helped many people with schizophrenia live more normal lives.

Studies have found physical abnormalities in the brains of people with schizophrenia, such as reduced size of some regions. Certain brain chemicals seem to be involved in the disorder. In addition, researchers are studying the genetic basis of schizophrenia to help create better means of treating the disorder. With the knowledge they gain, psychologists hope someday to develop a cure for schizophrenia.

▶ **CRITICAL THINKING**

1. ***Summarizing*** How has the understanding of schizophrenia changed over time?

2. ***Making Connections*** How might research into possible genetic causes of schizophrenia affect other psychological disorders that have a genetic basis?

Autism

Schizophrenia and autism involve neurons in specialized areas of the brain. In autism, errors in the final stages of brain development affect the amygdala, limbic system, and possibly the cerebellum. These regions are related to language, information processing, and the emotional coloration of those processes.

Obvious to the parents in haunting ways soon after birth, *infantile autism* causes children to differ from normal children in three ways. First, children with autism do not respond to other people. If you pick up an autistic child, he or she is stiff or limp; the child will not cling to you as normal children will. Second, an autistic child is very slow in developing language and communication skills. By age 5 or 6, they may simply repeat what has been said, a condition called *echolalia*. Third, autistic children are very limited in their interests and behavior. They may flap their hands or rock back and forth for hours without ceasing. They may injure themselves.

Autism now affects one in 88 children. Males are four times as likely as females to be affected. Explaining autism's cause has been difficult, partly because the symptoms range widely. Learning-based and psychoanalytic attempts have failed. People with high-functioning autism usually have average or above-average intelligence.

No single cause of autism has been identified. It seems likely that there is a genetic predisposition to autism. In cases of identical twins, if one has autism, so does the other twin 90 percent of the time, making it clear that genetics play a role. An inborn defect may interact with later environmental or biological events to produce autism.

Asperger's Syndrome

Asperger's syndrome (AS) is an autism spectrum disorder characterized by impairment in communication skills, as well as restrictive patterns of thought and behavior. Unlike children with autism, children with AS retain their early language skills and do not withdraw from the world, although the limited interests and poor social skills associated with AS often result in isolation from other people.

The most distinctive symptom of AS is an obsession with a single topic to the exclusion of everything else. People with AS will collect enormous amounts of information about the topic they are interested in, and will talk about little else. Other symptoms include eccentric or repetitive behaviors, unusual rituals, problems with communication and coordination, and poor social skills.

Children with AS are at risk for developing other mental illnesses over time. Asperger's syndrome has been linked to such disorders as depression, attention deficit hyperactivity disorder (ADHD), obsessive-compulsive disorder, and schizophrenia.

The cause of Asperger's syndrome is not known, although current research points to brain abnormalities. Because it tends to run in families, scientists know that there is a genetic component to AS. Boys are three to four times as likely to be affected as girls.

Many people with AS are very skilled or talented in a particular area, such as math or music. Because people with AS usually have average or above-average intelligence, many of them are able to function very well in academic and work environments. However, because of the impairment in communication skills so characteristic of this disorder, people with AS may continue to have problems with building and maintaining relationships, as well as in other areas of socialization, throughout their lives.

✓ READING PROGRESS CHECK

Contrasting How does Asperger's syndrome differ from autism?

More ABOUT...

Pervasive Development Disorders

There is currently no cure for pervasive development disorders such as autism or Asperger's syndrome. Because of the wide range of symptoms and abilities they display, each child's specific needs must be taken into consideration in developing a therapy plan. Such a plan may include special education, behavior modification, and speech or physical therapy. There are no medications to treat PDDs, although medications may be prescribed for specific symptoms, such as anxiety or ADHD.

Mood Disorders

GUIDING QUESTION *How do major depressive disorders and bipolar disorder differ?*

Occasional depression is common. For some, however, these moods are more intense and tend to last for longer periods. These individuals often get the sense that their depression will go on forever and believe that there is nothing they can do to change it. As a result, their emotions hamper their ability to function effectively or to seek help for their disorder. In extreme cases, a mood may cause individuals to lose touch with reality or seriously threaten their health or lives.

Major Depressive Disorder

Individuals suffering from **major depressive disorder** spend at least two weeks feeling depressed, sad, anxious, fatigued, and agitated, experiencing a reduced ability to function and interact with others. The depression ranges from mild feelings of uneasiness, sadness, and apathy to intense suicidal despair. To be diagnosed as depression, these feelings cannot be attributed to bereavement (the loss of a loved one). This disorder is marked by at least four of the following symptoms: problems with eating too much or too little; trouble with sleeping too much or too little; difficulty with thinking, concentrating, or decision making; lacking energy; thinking about suicide; and feeling worthless or guilty.

Bipolar Disorder

One type of mood disorder is **bipolar disorder**, in which individuals are excessively and inappropriately happy or unhappy. These reactions may take the form of high elation, hopeless depression, or an alternation between the two. In the *manic phase*, a person experiences elation, extreme confusion, distractibility, and racing thoughts. Often the person has an exaggerated sense of self-esteem and engages in irresponsible behavior. This state is not as easy to detect as the person seems to be in touch with reality and blessed with an unending sense of optimism. During a manic episode, one may behave as if they need less sleep. Activity levels typically increase, as does the volume and frequency in which they speak.

In a screening for a history of manic episodes, there must be a differentiation between evidence of normal euphoria or high energy from a true manic state. The following mnemonic, "DIG-FAST," can be used to recall the classic symptoms of a manic state: **D**istractability; **I**ndiscretion; **G**randiosity; **F**light of ideas; **A**ctivity increase; **S**leep deficit; **T**alkativeness.

Steve West/Taxi/Getty Images

major depressive disorder severe form of lowered mood in which a person experiences feelings of worthlessness and diminished pleasure or interest in many activities

bipolar disorder disorder in which an individual alternates between feelings of mania (euphoria) and depression

A depressed person often feels empty and alone.

▶ **CRITICAL THINKING**

Specifying When does depression become a psychological disorder?

In the *depressive phase*, the individual is overcome by feelings of failure, worthlessness, and despair. In contrast to the optimism and high activity of a manic-type reaction, a depressive-type reaction is marked by lethargy, despair, sadness, and unresponsiveness. The behavior of one who is depressed in a bipolar disorder is essentially the same as one who has a major depressive disorder.

In some cases a person with a bipolar disorder will alternate between frantic action and motionless despair. Some experience occasional episodes of a manic-type or depressive-type reaction, separated by long intervals of relatively normal behavior. Others exhibit almost no normal behavior, cycling instead from periods of manic-type reactions to equally intense depressive-type reactions. Some theorists have speculated that the manic periods serve as an attempt to ward off the underlying hopelessness of the depressive periods. Others believe that mania can be traced to the same biochemical disorder responsible for depression.

Seasonal Affective Disorder

Many feel a tinge of sadness when looking at a winter landscape of dull grays and browns. However, some develop a deep depression in the midst of winter known as *seasonal affective disorder*, or *SAD*. Throughout the winter they struggle with depression; their spirits lift only with the coming of spring. People suffering from SAD tend to sleep and eat excessively during their depressed periods.

Researchers have proposed that the hormone melatonin may play a role. The less light available (in winter), the more melatonin is secreted by the brain's pineal gland. A higher level of melatonin in their blood levels may cause some people to suffer from SAD. Researchers do not know why higher levels of melatonin lead to SAD in some people and not in others. Many SAD sufferers can be treated by facing bright lights for approximately 30 minutes during the early morning.

Explaining Mood Disorders

Psychological factors underlying mood disorders include certain personality traits (such as self-esteem), amount of social support, and the ability to deal with stressful situations. The cognitive theories of Aaron Beck and Martin Seligman have often served as the basis for research on depression. Beck believes that depressed people draw illogical conclusions about themselves; they blame themselves for normal problems and consider every minor failure a catastrophe. Seligman believes that depression is caused by a feeling of learned helplessness. The depressed person learns to believe that he has no control over events in his life and that it is useless even to try.

Researchers looking for a physiological or biological explanation of depression are currently searching for the neurotransmitters (such as serotonin and noradrenaline) that might cause mood disorders. They are also looking at genetic factors and faulty brain structure and function as possible causes.

Suicide and Depression

Not all who commit suicide are depressed, and not all depressed people attempt suicide. Many do think about suicide, and some translate those thoughts into action. Research indicates that the brains of people who have attempted suicide have low levels of serotonin, a chemical that helps control impulsive behavior. More research needs to be done before a definite link can be established.

People may take their lives for any number of reasons. It may be to escape from physical or emotional pain—perhaps a terminal illness or the loneliness of old age. It might be an effort to end the torment of unacceptable feelings, to punish themselves for wrongs they think they have committed, or to punish others who have not perceived their needs. In many cases we simply do not know why the suicide occurred.

Psychology & YOU

What Should You Do?

If you suspect someone you know is thinking about suicide, what should you do? Treat them like a normal human being. (Meanwhile, contact a professional psychologist or trusted teacher on how to guide your own behavior.) Do not assume that you will upset them—just talk to them. Do not be afraid to ask them about their thoughts (even suicidal ones). Listen to them—they might be relieved to have someone just listen. Urge them to get professional help. Most cities have suicide prevention hot lines.

SUICIDE RATES

Suicide rates vary according to age and gender.

▶ **CRITICAL THINKING**

1. *Analyzing Visuals* Which age group has the highest suicide rate?

2. *Comparing and Contrasting* Which gender has the higher suicide rate?

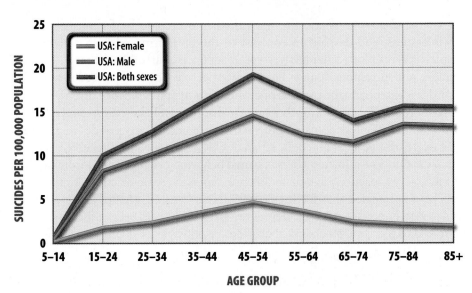

SUICIDES PER 100,000 POPULATION

— USA: Female
— USA: Male
— USA: Both sexes

AGE GROUP

5–14 15–24 25–34 35–44 45–54 55–64 65–74 75–84 85+

Source: National Vital Statistics Reports, Centers for Disease Control and Prevention, 2009

Every year more than 30,000 Americans end their lives—about 1 every 15 minutes. More women than men attempt suicide, but men more often succeed due in part to the means chosen to carry out the suicide. Suicide is common among older people but also ranks as the fourth most common cause of death among those ages 18 and 65 in the United States.

Contrary to popular belief, people who threaten suicide or make an unsuccessful attempt usually *are* serious. Studies show that about 70 percent of people who kill themselves had threatened to do so within the three months prior to the suicide. An unsuccessful attempt is often a trial run.

Among youth, bullying—including cyberbullying—has become a major public health problem. Studies show that victims of bullying show a high incidence of depression, suicidal thought, and suicide attempts. These tendencies have been found in youth of all ages, from elementary school through high school. Some studies have shown that bullies often suffer from depression as well, and are also at increased risk for suicide.

☑ **READING PROGRESS CHECK**

Contrasting How does depressive disorder differ from occasional depression?

LESSON 4 REVIEW

Reviewing Vocabulary

1. *Defining* Define schizophrenia and list five symptoms of the disorder.

Using Your Notes

2. *Describing* Use the notes you completed during the lesson to describe each of the types of schizophrenia you identified.

Answering the Guiding Questions

3. *Explaining* How is schizophrenia a split between the emotional and intellectual parts of a person?

4. *Defining* What is the diathesis-stress hypothesis?

5. *Analyzing* How are autism and Asperger's syndrome similar?

6. *Contrasting* How do major depressive disorders and bipolar disorder differ?

Writing Activity

7. *Informative/Explanatory* Schizophrenia often is misunderstood. Research facts about schizophrenia or the life of someone who has been diagnosed with schizophrenia. Write a brief report about their case, making comparisons with the information presented in the text.

netw⊙rks

There's More Online!

☑ **DIAGRAM** Effects of Alcohol Use

☑ **SELF-CHECK QUIZ**

☑ **TABLE** Types of Personality
Disorders

Personality Disorders and Drug Addiction

Reading **HELP**DESK (CCSS)

Academic Vocabulary
• **constrain** • **vary**

Content Vocabulary
• personality disorders
• antisocial personality
• psychological dependence
• tolerance
• withdrawal

TAKING NOTES:
Key Ideas and Details

ORGANIZING Use a graphic organizer like the one below to list characteristics of an antisocial personality.

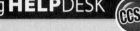

```
1. Characteristics of an
   Antisocial Personality
   A. _____
   B. _____
   C. _____
   D. _____
```

ESSENTIAL QUESTION • *What happens when psychological processes break down?*

◯ IT MATTERS BECAUSE
Drug abuse has become a major psychological problem in American society. The Department of Health and Human Services estimates that approximately 10 percent of the population experiences alcoholism, while another 5 percent are addicted to drugs. Millions of Americans depend so heavily on drugs and alcohol that they hurt themselves physically, socially, and psychologically.

Personality Disorders

GUIDING QUESTION *How are personality disorders different from anxiety disorders?*

The American Psychological Association defines personality as "the unique psychological qualities of an individual that influence a variety of characteristic behavior patterns (both overt and covert) across different situations and over time." Our personality affects the way we view the world. Our attitudes, thoughts, and feelings are all part of our personality. People with healthy personalities are able to form personal relationships with family, friends, and co-workers and to deal with normal stresses. People who are unable to function normally in these areas may be suffering from personality disorders.

Personality disorders are different from the problems we have been discussing. People with personality disorders generally do not suffer from acute anxiety nor do they behave in bizarre, incomprehensible ways. Psychologists consider these people to have a disorder because they seem unable to establish meaningful relationships with other people, to assume social responsibilities, or to adapt to their social environment. This diagnostic category includes a wide range of self-defeating personality patterns, from painfully shy, lonely types to vain, pushy show-offs.

Symptoms vary widely, depending on the type of disorder, and range from mild to severe. They may lead to problems at work and in social settings. Personality disorders are diagnosed based on a psychological evaluation and the history and severity of symptoms.

TYPES OF PERSONALITY DISORDERS

An individual with a personality disorder displays an inflexible, longstanding, and maladaptive way of dealing with the environment and other people.

▶ **CRITICAL THINKING**

1. *Describing* What are the characteristics of an individual with a paranoid personality disorder?

2. *Contrasting* How do the characteristics of a schizoid and a schizotypal disorder differ from each other?

Disorder	Characteristics Displayed
Antisocial	pattern of disregarding and violating the rights of others without feeling remorse
Avoidant	pattern of self-consciousness in social situations, feelings of inadequacy, and extreme sensitivity to criticism
Borderline	instability in interpersonal relationships and self-image and marked impulsivity
Dependent	pattern of submissiveness and excessive need to be taken care of
Histrionic	excessive emotions; excessively seeks attention
Narcissistic	exaggerated sense of self-importance, need for admiration, and lack of empathy
Obsessive-Compulsive	has an intense interest in being orderly, having control, and achieving perfection
Paranoid	distrusts others; perceives others as having evil motives
Schizoid	pattern of detachment from social relationships and limited range of emotional expression
Schizotypal	feels intense discomfort in close relationships; has distorted thinking and eccentric behavior

personality disorders
maladaptive or inflexible ways of dealing with others and one's environment

Diagnosing Personality Disorders

In making their diagnosis, mental health professionals look for four core features that characterize personality disorders:

1. Extreme and distorted thinking patterns
2. Problematic emotional response patterns
3. Impulse control problems
4. Significant interpersonal problems

A person must exhibit at least two of these four features in order to be diagnosed with a personality disorder. DSM-IV-TR recognized ten personality disorders, which were grouped into three clusters. Cluster A (odd or eccentric behavior) included paranoid, schizoid, and schizotypal disorders. Cluster B (dramatic, emotional, or erratic behavior) included antisocial, borderline, histrionic, and narcissistic disorders. Cluster C (anxious or fearful behavior) included avoidant, dependent, and obsessive-compulsive disorders.

Personality disorders are usually recognizable by adolescence and become less obvious in middle age. There are many different types of help available for people with personality disorders. Treatment depends on the type of disorder, and may include individual, group, or family therapy. Medications may be prescribed to relieve some of the symptoms, including anxiety or problems with perceptions.

Antisocial Personality

antisocial personality
a personality disorder characterized by irresponsibility, shallow emotions, and lack of conscience

In this section we focus on people with **antisocial personalities**, who in the past were referred to as sociopaths or psychopaths. Individuals with antisocial personalities exhibit a persistent disregard for and violation of others' rights. They treat people as objects—as things to be used for their gratification and to be cast aside coldly when they are no longer wanted. Intolerant of everyday frustrations and unable to save or plan or wait, they live for the moment. Seeking thrills is their major occupation. If they should injure other people along the way or break social rules, they do not seem to feel any shame or guilt. Getting caught does not seem to **constrain** them, either. Multiple reprimands, punishments, or jailing, do not lead to them staying out of trouble. They simply do not profit from experience.

constrain to hold back as if by force; to restrict

Many individuals with antisocial personalities can get away with destructive behavior because they are intelligent, entertaining, and able to feign emotions they do not feel. They win affection and confidence from others of whom they then take advantage. If caught, these individuals will either spin a fantastic lie or simply insist, with wide-eyed sincerity, that their intentions were utterly pure. Guilt and anxiety have no place in the antisocial personality.

For example, Hugh Johnson was caught after defrauding people out of thousands of dollars in 64 separate swindles. Researchers reported the following when they asked Johnson why he had victimized so many people: "He replied with some heat that he never took more from a person than the person could afford to lose, and further, that he was only reducing the likelihood that other more dangerous criminals would use force to achieve the same ends."

How do psychologists explain such a lack of ordinary human decency? According to one theory, individuals with antisocial personalities have simply imitated their own antisocial parents. Other theories point to lack of discipline or inconsistent discipline or other problems during childhood. Finally, some researchers believe that these individuals have a dysfunction of the nervous system. Psychologists are still investigating the relationship between genes and antisocial behavior. While most of us get very nervous when we do something that we have been punished for in the past, those with antisocial personalities never seem to learn to anticipate punishment and remain calm while committing antisocial acts.

Recent research has shown the importance of callous-unemotional (CU) traits and conduct problems in helping to identify children at risk of antisocial behavior. CU traits include a lack of emotion and a lack of guilt or empathy. These traits are exhibited by a small number of children with persistent conduct problems. CU traits appear to be influenced by genetic factors, especially in boys. Far fewer girls exhibit high levels of CU traits, and environmental factors appear to play a more significant role in those cases. High levels of CU traits and conduct problems between the ages of seven and twelve are predictors for severe antisocial behavior. Evidence suggests that this behavior can be changed by early intervention. Low levels of physical punishment have been shown to decrease CU traits over time. More significantly, increased levels of parental affection and involvement have been shown to decrease both CU traits and antisocial behavior over time, as well as to lower levels of anxiety.

☑ **READING PROGRESS CHECK**

Contrasting How do personality disorders differ from other psychological disorders?

Drug Addiction

GUIDING QUESTION *How does dependence make an addiction difficult to overcome?*

Drug addiction and alcoholism are covered in the DSM-IV. Abuse of drugs invariably involves **psychological dependence**. Users come to depend so much on the feeling of well-being they obtain from the drug that they feel compelled to continue using it. People can become psychologically dependent on a wide variety of drugs, including alcohol, caffeine, nicotine (in cigarettes), cocaine, marijuana, prescription pain pills, and amphetamines. When deprived of the drug, a psychologically dependent person becomes restless, irritable, and uneasy.

In addition to psychological dependence, drugs can lead to physiological addiction. A person is addicted when his system has become so used to the drug that the drugged state becomes the body's normal state. If the drug is not

Psychopaths and Sociopaths

DSM-IV designates both psychopaths and sociopaths as antisocial behavior personalities. Both disorders usually develop by age 15, and may begin with cruelty to animals. They are characterized by a lack of conscience, inability to feel empathy toward others, and lack of respect for the law.

Psychopaths are often well educated and successful in their careers. They tend to be obsessively organized. Sociopaths are frequently homeless and either out of work or unable to keep a job.

Psychopaths may be able to have normal relationships. They understand normal human emotions and empathy, but manipulate them. Sociopaths, on the other hand, are unable to understand empathy and have difficulty maintaining relationships. They may use people, and have no qualms about humiliating supposed friends. They tend to be habitual liars.

Both types are violent and deceitful. Psychopaths may spend years planning a crime, whereas sociopaths often explode into violence and are more likely to be caught. When caught, psychopaths often blame their victims or circumstances, whereas sociopaths tend to lie about their crimes.

Both disorders can be treated with therapy and psychiatric drugs.

psychological dependence use of a drug to such an extent that a person feels nervous and anxious without it

in the body, the person experiences extreme physical discomfort as he would if he were deprived of oxygen or water.

Just as dependence causes a psychological need for the drug, addiction causes a physical need. Furthermore, once a person is addicted to a drug, he develops **tolerance**; that is, his body becomes so accustomed to the drug that he has to keep increasing his dosage to obtain the high achieved with smaller doses. With certain sleeping pills, for example, a person can rapidly develop a tolerance for up to sixteen times the original dose. Further, an addict must have his drug to retain what little physical and psychological balance he has left. If he does not get it, he is likely to go through the dreaded experience of withdrawal.

Withdrawal is a state of physical and psychological upset during which the body and the mind revolt against and finally get used to the absence of the drug. Withdrawal symptoms **vary** from person to person and from drug to drug. They range from a mild case of nausea and the shakes to hallucinations, convulsions, coma, and death.

Alcoholism

This country's most serious drug problem is alcoholism. In American society, consumption of alcohol often begins at an early age. Researchers estimate that 71 percent of all high school seniors have consumed alcohol at some point in their lifetimes and that 41 percent of seniors have consumed it within the past month—down from 54 percent in 1991. Approximately 36 percent of all students entering high school have tried alcohol. An estimated 23 percent report having consumed five or more drinks in a row within the past two weeks, and nearly 3 percent of graduating seniors are drinking alcohol daily. Binge drinking is associated with college students, but 70 percent of all cases are in adults over age 26.

In small doses, alcohol is often called a social drug. It is often an activity some want to do or feel comfortable doing in the company of others. The first psychological function that it slows down is our social inhibitions. One or two drinks can make a person relaxed, talkative, playful, even giggly. It is for this reason that many people consider alcohol a stimulant, when it is really a depressant.

tolerance physical adaptation to a drug so that a person needs an increased amount in order to produce the original effect

withdrawal the symptoms that occur after a person discontinues the use of a drug to which he or she has become addicted

vary to exhibit a deviation from the typical form

Alcohol abuse is responsible for the deaths of approximately 75,000 Americans each year.

▶ **CRITICAL THINKING**

Specifying When does alcohol use become a problem?

As the number of drinks increases, problems multiply. One by one, the person's psychological and physiological functions begin to shut down. Perceptions and sensations become distorted, and behavior may become obnoxious. The person begins to stumble and weave, speech becomes slurred, and reactions, to a stop sign, for example, become sluggish or disappear. If enough alcohol accumulates in the body, it leads to unconsciousness and, in some cases, coma and death. It all depends on how much and how rapidly alcohol enters the bloodstream, which, in turn, depend on a person's weight, body chemistry, how much he or she drinks and how quickly, and his or her past experience with drinking.

Alcohol can produce psychological dependence, tolerance, and physiological dependence. One researcher outlined four stages of a Disease Model of Alcoholism. In Stage I, the individual drinks and relaxation encourages more drinking. In Stage II, secret drinking occurs, with blackouts and no memory of drinking. Stage III features rationalization to justify the drinking, and Stage IV shows impaired thinking and compulsive drinking. The disease model is no longer favored. Other researchers have noted that if alcoholism is a disease, how many among those who never decide to drink would "catch" the "disease"? Those supporting an Adaptive Model suggest that choosing to drink is a voluntary process influenced by alcoholism as a response to individual psychological and environmental factors. Those with a former substance abuse problem have no problem because they choose not to.

Alcoholism may develop from both environmental and genetic factors. A person's risk of becoming an alcoholic is three to four times higher if a member of the family is an alcoholic. Children of alcoholic parents may also be raised in an atmosphere of distrust, overdependence, and stress, which contributes to the possible development of alcoholism.

Societal Effects of Alcoholism

Alcoholism does not just affect the alcoholic. It affects his or her entire family. Just how it affects the family depends on the degree and type of alcoholism. Some alcoholics are able to function socially and to perform their normal duties. Some may become very jolly and good-humored after drinking. Others become verbally, emotionally, or physically abusive.

Children of alcoholics often experience high levels of stress, anxiety, depression, anger, and other emotional distress. They may blame themselves for their parents' behavior. They often worry about what is going on at home even when they are at school or social events. Because of this, their grades and relationships with others often suffer. The effects often continue into adulthood. Adult children of alcoholics may exhibit depression, anxiety, and obsessive or impulsive behavior. They may have difficulty in forming intimate relationships. They may have low self-esteem, and tend to have higher rates of eating disorders. Other family members, such as spouses, siblings, and parents of alcoholics, are also affected. Alcoholism often leads to marital problems. Members of an alcoholic's family often become codependent.

About 24 percent of the drivers' deaths in automobile and motorcycle accidents each year can be traced back to alcohol. Excessive alcohol use is the third leading lifestyle-related cause of death in the United States. The cost in human suffering to the individual, as well as to his or her family, is impossible to measure.

A number of organizations help the families of alcoholics. Al-Anon Family Groups provide support for family members and friends of problem drinkers. Alateen is part of Al-Anon, and provides support for young Al-Anon members whose lives have been affected by someone else's drinking. For more information about these groups, to find a local meeting, or to find an electronic meeting, you can visit www.al-anon.alateen.org.

More
ABOUT...

Teenage Drinking

How do you know if a friend or classmate has a problem with alcohol? The following physical, emotional, and social changes can provide clues:

- Smell of alcohol
- Staggered walking or other coordination problems
- Depression
- Low self-esteem
- Tendency to argue
- Tendency to be destructive
- Drop in grades
- Associating with others who condone drinking
- Participation in reckless behavior
- Lack of interest in sports or other activities

If you have a friend who you suspect has a drinking problem, you can help by showing your concern. Tell your friend that you are worried. Make sure your friend knows that it is the drinking, not your friend, that you dislike. Tell your friend how his or her drinking affects you. If your friend admits having a drinking problem, talk to them about why they drink, what they think they can do about it, and what you are willing to do to help them. You may also want to help them find a local group such as Alcoholics Anonymous that can provide support.

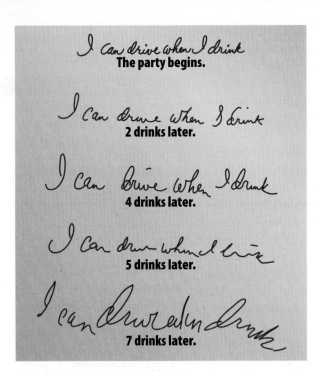

I can drive when I drink

The party begins.

I Can drive when I drink

2 drinks later.

I can drive when I drink

4 drinks later.

I can drive when I drive

5 drinks later.

I can drive when I drink

7 drinks later.

DIAGRAM ∧

EFFECTS OF ALCOHOL USE OVER TIME

As a person consumes more and more alcohol, psychological and physiological functions begin to shut down, as shown in these handwriting samples.

▶ **CRITICAL THINKING**

1. *Explaining* What is the treatment for alcoholism?

2. *Drawing Inferences* Based on the diagram, after how many drinks does the use of alcohol appear to have the greatest effect on motor skills?

Treatment

The first step in treating the alcoholic is to help him or her through the violent withdrawal, called *delirium tremens*, typical of alcohol addiction. Delirium tremens, commonly referred to as "the DTs," usually begin within 72 hours after the last drink. Body tremors, delirium, hallucinations, seizures, anxiety, depression, loss of appetite, nausea, palpitations, and heavy sweating are just a few of the symptoms associated with the DTs.

Delirium tremens is a serious condition. A person suffering from the DTs needs to be hospitalized; symptoms may get worse quickly. The first objective of treatment is to save the patient's life. Other treatment goals include relieving the symptoms and preventing any further complications. Phenobarbitol may be administered to control convulsions. Seizures, anxiety, and tremors may be treated with diazepam or lorazepam. Antipsychotic medications are usually avoided when possible because they can lead to seizures.

The next step is to try to make him or her healthier. He or she may be given a variety of treatments, from drugs to psychotherapy. Long-term preventive treatment includes therapy and counseling. People who have gone through alcohol withdrawal should try to avoid alcohol for the rest of their lives. Alcoholics Anonymous (AA), an organization for alcoholics run by people who have had a drinking problem in the past, has been more successful than most organizations in helping people stop drinking. Some alcoholics may have to turn to medical treatment. Doctors may prescribe *Antabuse* or other drugs to alcoholics.

Antabuse, or disulfiram, is a chemical that blocks the conversion of acetaldehyde to acetic acid. (Ordinarily, the liver converts alcohol into acetaldehyde, a toxic substance, and then converts acetaldehyde into acetic acid, a harmless substance.) When alcoholics take a daily Antabuse pill, they become violently sick if they have a drink of alcohol. The threat of the violent sickness may become an effective prevention. There is, however, no certain cure for alcoholism. One problem is that our society tends to encourage social drinking and to tolerate the first stage of alcoholism.

✓ **READING PROGRESS CHECK**

Listing What are the four stages of alcoholism?

LESSON 5 REVIEW

Reviewing Vocabulary

1. *Making Connections* How are addiction, tolerance, and withdrawal related to drug abuse?

Using Your Notes

2. *Analyzing* Use the notes you completed during the lesson to analyze the behavior of a real person from history or the news who demonstrated an antisocial personality.

Answering the Guiding Questions

3. *Contrasting* How are personality disorders different from anxiety disorders?

4. *Explaining* How does dependence make an addiction difficult to overcome?

Writing Activity

5. *Informative/Explanatory* Write a brief essay describing how the antisocial personality and the alcoholic impinge on others' freedom and when and why society might take steps to stop them.

Directions: On a separate sheet of paper, answer the questions below. Make sure you read carefully and answer all parts of the question.

Lesson Review

Lesson 1

1 *Contrasting* In what way does the system psychologists currently use to classify abnormal behavior differ from the one that preceded it?

2 *Stating* What is the purpose of axes in the DSM-IV?

Lesson 2

3 *Describing* Describe the symptoms associated with anxiety. Give two explanations for the occurrence of anxiety.

4 *Explaining* What is the cause of post-traumatic stress disorder?

Lesson 3

5 *Defining* What is *la belle indifférence?* How can this help determine the cause of a person's disability?

6 *Defining* What is a dissociative fugue? What psychological function might it serve? How does it differ from dissociative amnesia?

Lesson 4

7 *Listing* List and explain three possible causes of schizophrenia.

8 *Identifying* What are the major early indicators that a child may have a developmental disorder?

Lesson 5

9 *Describing* How would you describe someone who is classified as having an antisocial personality disorder?

10 *Explaining* How does the Adaptive Model explain drinking?

21st Century Skills

Interpreting a Graph Review the graph below, then answer the questions that follow.

Reported Anxiety Disorders in the United States

Any Anxiety Disorder	18%
Phobic Disorders	9%
Social Anxiety Disorder	7%
Post-Traumatic Stress Disorder	3%
Generalized Anxiety Disorder	3%
Panic Disorder	3%
Obsessive-Compulsive Disorder	1%

Source: National Institute of Mental Health, 2012

11 *Evaluating* According to the graph, what is the most common anxiety disorder reported in the United States?

12 *Drawing Conclusions* If the U.S. population is more than 311 million people, approximately how many people report obsessive-compulsive disorder?

13 *Assessing* Approximately how many people in the United States report a generalized anxiety disorder? How does that compare to the number with panic disorder?

14 *Interpreting* Do you think that suffering from an anxiety disorder is a common occurrence? Explain.

Critical Thinking Questions

15 *Defining* Develop your own definition of *psychological disorder*. Is your definition free of social values, or are values a necessary part of such a definition? Explain.

16 *Speculating* What factors might prompt members of an ethnic minority group to continue or discontinue treatment provided in state or county mental health programs? How might a doctor's cultural perceptions affect treatment?

Need Extra Help?

If You've Missed Question	**1**	**2**	**3**	**4**	**5**	**6**	**7**	**8**	**9**	**10**	**11**	**12**	**13**	**14**	**15**	**16**
Go to page	455	456	460	463	467	468	474	476	482	485	459	463	459	459	452	458

Directions: On a separate sheet of paper, answer the questions below. Make sure you read carefully and answer all parts of the question.

17 *Drawing Inferences* Why do you think it can be difficult for people suffering from major depressive disorder to take action to overcome the disorder?

18 *Assessing* Why might using drugs to treat schizophrenia be more effective than psychotherapy?

19 *Synthesizing* Why do you think people who have been treated for alcohol or drug abuse run the risk of a relapse?

Exploring the Essential Question

20 *Organizing* Create a graphic organizer for the major types of abnormal behavior described in this chapter. Look for the symptoms and causes of each abnormal behavior and categorize them along with the name of the disorder.

College and Career Readiness

21 *Research Skills* Research magazine articles about programs available to help people combat anxiety disorders. For example, you might find out about classes that airlines provide to help people overcome their fear of flying. Use software to create an informational pamphlet in which you summarize and evaluate your findings. Use standard grammar, spelling, sentence structure, and punctuation. Revise your pamphlet based on critical response from your classmates and teacher.

22 *Research and Methods* The artist Vincent van Gogh suffered from a mood disorder. Find out how his disorder affected his work. You might provide examples of paintings that he created when he was psychologically healthy and those that he created when he was suffering from the disorder. Create a biography of 2–5 pages that details your findings.

DBQ Analyzing Primary Sources

Use the document below to answer the following questions.

PRIMARY SOURCE

❝[D]epending on which figures you believe, between 20 and 84 percent of people who consult a doctor do so for some form of somatization. Hypochondria alone is said to be present in 9 percent of patients who consult their family physicians.

...Peering ahead, I think the number of people with somatization symptoms will increase dramatically as we enter the next century. Their individual dramas will be played out on a stage dominated by an increasingly stress-filled world and a backdrop of frequent family disruption, rapid cultural change, and...increased attention to, and care of, the body.❞

—Dr. Berney Goodman, *When the Body Speaks its Mind* (1994)

23 *Exploring the Main Idea* Why does the author believe that symptoms of somatization will increase?

24 *Drawing Inferences* What effect does somatization have on health care systems?

Research and Technology

25 *Identifying Cause and Effect* Conduct research to determine how television coverage of global conflict can influence anxiety, depression, or other disorders. Put your findings in a written report, including specific examples.

Psychology Journal Activity

26 *Informative/Explanatory* Review your entry in your Psychology Journal for this chapter. Were your ideas about how to identify an "excessive" amount of time doing an activity accurate? How did they compare with the standard methods of identifying a psychological disorder?

TEXT: From WHEN THE BODY SPEAKS ITS MIND by Berney Goodman, copyright © 1994 by Berney Goodman, MD. Used by permission of Jermey P. Tarcher, an imprint of Penguin Group (USA) Inc.

Need Extra Help?

If You've Missed Question	**17**	**18**	**19**	**20**	**21**	**22**	**23**	**24**	**25**	**26**
Go to page	478	471	483	459	459	478	466	466	459	450

Therapy and Change

ESSENTIAL QUESTIONS • *How can therapists modify behaviors?* • *How do changes to the body change the mind?*

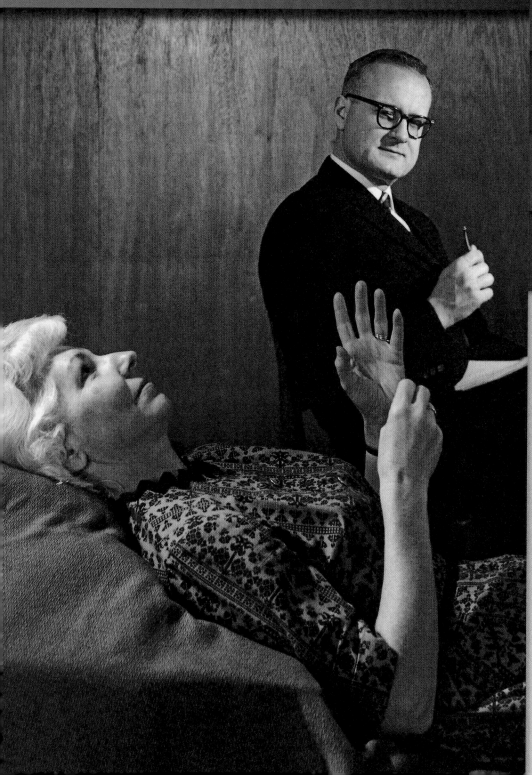

Psychology Matters...

Throughout history humanity has sought explanations for mental illness. Historically, many societies attributed mental illness to evil spirits or other myths. Even in our modern world, there are misconceptions and prejudices against those with psychological disorders. Today, disorders are treatable through the use of well established, proven psychotherapies. These therapies can help people lead happy, productive lives.

◄ Classic psychoanalysis, seen at left, is what many think of when they think of therapy. Therapy has changed in many ways over the years. Today therapy takes many different forms designed around the needs of the client.

SuperStock

489

Lab Activity

Speaking Freely

THE QUESTION...

RESEARCH QUESTION What is the best conversational style to encourage someone to share his or her feelings?

Imagine your friend is upset and you want to help her. You ask her what's wrong, and she says, "Nothing." You know that's not true, but what do you do next? You know that it would be best if she shared what's going on with her. But not everyone is comfortable sharing information about themselves, especially when the topic is emotional. You're not sure where to begin, but you assume that some methods are better than others.

In this experiment, we will investigate different conversational styles and the ways in which they encourage individuals to share information.

Psychology Journal Activity

Do you like sharing your feelings with others or does it make you nervous? Write about this in your Psychology Journal. Consider the following issues: Has it ever been beneficial to share your feelings with someone else? In what ways can it be helpful?

FINDING THE ANSWER...

HYPOTHESIS A positive, supportive conversational style encourages people to speak more freely.

THE METHOD OF YOUR EXPERIMENT

MATERIALS   sheets of paper, pens

PROCEDURE   Recruit as many participants as you are comfortable working with, but no fewer than two participants. In this experiment, you will play the role of listener. Ask each participant a simple question, such as "How was your day?" or "What did you do yesterday?" With each participant, ask the question using a different conversational style, such as supportive, argumentative, disinterested, inquisitive, and so forth. Continue talking with the participant, using the same style throughout the conversation. Be sure to use body language to help convey each conversational style. Once your conversation is over, have the participant rate you, the listener, on 10 different rubrics you have prepared. Your rubrics can include items such as: felt respected by the listener, felt that the listener was interested in what I had to say, felt that the listener spoke in an appropriate tone of voice, felt that the listener's body language showed his or her interest, felt that I could freely express myself with the listener.

DATA COLLECTION   Compare each participant's answers to the rubrics. Create a table that compares their answers. Make sure you preserve the confidentiality of each participant.

ANALYSIS & APPLICATION

1. Did your results support the hypothesis?
2. What are some of the possible obstacles that people must overcome to share information about themselves?
3. What conclusions can you draw about the style of communication that encouraged the participants to speak more freely?

networks   ONLINE LAB RESOURCES

Online you will find:

- An **interactive lab experience,** allowing you to put principles from this chapter into practice in a digital psychology lab environment. This chapter's lab will include an experiment related to therapy and change.

- A **Skills Handbook** that includes a guide for using the scientific method, creating experiments, and analyzing data.

- A **Notebook** where you can complete your Psychology Journal and record and analyze data from your experiment.

net**w**orks

There's More Online!

- ☑ **IMAGE** Group Therapy
- ☑ **TABLE** Kinds of Therapists
- ☑ **TABLE** Types of Psychotherapies
- ☑ **SELF-CHECK QUIZ**

Reading **HELP**DESK

Academic Vocabulary

- **imply**
- **assessment**

Content Vocabulary

- **psychotherapy**
- **eclectic approach**
- **group therapy**

TAKING NOTES:

Integration of Knowledge and Ideas

IDENTIFYING CAUSE AND EFFECT In the diagram below, place the primary goal of therapy in the center rectangle. In each surrounding rectangle, enter a factor that can help achieve this goal.

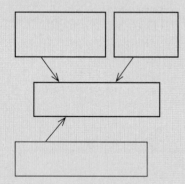

LESSON 1

What Is Psychotherapy?

ESSENTIAL QUESTION • *How can therapists modify behaviors?*

IT MATTERS BECAUSE

Have you ever had a problem that seemed so serious you were unsure if you could handle it yourself? At certain times of transition and crisis, we may need to find someone trustworthy with whom to share our doubts and problems. A parent, relative, or close friend is often helpful at these times. When psychological problems are too bewildering and complex to be solved in this way, psychotherapy can be helpful.

The Nature of Psychotherapy

GUIDING QUESTION *What is the goal of psychotherapy?*

When adults become dissatisfied or distraught with life and suspect that the reason lies within themselves, they are likely to seek help from someone with training and experience in such matters. These people seek *therapy*, which refers to treatment of behavioral, bodily, or psychological disorders. Mental health professionals who have been trained to deal with the psychological problems of others include clinical, counseling, and school psychologists, and psychiatrists. The special kind of help they provide is called psychotherapy. **Psychotherapy** involves three things: verbal interaction between a therapist and client; the development of a supportive and trusting relationship; and an analysis by the therapist of the client's problems, including suggestions for overcoming those problems.

Psychotherapy literally means "healing of the soul." In early times, people often thought that psychological disturbances represented some sort of moral or religious shortcoming. People with personal problems were sometimes viewed as being inhabited by demons, and treatment consisted of exorcism—the driving out of these demons by religious ceremonies—or physical punishment. Within the past 200 years, however, views of psychological disorders have changed. Psychological disorders slowly came to be thought of as diseases, and the term *mental illness* was applied to many psychological problems.

One of the earliest reformers was Philippe Pinel (1745–1826) who, in 1792, became the chief physician at the Paris asylum Bicêtre. His unprecedented step of unchaining mental patients who were shackled to the walls changed society's view of people with psychological disturbances.

(l)Library of Congress Prints & Photographs Division (LC-USZ62-9797); (r)Jon Bradley/Stone/Getty Images

Society began to see that the psychologically disturbed were not possessed by demons, but rather needed care and treatment for their illnesses. Pinel believed that extreme social and psychological stresses were a major cause of psychological disorders. He encouraged close contact with patients and encouraged them to discuss their personal problems.

Nevertheless, many psychotherapists feel that the term *mental illness* has outlived its usefulness and that, in fact, it may now be doing more harm than good. The trouble with letting a person think of himself as mentally ill is that he sees himself in a passive, helpless position. He sees his troubles as being caused by forces over which he has no control. By thinking of himself in this way, the person can avoid taking responsibility for his own situation and for helping himself change.

Development of Psychotherapy

Different types of psychotherapy developed over the years. Sigmund Freud, who created psychoanalysis, began his career in the late 1800s as a neurologist. A neurologist is a physician who studies the physical structure and function of the neurons and brain. Freud became interested in hypnosis, which led him to explore the unconscious mind. Ultimately his education in medicine led him to develop psychoanalysis, the first "talk" therapy in the Western world. For many years, psychoanalysis was the primary method of therapy for individuals with psychological disorders. In psychoanalysis, power revolves around the physician. The physician tells the patient what is wrong with him or her. Patients are expected to follow the psychoanalyst's instructions on how to improve their lives.

Following World War II, the number of psychologists in the United States increased dramatically. In the mid-1900s, people were less willing to rely on authority. The 1960s saw a boom in the "human potential" movement—people believed they were in charge of their own destinies. They would not be controlled by some aloof authority such as a remote psychotherapist. This led to the creation of humanistic therapy, which believed that, under the right circumstances, individuals could heal themselves. During this time, a number of philosophers, including Jean-Paul Sartre, wrote about the meaning of life for the individual. Humanistic therapy, with its emphasis on self, drew on this thinking. Carl Rogers's client-centered therapy, which worked to help people reach their full potential, was the most influential form of humanistic therapy. The introduction of humanistic therapy had long-term effects. No longer was the therapist in complete control of treatment. From this point forward, dealing with psychological disorders was seen as a team effort between the professional and the individual.

While humanistic therapy could help people make important changes, some psychologists thought the results were not measurable and that humanistic therapies focused too much on people's feelings and not enough on correcting illogical thought processes. This led to the development of cognitive therapy. The word cognition means "reason" or "intellect." These techniques focus on helping individuals to think, and then behave, in ways that can help them reach their goals. The late 1960s saw the introduction of behavior therapy. This method focused on changing people's actual behavior, rather than delving into its causes. Many therapists combined cognitive and behavior therapy methods. This led to cognitive-behavior therapy, which is widely used today.

Mental health professionals began to realize that many individuals with psychological challenges needed practice with interpersonal skills. This led to the beginning of group therapy. Another reason for the increasing use of group therapy is the high cost of individual therapy. Today, many people find group therapy helpful. In self-help groups, such as Alcoholics Anonymous, members with similar challenges work together, often with a leader, to provide support for one another.

Dorothea Dix (1802–1887)
In 1841 Dorothea Dix began teaching a Sunday school class at a local prison in Massachusetts. She was horrified to find mentally ill patients locked up with criminals in dark, unheated, and filthy rooms. She saw people being chained and beaten whose only "crime" was of having a psychological disorder; men, women, and children were thrown into the same jail cell.

Dix set out on a crusade that would last a lifetime. She toured similar jails in several states, reporting the appalling things she witnessed to the state legislators. Her struggles resulted in reforms in the treatment of prisoners and people with psychological disorders.

▶ **CRITICAL THINKING**

Speculate What personal characteristics do you think Dorothea Dix had?

psychotherapy any treatment used by therapists to help troubled individuals overcome their problems

Therapy Method	Main Techniques	Main Goal	Means of Achieving Goal
Psychoanalysis	free association, dream analysis, transference	reduce anxiety and guilt from unconscious urges	verbal processes
Humanistic Therapy	active listening, acceptance, support	fulfill one's potential and improve self-concept	verbal processes
Cognitive Therapy	talking, listening, role-playing, and completion of assignments	unite behaviors and thought	revising thoughts
Behavior Therapy	counterconditioning, operant conditioning, systematic desensitization	change one's unwanted or abnormal behaviors and acquire desirable behaviors	behavioral training

TABLE ∧

TYPES OF PSYCHOTHERAPIES
There are many types of therapies. The ones listed in this chart are common methods in use today.

▶ **CRITICAL THINKING**

1. *Differentiating* Which method would probably be most effective for treating someone with an eating disorder?

2. *Contrasting* In which method of therapy would the therapist be most likely to ask the individual to act out a situation that makes her feel uncomfortable?

As medicine advanced, many diseases and conditions that used to be untreatable could be treated with drug therapy. Epilepsy, for example, is an example of such a condition. Scientists also developed drugs that helped control psychological disorders. While these drugs are not cures, they can control symptoms. The are often used in conjunction with psychotherapy. The use of drugs has greatly changed the treatment of psychological disorders.

Today's psychotherapy has benefited from all of the methods discussed here. No one method of therapy has convincingly proven to be better than the others. However, several factors have been shown to be important. These factors include identifying the issue to be addressed, the relationship between the individual and the therapist, and the importance of focusing on changing the individual's behavior.

Functions of Psychotherapy

One of the functions of psychotherapy is to help people realize that they are responsible for their own problems and that, even more importantly, they are the only ones who can really solve these problems. This approach does not imply that people become disturbed on purpose or that no one should need outside help. People often adopt certain techniques for getting along in life that seem appropriate at the time but lead to trouble in the long run. Such patterns can be difficult for the individual to recognize or change. The major task of the therapist, therefore, is to help people examine their way of living, to understand how their present way of living causes problems, and to start living in new, more beneficial ways. The therapist can be thought of as a professional hired by the individual to help him find the source of his problems and investigate appropriate solutions.

Approaches to Psychotherapy

There are many different kinds of therapy. However, only a few of them will be described in this chapter, including psychoanalysis, humanistic, cognitive, behavioral, and biological approaches to treatment (see table, Types of Psychotherapies). Each one is based on different theories about how human personality works, and each one is carried out in a different style. Some psychotherapists stick primarily to one style and consider the other styles less useful. Other psychotherapists use an **eclectic approach** to therapy, choosing methods from many different kinds of therapy and using the ones that work best. Whatever the style or philosophy, all types of psychotherapy have certain characteristics in common.

The primary goal of psychotherapy is to strengthen the patient's control over his or her life. People seeking psychotherapy need to change their thoughts, feelings, and behaviors. Over the years, they have developed not only certain feelings about themselves but also behaviors that strengthen those feelings. Their behaviors and feelings make it difficult, if not impossible for them to reach their goals.

eclectic approach method that combines various kinds of therapy or combinations of therapies

One of the most important factors in effective treatment is the patient's belief or hope that he can change. The influence that a patient's hopes and expectations have on his improvement is often called the *placebo effect*. This name comes from giving medical patients placebos, inert sugar pills, when they complain of ailments that do not seem to have any physiological basis. The patients take the tablets, and their symptoms disappear.

The placebo effect does not **imply** that problems can be solved simply by fooling the patient. It does demonstrate, however, the tremendous importance of the patient's attitude in finding ways to change. A patient who does not believe he can be helped probably cannot be. A patient who believes he can change and that he has the power to change will find a way. Therapy goes beyond the placebo effect. It combines the patient's belief that he can change with hard work and professional guidance.

imply to suggest

Qualities of a Therapist

In American society, there are many practitioners of psychotherapy. Some, like clinical psychologists, are trained in psychological testing, **assessment**, and diagnosis. Counseling psychologists have been trained to deal with problems of adjustment. Various kinds of therapists and the training that each goes through before practicing psychotherapy are shown in the table, Kinds of Therapists.

assessment a judgment or opinion about someone or something

Before going to a professional therapist, most people first turn to a friend or other nonprofessional for help and advice. Sometimes, this is exactly what's needed. Professional therapists, however, are likely to be more skillful in encouraging the person to examine uncomfortable feelings and problems.

There are three characteristics found in effective therapists. First, a therapist needs to be psychologically healthy. A therapist who is anxious, defensive, and withdrawn will not be able to see the patient's problems clearly nor able to aid in the development of solutions. A second important characteristic is empathy.

Clinical psychologists are therapists with a PhD or a PsyD, a Doctor of Psychology. They treat people with psychological disorders in hospitals, clinics, and community health centers.

Counseling psychologists generally have a master's or PhD degree in counseling psychology. They usually work in educational institutions, where they are available for consultation about personal problems. They customarily refer clients with serious problems to clinical psychologists or psychiatrists.

Clinical Neuropsychologists have PhD degrees. They have extensive education in neurophysiology regarding the mechanisms and operation of the brain. They typically work with patients who have a brain injury that is interfering with normal behavior. Such damage may result from drug use, accidents, or normal aging. Their primary role has been in assessing neurological damage; some are now involved in therapy, and some prescribe medicine.

Psychiatrists are medical doctors. They take postgraduate training in the causes and treatment of abnormal behavior. Because of their medical background, psychiatrists are licensed to prescribe medicines and are the only group that can perform operations.

Psychoanalysts are usually medical doctors who have taken special training in the theory of personality and techniques of psychotherapy of Sigmund Freud, typically at a psychoanalytic institute. They must themselves be psychoanalyzed before they can practice. Declining numbers of psychoanalysts still practice.

Psychiatric social workers are people with a master's degree in social work. They counsel people with everyday problems.

Psychiatric nurses have a standard nursing license and advanced training in psychology. They dispense medicine and act as a contact person between counseling sessions.

Counselors have a master's degree from a counseling program. They dispense advice and may or may not have any training in psychology. Nevertheless, more troubled people turn to counselors than to other kinds of therapists.

< TABLE

KINDS OF THERAPISTS
Several groups of people practice psychotherapy. Not all of them have professional training in psychology.

▶ CRITICAL THINKING

1. **Contrasting** What is the difference between a counselor and a psychoanalyst?

2. **Evaluating** What kinds of therapists are *most* likely to have PhD degrees?

Empathy is the capacity for warmth and understanding. Troubled people are usually fearful and confused about explaining their problems. The therapist needs to be able to give the patient confidence that he is capable of caring and understanding. Finally, a good therapist must be experienced in dealing with people and understanding their complexities. Only by having worked with many people can a therapist learn when to give support, when to insist that the patient stand on his own feet, and how to make sense of the things people say.

✓ READING PROGRESS CHECK

Describing What are three characteristics that make a good, effective therapist?

Group Therapies

GUIDING QUESTION *What are the advantages of group therapy?*

group therapy patients work together with the aid of a leader to resolve interpersonal problems

In some forms of therapy, the patient is alone with the therapist. In **group therapy**, however, she is in the company of other patients. There are several advantages to this situation. Sometimes individuals with psychological challenges think they are somehow strange or abnormal. A person in group therapy has the chance to see other people struggling with problems similar to her own. She discovers what other people think of her, and, in turn, can express what she thinks of them. In this exchange she discovers where she is mistaken in her views of herself and of other people and where she is correct. Within the group, the patient can practice different ways of interacting with others in a safe environment. In this way, she can see which techniques work for her and which ones do not. She also can see other people with similar problems recovering, giving her the hope of recovery.

Another advantage to group therapy is that one therapist can help a large number of people at a reduced cost. Most group-therapy sessions are led by a trained therapist who makes suggestions, clarifies points, and keeps activities from getting out of hand. In this way, her training and experience are used to help as many as 20 people at once, although 8–10 is a more comfortable number. It is possible to use psychoanalytical, cognitive, and behavioral techniques in a group setting. What is discussed in group therapy is confidential. To safeguard this confidentiality, members agree not to disclose names of group members or topics of group discussion outside of session meetings.

Group therapy sessions give people the opportunity to see that they are not the only one struggling with a problem.

▶ **CRITICAL THINKING**

Identifying What are some situations where someone might benefit from receiving group therapy?

Family Therapy

Therapists often suggest, after talking to a patient, that the entire family unit should work at group therapy. In *family therapy*, the focus is on the interactions among the family members. This method is particularly useful because it untangles the twisted web of relationships that has led one or more members of the family to experience emotional suffering.

Often family members are unhappy because they are mistreating or are being mistreated by other family members in ways no one understands or wants to talk about. Each one also has a subjective viewpoint.

Jon Bradley/Stone/Getty Images

496

The family therapist can point out what is happening from an objective viewpoint and can suggest ways of improving communication and fairness in the family. An important goal for the therapist is to help the members create an alliance in which they all work together to achieve common goals. One way that the therapist can do this is by making certain that each family member receives his or her turn to be heard. This encourages the family members to be respectful toward one another and ensures that everyone has an opportunity to share their viewpoint. While the therapist avoids directly telling members how to change their behavior, the therapist encourages the family members to see events from each others' point of view. The therapist may also suggest several ways of improving communication and fairness within the family. For example, if a child is angry because her sister borrows her clothes or other personal items without asking her permission, the family can work together on a solution. By working together, they strengthen their ability to communicate, which will help them resolve future, and possibly more difficult, challenges.

Self-Help Groups

Not all group therapies are run by professional therapists. Some of the most successful examples are provided in nonprofessional organizations, such as self-help groups. An increasing number of *self-help groups* have emerged in recent years. These voluntary groups, composed of people who share a particular problem, are often conducted without the active involvement of a professional therapist. During regularly scheduled meetings, members of the group come together to discuss their difficulties and to provide one another with support and possible solutions. Self-help groups have been formed to deal with problems ranging from alcoholism, overeating, and drug addiction to child abuse, widowhood, single parenting, adjusting to cancer, and gambling.

The best-known self-help group is Alcoholics Anonymous (AA), which was founded in 1935. Far more people find treatment for their drinking problems through AA than in psychotherapy or treatment centers.

The purpose of Alcoholics Anonymous is "to carry the AA message to the sick alcoholic who wants it." The only requirement to join is "a desire to stop drinking." According to AA, the only way for alcoholics to change is to admit that they are powerless over alcohol and that their lives have become unmanageable. Those who think they can battle the problem alone will not be successful. There are also AA-based groups, such as Al-Anon and Alateen, for family members for mutual support.

Members of AA usually meet at least once a week to discuss the meaning of this message, to talk about their experiences with alcohol, and to describe the new hope they have found with AA. Mutual encouragement, friendship, and an emphasis on personal responsibility are used to keep an individual sober.

Many self-help groups, such as Narcotics Anonymous and Overeaters Anonymous, base their organizations on the AA model. Together, these organizations are referred to as "twelve-step" programs because members abide by twelve steps to reach recovery. These steps are fundamentally the same for all the organizations. In Overeaters Anonymous, for example, the first step is "We admitted we were powerless over food — that our lives had become unmanageable."

National and community organizations such as NAMI (National Alliance on Mental Illness) strive to improve the lives of individuals with psychological difficulties. All of these organizations work to aid those with challenges they are working to overcome.

☑ READING PROGRESS CHECK

Comparing How is traditional group therapy different from self-help groups?

More
ABOUT...

Conducting Therapy

There are four areas of concern that a therapist might discuss with the patient.

1. Identify the problem behavior based on the classification scheme for psychological disorders. This document, known as the *Diagnostic and Statistical Manual of Mental Disorders*, is published by the American Psychiatric Association and is periodically updated.

2. Propose some ideas about the history and cause of the problem.

3. Explain the details of what is included in the treatment program.

4. Make a time line for the course of treatment. Identifying a distinct ending point encourages both the therapist and the patient to work hard to achieve their goal, often not more than 10 hour-long sessions.

Recent economic trends and steeply rising healthcare costs have caused so-called "third-party payers" to limit individuals' access to psychotherapy and other treatments. Third-party payers include traditional health insurance companies and HMOs (health maintenance organizations.) In particular, insurers are concerned about paying for group therapy. These companies want a clear explanation of the purpose for the treatment, a specific plan of treatment, and will generally only pay for short-term therapy. As a result, individuals who require extensive therapy may not be able to receive it unless they pay for it on their own.

Does Psychotherapy Work?

GUIDING QUESTION *What are the arguments against psychotherapy?*

In 1952 Hans Eysenck published a review of 24 different studies on the effectiveness of psychoanalytic treatment and eclectic psychotherapy, treatment in which several different therapeutic approaches are combined. Eysenck concluded that psychotherapy was no more effective than no treatment at all. According to his interpretation of these 24 studies, only 44 percent of the psychoanalytic patients improved with treatment, while 64 percent of those given eclectic psychotherapy had improved. Most startling, Eysenck argued that even this 64 percent improvement rate did not demonstrate the effectiveness of psychotherapy, since it has been reported that 72 percent of a group of hospitalized neurotics improved without treatment. If no treatment at all leads to as much improvement as psychotherapy, the obvious conclusion is that psychotherapy is not effective.

In 1970, Allen Bergin wrote a carefully reasoned review that leads one to question the validity of Eysenck's sweeping generalization. Much of Bergin's argument is based on how patients should be classified. Precise criteria for improvement are difficult to define and apply. Some people may experience spontaneous remission, or the sudden, unaccountable disappearance of symptoms without any therapy at all. However, it is important to realize that these people may have received help from unacknowledged sources. If the prime ingredient in therapy is to establish a close relationship, then spontaneous remission in people who have received continuing help from such sources is not spontaneous at all.

An analysis of nearly 400 studies on the effectiveness of psychotherapy, conducted by Mary Lee Smith and Gene V. Glass, used elaborate statistical procedures to estimate the effects of psychotherapy. They found that therapy is generally more effective than no treatment and on the average most forms of therapy have similar effects; that is, therapy may improve the quality of life for the patients. Smith and Glass were able to show that for some specific clients and situations, some forms of therapy would be expected to result in a greater improvement than others. As a result, the psychologist and client may work together to discuss the appropriate form of psychotherapy to achieve a cure.

☑ **READING PROGRESS CHECK**

Summarizing What conclusions did Hans Eysenck reach regarding the effectiveness of psychotherapy? How did others respond to these conclusions?

LESSON 1 REVIEW

Reviewing Vocabulary

1. *Explaining* How can the placebo effect be responsible for a patient's improvement during therapy?

2. *Describing* Cite and describe two examples of group therapy and how these types of therapy help patients.

Using Your Notes

3. *Making Connections* Review the notes that you completed during the lesson to discuss the ways in which psychotherapists can help people gain control over their lives.

Answering the Guiding Questions

4. *Identifying* What is the goal of psychotherapy?

5. *Considering Advantages* What are the advantages of group therapy?

6. *Recognizing Counter Arguments* What are the arguments against psychotherapy?

Writing Activity

7. *Informative/Explanatory* Conduct research to learn more about five local and national self-help organizations. Then create an illustrated brochure in which you summarize the methods and goals of each group. The brochure should be aimed at the average person who wants to learn more about the different kinds of help that are available.

networks

There's More Online!

☑ **CARTOON** Humanistic Approaches to Therapy

☑ **SELF-CHECK QUIZ**

Psychoanalysis and Humanistic Therapy

Reading HELPDESK (ccss)

Academic Vocabulary
• **authoritative**   • **indicate**

Content Vocabulary
• **psychoanalysis**
• **free association**
• **resistance**
• **dream analysis**
• **transference**
• **humanistic therapy**
• **client-centered therapy**
• **nondirective therapy**
• **active listening**

TAKING NOTES:
Key Ideas and Details

CATEGORIZING Fill in the diagram below by listing the psychotherapies discussed in this lesson and the major therapeutic methods used in each.

(l)Kerstin Waurick/Vetta/Getty Images; (r)Andrea Morini/Digital Vision/Getty Images

ESSENTIAL QUESTION • *How can therapists modify behavior?*

IT MATTERS BECAUSE

Freud's new practice of psychotherapy destroyed a barrier. By showing that psychological problems could be successfully treated, he changed the public's perception of individuals with these challenges. Eventually, new forms of psychotherapies evolved from Freud's innovative idea.

What Is Psychoanalysis?

GUIDING QUESTION *What is the objective of the psychoanalyst?*

For a long time **psychoanalysis** was the only formalized psychotherapy practiced in Western society. Psychoanalysis is based on the theories of Sigmund Freud, whose connection to the therapy gave rise to the classic picture of a bearded doctor seated behind a patient lying on a couch. According to Freud, psychological disturbances are due to anxiety caused by conflicts among the unconscious components of one's personality. One job of the psychoanalyst is to make patients aware of the unconscious impulses, desires, and fears that cause their anxiety. Psychoanalysts believe that if patients can understand their unconscious motives, they have taken the first step toward freeing themselves of their problems. Such understanding is called insight. The following dream was experienced by an elderly woman who was fighting a serious illness:

PRIMARY SOURCE

"*I was a child again, and riding my bicycle along the village street, but its wheels began to sink into sticky, muddy earth, so that I could barely move. Finally, however, the earth began to dry, and I found that I was able to cycle along quite easily once more.*"

— Julia and Derek Parker, *Parker's Complete Book of Dreams* (1995)

Psychoanalysts might interpret the dream in the following manner: the muddy earth symbolized the illness as well as the woman's fear of death. As a child, she had never been allowed to own a bicycle, so having one represented freedom. The bike also symbolized the good health she hoped to regain. Psychoanalysts would then use this dream interpretation to help the woman understand the psychological dilemmas she faces.

Free Association

psychoanalysis therapy aimed at making patients aware of their unconscious motives so that they can gain control over their behavior

free association a method used to examine the unconscious; the patient is instructed to say whatever comes into his or her mind

Psychoanalysis is a slow procedure. It may take several years of 50-minute sessions once or twice a week before the patient is able to make fundamental changes. Throughout this time, the analyst helps the patient thoroughly understand the unconscious motives behind his or her behavior. This task begins with the analyst telling the patient to relax and talk about everything that comes to mind. This method is called **free association**. The patient may consider some passing thoughts too unimportant or too embarrassing to mention. The analyst suggests that everything should be expressed without censoring them first—the thought that seems most inconsequential may, in fact, offer insight into the patient's unconscious.

As the patient lies on the couch, he or she describes dreams, discusses private thoughts, or recalls long-forgotten experiences. The psychoanalyst often says nothing for long periods of time. The psychoanalyst occasionally makes remarks or asks questions that guide the patient. The analyst also may suggest an unconscious motive or factor that explains something the patient has been talking about. However, most of the work is done by the patient.

resistance the reluctance of a patient either to reveal painful feelings or to examine longstanding behavior patterns

The patient is understandably reluctant to reveal painful feelings and to examine lifelong patterns that need to be changed. As the analysis proceeds, the patient is likely to try unconsciously to hold back the flow of information. This phenomenon—in fact, any behavior that impedes the course of therapy—is called **resistance**. The patient may agree to cooperate fully, yet at times the patient's mind seems blank. He feels powerless and can no longer think of anything to say. At such times the analyst will simply point out what is happening and wait for the patient to continue. The analyst may also suggest another way of approaching the area of resistance. By analyzing the patient's resistances, both the therapist and the patient can understand the source of the anxieties and how the patient deals with anxiety-provoking material.

dream analysis a technique used by psychoanalysts to interpret the content of patients' dreams

Dream Analysis

Freud believed that dreams express unconscious thoughts and feelings. In a technique known as **dream analysis**, the psychoanalyst interprets the patient's dream to find the unconscious thoughts and feelings in it.

When we sleep, our dreams probably do not follow logical thought patterns. Because of this, Freud considered dreams the purest form of free association.

▶ **CRITICAL THINKING**

Drawing Conclusions What do therapists hope to learn from analyzing dreams?

Freud believed that dreams contain manifest and latent content. *Manifest content* refers to what you remember about your dream. For instance, you recall seeing your house fall apart, brick by brick, in last night's dream. *Latent content* refers to the hidden meanings represented symbolically in the dream that the therapist interprets from the manifest content. Although a therapist might link your dream to your current health concerns, there is little research evidence linking dream content to a person's existing life-problems.

Transference

Sooner or later, the analyst begins to appear in the patient's associations and dreams. The patient may begin feeling toward the analyst the way she feels toward some other important figure in her life. This process is called **transference**.

If the patient can recognize what is happening, transference may allow her to experience her true feelings toward the important person. Often, instead of experiencing and understanding her feelings, the patient simply begins acting toward the therapist in the same way she used to act toward the important person, usually one of her parents.

The therapist does not allow the patient to resort to these tactics. Remaining impersonal and anonymous, the therapist always directs the patient back to herself. The therapist may ask, for example, "What do you see when you imagine my face?" The patient may see the therapist as an angry, frowning, unpleasant figure. The therapist never takes this personally, instead asking, "What does this make you think of?" Gradually, it will become clear to both patient and therapist that the patient is reacting to the neutral therapist as though he or she were, for example, a threatening parent.

By understanding transference, the patient becomes aware of hidden feelings and motivations. She may begin to understand, for example, the roots of trouble with her boss at work. The boss, the therapist, or any **authoritative** person may be viewed in the same way that, as a child, she saw her parents.

The purpose of psychoanalysis is to show the role of the unconscious and to provide insight for the client. This type of classical psyche (mind) analysis, however, is not for everyone. It requires an average of 600 sessions and years of meeting with a psychoanalyst. Psychoanalysis has changed with patients, disorders, and the prevailing cultures. Today, many versions of classical psychoanalysis are available. For example, *short-term dynamic psychotherapy* is a shortened version of psychoanalysis. This type of therapy focuses on a client's problems. The therapist uses a direct and more active approach in identifying and resolving the problems. This approach to therapy, along with psychoanalysis, works well for clients who are able to gain insight into their behavior. People who lose touch with reality—for instance, a person suffering from schizophrenia—will probably not benefit from psychoanalysis, though.

✓ READING PROGRESS CHECK

Making Connections How do psychoanalysts use dream analysis to help patients gain insight?

When a patient understands the process of transference, she becomes aware of hidden feelings and motivations.

▶ **CRITICAL THINKING**

Describing How should a therapist respond when working with a patient who uses transference tactics?

transference the process, experienced by the patient, of feeling toward an analyst or therapist the way he or she feels or felt toward some other important figure in his or her life

authoritative proceeding from authority

Humanistic Therapy

GUIDING QUESTION *Why did Rogers choose the word* client *over the word* patient?

The goal of **humanistic therapy** is to help people fulfill their human potential. Humanistic psychology has given rise to several approaches to psychotherapy, known collectively as **client-centered therapy**. Humanistic psychologists stress the actualization of one's unique potentials through personal responsibility, freedom of choice, and authentic relationships.

Client-centered therapy, or person-centered therapy, is based on the theories of Carl Rogers. This therapy depends on the person's own motivation toward growth and self-actualization. The use of the term *person* or *client* instead of *patient* gives one an insight into the reasoning behind Rogers's method. *Patient* may suggest inferiority or passivity, whereas *person* or *client* implies an equal relationship between the therapist and the individual seeking help. According to Rogers, this equal relationship reflects three therapeutic components—positive regard, empathy, and genuineness. Positive regard refers to the therapist's ability to demonstrate caring and respect for the client. Empathy is the ability to understand what the client is feeling. Genuineness refers to the therapist's ability to act toward the client in a real and non-defensive manner.

Client-centered therapists assume that people are basically good and capable of handling their own lives. We are all free to make choices; if we can become less defensive, we are likely to make better choices. Psychological problems arise when the true self becomes lost and the individual comes to view himself or herself according to the standards of others. One of the goals of therapy is to help clients recognize their own strength and confidence, thereby learning to be true to their own standards and ideas about how to live effectively.

In the course of an interview, the client is encouraged to speak freely about any troubling matters. The topics discussed are entirely up to the client. This method is called **nondirective therapy** because the therapist does not direct, or guide, it. The therapist listens and encourages conversation but tries to avoid giving opinions. Many experienced therapists told Rogers that in promoting nondirective therapy, he had put into words something they had learned from their own experiences in helping others. These therapists realized that the client knows best what direction their therapy should take.

As the client talks, the therapist tries to echo back, as clearly as possible, the feelings the client has expressed. This communication technique is called **active listening**. The therapist tries to extract the main points from the client's hesitant or rambling explanations and then repeat these points. The client is instructed to correct the therapist if the client thinks he has been misunderstood. Between them, the client and therapist form a clearer picture of how the client really feels about self, life, and important others. Rogers stated that the therapist will begin to see the client as the client sees himself. The therapist's role is no longer to diagnose and evaluate the client, but rather to provide a deep understanding of the attitudes that the client holds.

Client-centered therapy is conducted in an atmosphere of emotional support that Rogers calls unconditional positive regard. The therapist never offers an opinion about the clients or what they have to say. Instead the therapist shows the clients that anything said is accepted without embarrassment, reservation, or anger. The therapist's main responsibility is to create a warm and accepting client relationship. This acceptance makes it easier for the clients to explore thoughts about themselves and their experiences. They are able to abandon old values without fear of disapproval, and can begin to see themselves, their situations, and their relationships with others in a new light and with new confidence.

As they reduce tensions and release emotions, the clients feel that they are becoming more complete people. They gain the courage to accept parts of their personalities that they had formerly considered weak or bad. By recognizing their self-worth, they can set up realistic goals and consider the steps necessary to reach them. The clients' movements toward independence **indicate** the end of their need for therapy, and they can assume the final steps to independence on their own.

Rogers attempted to evaluate the effectiveness of the client-centered approach. He tried to measure the gap between the clients' "real self" and what they saw as their "ideal self." More recent research has emphasized the importance of the therapist being able to create a team relationship with the client. Although client-centered therapy has proved more effective than no treatment, it seems to be no more or less effective than other types of therapy. However, client-centered therapy has helped make therapists aware of the importance of developing supportive relations with their clients.

☑ **READING PROGRESS CHECK**

Evaluate How do you think unconditional positive regard might influence how the client responds to therapy?

∧ **CARTOON**

HUMANISTIC APPROACHES TO THERAPY
Humanistic therapies attempt to help clients recognize their own strengths rather than trying to live up to the standards of others.

▶ **CRITICAL THINKING**

1. *Analyzing Visuals* How does this cartoon reflect a humanistic approach to therapy?

2. *Describing* Describe the methods a therapist would use in a session with this client.

indicate a sign that shows that something is happening

LESSON 2 REVIEW

Reviewing Vocabulary

1. *Identifying* In psychoanalysis, what does the term *resistance* mean?

Using Your Notes

2. *Analyzing* Review the notes that you completed during the lesson to discuss the importance of three techniques used by humanistic therapists.

Answering the Guiding Questions

3. *Analyzing* What is the objective of the psychoanalyst?

4. *Contrasting* Why did Rogers choose the word *client* over *patient*?

Writing Activity

5. *Informative/Explanatory* Some therapists may view therapy as a process of teaching a philosophy of life. Do you think this goal is appropriate? Does this goal assume the therapist has the *better* philosophy of life? Write an essay in which you argue your point.

Case Study

The Case of Rat Man

Period of Study: Early 1900s

PRIMARY SOURCE

❝ *The therapist, like the patient, is viewed as a unique individual, with his own theory of how therapy works, his own idiosyncrasies, his own conflicts, and his own past, all of which contribute to the unfolding of transference. Thus the* transference *is seen as a joint creation between patient and therapist. It is a joint creation between two individuals, both with their own unique personalities, values, and subjectivities.* ❞

—*William C. Goldstein*, The transference in psychotherapy: The old vs. the new, analytic vs. dynamic, *(2000)*

Introduction: Sigmund Freud used psychoanalysis with a patient he referred to as *Rat Man*. A 29-year-old man came to Freud complaining of various fears, obsessions, and compulsions, or cravings, which had kept the man from any achievement. Freud focused on Rat Man's uncontrollable fantasy in which the man would see his father and girlfriend tied down and being tortured by hungry rats strapped to their flesh.

Hypothesis: Freud's earliest hypothesis was that Rat Man maintained a conflict over whether he should marry his girlfriend or not. Since Rat Man was unable to decide consciously, he resolved this issue through his unconscious mind, which produced disturbing pictures. Freud theorized that past love and hate issues between Rat Man and his father caused the father to be in Rat Man's dreams and fantasies.

Method: Freud began therapy with Rat Man by using a psychoanalytic technique called *free association*. Freud asked Rat Man to free associate with the word *rats*. Rat Man came up with the word *rates*, referring to installments or money. In an earlier session, Rat Man indicated his girlfriend had little money and his father had wanted him to marry a wealthy woman. Freud deduced the rat fantasies were related to the father's opposition to the girlfriend.

In another session, Rat Man described an event relayed to him by his mother, which had taken place when he was around four years of age. Rat Man claimed his mother had told him that as a little boy he had

bitten the nurse who was taking care of his father. Rat Man's father began to beat him immediately after the incident occurred. Rat Man responded to the beatings with a multitude of harsh words directed toward his father. After hearing those words, Rat Man's father never beat him again. Freud suggested that the act of Rat Man biting the nurse was a sexual action. Since his father beat him for indulging in his sexual needs (biting), Rat Man's fear of fulfilling his needs for a relationship stemmed from fear he would be punished.

A major breakthrough occurred when Rat Man revealed a fantasy in which he was persuaded to marry Freud's daughter. These wishes came directly from Freud himself (according to Rat Man's fantasy). Freud immediately interrupted and stated that Rat Man was replacing the role of his father with Freud. Moments later Rat Man became emotionally enraged at his therapist. This rage ended with an intense fear that Freud would beat him. This signified a chief discovery. Freud convinced Rat Man he was reliving the event with his father by placing the therapist in the father's role.

Results: Before therapy, Rat Man had never consciously experienced anger toward his father. This anger came out in therapy sessions. To Freud, the rats biting into and destroying Rat Man's father and girlfriend symbolized significant past events—Rat Man biting his first love, or the nurse, and in another essence *biting* his father with angry words. According to Freud, Rat Man's conscious acceptance of the feelings of fear and anger toward his father would lead to a recovery.

Analyzing the Case Study

1. *Interpreting Significance* How did Rat Man demonstrate transference? How was this transference important in his therapy?

2. *Analyzing Primary Sources* How does the quote by Goldstein differ in its opinion on transference from the discussion of transference in the Rat Man case study?

3. *Drawing Conclusions* Did Freud think that Rat Man's changing feelings toward his father was a positive or negative outcome of therapy? Why?

Cognitive and Behavior Therapies

Matt McClain/The Washington Post/Getty Images

Reading **HELP**DESK (CCSS)

Academic Vocabulary
- **logic**
- **widespread**

Content Vocabulary
- **cognitive therapies**
- **rational-emotive therapy (RET)**
- **behavior therapy**
- **behavior modification**
- **systematic desensitization**
- **aversive conditioning**
- **contingency management**
- **cognitive-behavior therapy**

TAKING NOTES:
Key Ideas and Details

DESCRIBING Fill in the graphic organizer below to describe the three basic types of therapy covered in this lesson.

Type of Therapy	Description

ESSENTIAL QUESTION • *How can therapists modify behaviors?*

◎ IT MATTERS BECAUSE

A friend has such a fear of snakes that he avoids going outdoors. You enjoy going on nature hikes, but he refuses to join you. Do you think it is important that he realize that his fear is irrational? Or do you just want to help him overcome it? Some psychotherapists believe that the individual must accept that their behavior makes no sense. Others simply work to help the individual overcome the undesirable behavior.

Cognitive Therapy

GUIDING QUESTION *What are the three principles followed by cognitive therapy?*

The goal of **cognitive therapies** is to change the way people think. The basic assumptions that cognitive therapies share are that faulty cognitions—our irrational or uninformed beliefs, expectations, and ways of thinking—distort our behaviors, attitudes, and emotions. To improve our lives, we must work to change our patterns of thinking, which will in turn affect how we feel emotionally. This is different from the psychoanalytic view in which individuals must first become aware of unconscious impulses and fears in order to free themselves from the difficulties these feelings cause.

In what other ways are cognitive therapies similar? According to some psychologists, all of these theories follow one or more of three principles—disconfirmation, reconceptualization, and insight. *Disconfirmation* occurs when clients are confronted with evidence that directly contradicts their existing beliefs. For example, a client who fears snakes may think that most are venomous, when, in fact, this is true of only about 5 percent of the snakes in the United States. In *reconceptualization*, clients work toward an alternative belief system to explain their experiences or current observations. In *insight*, clients work toward understanding and deriving new or revised beliefs.

In contrast to some forms of psychotherapy, such as psychoanalysis, cognitive therapy has developed an approach more focused on problem-solving. Additionally, cognitive therapy is most often focused on present, rather than past, events. Finally, compared to the lengthy process of psychoanalysis, cognitive therapy is relatively short-term.

Rational-Emotive Therapy

cognitive therapies using thoughts to control emotions and behaviors

rational-emotive therapy (RET) a form of psychological help aimed at changing unrealistic assumptions about oneself and other people

Albert Ellis developed a form of therapy called **rational-emotive therapy (RET)**. Ellis believed that people behave in deliberate and rational ways, given their assumptions about life. Most people want to be happy and get along with others. When these goals are blocked, they often respond in healthy ways. At other times, their responses may be unhealthy and cause difficulties. These unhealthy responses arise when an individual's assumptions are unrealistic.

Suppose a man seeks therapy when a woman leaves him. He cannot stand her rejection. Without her, his life is empty and miserable. She has made him feel utterly worthless. He must get her back. Like a spoiled child, the man is demanding that the woman love him. He expects, even insists, that things will always go his way. Given this assumption, the only possible explanation for her behavior is that something is dreadfully wrong, either with him or with her.

What is wrong, in the therapist's view, is the man's thinking. By defining his feelings for the woman as need rather than desire, he—not she—is causing his depression. When you convince yourself that you need someone, you will in fact be unable to carry on without that person in your life. When you believe that you cannot stand rejection, you will in fact fall apart when you encounter rejection. This kind of faulty thinking is based on unreasonable attitudes, false premises, and rigid roles for behaviors.

The goal of rational-emotive therapy is to correct these false and self-defeating beliefs. Rejection is unpleasant, but not unbearable. A relationship may be desirable, but it is not irreplaceable. To teach the individual to think in realistic terms, RET therapists may use a number of techniques. One is *role-playing* so that the person can see how his beliefs affect his relationships. Another technique is *modeling* to demonstrate other ways of thinking and acting. A third is *humor* to underline the absurdity of his beliefs. Still another is simple *persuasion*. The therapist may also assign homework to give practice in more reasonable forms of action.

Ellis liked to teach that behaviors are the result of the ABCs. *A* refers to the *Activating* event, the event that led to the undesirable behavior. *B* is the person's *Belief* system about the event. This belief system typically involved irrational thinking. *C* refers to the *Consequences* that follow. These consequences are a result of the irrational thinking. Ellis claimed it is not the event that causes trouble but rather the way a person thinks about the event. In other words, A does not cause C, but instead B causes C.

TABLE >

EXAMPLES OF IRRATIONAL THINKING

Albert Ellis (1961) asserted that the irrational ideas we believe stand in the way of achieving lives that are free of anxiety.

▶ **CRITICAL THINKING**

1. *Analyzing* How might a RET therapist counter these irrational beliefs?

2. *Evaluating* Why is the second statement an example of irrational thinking?

Everything I do must be approved and loved by virtually everybody.
I have to be completely competent, totally in control, and successful in everything I do.
It is catastrophic when things are not going the way I want them to go.
My unhappiness is not my fault. People and events over which I have no control are responsible.
Anytime I encounter something that I fear, I need to be consumed with worries and upset about it.
It is easier to avoid life's difficulties and responsibilities than to develop a better system for meeting them.
My life and the people with whom I work should be changed from the way they are.
The best I can do for myself is to relax and enjoy life. Inaction and passivity are the best bet to maximize my own enjoyment.

In therapy, the therapist and client work to change B, the belief. Ellis believes that the individual must take three steps in order to cure or correct himself. First, he must realize that some of his assumptions are false. Second, he must see that he is making himself disturbed by acting on false beliefs. Finally, he must work to break old habits of thought and behavior. He has to practice self-discipline and learn to take risks.

Beck's Cognitive Therapy

Aaron T. Beck introduced another form of cognitive therapy that is similar to Ellis's rational-emotive therapy. The primary difference in Beck's therapy is the focus on illogical thought processes. These therapists—through using persuasion and **logic** to change clients' existing beliefs—also encourage clients to engage in actual tests of their own beliefs. For example, if a client believes that "I never have a good time," the therapist might point out that this is a hypothesis and not a fact. The therapist might then ask the client to test her own hypothesis by looking at the evidence differently and by identifying the times in her life when she actually did have a good time. The therapist's goal is to demonstrate to the client that her automatic negative thinking may be incorrect and that things are not as bad as she believes them to be.

logic a way of thinking or explaining something

Overgeneralization	Making blanket judgments about oneself	I'm a failure.
Polarized Thinking	Categorizing information into two categories	Most people don't like me.
Selective Attention	Focusing on only one detail of many	People always criticize me

Beck's work has been very successful with people who are depressed. He believed that depressed people blame themselves instead of their circumstances and focus on only negative events, ignoring the positive events occurring in their lives. They make pessimistic projections about the future. Finally, he believed they make negative conclusions about their self-worth based on events that are not significant.

To work at alleviating their depression, clients are first taught to identify and then write down any negative thoughts they may have. This helps them realize how these thoughts affect their feelings and behavior. They learn to evaluate whether the thoughts are valid and how to change them to a more positive viewpoint. Clients eventually learn to modify their underlying assumptions. The therapist also teaches the clients how to cope with events by dividing large, difficult problems into smaller steps that are more manageable and less intimidating. Clients are often given homework assignments to assess the true value of their beliefs. They may be asked to engage in behaviors that test these beliefs outside of the office. For example, a person who is not very assertive may be asked to find situations to speak up for themselves, to strike up a conversation with a stranger, or to ask someone for a favor.

The goal of Beck's cognitive therapy is that by focusing on people's thought patterns, you can change the way people think. The therapist's job is to determine the pace and direction of the therapy and to help the client detect negative thinking patterns. Therapists also help the client use more reasonable standards for self-evaluation.

✓ READING PROGRESS CHECK

Drawing Inferences Why do you think Beck gave clients homework assignments?

< TABLE

BECK'S DYSFUNCTIONAL THOUGHT PATTERN
Beck believed that dysfunctional thought patterns cause a distorted view of oneself and one's world, leading to various psychological problems.

▶ CRITICAL THINKING

1. ***Finding the Main Idea*** What is polarized thinking?

2. ***Contrasting*** How is *selective attention* different from *polarized thinking*?

Behavior Therapy

GUIDING QUESTION *How does aversive conditioning differ from counterconditioning?*

In **behavior therapy** there is emphasis on one's behavior rather than one's thoughts, as in cognitive therapy. Rather than spending large amounts of time going into the patient's past or the details of his or her dreams, the behavior therapist concentrates on determining what is specifically troubling in the patient's life and takes steps to change it. Behavior therapy uses a method called **behavior modification** to systematically change how a person acts and feels.

The idea behind behavior therapy is that a disturbed person is one who has learned to behave in an undesirable way and that any behavior that is learned can be unlearned. The therapist's job, therefore, is to help the patient learn new behaviors. The reasons for the patient's undesirable behavior are not important, what is important is to change the behavior. By changing one's behavior, one's thoughts change as well. The person is asked to list concrete examples of desired behaviors and behavioral goals. Once these behaviors have been targeted, a program to achieve these goals is developed. To bring about such changes, the therapist uses conditioning techniques first discovered in animal laboratories.

Counterconditioning

One technique used by behavior therapists is counterconditioning. This technique pairs the stimulus that triggers an unwanted behavior, like a fear of public speaking, with a new, more desirable behavior. The therapist helps the client reduce anxiety by pairing relaxation with anxiety-producing situations. Counterconditioning is a three-step process: (1) the person builds an anxiety hierarchy with the least feared situation on the bottom and the most feared situation on top;

DIAGRAM ∨

LOSING FEARS
Counterconditioning techniques, such as systematic desensitization, are used to help people overcome their irrational fears and anxieties.

▶ **CRITICAL THINKING**

1. *Sequencing* What steps might be used to desensitize a child's fear of the dark?

2. *Drawing Inferences* Why is this technique referred to as *systematic* desensitization?

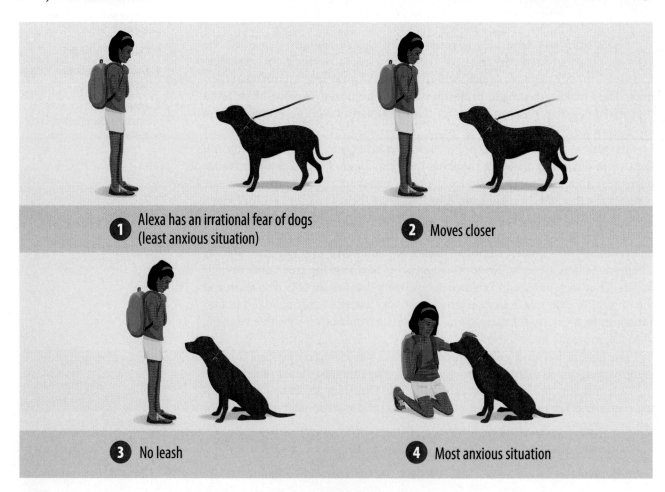

① Alexa has an irrational fear of dogs (least anxious situation)

② Moves closer

③ No leash

④ Most anxious situation

508

(2) the person learns deep muscle relaxation; (3) the person imagines or experiences each step in the hierarchy, starting with the least anxiety-provoking situation, while learning to be relaxed. Since it is impossible to maintain both relaxation and anxiety, the idea is to teach the person that the situation does not have to be anxiety producing. Using the anxiety hierarchy, the person progresses through each step after successfully completing the previous one.

Systematic desensitization is a counterconditioning technique used to overcome irrational fears and anxieties the client has learned. The goal of systematic desensitization therapy is to encourage people to imagine the feared situation while relaxing, thus extinguishing the fear response (see diagram, Losing Fears). For example, suppose a student is terrified of speaking in front of large groups—that, in fact, his stage fright is so tremendous that he is unable to speak when called upon in class. How would systematic desensitization therapy effectively change this person's behavior?

The therapist might have the student make a list of the frightening aspects of talking to others. Perhaps the most frightening aspect is actually standing before an audience, whereas the least frightening is speaking to a single other person. The client ranks these fears, from the most frightening on down. Then the therapist begins teaching the client muscle relaxation. Once he knows how to relax completely, the client is ready for the next step. The client tries to imagine as vividly as possible the least disturbing scene on his list of fears. Thinking about speaking to a single stranger may cause mild anxiety. Because the therapist has taught him how to relax, he learns to think about the experience without feeling anxious. The basic logic is that a person cannot feel anxious and relaxed at the same time. The therapist attempts to replace anxiety with its opposite, relaxation, through counterconditioning.

The client and therapist then progress step-by-step through the list of anxiety-arousing events. The client reaches a point where he is able to imagine the most threatening situations without feeling anxiety. Now the therapist starts to expose the person to real-life situations that have previously frightened him. Therapy finally reaches the point where the student is able to deliver an unrehearsed speech to a full auditorium.

Flooding refers to another treatment in which a therapist exposes the client to a feared object or situation. For example, let's say that you are deathly afraid of snakes. Your therapist might have you imagine yourself in a room full of snakes or have you hold a snake. This makes your heart rate soar, but it cannot stay that way forever. Eventually your heart rate returns to normal, and you realize that you have survived this test. You have begun to overcome your fear by facing it.

Behavior therapists also use *modeling* to teach a client to do something by watching someone else do it. For example, when teaching a client how to be assertive, a therapist might demonstrate ways to be assertive. The client watches and then tries to imitate the behavior.

Quick Lab

HOW CAN SOMEONE OVERCOME AN IRRATIONAL FEAR?
Systematic desensitization is most often used to help individuals overcome fears and anxieties. How is this technique applied?

Procedure
1. Identify a situation that makes someone you know fearful, or you can make up a fear for an imaginary person.
2. Imagine that you are that person. List all the aspects of the situation that you find frightening and rank them in order from the most frightening to least frightening.
3. Suggest a step-by-step plan. Apply the systematic desensitization technique to help overcome the fear.

Analysis
1. Prepare a flowchart showing the steps you would use to help the individual change his or her behavior.
2. Why do you think this technique is often effective in overcoming irrational fears?

systematic desensitization a technique to help a patient overcome irrational fears and anxieties

Imagine that you are scared to death of heights. Suddenly you discover yourself riding a glass elevator to the 74th floor of a building. However, this is not a "real" building, instead you are in the make-believe world of virtual reality (VR). Some psychotherapists use VR to help clients overcome intense fears. The therapist can closely monitor the situation and turn off the virtual display if the client becomes too agitated.

VR is also being used to help people mentally escape painful medical procedures, such as the excruciating treatments for severe burns. While wearing a VR helmet, which completely covers their eyes and ears, patients can select an "environment" to explore—such as diving underwater and searching for treasure–which mentally distracts them from their present reality.

aversive conditioning links an unpleasant state with an unwanted behavior in an attempt to eliminate the behavior

contingency management undesirable behavior is not reinforced, while desirable behavior is reinforced

In **aversive conditioning**, the goal is to make certain acts unpleasant so that they will be avoided. For example, alcoholics can be given medication that will make them sick when they take alcohol. The relearning process involved is to try to associate the aversive (negative) feeling with taking the alcohol and hence reduce its appeal and use. The rate of improvement for this method is about 50 percent, with the effect lasting about six months. Thus it is not a solution as much as a good beginning for a number of alcoholics.

Operant Conditioning

Operant conditioning is based on the assumption that behavior that is reinforced tends to be repeated, whereas behavior that is not reinforced tends to be extinguished. In **contingency management** the therapist and patient decide what old, undesirable behavior needs to be eliminated and what new, desirable behavior needs to appear.

Arrangements are then made for the old behavior to go unrewarded and for the desired behavior to be positively reinforced. In its simplest form, contingency management consists of the therapist agreeing with the patient: "If you do X, I will give you Y." This form of agreement is similar to systems of reward that people often use on themselves or parents use on children. For instance, a student may think, "If I get a good grade on the exam, I'll treat myself to a new video game." The reward is contingent (dependent) upon getting a good grade.

Contingency management is used in prisons, psychiatric hospitals, schools, army bases, and with individual patients. In these situations it is possible to set up whole miniature systems of rewards, called *token economies*. For example, psychologists in some psychiatric hospitals select behavior they judge desirable. Patients are then rewarded for these behaviors with tokens. Thus if a patient cleans his room or works in the hospital garden, he is rewarded with token money. The patients are able to cash in their token money for things they want, such as candy or toiletry items, or for certain privileges, such as time away from the ward.

These methods are successful in inducing patients to begin leading active lives. Token economies have a number of advantages. They can help individuals learn to take care of themselves instead of having to be cared for constantly. They allow for immediate reinforcement; however, if desired, the reinforcement can be delayed. The quantity and frequency of the reinforcement can be changed over time. Once the desired behavior becomes routine, the reinforcement can be gradually phased out. Another advantage is that token economies are easy to generalize. For example, individuals in a prison will need different rewards than children in a special education classroom. The individual has control over how to redeem the tokens. However, there also are some disadvantages. A major one is that the individuals in charge of the program must be consistent. This means that token economies are time-consuming to set up and maintain. Specific concrete goals must be established. Token economies can also lead to dependency and can be expensive, depending on the rewards given. Nonetheless, token economies have proven to be useful in many situations, especially in institutions.

Cognitive-Behavior Therapy

Many therapists combine aspects of cognitive and behavior therapies. **Cognitive-behavior therapy** focuses on setting goals for changing a client's behavior and then, unlike other behavior therapies, placing more emphasis on changing the client's interpretation of his or her situation. This type of therapy seeks to help clients differentiate between serious, real problems and imagined or distorted problems. A cognitive-behavior therapist might work with a client to change certain behaviors by monitoring current behaviors and thought patterns, setting progressively difficult goals, reinforcing positive changes, substituting positive

This woman is a counselor at a camp for burn survivors. She cheers on her team of campers as they participate in a competition. Campers take part in various activities, such as swimming, horseback riding, and arts and crafts. The camp is designed to help build the campers' self-esteem in a safe setting.

▶ **CRITICAL THINKING**

Assessing Why would cognitive-behavior therapy be used at a camp such as this one?

cognitive-behavior therapy based on a combination of substituting healthy thoughts for negative thoughts and beliefs and changing disruptive behaviors in favor of healthy behaviors

thoughts for negative thoughts, and practicing new behaviors in a safe setting. Many self-help programs use this approach. For example, you might begin a program of developing positive self-esteem by using these techniques. Cognitive behavior therapies are becoming increasingly **widespread** and have proven effective for treating a wide range of problems.

widespread extensive or prevalent

 READING PROGRESS CHECK

Making Connections Why are token economies an important part of contingency management therapy?

Matt McClain/The Washington Post/Getty Images

LESSON 3 REVIEW (CCSS)

Reviewing Vocabulary

1. *Speculating* Why might a therapist use cognitive-behavior therapy?

2. *Identifying* What steps does a rational-emotive therapist expect the client to take to solve his or her problems?

3. *Classify* What type of therapy is systematic desensitization associated with? Why?

Using Your Notes

4. *Diagramming* Review the notes you completed during the lesson. Create a diagram that lists each of the three therapies presented in this lesson: cognitive therapy, behavior therapy, and cognitive-behavior therapy. State the major goal of each therapy. Include two or three techniques used in this therapy to achieve its goal.

Answering the Guiding Questions

5. *Naming* What are the three principles followed by cognitive therapy?

6. *Contrasting* How does aversive conditioning differ from counterconditioning?

Writing Activity

7. *Informative/Explanatory* Conduct research to learn more about counterconditioning, aversive conditioning, and operant conditioning. Then choose a common undesirable behavior, such as chewing fingernails. Write a narrative in which you describe an individual with this behavior seeking out a therapist. Discuss how the therapist might decide which type of conditioning to use in helping the individual eliminate the behavior. Make certain that your narrative is well organized and that the comparisons you make between the therapies are thorough and clearly written.

Reader's Dictionary (CCSS)

alcove: *a small recessed section of a room*

foreboding: *a strong feeling that something unpleasant or dangerous is going to happen*

electrotherapy: *treatment or therapy that uses electricity; electroconvulsive therapy (ECT)*

pallid: *lacking sparkle or liveliness*

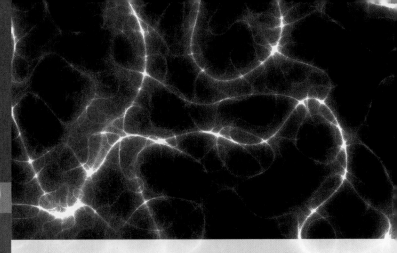

In the novel *The Bell Jar*, 19-year-old Esther Greenwood wins a dream assignment on a New York fashion magazine, but she quickly finds herself sinking into despair. In this excerpt, Esther receives electroshock therapy at Belsize hospital after attempting to commit suicide. This novel is largely autobiographical—poet-author Sylvia Plath ended her own life a month after the book's publication in 1963.

The
Bell Jar

by Sylvia Plath

PRIMARY SOURCE

The nurse rapped on my door and, without waiting for an answer, breezed in.

It was a new nurse—they were always changing—with a lean, sand-colored face and sandy hair, and large freckles polka-dotting her bony nose. For some reason the sight of this nurse made me sick at heart, and it was only as she strode across the room to snap up the green blind that I realized part of her strangeness came from being empty-handed.

I opened my mouth to ask for my breakfast tray, but silenced myself immediately. The nurse would be mistaking me for somebody else. New nurses often did that. Somebody in Belsize must be having shock treatments, unknown to me, and the nurse had, quite understandably, confused me with her.

I waited until the nurse had made her little circuit of my room, patting, straightening, arranging, and taken the next tray in to Loubelle one door farther down the hall.

Then I shoved my feet into my slippers, dragging my blanket with me, for the morning was bright, but very cold, and crossed quickly to the kitchen. The pink-uniformed maid was filling a row of blue china coffee pitchers from a great, battered kettle on the stove. . . .

"There's been a mistake," I told the maid, leaning over the counter and speaking in a low, confidential tone. "The new nurse forgot to bring me in my breakfast tray today."

I managed a bright smile, to show there were no hard feelings.

"What's the name?"

"Greenwood. Esther Greenwood."

"Greenwood, Greenwood, Greenwood." The maid's warty index finger slid down the list of names of the patients in Belsize tacked upon the kitchen wall. "Greenwood, no breakfast today."

I caught the rim of the counter with both hands. . . .

I strode blindly out into the hall, not to my room, because that was where they would come to get me, but to the alcove. . . .

I curled up in the far corner of the **alcove** with the blanket over my head. It wasn't the shock treatment that struck me, so much as the bare-faced treachery of Doctor Nolan. I liked Doctor Nolan, I loved her, I had given her my trust on a platter and told her everything, and she had promised, faithfully, to warn me ahead of time if ever I had to have another shock treatment.

If she had told me the night before I would have lain awake all night, of course, full of dread and **foreboding**,

512

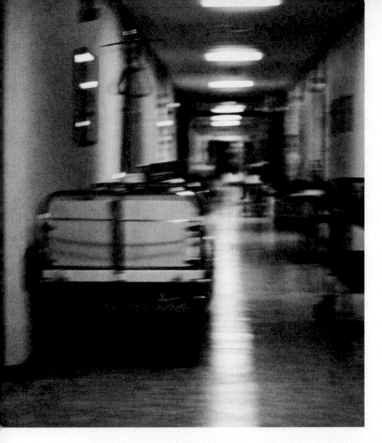

Markus Moellenberg/Corbis

but by morning I would have been composed and ready. I would have gone down the hall between two nurses, past DeeDee and Loubelle and Mrs. Savage and Joan, with dignity, like a person coolly resigned to execution.

The nurse bent over me and called my name.

I pulled away and crouched farther into the corner. The nurse disappeared. I knew she would return, in a minute, with two burly men attendants, and they would bear me, howling and hitting, past the smiling audience now gathered in the lounge.

Doctor Nolan put her arm around me and hugged me like a mother.

"You said you'd tell me!" I shouted at her through the dishevelled blanket.

"But I am telling you," Doctor Nolan said. "I've come specially early to tell you, and I'm taking you over myself."

I peered at her through swollen lids. "Why didn't you tell me last night?"

"I only thought it would keep you awake. If I'd known . . ."

"You said you'd tell me."

"Listen, Esther," Doctor Nolan said. "I'm going over with you. I'll be there the whole time, so everything will happen right, the way I promised. I'll be there when you wake up, and I'll bring you back again."

I looked at her. She seemed very upset.

I waited a minute. Then I said, "Promise you'll be there."

"I promise."

Doctor Nolan . . . led me down a flight of stairs into the mysterious basement corridors that linked, in an elaborate network of tunnels and burrows, all the various buildings of the hospital. The walls were bright, white lavatory tile with bald bulbs set at intervals in the black ceiling. Stretchers and wheelchairs were beached here and there against the hissing, knocking pipes that ran and branched in an intricate nervous system along the glittering walls. I hung on to Doctor Nolan's arm like death, and every so often she gave me an encouraging squeeze.

Finally, we stopped at a green door with **Electrotherapy** printed on it in black letters. I held back, and Doctor Nolan waited. Then I said, "Let's get it over with," and we went in.

The only people in the waiting room besides Doctor Nolan and me were a **pallid** man in a shabby maroon bathrobe and his accompanying nurse. . . .

"Do you want to sit down?" Doctor Nolan pointed at a wooden bench, but my legs felt full of heaviness, and I thought how hard it would be to hoist myself from a sitting position when the shock treatment people came in.

"I'd rather stand."

At last a tall, cadaverous woman in a white smock entered the room from an inner door. I thought that she would go up and take the man in the maroon bathrobe, as he was first, so I was surprised when she came toward me. . . .

Through the slits of my eyes, which I didn't dare open too far, lest the full view strike me dead, I saw the high bed with its white, drumtight sheet, and the machine behind the bed, and the masked person—I couldn't tell whether it was a man or a woman—behind the machine, and other masked people flanking the bed on both sides.

Miss Huey helped me climb up and lie down on my back.

"Talk to me," I said.

Miss Huey began to talk in a low, soothing voice, smoothing the salve on my temples and fitting the small electric buttons on either side of my head. "You'll be perfectly all right, you won't feel a thing, just bite down. . . ." And she set something on my tongue and in panic I bit down, and darkness wiped me out like chalk on a blackboard.

Analyzing Primary Sources

1. *Identifying* What is the setting of this excerpt?

2. *Inferring* How does Esther realize that she is scheduled for a shock treatment that morning?

3. *Exploring Issues* Despite its risks, ECT is still used to treat severe depression. Do you think this is ethical? Under what circumstances would such treatment be administered?

networks

There's More Online!

☑ **GRAPHIC ORGANIZER**

☑ **SELF-CHECK QUIZ**

LESSON 4
Biological Approaches to Treatment

Reading **HELP**DESK

Academic Vocabulary

• **expert**   • **consist**

Content Vocabulary

• **drug therapy**
• **antipsychotic drugs**
• **antidepressants**
• **lithium carbonate**
• **electroconvulsive therapy (ECT)**
• **psychosurgery**
• **prefrontal lobotomy**

TAKING NOTES:

Key Ideas and Details

IDENTIFYING ADVANTAGES AND DISADVANTAGES Fill in the table below with the desired outcomes and possible negative outcomes for each approach.

Approach	Desired Outcomes	Possible Negative Outcomes
Antipsychotic Drugs		
Antidepressant Drugs		
Mood Stabilizers		
Antianxiety Drugs		
Electroconvulsive Therapy		
Psychosurgery		

514

ESSENTIAL QUESTION • *How do changes to the body change the mind?*

IT MATTERS BECAUSE

The idea of using drugs, brain surgery, or" shock" treatments to alter a person's mind may conjure up images of a horror movie. Psychologists report, however, that nearly 40 percent of clients receive drug therapy. Most therapists think the use of drugs will grow in coming years—and electroconvulsive (shock) therapy has successfully treated severely depressed people who have failed to respond to psychotherapy.

Biological Therapy

GUIDING QUESTION *What is the major effect of antianxiety drugs?*

People with ear infections are given antibiotics, and within 10 days, most of the infections have disappeared. Could the same approach be used for people with psychological problems? Today, medications are widely prescribed for psychological disorders. Unlike antibiotics, these medications do not "cure" the condition, but rather control the symptoms. Some **experts** believe that biological therapies should be reserved for people who fail to respond to psychotherapy. Other experts believe that a combination of psychotherapy and biological therapy is the answer for many patients.

Biological approaches to treatment assume there is an underlying physiological reason for the disturbed behavior, the faulty thinking, and the inappropriate emotions the person displays. Biological therapy uses methods such as medication, electric shock, and surgery to help people with psychological disorders. Since these treatments are medical in nature, physicians or psychiatrists typically administer them. In recent years qualified psychologists also have begun prescribing drugs. However, decisions regarding whether or not a biological approach to treatment is appropriate for patients can be made by all qualified psychiatrists.

The most widely used biological therapy for psychological disorders is **drug therapy**. Drug therapy involves four main types of psychoactive medications: antipsychotic drugs, antidepressant drugs, mood stabilizers, and antianxiety drugs. Prescribed drug therapy medications relieve psychiatric symptoms and increase the usefulness of other forms of psychotherapy. Their effectiveness is temporary, however. They are not a cure.

(l)Digital Vision/Getty Images; (r)Mitchell Funk/Photographer's Choice/Getty Images

When patients undergoing drug therapy stop taking the medication, symptoms typically reappear. Typically, drugs treat only the symptoms; drug therapy does not remove the causes of the disorder.

Antipsychotic Drugs

For a long time the most common method of helping dangerous or overactive schizophrenic patients was physical restraint—the straitjacket, wet-sheet wrapping, and isolation. Doctors calmed the patient by means of psychosurgery or electroconvulsive shock, which is discussed later.

Today, patients with schizophrenia are usually prescribed **antipsychotic drugs**. These drugs have helped schizophrenics stay out of mental institutions. Many patients with schizophrenia who take these drugs improve in a number of ways: they become more vigilant and attentive, with improved problem-solving and organization skills. Even so, it may reduce their fine motor skills. One theory of schizophrenia proposes that when a person's dopamine neurotransmitter system somehow becomes overactive, that person develops schizophrenia. These medicines inhibit dopamine receptor sites. Drugs like chlorpromazine (such as Thorazine) and haloperidol (such as Haldol) block or reduce the sensitivity of dopamine receptors. Clozapine (such as Closaril) decreases dopamine activity and increases the serotonin level, which inhibits the dopamine system. While these drugs reduce symptoms, there can be unpleasant side effects including muscular rigidity, impaired coordination, and tremors.

Antidepressants

Another class of drugs, called **antidepressants**, relieves depression. Depression is accompanied by imbalances in the neurotransmitters serotonin and norepinephrine. The most popular antidepressants are the selective serotonin reuptake inhibitors (SSRIs) and include fluoxetine (Prozac), sertraline (Zoloft), and paroxetine (Paxil). Others inhibit the reuptake of both serotonin and norepinephrine and include venlafaxine (Effexor) and duloxetine (Cymbalta.) Antidepressants may have unpleasant side effects such as headache, nausea, drowsiness, and sleeplessness.

Mood Stabilizers

People with bipolar disorder have extremely intense mood swings. While there is no cure for this condition, mood stabilizers help to minimize these extreme shifts. The most widely used drug in this category is lithium carbonate. The fact that lithium carbonate could stabilize moods in agitated individuals was discovered in 1949. **Lithium carbonate** is a natural chemical element that works by controlling levels of the neurotransmitter norepinephrine. If the norepinephrine levels are too low, it raises the levels; if they are too high, the levels are lowered. If it is not administered under proper supervision, lithium carbonate can cause side effects, such as loss of coordination and seizures. Lithium salts reduce the symptoms of people with a bipolar disorder more so than for those with a unipolar depression. Studies have shown that lithium carbonate decreases bipolar episodes by 80 percent as compared to 40 percent for a placebo. Besides its high degree of effectiveness, lithium carbonate also has the advantage of being relatively inexpensive.

expert someone having special skill or knowledge

drug therapy biological therapy that uses medications

antipsychotic drug medication to reduce agitation, delusions, and hallucinations by blocking the activity of dopamine in the brain; tranquilizers

antidepressant medication to treat major depression by increasing the amount of one or both of the neurotransmitters noradrenaline and serotonin

lithium carbonate a chemical used to counteract mood swings of bipolar disorder.

A patient consults his doctor about his treatment. Together they evaluate how he is doing and what should happen next.

▶ **CRITICAL THINKING**

Sequencing When would a psychiatrist suggest that a patient try medication?

Anticonvulsant drugs are also used as mood stabilizers. Anticonvulsant drugs were originally developed to control seizures, but it has been shown that they also can regulate mood swings. They are used to treat bipolar disorders when lithium carbonate does not work or the individual is unable to tolerate it. In addition, anticonvulsant drugs may be used in combination with lithium carbonate. Drugs in this category include valproic acid (Depakote) and carbamazepine (Tegretol.) Like lithium carbonate, these drugs can have serious side effects. For example, valproic acid is capable of causing liver damage.

Connecting Psychology to Economics

SOCIAL COSTS OF MENTAL ILLNESS

Individuals with serious psychological disorders, such as schizophrenia, face numerous social, physical, mental, and economic problems. About 6 percent of American adults are affected by serious psychological disorders. The *American Journal of Psychiatry* estimates that this results in $193 billion in lost earnings a year. This causes hardships for the individuals involved and hurts our overall economy.

Many individuals with major psychological disorders must be on expensive medications. Sometimes these expenses are covered by health insurance or government programs. However, in many cases, individuals either do not have these options or do not understand how to gain access to them. A 2010 research project found that 46 percent of Medicaid recipients had problems getting access to needed medications within the last year. Many ended up in hospital emergency rooms, an expensive way of handling a complex situation.

Up until the 1950s and 1960s, institutions housed most people with severe psychological disorders. With the introduction of antipsychotic drugs, such individuals could function in society and were often quickly released in a process called *deinstitutionalization*. Because many of the deinstitutionalized cannot hold a job or live alone, they may find themselves without a place to live. The Substance Abuse and Mental Health Services Administration reports that 20 to 25 percent of homeless individuals suffer from severe psychological disorders. In part due to deinstitutionalization, these new percentages are largely due to the availability of fewer alternative housing options. Declining government resources mean that less money is allocated to meet the special housing needs of this group.

The increased likelihood of being homeless may cause this group to have poor personal hygiene. Employers are less likely to hire them and they may be discriminated against in public places such as restaurants and stores. A large percentage ends up in the lower socioeconomic classes. These problems can cause them to further withdraw from interacting with others. This group should not face discrimination when interacting with psychologists. As stated in the American Psychological Association's Ethics Code, psychologists are bound to treat all clients the same, regardless of socioeconomic status, race, and similar factors. When working with these individuals, psychotherapists must carefully guard against such discrimination.

▲ The social and economic impact of mental disorders can be extreme.

Racial and ethnic minorities have special problems, partly because they tend to live in areas that have the lowest levels of mental health care. Another group, veterans of the armed services, make up 45 percent of those struggling with mental illness and about one-third of homeless people. About 56 percent of homeless veterans are African American or Latino, even though these two groups make up 12.8 percent and 15.4 percent of the population, respectively.

It is not enough to simply find these individuals a place to live. If they do not receive mental health care and support, they are likely to return to the streets. Research by the National Mental Health Association has shown that supported housing is effective for people with mental illnesses. In addition to housing, supported housing programs offer services such as mental and physical health treatment, education and employment opportunities, peer support, and daily living skills training. This broad-ranging support system provides hope for reducing homelessness among those with major psychological disorders.

▶ **CRITICAL THINKING**

1. *Identifying Cause and Effect* What is one cause of the high homeless rate for individuals with severe psychological disorders?

2. *Explaining* How does homelessness affect individuals with severe psychological disorders both socially and economically?

Mitchell Funk/Photographer's Choice/Getty Images

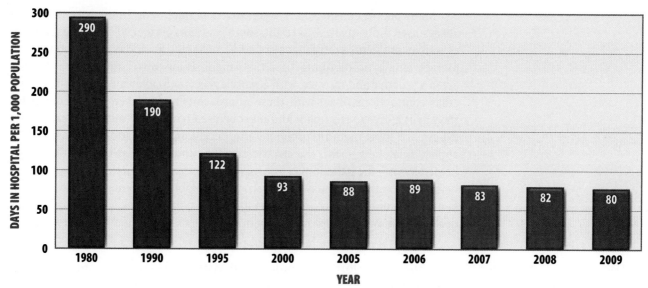

Source: U.S. Bureau of the Census, *Statistical Abstract of the United States* 2003, 2006, 2012.

Antianxiety Drugs

Commonly known as sedatives or mild tranquilizers, antianxiety drugs are used to reduce excitability and cause drowsiness. First the barbiturates, then Miltown (meprobamate), and eventually the benzodiazepines have been very popular prescriptions in recent decades. At one time Valium (diazepam) was the most popular prescription drug in the country. Now several benzodiazepines, including alprazolam (Xanax) and lorazepam (Ativan), have joined it. While these drugs are effective for helping normal people cope with difficult periods in their lives, they are also prescribed for the alleviation of various anxiety-based symptoms, psychosomatic problems, and symptoms of alcohol withdrawal.

If antianxiety drugs are taken properly, the side effects are few and **consist** mainly of drowsiness and dizziness. However, prolonged use may lead to dependence, and heavy doses taken along with alcohol can result in death. These drugs do reduce anxiety, but the best use seems to be for dealing with acute (temporary) rather than chronic (long-term) anxiety.

☑ **READING PROGRESS CHECK**

Explaining How do the SSRIs work to alleviate depression?

Other Procedures

GUIDING QUESTION *Why are electroconvulsive therapy and psychosurgery considered controversial treatments?*

Psychotherapy and drug therapy are the two most common treatments for psychological disorders. However, when these methods do not achieve the desired results, mental health care professionals may turn to other treatments.

Electroconvulsive Therapy

Electroconvulsive therapy (ECT), commonly called shock treatment, has proved extremely effective in the treatment of severe depression, acute mania, and some types of schizophrenia. For example, research has found an 86 percent remission rate for those with major depression. No one understands exactly how it works, but it involves administering, over several weeks, a series of brief electrical shocks. The shock induces a convulsion in the brain similar to an epileptic seizure that may last up to a minute.

^ GRAPH

DEINSTITUTIONALIZATION

Over the past three decades the national policy has been one of deinstitutionalization. Deinstitutionalization refers to the release of patients from psychiatric hospitals. These patients rejoin the community to attempt to lead independent lives.

▶ **CRITICAL THINKING**

1. *Comparing* How has the number of days patients spend in psychiatric hospitals changed since 1980?

2. *Contrasting* Which decade saw the biggest drop?

consist to involve

electroconvulsive therapy (ECT) therapeutic method in which an electrical shock is sent through the brain to try to reduce symptoms of mental disturbance

Therapy and Change **517**

Many people consider ECT a controversial treatment. In the past, it was not always used judiciously. As a result, some people experienced extensive amnesia, as well as problems with language and verbal abilities. Today, electroconvulsive therapy entails no discomfort for the patient. Prior to treatment, the patient is given a sedative and injected with a muscle relaxant to alleviate involuntary muscular contractions. Even with these improvements, however, electroconvulsive therapy is a drastic treatment and must be used with great caution. Many people experience some memory problems after receiving this treatment. When ECT is applied bilaterally—with the electric current running across both of the brain's hemispheres—the patient may lose memory for events occurring one to two days before the treatment. Today physicians usually apply ECT unilaterally to the right hemisphere only. This technique results in little memory loss. The use of ECT has declined somewhat, but it remains a highly effective treatment for depression.

Psychosurgery

Brain surgery performed in order to alleviate psychological disorders is called **psychosurgery**. Historically, the most common procedure has been **prefrontal lobotomy**, which destroys the front portion of the brain, just behind the forehead. This part of the brain, the frontal lobe, contains most of the nerve connections that control emotions. From the late 1930s to the early 1950s, doctors performed prefrontal lobotomies on people who were extremely violent or diagnosed with schizophrenia, depression, bipolar disorder, and obsessive-compulsive disorder.

However, because of severe side effects, such as epilepsy and undesirable personality changes, prefrontal lobotomies are only rarely performed. Today, drug therapy is commonly used with these patients. For patients who do not respond to drug therapy, surgical techniques involving inserting metal probes into specific areas of the brain may be used. Precise portions can then be destroyed. This high level of precision reduces the possibility of damaging side effects. Proponents of psychosurgery claim that it can benefit violent patients and those with severe obsessive-compulsive disorders. However, psychosurgery is generally used as a last resort and therefore is a very small part of today's treatment for psychological disorders.

☑ READING PROGRESS CHECK

Analyzing Why is psychosurgery only a small part of the treatment for psychological disorders?

psychosurgery a medical operation that destroys part of the brain to make the patient calmer and freer of symptoms

prefrontal lobotomy a radical form of psychosurgery in which a section of the frontal lobe of the brain is destroyed

---

LESSON 4 REVIEW

Reviewing Vocabulary
1. *Listing* What are two different ways that antidepressants function?
2. *Explaining* Why might a person take a mood stabilizer?

Using Your Notes
3. *Categorizing* Review the notes that you completed during the lesson to create a list of those drugs that are used for a specific psychological disorder. These disorders might include schizophrenia, major depressive disorder, bipolar disorder, or anxiety.

Answering the Guiding Questions
4. *Identifying* What is the major effect of antianxiety drugs?
5. *Identifying Central Issues* Why are electroconvulsive therapy and psychosurgery considered controversial treatments?

Writing Activity
6. *Informative/Explanatory* Conduct research to learn more about the current uses of either electroconvulsive therapy or psychosurgery. Write a report in which you describe the circumstances under which your chosen treatment is used. The report should be well organized and use formal language.

Directions: On a separate sheet of paper, answer the questions below. Make sure you read carefully and answer all parts of the question.

Lesson Review

Lesson 1

❶ *Drawing Conclusions* What difficulties might occur if a client considers himself or herself as mentally ill?

❷ *Explaining* What is an important advantage to using an eclectic approach to therapy?

Lesson 2

❸ *Analyzing* Why do psychoanalysts use free association and dream therapy?

❹ *Drawing Inferences* What is active listening? Do you think active listening might help improve day-to-day communication between people? Explain your answer.

Lesson 3

❺ *Applying* Make a list of a few fears that you have. Do you think any of your fears are based on conditioning? Describe a method of counterconditioning that you think would remove one of the fears or make it less intense.

❻ *Constructing Arguments* Do you agree with Albert Ellis that it is not the event in a person's life that causes trouble but rather the way a person thinks about the event? Explain your answer.

Lesson 4

❼ *Describing* What is the purpose of each of these: antipsychotic drugs, antidepressant drugs, mood stabilizers, antianxiety drugs?

❽ *Finding the Main Idea* In a graphic organizer similar to the one below, list and explain the biological approaches to treatment.

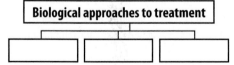

Exploring the Essential Questions

❾ *Organizing* Create a table. In the first column, list the following therapies and treatments: psychoanalysis, humanistic therapy, cognitive therapy, behavior therapy, drug therapy, electroconvulsive therapy, and psychosurgery. In the second column, briefly describe each one and explain how each can be used to modify behavior.

College and Career Readiness

The following table compares the percentage of psychologists using various therapeutic approaches. Use this information to answer the questions below.

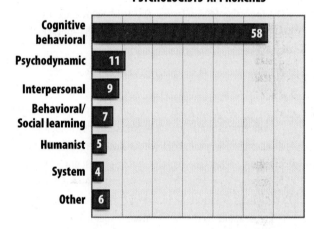

Source: Study of the Practice of Licensed Psychologists in the United States and Canada, by P*E*S, Dr. Greenberg, Dr. Caro, and Dr. Smith, © 2012 by the Association of State and Provincial Psychology Boards.

❿ *Examining Information* Which type of therapy is used by the greatest percentage of psychologists? Why do you think that is so?

⓫ *Reaching Conclusions* Psychodynamic therapy (or short-term dynamic psychotherapy) is an approach that is similar to psychoanalysis. Why do you think more therapists today practice psychodynamic therapy rather than classical psychoanalysis?

Need Extra Help?

If You've Missed Question	❶	❷	❸	❹	❺	❻	❼	❽	❾	❿	⓫
Go to page	493	494	500	502	508	506	515	514	494	519	501

Directions: On a separate sheet of paper, answer the questions below. Make sure you read carefully and answer all parts of the question.

Research and Technology

12 Gathering Information Imagine you are a reporter with an assignment to cover psychosurgery. Conduct a Web quest to learn more about psychosurgery, including how it helps individuals and when individuals would need this type of treatment. Using your information, write a news article that could appear in your local newspaper.

Critical Thinking Questions

13 Evaluating Counter Arguments While many people think psychotherapy can improve people's lives, others have specific arguments against it. Describe some of these arguments and discuss whether you think they are valid.

14 Analyzing Ethical Issues Discuss the pros and cons to using drug therapy and ECT. Also discuss the ethical issues that surround these treatments.

21ˢᵗ Century Skills

15 Identifying Perspectives Factors such as culture and age influence attitudes toward treatment for psychological disorders. For example, a cultural group might think psychotherapy is acceptable, but be against drug therapy. Conduct Web research to learn the attitudes of different cultures or age groups to various treatments. Create an oral presentation with graphics to share your findings.

16 Time, Chronology, and Sequencing Conduct Web research to create a time line showing major developments for treatment of psychological disorders over the past 300 years. Create a digital slide show to present your time line.

17 Identifying Perspectives Some of what we know about the brain and its functioning has come from studies and experiments performed on animals. Work with a partner to create a script for a role-play between two researchers. If class time allows, perform the scenario; one of you should act the part of the researcher who supports using animals for psychological research while the other opposes their use. Be sure to include information on the APA's stand on this issue.

DBQ Analyzing Primary Sources

The following is an excerpt from an article in the APA's Monitor on Psychology *concerning the use of psychotropic drugs on psychotherapy patients. Use the document to answer the following questions.*

PRIMARY SOURCE

"*On average, 39 percent of the respondents' patients are on drug therapy. Respondents who see children less than 13 years old said that about 22 percent of patients in that age group take psychotropic medications. Survey respondents report that 29 percent of their teenage patients—those 13 to 19 years old—are taking psychotropic medications. However, responding psychologists report that adult patients are more likely to be on drug therapy—46 percent of patients 20 to 59 years old and 43 percent of patients older than 60 years. Participating psychologists expect that these numbers will increase: 62 percent think that medication will play a greater role in treating mental health disorders over the next three to five years. . .*"

—from "Psychologists and Psychotropic Medication," Monitor on Psychology, *May, 2006.*

18 Making Generalizations What statements can you make concerning the use of psychotropic drugs in different age groups?

19 Analyzing What trends do psychologists see for the use of psychotropic drugs in the future?

Psychology Journal Activity

20 Informative/Explanatory Review your entry in your Psychology Journal for this chapter. Does learning about the methods of psychoanalysis make you more or less willing to share information about yourself with others? What are some benefits of sharing information?

Need Extra Help?

If You've Missed Question	12	13	14	15	16	17	18	19	20
Go to page	518	493	517	492	492	518	514	514	490

TEXT: Laurie Meyers, Psychologists and psychotropic medication, the *Monitor*, June 2006, Vol 37, No. 6, pp. 46, American Psychological Association, © 2006, adapted with permission.

Individual Interaction

networks

There's More Online about individual interactions.

CHAPTER 18

ESSENTIAL QUESTIONS • *Why do people form bonds?* • *How do individuals develop judgments?*

Psychology Matters...

Who are the key people in your life? Who are the people who influence your decisions? Why are these people important to you? Have you thought about why you choose to interact with certain people and not with others? Some of these people are in your life due to circumstance. Others are in your life because you have chosen for them to be. In this chapter, we will learn more about the people who are part of our lives and how we interact with them.

◄ Friends. We often take them for granted, but our relationships impact how we feel about ourselves and our activities.

©Tanya Constantine/Corbis

521

Lab Activity

Choosing Your Friends

THE QUESTION...

RESEARCH QUESTION What factors guide our interactions with each other?

Imagine you move to a new school and want to make some new friends. How will you decide who you'd like your friends to be? Do you talk to Carlos, who wears the coolest clothes? Or do you talk to Emma, who makes short films after school? Or do you talk to Jacob, who always opens the door for people? It might feel like friendships "just happen" and that you don't spend much time thinking about how they form, but many factors shape how we interact with each other.

This experiment explores some of the factors that shape social interactions. Will this experiment make you more popular? That's hard to say, but it might shed some light on what traits are more popular.

Psychology Journal Activity

What do you get out of friendships? Write about this in your Psychology Journal. Consider the following issues: What personality traits do you look for in your friends? What personality traits do you tend to avoid? Why? What are the short-term and long-term benefits of having friends?

FINDING THE ANSWER...

HYPOTHESIS We choose friends with personalities that are similar to our own.

THE METHOD OF YOUR EXPERIMENT

MATERIALS 20 surveys, 20 collections of images, 20 pens

PROCEDURE Create a list of five positive and common personality traits, such as athletic, intelligent, friendly, responsible, and fun. Then use the Internet to find five images for each trait that show different people representing that trait. Create a document with the images randomly ordered by trait and place a 1 to 5 scale beside or under each image. Gather 20 participants. Give the participants a brief survey in which they rate their own personality by identifying with one of the four personality traits you are testing. Then present the participants with the collection of 20 images. Ask them to rate how much they would like to be friends with each photo subject; have them use a scale of 1 to 5, with 1 meaning "not interested" and 5 meaning "very interested."

DATA COLLECTION Collect the participants' scores for the two surveys. Determine which personality trait received the highest score on the brief survey. Then average the scores for the image surveys and draw conclusions about the participants' preferences. Be sure to protect participant confidentiality.

ANALYSIS & APPLICATION

1. Did your results support the hypothesis?

2. How could the methods of this experiment be improved to produce better data?

3. What other personal qualities could be tested using the methods in this experiment?

networks ONLINE LAB RESOURCES

Online you will find:

- An **interactive lab experience,** allowing you to put principles from this chapter into practice in a digital psychology lab environment. This chapter's lab will include an experiment on issues related to individual interactions.

- A **Skills Handbook** that includes a guide for using the scientific method, creating experiments, and analyzing data.

- A **Notebook** where you can complete your Psychology Journal and record and analyze your experiment data.

networks

There's More Online!

☑ **GRAPHIC ORGANIZER**

☑ **SELF-CHECK QUIZ**

Reading **HELP**DESK **CCSS**

Academic Vocabulary

• appropriate • similarity

Content Vocabulary

• social psychology
• social cognition
• physical proximity
• stimulation value
• utility value
• ego-support value
• complementarity

TAKING NOTES:

Key Ideas and Details

ORGANIZING Use a graphic organizer like the one below to list and describe the factors involved in choosing friends.

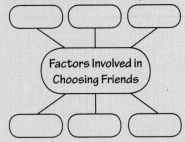

Factors Involved in Choosing Friends

LESSON 1

Interpersonal Attraction

ESSENTIAL QUESTIONS • *Why do people form bonds?* • *How do individuals develop judgments?*

IT MATTERS BECAUSE

Have you ever been discouraged and overwhelmed by events, and then been encouraged by the words or presence of a friend? How did it feel to be reminded that you were not alone? John Donne, the seventeenth-century poet wrote, "No man is an island, entire of itself; every man is a piece of the continent, a part of the main . . ." His words are still true today.

Why You Need Friends

GUIDING QUESTION *How do friends reduce uncertainty?*

Is it possible to shut away the world, or isolate ourselves in order to remain safe, and yet still remain happy? Isolation has a price. Being with other people may not always be safe, but it is often preferable. That is why we choose friends. This topic is the concern of **social psychology**—the study of how our thoughts, feelings, perceptions, and behaviors are influenced by our interactions with others. **Social cognition**, a subfield of social psychology, is the study of how we perceive, store, and retrieve information about these social interactions. Social psychologists might ask: Why did we choose the friends we have? What attracted us to them in the first place? Every day we are making judgments about others based on our perceptions of who they are. Then, when we interact with these people, we must adjust our judgments to explain their behavior and ours.

During infancy we depend on others to satisfy our basic needs. In this relationship we learn to associate close personal contact with the satisfaction of basic needs. Later in life we seek personal contact for the same reason, even though we can now care for ourselves.

Being around other human beings—interacting with others—has become a habit that would be difficult to break. Moreover, we have developed needs for praise, respect, love and affection, the sense of achievement, and other rewarding experiences. These needs, acquired through social learning, can only be satisfied by other human beings. On the other hand, failing to form social connections or being rejected by others, particularly those with whom we have formed connections, is painful.

(l-r)DLILLC/Corbis; Photodisc/Getty Images; ace stock/Alamy; ©Hugh Sitton/Corbis; Jeremy Hoarey/age fotostock

524

Anxiety and Companionship

Social psychologists are interested in discovering what circumstances intensify our desire for human contact. It seems that we need company most when we are afraid or anxious, and we also need company when we are unsure of ourselves and want to compare our feelings with those of other people.

Psychologist Stanley Schachter in 1959 decided to test the old saying "Misery loves company." His experiment showed that people suffering from a high level of anxiety are more likely to seek out company than are those who feel less anxious.

Schachter arranged for a number of college women to come to his laboratory as participants in an experiment. He separated the women into two groups. One group of women was greeted by a frightening-looking man in a white coat who identified himself as Dr. Gregor Zilstein of the medical school. Dr. Zilstein told each woman that she would be given electric shocks to study the effect of electricity on the body. He told the women, in an ominous tone, that the shocks would be extremely painful. With a devilish smile, he added that the shocks would cause no permanent skin damage. For obvious reasons, this group of women was referred to as the high-anxiety group. The doctor was friendly to the other group and told them that the shocks would produce only ticklish, tingling sensations, which they might even find pleasant. These women were referred to as the low-anxiety group.

Zilstein told the participants that they would have to leave the laboratory while he set up the equipment. He then asked each woman to indicate on a questionnaire whether she wished to wait alone in a private room or with other participants in a larger room. Most women in the low-anxiety group chose to wait alone. The majority of high-anxiety women, however, preferred to wait with others. Thus, the experiment demonstrated that high anxiety tends to produce a need for companionship.

Comparing Experiences and Reducing Uncertainty

People also like to get together with one another to reduce their uncertainties about themselves. For example, after competing in a sporting event, you expect to find out how the other competitors fared. When you get a test back, you probably ask your friends how they did. You try to understand your own situation by comparing it to other people's. You learn your strengths and weaknesses by asking: Can other people do what I can do? Do they do it better or worse?

social psychology the study of how our thoughts, feelings, perceptions, and behaviors are influenced by interactions with others

social cognition the perception, storage, and retrieval of information about social interactions

Some animals, like snakes, are solitary throughout their lives; other animals, like elephants and humans, remain highly social even after they become self-sufficient.

▶ CRITICAL THINKING

Identifying Central Issues Why do we need friends?

(l)Creatas/PunchStock; (c)©DLILLC/Corbis; ©Roy Morsch/Corbis

LOW ANXIETY   HIGH ANXIETY

22

10

20

12

■ Number of women who chose
to be alone or did not care
■ Number of women who
chose to affiliate

GRAPH ∧

SCHACHTER'S RESULTS
These graphs show the results of Schachter's experiment about the effects of anxiety on affiliation, or the likelihood of joining or connecting with others.

▶ CRITICAL THINKING

1. *Analyzing Visuals* Which group was more likely to seek company? Why?

2. *Identifying Central Issues* What benefit did the high-anxiety women gain from company?

appropriate suitable, acceptable, or correct for the particular circumstances

Many individuals use the performance of others as a basis for self-evaluation. According to this theory, one of the reasons why the women in the shock experiment sought company was to find out how they should respond to Dr. Zilstein. Should they feel fear or anger, or should they take the whole thing in stride? One way to get this information was to talk to others.

Schachter conducted another experiment to test this idea. It was essentially the same as the Dr. Zilstein experiment, but this time all the women were made anxious. Half of them were then given the choice between waiting alone and waiting with other women about to take part in the same experiment. The other half were given the choice between waiting alone and passing the time in a room where students were waiting to see their academic advisers.

As you might expect, the women who had a chance to be with other women in the same predicament seized the opportunity. These women wanted to compare their dilemma with others. Yet most of the women in the second group chose to spend the time alone rather than with the unconcerned students. As the experimenter put it, "Misery doesn't love just any kind of company; it loves only miserable company."

Other researchers have shown that the more uncertain a person is, the more likely he or she is to seek out other people. Like Schachter, Harold Gerard and J.M. Rabbie, in a study in 1961, recruited volunteers for an experiment. When the volunteers arrived, some of them were escorted to a booth and attached to a machine that was supposed to measure emotionality. The machine was turned on, and the participants were able to see not only their own ratings but also the ratings of three other participants. In each case the dial for the participant registered 82 on a scale of 100; the dials for the other participants registered 79, 80, and 81. For this first group of participants, the machine was rigged to display only those numbers. A second group of participants was attached to a similar machine and shown their own ratings but not those of other participants. A third group was not given any information about themselves or other participants in the experiment. When asked whether they wanted to wait alone or with other participants, most of the people in the first group chose to wait alone. They had seen how they compared to others and felt they were reacting **appropriately**. Most of the participants in the other two groups, who had no basis for evaluating themselves, however, chose to wait with other people.

Friendship also offers support in trying times. Friends may serve as mediators if you have problems with another person. Friends are there to react to your ideas. In your social network, friends are your connections to a broad array of available support.

Yet, as we will see, predicting the effects of friendship can be quite complex. Karen Rook, in a 1987 study, found that having friends who offer support helped reduce very high stress. On the other hand, friends were no significant help in dealing with average amounts of stress. Perhaps, most surprisingly, the support of friends actually hindered people's ability to deal with low levels of stress. Rook theorizes that reviewing smaller problems again and again with your friends may actually increase your sensitivity to those problems.

☑ READING PROGRESS CHECK

Explaining Why do people want companionship in times of anxiety?

How You Choose Friends

GUIDING QUESTION *What factors play a role in friend selection?*

How do you choose your friends? Do you find that you choose to be friends with the people who live closest to you? Maybe you choose your friends because of specific ways they can benefit you—you are attracted to their appearance, you feel good when you are around them, you have similar interests, you find their differences appealing, or you are in several classes with that person every day at school. All of these factors may come into play when you choose your friends.

Most people feel they have a great deal of latitude in their choice of friends. The convenient transportation, wealth of communication devices, social media options, and spare time available to many Americans should make it easy for them to get acquainted, make friends, and engage in activities with a wide range of individuals in many locations. The greater the effort required, the less likely a friendship will be established.

Proximity

Would it surprise you to learn that one of the most important factors in determining whether two people will become friends is **physical proximity**—the distance from one another that people live or work? In general, the closer two individuals are to one another geographically, the more likely they are to become attracted to each other. Yet it is more than just the opportunity for interaction that makes the difference.

Psychologists have found that even in a small two-story apartment building where each resident was in easy reach of everyone else, people were more likely to become close friends with the person next door than with anyone else. Psychologists believe that this is a result of the fears and embarrassments most people have about making contact with strangers. When two people live next door to one another, go to the same class, or work in the same place, they are able to get used to one another and to find reasons to talk to one another without embarrassment.

physical proximity the distance of one person to another person

Even if others are within relatively close proximity, people are more likely to become good friends with their next-door neighbor than with anyone else.

▶ **CRITICAL THINKING**

Making Connections How does physical proximity affect your choice of friends?

Photodisc/Getty Images

Standards of physical attractiveness vary widely internationally. These photos are of people considered beautiful from Kenya, Peru, and Japan.

▶ **CRITICAL THINKING**

Assessing Do you believe that your ideal of physical beauty is dependent on your culture? Explain.

stimulation value the ability of a person to interest you in or to expose you to new ideas and experiences

utility value the ability of a person to help another achieve his or her goals

ego-support value the ability of a person to provide another person with sympathy, encouragement, and approval

They never seriously have to risk rejection. To make friends with someone you do not see routinely is much more difficult. You have to make it clear that you are interested and thus run the risk of making a fool of yourself—either because the other person turns out to be less interesting than he or she seemed at a distance or because that person expresses no interest in you. Of course, it may turn out that both of you are very glad someone spoke up.

Reward Values

Proximity helps people make friends, but it does not make certain, or ensure, that a friendship will last. Sometimes people who are forced together in a situation take a dislike to one another that develops into hatred. Furthermore, once people have made friends, physical separation does not necessarily bring an end to their relationship. What are the factors that determine whether people will remain friends once they come into contact?

Psychologists have studied the reward value of friendship. There are inherent benefits in friendship. These benefits may be tangible, such as financial assistance, or intangible, such as encouragement and companionship. Scholars have grouped these benefits into two categories: instrumental and expressive. Instrumental rewards are those things such as goods, money, or assistance toward goals. This would include people you befriend because they can help you study for a test or assist you in your career. Expressive rewards are the intangible benefits of companionship, encouragement, and emotional support.

One reward of friendship is stimulation. A friend has **stimulation value** if he or she is interesting or imaginative or can introduce you to new ideas or experiences. A friend who is cooperative and helpful has **utility value**; he or she is willing to give time and resources to help you achieve your goals. A third type of value in friendship is **ego-support value**—sympathy and encouragement when things go badly, appreciation and approval when things go well.

These three kinds of rewards—stimulation, utility, and ego support—are evaluated consciously or unconsciously in every friendship. One person may like another because the second is a witty conversationalist (stimulation value) and knows a lot about gardening (utility value). You may like some people because they value your opinions (ego-support value) and because you have an exciting time with them (stimulation value). By considering the three kinds of rewards that a person may look for in friendship, it is possible to understand other factors that affect liking and loving.

Thinking about the value rewards that your friends offer you can also help you to determine whether your friendships have true value at all. If your friends don't support you in any way, consider why this might be. Think about what it is that you like about your friends and what they offer to your relationship. You should be able to come up with some kind of reward for your relationship, whether the reward is stimulation, utility, or ego support.

Physical Appearance

A person's physical appearance greatly influences others' impressions of him or her. People feel better about themselves when they associate with people whom others consider desirable. People may think about physical appearance when they choose friends because they consider their friends to be a reflection of themselves. Socializing with attractive people may mean that society considers them attractive as well. In addition, a 1995 study by Longo and Ashmore showed that we often consider those with physical beauty to be more responsive, interesting, sociable, intelligent, kind, outgoing, and poised. This is true of same-sex as well as opposite-sex relationships. Physical attractiveness influences who we choose as friends as well as romantic partners.

In a 1972 study by Dion, Berscheid, and Walster, participants were shown pictures of men and women of varying degrees of physical attractiveness and were asked to rate their personality traits. The physically attractive people were consistently viewed more positively than the less attractive ones. They were seen as more sensitive, kind, interesting, strong, poised, modest, and sociable. It appears, therefore, that although we have heard that "beauty is only skin deep," we act as if it permeates one's entire personality.

Fashion and styles also contribute to a person's physical appearance. People sometimes choose their friends based on the way others dress or present themselves. A young person who dresses to show their interest in a particular sport, fashion, or kind of music may attract the attention of others who are interested in the same things. Friendships may form based on these assumptions about physical appearance.

People who do not meet society's standards for attractiveness are often viewed in an unfavorable light. Research has shown that obese adults are often discriminated against when they apply for jobs. Even children are targets of prejudice. In their 1972 study, Dion, Berscheid, and Walster found that an unattractive child is far more likely to be judged to be bad or cruel for an act of misbehavior than is a more attractive peer. These discriminations are unfair, so why do they happen? The *just-world bias* states that people have the misconception that the world should be a fair and just place. In reality, good people may very well be mistreated and those who mistreat them may get away with their actions with no consequence.

Interestingly, psychologists have found that both men and women pay much less attention to physical appearance when choosing a marriage partner or a close friend than when inviting someone to go to a movie or a party. Yet neither men nor women necessarily seek out the most attractive member of their social world. Rather, people usually seek out others whom they consider their equals on the scale of attractiveness.

Adult participants in a study saw the behaviors committed by unattractive children as more antisocial and attributed a negative moral character to these children compared to the attractive ones.

▶ **CRITICAL THINKING**

Making Connections Why are we attracted to good-looking people?

ace stock/Alamy

Approval

Another factor that affects a person's choice of friends is approval. All of us tend to like people who agree with and support us because they make us feel better about ourselves—they provide ego-support value.

Some studies suggest that other people's evaluations of themselves are more meaningful when they are a mixture of praise and criticism than when they are extreme in either direction. No one believes that he or she is all good or all bad. As a result, one can take more seriously a person who sees some good points and some bad points. When the good points come first, hearing the bad can make one disappointed and angry at the person who made them. When the bad points come first, the effect is opposite.

Similarity

People tend to choose friends whose backgrounds, attitudes, and interests are similar to their own. Often, husbands and wives have similar economic, religious, and educational backgrounds. The couples may have chosen to date each other based on these **similarities**. These similarities are what help to make the relationship last.

There are several explanations for the power of shared attitudes. First, agreement about what is stimulating, worthwhile, or fun provides the basis for sharing activities. People who have similar interests are likely to do more things together, providing more time to get to know one another.

Second, most of us feel uneasy around people who are constantly challenging our views, and we translate our uneasiness into hostility or avoidance. We are more comfortable around people who support us. A friend's agreement bolsters our confidence and contributes to our self-esteem. In addition, most of us are self-centered enough to assume that people who share our values are basically decent and intelligent.

Finally, people who agree about things usually find it easier to communicate with each other. They have fewer arguments and misunderstandings, and they are better able to predict one another's behavior and thus feel at ease with each other. People with differing views may indeed have a lot to discuss through healthy debates, but people with the similar core values and opinions often have lasting relationships due to the ease of communication.

similarity the state of being like someone or something but not exactly the same

People tend to choose friends whose backgrounds, attitudes, and interests are similar. A shared sense of humor can enhance friendship.

▶ CRITICAL THINKING

Synthesizing Think about your friends. Identify one friend and state whether this is a friendship based on similarity or on complementarity. Explain your answer.

©Phillip Graybill/Corbis

Complementarity

Despite the power of similarity, an attraction between opposite types of people—**complementarity**—is not unusual. For example, a dominant person might be happy with a submissive mate. A shy person might feel comfortable being with a person who is more outgoing. Both people may feel happy with the social dynamic between them because one person naturally displays qualities that the other has trouble exhibiting. Sigmund Freud believed that people who are dissatisfied with themselves make up for personal weaknesses by loving people who exhibit strengths in those areas, which is a form of complementarity. Nonetheless, most psychologists agree that similarity is a much more important factor. Although the old idea that opposites attract seems reasonable, researchers continue to be unable to verify it.

complementarity the attraction that often develops between opposite types of people because of the ability of one to supply what the other lacks

Mere Exposure

Another way that people make friends is through repeated exposure. Beginning in the 1960s, psychologist Robert Zajonc initiated a series of experiments in which people were repeatedly exposed to a particular stimulus. Over time, a preference emerged for that object over other newer objects. This "mere-exposure effect" (also called the "familiarity principle") has been demonstrated across cultures and can serve as an explanation of why and how some relationships form. For example, you may meet someone in school with whom you have nothing in common. After repeated exposure day after day at school, your sense of familiarity with that person grows. Repeated exposure may create a positive feeling. Over time, you may create common experiences and memories with that person, eventually solidifying a friendship between the two of you.

In a similar way people working in the same job environment may form friendships. People of different cultures, backgrounds, and age groups can become friendly merely based on their daily exposure to each other. Some work friendships can become very strong, offering an outlet for people to talk about their home lives or other life experiences.

There are exceptions to the mere-exposure effect. If a person's first exposure to a stimulus is negative, that negative impression may last into repeated exposures. Similarly, you may meet someone who makes a bad first impression on you. That bad impression may affect your readiness to become comfortable with the person in the future, even after repeated exposure to the person.

✓ READING PROGRESS CHECK

Describing What is the concept of reward value in friendship?

LESSON 1 REVIEW

Reviewing Vocabulary

1. *Identifying* Explain the differences among stimulation value, utility value, and ego-support value.

Using Your Notes

2. *Organizing* Use the notes from your graphic organizer to write a paragraph describing the factors involved in choosing friends.

Answering the Guiding Questions

3. *Explaining* How do friends reduce uncertainty?

4. *Identifying* What factors play a role in friend selection?

Writing Activity

5. *Argument* Go to a greeting card store and examine several types of cards to send to important people in your life. In a brief essay analyze the following question: What factors of interpersonal attraction do you find are emphasized in the cards?

FOCUS on research

Case Study CCSS

What You See Is What You Get?

Period of Study: 1992

Introduction: Even though people are taught that "looks aren't everything" and "beauty is in the eye of the beholder," these beliefs do not always seem to be upheld within American society. For many years psychologists have disputed whether the importance of physical appearance is a learned concept, from such influences as television, the Internet, or magazines, or has a biological explanation. One consistency found is that physical attractiveness becomes less important as individuals mature.

There have been many studies focusing on the link between physical attractiveness and the behavior of individuals. Some researchers studied the link between physical appearance and perceived personality. Others researched the feelings and perceptions of adults about the "cuteness" of an assorted group of newborn infants. One study had men rate pictures of attractive and unattractive women on different personality traits. Studies have also compared the annual salaries of men and women who had like qualifications but contrasting physical appearance. The results from all of these studies were similar—physical attractiveness was a key factor. Studies have also shown that the perception of attractiveness is based on the needs of the observer.

PRIMARY SOURCE

❝ *For sociability, dominance, general mental health, and intelligence, good-looking people are not what we think: . . . correlational research indicated no notable differences in these characteristics between attractive and unattractive people.* ❞

—*Feingold, Psychological Bulletin (1992)*

Hypothesis: Alan Feingold set out to study and compare personality traits of those individuals who were considered to be physically attractive with those who were not considered physically attractive. Feingold wanted to access the belief that attractive or good-looking individuals could possess superior personality traits.

Method: Defining the attractiveness of individuals for this type of research is not a simple task. There are many bases in terms of in which people can be classified in terms of beauty and personality. Much of this involves the personal preferences of others. Feingold combined the results of numerous studies dealing with this issue.

Results: Feingold's research indicated that there were no significant relationships between physical attractiveness and such traits as intelligence, leadership ability, self-esteem, and mental health. Physical attractiveness has always been a starting point in typical discussions among late adolescents. The discussion usually involves relationships between attractiveness and the features of an individuals personality and character. When physical attractiveness dominates in such discussions, it demonstrates shallowness in judgment. The saying "beauty is only skin deep" emphasizes the need to include other, more personal, factors and abilities in such discussions. Even Feingold's somewhat dated research demonstrated that those individuals who are considered attractive generally are more comfortable in social settings and are less likely to be lonely and anxious. They seem to be more socially skilled than their counterparts. Therefore, what seems to be important is how we define physical attractiveness and our perceptions of the personalities of those attractive people.

Analyzing the Case Study

1. ***Identifying*** What connection between personality and physical attractiveness did Feingold set out to study?

2. ***Summarizing*** What connections between physical attractiveness and personality did Feingold discover?

3. ***Drawing Conclusions*** Do you think physical beauty influences a person's personality? Explain.

4. ***Synthesizing*** Relate the motivational analysis of attractiveness to Feingold's results.

Reading **HELP**DESK CCSS

Academic Vocabulary

- outcome • initial

Content Vocabulary

- primacy effect
- stereotype
- attribution theory
- fundamental attribution error
- actor–observer bias
- self-serving bias
- nonverbal communication

TAKING NOTES:

Key Ideas and Details

GATHERING INFORMATION Use a graphic organizer like the one below to take notes on the key concepts and ideas in this lesson.

First Impressions	Attribution Theory	Nonverbal Communication

LESSON 2

Social Perception

ESSENTIAL QUESTIONS • *Why do people form bonds?* • *How do individuals develop judgments?*

IT MATTERS BECAUSE

Have you ever known the moment you met someone that the two of you could be best friends? As you got to know that person better, did that impression grow or fade? What about the person you knew instantly you would not get along with? Did that relationship develop as expected? Sometimes our first impressions turn out to be correct, and other times they are not so accurate.

First Impressions

GUIDING QUESTION *How do first impressions help us form schemas?*

Sometimes we cannot explain our own behaviors. How then do we explain the behavior of others? It takes people very little time to make judgments about one another. From one brief conversation or even by watching a person across a room, you may form an impression of what someone is like, and first impressions influence the future of a relationship. If a person seems interesting, he or she becomes a candidate for future interaction. A person who seems to have nothing interesting to say—or too much to say—does not. We tend to be sympathetic toward someone who seems shy, to expect a lot from someone who impresses us as intelligent, and to be wary of a person who strikes us as aggressive.

Forming an impression of a person is not a passive process in which certain characteristics of the individual are the input and a certain impression is the automatic **outcome**. If impressions varied only when input varied, then everyone meeting a particular stranger would form the same impression of him or her.

This, of course, is not what happens. One individual may judge a newcomer to be quiet, another may judge the same person to be dull, and still another person may think the person mysterious. These various impressions lead to different expectations of the newcomer and to different interactions with him or her.

When you are meeting someone for the first time, how do you treat that person? Why? Your first impression of someone is usually based on that person's physical appearance. You instantly make certain judgments.

Are you drawn to the people in these photos, or is your impression less favorable? Think about what you noticed about each image and what led to your first impression. Your answer depends in large part on the schemas you have developed.

▶ **CRITICAL THINKING**

Evaluating How do we use our schemas of people?

outcome the way that something turns out in the end; an expected or likely final state, achievement, or result

initial coming first, or present at the beginning of an event or process

primacy effect the tendency to form opinions about others based on first impressions

Your judgments are based on how that person looks. For example, if you meet a well-dressed woman in an office building, you might assume that she is a well-paid corporate executive. Should you meet a waiter in a local restaurant, you might assume that he does not make as much money as the corporate executive. You might interact with these people differently, just as you might interact differently with people of different genders, races, or socioeconomic classes.

These **initial** judgments may influence us more than later information does. For example, in a 1950 study, a researcher invited a guest lecturer to a psychology class. Beforehand, all the students were given a brief description of the visitor. The descriptions were identical in all traits but one. Half the students were told that the speaker was a rather cold person, as well as being industrious, critical, practical, and determined; the others were told he was a very warm person, along with the other four attributes.

Primacy Effect

After the lecture, the researcher asked all the students to evaluate the lecturer. Reading their impressions, you would hardly know that the two groups of students were describing the same person. The students who had been told he was cold saw a humorless, ruthless, self-centered person. The other students saw a relaxed, friendly, concerned person. The students used cold or warm to influence the meaning they assigned to the other four words, so cold and warm—the first words heard—exhibited a **primacy effect** on the other, previously neutral, words. The students interpreted the common words practical and determined in terms of the different words warm or cold, giving them greater, or primary, impact. Thus, to be warm and determined was perceived as dedicated; to be cold and determined was perceived as rigid. It also affected their behavior. Students in the "warm group" were warm themselves, initiating more conversations with the speaker than did the students in the other group.

What was your first impression of your teacher? Did that first impression ever change? These impressions sometimes become a self-fulfilling prophecy; that is, the way you act toward someone changes depending on your impression of him or her, and this in turn affects how that person interacts with you. For instance, suppose you showed up on the first day of class in a terrible mood. During the class period, you did not really pay attention to the lecture and even made a few jokes in class. Your teacher immediately labeled you as the class trouble-maker and, therefore, did not treat you as an attentive and good student.

How would that treatment have impacted your school performance? You may have responded to that treatment by not studying nor caring about your grade in class. In reality, you may be a great student; you just had a bad day on the first day of class and now cannot seem to please your teacher. On many occasions we take the first impressions of others into account in our behavior. For example, when you first start dating someone, you try to look nice. When going for a job interview, you dress well.

Schemas

Forming impressions about others helps us place these people into categories. The knowledge or set of assumptions that we develop about any person or event is known as a schema. We develop a schema for every person we know. When you meet someone who seems unusually intelligent, you may assume she is also active, highly motivated, and conscientious. Another person in the group may have an altogether different schema for highly intelligent people—that they are boring, boastful, unfriendly, and the like. Whatever the person does can be interpreted as support for either theory. You are impressed by how animated your intelligent friend becomes when talking about work; another person does not care for how little attention your friend pays to other people. Both of you are filling in gaps in what you know about the person, fitting her into a type you have constructed in your mind.

Sometimes we develop schemas for people we do not know but have heard about. Schemas can influence and distort our thoughts, perceptions, and behaviors. Think of a person you like. If that person smiles as you pass in the hallway, that smile looks friendly to you. Now think of a person whom you mistrust or do not really like. If that person smiles at you in the hallway, you may not interpret the smile as friendly but instead think of it as a guilty or fake smile. We develop schemas for people and events. The schemas associated with people are judgments about the traits people possess or the jobs they perform.

Schemas about events consist of behaviors that we associate with certain events. For example, we know that we can yell and cheer at the basketball game but that we should be quiet and subdued at funerals. What is the purpose of developing these schemas? With your schemas you are able to explain a person's past behavior and to predict his future behavior. Schemas allow us to organize information so that we can respond appropriately in social situations.

Stereotypes

Sometimes we develop schemas for entire groups of people. You may have schemas for men, women, Asian Americans, African Americans, or certain religious groups. Such schemas are called stereotypes. A **stereotype** is a set of assumptions about an identifiable group of people. The belief that males are dominant and independent or that females are nurturing and emotional are examples. Stereotypes may contain positive or negative information, but primacy effects may cause stereotypes that result in a bias. If stereotypes influence our information about people and are not modified by experience, they may become self-fulfilling prophecies. Schemas are useful because they help us predict with some degree of accuracy how people will behave. Without them, we would spend considerable energy observing and testing people to find out what they are like, whether we want to pursue a relationship with them, and so on. Like stereotypes, if the assumptions we make about people from our first impressions do not change as we get to know them better, then we are guilty of harboring prejudice.

stereotype a set of assumptions about people in a given category summarizing our experience and beliefs about groups of people

☑ **READING PROGRESS CHECK**

Summarizing Why are first impressions not always reliable?

Shyness

A 1996 study by Henderson and Zimbardo showed that about 40 percent of adults are shy. Shyness is a feeling of distress that results from feeling awkward in social situations and from fearing rejection. People may feel shy in front of authority figures, in one-on-one dating scenarios, with strangers, or in groups of people. Shyness is really a form of excessive self-focus. The shy person is preoccupied with his or her own thoughts, feelings, or physical reactions.

Shy people differ from others in how they attribute their own successes and failures. Whereas most people demonstrate the self-serving bias—taking credit for success and blaming failures on external causes—shy people reverse this bias and blame themselves for failure and externalize the causes of success. For example, whereas Roger may credit his strength and skill for winning a tennis match, shy Jackie may attribute her win to luck or to her opponent's poor performance.

Psychologists often treat shyness by exposing the patient to feared situations and teaching the patient how to control anxiety. In addition, psychologists may lead a patient to restructure his or her negative thoughts into positive affirmations.

attribution theory the process by which we interpret and explain others' behaviors

Attribution Theory

GUIDING QUESTION *How do our previous experiences apply to attribution theory?*

You are waiting in the right lane at a traffic light. Somebody behind you honks and gestures frantically for you to get out of the way. Not sure what is happening, you move your car—slowly, so they will not think you are a pushover—into the middle lane to allow the driver to turn right. As he does, the driver looks across at you and says, "Thanks. My wife's in labor. We're in a hurry!"

If you are like most of us, you feel foolish, but everyone has moments like that. You were facing a situation many social psychologists study—trying to interpret and explain people's behavior by identifying what caused the behavior. The focus of study in this circumstance is called **attribution theory**, an analysis of how we interpret and understand other people's behavior. When you first heard the horn, you undoubtedly attributed the man's behavior to personal characteristics—often called an *internal attribution*. In this case, you might have thought the man was impatient by nature. Once he thanked you and gave a reason for his urgency, your analysis immediately changed to credit his behavior to the situation—often called an *external attribution*. In this case, you might have decided that the man was acting on behalf of his wife's needs. Internal attributions are also known as *dispositional*, while external attributions are sometimes referred to as *situational*.

Fundamental Attribution Error

We can make errors when we decide whether behavior is caused by internal or external factors. A prominent example, the **fundamental attribution error**, is the tendency to attribute the behavior of other people to their disposition, rather than taking into account their situation. In the traffic light example, you probably attributed the man's honking to pushiness, an internal cause, without considering possible external causes. Whether and how often we engage in the fundamental attribution error varies to some extent on whether we are from a culture that emphasizes individual behavior over group behavior. People from individualistic cultures, such as in the United States, in which personal accomplishments are highly valued, are more susceptible to making fundamental attribution errors than are people from collectivistic cultures, such as in Japan, in which group accomplishments are more highly valued. That is, those of us raised in an individualist culture have a tendency to attribute another person's behavior to internal factors (their disposition); someone from a collectivist culture is more likely to attribute another person's behavior to some external cause (their situation).

Assumed-Similarity Bias

An assumed-similarity bias is the tendency to think of someone as similar to ourselves. We may assume a person will act the same way we do because they are of the same race, gender, or socioeconomic class. We may think someone will be friendly because the person looks like us or reminds us of ourselves in some way. This bias has implications both on the way we view others as well as the way we view ourselves. The bias may be especially apparent during interviews. Based on an interviewee's appearance or background, the interviewer may assume that the interviewee will answer questions or have a similar work ethic as the interviewer.

The Halo Effect

In 1920 psychologist Edward Thorndike described the phenomenon known as the halo effect. The effect is a bias that states that our judgments of a person's character are influenced by the way we perceive them in other respects. For instance, if we have an overall positive impression of someone, we may dismiss or not believe negative information we hear about them. Thorndike conducted a study in which soldiers were ranked in various categories such as intelligence, leadership, loyalty, and so on. He found that the ratings in one area affected their ratings in another area. Soldiers who were rated highly in leadership might by association also be rated highly in intelligence, dependability, and cooperation because they were perceived as being overall good soldiers.

Actor–Observer Bias

We tend to focus on internal factors when explaining the behavior of others; however, we focus more on external factors when explaining our own behavior. This is called the **actor–observer bias**. When explaining our own actions, we are the actor. Our focus is external, on the situation and how it caused our behavior—"I cut that car off in traffic because I didn't see it and I'm running late." When functioning as an observer, however, we focus on the other person, seeing their behavior as a reflection of who they are and attributing it to internal causes—"That driver cut me off in traffic because he doesn't know how to drive and he shouldn't be on the road."

Why do we have this bias? Some psychologists propose that we realize our behavior changes from situation to situation, because as an actor our attention is on the situation; we may not believe the same is true of others, because as the observer our attention is on the other individual doing the behavior. The point is that we all actively perceive other people's actions. What we conclude about other people depends not only on what they do but also on our interpretations. This is true not just when we deal with individuals but also when we react to groups.

Self-Serving Bias

When there is glory to be claimed, we often demonstrate another form of error called a **self-serving bias**. In victory, we are quick to claim personal responsibility (internal attribution); in defeat, we pin the blame on circumstances beyond our control (external attribution). For example if we receive an A on a test, we attribute our good grade to our hard work and intelligence. When we get a D on the test, however, we blame a biased test for our poor performance. In this way we try to see ourselves in the best possible light.

✔ **READING PROGRESS CHECK**

Comparing How do actor-observer bias and self-serving bias relate to attribution theory?

---

fundamental attribution error an inclination to over attribute others' behavior to internal causes (dispositional factors) and discount the situational factors contributing to their behavior

actor–observer bias tendency to attribute one's own behavior to outside causes but attribute the behavior of others to internal causes

We make different attributions depending on whether we are the "actor" or the "observer." When we are the "actor" and judge our own behavior, we tend to take situational factors more into account than we do when we are the "observer" and judge others' behavior.

▶ **CRITICAL THINKING**

Identifying Central Issues Why do we attribute internal, or dispositional, causes to others' actions?

self-serving bias a tendency to claim success is due to our efforts, while failure is due to circumstances beyond our control

Nonverbal Communication

GUIDING QUESTION *How do we communicate emotion with body language?*

Communication helps us move past our ideas of what caused another person's behavior. In the incident with the man at the traffic light, verbal communication explained his impatient behavior. Central to the development and maintenance of a relationship is the willingness to communicate aspects of yourself to others. Communication involves at least two people: a person who sends a message and a person who receives it. The message sent consists of an idea and some emotional component. Messages are sent verbally and nonverbally. "I like to watch you dance" is a verbal message, while a warm smile is an example of **nonverbal communication**.

nonverbal communication the process through which messages are conveyed using space, body language, and facial expression

Expression

Although most people are aware of what they are saying verbally, they are often unaware of their nonverbal messages. They are more aware of the nonverbal messages when they are on the receiving end of them. You have probably heard someone say, "It doesn't matter," speaking in a low voice and looking away; the unspoken message is "My feelings are hurt." You do not need to be told in so many words that a friend is elated or depressed, angry or pleased, nervous or content. You sense these things. People communicate nonverbally, not only through facial expressions but also through their use of space and body language, their posture and gestures.

We even use symbols in technology to express ourselves nonverbally. When we write a text message, chat online, or post a comment in a social networking environment, we may use nonverbal "emoticons" to express our emotions. An emoticon describes our mood by using keyboard characters to show a facial expression. Since we cannot give visual clues when we are chatting or texting, a smiley face, a wink, or an unhappy face built using keyboard characters can help us indicate when we are joking, happy, confused, or angry.

CARTOON ›

BODY LANGUAGE
Whether we know it or not, our bodies are talking.

▶ CRITICAL THINKING

1. *Analyzing Visuals* What does body language tell you about another person's feelings in this cartoon?

2. *Speculating* Is body language always more correct than words? Explain your answer.

"I almost get the sense that you're upset."

Body Language

The way you carry your body also communicates information about you to others. This is your *body language*. If you stand tall and erect, you convey the impression of self-assurance. If you sit and talk with your arms folded and legs crossed—a closed body position—you communicate that you are protecting yourself. When you unfold your arms and stretch out, your open body position may be saying that you are open to people.

Although the use of body language is often unconscious, many of the postures we adopt and gestures we make are governed by *social rules*. These rules are very subtle. Touching, for example, has rules involving which people you may touch and where and when a touch is acceptable. Your teacher or boss is much more likely to touch you than you are to touch him or her. Touching is considered a privilege of higher status, although the rules are changing.

There are even social rules to body language. The distance we stand or sit from other people in social situations indicates our understanding of whether our relationship with the other person is formal or informal. It also indicates whether a conversation is serious or casual. The term *proxemics* was coined in the 1950s to describe this physical comfort zone between people. It includes the physical space we prefer between us and a speaker, teacher, friend, family member, or other person. It even includes the personal territory we prefer to have between ourselves and the next person in a public line, such as at a grocery store or movie theater. Studies have found that in the United States, people are used to 10 or more feet between themselves and a public speaker, about 3 to 10 feet in a social or business situation with friends or strangers, 18 inches to 4 feet between family members or friends, and 18 or fewer inches between themselves and people with whom they are intimate.

There can be great cultural differences in proxemics from country to country. For example, people in Latin American countries require less personal space between themselves and the person they are interacting with. As a result, an American interacting with a Latin American may find himself feeling uncomfortable in a conversation because he does not have enough personal space. People in some Western cultures may shake hands or hug upon greeting someone, while people in Asian cultures may feel that bowing is more acceptable so that human contact is avoided and a greater personal space is maintained. People unaware of the cultural and gender differences may be offended if others do not express the same proxemics they are accustomed to from their own culture.

✓ **READING PROGRESS CHECK**

Defining What is needed for communication?

LESSON 2 REVIEW

Reviewing Vocabulary
1. *Understanding Relationships* Explain the relationship between schemas and stereotypes.

Using Your Notes
2. *Identifying Central Issues* Using the notes you took during this lesson, list and describe the two components of attribution theory.

Answering the Guiding Questions
3. *Describing* How do first impressions help us form schemas?

4. *Interpreting* How do our previous experiences apply to attribution theory?

5. *Explaining* How do we communicate emotion with body language?

Writing Activity
6. *Informative/Explanatory* Use information found in the library, on the Internet, or through personal interviews to find examples of nonverbal communication in other cultures. Be prepared to show at least two such examples to the class.

Analyzing
Readings in Psychology

PHOTO: chrisgorgio/age fotostock; TEXT: ©2012 National Public Radio, Inc. NPR® news report titled "Why Compromise Is A Bad Word In Politics" by Steve Inskeep and Shankar Vedantam was originally broadcast on NPR's Morning Edition® on March 13, 2012, and is used with the permission of NPR. Any unauthorized duplication is strictly prohibited.

Reader's Dictionary

cognitive: relating to or involving thinking, reasoning, or remembering

uncharitable: unkind; unsympathetic

disposition: the tendency to act in a certain manner under given circumstances or based on personality

craven: lacking the least bit of courage, cowardly

How does the fundamental attribution error play out in politics? In this NPR interview transcript, social scientist Shankar Vedantam discusses why the tendency to "stick to one's guns" is more attractive in American politics than changing one's mind or an approach based on context—what some might refer to as "flip-flopping."

Why Compromise Is a
Bad Word
in Politics

An NPR Interview by Steve Inskeep
and Shankar Vedantam

PRIMARY SOURCE

Why do voters want leaders who are adaptable, but detest those who don't stick to their guns? Social science research indicates voters want compromise but only when the other side is caving in.

STEVE INSKEEP, HOST: Here's one thing that many people mean when they say Washington is broken. They may mean that politicians from different parties seem unable or totally unwilling to compromise, and many voters hate that. And yet many voters also hate it if politicians from their own party should compromise with the other side. That could be considered giving in. NPR's science correspondent Shankar Vedantam joins us regularly to talk about social science research, and he's found some that relates to this political problem.

INSKEEP: Hi, Shankar.

SHANKAR VEDANTAM, BYLINE: Hi, Steve, thanks for having me.

INSKEEP: OK. So voters want compromise, they just don't want their guys to compromise. Is this correct?

VEDANTAM: Yeah, I think so, because if you look at the ratings that Congress enjoys among the American people today, it's in the very low double digits.

INSKEEP: Eleven, twelve percent around.

VEDANTAM: Right. And at least at a **cognitive** level, people believe that getting stuff done requires compromise. Now, I talked with this psychologist who studies politics at the University of Montana. His name is Luke Conway, and he told me the problem is that compromise is really, really terrible politics. Here he is.

LUKE CONWAY: The view from 30,000 feet is that simplicity sells. Few people march under a banner that says, we may be right, we may be wrong, let's compromise! You know, that's not good politics.

VEDANTAM: So basically, people want compromise, but when they see compromise, they see it as caving in.

INSKEEP: Or we want compromise in the general sense, but on a particular issue, we want our side to win. Is that what's being said here?

VEDANTAM: The **uncharitable** view is that we want compromise so long as it's the other side that's compromising.

INSKEEP: So why is it that voters would see compromise as bad?

VEDANTAM: You know, I've talked with different psychologists about this, and one of the dominant opinions is that we believe that consistency and the ability to hold firm is a core trait of leadership, that

dispositional. And what Conway is suggesting is that Americans may have a tendency to see human behavior as more **disposition** or driven by the individual as opposed to driven by the context.

INSKEEP: Oh, meaning I understand that I have to make compromises in my own life, but if I see some politician flip-flop or change his views or sign onto something he doesn't totally agree with, that means the politician is **craven**, he's terrible.

VEDANTAM: Exactly, that we see people who change their minds on issues as fundamentally lacking core principles, which is really, really important to us.

INSKEEP: OK. Does Conway have an example where people have different attitudes about consistency depending on the situation here?

VEDANTAM: He does. He actually thinks that there's research suggesting that in non-Western countries—he actually cited the example of Japan in particular—people are more willing to see behavior as contextually driven as opposed to dispositionally driven. The point that Conway is making is not, you know, a universal blanket statement about how Japanese are different from Americans, but he's saying there are tendencies that are driven by the culture that make some people more willing to tolerate inconsistency than we Americans do.

INSKEEP: Well, now, what about inside this country? Because there have been any number of polls that have suggested that for whatever reason, in this current political situation more Democrats have been willing to say I want my politicians to compromise than Republicans.

VEDANTAM: You know, I've seen the same survey, Steve. I'm not sure I know of good psychological research that explains that, but it could be that the same patterns we're seeing between Western and non-Western countries at the global level are also playing themselves out at the domestic level, meaning that one party tends to be more willing to compromise while the other party tends to see compromise as being a really bad thing.

INSKEEP: It's a cultural difference, in other words.

VEDANTAM: Exactly.

great leaders are people who can look out into the horizon steer towards a distant point and not get sidetracked by all manner of differences.

INSKEEP: You were talking about this just the other day, the hedgehog theory of leadership.

VEDANTAM: Exactly.

INSKEEP: You stay right on target regardless, or you at least appear to be staying right on target at all times.

VEDANTAM: Exactly. But there's also some evidence that the fact that Americans are so unable to see compromise might at least partially have something to do with American culture. Here's Luke Conway again.

CONWAY: It's partially based on our hyper-individualistic norm that says the person is more important. So I can't go from situation A to situation B and be a different person.

INSKEEP: Hyper-individualistic norm?

VEDANTAM: Yeah, he's basically saying that in the United States we tend to see human behavior as driven by individuals. So psychologists have this term, they call it the fundamental attribution error. And the fundamental attribution error says when I do something, when I look at my own behavior, I tend to see it in context. So I think of myself as being a safe driver, but if I'm driving fast today, it's because I'm running late for an appointment.

But when I look at another person driving quickly, I say this person is a reckless driver, so I see it as being

Analyzing Primary Sources

1. *Identifying* How do American voters tend to view compromise?

2. *Drawing Conclusions* Based on the information in the selection, would a political ad addressing inconsistencies in a candidate's decisions be successful in China? Why or why not?

3. *Theorizing* What problems might the American political value of consistency cause?

Personal Relationships

Reading **HELP**DESK

Academic Vocabulary
- define
- identity

Content Vocabulary
- generational identity

TAKING NOTES:
Key Ideas and Details

CATEGORIZING Use a graphic organizer like the one below to name the three components of romantic love.

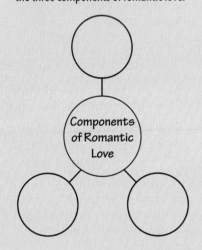

ESSENTIAL QUESTIONS • *Why do people form bonds?* • *How do individuals develop judgments?*

IT MATTERS BECAUSE

When your parents were growing up, they learned how to relate to others by interacting with their parents. You have learned the same relational skills from your own parents and will someday teach them to your children. Your personal relationships with your family members have a significant impact on your life and who you will become.

Parent-Child Relationships

GUIDING QUESTION *How do parent-child relationships affect the child's relationships with those outside their family?*

The relationships we have with our grandparents, parents, guardians, and others can influence and enrich our lives. Our personal relationships with others within and beyond our families can bring meaning and substance to our everyday experiences. Do our family relationships influence our relationships outside of our families? Some noted psychologists, including Erik Erikson, contend that early and persistent patterns of parent-child interaction influence people's later adult expectations about their relationships with the significant people in their lives.

If a young infant's first relationship with a caregiver is a loving, responsive, and consistent relationship, the child will develop a trust in the ability of other people to meet his or her needs. In turn, this trusting will encourage the person to be receptive to others. However, a child who has experienced unresponsive, inconsistent, or unaffectionate care in infancy will most likely be more wary or mistrustful of other people. Within the parent-child relationship, we learn how to interact with others to have our needs met. A parent is likely to satisfy the wishes of a child who is well behaved and who does what the parent asks. A child may also learn to get attention by pouting or having temper tantrums.

As children develop and form relationships with people outside their families, they apply what they have learned about relationships. As a result of childhood experiences, an individual might, for example, believe that the only way to establish and maintain good relationships with friends is always to say what pleases those friends rather than speak the truth.

(l)Ingram Publishing; (c)Ron Levine/Digital Vision/Getty Images; (r)Peter Dazeley/Photographer's Choice RF/Getty Images

Your parents influenced the quality of your adult relationships in other ways. They provided you with your first model of a marital relationship. As you watched your mother and father interacting with one another as husband and wife, you were most likely forming some tentative conclusions about the nature of relationships. Later on, you might use their example as a guide in selecting a future mate or in evaluating your relationships.

If your parents have a happy marriage, you will most likely seek to duplicate it by imitating their patterns. Sadly, the reverse may also be true. Evidence provided in a 2005 study by DeGenova and Rice suggests that being part of a violent family in childhood increases the likelihood that someone will use violence against his or her children and spouse.

In our society, parent-child conflict may develop during adolescence. Adolescence may be a period of inner struggles. The desire to set and achieve goals battles the fear of the inability to accomplish them. Desire for independence struggles against the realization that we are only human and have limitations. An adolescent needs parents who are sure of themselves, their identities, and their values. Such parents serve not only as models but also as sources of stability in a world that has become complicated and full of choices.

Each generation has a **generational identity**. This refers to the simple fact that adolescents and their parents tend to think differently about some things. Why does this happen? Each generation has shared formative experiences that are different from those of other generations. For example, author Tom Brokaw refers to the children that grew up in the 1920s and 1930s as "the greatest generation" because of their shared experience persevering through the Great Depression and World War II. Youth of the 1960s complained of the "generation gap" between themselves and their parents. The Vietnam War and political upheavals such as the civil rights movement of the 1960s shaped your grandparents' ideas.

You are part of a generation that is distinct from the ones that have gone before and the ones that will follow yours. Situations such as economic uncertainty and conflict in Afghanistan and Iraq may shape your generations' views.

generational identity the theory that people of different ages tend to think differently about certain issues because of different formative experiences

Parenting styles vary among different families and different ethnic groups.

▶ **CRITICAL THINKING**

Making Connections Do you think adolescents all over the world experience the same types of conflicts with their parents? Explain.

Sigmund Freud
(1856–1939)

It has been said that a person in love does not see his or her lover as others do. Freud spoke of his wife Martha Bernays with affection and respect. Freud believed that we see the lover as our ideal, and the more dissatisfied with ourselves we are, the more we need a lover to make up for our weaknesses, and the more inclined we are to idealize our lover.

Why do we do this? Freud believed that whenever we make a choice—such as choosing a romantic partner—we are governed by hidden mental processes of which we are unaware and over which we have no control. Freud's contributions to psychology are controversial. Although his ideas greatly influenced the development of the field of psychology, critics claim that Freud saw people as foolish, weak, and self-deluded. Others argue it may be better to view people as basically good, though injured.

▶ **CRITICAL THINKING**

Synthesizing How are Freud's beliefs about people reflected in his view on love?

So might the prevalence of divorce, new technology, or a low sense of security. The events of September 11, 2001 are likely a flashbulb memory for your parents' generation but may be as indistinct a memory for your generation as the attack on Pearl Harbor was for theirs. The flashbulb memories of your generation, regardless of how deeply they impact you, will not be those of the generations that follow yours. Such differences do not automatically lead to conflict. The conflicts that adolescents may experience with their parents may result from their changing parent-child relationship, as well as from different ideologies and concerns.

☑ **READING PROGRESS CHECK**

Summarizing How does generational identity separate you from your parents?

Love Relationships

GUIDING QUESTION *What is the difference between passionate and companionate love?*

While most people say that they love their parents, their friends, and maybe even their brothers and sisters, they attach a different meaning to love when referring to a boyfriend, girlfriend, or spouse. Some love relationships, as explained later, are very passionate and all-consuming. Other relationships are compassionate and stable, involving more complex feelings of commitment and trust. Love means different things to different people and within different relationships.

Love and Marriage

The idea of love without marriage is no longer shocking. The fact that a couple is developing a close and intimate relationship or even living together does not necessarily mean that they are contemplating marriage. The idea of marriage without love, however, remains unpopular to most Americans. Marrying for convenience, companionship, financial security, or any reason that does not include love strikes most of us as impossible or at least unfortunate.

This, according to psychologist Zick Rubin in a 1973 study, is one of the main reasons it is difficult for many people to adjust to love and marriage. Exaggerated ideas about love may also help explain the increasing frequency of divorce. Fewer couples who no longer love one another are staying together for the sake of the children or to avoid gossip than did in the past. Let us begin at the beginning, though, with love.

Reflecting on almost two decades of studies, one team of psychologists identified two common types of love: passionate love and companionate love. *Passionate love* is very intense, sensual, and all-consuming. It couples feelings of great excitement and intense sexuality with the fear that it might be endangered and suddenly disappear. Passionate love does usually fade in any romantic relationship. When passionate love subsides, it may grow into *companionate love*, a more stable love, which includes commitment, intimacy, friendship, mutual trust, and the desire to be with one another. There are other views of love, however.

In the same 1973 study, Rubin surveyed University of Michigan student volunteers. Couples who had been together for anywhere from a few weeks to six or seven years filled out questionnaires about their feelings toward their partners and their same-sex friends. The answers enabled Rubin to distinguish between liking and loving.

Liking is based primarily on respect for another person and the feeling that he or she is similar to you. Loving is rather different. As Rubin wrote in 1973, "There are probably as many reasons for loving as there are people who love. In each case there is a different constellation of needs to be gratified, a different set of characteristics that are found to be rewarding, a different ideal to be fulfilled."

Components of Love

Looking beyond these differences, however, Rubin identified three major components of romantic love: *need* or attachment, *caring* or the desire to give, and *intimacy*. People in love feel strong desires to be with the other person, to touch, to be praised and cared for, to fulfill and be fulfilled. The role *need* plays in love can be seen in the frequency with which romantic love is described as a longing, a hunger, a desire to possess, or a sickness that only one person can heal.

Equally central to love is the desire to give. Love goes beyond the cost-reward level of human interaction. Fromm **defined** love in 1956 as "the active concern for the life and growth of that which we love." Heinlein, in 1972, described love as "that state in which the happiness of another person is essential to our own." This kind of love is very altruistic, very giving. Without caring, need becomes a series of self-centered, desperate demands; without need, caring is charity or kindness. In love, the two are intertwined.

Need and caring take various forms, depending on individual situations. What all people in love share is intimacy—a special knowledge of each other derived from uncensored self-disclosure. Exposing your true self to another person is always risky. It does not hurt so much if a person rejects a role you are trying to play, but it can be devastating if a person rejects the secret longings and fears you ordinarily disguise or keep hidden. It hurts deeply if he or she uses that private information to manipulate you. This is one of the reasons why love so often brings out violent emotions—the highs and lows of our lives.

What may be difficult to maintain in a loving relationship is the balance between needing and giving. One person in the relationship may tend to have a greater emotional need for, or attachment to, their partner. One partner may tend to be more giving of himself or herself in the relationship. Each partner may feel his or her needs are being met when the relationship is in its early stages. Over time, however, an imbalance may become apparent that makes one or both feel slighted, unappreciated, or misunderstood. The person with the greater emotional need might feel abandoned but be seen by the partner as clingy or difficult. The person who gave more to the relationship might start to feel used but be seen by the partner as manipulative or controlling. Communication with a partner is an important part of maintaining a healthy and intimate relationship.

define to state or describe something exactly

It is easy to think of love in a narrow context and consider only the sexual relationship that exists between a man and a woman. This view, however, omits the kinds of love that exist between children and grandparents, between people and their pets, between siblings and friends, and so on.

▶ **CRITICAL THINKING**

Finding the Main Idea Why are caring and need important in love?

(l)Ron Levine/Digital Vision/Getty Images; (r)©Andersen Ross/Blend Images LLC; (c)©Ariel Skelley/Blend Images LLC

The Behavior of Love

Rubin conducted a number of experiments to test common assumptions about the way that people who are in love feel and act. He found that couples who rated high on his "love scale" did, indeed, spend more time gazing into each other's eyes (while waiting for the experimenter) than other couples did. He was unable, however, to prove that romantic partners sacrifice their own comfort for that of their partners.

Perhaps the most interesting discoveries in love research concern the differences between men and women. Rubin found that most couples were equal on the love scale; the woman expressed the same degree of love for her partner as he did for her. Women, however, tended to like their boyfriends—to respect and identify with them—more than their boyfriends liked them. Women also tended to love and share intimacies with their same-sex friends more often than men did with theirs.

As Rubin suggested, women in our society tend to specialize in the social and emotional dimensions of life. One revelation—that men carry out more romantic gestures than women—may seem surprising, but perhaps it should not. At a time when women usually worked at home, marriage basically determined their style of living. Now earning power is no longer such a powerful concern. More than half of all married women work outside the home, so both men and women contribute to their family's finances and have the ability to perform more romantic gestures. In fact, two psychologists, Fehr and Russell, reported that women are no longer different from men as to how "romantic" they are. Men and women participate equally in varying forms of passionate and companionate love.

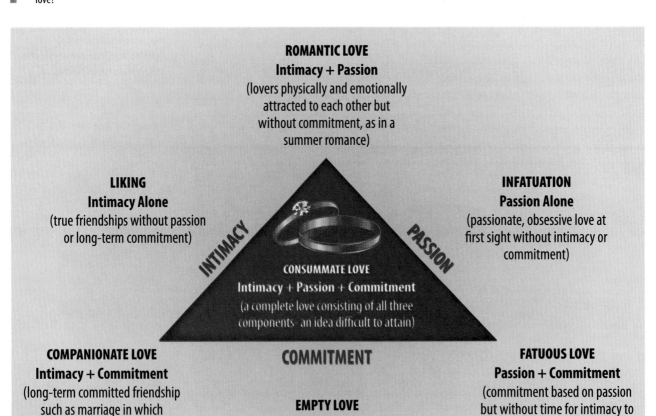

ROMANTIC LOVE
Intimacy + Passion
(lovers physically and emotionally attracted to each other but without commitment, as in a summer romance)

LIKING
Intimacy Alone
(true friendships without passion or long-term commitment)

INFATUATION
Passion Alone
(passionate, obsessive love at first sight without intimacy or commitment)

INTIMACY

PASSION

CONSUMMATE LOVE
Intimacy + Passion + Commitment
(a complete love consisting of all three components- an idea difficult to attain)

COMPANIONATE LOVE
Intimacy + Commitment
(long-term committed friendship such as marriage in which the passion has faded)

COMMITMENT

FATUOUS LOVE
Passion + Commitment
(commitment based on passion but without time for intimacy to develop; shallow relationship such as a whirlwind courtship)

EMPTY LOVE
Commitment Alone
(decision to love each other without intimacy or passion)

A follow-up questionnaire, sent a year after Rubin's original study, indicated that when both a man and a woman express their interest in each other, the relationship is more likely to progress; that is, they become more intimate and committed to each other. What is the implication of this finding? Love is not something that happens to you; it is something you seek and create. You must work at it and nurture it.

Triangular Theory of Love

A more comprehensive theory of the many forms of love has been proposed by Robert Sternberg. Sternberg's triangular theory of love contends that love is made up of three parts: intimacy, passion, and commitment. These parts can be conceptualized as a "love triangle." The various combinations of these parts account for the many different ways that love is experienced.

Using Sternberg's model, we can see how different kinds of love are made of different degrees of intimacy, passion, and commitment. The love-at-first-sight felt on a first date has a lot of passion but little commitment, whereas the love felt by a couple celebrating their fiftieth wedding anniversary has much commitment, and may have intimacy, but probably less passion. Yet, each combination yields a satisfying love for those experiencing it.

Marriage

A couple decides to make a formal and public commitment to each other. They marry. Will they "live happily ever after"? Their chances are good if they come from similar cultural and economic backgrounds, have about the same level of education, and practice (or reject) the same religion. Their chances are better still if their parents were happily married, they had happy childhoods, and they maintain good relations with their families. All of these are good predictors of marital success. Two principles tend to govern behavior leading to successful marriages: endogamy and homogamy.

Endogamy identifies the tendency to marry someone who is from one's own social group. Marriages are more likely to be successful when we marry someone similar to us. In addition, *homogamy* identifies our tendency to marry someone who has similar attributes to our own, including physical attractiveness, age, and physique. A common observation is that people who marry tend to look similar to one another. It is now suspected that some social processes tend to cause this matching to happen. At a dance held at the University of Minnesota a number of years ago, a computer randomly matched students. Physical attractiveness was the only predictor of the likelihood that two randomly matched people would continue dating.

This is not to say that couples must be of the same cultural or socioeconomic background in order to have a successful marriage, or that they must have similar degrees of physical attractiveness. In American families, there is a vast amount of diversity involving people's race, culture, socioeconomic background, level of education, religion, and so on. The feelings that two people have about each other can transcend these differences.

Quick Lab

WHAT TRAITS ARE IMPORTANT IN A POTENTIAL MARRIAGE PARTNER?
The majority of adults in the United States eventually marry. How do they decide which person is right for them?

Procedure
1. Ask at least 30 of your classmates and friends to identify one quality they consider essential in a potential mate.
2. Separate the results into responses from females and those from males. Tally the results in a chart.

Analysis
1. What traits did females consider most important in a potential partner? Males?
2. Based on the information in the chapter regarding love and marriage, do you think the traits listed by the people you surveyed are ones that are likely to result in a successful marriage? Explain.

Marital Problems

What helps make a marriage last? In general, healthy adjustment to marriage seems to depend on three factors: whether the couple's needs are compatible, whether the couple's images of themselves coincide with their images of each other, and whether they agree on what their roles in the marriage are.

External factors, including gender role expectations or environment, may make it impossible for one or both to live up to their own role expectations. A man who is unemployed cannot be the good provider he wants to be. As a consequence he may take out his frustrations on his spouse, children or other family members, whose presence and own disappointments constantly remind him of his own perceived failings. A woman holding one or multiple jobs while also helping raise a family in a poorer environment may have trouble keeping the kitchen clean with a broken sink, providing frequent and nutritious meals for her family, or keeping her children safe.

These circumstances, or a combination of some much like them often result in mutual frustrations. Both spouses feel personal disappointment in themselves and at times in one another. This can lead to strife in the form of resentments, arguments, and at times verbal or physical abuse.

No couple is immune to problems in a marriage. Often couples just grow apart. The husband or wife may become totally engrossed in work, a social life independent of their spouse, a personal hobby, raising the children, or community affairs. Let us suppose they are either unable or unwilling to fill each other's needs and role expectations through accommodation or compromise. Perhaps they cannot face their problems. For whatever reasons, they decide to end their marriage and to get a divorce. What happens to the couple's relationship then?

Divorce

In many ways, adjusting to divorce is like adjusting to death—the death of a relationship. Almost inevitably, divorce releases a torrent of emotions: anger (even if the person wanted a divorce), resentment, fear, loneliness, anxiety, and, above all, the feeling of failure. Both individuals are suddenly thrust into a variety of unfamiliar situations. If one spouse had consistently filled the role of cook, the other may be overwhelmed by the task of fixing meals for the first time in years. If one partner has done all of the home maintenance, the other may be daunted by the first leaky faucet.

Friends of the couple may feel they have to choose sides in the dispute, so one partner or the other may lose friends in the process. Dating for the first time in five or ten years can make a formerly married person feel like an adolescent. Some divorcing people may find it unsettling to think of giving up on a marriage or being unattached and free to do whatever they like. One of the biggest problems may be time—the free time a person so desperately wanted but now has no idea how to fill.

As positive as the emotions usually leading to a marriage may be, divorce results from a much wider array of emotions. Both former partners must establish new homes and living styles. Any children typically become the responsibility of one parent with the establishment of visitation rights. These children must establish new ways of relating to their parents and perhaps a stepparent.

▶ **CRITICAL THINKING**

Comparing How does the adjustment to divorce differ between young children and adolescents?

HOW TO HELP A FRIEND

Your high school years can be among the most memorable of your life. Upon graduation, you are usually preparing to move away from your home and family, looking toward college, career, and perhaps your own home and family. Many choices lie before you, and the world is filled with hopes, dreams, and promises.

At least that is the way one would like it to be. However, for many young people this is a time of stress and hardship. The decisions for the future may seem overwhelming rather than exciting. The environment at home may not be supportive. Parents may be dealing with marital stress and even divorce. The strain of living between two households, with parents and stepparents, may be exhausting. Sometimes exposure to drugs and alcohol in the high school years turns a teen from a path of hope to an alley of despair.

If you have a friend whose world is filled with stress and despair, or who may be struggling with mental illness, what can you do to help? Most of all, listen. Sometimes your friend just needs to know someone cares. As you listen, think about what your friend wants and needs. Are there deeper issues that require professional help? A good place to start is the National Association for the Mentally Ill (NAMI). NAMI is an umbrella organization that provides information and support to individuals and family members dealing with mental illness. You can learn about NAMI by visiting the Web site www.nami.org. There you will find information on mental illnesses, support groups, and phone numbers for hotlines to provide you with instant access to help and information. If your friend is dealing with alcohol or drug abuse, a visit to www.al-anon.alateen.org can provide you with contact numbers and information to help your friend. You can also visit the National Institute on Drug Abuse (NIDA) Web site at www.drugabuse.gov, which provides information on drug abuse and treatment.

What if your friend is struggling with family issues? As a teen, your friend may feel powerless to change the events impacting his or her life. Conflicts are especially difficult to resolve in situations in which there are few choices and little room for compromise. Contact a teacher, counselor, mentor, or clergyperson whom you think would be willing to help.

▲ Active, empathetic listening is the first step in helping a troubled friend.

▶ **CRITICAL THINKING**

1. *Formulating Questions* If your friend tells you that he or she is worried about a parent's drinking problem, what questions could you ask in order to best help your friend?

2. *Simulating* Suppose your friend has become very discouraged and is now questioning whether there is really any point in getting up and going to school each day. Outline some steps you could take to help your friend.

All of this adds up to what Mel Krantzler in 1973 referred to as "separation shock." Whatever the circumstances, most divorced people go through a period of mourning that lasts until the person suddenly realizes that he or she has survived. This realization is the first step toward adjusting to the divorce. Resentment of his or her former spouse begins to subside. The pain left over from the past no longer dominates the present. The divorced person begins calling old friends, making new ones, and enjoying the fact that he or she can base their decisions on his or her own personal interests. In effect, the divorcee leaves behind their identity as a married person and has begun to construct a new identity as a single person.

Elena Elisseeva/Alamy

Children and Divorce

Adjusting to divorce is usually far more difficult for children than it is for their parents. First, rarely do children want a divorce to occur; the conflict is not theirs but their parents'. Second, while the parents may have good reasons for the separation, children (especially very young children) are unlikely to understand those reasons. Third, children themselves rarely have any control over the outcome of a divorce. Such decisions as with whom they will live and how frequently they will be able to see the separated parent are out of their hands. Finally, children, especially young ones, cannot muster as much emotional maturity as their parents to help them through such an overwhelming experience.

A child of parents who divorce may exhibit behaviors ranging from emotional outbursts to depression or rebellion. According to a study by Berger in 2005, the longevity of these behaviors may be determined by "the harmony of the parents' ongoing relationship, the stability of the child's life, and the adequacy of the care giving arrangement." In other words, the trauma of divorce on children can be made worse by parents who continue to battle during the divorce process or once the divorce is final. Children whose divorcing parents are willing to set aside their differences enough to provide a stable transition for their children will move through the process with fewer emotional side effects.

Adolescents experience special problems as a result of their parents' divorce. This is largely because the adolescence developmental stage already involves the process of redefining their **identity** by breaking family ties. If that family separation takes place before the adolescent is ready to actively begin that separation as a part of their identity formation, then the experience can be terribly unsettling. As one young person said in a 1974 study, "[It was] like having the rug pulled out from under me."

The issues that children of divorcing parents must face are not insurmountable. Like their parents, most children do eventually come to terms with divorce. They learn to put some distance between themselves and their parents' conflict, and they learn to be realistic about the situation and make the best of it. Adjustment is made easier when parents take special care to explain the divorce and allow their children to express their feelings. Divorce is becoming a problem with which more and more children will have to cope.

identity who or what someone or something is

✓ READING PROGRESS CHECK

Explaining Explain the three aspects of the triangular theory of love.

LESSON 3 REVIEW

Reviewing Vocabulary
1. *Identifying* What is generational identity?

Using Your Notes
2. *Diagramming* Use the notes you took during this lesson to explain why children may have difficulty adjusting to their parents' divorce.

Answering the Guiding Questions
3. *Differentiating* How do parent-child relationships affect the child's relationships with those outside their family?

4. *Contrasting* What is the difference between passionate and companionate love?

Writing Activity
5. *Argument* Have you heard of "love at first sight"? Write a paragraph explaining what you think this phrase means. Interview an adult about their experience of love in terms of intimacy and commitment.

Directions: On a separate sheet of paper, answer the questions below. Make sure you read carefully and answer all parts of the question.

Lesson Review

Lesson 1

1 *Explaining* Is the saying "misery loves company" accurate? Explain.

2 *Analyzing* There is a saying stating that "beauty is only skin deep." Do you think it is true? Do people act as if it is true? Explain.

Lesson 2

3 *Summarizing* What are *social rules*? Give an example of such a rule.

4 *Assessing* If you want people to think that you are smart, should you try to do your best on the first, second, or last test in a class? Why?

5 *Labeling* Rate the following situations as external or internal attributions:
(a) Your friend helped you wash your car because she is nice. (b) Your friend helped you wash your car because she wanted to impress your parents, who were watching. (c) Your friend helped you wash your car because she owed you a favor.

Lesson 3

6 *Differentiating* What is the difference between *endogamy* and *homogamy*? Explain.

7 *Contrasting* In what ways are *liking* and *loving* different? Explain.

8 *Listing* Identify three factors upon which marital happiness depends.

21st Century Skills

Using Charts Ten thousand people from different countries in the world were surveyed about the characteristics they look for in a mate. Review the results in the chart below (1 is most important; 18 is least important), then answer the questions that follow.

9 *Using Tables* In which country were males and females most in agreement about the kinds of characteristics they looked for in a mate?

10 *Understanding Relationships Among Events* Which characteristic ranked the lowest among both males and females in each of the three countries included in the chart? How do you explain this?

Rank Ordering of Desired Characteristics in a Mate													
	United States		China		South Africa Zulu			United States		China		South Africa Zulu	
	Females	Males	Females	Males	Females	Males		Females	Males	Females	Males	Females	Males
Mutual attraction—love	1	1	8	4	5	10	Refinement, neatness	12	10	10	7	10	7
Emotional stability and maturity	2	2	1	5	2	1	Ambition and industriousness	6	11	5	10	7	8
Dependable character	3	3	7	6	1	3	Similar education	10	12	12	15	12	12
Pleasing disposition	4	4	16	13	3	4	Good cook and housekeeper	16	13	11	9	15	2
Education and intelligence	5	5	4	8	6	6	Favorable social status or rating	14	14	13	14	14	17
Good health	9	6	3	1	4	5	Similar religious background	15	15	18	18	11	16
Good looks	13	7	15	11	16	14	Good financial prospect	11	16	14	16	13	18
Sociability	8	8	9	12	8	11	Chastity (no prior sexual intercourse)	18	17	6	3	18	13
Desire for home and children	7	9	2	2	9	9	Similar political background	17	18	17	17	17	15

Source: Feldman, Robert. *Understanding Psychology*. New York: McGraw-Hill. 2011.

Need Extra Help?

If You've Missed Question	**1**	**2**	**3**	**4**	**5**	**6**	**7**	**8**	**9**	**10**
Go to page	525	529	539	534	536	547	546	547	530	530

Directions: On a separate sheet of paper, answer the questions below. Make sure you read carefully and answer all parts of the question.

Critical Thinking Questions

11 *Evaluating* Think of people with whom you are friends. Which rewards do you get from these friendships?

12 *Analyzing* We may think that stereotyping does not influence us. Watch a television program about (a) a detective, (b) an African American family, (c) a white family, and (d) an independent woman. What traits does each character have? Are these stereotypes?

13 *Drawing Conclusions* People sometimes are accused of saying one thing but meaning another. Do you think people's nonverbal communication sometimes conflicts with their verbal communication? Explain.

14 *Synthesizing* Pretend someone has just asked you, "How do I know if I'm in love?" How would you respond?

15 *Making Connections* How could understanding fundamental attribution error help you better explain the behavior of others?

College and Career Readiness

16 *Decision Making* Prepare a want ad in which you advertise for a friend. Include the main characteristics you look for in a friend in the advertisement.

17 *Reaching Conclusions* In an essay, support or refute the following popular sayings with information you learned from the chapter:

"Birds of a feather flock together."
"Opposites attract."
"Familiarity breeds contempt."
"Beauty is only skin deep."
"Absence makes the heart grow fonder."

Exploring the Essential Questions

18 *Identifying Central Issues* Why do people form bonds and how do individuals develop judgments?

Research and Technology

19 *Evaluating* Several sites on the Internet are designed to help parents and teenagers deal with conflicts. Find these Web sites and evaluate the suggestions they offer.

DBQ Analyzing Primary Sources

Use the document to answer the following questions.

PRIMARY SOURCE

" *Friendship is, strictly speaking, reciprocal benevolence, which inclines each party to be as solicitous for the welfare of the other as for his own. This equality of affection is created and preserved by a similarity of disposition and manners.* "

—*Plato*

20 *Applying* Agree or disagree with Plato's description of friendship. Support your opinion with information regarding interpersonal attraction learned in the chapter.

21 *Differentiating* In general, are you likely to choose as a friend a person who is similar to you or a person who complements your strengths and weaknesses?

Psychology Journal

22 *Argument* Review your entry in your Psychology Journal for this chapter. Why do you think "comparing experiences" and "reducing uncertainty" are benefits of friendships?

Need Extra Help?

If You've Missed Question	⓫	⓬	⓭	⓮	⓯	⓰	⓱	⓲	⓳	⓴	㉑	㉒
Go to page	528	535	538	545	536	527	527	527	543	527	530–531	525

Group Interaction

ESSENTIAL QUESTION • *How can groups shape the behavior of individuals?*

Psychology Matters...

We may be unaware of our membership, but we all belong to many different groups. We are a part of school groups, sports groups, groups of friends, and groups of family members. Each of these groups expects something different from us and we somehow know how to act in each one. What makes us act differently in groups than we do on our own? Understanding group behaviors can help us understand the importance of teamwork and overcoming conflicts with others.

◀ An orchestra is a social group that also has a common goal. Each member works for the good of the group.

Hill Street Studios/Blend Images/Getty Images

Strength in Numbers

THE QUESTION...

RESEARCH QUESTION How does being in a group affect our behavior?

Have you ever noticed how people sometimes behave differently in a group than they behave individually? Some people tend to become louder or more extraverted, while some get quieter or more reserved. Whether the setting is a movie, a football game, or a street festival, individuals often act differently in a group than they would if they were alone. Being in a group can even influence how people think. You might have observed this in your daily life, but we can use the scientific method to find measurable evidence of it.

In this experiment, we will put people in groups, inject an idea, and measure the results.

Psychology Journal Activity

How do you behave in a group? Write about this in your Psychology Journal. Consider the following issues: Have you ever experienced pressure to conform while in a group? How have you handled this pressure?

FINDING THE ANSWER...

HYPOTHESIS Being in a group of like-minded people causes one's views to become more extreme.

THE METHOD OF YOUR EXPERIMENT

MATERIALS   paper, pens or pencils, calculator

PROCEDURE   Gather a group of at least ten participants and ask if they agree or disagree with the following proposition: "The school day should be longer but there should only be four school days per week." Have them write their answers on signed slips of paper, using a scale of 1 to 10, where 1 represents "strongly disagree" and 10 represents "strongly agree." Collect the responses and separate them into those that agree and those that disagree. Divide the participants into two groups according to the results. Pose the proposition again to the two groups and instruct the groups to come up with five reasons to support their position. Have the groups share their reasons. Then ask all participants to once again decide if they agree or disagree with the proposition and have them rate their agreement on the previous scale of 1 to 10 on signed slips of paper.

DATA COLLECTION   Gather the final results and calculate the averages of those who agree and those who did not. Compare those numbers to the results from the first round of answers.

ANALYSIS & APPLICATION

1. Did your results support the hypothesis? If so, what does the data tell us about the hypothesis?

2. Why do you think participants' views changed after having a group discussion?

3. What do these results mean for the behavior of voters who belong to political parties?

netw⦿rks   ONLINE LAB RESOURCES

Online you will find:

- An **interactive lab experience**, allowing you to put principles from this chapter into practice in a digital psychology lab environment. This chapter's lab will include an experiment on issues related to group behavior.

- A **Skills Handbook** that includes a guide for using the scientific method, creating experiments, and analyzing data.

- A **Notebook** where you can complete your Psychology Journal and record and analyze data from your experiment.

There's More Online!

☑ **DIAGRAM** Group Polarization

☑ **DIAGRAM** Sociograms

☑ **GRAPHIC ORGANIZER**

☑ **SELF-CHECK QUIZ**

Circle

LESSON 1

Group Behavior

Reading HELPDESK CCSS

Academic Vocabulary
- **differentiate** • **instance**

Content Vocabulary
- **group**
- **task functions**
- **social functions**
- **ideology**
- **social facilitation**
- **social inhibition**
- **group polarization**
- **groupthink**
- **sociogram**

TAKING NOTES:
Key Ideas and Details

CATEGORIZING Use a graphic organizer like the one below to describe three styles of leadership and list both positive and negative aspects about each leadership style.

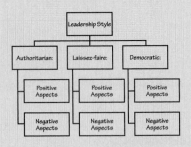

ESSENTIAL QUESTION • *How can groups shape the behavior of individuals?*

IT MATTERS BECAUSE
We interact with people every day. We see people at school, on the playing field, at the store, and in our homes. Each situation requires different behavior from us. When we realize our role in each social group, we can better understand why people act the way they do in public and among others.

Groups

GUIDING QUESTION *What are some primary and secondary groups with which you are involved?*

Social psychologists are interested in what happens between groups of people. Groups can be **differentiated** by in-groups and out-groups and primary and secondary groups. When a group's members identify with their group, they are referred to as the *in-group*. The *out-group* includes everyone who is not a member of the in-group. Members of the out-group may be rejected by and could be hostile to the in-group.

A *primary* group is a group of people who interact face-to-face daily. As these interactions happen frequently, some may become emotionally charged. For example, you see your family members every day. You eat, sleep, have fun with them, and also fight with them. A *secondary* group is a larger group of people with whom you might have more impersonal relationships. For example, your psychology class is a secondary group.

Types of Groups
What do the St. Olaf Parish Bowling Team, Chess Club, and Rascal Flatts have in common? Each can be classified as a group. A **group** is a collection of people who interact, share common goals, and influence how members think and act. In general, members of a *group* are interdependent, have shared goals, and communicate with one another. People who congregate but do not interact are not a group but an *aggregate*. For example, a collection of people waiting to cross the street is an aggregate. If the light refuses to change and more people join, there is a common goal and there is interaction. When one person starts to cross, usually the group will follow, showing interdependence. *Interaction* is the key factor in forming a group.

(l)Spencer Grant/Alamy; (r)Brand X Pictures/PunchStock

556

Interdependence

To be classified as a group, a collection of people must be interdependent. Interdependence occurs when any action by one member will affect or influence the other members. For **instance**, in groups of athletes or family members, each member has a certain responsibility to the rest of the group, and if he or she does not fulfill it, the other members will be affected. For the athletes, the consequence may be losing the game; for the family members, a messy house. A person may be the group leader, the decision maker, the one who is the listener, or so on. If any person does not fulfill his or her role, the rest of the group is affected.

In small groups, members usually have a direct influence on one another: one member communicates directly with another. In larger groups, the influence may be indirect. The interdependence between you and the president of the United States is not a result of personal contact. Nevertheless, one of the things that makes the people of the United States a group is that the president's actions affect us, and of equal importance, our actions affect the president.

Communication

Communication is crucial to the functions of a group. In some cases, the communication is directed outward as a declaration of group membership, such as when a member of the band wears a T-shirt or jacket with the school's logo or name. In other instances, the communication is internal, intended for group members to discuss group activities and share common experiences. Direct communication aids members' feelings of belonging and does not isolate members of the group. It increases the likelihood that group members will respond differently to one another than to those who do not belong to the group. Communication encourages debate among members regarding individual goals and increases members' feelings of commitment to group goals.

Shared Goals

Group members become interdependent because they share common goals. Groups are usually created to perform tasks or to organize activities that no individual could handle alone. Members of a consumer group, for example, share the common goal of working for consumer protection. Members of ethnic and religious groups desire to perpetuate a common heritage or set of beliefs.

The purposes groups serve are of two general kinds: **task functions**, those directed toward getting some job done; and **social functions**, those directed toward filling the emotional needs of members. In most groups, task and social functions are combined naturally and cannot be separated easily, although one dominates in any given group.

Political parties, teams of surgeons, and crews of construction workers are all task-oriented groups. Although social interactions occur within each of these groups, their main purpose is to complete a project or achieve some change in the environment. Social functions are emphasized in more informal, temporary groups. When people take walks together, attend parties, or participate in conversations, they have formed a group to gain social rewards such as companionship and emotional support. Yet again, every group involves both task and social functions.

✔ READING PROGRESS CHECK

Assessing Why is communication important among group members?

---

differentiate to make different in some way

group a collection of people who have shared goals, a degree of interdependence, and some amount of communication

instance an example of a particular type or action

task functions activities directed toward getting a job done

social functions responses directed toward satisfying the emotional needs of members

Whether or not the members of this surgical team get along outside the operating room does not matter. Their main purpose is to do a certain job.

▶ CRITICAL THINKING

Identifying What are the features that groups share?

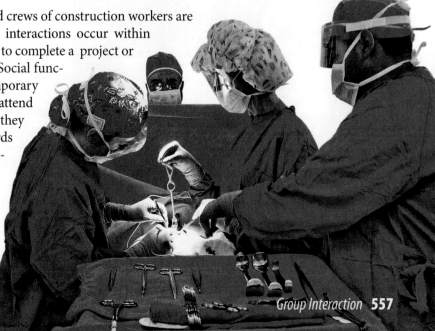

How Groups Are Held Together

GUIDING QUESTION *How do groups achieve cohesiveness?*

Some groups function well, with members interested and committed to the group. Other groups may display a lack of interest among its members, leaving the group in danger of falling apart. The factors that work to hold a group together—that increase the group's *cohesiveness*—include shared attitudes and standards and the group's commitment to them.

Norms

ideology the set of principles, attitudes, and defined objectives for which a group stands

Norms are usually unwritten rules that govern the behavior and attitudes of group members. They include rules—shared beliefs about the correct way to behave and what to believe. For example, there are rules about how to behave at home, at school, and at an amusement park. There are rules about what to say and how to communicate with brothers, sisters, parents, and friends. Would you use the same words and expressions with both your friends and your parents? Most people would not. These rules are not necessarily like rigid laws. They may be more like tendencies or habits, but group members are expected to act in accordance with group norms and may be punished in some way if they do not. If a student consistently sneaks to the front of the lunch line, her friends would not hesitate to say something about it to ensure that it does not happen again. Strangers might point and grow angry—simply because she violated a norm that you wait in line after the people who arrived before you. Thus, the punishment may take the form of coldness or criticism from other group members. If the norm is very important to the group, a member who violates it may endure a more severe social reaction or may be excluded from the group.

Social norms can be formal or informal. Formal norms are rules such as traffic laws. Informal norms are unwritten rules, such as greeting friends and shaking your opponents' hands at the end of a game.

▶ **CRITICAL THINKING**

Analyzing What norms might be important to a group organized to serve social functions?

The most common group norms are those that acknowledge all members of the group. For example, in a high school, the social norms include helping, respecting, and protecting the other students in the school. In this kind of situation, it is easier for the members of the group to make healthy social decisions. In sports groups, social norms include encouraging teammates to contribute their best work to the group.

Ideology

For a group to be cohesive, members must share the same values. In some cases, people are drawn together because they discover they have common ideas, attitudes, and goals—that is, they have a common **ideology**. In other instances, people are attracted to a group because its ideology provides them with a new way of looking at themselves and interpreting events and a new set of goals and means for achieving them. The National Organization for Women (NOW), for example, has provided a focal point for resistance to discrimination on the basis of gender. AARP is an organization that lobbies for the rights of older people and retirees. Leaders, heroes and heroines, rallies, books and pamphlets, slogans, and symbols all help popularize an ideology, win converts, and create feelings of solidarity among group members.

Commitment

One factor that increases individual commitment to a group is the requirement of personal sacrifice. If a person is willing to pay money, endure hardship, or undergo humiliation to join a group, he or she is likely to continue with it. For example, some groups in high school require initiation rites in order to join the group. College students who undergo embarrassing initiation rites to join sororities or fraternities tend to develop a loyalty to the group that lasts well beyond their college years. During your first year of high school, you also go through initiation rites. Seniors may tell new students about elevators that do not exist, stairwells that are blocked, or directions that lead to the wrong place. These common ordeals bind people to others in the group.

Another factor that strengthens group commitment is participation. When people actively participate in group decisions and share the rewards of the group's accomplishments, their feeling of membership increases—they feel that they have helped make the group what it is. For example, social psychologists have compared groups of workers who participate in decisions that affect their jobs with other workers who elect representatives to decision making committees or workers who are simply told what to do. Those who participate have higher morale and accept change more readily than do the other workers. Other studies have highlighted the importance of supportive managers in maintaining such worker involvement.

The processes that hold a group together must work both ways. The individual must be responsive to the norms of the group, subscribe to its ideology, and be prepared to make sacrifices to be part of it. The group must also respond to the needs of its members. It cannot achieve cohesiveness if its norms are unenforceable, if its ideology is inconsistent with the beliefs of its members, or if the rewards it offers do not outweigh the sacrifices it requires.

✅ **READING PROGRESS CHECK**

Drawing Conclusion Why is it important for social groups to have norms?

Social Facilitation and Interaction

GUIDING QUESTION *What purpose do "roles" serve in group interactions?*

Do you perform better or worse in front of a crowd? Have you heard of the "home team advantage"? This is another term for social facilitation. **Social facilitation** refers to the tendency to perform better in the presence of a group. When you have the home team advantage, you tend to play better because you know the crowd is on your side. At times, however, you may perform poorly in front of crowds. This is an example of **social inhibition**. The away team might suffer from social inhibition. Social facilitation and social inhibition may occur because the presence of a crowd increases one's drive or arousal.

In one study, psychologist Robert Zajonc noticed that social facilitation seemed to occur when participants performed simple or well-learned tasks, whereas social inhibition occurred when participants performed more complex tasks or tasks that involved unfamiliar factors. So, in effect, how you perform in front of a crowd depends on what you are doing and your experience in doing it. For example, if you are an expert tennis player but a novice piano player, you might perform well in front of others when you are playing in a tennis tournament but poorly in front of others when you are trying to play the piano at a party. The effect of a crowd on your behavior may also be a reflection of your concern about being evaluated. For example, you might play an excellent game of tennis in front of your friends and parents, but your performance might slip when you play in front of college recruiters.

Social Norms

Visual behavior illustrates the effects of norms on our behavior. When you walk by someone you do not know, you have two choices: to speak or not to speak.

In both instances, when you are between 10 and 18 feet in front of the person, accepted social rules are that you divert your eyes to the right. If you look at the person until your head is turned 90 degrees, it is considered pushy. If you turn and continue looking at the person as you walk down the hallway, it might be viewed as harassment or a challenge.

Similar norms operate in many different situations. For instance, it is customary for elevator riders to redistribute floor space more or less equally each time someone gets on or off. These norms are the unwritten rules that govern our social behavior.

social facilitation an increase in performance in front of a crowd

social inhibition a decrease in performance in front of a crowd

Providing an individual with values and a sense of identity is only one aspect of the group's meaning to him or her. The particular role he or she plays in the group's activities is also important. Each group member has certain unique abilities and interests, and the group has a number of different tasks that need to be performed. The study of the roles various members play in the group and how these roles are interrelated is the study of *group structure*.

There are many aspects to group structure: the personal relationships between individual members, such as liking relationships and trusting relationships; the rank of each member on a particular dimension, such as power, popularity, status, or amount of resources; and the roles various members play. A *role* is behavior expected of an individual because of his or her membership in a particular group. Thus, when your class meets, someone has the role of teacher, and others have the role of students. Is someone a student leader in your class? Does someone always remain silent? Is another person always making jokes? Each of us has *multiple roles* that shift as we merge with different groups. Occasionally, we may find ourselves in *role conflict*, such as if you switch schools and your old school plays your new school in football.

Decision Making

Most groups must make decisions. For example, you and your friends must decide what to do Saturday night. Jurors must decide whether a defendant is guilty or not guilty. A president's advisory committee must determine the proper solution to a company crisis. Group polarization and groupthink are two processes that affect group decision making.

Have you ever expressed an opinion and discussed it with a group of friends? How did the discussion affect the strength of your opinion? In the process of **group polarization**, when a group of people discuss their opinions about an issue and a majority of the members argue for one side of the issue, engaging in the discussion typically pushes the members of the majority to a more extreme view than they held before the discussion occurred. In this process, the majority's point of view is reinforced. The repetition of the same arguments results in stronger attitudes in support of the majority's view. If opinions of a group are equally split on an issue before a discussion, though, the group discussion usually results in compromise.

group polarization theory that group discussion reinforces the majority's point of view and shifts group members' opinions to a more extreme position

DIAGRAM >

GROUP POLARIZATION
Each triangle represents the opinion of one individual. Before the group discussion, individuals are divided in the content and strength of their opinions. After the group discussion, individuals' opinions move toward a more extreme version from their initial opinions.

▶ **CRITICAL THINKING**

1. *Evaluating* Why do opinions become more extreme during group polarization?

2. *Comparing* How is group polarization similar to groupthink?

BEFORE GROUP DISCUSSION

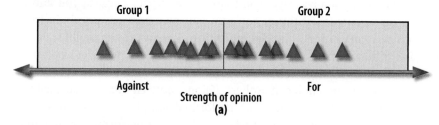

Group 1   Group 2

Against   For
Strength of opinion
(a)

AFTER GROUP DISCUSSION

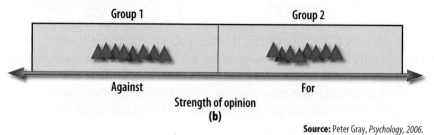

Group 1   Group 2

Against   For
Strength of opinion
(b)

Source: Peter Gray, *Psychology*, 2006.

For example, say you think that bikers should wear helmets. One afternoon at lunch, the subject of bikers and helmets comes up. Most of your friends also believe that bikers should wear helmets. As your group discusses the issue, you and your friends use examples and your own reasoning to argue the point. You come away from the discussion feeling very strongly about the issue—much more strongly than before the discussion. You feel that it should be mandatory for bikers to wear helmets.

Throughout history, government leaders have sometimes made poor decisions. When John F. Kennedy became president of the United States in 1961, he faced the problem of Fidel Castro, the Communist leader of Cuba. Castro formed a close alliance with the Soviet Union, and this alliance threatened the security of the United States. Kennedy ordered a secret invasion of Cuba to overthrow Castro. The invasion at the Bay of Pigs failed miserably, making Kennedy's administration look weak and bringing the world close to nuclear war. Why did Kennedy make this ill-fated decision? Kennedy and his administration were probably the victims of groupthink.

When groups stick together and fail to adequately appraise alternative courses of action, they are guilty of **groupthink**. When engaged in groupthink, the members of a group do not make the best decisions. Group members may refrain from criticizing one another, and they may not discuss opposing viewpoints sufficiently or evaluate the situation critically.

The ill-fated Bay of Pigs invasion is a good example of groupthink in action. The invasion plan had numerous flaws, but was popular among the president's advisers. This group of advisers believed they were strongly unified, and each adviser was reluctant to offer opposing viewpoints or challenge bad ideas because it might disturb group unity. While some advisers privately told the president they disagreed with the invasion, no one would oppose it in front of the group. As a result, many of the flaws in the plan, like an underestimation of the size of Cuba's army, went unquestioned. Had these flaws been questioned or criticized, they could have been corrected. The costs were high. Several hundred members of the invading force lost their lives. Recognizing a problem, President Kennedy then began to encourage his advisers to offer opposing views more openly.

Groups can improve decision quality. Group leaders should avoid strongly advocating their own views and encourage group discussion. During discussion, group members should hear all viewpoints and challenge one another's views. Minority viewpoints should be expressed and discussed. Also, group members should focus on the task at hand. Groups should not focus on unity when making decisions. They should focus on keeping the lines of communication open and gathering enough information to make an unbiased decision.

Communication Patterns

In studying groups, social psychologists use a technique called the **sociogram** to analyze group structure. All members of a group are asked to name those people with whom they would like to interact, those they like best, and those with whom they'd rather not work. For example, the members may be asked with whom they would like to go to a party, to discuss politics, to spend a vacation, or to complete a task. Their choices can then be diagrammed. Sociograms can help psychologists predict how that individual is likely to communicate with other group members. Another way to discover the structure of a group is to examine the communication patterns in the group—who says what to whom and how often individuals speak.

- They satisfy our need to belong.
- We must compare ourselves to others who are similar to us.
- We must compare our experiences with those of others who are similar to us.
- We use group members as standards against which to evaluate ourselves.
- Groups reduce our uncertainty.
- Group members may offer us support in trying times.
- Groups provide us with companionship.
- Groups provide comfort and lessen our anxiety.
- Groups help us accomplish things that we could not do alone.

∧ **TABLE**

WHY DO WE JOIN GROUPS?
Psychologists have proposed various reasons why we join groups.

▶ **CRITICAL THINKING**

1. *Drawing Inferences* For what reason would you join a task-oriented group?

2. *Making Connections* How might a group benefit someone who may have just lost a loved one?

groupthink poor group decision making that occurs as a result of a group emphasizing unity over critical thinking

sociogram a diagram that represents relationships within a group, especially likes and dislikes of members for other members

An experiment on communication patterns in problem solving was conducted by Harold Leavitt in 1951. He gave a card with several symbols on it to each person in a group of five and put each person in a separate room or booth. By allowing group members to communicate only by written messages in a certain configuration, he was able to create a network of interactions (see Leavitt's Communication System diagram). Each circle represents a person, and the lines represent open channels. Participants placed in each position could exchange messages only with the person to whom they were connected by channels.

The people who were organized into a "circle" were the slowest at solving the problem presented on the cards but the happiest at doing it. In this group everyone sent and received a large number of messages until someone solved the problem and passed the information on. In the "wheel," by contrast, everyone sent a few messages to one central person, who solved the puzzle and told the rest. These groups found the answer quickly, but the people on the outside of the wheel did not enjoy the job.

Following the experiment, the members in each group were asked to identify the leader of their group. In the centralized groups (wheel, Y, and chain), the person in the center was usually chosen as the group leader. In the circle network, however, half the group members said they thought there was no real leader, and those who did say there was a leader disagreed on who that leader was. Thus a centralized organization seems more useful for task-oriented groups, whereas a decentralized network is more useful in socially oriented groups.

Social Networking

Social networking sites on the Internet have also helped psychologists learn about how people communicate and interact in groups. A social networking site, such as Facebook, typically allows users to collect friends and update them on their social life by way of status updates and photographs.

Not many studies have been done to test the impact a social networking site has on its users. However, one study at Stanford University examined the effect of such sites on the mood of some of its users. That study has shown that users consistently felt dejected and unhappy with their own lives after viewing the photos and updates of others. The study also showed that an image of unrealistic happiness was often displayed on a site, which caused some viewers to feel inadequate about their own lives.

However, social networking sites can also bring people together and allow them to keep in touch and share their lives. They can keep updated on subjects they like by subscribing to groups that will allow them to communicate with people who share similar interests. Forums on many Web sites also allow communication and social networking between people. From sports to car mechanics to knitting to residence in a particular urban area, social online forums provide an opportunity to communicate with others who are also interested in a topic, allowing the users to ask advice, share information, and compare experiences.

Leadership

Most groups, whether made up of students, workers, club members, or politicians, have leaders. A leader embodies the norms and ideals of the group and represents the group to outsiders. Within the group, a leader initiates action, gives orders, makes decisions, and settles disputes. An effective leader has a great deal of influence on the other members.

Leadership may be defined in several ways. Most of us think of leadership as a *personality trait*. To an extent, this is true. One psychologist identified leadership as being an aspect of personality—the ability to get people to comply. It can be thought of as skills in social influence or persuasion or simply as social power.

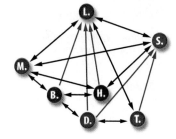

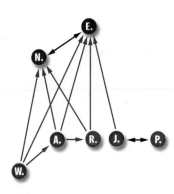

DIAGRAM ∧

SOCIOGRAMS

In these sociograms, the blue arrows indicate admiration that is not returned, and the black arrows indicate a two-way friendship. The more a person is liked, the higher in the pattern he or she appears. The pattern of the bottom group shows a hierarchical structure.

▶ **CRITICAL THINKING**

1. *Analyzing Visuals* Who are the leaders in the bottom group?

2. *Evaluating* Why is the top group more likely a social group?

SUPREME COURT DECISIONS

Authority figures must consider how their decisions affect the lives of people of different social and economic backgrounds. In 1954, the United States Supreme Court helped to protect the rights of African Americans in the landmark case, *Brown* v. *Board of Education*. In that case, attorney Thurgood Marshall helped to convince the court that a law that demanded separate schools for black and white students was unconstitutional. The decision ended more than 50 years of segregation in the United States.

In 1896, Supreme Court Justice Henry Brown had helped to convince the Supreme Court in a similar case called *Plessy* v. *Ferguson* that "separate" but "equal" facilities for blacks and whites was constitutional. The case occurred in response to the jailing of a black man who sat in a railroad car reserved for whites. The differing decisions of the court show how the attitudes and personalities of the people in power have a great effect on the members of society, with Henry Brown accepting or justifying an oppressive system and Thurgood Marshall taking steps to oppose such a system.

▶ **CRITICAL THINKING**

1. *Analyzing* In 1954, how do you think the Supreme Court showed an understanding of the needs of the nation as a whole?

2. *Defending* From the standpoint of a sociocultural psychologist, how would you analyze individuals or groups who opposed the Supreme Court's 1954 decision?

▲ The leadership of the attorneys who argued the case against segregation, George Hayes, Thurgood Marshall, and James Nabrit, Jr., resulted in the Supreme Court ruling that segregation in public schools is unconstitutional.

It has been found that leaders tend to be better adjusted, more self-confident, more energetic and outgoing, and slightly more intelligent than other members of their group.

Other researchers proposed a different model. They argued that leaders are concerned to some degree with both output (that is, the task) and the welfare of the people. Each dimension is separate, and any leader can be at any level on either dimension. A leader deeply concerned with both output and welfare would likely develop a team management program so that workers contribute to the group's goals. A leader concerned solely with output would stress obedience, and a leader whose primary concern was the worker might create a stress-free atmosphere with a friendly organization. A leader who cared little for output or welfare might encourage workers to do the minimum to keep things functioning.

Another way to think of leadership is as the *end product of the reinforcements of the group* being led. In this way, leadership is simply the center or focus of group action, an instrument for achieving the group's goal, or a result of group interaction. In this sense, the nature of the group itself in part determines who will lead.

Different circumstances call for different kinds of leaders. A group that is threatened by internal conflict requires a leader who is good at handling people, settling disputes, and soothing tempers. A group that has a complex task to perform needs a leader with special experience in setting goals and planning strategies relative to the task for achieving those goals.

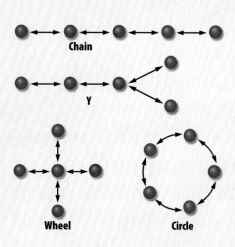

DIAGRAM ∧

LEAVITT'S COMMUNICATION NETWORK SYSTEM

Each dot represents a person. The lines represent open channels. Participants could exchange messages only with the person to whom they were connected by channels.

▶ **CRITICAL THINKING**

1. *Analyzing* What were Leavitt's findings regarding centralized organizations?

2. *Contrasting* How is the chain network system different from the circle network system?

Another kind of leadership is called *transformational leadership*. This leadership produces large-scale organizational change by changing the goals of group members and deepening their commitment. Transformational leaders are charismatic. They provide individualized attention to group members, and they are able to enthuse and intellectually stimulate group members. *Charisma* refers to a leader's persuasive powers and popularity. This, in turn, is based on the followers' perceptions of the leader's talents and expertise. When a leader is charismatic, followers trust the correctness of the leader's views, obey the leader willingly, feel affection for the leader, and are motivated to perform at peak levels. Presidents Franklin D. Roosevelt and John F. Kennedy have been called charismatic leaders.

Early studies in leadership established three major leadership styles. The three leadership styles are authoritarian, laissez-faire (LEH • SAY • FEHR), and democratic. An *authoritarian* leader makes all the decisions and assigns tasks to group members. These leaders are focused on completion of tasks and compliance with group goals. Authoritarian leaders, such as political dictators, military commanders, or autocratic business executives, tell other group members what to do and demand obedience. A *laissez-faire* leader allows group members to set their own goals and make their own decisions but is available to answer questions and provide feedback. When leading a discussion, your teacher may be a good example of a laissez-faire leader—one who encourages group members to explore their own ideas. In corporate life, laissez-faire leadership can work well with highly skilled, creative groups but may not work well with groups that require managerial involvement and direction. A *democratic* leader encourages group members to come to decisions through consensus. These leaders are often viewed as supportive but not good decision makers. Democratic leaders, such as the members of the U.S. Congress, try to build a consensus among group members.

☑ **READING PROGRESS CHECK**

Drawing Conclusions What makes people trust a charismatic leader?

LESSON 1 REVIEW

Reviewing Vocabulary

1. *Understanding Relationships* Give an example of groupthink that could occur at a task function and explain how members of that group could avoid groupthink.

Using Your Notes

2. *Applying* Use your notes to describe three styles of leadership and explain both positive and negative aspects of the three styles.

Answering the Guiding Questions

3. *Examining* What are some primary and secondary groups with which you are involved?

4. *Explaining* How do groups achieve cohesiveness?

5. *Describing* What purpose do "roles" serve in group interactions?

Writing Activity

6. *Informative/Explanatory* Describe an activity that you did in the past month in front of a crowd. How did you perform? Analyze in a brief report whether you experienced social inhibition and when you think social inhibition might occur.

net**w**⊚rks

There's More Online!

- ☑ **CARTOON** Conformity and Obedience
- ☑ **GRAPHIC ORGANIZER**
- ☑ **SELF-CHECK QUIZ**

Reading **HELP**DESK (CCSS)

Academic Vocabulary

- persist
- comment

Content Vocabulary

- obedience
- debriefing

TAKING NOTES:

Key Ideas and Details

DESCRIBING Use a graphic organizer like the one below to describe the Asch Experiment.

The Asch Experiment

Hypothesis:	
Method:	
Results:	

LESSON 2

Conformity and Obedience

ESSENTIAL QUESTION • *How can groups shape the behavior of individuals?*

IT MATTERS BECAUSE

Everyone wants to be part of a group and have a sense of belonging. Being a part of a group can be a desire that is so strong that people may do questionable things in order to feel like they belong. People also work hard to uphold the expectations of the group and do what others in the group do. Understanding why people conform to group thinking and norms can help us to understand the importance of groups in our lives.

Pressure to Conform

GUIDING QUESTION *Why did the "yielders" conform in Asch's experiment?*

Have you ever come home and surprised your parents by wearing the latest fad in clothing? Possibly the conversation that followed went something like this:

"How can you go around looking like that?"

"But everyone dresses like this."

The pressure to conform to the way other people look and act can be strong, especially for young people. *Conformity* is the act of behaving in accordance with socially accepted conventions, even if the behavior does not feel natural. In the workforce, people are required to conform to rules that require wearing business attire, attending meetings, performing assigned tasks, and interacting in a professional way with co-workers. Not all of these things may be easy for an employee to do, but the employee must do them in order to keep the job. For example, an employee who always wears jeans willingly conforms by investing in a work wardrobe.

Not all conformity is required, however. Teens do not need to conform to the group norms or activities of others. They may do it because they want to, or they may do it because of pressure from others. Peer pressure to wear certain styles of clothes or to drink or do drugs can interfere with people's lives and sense of self and happiness. To a certain degree, we all conform by doing what is expected of us in society. But the pressure to conform socially can be a stressor for individuals. Psychologists have conducted studies designed to observe people's behaviors when they are presented with pressures to conform.

Asch Conformity Experiments

Psychologist Solomon Asch designed what has become a classic experiment to test conformity to pressure from one's peers. Conformity involves any behavior that you engage in because of direct or indirect group pressure. He found that people may conform to other people's ideas of the truth, even when they disagree. The following is what you would have experienced if you had been a participant in this experiment.

You and six other students meet in a classroom for an experiment on visual judgment. A line is projected on a screen in front of all seven participants. You are then shown another view of three lines and are asked to pick the one that is the same length as the first line. One of the three is exactly the same length. The other two lines are obviously different.

The experiment begins uneventfully. The participants announce their answers in the order in which they are seated in the room. You happen to be sixth, and one person follows you. On the first comparison, every person chooses the same matching line.

The second set of lines is displayed, and once again the group is unanimous. The discriminations seem simple and easy, and you prepare for what you expect will be a rather boring experiment.

On the third trial, you are unexpectedly disturbed. You are quite certain that line 2 is the one that matches the standard. Yet the first person in the group announces confidently that line 1 is the correct match. Then the second person follows suit, and he, too, declares that the answer is line 1; so do the third, fourth, and fifth participants. Now it is your turn. You are suddenly faced with two contradictory pieces of information; the evidence of your own senses tells you that one answer is clearly correct, but the unanimous and confident judgments of the five preceding participants tell you that you are wrong.

The dilemma **persists** through 18 trials. On 12 of the trials, the other group members unanimously give an answer that differs from what you clearly perceive to be correct. It is only at the end of the experimental session that you learn the explanation for the confusion. The six other participants were all actors, and they had been instructed to give incorrect answers on those 12 trials.

How do most participants react to this situation? Asch found that about 75 percent of his participants conformed some of the time. These conformers he called the "yielders." Most yielders explained to Asch afterward that they knew which line was correct but they yielded to group pressure to not appear different from the others. Asch called those who did not conform "independents." About 25 percent of the participants were independents. They gave the correct answer despite group pressure. Why so much conformity? According to one theory, most children are taught the overriding importance of being liked and of being accepted. Conformity is the standard means of gaining this approval.

Asch sometimes varied the experiment by having one or two actors give a different answer than the rest of the actors. When they did this, Asch found that a participant was less likely to yield—even if the different answer was not correct. This seems to prove that independents can have an influence within a group. Minority social influence occurs when a subgroup rejects the established norm of the majority but still maintains an impact over others. An independent may be able to influence a yielder in a group to adhere to a viewpoint.

Minority social influence can occur in situations such as Asch's experiment in which it is obvious that the majority is incorrect. In social situations, when the majority group is mistreating others, an independent may be able to influence some yielders to behave appropriately instead of yielding unquestioningly to the majority group. Those who stand alone in a group are of interest to study.

Standard Line

A ————————

Comparison Lines

1   ————————

2   ————————————

3   ——————

DIAGRAM ∧

ASCH'S EXPERIMENT

These two choices were shown to participants in one trial of Asch's experiment on conformity. The participants' task was to determine whether the length of the standard line matches the length of the comparison lines. The actual discrimination is easy.

▶ **CRITICAL THINKING**

1. *Analyzing* What was the purpose of Asch's experiment?

2. *Identifying* Why were a majority of participants in Asch's experiment labeled as "yielders"?

persist to continue to occur beyond the expected time

Patrick Riviere/Getty Images Entertainment/Getty Images

In the dramatic play *Twelve Angry Men*, eleven jurors believe the defendant in a murder trial is guilty, while one juror fights against the tide of conformity to try to persuade the others to vote not guilty.

▶ **CRITICAL THINKING**

Drawing Conclusions In what way does this play's topic illustrate the concepts of minority influence, dissent, and compliance?

Minority Dissent and Compliance

One of the most important findings of Asch's experiment was that if even one person among the first five failed to conform to the group's judgment, the participant would always stick to his own perceptions. It seems that it is hardest to stand alone. Later researchers have shown that under some conditions, a minority view can come to win over the larger group. By disagreeing with the majority view, a person can actually reduce the pressure that others feel to conform. A minority dissenter may also serve an informational purpose by making others question whether the majority view is actually right. When people hear a dissenting opinion, they are more likely to examine the issue more closely, which can lead to a different outcome.

In Asch's experiment, participants conformed; they responded to match the other group members' responses. Outside of the group setting, however, they might not have actually changed their beliefs. This contrast between public behavior and private belief often characterizes *compliance*. Compliance occurs when we respond to the request of another person without necessarily changing our beliefs. A method of gaining compliance is the *foot-in-the-door technique*. This occurs when you get a person to agree to a relatively minor request. This minor request, which the participant is likely to agree with, is really a set-up for a major request. For example, a car salesperson might get customers into the showroom by saying, "Just come in, and we'll run a few numbers—no obligation." Once the prospects are in the showroom, though, they are more likely to develop the attitude that they need new cars. Their initial minor commitment becomes intense.

There are several factors that increase conforming behavior in people. The factors include:

- belonging to a group that emphasizes the role of groups rather than individuals
- the desire to be liked by other members of the group
- low self-esteem
- social shyness
- lack of familiarity with a task
- group size (Conformity increases as the size of the group grows to five or six people. After that, conformity levels off.)
- cultural influences

☑ **READING PROGRESS CHECK**

Assessing In a social situation, what would make someone give an answer they feel is incorrect?

Obedience to Authority

GUIDING QUESTION *What does the Milgram Experiment reveal about obedience to authority?*

The influence other people have on your attitudes and actions is considerable. Sometimes this influence is indirect and subtle, and at other times it is quite direct. People may simply tell you what to believe and what to do. Under what conditions do you obey them?

Everyone in this society has had experiences with authorities such as parents, teachers, police officers, managers, judges, clergy, or military officers. Behavior in response to orders given by these authorities, or **obedience**, can be either useful or destructive. For instance, obeying the orders of a doctor or firefighter in an emergency would be constructive. Psychologists are more interested, however, in the negative aspects of obedience. They know from historical events such as the barbarities of German Nazism that individuals can be casued to obey irrational commands. In fact, people often obey authority even when obedience goes against their conscience and their system of morality.

The Milgram Experiment

Psychologist Stanley Milgram conducted the most famous investigation of obedience in the early 1960s. Milgram set up the experiment as follows. Two participants appeared for each session. They were told that they would be participating in an experiment to test the effects of punishment on memory. One of the participants was to be the "teacher" and the other the "learner." In reality, the learner was not a volunteer participant; he was Milgram's accomplice. The teacher was to read into a microphone a list of words to be memorized by the learner, who would be in a nearby room. If the learner failed to recite the list back correctly, the teacher was to administer an electric shock. The alleged purpose of the experiment was to test whether the shock would have any effect on learning. In actuality, however, Milgram wanted to discover how far the teacher would follow his instructions and how much shock the teacher would be willing to give another human being. Milgram surveyed a group of psychology students before the experiment. All respondents predicted that very few participants would be willing to shock the learner.

obedience a change in attitude or behavior brought about by social pressure to comply with people perceived to be authorities

(A) In Milgram's experiment on obedience, the "learner" is connected to the shock apparatus. (B) Milgram explains the procedure to the "teacher." (C) This participant refuses to administer shocks any further and angrily rises in protest. (D) Milgram explains the truth about the experiment.

▶ **CRITICAL THINKING**

Interpreting Why did many participants continue to administer shocks to the learner?

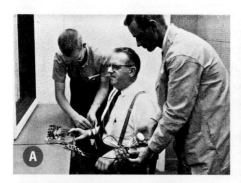

From the Film Obedience ©1968 by Stanley Milgram, © renewed 1993 by Alexandra Milgram

As the experiment began, the learner continually gave wrong answers, and the teacher began to administer the prescribed shocks from an impressive-looking shock generator. The generator had a dial that ranged from 15 volts, which was labeled "Slight Shock," to 450 volts, which was labeled "Danger: Severe Shock." After each of the learner's mistakes, the teacher was told to increase the voltage by one level. The teacher believed that the learner was indeed receiving these shocks because he himself had experienced a mild sample shock, had seen the learner being strapped into a chair, and had watched electrodes being attached to the learner's hands. While the learner acted as if he'd been shocked, in actuality the learner received no shocks at all.

As the experiment progressed, the learner made many mistakes, and the teacher was instructed to give increasingly severe shocks. At 300 volts the learner pounded on the wall and refused to provide any further answers. At this point the experimenter (who wore a white lab coat) instructed the participant to treat no answer as a wrong answer and to continue the procedure. The experiment ended either when the maximum 450 volts was administered or when the teacher refused to administer any more shocks. If at any point the teacher indicated a desire to stop, the experimenter calmly said, "Whether the learner likes it or not, you must go on until he has learned all the word pairs correctly."

Sixty-five percent of the participants delivered the full range of shocks. These participants were not sadists, or people who enjoy inflicting pain. Many of them showed signs of extreme tension and discomfort during the session, and they often told the experimenter that they would like to stop. Despite these feelings, most continued to obey the experimenter's commands. They were ordinary people—salespeople, engineers, and postal workers—placed in an unusual situation. What accounts for this surprisingly high level of obedience? Part of the answer is that the experimenter represents a legitimate authority. People assume that such authorities know what they are doing, even when their instructions seem to run counter to standards of moral behavior.

"Yesterday we asked you to follow the dress code. Today we're doing this. Is that a problem?"

‹ CARTOON

CONFORMITY AND OBEDIENCE

Conforming to a group and obedience to authority has practical explanations. If you see people running out of a building, you may assume that they know something you do not—that the building is on fire, for example.

▶ **CRITICAL THINKING**

1. *Defending* What are other reasons for conforming with a group?

2. *Comparing* Under what circumstances do you think this new employee would disobey his superiors?

HOW DO WE CONFORM TO GROUP NORMS?

Norms are formalized rules for how members of groups should behave. Those who are part of the in-group identify with the group. Those who are not members are part of the out-group. The in-group can exert strong influences on other members' behaviors. How do people react when group norms are not adhered to?

Procedure

1. Think of a norm that regulates what an individual should or should not do in a given in-group. Examples include celebrating a friend's birthday, or calling or getting together on a weekend.
2. Design and act out an experiment in which you do not adhere to the norm.

Analysis

1. What were the general reactions of other group members to you not adhering to the particular norm? How would you describe your experience of being part of the out-group?
2. Do you think norms are always useful? Can they be harmful? Why do you think so?

debriefing a procedure conducted at the end of an experiment to reveal the details of the study so that participants do not leave feeling confused or upset

Milgram's participants could have walked out at any time; they had nothing to lose by leaving. Nevertheless, social conditioning for obeying legitimate authorities is so strongly ingrained that people often lack the words or the ways to do otherwise. Getting up and leaving would have violated powerful unwritten rules of acceptable social behavior.

Milgram's experiment is important because it questions so many different aspects of human behavior. The experiment also raised questions about the ethics of some psychological experiments. How would you feel if you had been one of Milgram's participants? How would you feel if you had been deceived into engaging in hurtful behavior? Since the experiment, the APA has changed its ethical standards for experiments. Today all experiments, especially those that have potential to cause psychological harm, are carefully screened by independent research committees. Informed consent prior to the experiment and a **debriefing** session—a complete disclosure of all design details after an experiment—are absolute rights of participants in modern-day psychological studies.

The Burger Experiment

The original obedience studies by Milgram were conducted as a means to investigate a rationale for Nazi soldiers obeying their superiors during the genocide committed during World War II. At the Nuremberg War Criminal trials, soldiers defended their behavior of killing innocent people by saying they were just following orders. Milgram's experiment could not be duplicated because of ethical concerns, but an increasing number of psychology students began to wonder if researchers would ever get the same results if the test were performed again. They wondered if people today would act in the same way when faced with orders to knowingly harm someone.

In 2009, psychology professor Jerry Burger modified Milgram's experiment so that it met today's ethical guidelines. The maximum shock that the participants were told they would be administering was 150 volts instead of the 450 volts involved in the original experiment. Also, participants went through a careful screening process. Those who viewed the idea of the experiment with a negative reaction were not considered for the study.

Some psychologists criticized Burger's study, stating that the differences between his study and the original study were too profound to be considered a duplication. Regardless, the study did yield some interesting results. The "teachers" in Burger's new study obeyed at the same rate as the teachers in Milgram's study in the 1960s. Even 40 years later, the same percentage of teachers simply obeyed the orders of their superior and followed the instructions of the study, administering shocks when the "learners" answered questions incorrectly. Other researchers believe that the results of Milgram's experiment have been successfully duplicated and Burger's procedures can be used to continue Milgram's research on obedience.

The Stanford Prison Experiment

One Sunday summer morning, a siren shattered the silence, awakening Tommy Whitlow. As Tommy opened his eyes, a police cruiser pulled up, screeching its tires to a halt. The police arrested Tommy, charging him with a felony. They informed him of his rights, frisked and handcuffed him, and placed him in the police vehicle. At the station, police fingerprinted and booked Tommy. They then blindfolded him and led him to the Stanford County Prison. Once he was there, guards stripped him naked and sprayed him down with a disinfectant. He was ordered to wear a beige smock uniform with his identification number patched on the front. Police arrested eight other students that morning as well.

Tommy and the other students were actually participants in another experiment that caused ordinary people to act in extraordinary ways. So as not to unduly surprise the participants, only volunteers were used. Tommy and the other volunteers had answered a newspaper ad; they had no idea that the experiment involved a staged arrest.

The researchers randomly divided the male volunteers into two groups—prisoners and prison guards. Both groups were sent to live in a simulated prison set up in the basement of a Stanford University building. The guards were instructed to maintain order. Within two days, most of the guards had become intoxicated with power. They acted cruelly toward the prisoners, often without reason. The guards expected the prisoners to follow the rules without question. If the prisoners did not follow the rules, they lost the privilege to read or write letters. As the prisoners disobeyed more rules, the punishments increased. Sometimes the guards subjected the prisoners to embarrassment, humiliation, and mindless tasks such as push-ups and washing toilets with their bare hands.

At the same time, the prisoners began showing signs of extreme stress, often acting subdued and depressed. Sometimes the prisoners refused to follow the rules. They yelled back at the guards, made negative **comments** about the jail, and later became passive from defeat. Some of the prisoners became angry and disillusioned, while others developed psychological illnesses and rashes. The emotional reactions were so extreme that experimenters ended the planned two-week experiment after only six days.

It seems that the prison environment was much stronger than individual personalities. Although the participants in this experiment were emotionally mature and stable (according to tests administered before the experiment), the roles these individuals adopted changed the way they acted. There may be other situations in everyday life that cause us to behave in ways we do not expect.

In follow-up interviews, none of the participants reported any lasting effects. Some of the participants had difficulty understanding how powerful the experiment had become. The experiment led to the development of the *Ethical Principles of Psychologists and Code of Conduct,* most recently revised in 2010. It also demonstrated the power that situations can have in changing how we feel, think, and behave. The social situation of being in the prison changed the rules, roles, and expectations of the students.

Why Do People Obey?

Why did the Germans obey Adolf Hitler's commands to commit genocide during World War II? Why do cult members sometimes consent to their leaders' orders to commit suicide? After all, these leaders' commands are clearly unreasonable, right? Psychologists have proposed that people learn to obey authority figures. Throughout our lives, we obey parents, doctors, teachers, and religious leaders. We also learn to obey the rules and follow orders. We follow traffic rules, school rules, and parental rules. However, we are more likely to follow these rules when the authority figure is actually present.

More
ABOUT...

Collectivism

Many Americans value individualism—a focus on defining oneself in individual terms and giving priority to personal goals. Other societies, though, focus on collectivism—defining oneself in terms of the groups to which one belongs and giving priority to the groups' goals. Individuals in collective societies, such as those in Africa, Asia, and Central and South America, work to control their behaviors and maintain harmonious relationships with others. These individuals are encouraged to be dependent on and submissive to the values of the group. People from collectivist cultures have different priorities and thus have different strategies in how they resolve conflicts and deal with others.

comment a statement that expresses an opinion

Some cultures, such as those found in rural Mexico, place greater emphasis on the group than on the individual. Individuals are viewed as part of the family and society and must work hard to maintain harmonious relationships with others.

▶ CRITICAL THINKING

Considering Point of View How do you think the American culture views individuals' roles in groups?

Do people's culture and economic class affect their level of obedience? Studies have shown that middle class parents put an emphasis on their children's independence, while working class families stress the importance of obedience. Cultures play a large part in the way a person learns to conform. A larger emphasis is placed on obedience in eastern cultures such as China or Japan. East African children have also been raised to have a great respect for their parents as well as other adults in general. While studies have shown that American children disobey the order of their own parents more often than the order of another child's parents, the East African children were found to fully obey all adults on the tasks they were given, whether the order came from their own parents or the parents of another child.

While Americans place an emphasis on independence and freedom, Asian cultures emphasize respect and discipline, and East African and South American cultures emphasize contributing to the home and family community. When people leave one culture for another, they may witness differing attitudes regarding obedience. They may choose to adopt these new ideas or remain loyal to the norms with which they were raised.

Education Images/Universal Images Group/Getty Images

✓ READING PROGRESS CHECK

Comparing How were Milgram's experiment and the Stanford prison experiment similar?

LESSON 2 REVIEW

Reviewing Vocabulary

1. *Identifying* Give an example of a way you show conformity.

Using Your Notes

2. *Defending* Use your notes to write an argument defending your position on whether or not the people who conformed in Asch's experiment always conform to groups.

Answering the Guiding Questions

3. *Explaining* Why did the "yielders" conform in Asch's experiment?

4. *Analyzing* What does the Milgram Experiment reveal about obedience to authority?

Writing Activity

5. *Informative/Explanatory* Try this experiment with your family or group of friends. Stare at the ceiling continuously for a time. Do other people start to look up at the ceiling also? Why or why not? Explain the principles behind this experiment in a short paragraph.

Case Study

Your Stripes or Your Morality

Period of Study: 1994

Introduction: Lawrence Rockwood, a captain in the United States Army, had served in the army for close to 20 years when he was ordered to lead a force of troops into Haiti. (A military government had come to power in Haiti. U.S. troops provided stability while the democratically elected government regained power.) Through the mission, President Bill Clinton intended to stop brutal crimes imposed on the Haitian people. Confident and eager about his mission, Rockwood strongly advocated human rights for people all over the world. Rockwood did not know, however, that his mission would clash intensely with his morals.

Hypothesis: Similar to the studies conducted by Asch and Milgram, the hypothesis was that when faced with pressure to conform, an individual would conform to the group or an authority.

Method: Immediately upon arrival in Haiti, U.S. leaders changed the mission from "stopping brutal crimes" to "forced protection," or keeping American troops safe from harm. Commanders ordered Captain Rockwood to survey local Haitian prisons and report on the conditions there. Rockwood found and reported horrible conditions in these prisons. Guards mistreated and tortured prisoners. Rockwood discovered that one of the prisons had about 30 inmates housed in one small cell and that one man had been confined in a position so long that portions of his skin had rotted off.

Outraged at these conditions, Captain Rockwood petitioned for special operations units to enter the prisons and enforce the rules and regulations involving prisoners of war. A senior officer listened to Rockwood's pleas. The officer recommended that special operations investigate the prisons. Special operations turned down the request.

This refusal prompted Rockwood to take matters into his own hands. Knowing his military career would be put on the line by way of court-martial, Rockwood disobeyed direct orders, climbed the outer fence of his base, and proceeded to a Haitian prison where he demanded to evaluate each prisoner. Four hours later,

a United States major arrived at the prison and ordered Rockwood to leave. When Rockwood resisted, troops forced him out of the prison. Army psychiatrists evaluated Rockwood twice and found him sane. The army then charged him with disobeying direct orders. One of the justifications for Rockwood's actions was as follows:

PRIMARY SOURCE

" *... Rockwood heard Clinton address the nation Sept. 15 and say that curbing human rights abuses would be one of the priorities of the U.S. operation. That was enough for Rockwood, who saw the statement as a higher order than any given him by lesser commanders.* "

Results: In 1995 the Army court-martialed Rockwood for his actions. The Army sentenced Rockwood to dismissal—equal to a dishonorable discharge—despite his perfect military record and stripped him of some pay and allowances. All of this occurred because Rockwood chose not to conform to the extreme pressures placed upon him by the military. He made the moral decision to come to the aid of his fellow human beings. Many people question the power the United States military possesses in making each and every soldier conform to and obey the ideology of each armed forces branch, no matter what the cost. The case of Captain Lawrence Rockwood and his squashed crusade for human rights demonstrates the power of an individual to resist conformity.

Analyzing the Case Study

1. *Explaining* Why did Rockwood refuse to conform to group pressure?

2. *Assessing* Should the quote from Rockwood have been enough of a defense to keep him from being dismissed from the Army? Explain your answer.

3. *Evaluating* Does this case study support the findings of Milgram and Asch? Explain.

4. *Speculating* Under what circumstances might Rockwood have obeyed his orders? Do you think that conformity depends upon the situation or the person? Or both? Explain your answer.

Analyzing
Readings in Psychology

PHOTO: Rubberball/Getty Images; TEXT: Republished with permission of ASSOCIATION FOR PSYCHOLOGICAL SCIENCE from Replicating Milgram by Jerry Burger, APS observer Vol. 20, No. 11 December 2007; permission conveyed through Copyright Clearance Center, Inc. APS observer by AMERICAN PSYCHOLOGICAL SOCIETY Copyright 2007 Reproduced with permission of ASSOCIATION FOR PSYCHOLOGICAL SCIENCE in the format Republish in "other" book via Copyright Clearance Center.

Reader's Dictionary ⒸⒸⓈⓈ

IRB: Institutional Review Board; a committee that has been formally designated to approve, monitor, and review research involving human subjects

atrocities: extremely wicked or cruel acts

assuage: make less intense; satisfy

juncture: a particular point in events or time

Students in psychology often learn about several key studies that have helped shape the field. One of the most well-known studies is the Milgram obedience study conducted in the early 1960s. This study soon became infamous, leading to increased focus on ethical issues in psychology. In this article, we learn about an attempt to replicate this controversial experiment.

Replicating
Milgram
By Jerry Burger

PRIMARY SOURCE

"It can't be done." These are the first words I said to Muriel Pearson, producer for ABC News' Primetime, when she approached me with the idea of replicating Stanley Milgram's famous obedience studies. Milgram's work was conducted in the early 1960s before the current system of professional guidelines and **IRBs** was in place. It is often held up as the prototypic example of why we need policies to protect the welfare of research participants. Milgram's participants were placed in an emotionally excruciating situation in which an experimenter instructed them to continue administering electric shocks to another individual despite hearing that person's agonizing screams of protest. The studies ignited a debate about the ethical treatment of participants. And the research became, as I often told my students, the study that can never be replicated.

Nonetheless, I was intrigued. Although more than four decades have passed since Milgram conducted his research, his obedience studies continue to occupy an important place in social psychology textbooks and classes. The haunting black-and-white images of ordinary citizens delivering what appear to be dangerous, if

not deadly, electric shocks and the implications of the findings for **atrocities** like the Holocaust and Abu Ghraib are not easily dismissed. Yet because Milgram's procedures are clearly out-of-bounds by today's ethical standards, many questions about the research have gone unanswered. Chief among these is one that inevitably surfaces when I present Milgram's findings to students: Would people still act that way today?

The challenge was to develop a variation of Milgram's procedures that would allow useful comparisons with the original investigations while protecting the well-being of the participants. But meeting this challenge would raise another: I would also need to **assuage** the apprehension my IRB would naturally experience when presented with a proposal to replicate the study that can never be replicated.

I went to great lengths to recreate Milgram's procedures...including such details as the words used in the memory test and the experimenter's lab coat. But I also made several substantial changes. First, we stopped the procedures at the 150-volt mark. This is the first time participants heard the learner's protests through the wall and his demands to be released. When we look at Milgram's data, we find that this point in the procedure is something of a "point of no return." Of the participants who continued past 150 volts, 79 percent went all the way to the highest level of the shock generator (450 volts). Knowing how people respond up to this point allowed us to make a reasonable estimate of what they would do if allowed to continue to the end.

574

Stopping the study at this **juncture** also avoided exposing participants to the intense stress Milgram's participants often experienced in the subsequent parts of the procedure.

Second, we used a two-step screening process for potential participants to exclude any individuals who might have a negative reaction to the experience. Potential participants were asked in an initial phone interview if they had ever been diagnosed with a psychiatric disorder; if they were currently receiving psychotherapy; if they were currently taking any medications for emotional difficulties; if they had any medical conditions that might be affected by stress; if they ever had any problems with alcohol or drug use; and if they had ever experienced serious trauma, such as child abuse, domestic violence, or combat. Individuals who responded "yes" to any of these questions (about 30 percent) were excluded from the study. During the second step in the screening process, participants completed measures of anxiety and depression and were interviewed in person by a licensed clinical psychologist. The clinicians were shown the anxiety and depression data and were allowed to interview participants for as long as needed...and to exclude anyone who they judged might have a negative reaction to the experiment procedures. More than 38 percent of the interviewed participants were excluded at this point.

Third, participants were told at least three times (twice in writing) that they could withdraw from the study at any time and still receive their $50 for participation. Fourth, like Milgram, we administered a sample shock to our participants (with their consent). However, we administered a very mild 15-volt shock rather than the 45-volt shock Milgram gave his participants. Fifth, we allowed virtually no time to elapse between ending the session and informing participants that the learner had received no shocks. Within a few seconds after ending the study, the learner entered the room to reassure the participant he was fine. Sixth, the experimenter who ran the study also was a clinical psychologist who was instructed to end the session immediately if he saw any signs of excessive stress. Although each of these safeguards came with a methodological price (e.g., the potential effect of screening out certain individuals, the effect of emphasizing that participants could leave at any time), I wanted to take every reasonable measure to ensure that our participants were treated in a humane and ethical manner.

Of course, I also needed IRB approval. I knew from my own participation on the IRB that the proposal would be met with concern and perhaps a little fear by the board's members....Given the possibility of a highly visible mistake, the easy response would have been to say "no." To address these concerns, I created a list of individuals who were experts on Milgram's studies and the ethical questions surrounding this research....More important, Steven Breckler,...executive director for science at the American Psychological Association, graciously provided an assessment of the proposal's ethical issues that I shared with the IRB.

In the end, all the extra steps and precautions paid off. The IRB carefully reviewed and then approved the procedures. More than a year after collecting the data, I have no indication that any participant was harmed by his or her participation in the study....We also produced some interesting findings. Among other things, we found that today people obey the experimenter in this situation at about the same rate they did 45 years ago....[I]t is my hope that other investigators will use the 150-volt procedure and thereby jump-start research on some of the important questions that motivated Stanley Milgram nearly half a century ago.

Analyzing Primary Sources

1. **Explaining** What do the results of the replicated study tell us about obedience behavior today?

2. **Theorizing** Besides ethical considerations, what is another reason why Milgram's experiment may be difficult to duplicate?

3. **Identifying Bias** What are some sources of possible error in the replicated study when making comparisons to the original study?

Hugh Threlfall/Alamy

netw⊙rks

There's More Online!

- ☑ **GRAPHIC ORGANIZER**
- ☑ **SELF-CHECK QUIZ**

Conflict and Cooperation

Reading **HELP**DESK (CCSS)

Academic Vocabulary
- **access**
- **participate**

Content Vocabulary
- **catharsis**
- **altruism**
- **diffusion of responsibility**
- **bystander effect**
- **social loafing**
- **deindividuation**

TAKING NOTES:
Key Ideas and Details

CATEGORIZING Use a graphic organizer like the one below to explain the different theories that are used to explain aggression.

Theories of Aggression	
Theory	
Theory	
Theory	
Theory	

ESSENTIAL QUESTION • *How can groups shape the behavior of individuals?*

IT MATTERS BECAUSE
Group interactions are not always positive experiences. Gangs and violence are the result of aggressive group behaviors. People involved in group interactions may find themselves in unintended situations and they may react in unexpected ways. Understanding different theories of aggression and how they affect people can help us learn more about how individuals handle conflict and cooperation in groups.

Aggression

GUIDING QUESTION *Why might excessive punishment not be the best response to childhood aggression?*

In April 1992, the media released footage of four white police officers beating an African American motorist. When jurors found the officers not guilty of charges including assault and excessive use of force, mob violence erupted in South Central Los Angeles. That violence continued for several days and fed on itself, resulting in 55 deaths and $1 billion in damages. In recent years, mobs have set fires and damaged property after athletic events and flash mobs have been called to violence in several major American cities. How do individuals find themselves engaging in group violence and harming other people?

Any overly forceful behavior with the desire to win can be considered aggression. People can be aggressive in sports, business, or other types of competition. And there is a difference between being aggressive and being *assertive*, or bold and confident in your behavior. Sometimes it is appropriate to be assertive, such as when you need to get something accomplished or to have your voice heard. This does not mean that a person is necessarily being aggressive. Being assertive may be stressful, particularly for individuals who are shy or reserved, although it is not dangerous or damaging. But aggression can cause physical or psychological harm. It seems that our society is being challenged by increasing violence and aggression. What causes humans to act in ways that harm others? Psychologists have proposed several theories to explain aggression.

Biological Influences

Some animals are naturally aggressive. For instance, you might know that when injured, some otherwise friendly dogs become vicious. This violent response is an innate biological reaction. Psychologists have proposed that humans also have innate biological factors that can cause aggression. Neurotransmitters, such as serotonin, influence a person's aggressive behavior. When a person has diminished serotonin levels in the brain, he or she may experience violent outbursts.

Studies indicate that mice whose genes have been altered so that their brains lack serotonin receptors attack other mice with more speed and intensity than normal mice do. Psychologists, though, warn against labeling aggression as caused by only biological factors.

You encounter a dangerous situation.

You feel threatened (have negative feelings).

Your initial reaction is to fight or flee.

You choose to fight.

‹ CHART

MODEL OF AGGRESSION
This is just one model of aggression. Psychologists have proposed various biological, cognitive, and environmental factors that influence a person's response to the fight-or-flight dilemma.

▶ **CRITICAL THINKING**

1. *Analyzing* What leads to aggression in this model?

2. *Drawing Inferences* What are some examples of dangerous situations that could lead to the fight-or-flight response?

There has been a popular belief that high levels of testosterone cause people to become aggressive. However, a 2009 study has found testosterone to be neutral and has no effect on behavior. People in the study who were told they were given testosterone exhibited more aggressive behavior, whether they had been given the hormone or not. It was the expectation, or myth, that the hormone produces aggression that made the subjects exhibit their behavior.

Cognitive Factors

Psychologist Albert Bandura proposes that children learn aggressive behavior by observing and imitating their parents. Bandura suggests that we watch models perform and then imitate the models' behavior. His social learning theory also proposes that aggressive behavior may be reinforced in several ways. Parents who use aggression to discipline their children may be teaching their children to use aggression. Bandura's studies show that children learn aggressive behavior by imitating adult models of aggression. He found that the children were more inclined to imitate the aggressive behavior if the person they were watching and learning from was rewarded for their behavior.

The media—television, movies, video games, and music—may also be teaching aggressive behavior to children. By 18 years of age, the average American has witnessed an estimated 200,000 acts of violence on television. As children witness media violence, they grow immune to the horror of violence, gradually accept violence as a way to solve problems, imitate the violence they observe, and identify with certain characters whether they are victims or victimizers.

Personality Factors

Certain personality traits, such as impulsiveness and having little empathy, combined with favoring domination, can turn a person into a bully. Aggressive people may also be arrogant and egotistical. People often strike out at others to affirm their sense of superiority. Can psychologists predict violent behavior based on personality factors? Past experience is usually the best predictor, as an aggressive child tends to become an aggressive adult.

Domestic violence is a pattern of behavior that is used to maintain control over another person in any relationship, whether it is a family or dating relationship. Consistent, unprovoked aggression toward another person can be a sign of violence in the home or in a relationship. Other indicators include signs of physical abuse and parents or dating partners who exhibit irrational, controlling behavior or have unprovoked, explosive reactions toward their teen or partner. Impulsive or explosive violence is not associated with discipline and has a great impact on a child or teen's psychological health.

Teens who are experiencing violence in the home or in a dating relationship can get help by reaching out to another trusted adult, guidance counselor, family member, doctor, or friend. There are also local and national domestic violence hotlines and Web sites that teens can contact to receive help.

catharsis releasing anger or aggression by letting out powerful negative emotions

Environmental Factors

Sometimes something provokes you and you become violent. Maybe your friend borrowed something without telling you. Maybe another driver refused to let you merge into traffic. Psychologists explain acts of violence that arise from such situations with the *frustration-aggression hypothesis*. This is the idea that frustration or a failure to obtain something expected leads to aggression. The hypothesis, though, fails to note that frustration does not always lead to aggressive behavior. For instance, if your friend trips and falls into you, knocking a soda out of your hands, you may not feel angry once you realize that it was an accident.

Leonard Berkowitz proposed a modified frustration-aggression hypothesis. Berkowitz proposes that frustration leads to aggression only in certain instances. For example, when a stranger bumps into you, you may strike that person if you have done so before or if the person does not intimidate you. Other reactions to frustration may include withdrawal, apathy, anxiety, stress, or simple tolerance.

Bullying

Social psychologists blame our culture for the increasing amount of aggression. Social changes may create feelings of isolation. Cultural influences also play a part, encouraging self-centeredness and a lack of empathy. Research has shown that the more time spent playing violent video games or watching violent movies and television the more likely children are to behave aggressively.

This can manifest itself in bullying, which is repeated unwanted aggressive behavior involving an imbalance of power between bully and victim. The three types of bullying—verbal (teasing or taunting), social (spreading rumors or embarrassing another in public), and physical (hitting, tripping, or pushing)—can occur in school and related areas as well as in the neighborhood or online. Twenty percent of students in grades 9–12 experienced bullying, according to a 2011 study.

The effects of bullying are widespread. Victims often experience depression and anxiety, health complaints, and decreased academic achievement. Bullies themselves are more likely to engage in other negative behaviors such as drug and alcohol abuse as well as criminal activities. Witnesses to bullying can also experience depression, anxiety, and increased negative behavior. Bullying creates a climate in which all students' academic achievement is affected, as a 2011 study of Virginia high schools showed.

Controlling Aggression

Aggression, then, is a combination of biological, cognitive, personality, and environmental factors. Knowing this, how do we limit and control aggression? One method is through catharsis. **Catharsis** involves releasing anger or aggression by expressing powerful negative emotions. For instance, when you are angry, you should "get it off your chest." This might mean talking to a friend, playing a tough game of soccer, or hitting a punching bag for a while. Unfortunately, critics of catharsis believe that any expression of aggression is negative. They point out that expressing your aggression may lead to more aggression.

Other strategies include punishing children for violent behavior and cutting down on the violence they observe. Excessive punishment, though, may trigger aggressive behavior. People can also be taught to control their aggression. Aggressive behavior can be controlled by teaching people to accept frustrations and move on and to react to disappointments in ways other than violence. If people do not view violence as an option, then they will not resort to violence.

☑ **READING PROGRESS CHECK**

Drawing Conclusions Is catharsis always reached through violent aggression? Why or why not?

Group Conflict vs. Cooperation

GUIDING QUESTION *How did experimenters create intergroup hostility at the Robbers Cave camp?*

Conflicts between groups are a fact of everyday life: some level of hostility does exist between women and men, young and old, workers and bosses, African Americans and whites, Catholics and Protestants, and students and teachers. Why do these conflicts exist, and why do they persist? Psychologists have found that even just the idea of competition between groups can make group members display more aggressive behaviors toward another group they view as a threat. Rather than work together to unite groups, members exhibited a desire to cooperate with and be accepted into their own group, and as a result, conflicts arise. Group conflicts may result in discriminating behaviors or even violence. These behaviors are especially apparent when looking at the group activities of gangs.

The Robbers Cave Experiment

Let us consider the findings of a group of psychologists who created a boys' camp to study intergroup relations. The camp at Robbers Cave offered all the usual activities, and the boys had no idea that they were part of an experiment. From the beginning of the experiment, the boys were divided into two groups. The boys hiked, swam, and played baseball only with members of their own group, and friendships and group spirit soon developed. After a while the experimenters (working as counselors) brought the groups together for a tournament. The psychologists had hypothesized that when these two groups of boys were placed in competitive situations, where one group could achieve its goals only at the expense of the other, hostility would develop. They were right.

Although the games began in a spirit of good sportsmanship, tension mounted as the tournament continued. Friendly competition gave way to name calling, fistfights, and raids on enemy cabins. The psychologists had demonstrated the ease with which they could produce unity within the two boys' groups and hatred between them. The experimenters then tried to see what might end the conflict and create civil relationships between the two groups. They tried to bring the groups together for enjoyable activities, such as a movie and a good meal. This approach failed. The campers shoved and pushed each other, threw food and insults, and generally continued their attacks.

Next, the psychologists staged a series of emergencies in which the boys would have to help one another or lose the chance to do or get something they all wanted. For instance, it was reported that the water line to the camp had broken.

Intergroup conflict results when a group no longer sees the enemy as individual humans and thus can treat them indecently.

▶ **CRITICAL THINKING**

Analyzing How does intergroup hostility develop?

Profiles in
Psychology

Lillian Comas-Díaz
(1950–)

Lillian Comas-Díaz was born in Chicago, Illinois, but moved to Puerto Rico when she was six. That early exposure led her to the recognition that cultural differences among people can influence their daily lives and decisions. She believes that sometimes cultural barriers must be broken through to help people in need.

Comas-Díaz takes an ethno-cultural approach to mental health. She believes that a clinician must be sensitive to a client's culture and socioeconomic experiences to be effective. She has shown that psychologists from varying cultural backgrounds are important in the field and can give a rich and informed perspective.

Comas-Díaz has developed community, educational, and media programs on cultural awareness and has worked in the areas of empowerment, antiracism, and violence prevention. She practices in the United States and feels that many minorities can be helped by an ethno-cultural approach.

▶ **CRITICAL THINKING**

Defending Why is it important for a clinician to try to understand a client's ethnic background?

The boys were told that unless they worked together to find the break and fix it, they would all have to leave camp. By afternoon, they had jointly found and fixed the damage. Gradually, through such cooperative activities, intergroup hostility and tensions lessened. Friendships began to develop between individuals of the opposing groups, and eventually the groups began to seek out occasions to mingle. At the end of the camp period, members of both groups requested that they ride home together on the same bus.

The results of this experiment were striking. Two groups of boys from identical backgrounds had developed considerable hostility toward each other simply because they were placed in competition. The crucial factor in eliminating group hostility was cooperation.

The question of conflict is not confined just to small groups. It applies to large communities, too, but then the possibility of a *social trap* is greater. A social trap occurs when individuals in a group decide not to cooperate. Instead, they act selfishly and create a bad situation for all. An illustration of the social trap can be seen in the way Americans have responded to the problems of pollution. We know that automobile exhaust pollutes the air. We know that one way to reduce air pollution is to carpool or use public transportation. Yet the driver who commutes 30 miles a day alone and who knows that he or she is polluting the air thinks: "Yes, I know my car exhaust is bad, but I am only one person. If I stop driving, it won't make any difference." As long as we fall into that social trap, we continue to destroy our environment.

Rather than simply requiring cleaner exhaust (which encourages continued driving), cities are offering priority lanes for buses and **access** to High Occupancy Vehicle lanes for cars with two or more occupants. Other ways to change people's behavior include educating them concerning the issues and communicating the idea that "Yes, you do make a difference." By publicizing the problems and solutions and organizing groups to act, individuals begin to believe that what they do does have an impact, and their actions are reinforced by the group. In this way, people find it more beneficial to cooperate than to act in a purely selfish manner.

Gangs

People who live in urban areas are likely familiar with the activity of gangs and visible indicators of gang activity. A gang is defined as a large social group with identifiable leadership and internal organization. Gangs are characterized by their violent behavior, often to claim control over territories. In addition to street gangs, there are also prison gangs, outlaw motorcycle gangs, and other crime groups with similar leadership and organization. Street gangs are often the most dangerous to their communities because of their territorial violence toward others. Young people may join street gangs hoping for social acceptance, or simply to ensure their own position in the social group. The Federal Bureau of Investigation estimates that there are about 1.4 million active gang members in the United States in 33,000 gangs. In hundreds of cities throughout the nation, these gangs are harming the communities in which they operate.

Police departments have identified three types of gangs. *Social* gangs are relatively permanent groups that hang out in a specific location. Members often engage in organized group activities. Members may hold the norms and values of society in general. *Delinquent* gangs are organized around the principle of monetary gain. Members depend on one another to carry out planned activities. The leader is usually the member most skilled at stealing. *Violent* gangs are organized to obtain emotional gratification from violent activities. Members spend their time carrying out violent acts. Leaders are usually emotionally unstable—they have a need to control others. Group members overestimate the importance and power of their group, and there may be violence within the group.

Anyone may become a victim of gang violence. Gang members are constantly recruiting members, focusing on younger and younger recruits. Many delinquent and violent gang members become career criminals. How do we stop the spread of gangs? Children can learn self-control; they can be taught how to deal with problems. Communities can develop greater opportunities to involve all citizens.

✓ **READING PROGRESS CHECK**

Identifying What are some other examples of social traps that people experience in large groups?

Altruism

GUIDING QUESTION *Why would deindividuation make a group member less likely to be altruistic?*

Altruism means helping another, often with a cost to oneself, for reasons other than the expectation of a reward. Consider the following scene: You are walking on a crowded street and suddenly hear a scuffle off to the side. You turn to see a man trying to rip a woman's purse from her grasp. Everyone else just keeps on walking past the scuffle. What do you do?

Diffusion of Responsibility

Sometimes when several people are faced with a common problem and there is no opponent, they may not even define themselves as a group. There have been many examples of muggings, rapes, and murders that were committed in public while some number of people watched without intervening or calling for help.

By studying artificial crises, psychologists have tried to find out why these people did not act. In one experiment, college students were asked to **participate** in a discussion of personal problems. They were asked to sit in separate rooms. Some were told that they would be communicating with only one other person, and others were given the impression that they would be talking with as many as five other people. All communication, the psychologist told each student, was to take place over microphones so that everyone would remain anonymous and thus would be able to speak more freely. Each person was to talk in turn.

In reality, there were no other people—all the voices presenting each problem were on tape. As discussion of solutions started, the participant heard one of the other "participants" go into what sounded like an epileptic seizure. The victim began to make choking sounds and call for help. The experimenters found that 85 percent of the people who thought they were alone with the victim came out of their room to help him. Of those who believed there were five other people nearby, however, only 31 percent did anything to help.

The experimenters suggested that this behavior was the result of **diffusion of responsibility**. In other words, because several people were present, each person assumed someone else would help. Researchers found that in experiments where people could see the other participants, the same pattern emerged. In addition, bystanders reassured one another that it would not be a good idea to interfere. The **bystander effect** occurs when a person refrains from taking action because of the presence of others. These findings suggest that the larger the crowd or group of bystanders, the more likely any given individual is to feel that he or she is not responsible for trying to alter whatever is going on.

Another influence that inhibits action is the tendency to minimize the need for any response. To act, you must admit that an emergency exists. You may not know exactly what is going on when you hear screams or loud thumps upstairs. You are likely to wait a while before risking the embarrassment of rushing to help.

access a way of getting near something or someone

altruism helping others, often at a cost or risk, for reasons other than rewards

participate to be involved with others in doing something

diffusion of responsibility the presence of others lessens an individual's feelings of responsibility for his or her actions or failure to act

bystander effect an individual does not take action because of the presence of others

Group Interaction **581**

You might feel silly or intrusive to rush in where help is not needed or wanted. It is easier to persuade yourself that nothing needs to be done if you look around and see other people behaving calmly. Not only can you see that they think nothing is wrong but you also can see that not doing anything is "the norm." Both the presence of a leader and being familiar with the person needing help, however, increase the likelihood and speed of help being offered. The same is true of knowing what kind of help is required, seeing the correct form of assistance being modeled, or expecting future interactions with the person needing help.

social loafing the tendency to work less hard when sharing the workload with others

Your evaluations of a situation also may lead to **social loafing**. Social loafing occurs when you allow your contributions to the group to slack off because you realize that individual contributions are not as apparent and easily measured in a group setting. When you are a member of a large group, for example, you may feel a reduced sense of accountability.

Deindividuation

deindividuation individuals behave irrationally when there is less chance of being personally identified

When people act as individuals, obey their consciences, and are concerned with self-evaluation, we think of them as *individualistic*. When **deindividuation** occurs, people lose their sense of self and follow group behaviors. The deindividuated person acts without thinking about self and goes along with the group. Why did normally pleasant people violently throw bottles and rocks at innocent people during the Los Angeles riots? Researchers believe that being in a crowd may reduce the feelings of guilt or self-awareness that one ordinarily feels. People in crowds are anonymous—there is little chance of pinpointing who threw the rock and of being identified.

Social pressure can affect us in positive ways, too. Most people care deeply about what others think of them. This can be a powerful source of pressure for individuals to do what others believe they should do. People may engage in polite, kind, or thoughtful behavior or refrain from rude, unkind, or thoughtless behavior because they would like others to think highly of them. The social influence of public opinion may have played a role in some of history's great acts of philanthropy.

☑ **READING PROGRESS CHECK**

Evaluating How does diffusion of responsibility affect our behavior in situations where another person needs help?

LESSON 3 REVIEW

Reviewing Vocabulary

1. *Explaining* How does diffusion of responsibility affect individuals in a group?

2. *Describing* Describe any personal experience you have had with ethnocentric conflict.

Using Your Notes

3. *Describing* Use the notes you took during the lesson to compare and contrast the different theories that explain aggression.

Answering the Guiding Questions

4. *Examining* Why might excessive punishment not be the best response to childhood aggression?

5. *Explaining* How did experimenters create intergroup hostility at the Robbers Cave camp?

6. *Identifying* Why would deindividuation make a group member less likely to be altruistic?

Writing Activity

7. *Informative/Explanatory* Some people like to listen to music at high volume. Describe how one person's right to exercise their freedom in this area may conflict with the freedom of others.

Directions: On a separate sheet of paper, answer the questions below. Make sure you read carefully and answer all parts of the question.

Lesson Review

Lesson 1

1 *Describing* What factors work to hold a group together? What factors increase the commitment of a person to the group?

2 *Contrasting* What is the difference between an in-group and an out-group? Give an example of each.

Lesson 2

3 *Examining* Why do people conform?

4 *Specifying* How is compliance related to conformity?

Lesson 3

5 *Discussing* How does the cognitive theory explain aggression?

6 *Summarizing* What is deindividuation, and how does it occur?

College and Career Readiness

7 *Personal and Group Identities* Use the Internet to research a few universities or colleges that most interest you. How many student organizations can you find at each one? What types of organizations are they? What is the purpose and makeup of each organization? Which ones interest you the most? Why? Would you consider joining that group if you attended that school? Create a report documenting your findings.

Research and Technology

8 *Researching* Think of a cause or an issue about which you feel strongly. Use the library and the Internet to find task-oriented groups that address this cause or issue. Find the e-mail address of the organization and send an e-mail to find out more about the group's goals and the ways that you might become involved. Share the information you collected, your sources, and any e-mail responses with the class.

21st Century Skills

Using Graphs Milgram was upset about the willingness of his participants to obey an authority. In later experiments, he tried to find ways to reduce obedience. He found that distance between the teacher and the learner had an effect. The graph shows the percentage of "teachers" who obeyed orders at three different physical distances. Review the graph, and then answer the questions below.

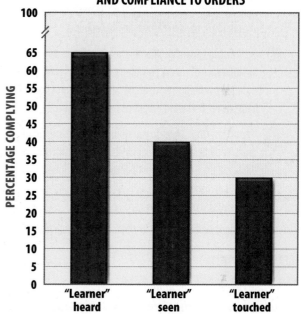

PHYSICAL DISTANCE FROM "LEARNER" AND COMPLIANCE TO ORDERS

9 *Analyzing Visuals* What percentage of teachers obeyed orders when they could only hear the learner?

10 *Analyzing Visuals* What happened to the percentage of teachers who obeyed orders when they were in the same room and could see the learner? When they were asked to touch the learner?

11 *Interpreting* What reasons can you give for the differences in the percentage of participants obeying authority in the three physical distances illustrated in the graph?

Need Extra Help?

If You've Missed Question	1	2	3	4	5	6	7	8	9	10	11
Go to page	558	556	565	567	577	582	557	559	568	568	568

Directions: On a separate sheet of paper, answer the questions below. Make sure you read carefully and answer all parts of the question.

Critical Thinking Questions

12 *Analyzing* Choose a person in your community whom you consider to be a leader. What qualities does this person have that make him or her a leader? How does the person demonstrate the characteristics of leadership?

13 *Speculating* Do you think it is possible for an individual to never have to conform to a group? Use online resources to find support for your answer.

14 *Defending* Which psychological theory discussed in the chapter do you think best explains the reasons for aggression? Provide reasons for your opinion.

15 *Explaining* Search online for professional opinions about the influence of media on violence. Report your results and explain how being aware of the causes of aggression can help people find ways to reduce violence in society.

16 *Hypothesizing* How do you think being a gang member can take away a person's social freedoms and power and at the same time increase hostility toward or from others?

DBQ Analyzing Primary Sources

Use the document below to answer the following questions.

PRIMARY SOURCE

"*Clinicians working with culturally diverse clients need to be of any color, the issue here is to be empathic, to aim to be culturally competent, to be present, and to have a willingness to understand the cultural background of the client. So yes, we all can work with culturally diverse clients if we are committed to becoming culturally competent, regardless of color.*"

—*Lillian Comas-Díaz*

17 *Analyzing* What makes Comas-Díaz's view a sociocultural view of psychology?

18 *Discussing* What do you think Comas-Díaz means by "culturally competent"? Explain your answer.

Exploring the Essential Question

19 *Researching* Groupthink occurs when group discussions stress agreement rather than critical thinking. The invasion of Iraq was one result of groupthink. Research other historical events that were the result of groupthink, such as the Bay of Pigs invasion, Watergate, or the *Challenger* disaster. Find out the background of these events and how groupthink contributed to the outcomes. Present your findings in an oral report.

20 *Researching* Research examples of extreme group conformity and obedience. You might find out about David Koresh and the Branch Davidians or Jim Jones and Peoples Temple. Research the general characteristics of the people who joined the groups and the reasons given for the leaders' ability to command such obedience. Share your findings in a documentary report or electronic slide show presentation.

21 *Exploring Issues* Create an illustrated and captioned poster that provides strategies for teenagers to use to control aggression and reduce conflict. Include persuasion, compromise, debate, and negotiation as possible strategies. Then role-play an improvised conflict and use the strategies in the poster to provide a resolution.

Psychology Journal Activity

22 *Informative/Explanatory* Review your entry in your Psychology Journal. Having learned in this chapter about the pressure to conform, describe an occasion when you felt this pressure.

Need Extra Help?

If You've Missed Question	**12**	**13**	**14**	**15**	**16**	**17**	**18**	**19**	**20**	**21**	**22**
Go to page	562	565	576	578	580	580	580	561	571	578	554

Attitudes and Social Influence

ESSENTIAL QUESTION • *How does culture influence behavior?*

netw⬤rks

There's More Online about attitudes and social influence.

CHAPTER 20

Lab Activity
Persuading People:
Emotions vs. Facts

Lesson 1
Attitude Formation

Lesson 2
Attitude Change
and Prejudice

Lesson 3
Persuasion

Psychology Matters...

If you have ever been asked, "How would you describe yourself? Do you see yourself as a hard worker? Are you open-minded? Do you have strong spiritual or political views?" then you have been asked to express your attitudes. Over the years, studying how people develop attitudes has been an important part of psychology. Understanding the factors that influence our beliefs and feelings helps us understand the factors that influence the way we think.

◄ Politicians use a variety of tactics to influence people's attitudes.

Digital Vision/Getty Images

585

Lab Activity

Persuading People:
Emotions vs. Facts

THE QUESTION...

RESEARCH QUESTION How important is emotional language in the process of persuasion?

If you wanted to protect a local forest from being turned into lumber, how would you try to persuade your fellow citizens? What would you put on your poster? Would you fill the poster with tables of data about the ecosystem? Or would you describe the beauty of the forest and how much people enjoy it? Both methods are valuable, but which is best? Advertisers and interest groups face this question every day, and the question remains a major topic in social psychological research.

In this experiment, we will explore the connection between emotion and persuasion.

Psychology Journal Activity

Do you think you are influenced by advertising? Write about this in your Psychology Journal. Consider the following issues: What methods and styles, in particular, do you find have the most influence on you?

FINDING THE ANSWER...

HYPOTHESIS Emotional language is more effective than dry facts in persuasive speeches.

THE METHOD OF YOUR EXPERIMENT

MATERIALS a factual speech, an emotional speech, paper, pen, calculator

PROCEDURE Write two short persuasive speeches on the same topic, such as why going to college is important or why one should avoid smoking. Speech #1 should consist of facts about the topic presented with dry logic, while Speech #2 should consist of facts about the topic presented with a strong emotional appeal. Recruit a fellow student to give both speeches in a similar manner and tone. Gather a group of ten or more listeners into a room. Have the student read both speeches. Then have the same student read the speeches in the opposite order to another group of ten listeners, as a control. After the speeches, have listeners write down how persuasive each speech was on a scale of 1 to 5, with 1 meaning "not persuasive" and 5 meaning "very persuasive."

DATA COLLECTION Gather the responses and calculate the average score for each rated speech.

ANALYSIS & APPLICATION

1. Did your results support the hypothesis? If so, why do you think Speech #2 was more persuasive?

2. Why was it important to deliver the two speeches in a similar manner and tone?

3. How else could you have measured the persuasiveness of the speeches?

netw⬤rks ONLINE LAB RESOURCES

Online you will find:

- An **interactive lab experience**, allowing you to put principles from this chapter into practice in a digital psychology lab environment. This chapter's lab will include an experiment on issues related to attitudes and social influence.

- A **Skills Handbook** that includes a guide for using the scientific method, creating experiments, and analyzing data.

- A **Notebook** where you can complete your Psychology Journal and record and analyze data from your experiment.

There's More Online!

☑ **CHART** A Theory of Planned
 Behavior

☑ **CHART** Attitude Formation
 Through Classical Conditioning

☑ **SELF-CHECK QUIZ**

Academic Vocabulary

• **exposure** • **maintain**

Content Vocabulary

• **attitude**
• **self-concept**

TAKING NOTES:
*Integration of Knowledge
and Ideas*

DIAGRAMMING Use a graphic
organizer like the one below to show
the three basic functions of attitudes.

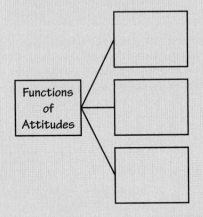

LESSON 1

Attitude Formation

ESSENTIAL QUESTION • *How does culture influence behavior?*

IT MATTERS BECAUSE

*We are constantly developing new attitudes or modifying existing ones.
For example, you may have a favorite brand of jeans. One day you try on
a different brand and decide they fit you better. Suddenly, your attitude
toward your old brand changes. Adjusting our attitudes helps us adapt
to our changing world. Understanding the factors that affect our
attitudes helps us to understand how we are influenced.*

The Source of Attitude

GUIDING QUESTION *What role does conditioning play in learning attitudes?*

What do you accept as fact? What do you call products of fantasy? Your
attitudes can lead you to believe that something is fact when it is really
imaginary or that something is not real when it really is fact. An **attitude**
is a predisposition to respond in particular ways toward specific things.
An attitude has three main elements: (1) a belief or opinion about something, (2) feelings about that thing, and (3) a tendency to act toward that
thing in certain ways. For example, what is your attitude toward the congressional representatives from your state? Do you *believe* they are doing
a good job? Do you *feel* that you trust or distrust them? Would you *act* to
vote for them?

 We have very definite beliefs, feelings, and responses to things about
which we have no firsthand knowledge. Where do these attitudes come
from? Attitudes are formed through conditioning, cognitive evaluation,
and other sources, such as observational learning.

Conditioning and Cognitive Evaluation

Classical conditioning can help you learn attitudes in different situations.
When a new stimulus (the conditioned stimulus, CS) is paired with a
stimulus that already causes a certain reaction (the unconditioned stimulus, US), the new stimulus begins to cause a reaction similar to the one
caused by the original stimulus. For instance, scientist Ivan Pavlov's dog
had a positive unconditioned response (UR) to meat—he liked to eat it.
When Pavlov paired the meat with the ringing of the tuning fork, the dog
formed a positive conditioned response (CR) to the sound of the tuning

fork. So when Pavlov's dog heard the sound of the tuning fork, he wagged his tail and salivated. We also acquire attitudes through operant conditioning; we receive praise, approval, or acceptance for expressing certain attitudes or we may be punished for expressing other attitudes.

Sometimes we develop attitudes toward something without thinking about it. For example, if our friend feels strongly about politics and uses many statistics or big words when speaking about a specific political issue, we may agree with her simply because she sounds like she knows what she is talking about. We have used a *heuristic,* a mental shortcut, to form an attitude.

However, we may sit down and systematically think about an issue that affects us directly. For example, if your friend speaks strongly about State College and its credentials, you may not simply accept her argument. You may evaluate the pros and cons of State College versus State University when selecting the college to attend. This matter is important, and you do not want to rely on shortcuts.

attitude predisposition to act, think, and feel in particular ways toward a class of people, objects, or an idea

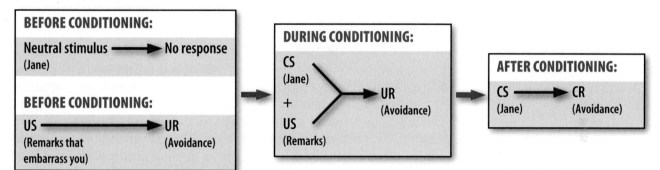

Other Sources

Your attitudes are also shaped by other forces. You may develop your attitudes by watching and imitating others—through observational learning. These forces are at work when you interact with others. For example, you may adopt your parents' political views or dress like your friends do. The culture in which you grew up, the people who raised you, and those with whom you associate all shape your attitudes. You also learn many of your attitudes through direct experience. For instance, you might have a negative attitude toward electric cars, but given the opportunity to drive one, you might develop a favorable attitude toward them.

Culture influences everything from our taste in food to our attitudes toward human relationships and our political opinions. For example, most Americans would consider eating grubs, curdled milk spiced with cattle blood, or monkey meat disgusting. Yet in some parts of the world these are considered delicacies. Indeed, it is only by traveling and reading about other ways of life that we discover how many of the things we take for granted are *attitudes,* not facts.

There is abundant evidence that all of us acquire many basic attitudes from our parents. How else would you account for the finding that a high percentage of elementary schoolchildren favor the same political party as their parents? As adults, more than two-thirds of all voters continue to favor the political party their parents supported. Parental influence wanes as children get older, of course.

It is not surprising that parental influence declines as children get older and their **exposure** to many other sources of influence increases. Starting in 1934, Theodore Newcomb questioned and requestioned students at Bennington College in Vermont about their political attitudes over a period of four years. Most of the young women came from wealthy, staunchly conservative families. In contrast, most of the Bennington faculty members were outspoken liberals.

exposure the act or condition of being subject to some effect or influence

maintain to make something continue at the same level or standard

Newcomb found that many of the students adopted the liberal point of view of the faculty. For instance, in 1936, 54 percent of the juniors and seniors supported the reelection of liberal president Franklin D. Roosevelt and his New Deal over the conservative Republican candidate Alf Landon.

Newcomb contacted the participants of his study 25 years after they had graduated and found that most had **maintained** the attitudes they had acquired in college. One reason was that they had chosen friends, spouses, and careers that supported liberal values. People tend to adopt the likes and dislikes of groups whose approval and acceptance they seek.

The Mere-Exposure Effect

One further determinant of attitudes is the mere-exposure effect—the more frequently people encounter an object or idea, the more favorably they evaluate it. You may have experienced this by listening to a song over and over again and growing to like that song even more. Another example occurs when we do not like foods when we first taste them, but after eating them more often, discover they have become some of our favorites.

The mere-exposure effect also applies to our attitudes toward other individuals. Friendly interactions with others make us feel more comfortable around them and lead to more favorable opinions of those individuals. Candidates for political office use the mere-exposure effect by constantly advertising during campaigns.

☑ **READING PROGRESS CHECK**

Analyzing How do family and peers affect our attitudes?

Functions of Attitudes

GUIDING QUESTION *How do our attitudes help us organize our reality?*

Why do we have attitudes? How do they help us in everyday functions and interactions with others? Attitudes reflect our beliefs and values as we define ourselves, help us to interpret the objects and events we encounter, and determine how we may act in given situations.

Attitudes As a Self-Defining Mechanism

Ask a friend to describe herself. How does she do it? Maybe she says she has long brown hair or green eyes. She may say she is a good soccer player or likes to dance. She also may include some of her attitudes, or values, saying that she likes to help others, or tries to be a good student, or supports equal rights. Her attitudes help her to define who she is, establishing her goals and her ideas about right and wrong. They make up her self-concept. Our **self-concept** refers to the way we see or describe ourselves. If you have a positive self-concept, you will tend to act and feel optimistically and constructively. If you have a negative self-concept, you will tend to act and feel pessimistically.

self-concept how we see or describe ourselves; our total perception of ourselves

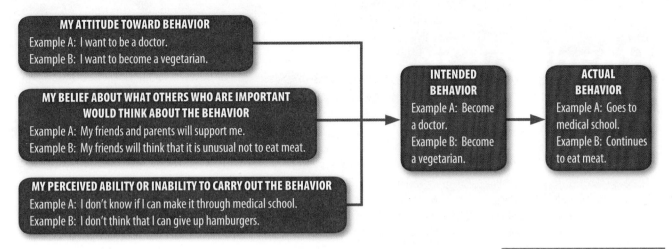

MY ATTITUDE TOWARD BEHAVIOR
Example A: I want to be a doctor.
Example B: I want to become a vegetarian.

MY BELIEF ABOUT WHAT OTHERS WHO ARE IMPORTANT
WOULD THINK ABOUT THE BEHAVIOR
Example A: My friends and parents will support me.
Example B: My friends will think that it is unusual not to eat meat.

MY PERCEIVED ABILITY OR INABILITY TO CARRY OUT THE BEHAVIOR
Example A: I don't know if I can make it through medical school.
Example B: I don't think that I can give up hamburgers.

INTENDED BEHAVIOR
Example A: Become a doctor.
Example B: Become a vegetarian.

ACTUAL BEHAVIOR
Example A: Goes to medical school.
Example B: Continues to eat meat.

Social groups as well as individuals hold attitudes. People who live the same way and who frequently communicate with one another tend to hold similar attitudes because they are exposed to the same information. People also form groups because they hold similar attitudes.

Attitudes As Cognitive Guidelines and Guides to Action

Attitudes affect the way we interpret and categorize people, objects, and events. They also affect our behavior, guiding us toward or away from certain people, objects, and events. We may link negative feelings with dark alleys and positive feelings with friendly people, so we avoid the former and approach the latter.

Our attitudes are not always consistent with our behaviors. You might agree that littering is wrong but still occasionally throw a candy wrapper on the ground. You may believe that bullying is wrong, and then join in—or pretend you do not notice—when your peers make fun of a younger student or taunt someone they do not like.

Behavior and attitudes will be more consistent if the attitudes were acquired through direct experience. If you do not eat meat because eating meat once made you sick, the smell of a grilled hamburger probably will not tempt you. If you do not eat meat for strictly moral reasons, you might give in and eat that grilled hamburger if you find the aroma tempting. So, attitudes do play a role in determining behavior, but this role varies according to different circumstances.

✔ READING PROGRESS CHECK

Analyzing How can attitudes help us determine what actions to take?

∧ CHART

A THEORY OF PLANNED BEHAVIOR
Psychologists have proposed a theory that three factors determine a person's behavior. The strength or weakness of each of these three factors explains why certain people behave differently despite shared attitudes.

▶ CRITICAL THINKING

1. *Identifying* What factors other than attitude determine a person's behavior?

2. *Making Connections* Give an example of when the third factor made a difference in your life.

LESSON 1 REVIEW

Reviewing Vocabulary
1. *Explaining* How do attitudes help us develop our self-concept?

Using Your Notes
2. *Applying* Review the notes that you completed during the lesson to give an example of how each of the three basic functions of attitudes works.

Answering the Guiding Questions
3. *Making Connections* What role does conditioning play in learning attitudes?

4. *Drawing Conclusions* How do our attitudes help us organize our reality?

Writing Activity
5. *Informative/Explanatory* Investigate how advertisers use classical conditioning to influence our attitudes. Locate an example of an advertisement that uses classical conditioning and, in a brief report, analyze the advertiser's technique. Use valid reasoning and specific evidence from the advertisement in your analysis.

Analyzing
Readings in Psychology

Reader's Dictionary

commissioned: ordered or authorized (a person or organization) to do or produce something

pilot study: a small scale preliminary study

attributes: qualities or features

interpretative: providing an explanation for or meaning of

definitive: done or reached decisively and with authority

How do attitudes about race form, and have these attitudes evolved since the era of the civil rights movement and desegregation of schools? According to a recently conducted pilot study, children, regardless of race, still show a bias towards lighter skin. This article examines the pilot study and its implications and questions lingering stereotypes.

Study: White and Black Children
Biased
Toward Lighter Skin

CNN U.S.

PRIMARY SOURCE

A white child looks at a picture of a black child and says she's bad because she's black. A black child says a white child is ugly because he's white. A white child says a black child is dumb because she has dark skin.

This isn't a schoolyard fight that takes a racial turn, not a vestige of the "Jim Crow" South; these are American schoolchildren in 2010.

Nearly 60 years after American schools were desegregated by the landmark Brown v. Board of Education ruling, and more than a year after the election of the country's first black president, white children have an overwhelming white bias, and black children also have a bias toward white, according to a new study **commissioned** by CNN.

Renowned child psychologist and University of Chicago professor Margaret Beale Spencer, a leading researcher in the field of child development, was hired as a consultant by CNN. She designed the **pilot study** and used a team of three psychologists to implement it:

two testers to execute the study and a statistician to help analyze the results.

Her team tested 133 children from schools that met very specific economic and demographic requirements. In total, eight schools participated: four in the greater New York City area and four in Georgia.

In each school, the psychologists tested children from two age groups: 4 to 5 and 9 to 10.

Since this is a pilot study and not a fully funded scientific study, the sample size and race selection were limited. But according to Spencer, it was satisfactory to yield conclusive results. A pilot study is normally the first step in creating a larger scientific study and often speaks to overall trends that require more research.

Spencer's test aimed to re-create the landmark Doll Test from the 1940s. Those tests, conducted by psychologists Kenneth and Mamie Clark, were designed to measure how segregation affected African-American children.

The Clarks asked black children to choose between a white doll and—because at the time, no brown dolls were available—a white doll painted brown. They asked black children a series of questions and found they overwhelmingly preferred white over brown. The study and its conclusions were used in the 1954 Brown v. Board of Education case, which led to the desegregation of American schools.

In the new study, Spencer's researchers asked the younger children a series of questions and had them

have that extra task of basically reframing messages that children get from society."

Spencer was also surprised that children's ideas about race, for the most part, don't evolve as they get older. The study showed that children's ideas about race change little from age 5 to age 10.

> "[T]he white youngsters are even more stereotypic in their responses concerning attitudes, beliefs and attitudes and preferences than the African-American children."

"The fact that there were no differences between younger children, who are very spontaneous because of where they are developmentally, versus older children, who are more thoughtful, given where they are in their thinking, I was a little surprised that we did not find differences."

Spencer said the study points to major trends but is not the **definitive** word on children and race. It does lead her to conclude that even in 2010, "we are still living in a society where dark things are devalued and white things are valued."

answer by pointing to one of five cartoon pictures that varied in skin color from light to dark. The older children were asked the same questions using the same cartoon pictures, and were then asked a series of questions about a color bar chart that showed light to dark skin tones.

The tests showed that white children, as a whole, responded with a high rate of what researchers call "white bias," identifying the color of their own skin with positive **attributes** and darker skin with negative attributes. Spencer said even black children, as a whole, have some bias toward whiteness, but far less than white children.

"All kids on the one hand are exposed to the stereotypes" she said. "What's really significant here is that white children are learning or maintaining those stereotypes much more strongly than the African-American children. Therefore, the white youngsters are even more stereotypic in their responses concerning attitudes, beliefs and attitudes and preferences than the African-American children."

Spencer says this may be happening because "parents of color in particular had the extra burden of helping to function as an **interpretative** wedge for their children. Parents have to reframe what children experience...and the fact that white children and families don't have to engage in that level of parenting, I think, does suggest a level of entitlement. You can spend more time on spelling, math and reading, because you don't

Analyzing Primary Sources

1. **Making Inferences** Why did the researchers decide to recreate a study from the 1940s?

2. **Interpreting** What does Spencer mean when she says, "parents of color in particular had the extra burden of helping to function as an interpretative wedge for their children"?

3. **Exploring Issues** How could the findings of this study be put to use in programs to combat racism and promote tolerance?

LESSON 2
Attitude Change and Prejudice

Reading **HELP**DESK (CCSS)

Academic Vocabulary

• injure   • status

Content Vocabulary

• compliance
• identification
• internalization
• cognitive dissonance
• counterattitudinal behavior
• self-justification
• prejudice

TAKING NOTES:
Integration of Knowledge and Ideas

IDENTIFYING CAUSE AND EFFECT
Use a graphic organizer like the one below to show the three main processes that cause people to develop attitudes.

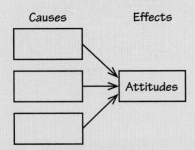

ESSENTIAL QUESTION • *How does culture influence behavior?*

IT MATTERS BECAUSE

Have you ever believed in one thing but done something else? Attitudes often influence our behavior, but the two are not as directly linked as you might think. Psychologists work to understand the connections between our beliefs and how we act on them. These connections are complex and are influenced by both internal and external factors.

Attitude Change

GUIDING QUESTION *Which attitude type is the most stable and long lasting?*

Suppose that you signed up for a class on American literature. You have taken other literature classes and enjoyed them. Plus your best friend will be in the class and he loves to talk about the books he is currently reading. So even before you start the class, you are looking forward to it—you have developed a positive attitude about the class.

People constantly develop and modify their attitudes. Understanding why we do this helps us understand how attitudes are formed. The three main processes involved in forming or changing attitudes are compliance, identification, and internalization. If you like a film director because everyone else does, you are complying. If you agree with everything a friend you admire says about the director, you are identifying. If you genuinely like the director's work and, regardless of what other people think, consider it brilliant, you are expressing an internalized attitude.

Compliance

One of the best measures of attitude is behavior. If a man settles back into his chair after dinner, launches into a discussion of his support for the women's rights movement, then shouts to his wife—who is in the kitchen washing dishes—to bring more coffee, you probably would not believe what he is saying. His actions speak louder than his words. Yet the same man might hire women for jobs he has always considered "men's work" because the law requires him to do so. He also might finally accept his wife's going to work because he knows that she, their children, and many of their friends would consider him old-fashioned if he did not. People often adapt their actions to the wishes of others to avoid discomfort or rejection and to gain support. This is called **compliance**. Under such circumstances, social pressure often results in temporary compliance, but attitudes do not really change. We shall see that compliance can sometimes affect one's beliefs.

Identification

One way in which attitudes may be formed or changed is through the process of **identification**. Suppose you have a favorite uncle who is everything you hope to be. He is a successful musician, has many famous friends, and seems to know a great deal about everything. In many ways you identify with him and copy his behavior. One night, during an intense conversation, your uncle asks you why you do not vote. At first, you feel defensive and argumentative. You say it does not matter, that your vote would not make a difference. As you listen to your uncle, however, you find yourself starting to agree with him. If a person as knowledgeable and respectable as your uncle believes it is important to vote, then perhaps you should, too. Later you find yourself eager to take part in the political process. You have adopted a new attitude because of your identification with your uncle.

Identification occurs when a person wants to define himself or herself in terms of a person or group and therefore adopts the person's or group's attitudes and ways of behaving. Identification is different from compliance because the individual actually believes the newly adopted views. Yet because these attitudes are based on emotional attachment to another person or group rather than the person's own assessment of the issues, they are fragile. If the person's attachment to that person or group fades, the attitudes may also weaken.

Previously, you read that adolescents move away from peer groups and toward independence as they grow older. If this is true, do attitudes stabilize with age? In 1989 two psychologists, Jon A. Krosnick and Duane F. Alwin, presented a study of the political and social attitudes of groups of people of various ages over an extended period. Those in the 18 to 25 age group were the most likely to change their attitudes; those age 34 and older held attitudes that were essentially stable. As self-critiquing and self-analysis decline through late adolescence and into adulthood, attitudes become more stable.

Internalization

The wholehearted acceptance of an attitude is **internalization**. The attitude becomes an integral part of the person. Internalization is most likely to occur when an attitude is consistent with a person's basic beliefs and values and supports his or her self-image. The person adopts a new attitude because he or she believes it is right to do so, not because he or she wants to be like someone else.

Internalization is the most lasting of the three sources of attitude formation or change. Your internalized attitudes will be more resistant to pressure from other people because your reasons for holding these views have nothing to do with other people. They are based on your own evaluation of the merits of the issue. In the study conducted by Newcomb at Bennington College, a student put it this way: "I became liberal at first because of its prestige value; I remain so because the problems around which my liberalism centers are important. What I want now is to be effective in solving problems."

As this example suggests, compliance or identification may lead to the internalization of an attitude. Often the three overlap. You may support a political candidate in part because you know your friends will approve, in part because someone you admire speaks highly of the candidate, and in part because you believe his or her ideals are consistent with your own.

☑ **READING PROGRESS CHECK**

Evaluating Why is identification an important way of shaping attitudes?

More
ABOUT...

The Just-World Bias

When watching movies, we expect the evil character to get punished. Psychologists label this tendency the *just-world bias*. We need to believe that life is fair and we have control over our environment. To think otherwise—that life is unfair, so something terrible could happen to us no matter what we do—makes us extremely uncomfortable. The just-world bias, then, motivates us to work hard and be good to ensure our well-being. However, the just-world bias may cause us to develop prejudice against those who suffer misfortunes.

To maintain our belief that life is fair, we reason that those who are worse off than we are somehow deserve their lot. We blame the victim. For example, we may say that the woman who was robbed last night should not have been walking alone at night.

compliance a change or maintenance of behavior to avoid discomfort or rejection and to gain approval

identification seeing oneself as similar to another person or group and accepting the attitudes of another person or group as one's own

internalization incorporating the values, ideas, and standards of others as a part of oneself

Cognitive Consistency

GUIDING QUESTION *What are some methods people use to reduce cognitive dissonance?*

Many social psychologists have theorized that people's attitudes change because they are always trying to get things to fit together logically inside their heads. The ability to avoid contradictions between or among our attitudes and behaviors is called *cognitive consistency.* Holding two opposing attitudes, or being in a state of cognitive inconsistency, can create great conflict in an individual, throwing him or her off balance. A doctor who smokes, a person who wants children but dislikes being around them, and a battered wife who believes her husband loves her have one thing in common: they are in cognitive conflict.

DIAGRAM >

BALANCE THEORY
According to Fritz Heider's Balance Theory—another means of analyzing cognitions related to attitudes—people are inclined to achieve consistency in their attitudes by balancing their beliefs and feelings about an object, person, or event against their attitudes about other people. When someone we care about strongly disagrees with us, an uncomfortable state of imbalance occurs.

▶ **CRITICAL THINKING**

1. Drawing Conclusions What do you think we do when we become involved in a state of imbalance?

2. Speculating According to Heider's theory, what might have happened if Rick had continued to like Latisha?

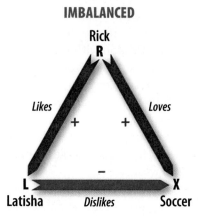

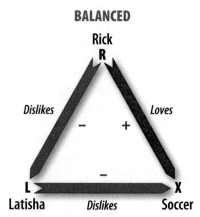

cognitive dissonance the uncomfortable feeling when a person experiences contradictory or conflicting thoughts, attitudes, beliefs, or feelings

Leon Festinger proposed the theory that people in these types of situations experience cognitive dissonance. **Cognitive dissonance** is the uncomfortable feeling that arises when a person's behavior conflicts with his or her other thoughts, beliefs, attitudes, feelings, or even other behaviors. To reduce dissonance, it is necessary to change either the behavior or the conflicting attitudes.

People reduce dissonance in several ways. Some deny the dissonance, pretending it did not happen. When faced with information on the health hazards of smoking, for instance, a smoker may convince himself that smoking has never been proven to cause health problems and discount the information as propaganda by antismoking groups.

Some people attempt to evade dissonance by avoiding exposure to information that would create conflict. For example, they may make a point of reading only newspapers and magazines that agree with their political attitudes, of surrounding themselves with people who share the same ideas. It is not surprising that such people get quite upset when a piece of conflicting information finally does get through.

Some people, when experiencing cognitive dissonance, decide to change their attitude and/or reevaluate the event that caused the dissonance. This might happen when a person is faced with new information that does not support her old beliefs or behaviors and she decides to revise and reform her attitude. For instance, a reformed smoker might have finally considered the evidence against smoking, decided to become health-conscious, and then quit smoking. The process of dissonance reduction does not always take place consciously, but it is a frequent and powerful occurrence.

☑ **READING PROGRESS CHECK**

Analyzing Why do people try to reduce cognitive dissonance?

Attitudes and Actions

GUIDING QUESTION *How can self-justification be used to justify prejudice?*

Social psychologists have discovered several interesting relationships between attitudes and actions. Obviously, attitudes affect actions: if a car buyer likes Fords, she will buy a Ford. Some of the other relationships are not so obvious. It turns out, for example, that if a person likes Fords but buys a Chevrolet for some reason (perhaps he was able to get a better deal on a Chevy), he will usually end up liking Fords less. In other words, actions affect attitudes.

In many instances, if you act and speak as though you have certain beliefs and feelings, you may begin to *really* feel and believe this way. This phenomenon is called **counterattitudinal behavior**, and it is a method of reducing cognitive dissonance. For example, people accused of a crime have confessed to crimes they did not commit. They confessed to relieve the pressure; but having said that they did the deed, they begin to believe that they really *are* guilty.

One explanation for this phenomenon comes from the theory of cognitive dissonance. If a person acts one way but thinks another, he or she will experience dissonance, or a conflict, between their thoughts and actions. To reduce the internal conflict presented by cognitive dissonance, the person will have to change either the behavior or the attitude. A similar explanation is that people have a need for **self-justification**—a need to justify their behavior.

In an experiment that demonstrated these principles, participants were paid either $1 or $20 (roughly $5 and $100 in today's currency) to tell another person that a boring experiment in which they both had to participate was really a lot of fun. Afterward, the experimenters asked the participants how they felt about the experiment. They found that the participants who had been paid $20 to lie about the experiment continued to believe that it had been boring. Those who had been paid $1, however, came to believe that the experiment had actually been fairly enjoyable. These people had less reason to tell the lie, so they experienced more dissonance when they did so. To justify their lie, they had to believe that they had actually enjoyed the experiment.

The phenomenon of self-justification has serious implications. For example, how would you justify to yourself that you had intentionally **injured** another human being? In another psychological experiment, participants were led to believe that they had injured or hurt other participants in some way. The aggressors were then asked how they felt about the victims they had just harmed. It was found that the aggressors had convinced themselves that they did not like the victims of their cruelty. In other words, the aggressors talked themselves into believing that their defenseless victims had deserved their injury. The aggressors also considered their victims to be less attractive after the experiment than before—their self-justification for hurting another person was something like "Oh, well, this person doesn't amount to much, anyway."

Self-Fulfilling Prophecy

Another relationship between attitudes and actions is rather subtle but extremely widespread. It is possible, it seems, for a person to act in such a way as to make his or her beliefs come true. This phenomenon is called a *self-fulfilling prophecy*. Self-fulfilling prophecies can influence all kinds of human activity. Suppose you believe that people are basically friendly and generous. Whenever you approach others you are friendly and open because you expect friendliness an openness in return. Because of your smile and positive attitude towards those that you meet, people respond to you in kind. Thus your belief that people are friendly produces your friendly behavior, which in turn causes people to respond favorably toward you. Your belief might not be correct, but your actions make it seem so.

Profiles in Psychology

Kenneth B. Clark
(1914–2005)

Kenneth B. Clark was an African American educator and psychologist. He spent his life fighting against racism because he believed the "racist system inevitably destroys and damages human beings; it brutalizes and dehumanizes them, black and white alike."

In 1950, Clark was involved in a study that showed school segregation seriously harmed both black and white students. This pioneering study was cited in the 1954 U.S. Supreme Court's ruling in *Brown v. Board of Education*, which declared that segregation is illegal in public schools.

▶ **CRITICAL THINKING**

Drawing Conclusions Why did Clark state that segregation damages both blacks and whites?

counterattitudinal behavior the process of taking a public position that contradicts one's private attitude

self-justification the need to rationalize one's attitude and behavior

injure to cause harm to or hurt

Suppose you turn this example around. Imagine that you believe people are selfish and cold. Because of your negative attitude, you avert your eyes from other people, act gloomy and withdrawn, and appear rather unfriendly. People think your actions are unpleasant or strange, and consequently, they avoid you or react coldly toward you. Your belief produced the behavior that made the belief come into being.

One type of self-fulfilling prophecy has been called the "Pygmalion effect." Pygmalion was an ancient Greek artist who created a sculpture of a woman that was so lifelike she became real. In the Pygmalion effect one person's expectations of another are validated when the other person's behavior conforms to the expectation. The Pygmalion effect has been studied frequently in classrooms and is the basis for many educational reforms in recent years. When teachers have high expectations for their students, the students will generally show above-average intellectual growth to meet those expectations. Conversely, when teachers have low expectations, students often perform at a lower level. In one famous example, called the Oak School experiment, researcher Robert Rosenthal told teachers that specific students (actually chosen at random), were expected to show signs of an intellectual growth spurt that year. By the end of the year those students did show significant gains, an average of more than 12 points on an IQ test compared to more than 8 points for the control group. This effect has been shown to operate at elementary, secondary, and college levels as well.

Prejudice

Prejudice means, literally, prejudgment. *Prejudice* means deciding beforehand what a person will be like instead of withholding judgment until it can be based on that individual's qualities or behavior. A *stereotype* is a generalization about all members of a group. All of us have stereotypes for the various people we meet, in which we make assumptions about them and have expectations about how they will behave. For instance, many of us have a stereotype for librarians that leads us to expect them to act a certain way in the library. To hold a stereotype about a group of people is not to be prejudiced, unless the stereotype contains biased information that is not revised after interacting with people from that group. Failing to revise a stereotype can result in prejudice.

Prejudice can be applied in both positive and negative ways—someone who is prejudiced against women is often equally prejudiced in favor of men, for example. However, negative prejudices pose a serious problem. Negative prejudices are often socially divisive. Negative prejudice can also result in personal harm when victims of prejudice are belittled, harassed, and excluded.

Prejudice is strengthened and maintained by inflexible stereotypes and rigid views of roles. Various racial, cultural, occupational, economic, and gender groups have been viewed and treated only as stereotypes rather than as individuals. A *role* is a response pattern structured by group membership.

prejudice preconceived attitudes toward a person or group that have been formed without sufficient evidence and are not easily changed

Racial groups are not the only targets for prejudicial attitudes and treatment. Gender, social or economic status, origin, age, ethnicity, religious belief, and physical or mental disability are also factors that may engender prejudice in some people.

▶ **CRITICAL THINKING**

Identifying Bias Describe how something that you have seen or heard in American media reinforces or counters prejudice.

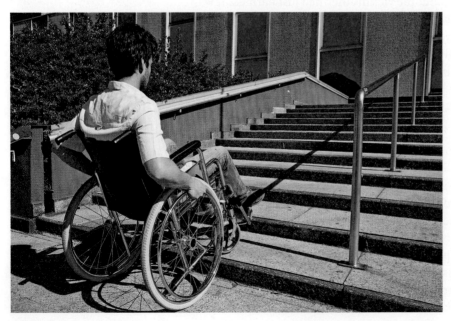
©Ocean/Corbis

Stereotypes and roles can act together in a way that makes them difficult to alter. For example, many whites once had a stereotype of minority racial groups, believing them to be irresponsible, superstitious, or unintelligent. Whites who believed this expected members of the racial group to act out a role that was consistent with a stereotype. Members of the targeted racial group were expected to be submissive, deferential, and respectful toward whites, who acted out the role of the superior, condescending parent. In the past, many people accepted these roles and looked at themselves and each other according to these stereotypes. Since the middle of the twentieth century, members of targeted racial groups have successfully stepped out of these roles and worked to eliminate the stereotypes.

In 1989, psychologist Patricia Devine proposed a model to explain the relationships between stereotypes and prejudice. She theorizes that if a specific stimulus is encountered, it automatically activates your stereotype mechanism. For example, if you see an elderly man or woman, it activates your stereotype of old people. Devine suggests that what separates prejudiced from nonprejudiced people is their ability to inhibit negative attitudes. If you can do so, your response will be nonprejudiced; if you cannot restrain your negative beliefs, you will respond in a prejudiced manner.

Diversity in Psychology

PREJUDICE IN TREATMENT

Members of some ethnic and racial groups may be hesitant to seek treatment for psychological difficulties. The reasons are varied and complex. For example, they may lack the financial resources or not know how to get help with the related expenses. They also may be concerned that, if they seek treatment, they will be misunderstood or treated differently than others. This concern may increase if the psychotherapist is a member of a different racial or ethnic group than the potential client.

A survey funded by the National Institute of Mental Health reported that older adult members of ethnic and racial minorities are less likely to be treated for depression than whites in the same age group. About 7.2 percent of Hispanics, 6.4 percent of whites, and 4.2 percent of African Americans were diagnosed with depression. In all cases, treatment consisted of antidepressants, psychotherapy, or both. There were significant differences in the percentages of minorities in this age group who received treatment. Seventy percent of the whites were treated as compared to 63.4 percent of the Hispanics and 60 percent of the African Americans. Overall, the minorities had lower socioeconomic status and poorer health insurance coverage. However, these financial and coverage differences did not seem to account for the lower treatment rates. Other studies have suggested that these differences may have to do with the shame or stigma associated with mental disorders among certain groups.

Cross-cultural training for health care workers, including psychotherapists, can make these professionals more aware of differences in attitudes among various cultural and racial groups and increase the chances that minority groups will get needed treatment.

▲ Some potential clients may be more inclined to seek help when they know the therapist will not be prejudiced.

▶ **CRITICAL THINKING**

1. **Synthesizing** Why do you think members of ethnic or racial minority groups are afraid they may be treated differently when asking for help with psychological problems?

2. **Gathering Information** Go to the World Health Organization's (WHO) Web site (www.who.org). Conduct research to learn what kinds of cultural considerations WHO recommends when diagnosing psychological disorders.

Spencer Grant/PhotoEdit

Illusory Correlation

An illusory correlation occurs when we see a relationship between variables that are not really related. Philip Zimbardo, former president of the American Psychological Association, gives an excellent example of this phenomenon. Many years ago a failure in a power station caused a blackout to sweep the East Coast one evening. At that precise moment, a Little Leaguer in Boston was on his way home from a game, swinging his bat at everything as he walked. Then, just as his bat hit a lamppost, the lights of the entire city blinked out before his disbelieving eyes. Did *he* do *that*? No, it was just an illusory correlation.

status position or rank in relation to others

Another psychologist, Thomas Pettigrew, suggests that in situations in which a dominant group and a deferential group can be identified, members of each one of the groups may play roles that foster and maintain their respective positions. A member of a dominating group, for example, will speak first, interrupt more often, and talk louder and longer. A member of the deferential group will show courtesy and concern for the dominant member and do more listening and less interrupting.

Prejudice can be based on social, economic, or physical factors. Psychologists have found that people may be prejudiced against those less well-off than themselves—these people seem to justify being better off by assuming that anyone of lower **status** or income must be inferior. People who have suffered economic setbacks also tend to be prejudiced; they blame others for their misfortune. Prejudice also arises from "guilt by association." People who dislike cities and urban living, for example, tend to distrust people associated with cities. Also, people may be prejudiced in favor of those they see as similar to themselves and against those who seem different.

Whatever the original factor, prejudice seems to persist. One reason is that children who grow up in an atmosphere of prejudice conform to the prejudicial norm. That is, they are encouraged to conform to the thoughts and practices of their parents and other teachers.

Prejudice, which is an attitude, should be distinguished from discrimination, which is a behavioral expression of a prejudice. Discrimination results in the unequal treatment of members of certain groups. It is possible for a prejudiced person not to discriminate. He or she may recognize his or her prejudice and try not to act on it. Similarly, a person may discriminate, not out of prejudice, but in compliance with social or economic pressures.

☑ **READING PROGRESS CHECK**

Contrasting How is prejudice different from discrimination?

LESSON 2 REVIEW

Reviewing Vocabulary

1. *Describing* What is the relationship between attitudes and behavior in counterattitudinal behavior, self-justification, and self-fulfilling prophecy?

2. *Categorizing* A friend refuses to wear a helmet while riding her bike. She states that accidents do not happen to careful cyclists like her. What method is she using to reduce cognitive dissonance?

3. *Explaining* How is status linked to prejudice?

Using Your Notes

4. *Applying* Use your notes to choose one of the three main processes that can cause people to develop attitudes (compliance, identification, and internalization). Describe in detail how this process might lead to the development of a specific attitude.

Answering the Guiding Questions

5. *Identifying* Which attitude type is the most stable and long lasting?

6. *Listing* What are some methods people use to reduce cognitive dissonance?

7. *Making Connections* How can self-justification be used to justify prejudice?

Writing Activity

8. *Argument* Attitudes come from a variety of sources. What source do you think is the most influential in establishing the attitudes of the average high school student? Write an essay in which you defend your choice. In your essay, you should give specific examples of why you think your chosen source is the most influential.

Case Study

Feelings vs. Actions

Period of Study: 1934

Introduction: In the early days of psychology, researchers assumed that people's behavior could be predicted by measuring their attitudes and opinions. In 1934, researcher Richard LaPiere conducted a study designed to evaluate a person's attitudes and actions with situations regarding race. He studied the social attitudes of individuals and examined the connection between real behavior and symbolic behavior. *Symbolic behavior* refers to a person's statements regarding his or her actions in a hypothetical situation. LaPiere set out to test individuals' symbolic racial responses compared with their actual racial responses.

Hypothesis: LaPiere came up with the idea of studying racial behavior when he traveled across the United States with a young Chinese couple to conduct research on a different topic. During the 1930s, much racial prejudice targeted Asian Americans. LaPiere wondered if his companions would encounter racism in the form of compromised or denied service.

Method: LaPiere and the couple visited various restaurants, attempted to check in to hotels, and frequented other public service businesses. During these times, the couple was always confident and well-mannered. LaPiere tried to distance himself from the couple when they were being served. For example, while the couple was checking into a motel, LaPiere would busy himself unloading luggage from the trunk of the car. He did this so that individuals' responses to the couple would not be influenced by the fact that they were accompanied by a white person.

LaPiere recorded significant data regarding how the couple was treated. Only one of the 251 establishments they visited refused service to his friends. Given the climate of prejudice against people from Asia, LaPiere was curious about this and investigated the issue by sending questionnaires to the establishments that they had visited. The questionnaires simply asked if that establishment would provide services to a Chinese husband and wife. He received 128 completed questionnaires, or 51 percent of the total mailed.

Results: Only one of the 128 responding businesses said that it would serve a Chinese couple. The vast majority (90 percent) said that they would not serve the couple. Yet only one establishment had actually denied LaPiere's companions service. The attitudes reported by the business owners (symbolic behavior) did not seem to match their actual behaviors.

Even though questionnaires are not the ideal way to measure these relationships, this study suggested that the attitudes people report do not necessarily predict behavior. Nor does behavior reflect reported attitudes. Later studies confirmed and refined this general conclusion. The relationship between attitudes and behavior has proven to be a rich topic of study for social psychologists.

PRIMARY SOURCE

" LaPiere's (1934) seminal research into the attitude-behavior relationship has been commonly misinterpreted as pointing out a discrepancy between attitudes and behaviors. In fact, the actual discrepancy uncovered was between true attitudes—the tendency to act in a certain way—and that which is measured by an attitude questionnaire. LaPiere's primary concern was to point out the danger of assuming that questionnaire-assessed 'attitudes' lead to actual behavior in specific situations. "

—Terry M. Dockery and Arthur G. Bedeian, "Attitudes Versus Actions: LaPiere's (1934) Classic Study Revisited" (1989)

Analyzing the Case Study

1. *Finding the Main Idea* Use formal language to write a clear and concise summary of LaPiere's study.

2. *Analyzing Primary Sources* How does the quote explain the discrepancy LaPiere found between people's actions and their responses to the questionnaire?

3. *Speculating* Do you think the couple's behavior when being waited on might be an example of a self-fulfilling prophesy? Explain your answer.

4. *Problem-Solving* How do you think a similar experiment could be conducted today? What would need to be changed? Why?

LESSON 3

Persuasion

(l)Alex Wong/Getty Images News/Getty Images; (c)FDA/Newscom; (r)Bill Aron/PhotoEdit

Academic Vocabulary

• **source**   • **reject**

Content Vocabulary

• **boomerang effect**
• **sleeper effect**
• **inoculation effect**
• **brainwashing**

TAKING NOTES:

Key Ideas and Details

IDENTIFYING CENTRAL ISSUES
Use a graphic organizer like the one below to identify the parts of the communication process.

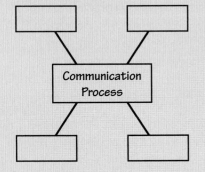

ESSENTIAL QUESTION • *How does culture influence behavior?*

⊙ IT MATTERS BECAUSE

Advertisers use persuasion to encourage consumers to buy their products. Psychologists have extensively studied the ways in which our attitudes can be influenced by these persuasive techniques. Because different methods affect us in unexpected ways, it is important that we are aware of them.

The Communication Process

GUIDING QUESTION *How does the foot-in-the-door technique differ from the door-in-the-face technique?*

Persuasion is a direct attempt to influence attitudes. At one time or another everyone engages in persuasion. Parents often attempt to persuade their children to conform to their values. Similarly, young people may try to persuade their parents that, for example, all their friends' parents are buying them smart phones. In both cases, the persuader's main hope is that by changing the other person's attitudes, he or she can change that person's behavior as well.

Enormous amounts of time, money, and effort go into campaigns to persuade people to change their attitudes and behavior. Some succeed on a grand scale, while others seem to have no effect. Discovering the elements of an effective persuasive communication is one of the most difficult problems confronted by social psychologists.

The communication process can be divided into four parts. The *message* itself is only one part. It is also important to consider the *source* of the message, the *channel* through which it is delivered, and the *audience* that receives it.

The Source

How a person sees the **source** of a message may be a critical factor in his or her acceptance of it. The person receiving the message asks three basic questions: Is the person giving the message trustworthy and sincere? Does he or she know anything about the subject? Is he or she likable? If the answers are yes, the message is more likely to be accepted.

Suppose, for example, that you wrote a paper criticizing a novel for your English class. A friend who reads the paper tells you about an article that praises the novel and asks you to reconsider your view. The article was written by a college student. You might change your opinion, or you might not. Suppose your friend tells you the same critique was written by the well-known author J.K. Rowling. Chances are that you would begin to doubt your own judgment.

The person receiving the message also asks, "Do I like the source?" If the communicator is respected and admired, people tend to go along with the message, often because they want to be like him or her. This identification phenomenon explains why athletes are used in advertisements. However, attempts to be friendly and personal can backfire. When people dislike the individual delivering a message, they may respond by taking the opposite point of view. This is known as the **boomerang effect**. For example, the sales of a product may go down if a well-known spokesperson for a product is arrested for breaking the law.

The Message

Suppose two people with opposing viewpoints are trying to persuade you to agree with them. You like and trust both of them. In this situation, the message becomes more important than the source. The persuasiveness of a message depends on the way in which it is composed and organized as well as on the actual content.

There are two ways to deliver a message. The *central route for persuasion* focuses on presenting information consisting of strong arguments and facts—it is a focus on logic. The *peripheral route for persuasion* is indirect, relies on emotional appeals, and may be devoid of facts or logic—it is a focus on feelings.

The most effective messages combine emotional appeal with factual information and argument. A message that deviates moderately from the attitudes of the target audience will tend to move that audience furthest. A communication that overemphasizes the emotional side of an issue may boomerang. The peripheral route sometimes arouses fear. For example, showing pictures of accident victims to people who have been arrested for drunken driving may convince them not to drive after drinking. Yet if the film is so bloody that people are frightened or disgusted, they may stop listening to the message. On the other hand, a communication that includes only logic and information may miss its mark because the audience does not relate the facts to their personal lives.

Communicators must also decide whether to present both sides of an issue. Presenting both sides is usually more effective because the audience tends to believe that the speaker is objective and fair-minded. However, presenting both sides can undercut the message or suggest that decision making might be too difficult.

People usually respond positively to a message that is structured and delivered in a dynamic way. A communication that is pushy, however, may produce negative results. People generally resent being pressured, and they may reject an opinion for this reason alone.

source origin

boomerang effect a change in attitude or behavior opposite of the one desired by the persuader

National newscasters, such as Brian Williams, appear attractive, honest, and credible. We are likely to believe sources that seem trustworthy and attractive.

▶ **CRITICAL THINKING**

Defining What is the identification phenomenon?

Advertisements, such as this anti-smoking ad, are effective only if you believe the danger is real and if you believe that you can do something to reduce the danger.

▶ **CRITICAL THINKING**

Making Connections Is this an example of a central or peripheral route for persuasion? Why?

The Channel

Where, when, and how a message is presented also influence response. Personal contact is usually the most effective approach to an audience. In one study in Ann Arbor, Michigan, 75 percent of voters who had been contacted personally voted in favor of a change in the city charter. Only 45 percent of those contacted by mail and 19 percent of those who saw only ads voted for the change.

Personal contact can boomerang; people may dislike the communicator or feel pressured. Many people have come to consider sales calls at their door and telemarketing calls as intrusive. Personal contact also reaches fewer numbers than do print or electronic media.

Television and films may be more effective persuasive tools than printed matter. In one experiment, 51 percent of people who had only watched a film could answer factual questions about the issue in question—compared to 29 percent of those who had only read about it. In addition, a greater number of the film viewers altered their viewpoints than did the readers.

Studies of the persuasiveness of Internet sources have been mixed. In general, the persuasive effects of similar Web-based and printed content appear to be similar. Users are influenced by different factors, such as the group or person responsible for the site and the site's domain (for example, *.edu* or *.com*.)

The Audience

Persuading people to alter their views depends heavily on knowing the audience and why its members hold the attitudes they do. Most people avoid information that does not support their beliefs. Suppose, for example, you are involved in a program to reduce the birthrate in a heavily populated area. To persuade them to practice family planning, you need to know why they value large families. In some areas of the world, people have as many children as they can because so many will not survive. In this case, you might tie the family-planning campaign to programs of prenatal and infant care. In some areas, children work to bring in needed income. In this case, you might promote an incentive system for families who limit themselves to two or three children. It is crucial to know who your audience is and what motivates its members.

Several strategies effectively involve the audience. One strategy that has been studied extensively is the *foot-in-the-door technique*, which involves first making a very small request that someone is almost sure to agree to and then making a much more demanding request. In one experiment, researchers asked residents for permission to place a small sign reading "Be a Safe Driver" in a window of their homes. They later asked residents for permission to stake a large "Drive Carefully" sign in the yard. Nearly 56 percent of those who had agreed to the first request also agreed to the second one. However, only 17 percent of the residents who heard the second request but not the first agreed to put the sign in their yard.

reject to refuse

Another strategy is sometimes called the *door-in-the-face technique*. It works like this: to encourage people to agree to a moderate request that might otherwise be **rejected**, you make a major request. When the major request is rejected, you follow up with a more minor request. For example, you might ask a friend, "Would you come over and help me move all day Saturday and Sunday? No? Well, then, could you come over Saturday morning and just help me move my bedroom furniture?" You now have a much higher likelihood of success.

☑ **READING PROGRESS CHECK**

Evaluating To research a paper on the views of a political candidate, which online source would you use: CNN or a blog created by a student at your school? Why?

FDA/Newscom

Models and Effects of Persuasion

GUIDING QUESTION *How do the different models of persuasion work in advertising?*

One model of persuasion is the heuristic model. This model states that attitudes can be changed either by heuristic processing or systematic processing. A *heuristic* is an informal rule or a shortcut that we use to make everyday decisions, as we cannot afford to expend a lot of time and energy on every single judgment in our life. Heuristics are a simplifying strategy or "rule of thumb" we use to make reasonable guesses in a limited amount of time.

If an individual is not terribly interested in the issue under discussion, he or she is likely to rely on heuristic processing—a very casual, low-attention form of analyzing evidence. The recipient tunes in to the peripheral aspects of the message, such as the likability of the source or the number of arguments. On the other hand, if the recipient is deeply interested in the topic, he or she is likely to use systematic processing—thoughtfully considering the issues and arguments.

Advertisers use heuristics to get you to buy their products. They may sprinkle their ads with convincing numbers or with nice-sounding, value-laden words, such as *integrity*. They might employ celebrities to endorse their products, or state that their product is the most popular one.

The Sleeper Effect

Changes in attitudes are not always permanent. Efforts at persuasion usually have their greatest impact immediately and then fade away. Sometimes people do seem to reach different conclusions about a message over time. This curious **sleeper effect**, or delayed attitude change, has been explained in several ways.

One explanation for the delayed impact depends on the tendency to retain the message but forget the source. As time goes by, a positive source no longer holds power to persuade nor does a negative source undercut the message. When the memory of the message's source fades, the message then stands on its own merit, and more people may accept it.

The problem is that this requires forgetting one thing and retaining another, with no obvious reason why that should occur. Researchers proposed an alternative explanation for the sleeper effect—the differential decay hypothesis—that the impact of the cue, or source, decays faster than the impact of the message. They found that the sleeper effect is more likely to come into play if a persuasive message is heard first and makes a big initial impact, and then is followed by the discounting cue (such as a disclaimer or a biased source). That is because over time we tend to forget that we had dismissed or discounted the content of the message because of its source, and are left with only the initial impact of the persuasive message.

The Inoculation Effect

Research has shown that people can be educated to resist attitude change. This technique can be compared to an inoculation, or vaccination. When a person is vaccinated, she is given a weakened or dead form of the disease-causing agent, which stimulates her body to manufacture defenses against the full-fledged disease.

sleeper effect the delayed impact on attitude change of a persuasive communication

We use heuristics, or shortcuts, to evaluate many messages. This saves us time and energy. We might evaluate this ad in this way: being healthy is good, and almonds help you be healthy, so almonds are good for me.

▶ **CRITICAL THINKING**

Analyzing Visuals Which heuristic is this advertiser using?

california almonds

How to improve your body by lifting an ounce a day.

Step 1: Take some tasty California Almonds to the gym.
Step 2: Snack on a handful before or after you work out.
Step 3: Get pumped up knowing that studies show that eating an ounce of almonds a day (about 23) can help you maintain a healthy cholesterol level.
Step 4: Repeat daily.

Remember: Snacking on almonds always gives you a powerful lift. They have protein, fiber and vitamin E, plus every crunch is cholesterol-free.

28g (1oz.) of almonds have 14g fat, of which only 1g is saturated.

almonds are in!
www.AlmondsAreIn.com

inoculation effect
developing resistance to persuasion by exposing a person to arguments that challenge his or her beliefs so that he or she can practice defending them

brainwashing extreme form of attitude change; uses peer pressure, physical suffering, threats, rewards, guilt, and intensive indoctrination

Similarly, a person who has resisted a mild attack on his beliefs is ready to defend them against an onslaught that might otherwise be overwhelming. This **inoculation effect** can be explained in two ways: it motivates individuals to defend their beliefs more strongly, and it gives them practice in defending those beliefs for the future.

Brainwashing

The most extreme means of changing attitudes involves a combination of psychological manipulation and physical torture called **brainwashing**. The most extensive studies of brainwashing have been done on Westerners captured by the Chinese during the Korean War and subjected to "thought reform." Psychiatrist Robert Jay Lifton interviewed several dozen prisoners released by the Chinese, and from their accounts, he outlined the methods used to break down people's convictions and introduce new patterns of belief, feeling, and behavior.

The aim in brainwashing is as much to create a new person as to change attitudes. The first step is to strip away all identity and then subject the person to intense social pressure and physical stress. A prisoner-of-war camp is a perfect setting for this process. So long as the prisoner holds out, he is treated with contempt or exhorted to confess. He is interrogated past the point of exhaustion and is humiliated and bound at all times. The prisoner is rewarded for cooperating. With every act of compliance, prison life is made a little more pleasant. Finally, by a combination of threat, peer pressure, systematic rewards, and other psychological means, the prisoner comes to believe that he is confessing to real crimes.

Knowing where persuasion ends and brainwashing begins can be important to the courts—especially in lawsuits involving the deprogramming of members of religious cults, or other groups that use mind-control techniques.

☑ **READING PROGRESS CHECK**

Analyzing When evaluating a message that is important you, do you rely on systematic processing or heuristics? Explain.

LESSON 3 REVIEW

Reviewing Vocabulary

1. *Explaining* How do the boomerang, sleeper, and inoculation effects influence your attitudes?

2. *Interpreting Significance* Why is brainwashing such a powerful tool in changing people's attitudes?

Using Your Notes

3. *Evaluating* Use your notes to reconsider the four parts of the communication process. Which of these parts influences you the most? For example, when viewing an advertisement, are you more influenced by its source, its message, its channel, or the audience at which it is aimed? Explain your answer.

Answering the Guiding Questions

4. *Contrasting* How does the foot-in-the-door technique differ from the door-in-the-face technique?

5. *Identifying Central Issues* How do the different models of persuasion work in advertising?

Writing Activity

6. *Informative/Explanatory* Imagine you are a car salesperson and are attempting to persuade a young couple to purchase an automobile. Write a brief script between the salesperson and the couple that incorporates aspects of persuasion techniques both might use. Then describe the techniques in a paragraph.

Directions: On a separate sheet of paper, answer the questions below. Make sure you read carefully and answer all parts of the question.

Lesson Review

Lesson 1

1 *Explaining* Why do people develop attitudes? Describe two ways in which attitudes help us to function every day.

2 *Categorizing* What method of shaping attitudes occurs when an attitude becomes an integral part of a person?

3 *Drawing Conclusions* How can attitudes help keep us out of dangerous situations?

Lesson 2

4 *Identifying* Which cognitive act are aggressors engaging in when they decide that they do not like their victim?

5 *Applying* Describe two short-term ways and two long-term ways that you think will help to reduce prejudice in your school or community.

6 *Analyzing* What might be a positive outcome of cognitive dissonance? What might be a negative outcome?

Lesson 3

7 *Making Predictions* How will listeners likely react if you pressure them to adopt your point of view? Why?

8 *Identifying* What is brainwashing?

Critical Thinking Questions

9 *Constructing Arguments* Take a pro or con position: It is easier to change an attitude that has a cognitive foundation than one that has a cultural foundation. Defend your point of view by including at least one example.

10 *Inferring* Do you think familiarity with brand names influences your choices in the store? Explain your answer.

11 *Synthesizing* Think of persuasive techniques used by candidates in a recent political campaign. How did they use central route processing? Peripheral route processing?

12 *Exploring Issues* How can self-fulfilling prophecies fuel stereotypes about racial and ethnic groups? Do you think such attitudes might affect the way that psychotherapists interact with clients? Why or why not?

College and Career Readiness

Study the cartoon below and then answer the questions that follow.

13 *Examining Information* What are the two conflicting views that result in the boss feeling cognitive dissonance?

14 *Reaching Conclusions* How does the boss attempt to reduce the dissonance he experiences in this situation?

Need Extra Help?

If You've Missed Question	**1**	**2**	**3**	**4**	**5**	**6**	**7**	**8**	**9**	**10**	**11**	**12**	**13**	**14**
Go to page	588	590	591	597	598	596	604	606	588	588	603	597	596	596

Directions: On a separate sheet of paper, answer the questions below. Make sure you read carefully and answer all parts of the question.

21st Century Skills

15 *Understanding Relationships Among Events*
Historically, members of ethnic and racial minority groups have encountered difficulties in getting elected to political office. However, those who have been elected have often brought about significant change, which has encouraged people to reexamine their prejudices and stereotypes. Think of a prominent political leader who is a member of a minority group, such as President Barack Obama. With a partner, investigate the challenges this person faced when campaigning for office. Present an oral report on your findings. In your report, discuss any long-term changes in social attitudes you think occurred as a result of this person's election.

16 *Using Correct Terminology and Grammar* Cults can be defined as relatively small groups of people that have religious beliefs others think are unusual or unacceptable. Cults often use intensive techniques in an attempt to control members' beliefs and attitudes. Conduct research on the Internet to learn more about these techniques and write a report describing them. In your report, take care to use correct psychology-related terminology. Your paper should be well organized and use proper grammar and spelling.

Research and Technology

17 *Identifying Bias* Work with a partner to conduct research that examines how portrayals in the media between the Civil War and modern times have created and reinforced cultural stereotypes. You may want to focus on a single stereotype, such as how portrayals of women, African Americans, Asian Americans, or Hispanics have changed over time. When you are done, prepare an electronic slide show to share what you have learned.

DBQ Analyzing Primary Sources

Use the document to answer the following questions.

The following is an excerpt from a paper on the techniques businesses frequently use when advertising to children.

PRIMARY SOURCE

"*Marketers who practice stealth advertising embed products within a program's content, use so-called viral (word-of-mouth) marketing, enable children to interact with online characters who promote specific brands, disguise advertisements as video news releases, and collect information from youth at online sites. All these practices are designed to create or enhance branded environments that foster user loyalty.*"

—Sandra L. Calvert, "Children as Consumers: Advertising and Marketing" (2008)

18 *Interpreting Significance* Why do you think stealth advertising is a powerful method of persuasion? Identify three techniques used in stealth advertising.

19 *Analyzing Ethical Issues* Do you think it is ethical to use persuasive techniques such as product placement with young children? Explain your answer.

Exploring the Essential Question

20 *Comparing and Contrasting* Use a variety of sources to find examples of the ways in which culture influences attitudes. Find out about attitudes in other places in the world and compare those attitudes to ones in this country. Present your findings in an illustrated, captioned poster.

Psychology Journal Activity

21 *Informative/Explanatory* Review your entry in your Psychology Journal for this chapter. Having read about the different models of persuasion that work in advertising, which model do you think impacts you the most? Provide specific examples.

Need Extra Help?

If You've Missed Question	**15**	**16**	**17**	**18**	**19**	**20**	**21**
Go to page	597	606	598	605	602	588	605

Psychology: Present and Future

ESSENTIAL QUESTION • *How does the field of psychology influence daily life?*

netw⊙rks

There's More Online about the field of psychology and its future.

CHAPTER 21

Lab Activity
The Intelligent Crowd?

Lesson 1
Psychology's Contributions

Lesson 2
Careers in Psychology

Psychology Matters...

At different points in our lives, we need some help and guidance from others. We may need help talking about problems or to find support for our friends or family. The field of psychology can be an important part of our lives. Many people choose careers in the field so that they can help others. Some psychology professionals specialize in certain areas so that they can assist people with specific aspects of their lives.

◀ A school psychologist is in tune with the challenges and stresses that teens and students face in their daily lives.

David Burch/UpperCut Images/Getty Images

Lab Activity

The Intelligent Crowd?

THE QUESTION...

RESEARCH QUESTION Can one person make a better guess than many individuals?

Imagine that you want to guess the weight of an elephant or the number of trees in a nearby forest. These numbers might be difficult to guess, but there is a key tool that could help you: other people. If you were to gather 100 people and tell everyone to guess the numbers, the average of their guesses will likely be close to the true numbers. This isn't group psychology because every person is making his or her guess individually, but the phenomenon might be called a "crowd" effect. The effect has been widely demonstrated but has yet to be fully explained.

Let's test this effect in a fun experiment. All you need is something to guess and a small crowd.

Psychology Journal Activity

How could this phenomenon be useful for society? Write about this in your Psychology Journal. List several questions that might be better answered by a crowd than by an individual. The topics might involve economics or civics.

FINDING THE ANSWER...

HYPOTHESIS The average of all the guesses made by many individuals is more accurate than a guess made by any one individual.

THE METHOD OF YOUR EXPERIMENT

MATERIALS   large jar; items such as marbles, cotton balls, or paper clips

PROCEDURE   Fill a large jar with small objects. The objects might be marbles, cotton balls, paper clips, or small candies. Count the objects before you put them in the jar. Ask 20 or more participants to guess how many objects are in the jar and record their answers.

DATA COLLECTION   The answers will most likely vary widely. Calculate an average of the data and compare it to the true number of objects. Determine the closest guess made by an individual. Compare the average to the closest guess.

ANALYSIS & APPLICATION

1. Did your results support the hypothesis?

2. Was anyone's guess more accurate than the averaged guesses of the crowd?

3. Why is it important for individuals to make their guesses independently rather than as a group?

net**w**orks   ONLINE LAB RESOURCES

Online you will find:

- An **interactive lab experience**, allowing you to put principles from this chapter into practice in a digital psychology lab environment. This chapter's lab will include an experiment allowing you to explore issues fundamental to the field of psychology and its future.

- A **Skills Handbook** that includes a guide for using the scientific method, creating experiments, and analyzing data.

- A **Notebook** where you can complete your Psychology Journal and record and analyze your experiment data.

5.7%
6.0%
8.1%
32.
24.9%

LESSON 1
Psychology's Contributions

Reading HELPDESK CCSS

Academic Vocabulary
• **prior**   • **professional**

Content Vocabulary
• 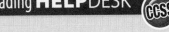 gerontology

TAKING NOTES:
Key Ideas and Details

CATEGORIZING Use a graphic organizer like the one below to outline the challenges that psychologists face today.

Challenges of Psychologists

ESSENTIAL QUESTION • *How does the field of psychology influence daily life?*

IT MATTERS BECAUSE
Psychologists have explored many topics having to do with human behavior and will face new challenges in the field. Learning about this field can help us understand our own behavior as well as the role that psychology plays in people's lives.

Psychology's Role

GUIDING QUESTION *What role does psychology play in standardized testing?*

Although most people seem to have an accurate idea of what doctors or lawyers do, many do not realize what psychologists do. Such people probably do not realize the many contributions that the science of human behavior has produced. Psychology is a varied field with psychologists filling many roles, from treating patients to consulting to researching.

Mental Health

The field of psychology as a helping effort began in the 1790s through the pioneering efforts of Philippe Pinel, a French physician and a founder of psychiatry. Pinel unchained patients who were held in mental wards, some of whom had been restrained for more than 20 years. Pinel argued against the prevailing belief that the mentally ill were possessed by demons. Moreover, he thought mental illness was just that—illness—and thus could be treated. Mainly due to his efforts, France became a leader in improving conditions for the mentally ill.

More than half a century passed before similar efforts were exerted in the United States. After discovering that the mentally ill were being jailed along with criminals, teacher and social reformer Dorothea Dix (1802–1887) became the chief spokesperson for reform. Her personal crusade in the 1840s led to more enlightened treatment of the mentally ill in Canada and Great Britain, as well as in the United States.

A former mental patient, Clifford Beers (1876–1943), became the guiding force in the early growth of the modern mental health movement. Beers's own account of his illness and recovery, *A Mind That Found Itself* (1908), has motivated a promotion of better psychological care in communities, schools, and hospitals.

Testing

Most students are given IQ tests or other tests at an early age. Psychologists have played a leading role in devising and updating these tests, as well as other tests in higher education and major standardized college entrance exams. The ACT, taken by nearly 1.6 million students each year, places greater emphasis on scientific concepts and abstract reading skills and less emphasis on factual material than earlier versions. An assessment of writing skills was added to the ACT in 2005. The SAT, taken by about 2 million students annually, was redesigned in 2005 and assesses critical reading, math concepts and reasoning, and development and expression of ideas in writing.

Everyday Life

With many parents working outside the home, caregiving by others has become a significant developmental issue. Researchers note that day care appears to have few negative effects on children and actually promotes the ongoing development of social skills. Children with experience in day care tend to be more assertive and aggressive. Alison Clarke-Stewart has suggested that this may result from the fact that children in day care tend to think at a more advanced level but have not yet developed sufficient social skills to smoothly implement their plans for action. Much remains to be learned about how children grow and learn.

Harry Harlow's work led to the idea that the attachment of children to their caregivers is made stronger by physical contact. That, in turn, led to the demonstration that breast-feeding versus bottle-feeding makes little difference in the parent-child attachment. It is the holding, not the feeding, that is most important. Studies have found that babies who are born prematurely and receive therapeutic touch from caregivers, such as the hospital nurses, progress better than babies who are not held or touched by their caregivers.

Psychologists play a role in designing and assessing tools for learning in a variety of media. Their understanding of the principles of learning contributed to the development of *Sesame Street*. Studies show that almost 60 percent of the preschool children who watch that program at least five times a week can recite the entire alphabet correctly. B.F. Skinner's ideas about feedback, **prior** knowledge, knowledge of results, and reinforcement have been implemented into computer software designs for games as well as educational programs.

☑ READING PROGRESS CHECK

Assessing Why do you think Clifford Beers was so successful in getting people to understand the need for better psychological care for patients?

Psychology Today

GUIDING QUESTION *How does the work of experimental and applied psychologists differ?*

Contemporary psychology can be grouped into experimental and applied fields. Experimental psychologists use a variety of scientific methods to study human and animal behavior. Applied psychologists put knowledge of psychology to work solving human problems. The distinction is not always sharp. Experimental and applied psychologists gather available evidence and offer the best explanation they find. Both study behavior and use similar processes. A major difference is that applied psychologists search for immediate solutions, experimental psychologists for long-range answers.

North Wind Picture Archives/Alamy

Funding

The United States federal government invests about one twenty-fifth of 1 percent of the national budget in psychological research. Psychological societies and organizations send representatives to Capitol Hill to appeal for more support. The government spends painfully little to study the nature of human behavior.

prior earlier in time

Often described as the father of scientific psychiatry, Philippe Pinel argued that the mentally ill required humane treatment, sympathy, and guidance, not the beatings, imprisonment, and ridicule they so often suffered.

▶ **CRITICAL THINKING**

Analyzing Why was Pinel's behavior considered revolutionary?

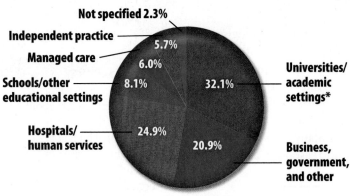

Not specified 2.3%

Independent practice — 5.7%

Managed care — 6.0%

Schools/other educational settings — 8.1%

Hospitals/ human services — 24.9%

20.9%

Universities/ academic settings* — 32.1%

Business, government, and other

*This category includes four-year colleges, medical school, and other academic settings.

Source: 2009 Doctorate Employment Survey, APA Center for Workforce Studies, June 2011

GRAPH ^

EMPLOYMENT OF PHD PSYCHOLOGISTS

Psychology is one of the most diverse fields to enter. Almost all psychologists are educated at colleges and universities, and therefore all psychologists are familiar with the academic setting.

▶ **CRITICAL THINKING**

1. *Identifying* Where did most people who obtained psychology PhDs in 2009 work?

2. *Analyzing Visuals* What percentage of PhD psychologists work in all forms of educational settings?

professional person engaged in a specific job

gerontology the study of aging

Current Trends

According to a recent survey completed by the APA Research Office, about 23 percent of those who studied psychology enrolled in master's degrees in counseling, 15 percent in clinical psychology, and 5 percent in school psychology. The remaining respondents surveyed obtained their degrees in traditional research and other subfields, such as industrial/organizational psychology, general and educational psychology, and experimental psychology.

The number of doctorates in psychology awarded to members of minority groups continues to increase. The proportion of women in the field of psychology is greater than in most other scientific disciplines, with women receiving about 73 percent of doctoral degrees awarded in psychology in 2010. Diversity in the discipline offers new perspectives on issues of psychology and behavior. Psi Chi, once the National Honor Society of Psychology, is now the International Honor Society of Psychology, and is gaining chapters all over the world.

The Challenges for Psychology

Social change, urban problems, early learning, the neural bases of behavior, psychology and minorities, and the reduction of violence are some of psychology's challenges today. One way to determine future directions for psychology is by analyzing the trends of age in the population. The average age of citizens in North America is going up; there are more people over age 65 in the United States and Canada now than at any time in the history of either country. That creates new problems for **professionals** in the field to study and new careers in both research and service. It also suggests a growing specialty in the field of developmental psychology—**gerontology**, the study of aging.

At the other end of the age spectrum are a different set of factors that may impact future jobs for psychologists. The top three killers of children and adolescents in our society now are accidents, violence, and drugs. Many of the dangers that face society today are rooted in social problems; that is, they can be solved through changing behavior and attitudes of individuals and communities.

☑ **READING PROGRESS CHECK**

Defending Why is it especially important for psychologists to help young people cope with their problems?

LESSON 1 REVIEW

Reviewing Vocabulary

1. *Explaining* Why has gerontology recently become an important branch of psychology?

Using Your Notes

2. *Visualizing* Use your notes to choose one of the challenges psychologists face today and explain how the challenge might be faced in the future.

Answering the Guiding Questions

3. *Applying* What role does psychology play in standardized testing?

4. *Identifying* How does the work of experimental and applied psychology differ?

Writing Activity

5. *Informative/Explanatory* Visit a large bookstore and browse through the titles of books dealing with psychology. What topics seem to be the most popular? Which books seem to be the most helpful? Which books seem most interesting to you? Why? Based on your observations, write an essay forecasting several topics that could result in new psychology books.

Parapsychology

Period of Study: 1882 and 1975

Introduction: Scientists sometimes investigate behavior or events that seem to have atypical origins. In psychology, this area of study is known as *parapsychology*, which means "alongside psychology." Parapsychology is not considered to be in the mainstream of psychology, but its controversial issues have attracted many people. Parapsychologists suggest that humans possess senses other than the known seven—vision, hearing, taste, smell, touch, balance, and body senses. People skeptical of this suggestion point to the fact that the evidence supporting parapsychology's claims never stands up to rigorous testing.

PRIMARY SOURCE

❝About three in four Americans profess at least one paranormal belief, according to a recent Gallup survey. The most popular is extrasensory perception (ESP), mentioned by 41%❞

—Gallup News Service, 2005

Hypothesis: Parapsychology's advocates often state their claims in such a way that they are not subject to disproof; in other words, the claims are not testable, scientific hypotheses. As a result, many investigators approach these claims by trying to eliminate all other reasonable explanations for the observed behaviors.

Method: In 1882, scientists established the first organization to study parapsychology, the Society of Psychical Research, in London. The American version of this society was formed in Boston three years later. These organizations focused on mediumship, or communication with those who have died. As time passed, other phenomena began to be studied, such as telepathy (the ability of people to communicate without using ordinary senses), clairvoyance (the ability to experience an event without physically being there), and psychokinesis (controlling objects with the mind).

Perhaps the most famous attempts to demonstrate psychokinesis were made by Uri Geller. Geller claimed he could bend and break metal objects by using his mind. On non-scientifically controlled occasions, Geller did appear to bend or break objects without

touching them. In 1974, psychologists filmed several encounters with Geller. In one instance, Geller unbalanced a precision scale, and in another, he appeared to bend a steel band. Many people believed Geller really did all this with psychokinetic power; however, skeptics and researchers debunked Geller's claims.

Results: The events surrounding Geller were highly controversial; for him, they were highly profitable. He began making appearances in various locations, bending spoons or similar objects. He eventually received an invitation to appear on national television, but when it was time to perform, Geller failed to deliver. It was discovered that he had access before all of his performances to the objects he was hoping to bend. On television, however, his personal set of objects had been switched with a new set, and Geller was left to claim that something was blocking his amazing "abilities."

Geller's claim that his abilities were blocked illustrates one difference between science and belief. Scientists accept the results of well-designed tests, whether their hypotheses are supported or not. Geller rejected the disconfirming observations, adding a vague explanation after the fact to explain unsatisfying results. The effects allegedly produced by parapsychological phenomena have much simpler explanations—sleight of hand or prior manipulation to bend spoons, hidden magnets to deflect compasses, and the like. Perhaps one day significant breakthroughs will occur in the study of parapsychology. However, for now, healthy skepticism properly prevails.

Analyzing the Case Study

1. ***Explaining*** What is parapsychology?

2. ***Identifying*** What abilities did Geller claim to have?

3. ***Making Connections*** Why does the likelihood of demonstrating psychic phenomena decrease when viewed under scientific controls?

4. ***Speculating*** Nearly 75 percent of Americans foster some belief in the paranormal. What might that indicate about parapsychological research continuing? Explain.

Analyzing
Readings in Psychology

Reader's Dictionary (CCSS)

sedentary: characterized by much sitting and little physical exercise

thwart: prevent (someone) from accomplishing something

plastic: the capacity for continuous alteration of the neural pathways and synapses of the living brain and nervous system in response to experience or injury

Exercise is good for more than just your body! In the studies outlined in this article, researchers have uncovered the healing and preventative benefits of physical exercise in helping prevent and reverse the effects of dementia in the elderly. Researchers and doctors are beginning to understand that brain health is closely related to physical health.

Exercise Can Shield the
Aging Brain,
Studies Show   By Jenifer Goodwin

PRIMARY SOURCE

Evidence is mounting that exercise provides some protection from memory loss and Alzheimer's disease, with three new studies showing that a variety of physical activities are associated with healthier brains in older adults.

One study found that normally **sedentary** older adults who walked at a moderate pace three times a week for a year boosted the size of the brain region involved with memory.

A second study found that twice-weekly resistance (weight) training helped women with mild signs of mental decline improve their scores on thinking and memory tests. And the third showed that exercise done for strength and balance also improved memory.

None of the findings offer a clear-cut prescription for **thwarting** mental declines and Alzheimer's, but taken together, the growing body of research strongly suggests that physical activity is essential for healthy brain aging, and may help prevent Alzheimer's, said

Heather Snyder, senior associate director of medical and scientific relations for the Alzheimer's Association.

"These studies really start to strengthen the literature about the impact that physical activity may have to reduce the risk of Alzheimer's disease," Snyder said.

The studies were to be presented Sunday at the Alzheimer's Association annual meeting in Vancouver.

In one study, U.S. researchers at three universities divided 120 older, sedentary adults without dementia into two groups. One group did aerobic exercise by walking on a track at a moderate pace for 30 to 45 minutes three times a week; the other group did stretching and toning exercises.

A year later, MRI brain scans showed that the size of the hippocampus, a region of the brain involved with memory, increased by 2 percent in the walking group. In the stretch-toning group, hippocampal brain volume declined by 1.5 percent.

After age 50 or 55, adults lose about 1 percent of brain volume per year, said lead study author Kirk Erickson, an assistant professor of psychology at the University of Pittsburgh. Marked shrinkage of the hippocampus can be a sign of Alzheimer's disease.

The new findings show that "the hippocampus remains very **plastic** throughout life, even in late life," Erickson said. "We can not only stop it from shrinking, but we can increase the size of the brain in a relatively short amount of time, just one year of getting people more active."

616

PHOTO: RubberBall/Alamy.; TEXT: *Exercise Can Shield the Aging Brain, Studies Show* by Jenifer Goodwin, © 2012 HealthDay, July 15, 2012.

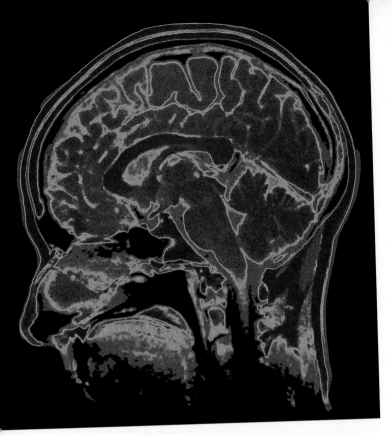

Mike Hill/Alamy

After six months, the resistance training group showed significantly improved performance on tests of attention and memory compared to the other two groups, the researchers found. Resistance training also led to functional changes in three brain regions involved in memory. The aerobic training group showed improvement in balance, mobility and cardio-vascular capacity.

The third study, by researchers at the National Center for Geriatrics and Gerontology in Japan, focused on 47 older adults with the mild memory impairment who were divided into two groups. One did 90 minutes of supervised exercise twice a week, while the other, the control group, sat through a few sessions of health education.

The exercise group did strength training, aerobics *and* exercises to improve balance, for one year. Those in the exercise group showed improvement on a memory task and tests gauging their ability to use language compared to those in the education group, although both groups showed memory improvements, the researchers said.

"There is a lot of evidence out there suggesting that exercises can be beneficial for you in a whole variety of ways, whether it's reducing risk of obesity and weight gain or reducing inflammation," Erickson said. "Exercise is associated with an increased lifespan, and repeatedly has been shown to be associated with reducing risk of dementia. There looks like there is a very direct link between physical activity and the integrity of the brain."

Because this research is being presented at a medical meeting, the data and conclusions should be viewed as preliminary until published in a peer-reviewed journal.

In addition, experts noted that while these studies found an association between exercise and healthier brain aging, the researchers didn't prove a cause-and-effect relationship.

Erickson and his colleagues also measured concentrations in the blood of brain-derived neurotrophic factor (BDNF), which is important in learning, memory and other brain functions, Erickson said.

They found that people who had greater increases in the size of their hippocampus also had a greater boost in BDNF, which suggests a healthier brain, he said.

Yet, how brain volume or BDNF levels relate to memory or thinking ability remains murky. The fact that both groups—those who did aerobic exercise and the stretch-tone group—performed better on thinking and memory tests after a year says that various types of exercise may act on different regions of the brain or different brain networks, Erickson said. Rather than saying one type of exercise is more important than another, the answer is likely more complex, with various types of physical activity affecting different aspects of brain health, Erickson said.

To test just that kind of theory, researchers from the University of British Columbia and the University of Illinois, Urbana, divided 86 women aged 70 to 80 who already showed signs of mild mental decline into three groups. One did twice-weekly resistance (weight) training, another did twice-weekly aerobic training (walking) and the third did twice-weekly balance and tone exercises.

Analyzing Primary Sources

1. *Finding the Main Idea* What is the main idea of this article?

2. *Summarizing* What are the distinct findings of each study?

3. *Analyzing* Why do experts say the researchers have not proven a cause-and-effect relationship?

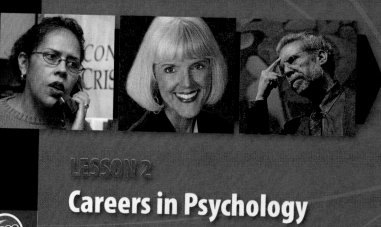

LESSON 2

Careers in Psychology

Reading **HELP**DESK **CCSS**

Academic Vocabulary

• **create** • **goal**

Content Vocabulary

• visualization
• crisis intervention program

TAKING NOTES:

Craft and Structure

CATEGORIZING Use a graphic organizer like the one below to name psychology careers in the fields of business, law, medicine, and psychology.

Business	
Law	
Medicine	
Psychology	

ESSENTIAL QUESTION • *How does the field of psychology influence daily life?*

IT MATTERS BECAUSE

Psychology is an important and growing field. Learning and thinking about opportunities available in the field of psychology can help young people decide how much education they want to pursue and the area of expertise they may be interested in focusing on as a career.

Careers in Psychology

GUIDING QUESTION *How is psychology both a science and a profession?*

Consider a typical conversation regarding the future: "What are you going to do when you get out of school?" "Beats me. My grandparents want me to learn the shoe business and take over when they retire. Mom and Dad want me to think about law as a career. I was leaning toward business administration, but my sister just graduated with an MBA. I don't want to be just like her. I've got more choices than I can handle."

This conversation is imaginary but typical for high school juniors and seniors. You do have many options. Since you have been studying psychology, it might be beneficial to respond to these questions: What will I do with what I have learned? Can I profit from just this one course? What careers in psychology are open to me? To help you find answers to these questions, this section offers descriptions of some of the many career opportunities in the vast field of psychology.

What Employers Are Looking For

Employers are most likely to hire someone who offers special skills. In psychology, as in many other fields, job choices are limited if you have only a high school diploma. Surprisingly, holders of a PhD also have relatively few choices, but they have chosen to fine-tune their education and experience for a specific kind of job; they are specialists.

Those with a bachelor's degree in psychology may have the highest number of options with the widest array of possible employers. Moreover, psychology is a logical undergraduate major for those planning graduate work in such fields as sociology, social work, law, medicine, or education. Many counselors and social workers hold their master's degree in psychology, which is often a two-year program that offers more training in

(l)Geri Engberg/The Image Works; (c)Linda L. McCarley, LCSW, ATR-BC, RPT-S; (r)David Adamson/Alamy

	1975	1995	2004	2010
Clinical/Counseling/School	35%	50%	53%	53%
Experimental/Comparative/Physiological	17%	16%	2%	1%
Developmental/Child/Social/Personality	14%	13%	2%	1%
Educational	5%	3%	7%	8%
Industrial/Organizational	3%	3%	2%	2%
Other psychology subfields	26%	15%	34%	34%

Sources: NSF/SRS Surveys of Doctorate Recipients; *Digest of Education Statistics*, 2005: U.S. Department of Education, National Center for Education Statistics, *Integrated Postsecondary Education Data System*, 2011.

‹ **TABLE**

AREAS OF EXPERTISE OF PHD PSYCHOLOGISTS
Over the past 30 years, the number of people receiving doctoral degrees in the field of psychology has grown by nearly 170 percent.

▶ **CRITICAL THINKING**

1. *Gathering Information* Which area of expertise has enjoyed the greatest growth?

2. *Interpreting* Why do you think clinical, counseling, and school psychologists are listed together in the chart?

dealing with individual patients. No matter the level of education, human behavior plays a key role in all psychological fields.

Fields of Psychology

Psychology is both a science and a profession. As scientists, psychologists study how people perceive, think, feel, and act. Professional careers that are based on psychological principles seek to predict how people will act, help people modify their behavior, and help organizations, businesses, and communities to bring about change.

Forensic psychology is a branch of applied psychology that studies and makes practical suggestions about the workings of the law. Many forensic psychologists study criminal behavior or the reliability of eyewitnesses, the effects on children who appear in court, victim counseling, and the jury selection process. A forensic psychologist often has a PhD and a law degree.

Work and the working environment are the provinces of industrial/organizational psychology, or, as the field is often called, organizational psychology. Psychologists in this field apply their findings to help businesses and industries operate more efficiently and humanely through improved methods of selection and training and new organizational and management strategies. Other industrial/organizational psychologists concentrate on such issues as labor-union relations, harassment, job satisfaction, and worker motivations and incentives.

Sports psychology, a field that developed during the 1980s, is an important part of training for many athletes. Sports psychologists apply the principles of psychology to sports activities. Some focus on maximizing athletic performance through **visualization**—mentally rehearsing the steps of a complete, successful performance—improving concentration or relaxation or reducing negative thoughts that may interfere with performance. Other areas of study include violence, the psychological and physiological benefits of sports participation, sports ethics, and equipment design.

visualization mentally rehearsing the steps involved in a successful performance or process

crisis intervention program short-term psychological first aid that helps individuals and families deal with emergencies or highly stressful situations

Volunteering at a crisis hotline requires specialized training.

▶ **CRITICAL THINKING**

Analyzing What are some issues that a teen crisis hotline volunteer might encounter?

Crisis Hotline Adviser A person holding this job might be a senior in high school. For **crisis intervention programs**, applicants must complete a comprehensive training program. A county hospital, for instance, might offer such training over three weekends. Following training, a typical assignment would involve two 4-hour shifts a week in a hospital.

Crisis hotline personnel respond primarily to two kinds of problems. One involves the immediate, possibly life-threatening situation that can result from a personal or family crisis—an argument, or the unexpected death of a loved one, or a drug overdose. The other kind is the crisis that results from long-term stress, such as that experienced in the family or on the job. Crises like these are not as threatening, but still need to be resolved.

Geri Engberg/The Image Works

A person handling a hotline will have a list of psychologists and counselors as well as information about a wide array of treatment facilities and programs operating in the vicinity. This job requires being able to calm the caller, identify his or her problem, and help that caller to see the wisdom—once the immediate crisis has been dealt with—of contacting the most appropriate agency or professional for long-term follow-up.

Mental Health Assistant This occupation usually requires at minimum an associate degree. An associate degree is awarded after a two-year course preparing for paraprofessional careers in nursing homes, community mental health centers, centers dealing with the intellectually disabled, or special education centers for the variously disabled in public schools. Mental health assistants work with children as well as seniors and may specialize in a certain developmental age group. An individual can volunteer in this area to explore what it is like to work with people who have mental and physical problems.

Typically supervised by a staff psychologist, an assistant helps with or conducts admission interviews. He or she may be responsible—under supervision—for administering various psychological tests to patients. People with business experience as well as experience caring for patients may be able to **create** their own small business and be self-employed in this area.

create to make something happen or exist

Connecting Psychology to Economics

FUNDING IN A CHANGING ECONOMY

Economics and changing economies can greatly affect the field of psychology. In a poor economy, less funding is available and psychological research grants from the government or private sector are often cut or eliminated. Mental health facilities may face staffing difficulties and have trouble properly treating their patients. Finally, fewer fellowships and scholarships may be given to students who want to enter the field.

The current recession has actually seen an increased demand for professionals in the field of psychology. There is need for psychologists in the areas of mental health for senior adults, veterans returning from overseas, and citizens coping with terror threats. Careers in fundraising may also help to provide psychological institutions the money they need to continue functioning. New developments in technology have also created opportunities for psychologists working in the fields of industrial/organizational psychology. These professionals consider all aspects of work-related psychology, from rethinking how teams of employees cooperate across cultural differences to preventing ill health through good job design and stress reduction.

▶ **CRITICAL THINKING**

1. *Drawing Conclusions* In what positive and negative ways can the field of psychology be affected by an economic recession?

2. *Researching* Do an online search to discover what the current job outlook is for careers in psychology. Write a brief paper that provides a synopsis of the overall job outlook as well as descriptions of the job outlook for specific psychology careers. Include their educational requirements and average salaries.

▲ An understanding of human behavior, and what influences it, is a valuable skill in almost every job.

Human Resources Director The successful applicant is likely to have a bachelor's degree in psychology, having concentrated on courses involving interviewing, test construction and interpretation, statistics, and law. Such a person would be employed in companies of any size. The person might also have minored in management courses in a college of Business Administration. He or she would stress organizational and quantitative skills. This is not an entry-level job, however. Prior experience with the employer's policies is a definite requirement.

A human resources director may participate in a wide array of activities, depending on the nature and interest of his or her employer. This person's responsibility would include some involvement in hiring and firing decisions, especially for the support staff in an organization. Such a person might also develop programs to improve or maintain staff skills in sales, interpersonal sensitivity, or any other area involved in conducting the company's business.

School Psychologist A master's degree is a must for this position; an undergraduate major in psychology is desirable. In addition, most school psychologists work on location in a school system and must be licensed or certified in their state of employment, which involves taking a test.

In bigger school districts you might work in one school, but many school psychologists divide their time among a number of schools. They usually work with children experiencing the normal array of problems in school. A school psychologist might give reading, aptitude, interest, or intelligence tests and must be skillful in interpreting them. At other times he or she might work directly with the children or young adults in school or with the families of those students.

Clinical Psychologist To use this title in most states requires a PhD (a Doctor of Philosophy) or a PsyD (a Doctor of Psychology). The PsyD is a degree developed in the 1970s. In a PsyD program, a student gains skill in psychotherapy, undergoing intensive training in testing, interviewing, and giving supervised therapy. Clinical psychologists may be self-employed, or they may work for a government, business, hospital, prison, or nonprofit organization.

A practicing clinical psychologist is often self-employed. Required skills include those needed to run any small business, in addition to practical experience with testing and various forms of therapy. He or she must develop working relations with other clinicians in the area—psychiatrists, medical doctors, and other contacts in local hospitals and mental health facilities—to obtain the patient/client referrals that are vital to success as a psychotherapist.

A typical day might involve 8 to 10 hours in various stages of psychotherapy with different individuals. The hours are determined to meet client needs, so this is not a typical 9-to-5 job. Other types of therapy a clinical psychologist might offer are group therapy or consultation with other therapeutic organizations, such as Alcoholics Anonymous. It is also possible, of course, to utilize clinical psychology skills in a state-supported psychiatric hospital, a Veterans Administration hospital, or a community mental health center.

Consulting Psychologist A PhD is required to be a consulting psychologist, whose services might be offered by a management consulting firm. Such a person might spend graduate school in an industrial/organizational psychology program learning management practices, testing strategies, interpersonal behavioral strategies, and intervention techniques in complex organizations.

Consultants usually work on short-term projects, offering clients a special array of skills. A consulting psychologist might, for instance, advise a company's top management on how to take human performance limits into account in the design of a control board for a factory. He or she might be involved in all aspects of the design of a new highway—signs, bridges, crossover devices, and lane-flow control.

Profiles in Psychology

Linda L. McCarley
(1946–)

Linda L. McCarley, an art therapist, founded the Art Therapy Institute in Dallas, Texas. Art therapy helps people create drawings, paintings, sculptures, and other art forms that provide a glimpse into their inner world.

How does art therapy work? Have you ever felt better after expressing yourself with music, dance, drama, or art? That is because words may not adequately express some of your deepest feelings or life experiences. Making art provides another avenue for self-expression, helps release tension, and is life enhancing. As we can see by studying the images etched on the walls of caves dating back to ancient times, people have always relied upon imagery to express their most significant life experiences.

Art therapists gain an understanding of their clients and foster self-discovery and healing by facilitating their clients' creative expressions.

▶ **CRITICAL THINKING**

Drawing Conclusions How might art therapy help a patient who was from a different culture than the therapist?

As you search the want ads in your local newspaper, you may not see very many entry-level job openings for psychologists. There are jobs, though, that can expose you to psychology-related work. Look for jobs that utilize people skills, such as communicating or relating to people; analytical skills, such as figuring out and resolving problems; writing skills, such as writing logical reports; and research skills, such as using statistics or tables to analyze issues. These skills are called for in a variety of jobs, such as working for case workers, business managers, probation or corrections officers, city managers, and human services.

goal something that you hope to achieve

He or she might consult with architects or builders to help design a space where people can work well together. These psychologists are consulted about the human factors in building and designing machines such as computer systems, cars, or office equipment.

Grief Counselor A grief counselor may have a bachelor's or master's degree in psychology and work with people who have suffered difficult losses in their lives, such as the loss of a friend or family member. The counselor may work with individuals or with groups. The counselor may work in schools after a tragic event occurs or in a community that is dealing with a catastrophe, such as a natural disaster in which people's lives were disrupted and a loss was experienced. Grief counselors are very familiar with the stages of loss, grieving, and dying, and their **goal** is to always be sensitive to the patient's feelings, experiences, and needs as they discuss their emotions. A grief counselor may refer a patient to a psychiatrist or other professional if they feel additional care is needed.

Substance Abuse Counselor Substance abuse counselors may have varying amounts of training, depending on the requirements of the state that the person is working in. Some may need a high school diploma or counseling certificate, while others may have a master's degree in psychology. Substance abuse counselors provide assistance to people addicted to drugs or alcohol. They may work with groups or individuals and may work in hospitals, mental health facilities, or residential centers. The counselor provides counseling sessions during a designated treatment plan and periodic drug tests on the patient. After rehabilitation, patients may need continued counseling to ensure that they have an outlet to discuss problems and stressors that may have contributed to their problem in the first place. These sessions may be on an individual basis or in a group setting.

Future Psychology Career Options

As psychologists in every specialty area meet new challenges, new areas of psychology develop. The field responds to emerging local, world, and cross-cultural issues with new research and new methods that open new career opportunities. For example, the relatively new area of health psychology combines aspects of physiological, social, counseling, and clinical psychology. Health psychologists focus on the role the psychological functions of an individual play on that person's health. They work with other health care professionals in both private practice and in hospitals to provide patients with complete health care. A health psychologist might research the origins of obesity to find effective treatments. A health psychologist might also deal with how stress is related to illness.

✓ **READING PROGRESS CHECK**

Analyzing What kind of qualities are most employers seeking in employees who work in the area of psychology?

LESSON 2 REVIEW

Reviewing Vocabulary
1. *Explaining* What types of situations does a crisis intervention program handle?

Using Your Notes
2. *Describing* Use your notes to choose a possible psychology career and describe how someone in that career might help improve the lives of others.

Answering the Guiding Question
3. *Analyzing* How is psychology both a science and a profession?

Writing Activity
4. *Informative/Explanatory* Explore your long-term goals by outlining a possible educational and career path that you might follow. In your outline, be sure to indicate your career goal and how you plan to achieve that goal. Explain why you have selected that goal.

Directions: On a separate sheet of paper, answer the questions below. Make sure you read carefully and answer all parts of the question.

Lesson Review

Lesson 1

❶ *Describing* Explain the findings of research about the effects of daycare on children.

❷ *Identifying* Explain the projections for the elderly population in the twenty-first century. How does this impact psychology?

❸ *Listing* List the similarities and differences in the work of applied psychologists and experimental psychologists.

Lesson 2

❹ *Identifying* Identify two careers that require a background in psychology and briefly describe the careers.

❺ *Specifying* What kind of psychological program might an individual be able to contact in the case of a life-threatening situation or to deal with long-term stress?

❻ *Locating* At what level of education can people begin to look for professional careers in psychology?

21st Century Skills

Using Graphs Job satisfaction—studied by industrial/organizational psychologists—is an issue for many people. Various factors contribute to job satisfaction. Review the graph, then answer the questions that follow.

❼ *Analyzing Visuals* According to this graph, what three job characteristics do most people find important for job satisfaction?

❽ *Identifying* With which three job characteristics were people most satisfied?

❾ *Identifying* With which three job characteristics were people least satisfied?

❿ *Evaluating* Select an area on the graph. How might an industrial/organizational psychologist help managers and/or employees in this area?

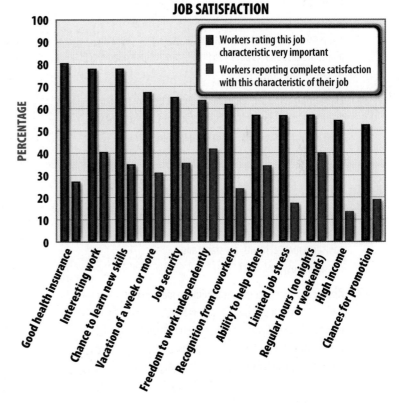

JOB SATISFACTION

■ Workers rating this job characteristic very important

■ Workers reporting complete satisfaction with this characteristic of their job

Need Extra Help?

If You've Missed Question	❶	❷	❸	❹	❺	❻	❼	❽	❾	❿
Go to page	613	614	613	619	620	618	619	619	619	619

Directions: On a separate sheet of paper, answer the questions below. Make sure you read carefully and answer all parts of the question.

Critical Thinking Questions

11 **Explaining** Define job satisfaction in your own words. Do you think it is possible to measure job satisfaction? Explain.

12 **Defending** Do college admission tests predict success in college? Why or why not?

13 **Comparing** There are many types of mental health professionals. What common characteristics do they all share?

14 **Discussing** Name three jobs in psychology that you think will offer good opportunities for employment and explain why. Name three jobs that you think will offer few opportunities and explain why.

Exploring the Essential Question

15 **Applying** Research different kinds of aptitude and intelligence tests given to high school students, such as the SAT. Find out what recent critics of the tests have claimed about the test and its ability to predict the future college success of students.

16 **Examining** Find out about the historical treatment of psychological problems. You might focus on the treatments used in the Middle Ages and in the early nineteenth century. Share your findings in an oral report.

College and Career Readiness

17 **Comparing and Contrasting** What are the educational requirements and the responsibilities of a crisis hotline adviser, a mental health assistant, and a consulting psychologist?

18 **Analyzing** Conduct research online to identify the following: Which psychology careers have developed as a result of domestic issues, such as the recession, and global issues, such as recent wars? What resources are available to help someone determine if those are careers they might want to pursue? Create a brief paper describing your findings. Be sure to provide a list of resources.

DBQ Analyzing Primary Sources

Use the document below to answer the following questions.

PRIMARY SOURCE

"*In my early professional years I was asking the question: How can I treat, or cure, or change this person? Now I would phrase the question in this way: How can I provide a relationship which this person may use for his own personal growth?*"

—*Carl Rogers*

19 **Analyzing** How do you think experience working as a psychologist changed Rogers's outlook about the field over time?

20 **Discussing** How can psychologists today learn from the work of Carl Rogers and other psychologists who worked in the past century?

Research and Technology

21 **Researching** In April and May, 2011, tornadoes ripped through Tuscaloosa, Alabama, and Joplin, Missouri, killing hundreds and destroying thousands of homes and businesses. Perform a Web quest to report on rebuilding efforts in these two towns. Use software to report on how the cities allocated resources, what improvements were made to the new structures in the area, and how the people of Joplin and Tuscaloosa have responded psychologically to these efforts.

Psychology Journal Activity

22 **Argument** Review your entry in your Psychology Journal for this chapter. How is the "crowd effect" phenomenon an example of applied psychology? Describe several ways that applied psychology can benefit society.

Need Extra Help?

If You've Missed Question	11	12	13	14	15	16	17	18	19	20	21	22
Go to page	618	613	619	620	613	612, 619	619	620	612	613	620	610

Psychology Handbook

Psychology Skills

Forming a Hypothesis

A researcher in the study of psychology analyzes information and asks a research question. The researcher then forms a **hypothesis,** or an educated guess that answers the research question. A hypothesis allows a person to make sense of unorganized, separate observations and bits of information by placing them within a structured and coherent framework. The researcher has some evidence for suspecting a specific answer. The hypothesis expresses the researcher's reasoning in such a way that it can be confirmed or not confirmed.

For example, a researcher may analyze the following information:

There are several different methods for trying to quit smoking. Most people, however, fail at their attempts to quit. Studies show that people who attend "quit smoking" clinics have a better chance of kicking the smoking habit.

Fear tactics, such as describing health hazards, have been used successfully to motivate people to modify their behavior.

The researcher asks:

Can fear tactics, such as describing the health hazards of smoking, increase the number of smokers who sign up for "quit smoking" clinics?

The researcher forms a hypothesis from this research question:

Using fear tactics, such as describing the health hazards of smoking, increases the number of smokers who sign up for "quit smoking" clinics.

Learn the Skill

1. Analyze information to identify a specific problem or question.
2. Use the specific problem or question to form a hypothesis.
3. Test the hypothesis by gathering additional information.
4. Use the additional information to reanalyze the original hypothesis. If necessary, restate the hypothesis.

Apply the Skill

Read the information below regarding two hypothetical behavioral scenarios. Once you have read both of them, form a hypothesis about these two different scenarios by using the four steps discussed above in the *Learn the Skill* section.

People who bathe in warm water relax more quickly than people who bathe in cold water.

Some mothers complain that they are unable to calm their babies in order to get them to sleep.

Interpreting Statistics

Statistics are mathematical processes used to organize, summarize, and analyze data collected by researchers. Interpreting statistics helps us use data to support a generalization or conclusion.

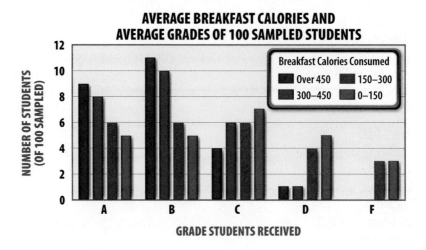

AVERAGE BREAKFAST CALORIES AND AVERAGE GRADES OF 100 SAMPLED STUDENTS

Learn the Skill

There are three things to consider when interpreting statistics: non-representative sample, correlation, and statistical significance.

1. Suppose that a psychologist wants to test the following hypothesis: *Teenagers who eat large breakfasts have high grades.* Since it is impossible to study all teenagers, the researcher must pick a **sample**, or a relatively small population, of students that represents the population of students as a whole. A **non-representative sample** is a sample that does not represent the entire population and, therefore, may affect the results of the study. For example, a sample that includes only females would be a non-representative sample. What information can you learn about the sample by looking at the Average Breakfast Calories graph?

2. A **correlation** is the association or relationship between two or more variables. For example, if data show that students who eat large breakfasts have high grades, this would be a positive correlation. If the data show that students who eat large breakfasts have low grades, this would be a negative correlation. What type of correlation do the statistics in the Average Breakfast Calories graph show?

3. When interpreting statistics, researchers must decide whether the data support a generalization or whether the data are due to chance. The results are called **statistically significant** if the probability that the data support a generalization is 95 percent or higher. Do you think the data in the Average Breakfast Calories graph support a generalization or are due to chance? Explain.

Apply the Skill

Develop a two-question survey for which you believe the data might show a correlation. For example, "Do you have a regular exercise routine that you follow?" and "Do you have enough energy to make it through the day?" Or, "Do you prefer a large group of friends or a small group of friends?" and "Are you the oldest, middle, youngest, or only child?" Pick a representative sample of people and conduct the survey. Organize and interpret your statistics.

Designing an Experiment

An **experiment** is a series of carefully planned steps that test a hypothesis. Psychologists establish cause-and-effect relationships by performing experiments. Experiments allow the researcher to control the situation and narrow the possibilities as to what can influence the results. In designing experiments, researchers think in terms of **variables**, or factors and conditions that can change or vary. Researchers test the relationship between two factors by deliberately producing a change in one factor and observing the effect the change has on the other factor. An **independent variable** is the factor that researchers change or alter so they can observe its effects. The **dependent variable** is the one that changes in response to manipulation of the independent variable.

Learn the Skill

Use the following steps to design an experiment:

1. Make a hypothesis. All experiments must start with a hypothesis. A **hypothesis** is an educated guess a researcher makes about some phenomenon. The researcher should state the hypothesis in clear, concrete language to rule out any confusion or error in its meaning. To be valid, a hypothesis must be testable by experimentation.

2. Brainstorm a list of ways to test the hypothesis. You might include surveys or questionnaires, but in order to be an experiment, one variable must be manipulated.

3. Identify the independent and dependent variables that will be measured.

4. From the list created in Step 2, design an experiment to test one variable identified in Step 3.

5. List materials needed for the experiment. This step includes determining the number of participants to be tested. Researchers should use at least two groups of participants in every experiment. The **experimental group** is the group of participants who is exposed to the independent variable. For example, if your hypothesis was that hot temperatures cause aggression in humans, then you would expose the members of the experimental group to hot temperatures and observe their reactions. Members of the **control group** are treated the same as the members of the experimental group in every way except they are not exposed to the independent variable (in this case hot temperatures).

6. Gather the data.

7. Decide how you can display the results. From the data collected, you will draw a conclusion and make a statement about your results. If your conclusion supports your hypothesis, then you may say that your hypothesis is confirmed. (Researchers use statistical procedures to determine if their results are statistically significant—that is, not due to chance.) If your conclusions did not support your hypothesis, then you would have to make additional observations, state a new hypothesis, and test it against the available data.

Researchers often repeat experiments many times before they are confident that the answers they found are correct. That is why the results of new studies and experiments are often questioned until other researchers have a chance to repeat the experiments and come up with the same conclusions.

Apply the Skill

Read the hypothesis below. Design an experiment using the steps discussed above.

People exposed to the smell of certain foods prior to eating a meal have a smaller appetite than people who are not exposed to the smell of those foods.

Using the Scientific Method

The **scientific method** is a series of planned steps used to solve problems. It is an objective, logical, and systematic way of collecting data and drawing conclusions. Psychology researchers use the scientific method to analyze data, to draw conclusions, and to prevent their own biases from interfering with the research process.

Researchers **analyze the data** collected in an experiment by looking for patterns and relationships in the facts obtained. Analyzing the data leads to **drawing conclusions**. After careful analysis of the data, the researcher asks: Was the hypothesis supported by the facts? Was it not supported? Are more data needed? **Inferences** are logical conclusions based on observations and are made after careful analysis of all the available data. Inferences are a means to explain or interpret observations.

Researchers also use reasoning to draw conclusions. **Inductive reasoning** involves first considering a number of specific statements or observations and then drawing a conclusion—reasoning from particular facts to a broad generalization. An example of inductive reasoning might be:

Observations: *That woman is a jogger. She is wearing sneakers.* Conclusion: *People who wear sneakers are joggers.*

However, just because someone is wearing sneakers does not necessarily mean that the person is a jogger. This generalization might be too broad.

Deductive reasoning involves using past knowledge or general rules to decide or predict how probable or accurate a certain conclusion is—reasoning from general to particular. An example of deductive reasoning might be:

General rule: *People who jog wear sneakers.* Past Knowledge: *That woman is a jogger.* Conclusion: *She probably wears sneakers when she jogs.*

Researchers must use both deductive and inductive reasoning in forming and testing hypotheses.

Learn the Skill

The following steps are used in the scientific method:

1. **Question** Ask a question about an observation you have made.
2. **Hypothesis** Make a hypothesis about the observation you have made.
3. **Experiment** Design an experiment that will test your hypothesis.
4. **Data** Collect data through observation and organize it into graphic form.
5. **Draw Conclusions** Analyze your data and determine if your hypothesis is true or false.

Apply the Skill

Read the hypothetical problem described below regarding Robert and his tuba. Using the steps in the scientific method outlined above, design a plan to investigate and solve this problem.

Robert is having difficulty learning to play the tuba. He is not sure if he learns better practicing by himself, with another tuba player, or with his tuba instructor.

What kind of experiment would help Robert find the answer to his question?

©Ariel Skelley/Corbis

Reading and Critical Thinking Skills

Identifying Cause-and-Effect Relationships

When reading information, it is important to determine cause-and-effect relationships in order to understand why an event occurred. A **cause** is the action or situation that produces an event. An **effect** is the result or consequence of an action or situation. The connection between what happens and what makes it happen is known as a **cause-and-effect relationship**.

Learn the Skill

1. Begin by asking questions about why events occur. Look for related problems and actions, since these are potential causes of the event.
2. Look for clue words that may help you identify whether one event caused the other. Words or phrases such as *because, led to, brought about, produced, as a result of, so that, for this reason, as a consequence, as an outgrowth, if, since,* and *therefore* indicate cause-and-effect relationships.
3. Identify the outcome or impact of the event or situation. Look for relationships between events. Be sure to check for other, more complex, connections beyond the immediate cause and effect. For example, in a chain of events, an event often becomes the cause of multiple events.

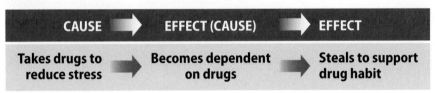

CAUSE	→	EFFECT (CAUSE)	→	EFFECT
Takes drugs to reduce stress	→	Becomes dependent on drugs	→	Steals to support drug habit

Apply the Skill

Read the following passage excerpted from an article in the *APA Monitor*. Then identify the causes and effects by creating a cause-and-effect diagram. In a paragraph, discuss the immediate effects and possible later effects.

In a recent study of 107 kindergarten students in New York City, [Dr. Carol] Dweck confirmed the notion that negative reactions to failure and criticism start early. Dweck asked the children to role-play a scene in which they pretended to give their teacher a gift they had made. Almost all of them were happy with the gift they gave. But, after the teacher found something wrong with it, nearly half of them decided the gift they had made was "bad," while the rest of them still considered the gift "good."

Comparing and Contrasting

Often it is necessary to compare and contrast to understand concepts, to make decisions, or to solve problems. Making comparisons is a good way to organize information, extend understanding, and learn more about the behavior of people. As long as two things share one common quality, they can be compared. To make a comparison, students must examine two or more groups, situations, events, or documents. Then students must identify **similarities**, or ways they are alike, and **differences**, or ways they are not alike. **Comparing** means identifying similarities. **Contrasting** means identifying differences.

Azar, Beth, *Schools the source of rough transitions* from *Close up on psychology: Supplemental readings from the APA Monitor* (Development pp. 58-71), Reich, Jill Nagy (Ed); Farberman, Rhea K. (Ed); Bulatao, Elizabeth Q. (Ed); VandenBos, Gary R. (Ed); American Psychological Association, Washington, DC, US (1997). Adapted with permission.

Learn the Skill

1. Identify what is being compared and contrasted.
2. Determine the purpose for comparing and contrasting. Ask: What do these events or items have in common? What would you compare using these two events or items? What is the purpose of this comparison? What question do you want to answer by comparing the events or items? By answering these questions, you are deciding what items are to be compared.
3. Now you must decide what characteristics will be used to compare the items. Note and list similarities in the characteristics of the items being compared. When comparing items, look for clue words that indicate two things are alike. Such clue words include *all, both, like, as, likewise,* and *similarly.*
4. List differences in the characteristics of the items. When contrasting, look for clue words that show how things differ, such as *different, differ, unlike, however,* and *on the other hand.*
5. At this point you should review the similarities and differences that you have found. Ask: Why are there similarities and differences in these items? What might have caused the differences? Point out information related to the similarities and differences found.
6. Finally, recall the research question or the purpose of comparing the events or items (from Step 2). Ask yourself: Does this comparison answer this research question? How?

Apply the Skill

Research to compare and contrast the theories and beliefs of any two of the following psychologists.

John B. Watson	Wilhelm Wundt	William James
Wolfgang Köhler	Sigmund Freud	Carl Rogers

Distinguishing Fact From Opinion

It is necessary to distinguish between fact and opinion in order to think critically and to make decisions. A **fact** is a statement that can be proved to be false or true and is supported by evidence. For example, the statement *In 2002, psychologist Daniel Kahneman won a Nobel Prize for applying psychological findings to economic theory* is a fact because it can be proved. An **opinion** expresses a personal belief, viewpoint, or emotion. For example, the statement *The best method to use to cope with stress is meditation* is an opinion since it cannot be proved and it is not supported with any evidence.

Learn the Skill

The following guidelines will help you distinguish between fact and opinion.

1. When listening to or reading a statement, keep in mind the meanings of *fact* and *opinion.* It is a fact if the statement is supported with evidence. It is an opinion if the statement is not or cannot be supported with evidence.
2. Identify facts by looking for words and phrases that indicate specific information about people, places, events, dates, times, and statistics.
3. Identify opinions by looking for words and phrases such as *I believe, I think, most likely, in my judgment, in my view, may, might, could,* and *seems to me.*

Apply the Skill

Find a newspaper or magazine article about a psychological study. Use the guidelines in *Learn the Skill* to help you identify five statements in the article as being either facts or opinions. Give a reason why each statement is either a fact or an opinion.

Research and Writing Skills

Using Critical Methods of Inquiry

It is important to use critical methods of inquiry when conducting research. Once you have decided on a topic for your research report, use the library, the Internet, or a computerized referral service to find suitable reference sources. Resource materials can be accessed through the World Wide Web. Information on the Web is organized according to category and is stored at an address, or *URL*—Universal Resource Locator. Web browsers and search engines help you locate material on the Internet.

Learn the Skill

There is a vast amount of information in libraries and on the Internet. Use the following steps in analyzing sources:

1. Determine if the material is a *primary source,* which is a firsthand account, or a *secondary source,* which is a description or interpretation of events. Primary sources are helpful because they provide a close-up view of research results. Secondary sources are helpful tools because the writer has the advantage of knowing what theories and research results were proved or disproved, thus providing a broad perspective.
2. Read the material to identify main ideas and supporting details. Consider the nature of the material. Is it scientific or is it telling a story?
3. Distinguish fact from opinion. Psychologists often express their beliefs, but make sure these beliefs are based on facts.
4. Check for bias or faulty reasoning. Search for evidence presented by the writer that supports the conclusion.
5. If possible, find more than one source to check for accuracy.
6. Consider the origin of the source. Does the writer have credibility in the field of psychology? Does the writer have a degree and experience in the subject area?
7. Search for information on the Internet written by a well-known source. Do not use information that does not list a source.

Apply the Skill

Select an article from a psychology magazine, journal, or book. Analyze the source by using the steps in *Learn the Skill.*

Organizing and Analyzing Information

Information for research reports must be organized and analyzed. To do this, it is important to know how to classify information you gather as you conduct your research, synthesize information from different sources and mediums, and create an outline of the information as it should appear in the research report.

Learn the Skill

1. **Classifying Information** As you read about your topic, identify information that has similar characteristics. List this information on separate note cards. Label the note cards with categories. Then classify this information by adding facts to the categories as you continue your research. Remember that when classifying your information, you are grouping objects or events for a purpose.

The purpose could be general, such as for ease of finding an item. Once you have classified the material, look for patterns and relationships among the facts. It is at this point that you may make comparisons, draw conclusions, and develop questions or hypotheses for further study.

2. **Synthesizing Information** When using more than one source for a research report, you need to synthesize, or combine, the information. Look for connections and relationships among different sources. You may want to include both primary and secondary sources in your report. Combine the information so that each source adds to the understanding of your topic.

3. **Outlining Information** Outlines are also very useful when researching and writing essays or reports. Use outlines to help clarify and organize your thoughts, to decide what main ideas to include, and to flesh out each main idea with subtopics and supporting details. A good outline summarizes information and shows how ideas and facts are connected. In an outline, information is arranged in three categories—main ideas; subtopics, or parts of each main idea; and supporting details. Outlines begin with broad ideas, followed by more specific ideas. Put your information in order. Determine what information will be part of the introduction, the body, and the conclusion of your report. Use main ideas as headings in your outline. Use supporting details as subheadings under the appropriate headings in your outline.

Apply the Skill

Select a topic for research. Organize and analyze the information you collect using the steps in *Learn the Skill*.

Writing a Research Report/Essay

You will be asked to write research reports and essays in most of the subjects you take in school, including psychology. There are basic steps to follow when writing research reports or essays. You can apply these steps to a report or essay written for any subject.

Writing and research skills apply to psychology and several other subjects.

Learn the Skill

1. Choose a topic and identify your purpose for the research report or essay.
2. Write several main idea questions you want to answer about your topic. Organize these questions into an outline.
3. Conduct research about the topic and take notes.
4. Organize and analyze your information. Classify, synthesize, and outline the information collected.
5. Write a first draft. A research report or essay has an introduction, a body, and a conclusion. The *introduction* explains the purpose of the report or essay. The *body* develops the main ideas of the report or essay. Be sure to use proper transitions between paragraphs in the body. The *conclusion* summarizes your findings.
6. Edit the first draft. Reorganize information, and use standard grammar, spelling, sentence structure, and punctuation.
7. Write your final report or essay.

Apply the Skill

Write a psychology research report on a subject of your choosing using the steps in *Learn the Skill*.

Visual Literacy Skills

Interpreting Charts, Tables, Graphs, and Diagrams

Data gathered in psychology research are often presented in charts, tables, graphs, and diagrams. These visual representations of data organize the information to make it quicker and easier to read, compare, and contrast.

Charts and tables are divided into columns and rows. The column title usually lists items to be compared. The row headings usually list the specific characteristics being compared among those items. There are three main types of graphs. A **line graph** shows the relationship between two variables. The independent variable usually goes on the x-axis, or the horizontal axis. The dependent variable usually goes on the y-axis, or the vertical axis. A **bar graph** is similar to a line graph, except bars are used to show comparisons between data or to display data that do not continuously change. Thick bars are used instead of dots and lines (see the Internet Usage graph below). A **circle graph** shows the parts of a whole (see the Marital Status graph below). Each section represents one part of the whole. A **diagram** is a drawing that shows what something is or how something is done. Diagrams may have several parts that show steps in a process. The parts of a diagram are usually labeled.

MARITAL STATUS OF POPULATION SEGMENTS, 2011

Source: U. S. Census Bureau, 2011

INTERNET USAGE BY AGE, LOCATION, AND DEVICE, 2010

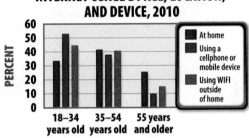

Source: U.S. Census Bureau, *Statistical Abstract of the United States,* 2012

Learn the Skill

1. **Read the title.** The title tells you the subject and purpose of the visual information being presented.
2. **Look for clues.** Study the parts of the visual information, paying close attention to labels and data types being presented.
3. **Analyze the information.** Ask yourself questions such as: How do the data relate to each other? How do the data change over time? What is the relationship of the parts to the whole? Can I identify or locate any trends presented by this data?
4. **Put the data to use.** Draw conclusions based on the data.

Apply the Skill

Find examples of visual information in your psychology text or by using the Internet. Use the steps in *Learn the Skill* to interpret the visual of your choice. Write a short paragraph about the conclusions you can draw from the data you review.

Reading and Making Graphic Organizers

A **graphic organizer** is a type of diagram that shows the relationship among ideas and helps you organize information in a visual context. A graphic organizer can make abstract ideas more concrete and help you better understand the ideas and terms you are studying. A graphic organizer can show the interaction of a series of events, present a hierarchy of procedures, or describe the steps in a process.

Graphic organizers come in many forms. There are network trees, concept webs, events chain maps, cycle concept maps, and others. There may be more than one way to construct a graphic organizer. As you make a graphic organizer, you may realize that there is a better way to show the information on a map. In that case, change the format or how the information is displayed. Graphic organizers can be used to help you review and study information.

The graphic organizer below is a network tree. To read it, begin by reading the term at the top of the network tree that shows the main concept—nervous system. Next, find the two divisions of the nervous system—central nervous system and peripheral nervous system—that branch out from the main concept. Now look at how the parts of these divisions branch out. Finally, see how the divisions of the autonomic system branch out.

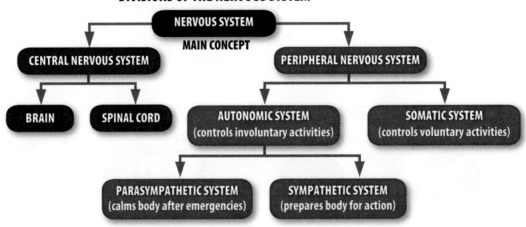

DIVISIONS OF THE NERVOUS SYSTEM

Learn the Skill

Follow the steps below when creating a graphic organizer.
1. State the main concept.
2. Branch the related concepts from the main concept. Use lines to connect the branches.
3. Continue to branch out more specific details from the related concepts.
4. You may write words on the lines to help explain the relationship of related concepts.

Apply the Skill

Construct a graphic organizer. Choose one of the following main concepts, or choose your own. Use information from your text and the steps in *Learn the Skill* to help you make your graphic organizer.

Endocrine System	Classical Conditioning
Processes of Memory	Development of Language
Changes in Old Age	Personality Theory

GLOSSARY/GLOSARIO

- Content vocabulary are words that relate to psychology content.
- Words that have an asterisk (*) are academic vocabulary. They help you understand your school subjects.
- All vocabulary words are **boldfaced** or highlighted in yellow in your textbook.

absolute threshold • alternative

ENGLISH — A — ESPAÑOL

absolute threshold the weakest amount of a stimulus that a person can detect half the time (p. 206)

umbral absoluto la magnitud más pequeña de un estímulo que una persona puede detectar la mitad de las veces (pág. 206)

*access a way of getting near something or someone (p. 580)

*acceder manera de acercarse a algo o alguien (pág. 580)

*accessibility capable of being easily used or seen (p. 214)

*accesibilidad cualidad de algo que puede usarse o verse fácilmente (pág. 214)

accommodation adjustment of one's schemas to include newly observed events and experiences (p. 61)

acomodamiento ajuste de los esquemas propios para incluir sucesos y experiencias de observación reciente (pág. 61)

*accurate correct or exact in its details (p. 398)

*preciso correcto o exacto en cuanto a los detalles (pág. 398)

achievement test measures how much a person has learned in a given subject or area (p. 366)

prueba de logros mide cuánto ha aprendido una persona en una materia o área determinada (pág. 366)

*acquire to get or obtain (p. 6)

*adquirir hacer u obtener (pág. 6)

active listening empathetic listening; a listener acknowledges, restates, and clarifies the speaker's thoughts and concerns (p. 502)

escucha activa escucha con empatía; un oyente reconoce, reformula y clarifica los pensamientos y las inquietudes del hablante (pág. 502)

acto-observer bias tendency to attribute one's own behavior to outside causes but attribute the behavior of others to internal causes (p. 537)

sesgo actor-observador tendencia a atribuir el comportamiento propio a causas externas, mientras que se atribuye el comportamiento de otros a causas internas (pág. 537)

*adapt to change in order to meet the demands of a certain environment or circumstance (p. 127)

*adaptarse cambiar para ajustarse a los requerimientos de cierto ambiente o circunstancia (pág. 127)

*adjust to change to fit new conditions (p. 125)

*ajustarse cambiar para adecuarse a nuevas condiciones (pág. 125)

*affected influenced or changed by a set of consequences (p. 244)

*afectado influido o cambiado por un conjunto de consecuencias (pág. 244)

ageism prejudice or discrimination against the elderly (p. 131)

discriminación por edad prejuicio o discriminación contra las personas mayores (pág. 131)

algorithm a step-by-step procedure for solving a problem (p. 297)

algoritmo procedimiento de varios pasos para resolver un problema (pág. 297)

*alleviate to ease or lessen pain or hardship (p. 259)

*aliviar calmar o atenuar un dolor o dificultad (pág. 259)

*alternative different (p. 11)

*alternativo diferente (pág. 11)

ENGLISH

altruism helping others, often at a cost or risk, for reasons other than rewards (p. 581)

Alzheimer's disease a condition that destroys a person's ability to think, remember, relate to others, and care for herself or himself (p. 135)

*analyze to study the nature of something by closely examining the parts that make it up (p. 18)

androgynous combining or blending traditionally male and female characteristics (p. 110)

anorexia nervosa a serious eating disorder characterized by a fear of gaining weight that results in prolonged self-starvation and dramatic weight loss (p. 104)

antidepressant medication to treat major depression by increasing the amount of one or both of the neurotransmitters noradrenaline and serotonin (p. 515)

antipsychotic drug medication to reduce agitation, delusions, and hallucinations by blocking the activity of dopamine in the brain; tranquilizers (p. 515)

antisocial personality a personality disorder characterized by irresponsibility, shallow emotions, and lack of conscience (p. 482)

anxiety a vague, generalized apprehension or feeling that one is in danger (p. 459)

applied science discovering ways to use scientific findings to accomplish practical goals (p. 7)

*approach a way of thinking about something (p. 294)

*appropriate suitable, acceptable, or correct for the particular circumstances (p. 526)

*approximate nearly correct or exact (p. 182)

aptitude test estimates the probability that a person will be successful in learning a specific new skill (p. 365)

archetype an inherited idea, based on the experiences of one's ancestors, which shapes one's perception of the world (p. 390)

*aspect a part or feature of something (p. 380)

ESPAÑOL

altruismo ayudar a los demás, generalmente con un costo o riesgo, por razones distintas de la búsqueda de recompensas (pág. 581)

mal de Alzheimer enfermedad que destruye la capacidad de una persona de pensar, recordar, relacionarse con los demás y cuidar de sí misma (pág. 135)

*analizar estudiar la naturaleza de una cosa por medio de un examen cuidadoso de las partes que la conforman (pág. 18)

andrógino que combina o fusiona características tradicionalmente femeninas y masculinas (pág. 110)

anorexia nerviosa trastorno alimenticio grave que se caracteriza por el miedo a subir de peso y que lleva al ayuno autoinfligido durante un período prolongado y a una pérdida drástica de peso (pág. 104)

antidepresivo medicación para tratar la depresión aguda por medio del aumento de la cantidad de uno o ambos de los neurotransmisores noradrenalina y serotonina (pág. 515)

antipsicótico medicación para reducir la agitación, los delirios y las alucinaciones por medio del bloqueo de la actividad de la dopamina en el encéfalo; tranquilizantes (pág. 515)

personalidad antisocial trastorno de la personalidad que se caracteriza por irresponsabilidad, emociones superficiales y falta de conciencia (pág. 482)

ansiedad aprensión vaga y generalizada o sentimiento de que se corre peligro (pág. 459)

ciencia aplicada descubrir maneras de usar los hallazgos científicos para lograr objetivos prácticos (pág. 7)

*enfoque manera de pensar acerca de algo (pág. 294)

*apropiado adecuado, aceptable o correcto para las circunstancias particulares (pág. 526)

*aproximado casi correcto o exacto (pág. 182)

prueba de aptitud estima la probabilidad de que una persona aprenda una destreza específica nueva correctamente (pág. 365)

arquetipo idea heredada, basada en las experiencias de los ancestros de una persona, que moldea la percepción que esa persona tiene del mundo (pág. 390)

*aspecto parte o característica de algo (pág. 380)

*assessment a judgment or opinion about someone or something (p. 495)

assimilation the process of fitting objects and experiences into one's schemas (p. 61)

*assume to think or accept that something is true but without having proof of it (p. 350)

*assumed thought to be true (p. 134)

asynchrony the condition during adolescence in which the growth or maturation of bodily parts is uneven (p. 88)

attitude predisposition to act, think, and feel in particular ways toward a class of people, objects, or an idea (p. 588)

attribution theory the process by which we interpret and explain others' behaviors (p. 536)

auditory nerve the nerve that carries impulses from the inner ear to the brain, resulting in the perception of sound (p. 215)

*augment to increase in number, size, or intensity (p. 194)

authoritative proceeding from authority (p. 501)

*authority a person who is in command or in charge (p. 95)

autonomic nervous system (ANS) the part of the peripheral nervous system that controls internal biological functions (p. 152)

autonomy ability to take care of oneself and make one's own decisions (p. 115)

aversive conditioning links an unpleasant state with an unwanted behavior in an attempt to eliminate the behavior (p. 510)

aversive control process of influencing behavior by means of unpleasant stimuli (p. 250)

avoidance conditioning training of an organism to respond so as to prevent the occurrence of an unpleasant stimulus (p. 251)

basic science the pursuit of knowledge about natural phenomena for its own sake (p. 7)

*evaluación juicio u opinión acerca de alguien o algo (pág. 495)

asimilación proceso en el que se insertan objetos y experiencias en los esquemas propios (pág. 61)

*suponer pensar o aceptar que algo es verdadero, pero sin tener pruebas de ello (pág. 350)

*supuesto considerado verdadero (pág. 134)

asincronía condición durante la adolescencia en la que el crecimiento o la maduración de distintas partes del cuerpo es desigual (pág. 88)

actitud predisposición para actuar, pensar y sentir de determinadas maneras respecto de una clase de personas, objetos o de una idea (pág. 588)

teoría de la atribución proceso por el cual interpretamos y explicamos los comportamientos de otros (pág. 536)

nervio auditivo nervio que transmite impulsos desde el oído interno hasta el encéfalo, lo cual causa la percepción del sonido (pág. 215)

*incrementar aumentar en cuanto al número, el tamaño o la intensidad (pág. 194)

autorizado que proviene de una autoridad (pág. 501)

*autoridad persona que está al mando o a cargo (pág. 95)

sistema nervioso autónomo (SNA) parte del sistema nervioso periférico que controla las funciones biológicas internas (pág. 152)

autonomía capacidad de cuidar de sí mismo y tomar decisiones por cuenta propia (pág. 115)

condicionamiento aversivo relaciona un estado desagradable con un comportamiento no deseado como método para eliminar ese comportamiento (pág. 510)

control aversivo proceso en el que se influye en el comportamiento por medio de un estímulo desagradable (pág. 250)

condicionamiento de evitación entrenamiento de un organismo para que responda y evite que ocurra un estímulo desagradable (pág. 251)

ciencia básica búsqueda del conocimiento sobre fenómenos naturales por el hecho en sí mismo (pág. 7)

ENGLISH	ESPAÑOL

B

behavior modification a systematic method of changing the way a person acts and feels (p. 508)

modificación del comportamiento método sistemático de cambiar la manera en la que una persona se comporta o se siente (pág. 508)

behavior therapy changing undesirable behavior through conditioning techniques (p. 508)

terapia conductual modificar un comportamiento no deseable por medio de técnicas de condicionamiento (pág. 508)

behaviorism belief that the proper subject matter of psychology is objectively observable behavior—and nothing else (p. 393)

conductismo creencia de que el verdadero objeto de estudio de la psicología es el comportamiento que se puede observar objetivamente y nada más que eso (pág. 393)

behaviorist a psychologist who analyzes how organisms learn or modify their behavior based on their response to events in the environment (p. 13)

conductista psicólogo que analiza de qué manera los organismos aprenden o modifican su comportamiento según su respuesta a lo que ocurre en el ambiente (pág. 13)

*beneficial having a helpful or useful effect (p. 164)

*beneficioso que tiene un efecto útil (pág. 164)

binocular fusion the process of combining the images received from the two eyes into a single, fused image (p. 212)

fusión binocular proceso en el que se combinan las imágenes recibidas por los dos ojos en una sola imagen fusionada (pág. 212)

biofeedback the process of learning to control bodily states by monitoring the states to be controlled (p. 444)

biorretroalimentación proceso de aprender a controlar los estados corporales mediante el monitoreo de esos estados que se quieren controlar (pág. 444)

biofeedback the process of learning to control bodily states with the help of machines monitoring the states to be controlled (p. 190)

biorretroalimentación proceso en el que se aprende a controlar los estados corporales con la ayuda de máquinas que monitorean los estados que deben controlarse (pág. 190)

bipolar disorder disorder in which an individual alternates between feelings of mania (euphoria) and depression (p. 478)

trastorno bipolar trastorno en el cual un individuo pasa de sentimientos de manía (euforia) a depresión y viceversa (pág. 478)

boomerang effect a change in attitude or behavior opposite of the one desired by the persuader (p. 603)

efecto búmeran cambio de actitud o comportamiento que es opuesto a la actitud o comportamiento deseados por quien quiere convencer a una persona (pág. 603)

brainwashing extreme form of attitude change; uses peer pressure, physical suffering, threats, rewards, guilt, and intensive indoctrination (p. 606)

lavado de cerebro forma extrema de cambio de actitud; se utilizan la presión de los pares, el sufrimiento físico, amenazas, recompensas, la culpa y un adoctrinamiento intensivo (pág. 606)

bystander effect an individual does not take action because of the presence of others (p. 581)

efecto espectador un individuoa no actúa debido a la presencia de otros (pág. 581)

C

*capacity an individual's mental or physical ability, aptitude, or skill (p. 54)

*capacidad habilidad, aptitud o destreza mental o física de un individuo (pág. 54)

cardinal trait a characteristic or feature that is so pervasive the person is almost identified with it (p. 410)

rasgo cardinal característica que es tan penetrante que la persona prácticamente se identifica con ella (pág. 410)

case study research method that involves an intensive investigation of one or more participants (p. 30)

estudio de caso método exhaustivo de investigación que implica un análisis intensivo de uno o más temas o sujetos (pág. 30)

catharsis releasing anger or aggression by letting out powerful negative emotions (p. 578)

catarsis dejar salir emociones negativas intensas para liberar sentimientos de enojo o agresión (pág. 578)

central nervous system (CNS) the brain and spinal cord (p. 148)

sistema nervioso central (SNC) el encéfalo y la médula espinal (pág. 148)

central tendency a number that describes something about the "average" score of a distribution variance (p. 42)

tendencia central número que describe algo que está por encima del resultado "promedio" de una varianza de la distribución (pág. 42)

*challenge to confront; to question formally (p. 466)

*desafiar confrontar; cuestionar formalmente (pág. 466)

chunking the process of grouping items to make them easier to remember (p. 271)

agrupamiento proceso en el que se agrupan elementos para que sean más fáciles de recordar (pág. 271)

circadian rhythm the rhythm of activity and inactivity lasting approximately one day (p. 183)

ritmo circadiano el ritmo de actividad e inactividad que dura aproximadamente un día (pág. 183)

classical conditioning a learning procedure in which associations are made between a neutral stimulus and an unconditioned stimulus (p. 236)

condicionamiento clásico procedimiento de aprendizaje en el que las asociaciones se hacen entre un estímulo neutral y un estímulo incondicionado (pág. 236)

client-centered therapy reflects the belief that the client and therapist are partners in therapy (p. 502)

terapia centrada en el cliente refleja la creencia de que el cliente y el terapeuta son compañeros en la terapia (pág. 502)

clique a small, exclusive group of people within a larger group (p. 101)

clan grupo pequeño y exclusivo de personas dentro de otro grupo más grande (pág. 101)

cognitive appraisal the interpretation of an event that helps determine its stress impact (p. 441)

evaluación cognitiva interpretación de un suceso que permite determinar su efecto estresante (pág. 441)

cognitive dissonance the uncomfortable feeling when a person experiences contradictory or conflicting thoughts, attitudes, beliefs, or feelings (p. 596)

disonancia cognitiva sentimiento incómodo que ocurre cuando una persona tiene pensamientos, actitudes, creencias o sentimientos contradictorios (pág. 596)

cognitive having to do with an organism's thinking and understanding (p. 4)

cognitivo relacionado con el razonamiento y la comprensión de un organismo (pág. 4)

cognitive learning form of altering behavior that involves mental processes and may result from observation or imitation (p. 256)

aprendizaje cognitivo forma de modificación del comportamiento que involucra procesos mentales y que puede deberse a la observación o la imitación (pág. 256)

cognitive map a mental picture of spatial relationships or relationships between events (p. 257)

mapa cognitivo imagen mental de relaciones espaciales o relaciones entre sucesos (pág. 257)

cognitive therapies using thoughts to control emotions and behaviors (p. 505)

terapias cognitivas usar los pensamientos para controlar las emociones y los comportamientos (pág. 505)

ENGLISH

ESPAÑOL

cognitive-behavior therapy based on a combination of substituting healthy thoughts for negative thoughts and beliefs and changing disruptive behaviors in favor of healthy behaviors (p. 511)

terapia conductual cognitiva tiene como base una combinación que implica reemplazar creencias y pensamientos negativos por pensamientos sanos y cambiar comportamientos disruptivos por comportamientos sanos (pág. 511)

cognitivist a psychologist who studies how we process, store, retrieve, and use information and how thought processes influence our behavior (p. 13)

cognitivista psicólogo que estudia de qué manera procesamos, almacenamos, recuperamos y usamos la información, y cómo los procesos del pensamiento influyen en nuestro comportamiento (pág. 13)

collective unconscious the part of the mind that contains inherited instincts, urges, and memories common to all people (p. 390)

inconsciente colectivo parte de la mente que contiene los instintos, impulsos y recuerdos heredados que comparten todas las personas (pág. 390)

*comment a statement that expresses an opinion (p. 571)

*comentario enunciado que expresa una opinión (pág. 571)

comparable worth the concept that women and men should receive equal pay for jobs calling for comparable skill and responsibility (p. 118)

valor comparable concepto de que los hombres y las mujeres deberían tener el mismo salario por hacer trabajos que demandan responsabilidades y destrezas comparables (pág. 118)

complementarity the attraction that often develops between opposite types of people because of the ability of one to supply what the other lacks (p. 531)

complementariedad atracción que se desarrolla a menudo entre tipos de personas opuestos por la capacidad de una de brindar a la otra algo que le falta (pág. 531)

*complex complicated (p. 395)

*complejo complicado (pág. 395)

compliance a change or maintenance of behavior to avoid discomfort or rejection and to gain approval (p. 595)

adecuación cambio o mantenimiento de comportamiento para evitar la incomodidad o el rechazo y obtener aprobación (pág. 595)

*component one of the parts of the whole (p. 140)

*componente una de las partes del todo (pág. 140)

*comprehensive covering completely (p. 455)

*integral que cubre por completo (pág. 455)

computerized axial tomography (CT) an imaging technique used to study the brain to pinpoint injuries and brain deterioration (p. 161)

tomografía axial computarizada (TC) técnica de diagnóstico por imágenes utilizada para estudiar el encéfalo con el objeto de localizar lesiones y deterioro cerebral (pág. 161)

*conclude to decide or believe something as a result of what you have heard or seen (p. 316)

*concluir decidir o creer algo como resultado de lo que se ha oído o visto (pág. 316)

conditioned response (CR) the learned reaction to a conditioned stimulus (p. 237)

respuesta condicionada (RC) reacción aprendida ante un estímulo condicionado (pág. 237)

conditioned stimulus (CS) a once-neutral event that elicits a given response after a period of training in which it has been paired with an unconditioned stimulus (p. 237)

estímulo condicionado (EC) suceso antes neutro que requiere una respuesta determinada después de un período de entrenamiento en el que se unió con un estímulo incondicionado (pág. 237)

conditions of worth the conditions a person must meet in order to regard himself or herself positively (p. 400)

condiciones de valor condiciones que una persona debe cumplir para considerarse de manera positiva (pág. 400)

*conduct a person's behaviior in a particular place or situation (p. 426)

*comportamiento el comportamiento de una persona en un lugar o un situación determinado (pág. 426)

confabulation the act of filling in memory gaps (p. 281)

confabulación acción de llenar vacíos en la memoria (pág. 281)

conflict situation when a person must choose between two or more options that tend to result from opposing motives (p. 422)

situación conflictiva cuando una persona debe escoger entre dos o más opciones que tienden a surgir de motivos opuestos (pág. 422)

*conflict a clash of opposing wishes or needs (p. 381)

*conflicto choque de deseos o necesidades opuestos (pág. 381)

*conform to act in accordance with prevailing standards or customs (p. 88)

*adecuarse actuar de acuerdo con los estándares o las costumbres predominantes (pág. 88)

conformity acting in accordance with some specified authority (p. 101)

adecuación actuar en conformidad con una autoridad específica (pág. 101)

consciousness a state of awareness, including a person's feelings, sensations, ideas, and perceptions (p. 180)

conciencia estado de conocimiento que incluye los sentimientos, las sensaciones, las ideas y las percepciones de una persona (pág. 180)

conservation the principle that a given quantity does not change when its appearance is changed (p. 62)

conservación principio de que una cantidad determinada no cambia cuando se cambia su apariencia (pág. 62)

*consist to involve (p. 517)

*consistir incluir (pág. 517)

constancy the tendency to perceive certain objects in the same way regardless of changing angle, distance, or lighting (p. 227)

constancia tendencia a percibir determinados objetos de la misma manera, independientemente de los cambios de ángulo, distancia o iluminación (pág. 227)

*constrain to hold back as if by force; to restrict (p. 482)

*reprimir retener como si fuera por la fuerza; restringir (pág. 482)

*constriction a narrowing of a channel or vessel, or a feeling of tightness or pressure (p. 191)

*constricción estrechamiento de un canal o vaso sanguíneo, o bien sensación de tensión o presión (pág. 191)

*contemporary modern or current (p. 12)

*contemporáneo moderno o actual (pág. 12)

contingencies of reinforcement the occurrence of rewards or punishments following particular behaviors (p. 394)

contingencias de refuerzo ocurrencia de recompensas o castigos después de comportamientos específicos (pág. 394)

contingency management undesirable behavior is not reinforced, while desirable behavior is reinforced (p. 510)

control de la contingencia el comportamiento no deseable no se refuerza, mientras que sí se refuerza el comportamiento deseable (pág. 510)

*contribute to give or supply along with others (p. 307)

*contribuir dar o proveer junto con otros (pág. 307)

control group the group that is treated in the same way as the experimental group except that the experimental treatment (the independent variable) is not applied (p. 32)

grupo de control grupo al que se trata de la misma manera que a un grupo experimental excepto por que no se aplica el tratamiento experimental (la variable independiente) (pág. 32)

conversion disorder changing emotional difficulties into a loss of a specific voluntary body function (p. 467)

trastorno de conversión trastorno en el cual las dificultades emocionales se convierten en la pérdida de una determinada función corporal voluntaria (pág. 467)

*core base or central part of something (p. 412)

*centro base o parte central de algo (pág. 412)

ENGLISH

correlation coefficient describes the direction and strength of the relationship between two sets of variables (p. 44)

correlation the measure of a relationship between two variables or sets of data (p. 31)

*correspond to be similar or equivalent to something (p. 367)

counterattitudinal behavior the process of taking a public position that contradicts one's private attitude (p. 597)

*create to make something happen or exist (p. 620)

crisis intervention program short-term psychological first aid that helps individuals and families deal with emergencies or highly stressful situations (p. 619)

cross-sectional study research method in which data are collected from groups of participants of different ages and compared so that conclusions can be drawn about differences due to age (p. 30)

cultural bias an aspect of an intelligence test in which the wording used in questions may be more familiar to people of one social group than to another group (p. 361)

*culture the beliefs, customs, practices, and social behavior of a particular nation or people (p. 362)

ESPAÑOL

coeficiente de correlación describe la dirección y el grado de la relación entre dos conjuntos de variables (pág. 44)

correlación medida de una relación entre dos variables o conjuntos de datos (pág. 31)

*corresponder ser similar o equivalente a algo (pág. 367)

comportamiento contraactitudinal proceso de tomar una posición pública que contradice la propia actitud privada (pág. 597)

*crear hacer que algo ocurra o exista (pág. 620)

programa de intervención en crisis primeros auxilios psicológicos a corto plazo que ayudan a individuos y familiares a lidiar con emergencias o situaciones sumamente estresantes (pág. 619)

estudio transversal método de investigación en el que se reúnen datos sobre grupos de participantes de diferentes edades que luego se comparan para poder sacar conclusiones acerca de las diferencias relacionadas con la edad (pág. 30)

sesgo cultural aspecto de una prueba de inteligencia en la cual la forma en la que se formulan las preguntas puede resultar más conocida para personas de un grupo social que de otro (pág. 361)

*cultura creencias, costumbres, prácticas y conductas sociales de una nación o pueblo en particular (pág. 362)

D

*data facts and statistics collected for study (p. 412)

debriefing a procedure conducted at the end of an experiment to reveal the details of the study so that participants do not leave feeling confused or upset (p. 570)

decay fading away of memory over time (p. 283)

declarative memory stored knowledge that can be called forth consciously as needed (p. 273)

*decline to drop or become less in amount (p. 472)

decremental model of aging idea that progressive physical and mental decline are inevitable with age (p. 131)

*datos hechos y estadísticas reunidos para un estudio (pág. 412)

informe posterior al sujeto procedimiento que se realiza al terminar un experimento para dar a conocer los detalles del estudio de manera que los participantes no se marchen confundidos ni disgustados (p. 570)

deterioro pérdida gradual de la memoria con el tiempo (pág. 283)

memoria declarativa conocimiento almacenado que puede recuperarse de manera consciente cuando es necesario (pág. 273)

*decrecer bajar o disminuir en cantidad (pág. 472)

modelo decremental del envejecimiento idea de que el deterioro físico y mental llega inevitablemente con la edad (pág. 131)

defense mechanisms certain specific means by which the ego unconsciously protects itself against unpleasant impulses or circumstances (p. 387)

mecanismos de defensa medios específicos por los cuales el yo inconscientemente se protege a sí mismo de impulsos o circunstancias desagradables (pág. 387)

*****define** to state or describe something exactly (p. 545)

*****definir** formular o describir algo exactamente (pág. 545)

deindividuation individuals behave irrationally when there is less chance of being personally identified (p. 582)

desindividuación los individuos se comportan de manera irracional cuando hay menos posibilidades de ser identificados personalmente (pág. 582)

delusions false beliefs that a person maintains in the face of contrary evidence (p. 472)

delirios creencias falsas que mantiene una persona ante pruebas que demuestran lo contrario (pág. 472)

dementia decreases in mental abilities, which can be experienced by some people in old age (p. 134)

demencia disminución de las habilidades mentales que puede afectar a algunas personas de edad avanzada (pág. 134)

*****demonstrate** to show something clearly by giving evidence (p. 241)

*****demostrar** mostrar algo claramente mediante pruebas (pág. 241)

descriptive statistics the listing and summarizing of data in a practical, efficient way (p. 41)

estadística descriptiva presentación y resumen de datos de manera práctica y eficiente (pág. 41)

*****detect** to find out or discover (p. 156)

*****detectar** descubrir (pág. 156)

developmental friendship friends force one another to reexamine their basic assumptions and perhaps adopt new ideas and beliefs (p. 116)

amistad del desarrollo los amigos se obligan entre sí a reevaluar sus suposiciones básicas y tal vez adoptar nuevas ideas y creencias (pág. 116)

developmental psychology the study of changes that occur as an individual matures (p. 52)

psicología del desarrollo estudio de los cambios que ocurren durante el proceso de maduración de un individuo (pág. 52)

*****device** something made or adapted for a particular purpose (p. 444)

*****dispositivo** algo hecho o adaptado para un propósito en particular (pág. 444)

difference threshold the smallest change in a physical stimulus that can be detected half the time (p. 206)

umbral diferencial el cambio más pequeño que puede detectarse en un estímulo físico la mitad de las veces (pág. 206)

*****differentiate** to make different in some way (p. 556)

*****diferenciar** hacer diferente de alguna manera (pág. 556)

diffusion of responsibility the presence of others lessens an individual's feelings of responsibility for his or her actions or failure to act (p. 581)

difusión de la responsabilidad la presencia de otras personas disminuye los sentimientos de responsabilidad que siente un individuo por sus acciones o su falta de acción (pág. 581)

discrimination the ability to respond differently to similar but distinct stimuli (p. 238)

discriminación capacidad de responder de manera diferente a estímulos similares pero singulares (pág. 238)

*****display** to exhibit (p. 463)

*****exponer** exhibir (pág. 463)

dissociative amnesia the inability to recall important personal events or information; is usually associated with stressful events (p. 468)

amnesia disociativa incapacidad de recordar información o sucesos personales importantes; por lo general, está asociada a sucesos estresantes (pág. 468)

Glossary/Glosario

ENGLISH

dissociative disorder a disorder in which a person experiences alterations in memory, identity, or consciousness (p. 468)

dissociative fugue a dissociative disorder in which a person suddenly and unexpectedly travels away from home or work and is unable to recall the past (p. 468)

dissociative identity disorder a person exhibits two or more personality states, each with its own patterns of thinking and behaving (p. 468)

*distort to twist out of true meaning or proportion (p. 228)

distress stress that stems from acute anxiety or pressure (p. 421)

*dominate to rule over or to stand out above all others (p. 328)

double-blind experiment an experiment in which neither the experimenter nor the participants know which participants received which treatment (p. 35)

dream analysis a technique used by psychoanalysts to interpret the content of patients' dreams (p. 500)

drive a state of tension produced by a need that motivates an organism toward a goal (p. 317)

drug therapy biological therapy that uses medications (p. 514)

DSM-5 current version of the American Psychiatric Association's *Diagnostic and Statistical Manual of Mental Disorders* (p. 455)

ESPAÑOL

trastorno disociativo trastorno en el cual una persona experimenta alteraciones en la memoria, la identidad o la conciencia (pág. 468)

fuga disociativa trastorno disociativo en el cual una persona se aleja de su casa o trabajo de repente y sin aviso, y no puede recordar el pasado (pág. 468)

trastorno de identidad disociativo trastorno en el cual una persona exhibe dos o más estados de personalidad, cada uno con patrones propios de razonamiento y comportamiento (pág. 468)

*distorsionar cambiar el verdadero significado o proporción de algo (pág. 228)

distrés estrés originado por ansiedad o presión agudas (pág. 421)

*dominar reinar o destacarse entre el resto (pág. 328)

experimento doble ciego experimento en el que ni el encargado del experimento ni los participantes saben qué participantes recibieron qué tratamiento (pág. 35)

análisis de los sueños técnica usada por los psicoanalistas para interpretar el contenido de los sueños de los pacientes (pág. 500)

impulso estado de tensión producido por una necesidad que motiva a un organismo hacia un objetivo (pág. 317)

terapia medicamentosa terapia biológica en la que se usan medicamentos (pág. 514)

DSM-5 versión actual del Manual diagnóstico y estadístico de los trastornos mentales de la Asociación Americana de Psiquiatría (pág. 455)

E

eclectic approach method that combines various kinds of therapy or combinations of therapies (p. 494)

ego the part of the personality that is in touch with reality and strives to meet the demands of the id and the superego in socially acceptable ways (p. 386)

ego-support value the ability of a person to provide another person with sympathy, encouragement, and approval (p. 528)

egocentric a young child's inability to understand another person's perspective (p. 62)

enfoque ecléctico método que combina varios tipos de terapia o combinaciones de terapias (pág. 494)

yo parte de la personalidad que está en contacto con la realidad y se esfuerza por satisfacer las exigencias del ello y del superyó de maneras socialmente aceptables (pág. 386)

valor de apoyo al yo capacidad de una persona de brindarle a otra su simpatía, ánimo y aprobación (pág. 528)

egocéntrico incapacidad de un niño joven de entender la perspectiva de otra persona (pág. 62)

eidetic memory the ability to remember with great accuracy visual information on the basis of short-term exposure (p. 282)

memoria eidética capacidad de recordar información visual con mucha precisión sobre la base de la exposición en el corto plazo (pág. 282)

elaborative rehearsal the linking of new information to material that is already known (p. 284)

ensayo elaborativo asociación de nueva información a otro material que ya se conoce (pág. 284)

electroconvulsive therapy (ECT) an electrical shock is sent through the brain to try to reduce symptoms of mental disturbance (p. 517)

terapia electroconvulsiva (TEC) se envía una corriente eléctrica a través del encéfalo para intentar reducir los síntomas de la alteración mental (pág. 517)

electroencephalograph (EEG) a machine used to record the electrical activity of large portions of the brain (p. 158)

electroencefalógrafo (EEG) máquina utilizada para registrar la actividad eléctrica de grandes porciones del encéfalo (pág. 158)

*eliminate to remove or get rid of (p. 35)

*eliminar quitar algo o deshacerse de algo (pág. 35)

*emerge to become known or apparent (p. 373)

*emerger hacerse conocido o aparente (pág. 373)

emotion a set of complex reactions to stimuli involving subjective feelings, physiological arousal, and observable behavior (p. 335)

emoción conjunto de reacciones complejas ante un estímulo que incluyen sentimientos subjetivos, la excitación fisiológica y el comportamiento observable (pág. 335)

emotional intelligence interpersonal and intrapersonal abilities needed to understand and use knowledge of emotions effectively (p. 356)

inteligencia emocional capacidades interpersonales e intrapersonales necesarias para comprender y utilizar eficazmente el conocimiento de las emociones (pág. 356)

empirical based on observation or experiment (p. 7)

empírico fundamentado por medio de la observación o la experimentación (pág. 7)

encoding the transforming of information so the nervous system can process it (p. 268)

codificación transformación de la información de manera que el sistema nervioso pueda procesarla (pág. 268)

*encounter to come upon or meet with, especially unexpectedly (p. 116)

*encontrar dar con algo o alguien, especialmente de forma inesperada (pág. 116)

endocrine system a chemical communication system, using hormones, by which messages are sent through the bloodstream (p. 164)

sistema endocrino sistema de comunicación química por el cual se envían mensajes a través del torrente sanguíneo por medio de hormonas (pág. 164)

*energy power or strength required to maintain activity (p. 385)

*energía poder o fuerza requeridos para mantener una actividad (pág. 385)

entrenched to establish solidly (p. 406)

arraigado establecerse firmemente (p. 406)

*environment the objects or conditions that surround something or someone (p. 20)

*ambiente objetos o condiciones que rodean algo o a alguien (pág. 20)

episodic memory chronological retention of the events of one's life (p. 273)

memoria episódica retención cronológica de los sucesos de la propia vida (pág. 273)

escape conditioning training of an organism to remove or terminate an unpleasant stimulus (p. 250)

condicionamiento de escape entrenamiento de un organismo para quitar o eliminar un estímulo desagradable (pág. 250)

ENGLISH

eustress positive stress, which results from motivating strivings and challenges (p. 421)

*evaluate to determine the significance of (p. 35)

*exhibit to demonstrate or show clearly (p. 434)

experimental group the group to which an independent variable is applied (p. 31)

*expert someone having special skill or knowledge (p. 514)

*exposure the act or condition of being subject to some effect or influence (p. 589)

extinction the gradual disappearance of a conditioned response when the conditioned stimulus is repeatedly presented without the unconditioned stimulus (p. 238)

extrasensory perception (ESP) an ability to gain information by some means other than the ordinary senses (p. 228)

extrinsic motivation engaging in activities that either reduce biological needs or help us obtain external incentives (p. 319)

ESPAÑOL

eustrés estrés positivo que resulta de impulsos y desafíos motivadores (pág. 421)

*evaluar determinar el significado de algo (pág. 35)

*exhibir demostrar o mostrar claramente (pág. 434)

grupo experimental grupo al que se aplica una variable independiente (pág. 31)

*experto alguien que tiene una destreza o un conocimiento especiales (pág. 514)

*exposición acto o condición de estar sujeto a un efecto o una influencia (pág. 589)

extinción desaparición gradual de una respuesta condicionada cuando el estímulo condicionado se presenta en varias ocasiones sin el estímulo incondicionado (pág. 238)

percepción extrasensorial (PES) capacidad de obtener información por medios distintos de los sentidos comunes (pág. 228)

motivación extrínseca realizar actividades que, o bien reducen necesidades biológicas, o bien nos ayudan a obtener incentivos externos (pág. 319)

F

factor analysis a complex statistical technique used to identify the underlying reasons variables are correlated (p. 411)

*factor something that contributes to producing a result; an ingredient (p. 306)

*flexibility able to change to meet new conditions or situations (p. 294)

*flexible able to change or be changed according to the circumstances (p. 371)

forebrain a part of the brain that covers the brain's central core, responsible for sensory and motor control and the processing of thinking and language (p. 153)

fraternal twins twins who come from two different eggs fertilized by two different sperm (p. 173)

análisis factorial técnica estadística compleja utilizada para identificar las razones subyacentes por las cuales las variables están correlacionadas (pág. 411)

*factor algo que contribuye a que se produzca un resultado; ingrediente (pág. 306)

*flexibilidad capacidad de cambiar para enfrentar nuevas condiciones o situaciones (pág. 294)

*flexible capaz de cambiar o de ser cambiado según las circunstancias (pág. 371)

cerebro anterior porción del encéfalo que cubre su parte central y se encarga de controlar las funciones sensoriales y motoras, y de procesar el pensamiento y el lenguaje (pág. 153)

gemelos fraternos gemelos que provienen de dos óvulos distintos, fecundados por dos espermatozoides diferentes (pág. 173)

free association a method used to examine the unconscious; the patient is instructed to say whatever comes into his or her mind (p. 500)

frequency distribution an arrangement of data that indicates how often a particular score or observation occurs (p. 41)

fully functioning having the person and self coincide (p. 401)

*__function__ use or purpose (p. 133)

functional fixedness the inability to imagine new uses for familiar objects (p. 298)

functionalist a psychologist who studies the function (rather than the structure) of consciousness (p. 11)

fundamental attribution error an inclination to over attribute others' behavior to internal causes (dispositional factors) and discount the situational factors contributing to their behavior (p. 536)

fundamental needs biological drives that must be satisfied to maintain life (p. 329)

*__fundamental__ central; forming the necessary basis of something (p. 367)

asociación libre método usado para examinar el inconsciente; se indica al paciente que diga cualquier cosa que le venga a la mente (pág. 500)

distribución de frecuencias ordenamiento de los datos que indica con qué frecuencia ocurre un resultado u observación particular (pág. 41)

plenamente funcional individuo cuya persona y autoconcepto coinciden (pág. 401)

*__función__ uso o propósito (pág. 133)

fijación funcional la incapacidad de pensar nuevos usos para objetos conocidos (pág. 298)

funcionalista psicólogo que estudia la función (más que la estructura) de la conciencia (pág. 11)

error fundamental de atribución inclinación a atribuir en exceso el comportamiento de otros a causas internas (factores de disposición) y descontar los factores situacionales que contribuyen a su comportamiento (pág. 536)

necesidades fundamentales impulsos biológicos que deben satisfacerse para mantener la vida (pág. 329)

*__fundamental__ central; que forma la base necesaria de algo (pág. 367)

G

gender identity the sex group (masculine or feminine) to which an individual biologically belongs (p. 108)

gender role the set of behaviors that society considers appropriate for each sex (p. 109)

gender schema a set of behaviors organized around how either a male or female should think and behave (p. 114)

gender stereotype an oversimplified or distorted generalization about the characteristics of men and women (p. 109)

*__gender__ relating to a person's sex, male or female (p. 108)

generalization responding similarly to a range of similar stimuli (p. 238)

identidad de género grupo sexual (masculino o femenino) al que biológicamente pertenece un individuo (pág. 108)

rol de género conjunto de comportamientos que la sociedad considera apropiados para cada sexo (pág. 109)

esquema de género conjunto de comportamientos organizados en función de cómo deben pensar y comportarse un hombre o una mujer (pág. 114)

estereotipo de género generalización distorsionada o excesivamente simplificada sobre las características de los hombres y las mujeres (pág. 109)

*__género__ relacionado con el sexo femenino o masculino de una persona (pág. 108)

generalización responder de manera similar a un rango de estímulos similares (pág. 238)

Glossary/Glosario

ENGLISH	ESPAÑOL
generational identity the theory that people of different ages tend to think differently about certain issues because of different formative experiences (p. 543)	**identidad generacional** teoría de que las personas de distintas edades tienden a pensar diferente acerca de ciertos asuntos porque tuvieron diferentes experiencias formativas (pág. 543)
generativity the desire, in middle age, to use one's accumulated wisdom to guide future generations (p. 129)	**generatividad** deseo, durante la mediana edad, de utilizar la propia sabiduría acumulada para guiar a las generaciones futuras (pág. 129)
genes the basic building blocks of heredity (p. 171)	**genes** componentes básicos de la herencia (pág. 171)
genotype the set of genes in an organism (p. 171)	**genotipo** conjunto de genes de un organismo (pág. 171)
gerontology the study of aging (p. 614)	**gerontología** estudio del envejecimiento (pág. 614)
Gestalt the experience that comes from organizing bits and pieces of information into meaningful wholes (p. 223)	**Gestalt** experiencia que proviene de la organización de fragmentos de información para formar un todo coherente (pág. 223)
*goal something that you hope to achieve (p. 622)	***meta** algo que se espera lograr (pág. 622)
grasping reflex an infant's clinging response to a touch on the palm of his or her hand (p. 54)	**reflejo de prensión** respuesta de agarre de un bebé al recibir un contacto en la palma de su mano (pág. 54)
group a collection of people who have shared goals, a degree of interdependence, and some amount of communication (p. 556)	**grupo** conjunto de personas que comparten objetivos, un grado de interdependencia y cierta cantidad de comunicación (pág. 556)
group polarization theory that group discussion reinforces the majority's point of view and shifts group members' opinions to a more extreme position (p. 560)	**polarización grupal** teoría de que los debates grupales refuerzan el punto de vista de la mayoría y llevan las opiniones de los miembros del grupo a una posición más extrema (pág. 560)
group therapy patients work together with the aid of a leader to resolve interpersonal problems (p. 496)	**terapia de grupo** los pacientes trabajan en conjunto con la ayuda de un líder para resolver problemas interpersonales (pág. 496)
groupthink poor group decision making that occurs as a result of a group emphasizing unity over critical thinking (p. 561)	**pensamiento grupal** en un grupo, toma de decisiones deficiente que ocurre porque se hace hincapié en la unidad en lugar del razonamiento crítico (pág. 561)

H

hallucinations perceptions that have no direct external cause (p. 472)	**alucinaciones** percepciones que no tienen una causa externa directa (pág. 472)
hallucinations perceptions that have no direct external cause (p. 195)	**alucinaciones** percepciones que no tienen causa externa directa (pág. 195)
hallucinogens drugs that often produce hallucinations (p. 195)	**alucinógenos** drogas que suelen producir alucinaciones (pág. 195)
*hence as a consequence (p. 393)	***por** tanto en consecuencia (pág. 393)

heredity the genetic transmission of characteristics from parents to their offspring (p. 170)

herencia transmisión genética de características de los padres a sus hijos (pág. 170)

heritability the degree to which a characteristic is related to inherited genetic factors (p. 360)

heredabilidad grado en el que una característica está relacionada con factores genéticos heredados (pág. 360)

heuristic a rule-of-thumb problem-solving strategy (p. 297)

heurística estrategia de resolución de problemas que es una regla de oro (pág. 297)

*hierarchy the classification of a group of people according to ability or to economic or social standing (p. 101)

*jerarquía clasificación de un grupo de personas según su capacidad o su estatus económico o social (pág. 101)

hindbrain a part of the brain located at the rear base of the skull that is involved in the basic processes of life (p. 153)

cerebro posterior porción del encéfalo ubicada en la fosa craneal posterior que controla los procesos básicos para el mantenimiento de la vida (pág. 153)

homeostasis the tendency of all organisms to correct imbalances and deviations from their normal state (p. 317)

homeostasis tendencia de todos los organismos de corregir desequilibrios y desviaciones de su estado normal (pág. 317)

hormones chemical substances that carry messages through the body in blood (p. 164)

hormonas sustancias químicas que llevan mensajes a todo el cuerpo a través de la sangre (pág. 164)

hospice a facility designed to care for the special needs of the dying (p. 140)

centro de cuidados paliativos institución orientada a atender las necesidades especiales de los enfermos terminales (pág. 140)

humanist a psychologist who believes that each person has freedom in directing his or her future and achieving personal growth (p. 13)

humanista psicólogo que cree que cada persona es libre de conducir su propio futuro y lograr un crecimiento personal (pág. 13)

humanistic psychology a school of psychology that emphasizes personal growth and the achievement of maximum potential by each unique individual (p. 397)

psicología humanista escuela de la psicología que hace hincapié en el crecimiento personal y el desarrollo del máximo potencial de cada individuo en particular (pág. 397)

humanistic therapy focuses on the value, dignity, and worth of each person; holds that healthy living is the result of realizing one's full potential (p. 502)

terapia humanista se enfoca en el valor, la dignidad y calidad de cada persona; sostiene que una vida sana es el resultado de la realización plena del propio potencial (pág. 502)

hypnosis a state of consciousness resulting from a narrowed focus of attention and characterized by heightened suggestibility (p. 188)

hipnosis estado de conciencia que se produce por un foco de atención reducido y se caracteriza por una alta sugestibilidad (pág. 188)

hypothesis an assumption or prediction about behavior that is tested through scientific research (p. 6)

hipótesis suposición o predicción sobre el comportamiento que se pone a prueba por medio de la investigación científica (pág. 6)

I

id the part of the unconscious personality that contains our needs, drives, instincts, and repressed material (p. 386)

ello parte de la personalidad inconsciente que contiene nuestras necesidades, impulsos, instintos y material reprimido (pág. 386)

identical twins twins who come from one fertilized egg; twins having the same heredity (p. 173)

gemelos idénticos gemelos que provienen de un solo óvulo fecundado; gemelos que poseen la misma herencia (pág. 173)

ENGLISH

identification seeing oneself as similar to another person or group and accepting the attitudes of another person or group as one's own (p. 595)

identification the process by which a child adopts the values and principles of the same-sex parent (p. 73)

identity crisis a period of inner conflict during which adolescents worry intensely about who they are (p. 97)

***identity** who or what someone or something is (p. 550)

ideology the set of principles, attitudes, and defined objectives for which a group stands (p. 558)

image a visual, mental representation of an event or object (p. 292)

***impact** to have a direct effect upon something (p. 165)

***imply** to suggest (p. 495)

imprinting inherited tendency of some newborn animals to follow the first moving object they see (p. 65)

inbred descended from ancestors with similar genetics (p. 172)

incentive an external stimulus, reinforcer, or reward that motivates behavior (p. 319)

***index** to enter into a sequential arrangement of material (p. 284)

***indicate** to show that something is happening (p. 503)

inferential statistics numerical methods used to determine whether research data support a hypothesis or whether results were due to chance (p. 45)

inferiority complex a pattern of avoiding feelings of inadequacy rather than trying to overcome their source (p. 390)

***inhibit** to discourage from spontaneous activity, especially through the operation of inner psychological or external social pressures (p. 197)

***initial** coming first, or present at the beginning of an event or process (p. 534)

ESPAÑOL

identificación verse a sí mismo como alguien similar a otra persona o grupo y aceptar las actitudes de otra persona o grupo como propias (pág. 595)

identificación proceso por el cual un niño adopta los valores y principios del progenitor de su mismo sexo (pág. 73)

crisis de identidad período de conflicto interno durante el cual los adolescentes sienten una intensa ansiedad por definir quiénes son (pág. 97)

***identidad** lo que es algo o quien es alguien (pág. 550)

ideología conjunto de principios, actitudes y objetivos definidos que representan a un grupo (pág. 558)

imagen representación visual y mental de un suceso u objeto (pág. 292)

***afectar** tener un efecto directo sobre algo (pág. 165)

***implicar** sugerir (pág. 495)

impronta tendencia heredada de algunos animales recién nacidos de seguir el primer objeto que ven en movimiento (pág. 65)

endogámico que desciende de ancestros que poseen una genética similar (pág. 172)

incentivo estímulo externo, refuerzo o recompensa que motiva el comportamiento (pág. 319)

***indizar** ingresar en una organización secuencial del material (pág. 284)

***indicador** para mostrar que algo está pasando (pág. 503)

estadística inferencial métodos numéricos que se utilizan para determinar si los datos de una investigación sustentan una hipótesis o si los resultados se obtuvieron por azar (pág. 45)

complejo de inferioridad patrón en el cual se evitan los sentimientos de inadecuación en lugar de intentar superar su origen (pág. 390)

***inhibir** no estimular la actividad espontánea, especialmente por medio de presiones psicológicas internas o presiones sociales externas (pág. 197)

***inicial** que viene primero o que está presente al principio de un suceso o proceso (pág. 534)

initiation rites ceremonies or rituals in which an individual is admitted to new status or accepted into a new position (p. 84)

ritos de iniciación ceremonias o rituales en los que un individuo obtiene un nuevo estatus o es aceptado en una nueva posición (pág. 84)

*injure to cause harm to or hurt (p. 597)

*dañar causar daño o lastimar (pág. 597)

inoculation effect developing resistance to persuasion by exposing a person to arguments that challenge his or her beliefs so that he or she can practice defending them (p. 606)

efecto de inoculación desarrollar una resistencia a la persuasión exponiendo a una persona a argumentos que ponen sus creencias en tela de juicio para que pueda practicar cómo defenderlas (pág. 606)

*insight the act or result of being aware of the inner nature of things (p. 5)

*discernimiento acción o resultado de tener conciencia de la naturaleza interna de las cosas (pág. 5)

insomnia the failure to get enough sleep at night in order to feel rested the next day (p. 183)

insomnio imposibilidad de dormir lo suficiente por la noche para sentirse descansado al día siguiente (pág. 183)

*instance an example of a particular type or action (p. 557)

*caso ejemplo de un tipo o una acción en particular (pág. 557)

instincts innate tendencies that determine behavior (p. 317)

instinto tendencias innatas que determinan el comportamiento (pág. 317)

intellectualization a coping mechanism in which the person analyzes a situation from an emotionally detached viewpoint (p. 441)

intelectualización mecanismo de defensa en el cual la persona analiza una situación desde un punto de vista desapegado de las emociones (pág. 441)

intelligence quotient (IQ) standardized measure of intelligence based on a scale in which 100 is average (p. 358)

coeficiente intelectual (CI) medida estandarizada de la inteligencia basada en una escala en la cual el promedio es 100 (pág. 358)

*intense to an extreme degree (p. 117)

*intenso en un grado extremo (pág. 117)

interest inventory measures a person's preferences and attitudes in a wide variety of activities to identify areas of likely success (p. 367)

inventario de intereses mide las preferencias y actitudes de una persona en cuanto a una amplia variedad de actividades para identificar las áreas en las que podría desempeñarse bien (pág. 367)

interference blockage of a memory by previous or subsequent memories or loss of a retrieval cue (p. 283)

interferencia bloqueo de un recuerdo causado por recuerdos anteriores o subsiguientes, o la pérdida de una clave de recuperación (pág. 283)

internalization incorporating the values, ideas, and standards of others as a part of oneself (p. 595)

internalización incorporación de los valores, las ideas y las normas de los demás como parte de sí mismo (pág. 595)

*interpret to tell the meaning of (p. 185)

*interpretar distinguir el significado de algo (pág. 185)

intrinsic motivation engaging in activities because they are personally rewarding or because they fulfill our beliefs and expectations (p. 319)

motivación intrínseca realizar actividades porque son gratificantes a nivel personal o porque se ajustan a nuestras creencias o cumplen con nuestras expectativas (pág. 319)

*invariably always (p. 66)

*invariablemente siempre (pág. 66)

*involve to contain or include something as a necessary element (p. 257)

*incluir contener algo como elemento necesario (pág. 257)

ENGLISH	ESPAÑOL
*isolating causing one to feel alone (p. 141)	***aislante** que causa sentimientos de soledad (pág. 141)
*issue a problem or worry (p. 74)	***problema** inconveniente o preocupación (pág. 74)

K

kinesthesis the sense of movement and body position (p. 219)	**sinestesia** sentido del movimiento y de la posición del cuerpo (pág. 219)

L

*label to describe or identify with a word or phrase (p. 452)	***rotular** describir o identificar con una palabra o frase (pág. 452)
language the expression of ideas through symbols and sounds that are arranged according to rules (p. 304)	**lenguaje** expresión de ideas por medio de símbolos y sonidos organizados de acuerdo con un conjunto de reglas (pág. 304)
latent learning alteration of a behavioral tendency that is not demonstrated by an immediate, observable change (p. 257)	**aprendizaje latente** alteración de una tendencia del comportamiento que no se demuestra con un cambio inmediato ni observable (pág. 257)
lateral hypothalamus (LH) the part of the hypothalamus that produces hunger signals (p. 323)	**hipotálamo lateral** (HL) parte del hipotálamo que produce las señales de hambre (pág. 323)
learned helplessness condition in which repeated attempts to control a situation fail, resulting in the belief that the situation is uncontrollable (p. 258)	**desesperanza aprendida** condición en la que fallan varios intentos de controlar una situación, lo que genera la creencia de que la situación es incontrolable (pág. 258)
lens a flexible, elastic, transparent structure in the eye that changes its shape to focus light on the retina (p. 210)	**lente** estructura transparente, elástica y flexible del ojo que cambia de forma para enfocar la luz sobre la retina (pág. 210)
*link a connection between two or more things (p. 431)	***conexión** relación entre dos o más cosas (pág. 431)
lithium carbonate a chemical used to counteract mood swings of bipolar disorder (p. 515)	**carbonato de litio** compuesto químico que se usa para contrarrestar los cambios bruscos del estado de ánimo del trastorno bipolar (pág. 515)
lobes the different regions into which the cerebral cortex is divided (p. 154)	**lóbulos** distintas regiones en las que se divide la corteza cerebral (pág. 154)
*logic reason (p. 507)	***lógica** razón (pág. 507)
longitudinal study research method in which data are collected about a group of participants over a number of years to assess how certain characteristics change or remain the same during development (p. 30)	**estudio longitudinal** método de investigación en el que se reúnen datos sobre un grupo de participantes a lo largo de una cantidad de años para evaluar de qué manera determinadas características cambian o se mantienen durante el desarrollo (pág. 30)

Glossary/Glosario

M

magnetic resonance imaging (MRI) a measuring technique used to study brain (p. 162)

imagen por resonancia magnética (IRM) técnica de medición utilizada para estudiar el encéfalo (pág. 162)

*maintain to make something continue at the same level or standard (p. 590)

*mantener hacer que algo continúe en el mismo nivel (pág. 590)

maintenance rehearsal a system for remembering that involves repeating information to oneself without attempting to find meaning in it (p. 270)

ensayo de mantenimiento sistema para recordar que incluye la repetición de la información para sí sin intentar otorgarle un sentido (pág. 270)

major depressive disorder severe form of lowered mood in which a person experiences feelings of worthlessness and diminished pleasure or interest in many activities (p. 478)

trastorno depresivo mayor forma grave de estado de ánimo disminuido en el cual una persona no se siente valorada y siente poco placer o interés por muchas actividades (pág. 478)

meditation the focusing of attention to clear one's mind and produce relaxation (p. 191)

meditación acto de concentrar la atención para despejar la mente y producir un estado de relajación (pág. 191)

menarche the first menstrual period (p. 87)

menarca primera menstruación (pág. 87)

menopause the biological event in which a woman's production of sex hormones is sharply reduced (p. 126)

menopausia suceso biológico en el que la producción de hormonas sexuales de una mujer tiene una reducción significativa (pág. 126)

mental set a habitual strategy or pattern of problem solving (p. 298)

disposición mental patrón o estrategia habitual de resolución de problemas (pág. 298)

*mental of or relating to the mind (p. 285)

*mental que pertenece a la mente o está relacionado con ella (pág. 285)

metacognition the awareness of or thinking about one's own cognitive processes (p. 295)

metacognición conciencia de los propios procesos cognitivos, o la reflexión acerca de ellos (pág. 295)

midbrain a small part of the brain above the pons that arouses the brain, integrates sensory information, and relays it upward (p. 153)

cerebro medio porción pequeña del encéfalo ubicada arriba de la protuberancia que activa el encéfalo; integra la información sensorial y la transmite hacia la parte superior (pág. 153)

modeling learning by imitating others; copying behavior (p. 259)

modelado aprender imitando a otros; copiar el comportamiento (pág. 259)

*modify to change something slightly (p. 171)

*modificar cambiar algo levemente (pág. 171)

morpheme the smallest unit of meaning in a given language (p. 305)

morfema unidad mínima de sentido de una lengua determinada (pág. 305)

motion parallax the apparent movement of stationary objects relative to one another that occurs when the observer changes position (p. 227)

paralaje de movimiento movimiento aparente de objetos estacionarios relacionados que ocurre cuando el observador cambia de posición (pág. 227)

motivation an internal state that activates behavior and directs it toward a goal (p. 316)

motivación estado interno que activa el comportamiento y lo dirige hacia un objetivo (pág. 316)

Glossary/Glosario

ENGLISH	ESPAÑOL
*motive a reason for doing something (p. 316)	*motivo razón para hacer algo (pág. 316)

N

narcolepsy a condition characterized by suddenly falling asleep or feeling very sleepy during the day (p. 183)	**narcolepsia** condición por la cual una persona se queda dormida repentinamente o siente mucho sueño durante el día (pág. 183)
naturalistic observation research method in which the psychologist observes the subject in a natural setting without interfering (p. 29)	**observación naturalista** método de investigación en el que el psicólogo observa al sujeto en un entorno natural sin interferir (pág. 29)
negative reinforcement increasing the strength of a given response by removing or preventing a painful stimulus when the response occurs (p. 250)	**refuerzo negativo** proceso en el que se aumenta la fuerza de una respuesta determinada quitando o evitando un estímulo doloroso cuando ocurre la respuesta (pág. 250)
neurons the long, thin cells of nerve tissue along which messages travel to and from the brain (p. 149)	**neuronas** células largas y delgadas de tejido nervioso por medio de las cuales se transmiten los mensajes que se envían al encéfalo y los que provienen de él (pág. 149)
neurotransmitters the chemicals released by neurons, which determine the rate at which other neurons fire (p. 150)	**neurotransmisores** sustancias químicas liberadas por las neuronas que determinan la tasa de disparo de otras neuronas (pág. 150)
neutral stimulus a stimulus that does not initially elicit any part of an unconditioned response (p. 236)	**estímulo neutro** estímulo que no requiere inicialmente ninguna parte de una respuesta incondicionada (pág. 236)
*neutral impartial; not belonging to one side or the other (p. 339)	*neutro imparcial; que no pertenece ni a un lado ni al otro (pág. 339)
night terrors sleep disruptions that occur during Stage IV of sleep, involving screaming, panic, or confusion (p. 184)	**terrores nocturnos** trastornos del sueño que ocurren durante la etapa IV del sueño y en los que se producen gritos, pánico o confusión (pág. 184)
nondirective therapy the free flow of images and ideas, with no particular direction (p. 502)	**terapia no directiva** la afluencia ilimitada de imágenes e ideas, sin una dirección particular (pág. 502)
nonverbal communication the process through which messages are conveyed using space, body language, and facial expression (p. 538)	**comunicación no verbal** proceso por el cual se transmiten los mensajes mediante el uso del espacio, el lenguaje corporal y la expresión facial (pág. 538)
normal curve a graph of frequency distribution shaped like a symmetrical, bell-shaped curve; a graph of normally distributed data (p. 42)	**curva normal** gráfica de distribución de frecuencias que se traza como una curva simétrica acampanada; gráfica con datos de distribución normal (pág. 42)
norms standard of comparison for test results developed by giving the test to large, well-defined groups of people (p. 351)	**normas** estándar de comparación de los resultados que se obtienen tras tomar una prueba a grupos grandes y bien definidos de personas (pág. 351)

O

obedience a change in attitude or behavior brought about by social pressure to comply with people perceived to be authorities (p. 568)

obediencia cambio de actitud o comportamiento causado por presiones sociales para cumplir con los requisitos de personas que se perciben como autoridades (pág. 568)

objective test a limited- or forced-choice test in which a person must select one of several answers (p. 369)

prueba objetiva prueba con opciones limitadas —o forzadas— en la cual una persona debe seleccionar una de varias respuestas (pág. 369)

*obtain to get possession of something, especially by making an effort or having the necessary qualifications (p. 246)

*obtener tomar posesión de algo, especialmente como resultado del esfuerzo o de tener las aptitudes necesarias (pág. 246)

olfactory nerve the nerve that carries smell impulses from the nerve to the brain (p. 217)

nervio olfativo nervio que transmite impulsos relacionados con los olores desde el nervio hasta el encéfalo (pág. 217)

operant conditioning learning in which a certain action is reinforced or punished, resulting in corresponding increases or decreases in occurrence (p. 244)

condicionamiento operante aprendizaje en el que cierta acción se refuerza o se castiga, lo que genera aumentos o disminuciones correspondientes de los casos (pág. 244)

optic nerve the nerve that carries impulses from the retina to the brain (p. 210)

nervio óptico nervio que transmite impulsos desde la retina hasta el encéfalo (pág. 210)

outbred descended from ancestors with dissimilar genetics (p. 172)

exogámico que desciende de ancestros que poseen una genética distinta (pág. 172)

*outcome the way that something turns out in the end; an expected or likely final state, achievement, or result (p. 533)

*resultado manera en la que algo acaba siendo; resultado, logro o estado final esperado o probable (pág. 533)

*overlap to extend over and cover part of something else (p. 226)

*superponerse extenderse sobre un objeto y cubrirlo en parte (pág. 226)

P

panic disorder an extreme anxiety that manifests itself in the form of panic attacks (p. 462)

trastorno de pánico ansiedad extrema que se manifiesta en la forma de ataques de pánico (pág. 462)

*participate to be involved with others in doing something (p. 581)

*participar formar parte de una actividad con otros (pág. 581)

*perceive to notice or be aware of (p. 206)

*percibir notar o ser consciente de algo (pág. 206)

percentile system ranking of test scores that indicates the ratio of scores lower and higher than a given score (p. 351)

sistema de percentiles clasificación de puntajes de pruebas que indica la proporción de puntuaciones que son mayores o menores que una puntuación dada (pág. 351)

perception the organization of sensory information into meaningful experiences (p. 205)

percepción organización de la información sensorial para formar experiencias significativas (pág. 205)

Glossary/Glosario

peripheral nervous system (PNS) nerves branching beyond the spinal cord into the body (p. 148)

sistema nervioso periférico (SNP) grupo de nervios que se extienden más allá de la médula espinal y recorren el cuerpo (pág. 148)

*persist to continue to occur beyond the expected time (p. 566)

*persistir seguir ocurriendo después del tiempo esperado (pág. 566)

personality disorders maladaptive or inflexible ways of dealing with others and one's environment (p. 481)

trastornos de la personalidad maneras inadaptivas o inflexibles de lidiar con los demás y con el ambiente propio (pág. 481)

personality test assesses an individual's characteristics and identifies problems (p. 369)

prueba de personalidad prueba que evalúa las características de un individuo e identifica problemas (pág. 369)

personality the consistent, enduring, and unique characteristics of a person (p. 380)

personalidad las características únicas, constantes y perdurables de una persona (pág. 380)

*phenomenon an observable event (p. 103)

*fenómeno suceso observable (pág. 103)

phenotype the expression of a particular trait in an organism (p. 172)

fenotipo expresión de un rasgo específico de un organismo (pág. 172)

phobia an intense and irrational fear of a particular object or situation (p. 461)

fobia miedo intenso e irracional a un objeto o situación en particular (pág. 461)

phoneme an individual sound that is a basic structural element of language (p. 304)

fonema sonido individual que es un elemento estructural básico del lenguaje (pág. 304)

physical proximity the distance of one person to another person (p. 527)

proximidad física la distancia de una persona a otra (pág. 527)

*physical of or relating to the body (p. 84)

*físico del cuerpo o relacionado con el cuerpo (pág. 84)

physiological having to do with an organism's physical processes (p. 4)

fisiológico relacionado con los procesos físicos de un organismo (pág. 4)

pituitary gland the center of control of the endocrine system that secretes a large number of hormones (p. 165)

glándula pituitaria centro de control del sistema endocrino que secreta una gran cantidad de hormonas (pág. 165)

placebo effect a change in a participant's illness or behavior that results from a belief that the treatment will have an effect rather than from the actual treatment (p. 35)

efecto placebo cambio en el comportamiento o la enfermedad de un participante que se produce por la creencia de que el tratamiento va a dar resultado más que por el tratamiento en sí (pág. 35)

positive regard viewing oneself in a favorable light due to supportive feedback received from interaction with other (p. 400)

consideración positiva visión de uno mismo desde una perspectiva favorable gracias a las respuestas positivas recibidas en la interacción con los demás (pág. 400)

positron emission tomography (PET) an imaging technique used to see which brain areas are being activated while performing tasks (p. 162)

tomografía por emisión de positrones (PET) técnica de diagnóstico por imágenes utilizada para ver qué áreas del encéfalo se activan mientras se realizan tareas determinadas (pág. 162)

post-traumatic stress disorder disorder in which victims of traumatic events experience the original event in the form of dreams or flashbacks (p. 463)

posthypnotic suggestion a suggestion made during hypnosis that influences the participant's behavior afterward (p. 190)

***precede** to come before in time, order or rank (p. 276)

prefrontal lobotomy a radical form of psychosurgery in which a section of the frontal lobe of the brain is destroyed (p. 518)

prejudice preconceived attitudes toward a person or group that have been formed without sufficient evidence and are not easily changed (p. 598)

***previous** existing or occurring before something else (p. 403)

primacy effect the tendency to form opinions about others based on first impressions (p. 534)

primary reinforcer stimulus that is naturally rewarding, such as food or water (p. 246)

***primary** of principle or chief importance (p. 386)

prior earlier in time (p. 613)

procedural memory permanent storage of learned skills that does not require conscious recollection (p. 273)

***process** a series of actions or operations directed toward a specific end (p. 236)

***professional** person engaged in a specific job (p. 614)

progressive relaxation lying down comfortably and tensing and releasing the tension in each major muscle group in turn (p. 443)

projective test an unstructured test in which a person is asked to respond freely, giving his or her own interpretation of various ambiguous stimulation (p. 372)

psychiatry a branch of medicine that deals with mental, emotional, or behavioral disorders (p. 18)

psychoactive drugs chemicals that affect the nervous system and result in altered consciousness (p. 193)

trastorno de estrés postraumático trastorno en el cual las víctimas de sucesos traumáticos experimentan el suceso original en la forma de sueños o reviviscencias (pág. 463)

sugestión posthipnótica sugestión realizada durante la hipnosis que luego influye en el comportamiento del participante (pág. 190)

***preceder** estar o aparecer antes en el tiempo, el orden o la jerarquía (pág. 276)

lobotomía prefrontal forma radical de psicocirugía en la que se destruye una sección del lóbulo frontal del encéfalo (pág. 518)

prejuicio actitudes preconcebidas dirigidas a una persona o grupo que se han formado sin pruebas suficientes y que no se cambian fácilmente (pág. 598)

***previo** que existe u ocurre antes de otra cosa (pág. 403)

efecto de primacía tendencia a formarse opiniones acerca de otros según la primera impresión (pág. 534)

refuerzo primario estímulo que es gratificante por naturaleza, como la comida o el agua (pág. 246)

***primario** principal o de suma importancia (pág. 386)

anterior anterior en el tiempo (pág. 613)

memoria procesal almacenamiento permanente de destrezas aprendidas que no requiere de la memoria consciente (pág. 273)

***proceso** serie de acciones u operaciones orientadas a conseguir un fin específico (pág. 236)

***profesional** persona que se dedica a un trabajo específico (pág. 614)

relajación progresiva proceso en el que una persona se recuesta cómodamente y luego tensiona y relaja un grupo muscular principal cada vez (pág. 443)

prueba proyectiva prueba desestructurada en la cual se pide a una persona que responda libremente y dé su propia interpretación de distintos estímulos ambiguos (pág. 372)

psiquiatría rama de la medicina que se ocupa de los trastornos mentales, emocionales y de comportamiento (pág. 18)

drogas psicoactivas sustancias químicas que afectan el sistema nervioso y generan una conciencia alterada (pág. 193)

Glossary/Glosario

ENGLISH

ESPAÑOL

psychoanalysis therapy aimed at making patients aware of their unconscious motives so that they can gain control over their behavior (p. 499)

psychoanalyst a psychologist who studies how unconscious motives and conflicts determine human behavior, feelings, and thoughts (p. 12)

psychobiologist a psychologist who studies how physical and chemical changes in our bodies influence our behavior (p. 13)

psychological dependence use of a drug to such an extent that a person feels nervous and anxious without it (p. 483)

psychological needs the urge to belong and to give and receive love, and the urge to acquire esteem (p. 330)

psychologist a scientist who studies the mind and behavior of humans and animals (p. 18)

psychology the scientific study of behavior that is tested through scientific research (p. 4)

psychophysics the study of the relationships between sensory experiences and the physical stimuli that cause them (p. 205)

psychosurgery a medical operation that destroys part of the brain to make the patient calmer and freer of symptoms (p. 518)

psychotherapy any treatment used by therapists to help troubled individuals overcome their problems (p. 492)

pupil the opening in the iris that regulates the amount of light entering the eye (p. 210)

*pursue to follow or seek (p. 335)

psicoanálisis terapia orientada a hacer que los pacientes descubran sus motivos inconscientes para que puedan tomar el control de su comportamiento (pág. 499)

psicoanalista psicólogo que estudia de qué manera ciertos motivos y conflictos inconscientes determinan el comportamiento, los sentimientos y los pensamientos de los seres humanos (pág. 12)

psicobiólogo psicólogo que estudia de qué manera los cambios físicos y químicos del cuerpo influyen en nuestro comportamiento (pág. 13)

dependencia psicológica consumo de una droga en tal medida que una persona se siente nerviosa y ansiosa si no la consume (pág. 483)

necesidades fisiológicas la necesidad imperiosa de pertenecer y de dar y recibir amor, y la necesidad imperiosa de adquirir estima (pág. 330)

psicólogo científico que estudia la mente y el comportamiento de los seres humanos y los animales (pág. 18)

psicología estudio científico del comportamiento que se pone a prueba por medio de la investigación científica (pág. 4)

psicofísica estudio de las relaciones entre las experiencias sensoriales y los estímulos físicos que las causan (pág. 205)

psicocirugía procedimiento médico que destruye parte del encéfalo para hacer que el paciente se sienta más calmo y presente menos síntomas (pág. 518)

psicoterapia cualquier tratamiento usado por un terapeuta para ayudar a los individuos angustiados a superar sus problemas (pág. 492)

pupila abertura en el iris que regula la cantidad de luz que llega al ojo (pág. 210)

*buscar intentar conseguir (pág. 335)

R

random without a particular pattern (p. 29)

aleatorio que no sigue un patrón específico (pág. 29)

*ratio relationship between two or more values (p. 207)

*proporción relación entre dos o más valores (pág. 207)

rational-emotive therapy (RET) a form of psychological help aimed at changing unrealistic assumptions about oneself and other people (p. 506)

terapia racional emotiva (TRE) forma de ayuda psicológica orientada a modificar suposiciones irrealistas sobre sí mismo y otras personas (pág. 506)

Glossary/Glosario

rationalization a process whereby an individual seeks to explain an often unpleasant emotion or behavior in a way that will preserve his or her self-esteem (p. 93)

racionalización proceso por el cual un individuo busca explicar una emoción o un sentimiento desagradable de una manera que le permita resguardar su autoestima (pág. 93)

recall memory retrieval in which a person reconstructs previously learned material (p. 281)

recordar recuperación de la memoria en la que una persona reconstruye material que ya ha aprendido antes (pág. 281)

recognition memory retrieval in which a person identifies an object, idea, or situation as one he or she has or has not experienced before (p. 280)

reconocimiento recuperación de la memoria en la que una persona identifica en un objeto, una idea o una situación algo que ya ha experimentado antes (pág. 280)

reconstructive processes the alteration of a recalled memory that may be simplified, enriched, or distorted, depending on an individual's experiences, attitudes, or inferences (p. 281)

procesos reconstructivos alteración de un recuerdo que puede simplificarse, enriquecerse o distorsionarse según las experiencias, actitudes o inferencias del individuo (pág. 281)

*regulate to control something (p. 148)

*regular controlar algo (pág. 148)

reinforcement stimulus or event that follows a response and increases the likelihood that the response will be repeated (p. 245)

refuerzo estímulo o suceso que sigue a una respuesta y aumenta la probabilidad de que la respuesta se repita (pág. 245)

*reject to refuse (p. 604)

*rechazar rehusar (pág. 604)

reliability the ability of a test to give the same results under similar conditions (p. 348)

fiabilidad capacidad de una prueba de arrojar los mismos resultados bajo condiciones similares (pág. 348)

REM sleep a stage of sleep characterized by rapid eye movements, a high level of brain activity, a deep relaxation of the muscles, and dreaming (p. 181)

sueño REM etapa del sueño que se caracteriza por movimientos oculares rápidos, sueños, un alto nivel de actividad cerebral y una relajación profunda de los músculos (pág. 181)

representational thought the intellectual ability of a child to picture something in his or her mind (p. 62)

pensamiento representacional capacidad intelectual de un niño de imaginar algo en la mente (pág. 62)

*research a careful study of a subject, especially in order to discover new facts or information (p. 66)

*investigación estudio cuidadoso de un sujeto, especialmente para descubrir nuevos datos o nueva información (pág. 66)

resistance the reluctance of a patient either to reveal painful feelings or to examine longstanding behavior patterns (p. 500)

resistencia reticencia de un paciente ya sea a revelar sentimientos dolorosos o a examinar patrones de comportamiento de larga data (pág. 500)

response chain learned reactions that follow one another in sequence, each reaction producing the signal for the next (p. 249)

cadena de respuestas reacciones aprendidas que ocurren en secuencia una después de otra; cada reacción produce la señal para la siguiente (pág. 249)

resynthesis combining old ideas with new ones and reorganizing feelings in order to renew one's identity (p. 117)

resintetizar combinar viejas ideas con otras nuevas y reorganizar los sentimientos para renovar la propia identidad (pág. 117)

retina the innermost coating of the back of the eye, containing the light-sensitive receptor cells (p. 210)

retina cubierta más profunda de la parte trasera del ojo que contiene células receptoras fotosensibles (pág. 210)

retinal disparity the differences between the images stimulating each eye (p. 212)

disparidad retiniana diferencias entre las imágenes que estimulan cada ojo (pág. 212)

Glossary/Glosario

Glossary/Glosario

retrieval the process of obtaining information that has been stored in memory (p. 268)

recuperación proceso en el que se obtiene información que se ha almacenado en la memoria (pág. 268)

*reveal to make generally known (p. 190)

*revelar dar a conocer en general (pág. 190)

*revise to change or update something to make it more accurate or realistic (p. 357)

*corregir cambiar o actualizar algo para que sea más preciso o realista (pág. 357)

role taking children's play that involves assuming adult roles, thus enabling the child to experience different points of view (p. 76)

juego de roles juego de niños que implica asumir roles adultos y que, en consecuencia, le permite al niño experimentar diferentes puntos de vista (pág. 76)

*role a part played by a person (p. 108)

*rol papel que desempeña una persona (pág. 108)

rooting reflex an infant's response in turning toward the source of touching that occurs anywhere around his or her mouth (p. 54)

reflejo de los puntos cardinales respuesta de un bebé de ponerse de frente a la fuente con la que ha entrado en contacto en la zona alrededor de su boca (pág. 54)

rule a statement of relation (p. 293)

regla enunciado de relación (pág. 293)

S

schema a conceptual framework a person uses to make sense of the world (p. 61)

esquema marco de referencia conceptual que una persona utiliza para comprender el mundo (pág. 61)

schemas conceptual frameworks a person uses to make sense of the world (p. 281)

esquemas marcos conceptuales que una persona usa para comprender el mundo (pág. 281)

*scheme a system for organizing or arranging things (p. 329)

*esquema sistema para organizar u ordenar cosas (pág. 329)

schizophrenia a group of disorders characterized by confused and disconnected thoughts, emotions, and perceptions (p. 471)

esquizofrenia grupo de trastornos caracterizados por emociones, percepciones y pensamientos confusos y desconectados (pág. 471)

secondary reinforcer stimulus such as money that becomes rewarding through its link with a primary reinforcer (p. 246)

refuerzo secundario estímulo tal como el dinero que se vuelve gratificante a causa de su asociación con un refuerzo primario (pág. 246)

self one's experience or image of oneself, developed through interaction with others (p. 400)

autoconcepto experiencia o imagen de uno mismo, desarrollada a partir de la interacción con los demás (pág. 400)

self-actualization needs the pursuit of knowledge and beauty or whatever else is required for the realization of one's unique potential (p. 330)

necesidades de autorrealización la búsqueda del conocimiento y la belleza o de lo que sea que se necesite para la realización del propio potencial singular (pág. 330)

self-actualization the humanist term for realizing one's unique potential (p. 398)

autorrealización término humanista que se refiere a la realización del potencial único de una persona (pág. 398)

self-concept how we see or describe ourselves; our total perception of ourselves (p. 590)

concepto de sí mismo cómo nos vemos o describimos; la percepción total que tenemos de nosotros mismos (pág. 590)

self-fulfilling prophecy a situation in which a researcher's expectations influence that person's own behavior, and thereby influence the participant's behavior (p. 34)

self-justification the need to rationalize one's attitude and behavior (p. 597)

self-serving bias a tendency to claim success is due to our efforts, while failure is due to circumstances beyond our control (p. 537)

semantic memory knowledge of language, including its rules, words, and meanings (p. 273)

semantics the study of meaning in language (p. 305)

sensation what occurs when a stimulus activates a receptor (p. 204)

sensory memory very brief memory storage immediately following initial stimulation of a receptor(p. 269)

*series a number of related or similar things arranged in a sequence (p. 271)

shaping technique in which the desired behavior is "molded" by first rewarding any act similar to that behavior and then requiring ever-closer approximations to the desired behavior before giving the reward (p. 249)

short-term memory memory that is limited in capacity to about seven items and in duration by the subject's active rehearsal (p. 270)

signal detection theory the study of people's tendencies to make correct judgments in detecting the presence of stimuli (p. 208)

*significant results that are unlikely to have occurred by chance (p. 45)

*similar alike but not exactly the same (p. 173)

*similarity the state of being like someone or something but not exactly the same (p. 530)

single-blind experiment an experiment in which the participants are unaware of who received the treatment (p. 34)

sleeper effect the delayed impact on attitude change of a persuasive communication (p. 605)

profecía autocumplida situación en la que las expectativas de un investigador influyen en su propio comportamiento y, por lo tanto, influyen en el comportamiento del participante (pág. 34)

autojustificación necesidad de racionalizar la actitud y el comportamiento propios (pág. 597)

sesgo favorable al yo tendencia a afirmar que el éxito es consecuencia de nuestros esfuerzos, mientras que el fracaso es consecuencia de circunstancias que escapan a nuestro control (pág. 537)

memoria semántica conocimiento de la lengua, incluidos sus reglas, palabras y significados (pág. 273)

semántica el estudio del significado en el lenguaje (pág. 305)

sensación lo que ocurre cuando un estímulo activa un receptor (pág. 204)

memoria sensorial almacenamiento de memoria muy breve que ocurre inmediatamente después de la estimulación inicial de un receptor (pág. 269)

*serie número de cosas relacionadas o similares ordenadas en secuencia (pág. 271)

moldeado técnica en la que el comportamiento deseado es "ajustado", primero, recompensando cualquier acción que sea similar a este comportamiento y, después, exigiendo aproximaciones cada vez más cercanas al comportamiento deseado antes de entregar la recompensa (pág. 249)

memoria a corto plazo memoria que se limita en cuanto a su capacidad a unos siete elementos y en cuanto a su duración en términos del ensayo activo del sujeto (pág. 270)

teoría de detección de señales estudio de la tendencia de las personas a tomar decisiones correctas tras detectar la presencia de un estímulo (pág. 208)

*significativos resultados que es improbable que hayan ocurrido por azar (pág. 45)

*similar parecido pero no exactamente igual (pág. 173)

*semejanza estado en el cual se es parecido a alguien o algo pero no exactamente lo mismo (pág. 530)

experimento simple ciego experimento en el que los participantes no saben quiénes recibieron el tratamiento (pág. 34)

efecto durmiente impacto retrasado que una comunicación persuasiva tiene en un cambio de actitud (pág. 605)

Glossary/Glosario

ENGLISH	ESPAÑOL
sleepwalking walking or carrying out behaviors while asleep (p. 184)	**sonambulismo** acto de caminar o realizar conductas mientras se está dormido (pág. 184)
social cognition the perception, storage, and retrieval of information about social interactions (p. 524)	**cognición social** percepción, almacenamiento y recuperación de información relacionada con las interacciones sociales (pág. 524)
social facilitation an increase in performance in front of a crowd (p. 559)	**facilitación social** mejora en el desempeño cuando se está frente a muchas personas (pág. 559)
social functions responses directed toward satisfying the emotional needs of members (p. 557)	**funciones sociales** respuestas dirigidas a la satisfacción de las necesidades sociales de los miembros (pág. 557)
social inhibition a decrease in performance in front of a crowd (p. 559)	**inhibición social** disminución del desempeño cuando se está frente a muchas personas (pág. 559)
social learning process of altering behavior by observing and imitating the behaviors of others (p. 256)	**aprendizaje social** proceso de modificación del comportamiento a partir de la observación e imitación del comportamiento de otras personas (pág. 256)
social learning theory Bandura's view of human development; emphasizes interaction (p. 99)	**teoría del aprendizaje social** enfoque de Bandura sobre el desarrollo humano; enfatiza la interacción (pág. 99)
social loafing the tendency to work less hard when sharing the workload with others (p. 582)	**holgazanería social** tendencia a trabajar menos cuando se comparte la carga de trabajo con otros (pág. 582)
social psychology the study of how our thoughts, feelings, perceptions, and behaviors are influenced by interactions with others (p. 524)	**psicología social** estudio de cómo nuestros pensamientos, sentimientos, percepciones y comportamientos están influidos por las interacciones con los demás (pág. 524)
social support information that leads someone to believe that he or she is cared for, loved, respected, and part of a network of communication and mutual obligation (p. 437)	**apoyo social** información que permite a una persona creer que la protegen, aman y respetan, y que es parte de una red de comunicación y obligaciones mutuas (pág. 437)
socialization the process of learning the rules of behavior of the culture within which an individual is born and will live (p. 72)	**socialización** proceso de aprendizaje de las reglas de comportamiento de la cultura en la que un individuo nace y vivirá (pág. 72)
sociogram a diagram that represents relationships within a group, especially likes and dislikes of members for other members (p. 561)	**sociograma** diagrama que representa las relaciones dentro de un grupo, especialmente lo que les gusta y lo que no a ciertos miembros en relación con otros (pág. 561)
somatic nervous system (SNS) the part of the peripheral nervous system that controls voluntary movement of skeletal muscles (p. 152)	**sistema nervioso somático** (SNS) parte del sistema nervioso periférico que controla el movimiento voluntario de los músculos esqueléticos (pág. 152)
somatoform disorder a condition in which there is no apparent physical cause (p. 466)	**trastorno somatoformo** condición en la cual no hay causa física aparente (pág. 466)
somesthesis the group of senses that includes balance, touch, and body positioning (p. 218)	**somestesia** grupo de sentidos como el equilibrio, el tacto y las posiciones del cuerpo (pág. 218)
***somewhat** slightly, to some extent (p. 471)	***de alguna** manera levemente, en cierta medida (pág. 471)

source trait a stable characteristic that can be considered to be at the core of personality (p. 411)

rasgo de origen característica estable que se puede considerar como el centro de la personalidad (pág. 411)

*source origin (p. 602)

*fuente origen (pág. 602)

*specific relating to a particular category (p. 28)

*específico relacionado con una categoría particular (pág. 28)

spermarche period during which males achieve first ejaculation (p. 87)

espermarca período durante el cual los machos logran su primera eyaculación (pág. 87)

spinal cord nerves that run up and down the length of the back and transmit most messages between the body and brain (p. 148)

médula espinal nervios que recorren toda la longitud de la espalda y transmiten la mayoría de los mensajes enviados entre el cuerpo y el encéfalo (pág. 148)

squandered to lose an advantage or opportunity through negligence or inaction (p. 406)

desperdiciar perder ventaja u oportunidad por negligencia o inacción (p. 406)

stagnation a discontinuation of development and desire to recapture the past (p. 129)

estancamiento discontinuación del desarrollo y deseo de recapturar el pasado (pág. 129)

standard deviation a measure of variability that describes an average distance of every score from the mean (p. 44)

desviación estándar medida de variabilidad que describe el promedio de distancia de cada resultado con respecto a la media (pág. 44)

standardization the administering and scoring of tests in the same way every time; establishing the average score made by a large group of people (p. 350)

estandarización proceso en el que se toman y califican pruebas de la misma manera todas las veces; proceso de establecer la puntuación promedio obtenida por un grupo grande de personas (pág. 350)

*statistics the branch of mathematics concerned with summarizing and making meaningful inferences from collections of data (p. 40)

*estadística rama de las matemáticas que se ocupa de resumir y hacer inferencias significativas (pág. 40)

*status position or rank in relation to others (p. 600)

*estatus posición o rango en relación con los demás (pág. 600)

stereotype set of assumptions about people in a given category summarizing our experience and beliefs about groups of people (p. 535)

estereotipo conjunto de suposiciones acerca de las personas de una categoría que resume nuestra experiencia y nuestras creencias acerca de los grupos de personas (pág. 535)

*stimulate to raise levels of interest, response, or activity (p. 156)

*estimular provocar determinados niveles de interés, respuesta o actividad (pág. 156)

stimulation value the ability of a person to interest you in or to expose you to new ideas and experiences (p. 528)

valor de estimulación capacidad de una persona de despertar el interés de otra o presentarle nuevas ideas y experiencias (pág. 528)

storage the process by which information is maintained over a period of time (p. 268)

almacenamiento proceso por el que se mantiene la información durante un período de tiempo (pág. 268)

stress a person's reaction to his or her inability to cope with a certain tense event or situation (p. 420)

estrés reacción de una persona a su incapacidad de lidiar con cierto suceso o situación de tensión (pág. 420)

stress reaction the body's response to a stressor (p. 421)

reacción de estrés respuesta del cuerpo a un estresor (pág. 421)

ENGLISH	ESPAÑOL
stressor a stress-producing event or situation (p. 421)	**estresor** suceso o situación que produce estrés (pág. 421)
structuralist a psychologist who studies the basic elements that make up conscious mental experiences (p. 8)	**estructuralista** psicólogo que estudia los elementos básicos que conforman las experiencias mentales conscientes (pág. 8)
sublimation the process of redirecting sexual impulses into learning tasks (p. 73)	**sublimación** proceso en el que se redirigen los impulsos sexuales al aprendizaje de tareas (pág. 73)
subliminal messages brief auditory or visual messages that are presented below the absolute threshold (p. 225)	**mensajes subliminales** mensajes auditivos o visuales breves presentados por debajo del umbral absoluto (pág. 225)
*summary a shortened version of something that has already been said or written, containing only the main points (p. 351)	***resumen** versión abreviada que solo contiene las ideas principales de algo que ya se ha dicho o escrito (pág. 351)
superego the part of the personality that is the source of conscience and counteracts the socially undesirable impulses of the id (p. 386)	**superyó** parte de la personalidad que es la fuente de la conciencia y contrarresta los impulsos del ello no deseables en la vida en sociedad (pág. 386)
surface trait a stable characteristic that can be observed in certain situations (p. 411)	**rasgo de superficie** característica estable que se puede observar en determinadas situaciones (pág. 411)
symbol an abstract unit of thought that represents an object or quality; anything that stands for or represents something else (p. 293)	**símbolo** unidad abstracta de pensamiento que representa un objeto o una cualidad; lo que representa otra cosa (pág. 293)
*symbol something that stands for or suggests something else; a visible sign of something invisible (p. 57)	***símbolo** algo que representa o sugiere otra cosa; un signo visible de algo invisible (pág. 57)
synapse the gap that exists between individual nerve cells (p. 150)	**sinapsis** espacio que separa una neurona de otra (pág. 150)
syntax language rules that govern how words can be combined to form meaningful phrases and sentences (p. 305)	**sintaxis** reglas lingüísticas que determinan cómo pueden combinarse las palabras para crear frases y oraciones que tengan sentido (pág. 305)
systematic desensitization a technique to help a patient overcome irrational fears and anxieties (p. 509)	**desensibilización sistemática** técnica para ayudar a un paciente a superar miedos y angustias irracionales (pág. 509)

T

ENGLISH	ESPAÑOL
task functions activities directed toward getting a job done (p. 557)	**funciones de tarea** actividades dirigidas a la finalización de un trabajo **funciones** (pág. 557)
telegraphic speech the kind of verbal utterances in which words are left out, but the meaning is usually clear (p. 57)	**discurso telegráfico** tipo de expresiones verbales en las que se omiten palabras, pero el significado suele ser claro (pág. 57)
thanatology the study of dying and death (p. 138)	**tanatología** estudio de la muerte (pág. 138)
theory a set of assumptions used to explain phenomena and offered for scientific study (p. 6)	**teoría** conjunto de suposiciones que se utilizan para explicar fenómenos y se ponen a disposición para el estudio científico (pág. 6)

*theory a plausible or scientifically acceptable general principle or body of principles offered to explain phenomena (p. 72)

*teoría principio o cuerpo de principios generales posibles o científicamente aceptables que se ponen a disposición para explicar fenómenos (pág. 72)

*thereby by or as a result of the situation or action mentioned (p. 443)

*de ese modo debido a la situación o acción mencionada, o como resultado de ella (pág. 443)

token economy conditioning in which desirable behavior is reinforced with valueless objects, which can be accumulated and exchanged for valued rewards (p. 261)

economía de fichas condicionamiento en el que un comportamiento deseable se refuerza con objetos sin valor, que pueden acumularse y cambiarse por recompensas de valor (pág. 261)

tolerance physical adaptation to a drug so that a person needs an increased amount in order to produce the original effect (p. 484)

tolerancia adaptación física a una droga de manera que una persona necesita una cantidad mayor para producir el efecto original (pág. 484)

trait a tendency to react to a situation in a way that remains stable over time (p. 409)

rasgo tendencia a reaccionar ante una situación de una manera estable a través del tiempo (pág. 409)

transference the process, experienced by the patient, of feeling toward an analyst or therapist the way he or she feels or felt toward some other important figure in his or her life (p. 501)

transferencia proceso, experimentado por el paciente, de tener los mismos sentimientos hacia el analista o terapeuta que los que tiene o tuvo hacia otra figura importante en su vida (pág. 501)

triarchic theory proposes that a person's intelligence involves analytical, creative, and practical thinking skills (p. 356)

teoría triárquica propone que la inteligencia de una persona implica destrezas analíticas, creativas, prácticas y de razonamiento (pág. 356)

two-factor theory proposes that a person's intelligence is composed of a general ability level and specific mental abilities (p. 355)

teoría de los dos factores propone que la inteligencia de una persona consiste en un nivel de capacidad general y capacidades mentales específicas (pág. 355)

U

*ultimate in the end; finally (p. 469)

*final que ocurrirá finalmente (pág. 469)

unconditional positive regard the perception that individuals' significant others value them for what they are, which leads the individuals to grant themselves the same favorable opinion or view (p. 401)

consideración positiva incondicional percepción de que las personas que son importantes para un individuo lo valoran por lo que es, lo cual lleva a ese individuo a tener la misma opinión o visión favorable de sí mismo (pág. 401)

unconditioned response (UR) an organism's automatic (or natural) reaction to a stimulus (p. 237)

respuesta incondicionada (RI) reacción automática (o natural) de un organismo ante un estímulo (pág. 237)

unconditioned stimulus (US) an event that elicits a certain predictable response typically without previous training (p. 237)

estímulo incondicionado (EI) suceso que requiere cierta respuesta predecible, habitualmente sin ningún entrenamiento previo (pág. 237)

unconscious the part of the mind that contains material of which we are unaware but that strongly influences conscious processes and behaviors (p. 384)

inconsciente parte de la mente que contiene material del cual no somos conscientes pero que tiene una gran influencia en las procesos y comportamientos conscientes (pág. 384)

*unique limited to a particular thing or person (p. 96)

*único limitado a una cosa o persona particular (pág. 96)

Glossary/Glosario

ENGLISH	ESPAÑOL

utility value the ability of a person to help another achieve his or her goals (p. 528)

valor de utilidad capacidad de una persona de ayudar a otra a alcanzar sus objetivos (pág. 528)

V

validity the ability of a test to measure what it is intended to measure (p. 350)

validez capacidad de una prueba de medir lo que se supone que debe medir (pág. 350)

variable any factor that is capable of change (p. 31)

variable cualquier factor que puede cambiar (pág. 31)

variance a measure of variability that is the mean of the squares of the deviations from the mean of the set of data (p. 44)

varianza medida de variabilidad que es igual a la media de los cuadrados de las desviaciones con respecto a la media de un conjunto de datos (pág. 44)

*vary to exhibit a deviation from the typical form (p. 484)

*variar exhibir una desviación de la forma típica (pág. 484)

ventromedial hypothalamus VMH) the part of the hypothalamus that can cause one to stop eating (p. 323)

hipotálamo ventromedial (HVM) parte del hipotálamo que puede causar que se deje de comer (pág. 323)

vestibular system three semicircular canals that provide the sense of balance, located in the inner ear and connected to the brain by a nerve (p. 218)

sistema vestibular tres canales semicirculares que están ubicados en el oído interno —conectados al encéfalo por medio de un nervio— y que proporcionan el sentido del equilibrio (pág. 218)

*violate to go against or refuse to obey a rule, law, or agreement (p. 425)

*viole para ir contra o rechazar obedecer una regla, una ley, o un acuerdo (pág. 425)

*visible capable of being seen (p. 212)

*visible capaz de ser visto (pág. 212)

visualization mentally rehearsing the steps involved in a successful performance or process (p. 619)

visualización ensayo mental de los pasos que llevan a un desempeño o proceso exitoso (pág. 619)

*voluntary proceeding from one's own consent (p. 152)

*voluntario acto realizado por consentimiento propio (pág. 152)

W

*widespread extensive or prevalent (p. 511)

*generalizado extensivo o prevaleciente (pág. 511)

withdrawal the symptoms that occur after a person discontinues the use of a drug to which he or she has become addicted (p. 484)

abstinencia síntomas que ocurren después de que una persona deja de consumir una droga a la cual se ha hecho adicta (pág. 484)

Italicized page numbers refer to illustrations. Preceding the page number, abbreviations refer to a cartoon (crt), chart (c), diagram (d), graph (g), photograph (p), and table (t). Quoted material is referenced with the abbreviation (q) before the page number.

A

B

Index

Index

Index

Index

Index

Index

Index

Index

Index

NAME INDEX

Index